Get started with your **Connected Casebook**

Redeem your code below to access the **e-book** with search, highlighting, and note-taking capabilities; **case briefing** and **outlining** tools to support efficient learning; and more.

1. Go to www.casebookconnect.com
2. Enter your access code in the box and click **Register**
3. Follow the steps to complete your registration and verify your email address

If you have already registered at CasebookConnect.com, simply log into your account and redeem additional access codes from your Dashboard.

ACCESS CODE:

Scratch off with care.

Is this a used casebook? Access code already redeemed? Purchase a digital version at **CasebookConnect.com/catalog**.

If you purchased a digital bundle with additional components, your additional access codes will appear below.

"I liked being able to search quickly while in class."

"Being able to highlight and easily create case briefs was a fantastic resource and time saver for me!"

"I loved it! I was able to study on the go and create a more effective outline."

PLEASE NOTE: Each access code can only be used once. Access codes expire one year after the discontinuation of the corresponding print or bundle title and must be redeemed before then. CCH reserves the right to discontinue this program at any time for any business reason. For further details, please see the CasebookConnect End User License Agreement at CasebookConnect.com/terms.

For technical support, please visit http://support.wklegaledu.com.

CHILDREN, PARENTS, AND THE LAW

ASPEN CASEBOOK SERIES

CHILDREN, PARENTS, AND THE LAW

Public and Private Authority in the Home, Schools, and Juvenile Courts

Fourth Edition

LESLIE J. HARRIS
Dorothy Kliks Fones Professor of Law Emerita
University of Oregon

LEE E. TEITELBAUM
Hugh B. Brown Professor of Law
Late, University of Utah

 Wolters Kluwer

Published by Wolters Kluwer in New York.

Wolters Kluwer Legal & Regulatory U.S. serves customers worldwide with CCH, Aspen Publishers, and Kluwer Law International products. (www.WKLegaledu.com)

To contact Customer Service, e-mail customer.service@wolterskluwer.com, call 1-800-234-1660, fax 1-800-901-9075, or mail correspondence to:

Wolters Kluwer
Attn: Order Department
PO Box 990
Frederick, MD 21705

Printed in the United States of America.

1 2 3 4 5 6 7 8 9 0

ISBN 978-1-5438-0171-2

Library of Congress Cataloging-in-Publication Data

Names: Harris, Leslie J., 1952- author. | Teitelbaum, Lee E., 1941-2004, author.
Title: Children, parents, and the law : public and private authority in the home, schools, and juvenile courts / Leslie J. Harris, Dorothy Kliks Fones Professor of Law Emerita, University of Oregon; Lee E. Teitelbaum, Hugh B. Brown Professor of Law, Late, University of Utah.
Description: Fourth edition. | New York : Wolters Kluwer, [2020] | Series: Aspen casebook series | Includes bibliographical references and index. | Summary: "Children and the law casebook for law school students enrolled in children and the law courses"—Provided by publisher.
Identifiers: LCCN 2019028430 | ISBN 9781543801712 (hardcover) | ISBN 9781543814743 (ebook)
Subjects: LCSH: Parent and child (Law)—United States. | Juvenile courts—United States. | Child abuse—Law and legislation—United States. | LCGFT: Casebooks (Law)
Classification: LCC KF540 .H375 2020 | DDC 346.7301/7—dc23
LC record available at https://lccn.loc.gov/2019028430

About Wolters Kluwer Legal & Regulatory U.S.

Wolters Kluwer Legal & Regulatory U.S. delivers expert content and solutions in the areas of law, corporate compliance, health compliance, reimbursement, and legal education. Its practical solutions help customers successfully navigate the demands of a changing environment to drive their daily activities, enhance decision quality and inspire confident outcomes.

Serving customers worldwide, its legal and regulatory portfolio includes products under the Aspen Publishers, CCH Incorporated, Kluwer Law International, ftwilliam.com, and MediRegs names. They are regarded as exceptional and trusted resources for general legal and practice-specific knowledge, compliance and risk management, dynamic workflow solutions, and expert commentary.

For my students.

Summary of Contents

Contents

Preface

This book is intended for a course in Children, Parents, and the State or for one dealing with juvenile courts. The books retains its original organization and structure while including the Supreme Court's newest decisions on special education and constitutional limits on punishing minors and new materials on conflicts between parents and state authorities over school curriculum, faith healing, and compulsory vaccination. The chapters on delinquency explore how the new understanding of how and when adolescents mature is revolutionizing the law, and the unit on child abuse and neglect and the child welfare system covers new state and federal legislation, as well as cases from around the country that examine the tension between protecting children's relationships with their families and protecting them from harm.

Unlike other books intended for a course in Children, Parents, and the State, this one contains extensive coverage of juvenile court jurisdiction and procedure in delinquency, status offense, and child protective matters. And unlike most books designed for a juvenile court course, this casebook offers a detailed consideration of the constitutional and other principles regarding public and private authority for decisions affecting the education, care, and rearing of young people.

The theoretical and practical issues that the book addresses are necessarily cross-disciplinary, and students must learn to become intelligent consumers of "non-legal" disciplines. The issues that the book explores are complex, value-laden, and contested, and it provides a wide range of perspectives on them, rather than privileging any one perspective.

Leslie Harris

July 2019

Editors' note: Throughout the book, footnotes to the text and to opinions and other quoted materials are numbered consecutively from the beginning of each chapter. Editors' footnotes added to quoted materials are indicated by the abbreviation: — Eds.

Acknowledgments

This book benefits greatly from materials created by co-authors of earlier editions, Tamar Birckhead and especially the late Lee Teitelbaum, and from the advice of Rachel Rebouché regarding adolescents' reproductive rights. Thanks very much to Paul Sobel, Kathy Langone, and their colleagues at The Froebe Group for editorial assistance and their endless patience.

The authors would also like to thank the following for granting permission to reprint materials:

Archard, David, Children: Rights and Childhood 98-104. Reprinted by permission of Routledge via Copyright Clearance Center.

Birckhead, Tamar R., Culture Clash: The Challenge of Lawyering Across Difference in Juvenile Court, 62 Rutgers Law Review 959 (2010). Reprinted by permission.

————, "The Youngest Profession": Consent, Autonomy, and Prostituted Children, 88 Washington University Law Review 1055 (2011). Reprinted by permission.

————, Toward a Theory of Procedural Justice for Juveniles, 57 Buffalo Law Review 1447 (2009). Reprinted by permission.

Buss, Emily, Do Children Have the Same First Amendment Rights as Adults?: The Speech-Enhancing Effect of Internet Regulation, 79 Chicago-Kent Law Review 103 (2004). Reprinted by permission via Copyright Clearance Center.

Buss, William G., School Newspapers, Public Forum, and the First Amendment, 74 Iowa Law Review 505 (1989). Reprinted with permission via Copyright Clearance Center.

Dwyer, James G., Spiritual Treatment Exemptions to Child Medical Neglect Laws: What We Outsiders Should Think, 76 Notre Dame Law Review 147 (November 2000). Copyright © Notre Dame Law Review, University of Notre Dame. Reprinted with permission.

Edwards, Jamie, A Lesson in Unintended Consequences: How Juvenile Justice and Domestic Violence Reforms Harm Girls in Violent Family Situations (and How to Help Them), 13 University of Pennsylvania Journal of Law & Social Change 219 (2009-2010). Reprinted by permission.

Emerson, Thomas L, The System of Freedom of Expression (1970), published by Random House.

Fagan, Jeffrey & Martin Guggenheim, Preventive Detention and the Judicial Prediction of Dangerousness for Juveniles: A Natural Experiment, 86 Journal of Criminal Law & Criminology 415 (1996). Reprinted by special permission of Northwestern University School of Law, Journal of Criminal Law and Criminology.

Feld, Barry C., Juvenile and Criminal Justice Systems' Responses to Youth Violence, 24 Crime and Justice 189 (1998). Copyright © The University of Chicago Press. Reprinted by permission via Copyright Clearance Center.

Filler, Daniel M. & Austin E. Smith, The New Rehabilitation, 91 Iowa Law Review 951 (2006). Reprinted by permission.

Findlater, Janet E. & Susan Kelly, Child Protective Services and Domestic Violence, 9(3) Future of Children 84 (1999). A publication of the Center for the Future of Children. Copyright © The Center for the Future of Children, the David and Lucile Packard Foundation.

Fondacaro, Mark R., Christopher Slobogin & Tricia Cross, Reconceptualizing Due Process in Juvenile Justice: Contributions from Law and Social Science, 57 Hastings L.J. 955 (2006). Reprinted by permission.

Galston, William A., Liberal Purposes: Goods, Virtues, and Diversity in the Liberal State, published by Cambridge University Press.

Geen, Rob, The Evolution of Kinship Care Policy and Practice, 14(1) Future of Children 131 (2004). This chapter first appeared in The Future of Children, a publication of The Woodrow Wilson School of Public and International Affairs at Princeton University and The Brookings Foundation.

Guggenheim, Martin, Somebody's Children: Sustaining the Family's Place in Child Welfare Policy, 113 Harvard Law Review 1716 (2000).

Gutmann, Amy, Democratic Education (1987) Reprinted by permission of Princeton University Press via Copyright Clearance Center.

Harris, Leslie Joan, An Empirical Study of Parental Responsibility Laws: Sending Messages, But What Kind and to Whom? 2006 Utah Law Review 5. Reprinted with permission.

————, Challenging the Overuse of Foster Care and Disrupting the Path to Delinquency and Prison in Justice for Kids: Keeping Kids *Out* of the Juvenile Justice System 62 (Nancy E. Dowd ed., 2011). Reprinted by permission.

Heise, Michael, From No Child Left Behind to Every Student Succeeds: Back to a Future for Education Federalism 117 Columbia Law Review 1859 (2017). Reprinted with permission by the author and Columbia Law Review via Copyright Clearance Center.

Hirschi, Travis & Michael Gottfredson, Rethinking the Juvenile Justice System, 39 Crime & Delinquency 262. Copyright © 1993. Reprinted by permission of Sage Publications, Inc.

IJA-ABA Juvenile Justice Standards Project, Standards Relating to Noncriminal Misbehavior 15-20 (Tent. Dr. 1977). Copyright © IJA/ABA. Reprinted with permission from the ABA Journal.

IJA-ABA Juvenile Justice Standards Project, Standards Relating to Counsel for Private Parties 1-8 (1979). Copyright © IJA/ABA. Reprinted with permission from the ABA Journal.

Jackson, Robert K. & Wesley D. McBride, Understanding Street Gangs 25, 31, 34-36, 40-41 (1985).

John D. and Catherine T. MacArthur Foundation, Juvenile Adjudicative Competence to Stand Trial: Executive Summary (2005). Available on the website of the MacArthur Foundation Research Network for Adolescent

Development and Juvenile Justice, http://www.adjj.org. Reprinted by permission.

Larson, Carol S. et al., Sexual Abuse of Children: Recommendations and Analysis, 4 The Future of Children: Sexual Abuse of Children 4 (1994). A publication of the Center for the Future of Children. Copyright © The Center for the Future of Children, the David and Lucile Packard Foundation.

Liang, Bryan & Wendy L. MacFarlane, Murder by Omission: Child Abuse and The Passive Parent, 36 Harvard Journal on Legislation 397 (1999). Copyright © (1990) by the President and Fellows of Harvard College and the Harvard Journal on Legislation. Reprinted with permission via Copyright Clearance Center.

Mahoney, Anne R., PINS and Parents in Beyond Control: Status Offenders in the Juvenile Court 161 (Lee E. Teitelbaum & Aidan Gough eds., 1977). Copyright © 1977 by Lee E. Teitelbaum. Reprinted by permission.

McConnell, Michael W., Old Liberalism, New Liberalism, and People of Faith in Christian Perspectives on Legal Thought 5 (Michael W. McConnell, Robert F. Cochran, Jr. & Angela C. Carmella eds., 2001). Copyright © by Yale University Press. Reprinted by permission of Yale University Press.

Melton, Gary B., Taking *Gault* Seriously: Toward a New Juvenile Court, 68 Nebraska Law Review 146 (1989).

Miccio, Kristian G., A Reasonable Battered Mother? Redefining, Reconstructing, and Recreating the Battered Mother in Child Protective Proceedings, 22 Harvard Women's Law Journal 89 (1999).

Myers, John E.B., The Legal Response to Child Abuse: In the Best Interest of Children, 24 Journal of Family Law 149 (1985). Reprinted by permission.

Schene, Patricia A., Past, Present and Future: Roles of Child Protective Services, 8(1) Future of Children 23 (1998). A publication of the Center for the Future of Children. Copyright © The Center for the Future of Children, the David and Lucile Packard Foundation.

Schoeman, Ferdinand, Rights of Children, Rights of Parents, and the Moral Basis of the Family, 91 Ethics 6 (1980). Copyright © 1980 by The University of Chicago Press. Reprinted by permission via Copyright Clearance Center.

Scott, Elizabeth S. & Thomas Grisso, Developmental Incompetence, Due Process and Juvenile Justice Policy, 81 Valparaiso University Law Review 2401 (1995). Reprinted by permission.

Sinden, Amy, "Why Won't Mom Cooperate?": A Critique of Informality in Child Welfare Proceedings, 11 Yale Journal of Law & Feminism 339 (1999).

Sprague, Marcia & Mark Hardin, Coordination of Juvenile and Criminal Court Child Abuse and Neglect Proceedings, 35 University of Louisville Journal of Family Law 239 (1997). Reprinted with permission of the Brandeis Law Journal.

Stapleton, W. Vaughan & Lee E. Teitelbaum, in Defense of Youth: A Study of the Role of Counsel in American Juvenile Courts (1972). Copyright © Lee E. Teitelbaum. Reprinted by permission.

Tanenhaus, David S., The Evolution of Juvenile Courts in the Early 20th Century: Beyond the Myth of Immaculate Conception in A Century of Juvenile Justice 42, 42-45 (Margaret Rosenheim et al. eds., 2002). Copyright © The University of Chicago Press 2002. Reprinted by permission.

Teitelbaum, Lee E., Family History and Family Law, 1985 Wisconsin Law Review 1135. Copyright © 1985 by The Board of Regents of the University of Wisconsin System. Reprinted by permission of the Wisconsin Law Review.

————, Foreword: The Meanings of Rights of Children, 10 New Mexico Law Review 235 (1980). Copyright © The New Mexico Law Review. Reprinted by permission of Lee E. Teitelbaum.

————, Juvenile Status Offenders, 3 Encyclopedia of Crime & Justice 983 (Sanford Kadish ed., 1983). Copyright © 1983 Encyclopedia of Crime and Justice. Reprinted by permission.

————, Status Offenses and Status Offenders, in A Century of Juvenile Justice 158 (Margaret Rosenheim et al. eds., 2002). Copyright © The University of Chicago Press 2002. Reprinted by permission.

Teitelbaum, Lee E. & James W. Ellis, The Liberty Interest of Children: Due Process Rights and Their Application, 12 Family Law Quarterly 153 (1978). Reprinted with permission from the ABA Journal.

Weinberger, Daniel R. et al., The Adolescent Brain: A Work in Progress (June 2005), available at http://www.teenpregnancy.org/resources/reading/pdf/BRAIN.pdf. Reprinted by permission.

Weisbrod, Carol, Communal Groups and the Larger Society: Legal Dilemmas in Communal Societies 1, 5-6, 9-11 (1992).

CHILDREN, PARENTS, AND THE LAW

PARENT, CHILD, AND STATE: RIGHTS AND INTERESTS

I

Providing and Controlling Children's Education

1

Defining the rights of children and parents and the authority of the state regarding those rights presents complexities not easily sorted out by organizations and constructs that serve well in analyses of other areas of human rights. Most traditional analysis of rights takes as its primary concern the moral and legal positions of individuals, standing apart from and in some sense opposed to all others. However, applying this approach is difficult if we cannot identify a single individual rights holder, as in the case of parents and children. If we look at the position of children, we cannot proceed far without implicating the rights of parents. If, on the other hand, we begin with the rights of parents, we know that analyzing those rights will also require consideration of the rights of children.

The various roles of government entities in connection with rights claims by children and parents add complications. On the one hand, state regulation is often intended to support the authority of parents over their children. This is true, for example, of laws granting parents the right to custody and control of their children and, to a less clear extent, laws that require notification of parents when a minor seeks an abortion. In other settings, state authority supports the interests of parents against others. Statutes restricting access by minors to sexually explicit or violent material or allowing parents to home school their children are justified this way.

On the other hand, state regulations often restrict parental choices. Compulsory education laws and child abuse and neglect laws are among the most familiar examples of such regulations. These laws can be explained on the ground that they protect the interests of children. Certainly, however, their enforcement does not depend on actual desires of children and thus must be understood as reflecting either the public's independent interest in child care and development or an interest otherwise imputed to children, but not as a "right" in the sense of an autonomy claim.

The first part of this chapter considers one meaning of the rights of children: to be provided for and taken care of, particularly the right to be provided with an education. The second part of the chapter focuses on parents' rights, examining situations in which courts and legislatures are required to resolve conflicts between parents and the state regarding children's education.

A.   CHILDREN'S RIGHT TO AN EDUCATION

Lee E. Teitelbaum, *Foreword: The Meanings of Rights of Children*

10 New Mexico L. Rev. 235, 236-242 (1980)

One theory of the rights of children may be called "integrative." . . .

Take, as an example of this theory, the notion of children's rights in connection with education. The United Nations Declaration of the Rights of the Child proclaims the following:

> Principle 7. The child is entitled to receive education, which shall be free and compulsory, at least in the elementary stages. He shall be given an education which will promote his general culture, and enable him, on the basis of equal opportunity, to develop his abilities, his individual judgment and his sense of moral and social responsibility, and to become a useful member of society.

This description of the child's right closely resembles the positions taken by educators who consider themselves advocates for their students and by mental health professionals and social workers in declaring rights to a good home. It may serve, accordingly, as a paradigm of the integrative approach to the rights of children.

The most apparent aspect of this notion of rights is its association with a duty on the part of others—specifically, a duty on the state to provide education for a certain period and of a certain quality. . . .

The United Nations' formulation of the child's right does not end, however, with creation of a governmental duty to provide education. It presumes not only that obligation, but also a corresponding duty on the child to accept the benefits of that right. Education is to be "compulsory" quite as much as it is to be "free," and both elements are part of the definition of the right itself.

The theory of "rights" embodied in the United Nations Declaration evidently is founded on a conviction about the needs of children, rather than their desires. In this respect, the Declaration further typifies the views held by many educators, social workers, mental health professionals, and even juvenile court judges in advocating children's rights, a fact that further confirms its paradigmatic value. For example, a child is entitled to psychiatric services because he needs them, not because he wants them. Social workers make their services available to and intervene on behalf of neglected children because, without that intervention, the children will not develop properly. It is not supposed that the client has a right not to become a ward of the court when that is necessary, however much he may want to stay at home. In the same tradition, the juvenile court has claimed to protect the child's "right . . . to custody." Judges acted when parents failed to exercise appropriate supervision over their young and did so to supply the latter's right to care and control, notwithstanding the fact that, in the usual case, the child's most urgent desire was to escape supervision.

A theory of rights that emphasizes needs rather than choice places its primary emphasis upon the integration of persons into society. That rights can serve an integrative function is revealed by a recent comparison of western and socialist legal theory which suggests that while "bourgeois" rights are "entitlements" conveying a measure of personal autonomy, socialist rights are considered declarations of public standards for desirable goals and behavior. "Socialist rights are thus not weapons (which would imply potential hostility between the individual and society) but rather like railroad tickets: they entitle the holder only to travel in the indicated direction." . . .

It should be obvious that the rights urged by social workers, mental health professionals, and the traditional juvenile court share this integrative purpose. . . .

[T]he integrative theory of rights . . . received its most comprehensive expression . . . throughout the Progressive era. . . .

. . . Educators saw clearly, for example, that education could not safely be left to parents, many of whom were themselves uneducated and most of whom were lacking in knowledge of how education should be conducted. Accordingly, the function of education was assumed by the state in order that children might progress beyond their parents' condition. Public schools would do "systematically and in a large, intelligent, and competent way what for various reasons can be done in most households only in a comparatively meager and haphazard manner." . . .[1]

. . . Public involvement with respect to education and socialization was viewed as a governmental duty and, correlatively, it came to be said that the child possessed a "right" to those things that the government undertook to provide. . . .

LESLIE JOAN HARRIS, *CHILD SUPPORT FOR POST-SECONDARY EDUCATION: EMPIRICAL AND HISTORICAL PERSPECTIVES*

29 J. Am. Acad. Matrim. Law. 299, 308–313 (2017)

. . . As early as 1642, the Massachusetts Bay Colony had laws requiring parents to teach their children religion, reading, and an "honest calling."[2] This was a minimal requirement, though, since through the early nineteenth century children were mostly seen as small adults whose labor was economically valuable. As a more romantic view of children as innocents to be protected developed, middle and upper-class parents increasingly kept their children out of the work force and

---

1. John Dewey, The School and Society 47-53, quoted in 2 Children and Youth in America 1119 (Robert Bremner ed., 1971).
2. Michael S. Katz, A History of Compulsory Education Laws 11-12 (1976). Massachusetts law later provided that communities of 50 households or more were to provide a teacher to instruct children in reading and writing, and communities of 100 households or more were to establish a grammar school. However, these laws were not effectively enforced. *Id.*

sent them to school, although working-class parents still needed their children's labor to support the family. Throughout the first half of the nineteenth century, the duty to educate a child remained firmly with the child's parent or master, and much education occurred outside schools.[3] Public schools and compulsory attendance laws gained ground from 1820 into the 1860s as a response to the growth of cities and immigration, as a means to stamp out crime and socialize the new residents. Massachusetts enacted the first compulsory attendance law in 1852, requiring parents to send children to public school for at least twelve weeks, but it was not enforced. By 1890 most states had compulsory attendance laws, but they were still not regularly enforced. . . .[4]

Over the first thirty years of the twentieth century, local school districts developed the administrative machinery to enforce school attendance laws, and child labor laws, which supported the school laws, were enacted and enforced. . . .[5]

While most children still did not attend school beyond the eighth grade at this time, the next battleground over children's education had already begun to emerge in the 1890s as high schools were developed to bridge between grammar school and the university. At first high schools were only for the elite. In 1922, sociologist and educator George Counts wrote that while public high schools existed, only the children of the professional and merchant classes were likely to attend and graduate, while other children were expected to go to work. . . .

The number of young people with high school degrees grew fivefold between 1910 and 1940, partly because of increasing demand for educated workers and lower demand for agricultural labor, and partly because of changes in educational and child labor laws. However, as late as 1976 one state, Mississippi, still did not have a compulsory education law, and only five states required compulsory school through age eighteen, although the general social expectation by then was that teens would complete high school.[6]

1. Is There a Constitutional Right to Education?

The extent of the obligation of the public to provide schools for all children has been and continues to be contested. The next case and the notes after it involve claims that states have a constitutional obligation to provide children with an education. As in other areas of constitutional decision making, the level of review applied to a state education law or practice is important.

---

3. Katz at 13.

4. Katz at 18-19.

5. At first the child labor laws were not enforced much, but by the 1920s they were. Adriana Lleras-Muney, Were Compulsory Attendance and Child Labor Laws Effective? An Analysis from 1915 to 1939, 45 J.L. & Econ. 401, 403 (2002).

6. Katz at 8. However, in 1974 only about 75 percent of all young people graduated from high school in the United States. *Id.* at 27.

SAN ANTONIO INDEPENDENT SCHOOL DISTRICT V. RODRIGUEZ

411 U.S. 1 (1972)

Mr. Justice POWELL delivered the opinion of the Court. This suit attacking the Texas system of financing public education was initiated by Mexican-American parents whose children attend the elementary and secondary schools in the Edgewood Independent School District, an urban school district in San Antonio, Texas. They brought a class action on behalf of schoolchildren throughout the State who are members of minority groups or who are poor and reside in school districts having a low property tax base. . . . The complaint was filed in the summer of 1968 and a three-judge court was impaneled in January 1969. In December 1971 the panel rendered its judgment in a per curiam opinion holding the Texas school finance system unconstitutional under the Equal Protection Clause of the Fourteenth Amendment. The State appealed, and we noted probable jurisdiction to consider the far-reaching constitutional questions presented. For the reasons stated in this opinion, we reverse the decision of the District Court. . . .

. . . Early in its history, Texas adopted a dual approach to the financing of its schools, relying on mutual participation by the local school districts and the State. As early as 1883, the state constitution was amended to provide for the creation of local school districts empowered to levy ad valorem taxes with the consent of local taxpayers for the 'erection . . . of school buildings' and for the 'further maintenance of public free schools.' Such local funds as were raised were supplemented by funds distributed to each district from the State's Permanent and Available School Funds. . . .

Recognizing the need for increased state funding to help offset disparities in local spending and to meet Texas' changing educational requirements, the state legislature in the late 1940s undertook a thorough evaluation of public education with an eye toward major reform. In 1947, an 18-member committee, composed of educators and legislators, was appointed to explore alternative systems in other States and to propose a funding scheme that would guarantee a minimum or basic educational offering to each child and that would help overcome interdistrict disparities in taxable resources. The Committee's efforts led to the passage of the Gilmer-Aikin bills, named for the Committee's co-chairmen, establishing the Texas Minimum Foundation School Program. Today, this Program accounts for approximately half of the total educational expenditures in Texas. . . .

The school district in which appellees reside, the Edgewood Independent School District, has been compared throughout this litigation with the Alamo Heights Independent School District. This comparison between the least and most affluent districts in the San Antonio area serves to illustrate the manner in which the dual system of finance operates and to indicate the extent to which substantial disparities exist despite the State's impressive progress in recent years. Edgewood is one of seven public school districts in the metropolitan area. Approximately 22,000 students are enrolled in its 25 elementary and secondary schools. The district is situated in the core-city sector of San Antonio in a residential neighborhood that has little commercial or industrial property. The residents are predominantly of Mexican-American descent: approximately 90% of the student population is Mexican-American and over 6% is Negro. The average assessed property value per pupil is $ 5,960 — the lowest in the metropolitan area — and the median family income ($4,686) is also the lowest. At an equalized tax rate of $1.05 per $100 of assessed property — the highest in the metropolitan area — the district contributed $26 to the education of each child for the 1967-1968 school years above its Local Fund Assignment for the Minimum Foundation Program. The Foundation Program contributed $222 per pupil for a state-local total of $248. Federal funds added another $108 for a total of $356 per pupil.

Alamo Heights is the most affluent school district in San Antonio. Its six schools, housing approximately 5,000 students, are situated in a residential community quite unlike the Edgewood District. The school population is predominantly 'Anglo,' having only 18% Mexican-Americans and less than 1% Negroes. The assessed property value per pupil exceeds $49,000, and the median family income is $8,001. In 1967–1968 the local tax rate of $.85 per $100 of valuation yielded $333 per pupil over and above its contribution to the Foundation Program. Coupled with the $225 provided from that Program, the district was able to supply $558 per student. Supplemented by a $36 per-pupil grant from federal sources, Alamo Heights spent $594 per pupil.. . . .

. . . [S]ubstantial interdistrict disparities in school expenditures found by the District Court to prevail in San Antonio and in varying degrees throughout the State still exist. And it was these disparities, largely attributable to differences in the amounts of money collected through local property taxation, that led the District Court to conclude that Texas' dual system of public school financing violated the Equal Protection Clause. . . .

Texas virtually concedes that its historically rooted dual system of financing education could not withstand the strict judicial scrutiny that this Court has found appropriate in reviewing legislative judgments that interfere with fundamental constitutional rights or that involve suspect classifications. . . .

This, then, establishes the framework for our analysis. We must decide, first, whether the Texas system of financing public education operates to the disadvantage of some suspect class or impinges upon a fundamental right explicitly or implicitly protected by the Constitution, thereby requiring strict judicial scrutiny. If so, the judgment of the District Court should be affirmed. If not, the Texas scheme must still be examined to determine whether it rationally furthers some legitimate, articulated state purpose and therefore does not constitute an invidious discrimination in violation of the Equal Protection Clause of the Fourteenth Amendment.

II

[The District Court concluded that strict scrutiny was required because the local property tax system discriminated on the basis of wealth and adversely affected what the court characterized as the fundamental right to education.]

We are unable to agree that this case, which in significant aspects is sui generis, may be so neatly fitted into the conventional mosaic of constitutional analysis under the Equal Protection Clause. Indeed, for the several reasons that follow, we find neither the suspect-classification nor the fundamental-interest analysis persuasive.

[The court rejected the conclusion that wealth is a suspect basis of classification, requiring strict or heightened scrutiny.]

We thus conclude that the Texas system does not operate to the peculiar disadvantage of any suspect class. But in recognition of the fact that this Court has never heretofore held that wealth discrimination alone provides an adequate basis for invoking strict scrutiny, appellees have not relied solely on this contention. They also assert that the State's system impermissibly interferes with the exercise of a 'fundamental' right and that accordingly the prior decisions of this Court require the application of the strict standard of judicial review. It is this question—whether education is a fundamental right, in the sense that it is among the rights and liberties protected by the Constitution—which has so consumed the attention of courts and commentators in recent years.

B

In Brown v. Board of Education, 347 U.S. 483 (1954), a unanimous Court recognized that 'education is perhaps the most important function of state and local governments.' What was said there in the context of racial discrimination has lost none of its vitality with the passage of time:

> 'Compulsory school attendance laws and the great expenditures for education both demonstrate our recognition of the importance of education to our democratic society. It is required in the performance of our most basic public responsibilities, even service in the armed forces. It is the very foundation of good citizenship. Today it is a principal instrument in awakening the child to cultural values, in preparing him for later professional training, and in helping him to adjust normally to his environment. In these days, it is doubtful that any child may reasonably be expected to succeed in life if he is denied the opportunity of an education. Such an opportunity, where the state has undertaken to provide it, is a right which must be made available to all on equal terms.'

This theme, expressing an abiding respect for the vital role of education in a free society, may be found in numerous opinions of Justices of this Court writing both before and after Brown was decided.

Nothing this Court holds today in any way detracts from our historic dedication to public education. We are in complete agreement with the conclusion of the three-judge panel below that 'the grave significance of education both to the individual and to our society' cannot be doubted. But the importance of a service performed by the State does not determine whether it must be regarded as fundamental for purposes of examination under the Equal Protection Clause. Mr. Justice Harlan, dissenting from the Court's application of strict scrutiny to a law impinging upon the right of interstate travel, admonished that '(v)irtually every state statute affects important rights.' Shapiro v. Thompson, 394 U.S., at 655, 661. In his view, if the degree of judicial scrutiny of state legislation fluctuated, depending on a majority's view of the importance of the interest affected, we would have gone "far toward making this Court a 'super-legislature.'" We would, indeed, then be assuming a legislative role and one for which the Court lacks both authority and competence. But Mr. Justice Stewart's response in Shapiro to Mr. Justice Harlan's concern correctly articulates the limits of the fundamental-rights rationale employed in the Court's equal protection decisions:

'The Court today does not 'pick out particular human activities, characterize them as 'fundamental,' and give them added protection. . . .' To the contrary, the Court simply recognizes, as it must, an established constitutional right, and gives to that right no less protection than the Constitution itself demands.'

. . . It is not the province of this Court to create substantive constitutional rights in the name of guaranteeing equal protection of the laws. Thus, the key to discovering whether education is 'fundamental' is not to be found in comparisons of the relative societal significance of education as opposed to subsistence or housing. Nor is it to be found by weighing whether education is as important as the right to travel. Rather, the answer lies in assessing whether there is a right to education explicitly or implicitly guaranteed by the Constitution.

Education, of course, is not among the rights afforded explicit protection under our Federal Constitution. Nor do we find any basis for saying it is implicitly so protected. . . . It is appellees' contention, however, that education is distinguishable from other services and benefits provided by the State because it bears a peculiarly close relationship to other rights and liberties accorded protection under the Constitution. Specifically, they insist that education is itself a fundamental personal right because it is essential to the effective exercise of First Amendment freedoms and to intelligent utilization of the right to vote. In asserting a nexus between speech and education, appellees urge that the right to speak is meaningless unless the speaker is capable of articulating his thoughts intelligently and persuasively. The 'marketplace of ideas' is an empty forum for those lacking basic communicative tools. Likewise, they argue that the corollary right to receive information becomes little more than a hollow privilege when the recipient has not been taught to read, assimilate, and utilize available knowledge.

A similar line of reasoning is pursued with respect to the right to vote. Exercise of the franchise, it is contended, cannot be divorced from the educational foundation of the voter. The electoral process, if reality is to conform to the democratic ideal, depends on an informed electorate: a voter cannot cast his ballot intelligently unless his reading skills and thought processes have been adequately developed.

We need not dispute any of these propositions. The Court has long afforded zealous protection against unjustifiable governmental interference with the individual's rights to speak and to vote. Yet we have never presumed to possess either the ability or the authority to guarantee to the citizenry the most effective speech or the most informed electoral choice. That these may be desirable goals of a system of freedom of expression and of a representative form of government is not to be doubted. These are indeed goals to be pursued by a people whose thoughts and beliefs are freed from governmental interference. But they are not values to be implemented by judicial instruction into otherwise legitimate state activities.

Even if it were conceded that some identifiable quantum of education is a constitutionally protected prerequisite to the meaningful exercise of either right, we have no indication that the present levels of educational expenditures in Texas provide an education that falls short. Whatever merit appellees' argument might have if a State's financing system occasioned an absolute denial of educational opportunities to any of its children, that argument provides no basis for finding an interference with fundamental rights where only relative differences in spending levels are involved and where—as is true in the present case—no charge fairly could be made that the system fails to provide each child with an opportunity to acquire the basic minimal skills necessary for the enjoyment of the rights of speech and of full participation in the political process.

Furthermore, the logical limitations on appellees' nexus theory are difficult to perceive. How, for instance, is education to be distinguished from the significant personal interests in the basics of decent food and shelter? . . .

. . . The present case, in another basic sense, is significantly different from any of the cases in which the Court has applied strict scrutiny to state or federal legislation touching upon constitutionally protected rights. Each of our prior cases involved legislation which 'deprived,' 'infringed,' or 'interfered' with the free exercise of some such fundamental personal right or liberty. A critical distinction between those cases and the one now before us lies in what Texas is endeavoring to do with respect to education. Mr. Justice Brennan, writing for the Court in Katzenbach v. Morgan, 384 U.S. 641 (1966), expresses well the salient point:

> 'This is not a complaint that Congress . . . has unconstitutionally denied or diluted anyone's right to vote but rather that Congress violated the Constitution by not extending the relief effected (to others similarly situated). . . .
>
> '(The federal law in question) does not restrict or deny the franchise but in effect extends the franchise to persons who otherwise would be denied it by state law. . . . We need only decide whether the challenged limitation on the relief effected . . . was permissible. In deciding that question, the principle that calls for the closest scrutiny of distinctions in laws denying fundamental rights. . . is inapplicable; for the distinction challenged by appellees is presented only as a limitation on a reform measure aimed at eliminating an existing barrier to the exercise of the franchise. Rather, in deciding the constitutional propriety of the limitations in such a reform measure we are guided by the familiar principles that a 'statute is not invalid under the Constitution because it might have gone farther than it did,' . . . that a legislature need not 'strike at all evils at the same time,' . . . and that 'reform may take one step at a time, addressing itself to the phase of the problem which seems most acute to the legislative mind. . . . '

The Texas system of school financing is not unlike the federal legislation involved in *Katzenbach* in this regard. Every step leading to the establishment of the system Texas utilizes today—including the decisions permitting localities to tax and expend locally, and creating and continuously expanding the state aid—was implemented in an effort to extend public education and to improve its quality. Of course, every reform that benefits some more than others may be criticized for what it fails to accomplish. But we think it plain that, in substance, the thrust of the Texas system is affirmative and reformatory and, therefore, should be scrutinized under judicial principles sensitive to the nature of the State's efforts and to the rights reserved to the States under the Constitution.

C

It should be clear, for the reasons stated above and in accord with the prior decisions of this Court, that this is not a case in which the challenged state action must be subjected to the searching judicial scrutiny reserved for laws that create suspect classifications or impinge upon constitutionally protected rights.

We need not rest our decision, however, solely on the inappropriateness of the strict-scrutiny test. A century of Supreme Court adjudication under the Equal Protection Clause affirmatively supports the application of the traditional standard of review, which requires only that the State's system be shown to bear some rational relationship to legitimate state purposes. This case represents far more than a challenge to the manner in which Texas provides for the education of its children. We have here nothing less than a direct attack on the way in which Texas has chosen to raise and disburse state and local tax revenues. We are asked to condemn the State's judgment in conferring on political subdivisions the power to tax local property to supply revenues for local interests. In so doing, appellees would have the Court intrude in an area in which it has traditionally deferred to state legislatures. . . .

In addition to matters of fiscal policy, this case also involves the most persistent and difficult questions of educational policy, another area in which this Court's lack of specialized knowledge and experience counsels against premature interference with the informed judgments made at the state and local levels. Education, perhaps even more than welfare assistance, presents a myriad of 'intractable economic, social, and even philosophical problems.' The very complexity of the problems of financing and managing a statewide public school system suggests that 'there will be more than one constitutionally permissible method of solving them,' and that, within the limits of rationality, 'the legislature's efforts to tackle the problems' should be entitled to respect.' On even the most basic questions in this area the scholars and educational experts are divided. Indeed, one of the major sources of controversy concerns the extent to which there is a demonstrable correlation between educational expenditures and the quality of education—an assumed correlation underlying virtually every legal conclusion drawn by the District Court in this case. Related to the questioned relationship between cost and quality is the equally unsettled controversy as to the proper goals of a system of public education. And the question regarding the most effective relationship between state boards of education and local school boards, in terms of their respective responsibilities and degrees of control, is now undergoing searching re-examination. The ultimate wisdom as to these and related problems of education is not likely to be divined for all time even by the scholars who now so earnestly debate the issues. In such circumstances, the judiciary is well advised to refrain from imposing on the States inflexible constitutional restraints that could circumscribe or handicap the continued research and experimentation so vital to finding even partial solutions to educational problems and to keeping abreast of ever-changing conditions. . . .

The foregoing considerations buttress our conclusion that Texas' system of public school finance is an inappropriate candidate for strict judicial scrutiny. These same considerations are relevant to the determination whether that system, with its conceded imperfections, nevertheless bears some rational relationship to a legitimate state purpose. It is to this question that we next turn our attention.

III

. . . In its reliance on state as well as local resources, the Texas system is comparable to the systems employed in virtually every other State. . . .

The 'foundation grant' theory upon which Texas legislators and educators based the Gilmer-Aikin bills was a product of the pioneering work of two New York educational reformers in the 1920s, George D. Strayer and Robert M. Haig. Their efforts were devoted to establishing a means of guaranteeing a minimum statewide educational program without sacrificing the vital element of local participation. . . .

The Texas system of school finance is responsive to these two forces. While assuring a basis education for every child in the State, it permits and encourages a large measure of participation in and control of each district's schools at the local level. In an era that has witnessed a consistent trend toward centralization of the functions of government, local sharing of responsibility for public education has survived. . . .

The persistence of attachment to government at the lowest level where education is concerned reflects the depth of commitment of its supporters. In part, local control means . . . the freedom to devote more money to the education of one's children. Equally important, however, is the opportunity it offers for participation in the decision making process that determines how those local tax dollars will be spent. Each locality is free to tailor local programs to local needs. Pluralism also affords some opportunity for experimentation, innovation, and a healthy competition for educational excellence. . . .

Appellees do not question the propriety of Texas' dedication to local control of education. To the contrary, they attack the school-financing system precisely because, in their view, it does not provide the same level of local control and fiscal flexibility in all districts. Appellees suggest that local control could be preserved and promoted under other financing systems that resulted in more equality in education expenditures. While it is no doubt true that reliance on local property taxation for school revenues provides less freedom of choice with respect to expenditures for some districts than for others, the existence of 'some inequality' in the manner in which the State's rationale is achieved is not alone a sufficient basis for striking down the entire system. It may not be condemned simply because it imperfectly effectuates the State's goals. Nor must the financing system fail because, as appellees suggest, other methods of satisfying the State's interest, which occasion 'less drastic' disparities in expenditures, might be conceived. Only where state action impinges on the exercise of fundamental constitutional rights or liberties must it be found to have chosen the least restrictive alternative. . . .

In sum, to the extent that the Texas system of school financing results in unequal expenditures between children who happen to reside in different districts, we cannot say that such disparities are the product of a system that is so irrational as to be invidiously discriminatory. . . . One also must remember that the system here challenged is not peculiar to Texas or to any other State. In its essential characteristics, the Texas plan for financing public education reflects what many educators for a half century have thought was an enlightened approach to a problem for which there is no perfect solution. We are unwilling to assume for ourselves a level of wisdom superior to that of legislators, scholars, and educational authorities in 50 States, especially where the alternatives proposed are only recently conceived and nowhere yet tested. The constitutional standard under the Equal Protection Clause is whether the challenged state action rationally furthers a legitimate state purpose or interest. We hold that the Texas plan abundantly satisfies this standard. . . .

(The concurring opinion of Mr. Justice STEWART and the dissenting opinions of Mr. Justice BRENNAN, Mr. Justice WHITE, and Mr. Justice MARSHALL are omitted.)

NOTES AND QUESTIONS

1. What would it mean to treat primary and secondary education as a fundamental right? Would it mean that courts would decide how much state money must be spent on education? Or what educational programs should be used in public schools?

The Court suggests that if education were a fundamental right requiring heightened scrutiny, the same would have to be true for the rights to food and shelter. Is this true?

2. The United States is the only country that has never ratified the UN Convention on the Rights of the Child. One of the reasons is that the Convention requires adopting countries to provide many social and economic rights, the kind of rights that Professor Teitelbaum describes as "integrative." If the United States were bound by treaty to provide such rights, it would affect the obligations of governments at all levels. The American constitution has generally been interpreted as protecting only individual rights to act autonomously and as restricting government actions that limit these rights, as the majority opinion in *Rodriguez* says.

3. The *Rodriguez* majority opinion concludes that the Texas system of school financing is rationally related to the goal of preserving local control over schools. What is the relationship between how schools are financed and what level of government controls schools? Why is local control of schools valued?

4. Even though the federal constitution does not protect the right to education, all state constitutions establish a right to a free public education, requiring the legislature to establish a system of public schools. "[S]ince *Rodriguez*, numerous state supreme court decisions and extensive statutory schemes have further defined, specified, and regulated this right. These cases dictate that education encompasses more than just the right to enter a school building; states must deliver a certain qualitative level of education therein." Derek Black, Unlocking the Power of State Constitutions with Equal Protection: The First Step Toward Education as a Federally Protected Right, 51 Wm. & Mary L. Rev. 1343, 1398 (2010). In the years after *Rodriguez*, most state legislatures adopted formulas for funding public schools that require wealth-equalization among districts to some extent. Jeffrey S. Sutton, San Antonio Independent School District v. Rodriguez and Its Aftermath, 94 Va. L. Rev. 1963 (2008).

5. Nine years after *Rodriguez*, the Supreme Court held that a Texas law denying undocumented resident children the right to attend public elementary and high schools without paying tuition violated equal protection. Plyler v. Doe, 457 U.S. 202 (1982). Applying heightened scrutiny, the Court rejected the state's arguments that the law was sufficiently closely tied to the state goals of preserving limited state resources, protecting the state from an influx of undocumented immigrants, improving the quality of public schools, and channeling state resources to children likely to remain in the state as adults.

While some language in *Plyler* suggests that the reason for using heightened scrutiny is the importance of education, the Court made clear in a subsequent decision that education is not a fundamental right that triggers increased scrutiny. Kadrmas v. Dickinson Public Schools, 487 U.S. 450 (1988). *Kadrmas* involved an equal protection challenge to a North Dakota law that permitted some school districts to charge a fee for bus transportation. Parents challenged the fee, relying on *Plyler*. The court distinguished *Plyler* on the bases that the Texas law penalized children for their parents' illegal conduct, promoted the creation and perpetuation of a subclass of illiterates, and completely denied access to education to the affected children.

6. Instances of state laws and policies that violate *Plyler* are regularly reported. In 2012, the Eleventh Circuit held that an Alabama statute enacted a year earlier conflicted with *Plyler*. The statute required all students enrolling in public school to show their birth certificates, or, if a child did not have a certificate, requiring the parents to reveal the child's citizenship in a notarized statement, and requiring schools to generate annual reports about the citizenship and immigration status of children in the schools. Hispanic Interest Coalition of Alabama v. Governor, 691 F.3d 1236 (11th Cir. 2012). In 2015, the New York Times reported that 20 school districts in mostly suburban areas would be required to remove barriers to undocumented children's access to school, pursuant to an agreement with the state attorney general. Benjamin Mueller, New York Compels 20 School Districts to Lower Barriers to Immigrants, Feb. 18, 2015.

7. On undocumented minors' access to post-secondary education, *see* Kate M. Manuel, Unauthorized Aliens, Higher Education, In-State Tuition, and Financial Aid: Legal Analysis (Cong. Res. Serv., Jan. 11, 2016).

NOTE: EDUCATION FOR ENGLISH LANGUAGE LEARNERS

English language learners (ELLs) are students who participate in school programs to help them become proficient in English and to succeed in school. In 2015, 9.5 percent of public school students were ELLs, an estimated 4.8 million children. The percentage of public school students who were ELLs increased between 2004–2005 and 2014–2015 in all but 15 states. In eight states 10 percent or more of the students were ELLs. California had the highest percentage of Ells, 21,0 percent. The other states were Alaska, Colorado, Kansas, Illinois, Nevada, New Mexico, Texas, and Washington. National Center for Education Statistics, https://nces.ed.gov/fastfacts/display.asp?id=96 (April 17, 2019).

The Supreme Court held in Lau v. Nichols, 414 U.S. 563 (1974), that Title VI of the Civil Rights Act of 1964 protects the rights of English language learners in public schools, applying regulations promulgated by the Department of Health, Education and Welfare in 1970. In *Lau* the court held that San Francisco violated Title VI when it provided Chinese-speaking students with the very same educational program provided to English-speaking students. The Court said, "There is no equality of treatment merely by providing students with the same facilities, textbooks, teachers and curriculum; for students who do not understand English are effectively foreclosed from any meaningful education." 414 U.S. at 566.

The next year, Congress codified this holding in the Equal Educational Opportunities Act of 1974, 20 U.S.C. § 1703(f) (EEOA), which requires states "to take appropriate action to overcome language barriers that impeded equal participation by its students in its instructional programs." Much of the litigation focused on claims that funding for English language learners was inadequate. However, the Supreme Court ruled in Horne v. Flores, 557 U.S. 433 (2009), that the EEOA does not require any particular level of funding because the law's focus "is on the quality of educational programming and services provided to students, not the amount of money spent on them." 557 U.S. at 466.

The Bush-era No Child Left Behind Act (NCLB), 20 U.S.C. §§ 6301-7941, required states to adopt standardized tests to measure student achievement and required states to demonstrate yearly progress as measured by students' performance on these tests. ELLs were included in the system, and the act made grants to schools to help students with limited command of English meet the achievement standards. In 2015 Congress repealed the NCLB and replaced it with the Every Child Succeeds Act (ESSA), 20 U.S.C. § 6301 et seq. ESSA continues to require that states maintain academic standards and measure students' achievement, but it repeals the specifics of NCLB and returns discretion and control to the states, including how to address the needs of ELLs. Ana A. Núñez Cárdenas, Note, Every English Learner Succeeds: The Need for Uniform Entry and Exit Requirements, 83 Brook. L. Rev. 755 (2018). On the changes from NCLB to ESSA generally, *see* Derek W. Black, Abandoning the Federal Role in Education: The Every Student Succeeds Act, 105 Calif. L. Rev. 1309 (2017); Michael Heise, From No Child Left Behind to Every Student Succeeds: Back to a Future for Education Federalism, 117 Col. L. Rev. 1859 (2017).

The most important and long-standing dispute about educating ELLs is whether schools should teach subjects other than English in a student's native language, supplemented by instruction in English as a second language (ESL), rather than teaching mostly in English with students pulled out for ESL classes as needed. Professor Martha Minow describes the dilemma in the following way:

> The contrast between [ESL] alone and bilingual-bicultural instruction illustrates a difficult choice between assimilation and preservation of group differences. It is especially difficult because it is also bound up with confusion about what constitutes equal opportunity. ESL proposes short-term segregation during part of the school day and long-term integration, abandoning minority identity within the school context. Its critics argue that the program reconfirms the association of difference with inferiority by refusing to recognize the positive experiences of minority difference and by failing to instruct either minority or majority children in the minority language and culture. Bilingual-bicultural programs, in attempting to meet this criticism, encounter the other side of the dilemma: by reinforcing minority difference and prolonging separation, such programs risk reconfirming the identification of difference with alien and inferior status. They also risk failing to prepare their students for a society in which mastery of English language and comfort with dominant American culture are made preconditions for success.

Martha Minow, Making All the Difference: Inclusion, Exclusion, and American Law 34 (1990).

The Third Circuit addressed a conflict over ELL teaching methodology in Issa v. School District of Lancaster, 847 F.3d 121 (3d Cir. 2017), one of the few cases interpreting the substantive requirements of the EEOA. Students who had immigrated to the United States in their late teens and who had very limited or no literacy in any language challenged a school district's requirement that immigrant students older than 17 who needed English language instruction attend a school offering an accelerated curriculum in which almost all of the classes were taught in English, with the exception of one 80-minute ESL course per day. The students could not understand much of what was going on in class and wanted to enroll in another ELL program in the district that provided much more intensive ESL instruction. The court affirmed the ruling in favor of the plaintiffs, agreeing that the district's program did not satisfy statutory requirements because it was not "informed by an educational theory recognized as sound by some experts in the field," (847 F.3d at 135) and "failed to produce results indicating that language barriers are actually being overcome" (847 F.3d at 137). Further, the court found that the plaintiff's lost educational opportunities stemmed from the plaintiffs' national origin. (847 F.3d at 140).

On state approaches to teaching ELLs and the impact of the English-only movement, *see* Matthew P. O'Sullivan, Laboratories for Inequality: State Experimentation and Educational Access for English-Language Learners, 64 Duke L.J. 671 (2015); Rachel F. Moran, Equal Liberties and English Language Learners: The Special Case of Structured Immersion Initiatives, 54 How. L.J. 397 (2011).

2. *Statutory Rights to Education: The Example of Children with Disabilities*

A second group of students traditionally denied the benefits of public schools is children with disabilities, who traditionally were excluded entirely or received only caretaking services from public schools.

ENDREW F. v. DOUGLAS COUNTY SCHOOL DISTRICT RE–1

137 S. Ct. 988 (2017)

Chief Justice ROBERTS delivered the opinion of the Court. . . . The Individuals with Disabilities Education Act (IDEA or Act) offers States federal funds to assist in educating children with disabilities. In exchange for the funds, a State pledges to comply with a number of statutory conditions. Among them, the State must provide a free appropriate public education—a FAPE, for short—to all eligible children.

A FAPE, as the Act defines it, includes both "special education" and "related services." "Special education" is "specially designed instruction . . . to meet the unique needs of a child with a disability"; "related services" are the support services "required to assist a child . . . to benefit from" that instruction. A State covered by the IDEA must provide a disabled child with such special education and related services "in conformity with the [child's] individualized education program," or IEP.

The IEP is "the centerpiece of the statute's education delivery system for disabled children." A comprehensive plan prepared by a child's "IEP Team" (which includes teachers, school officials, and the child's parents), an IEP must be drafted in compliance with a detailed set of procedures. These procedures emphasize collaboration among parents and educators and require careful consideration of the child's individual circumstances. The IEP is the means by which special education and related services are "tailored to the unique needs" of a particular child.

The IDEA requires that every IEP include "a statement of the child's present levels of academic achievement and functional performance," describe "how the child's disability affects the child's involvement and progress in the general education curriculum," and set out "measurable annual goals, including academic and functional goals," along with a "description of how the child's progress toward meeting" those goals will be gauged. The IEP must also describe the "special education and related services . . . that will be provided" so that the child may "advance appropriately toward attaining the annual goals" and, when possible, "be involved in and make progress in the general education curriculum."

Parents and educators often agree about what a child's IEP should contain. But not always. When disagreement arises, parents may turn to dispute resolution procedures established by the IDEA. The parties may resolve their differences informally, through a "[p]reliminary meeting," or, somewhat more formally, through mediation. If these measures fail to produce accord, the parties may proceed to what the Act calls a "due process hearing" before a state or local educational agency. And at the conclusion of the administrative process, the losing party may seek redress in state or federal court.

B

This Court first addressed the FAPE requirement in [Board of Ed. v. Rowley, 458 U. S. 176 (1982)]. Plaintiff Amy Rowley was a first grader with impaired hearing. Her school district offered an IEP under which Amy would receive instruction in the regular classroom and spend time each week with a special tutor and a speech therapist. The district proposed that Amy's classroom teacher speak into a wireless transmitter and that Amy use an FM hearing aid designed to amplify her teacher's words; the district offered to supply both components of this system. But Amy's parents argued that the IEP should go further and provide a sign-language interpreter in all of her classes. Contending that the school district's refusal to furnish an interpreter denied Amy a FAPE, Amy's parents initiated administrative proceedings, then filed a lawsuit under the Act.

The District Court agreed that Amy had been denied a FAPE. The court acknowledged that Amy was making excellent progress in school: She was "perform[ing] better than the average child in her class" and "advancing easily from grade to grade." At the same time, Amy "under[stood] considerably less of what goes on in class than she could if she were not deaf." Concluding that "it has been left entirely to the courts and the hearings officers to give content to the requirement of an 'appropriate education,'" the District Court ruled that Amy's education was not "appropriate" unless it provided her "an opportunity to achieve [her] full potential commensurate with the opportunity provided to other children." . . .

In this Court, the parties advanced starkly different understandings of the FAPE requirement. Amy's parents defended the approach of the lower courts, arguing that the school district was required to provide instruction and services that would provide Amy an "equal educational opportunity" relative to children without disabilities. The school district, for its part, contended that the IDEA "did not create substantive individual rights"; the FAPE provision was instead merely aspirational.

Neither position carried the day. On the one hand, this Court rejected the view that the IDEA gives "courts *carte blanche* to impose upon the States whatever burden their various judgments indicate should be imposed." After all, the statutory phrase "free appropriate public education" was expressly defined in the Act, even if the definition "tend[ed] toward the cryptic rather than the comprehensive." This Court went on to reject the "equal opportunity" standard adopted by the lower courts, concluding that "free appropriate public education" was a phrase "too complex to be captured by the word 'equal' whether one is speaking of opportunities or services." The Court also viewed the standard as "entirely unworkable," apt to require "impossible measurements and comparisons" that courts were ill suited to make.

On the other hand, the Court also rejected the school district's argument that the FAPE requirement was actually no requirement at all. Instead, the Court carefully charted a middle path. Even though "Congress was rather sketchy in establishing substantive requirements" under the Act the Court nonetheless made clear that the Act guarantees a substantively adequate program of education to all eligible children. We explained that this requirement is satisfied, and a child has received a FAPE, if the child's IEP sets out an educational program that is "reasonably calculated to enable the child to receive educational benefits." For children receiving instruction in the regular classroom, this would generally require an IEP "reasonably calculated to enable the child to achieve passing marks and advance from grade to grade."

In view of Amy Rowley's excellent progress and the "substantial" suite of specialized instruction and services offered in her IEP, we concluded that her program satisfied the FAPE requirement. But we went no further. Instead, we expressly "confine[d] our analysis" to the facts of the case before us. Observing that the Act requires States to "educate a wide spectrum" of children with disabilities and that "the benefits obtainable by children at one end of the spectrum will differ dramatically from those obtainable by children at the other end," we declined "to establish any one test for determining the adequacy of educational benefits conferred upon all children covered by the Act."

C

Petitioner Endrew F. was diagnosed with autism at age two. Autism is a neurodevelopmental disorder generally marked by impaired social and communicative skills, "engagement in repetitive activities and stereotyped movements, resistance to environmental change or change in daily routines, and unusual responses to sensory experiences." A child with autism qualifies as a "[c]hild with a disability" under the IDEA, and Colorado (where Endrew resides) accepts IDEA funding. Endrew is therefore entitled to the benefits of the Act, including a FAPE provided by the State.

Endrew attended school in respondent Douglas County School District from preschool through fourth grade. Each year, his IEP Team drafted an IEP addressed to his educational and functional needs. By Endrew's fourth grade year, however, his parents had become dissatisfied with his progress. Although Endrew displayed a number of strengths—his teachers described him as a humorous child with a "sweet disposition" who "show[ed] concern[]" for friends"—he still "exhibited multiple behaviors that inhibited his ability to access learning in the classroom." Endrew would scream in class, climb over furniture and other students, and occasionally run away from school. He was afflicted by severe fears of commonplace things like flies, spills, and public restrooms. As Endrew's parents saw it, his academic and functional progress had essentially stalled: Endrew's IEPs largely carried over the same basic goals and objectives from one year to the next, indicating that he was failing to make meaningful progress toward his aims. His parents believed that only a thorough overhaul of the school district's approach to Endrew's behavioral problems could reverse the trend. But in April 2010, the school district presented Endrew's parents with a proposed fifth grade IEP that was, in their view, pretty much the same as his past ones. So his parents removed Endrew from public school and enrolled him at Firefly Autism House, a private school that specializes in educating children with autism.

Endrew did much better at Firefly. The school developed a "behavioral intervention plan" that identified Endrew's most problematic behaviors and set out particular strategies for addressing them. Firefly also added heft to Endrew's academic goals. Within months, Endrew's behavior improved significantly, permitting him to make a degree of academic progress that had eluded him in public school.

In November 2010, some six months after Endrew started classes at Firefly, his parents again met with representatives of the Douglas County School District. The district presented a new IEP. Endrew's parents considered the IEP no more adequate than the one proposed in April, and rejected it. They were particularly concerned that the stated plan for addressing Endrew's behavior did not differ meaningfully from the plan in his fourth grade IEP, despite the fact that his experience at Firefly suggested that he would benefit from a different approach.

In February 2012, Endrew's parents filed a complaint with the Colorado Department of Education seeking reimbursement for Endrew's tuition at Firefly. To qualify for such relief, they were required to show that the school district had not provided Endrew a FAPE in a timely manner prior to his enrollment at the private school. Endrew's parents contended that the final IEP proposed by the school district was not "reasonably calculated to enable [Endrew] to receive educational benefits" and that Endrew had therefore been denied a FAPE. An Administrative Law Judge (ALJ) disagreed and denied relief.

Endrew's parents sought review in Federal District Court. Giving "due weight" to the decision of the ALJ, the District Court affirmed. The court acknowledged that Endrew's performance under past IEPs "did not reveal immense educational growth." But it concluded that annual modifications to Endrew's IEP objectives were "sufficient to show a pattern of, at the least, minimal progress." Because Endrew's previous IEPs had enabled him to make this sort of progress, the court reasoned, his latest, similar IEP was reasonably calculated to do the same thing. In the court's view, that was all *Rowley* demanded.

   The Tenth Circuit affirmed. The Court of Appeals recited language from *Rowley* stating that the instruction and services furnished to children with disabilities must be calculated to confer "*some* educational benefit." The court noted that it had long interpreted this language to mean that a child's IEP is adequate as long as it is calculated to confer an "educational benefit [that is] merely . . . more than *de minimis.*" Applying this standard, the Tenth Circuit held that Endrew's IEP had been "reasonably calculated to enable [him] to make *some* progress." Accordingly, he had not been denied a FAPE.

   We granted certiorari.

II

A

   The Court in *Rowley* declined "to establish any one test for determining the adequacy of educational benefits conferred upon all children covered by the Act." The school district, however, contends that *Rowley* nonetheless established that "an IEP need not promise any particular *level* of benefit," so long as it is "'reasonably calculated' to provide *some* benefit, as opposed to *none.*"

   The district relies on several passages from *Rowley* to make its case. It points to our observation that "any substantive standard prescribing the level of education to be accorded" children with disabilities was "[n]oticeably absent from the language of the statute." The district also emphasizes the Court's statement that the Act requires States to provide access to instruction "sufficient to confer *some* educational benefit," reasoning that any benefit, however minimal, satisfies this mandate. Finally, the district urges that the Court conclusively adopted a "some educational benefit" standard when it wrote that "the intent of the Act was more to open the door of public education to handicapped children . . . than to guarantee any particular level of education."

   These statements in isolation do support the school district's argument. But the district makes too much of them. Our statement that the face of the IDEA imposed no explicit substantive standard must be evaluated alongside our statement that a substantive standard was "implicit in the Act." Similarly, we find little significance in the Court's language concerning the requirement that States provide instruction calculated to "confer some educational benefit." The Court had no need to say anything more particular, since the case before it involved a child whose progress plainly demonstrated that her IEP was designed to deliver more than adequate educational benefits. The Court's principal concern was to correct what it viewed as the surprising rulings below: that the IDEA effectively empowers judges to elaborate a federal common law of public education, and that a child performing *better* than most in her class had been denied a FAPE. The Court was not concerned with precisely articulating a governing standard for closer cases. And the statement that the Act did not "guarantee any particular level of education" simply reflects the unobjectionable proposition that the IDEA cannot and does not promise "any particular [educational] outcome." No law could do that—for any child.

   More important, the school district's reading of these isolated statements runs headlong into several points on which *Rowley* is crystal clear. For instance—just after saying that the Act requires instruction that is "sufficient to confer some educational benefit"—we noted that "[t]he determination of when handicapped children are receiving *sufficient* educational benefits . . . presents a . . . difficult problem." And then we expressly declined "to establish any one test for determining the *adequacy* of educational benefits" under the Act. It would not have been "difficult" for us to say when educational benefits are sufficient if we had just said that *any* educational benefit was enough. And it would have been strange to refuse to set out a test for the adequacy of educational benefits if we had just done exactly that. We cannot accept the school district's reading of *Rowley*.

B

While *Rowley* declined to articulate an overarching standard to evaluate the adequacy of the education provided under the Act, the decision and the statutory language point to a general approach: To meet its substantive obligation under the IDEA, a school must offer an IEP reasonably calculated to enable a child to make progress appropriate in light of the child's circumstances.

The "reasonably calculated" qualification reflects a recognition that crafting an appropriate program of education requires a prospective judgment by school officials. The Act contemplates that this fact-intensive exercise will be informed not only by the expertise of school officials, but also by the input of the child's parents or guardians. Any review of an IEP must appreciate that the question is whether the IEP is *reasonable*, not whether the court regards it as ideal.

The IEP must aim to enable the child to make progress. After all, the essential function of an IEP is to set out a plan for pursuing academic and functional advancement. This reflects the broad purpose of the IDEA, an "ambitious" piece of legislation enacted "in response to Congress' perception that a majority of handicapped children in the United States 'were either totally excluded from schools or [were] sitting idly in regular classrooms awaiting the time when they were old enough to drop out.'" A substantive standard not focused on student progress would do little to remedy the pervasive and tragic academic stagnation that prompted Congress to act.

That the progress contemplated by the IEP must be appropriate in light of the child's circumstances should come as no surprise. A focus on the particular child is at the core of the IDEA. The instruction offered must be "*specially* designed" to meet a child's "*unique* needs" through an "[*i*]*ndividualized* education program." An IEP is not a form document. It is constructed only after careful consideration of the child's present levels of achievement, disability, and potential for growth. As we observed in *Rowley*, the IDEA "requires participating States to educate a wide spectrum of handicapped children," and "the benefits obtainable by children at one end of the spectrum will differ dramatically from those obtainable by children at the other end, with infinite variations in between."

Rowley sheds light on what appropriate progress will look like in many cases. There, the Court recognized that the IDEA requires that children with disabilities receive education in the regular classroom "whenever possible." When this preference is met, "the system itself monitors the educational progress of the child." "Regular examinations are administered, grades are awarded, and yearly advancement to higher grade levels is permitted for those children who attain an adequate knowledge of the course material." Progress through this system is what our society generally means by an "education." And access to an "education" is what the IDEA promises. Accordingly, for a child fully integrated in the regular classroom, an IEP typically should, as *Rowley* put it, be "reasonably calculated to enable the child to achieve passing marks and advance from grade to grade."

This guidance is grounded in the statutory definition of a FAPE. One of the components of a FAPE is "special education," defined as "specially designed instruction . . . to meet the unique needs of a child with a disability." In determining what it means to "meet the unique needs" of a child with a disability, the provisions governing the IEP development process are a natural source of guidance: It is through the IEP that "[t]he 'free appropriate public education' required by the Act is tailored to the unique needs of" a particular child.

The IEP provisions reflect *Rowley*'s expectation that, for most children, a FAPE will involve integration in the regular classroom and individualized special education calculated to achieve advancement from grade to grade. Every IEP begins by describing a child's present level of achievement, including explaining "how the child's disability affects the child's involvement and progress in the general education curriculum." It then sets out "a statement of measurable annual goals . . . designed to . . . enable the child to be involved in and make progress in the general education curriculum," along with a description of specialized instruction and services that the child will receive. The instruction and services must likewise be provided with an eye toward "progress in the general education curriculum." Similar IEP requirements have been in place since the time the States began accepting funding under the IDEA.

The school district protests that these provisions impose only procedural requirements—a checklist of items the IEP must address—not a substantive standard enforceable in court. But the procedures are there for a reason, and their focus provides insight into what it means, for purposes of the FAPE definition, to "meet the unique needs" of a child with a disability. When a child is fully integrated in the regular classroom, as the Act prefers, what that typically means is providing a level of instruction reasonably calculated to permit advancement through the general curriculum.[7]

Rowley had no need to provide concrete guidance with respect to a child who is not fully integrated in the regular classroom and not able to achieve on grade level. That case concerned a young girl who was progressing smoothly through the regular curriculum. If that is not a reasonable prospect for a child, his IEP need not aim for grade-level advancement. But his educational program must be appropriately ambitious in light of his circumstances, just as advancement from grade to grade is appropriately ambitious for most children in the regular classroom. The goals may differ, but every child should have the chance to meet challenging objectives.

---

7. This guidance should not be interpreted as an inflexible rule. We declined to hold in *Rowley*, and do not hold today, that "every handicapped child who is advancing from grade to grade . . . is automatically receiving a [FAPE]."

Of course this describes a general standard, not a formula. But whatever else can be said about it, this standard is markedly more demanding than the "merely more than *de minimis*" test applied by the Tenth Circuit. It cannot be the case that the Act typically aims for grade-level advancement for children with disabilities who can be educated in the regular classroom, but is satisfied with barely more than *de minimis* progress for those who cannot.

When all is said and done, a student offered an educational program providing "merely more than *de minimis*" progress from year to year can hardly be said to have been offered an education at all. For children with disabilities, receiving instruction that aims so low would be tantamount to "sitting idly . . . awaiting the time when they were old enough to 'drop out.'" The IDEA demands more. It requires an educational program reasonably calculated to enable a child to make progress appropriate in light of the child's circumstances.

C

Endrew's parents argue that the Act goes even further. In their view, a FAPE is "an education that aims to provide a child with a disability opportunities to achieve academic success, attain self-sufficiency, and contribute to society that are substantially equal to the opportunities afforded children without disabilities."

This standard is strikingly similar to the one the lower courts adopted in *Rowley*, and it is virtually identical to the formulation advanced by Justice Blackmun in his separate writing in that case. ("[T]he question is whether Amy's program . . . offered her an opportunity to understand and participate in the class-room that was substantially equal to that given her non-handicapped classmates"). But the majority rejected any such standard in clear terms. ("The requirement that States provide 'equal' educational opportunities would . . . seem to present an entirely unworkable standard requiring impossible measurements and com-parisons"). Mindful that Congress (despite several intervening amendments to the IDEA) has not materially changed the statutory definition of a FAPE since *Rowley* was decided, we decline to interpret the FAPE provision in a manner so plainly at odds with the Court's analysis in that case.

D

We will not attempt to elaborate on what "appropriate" progress will look like from case to case. It is in the nature of the Act and the standard we adopt to resist such an effort: The adequacy of a given IEP turns on the unique circum-stances of the child for whom it was created. This absence of a bright-line rule, however, should not be mistaken for "an invitation to the courts to substitute their own notions of sound educational policy for those of the school authorities which they review."

At the same time, deference is based on the application of expertise and the exercise of judgment by school authorities. The Act vests these officials with responsibility for decisions of critical importance to the life of a disabled child. The nature of the IEP process, from the initial consultation through state admin-istrative proceedings, ensures that parents and school representatives will fully air their respective opinions on the degree of progress a child's IEP should pursue. By the time any dispute reaches court, school authorities will have had a complete opportunity to bring their expertise and judgment to bear on areas of disagreement. A reviewing court may fairly expect those authorities to be able to offer a cogent and responsive explanation for their decisions that shows the IEP is reasonably calculated to enable the child to make progress appropriate in light of his circumstances.

The judgment of the United States Court of Appeals for the Tenth Circuit is vacated, and the case is remanded for further proceedings consistent with this opinion.

NOTES AND QUESTIONS

1. *Rowley* and *Endrew F.* concern the meaning of a concept central to special education, a "free appropriate public education" or FAPE. How does the *Endrew F.* standard differ from the one adopted in *Rowley*? Why isn't a child eligible for services under the IDEA entitled to an education that provides the child with "opportunities to achieve academic success, attain self-sufficiency, and contribute to society that are substantially equal to the opportunities afforded children without disabilities," as Endrew's parents argued?

Amy Rowley became a professor of modern languages and literature, and she published an article reflecting on her response to the litigation about her education. Amy June Rowley, *Rowley* Revisited: A Personal Narrative, 37 J.L. & Educ. 311 (2008). Both Amy's parents were deaf, and her mother was a teacher in a school for deaf students before her children were born. Amy's parents chose to enroll her in public school rather than the specialized school for the deaf in part because they found that many students in the school for the deaf were language-delayed because their hearing parents did not teach them in American Sign Language before they went to school, as Amy's parents had done. Amy wrote that during the litigation she resisted having an interpreter or being pulled out of class for special instruction because it made her stand out, and she always insisted that she understood everything, even when she did not, trying to make people leave her alone. She also said that the FM amplifier system provided to her as part of her IEP did not help her at all, but having an interpreter was very important because it allowed her to communicate and interact with the other children. As the litigation progressed, the situation in the school became more and more tense, and her brother had to leave the school because so much hostility was directed toward him. After the Supreme Court decision, her family moved to New Jersey, and Amy went to school with other deaf children. Her article concludes,

> People ask me if this was all worth it. Would I do this again? I was faced with that decision with my own children who are deaf. The school district I first worked with informed me that they wanted my oldest daughter to be able to function without an interpreter by the time she entered school. In my mind I was thinking that the school wanted to make her hearing. They wanted to deprive me and her of communication. I had to explain to the school that American Sign Language is not a detriment to my daughter's education but actually an advantage that helps her thrive in school. Twenty-five years ago my parents asked for an interpreter for the exact same reasons.

Twenty-five years later I know there has been progress, but it is not always evident. So would I do it again? Not at the expense of my children.

37 J.L. & Educ. at 328.

2. The IDEA also requires schools to provide noneducational "related services" to children eligible for special education to enable them to attend school, so long as the service does not have to be provided by a medical doctor. Cedar Rapids Community School District v. Garret F., 526 U.S. 66 (1999). These services could be as or more expensive than services that are not required under *Rowley* and *Endrew F.* In *Garret F.*, for example, the child was quadriplegic and needed to have a medically-trained person available to assist him at all times. The Court held that the IDEA required the school to pay for this service. How can the holdings of the three cases be squared?

3. The IDEA requires states to educate children with disabilities with children who are not disabled "to the maximum extent possible." IDEA expresses this requirement in terms of providing a student with a disability with a free appropriate education "in the least restrictive environment." The preference for "mainstreaming" is certainly a substantive element in the statute.

Is mainstreaming consistent with a desire to provide the best possible academic education? The dilemma articulated by Professor Minow in connection with bilingual and bicultural educational theories applies here as well:

> Identifying a child as handicapped entitles her to individualized educational planning and special services but also labels the child as handicapped and may expose her to attributions of inferiority, risks of stigma, isolation, and reduced self-esteem. Nonidentification frees a child from the risks associated with labeling but also denies him specialized attention and services.

Martha Minow, Making All the Difference: Inclusion, Exclusion, and American Law 36 (1990).

4. Is the IDEA's mainstreaming requirement consistent with school discipline? In Honig v. Doe, 484 U.S. 305 (1988), the Supreme Court interpreted the IDEA as preventing schools from expelling special education students for behavior that is a manifestation of their disability. The IDEA allows a school to suspend a special education student for no more than ten days without going through a due process hearing. If at the hearing the child's behavior is found to be a manifestation of the disability, the child's placement cannot be changed. If the behavior is independent of the disability, the child may be suspended but must be provided with educational services in an alternative setting that is consistent with the IEP.

The IDEA allows a school to remove a child with a disability from the classroom and to place him or her in an alternative education setting for 45 school days in addition to the regular ten-day limit on such a removal if the child carries any weapon; has, uses, solicits the sale of, or sells medications or illegal drugs; or inflicts serious bodily injury on another person while at school. The removal, which must be authorized by a hearing officer, is permitted when the officer finds that maintaining the current placement is substantially likely to result in injury to the child or to others.

Studies consistently show that students with disabilities are greatly overrepresented in children who are suspended and otherwise disciplined for behavior. Data from the United States Department of Education show that public schools suspended 2.8 million students, about 6 percent of all public school students, during 2013-2015. Of these, about 25 percent were students with disabilities receiving services under IDEA, and about 39 percent were African American. Students of color with disabilities were more likely to be suspended than white students with disabilities, and male students of color with disabilities were suspended at the highest rates. Kate Mitchell, "We Can't Tolerate that Behavior in this School!": The Consequences of Excluding Children with Behavioral Health Conditions and the Limits of the Law, 41 NYU Rev. L & Soc. Change 407, 410 (2017). *See also* Office for Civil Rights, Dept. of Education, Revealing New Truths About Our Nation's Schools 1, 3 (2012) (Nationwide, students who are eligible for special education are twice as likely to be suspended as students who are not eligible.); Justice Center & Public Policy Research Institute, Breaking Schools' Rules: A Statewide Study of How School Discipline Relates to Students' Success and Juvenile Justice Involvement at x-xi, 66 (2011) (Of all Texas children in seventh grade public schools who qualified for special education, 75 percent had been suspended or expelled at least once.)

5. IDEA also imposes an affirmative obligation on schools to locate, evaluate, and identify students with disabilities (the "child find" duty). 20 U.S.C. § 1412(a)(3)(A). Parents may, however, resist having their children identified as eligible for services because they believe that the special education label is stigmatizing or because they fear that their child will receive an inferior education. Professor Raj has written that such a fear may be well-founded.

> Special education, despite being a uniform federal mandate, is often implemented drastically differently depending on the school system delivering services, the particular category of disability, and the race or ethnicity of students. Affluent white children who attend well-managed school districts tend to benefit from special education services. In the under-funded and over-tasked districts where most minorities attend school, the special education system does not always provide the same benefits. In these schools, special education, too often, operates as a dumping ground for those students the general education system cannot or refuses to serve. In these instances, the label of "special education" may carry harms that outweigh its benefits. For instance, African-American and American-Indian boys are the most likely to be removed from the general education classroom, be educated in more restrictive or separate environments, drop out of school, and be tracked into lower achieving classes. Consequently, they have the least access to higher education and post-high school employment. In short, special education does not appear to be helping many of these students overcome the challenges they face, and it can sometimes make matters worse.

Claire Raj, The Misidentification of Children with Disabilities: A Harm with No Foul, 48 Ariz. St. L.J. 373, 374-375 (2016). Since the inception of the federal special education program, African-American and other children of color have been overrepresented in special education. Russell J. Skiba et al., Achieving Equity in Special Education: History, Status, and Current Challenges, 74 Exceptional Children 264 (2008).

6. An individualized education program (IEP) may require placement of children with disabilities in private schools with programs specially designed for their needs. In Florence County School District No. 4 v. Carter, 510 U.S. 7 (1993), a ninth-grade student, Shannon Carter, was classified as learning-disabled. School officials met with Shannon's parents to formulate an IEP, as required by the statute. The parents were dissatisfied with the plan and then enrolled her in a private school specializing in educating children with disabilities, just as Endrew's parents did. The parents successfully sued the school district for failing to provide Shannon with a FAPE. The Supreme Court affirmed the trial court's order requiring the school district to reimburse the parents for the private school tuition. The *Carter* reimbursement remedy may be claimed even if a child was not receiving special education services before the parents placed the child in private school, provided that the other conditions of the IDEA are satisfied. Forest Grove School District v. T.A., 557 U.S. 230 (2009).

However, parents who rely on *Carter* run the risk that they will be responsible for educational costs if the IEP is held adequate or the alternative is held inappropriate. A state may reduce or deny reimbursement to parents for a child placed in a private school without state consent if the parents (1) did not notify the state agency of the planned placement in writing, expressing their concerns, at least ten days before the child was removed from public school or (2) did not make the child available for an initial assessment and evaluation by the public school before removing the child from public school, or otherwise in the judge's discretion.

7. If a school fails to implement an IEP, parents may invoke the administrative review process, seeking compensatory education. However, most courts have held that relief is available only if the failure is "material." Van Duyn v. Baker School District 5J, 502 F.3d 811 (9th Cir. 2007); Neosho R-V School District v. Clark, 315 F.3d 1022 (8th Cir. 2003); Houston Indep. School District v. Bobby R., 200 F.3d 341 (5th Cir. 2000). A "material failure occurs when there is more than a minor discrepancy between the services a school provides to a disabled child and the services required by the child's IEP." *Van Duyn*, 502 F.3d at 822. The Second Circuit has rejected the material failure test and instead holds that any discrepancy can be the basis for relief. D.D. ex rel. V.C. v. New York City Board of Education, 465 F.3d 503 (2d Cir. 2006). For more information, *see* David Ferster, Broken Promises: When Does a School's Failure to Implement an Individualized Education Program Deny a Disabled Student a Free and Appropriate Public Education, 28 Buff. Pub. Int. L.J. 71 (2009-2010).

The party who challenges an IEP in an administrative hearing has the burden of persuading the factfinder that the IEP is not adequate. Schaffer v. Weast, 546 U.S. 49 (2005). The IDEA allows a court to order the state to reimburse parents who prevail on appeal for costs and attorney's fees. However, in Arlington Central School District Board of Education v. Murphy, 548 U.S. 291 (2006), the court held that this provision did not cover the fees of an expert educational consultant who helped parents through the appeals process. A court may also award attorneys' fees to the state if the parent filed a complaint for any improper purpose or if the parent's attorney filed a frivolous, unreasonable, or foundationless complaint or continued to litigate after the case clearly became frivolous, unreasonable, or without foundation. A parent who wishes to proceed *pro se* is entitled to do so, the Supreme Court held in Winkelman v. Parma City School District, 550 U.S. 516 (2007), because the parent has his or her own interests at stake that are independent of the child's. If the parents acted only on behalf of their children, their attempt to proceed without an attorney would constitute practicing law without a license.

8. Two other federal statutes, § 504 of the Rehabilitation Act of 1973, 29 U.S.C. § 794, and the Americans with Disabilities Act (ADA), 42 U.S.C. §§ 12131-12150, also protect children with disabilities. In contrast to the IDEA, which protects access to education, these statutes prohibit discrimination against people with disabilities in programs or services that receive federal funds. The courts have generally held that the protections provided by the ADA and by § 504 are the same. Mark C. Weber, The IDEA Eligibility Mess, 57 Buff. L. Rev. 83 (2009). Children may be eligible for services under § 504 without going through the special education eligibility process or even if they do not meet the specific requirements of an IDEA eligibility category. The Supreme Court held in Fry v. Napoleon Community Schools, _ U.S. _, 137 S. Ct. 743 (2017), that a child does not have to exhaust the administrative remedies of the IDEA before suing under § 504 unless the child is claiming that the school has not provided a FAPE. Section 504's protections may also be important for children with disabilities who do not need special education or related services, even though they have disabilities. 57 Buff. L. Rev. at 99-100. On the other hand, only the IDEA requires parental participation in the child's education planning and, under the IDEA a court cannot award damages, while it can award compensatory damages for some violations of § 504. *See also* Mark C. Weber, A New Look at Section 504 and the ADA in Special Education Cases, 16 Tex. J. C.L. & C.R. 1 (2010).

For more on *Endrew F.* and *Fry, see* the fall 2017 issue of the Journal of Law and Education, which has articles by Ruth Colker, Robert Garda, Terry Jean Seligmann, Claire Raj and Emily Suski, Julie Waterstone, and Maureen A. MacFarlane.

9. On the duties and role of attorneys in special education cases *see* Cynthia Godsoe, All in the Family: Towards a New Representational Model for Parents And Children, 24 Geo. J. Legal Ethics 303 (2011); Joseph B. Tulman & Kylie A. Schofield, Reversing the School-to-Prison Pipeline: Initial Findings from the District of Columbia on the Efficacy of Training and Mobilizing Court-Appointed Lawyers to Use Special Education Advocacy on Behalf of At-Risk Youth, 18 U.D.C. L. Rev. 215 (2015).

PROBLEMS

1. Alice Robinson, a profoundly deaf child, is a third-grader in the local public school. Her school has few services in place for deaf children, and school officials sought to have her transferred to the state residential school for the deaf, located 120 miles from Alice's home. The residential school has better programs and a larger, more expert staff than is or can be made available in the local school and will provide Alice the best educational opportunities. Her parents, however, wish Alice to remain at the local school. What arguments might be made for the school and the parents?

2. The parents of Warren, a child with a mild cognitive disability, have asked the school to supply a tutor for Warren so that he can remain in the regular

classroom. The school proposes instead that Warren be placed in a special education class. The parents nonetheless engaged a tutor and seek reimbursement for that expense. There is evidence that the special education class will benefit Warren but that a tutor may provide greater benefit. Should reimbursement under *Carter* be ordered, assuming that the parents satisfied the procedural requirements for reimbursement?

B. PARENT-STATE CONFLICTS OVER EDUCATION

So far we have been discussing the state's obligation to provide children with an education. Now we turn to questions about who controls the content of that education, the state, which provides it, or the child's parents', as part of parents' general rights to raise and control their children. Why might the state or local school board assert a claim to control what happens in school? What happens if parents object? This section begins with readings about the claims of society to direct the upbringing of children and the foundations of parental rights.

LEE E. TEITELBAUM, *FAMILY HISTORY AND FAMILY LAW*

1985 Wis. L. Rev. 1135, 1150-1152

. . . During the early 1800's, common schools arose to educate poor children whose parents could not afford to send them to academies and could not themselves perform that function. In Boston, where concern for the capacity of families to educate their children had long existed, school attendance became compulsory during the first part of the nineteenth century, and the New York Public School Society asked for similar legislation in 1832. That this step would involve substantial intervention in parental control of children was frankly conceded. . . .

> . . . Every Political compact supposes a surrender of some individual rights for the general good. In a government like ours, "founded on the principle that the only true sovereignty is the will of the people," universal education is acknowledged by all, to be, not only of the first importance, but necessary to the permanency of our free institutions. If then persons are found so reckless of the best interests of their children, and so indifferent to the public good, as to withhold from them that instruction, without which they cannot beneficially discharge those civil and political duties which devolve on them in after life, it becomes a serious and important question, whether so much of the natural right of controlling their children may not be alienated as is necessary to qualify them for usefulness, and render them safe and consistent members of the political body.

By the middle of the nineteenth century, public schools, houses of refuge, state reformatories, and similar institutions were widely relied on to mold poor and wayward children "into the form and character which the peculiar nature of the edifice [of American society] demands. . . ."

As the nineteenth century wore on, this development was confirmed and expanded. Although compulsory education had been adopted in some localities before the Civil War, it gained far broader acceptance in the last third of the century. The reasons for its spread were much the same at the end of the century as at the beginning: the felt importance of education for good citizenship and social order together with the implicit conviction that parents could not routinely be trusted to discharge that function. Compulsory education laws were considered to "belong to the class of laws which are intended for the suppression of vice. . . ."

During the same time, the implications of Enlightenment theory for the manner of education were also developed more fully. . . . The traditional method of education by mastery of bodies of knowledge was replaced by one that emphasized the individual growth and development of students. "If," as Richard Hofstadter observed of the views of [John] Dewey, "a democratic society is truly to serve all its members, it must devise schools in which, at the germinal point in childhood, these members will be able to cultivate their capacities and, instead of simply reproducing the qualities of the larger society, will learn how to improve them." So sophisticated an approach entailed trained educators in place of parental instruction. Public schools, Dewey observed, would do "systematically and in a large, intelligent, and competent way what for various reasons can be done in most households only in a comparatively meager and haphazard manner."

WILLIAM A. GALSTON, *LIBERAL PURPOSES*
248-255 (1991)

Civic education poses a special difficulty for liberal democracy. . . . For [most] political communities, the government's authority to conduct civic education is unquestioned, because conflicts between political and sub-political commitments are resolved by the belief that the political enjoys a principled primacy. In liberal societies, by contrast, the resolution of such conflicts is far less clear-cut. Reservations against public authority in the name of individual autonomy, parental rights, and religious conscience are both frequent and respectable. The liberal tradition is animated by the effort to carve out spheres that are substantially impervious to government—an effort set in motion by the historical lesson that the attempt to impose religious uniformity through public fiat undermines civil order as well as historical conscience. . . .

Perhaps the most poignant problem raised by liberal civic education is the clash between the content of that education and the desire of parents to pass on their way of life to their children. Few parents, I suspect, are unaware of or immune to the force of this desire. What could be more natural? If you believe that you are fit to be a parent, you must also believe that at least some of the choices you have made are worthy of emulation by your children, and the freedom to pass on the fruits of those choices must be highly valued. Conversely, who can contemplate without horror totalitarian societies in which families are compelled to yield all moral authority to the state?

Still, your child is at once a future adult and a future citizen. Your authority as a parent is limited by both these facts. For example, you are not free to treat your child in a manner that impedes normal development. You may not legitimately starve or beat your child or thwart the acquisition of basic linguistic and social skills. The systematic violation of these and related norms suffices to warrant state intervention. Similarly, you are not free to impede the child's acquisition of a basic civic education—the beliefs and habits that support the polity and enable individuals to function competently in public affairs. In particular, you are not free to act in ways that will lead your child to impose significant and avoidable burdens on the community. For example, the liberal state has a right to teach all children respect for the law, and you have no opposing right as a parent to undermine that respect. . . .

Thus far, I think, the argument is reasonably strong and uncontroversial. But how much farther can the liberal state go. . . .

Amy Gutmann, *Democratic Education*

22-46 (1987)

[President Gutmann identifies several normative theories of the relation between education and the family. She begins with the Platonic "family state," in which educational authority rests with the state, whose responsibility is to teach children to associate their own good with the social good and then to pursue that good. She then discusses a second theory, which she calls "the state of families."]

States that aspire to the moral unity of families underestimate the strength and deny the legitimacy of the parental impulse to pass values on to children. Radically opposed to the family state is the state of families, which places educational authority exclusively in the hands of parents, thereby permitting parents to predispose their children, through education, to choose a way of life consistent with their familial heritage. Theorists of the state of families typically justify placing educational authority in the hands of parents on grounds either of consequences or of rights. John Locke maintained that parents are the best protectors of their children's future interests. Some Catholic theologians, following Thomas Aquinas, claim that parents have a natural right to educational authority. Many modern-day defenders of the state of families maintain both, and add another argument: if the state is committed to the freedom of individuals, then it must cede educational authority to parents whose freedom includes the right to pass their own way of life on to their children.

. . . [N]one of these theoretical arguments justifies resting educational authority exclusively—or even primarily—in the hands of parents. It is one thing to recognize the right (and responsibility) of parents to educate their children as members of a family, quite another to claim that this right of familial education extends to a right of parents to insulate their children from exposure to ways of life or thinking that conflict with their own. The consequentialist argument is surely unconvincing; parents cannot be counted upon to equip their children with the intellectual skills necessary for rational deliberation.

Some parents, such as the Old Order Amish in America, are morally committed to shielding their children from all knowledge that might lead them to doubt and all worldly influences that might weaken their religious beliefs. Many other parents, less radical in their rejection of modern society, are committed to teaching their children religious and racial intolerance. . . .

The same principle that requires a state to grant adults personal and political freedom also commits it to assuring children an education that makes those freedoms both possible and meaningful in the future. A state makes choice possible by teaching its future citizens respect for opposing points of view and ways of life. It makes choice meaningful by equipping children with the intellectual skills necessary to evaluate ways of life different from that of their parents. History suggests that without state provision or regulation of education, children will be taught neither mutual respect among persons nor rational deliberation among ways of life. To save their children from future pain, especially the pain of eternal damnation, parents have historically shielded their children from diverse associations, convinced them that all other ways of life are sinful, and implicitly fostered (if not explicitly taught them) disrespect for people who are different. . . .

The state of families mistakenly conflates the welfare of children with the freedom of parents when it assumes that the welfare of children is best defined or secured by the freedom of parents. But the state of families rightly recognizes, as the family state does not, the value of parental freedom, at least to the extent that such freedom does not interfere with the interests of children in becoming mutually respectful citizens of a society that sustains family life. There is no simple solution to the tension between the freedom of parents and the welfare of children. . . .

The attractions of the state of families are apparent to most Americans: by letting parents educate their own children as they see fit, the state avoids all the political battles that rage over the content of public education. The state of families also appears to foster pluralism by permitting many ways of life to be perpetuated in its midst. But both these attractions are only superficial in a society where many parents would teach racism, for example, in the absence of political pressure to do otherwise. . . .

The "pluralism" commonly identified with the state of families is superficial because its internal variety serves as little more than an ornament for onlookers. Pluralism is an important political value insofar as social diversity enriches our lives by expanding our understanding of different ways of life. To reap the benefits of social diversity, children must be exposed to ways of life different from their parents and—in the course of their exposure—must embrace certain values, such as mutual respect among persons, that make social diversity both possible and desirable. There is no reason to assume that placing educational authority exclusively in the hands of parents is the best way of achieving these ends. . . .

A DEMOCRATIC STATE OF EDUCATION . . .

None [of the theories discussed earlier] provides an adequate foundation for educational authority. Yet each contains a partial truth. States, parents, and professional educators all have important roles to play in cultivating moral character. A democratic state of education recognizes that educational authority must be shared . . . even though such sharing does not guarantee that power will be wedded to knowledge, that parents can successfully pass their prejudices to their children, or that education will be neutral among competing conceptions of the good life. . . .

A democratic state is therefore committed to allocating educational authority in such a way as to provide its members with an education adequate to participating in democratic politics, to choosing among (a limited range of) good lives, and to sharing in the several sub-communities, such as families, that impart identity to the lives of its citizens.

A democratic state of education constrains choice among good lives . . . out of a concern for civic virtue. Democratic states can acknowledge two reasons for permitting communities to use education to predispose children toward some ways of life and away from others. One reason is grounded on the value of moral freedom. . . . All societies of self-reflective beings must admit the moral value of enabling their members to discern the difference between good and bad ways of life. Children do not learn to discern this difference on the basis of an education that strives for neutrality among ways of life. Children are not taught that bigotry is bad, for example, by offering it as one among many competing concepts of the good life. . . .

The second, more specifically democratic, reason for supporting the non-neutral education of states and families is that the good of children includes not just freedom of choice, but also identification with and participation in the good of their family and the politics of their society. . . . To focus exclusively on the value of freedom, or even on the value of moral freedom, neglects the value that parents and citizens may legitimately place on *partially* prejudicing the choices of children by their familial and political heritage.

MICHAEL W. MCCONNELL, *OLD LIBERALISM, NEW LIBERALISM, AND PEOPLE OF FAITH*

Christian Perspectives on Legal Thought 5, 17-20
(Michael W. McConnell, Robert F. Cochran, Jr. &
Angela C. Carmella, eds., 2001)

In its early phase, liberalism was not a comprehensive ideology, in the sense of offering answers to questions about the nature of the good life. To borrow a distinction from John Rawls without necessarily embracing his conception of it, early liberalism was a "political" liberalism. A "political" conception of justice, according to Rawls, is one that applies only to "the framework of basic institutions," whereas a "comprehensive" doctrine is one that addresses nonpolitical life as well, including "conceptions of what is of value in human life, and ideals of personal character, as well as ideals of friendship and of familial and associational relationships, and much else that is to inform our conduct." The constitutional principles of the early American republic were a form of political liberalism because they did not purport to direct the people how they should live. They solely limited the government in the way it should conduct the public business. The First Amendment, for example, begins "*Congress* shall make no law. . . ." It did not restrict — indeed, it protected — the ability of citizens to take sides in religious disputes, and to be prejudiced or enlightened in accordance with their own lights. . . .

Elements of this liberal polity were state neutrality, tolerance, and the guarantee of equality before the law. Neutrality meant, fundamentally, that government would not take sides in the religious and philosophical disagreements among the people. "If there is any fixed star in our constitutional constellation," wrote

Justice Robert Jackson, "it is that no official, high or petty, can prescribe what shall be orthodox in politics, nationalism, religion, or other matters of opinion." Tolerance meant something like "live and let live." It did not mean that everyone in the nation was expected to approve of the conduct or beliefs of everyone else. It meant that everyone would refrain from using public or private violence to force one another to conform. . . .

It seems obvious that something has changed. Today there is a widespread sense not only that the government should be neutral, tolerant, and egalitarian, but so should all of us, and so should our private associations. Open-mindedness, not conviction, is the mark of the good liberal citizen. Indeed, there is something suspect in those who are sure that they are right, since it might imply that someone else is wrong. From a religious point of view, however, open-mindedness in itself is a largely instrumental virtue—a way station in the search for Truth. . . . [T]he new ideal of the liberal citizen seems to conflict with the ideal believer in religion or any other comprehensive faith or ideology. To the extent that the state uses its power to inculcate and enforce this new vision of the liberal citizen, religious freedom is gravely endangered. Indeed, liberalism in the old sense is itself endangered, for liberal government becomes not a set of political arrangements by which persons of widely differing views can live together in relative harmony, but a narrow and sectarian program enforcing its dogmas by force. . . .

We can see the origins of this new secular liberalism—this liberalism as a comprehensive ideology—in Rousseau. . . .

In America, we do not live up to Rousseau's [insistence that only religions that embrace toleration be themselves tolerated]. But there is more than a hint of Rousseau in Amy Gutmann's argument that all schools, including private religious schools, should be forced to teach liberal dogma concerning "toleration" and "mutual respect." . . .

The logical misstep here is not in the identification of neutrality, tolerance, and equality as proper guiding principles for liberal government. It is the projection of political principles onto private persons and associations. It is not merely overextension. It is inversion. When government comes to insist that all citizens should be neutral, tolerant, and egalitarian, it ceases to be a liberal government.

The compulsory aspect of public education laws presents the possibility of a contest between the state and parents regarding the extent of the requirement and the program to which children will be compulsorily exposed. This conflict is often expressed by parents' claims that the education provided by the state unconstitutionally limits their authority. The first cases in this part provide the constitutional foundation for parental rights, but before reading them, we should think about why parents would be regarded as having rights to control their children.

DAVID ARCHARD, *CHILDREN: RIGHTS AND CHILDHOOD*

98-104 (1993)

The "proprietarian" argument [for parental rights] reasons that a natural parent owns its children and the right to rear would be included within a right to dispose of what is rightfully owned. The ownership of a child by its parents is in some way grounded in its production by them. The thesis first found expression in Aristotle who spoke of children as belonging to their parents: for the product belongs to the producer (e.g., a tooth or hair or anything else to him whose it is). In fact Aristotle's examples suggest something more than the relation of producer to product, namely that of part to whole. A child is, in some sense, a part of the parent's body. This could be taken as applying, if at all, during pregnancy, and even this claim is deeply controversial.

It is in Locke that there is a more credible version of the proprietarian argument which derives from a general theory of property. For Locke one owns the product of one's labour in virtue of owning one's body and thus one's labour. The felicitous association of "labour" with childbirth helps support the idea that one's child is owned because it is one's product. . . .

There are then two ways of responding to the "proprietarian argument." The first is to deny the general validity of the Lockean thesis about labour generating ownership; the second is to show that there are good reasons, other than Locke's own, to exempt children from the scope of that thesis.

Locke's argument that people own that with which they have "mixed" their labour is subject to a number of familiar criticisms. The move from owning one's own "self" to owning what that self works on is not obviously valid, and may depend upon conflating labour as an activity with labour as a product. . . . Why should the act of labouring be thought of as a process whereby entitlement passes from labourer to laboured upon, rather than a loss of labour in its object? . . .

Procreation illustrates many of these difficulties only too well. . . . Can begetting be construed as improving something? If so, are there degrees of improvement such that parents might be entitled only the equivalent of the amount by which their particular procreation is improving? . . . Strictly speaking, only the mother "labours" to produce the child, and the father's contribution may be seen as a freely given gift (this may be explicit in the case of semen donation and artificial insemination). . . .

Such problems notwithstanding, if Locke's argument is valid is there then a good reason to exempt children from its scope? . . . [M]odern critics have suggested one. This is that the child has, as a new human being, a right to liberty. It is this right which, in the case of adults, underpins the right to dispose of one's body as one chooses and thus the right to own the product of that body's exertions. Since the right to own derives from a right of liberty the former could not conceivably trump the latter. The child's liberty undercuts any presumptive rights of another to its ownership.

This reasoning is not *ad hoc* since it derives from the general presumption of self-ownership. However, it can seem paradoxical since it denies precisely what the labour thesis affirms, namely that you own what you produce. . . . The paradox is not vicious. Rather it seems to be a case of a principle or thesis limiting itself. Self-ownership is universal and universally generates ownership in things other than oneself, except when the products of labour happen to be human beings.

A defender of the "proprietarian thesis" may simply insist that this is to beg the question. If children *are* owned then this is not a case of self-ownership failing to be universal. It is rather that children are not the sorts of things that can be self-owning, any more than domestic animals are. Children *become* self-owning when they reach adulthood. Thinking this way seems to fly in the face of deep moral convictions. But previous cultures have not felt as we do. A major principle of

Roman law was that of *patria potestas*. The father as head of the family, *paterfamilias*, had the absolute power of life and death over his son; he completely controlled his person and his property. The son was released from this state only by his father's death or manumission. In practice the son exercised de facto administration of his own property, *peculium*, and instances of his father exercising his *potestas* to the limit seem to have been rare. . . .

This shows that the idea of a child as something over which parents have total power has been seriously entertained. In the last analysis, consequently, rejection of the "proprietarian" argument requires that one either be skeptical of Locke's general labour theory . . . or insist that children are just like adults in being self-owning and thus exempt from that thesis' scope.

For all of that the "proprietarian argument" casts a long shadow over much thinking about parental rights, and it is easy to find modern examples of arguments or claims which appear to make proprietarian assumptions. The talk of "owner-ship" may not be explicit but something very like it seems to be argued for. Charles Fried, for instance, writes that "the rights to form one's child's values . . . are exten-sions of the basic right not to be interfered with in doing these things for oneself. In other words the rightful exercise of parental control over one's children is just a part of one's rightful self-disposition. . . ."

FERDINAND SCHOEMAN, *RIGHTS OF CHILDREN, RIGHTS OF PARENTS, AND THE MORAL BASIS OF THE FAMILY*

91 Ethics 6, 14-19 (1980)

We have yet to supply the justification of three institutions which we, for the most part, take for granted. Why should the family be accorded rights to privacy and autonomy? Why should the family be given extensive responsibilities for the development of children? Why should the biological parent be thought entitled to be in charge of a family? I believe that the notion of intimacy supplies the basis for these presumptions. . . .

At an earlier point in this paper, I described an intimate relationship as one in which one shares one's self with one or more others. It was suggested that, via intimate relationships, one transcends abstract and rather impersonal associ-ations with others and enters personal and meaningful relationships or unions. Such relationships are meaningful because of the personal commitments to others which are constitutive of such relationships. For most people, not only are such unions central to defining who one is, but human existence would have little or no meaning if cut off from all possibility of maintaining or reestablishing such relationships. . . .

. . . Friendship, love, and family represent institutions in which intimacy is central to the relationships. Because of the importance of these relationships to the self-image and meaningful existence of most people, the state, before intruding, should impose high standards like the clear-and-present danger test. . . . The state should be very chary in trying to alter the terms of such relationships to serve social ends. As has been noted by others, while the state is quite limited in its abil-ity to promote relationships, it can do much to destroy them. The state threatens relationships by requiring the parties to think of themselves as primarily serving public ends and as having public duties. This intrusion beclouds the integrity of the trust and devotion that can arise between people. . . .

Yet to show the importance of intimate relationships, even family relationships as characterized in this paper, is not yet to show that parents have any rights to their children. After all, adults can establish intimate relationships with other consenting adults. Insuring that children become part of an intimate and secure setting is not the same as assuring the biological parents of these children that they (the parents) will be part of this same setting.

The alternative to the natural and customary distribution of children to their parents is some kind of social decision determining who goes with whom. Such distribution schemes are not necessarily, from the perspective of the infant, inimical to intimacy, as the institution of early adoption establishes. But it does or may preclude such kinds of intimacy for those who are determined by popular social criteria to be not maximally fit or not maximally competent to really provide children with all that they need or can use. But such a preclusion would, I believe, represent an interference with a practice from which intimacy and with it life meaning typically emerge. . . .

Though the infant is nonconsenting, it does not represent a denial of its rights for it to be entrusted to its parents even if better surroundings are available, since we are assuming that minimal conditions for adequate upbringing will be met. (We are, after all, utilizing something like the clear-and-present-danger test to protect children from abuse and neglect, though of course such standards raise problems of their own.) To set terms for emotional parenting more stringent than required for the protection of children from abuse and neglect constitutes an interference in a person's claim to establish intimate relations except on the society's terms. We have already indicated reasons for thinking that such regulation transforms relationships into less intimate ones. Such allocation schemes could redefine the parenting role as one in which the objective is abstract social well-being, not intimacy and the kind of meaning found in commitment to particular others.

The practice of entrusting children to their parents ultimately limits the control of society to determine the life-style and beliefs of persons because it means there would be one important relationship a person could be in without the requirement of prior social approval. Since society cannot determine and should not try to determine who may have intimate relationships with whom, if a person chooses to have his relationships in a family setting, society should not interfere, since that kind of choice is essential to intimate relationships in general.

Thus, as a way of transcending oneself and the boundaries of abstract others, as a way of finding meaning in life, and as a means of maintaining some kind of social and moral autonomy, the claim to freedom from scrutiny and control in one's relations with others should be thought of as a moral claim as important as any other that can be envisioned. It must not be up to society in general, without there being some special cause, to decide whom one can relate to and on what terms. Other things being equal, parents consequently are entitled to maintain their offspring and seek meaning with and through them. . . .

Most justifications of family autonomy that one finds in the literature have concentrated on the child's perspective and stressed the point that families, as we know them, represent the least-detrimental means we have of child rearing. In contrast, my arguments on behalf of the family, though concerned with the well-being of children, have had as their chief focus an idea of human relationships. Consequently, even if someone could demonstrate that there were some more efficient and effective institution for promoting the interests of children than the traditional family, I would still think that the family would have a strong, though rebuttable, moral presumption in its favor. The implications of such a presumption extend beyond requiring high threshold conditions before the state intervenes coercively into family affairs. The presumption would seem to imply that the state should not, to the extent possible, make the family and parental responsibility otiose through the provision directly to children of services which parents are in a position to supply.

Joseph Goldstein, Anna Freud & Albert Solnit, *Beyond the Best Interests of the Child*

6-8 (1973)

Psychoanalytic theory [and] developmental studies of other orientations [emphasize] the need of every child for unbroken continuity of affection and stimulating relationships with an adult. . . .

To safeguard the right of parents to raise their children as they see fit, free of government intrusion, except in cases of neglect and abandonment, is to safeguard each child's need for continuity. The preference for minimum state intervention and for leaving well enough alone is reinforced by our recognition that law is incapable of effectively managing, except in a very gross sense, so delicate and complex a relationship as that between parent and child.

Elisabeth S. Scott & Robert E. Scott, *Parents as Fiduciaries*

81 Val. L. Rev. 2401, 2401-2402 (1995)

Traditionally, the law has deferred to the rights of biological parents in regulating the parent-child relationship. More recently, as the emphasis of legal regulation has shifted to protecting children's interests, critics have targeted the traditional focus on parents' rights as impeding the goal of promoting children's welfare. Some contemporary scholars argue instead for a "child-centered perspective," in contrast to the current regime under which biological parents continue to have important legal interests in their relationship with their children. The underlying assumption of this claim is that the rights of parents and the interests of children often are conflicting, and that greater recognition of one interest means diminished importance to the other.

One way of thinking about a legal regime that seeks to harmonize this conflict is to imagine that the parent's legal relationship to the child is shaped by fiduciary responsibilities toward the child rather than by inherent rights derived from status. Fiduciaries in law are agents who occupy a position of special confidence, superiority, or influence, and thus are subject to strict and non-negotiable duties of loyalty and reasonable diligence in acting on behalf of their principals. Characterizing parents as fiduciaries suggests that the parent-child relationship shares important features with other legal relationships that have been similarly defined, such as trustees and trust beneficiaries, corporate directors and share-holders, executors and legatees, and guardians and wards. Basic structural similar-ities are apparent. There are information asymmetries in this family relationship that are analogous to those of other fiduciary relationships. Moreover, satisfactory performance by parents, like that of other fiduciaries, requires considerable discre-tion, and children, like other principals, are not in a position to direct or control that performance. Here, as in other contexts, the challenge for legal regulation is to encourage the parent to act so as to serve the interests of the child rather than her own conflicting interests, and yet to do so in a context in which monitoring parental behavior is difficult.

1.   *The Constitutional Foundations*

MEYER V. NEBRASKA

---

262 U.S. 390 (1923)

McReynolds, J. Plaintiff in error was tried and convicted in the district court for Hamilton County, Nebraska, under an information which charged that on May 25, 1920, while an instructor in Zion Parochial School he unlawfully taught the subject of reading in the German language to Raymond Parpart, a child of ten years, who had not attained and successfully passed the eighth grade. The information is based upon "An act relating to the teaching of foreign languages in the state of Nebraska," approved April 9, 1919, which follows:

> Section 1. No person, individually or as a teacher, shall, in any private, denomina-tional, parochial or public school, teach any subject to any person in any language other than the English language.

. . . The problem for our determination is whether the statute as construed and applied unreasonably infringes the liberty guaranteed to the plaintiff in error by the Fourteenth Amendment: "No state . . . shall deprive any person of life, liberty, or property, without due process of law."

While this court has not attempted to define with exactness the liberty thus guaranteed, the term has received much consideration and some of the included things have been definitely stated. Without doubt, it denotes not merely freedom from bodily restraint but also the right of the individual to contract, to engage in any of the common occupations of life, to acquire useful knowledge, to marry, establish a home and bring up children, to worship God according to the dictates of his own conscience, and generally to enjoy those privileges long recognized at common law as essential to the orderly pursuit of happiness by free men. The established doctrine is that this liberty may not be interfered with, under the guise of protecting the public interest, by legislative action which is arbitrary or without reasonable relation to some purpose within the competency of the state to effect. Determination by the Legislature of what constitutes proper exercise of police power is not final or conclusive but is subject to supervision by the courts.

The American people have always regarded education and acquisition of knowledge as matters of supreme importance which should be diligently promoted. The Ordinance of 1787 declares: "Religion, morality and knowledge being necessary to good government and the happiness of mankind, schools and the means of education shall forever be encouraged." Corresponding to the right of control, it is the natural duty of the parent to give his children education suitable to their station in life; and nearly all the states, including Nebraska, enforce this obligation by compulsory laws.

Practically, education of the young is only possible in schools conducted by especially qualified persons who devote themselves thereto. The calling always has been regarded as useful and honorable, essential, indeed, to the public welfare. Mere knowledge of the German language cannot reasonably be regarded as harmful. Heretofore it has been commonly looked upon as helpful and desirable. Plaintiff in error taught this language in school as part of his occupation. His right thus to teach and the right of parents to engage him so to instruct their children, we think, are within the liberty of the Amendment. . . .

It is said the purpose of the legislation was to promote civic development by inhibiting training and education of the immature in foreign tongues and ideals before they could learn English and acquire American ideals; and "that the English language should be and become the mother tongue of all children reared in this state." It is also affirmed that the foreign-born population is very large, that certain communities commonly use foreign words, follow foreign leaders, move in a foreign atmosphere, and that the children are thereby hindered from becoming citizens of the most useful type and the public safety is imperiled.

That the state may do much, go very far, indeed, in order to improve the quality of its citizens, physically, mentally and morally, is clear; but the individual has certain fundamental rights which must be respected. The protection of the Constitution extends to all, to those who speak other languages as well as to those born with English on the tongue. Perhaps it would be highly advantageous if all had ready understanding of our ordinary speech, but this cannot be coerced by methods which conflict with the Constitution—a desirable end cannot be promoted by prohibited means.

For the welfare of his Ideal Commonwealth, Plato suggested a law which should provide: "That the wives of our guardians are to be common, and their children are to be common, and no parent is to know his own child, nor any child his parent. . . . The proper officers will take the offspring of the good parents to the pen or fold, and there they will deposit them with certain nurses who dwell in a separate quarter; but the offspring of the inferior, or of the better when they chance to be deformed, will be put away in some mysterious, unknown place, as they should be." In order to submerge the individual and develop ideal citizens, Sparta assembled the males at seven into barracks and entrusted their subsequent education and training to official guardians. Although such measures have been deliberately approved by men of great genius, their ideas touching the relation between individual and State were wholly different from those upon which our institutions rest; and it hardly will be affirmed that any legislature could impose such restrictions upon the people of a State without doing violence to both letter and spirit of the Constitution.

The desire of the Legislature to foster a homogeneous people with American ideals prepared readily to understand current discussions of civic matters is easy to appreciate. Unfortunate experiences during the late war and aversion toward every character of truculent adversaries were certainly enough to quicken that aspiration. But the means adopted, we think, exceed the limitations upon the power of the State and conflict with rights assured to plaintiff in error. The interference is plain enough and no adequate reason therefor in time of peace and domestic tranquility has been shown.

The power of the State to compel attendance at some school and to make reasonable regulations for all schools, including a requirement that they shall give instructions in English, is not questioned. Nor has challenge been made of the State's power to prescribe a curriculum for institutions which it supports. Those matters are not within the present controversy. . . . No emergency has arisen which renders knowledge by a child of some language other than English so clearly harmful as to justify its inhibition with the consequent infringement of rights long freely enjoyed. We are constrained to conclude that the statute as applied is arbitrary and without reasonable relation to any end within the competency of the state.

PIERCE v. SOCIETY OF SISTERS

268 U.S. 510 (1925)

[The Oregon Compulsory Education Act of 1922 required, with certain exceptions, every parent of a child between the ages of eight and sixteen years to send the child to a public school. An injunction against the enforcement of this statute was brought by the Society of Sisters of the Holy Names of Jesus and Mary, which had operated parochial schools in Oregon since 1880, and the Hill Military Academy, which conducted for profit an elementary, college preparatory, and military training school for boys between the ages of five and twenty-one years. Petitioners claimed that the act's requirement of attendance at public school violated their rights under the due process clause.]

McREYNOLDS, J. . . . No question is raised concerning the power of the State reasonably to regulate all schools, to inspect, supervise and examine them, their teachers and pupils; to require that all children of proper age attend some school, that teachers shall be of good moral character and patriotic disposition, that certain studies plainly essential to good citizenship must be taught, and that nothing be taught which is manifestly inimical to the public welfare.

The inevitable practical result of enforcing the Act under consideration would be destruction of appellee's primary schools, and perhaps all other private primary schools for normal children within the State of Oregon. These parties are engaged in a kind of undertaking not inherently harmful, but long regarded as useful and meritorious. Certainly there is nothing in the present records to indicate that they have failed to discharge their obligations to patrons, students, or the State. . . .

Under the doctrine of Meyer v. Nebraska, 262 U.S. 390, we think it entirely plain that the Act of 1922 unreasonably interferes with the liberty of parents and guardians to direct the upbringing and education of children under their control.

As often heretofore pointed out, rights guaranteed by the Constitution may not be abridged by legislation which has no reasonable relation to some purpose within the competency of the State. The fundamental theory of liberty upon which all governments in this Union repose excludes any general power of the State to standardize its children by forcing them to accept instruction from public teachers only. The child is not the mere creature of the State; those who nurture him and direct his destiny have the right, coupled with the high duty, to recognize and prepare him for additional obligations.

Barbara Bennett Woodhouse, *"Who Owns the Child?": Meyer and Pierce and the Child as Property*

33 Wm. & Mary L. Rev. 995, 1017-1021 (1992)

The Oregon initiative originated with the national organization of the Scottish Rite Masons and was sponsored by a variety of organizations, including the American Legion and the respected Federation of Patriotic Societies. The Ku Klux Klan, though not an official sponsor, was instrumental in its passage. Quality of instruction, problems with teacher certification, and neglect of English in parochial and private schools had drawn some criticism in educational journals. The guiding sentiment behind the Oregon law, however, seems to have been an odd commingling of patriotic fervor, blind faith in the cure-all powers of common schooling, anti-Catholic and anti-foreign prejudice, and the conviction that private and parochial schools were breeding grounds of Bolshevism.

Another motive, however, was largely neglected by historians but noted by contemporaries. The argument in favor of the initiative printed in the Official Ballot added a second theme—that of class leveling—to the cultural assimilationism of the language laws.

> Mix the children of the foreign-born with the native-born, and the rich with the poor. Mix those with prejudices in the public school melting pot for a few years while their minds are plastic, and finally bring out the finished product—a true American.
>
> The permanency of this nation rests in the education of its youth in the public schools . . . where all shall stand upon one common level.
>
> When every parent in our land has a child in our public schools, then and only then will there be a united interest in the growth and higher efficiency of our schools.
>
> Our children must not under any pretext, be it based upon money, creed or social status, be divided into antagonistic groups, there to absorb the narrow views of life, as they are taught. If they are so divided, we will find our citizenship composed and made up of cliques, cults and factions, each striving, not for the good of the whole, but for the supremacy of themselves.

Voters rallied behind such slogans as "Free Public Schools—Open to All, Good Enough for All, Attended by All. All for the Public School and the Public School for All. One Flag, One School, One Language." The Exalted Cyclops of the Klan, Frederick Gifford, declared: "We do not believe in snobbery and are just as much opposed to private schools of the so-called 'select' kind as we are to denominational private schools. All American children should be educated on the same basis."

This strange coalition of ideologies defies any easy synthesis. It mixed the leveling spirit of populism with a frontier brand of Klan bigotry and a western strain of meliorist assimilationism. Blending elements of bias, redemption, and unity, the Oregon law was an incongruous recipe for radical change. One thing is certain, the strong flavor of class and status leveling was not lost on the establishment observers from the East. The editors of the *New York Times* commented on the Oregon law: "A further motive was resentment of special educational opportunities maintained for their children by the rich or well-to-do. 'What is good enough for my children is good enough for anybody's children' — this became a slogan in the period of discussion." . . .

The goal of equality through common schooling had been voiced before, from the Working Men's Committee in 1830, to Horace Mann and other school reformers of the Progressive era, to John Dewey in the first decades of the twentieth century. Although modern scholars have questioned whether common schools actually achieved these goals, certainly the egalitarian rhetoric of common schooling contrasted markedly with the manifest role of private schools in maintaining class and cultural divisions. In the past, however, proponents of common schooling had used price and product competition to entice private school students into the melting pot. Now public education was to be not only free but universal, bringing everyone's children, rich and poor alike, into a melting pot which would obliterate class as well as ethnicity. This rhetoric of social leveling and classless unity has been overshadowed by the divisive, anti-Catholic biases of some of the Oregon law's key supporters. It should not be dismissed as an aberration, however, for it has roots in the rhetoric of the agrarian revolts of the 1800's and rekindles a Populist vision in which divisions of class, race, and religion would give way to one unified community.

NOTES AND QUESTIONS

1. What is the "liberty" involved in *Meyer* and *Pierce*? What is the constitutional basis for recognizing that interest? Does the Court seem to understand protecting parental rights as a means to some end, and, if so, to what end(s)? Or does the Court say that parental rights are inherently valuable?

2. Professors Kirp and Yudof describe *Pierce* as a compromise decision:

> [The Court] could have upheld the right of the state to compel public school attendance, or it could have struck down compulsory attendance laws (an issue which was not, however, raised in the litigation), giving complete control over the child's education to the family. The formula it adopted was a compromise between these two positions: the state may compel attendance at some school, but it is the parent's right to choose between public and private schools.

David Kirp & Mark G. Yudof, Educational Policy and the Law 134 (1982). How does one explain this compromise?

3. The state in both *Meyer* and *Pierce* invoked a "melting pot" argument, which the court of appeals in *Pierce* addressed briefly: "The melting pot idea, applied to the common schools of the state . . . is an extravagance in simile.

A careful analysis of the attendance of children of school age, foreign-born and of foreign-born parentage, would undoubtedly show that the number is negligible, and the assimilation problem could afford no reasonable basis for the adoption of the measure. But if it be that the incentive is political, and arises out of war exigencies and conditions following thereupon, then the assimilation idea is pointedly answered by the opinion rendered in the *Meyer* Case. . . ." Society of Sisters v. Pierce, 296 F.2d 928, 938 (D. Or. 1924).

Suppose that the state's argument was expressed in more explicit civic educational terms—that is, to educate children to understand and perhaps respect difference, and to evaluate competing versions of the good life. Would this argument justify refusal to approve enrollment in schools that did not seek or were not likely to develop those values?

4. *Meyer* and *Pierce* support the authority of the state to require that teachers have a "patriotic disposition" and that the curriculum include "studies plainly essential to good citizenship." How far does this authority go? A number of states have enacted legislation requiring schools to teach "patriotism." For example, the first paragraph of Neb. Rev. Stat. § 79-724, which was enacted in 1949 and amended several times, most recently in 2011, includes this language:

> Since youth is the time most susceptible to the acceptance of principles and doctrines that will influence men and women throughout their lives, it is one of the first duties of our educational system to conduct its activities, choose its textbooks, and arrange its curriculum in such a way that the love of liberty, justice, democracy, and America will be instilled in the hearts and minds of the youth of the state.
>
> (1) Every school board shall, at the beginning of each school year, appoint from its members a committee of three, to be known as the committee on Americanism. The committee on Americanism shall:
>
> (a) Carefully examine, inspect, and approve all textbooks used in the teaching of American history and civil government in the school. Such textbooks shall adequately stress the services of the men and women who achieved our national independence, established our constitutional government, and preserved our union and shall be so written to include contributions by ethnic groups as to develop a pride and respect for our institutions and not be a mere recital of events and dates;
>
> (b) Assure themselves as to the character of all teachers employed and their knowledge and acceptance of the American form of government; . . .
>
> (3) All grades of all public, private, denominational, and parochial schools, below the sixth grade, shall devote at least one hour per week to exercises or teaching periods for the following purpose:
>
> (a) The recital of stories having to do with American history or the deeds and exploits of American heroes;
>
> (b) The singing of patriotic songs and the insistence that every pupil memorize the Star-Spangled Banner and America; and
>
> (c) The development of reverence for the flag and instruction as to proper conduct in its presentation.
>
> (4) In at least two of the three grades from the fifth grade to the eighth grade in all public, private, denominational, and parochial schools, at least three periods per week shall be set aside to be devoted to the teaching of American history from approved textbooks, taught in such a way as to make the course interesting and attractive and to develop a love of country.

(5) In at least two grades of every high school, at least three periods per week shall be devoted to the teaching of civics, during which courses specific attention shall be given to the following matters:

(a) The United States Constitution and the Constitution of Nebraska;

(b) The benefits and advantages of our form of government and the dangers and fallacies of Nazism, Communism, and similar ideologies; and

(c) The duties of citizenship, including active participation in the improvement of a citizen's community, state, country, and world and the value and practice of civil discourse between opposing interests.

(6) Appropriate patriotic exercises suitable to the occasion shall be held under the direction of the superintendent in every public, private, denominational, and parochial school on Lincoln's birthday, Washington's birthday, Flag Day, Memorial Day, and Veterans Day, or on the day preceding or following such holiday, if the school is in session. . . .

What are the limits on the authority of the state to require that schools teach patriotism? And indeed, what does it mean to teach patriotism?

PRINCE V. COMMONWEALTH OF MASSACHUSETTS

321 U.S. 158 (1944)

RUTLEDGE, J. The case brings for review another episode in the conflict between Jehovah's Witnesses and state authority. This time Sarah Prince appeals from convictions for violating Massachusetts' child labor laws, by acts said to be a rightful exercise of her religious convictions.

When the offenses were committed she was the aunt and custodian of Betty M. Simmons, a girl nine years of age. Originally there were three separate complaints. They were, shortly, for (1) refusal to disclose Betty's identity and age to a public officer whose duty was to enforce the statutes; (2) furnishing her with magazines, knowing she was to sell them unlawfully, that is, on the street; and (3) as Betty's custodian, permitting her to work contrary to law. . . .

. . . Mrs. Prince, living in Brockton, is the mother of two young sons. She also has legal custody of Betty Simmons who lives with them. The children too are Jehovah's Witnesses and both Mrs. Prince and Betty testified they were ordained ministers. The former was accustomed to go each week on the streets of Brockton to distribute "Watchtower" and "Consolation," according to the usual plan. She had permitted the children to engage in this activity previously, and had been warned against doing so by the school attendance officer, Mr. Perkins. But, until December 18, 1941, she generally did not take them with her at night.

That evening, as Mrs. Prince was preparing to leave her home, the children asked to go. She at first refused. Childlike, they resorted to tears and, motherlike, she yielded. Arriving downtown, Mrs. Prince permitted the children "to engage in the preaching work with her upon the sidewalks." That is, with specific reference to Betty, she and Mrs. Prince took positions about twenty feet apart near a street intersection. Betty held up in her hand, for passersby to see, copies of "Watch Tower" and "Consolation." . . .

Mrs. Prince and Betty remained until 8:45 P.M. A few minutes before this Mr. Perkins approached Mrs. Prince. A discussion ensued. He inquired and she refused to give Betty's name. However, she stated the child attended the Shaw School. Mr. Perkins referred to his previous warnings and said he would allow five minutes for them to get off the street. Mrs. Prince admitted she supplied Betty with the magazines and said, "[N]either you nor anybody else can stop me. . . . This child is exercising her God-given right and her constitutional right to preach the gospel, and no creature has a right to interfere with God's commands." However, Mrs. Prince and Betty departed. . . . It may be added that testimony, by Betty, her aunt and others, was offered at the trials, and was excluded, to show that Betty believed it was her religious duty to perform this work and failure would bring condemnation "to everlasting destruction at Armageddon." . . .

Appellant . . . rests squarely on freedom of religion under the First Amendment, applied by the Fourteenth to the states. She buttresses this foundation, however, with a claim of parental right as secured by the due process clause of the latter Amendment. *Cf.* Meyer v. Nebraska, 262 U.S. 390. These guaranties, she thinks, guard alike herself and the child in what they have done. Thus, two claimed liberties are at stake. One is the parent's, to bring up the child in the way he should go, which for appellant means to teach him the tenets and the practices of their faith. The other freedom is the child's, to observe these; and among them is "to preach the gospel . . . by public distribution" of "Watchtower" and "Consolation," in conformity with the scripture: "A little child shall lead them." . . .

To make accommodation between these freedoms and an exercise of state authority always is delicate. It hardly could be more so than in such a clash as this case presents. On one side is the obviously earnest claim for freedom of conscience and religious practice. With it is allied the parent's claim to authority in her own household and in the rearing of her children. The parent's conflict with the state over control of the child and his training is serious enough when only secular matters are concerned. It becomes the more so when an element of religious conviction enters. Against these sacred private interests, basic in a democracy, stand the interests of society to protect the welfare of children, and the state's assertion of authority to that end, made here in a manner conceded valid if only secular things were involved. The last is no mere corporate concern of official authority. It is the interest of youth itself, and of the whole community, that children be both safeguarded from abuses and given opportunities for growth into free and independent well-developed men and citizens. Between contrary pulls of such weight, the safest and most objective recourse is to the lines already marked out, not precisely but for guides, in narrowing the no man's land where this battle has gone on.

The rights of children to exercise their religion, and of parents to give them religious training and to encourage them in the practice of religious belief, as against preponderant sentiment and assertion of state power voicing it, have had recognition here. . . . It is cardinal with us that the custody, care and nurture of the child reside first in the parents, whose primary function and freedom include preparation for obligations the state can neither supply nor hinder. Pierce

v. Society of Sisters, *supra*. And it is in recognition of this that these decisions have respected the private realm of family life which the state cannot enter.

But the family itself is not beyond regulation in the public interest, as against a claim of religious liberty. And neither rights of religion nor rights of parenthood are beyond limitation. Acting to guard the general interest in youth's well being, the state as *parens patriae* may restrict the parent's control by requiring school attendance, regulating or prohibiting the child's labor, and in many other ways. Its authority is not nullified merely because the parent grounds his claim to control the child's course of conduct on religion or conscience. Thus, he cannot claim freedom from compulsory vaccination for the child more than for himself on religious grounds. The right to practice religion freely does not include liberty to expose the community or the child to communicable disease or the latter to ill health or death. The catalogue need not be lengthened. It is sufficient to show what indeed appellant hardly disputes, that the state has a wide range of power for limiting parental freedom and authority in things affecting the child's welfare; and that this includes, to some extent, matters of conscience and religious conviction.

But it is said the state cannot do so here. This, first, because when state action impinges upon a claimed religious freedom, it must fall unless shown to be necessary for or conducive to the child's protection against some clear and present danger, and, it is added, there was no such showing here. The child's presence on the street, with her guardian, distributing or offering to distribute the magazines, it is urged, was in no way harmful to her, nor in any event more so than the presence of many other children at the same time and place, engaged in shopping and other activities not prohibited. Accordingly, in view of the preferred position the freedoms of the First Article occupy, the statute in its present application must fall. It cannot be sustained by any presumption of validity. And, finally, it is said, the statute is, as to children, an absolute prohibition, not merely a reasonable regulation, of the denounced activity.

Concededly a statute or ordinance identical in terms with Section 69, except that it is applicable to adults or all persons generally, would be invalid. But the mere fact a state could not wholly prohibit this form of adult activity, whether characterized locally as a "sale" or otherwise, does not mean it cannot do so for children. Such a conclusion granted would mean that a state could impose no greater limitation upon child labor than upon adult labor. Or, if an adult were free to enter dance halls, saloons, and disreputable places generally, in order to discharge his conceived religious duty to admonish or dissuade persons from frequenting such places, so would be a child with similar convictions and objectives, if not alone then in the parent's company, against the state's command.

The state's authority over children's activities is broader than over like actions of adults. This is peculiarly true of public activities and matters of employment. A democratic society rests, for its continuance, upon the healthy, well-rounded growth of young people into full maturity as citizens, with all that implies. It may secure this against impeding restraints and dangers, within a broad range of selection. Among evils most appropriate for such action are the crippling effects of child employment, more especially in public places, and the possible harms arising from other activities subject to all the diverse influences of the street. It is too late now to doubt that legislation appropriately designed to reach such evils is within the state's police power, whether against the parents' claim to control of the child or one that religious scruples dictate contrary action.

It is true children have rights, in common with older people, in the primary use of highways. But even in such use streets afford dangers for them not affecting adults. And in other uses, whether in work or in other things, this difference may be magnified. This is so not only when children are unaccompanied but certainly to some extent when they are with their parents. What may be wholly permissible for adults therefore may not be so for children, either with or without their parents' presence. . . .

. . . The zealous though lawful exercise of the right to engage in propagandizing the community, whether in religious, political, or other matters, may and at times does create situations difficult enough for adults to cope with and wholly inappropriate for children, especially of tender years, to face. Other harmful possibilities could be stated, of emotional excitement and psychological or physical injury. Parents may be free to become martyrs themselves. But it does not follow they are free, in identical circumstances, to make martyrs of their children before they have reached the age of full and legal discretion when they can make that choice for themselves. Massachusetts has determined that an absolute prohibition, though one limited to streets and public places and to the incidental uses proscribed, is necessary to accomplish its legitimate objectives. Its power to attain them is broad enough to reach these peripheral instances in which the parent's supervision may reduce but cannot eliminate entirely the ill effects of the prohibited conduct. We think that with reference to the public proclaiming of religion, upon the streets and in other similar public places, the power of the state to control the conduct of children reaches beyond the scope of its authority over adults, as is true in the case of other freedoms, and the rightful boundary of its power has not been crossed in this case. . . .

The judgment is affirmed.

NOTES AND QUESTIONS

1. A statute prohibiting adults from distributing religious magazines on the street would surely be unconstitutional. Why is the statute valid when directed to children? What does the Court assume in upholding this regulation?

2. Against what evils is the child being protected? Against the parents themselves, as the quotation regarding martyrdom seems to suggest? But why is the parents' behavior dangerous?

3. What interest of the child is served by the statute? Against what values is the desirability of distributing religious literature measured?

4. In what sense is this a children's rights case? In what sense a parental rights case?

5. To the extent that parental rights are involved, are they founded on the First Amendment or on some other constitutional basis? As the Court analyzes the issues, does it make any difference?

WISCONSIN V. YODER

406 U.S. 205 (1972)

BURGER, J. . . . Respondents Jonas Yoder and Wallace Miller are members of the Old Order Amish religion, and respondent Adin Yutzy is a member of the Conservative Amish Mennonite Church. They and their families are residents of Green County, Wisconsin. Wisconsin's compulsory school-attendance law required them to cause their children to attend public or private school until reaching age 16 but the respondents declined to send their children, ages 14 and 15, to public school after they completed the eighth grade. The children were not enrolled in any private school, or within any recognized exception to the compulsory-attendance law, and they are conceded to be subject to the Wisconsin statute.

On complaint of the school district administrator for the public schools, respondents were charged, tried, and convicted of violating the compulsory-attendance law in Green County Court and were fined the sum of $5 each. Respondents defended on the ground that the application of the compulsory-attendance law violated their rights under the First and Fourteenth Amendments. The trial testimony showed that respondents believed, in accordance with the tenets of Old Order Amish communities generally, that their children's attendance at high school, public or private, was contrary to the Amish religion and way of life. They believed that by sending their children to high school, they would not only expose themselves to the danger of the censure of the church community, but, as found by the county court, also endanger their own salvation and that of their children. The State stipulated that respondents' religious beliefs were sincere.

In support of their position, respondents presented as expert witnesses scholars on religion and education whose testimony is uncontradicted. They expressed their opinions on the relationship of the Amish belief concerning school attendance to the more general tenets of their religion, and described the impact that compulsory high school attendance could have on the continued survival of Amish communities as they exist in the United States today. The history of the Amish sect was given in some detail, beginning with the Swiss Anabaptists of the 16th century who rejected institutionalized churches and sought to return to the early, simple, Christian life de-emphasizing material success, rejecting the competitive spirit, and seeking to insulate themselves from the modern world. As a result of their common heritage, Old Order Amish communities today are characterized by a fundamental belief that salvation requires life in a church community separate and apart from the world and worldly influence. This concept of life aloof from the world and its values is central to their faith.

A related feature of Old Order Amish communities is their devotion to a life in harmony with nature and the soil, as exemplified by the simple life of the early Christian era that continued in America during much of our early national life. Amish beliefs require members of the community to make their living by farming or closely related activities. Broadly speaking, the Old Order Amish religion pervades and determines the entire mode of life of its adherents. Their conduct is regulated in great detail by the *Ordnung*, or rules, of the church community. Adult baptism, which occurs in late adolescence, is the time at which Amish young people voluntarily undertake heavy obligations, not unlike the Bar Mitzvah of the Jews, to abide by the rules of the church community.

Amish objection to formal education beyond the eighth grade is firmly grounded in these central religious concepts. They object to the high school, and higher education generally, because the values they teach are in marked variance with Amish values and the Amish way of life; they view secondary school education as an impermissible exposure of their children to a "worldly" influence in conflict with their beliefs. The high school tends to emphasize intellectual and scientific accomplishments, self-distinction, competitiveness, worldly success, and social life with other students. Amish society emphasizes informal learning-through-doing; a life of "goodness," rather than a life of intellect; wisdom, rather than technical knowledge; community welfare, rather than competition; and separation from, rather than integration with, contemporary worldly society.

Formal high school education beyond the eighth grade is contrary to Amish beliefs, not only because it places Amish children in an environment hostile to Amish beliefs with increasing emphasis on competition in class work and sports and with pressure to conform to the styles, manners, and ways of the peer group, but also because it takes them away from their community, physically and emotionally, during the crucial and formative adolescent period of life. During this period, the children must acquire Amish attitudes favoring manual work and self-reliance and the specific skills needed to perform the adult role of an Amish farmer or housewife. They must learn to enjoy physical labor. Once a child has learned basic reading, writing, and elementary mathematics, these traits, skills, and attitudes admittedly fall within the category of those best learned through example and "doing" rather than in a classroom. And, at this time in life, the Amish child must also grow in his faith and his relationship to the Amish community if he is to be prepared to accept the heavy obligations imposed by adult baptism. In short, high school attendance with teachers who are not of the Amish faith—and may even be hostile to it—interposes a serious barrier to the integration of the Amish child into the Amish religious community. Dr. John Hostetler, one of the experts on Amish society, testified that the modern high school is not equipped, in curriculum or social environment, to impart the values promoted by Amish society....

On the basis of such considerations, Dr. Hostetler testified that compulsory high school attendance could not only result in great psychological harm to Amish children, because of the conflicts it would produce, but would also, in his opinion, ultimately result in the destruction of the Old Order Amish church community as it exists in the United States today.... The evidence also showed that the Amish have an excellent record as law-abiding and generally self-sufficient members of society....

I

There is no doubt as to the power of a State, having a high responsibility for education of its citizens, to impose reasonable regulations for the control and duration of basic education. *See, e.g.,* Pierce v. Society of Sisters, 268 U.S. 510 (1925). Providing public schools ranks at the very apex of the function of a State.

Yet even this paramount responsibility was, in *Pierce*, made to yield to the right of parents to provide an equivalent education in a privately operated system. . . . As that case suggests, the values of parental direction of the religious upbringing and education of their children in their early and formative years have a high place in our society. Thus, a State's interest in universal education, however highly we rank it, is not totally free from a balancing process when it impinges on fundamental rights and interests, such as those specifically protected by the Free Exercise Clause of the First Amendment, and the traditional interest of parents with respect to the religious upbringing of their children so long as they, in the words of *Pierce*, "prepare [them] for additional obligations."

The essence of all that has been said and written on the subject is that only those interests of the highest order and those not otherwise served can overbalance legitimate claims to the free exercise of religion. We can accept it as settled, therefore, that, however strong the State's interest in universal compulsory education, it is by no means absolute to the exclusion or subordination of all other interests.

II

We come then to the quality of the claims of the respondents concerning the alleged encroachment of Wisconsin's compulsory school-attendance statute on their rights and the rights of their children to the free exercise of the religious beliefs they and their forbears have adhered to for almost three centuries. In evaluating those claims we must be careful to determine whether the Amish religious faith and their mode of life are, as they claim, inseparable and interdependent. A way of life, however virtuous and admirable, may not be interposed as a barrier to reasonable state regulation of education if it is based on purely secular considerations; to have the protection of the Religion Clauses, the claims must be rooted in religious belief. Although a determination of what is a "religious" belief or practice entitled to constitutional protection may present a most delicate question, the very concept of ordered liberty precludes allowing every person to make his own standards on matters of conduct in which society as a whole has important interests. Thus, if the Amish asserted their claims because of their subjective evaluation and rejection of the contemporary secular values accepted by the majority, much as Thoreau rejected the social values of his time and isolated himself at Walden Pond, their claims would not rest on a religious basis. Thoreau's choice was philosophical and personal rather than religious, and such belief does not rise to the demands of the Religion Clauses. Giving no weight to such secular considerations, however, we see that the record in this case abundantly supports the claim that the traditional way of life of the Amish is not merely a matter of personal preference, but one of deep religious conviction, shared by an organized group, and intimately related to daily living. . . . As the expert witnesses explained, the Old Order Amish religion pervades and determines virtually their entire way of life. . . .

We turn, then, to the State's broader contention that its interest in its system of compulsory education is so compelling that even the established religious practices of the Amish must give way. Where fundamental claims of religious freedom are at stake, however, we cannot accept such a sweeping claim; despite its admitted validity in the generality of cases, we must searchingly examine the interests that the State seeks to promote by its requirement for compulsory education to age 16, and the impediment to those objectives that would flow from recognizing the claimed Amish exemption.

The State advances two primary arguments in support of its system of compulsory education. It notes, as Thomas Jefferson pointed out early in our history, that some degree of education is necessary to prepare citizens to participate effectively and intelligently in our open political system if we are to preserve freedom and independence. Further, education prepares individuals to be self-reliant and self-sufficient participants in society. We accept these propositions.

However, the evidence adduced by the Amish in this case is persuasively to the effect that an additional one or two years of formal high school for Amish children in place of their long-established program of informal vocational education would do little to serve those interests. Respondents' experts testified at trial, without challenge, that the value of all education must be assessed in terms of its capacity to prepare the child for life. It is one thing to say that compulsory education for a year or two beyond the eighth grade may be necessary when its goal is the preparation of the child for life in modern society as the majority live, but it is quite another if the goal of education be viewed as the preparation of the child for life in the separated agrarian community that is the keystone of the Amish faith. *See* Meyer v. Nebraska, 262 U.S., at 400.

The State attacks respondents' position as one fostering "ignorance" from which the child must be protected by the State. No one can question the State's duty to protect children from ignorance but this argument does not square with the facts disclosed in the record. Whatever their idiosyncrasies as seen by the majority, this record strongly shows that the Amish community has been a highly successful social unit within our society, even if apart from the conventional "mainstream." Its members are productive and very law-abiding members of society; they reject public welfare in any of its usual modern forms. The Congress itself recognized their self-sufficiency by authorizing exemption of such groups as the Amish from the obligation to pay social security taxes.

It is neither fair nor correct to suggest that the Amish are opposed to education beyond the eighth grade level. What this record shows is that they are opposed to conventional formal education of the type provided by a certified high school because it comes at the child's crucial adolescent period of religious development. Dr. Donald Erickson, for example, testified that their system of learning-by-doing was an "ideal system" of education in terms of preparing Amish children for life as adults in the Amish community, and that "I would be inclined to say they do a better job in this than most of the rest of us do." As he put it, "These people aren't purporting to be learned people, and it seems to me the self-sufficiency of the community is the best evidence I can point to—whatever is being done seems to function well.". . .

The State, however, supports its interest in providing an additional one or two years of compulsory high school education to Amish children because of the possibility that some such children will choose to leave the Amish community, and that if this occurs they will be ill-equipped for life. The State argues that if Amish children leave their church they should not be in the position of making their way in the world without the education available in the one or two additional years the State requires. However, on this record, that argument is highly speculative. There is no specific evidence of the loss of Amish adherents by attrition, nor is there any showing that upon leaving the Amish community Amish children, with their practical agricultural training and habits of industry and self-reliance, would become burdens on society because of educational shortcomings. Indeed, this argument of the State appears to rest primarily on the State's mistaken assumption, already noted, that the Amish do not provide any education for their children beyond the eighth grade, but allow them to grow in "ignorance." To the contrary, not only do the Amish accept the necessity for formal schooling through the eighth grade level, but continue to provide what has been characterized by the undisputed testimony of expert educators as an "ideal" vocational education for their children in the adolescent years.

There is nothing in this record to suggest that the Amish qualities of reliability, self-reliance, and dedication to work would fail to find ready markets in today's society. Absent some contrary evidence supporting the State's position, we are unwilling to assume that persons possessing such valuable vocational skills and habits are doomed to become burdens on society should they determine to leave the Amish faith, nor is there any basis in the record to warrant a finding that an additional one or two years of formal school education beyond the eighth grade would serve to eliminate any such problem that might exist.

Insofar as the State's claim rests on the view that a brief additional period of formal education is imperative to enable the Amish to participate effectively and intelligently in our democratic process, it must fall. The Amish alternative to formal secondary school education has enabled them to function effectively in their day-to-day life under self-imposed limitations on relations with the world, and to survive and prosper in contemporary society as a separate, sharply identifiable and highly self-sufficient community for more than 200 years in this country. In itself this is strong evidence that they are capable of fulfilling the social and political responsibilities of citizenship without compelled attendance beyond the eighth grade at the price of jeopardizing their free exercise of religious belief. . . . Even their idiosyncratic separateness exemplifies the diversity we profess to admire and encourage. . . .

The requirement of compulsory schooling to age 16 must . . . be viewed as aimed not merely at providing educational opportunities for children, but as an alternative to the equally undesirable consequence of unhealthful child labor displacing adult workers, or, on the other hand, forced idleness. The two kinds of statutes — compulsory school attendance and child labor laws — tend to keep children of certain ages off the labor market and in school; this regimen in turn provides opportunity to prepare for a livelihood of a higher order than that which children could pursue without education and protects their health in adolescence.

In these terms, Wisconsin's interest in compelling the school attendance of Amish children to age 16 emerges as somewhat less substantial than requiring such attendance for children generally. For, while agricultural employment is not totally outside the legitimate concerns of the child labor laws, employment of children under parental guidance and on the family farm from age 14 to age 16 is an ancient tradition that lies at the periphery of the objectives of such laws. There is no intimation that the Amish employment of their children on family farms is in any way deleterious to their health or that Amish parents exploit children at tender years. Any such inference would be contrary to the record before us. Moreover, employment of Amish children on the family farm does not present the undesirable economic aspects of eliminating jobs that might otherwise be held by adults.

IV

Finally, the State, on authority of Prince v. Massachusetts, argues that a decision exempting Amish children from the State's requirement fails to recognize the substantive right of the Amish child to a secondary education, and fails to give due regard to the power of the State as *parens patriae* to extend the benefit of secondary education to children regardless of the wishes of their parents. Taken at its broadest sweep, the Court's language in *Prince* might be read to give support to the State's position. However, the Court was not confronted in *Prince* with a situation comparable to that of the Amish as revealed in this record; this is shown by the Court's severe characterization of the evils that it thought the legislature could legitimately associate with child labor, even when performed in the company of an adult. 321 U.S., at 169-170. . . .

This case, of course, is not one in which any harm to the physical or mental health of the child or to the public safety, peace, order, or welfare has been demonstrated or may be properly inferred. The record is to the contrary, and any reliance on that theory would find no support in the evidence. . . .

Our holding in no way determines the proper resolution of possible competing interests of parents, children, and the State in an appropriate state court proceeding in which the power of the State is asserted on the theory that Amish parents are preventing their minor children from attending high school despite their expressed desires to the contrary. Recognition of the claim of the State in such a proceeding would, of course, call into question traditional concepts of parental control over the religious upbringing and education of their minor children recognized in this Court's past decisions. It is clear that such an intrusion by a State into family decisions in the area of religious training would give rise to grave questions of religious freedom comparable to those raised here and those presented in Pierce v. Society of Sisters, 268 U.S. 510 (1925). On this record we neither reach nor decide those issues.

The State's argument proceeds without reliance on any actual conflict between the wishes of parents and children. It appears to rest on the potential that exemption of Amish parents from the requirements of the compulsory-education law might allow some parents to act contrary to the best interests of their children by foreclosing their opportunity to make an intelligent choice between the Amish way of life and that of the outside world. The same argument could, of course, be made with respect to all church schools short of college. There is nothing in the record or in the ordinary course of human experience to suggest that non-Amish parents generally consult with children of ages 14-16 if they are placed in a church school of the parents' faith.

Indeed it seems clear that if the State is empowered, as *parens patriae*, to "save" a child from himself or his Amish parents by requiring an additional two years of compulsory formal high school education, the State will in large measure influence, if not determine, the religious future of the child. Even more markedly than in *Prince*, therefore, this case involves the fundamental interest of parents, as contrasted with that of the State, to guide the religious future and education of their children. The history and culture of Western civilization reflect a strong tradition of parental concern for the nurture and upbringing of their children. This primary role of the parents in the upbringing of their children is now established beyond debate as an enduring American tradition. If not the first, perhaps the most significant statements of the Court in this area are found in Pierce v. Society of Sisters. . . .

The duty to prepare the child for "additional obligations," referred to by the Court, must be read to include the inculcation of moral standards, religious beliefs, and elements of good citizenship. *Pierce*, of course, recognized that where nothing more than the general interest of the parent in the nurture and education of his children is involved, it is beyond dispute that the State acts "reasonably" and constitutionally in requiring education to age 16 in some public or private school meeting the standards prescribed by the State. . . .

Affirmed.

WHITE, J., with whom Mr. Justice BRENNAN and Mr. Justice STEWART join, concurring. Cases such as this one inevitably call for a delicate balancing of important but conflicting interests. I join the opinion and judgment of the Court because I cannot say that the State's interest in requiring two more years of compulsory education in the ninth and tenth grades outweighs the importance of the concededly sincere Amish religious practice to the survival of that sect.

This would be a very different case for me if respondents' claim were that their religion forbade their children from attending any school at any time and from complying in any way with the educational standards set by the State. Since the Amish children are permitted to acquire the basic tools of literacy to survive in modern society by attending grades one through eight and since the deviation from the State's compulsory-education law is relatively slight, I conclude that respondents' claim must prevail, largely because "religious freedom—the freedom to believe and to practice strange and, it may be, foreign creeds—has classically been one of the highest values of our society."

DOUGLAS, J., dissenting in part. . . . The Court's analysis assumes that the only interests at stake in the case are those of the Amish parents on the one hand, and those of the State on the other. The difficulty with this approach is that, despite the Court's claim, the parents are seeking to vindicate not only their own free exercise claims, but also those of their high-school-age children.

It is argued that the right of the Amish children to religious freedom is not presented by the facts of the case, as the issue before the Court involves only the Amish parents' religious freedom to defy a state criminal statute imposing upon them an affirmative duty to cause their children to attend high school. . . .

[I]t is essential to reach the question to decide the case, not only because the question was squarely raised in the motion to dismiss, but also because no analysis of religious-liberty claims can take place in a vacuum. If the parents in this case are allowed a religious exemption, the inevitable effect is to impose the parents' notions of religious duty upon their children. Where the child is mature enough to express potentially conflicting desires, it would be an invasion of the child's rights to permit such an imposition without canvassing his views. As in Prince v. Massachusetts, 321 U.S. 158, it is an imposition resulting from this very litigation. As the child has no other effective forum, it is in this litigation that his rights should be considered. And, if an Amish child desires to attend high school, and is mature enough to have that desire respected, the State may well be able to override the parents' religiously motivated objections. . . .

II

This issue has never been squarely presented before today. Our opinions are full of talk about the power of the parents over the child's education. *See* Pierce v. Society of Sisters, 268 U.S. 510; Meyer v. Nebraska, 262 U.S. 390. And we have in the past analyzed similar conflicts between parent and State with little regard for the views of the child. *See* Prince v. Massachusetts, *supra*. Recent cases, however, have clearly held that the children themselves have constitutionally protectible interests. . . .

On this important and vital matter of education, I think the children should be entitled to be heard. While the parents, absent dissent, normally speak for the entire family, the education of the child is a matter on which the child will often have decided views. He may want to be a pianist or an astronaut or an oceanographer. To do so he will have to break from the Amish tradition.

It is the future of the student, not the future of the parents, that is imperiled by today's decision. If a parent keeps his child out of school beyond the grade school, then the child will be forever barred from entry into the new and amazing world of diversity that we have today. The child may decide that that is the preferred course, or he may rebel. It is the student's judgment, not his parents', that is essential if we are to give full meaning to what we have said about the Bill of Rights and of the right of students to be masters of their own destiny. If he is harnessed to the Amish way of life by those in authority over him and if his education is truncated, his entire life may be stunted and deformed. The child, therefore, should be given an opportunity to be heard before the State gives the exemption which we honor today.

The views of the two children in question were not canvassed by the Wisconsin courts. The matter should be explicitly reserved so that new hearings can be held on remand of the case. . . .

NOTES AND QUESTIONS

1. *Meyer*, *Pierce*, and *Yoder* indicate the legal and moral complexity of parent-child relations. Are these cases about parents' rights, children's rights, or both?

2. How strongly do these cases support parental rights as against state authority? How far do the holdings of these cases restrict the state's power to require education in schools the state approves?

3. Chief Justice Burger concedes that the state would have a substantial interest in protecting children from "ignorance" but states that this principle is irrelevant in *Yoder*. Why is it irrelevant? How is "ignorance" or "education" understood by the state, the Amish, and Chief Justice Burger? Is the Amish position not precisely that ignorance in some respects is bliss?

What is the conflict really about? What happens between the eighth and tenth grades in high school that is either valuable or harmful, depending on one's perspective? Do other things happen?

4. To what extent is *Yoder*'s acceptance of the Amish wish to withdraw children from public school after eighth grade tied to the traditional Amish farming way of life?

Today, instead of farming, most Amish boys and men work in sawmills and factories making wooden furniture to sell to outsiders. Federal child labor laws prohibit children younger than 18 from working in sawmills, which are one of the most dangerous workplaces, but in 2004 Senator Arlen Specter of Pennsylvania successfully sponsored an exemption to the laws for the Amish. Girls make quilts and work in Amish shops and restaurants. Louise Weinberg, The McReynolds Mystery Solved, 90 Denv. U. L. Rev. 133, 153-155 (2011).

Professor Weinberg described the experience of Amish teenagers in today's world:

It is increasingly understood that these children have few options. Some Amish, whether remaining within or departing from their communities, have begun to write books about Amish life. Although some Amish authors praise the serenity of the lives they led or are leading, others explain that the denial to them of an education when they were young made it difficult for them to live outside the community. Some charge that the children are kept uneducated for the very purpose of binding them to the community.

Other facts have been coming to light as well. The strongest measure of the community's confidence in its ultimate control over its children is the practice of *rumspringa*, a traditional "running around" period allotted to youngsters. At about the age of eighteen, Amish youngsters are permitted, if they wish, to go off and do anything they like. Because the Amish are Anabaptists who believe in adult baptism, these youngsters are not yet baptized, and therefore, technically, their sins somehow do not "count." *Rumspringa* can be imagined as a time to sew wild oats before taking on the heavy responsibilities baptism imposes on the Amish.

Rumspringa can last as long as a youngster likes, postponing baptism indefinitely. Many Amish youngsters prefer to stay home under the supervision of their parents, and at most may attend a dance or party, or an overnight visit to a friend. These youngsters submit to baptism eagerly. Many others go off in groups, interesting themselves in fornication, alcohol, and narcotics.

Looked at functionally, *rumspringa* is the ultimate demonstration to the children that they are substantially unable to leave the community, that for them there is no such thing as freedom. There is little room for these undereducated waifs in modern society. Such employment as they can find outside their community, even in good times, does not often improve on the labor awaiting them at home. Although statistics vary widely, it appears that Chief Justice Burger's observation remains more true than he knew: There is very little attrition among the Amish.

Id. at 156-157. If *Yoder* were decided in light of these changed conditions and this additional information, would the outcome be the same?

5. Do *Meyer, Pierce, Prince,* and *Yoder* recognize any independent role for the child? Consider the following observations in Barbara Bennett Woodhouse, "Who Owns the Child?": *Meyer* and *Pierce* and the Child as Property, 33 Wm. & Mary L. Rev. 995, 1114-1115 (1992):

> [O]ur legal system fails to respect children. Children are often used as instruments, as in *Meyer* and *Pierce*. The child is denied her own voice and identity and becomes a conduit for the parents' religious expression, cultural identity, and class aspirations. The parents' authority to speak for and through the child is explicit in *Meyer*'s "right of control" and *Pierce*'s "high duty" of the parent to direct his child's destiny. Later cases, like Wisconsin v. Yoder, seem to ratify this instrumentalism. The minor child is a key tool of the parents' free exercise but has no independent free exercise protections. Even when *Meyer* and *Pierce* lead to the vindication of First Amendment liberties, it is thus the parent's voice and choice that we hear and not the child's. Obviously, good reasons exist for presuming that the parent speaks for the child. I am sure that Brandeis and McReynolds would both agree that, ordinarily, the best guardian of the child's intellectual liberty and welfare is the parent. But constitutionalizing this presumption as the parents' "right" to speak, choose, and live through the child has led to its being too often invoked in situations in which it is, at best, unnecessary or, at worst, oppressive.

6. The Court in *Yoder* insists that its decision is not inconsistent with *Prince*. Are you convinced? How can we avoid saying that the parents in *Yoder* are permitted to make martyrs of their children in pursuit of their (the parents') beliefs? On the other hand, how much weight should be placed on the preference of a 15-year-old?

PROBLEM

You represent the Swivet County School Board. The principal of Swivet Junior High School has approached you with the following problem.

The parents of two of her students who are finishing eighth grade belong to the Old Order Amish religion. They wish to withdraw their children from her school. Both children are 14 years of age and have said that they would like to continue in school.

One of these children is Adolph. Adolph has been a very fine student, at the top of his class, and has demonstrated unusually good abilities in mathematics and science. His standardized test scores in those subjects place him in the top 1 percent of the country. Adolph has said that he wants to be a scientist when he grows up, and the principal is confident that he has great promise.

The other student is Rudolph. Rudolph is a good, although not outstanding, student. He is, however, very popular with members of his class, although his beliefs seem a bit odd to some of his classmates. In fact, Rudolph was elected class president and is active in the school choir and other programs. Rudolph would like to stay in school to be with his friends.

The principal would like your assistance in helping both Adolph and Rudolph to stay in school. How would you advise her?

2.   *Regulation of Homeschooling*

One way of understanding *Yoder* is that the Amish parents wanted to home-school their children after the eighth grade and that the Supreme Court held they were constitutionally entitled to do so. While today all states permit homeschooling, the opposite was true as recently as 1981. A movement supporting homeschooling emerged in the 1970s among parents from both ends of the political spectrum who wished to "withdraw from mainstream secular life." Martha Albertson Fineman & George Shepherd, Homeschooling: Choosing Parental Rights Over Children's Interests, 46 U. Balt. L. Rev. 57, 64 (2016). Two advocacy organizations successfully lobbied for legislation legalizing homeschooling with minimal regulation in most states. The website of one of these groups says that its mission is "To preserve and advance the fundamental, God-given, constitutional right of parents and others legally responsible for their children to direct their education. In so doing, we rely on two fundamental freedoms—parental rights and religious freedom." Home School Legal Defense Association, Mission Statement, https://hslda.org/content/about/mission.asp (June 26, 2018). The next case concerns an effort to apply *Meyer*, *Pierce*, and *Yoder* to invalidate regulations on homeschooling.

COMBS V. HOME-CENTER SCHOOL DISTRICT

540 F.3d 231 (3rd Cir. 2008)

PER CURIAM. . . . The Commonwealth of Pennsylvania's education system, as enacted by the General Assembly, allows parents to satisfy the compulsory attendance requirement through "home education programs." Parents supervising the home education programs must provide instruction for a minimum number of days and hours in certain subjects and submit a portfolio of teaching logs and the children's work product for review. The local school district reviews the home education programs for compliance with the minimum hours of instruction and course requirements and determines whether each student demonstrates progress in the overall program. The school district does not review the educational content, textbooks, curriculum, instructional materials, or methodology of the program. . . .

Parents have home-schooled their children for many years. All six families are Christians, but of different denominations. They hold in common a religious belief that "education of their children, not merely the religious education, is religion" and that God has assigned religious matters to the exclusive jurisdiction of the family. Accordingly, because God has given Parents the sole responsibility for educating their children, the school districts' reporting requirements and "discretionary review" over their home education programs violate their free exercise of religion. . . .

. . . Parents sued the school districts in various state and federal courts seeking declaratory and injunctive relief under the First and Fourteenth Amendments to the United States Constitution, 42 U.S.C. § 1983. . . . The District Court engaged in two rounds of summary judgment motions.

The first round addressed facial challenges to Act 169. Parents filed a consolidated motion for summary judgment and the school districts filed a consolidated opposition, but did not file a cross-motion for summary judgment. The District Court denied Parents' motion. In the second round, the school districts filed a motion for summary judgment addressing both Parents' facial and "as applied" challenges to Act 169. The District Court granted the school districts' motion, concluding that . . . Act 169 is a neutral law of general applicability, satisfying rational basis review. . . .

The Pennsylvania Constitution mandates that the General Assembly "provide for the maintenance and support of a thorough and efficient system of public education to serve the needs of the Commonwealth." The General Assembly has carried out its constitutional charge by enacting the Public School Code.

The Public School Code requires "every child of compulsory school age having a legal residence in this Commonwealth . . . to attend a day school in which the subjects and activities prescribed by the standards of the State Board of Education are taught in the English language.". . .

The Pennsylvania General Assembly currently permits parents to choose among four alternative categories of education to satisfy the compulsory attendance requirement: (1) a public school with certain trade school options, (2) a private academic day school or private tutoring, (3) a day school operated by a "bona fide church or other religious body," or (4) a "home education program."

. . . A home education program must satisfy the same minimum hours of instruction requirements and almost all of the same subject matter requirements as a school operated by a bona fide church or religious body. . . .

The superintendent of the public school district of the child's residence is charged with ensuring that each child is receiving "appropriate education," which is defined by Act 169 as "a program consisting of instruction in the required subjects for the time required in this act and in which the student demonstrates sustained progress in the overall program." In order to demonstrate to the superintendent that "appropriate education" is taking place, at the end of each public school year the supervisor of the home education program must submit a file with two types of documentation. First, the file must contain a portfolio of records and materials:

> The portfolio shall consist of a log, made contemporaneously with the instruction, which designates by title the reading materials used, samples of any writings, worksheets, workbooks or creative materials used or developed by the student and in grades three, five and eight results of nationally normed standardized achievement tests in reading/language arts and mathematics or the results of Statewide tests administered in these grade levels. The department shall establish a list, with a minimum of five tests, of nationally normed standardized tests from which the supervisor of the home education program shall select a test to be administered if the supervisor does not choose the Statewide tests. At the discretion of the supervisor, the portfolio may include the results of nationally normed standardized achievement tests for other subject areas or grade levels. The supervisor shall ensure that the nationally normed standardized tests or the Statewide tests shall not be administered by the child's parent or guardian.

Second, the supervisor of the home education program must obtain an annual written evaluation of the child's work. The supervisor may choose any person qualified under Act 169 to make the evaluation. The evaluation measures:

> the student's educational progress. . . . The evaluation shall also be based on an interview of the child and a review of the portfolio required in clause (1) and shall certify whether or not an appropriate education is occurring.

Based upon the entire file—the portfolio of records and materials and the third-party evaluation—the superintendent determines whether the home education program provides the child with an "appropriate education." . . .

In practice, the school districts engage in a limited level of oversight. . . . Deposition testimony reveals that school officials do not check in on the progress of home education programs during the school year. Furthermore, all school officials deposed acknowledged that they never disagreed with or rejected an independent evaluator's assessment of the home education program. School officials reviewed the disclosures for compliance with the statute and, if all the required disclosures were presented, the home education program would be approved. . . .

We address Parents' federal constitutional claim. Parents contend Act 169 imposes a substantial burden on the free exercise of religion as protected by the First and Fourteenth Amendments. . . .

In Employment Division, Department of Human Resources of Oregon v. Smith, 494 U.S. 872, 890 (1990), the Supreme Court held "a law that is neutral and of general applicability need not be justified by a compelling governmental interest even if the law has the incidental effect of burdening a particular religious practice." . . .

Act 169 is a neutral law of general applicability. It neither targets religious practice nor selectively imposes burdens on religiously motivated conduct. Instead, it imposes the same requirements on parents who home-school for secular reasons as on parents who do so for religious reasons. Furthermore, nothing in the record suggests Commonwealth school officials discriminate against religiously motivated home education programs (e.g., denying approval of home education programs because they include faith-based curriculum materials). . . .

Since Act 169 is a neutral law of general applicability, we will apply rational basis review unless an exception to the *Smith* rule applies. "[R]ational basis review requires merely that the action be rationally related to a legitimate government objective." "Under rational basis review, 'a statute is presumed constitutional, and the burden is on the one attacking the legislative arrangement to negative every conceivable basis which might support it, whether or not that basis has a foundation in the record.'"

The Commonwealth has a legitimate interest in ensuring children taught under home education programs are achieving minimum educational standards and are demonstrating sustained progress in their educational program. *See, e.g.,* Pierce v. Soc.'y of Sisters of the Holy Names of Jesus and Mary, 268 U.S. 510, 534 (1925) (acknowledging the "power of the State reasonably to regulate all schools, to inspect, supervise and examine them, their teachers and pupils"). In *Brown v. Board of Education,* the Supreme Court noted the importance of education and the meaningful role the state plays in preparing a child for citizenship and adult life:

> Today, education is perhaps the most important function of state and local governments. Compulsory school attendance laws and the great expenditures for education both demonstrate our recognition of the importance of education to our democratic society. It is required in the performance of our most basic public responsibilities, even service in the armed forces. It is the very foundation of good citizenship. Today it is a principal instrument in awakening the child to cultural values, in preparing him for later professional training, and in helping him to adjust normally to his environment. In these days, it is doubtful that any child may reasonably be expected to succeed in life if he is denied the opportunity of an education.

347 U.S. 483, 493 (1954). Act 169's disclosure requirements and corresponding school district review rationally further these legitimate state interests. Accordingly, Act 169 survives rational basis review.

Parents assert their claim falls within a "hybrid-rights" exception the Supreme Court discussed in *Smith:*

> The only decisions in which we have held that the First Amendment bars application of a neutral, generally applicable law to religiously motivated action have involved not the Free Exercise Clause alone, but the Free Exercise Clause in conjunction with other constitutional protections, such as freedom of speech and of the press, or the right of parents, acknowledged in Pierce v. Society of Sisters, [268 U.S. 510 (1925)], to direct the education of their children, *see* Wisconsin v. Yoder, [406 U.S. 205 (1972)] (invalidating compulsory school-attendance laws as applied to Amish parents who refused on religious grounds to send their children to school).

Parents contend Act 169 substantially burdens both their free exercise of religion and their fundamental right as parents, under the Fourteenth Amendment, to direct the education and upbringing of their children. Accordingly, they invoke the hybrid-rights exception of *Smith*, seeking strict scrutiny review. Alternatively, Parents contend that, notwithstanding our hybrid-rights determination, Wisconsin v. Yoder remains good law and the same constitutional test applies here.

Although we have discussed the *Smith* hybrid-rights theory in prior opinions, its meaning and application remains an open question in our circuit. We have never decided a case based on a hybrid-rights claim, let alone the type of a hybrid-rights claim invoked here—one based on the Free Exercise Clause and the companion right to direct a child's upbringing.

Smith's hybrid-rights theory has divided our sister circuits. Some characterize the theory as dicta and others use different standards to decide whether a plaintiff has asserted a cognizable hybrid-rights claim. The United States Courts of Appeals for the Second and Sixth Circuits have concluded the hybrid-rights language in *Smith* is dicta. Furthermore, the United States Court of Appeals for the Sixth Circuit views the hybrid-rights exception as "completely illogical," and the United States Court of Appeals for the Second Circuit "can think of no good reason for the standard of review to vary simply with the number of constitutional rights that the plaintiff asserts have been violated." Accordingly, when faced with a neutral law of general applicability, both appellate courts decline to allow the application of strict scrutiny to hybrid-rights claims and instead apply *Smith*'s rational basis standard.

The United States Courts of Appeals for the First Circuit and District of Columbia have acknowledged that hybrid-rights claims may warrant heightened scrutiny, but have suggested that a plaintiff must meet a stringent standard: the free exercise claim must be conjoined with an independently viable companion right.

This stringent approach requiring an independently valid companion claim has received criticism, most notably that such a requirement would make the free exercise claim superfluous.

The United States Courts of Appeals for the Ninth and Tenth Circuits recognize hybrid rights and require a plaintiff to raise a "colorable claim that a companion right has been violated." They define colorable as "a fair probability or a likelihood, but not a certitude, of success on the merits." They characterize this fact-driven, case-by-case inquiry as "a middle ground between two of the extremes of painting hybrid-rights claims too generously and construing them too narrowly." A plaintiff cannot "simply invoke the parental rights doctrine, combine it with a claimed free-exercise right, and thereby force the government to demonstrate the presence of a compelling state interest." Nor is one required to establish that the challenged law independently violates a companion constitutional right alone, without any recognition of the Free Exercise Clause.

By requiring a "colorable claim" that a companion right has been violated, the United States Courts of Appeals for the Ninth and Tenth Circuits examine "the claimed infringements on the party's claimed rights to determine whether either the claimed rights or the claimed infringements are genuine." Thus, in order to trigger heightened scrutiny, a hybrid-rights plaintiff must show a fair probability or likelihood, but not a certitude, of success on the merits of his companion constitutional claim.

In *Smith*, the Court asserted that the case before it "[did] not present . . . a hybrid situation, but a free exercise claim unconnected with any communicative activity or parental right." The criterion applicable to a free exercise claim combined with a companion constitutional right was left undefined. Since *Smith*, a majority of the Court has not confirmed the viability of the hybrid-rights theory. Until the Supreme Court provides direction, we believe the hybrid-rights theory to be dicta.

Even if we were to apply the approaches used by our sister circuits—"colorable" claim approach and independently viable claim approach—we would find Parents' arguments unconvincing. Under either approach, we must determine whether Parents can establish a hybrid-rights claim by asserting combined violations of the Free Exercise Clause and the companion right of a parent under the Fourteenth Amendment to direct a child's education. Parents have not presented an independent or colorable companion claim and, accordingly, cannot establish a valid hybrid-rights claim.

"The Due Process Clause guarantees more than fair process. . . . The Clause also provides heightened protection against government interference with certain fundamental rights and liberty interests." Washington v. Glucksberg, 521 U.S. 702, 719–20 (1997). In *Glucksberg*, the Supreme Court articulated the fundamental rights protected by the Due Process Clause. Included in the list was the right "to direct the education and upbringing of one's children."

Parents rely on three Supreme Court cases to generally identify a parent's constitutional right to direct a child's education. *See* Meyer v. Nebraska, 262 U.S. 390, 401–03 (1923) (holding state law prohibiting foreign language instruction violated the "power of parents to control the education of their own"); *Pierce*, 268 U.S. at 535–36 (holding state compulsory education law requiring students to attend solely public schools "unreasonably interferes with the liberty of parents . . . to direct the upbringing and education of children under their control"); Wisconsin v. Yoder, 406 U.S. 205, 214 (1972) (finding a compulsory education system, as applied to the Amish, to violate the Free Exercise Clause and the "traditional interest of parents with respect to the religious upbringing of their children so long as they, in the words of *Pierce*, 'prepare (them) for additional obligations' "). But the particular right asserted in this case—the right to be free from all reporting requirements and "discretionary" state oversight of a child's home-school education—has never been recognized.

Although Parents assert the fundamental nature of their general right, it is a limited one. We have noted "[t]he Supreme Court has never been called upon to define the precise boundaries of a parent's right to control a child's upbringing and education. It is clear, however, that the right is neither absolute nor unqualified." "The case law in this area establishes that parents simply do not have a constitutional right to control each and every aspect of their children's education and oust the state's authority over that subject." Furthermore,

> [t]he Court has repeatedly stressed that while parents have a constitutional right to send their children to private schools and a constitutional right to select private schools that offer specialized instruction, they have no constitutional right to provide their children with private school education unfettered by reasonable government regulation.

In addition to *Yoder*, discussed *infra*, Parents rely on *Meyer* and *Pierce* for foundational support. Read together, the cases

> evince the principle that the state cannot prevent parents from choosing a specific educational program—whether it be religious instruction at a private school or instruction in a foreign language. That is, the state does not have the power to "standardize its children" or "foster a homogenous people" by completely foreclosing the opportunity of individuals and groups to choose a different path of education.

In the present case, Parents are given the freedom to choose a "different path of education"—home-schooling—subject only to the Act 169 requirements. The school districts do not have any role in selecting the program Parents wish to follow. Parents are unable to point to a single instance in which the school districts have limited or interfered with their religious teachings and/or materials. . . .

Parents nevertheless contend that the Commonwealth's "subjective" and "discretionary" review over the Act 169 disclosures violates their right to control their children's education. They insist any review of the home education programs must be purely "objective." In other words, they contend the Commonwealth usurps the religious and parental rights of parents when an official makes a limited determination of whether a child has "sustained progress in the overall program." Parents have not articulated their definition of "objective" in their brief. When questioned during oral argument, Parents' counsel was unable or unwilling to provide a concrete explanation or example of an "objective" review. Furthermore, it is difficult to accept Parents' assertion that review of a child's educational progress can truly be objective. The grading of an essay, even on a pass/fail scale, will always be imbued with some element of subjectivity.

As noted, there is no recognized right for parents to educate their children "unfettered by reasonable government regulation." The Court in *Pierce* expressly acknowledged "'the power of the State reasonably to regulate all schools, to inspect, supervise and examine them, their teachers and pupils.'" Furthermore, there is "a distinction between actions that strike at the heart of parental decision-making authority on matters of the greatest importance and other actions that . . . are not of constitutional dimension." Parents identify the general right to control the education of one's child. But Parents do not have a constitutional right to avoid reasonable state regulation of their children's education. Act 169's reporting and superintendent review requirements ensure children taught in home education programs demonstrate progress in the educational program. The statute does not interfere, or authorize any interference, with Parents' religious teachings and/or use of religious materials. Parents' claim under the Fourteenth Amendment is of insufficient constitutional dimension to state either an independently viable or colorable claim. Accordingly, under both the stringent and colorable hybrid-rights approaches of our sister circuits, Parents have not asserted a "hybrid-rights claim."

Parents also contend that, notwithstanding the different standards articulated by the circuits regarding hybrid-rights claims, they raise the same type of claim as the parents in *Yoder*. They contend that since *Yoder* is still good law, parents claiming a religious-parental exemption to a neutral law of general applicability get the benefit of the traditional Free Exercise test. Parents assert that "it is beyond legitimate question that the same constitutional tests employed in *Yoder* must be used here to evaluate these Parents' religious-parental claims."

In *Yoder*, the Court granted a religious-based exception to a regulation of general applicability. But the unique burden suffered by the Amish, combined with the Supreme Court's limiting language, distinguish *Yoder* from this case.

In response to objections by Amish citizens, the *Yoder* Court held that the First Amendment required a partial exemption from a Wisconsin compulsory high-school education law requiring children to attend public or private school until age 16. The Amish refused to send their children, ages 14 and 15, to school after completion of the eighth grade of schooling. The Court noted the Amish's "convincing showing":

> the Amish in this case have convincingly demonstrated the sincerity of their religious beliefs, the interrelationship of belief with their mode of life, the vital role that belief and daily conduct play in the continued survival of Old Order Amish communities and their religious organization, and the hazards presented by the State's enforcement of a statute generally valid as to others.

The Court applied a heightened level of scrutiny and found the State's interest lacking.

Parents favor a broad reading of *Yoder* and insist that it applies to all citizens. But *Yoder*'s reach is restricted by the Court's limiting language and the facts suggesting an exceptional burden imposed on the plaintiffs. In *Yoder,* the religious beliefs of the Amish were completely integrated with their community and "mode of life." As a result, compulsory attendance would "substantially interfer[e] with the religious development of the Amish child and his integration into the way of life of the Amish faith community." Accordingly, the Wisconsin law carried "a very real threat of undermining the Amish community and religious practice," and placed the continued survival of Amish communities in "danger." Compulsory attendance "prevented these Amish parents from making *fundamental* decisions regarding their children's religious upbringing and effectively overrode their ability to pass their religion on to their children, as their faith required."

Before applying a heightened level of scrutiny, the Court wanted to ensure that the "Amish religious faith and their mode of life are, as they claim, inseparable and interdependent." Recognizing the exceptional nature of the Amish's showing, the Court held: "when the interests of parenthood are combined with a free exercise claim of the nature revealed by this record, more than merely a 'reasonable relation to some purpose within the competency of the State' is required to sustain the validity of the State's requirement under the First Amendment."

The United States Court of Appeals for the Second Circuit has interpreted the central underpinning of *Yoder* to be the "threat to the Amish community's way of life, posed by a compulsory school attendance statute." *Leebaert,* 332 F.3d at 144. In *Leebaert,* a parent alleged a violation of the First and Fourteenth Amendments because a school refused to excuse his son from a mandatory health and education course. While not questioning the sincerity of the parent's beliefs, the Second Circuit found the claims were not governed by *Yoder.*

In the pre-*Smith* case New Life Baptist Church Academy v. East Longmeadow, 885 F.2d 940 (1st Cir.1989), a religious school asserted a remarkably similar claim to Parents' claim. The New Life Baptist Church Academy refused to comply with state rules and procedures for determining the adequacy of the secular education provided by the school because it believed "it is a sin to 'submit' [its] educational enterprise to a secular authority for approval." Finding that "the weight of legal precedent is strongly against the Academy's position," the United States Court of Appeals for the First Circuit concluded that "this case differs significantly from [*Yoder*]." It noted that the state's procedures

> do not threaten interference with religious practices, prayer, or religious teaching; and the record, while indicating a sincere religious scruple, does not suggest that enforcement of the [state] procedures would destroy a religious community's way of life. Nor does the record support the view that the Academy, left on its own, would provide "ideal" or even adequate secular education. All these factors make this case quite unlike *Yoder.*

Similarly, the claim raised by the Amish parents in *Yoder* can be distinguished from the claim raised by Parents here. Act 169 does not threaten Parents' or their community's entire mode of life. Even though Parents are required to keep records and submit them for review, they are in complete control of the religious upbringing of their children. In fact, Parents are unable to point to even one occasion in which the school districts have questioned their religious beliefs, texts, or teachings. . . .

Since Act 169 survives rational basis review and since Parents have failed to establish that an exception to *Smith*'s neutral law of general applicability rule applies, Parents' federal constitutional claims fail. . . .

NOTES AND QUESTIONS

1. Why doesn't the *Combs* court employ heightened scrutiny? How does it distinguish *Yoder*? *Meyer* and *Pierce*?

2. Given the history of how uncritically the state implemented the home-schooling law, why do the parents in *Combs* object to the regulations? What reasons does the state give for imposing the regulations? Is the information that parents must submit well-suited to achieving the state's goals?

Most schools do not assert as much control over homeschooling as Pennsylvania does. According to an advocacy organization, the Home School Legal Defense Association, eleven states impose no regulations on homeschoolers, not even a requirement that parents notify school officials that a child is being homeschooled. Fifteen states only require parents to notify the state that they are homeschooling, and nineteen require that parents provide test scores or other evaluations of their children's academic progress. Only five states (including Pennsylvania) regulate homeschooling more extensively, requiring reports of test scores or professional evaluations and test scores and/or professional evaluation and imposing requirements regarding curriculum or teacher qualifications. HSLDA, Home School Laws in Your State, https://hslda.org/content/laws/ (June 26, 2018).

3. What is the attraction of homeschooling? A 2016 survey estimated that almost 1.7 million students (3.3 percent of all school-aged children) were being homeschooled, an increase from 850,000 in 1999, the first year when estimates were first reported. In 2016, the most common reason that parents gave for home-schooling was their desire to provide religious or moral instruction; the next two most important reasons were concern about the school environment, including safety, drugs, or negative peer pressure, and dissatisfaction with academic instruction at other schools. Eighty-three percent of parents said that one of the reasons they homeschooled was to provide religious or moral instruction. National Center for Education Statistics, Parent and Family Involvement in Education, from the National Household Education Surveys Program of 2016 (June 2016), https://nces.ed.gov/pubs2017/2017102.pdf (June 26, 2018).

"In addition to homeschooling growth trends, another notable wrinkle in the homeschool context is the evolving composition of households engaged in homeschooling and its deeper penetration into American society. Between 2003 and 2012, the percentage of homeschooling parents possessing a graduate or professional degree increased and the percentage of parents with no more than a high school diploma decreased. Similarly, the median household income of homeschooled children has increased. The broadening of the pool of families engaged in homeschooling has led some to characterize homeschools as 'mainstream.'" Michael Heise, From No Child Left Behind to Every Student Succeeds: Back to a Future for Education Federalism, 117 Colum. L. Rev. 1859, 1888 (2017).

4. Professors Fineman and Shepherd assert that homeschooling should be outlawed. They argue, "It is an unreliable way to ensure children gain the necessary resilience they need to take advantage of future opportunities in both education and the workplace. It also may impair their sense of solidarity and citizenship by eliminating empathy-building encounters with people who are different demographically or ideologically." Martha Albertson Fineman & George Shepherd, Homeschooling: Choosing Parental Rights Over Children's Interests, 46 U. Balt. L. Rev. 57, 96 (2016). *See also* James G. Dwyer, Religious Schooling and Homeschooling Before and After Hobby Lobby, 2016 U. Ill. L. Rev. 1393; Kimberly A. Yuracko, Education Off the Grid: Constitutional Constraints on Homeschooling, 96 Cal. L. Rev 123 (2008). Would it be constitutional to ban homeschooling altogether?

5. The curriculum of private schools and homeschooling parents may be insufficient to satisfy university admission requirements. For example, the University of California system reviews the syllabi of high school courses in required subjects; applicants to the universities may only count courses that are approved through this process toward their required high school prerequisites. After the UC system rejected some courses that used conservative Christian texts from Bob Jones University Press and A Beka Book, the Calvary Chapel Christian School and an association of Christian schools sued the system, claiming that it had violated the First Amendment Free Speech and Religion Clauses and equal protection. The federal district court granted the system's motion for summary judgment, and the Ninth Circuit affirmed. Assn. of Christian School International v. Stearns, 362 Fed. Appx. 640 (9th Cir. 2010). The court applied rational basis scrutiny and concluded that the UC regulations on their face and as applied were reasonable and did not constitute viewpoint discrimination. For more about the litigation, *see* Anna M. Sewell, Comment: Moving Beyond Monkeys: The Expansion and Relocation of the Religious Curriculum Debate, 114 Pa. St. L. Rev. 1067 (2010).

6. Several courts have upheld juvenile court orders prohibiting homeschooling by parents who have been found to have neglected or abused their children. *See, e.g.,* In re Cassandra B., 861 N.W.2d 398 (Neb. 2015); Jonathan L. v. Superior Court, 81 Cal. Rptr. 3d 571 (Cal. App. 2008). In light of reports from around the country of homeschooled children being severely abused and neglected, popular and legal commentators have called for greater regulation of homeschooling to ensure that authorities know that the children exist, to allow greater monitoring of their educational achievement, and to allow safety checks under some circumstances. *See* Tyler Barnett, Student Note & Comment: Pulling Back the Curtains: Undetected Child Abuse and the Need for Increased Regulation of Home Schools in Missouri, 2013 BYU Educ. & L.J. 341; Timothy Brandon Waddell, Note, Bringing It All Back Home: Establishing a Coherent Constitutional Framework for the Re-Regulation of Homeschooling, 63 Van. L. Rev. 541 (2010).

7. Some homeschooling families seek permission for their children to participate in selected classes or extracurricular activities of a public school. Paul J. Batista & Lance C. Hatfield, Learn at Home, Play at School: A State-by-State Examination of Legislation, Litigation and Athletic Association Rules Governing Public School Athletic Participation by Homeschool Students, 15 J. Legal Aspects Sport 213 (2005); David W. Fuller, Public School Access: The Constitutional

Right of Home Schoolers to "Opt In" to Public Education on a Part-Time Basis, 82 Minn. L. Rev. 1599, 1601 (1998). Like cases where parents and students seek to opt out of some part of a public school curriculum, suits to "opt in" by students in private or home schools rarely succeed. *See* Swanson v. Guthrie Independent School District No. 1-L, 135 F.3d 694 (10th Cir. 1998); Parents' Assn. of P.S. 16 v. Quinones, 803 F.2d 1235 (2d Cir. 1986). However, some states do provide a degree of access. Fuller, *supra* at 1615-1616.

Are the issues in opt-out cases parallel to those where students seek to opt in? If public schools are a vehicle for civic education, what is the legitimate governmental purpose in excluding part-time students from access to public school programs?

PROBLEMS

1. Alex Williams has homeschooled his 9-year-old son for the last two years. State law requires that homeschooled children take a standardized examination and perform above a certain minimum. In this case, the state minimum is the 40th percentile. At the end of the second year, the boy achieved a score in the 37th percentile. Mr. Williams was then informed that his child is no longer eligible for homeschooling. He has challenged the examination score requirement on constitutional grounds.

What arguments would be made for and against his position? Would the reason for Mr. Williams's decision to engage in homeschooling matter?

2. Carl and Judy Smith have three children, Ida (age 15), Willa (age 13), and Alphonse (age 9). Carl and Judy belong to a small religious group, Christ Church of the First Born, which does not believe in conventional medicine but rather practices faith healing. The members of the group live in an isolated community consisting entirely of church members. The adults have as little to do with people outside the group as possible, homeschool their children, and never take their children outside the community.

Consistently with their religious beliefs, the women of the group have their babies at home without medical assistance, and the group does not register births or deaths with the state office of vital statistics. Rumors have circulated in the county that ten or more children have died in the community over the last five years from treatable medical conditions, and the state police have confirmed two of these deaths. Under state law, which has been held to be constitutional, if parents fail to seek regular medical care for their children and the children die, the parents can be convicted of manslaughter.

The state compulsory education law allows homeschooling, and it does not regulate the practice in any way. Until the news about the deaths of children in the Christ Church community, no one had interfered with the parents' decision to keep their children within the community and teach them at home. However, last month the Department of Human Services announced that all the children from the Christ Church of the First Born community must attend a public or private school in the county so that they will be under the watchful eye of teachers, who are mandatory child abuse reporters. They based this announcement on an interpretation of the compulsory education law by the state Attorney General. The Smiths did not send their children to school, and the Department has filed child neglect charges in juvenile court against them, alleging that their failure to send their children to a public or private school violates the compulsory education law as construed. The Smiths have filed a motion to dismiss the neglect charges, claiming that the compulsory education statute is unconstitutional as applied to their family.

The juvenile court judge, for whom you clerk, has asked you to draft a memorandum analyzing the arguments that can be made for and against the motion to dismiss.

3.   *Disputes over Public School Education*

Parents of children attending public schools sometimes seek to have their children excused from specific classes or even from whole courses because they believe the subject matter conflicts with their religious or other values. As you might expect from *Combs*, courts generally are not receptive to these pleas. For example, in Parker v. Hurley, 514 F.3d 87 (1st Cir. 2008), parents claimed that an elementary school violated their parental and free exercise rights by including favorable depictions of same-sex relationships in books in the classroom library and in a book that a teacher read to her class. The court rejected arguments for heightened scrutiny and held that the parents' rights were not violated. The court distinguished *Yoder*, saying, "*Yoder* emphasized that its holding was essentially *sui generis*, as few sects could make a similar showing of a unique and demanding religious way of life that is fundamentally incompatible with any schooling system." 514 F.3d at 100. It then continued:

> . . . Plaintiffs argue their request for notice and exemption is simply a logical extension of their parental rights under *Meyer* and *Pierce*, as reinforced by their free exercise rights.
>   Defendants respond that plaintiffs' argument runs afoul of the general proposition that, while parents can choose between public and private schools, they do not have a constitutional right to "direct how a public school teaches their child." That proposition is well recognized. *(citations omitted)* Indeed, *Meyer* and *Pierce* specified that the parental interests they recognized would not interfere with the general power of the state to regulate education, including "the state's power to prescribe a curriculum for institutions which it supports."
>   Plaintiffs say, in response, that they are not attempting to control the school's power to prescribe a curriculum. The plaintiffs accept that the school system "has a legitimate secular interest in seeking to eradicate bias against same-gender couples and to ensure the safety of all public school students." They assert that they have an equally sincere interest in the accommodation of their own religious beliefs and of the diversity represented by their contrary views. Plaintiffs specifically disclaim any intent to seek control of the school's curriculum or to impose their will on others. They do not seek to change the choice of books available to others but only to

require notice of the books and an exemption, and even then only up to the seventh grade. Nonetheless, we have found no federal case under the Due Process Clause which has permitted parents to demand an exemption for their children from exposure to certain books used in public schools. . . .

. . . We turn then to whether the combination of substantive due process and free exercise interests give the parents a cause of action. . . .

The heart of the plaintiffs' free exercise claim is a claim of "indoctrination": that the state has put pressure on their children to endorse an affirmative view of gay marriage and has thus undercut the parents' efforts to inculcate their children with their own opposing religious views. The Supreme Court, we believe, has never utilized an indoctrination test under the Free Exercise Clause, much less in the public school context. . . . We do not address whether or not an indoctrination theory under the Free Exercise Clause is sound. Plaintiffs' pleadings do not establish a viable case of indoctrination, even assuming that extreme indoctrination can be a form of coercion.

First, as to the parents' free exercise rights, the mere fact that a child is exposed on occasion in public school to a concept offensive to a parent's religious belief does not inhibit the parent from instructing the child differently. A parent whose "child is exposed to sensitive topics or information [at school] remains free to discuss these matters and to place them in the family's moral or religious context, or to supplement the information with more appropriate materials." The parents here did in fact have notice, if not prior notice, of the books and of the school's overall intent to promote toleration of same-sex marriage, and they retained their ability to discuss the material and subject matter with their children. Our outcome does not turn, however, on whether the parents had notice. . . .

Public schools are not obliged to shield individual students from ideas which potentially are religiously offensive, particularly when the school imposes no requirement that the student agree with or affirm those ideas, or even participate in discussions about them. The reading of [the book during class] was not instruction in religion or religious beliefs.

On the facts, there is no viable claim of "indoctrination" here. Without suggesting that such showings would suffice to establish a claim of indoctrination, we note the plaintiffs' children were not forced to read the books on pain of suspension. Nor were they subject to a constant stream of like materials. There is no allegation here of a formalized curriculum requiring students to read many books affirming gay marriage. The reading by a teacher of one book, or even three, and even if to a young and impressionable child, does not constitute "indoctrination."

Because plaintiffs do not allege facts that give rise to claims of constitutional magnitude, the district court did not err in granting defendants' motion to dismiss the claims under the U.S. Constitution. . . .

514 F.3d at 101- 107. What, though, of other parental requests, such as to exempt a child from a school dress code for religious reasons?

A.A. EX REL. BETENBAUGH V. NEEDVILLE INDEPENDENT SCHOOL DISTRICT

611 F.3d 248 (5th Cir. 2010)

PATRICK E. HIGGINBOTHAM, Circuit Judge. When this dispute began, A.A. was a five-year-old prospective kindergartner whose parents were planning to move to Needville, Texas, a small town located forty-five miles southwest of downtown Houston. The school district in Needville has long had a grooming policy, which, among other things, provides that "[b]oys' hair shall not cover any part of the ear or touch the top of the standard collar in back." The policy's stated design is "to teach hygiene, instill discipline, prevent disruption, avoid safety hazards, and assert authority." In keeping with his Native American religious beliefs, A.A. has never cut his hair, which he has at times kept unbraided, and in one and two braids.

Like most young children, A.A.'s beliefs hitch to those of his parents, Kenney Arocha and Michelle Betenbaugh. Arocha identifies as Native American and both he and his son are members of the state-recognized Lipan Apache Tribe of Texas. . . .

Long hair is part of Arocha's religious beliefs. He wears his hair long, as he did as a young child before he was forced to cut it for school—an experience he describes as "unsettling." His grandfather wore his hair short, but his uncle wore his hair long and in one or two braids. As an adult and over time Arocha came to find religious meaning in wearing his hair long as he gained greater understanding of his grandfather and uncle's teachings. The result is that, as with other aspects of Arocha's religious experience, "something he has been doing for a long time winds up being something that's more significant," and for more than a decade he has seen his long hair as "a symbol, an outward extension of who we are and where we come from, our ancestry and where we're going in life" and "a constant reminder to us of who we are." Arocha last cut his hair's *length* about ten or eleven years ago, though he does trim the sides on occasion because of the summer heat. He will not cut his hair's length unless he is mourning for a loved one. An employer once threatened to terminate him if he did not cut his hair, but Arocha refused. And, when he underwent brain surgery a few years ago, he worked with his doctors to keep his long braids.

Arocha and Betenbaugh have passed these familial religious traditions on to their son and so, as we have noted, A.A.'s hair has never been cut. A.A.'s parents have explained to him that his hair is a connection to his ancestors, as well as a reminder of "how long he has been here and an extension of who he is." When others ask about his long hair, A.A. responds that he is Native American. He once refused to wear a wig as part of a Halloween costume because he did not want it to cover his braids. While A.A. "customarily keeps" his hair "in two 13-inch-long braids," he does not always do so.

[The parents requested that A.A. be exempted from the school's policy regarding boys' hair length on religious grounds. At the recommendation of the superintendent, the school board granted him an exemption allowing him to wear his hair in a single braid tucked into the collar of his shirt. The boy did not comply but came to school wearing two braids outside his shirt. He was placed in in-school suspension, and the parents filed suit in federal district court.]

. . . During the litigation and responsive to the bun or tucked braid requirement, Arocha expressed religious significance in braiding his long hair. As the district court found, Arocha "feels that his hair is 'a symbol, an outward extension of who we are and where we come from, our ancestry and where we're going in life.'" The court explained that "[h]e believes that each braid and each plait has a deep meaning" and "that the very act of braiding helps him feel connected to who he is." Arocha says that braids should be worn "in plain sight" and that "each braid has its own significance and . . . that's the way it should be presented."

. . . The District conceded that A.A. has a right to some form of exemption from its grooming policy, but argued that either of the two proffered options—a single "tightly woven" braid tucked behind A.A.'s shirt or a bun on top of his head—would be legally sufficient. The district court found for the family on all four grounds and issued a permanent injunction against the District preventing the grooming policy's application to A.A. The District timely appealed to this court.

Because we do not decide constitutional claims when a case can be footed on alternative grounds, our analysis begins with state law—specifically, the Texas Religious Freedom Restoration Act.

That act—often abbreviated as TRFRA—prevents any government agency in Texas from "substantially burden[ing] a person's free exercise of religion" unless it "demonstrates that the application of the burden to the person . . . is in further-ance of a compelling governmental interest; and . . . is the least restrictive means of furthering that interest." . . .

Texas did not enact TRFRA on a clean slate. The act is a response to a twenty-year federal kerfuffle over the level of scrutiny to apply to free exercise claims under the First Amendment of the United States Constitution. Nine years before TRFRA's enactment, the Supreme Court held, in Employment Division, Department of Human Resources of Oregon v. Smith, that the First Amendment's Free Exercise Clause does not inhibit enforcement of otherwise valid laws of gen-eral application that incidentally burden religious conduct. Responding to *Smith*, Congress enacted the Religious Freedom Restoration Act of 1993 (RFRA). RFRA expressly adopted the compelling interest test as set forth in a pair of Supreme Court cases, Sherbert v. Verner and Wisconsin v. Yoder. That test "prohibits '[g]overnment' from 'substantially burden[ing]' a person's exercise of religion even if the burden results from a rule of general applicability unless the government can demonstrate the burden '(1) is in furtherance of a compelling governmental interest; and (2) is the least restrictive means of furthering that compelling gov-ernmental interest.'"

As originally enacted, RFRA applied to both federal and state governments, "but notably lacked a Commerce Clause underpinning or a Spending Clause lim-itation to recipients of federal funds." In City of Boerne v. Flores, the Supreme Court invalidated RFRA as applied to the states and their subdivisions, finding that Congress had exceeded its remedial power under the Fourteenth Amendment to delineate the scope of constitutional violations.

Congress again responded. This time it enacted the Religious Exercise in Land Use and Institutionalized Persons Act of 2000 (RLUIPA), which "is largely a reprisal of the provisions of . . . RFRA," though "its scope is limited to laws and regulations that govern (1) land use and (2) institutions such as prisons that receive federal funds."

Unhappy with the federal government's solution, thirteen states took matters into their own hands, including Texas, which enacted TRFRA to "provide [] the same protections to religious free exercise envisioned by the framers of its federal counterpart, RFRA." In other words, TRFRA provides protections to religious freedom "in addition to the protections provided under federal law" and the Texas and United States constitutions. Because TRFRA and its federal cousins—RFRA and RLUIPA—"were all enacted in response to *Smith* and were animated in their common history, language and purpose by the same spirit of religious freedom,"

Texas courts "consider decisions applying the federal statutes germane in applying the Texas statute." . . .

. . . To succeed on a claim under TRFRA, a plaintiff must demonstrate (1) that the government's regulations burden the plaintiff's free exercise of religion and (2) that the burden is substantial. If the plaintiff manages that showing, the government can still prevail if it establishes that (3) its regulations further a compelling governmental interest and (4) that the regulations are the least restrictive means of furthering that interest. . . .

. . . Under TRFRA, a burden is substantial if it is "real vs. merely perceived, and significant vs. trivial"—two limitations that "leave a broad range of things covered." The focus of the inquiry is on "the degree to which a person's religious conduct is curtailed and the resulting impact on his religious expression," as "measured . . . from the person's perspective, not from the government's." This inquiry is "case-by-case" and "fact-specific" and must take into account "individual circumstances."

From federal precedent, we know that "at a minimum, the government's *ban* of conduct sincerely motivated by religious belief substantially burdens an adherent's free exercise of that religion." When conduct is subject to an outright ban, "alternative accommodations do not alter 'the fact that the rituals which [the adherent] claims are important to *him*—without apparent contradiction—are now completely forbidden.'" . . .

Requiring A.A. to cut his hair—a total ban of conduct—would also likely constitute a substantial burden. But that is not what the District's proposed exemptions require so the bar is incomplete. Whereas forceably cutting his hair would limit his free exercise at all times, the exemptions permit the District to control A.A.'s hair only while he is at school. At home he may wear his hair however he likes.

When a restriction is not completely prohibitive, Texas law still considers it substantial if "alternatives for the religious exercise are severely restricted." . . . Here, that standard is met.

First, the burden on A.A. is significant. The exemptions place a direct burden on A.A.'s religious conduct and expression by, as the district court put it, "deny[ing] A.A. the opportunity to express a religious practice that is very dear to him and his father." While the District's policy and exemptions do not completely bar A.A.'s free exercise, the bar is complete in the sense that he cannot wear his hair visibly long at all during the school day, a critical period of time in a young child's development. The stricture will define his days as a student. As other courts have recognized in analogous contexts, depriving children of religious exercise during the school day is a significant burden. . . .

The exemptions would also indirectly burden A.A.'s religious conduct and expression. If A.A. complies with either of them, he will stand out as someone subject to official stigma. If he does not, he will be exposed to punishment. The district court believed these "terms of existence" would force A.A. to choose between attending Needville public schools and following his religious beliefs.

Not only is the burden on A.A. significant, it is real. As the district court found, A.A. has already recognized that he has been treated differently because of his hair. And, given that A.A. understands that his hair is part of the practice and expression of his Native American beliefs, the obvious lesson is that he is being treated differently because of his religion. This recognition risks feelings of shame and resentment, a risk that, while real now, will continue to grow. A.A. will also be subject to constant threat of punishment should his hair fall out of a bun, or escape his shirt. This threat is real.

"To say that a person's right to free exercise has been burdened, of course, does not mean that he has an absolute right to engage in the conduct." TRFRA permits the regulation of free exercise if the government can establish a compelling interest that justifies the burden, and that it has adopted the least restrictive means of achieving that interest. "Because religious exercise is a fundamental right . . . justification can be found only in 'interests of the highest order.'"

On these counts, the District's amicus, the Texas Association of School Boards Legal Assistance Fund takes the lead. The Fund argues that the District's grooming policy is supported by five goals: to teach hygiene, instill discipline, prevent disruption, avoid safety hazards, and assert authority. The Fund relies on a handful of Texas cases that find these interests sufficient to overcome challenges to student and teacher dress codes. From this precedent, the Fund would extract a principle that "maintaining order in a school [is] a compelling state interest" that always justifies hair and clothing regulation no matter the constitutional interest. This principle is not the law.

While the advanced scholastic concerns are no doubt legitimate, the Fund's argument suffers from two critical defects. . . .

Here, the District makes only cursory attempts to translate the abstract goals of its grooming policy into an interest sufficiently compelling to justify requiring a Native American kindergartner to confine his hair to a bun or to a braid tucked behind his shirt. In the words of *Yoder*, one of the two Supreme Court decisions on which TRFRA's compelling interest test is based, the District has failed "to show with more particularity how its admittedly strong interest . . . would be adversely affected by granting an exemption" to A.A.

We can quickly discard hygienic concern: the District does not dispute that A.A.'s hair is kept clean, nor does it explain why its "one braid down the back" exemption would foster hygiene as compared to two braids.

Safety concerns are insufficient, too. The hazard of long hair in an elementary school setting does not rise to the level of, say, the danger posed by the wearing of insecurely fastened yarmulkes by Orthodox Jews during high school basketball games, a situation examined by the Seventh Circuit nearly thirty years ago. And, as Judge Posner found, even that danger was "not great" (though "not wholly trivial either"). Moreover, to say the District's safety concerns are not compelling, we need not go so far as a divided Ninth Circuit panel did in Cheema v. Thompson. There, the panel majority held under RFRA that a school did not have a compelling interest in a wholesale ban on ceremonial knives worn by some Sikhs. The court remedied the violation by crafting an exemption that allowed the knives in slightly modified form. To the extent A.A.'s long hair poses a cognizable safety concern, it is of course far from those associated with a knife of any size or shape.

Any risk of disruption and its potential degree are less readily predicted. While there is evidence that A.A. has twice been mistaken for a girl while at school, there is no indication that these occasional cases of mistaken gender identity were disruptive and certainly not such to constitute a compelling interest; the confusion was easily resolved and the District did not even bother informing his parents when a misunderstanding did arise.

The district court did find that A.A.'s hair "sometimes falls in his eyes and his teacher has to tell him to tuck it behind his ear," but explained that the teacher occasionally has to make the same suggestion to girls and A.A.'s presence has not interfered with the teacher's ability to teach. The District provides no argument or evidence to the contrary. . . .

We are left then with the District's stated interests in instilling discipline and asserting authority. To this list, Superintendent Rhodes would add one last concern, explaining that in crafting the "tucked braid" exemption, he did not necessarily seek to effect the goals of the grooming policy at all, but to "try to have [A.A.'s] hair resemble the rest of the student body in Needville."

Under the compelling interest test, the District's support for these concerns quickly dissolves. For one, the District has failed to put forth a single case in which a school's interests in discipline, authority, and uniformity have proved enough when subject to strict scrutiny. Yes, courts, including the Supreme Court, have found similar interests sufficient—under varying levels of scrutiny—to override an adherent's right to a religiously informed appearance in different circumstances. But, when applying a compelling interest standard, "[c]ontext matters." . . .

. . . What we have in the present case is an elementary school, which, even in its most authoritarian form, is neither a military operation nor an incarceration facility. A.A.'s religious expression does not jeopardize a school's interest in authority and discipline in the same way that it might impinge on the military's need for instinctive obedience, a police department's desire to present an impartial public face, or the penological goal of keeping prisoners in prison. Regulation of hair and dress in public schools is meant in part to instill discipline and to teach respect for authority—not because a kindergartner is a flight risk or because he will need to take direction from superiors in a war zone—but because a grooming policy preserves order in the classroom and prepares students to become society's next generation of citizens. These goals are legitimate, but they are not served by applying the District's hair regulation to A.A. That legitimacy accepts that the wearing of long hair and unconventional dress by most boys may be seen as an act of defiance—and a rejection of authority. Well and good, but A.A.'s long hair is conceded to be an exercise, not of rebellion, but of adherence to religious belief. That adherence does not thwart the school's pedagogical mission, a teacher's dominion over her classroom, or a principal's ability to maintain an environment conducive to learning. As the District has conceded, it is an acknowledgment of piety to religion and fealty to an authority superior to individual whim. The District's regulation aimed at this acknowledgment—in the name of authority and discipline—is not a compelling interest.

With no evidence specific to A.A.'s request for exemption, the District makes no suggestion that A.A.'s visibly long hair will erode obedience and discipline among the general student population. It also puts forth no claim that a grant of an exemption here will lead to future claims destructive of the District's general policy. The evidence is all to the contrary: A.A.'s religious exemption request is just the second ever received by the District (as we have noted, the first request was granted). Treating A.A.'s exemption request as an outlier, it is, in the district court's words, "difficult to imagine that allowing one male child to wear long hair, as part of his religious beliefs, would disturb the school's sense of order."

So seen, Superintendent Rhodes's concern for aesthetic homogeneity, like the others, is insufficiently compelling to overtake the sincere exercise of religious belief. Regardless, the District's exemptions do not serve it: A.A. would still be non-conforming in appearance—either as the only child wearing a thirteen-inch braid tucked inside his shirt or the only male child wearing a bun.

Had the District succeeded in presenting specific evidence connecting its concerns to A.A.'s request for exemption, any connection would be weakened by the District's decision to permit *girls* to wear their hair visibly long. The District has not shown that girls with long hair are less prone to accidents or that they are better able to conform with the District's hygienic standards. Nor does the District explain why any gender confusion issues associated with A.A.'s long hair would not also be true for a girl who chose to wear her hair short, as the grooming policy allows. At the same time, the District's decision to allow some girls to wear short hair is a judgment call that "undoubtedly undermines" any "interest in fostering a uniform appearance" through its policy. That the District itself contemplates secular, gender-based exceptions indicates that none of the generalized interests purportedly advanced through the grooming policy should carry "determinative weight" for TRFRA purposes. More to the point, it makes plain that it is non-conforming appearance evincing resistance to school authority that justifies the District's grooming policy; that it misses the mark to turn that code to dress and hair conceded to be born of sincere religious belief.

To review, while a school may set grooming standards for its students, when those standards substantially burden the free exercise of religion, they must accomplish *something*. Under TRFRA, that "something" is a compelling interest. The District only invokes the same five generalized interests without explaining the play of those interests here. TRFRA demands more. The questions of detail and degree that the District would answer for its students do not rise to the level of compelling interest, and are therefore left to the adherent alone. . . .

NOTES AND QUESTIONS

1. While this case was brought in the name of A.A., a 5-year-old child, it's clear that the parents are actually the ones pursuing the action. As a doctrinal matter, the level of scrutiny would be the same, regardless of who brought the claim, since the state Religious Freedom Restoration Act (RFRA) requires strict scrutiny. Why did the school's refusal to make an exception from the hair-length policy fail to survive strict scrutiny?

The Supreme Court held in City of Boerne v. Flores, 521 U.S. 507 (1997), that the federal RFRA, 42 U.S.C. § 2000bb *et seq.*, which purported to overrule Employment Division v. Smith, 494 U.S. 872 (1990), could not constitutionally be applied when state laws and policies are challenged on free exercise grounds. However, the federal RFRA does apply when federal laws and policies are at stake. Burwell v. Hobby Lobby Stores, Inc., 573 U.S. 682 (2014).

2. As you saw in *Combs*, if the challenge in *A.A.* had been brought under the Free Exercise Clause of the federal Constitution, Employment Division v. Smith

would provide that the school policy would only have been subject to rational basis scrutiny, since the policy was neutral and of general applicability. What would be the result if that standard were applied in *A.A.*?

3. What assumptions about the role of schools undergird opinions rejecting parents' challenges to curricular matters? How are a school's interests in having students take the same classes, the result protected in Parker v. Hurley, different from the school's interests in a uniform dress code, asserted in *A.A.*? In the era before *Employment Division*, courts generally found the school's interests in curriculum cases sufficiently strong to survive parents' Fourteenth Amendment and free exercise claims. They usually distinguish *Yoder* in the way that *Combs* does. *See, e.g.*, Mozert v. Hawkins, 827 F.2d 1058 (6ᵗʰ Cir. 1987).

4. Parents' challenges to other school policies based on parental rights and free exercise also rarely succeed. For example, Herndon v. Chapel Hill-Carrboro City Board of Education, 89 F.3d 174 (4ᵗʰ Cir. 1996), rejected a challenge to a requirement that all students perform 50 hours of community service as a condition of graduation. The students alleged that the requirement violated their constitutional freedom from involuntary servitude, and rights for personal liberty and privacy; the parents claimed an invasion of their constitutional right to direct the rearing and education of their children. The Fourth Circuit found no constitutionally based freedom from compulsory charitable service. It also held that limits on graduation from high school do not rise to the level of "physical or legal coercion" necessary to invoke the Thirteenth Amendment and that, in any event, a community service requirement was in no way comparable to slavery. With respect to the parental claim, the court applied rational basis scrutiny. Since the claimants acknowledged the "basic legitimacy" of the district's interest in teaching students the value of public service, the requirement was upheld.

Parents' *Meyer-Pierce* challenges to schools administering surveys to students that included questions on highly personal topics, including sexual attitudes and concerns, drug and alcohol use, and relations between the children and their parents, have also failed. C.N. v. Ridgewood Board of Education, 430 F.3d 159 (3d Cir. 2005); Fields v. Palmdale School District, 427 F.3d 1197 (2005), *amended by, reaffirmed* 447 F.3d 1187 (9th Cir. 2006). For a discussion of the broader issues, based on *Fields*, *see* Maxine Eichner, School Surveys and Children's Education: The Argument for Shared Authority Between Parents and the State, 38 J.L. & Educ. 459 (2009).

5. The problem of conflicting world views between the majority in a community and some parents expresses itself in many other ways. For example, in some public schools today, recognition of Christian holidays such as Christmas and Easter is so taboo that schools do not permit such secular displays as holiday trees. The New York City Department of Education took a different approach, using a variety of end-of-the-year holidays, including Christmas, Chanukah, Ramadan, and Kwanzaa, "to teach children about and to encourage respect for the different cultures in their community." The department issued a holiday display policy that permitted "secular" symbols such as "Christmas trees, Menorahs, and the Star and Crescent." The policy banned symbols that it regarded as too sectarian, including crèches. In Skoros v. City of New York, 437 F.3d 1 (2d Cir. 2006), a parent unsuccessfully challenged the policy, claiming that it violated the Establishment Clause by favoring Judaism and Islam over Christianity. Is this solution to the problem more satisfactory? What are its limits?

6. Rather than simply rejecting dissenting parents' views as losers in the political tug-of-war, many schools allow parents to excuse their children from particular lessons. *See* Noa Ben-Asher, The Lawmaking Family, 90 Wash. U. L. Rev. 363, 398 (2012). Professor Ben-Asher argues that these laws reinstate a relationship between public schools and parents that predominated early in the twentieth century, when parents' efforts to exempt their children from particular lessons usually succeeded. According to Ben-Asher, at that time schools were understood as providing a service to parents, rather than as government agencies with primary responsibility for children's schooling, and courts understood the issue when parents and schools clashed as whether a school could prescribe the education of children, not whether parents could dictate to schools. The article proposes a limited return to this model. What are the practical limits to this solution? Are there principled limits as well?

PROBLEM

Plaintiffs are members of a religious group, the Plymouth Brethren, who challenge a Board of Education regulation requiring all primary and secondary school students to receive instruction about acquired immunodeficiency syndrome (AIDS). The curriculum of which they complain includes instruction in the nature of the disease, methods of transmission, and methods of prevention. The Board of Education has moved for summary judgment against the plaintiffs, who seek an exemption from participation by their children in this or any AIDS or sex education curriculum.

The Plymouth Brethren are a worldwide religious organization with approximately 35,000 adherents, some 2,000 of whom live in the United States. Plaintiffs' factual allegations may be summarized as follows:

1. The Plymouth Brethren are a religious group with a long history of maintaining a cohesive community separated and insulated from society. Members—who have been accorded "conscientious objector" status by the Selective Service System—are strongly moral and principled individuals practicing and reinforcing personal purity and other exemplary moral behavior. Apart from the practical necessity for this very small group to attend public school and earn a livelihood in the community, members' associations are limited to other Brethren.

2. Plaintiffs' children are not permitted to socialize with nonmember children after school, or even to eat with them at school. The Brethren do not allow television or radio, and they do not see movies or read magazines. Their lives are spent in worship or in social activities limited to association with other members under the constant moral guidance and supervision of parents and other community adults in an "extended family."

3. Insistence upon rigorous morality is interwoven with the movement's strong sense of separateness. The central principle of the Brethren's religion is the obligation to "separate from evil." Even to know the details of evil is regarded as subversive. This injunction forms the basis of their teaching and practice.

4. Brethren religious tenets entirely forbid exposure to instruction concerning sexual relations and moral teachings other than those imparted by members

of the community to members of the community. Consequently, plaintiffs believe that their children's exposure to the contents of the AIDS curriculum is inimical to their religious, moral, ethical, and personal well-being.

5. Exposure to the AIDS curriculum would undermine the Brethren's ability to guide their children's moral lives in accordance with their faith. In short, as plaintiffs affirmed, such exposure "carries with it the very real threat of undermining [plaintiffs'] religious community and religious practice."

6. Brethren children have been exposed to school disciplinary sanction by reason of their refusal to participate in mandatory AIDS-related instruction.

Frame the arguments that would be made for and against the motion for summary judgment.

Where home education or efforts to be excused from a part of public school programs are involved, parents and their children who claim exemption on religious or moral grounds are "outsiders." Sometimes, though, parents who want the public schools to incorporate religious teaching of various kinds gain control of the school board, which enacts policies that implement this perspective. Then parents who do not share these beliefs may challenge the school board action, but not on free exercise grounds. Instead, they claim that the school is violating another provision of the First Amendment, the prohibition on establishment of religion. A famous example of such a conflict is the 1925 Scopes monkey trial, dealing with whether states may prohibit the teaching of evolution or require the teaching of creationism (or, sometimes, "creation science"). *See* Edward J. Larson, Summer for the Gods: The Scopes Trial and America's Continuing Debate over Science and Religion (1997).

Many years later, parents challenged another state's law requiring the teaching of creation of science in Edwards v. Aguillard, 482 U.S. 578 (1987). The Court held the law unconstitutional, finding that despite the state's claim that the act intended only to protect academic freedom, its real purpose was to promote the religious beliefs of a particular group.

Schools' efforts to incorporate prayer into official activities have also been a fertile ground for Establishment Clause challenges.

Santa Fe Independent School District v. Doe

530 U.S. 290 (2000)

Stevens, J. Prior to 1995, the Santa Fe High School student who occupied the school's elective office of student council chaplain delivered a prayer over the public address system before each varsity football game for the entire season. This practice, along with others, was challenged in District Court as a violation of the Establishment Clause of the First Amendment. While these proceedings were pending in the District Court, the school district adopted a different policy that permits, but does not require, prayer initiated and led by a student at all home games. The District Court entered an order modifying that policy to permit only nonsectarian, nonproselytizing prayer. The Court of Appeals held that, even as modified by the District Court, the football prayer policy was invalid. . . .

We granted the District's petition for certiorari, limited to the following question: "Whether petitioner's policy permitting student-led, student-initiated prayer at football games violates the Establishment Clause." We conclude, as did the Court of Appeals, that it does.

The first Clause in the First Amendment to the Federal Constitution provides that "Congress shall make no law respecting an establishment of religion, or prohibiting the free exercise thereof." The Fourteenth Amendment imposes those substantive limitations on the legislative power of the States and their political subdivisions. In Lee v. Weisman, 505 U.S. 577 (1992), we held that a prayer delivered by a rabbi at a middle school graduation ceremony violated that Clause. Although this case involves student prayer at a different type of school function, our analysis is properly guided by the principles that we endorsed in *Lee*.

As we held in that case:

> The principle that government may accommodate the free exercise of religion does not supersede the fundamental limitations imposed by the Establishment Clause. It is beyond dispute that, at a minimum, the Constitution guarantees that government may not coerce anyone to support or participate in religion or its exercise, or otherwise act in a way which "establishes a [state] religion or religious faith, or tends to do so."

In this case the District first argues that this principle is inapplicable to its October policy because the messages are private student speech, not public speech. It reminds us that "there is a crucial difference between government speech endorsing religion, which the Establishment Clause forbids, and private speech endorsing religion, which the Free Speech and Free Exercise Clauses protect." We certainly agree with that distinction, but we are not persuaded that the pregame invocations should be regarded as "private speech."

These invocations are authorized by a government policy and take place on government property at government-sponsored school-related events. Of course, not every message delivered under such circumstances is the government's own. We have held, for example, that an individual's contribution to a government-created forum was not government speech. *See* Rosenberger v. Rector and Visitors of Univ. of Va., 515 U.S. 819 (1995). Although the District relies heavily on *Rosenberger* and similar cases involving such forums, it is clear that the pregame ceremony is not the type of forum discussed in those cases. The Santa Fe school officials simply do not "evince either 'by policy or by practice,' any intent to open the [pregame ceremony] to 'indiscriminate use,' . . . by the student body generally." Hazelwood School Dist. v. Kuhlmeier, 484 U.S. 260 (1988) (quoting Perry Ed. Assn. v. Perry Local Educators' Assn., 460 U.S. 260 (1983)). Rather, the school allows only one student, the same student for the entire season, to give the invocation. The statement or invocation, moreover, is subject to particular regulations that confine the content and topic of the student's message. By comparison, in *Perry* we rejected a claim that the school had created a limited public forum in its school mail system despite the fact that it had allowed far more speakers to address a much broader range of topics than the policy at issue here. As we concluded in *Perry*, "selective access does not transform government property into a public forum."

Granting only one student access to the stage at a time does not, of course, necessarily preclude a finding that a school has created a limited public forum. Here, however, Santa Fe's student election system ensures that only those messages deemed "appropriate" under the District's policy may be delivered. That is, the majoritarian process implemented by the District guarantees, by definition, that minority candidates will never prevail and that their views will be effectively silenced. . . .

In *Lee*, the school district made the related argument that its policy of endorsing only "civic or nonsectarian" prayer was acceptable because it minimized the intrusion on the audience as a whole. We rejected that claim by explaining that such a majoritarian policy "does not lessen the offense or isolation to the objectors. At best it narrows their number, at worst increases their sense of isolation and affront." Similarly, while Santa Fe's majoritarian election might ensure that most of the students are represented, it does nothing to protect the minority; indeed, it likely serves to intensify their offense.

Moreover, the District has failed to divorce itself from the religious content in the invocations. It has not succeeded in doing so, either by claiming that its policy is "'one of neutrality rather than endorsement'" or by characterizing the individual student as the "circuit-breaker" in the process. Contrary to the District's repeated assertions that it has adopted a "hands-off" approach to the pregame invocation, the realities of the situation plainly reveal that its policy involves both perceived and actual endorsement of religion. In this case, as we found in *Lee*, the "degree of school involvement" makes it clear that the pregame prayers bear "the imprint of the State and thus put school-age children who objected in an untenable position." . . .

In this context the members of the listening audience must perceive the pregame message as a public expression of the views of the majority of the student body delivered with the approval of the school administration. In cases involving state participation in a religious activity, one of the relevant questions is "whether an objective observer, acquainted with the text, legislative history, and implementation of the statute, would perceive it as a state endorsement of prayer in public schools." Regardless of the listener's support for, or objection to, the message, an objective Santa Fe High School student will unquestionably perceive the inevitable pregame prayer as stamped with her school's seal of approval. . . .

School sponsorship of a religious message is impermissible because it sends the ancillary message to members of the audience who are nonadherents "that they are outsiders, not full members of the political community, and an accompanying message to adherents that they are insiders, favored members of the political community." The delivery of such a message—over the school's public address system, by a speaker representing the student body, under the supervision of school faculty, and pursuant to a school policy that explicitly and implicitly encourages public prayer—is not properly characterized as "private" speech.

The District next argues that its football policy is distinguishable from the graduation prayer in *Lee* because it does not coerce students to participate in religious observances. Its argument has two parts: first, that there is no impermissible government coercion because the pregame messages are the product of student choices; and second, that there is really no coercion at all because attendance at an extracurricular event, unlike a graduation ceremony, is voluntary.

The reasons just discussed explaining why the alleged "circuit-breaker" mechanism of the dual elections and student speaker do not turn public speech into private speech also demonstrate why these mechanisms do not insulate the school from the coercive element of the final message. In fact, this aspect of the District's argument exposes anew the concerns that are created by the majoritarian election system. The parties' stipulation clearly states that the issue resolved in the first election was "whether a student would deliver prayer at varsity football games," and the controversy in this case demonstrates that the views of the students are not unanimous on that issue.

One of the purposes served by the Establishment Clause is to remove debate over this kind of issue from governmental supervision or control. We explained in *Lee* that the "preservation and transmission of religious beliefs and worship is a responsibility and a choice committed to the private sphere." The two student elections authorized by the policy, coupled with the debates that presumably must precede each, impermissibly invade that private sphere. The election mechanism, when considered in light of the history in which the policy in question evolved, reflects a device the District put in place that determines whether religious messages will be delivered at home football games. The mechanism encourages divisiveness along religious lines in a public school setting, a result at odds with the Establishment Clause. Although it is true that the ultimate choice of student speaker is "attributable to the students," the District's decision to hold the constitutionally problematic election is clearly "a choice attributable to the State." . . .

Even if we regard every high school student's decision to attend a home football game as purely voluntary, we are nevertheless persuaded that the delivery of a pregame prayer has the improper effect of coercing those present to participate in an act of religious worship. For "the government may no more use social pressure to enforce orthodoxy than it may use more direct means." As in *Lee*, "[w]hat to most believers may seem nothing more than a reasonable request that the non-believer respect their religious practices, in a school context may appear to the nonbeliever or dissenter to be an attempt to employ the machinery of the State to enforce a religious orthodoxy." The constitutional command will not permit the District "to exact religious conformity from a student as the price" of joining her classmates at a varsity football game.

The Religion Clauses of the First Amendment prevent the government from making any law respecting the establishment of religion or prohibiting the free exercise thereof. By no means do these commands impose a prohibition on all religious activity in our public schools. Indeed, the common purpose of the Religion Clauses "is to secure religious liberty." Thus, nothing in the Constitution as interpreted by this Court prohibits any public school student from voluntarily praying at any time before, during, or after the school day. But the religious liberty protected by the Constitution is abridged when the State affirmatively sponsors the particular religious practice of prayer. . . .

NOTES AND QUESTIONS

1. The majority in *Santa Fe Independent School District* regards religious beliefs and worship as a choice committed to the "private" sphere, which government may not invade. Does instruction in evolution but not creationism "invade"

the private sphere for some families? Does failure to say grace during lunch at school do so?

2. The Supreme Court has drawn a sharp line between government speech, which cannot endorse religion, and private speech, including religious speech, which is protected by the First Amendment's guarantees of freedom of speech and religion. Since the prayers at the football game were initiated and given by students, why didn't the Court categorize them as private speech?

3. One of the functions that the majority attributes to the Free Exercise Clause is avoidance of divisiveness within the school. This claim follows the view of Justice Brennan, who observed that "[i]t is implicit in the history and character of American public education that the public schools serve a uniquely *public* function: the training of American citizens in an atmosphere free of parochial, divisive, or separatist influences of any sort. . . . This is a heritage neither theistic nor atheistic, but simply civic and patriotic." Abington Township v. Schempp, 374 U.S. 203, 241-242 (1963) (Brennan, J., concurring).

What does it mean for prayers to be divisive if the community overwhelmingly supports them? The main case arose in Santa Fe, Texas, a small town 30 miles south of Houston with a population of about 9,500 people. The community is deeply religious, with large numbers of Protestants and Catholics. It has one Jewish family. Paul Horwitz, Of Football, "Footnote One," and the Counter-Jurisdictional Establishment Clause: The Story of Santa Fe Independent School District v. Doe, in First Amendment Stories (Andrew Koppelman, ed., 2011), available at http:// ssrn.com/abstract=1589757. "To say football is important in this Texas town is almost redundant. . . . Football . . . is Texas's unofficial religion. . . . [I]n Texas, high school football is the official and established religion of the state." *Id.* at 10. The federal district court in the case issued an order forbidding the school district, school officials, and others from attempting to find out the identities of the plaintiffs in the case "by means of bogus petitions, questionnaires, individual interrogation, or downright 'snooping.'" *Id.* at 8. The suit against the football prayers was denounced from the pulpit in the plaintiffs' church, and the family who objected to the prayers received threatening phone calls. *Id.* at 12.

4. Wallace v. Jaffree, 472 U.S. 38 (1985), held unconstitutional an Alabama law authorizing a period of silence "for meditation or voluntary prayer." The state did not allege any secular purpose for the "moment of silence," and the legislative history revealed a desire to return voluntary prayer to the schools. Justice O'Connor concurred, saying that nothing in the Constitution prevents public school students from praying voluntarily in school and suggesting that similar statutes not motivated by the wish to return prayer to schools might be sustained. Sherman ex rel. Sherman v. Koch, 623 F.3d 501 (7th Cir. 2010), held that an Illinois statute mandating a period of silence in public schools did not violate the Establishment Clause. The court distinguished *Wallace* on the basis of the statute's avowed secular purpose, set forth in the first section: "This period shall not be conducted as a religious exercise but shall be an opportunity for silent prayer or for silent reflection on the anticipated activities of the day." The court rejected the challengers' claim that this was a sham.

5. In Newdow v. U.S. Congress, 328 F.3d 466 (9th Cir. 2002), the court held that requiring students to recite the Pledge of Allegiance in school violates the Establishment Clause because of the phrase "under God." The Supreme Court

granted certiorari and held that the federal courts should not have entertained the suit because Newdow, a noncustodial father, lacked standing. Elk Grove Unified School District v. Newdow, 542 U.S. 1 (2004). Other parents who did have standing filed the same claim in the same federal district court, which ruled in their favor. The Ninth Circuit reversed, holding that the Pledge is a patriotic, rather than a religious activity, and, therefore, that a policy providing for students to recite the Pledge voluntarily does not violate the Establishment Clause. Newdow v. Rio Linda Union School Dist., 597 F.3d 1007 (9th Cir. 2010). Other cases rejecting Establishment Clause and other constitutional objections to Pledge of Allegiance laws include American Humanist Ass'n v. Matawan-Aberdeen Regional School Dist., 115 A.3d 292 (N.J. Super. L. 2015); Doe v. Acton-Boxborough Regional School Dist., 8 N.E.3d 737 (Mass. 2014); Freedom from Religion Foundation v. Hanover School Dist., 665 F. Supp.2d 58 (D.N.H. 2009); Myers v. Loudoun County Public Schools, 418 F.3d 395 (4th Cir. 2005).

MICHAEL HEISE, *FROM NO CHILD LEFT BEHIND TO EVERY STUDENT SUCCEEDS: BACK TO A FUTURE FOR EDUCATION FEDERALISM*

117 Colum. L. Rev. 1859, 1881-1888, 1894-1896 (2017)

Given the plethora of school choice options—options that exist within the public school sphere as well as options between the public and non-public school markets—one important, though broad, barometer of interest in school choice involves changes over time in the percentage of students attending their government "assigned" public schools. Data from the U.S. Department of Education make clear that this percentage has declined from 80% in 1993 to 73% in 2007. To put this 7% decline into some context, the Department of Education reports that in 2013 just over fifty million students attended public K-12 schools. A 7% decline in students attending their traditional government "assigned" public schools implies an approximate drop of 3.5 million students over a fifteen-year period.

Interestingly, the increased availability and flexibility of *public* funding helps fuel some of the attendance decline in students' assigned public schools. To be sure, flexible public funding enables some families to attend alternative public school options, such as charter and magnet schools, which are inter- and intra-district school choices. Other families, by contrast, use public funds to exercise their *Pierce* rights and seek out various non-public school options, including private and private religious schools, homeschooling, and virtual schools. . . .

1. Charter and Magnet Schools. Public charter schools' importance in the school choice movement continues to increase over time. Between 2000 and 2014, the raw number of charter schools more than quadrupled, from 1,525 to 6,465. Not surprisingly, an increase in the number of charter schools helped fuel a similar increase in the number of students attending charter schools. Indeed, during these same years, 2000 to 2014, charter school enrollment increased by more than 740%. Finally, and perhaps most saliently, charter school enrollments grew as a percentage of total public school enrollment. In 2000, charter school enrollment accounted for less than 1% of total public school enrollment. By 2014, that percentage grew to 5.1%. When one adds public magnet schools into this mix, the drain on traditional "assigned" public school enrollment doubles. In 2014, of the 49.7 million students attending public schools, more than 5 million, or 10 percent of, students chose to attend charter or magnet public schools—that is, to attend a public school *other* than a student's "assigned" public school.

Not surprisingly, charter schools vary—sometimes tremendously—both within and across states. Although charter schools are, in a formal legal sense, public institutions, one trend within the public-charter-school market includes the growing use of private management companies to operate public charter schools. Interestingly, the lurch toward privatization straddles traditional political labels. The cumulative effect of multiple administrations over time, both Republican and Democratic, is that "there are about seven thousand publicly-funded, privately-managed charter schools, enrolling nearly three million students."

Charter schools' significant growth should not deflect attention from another genre of intra-district school choice: magnet schools. Historically, magnet schools' origins partly reflect public school districts' (typically larger urban public districts) desire to increase desegregation and student achievement through schools that usually feature particular academic focus or curricular orientation. While magnet schools vary in terms of their focus and efficacy, they remain an attractive option for many families. Indeed, both the raw number of magnet schools as well as the number of students attending them more than doubled between 2001 and 2014. Despite magnet schools' variety, for purposes of this Essay, the two key characteristics that bind them are that they dislodge students away from geographically assigned public schools and provide parents and students with additional education options.

2. Private Schools and Voucher Programs – Once-stable private religious and secular school enrollment (as measured by private school enrollment as a percentage of total school enrollment) has, since the 2008 financial crisis, displayed evidence of a slight decline. Between 1995 and 2007, the private school enrollment percentage decreased from 11.7% to 10.7%. Beginning in 2009, and through 2013, the percentage dipped to 9.8%. The percentage decline, however, should not obscure private school's important market share of America's school children. Despite any recent minor comparative market-share decline, the total number of students participating in private school choice programs "has more than tripled in the last decade to 350,000 students in 2014-2015." Among private school selections in 2013, families overwhelmingly chose religious-affiliated schools over sectarian schools (68.1% versus 31.9%, respectively).

Voucher programs, both publicly and privately funded, seek, in part, to reduce barriers to the private school market for families. Early voucher programs tended to focus on either students from low-income households or students assigned to struggling public schools or both. ...

Contributing much to the recent growth in publicly funded voucher programs is a shift in voucher programs' initial focus on students from low-income households and those assigned to struggling public schools to a broader slice of middle-class students. While political realities typically prompted publicly and privately funded voucher programs to focus on those students most in need of additional school choices, as the politics surrounding school choice has evolved so too has voucher programs' focus. Now, ironically, successful political support for voucher programs typically requires that the programs include middle-class families as well. . . .

. . . School choice, in all its various forms exercised by parents and students, continues to increase in both absolute and relative terms. One inevitable consequence of school choice policies is that they reduce governmental control over the education enterprise in a fundamental manner. An increase in school choice results in an unmistakable shift in power over critical educational decisions concerning elementary and secondary schooling away from government (at all levels) and toward parents and their schoolchildren. . . .

Given the explosive market developments, homeschooling, with its potential to disrupt traditional education markets and further contribute to the diminished relevance of current education federalism turbulence, warrants particular attention. While it is difficult to accurately assess how the dramatic growth of quality online curricula and resources will continue to inform homeschooling's popularity over time, a few points are already clear. First, at its core, education remains a labor-intensive activity, whether delivered in traditional schools or in the home. On this point, status quo largely endures, and homeschooling remains limited only to those who can absorb (or organize) and meet the intensive labor requirements. While technology, including online instruction, can reduce this burden, technology cannot — at least not yet — substantially eliminate the fixed labor requirements. Technological developments can reduce, however, other traditional market barriers, including, for example, access to instructional material. The potentially significant reduction of one traditional barrier to the homeschooling market will likely steepen homeschooling's growth trend going forward. . . .

Given the importance of education to an individual's ability to participate fully in the nation's economic, political, and social realms, that states compel some amount of education is unremarkable. Equally unremarkable, however, is that our constitutional values, expressed by the Court in Pierce v. Society of Sisters, allow individuals the ability to discharge their affirmative schooling obligations through public- *and* non-public-school attendance. The distribution of families able to fully exercise their *Pierce* rights, however, predictably skews in a direction that favors the wealthy over the poor. To the extent that school choice policies increase education autonomy for a greater number and percentage of families, a corresponding shift in power from governments to families will result.

NOTES AND QUESTIONS

1. How does the school-choice movement undermine the social values that support public schools in the traditional sense? How does it support these values? How do the challenges and advantages presented by school vouchers differ from those presented by charter schools?

The Washington Supreme Court held in League of Women Voters v. State, 355 P.3d 1131 (Wash. 2015) (en banc), that an initiative providing for charter schools that were not subject to local voter control are not public schools under state law, and that, therefore state taxes collected to support public schools cannot be shifted to support them under the state constitutional provision requiring the legislature to establish a general and uniform system of public schools and to devote schools taxes exclusively to such schools. The outcome of constitutional challenges to charter schools under such provisions varies with the language of the clauses and the various states' interpretations of the requirements they impose. These limits are discussed in Nicole Stelle Garnett, The Legal Landscape of Parental Choice Policy, American Enterprise Institute (2015), https://papers.ssrn.com/sol3/papers.cfm?abstract_id=2699296.

2. Local governments first issued vouchers to parents to finance private school education on a large scale after the Supreme Court's decision in Brown v. Board of Education, 347 U.S. 483 (1955), which required the desegregation of public schools. Several southern states offered the vouchers as part of the systematic resistance to desegregation. A dramatic increase in the number of Protestant church schools was also part of the response. By the late 1970s conservative religious leaders were strong supporters of vouchers to aid private schools. John C. Jeffries, Jr. & James E. Ryan, A Political History of the Establishment Clause, 100 Mich. L. Rev. 279, 330 - 333 (2001). Seeking broader political support for vouchers, the original proponents began to forge an alliance in the 1990s with African-American and Latino parents seeking better schools for their children. James Forman, Jr., The Rise and Fall of School Vouchers: A Story of Religion, Race, and Politics, 54 UCLA L. Rev. 547, 568-574 (2007).

3. In practice, voucher programs have not posed the threat to public schools that many feared. Charter schools have been much more successful and present a much greater challenge to the traditional public school. Charter school students have proportionately fewer white students than other public schools, and their parents have proportionately lower levels of educational attainment. Aaron Jay Saiger, The Last Wave: The Rise of the Contingent School District, 84 N.C. L. Rev. 857, 880-881 (2006). About half of charter school students are poor, and 42 percent live in one-parent families. Sarah Grady, Stacey Bielick & Susan Aud, Trends in the Use of School Choice: 1993 to 2007, at 18 (U.S. Dept. Ed. Apr. 2010). Professor James Ryan observes, "This is not altogether surprising. Charter schools are naturally most attractive to parents and students who are not satisfied with their current public schools. There is a higher degree of dissatisfaction with urban than suburban schools. Charter schools are thus concentrated in central cities. Central city schools, in turn, educate a disproportionate number of poor and minority students." James E. Ryan, Charter Schools and Public Education, 4 Stan. J. C.R. & C.L. 393 (2008).

4. Most charter schools' students do not perform better than public school students. A comprehensive study published in 2004 found that the students in 17 percent of the schools performed better, students in 37 percent performed worse, and in the remainder the students performed about the same as public school students. Blacks and Latinos experienced significantly worse learning gains in charter schools than their peers in public schools. (Osamudia R. James, Opt-Out Education: School Choice as Racial Subordination, 99 Iowa L. Rev. 1083, 1096, 1101 (2014)). The majority of charter schools are in inner-city areas, and minority students enroll in them at disproportionately higher rates than white children. *Id.* at 1118. Prof. James argues that the school choice movement masks continuing racial subordination in public schools and undermines democratic values.

5. Most school vouchers are used to pay for tuition in church-affiliated schools. As a result, voucher programs have been challenged as violating the Establishment Clause. However, the Supreme Court rejected this argument in Zelman v. Simmons-Harris, 536 U.S. 639 (2002), and in the process revised Establishment Clause jurisprudence. The plaintiffs challenged the program in Cleveland, which had been enacted because its public schools had "been among the worst performing public schools in the Nation." 536 U.S. at 644. The program provided vouchers for low-income students that could be used at any private school within the district that satisfied statewide educational standards and agreed not to discriminate on the basis of race, religion, or ethnic background, or to "advocate or foster unlawful behavior or teach hatred of any person or group on the basis of race, ethnicity, national origin, or religion." Id. at 645. Of the private schools that participated in the program, 82 percent were religiously affiliated, and 96 percent of the 3,700 students in the program attended a religious school. Approximately 1,400 students received money for tutors.

The Supreme Court held that the program did not violate the Establishment Clause because it was created for a valid secular purpose and on its face was neutral with respect to religion, and because parents decided where to spend the vouchers and thus were making the choice about whether religious or nonreligious schools received the money. The Court said, "The incidental advancement of a religious mission, or the perceived endorsement of a religious message, is reasonably attributable to the individual recipient, not to the government, whose role ends with the disbursement of benefits." Id. at 652.

6. Even though Zelman provides a model for voucher programs that include religious schools that do not violate the Establishment Clause, many state constitutions create an additional barrier. These provisions, called Blaine Amendments, prohibit public funding of religious institutions. Courts in several states have interpreted them as precluding voucher programs from supporting children in religious schools. Bush v. Holmes, 919 So. 2d 392 (Fla. 2006); Opinion of the Justices (Choice in Education), 616 A.2d 478 (N.H. 1992); Opinion of the Justices to the Senate, 514 N.E.2d 353 (Mass. 1987). In Locke v. Davey, 540 U.S. 712 (2004), the Supreme Court held that the State of Washington's application of its constitutional provision to deny a state scholarship to a student studying theology did not violate the Free Exercise Clause. The Court found that the motivation for the provision was not to discriminate against religion but to provide greater protection for religious freedom to its citizens than the federal constitution does, a permissible state goal.

However, Trinity Lutheran Church of Columbia, Inc. v. Comer, __ U.S. __, 137 S. Ct. 2012 (2017), limited the broad language of Locke. A Missouri state agency applied its state Blaine Amendment to deny the application of a church-sponsored preschool to participate in a program that provided grants to nonprofit organizations to purchase playground surfaces made from recycled tires. The church successfully challenged the ruling as violating the Free Exercise Clause. Applying strict scrutiny, the Court held that the state's interest in avoiding a state establishment of religion was not sufficiently compelling to justify the denial of a benefit solely because of the church's religious character. The Court distinguished Locke on the basis that there the state law was applied to deny a benefit to the student because of what he proposed to do, while the law here applied because of what the church was.

This decision invokes the Free Exercise principles of an earlier line of cases that make clear that a school cannot discriminate against religious groups when it has opened its facilities to nonreligious groups. In Good News Club v. Milford Central School, 533 U.S. 98 (2001), the Milford Public School conceded that it had created a limited public forum by opening its facilities to activities that served a variety of purposes, including events "pertaining to the welfare of the community." Any group that "promote[s] the moral and character development of children" was eligible to use the school building. Milford excluded religious groups from those facilities out of concern for encountering Establishment Clause issues. The Supreme Court held that the exclusion of religious schools in a public or limited public forum constituted forbidden viewpoint discrimination and that there was no valid Establishment Clause concern that might constitute a compelling interest justifying viewpoint discrimination.

However, in 2010, the Supreme Court held that a university can constitutionally deny official recognition to a student group unless it allowed any student to join. The rule was challenged by a religious student group that excluded anyone who did not adhere to its statement of faith, as well as gays and lesbians (because one of the group's tenets is that sex outside of marriage between a man and a woman is forbidden). The Court held that the rule operated as a reasonable, viewpoint neutral condition on access to a limited public forum. Christian Legal Society v. Martinez, 561 U.S. 661 (2010).

Professors Thro and Russo interpret *Trinity Lutheran Church* as prohibiting the granting or denial of a benefit because of a person or entity's religious character unless to do so would violate the Establishment Clause. They say that in most situations states may not interpret state anti-establishment provisions more broadly than the federal limits, with the limited exception applied in *Locke*. William E. Thro & Charles J. Russo, Odious to the Constitution: The Educational Implications of Trinity Lutheran Church v. Comer, 346 Educ. L. Reptr. 1 (2017), https://papers.ssrn.com/sol3/papers.cfm?abstract_id=3033967.

Children's Rights as Autonomy Claims

2

The materials we have considered to this point primarily concern the allocation of child-rearing responsibility between parents and the state. While there was talk about the "rights of children," those rights (with a few exceptions) are understood as claims to shelter, education, nutrition, and physical safety.

The materials that follow deal with the rights of children as they are usually invoked when we talk about the rights of persons generally—that is, claims to autonomous decision making and to physical liberty. The special questions that arise are why, when, and to what extent minors are entitled to make decisions as a matter of individual choice, without being bound by the views of parents or state agencies about what is in their interests.

The broad agreement that rational persons are entitled to decide how to lead their lives is matched by wide acceptance of the idea that persons who lack the capacity for rational choice are not entitled to that claim to respect or the opportunity for self-realization. The term "paternalism" itself suggests that what is wrong in making decisions for others lies in treating them as if they were children. But if those to whom coercion is directed are indeed children, paternalism seems the natural course. Consider the following views.

JOHN STUART MILL, *ON LIBERTY*: [T]he only purpose for which power can be rightfully exercised over any member of a civilized community, against his will, is to prevent harm to others. His own good, either physical or moral, is not a sufficient warrant. . . . It is perhaps hardly necessary to say that this doctrine is meant to apply only to human beings in the maturity of their faculties. We are not speaking of children, of young persons below the age which the law may fix as that of manhood or womanhood. Those who are still in a state to require being taken care of by others, must be protected against their own actions as well as against external injury. For the same reason, we may leave out of consideration those backward states of society, in which the race itself may be considered in its nonage. . . . Despotism is a legitimate mode of government in dealing with barbarians, provided the end be their improvement, and the means justified by actually effecting that end. Liberty, as a principle, has no application to any state of things anterior to the time when mankind have become capable of being improved by free and equal discussion.

JOHN LOCKE, *THE SECOND TREATISE ON GOVERNMENT*, §§ 54-55: I have said . . . *[t]hat all Men by Nature are equal. . . . Children*, I confess, are not born in this full state of *Equality*, though they are born to it. Their Parents have a sort of Rule and Jurisdiction over them when they come into the World, and for some time after, but 'tis but a temporary one. . . .

The Law that was to govern *Adam*, was the same that was to govern all his Posterity, the *Law of Reason. . . .* [T]his law being promulgated or made known by *Reason* only, he that is not come to the Use of his Reason, cannot be said to be *under this Law. . . .*

H.L.A. HART, *ARE THERE ANY NATURAL RIGHTS?*, in Political Philosophy 53, 57-58 (A. Quinton ed., 1967): I shall advance the thesis that if there are any moral rights at all, it follows that there is at least one natural right, the equal right of all men to be free. By saying that there is this right, I meant that in the absence of certain conditions . . ., any adult human being capable of choice (1) has the right to forbearance on the part of all others from the use of coercion or restraint against him save to hinder coercion or restraint and (2) is at liberty to do (i.e., is under no obligation to abstain from) any action which is not one coercing or restraining or designed to injure other persons. . . .

[Although it is sometimes said that because we have a duty not to ill-treat animals and babies, they have rights to proper treatment, we should not] extend to animals and babies whom it is wrong to ill-treat the notion of a right to proper treatment, for the moral situation can be simply and adequately described here by saying that it is wrong or that we ought not to ill-treat them or, in the philosopher's generalized sense of "duty," that we have a duty not to ill-treat them. If common usage sanctions talk of the rights of animals or babies it makes an idle use of the expression "a right," which will confuse the situation with other different moral situations where the expression "a right" has a specific force and cannot be replaced by other moral expressions which I have mentioned.

How, though, do we decide that a young person is a "child" not entitled to make autonomous decisions? And should the answer to this question be the same for all decisions? The rest of this chapter explores these issues, first in the context of rights to free expression and then to reproductive choices.

A. THE FREE EXPRESSION RIGHTS OF MINORS

THOMAS I. EMERSON, *THE SYSTEM OF FREEDOM OF EXPRESSION*

6-7 (1970)

The system of freedom of expression in a democratic society rests upon four main premises. These may be stated, in capsule form, as follows:

First, freedom of expression is essential as a means of assuring individual self-fulfillment. The proper end of man is the realization of his character and potentialities as a human being. For the achievement of this self-realization the mind must be free. Hence suppression of belief, opinion, or other expression is an affront to the dignity of man, a negation of man's essential nature. Moreover, man in his capacity as a member of society has a right to share in the common decisions that affect him. To cut off his search for truth, or his expression of it, is to elevate society and the state to despotic command over him and to place him under the control of others.

Second, freedom of expression is an essential process for advancing knowledge and discovering truth. An individual who seeks knowledge and truth must hear all sides of the question, consider all alternatives, test his judgment by exposing it to opposition, and make full use of different minds. Discussion must be kept open no matter how certainly true an accepted opinion may seem to be; many of the most widely acknowledged truths have turned out to be erroneous. Conversely, the same principle applies no matter how false or pernicious the new opinion appears to be; for the unaccepted opinion may be true or partially true and, even if wholly false, its presentation and open discussion compel a rethinking and retesting of the accepted opinion. . . .

Third, freedom of expression is essential to provide for participation in decision making by all members of society. This is particularly significant for political decisions. . . . The principle also carries beyond the political realm. It embraces the right to participate in the building of the whole culture, and includes freedom of expression in religion, literature, art, science, and all areas of human learning and knowledge.

Finally, freedom of expression is a method of achieving a more adaptable and hence a more stable community, of maintaining the precarious balance between healthy cleavage and necessary consensus. This follows because suppression of discussion makes a rational judgment impossible, substituting force for reason. . . . At the same time the process of open discussion promotes greater cohesion in a society because people are more ready to accept decisions that go against them if they have a part in the decision-making process. . . .

NOTES AND QUESTIONS

1. Professor Emerson's summary of the values associated with free speech reflects several possible bases. The first—that freedom of speech is an essential element of self-realization—might rest on the claim that expression, and the right to hear the expressions of others, is an essential aspect of human autonomy. Professor Baker, among others, argued that such a view provides the most coherent theory of the First Amendment:

The liberty model holds that the free speech clause protects not a marketplace but rather an arena of individual liberty from certain types of governmental restrictions. Speech is protected not as a means to a collective good but because of the value of speech conduct to the individual. The liberty theory justifies protection because of the way the protected conduct fosters individual self-realization and self-determination without improperly interfering with the legitimate claims of others.

C. Edwin Baker, Scope of the First Amendment Freedom of Speech, 25 UCLA L. Rev. 964, 966 (1978).

2. The second value identified by Professor Emerson is that free expression contributes to the "marketplace of ideas." That phrase seems first to have been used, almost inevitably, by Justice Holmes, dissenting in Abrams v. United States, 250 U.S. 616 (1919):

> But when men have realized that time has upset many fighting faiths, they may come to believe even more than they believe the very foundations of their own conduct that the ultimate good desired is better reached by free trade in ideas — that the best test of truth is the power of the thought to get itself accepted in the competition of the market.

Id. at 630. The idea itself is, of course, far older, having been expressed by John Milton in the Areopagitica (1644) and by Mill in On Liberty (1859).

The foundation of the "marketplace" notion is obviously utilitarian; free expression is important not because it is an aspect of individual self-realization but because, on balance, good results (that is, greater truth) will flow from it. Despite its popular acceptance, the marketplace theory has been widely criticized on a variety of grounds. *See, e.g.*, Martin H. Redish, The Value of Free Speech, 130 U. Pa. L. Rev. 591 (1982); Baker, above.

3. The third value emphasizes the relationship of speech to effective citizenship and is, like the second, apparently founded on utilitarianism. The same may be said of the social cohesion aspect to speech, reflected in the fourth point.

As you consider the following materials, the relationship of these various theories to the regulation of children's speech will be a recurring concern.

GINSBERG v. NEW YORK

390 U.S. 629 (1968)

BRENNAN, J. This case presents the question of the constitutionality on its face of a New York criminal obscenity statute which prohibits the sale to minors under 17 years of age of material defined to be obscene on the basis of its appeal to them whether or not it would be obscene to adults.

Appellant and his wife operate "Sam's Stationery and Luncheonette" in Bellmore, Long Island. They have a lunch counter, and, among other things, also sell magazines including some so-called "girlie" magazines. Appellant was prosecuted under two informations, each in two counts, which charged that he personally sold a 16-year-old boy two "girlie" magazines on each of two dates in October 1965, in violation of § 484-h of the New York Penal Law. He was tried before a judge without a jury in Nassau County District Court and was found guilty on both counts. The judge found (1) that the magazines contained pictures which depicted female "nudity" in a manner defined in subsection 1(b), . . . and (2) that the pictures were "harmful to minors" in that they had, within the meaning of subsection 1(f) "that quality of . . . representation . . . of nudity. . . ."

The "girlie" picture magazines involved in the sales here are not obscene for adults. . . .

The New York Court of Appeals "upheld the Legislature's power to employ variable concepts of obscenity" in a case in which the same challenge to state power to enact such a law was also addressed to § 484-h. In sustaining state power to enact the law, the Court of Appeals said, Bookcase, Inc. v. Broderick, 18 N.Y.2d 71, at 75, 218 N.E.2d 668, p. 671:

> [M]aterial which is protected for distribution to adults is not necessarily constitution-ally protected from restriction upon its dissemination to children. In other words, the concept of obscenity or of unprotected matter may vary according to the group to whom the questionable material is directed or from whom it is quarantined. Because of the State's exigent interest in preventing distribution to children of objectionable material, it can exercise its power to protect the health, safety, welfare and morals of its community by barring the distribution to children of books recognized to be suitable for adults.

Appellant's . . . contention is the broad proposition that the scope of the constitutional freedom of expression secured to a citizen to read or see material concerned with sex cannot be made to depend upon whether the citizen is an adult or a minor. . . .

We have no occasion in this case to consider the impact of the guarantees of freedom of expression upon the totality of the relationship of the minor and the State. It is enough for the purposes of this case that we inquire whether it was constitutionally impermissible for New York, insofar as § 484-h does so, to accord minors under 17 a more restricted right than that assured to adults to judge and determine for themselves what sex material they may read or see. We conclude that we cannot say that the statute invades the area of freedom of expression con-stitutionally secured to minors.

Appellant argues that there is an invasion of protected rights under § 484-h constitutionally indistinguishable from the invasions under the Nebraska statute forbidding children to study German, which was struck down in Meyer v. State of Nebraska, 262 U.S. 390; the Oregon statute interfering with children's attendance at private and parochial schools, which was struck down in Pierce v. Society of Sisters, 268 U.S. 510; and the statute compelling children against their religious scruples to give the flag salute, which was struck down in West Virginia State Board of Education v. Barnette, 319 U.S. 624. We reject that argument. We do not regard New York's regulation in defining obscenity on the basis of its appeal to minors under 17 as involving an invasion of such minors' constitutionally pro-tected freedoms. Rather § 484-h simply adjusts the definition of obscenity "to social realities by permitting the appeal of this type of material to be assessed in term of the sexual interests . . ." of such minors. That the State has power to make that adjustment seems clear, for we have recognized that even where there is an invasion of protected freedoms "the power of the state to control the conduct of children reaches beyond the scope of its authority over adults. . . . " Prince v. Commonwealth of Massachusetts, 321 U.S. 158, 170. . .

The well-being of its children is of course a subject within the State's consti-tutional power to regulate, and, in our view, two interests justify the limitations in § 484-h upon the availability of sex material to minors under 17, at least if it was rational for the legislature to find that the minors' exposure to such material might be harmful. First of all, constitutional interpretation has consistently recognized that the parents' claim to authority in their own household to direct the rearing of their children is basic in the structure of our society. "It is cardinal with us that the custody, care and nurture of the child reside first in the parents, whose primary function and freedom include preparation for obligations the state can neither supply nor hinder." Prince v. Commonwealth of Massachusetts, *supra*, at 166. The legislature could properly conclude that parents and others, teachers for example, who have this primary responsibility for children's well-being are entitled to the support of laws designed to aid discharge of that responsibility. Indeed, subsection 1(f)(ii) of § 484-h expressly recognizes the parental role in assessing sex-related material harmful to minors according "to prevailing standards in the adult community as a whole with respect to what is suitable material for minors." Moreover, the prohibition against sales to minors does not bar parents who so desire from purchasing the magazines for their children.

The State also has an independent interest in the well-being of its youth. . . .

In Prince v. Massachusetts, *supra*, at 165, this Court, too, recognized that the State has an interest "to protect the welfare of children" and to see that they are "safeguarded from abuses" which might prevent their "growth into free and independent well-developed men and citizens." The only question remaining, therefore, is whether the New York Legislature might rationally conclude, as it has, that exposure to the materials proscribed by § 484-h constitutes such an "abuse."

Section 484-e of the law states a legislative finding that the material condemned by § 484-h is "a basic factor in impairing the ethical and moral development of our youth and a clear and present danger to the people of the state." It is very doubtful that this finding expresses an accepted scientific fact. But obscenity is not protected expression and may be suppressed without a showing of the circumstances which lie behind the phrase "clear and present danger" in its application to protected speech. . . . We do not demand of legislatures "scientifically certain criteria of legislation." Noble State Bank v. Haskell, 219 U.S. 104, 110. We therefore cannot say that § 484-h, in defining the obscenity of material on the basis of its appeal to minors under 17, has no rational relation to the objective of safeguarding such minors from harm.

STEWART, J., concurring. . . . I think a State may permissibly determine that, at least in some precisely delineated areas, a child—like someone in a captive audience—is not possessed of that full capacity for individual choice which is the presupposition of First Amendment guarantees. It is only upon such a premise, I should suppose, that a State may deprive children of other rights—the right to marry, for example, or the right to vote—deprivations that would be constitutionally intolerable for adults.

NOTES AND QUESTIONS

1. To what extent does *Ginsberg* recognize First Amendment rights for minors? Are those rights coextensive with the rights of adults? What explains the broader scope of state power to limit minors' First Amendment rights and the more deferential standard of review applicable to state regulations affecting their rights?

2. Appellant relied on *Meyer*, *Pierce*, and *Barnette* to support a right to distribute "girlie" magazines to minors. *Barnette* involved a challenge by Jehovah's Witnesses to a state law requiring school children to salute the flag, a practice offensive to their religious beliefs. The Court held the statute invalid, stating that "[i]f there is any fixed star in our constitutional constellation, it is that no official, high or petty, can prescribe what shall be orthodox in politics, nationalism, religion, or other matters of opinion. . . . " 319 U.S. 624, 642 (1943). How far do these three cases support the appellant's position?

Most states still have laws requiring that the Pledge of Allegiance be recited in schools, and most permit parents to excuse their children from the exercise. Courts are divided about whether the parental permission requirement violates minors' first amendment right to decide for themselves whether to recite the pledge. *Compare* Frazier ex rel. Frazier v. Winn, 535 F.3d 1279, 1283 (11th Cir. 2008) (upholding statute), and Circle Schools v. Pappert, 381 F.3d 172 (3d Cir. 2004) (striking down statute). Schools continue to discipline or harass students who refuse to recite the pledge with parental permission, which courts consistently hold is unconstitutional under *Barnette*. *See, e.g.,* Arceneaux v. Klein Independent School District, 2018 WL 2317565 (S.D. Tex. 2018).

3. The Court explains the state interest protected by the statute in *Ginsberg* partly in terms of support for parental authority, on the assumption that parents would not want their children exposed to lewd magazines. Moreover, the Court says, parents may (if they hold a different view) buy these magazines for their children. Would the statute be unconstitutional if it prohibited the sale of obscene magazines "to or for the use of" minors? Does *Prince*, cited by the majority, suggest that such a statute is valid?

4. The Court in *Ginsberg* adopts the variable obscenity test employed by the New York Court of Appeals. What makes material "obscene" (or at least proscribable) for one audience but not for another? Is it a matter of the impact of the speech? Is it that minors have not made a mature judgment to be exposed to sexually oriented material? What does it mean to say that an adult has made a mature judgment to read (if that is the term) *Hustler* magazine?

BROWN v. ENTERTAINMENT MERCHANTS ASSOCIATION

564 U.S. 786 (2011)

Justice SCALIA delivered the opinion of the Court. . . . Cal. Civ. Code Ann. §§ 1746-1746.5 (West 2009) (Act), prohibits the sale or rental of "violent video games" to minors, and requires their packaging to be labeled "18." The Act covers games "in which the range of options available to a player includes killing, maiming, dismembering, or sexually assaulting an image of a human being, if those acts are depicted" in a manner that "[a] reasonable person, considering the game as a whole, would find appeals to a deviant or morbid interest of minors," that is "patently offensive to prevailing standards in the community as to what is suitable for minors," and that "causes the game, as a whole, to lack serious literary, artistic, political, or scientific value for minors." Violation of the Act is punishable by a civil fine of up to $1,000.

Respondents, representing the video-game and software industries, brought a preenforcement challenge to the Act in the United States District Court for the Northern District of California. That court concluded that the Act violated the First Amendment and permanently enjoined its enforcement. The Court of Appeals affirmed, and we granted certiorari.

II

California correctly acknowledges that video games qualify for First Amendment protection. The Free Speech Clause exists principally to protect discourse on public matters, but we have long recognized that it is difficult to distinguish politics from entertainment, and dangerous to try. "Everyone is familiar with instances of propaganda through fiction. What is one man's amusement, teaches another's doctrine. Like the protected books, plays, and movies that preceded them, video games communicate ideas—and even social messages—through many familiar literary devices (such as characters, dialogue, plot, and music) and through features distinctive to the medium (such as the player's interaction with the virtual world). That suffices to confer First Amendment protection. Under our Constitution, "esthetic and moral judgments about art and literature . . . are for the individual to make, not for the Government to decree, even with the mandate or approval of a majority." United States v. Playboy Entertainment Group, Inc., 529 U.S. 803, 818 (2000). And whatever the challenges of applying the Constitution to ever-advancing technology, "the basic principles of freedom of speech and the press, like the First Amendment's command, do not vary" when a new and different medium for communication appears.

The most basic of those principles is this: "[A]s a general matter, . . . government has no power to restrict expression because of its message, its ideas, its subject matter, or its content." There are of course exceptions. " 'From 1791 to the present,' . . . the First Amendment has 'permitted restrictions upon the content of speech in a few limited areas,' and has never 'include[d] a freedom to disregard these traditional limitations.' " These limited areas—such as obscenity, incitement, and fighting words—represent "well-defined and narrowly limited classes of speech, the prevention and punishment of which have never been thought to raise any Constitutional problem."

Last Term, in *Stevens*, we held that new categories of unprotected speech may not be added to the list by a legislature that concludes certain speech is too harmful to be tolerated. *Stevens* concerned a federal statute purporting to criminalize the creation, sale, or possession of certain depictions of animal cruelty. . . . A saving clause largely borrowed from our obscenity jurisprudence, see Miller v. California, 413 U.S. 15, 24 (1973), exempted depictions with "serious religious, political, scientific, educational, journalistic, historical, or artistic value." We held that statute to be an impermissible content-based restriction on speech. There was no American tradition of forbidding the *depiction of* animal cruelty—though States have long had laws against *committing* it. . . . .

That holding controls this case. As in *Stevens*, California has tried to make violent-speech regulation look like obscenity regulation by appending a saving clause required for the latter. That does not suffice. Our cases have been clear that the obscenity exception to the First Amendment does not cover whatever a legislature finds shocking, but only depictions of "sexual conduct." . . .

Because speech about violence is not obscene, it is of no consequence that California's statute mimics the New York statute regulating obscenity-for-minors that we upheld in Ginsberg v. New York, 390 U.S. 629 (1968). That case approved a prohibition on the sale to minors of *sexual* material that would be obscene from the perspective of a child. . . .

The California Act is something else entirely. It does not adjust the boundaries of an existing category of unprotected speech to ensure that a definition designed for adults is not uncritically applied to children. California does not argue that it is empowered to prohibit selling offensively violent works *to adults*—and it is wise not to, since that is but a hair's breadth from the argument rejected in *Stevens*. Instead, it wishes to create a wholly new category of content-based regulation that is permissible only for speech directed at children.

That is unprecedented and mistaken. "[M]inors are entitled to a significant measure of First Amendment protection, and only in relatively narrow and well-defined circumstances may government bar public dissemination of protected materials to them." Erznoznik v. Jacksonville, 422 U.S. 205, 212-213 (1975) (citation omitted). No doubt a State possesses legitimate power to protect children from harm, but that does not include a free-floating power to restrict the ideas to which children may be exposed. "Speech that is neither obscene as to youths nor subject to some other legitimate proscription cannot be suppressed solely to protect the young from ideas or images that a legislative body thinks unsuitable for them." *Erznoznik, supra*, at 213-214.

California's argument would fare better if there were a longstanding tradition in this country of specially restricting children's access to depictions of violence, but there is none. Certainly the *books* we give children to read—or read to them when they are younger—contain no shortage of gore. Grimm's Fairy Tales, for example, are grim indeed. As her just deserts for trying to poison Snow White, the wicked queen is made to dance in red hot slippers "till she fell dead on the floor, a sad example of envy and jealousy." Cinderella's evil stepsisters have their eyes pecked out by doves. And Hansel and Gretel (children!) kill their captor by baking her in an oven.

High-school reading lists are full of similar fare. Homer's Odysseus blinds Polyphemus the Cyclops by grinding out his eye with a heated stake. In the Inferno, Dante and Virgil watch corrupt politicians struggle to stay submerged beneath a lake of boiling pitch, lest they be skewered by devils above the surface. And Golding's Lord of the Flies recounts how a schoolboy called Piggy is savagely murdered *by other children* while marooned on an island.

This is not to say that minors' consumption of violent entertainment has never encountered resistance. In the 1800's, dime novels depicting crime and "penny dreadfuls" (named for their price and content) were blamed in some quarters for juvenile delinquency. When motion pictures came along, they became the villains instead. "The days when the police looked upon dime novels as the most dangerous of textbooks in the school for crime are drawing to a close. . . . They say that the moving picture machine . . . tends even more than did the dime novel to turn the thoughts of the easily influenced to paths which sometimes lead to prison." For a time, our Court did permit broad censorship of movies because of their capacity to be "used for evil," but we eventually reversed course. Radio dramas were next, and then came comic books. Many in the late 1940's and early 1950's blamed comic books for fostering a "preoccupation with violence and horror" among the young, leading to a rising juvenile crime rate. But efforts to convince Congress to restrict comic books failed. And, of course, after comic books came television and music lyrics.

California claims that video games present special problems because they are "interactive," in that the player participates in the violent action on screen and determines its outcome. . . . As Judge Posner has observed, all literature is interactive. "[T]he better it is, the more interactive. Literature when it is successful draws the reader into the story, makes him identify with the characters, invites him to judge them and quarrel with them, to experience their joys and sufferings as the reader's own." . . .

Because the Act imposes a restriction on the content of protected speech, it is invalid unless California can demonstrate that it passes strict scrutiny — that is, unless it is justified by a compelling government interest and is narrowly drawn to serve that interest. The State must specifically identify an "actual problem" in need of solving, and the curtailment of free speech must be actually necessary to the solution. That is a demanding standard. "It is rare that a regulation restricting speech because of its content will ever be permissible."

California cannot meet that standard. At the outset, it acknowledges that it cannot show a direct causal link between violent video games and harm to minors. . . .

The State's evidence is not compelling. California relies primarily on the research of Dr. Craig Anderson and a few other research psychologists whose studies purport to show a connection between exposure to violent video games and harmful effects on children. These studies have been rejected by every court to consider them,[1] and with good reason: They do not prove that violent video games *cause* minors to *act* aggressively (which would at least be a beginning). Instead, "[n]early all of the research is based on correlation, not evidence of causation, and most of the studies suffer from significant, admitted flaws in methodology." They show at best some correlation between exposure to violent entertainment and minuscule real-world effects, such as children's feeling more aggressive or making louder noises in the few minutes after playing a violent game than after playing a nonviolent game.

Even taking for granted Dr. Anderson's conclusions that violent video games produce some effect on children's feelings of aggression, those effects are both small and indistinguishable from effects produced by other media. In his testimony

---

1. *See* Video Software Dealers Assn. v. Schwarzenegger, 556 F.3d 950, 963-964 (C.A. 9 2009); Interactive Digital Software Assn. v. St. Louis County, 329 F.3d 954 (C.A. 8 2003); American Amusement Machine Assn. v. Kendrick, 244 F.3d 572, 578-579 (C.A. 7 2001); Entertainment Software Assn. v. Foti, 451 F. Supp. 2d 823, 832-833 (M.D. La. 2006); Entertainment Software Assn. v. Hatch, 443 F. Supp. 2d 1065, 1070 (Minn. 2006), *aff'd*, 519 F.3d 768 (C.A. 8 2008); Entertainment Software Assn. v. Granholm, 426 F. Supp. 2d 646, 653 (E.D. Mich. 2006); Entertainment Software Assn. v. Blagojevich, 404 F. Supp. 2d 1051, 1063 (N.D. Ill. 2005), *aff'd*, 469 F.3d 641 (C.A. 7 2006).

in a similar lawsuit, Dr. Anderson admitted that the "effect sizes" of children's exposure to violent video games are "about the same" as that produced by their exposure to violence on television. And he admits that the *same* effects have been found when children watch cartoons starring Bugs Bunny or the Road Runner, or when they play video games like Sonic the Hedgehog that are rated "E" (appropriate for all ages), or even when they "vie[w] a picture of a gun."

Of course, California has (wisely) declined to restrict Saturday morning cartoons, the sale of games rated for young children, or the distribution of pictures of guns. The consequence is that its regulation is wildly underinclusive when judged against its asserted justification, which in our view is alone enough to defeat it. Underinclusiveness raises serious doubts about whether the government is in fact pursuing the interest it invokes, rather than disfavoring a particular speaker or viewpoint. Here, California has singled out the purveyors of video games for disfavored treatment—at least when compared to booksellers, cartoonists, and movie producers—and has given no persuasive reason why.

The Act is also seriously underinclusive in another respect—and a respect that renders irrelevant the contentions of the concurrence and the dissents that video games are qualitatively different from other portrayals of violence. The California Legislature is perfectly willing to leave this dangerous, mind-altering material in the hands of children so long as one parent (or even an aunt or uncle) says it's OK. And there are not even any requirements as to how this parental or avuncular relationship is to be verified; apparently the child's or putative parent's, aunt's, or uncle's say-so suffices. That is not how one addresses a serious social problem.

California claims that the Act is justified in aid of parental authority: By requiring that the purchase of violent video games can be made only by adults, the Act ensures that parents can decide what games are appropriate. . . .

. . . California cannot show that the Act's restrictions meet a substantial need of parents who wish to restrict their children's access to violent video games but cannot do so. The video-game industry has in place a voluntary rating system designed to inform consumers about the content of games. The system, implemented by the Entertainment Software Rating Board (ESRB), assigns age-specific ratings to each video game submitted: EC (Early Childhood); E (Everyone); E10+ (Everyone 10 and older); T (Teens); M (17 and older); and AO (Adults Only—18 and older). The Video Software Dealers Association encourages retailers to prominently display information about the ESRB system in their stores; to refrain from renting or selling adults-only games to minors; and to rent or sell "M" rated games to minors only with parental consent. In 2009, the Federal Trade Commission (FTC) found that, as a result of this system, "the video game industry outpaces the movie and music industries" in "(1) restricting target-marketing of mature-rated products to children; (2) clearly and prominently disclosing rating information; and (3) restricting children's access to mature-rated products at retail." This system does much to ensure that minors cannot purchase seriously violent games on their own, and that parents who care about the matter can readily evaluate the games their children bring home. Filling the remaining modest gap in concerned-parents' control can hardly be a compelling state interest.

And finally, the Act's purported aid to parental authority is vastly overinclusive. Not all of the children who are forbidden to purchase violent video games on their own have parents who *care* whether they purchase violent video games.

While some of the legislation's effect may indeed be in support of what some parents of the restricted children actually want, its entire effect is only in support of what the State thinks parents *ought* to want. This is not the narrow tailoring to "assisting parents" that restriction of First Amendment rights requires. . . .

We affirm the judgment below.

Justice ALITO, with whom THE CHIEF JUSTICE joins, concurring in the judgment. . . . Respondents in this case, representing the video-game industry, ask us to strike down the California law on two grounds: The broad ground adopted by the Court and the narrower ground that the law's definition of "violent video game," is impermissibly vague. Because I agree with the latter argument, I see no need to reach the broader First Amendment issues addressed by the Court. . . .

The Court's opinion distorts the effect of the California law. I certainly agree with the Court that the government has no "free-floating power to restrict the ideas to which children may be exposed," but the California law does not exercise such a power. If parents want their child to have a violent video game, the California law does not interfere with that parental prerogative. Instead, the California law reinforces parental decisionmaking in exactly the same way as the New York statute upheld in *Ginsberg*. Under both laws, minors are prevented from purchasing certain materials; and under both laws, parents are free to supply their children with these items if that is their wish.

Citing the video-game industry's voluntary rating system, the Court argues that the California law does not "meet a substantial need of parents who wish to restrict their children's access to violent video games but cannot do so." The Court does not mention the fact that the industry adopted this system in response to the threat of federal regulation, a threat that the Court's opinion may now be seen as largely eliminating. Nor does the Court acknowledge that compliance with this system at the time of the enactment of the California law left much to be desired — or that future enforcement may decline if the video-game industry perceives that any threat of government regulation has vanished. Nor does the Court note, as Justice Breyer points out, that many parents today are simply not able to monitor their children's use of computers and gaming devices.

C

Finally, the Court is far too quick to dismiss the possibility that the experience of playing video games (and the effects on minors of playing violent video games) may be very different from anything that we have seen before. Any assessment of the experience of playing video games must take into account certain characteristics of the video games that are now on the market and those that are likely to be available in the near future.

Today's most advanced video games create realistic alternative worlds in which millions of players immerse themselves for hours on end. These games feature visual imagery and sounds that are strikingly realistic, and in the near future video-game graphics may be virtually indistinguishable from actual video footage. . . .

Persons who play video games also have an unprecedented ability to participate in the events that take place in the virtual worlds that these games create.

Players can create their own video-game characters and can use photos to produce characters that closely resemble actual people. A person playing a sophisticated game can make a multitude of choices and can thereby alter the course of the action in the game. In addition, the means by which players control the action in video games now bear a closer relationship to the means by which people control action in the real world. . . .

These present-day and emerging characteristics of video games must be considered together with characteristics of the violent games that have already been marketed.

In some of these games, the violence is astounding. Victims by the dozens are killed with every imaginable implement, including machine guns, shotguns, clubs, hammers, axes, swords, and chainsaws. Victims are dismembered, decapitated, disemboweled, set on fire, and chopped into little pieces. They cry out in agony and beg for mercy. Blood gushes, splatters, and pools. Severed body parts and gobs of human remains are graphically shown. In some games, points are awarded based, not only on the number of victims killed, but on the killing technique employed.

It also appears that there is no antisocial theme too base for some in the video-game industry to exploit. There are games in which a player can take on the identity and reenact the killings carried out by the perpetrators of the murders at Columbine High School and Virginia Tech. The objective of one game is to rape a mother and her daughters; in another, the goal is to rape Native American women. There is a game in which players engage in "ethnic cleansing" and can choose to gun down African-Americans, Latinos, or Jews. In still another game, players attempt to fire a rifle shot into the head of President Kennedy as his motorcade passes by the Texas School Book Depository.

If the technological characteristics of the sophisticated games that are likely to be available in the near future are combined with the characteristics of the most violent games already marketed, the result will be games that allow troubled teens to experience in an extraordinarily personal and vivid way what it would be like to carry out unspeakable acts of violence.

The Court is untroubled by this possibility. According to the Court, the "interactive" nature of video games is "nothing new" because "all literature is interactive." Disagreeing with this assessment, the International Game Developers Association (IGDA)—a group that presumably understands the nature of video games and that supports respondents—tells us that video games are "far more concretely interactive." And on this point, the game developers are surely correct.

It is certainly true, as the Court notes, that "'[l]iterature, when it is successful, draws the reader into the story, makes him identify with the characters, invites him to judge them and quarrel with them, to experience their joys and sufferings as the reader's own.'" But only an extraordinarily imaginative reader who reads a description of a killing in a literary work will experience that event as vividly as he might if he played the role of the killer in a video game. To take an example, think of a person who reads the passage in Crime and Punishment in which Raskolnikov kills the old pawn broker with an axe. Compare that reader with a video-game player who creates an avatar that bears his own image; who sees a realistic image of the victim and the scene of the killing in high definition and in three dimensions; who is forced to decide whether or not to kill the victim and decides to do so; who then pretends to grasp an axe, to raise it above the head of the victim, and then to bring it down; who hears the thud of the axe hitting her head and her cry of pain; who sees her split skull and feels the sensation of blood on his face and hands. For most people, the two experiences will not be the same.

When all of the characteristics of video games are taken into account, there is certainly a reasonable basis for thinking that the experience of playing a video game may be quite different from the experience of reading a book, listening to a radio broadcast, or viewing a movie. And if this is so, then for at least some minors, the effects of playing violent video games may also be quite different. The Court acts prematurely in dismissing this possibility out of hand. . . .

Justice THOMAS, dissenting. The Court's decision today does not comport with the original public understanding of the First Amendment. The majority strikes down, as facially unconstitutional, a state law that prohibits the direct sale or rental of certain video games to minors because the law "abridg[es] the freedom of speech." But I do not think the First Amendment stretches that far. . . . I would hold that the law at issue is not facially unconstitutional under the First Amendment, and reverse and remand for further proceedings. . . .

. . . The historical evidence shows that the founding generation believed parents had absolute authority over their minor children and expected parents to use that authority to direct the proper development of their children. It would be absurd to suggest that such a society understood "the freedom of speech" to include a right to speak to minors (or a corresponding right of minors to access speech) without going through the minors' parents. The founding generation would not have considered it an abridgment of "the freedom of speech" to support parental authority by restricting speech that bypasses minors' parents. . . .

. . . Although much has changed in this country since the Revolution, the notion that parents have authority over their children and that the law can support that authority persists today. For example, at least some States make it a crime to lure or entice a minor away from the minor's parent. Every State in the Union still establishes a minimum age for marriage without parental or judicial consent. Individuals less than 18 years old cannot enlist in the military without parental consent. And minors remain subject to curfew laws across the country and cannot unilaterally consent to most medical procedures.

Moreover, there are many things minors today cannot do at all, whether they have parental consent or not. State laws set minimum ages for voting and jury duty. In California (the State at issue here), minors cannot drive for hire or drive a school bus, purchase tobacco, play bingo for money, or execute a will.

My understanding of "the freedom of speech" is also consistent with this Court's precedents. To be sure, the Court has held that children are entitled to the protection of the First Amendment, *see, e.g.*, Erznoznik v. Jacksonville, 422 U.S. 205, 212-213 (1975), and the government may not unilaterally dictate what children can say or hear, *see id.* at 213-214; Tinker v. Des Moines Independent Community School Dist., 393 U.S. 503, 511 (1969). But this Court has never held, until today, that "the freedom of speech" includes a right to speak to minors (or a right of minors to access speech) without going through the minors' parents. To the contrary, "[i]t is well settled that a State or municipality can adopt more stringent controls on communicative materials available to youths than on those available to adults."

The Court's constitutional jurisprudence "historically has reflected Western civilization concepts of the family as a unit with broad parental authority over minor children." Parham v. J.R., 442 U.S. 584, 602 (1979). Under that case law, "legislature[s] [can] properly conclude that parents and others, teachers for example, who have . . . primary responsibility for children's well-being are entitled to the support of laws designed to aid discharge of that responsibility." Ginsberg v. New York, 390 U.S. 629, 639 (1968); see also Bellotti v. Baird, 443 U.S. 622, 635 (1979) (opinion of Powell, J.). . . .

. . . Even assuming that video games are speech, in most applications the California law does not implicate the First Amendment. All that the law does is prohibit the direct sale or rental of a violent video game to a minor by someone other than the minor's parent, grandparent, aunt, uncle, or legal guardian. Where a minor has a parent or guardian, as is usually true, the law does not prevent that minor from obtaining a violent video game with his parent's or guardian's help. In the typical case, the only speech affected is speech that bypasses a minor's parent or guardian. Because such speech does not fall within "the freedom of speech" as originally understood, California's law does not ordinarily implicate the First Amendment and is not facially unconstitutional. . . .

I respectfully dissent.

Justice BREYER, dissenting. . . . In determining whether the statute is unconstitutional, I would apply both this Court's "vagueness" precedents and a strict form of First Amendment scrutiny. In doing so, the special First Amendment category I find relevant is not (as the Court claims) the category of "depictions of violence," but rather the category of "protection of children." This Court has held that the "power of the state to control the conduct of children reaches beyond the scope of its authority over adults." Prince v. Massachusetts, 321 U.S. 158, 170 (1944). And the "'regulatio[n] of communication addressed to [children] need not conform to the requirements of the [F]irst [A]mendment in the same way as those applicable to adults.'" Ginsberg v. New York, 390 U.S. 629, 638, n.6 (1968) (quoting Emerson, Toward a General Theory of the First Amendment, 72 Yale L.J. 877, 939 (1963)).

The majority's claim that the California statute, if upheld, would create a "new categor[y] of unprotected speech" is overstated. No one here argues that depictions of violence, even extreme violence, *automatically* fall outside the First Amendment's protective scope as, for example, do obscenity and depictions of child pornography. We properly speak of *categories* of expression that lack protection when, like "child pornography," the category is broad, when it applies automatically, and when the State can prohibit everyone, including adults, from obtaining access to the material within it. But where, as here, careful analysis must precede a narrower judicial conclusion (say, denying protection to a shout of "fire" in a crowded theater, or to an effort to teach a terrorist group how to peacefully petition the United Nations), we do not normally describe the result as creating a "new category of unprotected speech." . . .

In my view, California's statute provides "fair notice of what is prohibited," and consequently it is not impermissibly vague. *Ginsberg* explains why that is so. . . .

. . . The five-Justice majority, in an opinion written by Justice Brennan, wrote that the statute was sufficiently clear. No Member of the Court voiced any vagueness objection.

Comparing the language of California's statute with the language of New York's statute, it is difficult to find any vagueness-related difference. Why are the words "kill," "maim," and "dismember" any more difficult to understand than the word "nudity"? Justice Alito objects that these words do "not perform the narrowing function" that this Court has required in adult obscenity cases, where statutes can only cover "'hard core'" depictions. But the relevant comparison is not to adult obscenity cases but to *Ginsberg*, which dealt with "nudity," a category no more "narrow" than killing and maiming. And in any event, *narrowness* and *vagueness* do not necessarily have anything to do with one another. All that is required for vagueness purposes is that the terms "kill," "maim," and "dismember" give fair notice as to what they cover, which they do.

The remainder of California's definition copies, almost word for word, the language this Court used in Miller v. California, 413 U.S. 15 (1973), in permitting a *total ban* on material that satisfied its definition (one enforced with *criminal* penalties). The California law's reliance on "community standards" adheres to *Miller* . . . California only departed from the *Miller* formulation in two significant respects: It substituted the word "deviant" for the words "prurient" and "shameful," and it three times added the words "for minors." The word "deviant" differs from "prurient" and "shameful," but it would seem no less suited to defining and narrowing the reach of the statute. And the addition of "for minors" to a version of the *Miller* standard was approved in *Ginsberg*, even though the New York law "dr[ew] no distinction between young children and adolescents who are nearing the age of majority."

Both the *Miller* standard and the law upheld in *Ginsberg* lack perfect clarity. But that fact reflects the difficulty of the Court's long search for words capable of protecting expression without depriving the State of a legitimate constitutional power to regulate. As is well known, at one point Justice Stewart thought he could do no better in defining obscenity than, "I know it when I see it." . . . Ultimately, however, this Court accepted the "community standards" tests used in *Miller* and *Ginsberg*. They reflect the fact that sometimes, even when a precise standard proves elusive, it is easy enough to identify instances that fall within a legitimate regulation. And they seek to draw a line, which, while favoring free expression, will nonetheless permit a legislature to find the words necessary to accomplish a legitimate constitutional objective.

What, then, is the difference between *Ginsberg* and *Miller* on the one hand and the California law on the other? . . .

There is, of course, one obvious difference: The *Ginsberg* statute concerned depictions of "nudity," while California's statute concerns extremely violent video games. But for purposes of vagueness, why should that matter? Justice Alito argues that the *Miller* standard sufficed because there are "certain generally accepted norms concerning expression related to sex," whereas there are no similarly "accepted standards regarding the suitability of violent entertainment." But there is no evidence that is so. The Court relied on "community standards" in *Miller* precisely because of the difficulty of articulating "accepted norms" about depictions of sex. I can find no difference—historical or otherwise—that is *relevant* to the vagueness question. Indeed, the majority's examples of literary descriptions of violence, on which Justice Alito relies, do not show anything relevant at all.

After all, one can find in literature as many (if not more) descriptions of physical love as descriptions of violence. Indeed, sex "has been a theme in art and literature throughout the ages." For every Homer, there is a Titian. For every Dante, there is an Ovid. And for all the teenagers who have read the original versions of Grimm's Fairy Tales, I suspect there are those who know the story of Lady Godiva.

Thus, I can find no meaningful vagueness-related differences between California's law and the New York law upheld in *Ginsberg*. . . . Consequently, for purposes of this facial challenge, I would not find the statute unconstitutionally vague.

. . . Like the majority, I believe that the California law must be "narrowly tailored" to further a "compelling interest," without there being a "less restrictive" alternative that would be "at least as effective." . . .

The interest that California advances in support of the statute is compelling. As this Court has previously described that interest, it consists of both (1) the "basic" parental claim "to authority in their own household to direct the rearing of their children," which makes it proper to enact "laws designed to aid discharge of [parental] responsibility," and (2) the State's "independent interest in the well-being of its youth." *Ginsberg*, 390 U.S., at 639-640. And where these interests work in tandem, it is not fatally "underinclusive" for a State to advance its interests in protecting children against the special harms present in an interactive video game medium through a default rule that still allows parents to provide their children with what their parents wish.

Both interests are present here. As to the need to help parents guide their children, the Court noted in 1968 that "'parental control or guidance cannot always be provided.'" . . .

As to the State's independent interest, we have pointed out that juveniles are more likely to show a "'lack of maturity'" and are "more vulnerable or susceptible to negative influences and outside pressures," and that their "character . . . is not as well formed as that of an adult." Roper v. Simmons, 543 U.S. 551, 569-570 (2005). And we have therefore recognized "a compelling interest in protecting the physical and psychological well-being of minors."

At the same time, there is considerable evidence that California's statute significantly furthers this compelling interest. That is, in part, because video games are excellent teaching tools. Learning a practical task often means developing habits, becoming accustomed to performing the task, and receiving positive reinforcement when performing that task well. Video games can help develop habits, accustom the player to performance of the task, and reward the player for performing that task well. Why else would the Armed Forces incorporate video games into its training?

. . . [E]xtremely violent games can harm children by rewarding them for being violently aggressive in play, and thereby often teaching them to be violently aggressive in life. And video games can cause more harm in this respect than can typically passive media, such as books or films or television programs.

There are many scientific studies that support California's views. . . .

Experts debate the conclusions of all these studies. Like many, perhaps most, studies of human behavior, each study has its critics, and some of those critics have produced studies of their own in which they reach different conclusions. (I list both sets of research in the appendixes.) I, like most judges, lack the social science expertise to say definitively who is right. But associations of public health professionals who do possess that expertise have reviewed many of these studies and found a significant risk that violent video games, when compared with more passive media, are particularly likely to cause children harm. . . .

[Six years ago] the American Psychological Association adopted a resolution that said:

[C]omprehensive analysis of violent interactive video game research suggests such exposure . . . increases aggressive behavior, . . . increases aggressive thoughts, . . . increases angry feelings, . . . decreases helpful behavior, and . . . increases physiological arousal.

The Association added:

[T]he practice, repetition, and rewards for acts of violence may be *more conducive* to increasing aggressive behavior among children and youth than passively watching violence on TV and in films.

Four years after that, in 2009, the American Academy of Pediatrics issued a statement in significant part about interactive media. It said:

Studies of these rapidly growing and ever-more-sophisticated types of media have indicated that the effects of child-initiated virtual violence may be *even more profound than those of passive media* such as television. In many games the child or teenager is 'embedded' in the game and uses a 'joystick' (handheld controller) that enhances both the experience and the aggressive feelings.

It added:

Correlational and experimental studies have revealed that violent video games lead to increases in aggressive behavior and aggressive thinking and decreases in prosocial behavior. Recent longitudinal studies . . . have revealed that in as little as 3 months, high exposure to violent video games increased physical aggression. Other recent longitudinal studies . . . have revealed similar effects across 2 years.

Unlike the majority, I would find sufficient grounds in these studies and expert opinions for this Court to defer to an elected legislature's conclusion that the video games in question are particularly likely to harm children. . . .

I can find no "less restrictive" alternative to California's law that would be "at least as effective." The majority points to a voluntary alternative: The industry tries to prevent those under 17 from buying extremely violent games by labeling those games with an "M" (Mature) and encouraging retailers to restrict their sales to those 17 and older. But this voluntary system has serious enforcement gaps. . . . [A]s of the FTC's most recent update to Congress, 20% of those under 17 are still able to buy M-rated video games, and, breaking down sales by store, one finds that this number rises to nearly 50% in the case of one large national chain. And the industry could easily revert back to the substantial noncompliance that existed in 2004, particularly after today's broad ruling reduces the industry's incentive to police itself.

The industry also argues for an alternative technological solution, namely "filtering at the console level." But it takes only a quick search of the Internet to find guides explaining how to circumvent any such technological controls. YouTube viewers, for example, have watched one of those guides (called "How to bypass parental controls on the Xbox 360") more than 47,000 times. . . .

California's statute is consequently constitutional on its face—though litigants remain free to challenge the statute as applied in particular instances, including any effort by the State to apply it to minors aged 17.

I add that the majority's different conclusion creates a serious anomaly in First Amendment law. *Ginsberg* makes clear that a State can prohibit the sale to minors of depictions of nudity; today the Court makes clear that a State cannot prohibit the sale to minors of the most violent interactive video games. But what sense does it make to forbid selling to a 13-year-old boy a magazine with an image of a nude woman, while protecting a sale to that 13-year-old of an interactive video game in which he actively, but virtually, binds and gags the woman, then tortures and kills her? What kind of First Amendment would permit the government to protect children by restricting sales of that extremely violent video game *only* when the woman—bound, gagged, tortured, and killed—is also topless? . . .

This anomaly is not compelled by the First Amendment. It disappears once one recognizes that extreme violence, where interactive, and *without literary, artistic, or similar justification*, can prove at least as, if not more, harmful to children as photographs of nudity. And the record here is more than adequate to support such a view. That is why I believe that *Ginsberg* controls the outcome here *a fortiori*. And it is why I believe California's law is constitutional on its face.

For these reasons, I respectfully dissent.

NOTES AND QUESTIONS

1. If the Supreme Court had struck down the California law on the ground of void for vagueness, as Justice Alito advocated, the legislature could have tried to redraft the law so that it was sufficiently clear. Does the rationale adopted by the Court leave redrafting as an option?

2. The *Brown* majority and Justice Breyer, who dissented, find the social science evidence about the impact of violent video games on children uncertain. Justice Breyer would "defer to the legislature" in this circumstance, but the majority did not. What explains the difference in these approaches to empirical uncertainty?

3. *Ginsberg* upheld the legislature's decision that the sale of some sexually oriented material to minors should be banned, even though adults are constitutionally entitled to have access to it. Why did the *Brown* majority reject a similar judgment about violent video games? Does *Brown* mean that minors have the same First Amendment right of access to speech that adults do?

4. In *Brown* the state argued that the statute was constitutional because it supported parents' childrearing authority. Professor Guggenheim argues that *Brown* decided the parents' rights claim wrongly. He regards parents as having

almost unlimited constitutionally protected authority over their children and concludes, "Parents have the constitutional right to deny their children access to materials for no better reason than they believe the material may be harmful to them." Martin Guggenheim, Violent Video Games and the Rights of Children and Parents: A Critique of *Brown v. Entertainment Merchants Association*, 41 Hastings Const. L. Q. 707, 756 (2014). Is this description of parental authority consistent with the Supreme Court decisions we have read? If so, does it mean that *Brown* was wrongly decided?

5. Erznoznik v. City of Jacksonville, 422 U.S. 205 (1975), which is discussed in *Brown*, involved a challenge to the validity of a city ordinance banning the showing of films containing nudity by a drive-in movie theater when its screen is visible from a public street or place. The Court struck down the ordinance, despite the city's argument that its ordinance was an exercise of its police power to protect children from this type of visual influence.

> It is well settled that a State or municipality can adopt more stringent controls on communicative materials available to youths than on those available to adults. *See, e.g.*, Ginsberg v. New York, 390 U.S. 629 (1968). Nevertheless, minors are entitled to a significant measure of First Amendment protection, *see* Tinker v. Des Moines School Dist., 393 U.S. 503 (1969), and only in relatively narrow and well-defined circumstances may government bar public dissemination of protected materials to them. In this case, assuming the ordinance is aimed at prohibiting youths from viewing the films, the restriction is broader than permissible. The ordinance is not directed against sexually explicit nudity, nor is it otherwise limited. Rather, it sweepingly forbids display of all films containing *any* uncovered buttocks or breasts, irrespective of context or pervasiveness. . . . Clearly all nudity cannot be deemed obscene even as to minors. *See* Ginsberg v. New York, *supra*. Nor can such a broad restriction be justified by any other governmental interest pertaining to minors. Speech that is neither obscene as to youths nor subject to some other legitimate proscription cannot be suppressed solely to protect the young from ideas or images that a legislative body thinks unsuitable for them. In most circumstances, the values protected by the First Amendment are no less applicable when government seeks to control the flow of information to minors.

422 U.S. at 212-214.

PROBLEMS

1. The state legislature has enacted a statute forbidding anyone to "distribute" video games to persons younger than 18 if they contain sexually oriented materials as defined in Ginsberg v. New York. The National Consortium of Video Game Manufacturers has filed suit to enjoin enforcement of the statute, contending that it violates the First Amendment rights of minors and the rights of parents protected by the Due Process Clause. What arguments should be made by the attorneys for the consortium and for the state?

2. The state has also enacted a statute identical to the one struck down in *Brown* except that the ban applies only to sales to children younger than 14, rather than to all minors. What arguments can be made in support of the law? Against it?

NOTE: CENSORING ELECTRONIC MEDIA TO PROTECT CHILDREN

In 1978 the Supreme Court upheld legislation granting authority to the Federal Communications Commission to regulate a radio broadcast described as "indecent but not obscene." Federal Communications Commn. v. Pacifica Foundation, 438 U.S. 726 (1978). The program in question, a satire of censorship by George Carlin entitled "Filthy Words," used a large number of four-letter words in a variety of ways. The FCC condemned the broadcast because it aired during the early afternoon when children were likely to be in the audience. The Supreme Court upheld the FCC's action. In doing so, the Court emphasized that the context in which speech occurs is important to deciding on the extent of protection it deserves. A broadcast is peculiarly intrusive in the sense that it confronts the citizen not only in public but also in the privacy of the home. Moreover, a listener may not be able to avoid some exposure to unexpected program content. And, finally,

> [B]roadcasting is uniquely accessible to children, even those too young to read. . . . We held in Ginsberg v. New York that the government's interest in the "well-being of its youth" and in supporting "parents' claim to authority in their own household" justified the regulation of otherwise protected expression. The ease with which children may obtain access to broadcast material, coupled with the concerns recognized in *Ginsberg*, amply justify special treatment of indecent broadcasting.

Id. at 749-750. In Federal Communications Commission v. Fox Television Stations, Inc., 567 U.S. 239 (2012), the Supreme Court was asked to reconsider *Pacifica*; the challengers claimed that the statute banning the broadcast of "obscene, indecent, or profane language" was unconstitutionally vague, but the Court resolved the case on other grounds. However, *Pacifica* has much less impact today than when it was decided because the FCC does not enforce the rules regarding "indecent" material against cable and other subscription services.

The Court distinguished *Pacifica* in Sable Communications of California, Inc. v. Federal Communications Commission, 492 U.S. 115 (1989), which concerned whether Congress could ban indecent as well as obscene interstate commercial telephone messages, i.e., dial-a-porn. While confirming *Pacifica*'s position that protecting children from indecent material is a compelling government interest, the Court held that the complete ban on sexually explicit messages for adults as well as children was not sufficiently narrowly tailored to achieving this goal. The Court distinguished *Pacifica* on the basis that, unlike radio broadcasting, telephones are not as accessible to children, and there is no captive audience.

Less than a decade later, Congress enacted the Communications Decency Act of 1996 (CDA), Title V of the Telecommunications Act of 1996, Pub. L. 104–104, the first of two failed attempts to regulate the Internet to prevent children from having access to obscene and indecent material. The CDA prohibited the knowing transmission of obscene or indecent messages to anyone under age 18. It granted an affirmative defense to anyone who took a good faith, effective action to restrict minors' access to such communications. Applying strict scrutiny because the statute limited the access of adults as well as children, the Court held the statute violated the First Amendment. Reno v. American Civil Liberties Union, 521 U.S. 844 (1997). The Court said that the Internet receives "full" First Amendment protection, distinguishing it from radio and TV, which are extensively regulated and much more "invasive." The Court distinguished *Ginsberg* and *Pacifica* on the bases that the CDA did not allow parents to consent to their children's access to restricted materials, was not limited to commercial transactions, and imposed a complete ban on the restricted materials on the basis of their content. Further, the statute's critical terms such as "indecent" were not sufficiently well-defined and were overbroad.

Congress responded in 1998 with the Child Online Protection Act (COPA), Pub. L. 105-277, which attempted to address the problems that *Reno* identified. It prohibited knowingly posting material that is harmful to minors on the Web for commercial purposes, with an affirmative defense similar to the one in the CDA. COPA defined "harmful to minors" by reference to contemporary community standards for minors. After two inconclusive trips to the Supreme Court and a trial on the merits of the petition to enjoin enforcement of the statute, the Third Circuit held that the statute was unconstitutionally vague and overbroad, that the definition of what was prohibited was not narrowly tailored to achieving the government's goal of protecting minors from sexually explicit materials, and that a ban was not the least restrictive alternative means of advancing the government interest, since other technologies such as blocking and filtering technologies could protect the interest without denying adults access. American Civil Liberties Union v. Mukasey, 534 F.3d 181 (3d Cir. 2008). The Supreme Court ended the saga when it declined to grant certiorari. 555 U.S. 1137 (2009). For a history of the COPA litigation, *see* Elizabeth Blanks Hindman, Protecting Childhood: Rights, Social Goals and the First Amendment in the Context of the Child Online Protection Act, 15 Comm. L. & Pol'y 1 (2010).

However, in United States v. American Library Association, 539 U.S. 194 (2003), the Supreme Court held that a different federal statute directed at preventing children from having access to inappropriate materials on the Internet is constitutional. The Children's Internet Protection Act, 47 U.S.C. § 254, requires public libraries and school districts that receive federal funds to have Internet safety policies, including required use of filtering software, without specifying the type of software. The statute also allows the filters to be turned off when adults are using the computers. The Court said that Congress may attach reasonable conditions to the receipt of federal funds, rejecting the claim that the filtering software prevents adults from having access to constitutionally protected materials.

EMILY BUSS, *DO CHILDREN HAVE THE SAME FIRST AMENDMENT RIGHTS AS ADULTS?: THE SPEECH-ENHANCING EFFECT OF INTERNET REGULATION*

79 Chi.-Kent L. Rev. 103, 113-115 (2004)

A strong argument can be made that the value to children of independent Internet access outweighs whatever loss of value to adults would be associated with regulations designed to afford children that independent access. The argument begins with the suggestion . . . that children, particularly adolescents, have a special, developmental interest in the free exploration of ideas. . . . [T]he potential to engage in unfettered and expansive exploration on the Internet makes it an especially suitable medium for this developmental work. Moreover, the wealth of information available to children in a successfully regulated world is vast, whereas the information lost to adults, while significant, is minor by comparison. Finally, adults have far more comprehensive means available to seek similar information elsewhere than do children, whose movements, finances, and schedule are controlled by the same people who will tightly control their Internet access in the absence of state regulation.

The scope of the Internet access restrictions imposed on many children in a regulation-free world can be expected to be far greater than the scope of those restrictions imposed on adults (or on children permitted full access) by well-tailored regulation. At worst, adults will lose access to sexually explicit materials that do not qualify as obscene, but are widely viewed as offensive. Children, in contrast, may lose access to the Internet altogether, or face severe curtailments on the freedom with which they use it. Put more starkly, adults risk the loss of a relatively small band of speech of questionable value, whereas children risk the loss of a vast amount of speech, much of high political, social, and scientific value. Moreover, where adults would be left free, in the regulated world, to explore what remains with abandon, many children still allowed access will be closely monitored by their parents in an unregulated world. . . .

The greater value of children's Internet access derives, also, from the relative scarcity of access opportunities for children when compared to those of adults. For children, Internet access in schools and libraries may be the only means available to them to explore vast bodies of information. Any other access to the Internet, or other sources of comparable information, will be significantly controlled by their parents: Their parents will determine whether there is Internet access at home at all, and, if so, whether, when, and under what circumstances their children can use it. Parents control their children's finances both directly (by controlling payment and allowance) and indirectly, in collaboration with the state (by controlling their employment). Parents also control their children's movements and associations, further diminishing children's opportunities to seek out information on their own. Adults, in contrast, have considerably more, though surely not absolute, control over all these aspects of their lives, and thus have far greater alternative access to the information in question. They can buy their own Internet access from home, buy books and images, and even arrange associations to facilitate access and exchange. . . .

On the Internet, children may have more to gain from regulation than adults have to lose. If we cannot protect children's independent Internet access by other means, the state might be justified in imposing regulations designed to encourage parents to allow this access.

We now turn our attention to other aspects of the right to freedom of expression—claims of rights to speak, publish, post, and upload. The Supreme Court cases on children's rights in these areas, as well as some but not all decisions from lower courts, have arisen in the context of efforts by schools to censor or punish student speech.

WILLIAM G. BUSS, *SCHOOL NEWSPAPERS, PUBLIC FORUM,
AND THE FIRST AMENDMENT*

74 Iowa L. Rev. 505, 505-506 (1989)

. . . [T]he role of values in American education has been ambiguous and controversial. Under one view, children must be indoctrinated in the values of the parents' generation. This "inculcation of values" view permits the majority of the people at various levels of government to decide which values are ours and which values are most important. A rival view has its starting point in the Bill of Rights, which protects individual liberty in general and freedom of speech in particular. Under this "marketplace of ideas" view, the essence of the American democratic system derives from the collective strength and wisdom of a multiplicity of uncoerced individual choices representing a wide variety of ideas of what is true, what is good, and what is right. This rival perspective looks with suspicion upon the indoctrination of values through government-operated schools as a hallmark of totalitarianism rather than democratic freedom.

The resulting conundrum has been and continues to be the puzzling heritage of the public schools: Schools should strengthen our democracy by inculcating the values identified by the majority while also strengthening our commitment to freedom by fostering pluralism and eschewing orthodoxy in religion or politics. This profound tension would exist even if we had no notion of judicial review. Individuals, communities, and government officials would have to find the golden mean between the inconsistent demands of these two powerful norms. The same tension resonates within the constitutional arguments that are invoked when the courts are asked to resolve the conflict between inculcation of values and the marketplace of ideas model.

TINKER V. DES MOINES INDEPENDENT COMMUNITY SCHOOL DISTRICT

393 U.S. 503 (1969)

FORTAS, J. Petitioner John F. Tinker, 15 years old, and petitioner Christopher Eckhardt, 16 years old, attended high schools in Des Moines, Iowa. Petitioner Mary Beth Tinker, John's sister, was a 13-year-old student in junior high school.

In December 1965, a group of adults and students in Des Moines held a meeting at the Eckhardt home. The group determined to publicize their objections to the hostilities in Vietnam and their support for a truce by wearing black armbands during the holiday season and by fasting on December 16 and New Year's Eve. Petitioners and their parents had previously engaged in similar activities, and they decided to participate in the program.

The principals of the Des Moines schools became aware of the plan to wear armbands. On December 14, 1965, they met and adopted a policy that any student wearing an armband to school would be asked to remove it, and if he refused he would be suspended until he returned without the armband. Petitioners were aware of the regulation that the school authorities adopted.

On December 16, Mary Beth and Christopher wore black armbands to their schools. John Tinker wore his armband the next day. They were all sent home and suspended from school until they would come back without their armbands. They did not return to school until after the planned period for wearing armbands had expired—that is, until after New Year's Day.

This complaint was filed in the United States District Court by petitioners, through their fathers, under § 1983 of Title 42 of the United States Code. It prayed for an injunction restraining the respondent school officials and the respondent members of the board of directors of the school district from disciplining the petitioners, and it sought nominal damages. After an evidentiary hearing the District Court dismissed the complaint. It upheld the constitutionality of the school authorities' action on the ground that it was reasonable in order to prevent disturbance of school discipline....

First Amendment rights, applied in light of the special characteristics of the school environment, are available to teachers and students. It can hardly be argued that either students or teachers shed their constitutional rights to freedom of speech or expression at the schoolhouse gate. This has been the unmistakable holding of this Court for almost 50 years. In Meyer v. Nebraska, 262 U.S. 390 (1923), and Bartels v. Iowa, 262 U.S. 404 (1923), this Court, in opinions by Mr. Justice McReynolds, held that the Due Process Clause of the Fourteenth Amendment prevents States from forbidding the teaching of a foreign language to young students. Statutes to this effect, the Court held, unconstitutionally interfere with the liberty of teacher, student, and parent.

In West Virginia v. Barnette, this Court held that under the First Amendment, the student in public school may not be compelled to salute the flag. Speaking through Mr. Justice Jackson, the Court said:

> The Fourteenth Amendment, as now applied to the States, protects the citizen against the State itself and all of its creatures—Boards of Education not excepted. These have, of course, important, delicate, and highly discretionary functions, but none that they may not perform within the limits of the Bill of Rights. That they are educating the young for citizenship is reason for scrupulous protection of Constitutional freedoms of the individual, if we are not to strangle the free mind at its source and teach youth to discount important principles of our government as mere platitudes. 319 U.S., at 637.

On the other hand, the Court has repeatedly emphasized the need for affirming the comprehensive authority of the States and of school officials, consistent with fundamental constitutional safeguards, to prescribe and control conduct in the schools. Our problem lies in the area where students in the exercise of First Amendment rights collide with the rules of the school authorities....

The school officials banned and sought to punish petitioners for a silent, passive expression of opinion, unaccompanied by any disorder or disturbance on the part of petitioners. There is here no evidence whatever of petitioners' interference, actual or nascent, with the schools' work or of collision with the rights of other students to be secure and to be let alone. Accordingly, this case does not concern speech or action that intrudes upon the work of the schools or the rights of other students....

In our system, state-operated schools may not be enclaves of totalitarianism. School officials do not possess absolute authority over their students. Students in school as well as out of school are "persons" under our Constitution. They are possessed of fundamental rights which the State must respect, just as they them-selves must respect their obligations to the State. In our system, students may not be regarded as closed-circuit recipients of only that which the State chooses to communicate. They may not be confined to the expression of those sentiments that are officially approved. In the absence of a specific showing of constitutionally valid reasons to regulate their speech, students are entitled to freedom of expres-sion of their views. . . .

This principle has been repeated by this Court on numerous occasions during the intervening years. In Keyishian v. Board of Regents, 385 U.S. 589, 603, Mr. Justice Brennan, speaking for the Court, said:

> "The vigilant protection of constitutional freedoms is nowhere more vital than in the community of American schools." Shelton v. Tucker, [364 U.S. 479], at 487. The classroom is peculiarly the "marketplace of ideas." The Nation's future depends upon leaders trained through wide exposure to that robust exchange of ideas which discov-ers truth "out of a multitude of tongues, [rather] than through any kind of authori-tative selection."

The principle of these cases is not confined to the supervised and ordained discussion which takes place in the classroom. The principal use to which the schools are dedicated is to accommodate students during prescribed hours for the purpose of certain types of activities. Among those activities is personal intercom-munication among the students. This is not only an inevitable part of the process of attending school; it is also an important part of the educational process. A stu-dent's rights, therefore, do not embrace merely the classroom hours. When he is in the cafeteria, or on the playing field, or on the campus during the authorized hours, he may express his opinions, even on controversial subjects like the conflict in Vietnam, if he does so without "materially and substantially interfer[ing] with the requirements of appropriate discipline in the operation of the school" and without colliding with the rights of others. But conduct by the student, in class or out of it, which for any reason—whether it stems from time, place, or type of behavior—materially disrupts classwork or involves substantial disorder or inva-sion of the rights of others is, of course, not immunized by the constitutional guarantee of freedom of speech. . . .

As we have discussed, the record does not demonstrate any facts which might reasonably have led school authorities to forecast substantial disruption of or material interference with school activities, and no disturbances or disorders on the school premises in fact occurred. . . .

Reversed and remanded.

BLACK, J., dissenting. . . . I deny, therefore, that it has been the "unmistakable holding of this Court for almost 50 years" that "students" and "teachers" take with them into the "schoolhouse gate" constitutional rights to "freedom of speech or expression." Even *Meyer* did not hold that. It makes no reference to "symbolic speech" at all; what it did was to strike down as "unreasonable" and therefore unconstitutional a Nebraska law barring the teaching of the German language before the children reached the eighth grade. One can well agree with Mr. Justice Holmes and Mr. Justice Sutherland, as I do, that such a law was no more unreason-able than it would be to bar the teaching of Latin and Greek to pupils who have not reached the eighth grade. In fact, I think the majority's reason for invalidating the Nebraska law was that it did not like it or in legal jargon that it "shocked the Court's conscience," "offended its sense of justice, or" was "contrary to fundamental concepts of the English-speaking world," as the Court has sometimes said. . . .

. . . [P]ublic school students [are not] sent to the schools at public expense to broadcast political or any other views to educate and inform the public. The original idea of schools, which I do not believe is yet abandoned as worthless or out of date, was that children had not yet reached the point of experience and wisdom which enabled them to teach all of their elders. It may be that the Nation has outworn the old-fashioned slogan that "children are to be seen not heard," but one may, I hope, be permitted to harbor the thought that taxpayers send children to school on the premise that at their age they need to learn, not teach. . . .

. . . School discipline, like parental discipline, is an integral and important part of training our children to be good citizens—to be better citizens. Here a very small number of students have crisply and summarily refused to obey a school order designed to give pupils who want to learn the opportunity to do so. One does not need to be a prophet or the son of a prophet to know that after the Court's holding today some students in Iowa schools and indeed in all schools will be ready, able, and willing to defy their teachers on practically all orders. . . . Turned loose with lawsuits for damages and injunctions against their teachers as they are here, it is nothing but wishful thinking to imagine that young, immature students will not soon believe it is their right to control the schools rather than the right of the States that collect the taxes to hire the teachers for the benefit of the pupils. This case, therefore, wholly without constitutional reasons in my judgment, subjects all the public schools in the country to the whims and caprices of their loudest-mouthed, but maybe not their brightest, students. I, for one, am not fully persuaded that school pupils are wise enough, even with this Court's expert help from Washington, to run the 23,390 public school systems in our 50 States. I wish, therefore, wholly to disclaim any purpose on my part to hold that the Federal Constitution compels the teachers, parents, and elected school officials to surrender control of the American public school system to public school students. I dissent.

NOTES AND QUESTIONS

1. Justice Stewart concurred but divorced himself from "the Court's uncritical assumption that, school discipline aside, the First Amendment rights of children are co-extensive with those of adults." Does the majority so hold? If so, can *Ginsberg* be distinguished?

2. Which of the values associated with free expression set forth by Professor Emerson at pages 94-95 are reflected in the majority's opinion? Does it establish the autonomy claims of the 8-year-old child? Are elementary school children entitled to "equal dignity and respect," as are adults?

Could the student's right to free speech be justified on other grounds? Even if we deny that a child is entitled to the same respect accorded adults because of the former's immaturity, we also expect that at some point (majority) the child will be able to exercise mature choice, and that is possible only if the child learns to choose during his or her minority. *See, e.g.,* John H. Garvey, Freedom and Choice in Constitutional Law, 94 Harv. L. Rev. 1756, 1771-1774 (1981):

> One part of the instrumental justification for freedom of speech for children is that liberty assists their development into mature adults capable of democratic self-government. . . . The second significant value attributed to freedom of speech in the adult model is the key role it plays in the process by which an individual defines himself. This position is less plausible with regard to children, since they can hardly be expected to develop their natural capacities in a socially acceptable fashion when allowed to act without interference. . . . But this does not mean that, for anyone not a fully competent adult, freedom of expression is completely subordinate to some social blueprint for the ideal citizen. Instead, we permit children to express them-selves — within limits — with the instrumental hope that they will grow up able to appreciate the extrinsic satisfactions of self-expression. Society has an interest in encouraging autonomy and diversity, and freedom of speech for children serves several values important to that end. Courts often note the value of freedom in teaching children the satisfactions that can result from expression of their own individual-ity; in ensuring the development of skills used for rational discourse; in instilling an appreciation of how speech can affect, assist, and injure others.

3. Justice Black's dissent in *Tinker* made the following observation about the parties:

> [A]pparently only seven out of the school system's 18,000 pupils deliberately refused to obey the [non-demonstration] order. One defying pupil was Paul Tinker, 8 years old, who was in the second grade; another, Hope Tinker, was 11 years old and in the fifth grade; a third member of the Tinker family was 13, in the eighth grade; and a fourth member of the same family was John Tinker, 15 years old, and an 11th grade high school pupil. Their father, a Methodist minister without a church, is paid a salary by the American Friends Service Committee [a pacifist organization]. Another stu-dent who defied the school order . . . was Christopher Eckhardt, an 11th grade pupil and a petitioner in this case. His mother is an official in the Women's International League for Peace and Freedom.

Tinker, 393 U.S. at 516.

What is the point of this observation? Does it strengthen or weaken the claim to freedom of speech? Does it make the case more or less closely resemble the values upon which *Meyer*, *Pierce*, and *Yoder* seem to rely?

In an article commemorating the fortieth anniversary of *Tinker*, Mary Beth Tinker, now a nurse, wrote an article describing her very socially conscious family and recalling the events that led to her expulsion from school:

> By Christmastime in 1965, about 1000 U.S. soldiers had been killed in Vietnam, with more and more boys in Des Moines being drafted. In November, my mother and John attended a march against the war in Washington D.C., along with Chris Eckhardt and his mother. . . . They heard of the idea of wearing black armbands, possibly from a Quaker named Herbert Hoover, who shared the famous name of his distant cousin, President Herbert Hoover. Students in the Unitarian youth group became interested, and one of them, Ross Peterson, wrote an article about the idea in the Roosevelt High School newspaper. Being upset about the war, especially the gruesome news on TV most nights as my sister and I cooked dinner, we wanted to wear armbands to school, too.

But on December 14, before we had made a decision on whether to wear the armbands, the school administrators ruled that we would be forbidden from wearing black armbands to school. This created a dilemma for me: I had been a good student with top grades who always followed rules. But I knew about the First Amendment's right to free speech and expression, and I thought students should have such rights, too. I was also influenced by a popular saying at the time, "Eichmann only followed orders," referring to the fact that Nazis were able to commit atrocious crimes because there were not enough courageous people to question the orders they received. And I was influenced by the examples of brave people like the Birmingham children and the people in Ruleville. So, I decided to wear the armband on December 16, along with my younger brother Paul and my sister Hope, and our family friend Chris Eckhardt. My brother John decided not to wear one that day, but to try and reason with the administrators first.

Mary Beth Tinker, Reflections on *Tinker*, 58 Am. U. L. Rev. 1119, 1124-1125 (2009).

4. In some cases, courts have avoided the problems of defining substantial disruption and how much risk of disruption must be foreseen to justify punishing student speech by invoking the "true threat" doctrine. *See, e.g.*, D.J.M. ex rel. D.M. v. Hannibal Public Sch. Dist. No. 60, 647 F.3d 754 (8th Cir. 2011); Riehm v. Engelking, 538 F.3d 952, 962 (8th Cir. 2008); Doe v. Pulaski Cnty. Special Sch. Dist., 306 F.3d 616 (8th Cir. 2002); *but see* J.S. ex rel. H.S. v. Bethlehem Area Sch. Dist., 807 A.2d 847 (Pa. 2002) (student's communication did not constitute a "true threat"). Language that constitutes a "true threat" is not protected speech under the First Amendment, just as obscenity is not. Watts v. United States, 394 U.S. 705 (1969), is the leading case on the meaning of "true threat." In that case, a man at a political rally was charged with the crime of making a threat against the president for saying "if they ever make me carry a rifle, the first man I want to get in my sights is L.B.J." The Supreme Court reversed the decision upholding his conviction:

We do not believe that the kind of political hyperbole indulged in by petitioner fits within that statutory term. For we must interpret the language Congress chose "against the background of a profound national commitment to the principle that debate on public issues should be uninhibited, robust, and wideopen, and that it may well include vehement, caustic, and sometimes unpleasantly sharp attacks on government and public officials." The language of the political arena, like the language used in labor disputes, is often vituperative, abusive, and inexact. We agree with petitioner that his only offense here was "a kind of very crude offensive method of stating a political opposition to the President." Taken in context, and regarding the expressly conditional nature of the statement and the reaction of the listeners, we do not see how it could be interpreted otherwise.

Other courts skip over the true threat analysis in cases of student speech and go straight to the *Tinker* analysis. *See, e.g.*, Cuff v. Valley Central Sch. Dist., 677 F.3d 109 (2d Cir. 2012); Wisniewski v. Weedsport Central Sch. Dist., 494 F.3d 34, 36 (2d Cir. 2007); Boim v. Fulton Cnty. Sch. Dist., 494 F.3d 978 (11th Cir. 2007). Many of these cases are discussed in R. George Wright, Doubtful Threats and the Limits of Student Speech Rights, 42 U.C. Davis L. Rev. 679 (2009). Professor Wright argues that the speech in many of the cases is not really threatening because of lack of specificity or imminence.

5. Does a student have a greater right to speak than to listen or read? Consider Board of Education v. Pico, 457 U.S. 853 (1982). A parent group submitted to the school board a list of books they deemed objectionable, including Slaughterhouse Five by Kurt Vonnegut, Best Short Stories of Negro Writers by Langston Hughes, Soul on Ice by Eldridge Cleaver, and Black Boy by Richard Wright. The board ordered the books removed from the shelves. When the decision became public, the board characterized the books as "anti-American, anti-Christian, anti-Sem[i]tic, and just plain filthy." Id. at 857.

Students brought suit to challenge the removal order. Writing for a plurality of the Court, Justice Brennan recognized the authority of schools to reflect community values in certain decisions. In considering the permissibility of removal of books from a school library, he said, "We are . . . in full agreement that local school boards must be permitted 'to establish and apply their curriculum in such a way as to transmit community values,' and that 'there is a legitimate and substantial interest in promoting respect for authority and traditional values be they social, moral, or political.'" Id. at 864. However,

> If petitioners *intended* by their removal decision to deny respondents access to ideas with which petitioners disagreed . . . then petitioners have exercised their discretion in violation of the Constitution. To permit such intentions to control official actions would be to encourage the precise sort of officially prescribed orthodoxy unequivocally condemned in *Barnette*.

Id. at 871.

If schools have the authority, and perhaps the responsibility, to convey traditional values, on what theory can their power to determine appropriate messages to students be limited?

6. While *Pico* suggests that challenges to curriculum are unlikely to succeed, there are limits on schools' authority even there. For example, in Arce v. Douglas, 793 F.3d 968 (9th Cir. 2015), the court found that a state law forbidding school boards from adopting certain kinds of curricula violated the First Amendment and equal protection. The legislation was enacted after the Tucson, Arizona, school board established a Mexican American Studies program for the public schools. The state legislation prohibited a school district from including in its program of instruction any course or class that (1) promotes the overthrow of the United States government, (2) promotes resentment toward a race or class of people, (3) is designed primarily for pupils of a particular ethnic group, or (4) advocates ethnic solidarity instead of the treatment of pupils as individuals. Ariz. Rev. Stat. § 15–112(A). The Tucson program was the first and only program found to violate the statute. When the school district eliminated the program, a student and her father sued the state superintendent of public instruction and others, claiming, *i.a.*, that the statute violates students' First Amendment rights because it was overbroad and expresses viewpoint discrimination, citing *Pico*. The trial court granted summary judgment in favor of the plaintiffs on the claim that limits based on the third criterion (designed primarily for pupils of a particular ethnic group) were overly broad. It granted the defendants' summary judgment motion on all other claims. The Ninth Circuit held that the legislation restricting curricular materials was unconstitutional unless it was reasonably related to legitimate pedagogical concerns. It then affirmed the trial court ruling in favor of the plaintiffs on the

overbreadth claim. It reversed and remanded the summary judgments in favor of the state on the viewpoint discrimination claim and the claim that the statute violated equal protection because it was motivated by discriminatory intent. On remand, the federal district court held that the enactment and enforcement of the law were motivated by racial animus and therefore violated equal protection, and that they violated students' First Amendment rights to receive information. Gonzalez v. Douglas, 269 F. Supp. 3d 948 (D. Ariz. 2017).

NOTE: PROCEDURAL DUE PROCESS IN PUBLIC SCHOOL DISCIPLINARY PROCEEDINGS

The children in *Tinker* were suspended from school until they agreed not to wear their armbands anymore, but the opinion does not indicate whether the principal summarily dismissed them or employed some kind of hearing to determine that they could be excluded. The Supreme Court first addressed public school students' procedural due process rights three years after *Tinker* in Goss v. Lopez, 419 U.S. 565 (1975). There the Court held that even though the federal Constitution does not guarantee a right to education, it does prohibit the states from depriving students of interests in receiving an education created by state law without due process. The specific procedural safeguards that are constitutionally required vary with the severity of the deprivation of the protected interest. Most fundamentally, the Court said, due process requires notice of the alleged basis for limiting the right and the opportunity to be heard on the issue. "At the very minimum, therefore, students facing suspension and the interference with a protected property interest must be given *some* kind of notice and afforded *some* kind of hearing." 419 U.S. at 579. For a suspension of 10 days or less, the Court held

> [T]he student must be given oral or written notice of the charges against him and, if he denies them, an explanation of the evidence the authorities have and an opportunity to present his side of the story. . . . There need be no delay between the time "notice" is given and the time of the hearing. In the great majority of cases the disciplinarian may informally discuss the alleged misconduct with the student minutes after it has occurred. . . .
>
> In holding as we do, we do not believe that we have imposed procedures on school disciplinarians which are inappropriate in a classroom setting. Instead we have imposed requirements which are, if anything, less than a fair-minded school principal would impose upon himself in order to avoid unfair suspensions. . . .
>
> We should also make it clear that we have addressed ourselves solely to the short suspension, not exceeding ten days. Longer suspensions or expulsions for the remainder of the school term, or permanently, may require more formal procedures.

419 U.S. at 581-584.

What is the significance of the Court's holding that due process requires notice and a hearing but that the notice and hearing can be no more than the informal conversation between a principal and a student just before the principal disciplines the student? As the Court observes, this holding did not change actual practice in most situations. What, if anything, did it accomplish, then?

Two years later, in Ingraham v. Wright, 430 U.S. 651 (1977), the Court held that corporal punishment of a student implicates a constitutionally protected liberty interest but that due process does not require notice or any kind of a hearing before a school official paddles a student. Instead, the Court said, common law remedies against an official who exceeds legal limits on corporal punishment are sufficient to satisfy due process. 430 U.S. at 672.

The Court also held that the Eighth Amendment prohibition of cruel and unusual punishment simply does not apply in the public school setting and so imposes no limits on school-administered corporal punishment. 430 U.S. at 664. The Court explained,

> The schoolchild has little need for the protection of the Eighth Amendment. . . . The openness of the public school and its supervision by the community afford significant safeguards against the kinds of abuses from which the Eighth Amendment protects the prisoner. In virtually every community where corporal punishment is permitted in the schools, these safeguards are reinforced by the legal constraints of the common law. Public school teachers and administrators are privileged at common law to inflict only such corporal punishment as is reasonably necessary for the proper education and discipline of the child; any punishment going beyond the privilege may result in both civil and criminal liability.

430 U.S. at 670.

How does the after-the-fact remedy of a tort suit vindicate a student's interest in being protected from unjustified corporal punishment?

PROBLEMS

1. Seventh-grader James wears a T-shirt portraying the U.S. president as a "chicken hawk" and a drug user through words and pictures. The shirt evokes comments from other students but no fights, and a student who disagrees with the views expressed on the shirt complains to the principal. Citing a school policy that prohibits wearing clothes that depict drugs or alcohol, the principal tells James to turn the shirt inside out, cover the pictures of drugs and alcohol with tape, or wear another shirt. James refuses and is suspended. What arguments might be made for and against him if he sues for readmission?

2. A high school that has had a number of troubling racial incidents over the last semester enacted a dress code forbidding students to wear clothing with messages that carry racist implications. A group of students wore T-shirts with a picture of a country singer on the front and Confederate flags on the back. When the principal told the students to remove the shirts, they objected, saying that they wore them to celebrate the singer's birthday and their Southern heritage. The students then sued to enjoin enforcement of the policy against them. What arguments should their attorneys and the attorney for the school make?

3. An eighth-grade student, David, helped his friend write a petition declaring that one of the teachers was "the devil." David and his friend circulated the petition among the students, threatening at least one that if he wouldn't sign, he would be beaten black and blue. The principal eventually discovered the petition and showed it to the teacher, who became upset and left school. The principal then summoned David and his father to his office, told them about the charges, and suspended David from school for five days. David sued, claiming that the principal's actions violated his procedural due process and First Amendment rights. What arguments should attorneys for each side make?

4. On the day that a Latino student at East High School was killed, Daniel, a tenth-grader, was overheard saying to a friend, "One down, 40,000 to go." When news about this spread among the student body, other students threatened Daniel; some said they would kill him or bomb his house. In the cafeteria a group of students confronted him, yelling that he was a racist. The vice principal escorted Daniel out of the high school and sent him home. As he left in the company of the vice principal, students yelled at him. The next day, Daniel and his mother asked the principal to read a statement over the school's public address system, explaining that Daniel had not said what had been reported and that he was innocent. The principal refused, saying that there was too great a risk of aggravating racial tensions in the school. In the next few days, Daniel received threatening phone calls at home, and police were assigned to patrol his house for the rest of the week. The principal also continued Daniel's suspension on the basis that it was still not safe for him to return to school. Daniel, through his parents, has filed suit against the school, alleging that its refusal to read his statement violated his right to freedom of speech. What arguments should be made?

5. Hayes High School has a mandatory civics course, which emphasizes the importance of democratic government and values. A student with Marxist views insists that the school include Das Kapital in the curriculum, or at least purchase it for the school library. She has threatened to bring suit if one of these is not done. The school principal has asked you if the suit would be likely to succeed. What advice would you give?

The next school speech case that reached the Supreme Court was Bethel School District No. 403 v. Fraser, 478 U.S. 675 (1986). High school student Matthew Fraser gave a speech nominating a classmate for a student council office during a voluntary, school-sponsored assembly. The speech was an extended, elaborate, sexually explicit metaphor, and some of the students hooted and yelled during the speech. Before the speech, teachers had advised Matthew not to give it, and afterward the assistant principal told him that the speech violated a school rule prohibiting conduct that substantially interfered with the education process. He was suspended for three days and was not allowed to be a candidate for student speaker at the upcoming graduation. He sued in federal district court, alleging that his free speech rights were violated. The Supreme Court ultimately ruled in favor of the school district, but not on the basis that the speech violated the *Tinker* standard. Instead, the Court said that the school could prohibit the use of "vulgar and offensive terms in public discourse" in pursuit of its mission to teach "the shared values of a civilized social order." 478 U.S. at 682. Citing *Ginsberg* and *Pacifica*, the Court said that the school was "entirely within its permissible authority in imposing sanctions upon Fraser in response to his offensively lewd and indecent speech." 478 U.S. at 685. The following decision was issued two years later.

HAZELWOOD SCHOOL DISTRICT V. KUHLMEIER

484 U.S. 260 (1988)

WHITE, J. . . . Petitioners are the Hazelwood School District in St. Louis County, Missouri; various school officials; Robert Eugene Reynolds, the principal of Hazelwood East High School, and Howard Emerson, a teacher in the school district. Respondents are three former Hazelwood East students who were staff members of Spectrum, the school newspaper. They contend that school officials violated their First Amendment rights by deleting two pages of articles from the May 13, 1983, issue of Spectrum.

Spectrum was written and edited by the Journalism II class at Hazelwood East. The newspaper was published every three weeks or so during the 1982-1983 school year. More than 4,500 copies of the newspaper were distributed during that year to students, school personnel, and members of the community.

The Board of Education allocated funds from its annual budget for the printing of Spectrum. These funds were supplemented by proceeds from sales of the newspaper. . . .

The practice at Hazelwood East during the spring 1983 semester was for the journalism teacher to submit page proofs of each Spectrum issue to Principal Reynolds for his review prior to publication. On May 10, Emerson delivered the proofs of the May 13 edition to Reynolds, who objected to two of the articles scheduled to appear in that edition. One of the stories described three Hazelwood East students' experiences with pregnancy; the other discussed the impact of divorce on students at the school.

Reynolds was concerned that, although the pregnancy story used false names "to keep the identity of these girls a secret," the pregnant students still might be identifiable from the text. He also believed that the article's references to sexual activity and birth control were inappropriate for some of the younger students at the school. In addition, Reynolds was concerned that a student identified by name in the divorce story had complained that her father "wasn't spending enough time with my mom, my sister and I" prior to the divorce, "was always out of town on business or out late playing cards with the guys," and "always argued about everything" with her mother. Reynolds believed that the student's parents should have been given an opportunity to respond to these remarks or to consent to their publication. He was unaware that Emerson had deleted the student's name from the final version of the article.

Reynolds believed that there was no time to make the necessary changes in the stories before the scheduled press run and that the newspaper would not appear before the end of the school year if printing were delayed to any significant extent. He concluded that his only options under the circumstances were to publish a four-page newspaper instead of the planned six-page newspaper, eliminating the two pages on which the offending stories appeared, or to publish no newspaper at all. Accordingly, he directed Emerson to withhold from publication the two pages containing the stories on pregnancy and divorce. He informed his superiors of the decision, and they concurred.

Respondents subsequently commenced this action in the United States District Court for the Eastern District of Missouri seeking a declaration that their First Amendment rights had been violated, injunctive relief, and monetary damages. After a bench trial, the District Court denied an injunction, holding that no First Amendment violation had occurred. . . .

The Court of Appeals for the Eighth Circuit reversed. . . .

. . . Students in the public schools do not "shed their constitutional rights to freedom of speech or expression at the schoolhouse gate." *Tinker, supra*, 393 U.S., at 506. They cannot be punished merely for expressing their personal views on the school premises—whether "in the cafeteria, or on the playing field, or on the campus during the authorized hours," unless school authorities have reason to believe that such expression will "substantially interfere with the work of the school or impinge upon the rights of other students." We have nonetheless recognized that the First Amendment rights of students in the public schools "are not automatically coextensive with the rights of adults in other settings," Bethel School District No. 403 v. Fraser, 478 U.S. 675, 682 (1986), and must be "applied in light of the special characteristics of the school environment." *Tinker, supra*, 393 U.S., at 506. A school need not tolerate student speech that is inconsistent with its "basic educational mission," *Fraser, supra* at 685, even though the government could not censor similar speech outside the school. ...

We deal first with the question whether Spectrum may appropriately be characterized as a forum for public expression. The public schools do not possess all of the attributes of streets, parks, and other traditional public forums that "time out of mind, have been used for purposes of assembly, communicating thoughts between citizens, and discussing public questions." Hence, school facilities may be deemed to be public forums only if school authorities have "by policy or by practice" opened those facilities "for indiscriminate use by the general public," or by some segment of the public, such as student organizations. If the facilities have instead been reserved for other intended purposes, "communicative or otherwise," then no public forum has been created, and school officials may impose reasonable restrictions on the speech of students, teachers, and other members of the school community. ...

The policy of school officials toward Spectrum was reflected in Hazelwood School Board Policy 348.51 and the Hazelwood East Curriculum Guide. Board Policy 348.51 provided that "[s]chool sponsored publications are developed within the adopted curriculum and its educational implications in regular classroom activities." The Hazelwood East Curriculum Guide described the Journalism II course as a "laboratory situation in which the students publish the school newspaper applying skills they have learned in Journalism I." The lessons that were to be learned from the Journalism II course, according to the Curriculum Guide, included development of journalistic skills under deadline pressure, "the legal, moral, and ethical restrictions imposed upon journalists within the school community," and "responsibility and acceptance of criticism for articles of opinion." Journalism II was taught by a faculty member during regular class hours. Students received grades and academic credit for their performance in the course.

School officials did not deviate in practice from their policy that production of Spectrum was to be part of the educational curriculum and a "regular classroom activit[y]." ...

The evidence relied upon by the Court of Appeals in finding Spectrum to be a public forum, is equivocal at best. For example, Board Policy 348.51, which stated in part that "(s)chool sponsored student publications will not restrict free expression or diverse viewpoints within the rules of responsible journalism," also stated that such publications were "developed within the adopted curriculum and its educational implications." One might reasonably infer from the full text of Policy 348.51 that school officials retained ultimate control over what constituted "responsible journalism" in a school-sponsored newspaper. Although the Statement of Policy published in the September 14, 1982, issue of Spectrum declared that

"Spectrum, as a student-press publication, accepts all rights implied by the First Amendment," this statement, understood in the context of the paper's role in the school's curriculum, suggests at most that the administration will not interfere with the students' exercise of those First Amendment rights that attend the publication of a school-sponsored newspaper. It does not reflect an intent to expand those rights by converting a curricular newspaper into a public forum. . . . [School officials] "reserve[d] the forum for its intended purpos[e]," as a supervised learning experience for journalism students. Accordingly, school officials were entitled to regulate the contents of Spectrum in any reasonable manner. It is this standard, rather than our decision in *Tinker*, that governs this case.

The question whether the First Amendment requires a school to tolerate particular student speech—the question that we addressed in *Tinker*—is different from the question whether the First Amendment requires a school affirmatively to promote particular student speech. The former question addresses educators' ability to silence a student's personal expression that happens to occur on the school premises. The latter question concerns educators' authority over school-sponsored publications, theatrical productions, and other expressive activities that students, parents, and members of the public might reasonably perceive to bear the imprimatur of the school. These activities may fairly be characterized as part of the school curriculum, whether or not they occur in a traditional classroom setting, so long as they are supervised by faculty members and designed to impart particular knowledge or skills to student participants and audiences.

Educators are entitled to exercise greater control over this second form of student expression to assure that participants learn whatever lessons the activity is designed to teach, that readers or listeners are not exposed to material that may be inappropriate for their level of maturity, and that the views of the individual speaker are not erroneously attributed to the school. . . . A school must be able to set high standards for the student speech that is disseminated under its auspices—standards that may be higher than those demanded by some newspaper publishers or theatrical producers in the "real" world—and may refuse to disseminate student speech that does not meet those standards. In addition, a school must be able to take into account the emotional maturity of the intended audience in determining whether to disseminate student speech on potentially sensitive topics, which might range from the existence of Santa Claus in an elementary school setting to the particulars of teenage sexual activity in a high school setting. A school must also retain the authority to refuse to sponsor student speech that might reasonably be perceived to advocate drug or alcohol use, irresponsible sex, or conduct otherwise inconsistent with "the shared values of a civilized social order," *Fraser, supra* at 683, or to associate the school with any position other than neutrality on matters of political controversy. Otherwise, the schools would be unduly constrained from fulfilling their role as "a principal instrument in awakening the child to cultural values, in preparing him for later professional training, and in helping him to adjust normally to his environment." Brown v. Board of Education, 347 U.S. 483, 493 (1954).

Accordingly, we conclude that the standard articulated in *Tinker* for determining when a school may punish student expression need not also be the standard for determining when a school may refuse to lend its name and resources to the dissemination of student expression. Instead, we hold that educators do not offend the First Amendment by exercising editorial control over the style and content of student speech in school-sponsored expressive activities so long as their actions are reasonably related to legitimate pedagogical concerns.

This standard is consistent with our oft-expressed view that the education of the Nation's youth is primarily the responsibility of parents, teachers, and state and local school officials, and not of federal judges. It is only when the decision to censor a school-sponsored publication, theatrical production, or other vehicle of student expression has no valid educational purpose that the First Amendment is so "directly and sharply implicate[d]," as to require judicial intervention to protect students' constitutional rights. . . .

BRENNAN, J., with whom MARSHALL, J., and BLACKMUN, J., join, dissenting. . . . Public education serves vital national interests in preparing the Nation's youth for life in our increasingly complex society and for the duties of citizenship in our democratic Republic. The public school conveys to our young the information and tools required not merely to survive in, but to contribute to, civilized society. It also inculcates in tomorrow's leaders the "fundamental values necessary to the maintenance of a democratic political system. . . . " All the while, the public educator nurtures students' social and moral development by transmitting to them an official dogma of " 'community values.' "

The public educator's task is weighty and delicate indeed. It demands particularized and supremely subjective choices among diverse curricula, moral values, and political stances to teach or inculcate in students, and among various methodologies for doing so. Accordingly, we have traditionally reserved the "daily operation of school systems" to the States and their local school boards. We have not, however, hesitated to intervene where their decisions run afoul of the Constitution. *See, e.g.,* Edwards v. Aguillard, 482 U.S. 578 (1987) (striking state statute that forbade teaching of evolution in public school unless accompanied by instruction on theory of "creation science"); West Virginia Board of Education v. Barnette, 319 U.S. 624 (1943) (public school may not compel student to salute flag); Meyer v. Nebraska, 262 U.S. 390 (1923) (state law prohibiting the teaching of foreign languages in public or private schools is unconstitutional). . . .

Free student expression undoubtedly sometimes interferes with the effectiveness of the school's pedagogical function. Some brands of student expression do so by directly preventing the school from pursuing its pedagogical mission: The young polemic who stands on a soapbox during calculus class to deliver an eloquent political diatribe interferes with the legitimate teaching of calculus. And the student who delivers a lewd endorsement of a student-government candidate might so extremely distract an impressionable high school audience as to interfere with the orderly operation of the school. *See* Bethel School Dist. No. 403 v. Fraser, 478 U.S. 675 (1986). Other student speech, however, frustrates the school's legitimate pedagogical purpose merely by expressing a message that conflicts with the school's, without directly interfering with the school's expression of its message. A student who responds to a political science teacher's question with the retort, "socialism is good," subverts the school's inculcation of the message that capitalism is better. Even the maverick who sits in class passively sporting a symbol of protest against a government policy, *cf.* Tinker v. Des Moines Independent Community School Dist., 393 U.S. 503 (1969), or the gossip who sits in the student commons swapping stories of sexual escapade could readily muddle a clear official message condoning the government policy or condemning teenage sex. Likewise, the student newspaper that, like Spectrum, conveys a moral position at odds with the school's official stance might subvert the administration's legitimate inculcation of its own perception of community values.

If mere incompatibility with the school's pedagogical message were a constitutionally sufficient justification for the suppression of student speech, school officials could censor each of the students or student organizations in the foregoing hypotheticals, converting our public schools into "enclaves of totalitarianism," that "strangle the free mind at its source," West Virginia State Board of Education v. Barnette, *supra* at 637. . . .

In *Tinker*, this Court struck the balance. We held that official censorship of student expression—there the suspension of several students until they removed their armbands protesting the Vietnam War—is unconstitutional unless the speech "materially disrupts classwork or involves substantial disorder or invasion of the rights of others." . . .

The Court is certainly correct that the First Amendment permits educators "to assure that participants learn whatever lessons the activity is designed to teach. . . . " That is, however, the essence of the *Tinker* test, not an excuse to abandon it. Under *Tinker*, school officials may censor only such student speech as would "materially disrup(t)" a legitimate curricular function. Manifestly, student speech is more likely to disrupt a curricular function when it arises in the context of a curricular activity—one that "is designed to teach" something—than when it arises in the context of a noncurricular activity. Thus, under *Tinker*, the school may constitutionally punish the budding political orator if he disrupts calculus class but not if he holds his tongue for the cafeteria. That is not because some more stringent standard applies in the curricular context. . . . It is because student speech in the noncurricular context is less likely to disrupt materially any legitimate pedagogical purpose.

I fully agree with the Court that the First Amendment should afford an educator the prerogative not to sponsor the publication of a newspaper article that is "ungrammatical, poorly written, inadequately researched, biased or prejudiced," or that falls short of the "high standards for . . . student speech that is disseminated under [the school's] auspices. . . . " But we need not abandon *Tinker* to reach that conclusion; we need only apply it. The enumerated criteria reflect the skills that the curricular newspaper "is designed to teach." The educator may, under *Tinker*, constitutionally "censor" poor grammar, writing, or research because to reward such expression would "materially disrup[t]" the newspaper's curricular purpose.

The same cannot be said of official censorship designed to shield the *audience* or dissociate the *sponsor* from the expression. Censorship so motivated . . . in no way furthers the curricular purposes of a student *newspaper*, unless one believes that the purpose of the school newspaper is to teach students that the press ought never report bad news, express unpopular views, or print a thought that might upset its sponsors. Unsurprisingly, Hazelwood East claims no such pedagogical purpose. . . .

The Court's second excuse for deviating from precedent is the school's interest in shielding an impressionable high school audience from material whose substance is "unsuitable for immature audiences." . . .

Tinker teaches us that the state educator's undeniable, and undeniably vital, mandate to inculcate moral and political values is not a general warrant to act as "thought police" stifling discussion of all but state-approved topics and advocacy of all but the official position. Otherwise educators could transform students into "closed-circuit recipients of only that which the State chooses to communicate," and cast a perverse and impermissible "pall of orthodoxy over the classroom." Thus, the State cannot constitutionally prohibit its high school students from recounting in the locker room "the particulars of (their) teen-age sexual activity," nor even from advocating "irresponsible se[x]" or other presumed abominations of "the shared values of a civilized social order." Even in its capacity as educator the State may not assume an Orwellian "guardianship of the public mind.". . .

NOTES AND QUESTIONS

1. Do *Tinker*, *Fraser*, and *Kuhlmeier* express similar First Amendment values in connection with speech? Do they express similar ideas about the functions of public schools?

2. The Supreme Court has not elaborated on just what can be censored under *Fraser*, and the lower courts are divided. For example, several have considered, with mixed results, whether a school can prohibit a school student from wearing a bracelet that says, "I (heart) boobies! Keep a breast!" as part of a breast cancer awareness campaign. *Compare* B.H. ex rel. Hawk v. Easton Area Sch. Dist., 725 F.3d 293 (3d Cir. 2013); J.A. v. Fort Wayne Community Schools, 2013 WL 4479229 (N.D. Ind. 2013); K.J. ex rel. Braun v. Sauk Prairie School District, 2012 WL 13055058 (W.D. Wisc. 2012). For discussion, *see* Clay Calvert, Mixed Messages, Muddled Meanings, Drunk Dicks, and Boobies Bracelets: Sexually Suggestive Student Speech and the Need to Overrule or Radically Refashion *Fraser*, 90 Denv. U. L. Rev. 131 (2012).

3. One issue expressly considered in *Kuhlmeier* is whether public schools or specific public school activities qualify as "public fora." This issue is important because the state can employ only reasonable regulations regarding the time, place, and manner of expression in a public forum; it may not otherwise deny access to the forum or, with few exceptions, regulate the content of speech in that forum. That the speech is offensive to an audience is not a sufficient basis for restriction or punishment unless it includes abusive epithets that are inherently likely to provoke violent reaction when addressed to the ordinary citizen. *See, e.g.*, Cohen v. California, 403 U.S. 15 (1971).

Whether a public setting constitutes a "public forum" depends on both tradition and governmental decisions. *See* Perry Education Assn. v. Perry Local Educators Assn., 460 U.S. 37 (1983), dealing with access to teachers' mailboxes:

> In places which by long tradition or by government fiat have been devoted to assembly and debate, the rights of the state to limit expressive activity are sharply circumscribed. At one end of the spectrum are streets and parks. In these quintessential public forums, the government may not prohibit all communicative activity. For the state to enforce a content-based exclusion it must show that its regulation is necessary to serve a compelling state interest and that it is narrowly drawn to achieve that end. The State may also enforce regulations of the time, place and manner of expression which are content neutral, are narrowly tailored to serve a significant governmental interest, and leave open ample alternative channels of communication.

A second category consists of public property which the state has opened for use by the public as a place of expressive activity. The Constitution forbids a state to enforce certain exclusions from a forum generally open to the public even if it was not required to create the forum in the first place. Although a state is not required to indefinitely retain the open character of the facility, as long as it does so it is bound by the same standards as apply in a traditional public forum. . . .

Public property which is not by tradition or designation a forum for public communication is governed by different standards. In addition to time, place, and manner regulations, the state may reserve the forum for its intended purposes, communicative or otherwise, as long as the regulation on speech is reasonable and not an effort to suppress expression merely because public officials oppose the speaker's view.

Id. at 44-46. The type of property referred to in the last paragraph of this excerpt is called a "limited public forum."

The Court plainly found in *Kuhlmeier* that the *Spectrum* was not a public forum. Why not? Is the conclusion to be drawn that school newspapers do not count as public fora or that this newspaper did not? Under what circumstances might a school newspaper be treated as a public forum?

4. Accepting the majority's conclusion that school officials in *Kuhlmeier* had not intended to treat the newspaper as a public forum, could the principal have banned publication of articles in the *Spectrum* calling for abolition of the draft? For a boycott of classes as a protest against the war in Vietnam? Could a student be punished for arguing in class that the draft should be abolished? The Second, Sixth, Ninth, and Eleventh Circuits have interpreted *Kuhlmeier* as requiring viewpoint neutrality in regulations of school-sponsored speech. Peck ex rel. Peck v. Baldwinsville Central Sch. Dist., 426 F.3d 617 (2d Cir. 2005); Kincaid v. Gibson, 236 F.3d 342 (6th Cir. 2001); Planned Parenthood of Southern Nevada, Inc. v. Clark Cnty. Sch. Dist., 941 F.2d 817 (9th Cir. 1991); Searcey v. Harris, 888 F.2d 1314 (11th Cir. 1989). The First, Third, and Tenth Circuits have held that *Kuhlmeier* permits schools to favor one viewpoint over another. Ward v. Hickey, 996 F.2d 448 (1st Cir. 1993); C.H. v. Oliva, 197 F.3d 63 (3d Cir. 1999), 226 F.3d 198 (3d Cir. 2000); Fleming v. Jefferson Cnty. School Dist., 298 F.3d 918, 926 (10th Cir. 2002).

5. In a number of cases, students who wished to express religious viewpoints at school in various contexts were censored by school officials, who feared that allowing the speech would violate the Establishment Clause or, in some situations, provoke a disruption in the school. The views of courts about how to analyze the situation vary greatly, as do the opinions of commentators.

For example, in Morgan v. Plano Independent Sch. Dist., 589 F.3d 740 (5th Cir. 2009), schools forbade students from distributing various religious materials, including pencils inscribed with "Jesus is the reason for the season," candy canes with cards describing their Christian origin, tickets to a church's religious musical programs, and tickets to a Christian play. Rejecting a free speech challenge, the court held that school rules which permitted students to distribute materials only during designated times and at designated tables were valid time, place, and manner restrictions. The same plaintiffs also sued the school district for damages for banning elementary school children from giving small gifts with religious messages to their classmates during winter break parties, birthday parties, between classes, and after school. Applying *Tinker*, the Fifth Circuit held that the after-school ban violated the children's first amendment rights but that school officials were entitled to qualified immunity because the rights were not clearly established at the time of their actions. The court declined to decide whether the other prohibitions were constitutional, since they raised closer questions of how to apply *Tinker* in the elementary school context. Morgan v. Swanson, 659 F.3d 359 (5th Cir. 2011). On the other hand, in K.A. ex rel. Ayers v. Pocono Mountain Sch. Dist, 710 F.3d 99 (3d Cir. 2013), the court affirmed a trial court order enjoining a school that prohibited a fifth grader from distributing invitations before class to a Christmas party at her church. Applying *Tinker*, the court said the evidence did not support a claim of material risk of substantial disruption, even in the elementary school context. *See also* Leal v. Everett Public Schools, 88 F. Supp. 3d 1220 (W.D. Wash. 2015) (applying time, place, and manner analysis to uphold rules allowing materials to be distributed only at beginning and end of school day and at entrances to school building and requiring that the material have been written by the student).

If the student's conduct occurs during a school-sponsored activity, the analyses can be more complex. *See, e.g.*, A.M. ex rel. McKay v. Taconic Hills Central Sch. Dist., 510 Fed. Appx. 3 (2d Cir. 2013) (applying *Kuhlmeier* legitimate pedagogical concerns test unless school's action was viewpoint based, in which case limitation on speech permitted only because of an "overriding" state interest); Fleming v. Jefferson County School District R-1, 298 F.3d 918 (10th Cir. 2002) (permitting school to censor message that is inconsistent with the school's position on an issue where message might be imputed to school). Discussions include Steven K. Green, All Things Not Being Equal: Reconciling Student Religious Expression in the Public Schools, 42 U.C. Davis L. Rev. 843 (2009); Frederick B. Jonassen, Free Speech and Establishment Clause Rights at Public School Graduation Ceremonies: A Disclaimer: The Preceding Speech Was Government Censored and Does Not Represent the Views of the Valedictorian, 55 Wayne L. Rev. 683 (2009); Emily Gold Waldman, A Post-*Morse* Framework for Students' Potentially Hurtful Speech (Religious and Otherwise), 37 J.L. & Educ. 463 (2008).

6. The United States courts of appeals are divided about whether *Kuhlmeier* applies to colleges. David L. Hudson, Jr., Thirty Years of *Hazelwood* and Its Spread to Colleges and University Campuses, 61 Howard L. J. 491 (2018).

PROBLEMS

1. West High publishes a school newspaper. Students who work on the newspaper meet after school on a volunteer basis; they receive no credit for contributing to the paper. An eighth-grader wrote reviews of two R-rated movies, and the school principal removed them from the publication. The student and his parents sued the school board and officials. What arguments might be made on each side?

2. The Emerald Valley School Board recently adopted a regulation requiring all students to wear uniforms; students must wear solid khaki-colored bottoms and solid-colored polo, tee, or button-down shirts (blue, red, or white) without logos. Kim, a high school freshman, repeatedly violated the policy by wearing shirts with printed messages, none of which the school claims were likely to cause substantial disruption. When she refused to cover the message on her shirt, she was suspended for 3 days. Through her parents, she has sued the school, alleging that the policy

violates the First Amendment. What arguments should her attorney and the attorney for the school make? If the policy included an exemption for students wearing a Boy Scout or Girl Scout uniform, how would the arguments change? If the school policy required students to wear a shirt that said "Tomorrow's Leaders," what additional arguments could Kim's lawyer make?

3. At Palmer High School graduation, the class valedictorian gives a speech, the text of which must be submitted in advance to the principal for approval. School policy prohibits student speech that "tends to create hostility or otherwise disrupt the orderly operation of the educational process." Valedictorian Erica submitted her graduation speech and had it approved. However, when she delivered it, she added a statement about her belief in Jesus, urging her fellow students to "find out more about the sacrifice He made for you so that you now have the opportunity to live in eternity with Him." At the end of the ceremony, the assistant principal told her that she would not receive her diploma unless she publicly apologized for the speech. She refused to apologize, though she did submit a statement saying that the statement expressed her own personal beliefs and was made without the principal's prior approval. The principal refused to give her the diploma, and she filed suit, alleging that the principal's action violated her right to free expression. What arguments should be made on her behalf? In support of the principal's action?

4. Members of the Golden Prairie High School football team decided to take a knee during playing of the national anthem at their homecoming game to protest racial discrimination and to express support for NFL players who had been forbidden by the NFL owners' association to take a knee at games. Upon learning of the plan, the principal told the students that this action would violate a school policy against students' expressing political opinions while they are engaged in activities in which they represent the school, and the principal said that if anyone on the team took a knee during the game, the game would be canceled and the offending student or students would be kicked off the team. The team members through their parents have sued, alleging a violation of the First Amendment. What arguments should the parties make?

MORSE v. FREDERICK

551 U.S. 393 (2007)

Chief Justice ROBERTS. . . . On January 24, 2002, the Olympic Torch Relay passed through Juneau, Alaska, on its way to the winter games in Salt Lake City, Utah. The torchbearers were to proceed along a street in front of Juneau-Douglas High School (JDHS) while school was in session. Petitioner Deborah Morse, the school principal, decided to permit staff and students to participate in the Torch Relay as an approved social event or class trip. Students were allowed to leave class to observe the relay from either side of the street. Teachers and administrative officials monitored the students' actions.

Respondent Joseph Frederick, a JDHS senior, was late to school that day. When he arrived, he joined his friends (all but one of whom were JDHS students) across the street from the school to watch the event. Not all the students waited patiently. Some became rambunctious, throwing plastic cola bottles and snowballs and scuffling with their classmates. As the torchbearers and camera crews passed by, Frederick and his friends unfurled a 14-foot banner bearing the phrase: "BONG HiTS 4 JESUS." The large banner was easily readable by the students on the other side of the street.

Principal Morse immediately crossed the street and demanded that the banner be taken down. Everyone but Frederick complied. Morse confiscated the banner and told Frederick to report to her office, where she suspended him for 10 days. Morse later explained that she told Frederick to take the banner down because she thought it encouraged illegal drug use, in violation of established school policy. . . .

Frederick then filed suit under 42 U.S.C. § 1983, alleging that the school board and Morse had violated his First Amendment rights. . . . The District Court granted summary judgment for the school board and Morse. . . .

The Ninth Circuit reversed. . . .

At the outset, we reject Frederick's argument that this is not a school speech case—as has every other authority to address the question. The event occurred during normal school hours. It was sanctioned by Principal Morse "as an approved social event or class trip," and the school district's rules expressly provide that pupils in "approved social events and class trips are subject to district rules for student conduct." Teachers and administrators were interspersed among the students and charged with supervising them. The high school band and cheerleaders performed. Frederick, standing among other JDHS students across the street from the school, directed his banner toward the school, making it plainly visible to most students. Under these circumstances, we agree with the superintendent that Frederick cannot "stand in the midst of his fellow students, during school hours, at a school-sanctioned activity and claim he is not at school." . . . . . . The message on Frederick's banner is cryptic. It is no doubt offensive to some, perhaps amusing to others. To still others, it probably means nothing at all. Frederick himself claimed "that the words were just nonsense meant to attract television cameras." But Principal Morse thought the banner would be interpreted by those viewing it as promoting illegal drug use, and that interpretation is plainly a reasonable one. . . .

The question thus becomes whether a principal may, consistent with the First Amendment, restrict student speech at a school event, when that speech is reasonably viewed as promoting illegal drug use. We hold that she may. . . .

Tinker held that student expression may not be suppressed unless school officials reasonably conclude that it will "materially and substantially disrupt the work and discipline of the school." The essential facts of *Tinker* are quite stark, implicating concerns at the heart of the First Amendment. The students sought to engage in political speech, using the armbands to express their "disapproval of the Vietnam hostilities and their advocacy of a truce, to make their views known, and, by their example, to influence others to adopt them." Political speech, of course, is "at the core of what the First Amendment is designed to protect." The only interest the Court discerned underlying the school's actions was the "mere desire to avoid the discomfort and unpleasantness that always accompany an unpopular viewpoint," or "an urgent wish to avoid the controversy which might result from the expression." That interest was not enough to justify banning "a silent, passive expression of opinion, unaccompanied by any disorder or disturbance."

This Court's next student speech case was *Fraser*. ... The mode of analysis employed in *Fraser* is not entirely clear. . . . For present purposes, it is enough to distill from *Fraser* two basic principles. First, *Fraser*'s holding demonstrates that "the constitutional rights of students in public school are not automatically coextensive with the rights of adults in other settings." Had Fraser delivered the same speech in a public forum outside the school context, it would have been protected. In school, however, Fraser's First Amendment rights were circumscribed "in light of the special characteristics of the school environment." Second, *Fraser* established that the mode of analysis set forth in *Tinker* is not absolute. Whatever approach *Fraser* employed, it certainly did not conduct the "substantial disruption" analysis prescribed by *Tinker*.

Our most recent student speech case, *Kuhlmeier*, concerned "expressive activities that students, parents, and members of the public might reasonably perceive to bear the imprimatur of the school." Staff members of a high school newspaper sued their school when it chose not to publish two of their articles. The Court of Appeals analyzed the case under *Tinker*, ruling in favor of the students because it found no evidence of material disruption to classwork or school discipline. This Court reversed, holding that "educators do not offend the First Amendment by exercising editorial control over the style and content of student speech in school-sponsored expressive activities so long as their actions are reasonably related to legitimate pedagogical concerns."

Kuhlmeier does not control this case because no one would reasonably believe that Frederick's banner bore the school's imprimatur. . . .

[Our recent cases about Fourth Amendment limits on school searches] recognize that deterring drug use by schoolchildren is an "important—indeed, perhaps compelling" interest. . . .

Congress has declared that part of a school's job is educating students about the dangers of illegal drug use. It has provided billions of dollars to support state and local drug-prevention programs and required that schools receiving federal funds under the Safe and Drug-Free Schools and Communities Act of 1994 certify that their drug prevention programs "convey a clear and consistent message that . . . the illegal use of drugs [is] wrong and harmful."

Thousands of school boards throughout the country—including JDHS—have adopted policies aimed at effectuating this message. Those school boards know that peer pressure is perhaps "the single most important factor leading schoolchildren to take drugs," and that students are more likely to use drugs when the norms in school appear to tolerate such behavior. Student speech celebrating illegal drug use at a school event, in the presence of school administrators and teachers, thus poses a particular challenge for school officials working to protect those entrusted to their care from the dangers of drug abuse.

The "special characteristics of the school environment," and the governmental interest in stopping student drug abuse—reflected in the policies of Congress and myriad school boards, including JDHS—allow schools to restrict student expression that they reasonably regard as promoting illegal drug use. . . .

Petitioners urge us to adopt the broader rule that Frederick's speech is proscribable because it is plainly "offensive" as that term is used in *Fraser*. We think this stretches *Fraser* too far; that case should not be read to encompass any speech that could fit under some definition of "offensive." After all, much political and religious speech might be perceived as offensive to some. The concern here is not that Frederick's speech was offensive, but that it was reasonably viewed as promoting illegal drug use. . . .

The judgment of the United States Court of Appeals for the Ninth Circuit is reversed, and the case is remanded for further proceedings consistent with this opinion.

Justice THOMAS, concurring. The Court today decides that a public school may prohibit speech advocating illegal drug use. I agree and therefore join its opinion in full. I write separately to state my view that the standard set forth in Tinker v. Des Moines Independent Community School Dist., 393 U.S. 503 (1969), is without basis in the Constitution.

. . . In my view, the history of public education suggests that the First Amendment, as originally understood, does not protect student speech in public schools. Although colonial schools were exclusively private, public education proliferated in the early 1800's. By the time the States ratified the Fourteenth Amendment, public schools had become relatively common. If students in public schools were originally understood as having free-speech rights, one would have expected 19th-century public schools to have respected those rights and courts to have enforced them. They did not. . . .

Tinker effected a sea change in students' speech rights, extending them well beyond traditional bounds. . . . [The opinion briefly discusses *Fraser* and *Kuhlmeier* as exceptions to *Tinker*.]

Today, the Court creates another exception. In doing so, we continue to distance ourselves from *Tinker*, but we neither overrule it nor offer an explanation of when it operates and when it does not. I am afraid that our jurisprudence now says that students have a right to speak in schools except when they don't—a standard continuously developed through litigation against local schools and their administrators. . . . .

Justice ALITO, with whom Justice KENNEDY joins, concurring. I join the opinion of the Court on the understanding that (a) it goes no further than to hold that a public school may restrict speech that a reasonable observer would interpret as advocating illegal drug use and (b) it provides no support for any restriction of speech that can plausibly be interpreted as commenting on any political or social issue, including speech on issues such as "the wisdom of the war on drugs or of legalizing marijuana for medicinal use." . . .

The opinion of the Court does not endorse the broad argument advanced by petitioners and the United States that the First Amendment permits public school officials to censor any student speech that interferes with a school's "educational mission." This argument can easily be manipulated in dangerous ways, and I would reject it before such abuse occurs. The "educational mission" of the public schools is defined by the elected and appointed public officials with authority over the schools and by the school administrators and faculty. As a result, some public schools have defined their educational missions as including the inculcation of whatever political and social views are held by the members of these groups.

During the *Tinker* era, a public school could have defined its educational mission to include solidarity with our soldiers and their families and thus could have attempted to outlaw the wearing of black armbands on the ground that they undermined this mission. Alternatively, a school could have defined its educational mission to include the promotion of world peace and could have sought to ban the wearing of buttons expressing support for the troops on the ground that the buttons signified approval of war. The "educational mission" argument would give public school authorities a license to suppress speech on political and social issues based on disagreement with the viewpoint expressed. The argument, therefore, strikes at the very heart of the First Amendment. . . .

Justice STEVENS, with whom Justice SOUTER and Justice GINSBURG join, dissenting. . . . Two cardinal First Amendment principles animate . . . *Tinker*. . . . First, censorship based on the content of speech, particularly censorship that depends on the viewpoint of the speaker, is subject to the most rigorous burden of justification. . . .

Second, punishing someone for advocating illegal conduct is constitutional only when the advocacy is likely to provoke the harm that the government seeks to avoid. . . .

Yet today the Court fashions a test that trivializes the two cardinal principles upon which *Tinker* rests. The Court's test invites stark viewpoint discrimination. In this case, for example, the principal has unabashedly acknowledged that she disciplined Frederick because she disagreed with the pro-drug viewpoint she ascribed to the message on the banner—a viewpoint, incidentally, that Frederick has disavowed. . . . [T]he Court's holding in this case strikes at "the heart of the First Amendment" because it upholds a punishment meted out on the basis of a listener's disagreement with her understanding (or, more likely, misunderstanding) of the speaker's viewpoint. "If there is a bedrock principle underlying the First Amendment, it is that the Government may not prohibit the expression of an idea simply because society finds the idea itself offensive or disagreeable."

It is also perfectly clear that "promoting illegal drug use" comes nowhere close to proscribable "incitement to imminent lawless action." Encouraging drug use might well increase the likelihood that a listener will try an illegal drug, but that hardly justifies censorship. . . .

The Court rejects outright these twin foundations of *Tinker* because, in its view, the unusual importance of protecting children from the scourge of drugs supports a ban on all speech in the school environment that promotes drug use. Whether or not such a rule is sensible as a matter of policy, carving out pro-drug speech for uniquely harsh treatment finds no support in our case law and is inimical to the values protected by the First Amendment.

I will nevertheless assume for the sake of argument that the school's concededly powerful interest in protecting its students adequately supports its restriction on "any assembly or public expression that . . . advocates the use of substances that are illegal to minors. . . . " . . .

But it is one thing to restrict speech that *advocates* drug use. It is another thing entirely to prohibit an obscure message with a drug theme that a third party subjectively—and not very reasonably—thinks is tantamount to express advocacy. . . .

Although this case began with a silly, nonsensical banner, it ends with the Court inventing out of whole cloth a special First Amendment rule permitting the censorship of any student speech that mentions drugs, at least so long as someone could perceive that speech to contain a latent pro-drug message. . . .

Even in high school, a rule that permits only one point of view to be expressed is less likely to produce correct answers than the open discussion of countervailing views. In the national debate about a serious issue, it is the expression of the minority's viewpoint that most demands the protection of the First Amendment.

Whatever the better policy may be, a full and frank discussion of the costs and benefits of the attempt to prohibit the use of marijuana is far wiser than suppression of speech because it is unpopular.

I respectfully dissent.

The opinion of Justice BREYER, concurring in part and dissenting in part, is omitted.

NOTES AND QUESTIONS

1. It's very unlikely that the principal would have punished Frederick if he had displayed a banner that read "D.A.R.E. To Keep Kids Off Drugs." By allowing her to punish him for his allegedly pro-drug speech, did *Morse* endorse viewpoint discrimination by public schools?

If Frederick's banner had read "Legalize Marijuana," could the school have banned it? Could the school adopt a rule prohibiting students from wearing clothing that advocates legalization of drugs?

2. Why didn't *Fraser* or *Kuhlmeier* control this case?

3. *Morse* might have shed light on schools' authority to regulate off-campus speech, but, instead, the Court held that the speech there was clearly on-campus. Why? What test did the opinion use to distinguish on-campus from off-campus speech? If Frederick lived across the street from the school and displayed the banner for the half hour before school started every morning for a week, hoping to attract the TV cameras' attention, could he have been disciplined under *Fraser*? Under the holding in *Morse*?

4. After *Morse*, may courts create additional categories of speech that schools may ban on a *per se* basis? Defoe ex rel. Defoe v. Spiva, 625 F.3d 324 (6th Cir. 2010), held that a school may ban "racially hostile or contemptuous" speech without having to show that it is likely to cause disturbances because such speech is inconsistent with the mission of schools. The case involved a high school's ban on clothing bearing the image of the Confederate flag. Ponce v. Socorro Independent School District, 508 F.3d 765 (5th Cir. 2007), upheld a policy prohibiting student speech that could reasonably be interpreted as advocating Columbine-style attacks on schools without proof that they created a reasonable risk of disruption.

BELL v. ITAWAMBA COUNTY SCHOOL BOARD

799 F.3d 379 (5th Cir. 2015) (en banc), cert. denied, 136 S. Ct. 1166 (2016)

RHESA HAWKINS BARKSDALE, Circuit Judge. . . On Wednesday, 5 January 2011, [Taylor] Bell, a high-school senior, posted a rap recording on his public Facebook profile page (and later on YouTube) . . . The recording, in part, alleges misconduct against female students by Coaches W. and R. . . .

At the very least, this incredibly profane and vulgar rap recording had at least four instances of threatening, harassing, and intimidating language against the two coaches . . .

A screenshot of Bell's Facebook profile page, taken approximately 16 hours after he posted the rap recording, shows his profile, including the rap recording, was open to, and viewable by, the public. In other words, anyone could listen to it.

On Thursday, 6 January, the day after the recording was posted, Coach W. received a text message from his wife, informing him about the recording; she had learned about it from a friend. After asking a student about the recording, the coach listened to it at school on the student's smartphone (providing access to the Internet). The coach immediately reported the rap recording to the school's principal, Wiygul, who informed the school-district superintendent, McNeece.

The next day, Friday, 7 January, Wiygul, McNeece, and the school-board attorney, Floyd, questioned Bell about the rap recording, including the veracity of the allegations, the extent of the alleged misconduct, and the identity of the students involved. Bell was then sent home for the remainder of the day.

Because of inclement weather, the school was closed through Thursday, 13 January. During Bell's resulting time away from school, and despite his having spoken with school officials about his rap recording, including the accusations against the two coaches, Bell created a finalized version of the recording (adding commentary and a picture slideshow), and uploaded it to YouTube for public viewing.

Bell returned to school when it reopened on Friday, 14 January; he was removed from class midday by the assistant principal and told he was suspended, pending a disciplinary-committee hearing . . . .

The hearing began with the principal's providing a summary of events, after which the YouTube version of the rap recording was played. Among the disciplinary-committee members' questions, one member asked Bell whether he had reported the alleged misconduct to school officials. Bell explained he had not done so because he believed they would ignore his complaints. Instead, he made the rap recording because he knew people were "gonna listen to it, somebody's gonna listen to it," acknowledging several times during the hearing that he posted the recording to Facebook because he knew it would be viewed and heard by students. Moreover, he explained that at least 2,000 people had contacted him about the rap recording in response to the Facebook and YouTube postings. . . .

Although Bell's attorney, at one point, attempted to discuss the misconduct of the coaches alleged in the rap recording, the school-board attorney redirected the proceeding to its purpose: to resolve whether Bell threatened, harassed, and intimidated the teachers; and, to decide whether his suspension should be upheld. In numerous instances, the school-board attorney emphasized this purpose, noting Bell's "comments made [in the recording that] 'you've fed with the wrong one / going to get a pistol down your mouth / POW'[,] those are threats to a teacher."

Bell contested the school-board attorney's interpretation, responding: "Well that ain't really what I said" and then provided what he described as the written "original copy" of what had been recorded. (It is unclear from the disciplinary-committee-hearing recording, or other parts of the summary-judgment record, which copy Bell provided.) Bell explained he did not mean *he* was going to shoot anyone, but that he was only "*foreshadowing* something that might happen." (Emphasis added.) But, he agreed that individuals "outside the school setting" had made "certain statements" to his mother that "'put a pistol down your mouth'[,] that is a direct threat." . . .

On 27 January, the day after the hearing, the school-board attorney informed Bell's mother by letter that: the disciplinary committee had determined "the issue of whether or not lyrics published by Taylor Bell constituted threats to school district teachers was vague," but that the publication of the recording constituted harassment and intimidation of two teachers, in violation of school-district policy and state law; as a result, the disciplinary committee recommended to the school board that Bell's seven-day suspension be upheld and that he be placed in the county's alternative school for the remainder of the nine-week grading period (approximately six weeks); Bell would not be "allowed to attend any school functions and [would] be subject to all rules imposed by the Alternative School;" and "[he would] be given time to make up any work missed while suspended or otherwise receive a 0, pursuant to Board policy."

On 7 February, the school board . . . found: Bell "threatened, harassed, and intimidated school employees." . . .

Approximately two weeks later, on 24 February, Bell and his mother filed this action, claiming, *inter alia*, the school board, superintendent, and principal (again, the school board) violated his First Amendment right to free speech. . . .

. . . On 15 March 2012, the district court denied the Bells' motion [for summary judgment] and granted the school board's. . . .

On appeal, only the summary judgment against Bell's First Amendment claim was challenged. A divided panel in December 2014 held, *inter alia*: the school board violated Bell's First Amendment right by disciplining him based on the language in the rap recording. En-banc review was granted in February 2015. . . .

Students *qua* students do not forfeit their First Amendment rights to freedom of speech and expression. *Tinker*, 393 U.S. at 506, 511. On the other hand, the First Amendment does not provide students absolute rights to such freedoms, and those rights must be tempered in the light of a school official's duty to, *inter alia*, "teach[] students the boundaries of socially appropriate behavior," Bethel Sch. Dist. No. 403 v. Fraser, 478 U.S. 675, 681 (1986), and "protect those entrusted to their care," Morse v. Frederick, 551 U.S. 393, 408 (2007). . . . Therefore, because "the constitutional rights of students in public school are not automatically coextensive with the rights of adults in other settings," *Fraser*, 478 U.S. at 682, certain speech, which would be protected in other settings, might not be afforded First Amendment protection in the school setting.

Balancing these competing interests, *Tinker* provided in 1969 the standard for evaluating whether the First Amendment protects a student's speech. . . . In holding the students' speech protected under the First Amendment, the Court, focusing primarily on the effect of that speech on the school community, held: A student "may express his opinions . . . if he does so without materially and substantially interfer[ing] with the requirements of *appropriate discipline in the operation of the school and without colliding with the rights of others*." Put another way, "conduct by the student, *in class or out of it*, which for any reason . . . materially disrupts classwork or involves substantial disorder or invasion of the rights of others is, of course, not immunized. . . ." Approximately three years after *Tinker*, our court held this standard can be satisfied either by showing a disruption has occurred, or by showing "demonstrable factors that would give rise to *any reasonable forecast* by the school administration of 'substantial and material' disruption." Shanley v. Ne. Indep. Sch. Dist., Bexar Cnty., Tex., 462 F.2d 960, 974 (5th Cir. 1972) (emphasis added) (holding school's suspension of students for their off-campus distribution of "underground" newspaper violated *Tinker*).

Since *Tinker*, the Court has revisited student speech on several occasions, each time carving out narrow exceptions to the general *Tinker* standard based on certain characteristics, or content, of the speech. In *Fraser*, the Court held the school board acted within its authority when it disciplined a student for an "offensively lewd and indecent" speech delivered at a student assembly. In *Hazelwood*, the Court upheld a school's right to "exercis[e] editorial control over the style and content of student speech" in a school-sponsored newspaper when the student engages in "expressive activities that students, parents, and members of the public might reasonably perceive to bear the imprimatur of the school" and the school officials' "actions are reasonably related to legitimate pedagogical concerns."

And, most recently in *Morse*, the Court considered whether a school infringed a student's First Amendment right of free speech when it disciplined him for holding up a banner that stated "BONG HiTS 4 JESUS" at a school-sponsored event. The Court, through Justice Alito's controlling concurrence (joined by Justice Kennedy), held a school may discipline a student for speech which poses a "grave and . . . unique threat to the physical safety of students," such as "advocating illegal drug use.". . .

For these exceptions, schools are not required to prove the occurrence of an actual disruption or one that reasonably could have been forecast. . . .

The parties do not assert, and the record does not show, that the school board disciplined Bell based on the lewdness of his speech or its potential perceived sponsorship by the school; therefore, *Fraser* and *Hazelwood* are not directly on point. Bell's speech likewise does not advocate illegal drug use or portend a Columbine-like mass, systematic school-shooting. And, as Justice Alito noted, when the type of violence threatened does not implicate "the special features of the school environment," *Tinker*'s "substantial disruption" standard is the appropriate vehicle for analyzing such claims. . . .

In claiming *Tinker* does not apply to off-campus speech, Bell asserts: *Tinker* limits its holding to speech inside the "schoolhouse gate"; and each of the Court's subsequent decisions reinforces this understanding.

. . . Over 45 years ago, when *Tinker* was decided, the Internet, cellphones, smartphones, and digital social media did not exist. The advent of these technologies and their sweeping adoption by students present new and evolving challenges for school administrators, confounding previously delineated boundaries of permissible regulations. Students now have the ability to disseminate instantaneously and communicate widely from any location via the Internet. These communications, which may reference events occurring, or to occur, at school, or be about members of the school community, can likewise be accessed anywhere, by anyone, at any time. Although, under other circumstances, such communications might be protected speech under the First Amendment, off-campus threats, harassment, and intimidation directed at teachers create a tension between a student's free-speech rights and a school official's duty to maintain discipline and protect the school community. These competing concerns, and differing standards applied to off-campus speech across circuits, as discussed *infra*, have drawn into question the scope of school officials' authority.

Greatly affecting this landscape is the recent rise in incidents of violence against school communities. School administrators must be vigilant and take seriously any statements by students resembling threats of violence, as well as harassment and intimidation posted online and made away from campus. This now-tragically common violence increases the importance of clarifying the school's authority to react to potential threats before violence erupts.

In the light of these competing interests and increasing concerns regarding school violence, it is necessary to establish the extent to which off-campus student speech may be restricted without offending the First Amendment. Our holding concerns the paramount need for school officials to be able to react quickly and efficiently to protect students and faculty from threats, intimidation, and harassment intentionally directed at the school community. . . .

Since *Tinker* was decided in 1969, courts have been required to define its scope. As discussed below, of the six circuits to have addressed whether *Tinker* applies to off-campus speech, five, *including our own*, have held it does. (For the other of the six circuits (the third circuit), there is an intra-circuit split. *See* Layshock v. Hermitage Sch. Dist., 650 F.3d 205, 219–220 (3d Cir. 2011) (en banc); *see also* J.S. ex rel. Snyder v. Blue Mountain Sch. Dist., 650 F.3d 915, 931 & n. 8 (3d Cir. 2011) (en banc) (divided court assuming, without deciding, that the *Tinker* substantial-disruption test applies to online speech harassing a school administrator). The remainder of the circuits (first, sixth, seventh, tenth, eleventh, D.C.) do not appear to have addressed this issue.

Although the Supreme Court has not expressly ruled on this issue, our court, 43 years ago, applied *Tinker* to analyze whether a school board's actions were constitutional in disciplining students based on their off-campus speech. . . .

Further, as noted *supra*, four other circuits have held that, under certain circumstances, *Tinker* applies to speech which originated, and was disseminated, off-campus. *See, e.g.*, Wynar [v. Douglas Cnty Sch. Dist.], 728 F.3d [1062,] 1069 [9th Cir. 2013); D.J.M. ex rel. D.M. v. Hannibal Pub. Sch. Dist. No. 60, 647 F.3d 754, 766–767 (8th Cir. 2011); Kowalski v. Berkeley Cnty. Schs., 652 F.3d 565, 573–574 (4th Cir. 2011); Doninger v. Niehoff, 527 F.3d 41, 48–50 (2d Cir. 2008). Therefore, based on our court's precedent and guided by that of our sister circuits, *Tinker* applies to off-campus speech in certain situations.

Therefore, the next question is under what circumstances may off-campus speech be restricted. . . .

Our court's . . . 2004 opinion in *Porter* . . . provides valuable insight in this regard. There, the school expelled a student after his brother brought to school a sketchpad containing a two-year-old drawing of the school's being attacked by armed personnel. The depiction, albeit violent in nature, "was completed [at] home, stored for two years, and *never intended* by [the creator of the drawing] to be brought to campus." After concluding *Tinker* applied to the school's regulations, our court held the speech was protected because the student never *intended* for the drawing to reach the school, describing its introduction to the school community as "accidental and unintentional." . . .

Porter instructs that a speaker's intent matters when determining whether the off-campus speech being addressed is subject to *Tinker*. A speaker's intention that his speech reach the school community, buttressed by his actions in bringing about that consequence, supports applying *Tinker*'s school-speech standard to that speech.

In addition, [other] courts to have considered the circumstances under which *Tinker* applies to off-campus speech have advocated varied approaches. *E.g.*, *Wynar*, 728 F.3d at 1069 (holding that, regardless of the location of the speech, "when faced with an identifiable threat of school violence [(threats communicated online via MySpace messages)], schools may take disciplinary action in response to off-campus speech that meets the requirements of *Tinker*"); *Snyder*, 650 F.3d at 940 (Smith, J., concurring) (noting that any standard adopted "cannot turn solely on where the speaker was sitting when the speech was originally uttered because such a standard would fail to accommodate the somewhat 'everywhere at once' nature of the [I]nternet," and advocating allowing schools to discipline off-campus speech "[r]egardless of its place of origin" so long as that speech was "intentionally directed towards a school"); *Kowalski*, 652 F.3d at 573 (applying *Tinker* when a "sufficiently strong" nexus exists between the student's speech and the school's pedagogical interests "to justify the action taken by school officials in carrying out their role as the trustees of the student body's well-being"); *D.J.M.*, 647 F.3d at 766 (applying *Tinker* because "it was reasonably foreseeable that [the student's] threats about shooting specific students in school would be brought to the attention of school authorities and create a risk of substantial disruption within the school environment"); *Doninger*, 527 F.3d at 48 (holding *Tinker* applies to speech originating off-campus if it "would foreseeably create a risk of substantial disruption within the school environment, at least when it was similarly foreseeable that the off-campus expression might also reach campus" (internal quotation marks omitted)).

. . . Accordingly, in the light of our court's precedent, we hold *Tinker* governs our analysis, as in this instance, when a student intentionally directs at the school community speech reasonably understood by school officials to threaten, harass, and intimidate a teacher, even when such speech originated, and was disseminated, off-campus without the use of school resources. . . .

Turning to the matter before us, there is no genuine dispute of material fact that Bell intended his rap recording to reach the school community. . . .

Further, regardless of whether Bell's statements in the rap recording qualify as "true threats," . . . they constitute threats, harassment, and intimidation, as a layperson would understand the terms. The Oxford English Dictionary defines: "threaten" as "to declare (usually conditionally) one's intention of inflicting injury upon" another, "harass" as "[t]o wear *out*, tire *out*, or exhaust with fatigue, care, [or] trouble," and "intimidate" as "[t]o render timid, inspire with fear; [or] to force to or deter from some action by threats or violence."

A reasonable understanding of Bell's statements satisfies these definitions; they: threatened violence against the two coaches, describing the injury to be inflicted (putting the pistol down their mouths and pulling the trigger, and "capping" them), described the specific weapon (a "rueger" [sic], which, as discussed *supra*, is a type of firearm), and encouraged others to engage in this action; and harassed and intimidated the coaches by forecasting the aforementioned violence, warning them to "watch [their] back[s]" and that they would "get no mercy" when such actions were taken. . . .

Having held *Tinker* applies in this instance, the next question is whether Bell's recording either caused an actual disruption or reasonably could be forecast to cause one. Taking the school board's decision into account, and the deference we must accord it, this question becomes whether a genuine dispute of material fact exists regarding . . . whether such language, as a matter of law, reasonably could have been forecast to cause a substantial disruption. . . .

"*Tinker* requires a specific and significant fear of disruption, not just some remote apprehension of disturbance." "School officials must be able to show that their actions were caused by something more than a mere desire to avoid the discomfort and unpleasantness that always accompany an unpopular viewpoint." "Officials must base their decisions on fact, not intuition," and those decisions are entitled to deference.

As our court has held: "While school officials must offer facts to support their proscription of student speech, *this is not a difficult burden, and their decisions will govern if they are within the range where reasonable minds will differ.*" Accordingly, school authorities are not required expressly to forecast a "substantial or material disruption"; rather, courts determine the possibility of a reasonable forecast based on the facts in the record.

Factors considered by other courts in determining, pursuant to *Tinker,* the substantiality *vel non* of an actual disruption, and the objective reasonableness *vel non* of a forecasted substantial disruption, include: the nature and content of the speech, the objective and subjective seriousness of the speech, and the severity of the possible consequences should the speaker take action; the relationship of the speech to the school, the intent of the speaker to disseminate, or keep private, the speech, and the nature, and severity, of the school's response in disciplining the student; whether the speaker expressly identified an educator or student by name or reference, and past incidents arising out of similar speech; the manner in which the speech reached the school community, the intent of the school in disciplining the student; and the occurrence of other in-school disturbances, including administrative disturbances involving the speaker, such as "[s]chool officials ha[ving] to spend considerable time dealing with these concerns and ensuring that appropriate safety measures were in place," brought about "because of the need to manage" concerns over the speech.

. . . Viewing the evidence in the requisite light most favorable to Bell, . . . the manner in which he voiced his concern—with threatening, intimidating, and harassing language—must be taken seriously by school officials, and reasonably could be forecast by them to cause a substantial disruption.

The speech pertained directly to events occurring at school, identified the two teachers by name, and was understood by one to threaten his safety and by neutral, third parties as threatening. . . . The possible consequences were grave—serious injury to, including the possible death of, two teachers. . . .

Further, even after finding Bell threatened, intimidated, and harassed two teachers, the school board's response was measured—temporarily suspending Bell and placing him in an alternative-education program for the remainder of the nine-week grading term (about six weeks). The reasonableness of, and amount of care given to, this decision is reinforced by the school board's finding, differently from the disciplinary committee's, that Bell's statements also constituted threats.

And finally, numerous, recent examples of school violence exist in which students have signaled potential violence through speech, writings, or actions, and then carried out violence against school communities, after school administrators and parents failed to properly identify warning signs.

In determining objective reasonableness *vel non* for forecasting a substantial disruption, the summary-judgment record and numerous related factors must be considered against the backdrop of the mission of schools to educate. It goes without saying that a teacher, which includes a coach, is the cornerstone of education. Without teaching, there can be little, if any, learning. Without learning, there can be little, if any, education. Without education, there can be little, if any, civilization.

It equally goes without saying that threatening, harassing, and intimidating a teacher impedes, if not destroys, the ability to teach; it impedes, if not destroys, the ability to educate. It disrupts, if not destroys, the discipline necessary for an environment in which education can take place. In addition, it encourages and incites other students to engage in similar disruptive conduct. Moreover, it can even cause a teacher to leave that profession. In sum, it disrupts, if not destroys, the very mission for which schools exist—to educate.

If there is to be education, such conduct cannot be permitted. In that regard, the real tragedy in this instance is that a high-school student thought he could, with impunity, direct speech at the school community which threatens, harasses, and intimidates teachers and, as a result, objected to being disciplined. . . .

For the foregoing reasons, the judgment is AFFIRMED.

E. GRADY JOLLY, specially concurring: . . . I would decide this case in the simplest way, consonant with our cases and the cases in other circuits, by saying as little as possible and holding:

Student speech is unprotected by the First Amendment and is subject to school discipline when that speech contains an actual threat to kill or physically harm personnel and/or students of the school; which actual threat is connected to the school environment; and which actual threat is communicated to the school, or its students, or its personnel. (boldface in original)

JAMES L. DENNIS, Circuit Judge, with whom GRAVES, Circuit Judge, joins in full, and with whom PRADO, Circuit Judge, joins except as to Parts I and II. B., dissenting: . . . Even in the most repressive of dictatorships, the citizenry is "free" to praise their leaders and other people of power or to espouse views consonant with those of their leaders. "Freedom of speech" is thus a hollow guarantee if it permits only praise or state-sponsored propaganda. Freedom of speech exists exactly to protect those who would criticize, passionately and vociferously, the actions of persons in power. But that freedom is denied to Bell by the majority opinion because the persons whose conduct he dared to criticize were school teachers. If left uncorrected, the majority opinion inevitably will encourage school officials to silence student speakers, like Taylor Bell, solely because they disagree with the content and form of their speech, particularly when such off-campus speech criticizes school personnel. Such a precedent thereby clearly contravenes the basic principle that, "[i]n our system, students may not be regarded as closed-circuit recipients of only that which the States chooses to communicate. They may not be confined to expression of those sentiments that are officially approved." . . .

The *en banc* majority opinion completely ignores Bell's argument that the School Board violated his First Amendment rights in punishing him for his rap song, which he contends was protected speech on "a matter of public concern." . . .

Speech on "matters of public concern" is "at the heart of the First Amendment's protection." "The First Amendment reflects 'a profound national commitment to the principle that debate on public issues should be uninhibited, robust, and wide-open.'" "That is because 'speech concerning public affairs is more than self-expression; it is the essence of self-government.'" "Accordingly, 'speech on public issues occupies the highest rung of the hierarchy of First Amendment values and is entitled to special protection.'". . .

Applying these principles to the instant case, the record indisputably reveals that Bell's speech addressed a matter of public concern. Bell composed his song after a number of his female friends at school informed him that Coaches Wildmon and Rainey had frequently sexually harassed them during school. . . . Although the song does contain some violent lyrics, the song's overall "content" is indisputably a darkly sardonic but impassioned protest of two teachers' alleged sexual misconduct, *e.g.*, opining that Rainey is "a fool/30 years old fucking with students at the school." That Bell's song may fall short of the School Board's aesthetic preferences for socio-political commentary is not relevant to determining whether the rap song's content addresses a matter of public concern. . . .

The "form" of Bell's speech, *i.e.*, a rap song, likewise militates in favor of finding that it addresses a matter of public concern. It is axiomatic that music, like other art forms, has historically functioned as a mechanism to raise awareness of contemporary social issues. Rap is no exception. "Over the past twenty years there has been extensive academic discourse on the role of rap music . . . as a form of political expression." A long aspiring rap artist himself, Bell invoked this same tradition by deploying the artistic conventions and style of the rap genre in order to critique the coaches' sexual harassment of female students.

Finally, the "context" of Bell's speech likewise evinces that it addresses a matter of public import. By releasing his song on the Internet, Bell sought to bring attention to the coaches' sexual misconduct against his female classmates . . .

The majority opinion, however, wholly ignores these critical aspects of Bell's speech, instead reflexively reducing Bell's rap song to "intimidating, harassing, and threatening" speech without any analysis whatsoever. Indeed, under the majority opinion's newfound approach, Bell's off-campus speech is regulable by school officials pursuant to *Tinker* because (i) Bell wanted his speech to be heard by community members *and* (ii) "a layperson" apparently would view some of the lyrics in the rap as "threatening," "harassing," and "intimidating." . . .

II.

The *en banc* majority opinion affirms the School Board's punishment of Bell pursuant to its new and unprecedented rule of constitutional law whereby schools may punish students' off-campus speech pursuant to *Tinker* if that speech is intentionally directed at the school community and is "threatening, harassing, and intimidating" to the ears of a "layperson" without any instruction on the meaning of these terms. The majority opinion's content-based, vague, and "layperson"-based restriction directly conflicts with the core principles underlying the First Amendment's guarantees. . . .

. . . As a general matter, the First Amendment prohibits the government from "restrict[ing] expression because of its message, its ideas, its subject matter, or its content." Ashcroft v. American Civil Liberties Union, 535 U.S. 564, 573 (2002). "From 1791 to the present, however, the First Amendment has permitted restrictions upon the content of speech in a few limited areas and has never included a freedom to disregard these traditional limitations." "These limited areas—such as obscenity, incitement, and fighting words—represent well-defined and narrowly limited classes of speech, the prevention and punishment of which has never been thought to raise any constitutional problem." Brown v. Entm't Merchants Ass'n., _ U.S. _, 131 S. Ct. 2729 (2011).

. . . [In *Brown*,] the Court outright rejected California's argument that the First Amendment permitted the state "to create a wholly new category of content-based regulation," *i.e.*, speech containing violent imagery, "that is permissible only for speech directed at children." Although acknowledging that the state "possesses legitimate power to protect children from harm," the Court concluded that such power "does not include a free-floating power to restrict the ideas to which children may be exposed." . . .

Applying these principles to the instant case, *Brown* represents a forceful reaffirmation by the Court that the First Amendment applies to minors, and that the government may only restrict that constitutional right in "narrow and well-defined circumstances." Indeed, after *Brown*, it cannot seriously be contested that minors enjoy the First Amendment right to engage in speech containing violent imagery when they are at home, away from school, so long as that speech does not rise to the level of a true threat, incitement or fighting words. Nevertheless, the majority opinion wholly fails to reckon with these important statements by the Court. Instead, by simply assuming that all children speak "*qua* students," its legal analysis begins with the false premise that the speech at issue constitutes "student speech" that must be "tempered in the light of a school official's duty" to teach students appropriate behavior. But the Supreme Court has never suggested that minors' constitutional rights *outside of school* are somehow qualified if they coincidentally are enrolled in a public school. To the contrary, *Brown* evinces that the majority opinion instead should have begun its analysis from the basic premise that children are entitled to "significant" First Amendment rights. . . .

The Court's opinion in Reno v. American Civil Liberties Union, 521 U.S. 844 (1997), further reveals the flaws in the majority opinion's holding that schools may regulate students' off-campus online speech, like Bell's. *Reno* was the first significant First Amendment case specifically pertaining to the Internet to reach the Supreme Court, and concerned a facial challenge to a congressional statute, the Communications Decency Act of 1996 ("CDA"), which was aimed at protecting minors from "indecent" and "patently offensive" material on the Internet by prohibiting the transmission of those materials to minors. In striking down the CDA as violative of the First Amendment, the Court articulated a number of principles that are directly pertinent to the instant case.

First, *Reno* reveals that the majority opinion here is in error in concluding that the advent of the Internet and other technologies necessitates expanding schools' authority to regulate students' off-campus speech. In direct contradiction to the majority opinion's logic, the Court in *Reno* held that Supreme Court precedents "provide no basis for qualifying the level of First Amendment scrutiny that should be applied to [the Internet]." . . .

In addition, the Court's analysis in *Reno* reveals how the majority opinion's ill-devised framework for regulating minors' off-campus Internet speech would be too vague altogether for the First Amendment to tolerate. . . .

Here, the *en banc* majority opinion similarly announces a new, categorical restriction upon students' off-campus speech that fails to "give people of ordinary intelligence fair notice of what is prohibited." Specifically, the majority opinion holds that school officials may punish students' off-campus speech when (i) it is intended to be heard by the school community; (ii) could be perceived by a layperson as "threatening," "harassing," and "intimidating;" and (iii) satisfies the *Tinker* "substantial-disruption" framework. As with the statute struck down in *Reno*, however, each one of these three prongs to the majority opinion's framework contains defects that fail to provide students, like Bell, with adequate notice of when their off-campus speech crosses the critical line between protected and punishable expression. *First*, the majority opinion's focus on whether the student "intended" his speech to reach the school community significantly burdens the ability of students to engage in online speech, because virtually any speech on the Internet can reach members of the school community. . . .

Second, the majority opinion's "threatening, harassing, and intimidating" test suffers from the precise same ambiguities that drove the Court to strike down the CDA in *Reno*. As with the CDA, the majority opinion fails to provide any meaningful definition of what constitutes "threatening," "harassing," or "intimidating" speech. Rather, the majority opinion merely concludes that if a "layperson would understand" speech to qualify as "threatening," "harassing," and "intimidating," then that speech is regulable under *Tinker*. In so holding, the majority opinion fails to apprehend that reasonable minds may differ about when speech qualifies as "threatening," "harassing," or "intimidating" . . .

Third, the aforementioned concerns are exacerbated by the fact that the *Tinker* standard itself could be viewed as somewhat vague. *Tinker* permits schools to regulate on-campus expressive activities *not only* when the speech, in fact, causes a substantial disruption, *but also* when school officials can "reasonably forecast" such a disruption. If this standard were applied off campus, how can a student or a student's parents know with any degree of certainty when off-campus online speech can be "forecasted" to cause a "substantial disruption"? Although *Tinker* is not a completely toothless standard, its framework inherently requires guesswork about how a third-party school official will prophesize over the effect of speech. Thus, in light of the majority opinion, before a student drafts an email or writes a blog entry, he hereinafter will be required to conjecture over whether his online speech *might* cause a "disruption" that is "substantial" in the eyes of school officials, or, alternatively, whether a school official *might* reasonably portend that a substantial disruption *might* happen. . . .

Further, by adopting a rule that focuses on whether a "layperson" would perceive Bell's speech as "threatening," "harassing," and "intimidating," the majority opinion also ignores Supreme Court case law that demands a more burdensome showing upon the government before levying penalties upon a speaker based on the content of his speech. . . .

In ultimately holding that the *Tinker* framework applies to off-campus speech like Bell's, the majority opinion ignores that *Tinker*'s holding and its *sui generis* "substantial-disruption" framework are expressly grounded in "the special characteristics of the school environment." . . . While recognizing that students do not "shed their constitutional rights to freedom of speech or expression at the schoolhouse gate," the Court also observed that students' exercise of their First Amendment rights at school must be calibrated against the competing need of school officials "to prescribe and control conduct *in the schools*." To reconcile the interests at stake that may collide when student speech occurs on campus, the Court articulated a rule that has become the lodestar for evaluating the scope of students' on-campus First Amendment rights ever since: while on campus, a student is free to "express his opinions, even on controversial subjects, if he does so without 'materially and substantially interfer(ing) with the requirements of appropriate discipline in the operation of the school' and without colliding with the rights of others."

. . . *Morse* and the Court's other post-*Tinker* precedents make crystal clear what the majority opinion and some of our sister circuits' decisions fail to follow: *Tinker* does not authorize school officials to regulate student speech that occurs off campus and not at a school-sponsored event, where the potential "collision" of interest upon which *Tinker*'s holding pivots simply is not present.

. . .[T]he *Tinker* standard was invented, in part, to counteract the consequences of speech that actually occurs within the school environment and to take account of school officials' competing interest to "control conduct in the schools." Specifically, in *Tinker*, the competing state interest was in avoiding the disruptive consequences of speech that occurs within school. Accordingly, the Supreme Court crafted a specific level of scrutiny (the "substantial-disruption" test) to evaluate restrictions on speech *within school* that strikes a balance between the competing interests at stake. Even assuming *arguendo* schools had some authority to punish students' off-campus speech, it is therefore simply a *non sequitur* for the majority opinion to reflexively assume that the same analysis should regulate the scope of schools' authority to punish students' expression *off campus*, where the consequences of the speech in question and the constitutional interests at stake are simply not the same as in *Tinker*.

The majority opinion's flawed logic in this regard stems naturally from a more fundamental error: the majority opinion fails to take seriously the significance of the various constitutional interests that are implicated by its decision to expand *Tinker*'s reach. As detailed above, the particular facts of this case principally concern the First Amendment right of students to speak out on "matters of public concern" when they are away from school by utilizing the unrivaled power of the Internet to make those messages heard. But narrowly focusing on this issue alone ignores the constellation of other constitutional interests that the majority opinion will negatively impact. For example, even when their off-campus expression does not have a "political" or "religious" dimension, children still maintain "significant" First Amendment rights, which indisputably include a right to express disrespect or disdain for their teachers when they are off campus. Further, for purposes of the First Amendment, it is simply irrelevant whether prevailing social mores deem a child's disrespect for his teacher to be contemptible. "The history of the law of free expression is one of vindication in cases involving speech that many citizens may find shabby, offensive, or even ugly." . . .

. . .[E]ven if *Tinker* were applicable to the instant case, the evidence does not support the conclusion, as would be required by *Tinker*, that Bell's Internet-posted song substantially disrupted the school's work and discipline or that the school officials reasonably could have forecasted that it would do so.

In considering the School Board's motion for summary judgment, we are required to view the evidence in the light most favorable to Bell, the non-movant. The majority opinion, however, wholly disclaims this duty by ignoring material facts and refusing to draw inferences in Bell's favor—particularly those facts and inferences clearly evincing that Bell's song was not and could not be regarded as a threat. For example, Bell has been an aspiring musician since he was a young boy. He began writing lyrics as a child and started to pursue a musical career in earnest while in his teens. . . . As he explained to the Disciplinary Committee, Bell considers himself "an artist," and, as explained above, he originally composed and publicized the song in an effort to "speak out" on and raise awareness of an important issue in his community, *i.e.*, sexual harassment of students. Moreover, consistent with his musical aspirations, Bell explained that the version of the song posted to YouTube was also intended to attract the attention of record labels. Further, the screenshot of Bell's Facebook page reveals that his friends who commented on the song viewed it as the product of Bell's musical talent as a rap musician rather than a threat of violence. . . . In addition, no one—neither Wildmon, Rainey, nor any other teacher or school official—testified that s/he thought Bell, himself, subjectively intended to cause anyone to fear that Bell personally would harm any person. Nor was there any evidence that Bell was a dangerous person or that he had ever engaged in violent or unlawful conduct. Although Bell in his rap song referred to a firearm, the evidence does not reflect that Bell had ever owned, possessed, or had any actual experience with firearms. Except for a single tardiness, Bell had an unblemished school conduct record. These crucial facts not only impeach the School Board's contention that Bell's song could reasonably be perceived as a legitimate threat of violence, but also illuminate the fallacies in the majority opinion's comparison between this case and other circuit decisions that have condoned punishment for intentionally violent student speech. . . .

Further, although the majority opinion emphasizes Wildmon's testimony that Bell's rap song allegedly scared him, the majority opinion refuses to acknowledge that Rainey testified that he viewed the song as "just a rap" and that "if [he] let it go, it will probably just die down." In addition to ignoring these material facts, the majority opinion likewise refuses to draw obvious inferences from the record which further evince the fact that school officials did not consider Bell's song to be threatening in nature. For example, in sharp contrast to other cases in which courts have upheld discipline for a student's purportedly "violent" speech, nothing in the record reflects that school officials ever contacted law enforcement about Bell's song. To the contrary, Bell's principal drove him home that day, and he thereafter was allowed to return to classes. Later, when Bell was suspended pending the outcome of the Disciplinary Committee hearing, he nevertheless was allowed to remain unattended in the school commons for the remainder of the day. These are simply not the actions of school officials who seriously or reasonably believe a student poses a threat of violence to school officials.

Had the majority opinion properly reviewed all the relevant facts and drawn the clear inferences therefrom, it would have been compelled to conclude that the evidence here does not support a finding, as would be required by *Tinker*, that a "substantial disruption" occurred or that school officials reasonably could have "forecast" a substantial disruption as a result of Bell's rap. . . .

In reaching the opposite conclusion, however, the majority opinion reasons that Bell's "threatening, intimidating, and harassing language . . . could be forecast by [school officials] to cause a substantial disruption." But, the "evidence" that the majority opinion cites for this conclusion is, at the very best, sorely lacking. . . . [N]o *reasonable* listener could perceive Bell's lyrics as threats in light of the particular context; nor did the particular listeners here. Critically, the speech at issue in this case occurred in a rap song, a musical genre in which hyperbolic and violent language is commonly used in order to convey emotion and meaning—not to make real threats of violence. *See, e.g.,* Andrea L. Dennis, Poetic (In)Justice? Rap Music Lyrics as Art, Life, and Criminal Evidence, 31 Colum. J.L. & Arts. 1, 22 (2007). . . . Bell's song was just that: a song, authored by a young and aspiring musical artist—not the calling card of a would-be killer. . . .

Viewed in the light of these longstanding principles, Bell's song was not a disruption of school activities but rather was an effort to participate as a citizen in our unique constitutional democracy by raising awareness of a serious matter of public concern. Yet, rather than commending Bell's efforts, the Itawamba County School Board punished him for the content of his speech, in effect teaching Bell that the First Amendment does not protect students who challenge those in power. The majority opinion teaches that same mistaken lesson to all the children in our Circuit. Indeed, in concluding that the First Amendment officially condones Bell's censoring and punishment by the School Board, instead of safeguarding his freedom of speech, the majority opinion undermines the rights of all students and adults to both speak and receive speech on matters of public concern through the Internet.

For these reasons, I respectfully and earnestly dissent.

(The concurring opinions of Judges Elrod and Costa and the dissenting opinions of Judges Prado, Haynes, and Graves are omitted.)

NOTES AND QUESTIONS

1. Including the principal case, the Supreme Court has denied certiorari in four cases questioning the constitutional limits on school authority to discipline students for off-campus social media activity. Kowalski v. Berkeley County Schools, 652 F.3d 565 (4th Cir. 2011), cert. denied, 132 S. Ct. 1095 (2012); J.S. ex rel. Snyder v. Blue Mountain Sch. Dist., 650 F.3d 915 (3d Cir. 2011), cert. denied 565 U.S. 1156 (2012); Doninger v. Niehoff, 642 F.3d 334 (2d Cir. 2011), cert. denied 799 F.3d 379 (2011).

2. The majority concludes that *Tinker* applies to this case. Is this because the speech occurred on campus, or because sometimes speech that occurs off campus is nevertheless subject to the *Tinker* rule? How does the dissent argue that *Tinker* does not apply? What test would the dissent use and why?

If Bell had shown the YouTube video to his friend on his tablet at home and his friend had viewed it at school, would his speech have occurred on campus? What if Bell had shown the site to no one, but a classmate browsing the Web at school found it?

Most courts confronting the issue have held that *Tinker* applies to student speech that does not literally occur on campus if it threatens a substantial disturbance of the educational environment. For analyses and proposals, *see* Elizabeth A. Shaver, Denying Certiorari in Bell v. Itawamba County School Board; A Missed Opportunity to Clarify Students' First Amendment Rights in the Digital Age, 82 Brooklyn L. Rev. 1539 (2017); Lee Goldman, Student Speech and the First Amendment: A Comprehensive Approach, 63 Fla. L. Rev. 395, 404-406 (2011); Mary-Rose Papandrea, Student Speech Rights in the Digital Age, 60 Fla. L. Rev. 1028, 1056-1065 (2008).

3. What meanings do the majority and the dissent give to the *Tinker* substantial disruption standard?

4. Why does Judge Jolly concur rather than joining the majority?

5. Given the majority's characterization of Bell's rap as "incredibly profane and vulgar," why didn't it apply *Fraser* to decide the case?

6. In addition to the principal case, at least nineteen other cases have discussed school shooting incidents in the course of determining whether student speech was protected by the First Amendment. The usual argument is that the danger of school violence justified strict school rules against any use of violent language. N.Z. v. Madison Board of Education, 94 N.E.3d 1198 (Ohio App. 2017); Kountze Independent School District v. Matthews, 2017 WL 4319908 (Tex. App. 2017); R.L. ex rel. Lordan v. Central York School District, 183 F. Supp. 3d 625 (M.D. Pa. 2016); CLM ex rel. McNeil v. Sherwood School District 88J, 2016 WL 894450 (D. Ore. 2016); Wynar v. Douglas County School District, 728 F.3d 1062 (9th Cir. 2013); D.J.M. ex rel. D.M. v. Hannibal Public Sch. Dist. No, 60, 647 F.3d 754 (8th Cir. 2011); Miller ex rel. Miller v. Penn Manor Sch. Dist., 588 F. Supp. 2d 606 (E.D. Pa. 2008); Ponce v. Socorro Ind. Sch. District, 508 F.3d 765 (5th Cir. 2007); Boim v. Fulton Cnty. Sch. Dist., 494 F.3d 978 (11th Cir. 2007); Governor Wentworth Regional Sch. Dist. v. Hendrickson, 421 F. Supp. 2d 410 (D.N.H. 2006); Douglass v. Londonderry Sch. Bd., 413 F. Supp. 2d 1 (D.N.H. 2005); Nixon v. Northern Local Sch. Dist. Bd. of Educ., 383 F. Supp. 2d 965 (S.D. Ohio 2005); Griggs ex rel. Griggs v. Fort Wayne Sch. Bd., 359 F. Supp. 2d 731 (N.D. Ind. 2005); In re George T., 93 P.3d 1007 (Cal. 2004); Hansen v. Ann Arbor Public Schs., 293 F. Supp. 2d 780 (E.D. Mich. 2003); Newsom ex rel. Newsom v. Albemarle Cnty. Sch. Bd., 354 F.3d 249 (4th Cir. 2003); Doe v. Pulaski Cnty. Spec. Sch. Dist., 306 F.3d 616 (8th Cir. 2002); J.S. ex rel. H.S. v. Bethlehem Area Sch. Dist., 807 A.2d 847 (Pa. 2002); LaVine v. Blaine Sch. Dist., 257 F.3d 981 (9th Cir. 2001).

This attention seems consistent with advice from the U.S. Secret Service, that plans to prevent school violence should "involve adults attending to concerns when someone poses a threat rather than waiting for a direct threat." Preventing School Shootings: A Summary of a U.S. Secret Service Safe School Initiative Report, NIJ Journal no. 248 (2002). The report continued,

> Most attackers engaged in some behavior prior to the incident that caused concern or indicated a need for help. . . . More than three-fourths of the attackers threatened to kill themselves, made suicidal gestures, or tried to kill themselves before their attacks. In one case, a student wrote several poems for English class that involved themes of homicide and suicide as possible solutions to feelings of hopelessness. School authorities ultimately determined that his was a family problem and did not intervene. He later went to school and killed two people. . . .

In contrast, the dissenting judge in *Pulaski* observed,

> Today's teenagers witness, experience, and hear violence on television, in music, in movies, in video games, and for some, in abusive relationships at home. It is hardly surprising that such violence is reflected in the way they express themselves and communicate with their peers, particularly where adult supervision is lacking. The shocking contents of the letter alone, however, do not warrant the finding of a true threat.

396 F.3d at 631 (Heaney, J., dissenting).

7. Most of the cases involving school authority to discipline students for electronic communications generated off campus have, like *Bell*, concerned school administrators. *See* Emily Gold Waldman, Badmouthing Authority: Hostile Speech about School Officials and the Limits of School Restrictions, 19 Wm. & Mary Bill Rts. J. 591 (2011). To protect students' rights to dissent while allowing schools to protect the authority of school officials, she proposes that the courts develop a distinction between dissenting and harassing speech and that they allow schools to punish speech that harasses authority figures but not speech that simply expresses dissent from school policies.

––––––––––

Cyberbullying of students by students has become a significant problem across the country. Estimates of the number of young people who have been cyberbullied vary from 10 to more than 40 percent, depending on the age of the group studied, how cyberbullying is defined, and the research methodology. Sameer Hinduja & Justin W. Patchin, Cyberbullying Identification, Prevention, and Response (2010), available at http://www.cyberbullying.us/cyberbullying_identification_prevention_ response.php. Lesbian, bisexual, transgender, and questioning youth are especially at risk; from 72 to 90 percent of them have been harassed at school because of their sexual orientation. Sameer Hinduja & Justin W. Patchin, Cyberbullying and Sexual Orientation (2011), available at http://www.cyberbullying.us/cyberbullying_and_ sexual_orientation.php. *See also* Michael J. Higdon, To Lynch a Child: Bullying and Gender Nonconformity in Our Nation's Schools, 86 Ind. L.J. 827 (2011).

States and local government units have enacted criminal statutes defining and punishing cyberbullying, which, not surprisingly, immediately elicited First Amendment challenges. This kind of case returns us to the question of whether minors' free speech rights outside school are coextensive with those of adults.

PEOPLE v. MARQUAN M.

19 N.E.3d 480 (N.Y. 2014)

GRAFFEO, J. Defendant, a 16–year–old high school student, anonymously posted sexual information about fellow classmates on a publicly-accessible Internet website. He was criminally prosecuted for "cyberbullying" under a local law enacted by the Albany County Legislature. We are asked to decide whether this cyberbullying statute comports with the Free Speech Clause of the First Amendment.

I

Bullying by children in schools has long been a prevalent problem but its psychological effects were not studied in earnest until the 1970s (*see* Hyojin Koo, A Time Line of the Evolution of School Bullying in Differing Social Contexts, 8 Asia Pac. Educ. Rev. 107 [2007], available at http://files.eric.ed. gov/fulltext/EJ768971. pdf). Since then, "[b]ullying among school-aged youth" has "increasingly be[en] recognized as an important problem affecting well-being and social functioning," as well as "a potentially more serious threat to healthy youth development" (Tonja R. Nansel et al., Bullying Behaviors among U.S. Youth, 285 JAMA 2094 [2001], available at http://jama.jamanetwork.com/article.aspx?articleid =193774). At its core, bullying represents an imbalance of power between the aggressor and victim that often manifests in behaviors that are "verbal (e.g., name-calling, threats), physical (e.g., hitting), or psychological (e.g., rumors, shunning/exclusion)." Based on the recognized harmful effects of bullying, many schools and communities now sponsor anti-bullying campaigns in order to reduce incidents of such damaging behaviors.

Educators and legislators across the nation have endeavored to craft policies designed to counter the adverse impact of bullying on children. New York, for example, enacted the "Dignity for All Students Act" in 2010 (see L. 2010, ch. 482, § 2; Education Law § 10 et seq.), declaring that our State must "afford all students in public schools an environment free of discrimination and harassment" caused by "bullying, taunting or intimidation." In furtherance of this objective, the State prohibited discrimination and bullying on public school property or at school functions. The Act relied on the creation and implementation of school board policies to reduce bullying in schools through the appropriate training of personnel, mandatory instruction for students on civility and tolerance, and reporting requirements. The Act did not criminalize bullying behaviors; instead, it incorporated educational penalties such as suspension from school.

Despite these efforts, the problem of bullying continues, and has been exacerbated by technological innovations and the widespread dissemination of electronic information using social media sites. The advent of the Internet with "twenty-four hour connectivity and social networking" means that "[b]ullying that begins in school follows students home every day" and "bullying through the use of technology can begin away from school property." Regardless of how or where bullying occurs, it "affects the school environment and disrupts the educational process, impeding the ability of students to learn and too often causing devastating effects on students' health and well-being" (id.; see, e.g., American Psychiatric Association, Resolution on Bullying among Children & Youth [2004], available at https://www.apa.org/about/policy/bullying.pdf). The use of computers and electronic devices to engage in this pernicious behavior is commonly referred to as "cyberbullying." Unlike traditional bullying, victims of cyberbullying can be "relentlessly and anonymously attack[ed] twenty-four hours a day for the whole world to witness. There is simply no escape."

The Dignity for All Students Act did not originally appear to encompass cyberbullying, particularly acts of bullying that occur off school premises. As the ramifications of cyberbullying on social networking sites spilled into the educational environment, in 2012, the state legislature amended the Act to expand the types of prohibited bullying conduct covered by its provisions. It added a proscription on bullying that applied to "any form of electronic communication," including any off-campus activities that "foreseeably create a risk of substantial disruption within the school environment, where it is foreseeable that the conduct, threats, intimidation or abuse might reach school property."

Before the addition of the 2012 amendments to the Dignity for All Students Act, elected officials in Albany County decided to tackle the problem of cyberbullying. They determined there was a need to criminalize such conduct because the "State Legislature ha[d] failed to address th[e] problem" of "non-physical bullying behaviors transmitted by electronic means" (Local Law No. 11 [2010] of County of Albany § 1). In 2010, the Albany County Legislature adopted a new crime—the offense of cyberbullying—which was defined as

> . . .any act of communicating or causing a communication to be sent by mechanical or electronic means, including posting statements on the internet or through a computer or email network, disseminating embarrassing or sexually explicit photographs; disseminating private, personal, false or sexual information, or sending hate mail, with no legitimate private, personal, or public purpose, with the intent to harass, annoy, threaten, abuse, taunt, intimidate, torment, humiliate, or otherwise inflict significant emotional harm on another person.

The provision outlawed cyberbullying against "any minor or person" situated in the county. Knowingly engaging in this activity was deemed to be a misdemeanor offense punishable by up to one year in jail and a $1,000 fine. . . .

A month later, defendant Marquan M., a student attending Cohoes High School in Albany County, used the social networking website "Facebook" to create a page bearing the pseudonym "Cohoes Flame." He anonymously posted photographs of high-school classmates and other adolescents, with detailed descriptions of their alleged sexual practices and predilections, sexual partners and other types of personal information. The descriptive captions, which were vulgar and offensive, prompted responsive electronic messages that threatened the creator of the website with physical harm.

A police investigation revealed that defendant was the author of the Cohoes Flame postings. He admitted his involvement and was charged with cyberbullying under Albany County's local law. Defendant moved to dismiss, arguing that the statute violated his right to free speech under the First Amendment. After City Court denied defendant's motion, he pleaded guilty to one count of cyberbullying but reserved his right to raise his constitutional arguments on appeal. County Court affirmed, concluding that the local law was constitutional to the extent it outlawed such activities directed at minors, and held that the application of the provision to defendant's Facebook posts did not contravene his First Amendment rights. A Judge of this Court granted defendant leave to appeal. . . .

Under the Free Speech Clause of the First Amendment, the government generally "has no power to restrict expression because of its message, its ideas, its subject matter, or its content." Consequently, it is well established that prohibitions of pure speech must be limited to communications that qualify as fighting words, true threats, incitement, obscenity, child pornography, fraud, defamation or statements integral to criminal conduct (*see.* . . Brown v. Entertainment Merchants Assn., 564 U.S. ____, ____, 131 S. Ct. 2729, 2733 [2011]; . . . Outside of such recognized categories, speech is presumptively protected and generally cannot be curtailed by the government.

Yet, the government unquestionably has a compelling interest in protecting children from harmful publications or materials (*see* Reno v. American Civil Liberties Union, 521 U.S. 844, 875 [1997]; *see also* Brown v. Entertainment Merchants Assn., 564 U.S. at ____, 131 S. Ct. at 2736; *see generally* Bethel School

Dist. No. 403 v. Fraser, 478 U.S. 675, 682 [1986]). Cyberbullying is not concep-
tually immune from government regulation, so we may assume, for the purposes
of this case, that the First Amendment permits the prohibition of cyberbullying
directed at children, depending on how that activity is defined. Our task therefore
is to determine whether the specific statutory language of the Albany County legislative enactment can comfortably coexist with the right to free speech.

Challenges to statutes under the Free Speech Clause are usually premised
on the overbreadth and vagueness doctrines. A regulation of speech is overbroad
if constitutionally-protected expression may be "chilled" by the provision because
it facially "prohibits a real and substantial amount of" expression guarded by
the First Amendment. This type of facial challenge, which is restricted to cases
implicating the First Amendment, requires a court to assess the wording of the
statute—"without reference to the defendant's conduct"—to decide whether "a
substantial number of its applications are unconstitutional, judged in relation to
the statute's plainly legitimate sweep." A law that is overbroad cannot be validly
applied against any individual. In contrast, a statute is seen by the courts as vague
if "it fails to give a citizen adequate notice of the nature of proscribed conduct
and permits arbitrary and discriminatory enforcement." Hence, the government
has the burden of demonstrating that a regulation of speech is constitutionally
permissible. . . .

Based on the text of the statute at issue, it is evident that Albany County
"create[d] a criminal prohibition of alarming breadth." The language of the local
law embraces a wide array of applications that prohibit types of protected speech
far beyond the cyberbullying of children. As written, the Albany County law in
its broadest sense criminalizes "any act of communicating . . . by mechanical or
electronic means . . . with no legitimate . . . personal . . . purpose, with the intent
to harass [or] annoy . . . another person." On its face, the law covers communications aimed at adults, and fictitious or corporate entities, even though the county
legislature justified passage of the provision based on the detrimental effects that
cyberbullying has on school-aged children. The county law also lists particular
examples of covered communications, such as "posting statements on the internet
or through a computer or email network, disseminating embarrassing or sexually
explicit photographs; disseminating private, personal, false, or sexual information,
or sending hate mail." But such methods of expression are not limited to instances
of cyberbullying—the law includes every conceivable form of electronic communication, such as telephone conversations, a ham radio transmission or even a
telegram. In addition, the provision pertains to electronic communications that
are meant to "harass, annoy . . . taunt . . . [or] humiliate" any person or entity,
not just those that are intended to "threaten, abuse . . . intimidate, torment . . . or
otherwise inflict significant emotional harm on" a child. In considering the facial
implications, it appears that the provision would criminalize a broad spectrum of
speech outside the popular understanding of cyberbullying, including, for example: an email disclosing private information about a corporation or a telephone
conversation meant to annoy an adult.

The County admits that the text of the statute is too broad and that certain aspects of its contents encroach on recognized areas of protected free speech.
Because the law "imposes a restriction on the content of protected speech, it is
invalid unless" the County "can demonstrate that it passes strict scrutiny—that is,

unless it is justified by a compelling government interest and is narrowly drawn to serve that interest." For this reason, the County asks us to sever the offending portions and declare that the remainder of the law survives strict scrutiny. What remains, in the County's view, is a tightly circumscribed cyberbullying law that includes only three types of electronic communications sent with the intent to inflict emotional harm on a child: (1) sexually explicit photographs; (2) private or personal sexual information; and (3) false sexual information with no legitimate public, personal, or private purpose.

It is true, as the County urges, that a court should strive to save a statute when confronted with a Free Speech challenge. But departure from a textual analysis is appropriate only if the statutory language is "fairly susceptible" to an interpretation that satisfies applicable First Amendment requirements. The doctrine of separation of governmental powers prevents a court from rewriting a legislative enactment through the creative use of a severability clause when the result is incompatible with the language of the statute. And special concerns arise in the First Amendment context—excessive judicial revision of an overbroad statute may lead to vagueness problems because

> . . .the statutory language would signify one thing but, as a matter of judicial decision, would stand for something entirely different. Under those circumstances, persons of ordinary intelligence reading [the law] could not know what it actually meant.

We conclude that it is not a permissible use of judicial authority for us to employ the severance doctrine to the extent suggested by the County or the dissent. It is possible to sever the portion of the cyberbullying law that applies to adults and other entities because this would require a simple deletion of the phrase "or person" from the definition of the offense. But doing so would not cure all of the law's constitutional ills. As we have recently made clear, the First Amendment protects annoying and embarrassing speech, even if a child may be exposed to it, so those references would also need to be excised from the definitional section. And, the First Amendment forbids the government from deciding whether protected speech qualifies as "legitimate," as Albany County has attempted to do.

It is undisputed that the Albany County statute was motivated by the laudable public purpose of shielding children from cyberbullying. The text of the cyberbullying law, however, does not adequately reflect an intent to restrict its reach to the three discrete types of electronic bullying of a sexual nature designed to cause emotional harm to children. Hence, to accept the County's proposed interpretation, we would need to significantly modify the applications of the county law, resulting in the amended scope bearing little resemblance to the actual language of the law. Such a judicial rewrite encroaches on the authority of the legislative body that crafted the provision and enters the realm of vagueness because any person who reads it would lack fair notice of what is legal and what constitutes a crime. Even if the First Amendment allows a cyberbullying statute of the limited nature proposed by Albany County, the local law here was not drafted in that manner. Albany County therefore has not met its burden of proving that the restrictions on speech contained in its cyberbullying law survive strict scrutiny.

There is undoubtedly general consensus that defendant's Facebook communications were repulsive and harmful to the subjects of his rants, and potentially created a risk of physical or emotional injury based on the private nature of the comments. He identified specific adolescents with photographs, described their purported sexual practices and posted the information on a website accessible world-wide. Unlike traditional bullying, which usually takes place by a face-to-face encounter, defendant used the advantages of the Internet to attack his victims from a safe distance, 24 hours a day, while cloaked in anonymity. Although the First Amendment may not give defendant the right to engage in these activities, the text of Albany County's law envelops far more than acts of cyberbullying against children by criminalizing a variety of constitutionally-protected modes of expression. We therefore hold that Albany County's Local Law No. 11 of 2010—as drafted—is overbroad and facially invalid under the Free Speech Clause of the First Amendment.

Accordingly, the order of County Court should be reversed and the accusatory instrument dismissed.

SMITH, J. (dissenting). Albany County has conceded that certain provisions of its Cyber–Bullying law are invalid. It seems to me that those provisions can be readily severed from the rest of the legislation and that what remains can, without any strain on its language, be interpreted in a way that renders it constitutionally valid.

The operative provision of the law says simply: "No person shall engage in cyber-bullying against any minor or person in the County of Albany." The County does not defend the law as it applies to adults, and the majority acknowledges that we may consider the statute as if the words "or person" were deleted. But the majority finds irreparable constitutional flaws in the definition of Cyber–Bullying, which is as follows:

> 'CYBER–BULLYING' shall mean any act of communicating or causing a communication to be sent by mechanical or electronic means, including posting statements on the internet or through a computer or email network, disseminating embarrassing or sexually explicit photographs; disseminating private, personal, false or sexual information, or sending hate mail, with no legitimate private, personal, or public purpose, with the intent to harass, annoy, threaten, abuse, taunt, intimidate, torment, humiliate, or otherwise inflict significant emotional harm on another person.

The County concedes that the words "embarrassing" and "hate mail" are "vague and thus unenforceable." It argues, correctly I think, that these terms can be dealt with in the same way as the reference to "person" in the operative section: simply by crossing them out. Once these deletions are made, I see nothing in the law that renders it unconstitutional.

The majority, it seems, is troubled by two other aspects of the definition of "Cyber–Bullying": the requirement that the forbidden communications be made "with no legitimate private, personal, or public purpose;" and the series of verbs—"harass, annoy, threaten, abuse, taunt, intimidate, torment, humiliate"—that precedes the words "or otherwise." Neither requires us to invalidate the law.

I grant that the words "no legitimate … purpose" are not remarkable for their precision. We have twice held, however, that they are clear enough to withstand a constitutional challenge for vagueness. We said in *Shack*:

...the phrase 'no purpose of legitimate communication' ... notwithstanding its subjective quality, would be understood to mean the absence of expression of ideas or thoughts other than threats and/or intimidating or coercive utterances.

Similarly here, the phrase "no legitimate purpose" should be understood to mean the absence of expression of ideas or thoughts other than the mere abuse that the law proscribes.

. . . The majority is also correct in saying that "the First Amendment forbids the government from deciding whether protected speech qualifies as 'legitimate,' but this begs the central question of what speech is "protected" and what is not. The Cyber–Bullying law prohibits a narrow category of valueless and harmful speech when the government proves, among other things, that the speaker had no legitimate purpose for engaging in it. The speech so prohibited is not protected speech.

As for the list of verbs beginning with "annoy" and ending with "humiliate," it is fair to read them, as the County urges, as "a non-exhaustive list of ways that the wrongdoer may formulate his or her intent to inflict emotional harm on the victim." In other words, the acts within the scope of the Cyber–Bullying law — disseminating sexually explicit photographs or private, personal, false or sexual information — are prohibited only where they are intended to "inflict significant emotional harm" on the victim, and the verbs merely serve as examples of ways in which significant emotional harm may be inflicted. That is not the only possible way to read the text of the law, but it is a perfectly reasonable way — indeed, the word "otherwise" seems to signal that the verbs preceding it are only illustrative. So read, the law does not prohibit conduct intended to harass, annoy, threaten or the like unless the actor specifically intended "significant emotional harm." I do not find such a prohibition to be unconstitutionally vague or overbroad.

. . . The crux of the case, in my view, is whether Albany County constitutionally may do what it is trying to do — to prohibit certain kinds of communication that have no legitimate purpose and are intended to inflict significant emotional injury on children. The answer to this question is not self-evident. The First Amendment protects some extremely obnoxious forms of speech, including insults offered to a dead soldier at his funeral (Snyder v. Phelps, 562 U.S. 443 [2011]) and horrifyingly violent video games marketed to teenagers (Brown v. Entertainment Merchants Assn., 564 U.S. ____, [2011]). But *Snyder* itself makes clear that speech designed to inflict serious emotional injury is protected only when, as in *Snyder*, the speech is directed at a matter of public concern:

> Whether the First Amendment prohibits holding Westboro liable for its speech in this case turns largely on whether that speech is of public or private concern, as determined by all the circumstances of the case. . . . [R]estricting speech on purely private matters does not implicate the same constitutional concerns as limiting speech on matters of public interest.

It is thus clear that the emotional abuse involved in *Snyder* would not have been constitutionally protected if, like Marquan's remarks about his fellow students, it had referred to no matter of public importance and had been uttered purely out of private rage or spite. And the victims of the abuse in *Snyder* were adults; in that respect, the present case is a fortiori. The Albany County Cyber–Bullying law is valid.

NOTES AND QUESTIONS

1. Does the majority's holding that the Albany County ordinance is unconstitutional depend on Marquan's youth?

State v. Bishop, 787 S.E.2d 814 (N.C. 2016), also reversed a conviction of cyberbullying on the ground of free speech. The North Carolina statute forbade posting private, personal, or sexual information pertaining to a minor with intent to intimidate or torment a minor. The court applied strict scrutiny because the statute imposed a content-based restriction on speech. While the goal of protecting children was sufficiently compelling, the court held that the statute was not sufficiently narrowly tailored. On the difficulties in using criminal sanctions against cyberbulling, *see* Lyrissa Lidsky & Andrea Pinzon Garcia, How Not to Criminalize Cyberbullying, 77 Mo. L. Rev. 693 (2012).

2. Parents of children who are the victims of other students' harassment often come to the schools for help, rather than going to the police or trying to handle the problem directly themselves. Jan Hoffman, Online Bullies Pull Schools into Fray, N.Y. Times, June 27, 2010. These cases squarely present the conflict between the policy of protecting young people from bullying, including cyberbullying, and free speech rights, as well as the extent of schools' authority to control students' activities outside the schoolhouse. Further complicating matters for schools is their potential tort liability for failing to protect students from harassment by other students. *See* Davis v. Monroe County Board of Education, 526 U.S. 629 (1999) (school can be held liable for a student's sexual harassment of another student on school grounds).

Would the First Amendment permit Marquan's school to adopt a rule worded identically to the county ordinance and to discipline him for the same conduct? Cases upholding school disciplinary actions under anti-cyberbullying rules and state statutes include Dunkley v. Bd. of Educ., 216 F. Supp. 3d 485 (D.J.H. 2016) (emphasizing that state law required schools to enact policies to protect against cyberbullying); C.R. ex rel. Rainville v. Eugene Sch. Dist. 4J, 835 F.3d 142 (9th Cir. 2016) (middle-school boy who sexually harassed disabled younger students invaded the rights of others within the meaning of *Tinker*); S.J.W. ex rel. Wilson v. Lee's Summit R-7 Sch. Dist., 696 F.3d 771 (8th Cir. 2012) (blog with offensive and racist and sexually explicit and degrading comments about female classmates identified by name created on-campus disturbance); Kowalski v. Berkeley Cnty. Schs, 652 F.3d 565 (4th Cir. 2011) (web pages ridiculing fellow student caused disruption under *Tinker*). *Contra:* J.C. v. Beverly Hills Unified Sch. Dist. 711 F. Supp. 2d 1094 (C.D. Cal. 2010) (video containing taunts did not present substantial risk of disruption). *See also* Benjamin A. Holder, *Tinker* Meets the Cyberbully: A Federal Circuit Conflict Round-Up and Proposed New Standard for Off-Campus Speech, 28 Fordham Intell. Prop. Media & Ent. L. J. 233 (2018).

3. Other civil remedies for bullying including cyberbullying may be available. For example, statutes that authorize restraining orders against people who stalk or harass others may be deployed against bullying in some situations. In A.T. v. C.R., 39 N.E.3d 744 (Mass. App. 2015), the appellate court upheld a "harassment prevention order" against a sixth-grade boy who made sexually suggestive comments to a girl in his class in the presence of other students and then threatened to "make her life a living hell" if she showed anyone the video of his comments and later

threatened to punch her in the breasts for having complained to school authorities. The majority rejected the boy's argument that the facts showed an 11-year-old boy displaying poor judgment rather than intentional efforts to intimate and cause fear. The dissent, relying on juvenile delinquency cases and the Supreme Court's decisions limiting life-without-parole sentences for minors, argued that the first two actions did not express an intent to physically harm the girl.

Boston v. Ahearn, 764 S.E.2d 582 (Ga. App. 2014), concerns parents' civil liability when their child engages in cyberbullying. A 13-year-old boy created a fake Facebook page for his classmate that included racist and sexual messages and implied that she was gay, took illegal drugs, and was on medication for mental health problems. Although the boy's parents acknowledged what he had done and disciplined him, they did nothing about the Facebook page, which remained up for 11 months. The girl and her parents sued the boy's parents. The appellate court reversed a grant of summary judgment to the defendants, ruling that the boy's parents could not be held vicariously liable for his tort but could be liable for their negligence in failing to supervise or control him, particularly their failure to make sure the page came down.

PROBLEMS

1. Two middle school students created a website called "Satan's Web Page" on their home computer that described "Satan's mission for you this week" as killing someone graphically; the site also included a list of "people I wish would die." The page ended with this message: "Now that you've read my Web page please don't go killing people and stuff then blaming it on me, OK?" Students accessed the page on their home computers, and one of their parents discovered it and called the police. The school expelled the students who created the page for violating a school policy against making threats. When the students sue the school, alleging violation of the First Amendment, what arguments should be made on their behalf? How should the school respond? Would it matter if the other students accessed the page on a school computer? If the web page did not have the "disclaimer" at the end?

2. High school student Jan used her home computer to post a video to YouTube that she had shot at a local restaurant. On the video, other students from the school make derogatory and sexual remarks about Calla, another student at the school, including taunts about her sexual orientation. Jan called several friends from home, telling them to look at the video, and then she called Calla to tell her about it. The next day, Calla and her mother came to school. Calla was crying, saying she was humiliated and hurt. The principal called Jan in, demanded that she take the video down, and suspended her for ten days. The school computers block YouTube, but students can access it using cell phones and other handheld devices. Jan has sued the school, alleging a violation of her First Amendment rights. What arguments should be made by both sides?

3. Bonnie, a sophomore high school cheerleader, was kicked off the cheerleading squad because she posted a photo of herself making an obscene gesture on Snapchat, accompanied by text that included profanity. School rules establish a code of conduct for cheerleaders at school and at out-of-school official events

which Bonnie's conduct violated. However, she took the photo on the weekend when she was not participating in a school activity, and she shared the posting only with her friends, rather than making it available to the public. However, she concedes that the snap could have reached 250 people. Bonnie sues the school, alleging a violation of her First Amendment rights. What arguments should be made?

B.   RIGHTS TO REPRODUCTIVE DECISION MAKING

Planned Parenthood of Central Missouri v. Danforth, 428 U.S. 52 (1976), decided only three years after Roe v. Wade, 410 U.S. 113 (1973), held that a rule requiring parental consent for an abortion for anyone younger than 18 violated due process, but the extent of permissible parental involvement required before a minor can have a legal abortion is still disputed. National polls consistently find that 70 to 75 percent of the public favors requiring parental consent for minors seeking abortions. Gallup News, Abortion, news.gallup.com/poll/1576/abortion.aspx (July 23, 2018). However, the major medical organizations (American Academy of Family Physicians, American Academy of Pediatrics, American College of Obstetricians and Gynecologists, American College of Physicians, American Medical Association, and Society for Adolescent Medicine) consistently oppose this policy. Cynthia Dailard & Chinue Turner Richardson, Teenagers' Access to Confidential Reproductive Health Services (Guttmacher Report Nov. 2005). The next case is the leading Supreme Court decision on this issue.

BELLOTTI V. BAIRD

443 U.S. 622 (1979)

POWELL, J. [A Massachusetts statute requires parental consent before an abortion can be performed on an unmarried woman under the age of 18. If one or both parents refuse such consent, however, the abortion may be obtained by order of a judge of the superior court "for good cause shown." In appellees' class action challenging the constitutionality of the statute, a three-judge district court held it unconstitutional. Subsequently, this Court vacated the district court's judgment, Bellotti v. Baird, 428 U.S. 132, holding that the district court should have abstained and certified to the Massachusetts Supreme Judicial Court appropriate questions concerning the meaning of the statute. On remand, the district court certified several questions to the Supreme Judicial Court. Among the questions certified was whether the statute permits any minors—mature or immature—to obtain judicial consent to an abortion without any parental consultation whatsoever. The Supreme Judicial Court answered that, in general, it does not; that consent must be obtained for every nonemergency abortion unless no parent is available; and that an available parent must be given notice of any judicial proceedings brought by a minor to obtain consent for an abortion. Another question certified was whether, if the superior court finds that the minor is capable of making and has in fact made and adhered to an informed and reasonable decision to have an abortion, the court may refuse its consent on a finding that a parent's, or its own, contrary decision is a better one. The Supreme Judicial Court answered in the affirmative. Following the Supreme Judicial Court's judgment, the district court again declared the statute unconstitutional and enjoined its enforcement.]

A child, merely on account of his minority, is not beyond the protection of the Constitution. As the Court said in In re Gault, 387 U.S. 1 (1967), "whatever may be their precise impact, neither the Fourteenth Amendment nor the Bill of Rights is for adults alone." This observation, of course, is but the beginning of the analysis. The Court long has recognized that the status of minors under the law is unique in many respects. . . . The unique role in our society of the family, the institution by which "we inculcate and pass down many of our most cherished values, moral and cultural," Moore v. East Cleveland, 431 U.S. 494, 503-504 (1977) (plurality opinion), requires that constitutional principles be applied with sensitivity and flexibility to the special needs of parents and children. We have recognized three reasons justifying the conclusion that the constitutional rights of children cannot be equated with those of adults: the peculiar vulnerability of children; their inability to make critical decisions in an informed, mature manner; and the importance of the parental role in child rearing. . . .

The Court's concern for the vulnerability of children is demonstrated in its decisions dealing with minors' claims to constitutional protection against deprivations of liberty or property interests by the State. With respect to many of these claims, we have concluded that the child's right is virtually coextensive with that of an adult. . . .

These rulings have not been made on the uncritical assumption that the constitutional rights of children are indistinguishable from those of adults. Indeed, our acceptance of juvenile courts distinct from the adult criminal justice system assumes that juvenile offenders constitutionally may be treated differently from adults. In order to preserve this separate avenue for dealing with minors, the Court has said that hearings in juvenile delinquency cases need not necessarily " 'conform with all of the requirements of a criminal trial or even of the usual administrative hearing.'" In re Gault, *supra*, at 30, quoting Kent v. United States, 383 U.S. 541, 562 (1966). Thus, juveniles are not constitutionally entitled to trial by jury in delinquency adjudications. McKeiver v. Pennsylvania, 403 U.S. 528 (1971). Viewed together, our cases show that although children generally are protected by the same constitutional guarantees against governmental deprivations as are adults, the State is entitled to adjust its legal system to account for children's vulnerability and their needs for "concern, . . . sympathy, and . . . paternal attention." . . .

Second, the Court has held that the States validly may limit the freedom of children to choose for themselves in the making of important, affirmative choices with potentially serious consequences. These rulings have been grounded in the recognition that, during the formative years of childhood and adolescence, minors often lack the experience, perspective, and judgment to recognize and avoid choices that could be detrimental to them.

Ginsberg v. New York, 390 U.S. 629 (1968), illustrates well the Court's concern over the inability of children to make mature choices, as the First Amendment rights involved are clear examples of constitutionally protected freedoms of choice. The Court was convinced that the New York Legislature rationally could conclude that the sale to children of the magazines in question presented a danger against which they should be guarded. Ginsberg, *supra*, at 641. It therefore rejected the argument that the New York law violated the constitutional rights of minors. . . .

Third, the guiding role of parents in the upbringing of their children justifies limitations on the freedoms of minors. The State commonly protects its youth from adverse governmental action and from their own immaturity by requiring parental consent to or involvement in important decisions by minors. But an additional and more important justification for state deference to parental control over children is that "[t]he child is not the mere creature of the state; those who nurture him and direct his destiny have the right, coupled with the high duty, to recognize and prepare him for additional obligations." Pierce v. Society of Sisters, 268 U.S. 510, 535 (1925). "The duty to prepare the child for 'additional obligations' . . . must be read to include the inculcation of moral standards, religious beliefs, and elements of good citizenship." Wisconsin v. Yoder, 406 U.S. 205, 233 (1972). This affirmative process of teaching, guiding, and inspiring by precept and example is essential to the growth of young people into mature, socially responsible citizens.

We have believed in this country that this process, in large part, is beyond the competence of impersonal political institutions. Indeed, affirmative sponsorship of particular ethical, religious, or political beliefs is something we expect the State not to attempt in a society constitutionally committed to the ideal of individual liberty and freedom of choice. Thus, "[i]t is cardinal with us that the custody, care and nurture of the child reside first in the parents, whose primary function and freedom include *preparation for obligations the state can neither supply nor hinder*." Prince v. Massachusetts, *supra*, 321 U.S., at 166 (emphasis added).

Unquestionably, there are many competing theories about the most effective way for parents to fulfill their central role in assisting their children on the way to responsible adulthood. While we do not pretend any special wisdom on this subject, we cannot ignore that central to many of these theories, and deeply rooted in our Nation's history and tradition, is the belief that the parental role implies a substantial measure of authority over one's children. Indeed, "constitutional interpretation has consistently recognized that the parents' claim to authority in their own household to direct the rearing of their children is basic in the structure of our society." Ginsberg v. New York, *supra*, at 639.

Properly understood, then, the tradition of parental authority is not inconsistent with our tradition of individual liberty; rather, the former is one of the basic presuppositions of the latter. Legal restrictions on minors, especially those supportive of the parental role, may be important to the child's chances for the full growth and maturity that make eventual participation in a free society meaningful and rewarding. Under the Constitution, the State can "properly conclude that parents and others, teachers for example, who have [the] primary responsibility for children's well-being are entitled to the support of laws designed to aid discharge of that responsibility." Ginsberg v. New York, 390 U.S., at 639.

With these principles in mind, we consider the specific constitutional questions presented by these appeals. In § 12S, Massachusetts has attempted to reconcile the constitutional right of a woman, in consultation with her physician, to choose to terminate her pregnancy as established by Roe v. Wade, 410 U.S. 113 (1973), and Doe v. Bolton, 410 U.S. 179 (1973), with the special interest of the State in encouraging an unmarried pregnant minor to seek the advice of her parents in making the important decision whether or not to bear a child. . . . The question before us—in light of what we have said in the prior cases—is whether § 12S, as authoritatively interpreted by the Supreme Judicial Court, provides for parental notice and consent in a manner that does not unduly burden the right to seek an abortion.

Appellees and intervenors contend that even as interpreted by the Supreme Judicial Court of Massachusetts, § 12S does unduly burden this right. They suggest, for example, that the mere requirement of parental notice constitutes such a burden. As stated in Part II above, however, parental notice and consent are qualifications that typically may be imposed by the State on a minor's right to make important decisions. As immature minors often lack the ability to make fully informed choices that take account of both immediate and long-range consequences, a State reasonably may determine that parental consultation often is desirable and in the best interest of the minor. It may further determine, as a general proposition, that such consultation is particularly desirable with respect to the abortion decision—one that for some people raises profound moral and religious concerns. . . .

But we are concerned here with a constitutional right to seek an abortion. The abortion decision differs in important ways from other decisions that may be made during minority. The need to preserve the constitutional right and the unique nature of the abortion decision, especially when made by a minor, require a State to act with particular sensitivity when it legislates to foster parental involvement in this matter.

. . . The pregnant minor's options are much different from those facing a minor in other situations, such as deciding whether to marry. A minor not permitted to marry before the age of majority is required simply to postpone her decision. She and her intended spouse may preserve the opportunity for later marriage should they continue to desire it. A pregnant adolescent, however, cannot preserve for long the possibility of aborting, which effectively expires in a matter of weeks from the onset of pregnancy.

Moreover, the potentially severe detriment facing a pregnant woman, see Roe v. Wade, 410 U.S., at 153, is not mitigated by her minority. Indeed, considering her probable education, employment skills, financial resources, and emotional maturity, unwanted motherhood may be exceptionally burdensome for a minor. In addition, the fact of having a child brings with it adult legal responsibility, for parenthood, like attainment of the age of majority, is one of the traditional criteria for the termination of the legal disabilities of minority. In sum, there are few situations in which denying a minor the right to make an important decision will have consequences so grave and indelible.

Yet, an abortion may not be the best choice for the minor. The circumstances in which this issue arises will vary widely. In a given case, alternatives to abortion, such as marriage to the father of the child, arranging for its adoption, or assuming the responsibilities of motherhood with the assured support of family, may be feasible and relevant to the minor's best interests. Nonetheless, the abortion decision is one that simply cannot be postponed, or it will be made by default with far-reaching consequences.

For these reasons, as we held in Planned Parenthood of Central Missouri v. Danforth, "the State may not impose a blanket provision . . . requiring the consent of a parent or person *in loco parentis* as a condition for abortion of an unmarried minor during the first 12 weeks of her pregnancy." Although, as stated in Part II, *supra*, such deference to parents may be permissible with respect to other choices facing a minor, the unique nature and consequences of the abortion decision make it inappropriate "to give a third party an absolute, and possibly arbitrary, veto over the decision of the physician and his patient to terminate the patient's pregnancy, regardless of the reason for withholding the consent." We therefore conclude that if the State decides to require a pregnant minor to obtain one or both parents' consent to an abortion, it also must provide an alternative procedure whereby authorization for the abortion can be obtained.

A pregnant minor is entitled in such a proceeding to show either: (1) that she is mature enough and well enough informed to make her abortion decision, in consultation with her physician, independently of her parents' wishes; or (2) that even if she is not able to make this decision independently, the desired abortion would be in her best interests. The proceeding in which this showing is made must assure that a resolution of the issue, and any appeals that may follow, will be completed with anonymity and sufficient expedition to provide an effective opportunity for an abortion to be obtained. In sum, the procedure must ensure that the provision requiring parental consent does not in fact amount to the "absolute, and possibly arbitrary, veto" that was found impermissible in *Danforth*.

Among the questions certified to the Supreme Judicial Court was whether § 12S permits any minors—mature or immature—to obtain judicial consent to an abortion without any parental consultation whatsoever. The state court answered that, in general, it does not. "[T]he consent required by [§ 12S must] be obtained for every nonemergency abortion where the mother is less than eighteen years of age and unmarried." . . .

We think that, construed in this manner, § 12S would impose an undue burden upon the exercise by minors of the right to seek an abortion. As the District Court recognized, "there are parents who would obstruct, and perhaps altogether prevent, the minor's right to go to court." There is no reason to believe that this would be so in the majority of cases where consent is withheld. But many parents hold strong views on the subject of abortion, and young pregnant minors, especially those living at home, are particularly vulnerable to their parents' efforts to obstruct both an abortion and their access to court. It would be unrealistic, therefore, to assume that the mere existence of a legal right to seek relief in superior court provides an effective avenue of relief for some of those who need it the most.

We conclude, therefore, that under state regulation such as that undertaken by Massachusetts, every minor must have the opportunity—if she so desires—to go directly to a court without first consulting or notifying her parents. If she satisfies the court that she is mature and well enough informed to make intelligently the abortion decision on her own, the court must authorize her to act without parental consultation or consent. If she fails to satisfy the court that she is competent to make this decision independently, she must be permitted to show that an abortion nevertheless would be in her best interests. If the court is persuaded that it is, the court must authorize the abortion. If, however, the court is not persuaded by the minor that she is mature or that the abortion would be in her best interests, it may decline to sanction the operation.

There is, however, an important state interest in encouraging a family rather than a judicial resolution of a minor's abortion decision. Also, as we have observed above, parents naturally take an interest in the welfare of their children—an interest that is particularly strong where a normal family relationship exists and where the child is living with one or both parents. These factors properly may be taken into account by a court called upon to determine whether an abortion in fact is in a minor's best interests. If, all things considered, the court determines that an abortion is in the minor's best interests, she is entitled to court authorization without any parental involvement. On the other hand, the court may deny the abortion request of an immature minor in the absence of parental consultation if it concludes that her best interests would be served thereby, or the court may in such a case defer decision until there is parental consultation in which the court may participate. But this is the full extent to which parental involvement may be required. For the reasons stated above, the constitutional right to seek an abortion may not be unduly burdened by state-imposed conditions upon initial access to court. . . .

Affirmed.

NOTES AND QUESTIONS

1. Does *Bellotti* actually protect a mature minor's right to make her own decision regarding abortion? Or, as Professor Guggenheim argues, does it simply shift power over minors from their parents to judges? Martin Guggenheim, Minor Rights: The Adolescent Abortion Cases, 30 Hofstra L. Rev. 589 (2002).

2. Compare *Bellotti*'s approach to minors' and parents' roles in making the abortion decision to the approach in Wisconsin v. Yoder. Is a decision regarding abortion more important for a child's development than a decision to remove her from a school and community after the eighth grade? On what basis would one distinguish these decisions?

The risk of death from complications related to childbirth is far higher than the risk from having an abortion. Moreover, teenagers have an even lower risk of experiencing complications associated with abortion. *See* Nancy E. Russo, Adolescent Abortion: The Epidemiological Context, in Adolescent Abortion: Psychological and Legal Issues 40, 59 (Gary Melton ed., 1986). The limited data on the psychological risks of abortion are not definitive, but they do not support a claim that abortion places most teens at higher risk of psychological problems in the long term. A 2010 study using data from the National Longitudinal Study of Adolescent Health found that teens who had had abortions were not at higher risk for depression or low self-esteem in the short term or for up to five years after the abortion. Jocelyn T. Warren, S. Marie Harvey & Jillian T. Henderson, Do Depression and Low Self-Esteem Follow Abortion Among Adolescents? Evidence from a National Study, 42 Persp. Sexual & Reprod. Health 230 (2010).

3. *Bellotti says* that minors' vulnerability justifies limiting their right to consent to an abortion. In this context, what does vulnerability mean? How does vulnerability differ from lack of capacity to make sound decisions? On the various meanings of "vulnerability" and how courts use it to explain why the law treats children differently from adults, *see* Lois A. Weithorn, A Constitutional Jurisprudence of Children's Vulnerability, 69 Hastings L. J. 179 (2017).

4. What role does *Bellotti* identify for parental rights? The Court refers to a parental role in protecting children from the consequences of their own immaturity and recognizes "an additional and more important justification for state deference to parental control over children: the parents' right to recognize and prepare [their child] for additional obligations." Can the holding in *Bellotti* be adequately explained on either of these principles?

If parental rights derive from parents' presumptive capacity to identify and promote the child's own interests, on what basis does the Court conclude that parents cannot be trusted to do so with respect to procreative decisions? Are decisions to prohibit an abortion equivalent to neglectful conduct, which is always regarded as an exception to the presumption that parents will promote their children's best interests?

If parents' rights are understood as rights to express the parents' own values and personalities through the way they raise their children, how does one justify a decision to deny that liberty with respect to a decision that draws on fundamental moral values?

5. *Bellotti* states that "[i]t seems unlikely that [a girl of tender years] will obtain adequate counsel and support from the attending physician at an abortion clinic. . . . " Why is that so unlikely? Will she receive better counsel and support from a court? From a pro-life counseling service? From her parents?

If medical advice from abortion clinics cannot be relied upon, is there an adequate reason for distinguishing between mature and immature minors?

6. Even if the state and parental interests must give way substantially to a mature minor's choice regarding abortion, why cannot the state give the parent such a veto when the minor is not sufficiently mature to choose for herself? Whose interests is the Court protecting in *Bellotti*? The child is, by hypothesis, too immature for a "right" (autonomy) claim to be recognized. The state, for its part, has sought to express its interest by relying on parental judgment and discretion. The parental interest, on whatever basis it may rest, seems therefore to coincide with the state's own definition of its interest in this area. What kind of interest remains to be enforced? How does the decision formulate that interest?

7. A number of cases since *Bellotti* have dealt with parental consent. All but one have resulted in a declaration that the statutory requirement is unconstitutional because it lacks some required exception to the consent requirement, *e.g.*, Akron v. Center for Reproductive Health, 462 U.S. 416 (1983) (no alternative judicial procedure for authorizing abortion); Wynn v. Carey, 582 F.2d 1375 (7th Cir. 1978) (no permission for judge to grant an abortion in the best interests of immature minor). Planned Parenthood of Kansas City, Mo. v. Ashcroft, 462 U.S. 476 (1983), held a parental consent statute modeled on Powell's *Bellotti* opinion constitutional. Planned Parenthood v. Casey, 505 U.S. 833 (1992), reaffirmed the previous decisions regarding parental consent.

8. Is a requirement of parental notice subject to the same constitutional limits as parental consent? In H.L. v. Matheson, 450 U.S. 398 (1981), the Court rejected a facial challenge to a statute requiring the doctor to notify parents if possible before performing an abortion on a minor. The Court said that the statute could be applied constitutionally to immature minors on the basis that it "plainly serves the important considerations of family integrity and protecting adolescents that we identified in *Bellotti II*. In addition, as applied to that class the statute serves

a significant state interest by providing an opportunity for parents to supply essential medical and other information to the physician. . . . " 450 U.S. at 411. The Court did not consider the constitutionality of requiring notice to the parents of a mature minor because there was no evidence about the petitioner's maturity, and it did not discuss the need for a bypass procedure because there was no evidence that notifying the petitioner's parents would not be in her best interests. Justices Powell and Stewart concurred on the bare record in this case but suggested that the State could not validly require notice to parents in all cases "without providing an independent decision maker to whom the minor can have recourse if she believes that she is mature enough to make the abortion decision independently or that notification otherwise would not be in her best interests." *Id.* at 413, 420. Justice Marshall, joined by Justices Brennan and Blackmun, dissented.

In Hodgson v. Minnesota, 497 U.S. 417 (1990), a fractured Court held unconstitutional a statute that required notice to both parents and did not include a bypass procedure unless parental abuse of the child had been reported to the authorities. The Court also held that a requirement of notice to both parents is constitutional if the statute provides a bypass option. A majority of the justices treated consent and notice as functionally equivalent for constitutional purposes under these circumstances, but Justices Kennedy, White, Rehnquist, and Scalia disagreed. While Justice Stevens argued that notice to both parents is not necessary to protect the child and so is unconstitutional even with a bypass provision, Justice Kennedy for the majority concluded that the provision protects parents' independent interests in participating in the care and rearing of their children.

Ayotte v. Planned Parenthood, 546 U.S. 320 (2006), concerned a statute that required parental notice unless the minor faced a risk of death and included a judicial bypass provision. The petitioner argued that the statute was unconstitutional because it did not include an exception for minors facing a risk of serious physical injury. The state conceded that it would be unconstitutional to apply the statute to a minor who faced a medical emergency involving a serious physical risk. The Supreme Court remanded the case for a determination of whether the constitutional infirmity could be cured by a remedy less drastic than enjoining enforcement of the whole statute. The legislature repealed the act in 2007.

9. How would a trial judge go about deciding whether a minor is sufficiently mature to make her own decision about abortion? Empirical studies agree that by age 15, minors engage in adult-like decision-making cognitive processes. Grisso & Vierling, Minors' Consent to Treatment: A Developmental Perspective, 9 Prof. Psych. 412 (1978). *See generally* Gary B. Melton, Children's Competence to Consent in Children's Competence to Consent 1 (Gary B. Melton, Gerald P. Koocher & Michael J. Saks eds., 1983).

Perhaps competence is a matter of moral judgment, not merely the cognitive ability to reason. Theorists describe moral development in terms how a person reasons based on ethical principles. A leading scholar argues that moral development occurs through distinct stages. At each stage, a person reasons differently about moral issues. Kohlberg identifies three general levels of moral judgment: preconventional, conventional, and post-conventional. At the preconventional level, a person understands "good" and "bad" only in terms of physical consequences and power. Good actions avoid punishment or, later on, produce satisfaction for oneself. At the conventional level, a person's moral reasoning is structured by the fixed rules of the person's society and family group. What one intends becomes important, as does "doing one's duty." Post-conventional moral judgment requires that a person develop moral principles for oneself, rather than relying on the authority of others. There are, of course, levels within the post-conventional stage, as there are for the other stages. Kohlberg places a "social contract" stage, with legalistic and utilitarian overtones, at the beginning, followed by development of conscientious decisions based not on legal authority but on a universal ethic, including notions of respect for individuals and the equality of human rights. Teens develop to the post-conventional stage by the end of high school, with further development typically during the mid-twenties. *See* June L. Tapp & Lawrence Kohlberg, Developing Sense of Law and Legal Justice, in Law, Justice, and the Individual in Society 89, 90-92 (June L. Tapp & Felice J. Levine eds., 1977).

Kohlberg's research has been criticized as specific to male moral development, most notably by Carol Gilligan, In a Different Voice: Psychological Theory and Women's Development (1982). The research supporting this theory includes a study of abortion, conducted from 1973 to 1975 in the immediate aftermath of Roe v. Wade, involving interviews with 29 women, ranging in age from 15 to 33, who came from diverse ethnic backgrounds and social classes. The study was "designed to clarify the ways in which women construct and resolve abortion decisions," and concluded that women were constructing the dilemma in a way that was completely at odds with the way in which issues were formulated in the public debate. Rather than a conflict between two individually grounded rights claims, opposing mothers and fetuses or women and men, Gilligan reports that the women she interviewed saw the question as a relational one in which harm would necessarily be done. The scope of interests included not only the woman and the fetus, but her parents and others who might be affected by the decision. *Id.* at 71-105. *See also* Carol Gilligan, Remembering Larry, 27 J. Moral Educ. 25 (1998) (reviewing this part of her research). Professor Gilligan argues that women tend to adopt a "caring" rather than hierarchical perspective. For a review and critique of that theory, *see* On In a Different Voice: An Interdisciplinary Forum, 11 Signs 304-333 (1986).

10. Researchers surveyed minors in Massachusetts who had been found mature enough in a bypass hearing to make their own decisions to learn why they chose to have an abortion and not to involve their parents. Roughly a third of the young women were white, a third black, and a third Latina. Their mean age was 16.3 years, three-fourths lived with one or both parents, and 85 percent were in school. The teens gave multiple reasons for having an abortion, most commonly not being ready to be a mother, future plans, life circumstances, and concerns about the children. About a quarter of the respondents thought their parents would be extremely upset and might harm them or kick them out. Others feared parental pressure to keep the baby or damage to their relationship with their parents. J. Shoshanna Ehrlich, Grounded in the Reality of Their Lives: Listening to Teens Who Make the Abortion Decision without Involving Their Parents, 18 Berkeley Women's L.J. 61 (2003).

11. What further inquiry should the court make if it decides that the minor is not sufficiently "mature"? A court would likely find that making the decision regarding abortion without involving parents would be in the minor's best interest if the evidence shows that she has been abused by her parents. In other

circumstances, how is a court to decide whether parental consultation is necessary to its resolution of the issue and, if not, whether an abortion is in the child's "best interests"? Is parental consultation important to learning something about the child or about the parents?

NOTE: PARENTAL INVOLVEMENT IN TEENAGE ABORTION AND THE JUDICIAL BYPASS OPTION

In 2018, 37 states required parental involvement in their minor daughters' abortions. Five states required both notice and consent, 21 required consent only, and 11 required notice only. Of those requiring consent, 3 required consent of both parents; 1 required notice to both parents. All but 1 of the states had judicial bypass procedures, although some applied only to consent requirements, and 7 also allowed grandparent or other adult relative involvement as an alternative to parental participation. Thirty-four states made an exception for medical emergencies, and 15 made an exception for cases of abuse, assault, incest, or neglect. Five more states have enacted laws requiring parental involvement in their minor daughters' abortions that have been temporarily or permanently enjoined. Guttmacher Institute, Parental Involvement in Minors' Abortions (July 1, 2018). Two states explicitly allow all minors to consent to abortion, and 5 states have no explicit statutory or case law. Guttmacher Institute, An Overview of Minors' Consent Law (July 1, 2018). For details on each state's laws, *see* http:// www.guttmacher.org/. The specifics of the bypass process vary significantly from state to state. *See* Rachel Rebouche, Parental Involvement Laws and New Governance, 34 Harv. J.L. & Gender 175, 183-188 (2011), for an overview.

Teenage abortion rates rose during the 1970s, stabilized during the 1980s at about 43 per 1,000 among women aged 15 to 19, and then declined to about 14 per 1,000 by 2011. The rate declined by 67 percent between 1990 and 2011. One reason for the decline is a drop in the incidence of teen pregnancy, but the proportion of teen pregnancies ending in abortion declined from a peak of 40 percent in 1985 to about 25 percent in 2011. Child Trends Data Bank, Teen Abortions 3 (Oct. 2016).

The relationship between parental involvement laws and teen abortion rates is not clear. In a literature review of 29 studies of the impact of parental involvement laws on a variety of outcomes, researchers found that the clearest documented effect is an increase in the number of minors who leave the state to go to another state that has fewer or no restrictions. Amanda Dennis et al., The Impact of Laws Requiring Parental Involvement for Abortion: A Literature Review 27 (Guttmacher Institute, Mar. 2009). The researchers point out methodological flaws with many of the studies; in particular, most of the studies did not account for young women who went out of state, which would cause lower reported abortion rates in states from which the minors left and higher rates in the states to which they went. The report summarized its findings:

> The state case studies yielded mixed results concerning effects of parental involvement laws on minors' abortion rates. In Massachusetts, the number of abortions was about what would have been expected if preexisting trends had continued and out-of-state abortions were counted. Similarly, the Mississippi law appeared to have little

effect on the number of abortions or births. In South Carolina, however, the abortion ratio among white 16-year-olds fell even in analyses that took into account out-of-state terminations. In Minnesota, the number of abortions also fell, with no corresponding increase in births, although the number of minors who sought services out of state is unknown. The clearest result is from Texas, where the abortion rate decreased and the birthrate increased among women slightly younger than age 18 in comparison with women slightly older than this age.

Taken together, these findings suggest that most parental involvement laws have little impact on minors' abortion rate and, by extension, on birthrates and pregnancy rates. However, the Texas study illustrates that in some cases, the laws may compel a small proportion of minors to continue unwanted pregnancies. The similar pattern found in Missouri could be real, or it could reflect missing data on residents' out-of-state abortions.

Id. at 27-28. A more recent study, conducted after it became more difficult for minors to travel to states with more liberal laws, found that imposing a parental notification requirement was associated with a decrease in the number of minors who had abortions, as well as delayed care for minors coming from out of state. Lauren J. Ralph, Ph.D. et al, The Impact of a Parental Notification Requirement on Illinois Minors' Access to and Decision-Making Around Abortion, 62 J. Adolescent Health 281 (2018). A study published in 2010 found that converting a parental notification requirement to a parental consent law was not associated with a change in the abortion rate. Ted Joyce, Parental Consent for Abortion and the Judicial Bypass Option in Arkansas: Effects and Correlates, 42(3) Perspect. Sex. Reprod. Health 168 (2010).

Aside from requiring notice to or consent of both parents, state statutes conditioning minors' abortion rights on parental involvement did not change very much until 2014. In that year Alabama amended its judicial bypass statute to require that the hearing on a minor's petition look very much like a trial and that more parties be involved in the hearing. The following trial court decision, which has been appealed to the Eleventh Circuit, considers the constitutionality of these provisions.

REPRODUCTIVE HEALTH SERVICES v. MARSHALL

268 F. Supp. 3d 1261 (M.D. Ala. 2017)

SUSAN RUSS WALKER, United States Magistrate Judge. . . . Alabama law mandates that "no physician shall perform an abortion upon an unemancipated minor unless the physician or his or her agents first obtain the written consent of either parent or the legal guardian of the minor." There are limited exceptions to the parental consent requirement, one of which is the judicial bypass exception. As a matter of law, states that have parental consent statutes must also enact a law that allows a minor to obtain a court order to bypass her parent's or guardian's consent. In *RHS I*, the court summarized the pertinent provisions of Alabama's judicial bypass law as follows.

Prior to the 2014 amendments, Alabama's judicial bypass statute allowed for an ex parte hearing which included as participants, in almost all instances, only the judge, the minor applicant, and her attorney. The new Act substantially alters the former bypass scheme; it is allegedly unique among all other states' judicial bypass laws.

Under Alabama's former judicial bypass law, which was enacted in 1987 and remained substantively unchanged for 27 years, the only necessary party to the bypass proceedings identified by statute was the minor petitioner. At his or her discretion, the presiding judge also could use a provision of the Alabama Rules of Civil procedure to appoint a guardian ad litem ("GAL") to represent the interests of the "infant unborn," but the judicial bypass law did not independently permit the appointment of a GAL or vest that person with the same rights as a party to the bypass proceedings. A minor petitioner was entitled to a decision from the reviewing court within 72 hours after filing her petition, excluding Saturdays, Sundays and legal holidays, unless the petitioner requested an extension of time and the court permitted the delay. The minor was the only person with standing to appeal the decision of the reviewing judge. "If notice of appeal [were] given, the record of appeal [was to] be completed and the appeal [was to be] perfected within five days from the filing of the notice of appeal."

The 2014 Act expands the number of potential parties to a judicial bypass proceeding and makes the inclusion of some of those parties mandatory. Those additional parties are either required or permitted to "examine" the petitioner and to represent interests in addition to those of the petitioner, including the interests of the State of Alabama, the unborn child, and the minor's parent(s) or legal guardian. For example, when a minor files a judicial bypass petition, the court now must immediately notify the district attorney ("DA") of the county in which the petition is filed or in which the petitioner resides, and the DA is then automatically joined as a necessary party to the bypass proceedings. The 2014 Act also allows the minor's parent(s) or legal guardian to be joined as parties if those individuals learn of the existence of the proceedings. The new law contains a statutory provision independent of Alabama Rule of Civil Procedure 17(c) which allows the reviewing court to appoint a GAL to represent "the interests of the unborn child[.]" The powers of the GAL are expansive, and that person also is joined as a party once appointed by the court.

In addition, the 2014 Act codifies the rights and obligations of the DA, GAL, and the parent(s) or legal guardian in their capacities as parties. The DA and the GAL are statutorily mandated to "participate as [advocates] for the state to examine the petitioner and any witnesses[.]" Alabama's interests, as explained by the Act, include "protecting minors from their own immaturity" and "protect[ing] the state's public policy to protect unborn life[.]" The minor's parents, once joined as parties, have the same rights as the DA, GAL, and the minor petitioner. All parties may be represented by an attorney, appeal the hearing judge's decision, request extensions of time, and have access to subpoena powers to compel witnesses to testify.

Moreover, the 2014 Act replaces the requirement in the former law that the hearing judge must issue a decision within 72 hours and the appeal must be "perfected" within five days. The law permits discretionary delays by the reviewing judge, either *sua sponte* or upon request by any party, "subject to the time constraints of the petitioner related to her medical condition."

The legal framework that applies to the substance of plaintiffs' *Bellotti II* claim begins with the well-established right of a minor to obtain an abortion of a non-viable fetus.

The Constitution protects a woman's right to terminate her pregnancy. This right, derived from the Due Process Clause of the Fourteenth Amendment, was reaffirmed by the U.S. Supreme Court in Planned Parenthood v. Casey, 505 U.S. 833 (1992), which left intact the essential holding of Roe v. Wade, 410 U.S. 113 (1973). This right is not limitless, however; the State has legitimate interests in protecting the health of the woman and the potential life of a fetus. Accordingly, the Court in *Casey* developed a standard to distinguish between lawful state regulation of abortion and regulation that violates due process. The Court held that when a regulation imposes a "substantial obstacle in the path of a woman seeking an abortion of a nonviable fetus," it unduly burdens the right to choose abortion. And "where state regulation imposes an undue burden . . . the power of the State reach[es] into the heart of the liberty protected by the Due Process Clause." . . .

"The rule announced in *Casey* . . . requires that courts consider the burdens a law imposes on abortion access together with the benefits those laws confer." Whole Woman's Health v. Hellerstedt, ___ U.S. ___, 136 S. Ct. 2292, 2309 (2016). . . .

The judicial bypass requirements espoused in *Bellotti II* are "strict standards." "Under *Bellotti*, a pregnant minor is entitled to show the court either: '(1) that she is mature enough and well enough informed to make her abortion decision, in consultation with her physician, independently of her parents' wishes; or (2) that even if she is not able to make this decision independently, the desired abortion would be in her best interests.'" Once the minor makes either showing, the bypass petition must be granted. The *Bellotti II* requirements, as summarized by the Supreme Court, consist of four factors that a judicial bypass law must satisfy to pass constitutional muster: (1) the bypass procedure must afford the minor an opportunity to demonstrate that she is sufficiently mature to make an informed decision to have an abortion "without regard to her parents' wishes"; (2) the abortion procedure must be authorized if the court finds that, despite a minor's inability to reach an abortion decision "by herself[,]" "the abortion is in the minor's best interests and in cases where the minor has shown a pattern of physical, sexual, or emotional abuse"; (3) the bypass procedure "must insure the minor's anonymity"; and (4) the bypass exception must allow the minor a court to conduct proceedings with the expediency necessary "to allow an effective opportunity to obtain the abortion." "Otherwise, the attendant bypass procedure is constitutionally invalid." . . .

The court is mindful that, in applying *Casey*'s undue burden test, it must "consider the burdens a law imposes on abortion access together with the benefits those laws confer," as noted above. *Hellerstedt*, 136 S. Ct. at 2309. . . . According to the Act, the purposes of the legislation are both "to . . . establish and protect the rights of the minor mother" and "to protect the state's public policy to protect unborn life"—and, specifically, to do so, "in part, by requiring judges to make determinations pursuant to the judicial by-pass procedure and [by requiring] judges [to] be provided with sufficient evidence and information upon which they may make informed and proper decisions. The Act also affirms the State's interest in enacting a constitutional bypass procedure. . . .

The court is also mindful, in considering the State interests articulated by the Legislature, that even if those interests are legitimate, the means chosen to further such interests are not constitutionally permissible if they place a substantial obstacle in the path of a woman's choice. *Casey*, 505 U.S. at 877 ("A finding of an undue burden is a shorthand for the conclusion that a state regulation has the purpose or effect of placing a substantial obstacle in the path of a woman seeking an abortion of a nonviable fetus. A statute with this purpose is invalid because the means chosen by the State to further the interest in potential life must be calculated to inform the woman's free choice, not hinder it. And a statute which, while furthering the interest in potential life or some other valid state interest, has the effect of placing a substantial obstacle in the path of a woman's choice cannot be considered a permissible means of serving its legitimate ends."). Indeed, the undue burden test itself embodies a balance between competing interests; it was expressly framed by the Supreme Court to accommodate the State's interest in protecting unborn life while also protecting a woman's right to choose.

Thus, while the State's legitimate interests and the Act's benefits are considered by the court below, these are not alone dispositive—a statute that restricts abortion access and that is justified by a legitimate State interest will fail constitutional scrutiny if it poses a "substantial obstacle" to a minor's liberty interest in reaching an abortion decision through a judicial bypass. . . .

1.   Parental involvement as parties to the bypass

The Act provides a mechanism for a minor petitioner's parent, parents, or legal guardian to participate as parties to the bypass proceeding.

> Although the court shall not be required or permitted to contact the minor's parent, parents, or legal guardian, in the event that the minor's parent, parents, or legal guardian are otherwise aware of the by-pass proceeding, they, he, or she shall be given notice of and be permitted to participate in the proceeding and be represented by counsel with all of the rights and obligations of any party to the proceeding.

The controlling opinion in *Bellotti II* is clear that "every pregnant minor is entitled in the first instance to go directly to the court for a judicial determination without prior parental notice, consultation, or consent[.]" . . . The requirement of the Act that parents who become aware of a judicial bypass proceeding be given formal notice of that proceeding and permitted to participate in it and be represented by counsel as parties, facilitates and, indeed, invites such obstruction, and oversteps the bounds of parental involvement set by *Bellotti II.*

Those bounds are clearly drawn. If a minor "satisfies the court that she is mature and well enough informed to make intelligently the abortion decision on her own, the court must authorize her to act without parental consultation or consent." If the minor "fails to satisfy the court that she is competent to make this decision independently, she must be permitted to show that an abortion nevertheless would be in her best interests." "If, all things considered, the court determines that an abortion is in the minor's best interests, she is entitled to court authorization without any parental involvement." Only if the court concludes that an immature minor's best interests would be served by denial of the abortion request may the court choose to defer decision until there is parental consultation, in which the court may participate. As the *Bellotti II* Court was at pains to emphasize, "this is the full extent to which parental involvement may be required." . . .

By providing a statutory mechanism for some parents or legal guardians to participate as parties to the bypass proceeding—and also to appeal any decision by the bypass court—the Act eviscerates the judicial bypass mandate of *Bellotti II* as to the minors affected. . . . Under the strict guidelines of *Bellotti II*, this section of the Act is unconstitutional.

2. *Anonymity of the petitioner and confidentiality of bypass proceeding*

Plaintiffs also argue that the Act is unconstitutional because it fails to ensure the affected minors' confidentiality. . . . Alabama Code § 26–21–4(c) provides, in relevant part, as follows:

> The minor's identity shall be kept confidential, but her identity may be made known to the judge, any guardian ad litem, the district attorney or any representative of the district attorney's office of the county where the minor is a resident or the county where the abortion is to be performed, any appropriate court personnel, any witness who has a need to know the minor's identity, or any other person determined by the court who needs to know. Any person who is given the identity of the minor shall keep her name confidential and shall not give it to any other person, unless otherwise ordered by the court.

If the court determines at the initial hearing on the petition that additional evidence or testimony is necessary, it may adjourn the hearing and "issue instanter subpoenas or otherwise permit any party or participant in the hearing to bring before the court admissible evidence or testimony either in support of or against the petition."

As to any appeal of the bypass court's decision, "[a]n expedited confidential and anonymous appeal shall be available to any minor to whom the court denies a waiver of consent, the district attorney's office, and any guardian ad litem, or the parent, parents, or legal guardian of the minor." The Act further provides that

> Records and information involving court proceedings conducted pursuant to [the Act] shall be confidential and shall not be disclosed other than to the minor, her attorney, and necessary court personnel. . . . Any person who shall disclose any records or information made confidential pursuant to [the foregoing sentence] shall be guilty of a Class C misdemeanor.

The defendants assert that these provisions, and particularly the fact that Alabama law criminalizes disclosure of information regarding a bypass proceeding, provide reasonable assurance of confidentiality.

Under *Bellotti II*, a minor is entitled to an "anonymous" judicial bypass to a state's parental consent law. Eleven years after *Bellotti II*, the plurality opinion in *Akron II* determined that "anonymity," as used by the *Bellotti II* plurality, did not mean "complete anonymity," and that a bypass statute is facially constitutional if it "takes reasonable steps to prevent the public from learning of the minor's identity." The Court distinguished between "complete anonymity" and the practical need to disclose a minor petitioner's identity to court personnel "for administrative purposes, not for public disclosure." . . .

Since *Akron II*, decisions from other courts have provided little in the way of guidance in interpreting the Supreme Court's holding that complete anonymity is not "critical," or in deciding what steps are "reasonable . . . to prevent the public from learning the minor's identity." Moreover, at no point has the word "public" been clearly defined in the context of a judicial bypass law. Still, it is clear that "confidentiality during and after [a judicial bypass] proceeding is essential to ensure that a minor will not be deterred from exercising her right to a hearing because of fear that her parents may be notified." Again, "[t]he [judicial bypass] proceeding . . . must assure that a resolution of the issue, and any appeals that may follow, will be completed with anonymity and sufficient expedition to provide an effective opportunity for an abortion to be obtained" and "the state must take reasonable steps to prevent the public from learning of the minor's identity."

The Act runs afoul of these essential requirements. As noted above, defendants argue that the statute does more than impose the kind of non-specific confidentiality requirement found insufficient by other federal courts, because Alabama Code § 26–21–8 makes disclosure of information about a judicial bypass proceeding a criminal act. . . .

Other provisions of the Act render § 26–21–8 impotent as an assurance of anonymity and confidentiality. Under the Act, the DA shall be notified and joined as a party and may designate a representative to participate in a bypass proceeding. A GAL for the fetus and the minors' parents or legal guardians may also be brought within the universe of persons authorized to learn about the minor's identity and the pendency of her judicial bypass petition and permitted to participate in the bypass proceeding. Thus, although § 26–21–8 prohibits and criminalizes disclosure of records and information involving court proceedings under § 26–21–4 other than "to the minor, her attorney, and necessary court personnel," disclosure concerning such proceedings to the office of the DA, to GALs, and to parents or guardians of affected minors clearly is permitted by other sections of the Act. The addition of these parties to the list of those to whom the petitioner's identity may be disclosed compromises the minor's anonymity to a degree well beyond the scope permitted by *Bellotti II* and any case decided in the intervening four decades.

The Act's provisions allowing parties or the court to investigate, gather evidence, and issue subpoenas, as well as the involvement of witnesses who have the right to participate in the proceedings for the purpose of presenting evidence and requesting delays, also breach the minors' anonymity and the confidentiality of the proceedings. In addition, the Act contains a catch-all exception to § 26–21–8: bypass information and the minor's identity may permissibly be shared with "any appropriate court personnel, any witness who has a need to know the minor's identity, or any other person determined by the court who needs to know. Any person who is given the identity of the minor shall keep her name confidential and shall not give it to any other person, unless otherwise ordered by the court." In other words, the bypass court acts wholly within its statutory discretion in authorizing disclosure to an unlimited number of people, including witnesses who may be called by the DA, the GAL, or a parent or guardian to offer "admissible evidence or testimony either in support of or against the petition." Of course, in order to possess relevant information on the subject of the minor's maturity, whether she is sufficiently informed about the abortion decision, and her best interests, such witnesses almost inevitably would have to be relatives, friends, or acquaintances of the petitioner herself—precisely those members of "the public" whom she is most likely not to want informed about her decision, and whose opposition to the petition could become coercive. Further, those who are privy to the protected information, although required to treat it as confidential themselves without further authorization, may disclose that information if the court so directs.

This is a very far cry from the strictly limited disclosure to court personnel for administrative purposes that was approved by *Akron II*. On the contrary, the Act "raise[s] the specter of public exposure and harassment of women who choose to exercise their personal, intensely private, right, with their physician, to end a pregnancy. Thus, [it poses] an unacceptable danger of deterring the exercise of that right and must be invalidated." . . .

3.   *Burdens of the Act*

In reaching the foregoing conclusions, the court has carefully considered the benefits conferred by the provisions in question together with the burdens they impose on abortion access, as directed by the Court in *Hellerstedt*. Defendants maintain that the purpose of the Act is "to provide Alabama bypass courts 'guidance in determining appropriate procedure and evidence'—so that the courts will have 'sufficient evidence and information' to 'make informed and proper decisions.'" "As a secondary goal, [the Act] also facilitate[s] the provision of 'guidance and assistance' to the girls who are attempting to make such a momentous decision on their own."

As to the latter, defendants do not indicate specifically how the challenged provisions of the Act offer pregnant minors any kind of guidance or assistance. The court can only speculate that defendants might be claiming some incidental—and unexplained—salutary effect emanating from the bypass proceeding itself, perhaps resulting from the minor's being cross-examined by the DA or the GAL for the fetus, or from her being privy to the testimony of a parent or a witness for an opposing party. But the Act itself is silent on this subject; it offers no clue at all as to how the challenged provisions might be designed to serve the Legislature's goal of "provid[ing] guidance and assistance to minors who find themselves in the unfortunate position of having to make [an abortion] decision[.]" . . .

Indeed, the bypass proceeding would be redundant as a tool for the counseling of the minor; the petitioner herself is charged by statute, in an unchallenged portion of the Act, with providing the court "probative and admissible evidence" that she has been informed of and understands the medical procedure and its consequences, and that she has been counseled by a "qualified person" as to the alternatives to abortion. She must "explain each of the foregoing to the court," and the court "shall be satisfied that she is making an informed judgment and shall document its finding in its order." The petitioner also must present "such additional probative evidence" to the court of her maturity as will demonstrate that she has "sufficient experience with and understanding of life" to enable her to make mature and informed decisions. These are prerequisites to the minor's obtaining relief. Charging the bypass court itself with the responsibility of providing the petitioner with an appropriate education concerning her choice via the addition of the parties and witnesses permitted by the Act—after the minor has already received expert counseling and has presented evidence to that effect and has also offered proof of her achievement of the requisite level of experience with and understanding of life—would be duplicative of these mandates.

Nor is it clear that a parent, guardian, DA, GAL, or witness would ordinarily represent a "qualified person" capable of educating the minor concerning the health risks, alternatives to abortion, and other factors that are material to an abortion decision. Finally, the bypass court is hardly the appropriate setting for such counseling, in any event; it is neither a physician's office, nor a classroom, nor any other such place of instruction or guidance. The only proper purpose of the bypass proceeding under *Belotti II* is the adjudication of the minor's maturity and whether she is well enough informed to make the abortion decision on her own, or, failing that, where her best interests lie.

Absent the Legislature's explicit expression of the intent to provide the minor guidance and assistance by means of the challenged portions of the Act, the court turns to the consideration of those provisions as they relate to the Legislature's stated objective of requiring judges in bypass proceedings "[to] be provided with sufficient evidence and information upon which they may make informed and proper decisions." In this regard, the Act says specifically that the DA, the GAL, and the witnesses called by the parties should present evidence for the purpose of assisting the court in making an informed decision and in doing substantial justice.

Notably, however, no such reason is given for the participation of parents or guardians who are "otherwise aware" of the bypass proceeding. Further, although the Act indicates generally that the DA, the GAL for the fetus, and the witnesses called by these parties should assist the court in making an informed decision and in doing substantial justice, it says little else on the subject. For example, it makes no finding that judicial bypass proceedings previously undertaken under Alabama's former bypass law—"which was enacted in 1987 and remained substantively unchanged for 27 years," and in which "the only necessary party to the bypass proceedings identified by statute was the minor petitioner"—were in fact deficient in developing the evidence necessary for bypass courts to decide the issues properly before them. Also, the necessity for these additional persons to help the court in making an informed and proper decision is called into question by the fact that some bypass proceedings will still go forward under the Act without any of the new participants; the statute permits, but does not mandate, the involvement of parents or a guardian who do not otherwise know of the petition, the GAL for the unborn child, and other unspecified additional witnesses. One must assume that the Legislature is satisfied that such petitions will proceed with sufficient evidence for the judge to adjudicate properly even without the required participation of these individuals.

In addition, the Act specifically directs the bypass court to deny an inadequately supported petition. And, indeed, the Alabama courts traditionally have not hesitated to deny a waiver when the minor failed to meet her burden of proof. Thus, the statute itself, the long-standing practice of the Alabama courts, and *Bellotti II* all ensure that any petition which the bypass court finds legally unsupported simply will not prevail.

Finally, the court has located *no other state* which either mandates or permits participation by a parent or guardian, the DA, a GAL for the fetus, or witnesses (other than those called by the minor) in bypass proceedings for the purpose of providing the court with assistance in arriving at informed and proper decisions—or, indeed, for any other purpose. Some states, either by choice or by court order, do not mandate parental consent or notification at all, and therefore have no bypass procedures. The 37 states that do have bypass statutes of some kind simply do not authorize such participation. Indeed, some states go so far as affirmatively to *prohibit* participation by parties other than the minor and her representatives. It would strain credulity to conclude that the bypass judges and other authorities in every other state that has a bypass statute are unable to make informed decisions and do substantial justice on the basis of their exclusively *ex parte* proceedings, and this court declines to do so.

Accordingly, the State's interest in the bypass court's having sufficient evidence and information upon which to make informed and proper decisions clearly is still well-served under the Act, even absent additional testimony or advocacy offered by participants other than the minor. And, even if in some way this state interest could plausibly be said to be incrementally better served by the addition of the new Alabama participants, the benefit of the Act is not outweighed by the burden it imposes.

Finally, for the reasons discussed above, the provisions which require or permit notice to, and the participation of, the minor's parents or legal guardians, the DA, a GAL for the unborn child, and unspecified witnesses or others who may be subpoenaed or otherwise need to know the minor's identity do not advance the State's express § 26–21–4(k) interest in enacting a constitutional bypass procedure. On the contrary, the Act clearly imposes an undue burden on the rights of the minor participants to whom it applies. Accordingly, even if the challenged portions of the Act addressed above furthered a valid state interest, those provisions have the effect of placing a substantial obstacle in the path of the affected minors' choice and, thus, cannot be considered a permissible means of serving any otherwise legitimate ends. . . .

Accordingly, the unconstitutional provisions of the Act will be severed from the remainder of the judicial bypass law. . . .

NOTES AND QUESTIONS

1. The sponsor of the Alabama statutory amendments said that they were needed because granting bypass petitions had become "a routine where any unsubstantiated claim from a minor would be grounds to keep her parents in the dark." J. Pepper Bryars, Alabama's New Parental Consent Law Protects Minors and the Unborn from Abortion: Opinion, https://www.al.com/opinion/index.ssf/2014/10/alabamas_new_parental_consent.html.

The limited available statistics seem to support this conclusion. The federal district court in *Hodgson* found that during the period for which statistics had been compiled, minors filed 3,753 bypass petitions in Minnesota courts; 6 petitions were withdrawn before decision, 9 petitions were denied, and 3,558 petitions were granted. Studies in other states have also found that petitions are routinely granted. Helena Silverstein, The Impact and Implementation of the Parental Consent Requirement for Minors Seeking Abortions 15 (paper presented at the Annual Meeting of the Law & Society Assn., July 1996) (Pennsylvania); Planned Parenthood League of Massachusetts v. Attorney General, 677 N.E.2d 101, 105 (Mass. 1997) ("judicial approval is a near certainty" in Massachusetts).

On the other hand, Silverstein reported that 40 percent of courts in Alabama, about 45 percent in Tennessee, and 73 percent in Pennsylvania "proved inadequately acquainted with their responsibilities" to implement bypass procedures. Helena Silverstein, Girls on the Stand: How Courts Fail Pregnant Minors 52 (2008). In an earlier article, Silverstein reported that many court officials in Alabama did not know the state bypass statute existed, and of those who knew of its existence, many had an inaccurate understanding of key provisions, including the duty of the court to appoint counsel for minors who were indigent. The study also found that several judges simply refused to implement the law. Helena Silverstein & Leanne Speitel, "Honey, I Have No Idea": Court Readiness to Handle Petitions to Waive Parental Consent for Abortion, 88 Iowa L. Rev. 75 (2002). *See also* Rebouche, at 188 ("In most states, the application of parental involvement laws is anything but effective, confidential, or timely.").

2. Professor Sanger has argued that even hearings that result in decisions allowing abortions are "a unique and rather clever form of punishment. They are intrusive, humiliating, and meant to punish." Carol Sanger, Regulating Teenage Abortion in the United States: Politics and Policy, 18 Int'l J.L. Pol'y & Fam. 305, 312 (2004). Quoting testimony from a hearing on the Texas parental notification law, she observes,

> The idea seems to be that rather than undergo a judicial bypass hearing — that is, sneak off to court during school hours to discuss one's pregnancy, sexual history, and life plans with a middle-aged stranger — girls will choose to talk to their parents, who will in turn persuade their daughters not to abort. While it is unclear that parents in general counsel against abortion, this is clearly the legislative expectation.
>
> This scheme — bypass hearing as threat — works only if the hearings are understood as a kind of ordeal. For girls who still refuse to involve parents, the hearings move from a threat to an experience. And the nature of the experience — humiliating, risky, intrusive — is properly understood as punishment. If some teenagers insist on aborting against the perceived wishes of their parents, bypass hearings at least make them pay a price for their decision.

Id. at 313-314. *See also* Helena Silverstein, *supra*; Carol Sanger, Decisional Dignity: Teenage Abortion, Bypass Hearings, and the Misuse of Law, 18 Colum. J. Gender & L. 409 (2009).

3. Under *Marshall*, when, if ever, could a state require that the DA appear at bypass hearings to contest petitions so as to provide the benefits of an adversarial, rather than an ex parte, hearing? If a minor's parents find out that she is pregnant and seek to intervene in an already-scheduled bypass hearing, does *Marshall* allow a court to grant their motion?

PROBLEM

You are the law clerk to Judge Schwartz of the Juvenile Court, who has the following case before him. Corinne, a 15-year-old young woman, is pregnant. She has sought judicial authorization for an abortion under the statutory bypass procedure. Corinne does not want to discuss her pregnancy with her parents because they are deeply religious people, and she is concerned that they will strongly oppose her terminating the pregnancy on moral grounds. She believes that they would encourage her to place the child for adoption and would no doubt pay any medical expenses. She is also certain that they will punish her for her immoral conduct.

Corinne became pregnant as the result of having sexual relations with a high school classmate during a party. She is an average student in high school and participates in various school activities.

Judge Schwartz would like your analysis of whether he can and should grant Corinne's petition.

Procreative decisions extend far beyond whether to have an abortion, of course, including whether to be sexually active at all and whether to use contraception. On average, young people have sex for the first time when they are 17. In 2011-2013, 44 percent of unmarried 15- to 19-year-old females had had sex, as had 49 percent of males. Guttmacher Institute, Adolescent Sexual and Reproductive Health in the United States (Sept. 2017). Guttmacher Institute, Facts on American Teens' Sexual and Reproductive Health (Aug. 2011). Of 18- to 19-year-olds, 3 percent of males and 8 percent of females reported their sexual orientation as homosexual or bisexual. *Id.* The proportion of high school students who had ever had sex was stable between 1995 and 2005, but decreased significantly, especially among ninth and tenth graders, between 2005 and 2015. Kathleen A. Ethier, PhD et al, Sexual Intercourse Among High School Students – 29 States and United States Overall, 2005-2015 (Centers for Disease Control and Prevention, Jan. 5, 2018).

One of the Supreme Court's early decisions regarding minors' autonomy rights concerns access to nonprescription contraceptives.

CAREY V. POPULATION SERVICES INTERNATIONAL
431 U.S. 678 (1977)

BRENNAN, J., delivered the opinion of the Court (Parts I, II, III, and V), together with an opinion (Part IV), in which STEWART, MARSHALL, and BLACKMUN, J.J., joined. Under New York Educ. Law § 6811(8) (McKinney 1972) it is a crime (1) for any person to sell or distribute any contraceptive of any kind to a minor under the age of 16 years; (2) for anyone other than a licensed pharmacist to distribute contraceptives to persons 16 or over; and (3) for anyone, including licensed pharmacists, to advertise or display contraceptives. A three-judge District Court for the Southern District of New York declared § 6811(8) unconstitutional in its entirety under the First and Fourteenth Amendments of the Federal Constitution insofar as it applies to nonprescription contraceptives, and enjoined its enforcement as so applied. We affirm. . . .

The District Court . . . held unconstitutional, as applied to nonprescription contraceptives, the provision of § 6811(8) prohibiting the distribution of contraceptives to those under 16 years of age. Appellants contend that this provision of the statute is constitutionally impermissible as a regulation of the morality of minors, in furtherance of the State's policy against promiscuous sexual intercourse among the young.

The question of the extent of state power to regulate conduct of minors not constitutionally regulable when committed by adults is a vexing one, perhaps not susceptible of precise answer. We have been reluctant to attempt to define "the totality of the relationship of the juvenile and the state." In re Gault, 387 U.S. 1, 13 (1967). Certain principles, however, have been recognized. "Minors, as well as adults, are protected by the Constitution and possess constitutional rights." Planned Parenthood of Central Missouri v. Danforth, 428 U.S., at 74. "[W]hatever may be their precise impact, neither the Fourteenth Amendment nor the Bill of Rights is for adults alone." In re Gault, *supra*, 387 U.S., at 13. On the other hand, "the power of the state to control the conduct of children reaches beyond the scope of its authority over adults." Prince v. Massachusetts, 321 U.S. 158, 170 (1944).

Of particular significance to the decision of this case, the right to privacy in connection with decisions affecting procreation extends to minors as well as to adults. Planned Parenthood of Central Missouri v. Danforth held that a State "may not impose a blanket provision . . . requiring the consent of a parent or person *in loco parentis* during the first 12 weeks of her pregnancy." . . . State restrictions inhibiting privacy rights of minors are valid only if they serve "any significant state interest . . . that is not present in the case of an adult." *Planned Parenthood* found no such interest justified a state requirement of parental consent.

Since the State may not impose a blanket prohibition, or even a blanket requirement of parental consent, on the choice of a minor to terminate her pregnancy, the constitutionality of a blanket prohibition of the distribution of contraceptives to minors is *a fortiori* foreclosed. The State's interests in protection of the mental and physical health of the pregnant minor, and in protection of potential life are clearly more implicated by the abortion decision than by the decision to use a nonhazardous contraceptive.

Appellants argue, however, that significant state interests are served by restricting minors' access to contraceptives, because free availability to minors of contraceptives would lead to increased sexual activity among the young. . . . The same argument, however, would support a ban on abortions for minors, or indeed support a prohibition on abortions, or access to contraceptives, for the unmarried, whose sexual activity is also against the public policy of many States. Yet, in each of these areas, the Court has rejected the argument. . . .

Moreover, there is substantial reason for doubt whether limiting access to contraceptives will in fact substantially discourage early sexual behavior. Appellants themselves concede that "there is no evidence that teenage extramarital sexual activity increases in proportion to the availability of contraceptives," and accordingly offered none, in the District Court or here. Appellees, on the other hand, cite a considerable body of evidence and opinion indicating that there is no such deterrent effect. Although we take judicial notice, as did the District Court, that with or without access to contraceptives, the incidence of sexual activity among minors is high, and the consequences of such activity are frequently devastating, the studies cited by appellees play no part in our decision. It is enough that we again confirm the principle that when a State, as here, burdens the exercise of a fundamental right, its attempt to justify that burden as a rational means for the accomplishment of some significant state policy requires more than a bare assertion . . . that the burden is connected to such a policy.

NOTES AND QUESTIONS

1. The plurality in *Carey* assumes that invalidation of the New York law restricting access to contraceptives follows a fortiori from *Danforth*. Is that evident?

2. The opinions in *Carey* suggest that the state has broader power with respect to minors than to adults. What standard of review does the opinion use to assess the constitutionality of the challenged regulations?

3. Is the minor's right to access to contraceptives based on respect for her decisions, on a balancing of benefits and costs, or both?

4. Twenty-six states and D.C. allow all minors 12 and older to consent to contraceptive services without parental involvement. Four states have no policy, and 20 allow minors to consent if they meet statutory conditions, which range from being married, being a mature minor, or having a child, to facing a health hazard. Thirty-two states and D.C. allow minors to consent to prenatal care, and four more allow a minor to consent if she is mature. Another state allows a minor to consent during the first trimester but requires parental consent thereafter. Thirteen of these states allow doctors to tell the minor's parents about the pregnancy if the doctor considers this to be in the patient's best interests. Guttmacher Institute, An Overview of Minors' Consent Law (July 1, 2018). All states and DC allow minors to consent to treatment for sexually transmitted infections, though 11 of them require the minor to be a certain age, usually 12 or 14, to consent. Guttmacher Institute, Minors' Access to STI Services (July 1, 2018).

5. Since 1970, Title X of the Public Health Service Act, which provides family planning services to low-income people, has provided confidential services to people regardless of their age. The federal Medicaid statute also requires that family planning services be provided to teenagers. Efforts to amend these laws to require parental involvement have been unsuccessful, but they do require clinics receiving federal funds to encourage teens to talk to their parents. Angela Napili, Title X (Public Health Service Act) Family Planning Program 24-26 (Cong. Res. Serv. Aug. 31, 2017).

6. Teens' use of contraceptives has risen significantly; in 1982 48 percent of females aged 15 to 19 used contraceptives the first time they had sex, compared to 79 percent in 2011-2013. The levels of sexual activity among teens in the United States and Europe are similar, but the Europeans are more likely to use contraceptives and to use effective contraceptives, and they have significantly lower pregnancy rates. Guttmacher Institute, Adolescent Sexual and Reproductive Health in the United States (Sept. 2017).

7. The major physical risks from unprotected sex are sexually transmitted infections (STIs) and pregnancy. Almost half of all new cases of sexually transmitted infections each year are in 15- to 24-year-olds, though they are only a quarter of the sexually active population. About 22 percent of newly diagnosed cases of HIV/AIDS in 2015 were among 13- to 24-year-olds. About two-thirds of the STI infections among young people are human papillomavirus (HPV) infections, which can cause cervical cancer if untreated. In 2015, 63 percent of young women and 50 percent of young men aged 13 to 17 had received at least one dose of HPV vaccine. Guttmacher Institute, Adolescent Sexual and Reproductive Health in the United States (Sept. 2017).

8. In 2013, the pregnancy rate among young women 15 to 19 years old in the United States was 43 births per 1,000, a decline from the peak of 118 per 1,000 in 1990. *Id.*

Most researchers believe that the main factors in the decline in adolescent pregnancy are increased use of contraceptives and better contraceptive methods.

Heather D. Boonstra, What Is Behind the Declines in Teen Pregnancy Rates?, 17(3) Guttmacher Policy Review 15 (2014). A second significant cause is the decrease in sexual activity among teens younger than 18 between 1995 and 2002. *Id.* at 16. One of the first programs to show a dramatic effect was a six-year-long Colorado program in which teens and poor women were offered free IUDs and long-lasting contraceptive implants. Between 2009 and 2013 the teen birthrate fell 40 percent, and the rate of abortions fell 42 percent. The birth and abortion rates for unmarried women younger than 25 saw similar declines. Sabrina Tavernise, Colorado's Effort Against Teenage Pregnancies Is a Startling Success, NY Times, July 5, 2015. While teen birthrates had been declining generally, "experts say the timing and magnitude of the reductions in Colorado are a strong indication that the state's program was a major driver." *Id.* The program was initially funded by a grant from Warren Buffett's family, and when the grant expired, the state legislature increased funding for family planning, and the Affordable Care Act expanded access as well. Jennifer Brown, IUD Program Leads to Big Decline in Teen Pregnancies, Abortions in Colorado, Denver Post, Nov. 30, 2017.

PROBLEM

Planix is a contraceptive that, when used as directed, reduces the risk of pregnancy by up to 89 percent. Planix does not have any known serious or long-term side effects, although it can have mild and short-term side effects, including nausea and abdominal pain. Almost all the FDA scientific review staff concluded that women of all ages could use Planix safely and effectively without a prescription. Nevertheless, the FDA rule restricts nonprescription access to women 17 and older, based on the agency's finding that adolescents have diminished capacity for sound decision making. If a young woman less than 17 years old wants the drug, she must obtain a doctor's prescription. If the rule denying nonprescription access to young women under the age of 17 were challenged under *Carey* and *Bellotti*, what arguments should be made in support of the challenge? How should the agency lawyers defend the rule?

**ANSPACH EX REL. ANSPACH v. CITY OF PHILADELPHIA,
DEPARTMENT OF PUBLIC HEALTH**

503 F.3d 256 (3d Cir. 2007)

McKEE, Circuit Judge. . . . On January 26, 2004, Melissa Anspach visited a health center operated by the City's Department of Public Health (the "Center"). Melissa had recently engaged in sexual intercourse and feared she may be pregnant. Upon arriving at the Center, she requested a pregnancy test, but a receptionist informed her that pregnancy tests were not being administered that day. Melissa then left the Center but returned a short time later after a friend prompted her to "ask for the morning after pill." Upon her return, Melissa was directed to the pediatric ward where she provided her name and date of birth, thereby disclosing that she was sixteen years of age.

Plaintiffs allege that Melissa then spoke with defendant Maria Fedorova, a social worker, for approximately ten minutes. They discussed sexually transmitted diseases, birth control, and emergency contraception. During the conversation, Fedorova confirmed that the Center could provide pills "that would prevent [Melissa] from getting pregnant," and Melissa requested the pills.

Defendant Mary Gilmore, a registered nurse, next took Melissa's temperature and blood pressure, and gave her four tablets of "Nordette." . . . Melissa then took the four Nordette pills in the nurse's presence, and went home.

Melissa took the second dose of pills at home at approximately 4:00 A.M. as she had been instructed. After taking the second dose, she experienced severe stomach pains and began vomiting. Melissa's father came to her room and found her lying on the floor. Upon learning that Melissa had taken emergency contraception, Mr. Anspach called their family physician and the poison control center, and then took Melissa to the emergency room of a nearby hospital. Melissa was treated there and released the same day, but subsequently returned because of sub-conjunctive hemorrhaging in her eye that was apparently caused by excessive vomiting. . . .

The District Court dismissed all of Plaintiffs' claims under [42 U.S.C.] § 1983 and remanded the remaining state law claims to state court. This appeal of the dismissal of the federal constitutional claims followed. . . .

Melissa's parents allege a substantive due process violation based on state interference with family relations. They argue that the Center's policies were aimed at preventing parents from learning of their minor daughter's possible pregnancies. In support of their contention, the Anspachs point to the fact that personnel at the Center knew Melissa's age, failed to ask Melissa if her parents knew of her predicament, and failed to encourage Melissa to consult with her parents before deciding whether to take emergency contraception. The Complaint alleges that these facts demonstrate that Defendants "engaged in a course of conduct that was intended to influence Melissa to refrain from discussing with her parents her possible pregnancy and what course of action was appropriate."

The Due Process Clause of the Fourteenth Amendment provides that "[n]o State shall . . . deprive any person of life, liberty, or property, without due process of law." To state a due process claim under § 1983, the Anspachs must identify a "recognized 'liberty or property' interest within the purview of the Fourteenth Amendment, and [show] that [they were] intentionally or recklessly deprived of that interest, even temporarily, under color of state law." . . .

. . . The type of "interference" that the Anspachs assert would impose a *constitutional* obligation on state actors to contact parents of a minor or to encourage minors to contact their parents. Either requirement would undermine the minor's right to privacy and exceed the scope of the familial liberty interest protected under the Constitution.

Courts have recognized the parental liberty interest only where the behavior of the state actor compelled interference in the parent-child relationship. These cases involve coercion that is absent from the allegations in Plaintiffs' Complaint. This point is perhaps best illustrated by Doe v. Irwin, 615 F.2d 1162 (6th Cir. 1980), a case very similar to the one before us here.

In *Doe*, a class of parents of minor children sued a publicly funded family planning center. They claimed that the distribution of contraceptives to minors without notice to the parents violated the parents' constitutional rights. The Family Planning Center in *Doe* served both adults and minors. "Neither the

Center nor any of its services related to minors [were] advertised, and minors [were] not sought out or encouraged to attend the Center. . . . " Minors were, however, "permitted to come to the Center either with or without parental consent." The Family Planning Center's services included prescription of contraceptives that were distributed to minors "both with and without parental knowledge or consent." . . .

The district court found that the distribution of contraceptives to minors without notice to parents violated the parents' constitutional rights. . . .

The Court of Appeals for the Sixth Circuit reversed. It relied on a line of Supreme Court cases involving the right of privacy, the authority of the state to regulate the conduct of children, and the scope of a minor's right of privacy and concluded that "[a]s with adults, the minor's right of privacy includes the right to obtain contraceptives." *Id.* at 1166 (citing Carey v. Population Services Int'l, 431 U.S. 678, 692–93 (1977)). . . . The court observed that the "one fundamental difference" between the case before it and cases where the state had interfered with the rights of parents or the rights of children was that "[i]n each of the Supreme Court cases the state was either requiring or prohibiting some activity." The court then explained its observation as follows:

> In Meyer v. Nebraska, [262 U.S. 390 (1923)] the state forbade the teaching of foreign languages to pupils who had not passed the eighth grade. The Court held the statute not reasonably related to any end within the competency of the state and violative of parents' Fourteenth Amendment right to liberty. In Pierce v. Society of Sisters, [268 U.S. 510 (1925)] the statute required all children between the ages of 8 and 16 to attend public schools. The Court found that the law unreasonably interfered with the liberty interest of parents to direct the upbringing and education of their children, including the right to send them to accredited private schools. Again in Wisconsin v. Yoder, [406 U.S. 205 (1972)] the law in question made school attendance compulsory. The Court held that Amish parents' First Amendment rights to the free exercise of their religion were infringed by the attendance requirement. In Prince v. Massachusetts, [321 U.S. 158 (1944)] child labor laws were construed to prohibit street sales of religious tracts by children. In that case the Court upheld the conviction of a parent who contended that these laws unreasonably interfered with her right of free exercise of religion and her parental rights. In so holding, the Court determined that a state's authority is not nullified merely because the parent grounds his claim to control the child's course of conduct on religion or conscience.

Viewed against this legal backdrop, it is clear that Plaintiffs cannot maintain a due process violation when the conduct complained of was devoid of any form of constraint or compulsion. . . .

. . . The Anspachs' allegation of coercion is merely that Nurse Gilmore "told Melissa to swallow the pills before leaving the center." However, Melissa was only given the pills because she asked for them. Arguing that coercion is established because a nurse said "take these," while handing Melissa a glass of water and the pills she had requested, ignores what really happened. Moreover, Plaintiffs' insistence that the atmosphere at the Center was sufficiently coercive to implicate the Due Process Clause is belied by the allegations in their Complaint. The Complaint states that, when she entered the Center for the second time, Melissa requested the morning after pill and was thereafter advised by Fedorova that the Center could provide pills that would prevent Melissa from becoming pregnant. Melissa responded that she would take the pills. "Nurse Gilmore then gave four of the pills to Melissa and instructed Melissa to take these pills with water, which Melissa did in Nurse Gilmore's presence." Simply being told when and how to take a pill that Melissa herself requested is not tantamount to coercion. . . .

The real problem alleged by Plaintiffs is not that the state actors *interfered* with the Anspachs as parents; rather, it is that the state actors did not *assist* the Anspachs as parents or affirmatively *foster* the parent/child relationship. However, the Anspachs are not entitled to that assistance under the Due Process Clause. Plaintiffs' arguments to the contrary ignore that the Constitution "does not require the Government to assist the holder of a constitutional right in the exercise of that right." . . .

. . . Although the Anspachs' moral and religious sensibilities may have been offended by their daughter seeking out and using emergency contraception, her decision was voluntary. The Constitution does not protect parental sensibilities, nor guarantee that a child will follow their parents' moral directives. Defendants' actions therefore do not "amount to unconstitutional interference with parental liberties. . . ."

We also hold that there is no constitutional right to parental notification of a minor child's exercise of reproductive privacy rights. Plaintiffs claim that their position is supported by parental notification requirements under Pennsylvania law in the context of medical treatment, school field trips, and blood donation. They argue that, just as the state can require parental notification in the context of a blood donation, the Center had an obligation to notify them when Melissa requested emergency contraception. In addition, the Anspachs argue that the Pennsylvania Minors' Consent Act, 35 P.S. § 10101, which allows minors to consent to certain types of medical treatment, prohibits minors from consenting to any form of medical treatment unspecified in the Act.

. . . The notifications Plaintiffs rely upon to fashion a federal constitutional right are all rooted in state law obligations rather than the Constitution. These statutes remain subject to constitutional limitations, including the minor's own privacy rights as well as the state's legitimate interest in the reproductive health of minors. Second, even if the Anspachs could ground their constitutional claim to notification in state parental consent law, they still could not prevail. The Minors' Consent Act specifically permits minors to "give effective consent for medical and health services to determine the presence of or treat pregnancy . . . and the consent of no other person shall be necessary."

We are also unpersuaded by Plaintiffs' reliance on Supreme Court cases that permit parental notification in the abortion context. They argue that parental consent is required for the distribution of emergency contraceptives in Pennsylvania unless the court allows the minor to "bypass" the parent when the court has determined that the minor is mature enough to make her own decision, or that the procedure is in the minor's best interest. However, the cases that Plaintiffs cite are fundamentally distinct from this case in both origin and application. They concern the constitutional limitations on a state to interfere with a minor's right to abortion, rather than a parent's affirmative right to be apprised of a minor's reproductive decisions generally. . . .

Though they cite no case law to support their position, Melissa's parents argue that Melissa's particular vulnerability as a 16-year-old minor requesting reproductive health services should tip the balance of liberty interests in their favor. However, allegations that minors seeking reproductive health services are particularly vulnerable can not negate the fact that minors are individuals who enjoy constitutional rights of privacy under substantive due process. *See Danforth,* 428 U.S. at 74 ("Constitutional rights do not mature and come into being magically only when one attains the state-defined age of majority."). While parental notification has been permitted in limited circumstances in the context of abortion, *see, e.g., Casey,* 505 U.S. 833, it has never been affirmatively required, nor extended to include other reproductive health services such as access to contraception. *See Carey,* 431 U.S. at 694 (holding that any absolute prohibition on the distribution of contraceptives to minors without parental consent was "*a fortiori* foreclosed."). We therefore reject Plaintiffs' claim to an affirmative constitutional right to notification. . . .

Because we agree that the allegations in Plaintiffs' complaint have failed to state a cause of action under § 1983, we will affirm the decision of the District Court.

NOTES AND QUESTIONS

1. If Melissa had not had a constitutional right of access to nonprescription contraceptives under *Carey,* would her parents have stated a viable claim? Consider that the background common law principle (as we'll discuss further in Chapter 3) is that parental consent is required for children's medical treatment. Did the Pennsylvania Minors' Consent Act exception cover the facts in this case?

2. If the clinic that provided Melissa with the morning after pill had been in her high school, would Melissa have been "coerced" into taking the medication, meaning that her consent was invalid, and that parental consent was, therefore, required? *Compare* Jackson v. Peekskill City Sch. Dist., 106 F. Supp. 3d 420 (S.D.N.Y. 2015) (parents stated claim for relief against school employees who secretly arranged for student to be transported to off-campus clinic to obtain emergency birth control in violation of parents' right to control upbringing of child, but employees had qualified immunity), and Alfanso v. Fernandez, 606 N.Y.S. 2d 259 (App. Div. 1993) (school condom distribution program with no parental consent requirement or parental opt-out provision violated parents' constitutional rights), with Curtis v. School Comm. of Falmouth, 652 N.E.2d 580 (Mass. 1995) (school condom distribution program did not violate parents' constitutional rights). *See also* Parents United for Better Schools, Inc. v. School District, 978 F. Supp. 197 (E.D. Pa. 1997), *aff'd,* 148 F.3d 260 (3d Cir. 1998) (school condom distribution program that allowed parents to veto children's participation did not violate parental rights).

3. *Anspach* distinguished two cases where courts found that schools had violated parental rights. In Arnold v. Bd. of Educ. of Escambia Cty., 800 F.2d 305 (11th Cir. 1989), high school officials who discovered that a student was pregnant called her and the father to the office to urge them to agree to an abortion, paid the students to do work at school to earn money to pay for the abortion, and paid a driver to take the teens to the abortion facility. The court held that the employees coerced the minor to obtain the abortion and not to discuss the matter with her parents. The court also found coercion in Gruenke v. Selp, 225 F.3d 290 (3d Cir. 2000), where the high school swim team coach insisted that a team member take a pregnancy test, had other coaches talk to her about having the test, and told her

through other members of the team that if she would not take the test, he would take her off the relay team.

4. Schools play an important role in educating young people about sex, sexuality, and sexually transmitted infections (STIs). In 2011-2013, more than 80 percent of 15- to 19-year-olds had received formal instruction about STIs, HIV, or how to say no to sex, but only 55 percent of males and 60 percent of females received formal instruction about birth control. These percentages were all significant declines from 2006-2010. Guttmacher Institute, American Adolescents' Sources of Sexual Health Information (Dec. 2017).

Twenty-two states and the District of Columbia require sex education and HIV education; 2 more require only sex education, and 12 more require only HIV education. Thirty-seven states require that when sex education is offered, it must include information on abstinence, while only 18 states and DC require that it include information on contraception, and only 13 require that the information be medically accurate. Twelve states require that sex education classes discuss sexual orientation, though 3 of these only require negative information. Guttmacher Institute, State Laws and Policies: Sex and HIV Education (July 1, 2018). Between 2000 and 2014, the percentage of schools requiring education about human sexuality dropped from 67 percent to 48 percent, and those requiring instruction about HIV prevention fell from 64 percent to 41 percent. In 2014, half of middle schools and about three-fourths of high schools taught abstinence as the best way to avoid pregnancy HIV, and STIs; only 61 percent of high schools taught about birth control generally. John S. Santelli, M.C., M.P.H. et al, Abstinence-Only-Until-Marriage: An Updated Review of US. Policies and Programs and Their Impact, 61 J. Adolescent Health 273, 276 (2017).

5. Federal funding plays an important role in school choices about how to provide sex education. During the 1990s and through the first half of the 2000s, the federal government provided substantial funds to the states for abstinence-only sex education. In 2009, Congress enacted a new law that allocated money to sex education programs with proven track records as well as to innovative programs, resulting in more emphasis on programs that taught about birth control generally. In 2018 the federal program was reoriented to emphasize abstinence-only sex education, abandoning the requirement that funded programs be evidence-based. Jesseca Boyer, The Teen Pregnancy Prevention Program Was on the Right Track, Now It's Being Dismantled (Guttmacher Institute, May 24, 2018); *see also* John E. Taylor, Family Values, Courts, and Culture War: The Case of Abstinence-Only Sex Education, 18 Wm. & Mary Bill Rts. J. 1053 (2010).

A comprehensive literature review concluded that while abstinence is theoretically effective, intentions to abstain from sexual activity often fail, and programs that teach abstinence only do not delay sexual activity or change sexual risk behaviors. John S. Santelli, M.C., M.P.H. et al, above.

DECISIONS ABOUT MEDICAL CARE

3

Since the late twentieth century, the law has evolved to allow competent adults to control their health care; they can even decline care necessary to save their own lives. Since children are by definition legally incompetent, they do not generally have similar authority. This chapter explores who should be able to make decisions about children's medical care and under what circumstances. Here, as in the situations considered in the first two chapters, parents generally have primary authority. A fundamental question is whether this deference to parents is justified as a way for parents to express their own values or as a means of protecting the interests of children. As you read these materials, consider whether value choices of the types considered in the first two chapters are at stake here or whether these cases simply involve disagreements over technical issues.

Parents' decisions regarding children's medical care are most commonly challenged when the parent refuses to take the child to a doctor or, having taken the child to the doctor, refuses to follow the doctor's advice. Sometimes parents do not provide necessary medical care for their children because of neglect or inattention, but this chapter does not deal with this kind of case. Instead, it concerns situations in which parents disagree with medical care providers about what kind of care is appropriate. In many of the high-profile cases, parents decline some or all kinds of conventional medical care because of their religious beliefs. However, parents may also disagree with doctors because they do not have faith in the efficacy of the proposed treatment or they think that the side effects of the treatment are not justified by the risk to the child.

The first section of this chapter examines the extent to which constitutional protection for parental authority requires that parents' choices regarding medical care prevail. The remaining sections consider how state law operates within this framework in a range of difficult situations. Sections B and C concern parents' refusal to authorize care recommended by doctors. Section D applies the principles we will have developed to medical decision making for severely disabled infants. In Section E, the role of adolescents in decisions about their own health is explored. Finally, Section F asks whether parents can ever decide to put their children at medical risk for altruistic purposes that do not obviously benefit the children themselves.

A. THE CONSTITUTIONAL FRAMEWORK

You have already read the Supreme Court decisions that concern minors' access to abortion, a type of medical care. The next case, which was decided the same year as Bellotti v. Baird, concerns mental hospitalization of minors. These two cases, which both have unique twists, are the only two from the Supreme Court concerning medical care for minors.

PARHAM v. J.R.

442 U.S. 584 (1979)

BURGER, C.J. . . . Appellee J.R., a child being treated in a Georgia state mental hospital, was a plaintiff in this class action based in 42 U.S.C. § 1983, in the District Court for the Middle District of Georgia. Appellants are the state's Commissioner of the Department of Human Resources, the Director of the Mental Health Division of the Department of Human Resources, and the Chief Medical Officer at the hospital where appellee was being treated. Appellee sought a declaratory judgment that Georgia's voluntary commitment procedures for children under the age of 18, Ga. Code §§ 88-503.1, 88-503.2 (1975),[1] violated the Due Process Clause of the Fourteenth Amendment and requested an injunction against their future enforcement.

A three-judge District Court was convened pursuant to 28 U.S.C. §§ 2281 and 2284 (1970 ed.). After considering expert and lay testimony and extensive exhibits and after visiting two of the state's regional mental health hospitals, the District Court held that Georgia's statutory scheme was unconstitutional because it failed to protect adequately the appellees' due process rights.

The parties agree that our prior holdings have set out a general approach for testing challenged state procedures under a due process claim. Assuming the existence of a protectible property or liberty interest, the Court has required a balancing of a number of factors:

> First, the private interest that will be affected by the official action; second, the risk of an erroneous deprivation of such interest through the procedures used, and the probable value, if any, of additional or substitute procedural safeguards; and finally, the

---

1. Section 88-503.1 provides:

   The superintendent of any facility may receive for observation and diagnosis . . . any individual under 18 years of age for whom such application is made by his parent or guardian. . . . If found to show evidence of mental illness and to be suitable for treatment, such person may be given care and treatment at such facility and such person may be detained by such facility for such period and under such conditions as may be authorized by law.

   Section 88-503.2 provides:

   The superintendent of the facility shall discharge any voluntary patient who has recovered from his mental illness or who has sufficiently improved that the superintendent determines that hospitalization of the patient is no longer desirable. . . . .

> Government's interest, including the function involved and the fiscal and administrative burdens that the additional or substitute procedural requirement would entail.

Mathews v. Eldridge, 424 U.S. 319, 335 (1976), *quoted in* Smith v. Organization of Foster Families, 431 U.S. 816, 848-849 (1977).

In applying these criteria, we must consider first the child's interest in not being committed. Normally, however, since this interest is inextricably linked with the parents' interest in and obligation for the welfare and health of the child, the private interest at stake is a combination of the child's and parents' concerns. Next, we must examine the State's interest in the procedures it has adopted for commitment and treatment of children. Finally, we must consider how well Georgia's procedures protect against arbitrariness in the decision to commit a child to a state mental hospital.

(a) It is not disputed that a child, in common with adults, has a substantial liberty interest in not being confined unnecessarily for medical treatment and that the state's involvement in the commitment decision constitutes state action under the Fourteenth Amendment. We also recognize that commitment sometimes produces adverse social consequences for the child because of the reaction of some to the discovery that the child has received psychiatric care.

This reaction, however, need not be equated with the community response resulting from being labeled by the state as delinquent, criminal, or mentally ill and possibly dangerous. The state through its voluntary commitment procedures does not "label" the child; it provides a diagnosis and treatment that medical specialists conclude the child requires. In terms of public reaction, the child who exhibits abnormal behavior may be seriously injured by an erroneous decision not to commit. Appellees overlook a significant source of the public reaction to the mentally ill, for what is truly "stigmatizing" is the symptomatology of a mental or emotional illness. . . .

However, we need not decide what effect these factors might have in a different case. For purposes of this decision, we assume that a child has a protectible interest not only in being free of unnecessary bodily restraints but also in not being labeled erroneously by some persons because of an improper decision by the state hospital superintendent.

(b) We next deal with the interests of the parents who have decided, on the basis of their observations and independent professional recommendations, that their child needs institutional care. Appellees argue that the constitutional rights of the child are of such magnitude and the likelihood of parental abuse is so great that the parents' traditional interests in and responsibility for the upbringing of their child must be subordinated at least to the extent of providing a formal adversary hearing prior to a voluntary commitment.

Our jurisprudence historically has reflected Western civilization concepts of the family as a unit with broad parental authority over minor children. Our cases have consistently followed that course; our constitutional system long ago rejected any notion that a child is "the mere creature of the State" and, on the contrary, asserted that parents generally "have the right, coupled with the high duty, to recognize and prepare [their children] for additional obligations." Pierce v. Society of Sisters, 268 U.S. 510, 535 (1925). *See also* Wisconsin v. Yoder, 406 U.S. 205, 213 (1972); Prince v. Massachusetts, 321 U.S. 158, 166 (1944); Meyer v. Nebraska, 262

U.S. 390, 400 (1923). Surely, this includes a "high duty" to recognize symptoms of illness and to seek and follow medical advice. The law's concept of the family rests on a presumption that parents possess what a child lacks in maturity, experience, and capacity for judgment required for making life's difficult decisions. More important, historically it has recognized that natural bonds of affection lead parents to act in the best interests of their children.

As with so many other legal presumptions, experience and reality may rebut what the law accepts as a starting point; the incidence of child neglect and abuse cases attests to this. That some parents "may at times be acting against the interests of their children" . . . creates a basis for caution, but is hardly a reason to discard wholesale those pages of human experience that teach that parents generally do act in the child's best interests. The statist notion that governmental power should supersede parental authority in *all* cases because *some* parents abuse and neglect children is repugnant to American tradition.

Nonetheless, we have recognized that a state is not without constitutional control over parental discretion in dealing with children when their physical or mental health is jeopardized. *See* Wisconsin v. Yoder, *supra*, at 230; Prince v. Massachusetts, *supra*, at 166. Moreover, the Court recently declared unconstitutional a state statute that granted parents an absolute veto over a minor child's decision to have an abortion. Planned Parenthood of Central Missouri v. Danforth, 428 U.S. 52 (1976). Appellees urge that these precedents limiting the traditional rights of parents, if viewed in the context of the liberty interest of the child and the likelihood of parental abuse, require us to hold that the parents' decision to have a child admitted to a mental hospital must be subjected to an exacting constitutional scrutiny, including a formal, adversary, pre-admission hearing.

Appellees' argument, however, sweeps too broadly. Simply because the decision of a parent is not agreeable to a child or because it involves risks does not automatically transfer the power to make that decision from the parents to some agency or officer of the state. The same characterizations can be made for a tonsillectomy, appendectomy, or other medical procedure. Most children, even in adolescence, simply are not able to make sound judgments concerning many decisions, including their need for medical care or treatment. Parents can and must make those judgments. Here, there is no finding by the District Court of even a single instance of bad faith by any parent of any member of appellees' class. We cannot assume that the result in Meyer v. Nebraska, *supra*, and Pierce v. Society of Sisters, *supra*, would have been different if the children there had announced a preference to learn only English or a preference to go to a public, rather than a church, school. The fact that a child may balk at hospitalization or complain about a parental refusal to provide cosmetic surgery does not diminish the parents' authority to decide what is best for the child. Neither state officials nor federal courts are equipped to review such parental decisions. . . .

In defining the respective rights and prerogatives of the child and parent in the voluntary commitment setting, we conclude that our precedents permit the parents to retain a substantial, if not the dominant, role in the decision, absent a finding of neglect or abuse, and that the traditional presumption that the parents act in the best interests of their child should apply. We also conclude, however, that the child's rights and the nature of the commitment decision are such that parents cannot always have absolute and unreviewable discretion to decide whether to have a child institutionalized. They, of course, retain plenary authority to seek such care for their children, subject to a physician's independent examination and medical judgment.

(c) The State obviously has a significant interest in confining the use of its costly mental health facilities to cases of genuine need. . . .

The State in performing its voluntarily assumed mission also has a significant interest in not imposing unnecessary procedural obstacles that may discourage the mentally ill or their families from seeking needed psychiatric assistance. The *parens patriae* interest in helping parents care for the mental health of their children cannot be fulfilled if the parents are unwilling to take advantage of the opportunities because the admission process is too onerous, too embarrassing, or too contentious. It is surely not idle to speculate as to how many parents who believe they are acting in good faith would forgo state-provided hospital care if such care is contingent on participation in an adversary proceeding designed to probe their motives and other private family matters in seeking the voluntary admission.

The State also has a genuine interest in allocating priority to the diagnosis and treatment of patients as soon as they are admitted to a hospital rather than to time-consuming procedural minutes before the admission. One factor that must be considered is the utilization of the time of psychiatrists, psychologists, and other behavioral specialists in preparing for and participating in hearings rather than performing the task for which their special training has fitted them. . . .

(d) We now turn to consideration of what process protects adequately the child's constitutional rights by reducing risks of error without unduly trenching on traditional parental authority and without undercutting "efforts to further the legitimate interests of both the state and the patient that are served by" voluntary commitments. Addington v. Texas, 441 U.S., at 430. *See also* Mathews v. Eldridge, 424 U.S., at 335. We conclude that the risk of error inherent in the parental decision to have a child institutionalized for mental health care is sufficiently great that some kind of inquiry should be made by a "neutral factfinder" to determine whether the statutory requirements for admission are satisfied. That inquiry must carefully probe the child's background using all available sources, including, but not limited to, parents, schools, and other social agencies. Of course, the review must also include an interview with the child. It is necessary that the decisionmaker have the authority to refuse to admit any child who does not satisfy the medical standards for admission. Finally, it is necessary that the child's continuing need for commitment be reviewed periodically by a similarly independent procedure.

We are satisfied that such procedures will protect the child from an erroneous admission decision in a way that neither unduly burdens the state nor inhibits parental decisions to seek state help.

Due process has never been thought to require that the neutral and detached trier of fact be law trained or a judicial or administrative officer. Surely, this is the case as to medical decisions, for "neither judges nor administrative hearing officers are better qualified than psychiatrists to render psychiatric judgments." In re Roger S., 19 Cal. 3d 921, 942, 569 P.2d 1286, 1299 (1977) (Clark, J., dissenting). Thus, a staff physician will suffice, so long as he or she is free to evaluate independently the child's mental and emotional condition and need for treatment.

It is not necessary that the deciding physician conduct a formal or quasi-formal hearing. A state is free to require such a hearing, but due process is not violated by use of informal traditional medical investigative techniques. Since well-established medical procedures already exist, we do not undertake to outline with specificity precisely what this investigation must involve. The mode and procedure of medical diagnostic procedures is not the business of judges. What is best for a child is an individual medical decision that must be left to the judgment of physicians in each case. We do no more than emphasize that the decision should represent an independent judgment of what the child requires and that all sources of information that are traditionally relied on by physicians and behavioral specialists should be consulted.

What process is constitutionally due cannot be divorced from the nature of the ultimate decision that is being made. Not every determination by state officers can be made most effectively by use of "the procedural tools of judicial or administrative decisionmaking."

Here, the questions are essentially medical in character: whether the child is mentally or emotionally ill and whether he can benefit from the treatment that is provided by the state. While facts are plainly necessary for a proper resolution of those questions, they are only a first step in the process. In an opinion for a unanimous Court, we recently stated in Addington v. Texas, 441 U.S., at 429, that the determination of whether a person is mentally ill "turns on the *meaning* of the facts which must be interpreted by expert psychiatrists and psychologists." . . .

Another problem with requiring a formalized, factfinding hearing lies in the danger it poses for significant intrusion into the parent-child relationship. Pitting the parents and child as adversaries often will be at odds with the presumption that parents and child act in the best interests of their child. It is one thing to require a neutral physician to make a careful review of the parents' decision in order to make sure it is proper from a medical standpoint; it is a wholly different matter to employ an adversary contest to ascertain whether the parents' motivation is consistent with the child's interests.

Moreover, it is appropriate to inquire into how such a hearing would contribute to the successful long-range treatment of the patient. Surely, there is a risk that it would exacerbate whatever tensions already exist between the child and the parents. . . . A confrontation over such intimate family relationships would distress the normal adult parents and the impact on a disturbed child almost certainly would be significantly greater.

It has been suggested that a hearing conducted by someone other than the admitting physician is necessary in order to detect instances where parents are "guilty of railroading their children into asylums" or are using "voluntary commitment procedures in order to sanction behavior of which they disapprov[e]." Ellis, Volunteering Children: Parental Commitment of Minors to Mental Institutions, 62 Calif. L. Rev. 840, 850-851 (1974). Curiously, it seems to be taken for granted that parents who seek to "dump" their children on the state will inevitably be able to conceal their motives and thus deceive the admitting psychiatrists and the other mental health professionals who make and review the admission decision. It is elementary that one early diagnostic inquiry into the cause of an emotional disturbance of a child is an examination into the environment of the child. It is unlikely, if not inconceivable, that a decision to abandon an emotionally normal, healthy child and thrust him into an institution will be a discrete act leaving no trail of circumstances. Evidence of such conflicts will emerge either in the interviews or from secondary sources. It is unrealistic to believe that trained psychiatrists, skilled in eliciting responses, sorting medically relevant facts, and sensing motivational nuances will often be deceived about the family situation surrounding a child's emotional disturbance. Surely a lay, or even law-trained, factfinder would be no more skilled in this process than the professional. . . .

IV

(a) Our discussion in Part III was directed at the situation where a child's natural parents request his admission to a state mental hospital. Some members of appellees' class, including J.R., were wards of the State of Georgia at the time of their admission. Obviously their situation differs from those members of the class who have natural parents. While the determination of what process is due varies somewhat when the state, rather than a natural parent, makes the request for commitment, we conclude that the differences in the two situations do not justify requiring different procedures at the time of the child's initial admission to the hospital.

For a ward of the state, there may well be no adult who knows him thoroughly and who cares for him deeply. . . . Contrary to the suggestion of the dissent, however, we cannot assume that when the State of Georgia has custody of a child it acts so differently from a natural parent in seeking medical assistance for the child. . . .

Once we accept that the State's application for a child's admission to a hospital is made in good faith, then the question is whether the medical decisionmaking approach of the admitting physician is adequate to satisfy due process. We have already recognized that an independent medical judgment made from the perspective of the best interests of the child after a careful investigation is an acceptable means of justifying a voluntary commitment. We do not believe that the soundness of this decisionmaking is any the less reasonable in this setting.

Lee E. Teitelbaum & James W. Ellis, *The Liberty Interest of Children: Due Process Rights and their Application*

12 Fam. L.Q. 153, 171-173, 191-194 (1978)

In [cases like *Meyer* and *Pierce*], there may be good reason to indulge a presumption that parents are better able than the state to determine what the child should do or believe. They are more familiar with the child's needs within the home and are prepared to teach other than orthodox doctrine. Their child's agreement or acquiescence affords some evidence that their judgment is correct or at least tolerable. Nor should the desirability of parental action be judged mechanically by the application of majoritarian norms. Disruption of a unified family is more likely to be destructive than helpful, and should occur only on a convincing showing of good cause. . . .

A different situation is presented, however, when the family is genuinely disunited or when the parents take action that will have that effect. In these instances, the very resort to public force changes the nature of the enterprise, both practically and in principle. . . . In the case of commitment . . . the family has reached the con-clusion that the child has a problem which cannot or can no longer be managed (treated) in the home. . . .

The magnitude of the problems faced by parents of a retarded child can-not be overstated. They do not resemble those of parents whose children present ordinary medical problems, or even serious but transient illness or injury. The dis-covery that a child is mentally retarded produces a number of emotional reactions, which one authority has summarized as "chronic sorrow." . . .

Together with these emotional burdens are the considerable—often over-whelming—practical and physical burdens imposed by everyday care of a retarded child. These problems are increased in the common situation where the child's mental disability is accompanied by serious physical handicap. It must also be kept in mind that, unlike occasional crises encountered by the parents of non-retarded children, the problems faced by the parents of the handicapped are chronic and unceasing. The strain these factors place upon parents is revealed by the fact that, when a child is placed in an institution, a sense of relief from the burdens created by the child's presence in the home is one of the most prominent reactions expe-rienced by parents.

. . . There is no reason for surprise at finding, therefore, that perhaps the most important factor in seeking commitment is the decision that the presence of the retarded child in the home has become an unacceptable disruption of family life and the realization that the parents have become too physically and emotion-ally weary to deal with the problems the child's presence brought to the fam-ily. Economic factors associated with the often considerable cost of caring for a retarded child play an important part, as does the perceived impact of the retarded child on the lives of his non-retarded brothers and sisters. The dominant theme in all studies, however, is the conviction of parents that the problem is one they cannot manage and for which they wish others to assume responsibility. . . .

These observations do not suggest that parents are ill-motivated or uncon-cerned about the needs of their retarded child. But the evidence clearly shows that they make a decision for the retarded child in a situation of considerable personal and familial stress and with a real need to ameliorate an unacceptable situation. . . . Commitment seems the end of a travail and frequently becomes just that. . . .

NOTES AND QUESTIONS

1. About a quarter of all adolescents have some kind of mental health disor-der between ages 13 and 18, and an estimated 10 percent of children have a serious mental disorder during their adolescence. National Institute of Mental Health, Health Information: Statistics: Mental Illness, https://www.nimh.nih.gov/health/statistics/mental-illness.shtml (July 30, 2018). Most of these children are not insti-tutionalized but are living at home, being treated with medications and therapy.

2. The Mathews v. Eldridge test requires the court to specify and ascribe weight to the interests of the person affected by a procedural arrangement and of the state. That test is easiest to apply in cases where the state seeks to regulate an individual's liberty and the individual seeks to require a more accurate or thorough procedure as a condition to such a limitation. How does the Court employ that

test in *Parham*, where two claimants are asserting an interest in the conduct or treatment of a third person, a child?

3. What approach does the Court seem to take to the claims of parents? Does it view those claims as founded on an autonomy claim inherent in parenthood? Are those claims founded instead on the empirical probability that children will best be served by parental decision making? What aspects of the Court's decision support one of these or some other interpretation of the rights of parents?

The Court talks of a "presumption that the parents act in the best interests of their children." What does this suggest about the basis for recognizing parental authority? If the Court's decisions "permit the parents to retain a substantial, if not the dominant, role in the [treatment] decision," does it follow that the state also has "a substantial, if not the dominant, role" in such decisions?

4. Bellotti v. Baird was decided only two weeks after *Parham*; however, it cites the latter case only once, and then with a "*Cf.*" signal at the end of a string citation. But don't the two cases have much to do with each other, at least insofar as *Bellotti* deals with minors not capable of mature decisions?

Consider, particularly, the "presumption that the parents act in the best interests of their children" recognized in *Parham*. Does *Bellotti* recognize such a presumption? Is there reason to believe that parents dealing with the abortion decision are likely to be more subject to what amounts to a conflict of interest with respect to their child's welfare than parents deciding whether to institutionalize their child? For that matter, does consideration of conflicting interests implicitly rely on some particular assumption about the nature of the parental right to rear a child?

5. What is the nature of the child's interest in *Parham*? While the Court speaks in terms of a "liberty interest" (the phrase used in *Mathews*), is it clear that the Court means to recognize a "rights" approach to the child's interest? What significance might attach to the Court's observation that "[w]e cannot assume that the result in [*Meyer* and *Pierce*] would have been different if the children there had announced a preference to learn only English or a preference to go to a public, rather than a church, school"?

Compare the approach to minors' interests in *Bellotti*. What explains the difference? Can *Bellotti* be distinguished on the ground that the abortion decision is peculiarly important for the future of the child? Confinement in a mental institution during a child's formative years may also have grave and indelible effects. There is considerable evidence that institutionalized children will fail to obtain the skills normally acquired in childhood or even lose some skills already possessed at the time of admission.

6. What process does the Court hold is minimally adequate to satisfy the Due Process Clause before a child is committed by parents to an inpatient psychiatric facility? Why does the Court say that this level of procedural formality is sufficient, even appropriate?

At the time *Parham* was decided, Professor Michael Perlin headed the New Jersey Mental Health Advocates Office, which represented children whose parents sought their institutionalization in psychiatric facilities. (New Jersey law provided children greater procedural safeguards than *Parham* required.) Perlin reported that the lawyers for children were often able to keep children out of institutions by finding less restrictive placements and funding for those placements, as well as exploring community-based alternatives, opening funding channels, and facilitating family contact with community services, including special education. Michael Perlin, An Invitation to the Dance: An Empirical Response to Chief Justice Warren Burger's 'Time-Consuming Procedural Minuets' Theory in Parham v. J.R., 9 Bull. Am. Acad. Psychiatry & L. 149 (1981).

More than 30 years later, advocates for children argue that failure to provide adequate community-based mental health services results in the unnecessary institutionalization of children. Yael Zakai Cannon, There's No Place Like Home: Realizing the Vision of Community-Based Mental Health Treatment for Children, 61 DePaul L. Rev. 1049 (2012).

7. Relying on both state and federal constitutional provisions, the California Supreme Court in In re Roger S., 569 P.2d 1286 (Cal. 1978), held that a child 14 or older is entitled to an administrative hearing before being committed to a state mental hospital by parents. The court said that the child must have adequate written notice of the proceedings, the right to counsel, and the rights to present evidence and cross-examine witnesses. The hearing officer must find that the grounds for commitment are proven by a preponderance of the evidence. To the extent the opinion relies on federal grounds, of course, *Parham* supplants it.

State ex rel. T.B. v. CPC Fairfax Hospital, 918 P.2d 497 (Wash. 1996), interpreted a Washington state statute as requiring public and private facilities to release a minor who does not consent to mental hospitalization within 24 hours of admission or to petition for a hearing. The opinion says that minors are also entitled to access to counsel and to their medical records. The decision was an interpretation of Washington's "Becca Bill," which was enacted after a 13-year-old runaway girl was murdered. Media coverage of her death highlighted parents' efforts to obtain help for and assistance with "out of control" adolescents. Part of the legislation amended statutes governing admission of adolescents 13 and older to mental hospitals. Before the bill, such a minor could be "voluntarily" admitted only with the consent of the parent and the minor himself or herself. The amendments removed the requirement that the children consent. Kelli Schmidt, Note & Comment: "Who Are You to Say What My Best Interest Is?" Minors' Due Process Rights When Admitted by Parents for Inpatient Mental Health Treatment, 71 Wash. L. Rev. 1187, 1193-1194 (1996).

8. Buried in the facts of *Parham* is an issue that raises special questions about the constitutional position of children and parents. The opinion does not discuss the difference between the positions of children placed in public facilities and those placed in private facilities. In fact, both situations were present in the group of cases consolidated for hearing in *Parham*, but it is far from clear that the same kind of analysis applies to both.

A claim under the Due Process Clause, such as the one presented in *Parham*, must be founded on some action undertaken by state authority. Private conduct, absent sufficient state involvement, might be the basis for a civil action for tort but does not present Fourteenth Amendment issues. Where public hospitals are involved, no substantial problem with state action exists. The state is involved because it maintains custody of the child, and confinement by the state in such institutions has, with respect to adults, been described by the Court as a "massive curtailment of liberty." Humphrey v. Cady, 405 U.S. 504, 509 (1972). *See* O'Connor v. Donaldson, 422 U.S. 563 (1975). But what about the situation where the parents drive their child to a privately owned and operated hospital and, as Georgia law contemplated and *Parham* apparently authorized, place the child there with the agreement of a staff mental health worker? Ordinarily, mere licensing of an otherwise private facility is not sufficient state involvement to subject its actions to constitutional review, nor does the absence of state restrictions (as opposed to state encouragement) itself amount to state action. *Cf.* Reitman v. Mulkey, 387 U.S. 369 (1967).

Since the last quarter of the twentieth century, the proportion of children admitted to private, rather than public, inpatient psychiatric facilities has increased dramatically. "In 1971, private hospital admissions accounted for 37.4 percent of juvenile mental hospitalizations. By 1980, the proportion of total psychiatric admissions that occurred in private facilities had risen to 61.2 percent. The rate of admission of minors to public facilities decreased 35.9 percent during this nine-year period while the rate of admission of minors to private facilities jumped 69.3 percent. Rates of admission to public facilities rose slightly in the 1980s and 1990s. Yet, private facility admissions continued to soar, and accounted for approximately three-quarters of juvenile psychiatric admissions by 1997." Lois A. Weithorn, Envisioning Second-Order Change in America's Responses to Troubled and Troublesome Youth, 33 Hofstra L. Rev. 1305, 1384-1385 (2005). Some evidence suggests that the risks of inappropriate commitment and of maltreatment are greater if parents take their children to private, for-profit institutions than if they take them to public facilities. Lenore Behar et al., Protecting Youth Placed in Unlicensed, Unregulated Residential "Treatment" Facilities, 45 Fam. Ct. Rev. 399 (2007); GAO, Residential Treatment Programs: Concerns Regarding Abuse and Death in Certain Programs for Troubled Youth (2007), https://www.gao.gov/new.items/d08146t.pdf (Aug. 6, 2018). Almost half of all children taken to private residential facilities were transported by professional services established for this purpose. Lenore Behar et al., Protecting Youth Placed in Unlicensed, Unregulated Residential "Treatment" Facilities, 45 Fam. Ct. Rev. 399, 404 (2007); *see also* Ira P. Robbins, Kidnapping Incorporated: The Unregulated Youth-Transportation Industry and the Potential for Abuse, 51 Am. Crim. L. Rev. 563 (2014).

9. In recent years, there have been a number of cases in which parents have consented to medical interventions for their children, even though the children were not ill or injured, making the procedures not medically necessary. The parents arranged for the treatments in the belief that they would provide the children with aesthetic, cultural, or social advantages. Professor Alicia Ouellette describes cases in which the eyes of adopted Asian children were surgically "Westernized," the facial features of children with Down syndrome were surgically "normalized," very tiny children were given human growth hormone, normal-sized children, usually boys, were given human growth hormone to make them bigger, and children as young as 12 were given liposuction. Alicia Ouellette, Shaping Parental Authority Over Children's Bodies, 85 Ind. L.J. 955 (2010). The law does not regulate these practices, and Professor Ouellette reports that prior judicial authorization was not sought in any of the cases. Does the parental authority protected in *Parham* extend to these decisions? Do these treatments affect children's constitutionally protected liberty interests? If so, what kind of process, if any, should be required before the treatments are administered? *See also* B. Jessie Hill, Constituting Children's Bodily Integrity, 64 Duke L.J. 1295 (2015).

PROBLEM[2]

Ashley is a six-year-old girl with profound developmental disabilities. She has the mental development of an infant, and she cannot sit up, walk, or talk. She has a stomach tube to provide her with nutrition. Her doctors believe that there is essentially no chance her condition will ever improve. She lives at home with her parents, who love her very much but who are very concerned about their ability to care for her as she grows older and larger and develops sexually. They want to keep her at home and hate the idea of placing her in an institution or care facility. In consultation with Ashley's doctors, her parents have decided to inhibit her sexual development and physical growth with three procedures: a hysterectomy, a mastectomy, and administration of high doses of estrogen (which will stunt her growth and keep her child-sized).

Ashley's parents believe that these procedures will not only enable them to continue to care for her at home, but will also save her from the trauma of menstruating, which she would not understand. Ashley's doctors support the parents, and they submitted the proposed treatment plan to the hospital ethics committee, which has also approved it, despite the substantial physical risks of all three procedures.

Because they realize that this treatment plan breaks new ground, the doctors and Ashley's parents have sought a declaratory judgment authorizing them to proceed. The court has appointed a guardian ad litem for Ashley whose obligation is to advocate for her best interests. The guardian ad litem has decided to oppose the proposed treatments as not medically necessary.

What arguments should the guardian ad litem make? The attorneys for Ashley's parents?

B. STATE AUTHORITY WHEN PARENTS DECLINE MEDICAL TREATMENT

The issue in *Parham* is whether parental consent is sufficient for a child to be treated in a mental hospital. More common are cases in which parents refuse to consent to medical care for a child, despite a doctor's recommendation. The next cases consider when a court may override the parents' decision and order that the medical care be provided. These cases are usually filed as neglect cases in juvenile court; all states' juvenile codes define a parent's failure to provide necessary medical care as neglect. The purpose of such a proceeding is not necessarily to remove the child from the parents' custody, but to allow the court to authorize the care over the parents' objection. If the child's life is in danger and the proposed medical

---

2. This problem is based on a case reported in Alicia Ouellette, Growth Attenuation, Parental Choice, the Rights of Disabled Children: Lessons from the Ashley X Case, 8 Houston J. Health L. & Pol'y 207 (2008). In the actual case, the treatment was undertaken without any kind of judicial review. The author also discusses this case in the article cited in Note 9 of the text, above.

care is generally regarded as safe and effective, virtually all courts will override the parents' decision.

Through the mid-twentieth century, the limited case law suggested that courts should not override parental decisions unless the child's life was at risk. Walter Wadlington, Medical Decision Making for and by Children: Tensions Between Parent, State, and Child, 1994 U. Ill. L. Rev. 311, 314-319. A famous pair of contrasting opinions from New York illustrates the evolution away from this rule. In In Matter of Seiferth, 127 N.E.2d 820 (N.Y. 1955), a 14-year-old boy had a cleft palate and a harelip. His father refused to authorize surgery for personal philosophical reasons, and the boy, who had been inculcated with his father's beliefs, also objected. The New York Court of Appeals ultimately upheld the trial court's decision not to authorize the surgery, saying:

> [T]here is no present emergency, time is less of the essence than it was a few years ago insofar as concerns the physical prognosis, and we are impressed by the circumstances that in order to benefit from the operation upon the cleft palate, it will almost certainly be necessary to enlist Martin's co-operation in developing normal speech patterns through a lengthy course in concentrated speech therapy. It will be almost impossible to secure his co-operation if he continues to believe, as he does now, that it will be necessary "to remedy the surgeon's distortion first and then go back to the primary task of healing the body." This is an aspect of the problem with which petitioner's plastic surgeon did not especially concern himself, for he did not attempt to view the case from the psychological viewpoint of this misguided youth. Upon the other hand, the Children's Court Judge, who saw and heard the witnesses, and arranged the conferences for the boy and his father which have been mentioned, appears to have been keenly aware of this aspect of the situation, and to have concluded that less would be lost by permitting the lapse of several more years, when the boy may make his own decision to submit to plastic surgery, than might be sacrificed if he were compelled to undergo it now against his sincere and frightened antagonism. One cannot be certain of being right under these circumstances, but this appears to be a situation where the discretion of the trier of the facts should be preferred to that of the Appellate Division.

In contrast, in In re Sampson, 278 N.E.2d 918 (N.Y. 1972), the trial court ordered a blood transfusion that was necessary for surgery to correct "massive disfigurement" to a 15-year-old boy's face and neck caused by Von Recklinghausen's disease. The disease did not pose an immediate threat to his life, and the doctors counseled waiting until the boy was older, as the risk from the surgery declined with age. Upholding the trial court, the New York Court of Appeals said that the decision was within the discretion of the trial judge, who had acted to protect the boy's right to grow up "normally."

Professor Wadlington says that two legislative trends during the 1970s — child abuse reporting statutes and statutes authorizing older minors to make certain kinds of medical decisions — contributed to courts' greater willingness to overrule parental decisions, even when the child's life is not endangered. Wadlington, above, at 322-324. By the mid-1980s, courts were consistently saying that judicial authority to override parental choices is not limited to circumstances in which the child's life is endangered, though they do not agree when this is appropriate.

In the Interest of M.R.R.

807 N.W.2d 158 (Iowa 2011)

SACKETT, C.J. . . . The child was born in January of 2002. The marriage of her parents was dissolved in 2005. The dissolution court approved the parties' stipulation that agreed they receive joint legal custody, the mother receive physical care, and the father receive specified reasonable visitation.

The child, at age four, began having seizures where there was a sudden onset of her rolling her eyes up in her head. The seizures were brief in duration, lasting about one second. The child was immediately back to normal or slightly confused for a short period of time. She has developmental delays and behavior difficulties. The parents sought medical advice, and in August 2006, the child was diagnosed with atypical epileptic seizure disorder. The child has been seen by her family doctor, as well as medical specialists in the areas of her problems at the University of Iowa Hospitals and Clinics, John Hopkins Medicine, Mayo Clinic, and a medical facility in Indiana. The child was put on special diets, which the mother successfully implemented,[3] and medications, which both parties administered. The child did not react well to the medication.[4]

The event that led to the Iowa Department of Human Services to intervene in the child's medical treatment was a call in October of 2010 to the department from Mayo Clinic where the child was being treated. Mayo Clinic reported there was a conflict between the parents as to how the child's treatment should proceed. As a result of the call, the State, in December of that year, filed a child-in-need-of-assistance petition, contending the child was in need of assistance under Iowa Code Section 232.2(6)(e).

The petition came on for hearing on January 12, 2010. The parents agreed to continue the adjudication hearing and to the entry of a temporary order by the

---

3. In the summer of 2000 the child went to John Hopkins Medicine and participated in the modified Atkins diet study. She was having about twenty seizures a day where she would stop, stare, roll her eyes, and be confused for several seconds with an EEG showing rapid, probably spike wave discharge. At the time she went to John Hopkins, the child was not on any anticonvulsant, and she was put on the modified Atkins diet. Seizures improved, and she went down to about two or four seizures a day, which the doctors approximated to be about a fifty percent improvement. In her second month on the study, the seizures remained under good control of approximately three or four a day. The doctors found, in September of 2009, there was no clear reason to stop the diet. The doctor did discuss with the mother that his next advice would probably be to add a dose of medication to see if they could get the child's seizures under better control. The doctor noted the decision to do so was ultimately up to the mother and he was of the impression that she was not particularly inclined to do so at that time.

4. In April of 2008, a doctor at the University of Iowa Hospitals and Clinics said,

Because [the child's] seizures are very brief and not very frequent, and because [the child] has had substantial side effects from Topamax therapy in the past, I recommend that [the child] be treated with no anticonvulsant at this time. If the seizures become more frequent or more severe, then strong consideration could be given to reinstituting anticonvulsant therapy.

juvenile court requiring both parties "to comply with the recommendations of the pediatric neurologist at Mayo Clinic, including any dietary and medication protocols for the child." The order also provided that either party could seek a second opinion, but that any contrary recommendations would not relieve the parents of complying with the recommendations of Mayo Clinic.

On February 8, 2010, the child went to Mayo Clinic for monitoring, which showed she had about two seizures per hour. The Mayo Clinic agreed with the mother putting the child on a ketogenic[5] diet at a ratio of 2.5 fats to 1 protein and carbohydrate. The Minnesota Epilepsy Group also concurred with the initiation of the ketogenic diet but noted that if the seizures were not completely controlled within a month, then medication should be initiated.

The child returned to the Mayo Clinic for a follow-up appointment on March 9, 2010. The Mayo Clinic reported:

> [The child] is currently on the ketogenic diet. The ketogenic diet is an excellent treatment for both symptomatic and primary generalized epilepsy. However, it is typically done as adjunctive therapy. The goal of the ketogenic diet is for a fifty percent reduction in seizures. Therefore, I suspect that [the child] will not likely be able to be seizure free with the ketogenic diet as monotherapy. I am hopeful that the diet will significantly decrease the seizure frequency, but I suspect it will not allow her seizures to resolve. [The child] will return to the Pediatric Epilepsy Monitoring Unit for continuous video EEG monitoring April 28–29 for seizure quantification. If [the child] continues to have frequent seizures, then I would recommend that she also be treated with an antiseizure medication in addition to the ketogenic diet.

The mother cancelled an appointment scheduled at the Mayo Clinic for late April. The appointment was rescheduled, and she cancelled it again. The State, in turn, filed a motion to compel the mother to take the child to the Mayo Clinic. The motion was granted, and the mother was ordered to take the child to the Mayo Clinic on May 17. The court further stated a failure to do so could result in a contempt finding.

At the May appointment, the Mayo Clinic reported a two-thirds reduction in the number of the child's seizures and agreed to give the diet an additional two months to see if any further progress could be made. However, the Mayo Clinic continued to say if complete seizure control was not obtained by the next appointment, medication would be ordered.

On June 29, 2010, Dr. Breitkreuz, on the parents' behalf, contacted Chareila N. Joshi, M.D. at the University of Iowa Hospitals and Clinics, requesting the doctor see the child prior to a scheduled appointment at the Mayo Clinic. An appointment at the University of Iowa was made for July 15, 2010, and both parents appeared with the child. Dr. Joshi had received certain medical reports and records addressing the child's diagnosis and treatment. Dr. Joshi was advised the parents were seeking another opinion regarding the child's treatment. Apparently,

---

5. The ketogenic diet is a very strict high-fat, low-carbohydrate diet. It is a more intensive version of the Atkins diet. By limiting carbohydrates, the ketogenic diet forces the body to use fat for energy. This results in the body having an abnormally high level of ketones (known as a state of ketosis), which reduces the frequency of seizures.

a separate report of the visit was requested by the father for himself, and he requested a second one for the department worker.

Dr. Joshi summarized the visit in a written report. The doctor noted that the father said he was very happy with the child's care at the Mayo Clinic, but he was there to support the mother, as the parents share custody. The child at the time was on the ketogenic diet, and the mother indicated, after speaking with other families that had used the diet, she felt more could be done with it for her child. The doctor also noted that:

> Mom's goal also seems to be to get [the child] better since according to a seizure chart that was brought and carefully kept by the family, at her worst [the child] was having upwards of 110 seizures a day, but since initiation of the diet and since maintenance of the diet there has been significant improvement such that there are days that the family sees no seizures.

The doctor also noted: "Both parents agree that seizures have definitely better controlled with the diet. Mom feels that [the child's] comprehension has improved."

The doctor was aware of the father's concern the child was not being treated. The doctor also was aware of the mother's wishes to continue to try diets. The doctor opined:

> [I]t would be very soon realized whether a 3.5 or 4.1 ratio will help keep [the child] seizure free longer especially given the fact that between February and May of 2010 [the child's] EEG as well as seizure count seems to have improved on the diet. I would possibly give [the child] a trial of the 3.5:1 therapy for 2–4 weeks. If [the child] has no side effects in the form of lethargy, vomiting, nausea, constipation, and if [the child] does not have hypertriglyceridemia or hypocholesterolemia on the same, I would be willing to push the diet to 4 as to 1, once again making sure that she does not have any side effects for a couple week period to see if [the child's] seizures go down to 0. Should that happen I think it would satisfy mother's curiosity since she feels that the diet is not tweaked enough to give [the child] the best potential.

The doctor also reported he told the parents:

> [A]ccording to articles written by Tassinari and Bureau, a combination of high dose of valproic acid and ethosuximide seems to be the best therapy for myoclonic absence. There is no reason to believe the above therapy cannot be used in conjunction with the diet. I would feel that probably given that the diet has done so well for [the child], we might be able to get away with a smaller dose of anticonvulsant medications for her, and according to a recent randomized trial by Tracy Glauser, et al, it seems that ethosuximide seems to give the best results in the treatment of absence epilepsy within approximately 16 weeks with the least possible side effects of inattention/clouding of attention.

The doctor further stated:

> Currently, since dad points to me that by court order they are only allowed to have a second opinion without making any changes, I will leave it to the family to decide whether they would want to change the diet over a brief duration of time.

The doctor then noted that:

I am the 6th or 7th doctor that [the child] has seen. . . . All doctors have felt that [the child's] epileptic encephalopathy needs treatment. I do not feel seeking multiple more medical opinions is in [the child's] best interest.

On August 10, 2010, the child returned to the Mayo Clinic for additional monitoring. The Clinic reported:

Overnight, [the child] did not have any absence seizures. She does continue to have innumerable myoclonic seizures. Her myoclonic seizures occur up to four times within a half hour. In addition, during sleep she has increased activation of epileptiform discharges that occur in bursts up to ten seconds in duration.

The Mayo Clinic determined a low dose of clonazepam should be initiated at bedtime to help decrease the epileptiform discharges during sleep. The mother apparently then told the Mayo Clinic that the University of Iowa had recommended maximizing the ketogenic diet. She did not give them the report from Dr. Joshi. Whether the father and the department provided Mayo Clinic a copy of the report is not clear. The Mayo Clinic stated it was willing to increase the diet ratio slowly to a ratio of 3.25:1, but it needed to be done in conjunction with the medication. The mother then told the Mayo Clinic she would discuss its recommendations with the child's father. Later that afternoon, she told the Mayo Clinic social worker she did not intend to give the child medication until it was decided in court. The social worker contacted the department, which in turn contacted the mother's attorney. The mother's attorney told the department the mother was willing to risk a finding of contempt rather than give her child medication. The father filled the prescription, and both parents have since been providing the child with the medication.

The petition came on for additional hearings on August 17 and October 20, 2010. At the hearings, the department caseworker and the father both testified that without court involvement, the mother would not be giving the child medication. The mother testified she was not against giving medication, but only wanted to see the ketogenic diet brought to "its full potential before adding any medication." Both parents acknowledged difficulties in communicating with each other. The father admitted he deferred getting treatment for the child, stating, "I don't feel that I have the ability to because of the placement." He also admitted he had stopped exercising visitation or talking to the mother because "the conflict between [the mother] and I is just too overwhelming for me."

The guardian ad litem recommended finding the child in need of assistance, opining the child has a "serious medical condition," proper medical treatment would not have occurred without the department's involvement, and the parents are "unable to get on the same page with regard to this child, who requires a lot of help from her parents."

On October 29, 2010, the juvenile court entered an adjudication order finding:

The overall consensus of medical opinion has been that this Child needs to take medication. The Child's mother has been resistive to this Child taking medication. The Child's father has been receptive to the Child taking medication.

Physicians have expressed concern that this Child has not been taken to follow-up appointments as needed. Physicians have expressed concern that the mother's continual search for a medical opinion that coincides with her own is detrimental to the Child; that the Child is in need of immediate treatment and that the Child's seizures need to be controlled.

The Child's mother has shopped this child around to different medical providers in an attempt to obtain a medical opinion which is consistent with her own non-medically-based opinion that this Child can be treated by diet alone. . . .

[The mother] has a pattern of only hearing what she wishes to hear with regard to recommendations made for this Child to undergo medical treatment and with regard to court orders regarding this Child's medical treatment.

Accordingly, the juvenile court found the child to meet the definition of a child in need of assistance under Iowa Code section 232.2(6)(e). On November 19, 2010, the juvenile court entered a dispositional order keeping primary physical placement of the child with her mother, subject to the existing visitation schedule, under the protective supervision of the department. The order further required the parents to comply with the recommendations of the Mayo Clinic, including any dietary and medication protocols for the child.

Child in Need of Assistance.   To prove its case, the State needs to prove by clear and convincing evidence that the child is in need of medical treatment to cure, alleviate, or prevent serious physical injury or illness, and the mother is unwilling to provide such treatment. The focus of the State's case is that the mother was apparently unwilling to agree to the child receiving medication to alleviate what the State contends is a serious physical illness.

The mother contends there is no medical evidence that the child was ever subject to a risk of a serious injury because she failed to provide the child with adequate care. In making this argument she recognizes a social worker with a B.A. degree testified to such things as "unless the seizures were reduced to zero [the child's] academic and behavior problems would increase and that the seizures caused brain damage," and "our fear at this point is critical care is denied if she does not follow the medical protocol." The mother contends these opinions should not be considered because they are contrary to the medical evidence. We agree that the social worker advanced medical opinions that are not supported by medical opinions advanced in medical reports. Therefore, we give any medical opinions advanced by the social worker little or no weight.

The evidence from medical experts came in by way of medical reports from doctors at respected medical facilities, all of which include certain medical opinions. Therefore, the usual testimony required to admit a medical opinion, including a recitation of the qualification of the doctor as well as his or her statement that his or her opinion is based on reasonable medical certainty, is not present. Nor have the parties had the opportunity to cross-examine the doctors. We consider these factors in interpreting the reports and determining the weight the opinions therein should be given.

The record clearly supports a finding the mother is dedicated to the child, provides for her needs, has sought opinions on her care from outstanding medical experts in the field of the child's problems, and has religiously implemented and monitored diets prescribed by experts, which have at times substantially reduced the child's seizures. What the record also clearly supports, is that the mother has not at all times been in favor of supplementing the child's diet with medication and has been extremely reluctant to do so. There also is evidence that the child had suffered reactions to medication in the past.

Assuming that the seizures will be stopped if the child takes medication, the question is what are the medical concerns if the medication is not administered. Finding no such opinion in any doctor's report to support the social worker's and father's claim that the child may suffer brain damage from seizures, we disregard this evidence. The testimony of Mayo Clinic's Elaine C. Wirrell, M.D., who opined "I am very concerned that with ongoing frequent seizures, her learning will continue to suffer." Yet the University of Iowa's Daniel Bonthius, M.D., Ph.D., opined, "However, I emphasized to [the child's] mother that the behavioral and academic problems are not caused by the seizures, per se." John Hopkins, in September of 2009, while discussing adding medication to the Atkins diet with the mother, indicated it was up to her what she wished to do. Dr. Joshi of the University of Iowa, who saw the child in July of 2010, and opined that a modified diet might be tried, while discussing with the parents certain drug therapy, indicated no concern in not having medication immediately prescribed.

Black's Law Dictionary 1398 (8th Ed. 2004), defines "serious" as to an injury or illness, accident, etc., "dangerous; potentially resulting in death or other severe consequences." We recognize the desires of the doctor and the father to assure that the child performs at her academic best, and until her seizures are totally controlled, she may not do so. We recognize there is competent medical evidence that seizures can have an undefined impact on the child's academic progress, and immediate medication is necessary. We also recognize there is other evidence that does not support this opinion. We also believe, even if we accept the fact that the seizures could be stopped with medication, there is not clear and convincing evidence to support the juvenile court's findings that the child was in need of medication to alleviate death or other serious consequences.

While as a state we are committed to seeing our children have adequate care, we should recognize that in most cases the child's parents are the best decision makers. The history of jurisprudence of this state on issues of child welfare shows, for the most part, the state and the courts do not involve themselves with medical decisions made by engaged and concerned parents. Making a decision to give one's child medication and/or treatment may find the parents faced with weighing the differing opinions of medical experts.

The mother knows her child better than anyone else knows this child. The mother was concerned about the side effects of medications the child takes. She wanted the diet explored fully before putting the child on more medication. There is no evidence as to the prognoses with medication and there is no evidence of side effects, if any, from the use of the medicine.

It is undeniable that the mother has continually sought treatments for the child. She also has successfully implemented diets that have decreased the child's seizures. She was giving the child medication at the time of the hearing. A child is in need of assistance under section 232.2(6)(e) when she is in need of treatment to cure a mental illness or emotional damage and her parent is unwilling or unable to provide such treatment. Upon our de novo review of the record, we find the evidence to support this ground of adjudication lacking. Both parents are willing and able to provide their daughter with treatment for her seizures. The mother has been active in assuring the child receives the directed diet and progress was made with the diet. She also testified that her reason for withholding the medicine is that she wanted to see the potential of the diet. Accordingly, we find clear and convincing evidence does not support the district court's adjudication of the child under section 232.2(6)(e) and reverse on this issue.

This said, we recognize that the father saw fit to agree to a finding the child was in need of assistance. Yet by his own admission, he has not been as involved in the care of his daughter as one would hope he would be. If issues as to the type of treatment this child should have continue to exist between the parents who have joint custody, those issues should be addressed in the district court in the context of the dissolution decree.

NOTES AND QUESTIONS

1. Most states recognize an emergency exception to the parental consent requirement for medical care. Why didn't the treatment proposed by the Mayo Clinic fall under this exception?

2. What test did the court use to decide whether to uphold the order for treatment over the mother's objection? Is the court's justification for deferring to the mother satisfactory?

3. The parents had joint legal custody, which ordinarily means that they share the right to make important decisions for the child, including major medical decisions. What role did the child's father play in making the decision about treatment? If he had been more insistent about wanting the child to have medications, how would the case have been different?

4. With regard to the consequences of failing to treat the epilepsy with medication, the state submitted testimony from an unqualified social worker. If a doctor with appropriate credentials had testified that the child was at serious risk for intellectual impairment and learning and social problems, giving specifics, would the outcome of the case have changed? Why or why not?

5. The doctors in *M.R.R.* had different opinions about the necessity of medicating the child. If, instead, all the doctors had agreed that medication was necessary, should the case have been decided differently? Why or why not? Does *M.R.R.* just recognize parental authority to choose between competing medical recommendations? Are parents in the best position to make this kind of choice? How does the doctor's role in this kind of case compare to the role of the doctors as described in *Parham*?

6. In some recent conflicts over children's medical treatment, the roles of doctors and parents have been reversed, with parents seeking treatments that doctors think are unnecessary, even though the parents are supported by other reputable doctors. In some of these cases, doctors opposing the treatments have reported the parents to child welfare and even criminal authorities, alleging that they have committed "medical child abuse." Maxine Eichner, Bad Medicine: Parents, the State, and the Charge of "Medical Child Abuse," 50 U.C. Davis L. Rev. 205, 210

(2016). Professor Eichner traces the label to an earlier claim, that some parents manufacture their children's medical symptoms and then seek medical care as a way of getting attention, the so-called Munchausen's Syndrome by Proxy (MSBP) cases. MSBP was always controversial and was discredited in England in the early 2000s. *Id.* at 214-218. In the United States MSBP was replaced beginning in the 1990s with the broader Medical Child Abuse diagnosis. Eichner criticizes the vagueness and breadth of the diagnosis, writing:

> [T]he terminology of "medical child abuse," and its association with MSBP, function to tar a vast range of parents as psychopaths intent on hurting their children. This is despite the fact that a large portion of behavior that falls within the broad definition of MCA might more accurately be considered simple differences of opinion between mothers and doctors, differences of opinions between two sets of doctors, or slight, within-the-bell-curve-of-normal exaggeration by a concerned parent. (This is not to say that the evaluating physicians always recognize the potentially broad possible range of motives a parent may have; instead, they often leap to assuming such a psychopathic motive exists based on scant evidence.) Rather than refer to this entire spectrum of behavior as "MCA," in many situations it would be far clearer for the evaluating pediatrician to specify the particular parental behavior deemed wrongful. For example, the physician might say simply "I think you were being overly anxious and didn't need to bring the child to the doctor." Or "I think you mistakenly gave the other doctor an incorrect picture of the child's symptoms. I don't think the child's nausea merited a prescription for Zofran." Yet framing the parent's behavior as "abuse" gives the evaluating doctor a potential legal lever to interfere coercively with the parent's decision-making. In contrast, framing the conflict as a simple disagreement between a doctor and a parent over what medical care the child needs gives a doctor no power to dictate the child's medical care, since parents are charged with the right to make health care decisions for their children absent abuse.

50 U.C. Davis L. Rev. at 224 – 225.

7. Parents are generally financially responsible for their children's needs, including payment for necessary medical care. If the parents do not pay voluntarily, a health care provider can recover the fair market value of services rendered under the common law necessaries doctrine. Greenspan v. Slate, 97 A.2d 390 (N.J. 1953). However, most parents do not pay for their children's medical care out of pocket. In 2016, 95 percent of all children were covered by health insurance. Private policies covered 63 percent of children, and public health insurance covered 42 percent of children. Child Trends, Health Care Coverage for Children, available at https://www.childtrends.org/indicators/health-care-coverage (July 28, 2018).

Children whose family income is no more than 133 percent of the poverty level qualify for Medicaid, the state-federal program that provides medical care for the poor, and in most states the qualifying income level is higher. The Children's Health Insurance Program (CHIP) covers most children in families with incomes at 200 percent of the poverty level, and in many states, families can have higher incomes and their children can still qualify. In addition, children with disabilities from poor families are eligible for cash assistance through the Supplemental Security Income (SSI) program, as well as for Medicaid. Medicaid provides children with periodic screening and diagnostic services and a range of services that includes services of health care providers, physical and other kinds of therapy, and medical equipment.

PROBLEM

Sara, who is 10 years old and in the fourth grade, is the third of eight children. She was recently diagnosed with T-Cell Lymphoblastic Lymphoma, a type of leukemia. On the recommendation of her doctors, her parents consented to the first phase of a series of chemotherapy treatments. The total course of treatments lasts two years, and with the treatment Sara would have a 55 percent chance of surviving for five years, when she would be considered cured. However, she responded very poorly to the chemotherapy; her parents described the side effects as horrible and terrible. Sara begged her parents to stop treatment. The parents did some research and learned that the adverse short- and long-term side effects of chemotherapy include nausea, fatigue, risk of uncontrolled bleeding, infections, infertility, cardiovascular disease, and other cancers. There is a small risk that the chemotherapy could be fatal. Because of concern about these effects and because they could not bear to see Sara suffer, the parents told the doctors to stop chemotherapy and that they would treat Sara with natural, holistic medicine.

At the juvenile court hearing on whether the parents' decision should be overridden, the doctor testified that no conventional medical treatment is as effective as the prescribed chemotherapy and that alternative treatments such as those her parents proposed would have no beneficial effect. The doctor testified that without treatment Sara would probably die within a year and that an interruption in her treatment risked reducing the efficacy of the treatment. You are a clerk to the trial judge who will decide this case. Please write a memo, based on the materials you have studied so far, analyzing this problem.

C. THE ROLE OF RELIGIOUS BELIEF

STATE V. BEAGLEY

305 P.3d 147 (Or. App. 2013)

SCHUMAN, P.J. . . . Defendants' son, Neil, had a rare congenital abnormality that caused the progressive loss of kidney function. The abnormality began to manifest, at the latest, in March 2008. Thereafter, Neil became increasingly weak, unable to hold down food, and unable to breathe freely. Because of their religious beliefs, and because Neil (who shared those beliefs) did not want to be medically treated, the family relied on what is commonly called "faith healing"—prayer, the laying on of hands, and anointment with oil. Neil rallied on one or two occasions but, on June 17, 2008, he died from complications of kidney failure. Medical intervention in the week before Neil died would have saved his life.

Defendants were each tried for criminally negligent homicide. The indictments charged each with causing the death of Neil "by failing to provide adequate medical care to [him], in violation of the duty of a parent." Defendants unsuccessfully demurred to the indictment, and a nine-day trial ensued. The jury returned guilty verdicts. Defendants now appeal.

A precise and complete definition of "criminal negligence" as it applies to this case will clarify several of the issues on appeal. A person commits criminally negligent homicide "when, with criminal negligence, the person causes the death of another person." "Criminal negligence," in turn, is defined in ORS 161.085(10):

> 'Criminal negligence' or 'criminally negligent,' when used with respect to a result or to a circumstance described by a statute defining an offense, means that a person fails to be aware of a substantial and unjustifiable risk that the result will occur or that the circumstance exists. The risk must be of such nature and degree that the failure to be aware of it constitutes a gross deviation from the standard of care that a reasonable person would observe in the situation.

Further, like all criminal offenses, criminally negligent homicide may be based on a person's "omission to perform an act which the person is capable of performing," if the act is one "the performance of which is required by law."

... The questions presented on appeal, then, cluster around three issues: first, whether the criminal negligence statute as charged in this case imposed, or constitutionally *could* impose, an obligation on defendants to provide life-sustaining medical care for Neil; second, whether the jury was properly instructed as to what facts it needed to find in order to return a guilty verdict; and third, whether the jury might have been prejudiced by hearing inadmissible evidence. ...

The issues raised by these arguments do not come to us on a blank slate. In *State v. Hays*, 964 P.2d 1042, *rev. den.*, 977 P.2d 1170 (1998), the defendant, following the teachings of his religion, relied on faith healing instead of medical care to treat his son's leukemia. When the son consequently died, the defendant was convicted of criminally negligent homicide. On appeal, he raised statutory and constitutional challenges to the prosecution. We affirmed the conviction, and in the process reached several conclusions that bear on the disposition of this case. We held that a parent has an "absolute" duty to "provide needed medical care to a child," subject only to legislatively established exceptions to accommodate the parent's belief in "treatment by spiritual means." The legislature, we observed, had enacted a statute relieving a parent of his or her duty to provide needed medical care for purposes of prosecution for criminal mistreatment, but not with respect to prosecutions for criminal negligence. Read together, we reasoned, the criminal negligence and criminal mistreatment statutes produce the following rule:

> [T]he statutes permit a parent to treat a child by prayer or other spiritual means so long as the illness is not life threatening. However, once a reasonable person should know that there is a substantial risk that the child will die without medical care, the parent must provide that care, or allow it to be provided, at the risk of criminal sanctions if the child does die.

That rule, we held, was not unconstitutionally vague, nor did it offend constitutional guarantees of due process or religious freedom.

Defendants acknowledge *Hays* and appear to recognize that a strict application of *stare decisis* would defeat their assignments of error challenging the denial of their demurrers. However, they have presented us with no compelling reason now to conclude that parents do *not* have a legal obligation to provide needed life-sustaining medical care for their children, nor that parents' constitutional right freely to exercise their religion encompasses a right unreasonably to fail to meet that obligation. . . .

We turn to defendants' arguments regarding jury instructions. In seven assignments of error, they contend that the court erroneously refused to give proffered instructions and erroneously gave objectionable instructions. . . .

After lengthy discussion with counsel, the court gave the following relevant jury instructions:

> A person acts with criminal negligence if that person fails to be aware of a substantial and unjustifiable risk that a particular result will occur and circumstance exists. The risk must be of such nature and degree that the failure to be aware of it constitutes a gross deviation from the standard of care that a reasonable person would observe in the situation.
>
> When used in the phrase 'did unlawfully and with criminal negligence cause the death of another human being, Neil Jeffrey Beagley, by failing to provide adequate medical care to a child, in violation of the duty of a parent,' criminal negligence or criminally negligent means that the person fails to be aware of a substantial and unjustifiable risk that the child will die without medical care. The risk must be of such nature and degree that the failure to be aware of it constitutes a gross deviation from the standard of care that a reasonable person would observe in the situation.
>
> Now, criminal negligence is also established if the State proves that the person acts recklessly. A person acts recklessly if the person is aware of and consciously disregards a substantial and unjustifiable risk either that a particular result will occur or that a particular circumstance exists.
>
> The risk must be of such nature and degree that disregarding it constitutes a gross deviation from the standard of care that a reasonable person would observe in the situation.
>
> Now, in connection with the phrase with regard to this case, that would mean that the particular result—in terms of measuring the definition of reckless conduct, that particular result would be the substantial and unjustifiable risk that the child would die without medical care. . . .
>
> Now, though it is true that our constitution generally protects free expression or religious practices and beliefs, these constitutional protections are limited when the safety and welfare of children are involved. It is not a defense to the charges of criminally negligent homicide that the defendants' care or treatment of their child was based solely upon spiritual means pursuant to the religious beliefs or practices of the defendants.
>
> Oregon law requires that a parent provide necessary and adequate medical care to a child. A child is defined as an unmarried person under 18 years of age. A person under the age of 18 years does not have a legal right to refuse medical care.

[D]efendants also argue that the court refused to give correct instructions. Defendants proposed, and the court rejected, the following instructions:

SPECIAL INSTRUCTION NO. 2

Oregon law permits a parent to treat a child by prayer or other spiritual means so long as the illness is not life threatening. However, if a reasonable person in the situation should know that there is a substantial and unjustifiable risk that the child will die without adequate medical care, then the parent must provide that care, or allow it to be provided.

SECOND ALTERNATIVE SPECIAL INSTRUCTION NO. 2

A parent has a right to direct the religious upbringing of his or her child.

Oregon law permits a parent to treat a child by prayer or other spiritual means so long as there is not an immediate threat to life. However, if a reasonable person in the situation should know that there is an immediate threat to life without adequate medical care, then the parent must provide that care, or allow it to be provided. . . .

[T]he court did not err in rejecting [second alternative special instruction no. 2]; it, too, does not correctly state the law. Nothing in *Hays* or any other source of law permits a parent to withhold medical care until the threat to life becomes *immediate*. Rather, under *Hays*, the obligation to provide life-saving medical care accrues when a reasonable person unreasonably and unjustifiably fails to recognize that failure to provide medical care creates a risk to life—regardless of the risk's immediacy. Thus, for example, the obligation to treat childhood leukemia would accrue when a parent learns that the child has the disease and that it is fatal without treatment—and not at the time when the disease has progressed to the point that death is imminent.

Defendants' special instruction No. [2], however, is an accurate and concise restatement of the holding in *Hays*. Thus, whether the court erred in rejecting the instruction depends on whether the instructions, taken as a whole, could have led the jury to return a guilty verdict under an erroneous impression of the law. For the reasons that follow, we conclude that the court did not err.

The thrust of defendants' challenges to the jury instructions is that, "[i]n sum, the trial court directed a verdict in favor of the state." By that, defendants mean that their theory of the case was that, because of the gradual onset of Neil's symptoms, the undramatic nature of those symptoms, and his periodic partial remissions, defendants' failure to recognize that his condition was life-threatening was not unreasonable—or, at least, not a gross deviation from the standard of care that a reasonable person would observe in the situation. To properly address that question, defendants argue, the jury had to know that defendants' obligation did not arise—that is, that their actions were not unlawful—until Neil's condition became obviously life-threatening. In order to make that determination, according to defendants, the jury had to know where the line was drawn between *permissible* treatment by spiritual means alone and *criminal* treatment by spiritual means alone. Defendants argue that the court's refusal to tell the jury where that line was, combined with the instructions that (1) Oregon law requires parents to provide necessary and adequate medical care to a child and (2) religious belief or practice is not a defense against criminally negligent homicide—this combination of instructions given and instructions refused misled the jury into believing that defendants could be convicted even if a reasonable person in their position would *not* have known that the omission created an unjustifiable risk of his death.

Defendants' argument is ultimately unpersuasive. Jurors must be correctly informed of what facts they need to find in order to return a guilty verdict. They do not need to know what facts, if found, will *not* suffice. The latter is implicit in the former. Thus, if a conviction for first-degree burglary requires the jury to find that a defendant entered a dwelling with the intent to commit a crime therein, the court does not need to instruct that a defendant is *not* guilty of first-degree burglary if she enters a dwelling without the requisite intent, or if the building she enters is not a dwelling. The instructions in this case correctly informed the jurors as to what 10 of them had to find in order to convict defendants of criminally negligent homicide: that defendants failed to be aware of a substantial and unjustifiable risk that Neil would die without medical care and that defendants' failure to be aware of that risk constituted a gross deviation from the standard of care that a reasonable person would observe in the situation. The jury was also correctly informed that defendants' religious beliefs were not a defense. Viewed as a whole, the instructions were free from error. . . .

CAROL WEISBROD, *COMMUNAL GROUPS AND THE LARGER SOCIETY: LEGAL DILEMMAS IN COMMUNAL SOCIETIES*

1, 5-6, 9-11 (1992)

. . . If a child is treated and returned home, what are the costs of the intervention in terms of the parent-child relations? We run the risk of trivializing religious beliefs which may result, for example, in the group's rejection of the healed child when the state has completed its temporary intervention. Finally on this point, we can note that the legal materials on the medical care problem include a Jehovah's Witness case[6] in which a judge went to the bedside of the patient—the mother of a young child—to interview her. The judge understood the mother to say, in effect, "You, the judge, can authorize the treatment where I cannot."[7] But this solution—let the sin be on the head of the legal system—may not be available in all cases. . . .

The point is that children are in effect members of the group and the state, the latter membership referred to as citizenship. Whatever their entitlements from the group, they have, as children, a right to protection by the state from others at certain times, even their parents. The language which is repeatedly quoted comes from the Supreme Court in Prince v. Massachusetts, a 1940's Jehovah's Witness case: "Parents may be free to become martyrs themselves. But it does not follow they are free, in identical circumstances, to make martyrs of their children before

---

6. Application of the President and Directors of Georgetown College, 331 F.2d 1000 (D.C. Cir. 1964).

7. *See id.* at 1007.

they have reached the age of full and legal discretion when they can make that choice for themselves."[8] But when is it martyrdom and when is it parental control? When is state intervention appropriate and when does it evoke that aspect of tyranny which uses as punishment the removal of children from their parents?

. . . Max Stirner's description of the shift from family to state authority stresses that the individual owes obedience to the family which has a kind of judicial function.[9] Thus a person may be expelled from the family as punishment. "Today, however," he writes,

> the arm of family power seldom reaches far enough to take seriously in hand the punishment of apostates. . . . The criminal against the family (family-criminal) flees into the domain of the State and is free, as the State criminal who gets away to America is no longer reached by the punishments of his State.[10]

Today, after Stirner, we associate the issue of discipline of children almost entirely with family pathology or dysfunction. We hardly relate it to the problem of the disciplinary power (working often through families) of intermediate groups within the state, unless the state intervention is seen as somehow too great. A large protective role for the state is generally conceded as to children.

James G. Dwyer, *Spiritual Treatment Exemptions to Child Medical Neglect Laws: What We Outsiders Should Think**

76 Notre Dame L. Rev. 147, 147-148, 151, 165-168, 172-173 (2000)

There are strongly opposing views as to whether parents should be exempted from the normal legal responsibility to secure medical treatment for sick or injured children when the parents have religious objections to medical care. . . . The division of opinion is not simply between the members of religious groups who want such an exemption for themselves and the rest of the world. There is division even among us "outsiders," we who are not members of a religious group with beliefs opposed to medical care and who therefore have no personal stake in the issue. . . .

Perhaps the greatest cause of the disagreement among outsiders, however, is confusion about the significance of the insiders' perspective. Supporters of exemptions point out that the insiders' perspective differs from ours in at least two ways. First, insiders perceive certain spiritual interests, of their own and of their children, that we outsiders do not perceive because we do not share their religious beliefs. Those spiritual interests count against medical care for their children, and insiders assign great weight to those spiritual interests. Second, some groups disagree with us outsiders on the relative efficacy of medical treatment in general. They think prayer is more effective in curing illness or healing injury and may even believe

---

8. Prince v. Massachusetts, 321 U.S. 158, 170 (1944).

9. Max Stirner, The Ego and His Own, trans. Steven T. Byington, 230 ff. (New York: Boni and Liveright, n.d.)

10. *Id.* at 232.

*The publisher bears responsibility for any errors that have occurred in reprinting or editing this article.

medical treatment to be counter-productive, because seeking it makes them less able to secure, or less worthy of, divine healing assistance. Many outsiders who support religious exemptions believe insider parents are entitled to act on the basis of their beliefs or that the State ought to defer to the insiders' perspective. . . .

Some supporters of spiritual treatment exemptions recognize that they cannot simply ignore the welfare and rights of the children involved and adopt an alternative strategy to support the conclusion that parents in these religious groups should be able to deny their children medical care. They ask, "Who determines what a child's interests are?" and answer this question by asserting that parents have a right to do so and the State does not. They then point out that the parents in these religious groups have a different perspective on human welfare and that, from the parents' perspective, the children are better off not receiving medical care.

This brings us, then, to the final issue—whether the State should defer to the insiders' perspective. Essentially, what most supporters of spiritual treatment exemptions to medical neglect laws argue is not that extensive exemptions are compelled by a proper balancing of interests as the State sees them, but rather that the State's view of what a child's interests are should not be controlling. They contend that the parents' view of what a child's interests are and of how best to promote them should instead be controlling in children's lives.

This is distinct from a claim simply for parental freedom, for noninterference with actions motivated by personal belief. . . . The claim here is about spheres of authority. It is essentially a claim about the proper domain of the State. It is a claim that parental control over children's lives is primordial, outside the public realm, and no business of the State.

Curiously, though, most proponents of this sort of "spheres of authority" position allow for state control over child rearing at the margins. The State may step in to prevent death. But they provide no real explanation for this qualification of the separate spheres position, for ceding some authority to the state. Instead, they may talk of bounds of reasonableness; parents' choices should control unless they are unreasonable, and a choice that will lead to a child's death is unreasonable. However, not only do supporters of exemptions fail to offer a coherent account of what "reasonable" means, but they also never explain why this or any other standard should limit parental authority within the private domain. If it is truly a separate domain, then how can the State ever legitimately intrude into child rearing? They do not tell us. Nor do they provide an argument for postulating separate spheres in the first place. Nor an explanation of why the "family as separate sphere" position would not also apply in non-religious child-rearing contexts, and indeed to relations between spouses. Should domestic violence laws contain a religious exemption on the theory that abusive husbands are entitled to determine what their wives' best interests are, at least so long as their wives do not object? If not, then supporters of spiritual treatment exemptions need to explain why not.

In any event, the reality is that the family is not a separate, primordial sphere that is or can be cordoned off from the power of the State. The law creates the family, and things could not be otherwise. The State assigns legal custody to particular adults for each and every child at the time of birth, reassigns custody at later points in the lives of a large percentage of children (for example, in connection with a divorce), and attaches to custody numerous legal rights and powers. Without the law creating and protecting parent-child relationships in this way, chaos would reign. So the separate spheres argument, in addition to being theoretically ungrounded, is out of touch with reality. It therefore fails as a basis for the position that the State should defer to the views of religious parents as to what constitutes the interests and rights of their children. The State does and must establish the rules for parental control over children's lives and, in doing so, must rest its judgment on assumptions about children's interests and rights as it sees them. In doing so, the State might justifiably conclude that parents should have presumptive authority to make decisions for children in many aspects of their lives, because the State has good reason to believe that it is, in general, best for children that their parents have that presumptive authority. What supporters of spiritual treatment exemptions need to argue is that the State has good reason to believe that it is best for children that their parents have authority to deny them medical care that the State deems necessary for the children's physical well-being whenever such care conflicts with the parents' religious beliefs. They have yet to offer any such reason. . . .

More relevant to the issue of who gets to define the ends of child rearing is the assertion that parents have a superior moral claim to that power than the State does. Some liberals—so called "liberal statists"—do appear to take the position that the State has a superior moral claim to that power in some areas of children's lives. Amy Gutmann has argued, for example, that society as a whole, acting through the instrumentality of the State, is entitled to control children's education to a substantial degree in order to serve certain collective ends—principally the reproduction of democratic culture from one generation to the next. But that is certainly not the only logical alternative to the position that parents are entitled to decide what the aims are for their children's lives. In my view, neither parents nor the State have any moral claim on their own behalf, any entitlement to decide what the ends of a child's life are. Rather, only children themselves have any moral claim or entitlement in connection with their upbringing, and we adults should be deliberating about how best to fulfill our obligation to them, not about which adults are entitled to determine how children's lives will go. Talk of superior moral claims of this sort effectively treats children and children's lives instrumentally, as means for satisfying the interests of one or another group of adults, and that is morally inappropriate. I have suggested in this Essay that the best way to fulfill the rights of children is to protect and promote their healthy development into adults, who can decide for themselves the aims for their lives. . . .

NOTES AND QUESTIONS

1. No American jurisdiction allows parents to deny a child medical care necessary to preserve the child's life because they believe in faith healing. On the other hand, as we have seen, in less serious circumstances parents have discretion to decide what kind of care their children receive. The problem that *Beagley* presents is at what point must parents provide conventional medical care, rather than employing spiritual healing practices. According to the jury instruction that was actually given, when does this duty arise? How is the rule in proposed Second

Alternative Special Jury Instruction No. 2 different? Under the instruction actually given, when were the Beagleys obliged to take Neil to the doctor?

Beagley is one of several recent Oregon cases on the extent of parents' right to decline medical care for their children for religious reasons. Several focus on the problem of exactly when a parent who believes in faith healing must provide conventional medical care to a sick child. In the most important case, State v. Hickman, 358 P.3d 987 (Or. 2015), parents were convicted of negligent homicide when they did not seek medical help for a child born two months prematurely. They unsuccessfully argued that under the Free Exercise Clause, they could be punished only if they knew that their child required conventional medical care to survive, i.e., that convicting them of negligent homicide would be unconstitutional.

2. If for religious reasons the parents in *M.R.R.* had refused to consent to the medication that the Mayo Clinic doctors recommended, would the standard applied in *Beagley* have allowed a court to override their decision? Should a parent's objection that is based on religion be accorded greater, less, or the same deference as one based on the parent's disagreement with the doctor about the medical risks and benefits of a proposed treatment? Why? *See* In the Matter of D.R., 20 P.3d 166 (Okla. App. 2001) (upholding order overriding parents' refusal to consent to medication for epilepsy on religious grounds and granting custody to child welfare agency where epilepsy was "severe," drug had few side effects, and only treatment proposed was prayer).

3. In Spiering v. Heineman, 448 F. Supp. 2d 1129 (D. Neb. 2006), parents challenged a state requirement that their newborn child be tested for a variety of metabolic conditions by having blood taken from a heel prick between 24 and 48 hours after birth. The Scientologist parents said the test was inconsistent with their belief in "Silent Birth," which requires that a child be protected from pain for seven days after birth. The parents essentially conceded that the requirement was rationally related to valid state interests but argued for strict scrutiny, relying on Wisconsin v. Yoder, 406 U.S. 205 (1972), as interpreted Employment Division v. Smith, 494 U.S. 872 (1989) (*see* discussion in Chapter 1, pages 60-68). The court refused to apply heightened scrutiny, saying that under *Smith*, heightened scrutiny is required only when parents couple a freedom of religion claim with a claim to control their children's education. The court added that even if the hybrid rights claim extended to this situation, the state may limit parental authority when a child's safety is at issue, citing Prince v. Massachusetts, 321 U.S. 158 (1944). "It is not plausible that the Supreme Court would apply 'strict scrutiny' and thus tilt the table in favor of the rights of parents and against the safety of children. This is all the more true where, as here, the medical evidence establishing a 'life and death' reason for testing infants is undisputed and, still further, where a parent's objection to either the test or treatment following the test will be resolved by a court after a hearing." 448 F. Supp. 2d at 1140. In 2005 the Nebraska Supreme Court reached a similar conclusion in Douglas County v. Anaya, 694 N.W.2d 601 (Neb. 2005). However, the court also held that the parents' refusal to consent to testing did not constitute neglect that supported juvenile court jurisdiction over the child. In re Interest of Anaya, 758 N.W.2d 10 (Neb. 2008). For a discussion of the impact of *Smith* on medical treatment decision cases, *see* B. Jessie Hill, Whose Body/ Whose Soul? Medical Decision-Making on Behalf of Children and the Free Exercise

Clause Before and After Employment Division v. Smith, 32 Cardozo L. Rev. 1857 (2011).

4. During the 1970s most states amended their child abuse and neglect statutes to provide exemptions from child abuse reporting laws and sometimes other laws for parents who practiced faith healing. The states enacted these laws so that they would be eligible for federal child welfare funds. The federal requirement was imposed after intense lobbying by religious groups, especially the Christian Scientists. While the federal requirement was abolished in 1983, as of 2016, 31 states and the District of Columbia still had laws exempting faith healing parents from child abuse reporting, and another 3 states had exemptions for Christian Science treatment. Sixteen of the 31 states allow juvenile courts to order medical treatment for children notwithstanding their parents' religious objections. Child Welfare Information Gateway, Definitions of Child Abuse and Neglect 4 (2016), (Aug. 7, 2018).

A typical statute was Cal. Welf. & Inst. Code § 300, which provided in 1987:

> No child who in good faith is under treatment solely by spiritual means through prayer in accordance with the tenets and practices of a recognized church or religious denomination by a duly accredited practitioner thereof shall, for that reason alone, be considered to have been neglected. . . .

Courts differ about whether such a statute prevents a juvenile court from finding a child medically neglected if the parents refuse to provide conventional medical care and instead seek spiritual treatment. In re Eric B., 235 Cal. Rptr. 22 (Ct. App. 1987), interpreted the statute as identifying one factor "to be considered by the juvenile court" and held that the statute permitted a court to conclude that a child who is receiving spiritual treatment was nevertheless medically neglected. The court then ordered that the child receive ongoing treatment for eye cancer over the objection of Christian Scientist parents. *See also* In the Matter of D.R., 20 P.3d 166 (Okla. App. 2001). In contrast, People in the Interest of D.L.E., 614 P.2d 873 (Colo. 1980), held that a similar statute precluded ordering surgery for a non-life-threatening condition over the parent's religious objections. The California statute has since been amended as follows:

> Whenever it is alleged that a child comes within the jurisdiction of the court on the basis of the parent's or guardian's willful failure to provide adequate medical treatment or specific decision to provide spiritual treatment through prayer, the court shall give deference to the parent's or guardian's medical treatment, nontreatment, or spiritual treatment through prayer alone in accordance with the tenets and practices of a recognized church or religious denomination, by an accredited practitioner thereof, and shall not assume jurisdiction unless necessary to protect the child from suffering serious physical harm or illness. In making its determination, the court shall consider (1) the nature of the treatment proposed by the parent or guardian, (2) the risks to the child posed by the course of treatment or nontreatment proposed by the parent or guardian, (3) the risk, if any, of the course of treatment being proposed by the petitioning agency, and (4) the likely success of the courses of treatment or nontreatment proposed by the parent or guardian and agency. The child shall continue to be a dependent child pursuant to this

subdivision only so long as is necessary to protect the child from risk of suffering serious physical harm or illness.

What is the significance of the statutory change?

5. If a spiritual treatment exemption statute precludes a juvenile court finding of neglect in non-life-threatening cases or a conviction of criminal child abuse, does this mean that parents cannot be criminally prosecuted for homicide if their child dies from a condition or illness that was medically treatable? While courts generally hold that the spiritual treatment exemption in itself does not preclude a homicide conviction, they are divided about whether such a conviction violates due process because parents are not on notice that spiritual treatment may subject them to criminal penalties if their child dies. Minnesota v. McKown, 475 N.W.2d 63 (Minn. 1991), and Hermanson v. Florida, 604 So. 2d 775 (Fla. 1992), held that due process was violated because the statutory scheme was sufficiently confusing to make the criminal statute unconstitutionally vague. Other courts have rejected the vagueness argument, however. *E.g.*, State v. Crank, 468 S.W.3d 15 (Tenn. 2015); State v. Neumann, 832 N.W.2d 560 (Wis. 2013); Walker v. Superior Court, 763 P.2d 852 (Cal. 1988), *cert. denied*, 491 U.S. 905 (1989).

BROWN V. SMITH

235 Cal. Rptr. 3d 218 (App. 2018)

GRIMES, J. . . . Plaintiffs Sharon Brown, Sarah Lucas, Dawnielle Selden, Serge Eustache, Tricia Eustache, and Nikki Jencen filed this lawsuit, seeking to invalidate amendments to California's public health laws governing immunization requirements against childhood diseases. These legislative changes were made by Senate Bill No. 277, approved by the Governor on June 30, 2015, effective January 1, 2016.

Senate Bill No. 277 eliminated the personal beliefs exemption from the requirement that children receive vaccines for specified infectious diseases before being admitted to any public or private elementary or secondary school, day care center or the like.[11] In addition to a medical exemption,[12] Senate Bill No. 277 contains exemptions for pupils in a home-based private school or independent

---

11. The childhood diseases specified are diphtheria, hepatitis B, haemophilus influenzae type b, measles, mumps, pertussis (whooping cough), poliomyelitis, rubella, tetanus, and varicella (chickenpox). The list also includes "[a]ny other disease deemed appropriate by the department, taking into consideration the recommendations of the Advisory Committee on Immunization Practices of the United States Department of Health and Human Services, the American Academy of Pediatrics, and the American Academy of Family Physicians." (*Id. at* subd. (a)(11).) As to the last item, immunization may be mandated before a pupil's first admission to any school or child care center only if exemptions are allowed for both medical reasons and personal beliefs. (§ 120338.)

12. The medical exemption, as amended by Senate Bill No. 277, states: "If the parent or guardian files with the governing authority a written statement by a licensed physician to the effect that the physical condition of the child is such, or medical circumstances relating to the child are such, that immunization is not considered safe, indicating the specific nature and probable duration of the medical condition or circumstances, including, but not limited to, family medical history, for which the physician does not recommend immunization, that child shall be exempt from the [immunization] requirements . . . to the extent indicated by the physician's statement."

study program who do not receive classroom-based instruction and for pupils previously allowed a personal beliefs exemption, until they enroll in the next grade span. Grade spans are "[b]irth to preschool," "[k]indergarten and grades 1 to 6," and "[g]rades 7 to 12." Also, pupils who qualify for an individualized education program are allowed access to any special education and related services required by that program. Otherwise, as of July 1, 2016, no pupil may be unconditionally admitted for the first time, or admitted or advanced to seventh grade level, unless immunized as required.

The legislative history of Senate Bill No. 277 includes an extensive analysis of the bill, the reasons the authors gave for proposing the bill, the diseases that vaccines prevent and their health risks to children, the legal considerations, and the support for and opposition to the bill.

Among many other things, the report from the Assembly Committee on Health discusses the protective effect of community immunity, which "wanes as large numbers of children do not receive some or all of the required vaccinations, resulting in the reemergence of vaccine preventable diseases in the U.S." The report explains that the vaccination rate in various communities "varies widely across the state," and some areas "become more susceptible to an outbreak than the state's overall vaccination levels may suggest," making it "difficult to control the spread of disease and mak[ing] us vulnerable to having the virus re-establish itself." Further, studies have found that "when belief exemptions to vaccination guidelines are permitted, vaccination rates decrease," and one analysis "found that more than a quarter of schools in California have measles-immunization rates below the 92-94% recommended by the CDC [(Center for Disease Control)]." The report describes the December 2014 outbreak of measles linked to Disneyland (131 confirmed cases); states that according to the CDC, "measles is one of the first diseases to reappear when vaccination coverage rates fall"; and states that in 2014, 600 cases were reported to the CDC, the highest in many years. . . .

The complaint described the plaintiffs, all of whom are parents with "sincerely held philosophic, conscientious, and religious objections to state-mandated immunization." The defendant named in the operative complaint is Karen Smith, sued in her capacity as director of the California Department of Public Health. The 38-page complaint consists principally of argument, alleging, for example, that plaintiffs "dispute the central hypothesis that drives vaccine theory," which "has never been proven and Plaintiffs are eager to disprove it"; that "[v]accines kill and maim children"; and that Senate Bill No. 277 "is a totalitarian mandate that expects parents to merrily sacrifice their children for the greater good." We will describe the complaint's allegations further as necessary in our discussion of plaintiffs' contentions on appeal.

Defendants demurred to the complaint, plaintiffs opposed, and the trial court sustained defendants' demurrer without leave to amend. The court entered an order dismissing plaintiffs' complaint with prejudice and plaintiffs appealed. . . .

Along with their respondents' brief, defendants filed a motion requesting judicial notice of several categories of documents. These include documents from the legislative history of Senate Bill No. 277; documents published by the World Health Organization, the CDC, the American Academy of Pediatrics, and the United States Department of Health and Human Services, plus other materials addressing the safety and effectiveness of vaccinations; and federal and state trial court decisions rejecting challenges to Senate Bill No. 277. In addition, defendants requested we take judicial notice "of the safety and effectiveness of vaccinations in preventing the spread of dangerous communicable diseases, a fact that is commonly known and accepted in the scientific community and the general public."

We grant defendants' request for judicial notice.

Plaintiffs do not object to the legislative history materials, but object to the materials on vaccination as hearsay, inadmissible opinion evidence, and "government propaganda." Plaintiffs further argue that we cannot take judicial notice of the safety and effectiveness of vaccines. They contend the proposition that "'protection of school children against crippling and deadly diseases by vaccinations is done effectively and safely'" is not common knowledge, and is the subject of reasonable dispute. But they cite no authority that supports their contention. The authorities are to the contrary. . . .

Accordingly, we conclude judicial notice of the safety and effectiveness of vaccinations is proper. . . .

Plaintiffs cite no pertinent authority for their assertion that Senate Bill No. 277 "violates freedom of religion." It does not.

As a preliminary matter, we note that three of the six plaintiffs describe themselves as Christians, two of whom are opposed to the use of fetal cells in vaccines; the third has children who have had most of the recommended vaccinations. The other three plaintiffs allege nothing about any religious basis for their objection to vaccination. A belief that is "philosophical and personal rather than religious . . . does not rise to the demands of the Religion Clauses."

Setting that point aside, in *Phillips v. City of New York* (2d Cir. 2015) 775 F.3d 538 (*Phillips*), the court held that "mandatory vaccination as a condition for admission to school does not violate the Free Exercise Clause." In *Phillips*, New York law required that students be immunized against various vaccine-preventable illnesses, and provided medical and religious exemptions. *Phillips* further stated: "New York could constitutionally require that all children be vaccinated in order to attend public school. New York law goes beyond what the Constitution requires by allowing an exemption for parents with genuine and sincere religious beliefs. [T]he State could bar [plaintiffs'] children from school altogether."

Phillips relied on the high court's "persuasive dictum" in *Prince v. Massachusetts* (1944) 321 U.S. 158. In *Prince*, the court observed: "[T]he family itself is not beyond regulation in the public interest, as against a claim of religious liberty. [Citations.] And neither rights of religion nor rights of parenthood are beyond limitation. ... [The state's] authority is not nullified merely because the parent grounds his claim to control the child's course of conduct on religion or conscience. Thus, he cannot claim freedom from compulsory vaccination for the child more than for himself on religious grounds. The right to practice religion freely does not include liberty to expose the community or the child to communicable disease or the latter to ill health or death."

Even if we were to assume that laws requiring vaccination substantially burden the free exercise of religion and therefore merit strict scrutiny, plaintiffs' claim fails. (Workman v. Mingo County Board of Education (4th Cir. 2011) 419 Fed. Appx. 348, 353 [West Virginia's mandatory immunization program withstands strict scrutiny].) Citing *Jacobson* and *Prince*, *Workman* rejected the contention "that because West Virginia law requires vaccination against diseases that are not very prevalent, no compelling state interest can exist." "On the contrary, the state's wish to prevent the spread of communicable diseases clearly constitutes a compelling interest."

We agree with these authorities, and plaintiffs point to no pertinent authority to the contrary. Plaintiffs cite *Yoder, supra*, 406 U.S. 205, but *Yoder* does not assist plaintiffs; it concerned compulsory school attendance, not immunization against contagious diseases. And, the court pointed out that the case was "not one in which any harm to the physical or mental health of the child or to the public safety, peace, order, or welfare has been demonstrated or may be properly inferred," and that a parent's power, "even when linked to a free exercise claim, may be subject to limitation under *Prince* if it appears that parental decisions will jeopardize the health or safety of the child, or have a potential for significant social burdens." Accordingly, plaintiffs' free exercise claim has no merit. . . .

NOTES AND QUESTIONS

1. What rationale does the court accept to justify vaccination requirements? How does this rationale differ from that asserted by the state in *M.R.R.* and *Beagley*? Would that rationale support a court order in *M.R.R.* authorizing medication for the child's epilepsy?

The Supreme Court rejected a man's challenge to a law requiring that he be vaccinated in Jacobson v. Massachusetts, 197 U.S. 11 (1905), long before the Court held that the Bill of Rights limits state and local governments. The challenger argued that the requirement violated the due process and privileges and immunities clauses of the Fourteenth Amendment. Justice Harlan wrote for the majority:

> The defendant insists that his liberty is invaded when the state subjects him to fine or imprisonment for neglecting or refusing to submit to vaccination; that a compulsory vaccination law is unreasonable, arbitrary, and oppressive, and, therefore, hostile to the inherent right of every freeman to care for his own body and health in such way as to him seems best; and that the execution of such a law against one who objects to vaccination, no matter for what reason, is nothing short of an assault upon his person. But the liberty secured by the Constitution of the United States to every person within its jurisdiction does not import an absolute right in each person to be, at all times and in all circumstances, wholly freed from restraint. There are manifold restraints to which every person is necessarily subject for the common good. On any other basis organized society could not exist with safety to its members. Society based on the rule that each one is a law unto himself would soon be confronted with disorder and anarchy. Real liberty for all could not exist under the operation of a principle which recognizes the right of each individual person to use his own, whether in respect of his person or his property, regardless of the injury that may be done to others. This court has more than once recognized it as a fundamental

principle that 'persons and property are subjected to all kinds of restraints and burdens in order to secure the general comfort, health, and prosperity of the state; of the perfect right of the legislature to do which no question ever was, or upon acknowledged general principles ever can be, made, so far as natural persons are concerned.' The possession and enjoyment of all rights are subject to such reasonable conditions as may be deemed by the governing authority of the country essential to the safety, health, peace, good order, and morals of the community. Even liberty itself, the greatest of all rights, is not unrestricted license to act according to one's own will. It is only freedom from restraint under conditions essential to the equal enjoyment of the same right by others. It is, then, liberty regulated by law.'

197 U.S. at 26-27. Zucht v. King, 260 U.S. 174 (1922), held that a local ordinance requiring all school children to be vaccinated was constitutional as well.

2. All states allow an exemption from compulsory school vaccination for children with medical conditions that put them at risk for serious side effects, and most states allow exemptions for religious or personal beliefs or both. When California enacted the law challenged in *Brown*, it joined Mississippi and West Virginia as the only states that recognized only medical exemptions, as of 2016. Erwin Chemerinsky & Michele Goodwin, Compulsory Vaccination Laws Are Constitutional, 110 Nw. U. L. Rev. 589, 593 (2016). A survey of all the people in New Mexico who received a religious or medical exemption found that more than half were not eligible for either exemption. These people opposed vaccinations because they believe them to be unsafe and lied to fit themselves into the exemption categories, since New Mexico does not have a personal belief exemption. Dorit Rubinstein Reiss, Thou Shalt Not Take the Name of the Lord Thy God in Vain: Use and Abuse of Religious Exemptions from School Immunization Requirements, 65 Hastings L.J. 1551, 1152-1553 (2014).

3. Michigan allows a parent to claim a religious exemption from mandatory school vaccinations but requires the parent to go to a county health office to discuss the objection with a health worker, and the exemption is granted only if the health worker certifies that the parent has "received education on the risks of not receiving the vaccines being waived and the benefits of vaccination to the individual and the community." The state has also published notes that workers use to respond to many common objections. A mother who participated in a meeting and was granted a waiver sued the state and county, alleging several constitutional violations in the course of her interview with the health worker. The Sixth Circuit held that she had standing to challenge the laws and practices under the Establishment Clause, since she alleged "direct and unwelcome contact with a government-sponsored religious object." Nikolao v. Lyon, 875 F.3d 310 (6th Cir. 2017). However, on the merits, the court upheld the law, since it had a secular purpose, did not advance or inhibit religion, and did not foster excessive government entanglement with religion.

4. In addition to the articles cited above, for more information *see* Linda C. Fentiman, Sex, Science, and the Age of Anxiety, 92 Neb. L. Rev. 455 (2014), discussing the controversy over requiring school-age children to be vaccinated against the human papillomavirus (HPV).

D.   DECISION MAKING AT THE END OF CHILDREN'S LIVES

A famous article published in the New England Journal of Medicine in 1973 acknowledged that doctors sometimes allow parents to choose not to authorize lifesaving care for seriously ill newborns, with the knowledge that the child's death is highly likely. Raymond Duff & A.G.M. Campbell, Moral and Ethical Dilemmas in the Special-Care Nursery, 289 New Eng. J. Med. 890 (Oct. 1973). The issue was brought to the public's attention dramatically early in the 1980s, when lawsuits were filed challenging decisions to deny critical surgery to conjoined twins born in Illinois and to a child with Down syndrome in Bloomington, Indiana. In both cases, the courts ultimately ruled in favor of the doctors and parents, but the public furor continued. In 1983, in what was known as the Baby Jane Doe case, an activist lawyer sued parents in New York, seeking to override their refusal to consent to surgery for a child born with spina bifida.[13] The trial judge appointed a guardian for the child to consent to the surgery, but on the parents' appeal, the decision was reversed on the ground that the plaintiff had no standing to bring the suit. Weber v. Stony Brook Hospital, 467 N.Y.S.2d 685, *aff'd*, 456 N.E.2d 1186, *cert. denied*, 464 U.S. 1026 (1983).

Beginning in 1982, the federal Department of Health and Human Services (DHHS) began to intervene and, by various routes, attempted to limit the practice of denying medical care to severely disabled newborns. In 1984, Congress amended the Child Abuse Prevention and Treatment Act to require states to establish programs and procedures to prevent medical neglect of infants with disabilities as a condition to receiving federal child welfare funds. 42 U.S.C. §§ 5101-5103. "Medical neglect" includes "withholding of medically indicated treatment," which is defined as:

> failure to respond to the infant's life-threatening conditions by providing treatment (including appropriate nutrition, hydration and medication) which, in the treating physician's (or physicians') reasonable medical judgment, will be most likely to be effective in ameliorating or correcting all such conditions, except that the term does not include the failure to provide treatment (other than appropriate nutrition, hydration or medication) to an infant when, in the treating physician's or physicians' reasonable medical judgment, (i) the infant is chronically and irreversibly comatose; (ii) the provision of such treatment would merely prolong dying, not be effective in ameliorating or correcting all of the infant's life-threatening conditions, or otherwise be futile in terms of the survival of the infant; or (iii) the provision of such treatment would be virtually futile in terms of the survival of the infant and the treatment itself would be inhumane.

---

13. Spina bifida is the common name for a medical condition, meningomyelocele, in which the spinal column fails to close properly during fetal development, often accompanied by hydrocephaly, the accumulation of cerebrospinal fluid in the cranium. Mild cases of spina bifida can be surgically corrected so that the child has only relatively minor permanent disabilities. In more severe cases, even with surgery the child may have major disabilities. If the spinal lesion is not closed soon after birth, though, the child is seriously at risk of meningitis, which can cause death. Gallo, Spina Bifida: The State of the Art of Medical Management, 14 Hastings Ctr. Rptr. 10, 10-11 (Feb. 1984).

45 C.F.R. § 1340.15(b)(2). In 2002, Congress enacted the Born-Alive Infants Protection Act, Pub. L. No. 107-207, which requires that resuscitation and other life-saving measures be initiated if an infant has a heartbeat or shows other signs of life.

Although the Baby Doe regulations were prompted by concerns about treatment of a full-term child with Down syndrome, today most of the cases in which there is a question whether to provide treatment involve premature babies, especially those born at 27 weeks of gestation or less and weighing two pounds or less. Craig A. Conway, Baby Doe and Beyond: Examining the Practical and Philosophical Influences Impacting Medical Decision-Making on Behalf of Marginally-Viable Newborns, 25 Ga. St. U. L. Rev. 1097, 1114 (2009).

A recent medical study concluded that the likelihood of a favorable outcome for extremely premature infants provided with intensive care can better be estimated by consideration of four factors in concert with gestational age: sex of the infant, exposure or non-exposure to antenatal corticosteroids, whether born as part of a single or multiple birth, and birth weight. If the infant was a single birth female with a slightly higher birth weight, the risk of death or impairment dramatically decreased. Also, each one-week increase in gestational age significantly increased the infant's chance of survival regardless of the sex of the child. The study, conducted on infants weighing less than 1000 grams [slightly over two pounds] at birth, reiterated physicians' practice of providing "comfort care" to infants born at twenty-two weeks of gestation or less and only providing more aggressive care to infants born twenty-three to twenty-four weeks of gestation with parental agreement.

> . . . Even if the newborn survives, long-term neurodevelopmental outcomes are poor. Often, the incidence of increased severe impairment including mental retardation, cerebral palsy, blindness and deafness accompanies survival. According to one medical study conducted in 2003, ninety-two percent of infants born at twenty-three to twenty-four weeks of gestation had some moderate to severe abnormal neurologic, psychomotor, or mental development problems. Rates of disability decreased with each additional gestation week of the newborn.

Id. at 1115-1116.

A number of commentators have concluded that an important effect of the federal rules is to shift medical standards of care toward more aggressive efforts to save the lives of compromised infants. See, e.g., Anita Silvers & Leslie Pickering Francis, Playing God with Baby Doe: Quality of Life and Unpredictable Life Standards at the Start of Life, 25 Ga. St. U. L. Rev. 1061, 1083-1084 (2009); Conway, Baby Doe and Beyond, above, 25 Ga. St. U. L. Rev. at 1108. The next case is one of a handful that have been litigated to the appellate level in which parents disagree with the doctors' wish to provide treatment.

MILLER v. HCA, INC.

118 S.W.3d 758 (Tex. 2003)

Justice ENOCH delivered the opinion of the Court. . . . The unfortunate circumstances of this case began in August 1990, when approximately four months before her due date, Karla Miller was admitted to Woman's Hospital of Texas (the "Hospital") in premature labor. An ultrasound revealed that Karla's fetus weighed about 629 grams or about 1.38 pounds and had a gestational age of approximately twenty-three weeks. Because of the fetus's prematurity, Karla's physicians began administering a drug designed to stop labor.

Karla's physicians subsequently discovered that Karla had an infection that could endanger her life and require them to induce delivery. Dr. Mark Jacobs, Karla's obstetrician, and Dr. Donald Kelley, a neonatologist at the Hospital, informed Karla and her husband, Mark Miller, that if they had to induce delivery, the infant had little chance of being born alive. The physicians also informed the Millers that if the infant was born alive, it would most probably suffer severe impairments, including cerebral palsy, brain hemorrhaging, blindness, lung disease, pulmonary infections, and mental retardation. Mark testified at trial that the physicians told him they had never had such a premature infant live and that anything they did to sustain the infant's life would be guesswork.

After their discussion, Drs. Jacobs and Kelley asked the Millers to decide whether physicians should treat the infant upon birth if they were forced to induce delivery. At approximately noon that day, the Millers informed Drs. Jacob and Kelley that they wanted no heroic measures performed on the infant and they wanted nature to take its course. Mark testified that he understood heroic measures to mean performing resuscitation, chest massage, and using life support machines. Dr. Kelley recorded the Millers' request in Karla's medical notes, and Dr. Jacobs informed the medical staff at the Hospital that no neonatologist would be needed at delivery. Mark then left the Hospital to make funeral arrangements for the infant.

In the meantime, the nursing staff informed other Hospital personnel of Dr. Jacobs' instruction that no neonatologist would be present in the delivery room when the Millers' infant was born. An afternoon of meetings involving Hospital administrators and physicians followed. Between approximately 4:00 P.M. and 4:30 P.M. that day, Anna Summerfield, the director of the Hospital's neonatal intensive care unit, and several physicians, including Dr. Jacobs, met with Mark upon his return to the Hospital to further discuss the situation. Mark testified that Ms. Summerfield announced at the meeting that the Hospital had a policy requiring resuscitation of any baby who was born weighing over 500 grams. Although Ms. Summerfield agreed that she said that, the only written Hospital policy produced described the Natural Death Act and did not mention resuscitating infants over 500 grams.

Moreover, the physicians at the meeting testified that they and Hospital administrators agreed only that a neonatologist would be present to evaluate the Millers' infant at birth and decide whether to resuscitate based on the infant's condition at that time. As Dr. Jacobs testified:

> [W]hat we finally decided that everyone wanted to do was to not make the call prior to the time we actually saw the baby. Deliver the baby, because you see there was this [question] is the baby really 23 weeks, or is the baby further along, how big is the baby, what are we dealing with. We decided to let the neonatologist make the call by looking directly at the baby at birth.

Another physician who attended the meeting agreed, testifying that to deny any attempts at resuscitation without seeing the infant's condition would be inappropriate and below the standard of care.

Although Dr. Eduardo Otero, the neonatologist present in the delivery room when Sidney was born, did not attend that meeting, he confirmed that he needed to actually see Sidney before deciding what treatment, if any, would be appropriate:

> *Q.* Can you . . . tell us from a worst case scenario to a best case scenario, what type of possibilities you've seen in your own personal practice?
>
> *A.* Well, the worst case scenario is . . . the baby comes out and it's dead, it has no heart rate. . . . Or you have babies that actually go through a rocky start then cruise through the rest and go home. And they may have small handicaps or they may have some problems but—learning disabilities or something like that, but in general, all babies are normal children or fairly normal children.
>
> *Q.* And is there any way that you could have made a prediction, at the time of Sidney's birth, where she would fall in that range of different options?
>
> *A.* No, sir.
>
> *Q.* Is there any way that you can make that decision, as to whether the newborn infant will be viable or not in a case such as Sidney's, before the time of delivery, an assessment at the time of delivery?
>
> *A.* No.

Mark testified that, after the meeting, Hospital administrators asked him to sign a consent form allowing resuscitation according to the Hospital's plan, but he refused. Mark further testified that when he asked how he could prevent resuscitation, Hospital administrators told him that he could do so by removing Karla from the Hospital, which was not a viable option given her condition. Dr. Jacobs then noted in Karla's medical charts that a plan for evaluating the infant upon her birth was discussed at that afternoon meeting.

That evening, Karla's condition worsened and her amniotic sac broke. Dr. Jacobs determined that he would have to augment labor so that the infant would be delivered before further complications to Karla's health developed. Dr. Jacobs accordingly stopped administering the drug to Karla that was designed to stop labor, substituting instead a drug designed to augment labor. At 11:30 P.M. that night, Karla delivered a premature female infant weighing 615 grams, which the Millers named Sidney. Sidney's actual gestational age was twenty-three and one-seventh weeks. And she was born alive.

Dr. Otero noted that Sidney had a heart beat, albeit at a rate below that normally found in full-term babies. He further noted that Sidney, although blue in color and limp, gasped for air, spontaneously cried, and grimaced. Dr. Otero also noted that Sidney displayed no dysmorphic features other than being premature. He immediately "bagged" and "intubated" Sidney to oxygenate her blood; he then placed her on ventilation. He explained why:

> Because this baby is alive and this is a baby that has a reasonable chance of living. And again, this is a baby that is not necessarily going to have problems later on. There are babies that survive at this gestational age that—with this birth weight, that later on go on and do well.

Neither Karla nor Mark objected at the time to the treatment provided.

Sidney initially responded well to the treatment, as reflected by her Apgar scores. An Apgar score records five different components of a new-born infant: respiratory effort, heart rate, reflex activity, color, and muscle tone. Each component gets a score of zero, one, or two, with a score of two representing the best condition. Sidney's total Apgar score improved from a three at one minute after birth to a six at five minutes after birth. But at some point during the first few days after birth, Sidney suffered a brain hemorrhage—a complication not uncommon in infants born so prematurely.

There was conflicting testimony about whether Sidney's hemorrhage occurred because of the treatment provided or in spite of it. Regardless of the cause, as predicted by Karla's physicians, the hemorrhage caused Sidney to suffer severe physical and mental impairments. At the time of trial, Sidney was seven years old and could not walk, talk, feed herself, or sit up on her own. The evidence demonstrated that Sidney was legally blind, suffered from severe mental retardation, cerebral palsy, seizures, and spastic quadriparesis in her limbs. She could not be toilet-trained and required a shunt in her brain to drain fluids that accumulate there and needed care twenty-four hours a day. The evidence further demonstrated that her circumstances will not change.

The Millers sued HCA, Inc., HCA–Hospital Corporation of America, Hospital Corporation of America, and Columbia/HCA Healthcare Corporation (collectively, "HCA"), and the Hospital, a subsidiary of HCA. They did not sue any physicians, including Dr. Otero, the physician that actually treated Sidney. Instead, the Millers asserted battery and negligence claims only against HCA and the Hospital.

The Millers' claims stemmed from their allegations that despite their instructions to the contrary, the Hospital not only resuscitated Sidney but performed experimental procedures and administered experimental drugs, without which, in all reasonable medical probability, Sidney would not have survived. The Millers also alleged that the Hospital's acts and/or omissions were performed with HCA's full knowledge and consent. Although the Millers did not sue Dr. Otero, they alleged that he and other Hospital personnel were the Hospital's apparent or ostensible agents. . . .

. . . The jury found that the Hospital, without the consent of Karla or Mark Miller, performed resuscitative treatment on Sidney. The jury also found that the Hospital's and HCA's negligence "proximately caused the occurrence in question." The jury concluded that HCA and the Hospital were grossly negligent and that the Hospital acted with malice. The jury also determined that Dr. Otero acted as the Hospital's agent in resuscitating Sidney and that HCA was responsible for the Hospital's conduct under alter ego and single business enterprise theories. The trial court rendered judgment jointly and severally against the HCA defendants on the jury's verdict of $29,400,000 in actual damages for medical expenses, $17,503,066 in prejudgment interest, and $13,500,000 in exemplary damages.

HCA appealed. The court of appeals, with one justice dissenting, reversed and rendered judgment that the Millers take nothing. The court concluded that the Texas Legislature allowed parents to withhold medical treatment, urgently needed or not, for a child whose medical condition is certifiably terminal under the Natural Death Act. But the court held that the Legislature had not extended that right to parents of children with non-terminal impairments, deformities, or disabilities, regardless of their severity. . . .

The court noted that when non-urgently-needed or non-life-sustaining medical treatment is proposed for a child, a court order is needed to override a parent's refusal to consent to the treatment because a determination of such issues as the child's safety, welfare, and best interest can vary under differing circumstances and alternatives. But the court held that when the need for life-sustaining medical treatment is or becomes urgent while a non-terminally ill child is under a health care provider's care, and when the child's parents refuse consent to treatment, a court order is unnecessary to override that refusal. According to the court, no legal or factual issue exists to decide about providing such treatment because a court cannot decide between impaired life versus no life at all.

Given this backdrop, the court concluded that the Millers had no right to deny the medical treatment given to Sidney and that no court order was necessary to overcome their refusal to consent. . . .

We granted the Millers' petition for review to consider this important and difficult matter. . . .

Generally speaking, the custody, care, and nurture of an infant resides in the first instance with the parents.[14] As the United States Supreme Court has acknowledged, parents are presumed to be the appropriate decision-makers for their infants:

> Our jurisprudence historically has reflected Western civilization concepts of the family as a unit with broad parental authority over minor children. Our cases have consistently followed that course; our constitutional system long ago rejected any notion that a child is "the mere creature of the State" and, on the contrary, asserted that parents generally "have the right, coupled with the high duty, to recognize and prepare [their children] for additional obligations." . . . Surely, this includes a "high duty" to recognize symptoms of illness and to seek and follow medical advice. The law's concept of the family rests on a presumption that parents possess what a child lacks in maturity, experience, and capacity for judgment required for making life's difficult decisions. More important, historically it has recognized that natural bonds of affection lead parents to act in the best interests of their children.[15]

The Texas Legislature has likewise recognized that parents are presumed to be appropriate decision-makers, giving parents the right to consent to their infant's medical care and surgical treatment. A logical corollary of that right, as the court of appeals here recognized, is that parents have the right not to consent to certain medical care for their infant, *i.e.*, parents have the right to refuse certain medical care.

Of course, this broad grant of parental decision-making authority is not without limits. The State's role as *parens patriae* permits it to intercede in parental decision-making under certain circumstances. As the United States Supreme Court has noted:

---

14. *See* Prince v. Massachusetts, 321 U.S. 158, 166 (1944).
15. Parham v. J.R., 442 U.S. 584, 602 (1979) (citations omitted).

[A]s persons unable to protect themselves, infants fall under the parens patriae power of the state. In the exercise of this authority, the state not only punishes parents whose conduct has amounted to abuse or neglect of their children but may also supervene parental decisions before they become operative to ensure that the choices made are not so detrimental to a child's interests as to amount to neglect and abuse.

But the Supreme Court has also pointed out:

[A]s long as parents choose from professionally accepted treatment options the choice is rarely reviewed in court and even less frequently supervened. The courts have exercised their authority to appoint a guardian for a child when the parents are not capable of participating in the decisionmaking or when they have made decisions that evidence substantial lack of concern for the child's interests.

The Texas Legislature has acknowledged the limitations on parental decision-making. For example, the Legislature has provided in the Family Code that the rights and duties of parents are subject to modification by court order. And Texas courts have recognized their authority to enter orders, under appropriate circumstances, appointing a temporary managing conservator who may consent to medical treatment refused by a child's parents. . . .

In Moss v. Rishworth, the court held that a physician commits a "legal wrong" by operating on a minor without parental consent when there is "an absolute necessity for a prompt operation, but not emergent in the sense that death would likely result immediately upon the failure to perform it." But the court in Moss expressly noted that "it [was] not contended [there] that any real danger would have resulted to the child had time been taken to consult the parent with reference to the operation." Moss therefore implicitly acknowledges that a physician does not commit a legal wrong by operating on a minor without consent when the operation is performed under emergent circumstances—i.e., when death is likely to result immediately upon the failure to perform it.

Moss guides us here. We hold that a physician, who is confronted with emergent circumstances and provides life-sustaining treatment to a minor child, is not liable for not first obtaining consent from the parents. . . .

Providing treatment to a child under emergent circumstances does not imply consent to treatment despite actual notice of refusal to consent. Rather, it is an exception to the general rule that a physician commits a battery by providing medical treatment without consent. As such, the exception is narrowly circumscribed and arises only in emergent circumstances when there is no time to consult the parents or seek court intervention if the parents withhold consent before death is likely to result to the child. Though in situations of this character, the physician should attempt to secure parental consent if possible, the physician will not be liable under a battery or negligence theory solely for proceeding with the treatment absent consent.

We recognize that the Restatement (Second) of Torts § 892D provides that an individual is not liable for providing emergency treatment without consent if that individual has no reason to believe that the other, if he or she had the opportunity to consent, would decline. But that requirement is inapplicable here because, as we have discussed, the emergent circumstances exception does not imply consent.

Further, the emergent circumstances exception acknowledges that the harm from failing to treat outweighs any harm threatened by the proposed treatment, because the harm from failing to provide life-sustaining treatment under emergent circumstances is death. . . .

Following these guiding principles, we now determine whether the Millers can maintain their battery and negligence claims against HCA. The jury found that the Hospital, through Dr. Otero, treated Sidney without the Millers' consent. The parties do not challenge that finding. Thus, we only address whether the Hospital was required to seek court intervention to overturn the lack of parental consent—which it undisputedly did not do—before Dr. Otero could treat Sidney without committing a battery.

The Millers acknowledge that numerous physicians at trial agreed that, absent an emergency situation, the proper course of action is court intervention when health care providers disagree with parents' refusal to consent to a child's treatment. And the Millers contend that, as a matter of law, no emergency existed that would excuse the Hospital's treatment of Sidney without their consent or a court order overriding their refusal to consent. The Millers point out that before Sidney's birth, Drs. Jacobs and Kelley discussed with them the possibility that Sidney might suffer from the numerous physical and mental infirmities that did, in fact, afflict her. And some eleven hours before Sidney's birth, the Millers indicated that they did not want any heroic measures performed on Sidney. The Millers note that these factors prompted the dissenting justice in the court of appeals to conclude that "[a]nytime a group of doctors and a hospital administration ha[ve] the luxury of multiple meetings to change the original doctors' medical opinions, without taking a more obvious course of action, there is no medical emergency."

We agree that a physician cannot create emergent circumstances from his or her own delay or inaction and escape liability for proceeding without consent. But the Millers' reasoning fails to recognize that, in this case, the evidence established that Sidney could only be properly evaluated when she was born. Any decision the Millers made before Sidney's birth concerning her treatment at or after her birth would necessarily be based on speculation. Therefore, we reject the Millers' argument that a decision could adequately be made pre-birth that denying all post-birth resuscitative treatment would be in Sidney's best interest. Such a decision could not control whether the circumstances facing Dr. Otero were emergent because it would not have been a fully informed one according to the evidence in this case. . . .

We acknowledge that certain physicians in this case initially asked the Millers to decide whether Sidney should be resuscitated some eleven hours before her birth. And certain physicians and Hospital administrators asked the Millers to consent to the subsequent plan developed to have a neonatologist present at Sidney's delivery to evaluate and possibly treat her. We agree that, whenever possible, obtaining consent in writing to evaluate a premature infant at birth and to render any warranted medical treatment is the best course of action. And physicians and hospitals should always strive to do so. But if such consent is not forthcoming, or is affirmatively denied, we decline to impose liability on a physician solely for providing life-sustaining treatment under emergent circumstances to a new-born infant without that consent. . . .

HCA argues that the federal "Baby Doe" regulations are part of Texas law and forbid any denial of medical care based on quality-of-life considerations. While we do not disagree with HCA's assertion as a general proposition, HCA cites 42 U.S.C. § 5106a(b)(2)(B) as support for its contention that the Baby Doe regulations were "scrupulously followed in this case" and "faithful adherence to the public policy established by the regulations should not be thwarted through civil liability in damages. . . ." But 42 U.S.C. § 5106a(b)(2)(B) provides that a federally-funded state must implement "procedures for responding to the reporting of medical neglect" which include:

> authority, under State law, for the State child protective services system to pursue any legal remedies, including the authority to initiate legal proceedings in a court of competent jurisdiction, as may be necessary to prevent the withholding of medically indicated treatment from disabled infants with life-threatening conditions.

Assuming that this provision applies here, it states that Texas must provide a mechanism by which the child protective services system can initiate legal proceedings to prevent the withholding of medical treatment from infants. And the Family Code and Texas Administrative Code contain such provisions.

But it is undisputed that neither the Hospital nor HCA initiated or requested child protective services to initiate legal proceedings to override the Millers' "withholding of medical treatment" by refusing to consent to Sidney's treatment. Thus, the federal funding regulations appear to contemplate legal proceedings to override the lack of parental consent, and they do not answer the question of whether Dr. Otero committed a battery by providing treatment without doing so. Further, we agree with the court of appeals' conclusion that the disposition of that issue "is governed by state law rather than federal funding authorities."

HCA also argues, and the court of appeals agreed, that parents can withhold "urgently-needed life-sustaining medical treatment" for their child only when the requirements of the Natural Death Act are satisfied—*i.e.*, only when the child is certifiably terminal. But the Act expressly states that it does not impair or supersede any legal right a person may have to withhold or withdraw life-sustaining treatment in a lawful manner. In any event, we need not decide this issue. The Millers asserted battery and negligence claims based on Dr. Otero treating Sidney without their consent. As we have discussed, when emergent circumstances exist, a physician cannot be held liable under either battery or negligence theories solely for providing life-sustaining medical treatment to a minor child without parental consent. . . .

We affirm the court of appeals' judgment.

DIALOG ON THE QUESTION OF BABY DOE, *COMMENTS BY* *BARBARA KATZ ROTHMAN*

Health-Pac-Bulletin 25 (1986)

. . . To refer to the needs of parents to do what they feel necessary for their babies as "wishes" trivializes the depths of their concern. I perceive the needs of people to prevent their child's death from being prolonged into months or lives of agony to be something more than "wishes." While some would have us think that the refusal of medical treatment is always destructive, others of us believe that it is something protective—even if it means choosing death over continued existence. . . .

I think that we are all wise enough to know that whenever there are difficult questions to be decided, mistakes are going to be made. Some babies, who by almost all standards, should have been allowed to die quickly and well, will be made to die slowly and in pain. And some babies, who by almost all standards, should have received medical treatment, will suffer or die needlessly because such treatment was refused. And we must all be wise enough to realize that we may never know whether the right decision was reached in any given case. . . .

It is not really a question of whose judgment we trust. We cannot know who will be right, but we do know that, inevitably, anyone making these decisions will sometimes be wrong. To me, it comes down not to *whose judgment* we trust, but whose *mistakes*.

Medicine has a long history of mistakes, especially mistakes in matters of disability. It is ironic that the disability rights movement seems so trusting of medical decision-making regarding necessary treatment; there has been so much *unnecessary* medical treatment to avoid or to repair disability. Medicine has long regarded disability, like death, as a sign of professional failure. . . .

Why, then, do I trust the idiosyncratic mistakes of parents? Precisely because they are idiosyncratic. The mistakes of medicine and those of the state are systematic, and that alone is reason not to trust. Medicine, and (perhaps even more so) the state, make their decisions in their own interests, in calculations of cost-benefit ratios, in definitions of "salvageability," in the very drawing of lines.

NOTES AND QUESTIONS

1. How do the legal analyses of the intermediate appellate court and the state supreme court differ in *Miller*? Under each approach, are doctors obliged to follow the instructions of parents not to treat a newborn? Under each approach, when can doctors decide not to treat? The Washington Supreme Court, on facts similar to those in *Miller*, reached the same conclusion, employing the same reasoning as the Texas Supreme Court. Stewart-Graves v. Vaughn, 170 P.3d 1151 (Wash. 2007) (en banc).

2. The original Baby Doe rules were antidiscrimination rules issued under § 504 of the Rehabilitation Act, 29 U.S.C. § 794. They prohibited withholding otherwise accepted treatment from babies just because they were disabled. 47 Fed. Reg. 26027 (June 16, 1982), 48 Fed. Reg. § 9630 (Mar. 7, 1983). These rules were invalidated because the courts found that Congress did not intend § 504 to apply to decisions about medical care for newborns with disabilities. United States v. University Hospital, 729 F.2d 144 (2d Cir. 1984). *See also* Bowen v. American Hospital Assn., 476 U.S. 610 (1986).

Do the CAPTA rules, which define withholding treatment as child neglect in some cases, express an antidiscrimination principle or a vitalist principle? The American Academy of Pediatrics has interpreted the rules as allowing doctors to exercise clinical judgment to deny treatment, but a number of critics disagree, arguing that the rules require maximal efforts to save the lives even of very premature infants. *See, e.g.*, Loretta M. Kopelman et al., Neonatalogists Judge the "Baby Doe" Regulations, 318 New Eng. J. Med. 677 (1988). *See also* Dionne Koller Fine, Government As God: An Update on Federal Intervention in the Treatment of Critically Ill Newborns, 34 New Eng. L. Rev. 343, 354-355 (2000). *But see* Thomas J. Balch, Are There Checks and Balances on Terminating the Lives of Children with Disabilities? Should There Be?, 25 Ga. St. U. L. Rev. 959 (2009).

In Montalvo v. Borkovec, 647 N.W.2d 413 (Wis. App. 2002), parents argued that doctors had failed to give them adequate information about their premature baby's prospects so that they could make an informed decision about whether to withhold treatment from him. Interpreting the CAPTA rules discussed above, the court of appeals said, "The implied choice of withholding treatment, proposed by the plaintiffs, is exactly what CAPTA prohibits." 647 N.W.2d at 419.

3. In Texas, as in many states, legislation allows surrogate decision makers for incompetent people to decide to withhold lifesaving treatment if the patient is near death. Some statutes allow the decision to be made in other circumstances as well. For example, in Oregon care may be withheld when a person is terminally ill, permanently unconscious, in a condition in which administration of life-sustaining procedures would not benefit the principal's medical condition and would cause permanent and severe pain, or when the person has a progressive illness that will be fatal and is in an advanced stage, the person is consistently and permanently unable to communicate by any means, swallow food and water safely, care for the person's self and recognize the person's family and other people, and it is very unlikely that the person's condition will substantially improve. Or. Rev. Stat. § 127.635.

Why didn't the Texas statute apply in *Miller*? If Sidney had developed a life-threatening but treatable illness when she was six, would the statute permit a decision to withhold treatment from her? What would the result be under the Oregan statute?

4. Some conflicts between doctors and parents over the treatment of infants arise when the doctors conclude that further treatment is futile but the parents insist on continued treatment. Professor Craig Conway identifies two belief systems that may prompt parents to reject physicians' recommendations against treating very premature babies — therapeutic illusions and vitalism. A therapeutic illusion is clinging to hope that treatment will be effective against all odds that it will not. Vitalism is the belief that all human life is precious and should be conserved, regardless of the costs, including pain and suffering of the person whose life is extended. Craig A. Conway, Baby Doe and Beyond: Examining the Practical and Philosophical Influences Impacting Medical Decision-Making on Behalf of Marginally-Viable Newborns, 25 Ga. St. U. L. Rev. 1097, 1121-1125 (2009).

In some of these cases, courts have held that juvenile courts have the authority to decide these cases under their general authority to make orders regarding medical care to serve the child's best interests. *See, e.g.*, Hunt v. Division of Family Services, 146 A.3d 1051 (2015). Others hold that unless grounds exist to terminate parents' parental rights, they have a due process right to make the decision about treatment. *See, e.g.,* In re Matthew W., 903 A.2d 333 (Me. 2006), overruled on other grounds In re B.C., 58 A.3d 1118 (Me. 2012); D.K. v. Commonwealth, 221 S.W.3d 382 (Ky. Ct. App. 2007); In re Guardianship of Stein, 821 N.E.2d 1008 (Ohio 2004). Other courts have applied their state natural death laws. *See, e.g.,* State ex rel. Juvenile Dept. of Multnomah County v. Smith, 133 P.3d 924 (Or. App. 2006). These issues are discussed in Daniel S. Goldberg, The Ethics of DNR Orders as to Neonatal & Pediatric Patients: The Ethical Dimension of Communication, 7 Hous. J. Health L. & Pol'y 57 (2006). *See also* John J. Paris et al., Has the Emphasis on Autonomy Gone Too Far? Insights from Dostoevsky on Parental Decisionmaking in the NICU, 15 Cambridge Q. Healthcare Ethics 15 (2006) (for some parents, deciding to stop treatment is psychologically or morally impossible, and therefore doctors should not frame the issue in this way when talking to them).

PROBLEM

Katie was born prematurely at 26 weeks gestation. She suffered from cerebral palsy and other problems, and, as a result, her heart stopped beating for 25 minutes. Efforts to resuscitate her succeeded, but because her brain had been deprived of oxygen for so long, she suffered severe brain damage. Doctors described her as "neurologically devastated," and they agreed that her chances of regaining cognitive ability were virtually nonexistent. They also agreed that any extraordinary attempts to resuscitate her would likely be highly invasive and painful and, therefore, recommended that a do not resuscitate (DNR) order be entered.

After Katie was discharged from the hospital to her mother, Barbara, Barbara did not bring Katie back to the hospital for scheduled appointments, took her off medical monitoring equipment, and ended her tube feeding. When Katie had a high fever and difficulty breathing, Barbara did not bring her to a doctor. The hospital successfully sought a juvenile court order that Katie was medically neglected because of Barbara's actions. After this finding, the hospital asked for the DNR order. Katie's father, who does not live with Barbara, consented to the order, but Barbara objected.

At the hearing on the hospital's motion to enter the DNR order, four doctors testified in support of the order. All the doctors agreed that Katie's prognosis for recovery was very grim and that efforts to resuscitate her would involve substantial pain and discomfort for her.

Barbara then testified. She wants the doctors to make all possible efforts to revive Katie if her heart or breathing stops. She testified, "I know Katie can make it. . . . It only matters if Katie is breathing. . . . There's a whole lot of them [like Katie] out there." When cross-examined regarding the relationship of benefits to burdens, ideas that the doctors testified about, Barbara said, "Any amount of pain is worth it as long as Katie breathes."

What arguments should the attorneys for each side make?

E.   ADOLESCENTS' VIEWS ABOUT THEIR OWN CARE

LESLIE JOAN HARRIS, *TEEN HEALTH CARE DECISIONS: HOW MATURITY AND SOCIAL POLICY AFFECT FOUR HARD CASES*

72 Studies in Law, Politics, and Society 185, 189-193 (2017), https://scholarsbank.uoregon.edu/xmlui/handle/1794/22433

Patient autonomy is the premiere governing principle of the law of medical consent for competent adults. Adults may legally reject medical care, even if the consequence will be death. This principle developed in response to remarkable medical developments in the last half of the 20th century that can save the lives of people who would surely have died in an earlier age, but which often have adverse side effects and result in people who are alive but with diminished quality of life. In this kind of situation, reasonable people can differ about whether the treatment is worthwhile, and the principle of patient autonomy allows individuals faced with these decisions to act on their own value judgments. However, to be able to make this decision, the patient must be competent, and the determination of whether a particular patient is competent to make a decision emphasizes cognitive capacity, in part because it avoids value judgments about the wisdom of the decisions themselves.

Medical decision-making, like all decision-making, is sometimes not wholly voluntary and uncoerced. In older areas of the law, legal doctrines such as undue influence and insane delusion in the law of wills deal with these problems. The law of medical decision-making has not developed similar doctrines. Perhaps the most important reason is that most of the time patients follow medical advice, and medical providers do not bother to question competence. So long as the patient-decision maker is acting in the legally preferred way, no one challenges the decision or the patient's capacity. Indeed, as a practical matter, health care providers routinely accept consents to proposed treatment from patients of questionable competence. The law of informed consent does not even require that patients accept information about their condition and proposed treatment before giving legally effective consent to a treatment.

. . . In practice, when adult patients disagree with medical advice, health care providers not infrequently ignore their wishes. Sometimes, health care providers frankly admit that they are ignoring what they regard as an ill-considered decision, and sometimes they are just more willing to challenge a dissenting patient's decision-making capacity. . . .

The law of medical decision-making for minors is consistent with the legal principles that govern adults' decisions. . . . Ordinarily parents have authority to make health care decisions for their children, consistent with the assumption that minors generally lack legal decision-making capacity. This rule works most of the time because most of the time parents accept medical advice, and their children do not object. . . .

A parent's consent may not be required if the child agrees to proposed medical care in one of three circumstances: (1) a special statute authorizes minors above a certain age or all minors to consent to the particular treatment; (2) the child is legally emancipated, or (3) in some states, the child is a "mature minor," that is, capable of making this particular decision. These exceptions to the requirement of parental consent solve problems that the usual legal rules do not address satisfactorily and are intended to insure that children, particularly teens, get medical care that they might forego if they had to tell their parents of the need for the care.

First, all states have special statutes that allow minors to consent to particular kinds of care that are both socially desirable and highly sensitive, such as contraception and prenatal care, and treatment for mental health problems, sexually transmitted infections, and drug and alcohol problems. In 32 states and the District of Columbia, all minors can consent to prenatal care, one more allows minors to consent during the first trimester, and four allow minors who are mature to consent. In 26 states and D.C., all minors can consent to contraceptive treatment, and 20 more allow some categories of minors to consent. All states and the District of Columbia allow minors to consent to treatment for sexually transmitted infections. In 47 states, minors acting alone can consent to outpatient drug treatment, and in 34 they can consent to outpatient mental health treatment. In 40 states, minors alone can consent to inpatient drug treatment, and in 28 states to inpatient mental health treatment. The minimum ages vary from no minimum to age 16.[16] ...

The second exception to the general rule allows emancipated minors and is explained by the nature of emancipation itself. These minors are, by definition, living separately and apart from their parents, who may not even be available. Again, allowing these minors to consent to their own care solves the problem.

Finally, in 14 states mature minors can consent to medical treatment in all or limited circumstances, and in three more states all minors can consent to treatment in all or limited circumstances. Thirty-four states have no exception for mature minors.[17] Broadly speaking, the mature minor rule allows a minor to consent to medical care even though he or she is not fully independent but is capable of making a reasoned decision. The rule requires an assessment of capacity on a case-by-case basis, and most discussions of the rule assume that the health care provider will make the assessment. However, courts may become involved if the provider seeks a judicial determination that the child has capacity, as a matter of caution, or if the child suffers harm or dies and the case comes to the attention of the authorities after the fact.

The mature minor doctrine was originally developed to protect health care providers against tort liability when they treated minors without parental consent when the providers had a sympathetic position, such as a reasonable belief that the young person was an adult. Since the 1980s, the doctrine has been extended to apply in other situations. For example, sometimes the parents and the doctors

16. [The sources of this information are Guttmacher Institute, An Overview of Minors' Consent Laws (June 1, 2016), and Mary Louise E. Kerwin et al., What Can Parents Do/ A Review of State Laws Regarding Decision Making for Adolescent Drug Abuse and Mental Health Treatment, 24(3) J. Adolescent Substance Abuse 166 (2015). – Ed.]

17. [The source of this information is Doriane Lambelet Coleman & Philip M. Rosoff, The Legal Authority of Mature Minors to Consent to General Medical Treatment, 131 Pediatrics 786 (2015).

disagree about treatment for the child, and it seems likely that if the doctors take the case to juvenile court, the parents will lose. The parents may claim that their child is old enough to make the decision under the mature minor rule, on the assumption that the child will make the same decision that the parents would. Parents have also sought to invoke the doctrine when they didn't take their children to doctors at all, the children suffered harm or died, and the parents were criminally prosecuted. In either situation, the parent will lose if the usual requirement of parental consent with the medical neglect limitation is applied, and they invoke the mature minor rule in an effort to avoid this outcome. The doctrine might also be invoked when the parents, child, and health care provider are in agreement, but the provider is concerned that the preferred course of treatment could be considered neglectful.

In re Cassandra C.

112 A.3d 158 (Conn. 2015)

Rogers, C.J. . . . Cassandra was born on September 30, 1997. From May 2014 through July 2014, when Cassandra was sixteen years old, she suffered from stomachaches, lower back pain, chest pain, and an enlarged and tender cervical gland. When antibiotic treatment failed to resolve her condition, her primary care physician, Hemant K. Panchal, referred Cassandra to another physician, Henry M. Feder, an infectious disease specialist. After an initial appointment on July 1, 2014, Feder attempted to follow up with the respondents to determine whether the treatment he had prescribed was effective, but Cassandra missed two scheduled appointments. Feder finally saw Cassandra in early August, at which time he ordered a chest X ray that revealed enlarged lymph nodes. At that point, Feder suspected that Cassandra might have cancer and he scheduled an appointment for a needle biopsy of her enlarged cervical gland. Cassandra did not attend the appointment, which concerned Feder. Feder scheduled a second appointment at which a needle biopsy was taken that was suspicious for lymphoma.

At that point, Cassandra was referred to the cancer and blood disorders services division of hematology and oncology at the Connecticut Children's Medical Center (medical center) in Hartford. An appointment was scheduled for September 4, 2014, but Cassandra did not show up. Another appointment was scheduled for September 9, at which Cassandra was examined by Eileen Gillan, a physician with the Connecticut Children's Specialty Group, who recommended that Cassandra undergo a biopsy procedure of an enlarged lymph node. On September 12, 2014, Brendan Campbell, a surgeon, performed an incisional biopsy on Cassandra's enlarged cervical gland. Pathological tests showed conclusively that Cassandra was suffering from Hodgkin's lymphoma, a type of cancer that is invariably fatal if not treated, but that has a high probability of cure if treated in a timely manner. Interrupting chemotherapy treatment of the disease can lead to resistance of the cancer to treatment. Delaying chemotherapy treatment may increase the risk of a poor outcome and may require radiation treatment, which has increased risks of harmful side effects, especially for young women.

On September 19, 2014, Gillan spoke by telephone with Cassandra's mother and informed her of the diagnosis. The mother was upset that Gillan had not called her earlier and by what she perceived as Gillan's attitude when she "nonchalantly" stated that she had been unsure how to break the bad news regarding Cassandra's diagnosis to the respondents. Gillan recommended that Cassandra undergo further evaluations to determine the stage of the cancer and to discuss treatment, but the mother refused.

At some point, Gillan asked her partner, Michael Isakoff, a pediatric oncologist, to take over Cassandra's treatment. Gillan told Isakoff that, on the basis of her interactions with the mother, she believed that Isakoff would be able to deal more effectively with her. Gillan also told Isakoff that the mother had been angry and hostile toward her and that the respondents were not interested in getting treatment or tests to determine the stage of the disease. Isakoff was able to schedule an appointment with the respondents to discuss these issues for October 7, 2014, but only Cassandra's mother and uncle attended that appointment. The mother was upset because she had been expecting to meet with Gillan. Isakoff explained the further testing and treatment that he recommended. When the mother expressed great concern about giving Cassandra "poisons," Isakoff acknowledged that the treatment had some toxic side effects but explained that chemotherapy was the only way to treat the disease and that there were ways to reduce the toxicity. The mother also complained about the manner in which information had been relayed to her and other "process" issues and was angry and hostile toward Isakoff. She further indicated that she did not believe the diagnosis and asked about getting a second opinion. Specifically, she questioned why the biopsy report showed no signs of the Epstein–Barr virus when, based on her research, that virus is always present with Hodgkin's lymphoma. Isakoff repeatedly assured the mother that that was not the case, but Isakoff was not convinced that she was comfortable with his response. Toward the end of the conversation, Isakoff told the mother bluntly that he was very concerned about the amount of time that had elapsed since the biopsy and that it was important for Cassandra to start treatment within two weeks. He asked the mother to contact him within two days to let him know how she wanted to proceed. At that point, the mother got up and walked out. On October 17, 2014, Isakoff wrote a letter to Cassandra's mother to express his concerns about the ongoing delays in the evaluation and treatment of Cassandra's disease and asked her to contact his office as soon as possible.

The respondents sought a second opinion about Cassandra's diagnosis from Matthew Richardson, a pediatric oncologist at Baystate Medical Center in Springfield, Massachusetts. Richardson examined Cassandra on October 14, 2014, and, after reviewing the scans and pathology reports from the medical center, agreed with the diagnosis that Cassandra had Hodgkin's lymphoma. Richardson attempted to contact the respondents seven times over two days and left telephone messages regarding his diagnosis and the urgency of the situation. The mother finally returned his calls on October 20, 2014, and Richardson told her that it was urgent that the staging of Cassandra's cancer be completed and that treatment be started. The mother indicated that she had not yet decided whether Richardson would be Cassandra's treating physician. Two days later, the mother called Richardson and indicated that she wanted Richardson to treat Cassandra.

On October 23, 2014, a PET scan was performed that revealed extensive stage three lymphoma in Cassandra's neck, chest, and abdomen. That same day, Richardson telephoned the mother and left a message on her telephone indicating that it was necessary to complete the staging evaluation and to start treatment, and that he was concerned that the period that had elapsed since the biopsy was beginning to be outside the standard of care. Richardson ultimately attempted to telephone the mother six times between October 25 and October 27, 2014, but received no answer. The mother finally telephoned Richardson on October 30, 2014, and stated that she had decided Cassandra would be receiving care from another physician. When Richardson asked where he should send Cassandra's medical records, the mother stated that she would pick them up. She also indicated that she did not have time to discuss the results of the PET scan and that Cassandra would not be following through with the pretreatment tests that had been scheduled.

Richardson spoke with Isakoff at some point and indicated that he had concerns about the mother's hostility and unwillingness to obtain treatment for Cassandra in a timely manner. In addition, Richardson told Isakoff that the respondents were seeking to have a second biopsy performed. Isakoff believed that a second biopsy was medically inappropriate because, even if it was negative, it would not invalidate the results of the first biopsy, and the biopsy procedure involves risk.

Meanwhile, on October 2, 2014, Feder had reported his concerns about the respondents' apparent unwillingness to obtain treatment for Cassandra's disease to the department. At that point, Margaret Nardelli, an investigator for the department, contacted the mother to discuss the referral. The mother indicated that she was not willing to meet with the department and that she was meeting Cassandra's needs. She also stated that she was obtaining a second opinion about Cassandra's condition. When Nardelli tried to follow up, the mother did not return her telephone calls. Finally, on October 21, 2014, Nardelli left a note at the respondents' residence. At that point, the mother called Nardelli. She was very upset and was yelling and swearing. The mother told Nardelli that she was not allowed to go to her home ever again, that Cassandra's needs were being met, and that she did not have to tell Nardelli anything or do anything that the department requested. The mother also told Nardelli that Cassandra felt fine and that she, the mother, did not think that Cassandra had cancer. Nardelli responded that if the mother did not want to meet with the department, Nardelli would speak with an attorney for the department about ways to ensure that Cassandra's needs were being met. The mother said that she did not care what the department did and hung up the telephone.

During Nardelli's investigation of the case, Richardson called her and indicated that he was concerned that the respondents were not moving quickly enough to obtain treatment for Cassandra's disease and that they were consistently not keeping medical appointments. Panchal also called Nardelli and stated that the respondents were not keeping scheduled appointments. In addition, Panchal reported that the mother had told him that he would no longer be Cassandra's physician and had demanded her medical records.

On the basis of this information, the department became concerned that the mother was not following through in a timely manner to obtain treatment for Cassandra's life threatening illness. The department also became concerned about the mother's "anxiety" and that the mother did not always remember information that previously had been provided to her. Although the mother eventually attended scheduled meetings with the department, she continued to question

Cassandra's diagnosis and to demand further assessments that Cassandra's medical providers had found to be inappropriate. On the basis of these concerns, the commissioner filed a neglect petition alleging that the mother had "failed to meet the medical needs" of Cassandra and sought an ex parte order of temporary custody pursuant to § 46b–129 (b). The trial court, *Westbrook, J.*, found that there was reason to believe that Cassandra was in immediate physical danger and granted an ex parte order of temporary custody on October 31, 2014. Immediately thereafter, the department brought Cassandra to the emergency room at the medical center for an evaluation. At that time, Cassandra was "very fearful" of staying in the hospital and of waking up with "tubes sticking out of her." She also expressed concerns about not wanting to anger her mother, who, she said, was very distrustful of physicians. Pursuant to Judge Westbrook's order, Cassandra was removed from her home and placed in the home of a cousin pending a hearing.

A preliminary hearing on the commissioner's request for an order of temporary custody was held on November 6, 2014, at which time Judge Westbrook ordered a guardian ad litem for Cassandra and scheduled an evidentiary hearing for November 12. At that evidentiary hearing, which took place before Judge Taylor, Nardelli, Feder, Campbell and Isakoff testified as to the foregoing facts. Cassandra's guardian ad litem, Jon David Anthony Reducha, testified that Cassandra had told him the previous day that she was willing to be treated for her disease, but that she would refuse treatment if she were not allowed to go home. Reducha acknowledged that Cassandra's decision to refuse treatment for her life threatening disease if she were not allowed to go home was not a rational decision. It was Reducha's understanding that Cassandra initially had resisted treatment because she was doing her own research and she needed time to absorb the information. Reducha believed that it would be in Cassandra's best interest to be allowed to go home so that she would agree to treatment.

Cassandra also testified at the November 12, 2014 hearing. Before she testified, her attorney requested the court's permission for her to testify from where she was sitting in the courtroom instead of from the witness stand, because she was nervous. When the trial court denied the request, the attorney requested permission to stand close to Cassandra "to give her a little comfort and moral support." The court also denied that request. Cassandra testified that her mother had told her many times that she did not want to lose a child and that she wanted her to undergo chemotherapy. Cassandra initially did not want to undergo chemotherapy because of "everything that happens when you go through chemo." After her best friend told Cassandra that she did not want to lose her and would "drag [her] to the hospital and make [her] do it," however, Cassandra changed her mind. Because the treatment was going to be very difficult, Cassandra wanted to be at home while she was undergoing chemotherapy. If she were not allowed to go home, she would refuse treatment. When told that the department was concerned that, if she were allowed to go home, she would still refuse treatment, Cassandra stated that "[i]f you let me go home today, I would start chemo tomorrow."

Cassandra's mother testified at the hearing that she had wanted to obtain a second opinion about Cassandra's condition because she had "a right to a second opinion" and the first diagnosis was serious. When the respondents went to Richardson, the mother asked him not to contact Isakoff because she wanted a "second opinion, not a second agreement. . . ." She was upset when she found out that Richardson had spoken to Isakoff. After she discontinued Cassandra's treatment with Isakoff, the mother decided not to comply with the department's request to "keep in touch" because she "was doing what [she] was supposed to be doing." The mother testified that, although she continued to believe that she had a right to a second and even a third opinion about Cassandra's diagnosis, she believed that Cassandra had cancer and that she would die without treatment. She further testified that she "[a]bsolutely" agreed that Cassandra should be treated as soon as possible.

On November 14, 2014, Judge Taylor issued an order sustaining Judge Westbrook's order of temporary custody. The court ordered that Cassandra be placed back in her home with her mother subject to certain conditions, including that the mother allow the department unfettered access to Cassandra and her home, that she cooperate with Cassandra's medical providers and that she keep all medical appointments and appointments with the department. The court also ordered that Isakoff would serve as Cassandra's treating physician and that treatment was required to begin within seventy-two hours after Cassandra returned home. In addition, the court ordered that Cassandra remain within the state for the duration of this case and that she not leave her home for more than twelve hours without the prior authorization of the department or the court.

On November 17 and 18, 2014, Cassandra underwent her first two chemotherapy treatments. Her mother did not attend the second treatment. After the second treatment, Isakoff observed bruising around the site of the intravenous infusion. At that point, he told Cassandra that, because her veins were fragile, she would have to have a "port-a-cath" surgically placed. Isakoff arranged for a surgeon to perform the procedure the next morning so that Cassandra could receive her scheduled treatment later that day. When a department employee arrived at the respondents' home on the morning of November 19, 2014, to transport Cassandra to her third chemotherapy treatment, Cassandra was not there. Her mother indicated that she did not know Cassandra's whereabouts. She made no efforts to find Cassandra and did not notify the police. The mother told the department that Cassandra would not be coming home. ... Several days after she disappeared, Cassandra's attorney called the department and stated that she wanted to return home.

Cassandra returned to her home on November 24, 2014, and, the next day, the department brought her to the medical center for an evaluation by Isakoff. ... Cassandra told Isakoff that she was adamant that she would not return for further chemotherapy. She stated that she did not feel sick and that when she started to feel sick she might reconsider her decision, but that she would not be treated at the medical center because she did not trust the physicians there. Isakoff told Cassandra that there was a danger that the cancer would become resistant if she interrupted the chemotherapy treatment. Cassandra then told Isakoff that she had never intended to start chemotherapy and that she had stated that she would do so in order to get the department and the court to agree to allow her to go home. She also stated that she was going to be eighteen years old soon, at which point she would not be in the position of being forced into treatment.

On December 1, 2014, the commissioner filed in the trial court a motion for reargument and reconsideration, for clarification and to reopen evidence. The commissioner requested that the trial court conduct a hearing "to consider evidence regarding [Cassandra's] subsequent behaviors and whether she is competent to make life/death decisions regarding her medical care." An evidentiary hearing for that purpose was held before Judge Quinn on December 9, 2014. Isakoff testified at the hearing that he did not believe that Cassandra was competent to make the decision to refuse chemotherapy treatment for her disease. Indeed, he testified that, if an adult were to make that decision, it would lead him to question that person's competence. Isakoff believed that it was unreasonable for Cassandra to subject herself to chemotherapy in order to be allowed to return home, especially if she intended to worsen her own prognosis by interrupting the treatment, but to refuse further chemotherapy to cure her fatal disease. He further testified that if Cassandra did not start chemotherapy within two weeks of the hearing, there would be a much higher probability that Cassandra would have to undergo radiation therapy. Isakoff also did not believe that Cassandra's mother was competent to make decisions regarding Cassandra's medical care. Although he understood the mother's concerns about putting "poisons" in Cassandra's body, the chemotherapy treatment provided Cassandra with her only chance of survival. Isakoff further testified that the mother's doubts about the diagnosis also were unreasonable, as the diagnosis had been repeatedly confirmed.

Cassandra's mother testified that she believed that Cassandra had cancer, that she believed that Cassandra needed chemotherapy, that she wanted Cassandra to have chemotherapy and that she had told Cassandra to undergo chemotherapy. She also testified, however, that she believed that it was Cassandra's "right as a human being" to refuse treatment and "to choose if she wants poisons that are going to affect her the rest of her life...." When asked whether she knew that Cassandra would die without treatment, the mother stated, "[t]hat's what they say, but there's no guarantee with treatment of cancer...."

At the conclusion of the hearing, Judge Quinn found that Cassandra's mother did not believe that Cassandra had Hodgkin's lymphoma or that she needed chemotherapy in order to have a chance to survive. Judge Quinn ordered that Cassandra remain in the custody of the department, that she be removed from her home and that the department make medical treatment decisions for her.

. . . The respondents then filed an application for certification to appeal to this court from both Judge Taylor's November 14, 2014 ruling and from Judge Quinn's December 9, 2014 ruling, pursuant to § 52–265a. . . . [W]e ordered that the respondents' appeal to the Appellate Court be transferred to this court and that it be heard on an expedited basis.

Thereafter, the commissioner filed a motion for an expedited articulation in which it requested that Judge Quinn articulate the basis for her December 9, 2014 ruling. . . . Judge Quinn issued an articulation in which she stated . . . that she had credited Isakoff's testimony that Cassandra did not have the capacity to make sound medical decisions concerning her cancer treatment based on "[Cassandra's] apparent willingness to undergo treatment [during the November 12, 2014 hearing before Judge Taylor] while secretly knowing she would not, the consequences of such behavior on the efficacy of the future treatment, and the totality of all the facts she knew. . . ." Judge Quinn also stated that she had observed Cassandra's behavior at trial and "saw how closely she followed her mother's testimony and hung on her every word." Judge Quinn then observed that the mother "did not appear to be in support of the chemotherapy and that Cassandra is concerned about going against what her mother would like to see happen." She further observed that "[t]he record is replete with [the] mother's arguments with physicians about the diagnosis, her seeking three separate opinions about the diagnosis, attempting to change pediatricians and delaying follow-up appointments and needed treatment." Judge Quinn concluded that the "mother has engaged in a passive refusal to follow reasonable medical advice for her mortally ill child." She further concluded that Cassandra "does not possess the necessary level of maturity or independence to make life and death decisions about her own medical care, as demonstrated both by her conduct and her behavior subsequent to the initial court order," and that Cassandra was "overshadowed by the strong negative opinions her mother holds about her cancer diagnosis and treatment, including chemotherapy." . . . Judge Quinn stated that Isakoff's "thoughtful assessment of [Cassandra's] capacity, the court's own observations of the parties and the witnesses, the observations of the [department's] investigations worker, and Cassandra's own actions all support the conclusion that she is an immature seventeen year old." Accordingly, she concluded that "Cassandra is not a mature minor. She is as yet incapable of acting independently concerning her own life threatening medical condition. And time is running out for the recommended course of treatment to have a positive outcome for her future."

. . . This court previously has not had the opportunity to address directly the question of whether and, if so, under what circumstances minors may be competent to make their own medical decisions. The United States Supreme Court has recognized, however, that "[m]ost children, even in adolescence, simply are not able to make sound judgments concerning many decisions, including their need for medical care or treatment. Parents can and must make those judgments." Parham v. J.R., 442 U.S. 584, 603 (1979). Accordingly, "[a]t common law, minors generally were considered to lack the legal capacity to give valid consent to medical treatment or services, and consequently a parent, guardian, or other legally authorized person generally was required to provide the requisite consent. In the absence of an emergency, a physician who provided medical care to a minor without such parental or other legally authorized consent could be sued for battery."

Although this general common-law principle has not been expressly recognized by this court, it has been implicitly recognized by our legislature. For example, pursuant to General Statutes § 46b–150d, "a minor [who] is *emancipated* . . . (1) . . . may consent to medical, dental or psychiatric care, without parental consent, knowledge or liability. . . ." (Emphasis added; footnote added.) Thus, under the "tenet of statutory construction referred to as expressio unius est exclusio alterius, which may be translated as the expression of one thing is the exclusion of another," it is implicit that unemancipated minors do not have this ability. Similarly, other statutes providing that under specific, narrowly limited circumstances, minors may make medical decisions clearly imply legislative recognition of the common-law principle that they generally are not competent to do so.[18] We conclude, therefore,

---

18. *See* General Statutes § 17a–688 (d) (minor may consent to treatment for drug and alcohol addiction); General Statutes § 19a–216 (a) (minor may obtain treatment for venereal disease without parental consent); General Statutes § 19a–285 (a) (minor may consent to medical treatment of minor's child); General Statutes § 19a–592 (a) (minor may be treated for human immunodeficiency virus infection without parental consent if notification of parent will result in treatment being denied or if minor will refuse treatment if parents are notified); General Statutes § 19a–601 (minor may have abortion without parental consent).

that the general rule in this state is that minors are presumed to be incompetent to make medical decisions. A number of courts have concluded, however, that there is an exception to this general common-law principle for *mature* minors.

With these principles in mind, we turn to the respondents' claims in the present case that Judge Quinn could not have determined that Cassandra was not a mature minor because that issue was not before her at the December 9, 2014 hearing and, even if the issue was before Judge Quinn, her finding that Cassandra was not a mature minor was not supported by the evidence. We disagree. For purposes of the mature minor doctrine, a mature minor is a minor who is competent to make medical decisions. As we have explained, the very reason that the commissioner asked for the December 9, 2014 hearing was to determine Cassandra's competence to refuse chemotherapy treatment for her cancer. Accordingly, the issue of whether Cassandra was sufficiently mature to make this decision despite the fact that she was a minor was squarely before the court. Under the authority previously set forth, there is a legal presumption that Cassandra was not competent to make the life or death decision whether to undergo chemotherapy treatment for her cancer because she was a minor, and the burden was therefore on the respondents to establish that she was sufficiently mature to do so. Because the respondents failed to produce any evidence on that factual issue, despite being on notice that that was the purpose of the hearing, there was no basis for Judge Quinn to find that Cassandra was a mature minor under any standard.[19] Accordingly, we conclude that her finding that Cassandra was not competent to make her own medical decisions was not clearly erroneous.

Moreover, although the burden was not on the department to show that Cassandra was *not* a mature minor, there was ample evidence to support Judge Quinn's express factual findings that Cassandra was not yet fully separated from or independent of her mother, that she was prone to engage in compulsive and risky actions, that she was unable or unwilling to speak her true mind to those in authority, and that she was reluctant to hold opinions that her mother did not share. Specifically, there was evidence: that Cassandra was extremely nervous and timid during the hearing before Judge Taylor, and that she was fearful during the medical evaluation at the medical center emergency room that followed the hearing; that the reasons that Cassandra did not want to undergo chemotherapy were that she was afraid of seeing "tubes sticking out of her" and that she did not yet feel sick, even though she had been told repeatedly that she would die without the treatment and that delaying treatment until she felt sick could have very serious consequences, potentially including her death; that Cassandra was very emotionally dependent on her mother, and was heavily influenced by her mother's distrust of physicians and other persons in positions of authority; that the respondents were influenced by their independent research into Hodgkin's lymphoma and its

---

19. Cassandra testified at the November 12, 2014 hearing that she has worked since she was fourteen years old and pays some of her own bills. This evidence has little bearing on her competence to make life and death medical decisions on her own. In addition, Cassandra's mother testified at the December 9, 2014 hearing that Cassandra was a "very bright, intelligent girl" who "can make her own decisions." This conclusory statement also provides little support for the respondents' position. Although Cassandra may be intelligent, intelligence, in and of itself, is not evidence of maturity, and she provided no reasoned argument for refusing chemotherapy treatment.

medical treatments, even after numerous physicians contradicted that research;[20] that Cassandra had intentionally misrepresented her intentions to Judge Taylor and the department when she stated that she was willing to undergo treatment; and that Cassandra intentionally violated Judge Taylor's order and placed her own health at serious risk when she interrupted chemotherapy and ran away from home. In turn, Judge Quinn's factual findings amply support her ultimate determination that Cassandra was not a mature seventeen year old and, therefore, was not competent to make her own medical decisions.

The respondents claim, however, that Judge Quinn improperly relied on Isakoff's testimony that Cassandra was not competent to make the decision rejecting treatment because that testimony was based on the "impossible position that an individual is proved incompetent to refuse medical care simply by the fact that she refuses medical care." The respondents concede that "[t]here is no dispute that Cassandra's refusal of treatment, if permitted, would be deleterious to her health," and they have pointed to no possible benefit that would have been gained if she had been permitted to refuse or delay treatment. Thus, they are effectively claiming that Cassandra had a right to reject lifesaving medical treatment for any reason or for no reason, and her assertion of this right had no bearing on the question of whether she was a mature minor. We disagree. Even if we were to assume that adults have the unfettered right to refuse lifesaving medical treatment, an issue that we need not address here, the law is clear that a seventeen year old does not have that right but, to the contrary, is presumed to be incompetent to do so, at least in the absence of proof of maturity. We conclude that it was well within Judge Quinn's discretion to credit Isakoff's eminently sensible opinion that Cassandra's assertion of her purported "right" to refuse the only treatment that could save her life for no reason except that it was her right to do so, did not constitute evidence of maturity, but its opposite. Accordingly, we conclude that the record amply supports Judge Quinn's ultimate finding that Cassandra was not a mature seventeen year old, and, therefore, was not competent to refuse a course of medical treatment that would provide her with her only chance of survival. Thus, there is no need for us to reach the question of whether we should adopt the mature minor doctrine because, even if we were inclined to do so, the doctrine would not apply to Cassandra. . . .

The judgment is affirmed.

NOTES AND QUESTIONS

1. If Cassandra was not mature enough to make her own decision (or if the state did not recognize the mature minor doctrine), her mother would have the legal authority to make medical decisions for her. Based on what you have read in

---

20. The mother's testimony that Cassandra did not want to put "poisons" in her body that could affect her for the rest of her life did not justify Cassandra's decision in any rational way. There was ample evidence that Cassandra would die within a relatively short period of time if she did not receive chemotherapy and that there was a high probability of cure if she received treatment. Even if the chemotherapy will have some long-term side effects, there was *no* evidence presented that there is a significant risk that those side effects will be worse than certain death in the near future.

this chapter, if the mother refused, would a court have been likely to override that decision on the petition of the child welfare agency? Why or why not?

Cassandra's doctors believed that she should have treatment for her cancer, but if the side effects had been worse or the chance of a cure less certain, they might have been willing to defer to Cassandra and her mother. In that situation, if Cassandra and her mother agreed that they did not want treatment, would there be any reason for the doctors to seek judicial approval of that course of action?

2. Why did the trial judge and the appellate court conclude that Cassandra was too immature to make her own decision about chemotherapy? What kind of evidence would have shown that Cassandra was mature enough to decide to refuse treatment?

3. Is the decision in Bellotti v. Baird an application of the mature minor rule? Does *Bellotti* suggest that mature minors are constitutionally entitled to make all treatment decisions for themselves?

Leading cases recognizing the mature minor doctrine include In re E.G., 549 N.E.2d 322 (Ill. 1989); In re Swan, 569 A.2d 1202, 1205 (Me. 1990); Cardwell v. Bechtol, 724 S.W.2d 739, 748 (Tenn. 1987); Belcher v. Charleston Area Medical Center, 422 S.E.2d 827 (W.Va. 1992).

4. As the introductory reading says, the mature minor doctrine has been invoked in a variety of situations. Would it make sense to recognize the doctrine for some legal purposes but not for others? Consider the following types of actions:

a. A juvenile court proceeding brought by a health care provider to challenge the child's and parent's refusal of treatment.
b. A criminal prosecution of the parents for homicide when the child dies from a treatable condition.
c. A wrongful death tort suit brought by the parents against the health care provider who honored the minor's and the parent's decision to forego treatment.

5. While it may seem that whether a minor is mature enough to make a decision about health care should not vary, depending on whether the minor accepts or rejects medical advice, courts in a number of jurisdictions require stronger evidence of competence before they will honor a refusal. English courts were the first to make this distinction. Section 8 of the English Family Law Reform Act of 1969 provides that 16- and 17-year-olds may consent to medical care even if their parents oppose it. The House of Lords held in Gillick v. West Norfolk & Wisbech Health Authority [1985] 3 All E.R. 402 (U.K. H.L.), that a mature minor younger than 16 also has the legal capacity to consent. However, the courts in In re R (A Minor) (Wardship: Consent to Treatment) [1991] 3 WLR 592, and In re W (A Minor) (Medical Treatment), [1992] 3 WLR 758, held that the Act does not give minors an absolute right to refuse treatment and that a court and perhaps parents acting alone may override the minor's refusal when necessary to protect the child's best interests. For discussions, *see* Robert L. Stenger, Exclusive or Concurrent Competence to Make Medical Decisions for Adolescents in the United States and United Kingdom, 14 J.L. & Health 209 (1999/2000); Judith Masson, Adolescent Crisis and Parental Power, [1991] Fam. L. 528; Hazel Houghton-James, The Child's Right to Die, [1992] Fam. L. 550.

The High Court of Australia recognized that mature minors can consent to medical care in Secretary (Dept. of Health & Community Serv.) v. J.W.B. (1992), 175 C.L.R. 218 (Australia H.C.), but state courts have held that courts can override a mature minor's refusal of treatment to protect a child's best interests. Director General (New South Wales Dept. Community Serv.) v. Y., [1999] NSWSC 644 (New South Wales S.C.); Minister for Health v. As, [2004] WASC 286 (Western Australia S.C.). Similarly, the Supreme Court of Canada said that a mature minor can consent to treatment but that a court can override a refusal of consent when necessary to protect the minor's best interests and that these rules are constitutional. Manitoba (Dir. Child & Fam. Serv.) v. C.(A.), (2009), 2009 SCC 30.

In State v. Beagley, above at p. 214, the parents claimed that their son was legally able to refuse treatment, relying on a statute that allows minors 15 years old and older to consent to all medical care. They argued that necessarily if a person can consent, that person can also refuse care. However, the appellate court rejected the argument, saying that no statute expressly authorizes minors to refuse medical care. It concluded, "Although we can imagine situations in which a mature minor might have the right to reject, for example, a parent's wish to have the child undergo an abortion, or plastic surgery, or circumcision, those situations do not bear on whether the instruction was correct in the context of a criminal homicide case where the supposed right of refusal involves necessary life-preserving care. The court's instruction was not error." 305 P.3d at 153-154.

What might explain the distinction that these courts draw between capacity to agree to treatment and to refuse it?

6. The American Academy of Pediatrics has issued a policy statement that supports respecting children's perspectives about their own health care. American Academy of Pediatrics Committee on Bioethics, Informed Consent, Parental Permission and Assent in Pediatric Practice, 95 Pediatrics 314 (1995), *aff'd*, AAP Committee on Bioethics, AAP Publications Retired or Reaffirmed, 119 Pediatrics 405 (2007).

7. Competent adults may execute advance directives to express their wishes regarding health care if they become incompetent. These directives are of two kinds. Living wills express a person's wishes regarding life-sustaining and other health care when the person is near death. Health care powers of attorney designate who is to make decisions on the principal's behalf if the principal becomes incompetent and so are used in a much broader set of circumstances. The federal Patient Self-Determination Act of 1990 requires health care institutions that receive federal funds to offer patients information about and the opportunity to create health care advance directives. However, it does not apply to patients younger than 18. Should adolescent patients younger than 18 be allowed to execute legally binding living wills? Powers of attorney for health care? If state law does not make a minor's advance directive legally binding, but a minor executes a directive, what weight should the family and health care provider give it?

8. Recent commentary on these issues includes Rhonda Gay Hartman, Noblesse Oblige: States' Obligations to Minors Living with Life-Limiting Conditions, 50 Duq. L. Rev. 333 (2012); B. Jessie Hill, Medical Decision Making by and on Behalf of Adolescents: Reconsidering First Principles, 15 J. Health Care L. & Pol'y 37 (2012); Constance MacIntosh, Carter, Medical Aid in Dying, and Mature Minors, 10 McGill J. L. & Health S1 (2016).

PROBLEMS

1. Ellen is a 17-year-old Jehovah's Witness with leukemia. She and her mother have refused blood transfusions for her, even though it is likely she will die within a month without them. The chances that Ellen's disease will go into remission are 80 percent if she receives transfusions and chemotherapy (to which they would consent). However, the long-term survival rate for minors with this disease is 20-25 percent. Ellen is a thoughtful, devout young woman who lives at home with her parents, does well in school, and is socially well adjusted. The only reason that she and her mother give for declining the transfusion is their religious beliefs. You know from materials earlier in this chapter that if Ellen were a young child, a court might well order the transfusion over the mother's objection. Ellen's doctor has filed a juvenile court petition asking that Ellen be found medically neglected and that the court order transfusions for her. What arguments should be made at the hearing on the petition?

2. Joe is a 16-year-old boy with cystic fibrosis who has been hospitalized four times within the last year for pneumonia. He knows that he is dying, has seen several of his friends die from the same disease, and fears that he will die slowly and painfully. He has strongly expressed his wish that he not be put on a ventilator. He is in the hospital, is unable to communicate any longer, and will soon die if he is not put on a ventilator. His parents adamantly insist that he be kept on a ventilator and intubated. His doctor asks you for advice. What advice do you give?

3. Mary is a 16-year-old girl who has had anorexia nervosa since the age of 12. Twice she has been in residential treatment arranged by her parents and has improved, but each time her condition has deteriorated after she was discharged. She is now in the hospital, receiving emergency treatment. She has run away from the hospital once. The police found her in a runaway shelter, and her parents returned her to the hospital. Her weight has been dangerously low for two weeks. Her doctors have gone to juvenile court, seeking an order requiring her to remain at the hospital and allowing them to use reasonable force to keep her there if need be. The doctors will testify that she is unable to make a reasoned judgment about whether to accept treatment because she cannot accept information about the amount of food she needs to consume to maintain weight. Her parents support treatment for Mary but are troubled by the doctors' requests. Assuming that a court would order treatment for Mary, does it necessarily follow that she can be forcibly detained for treatment? Does *Parham* illuminate this problem?

F. BEYOND TREATMENT — ORGAN DONATION AND MEDICAL EXPERIMENTATION

In all the materials that you have read so far, medical interventions were proposed for the purpose of curing the child of a disease, repairing an injury to the child, or the like. This section deals with the question of whether a child can ever volunteer or be volunteered to undergo a medical procedure for the sake of helping someone else that does not promise this kind of direct benefit. Adults donate organs and participate in medical experiments for purely altruistic reasons. Children lack the legal capacity to make such a choice. Can parents or others make it for them?

1.   Organ Donation

The first reported case in the United States involving a minor as an organ donor was Bonner v. Moran, 126 F.2d 121 (D.C. Cir. 1941), in which the aunt of 15-year-old John Bonner convinced him to donate skin for his badly burned cousin. John's mother was not asked for her consent. John suffered serious effects from the procedure, requiring blood transfusions, missed two months of school, and bore permanent scars. He sued the doctor for battery, claiming that the surgery had been done without adequate consent, particularly without the consent of his mother. The jury applied the mature minor rule and decided for the doctor. The appellate court reversed, saying that minors could not consent, at least not to this kind of procedure. Doctors in Boston transplanted kidneys and bone marrow between identical twins during the 1950s with court approval, but the opinions were not published or made publicly available. Doriane Lambelet Coleman, Testing the Boundaries of Family Privacy: The Special Case of Pediatric Sibling Transplants, 35 Cardozo L. Rev. 1289, 1299 - 1300 (2014). The next case, which is much more recent, concerns the extent of parental authority to consent to organ donation.

CURRAN V. BOSZE

---

566 N.E.2d 1319 (Ill. 1990)

Justice CALVO delivered the opinion of the court. Allison and James Curran are 3½-year-old twins. Their mother is Nancy Curran. The twins have lived with Ms. Curran and their maternal grandmother since their birth on January 27, 1987.

The twins' father is Tamas Bosze. Ms. Curran and Mr. Bosze have never been married. . . .

Mr. Bosze is the father of three other children: a son, age 23; Jean Pierre Bosze, age 12; and a one-year-old daughter. Ms. Curran is not the mother of any of these children. Each of these children has a different mother. Jean Pierre and the twins are half-siblings. The twins have met Jean Pierre on two occasions. Each meeting lasted approximately two hours.

Jean Pierre is suffering from acute undifferentiated leukemia (AUL), also known as mixed lineage leukemia. Mixed lineage leukemia is a rare form of leukemia which is difficult to treat. . . . Jean Pierre was treated with chemotherapy and went into remission. Jean Pierre experienced a testicular relapse in January 1990, and a bone marrow relapse in mid-June 1990. Dr. Kwon has recommended a bone marrow transplant for Jean Pierre.

Mr. Bosze asked Ms. Curran to consent to a blood test for the twins in order to determine whether the twins were compatible to serve as bone marrow donors for a transplant to Jean Pierre. Mr. Bosze asked Ms. Curran to consent to the twins' undergoing a bone marrow harvesting procedure if the twins were found to be compatible. After consulting with the twins' pediatrician, family members, parents of bone marrow donors and bone marrow donors, Ms. Curran refused to give consent to the twins' undergoing either the blood test or the bone marrow harvesting procedure.

On June 28, 1990, Mr. Bosze filed an emergency petition in the circuit court of Cook County. The petition informed the court that Jean Pierre "suffers from leukemia and urgently requires a [bone] marrow transplant from a compatible donor. Without the transplant he will die in a short period of time, thereby creating an emergency involving life and death." . . .

[The court determined that the doctrine of substituted judgment, used in Illinois to make health care decisions on behalf of an incompetent adult who has formerly been competent, could not be used in this case because it is impossible to determine whether 3½-year-old children would consent if they were competent.]

Several courts from sister jurisdictions have addressed the issue whether the consent of a court, parent or guardian, for the removal of a kidney from an incompetent person for transplantation to a sibling, may be legally effective. . . .

In Strunk v. Strunk (Ky. 1969), 445 S.W.2d 145, the Kentucky Court of Appeals, in a 4 to 3 decision, determined that a court of equity had the power to permit a kidney to be removed from a mentally incompetent ward of the State, upon the petition of his committee, his mother, for transplantation into his 28-year-old brother who was dying from a kidney disease. The ward of the State was a 27-year-old man who had the mental capacity of a six-year-old. The mother petitioned the county court for authority to proceed with the kidney transplant. The county court "found that the operation was necessary, that under the peculiar circumstances of this case it would not only be beneficial to [the ward's brother] but also beneficial to [the ward] because [the ward] was greatly dependent upon [his brother], emotionally and psychologically, and that [the ward's] well-being would be jeopardized more severely by the loss of his brother than by the removal of a kidney." *Strunk*, 445 S.W.2d at 146.

. . . Appeal was taken to the circuit court, which adopted the findings of the county court. The circuit court "found that it would be to the best interest of the ward of the state that the procedure be carried out." *Strunk*, 445 S.W.2d at 147. . . .

In Hart v. Brown (Super. 1972), 29 Conn. Supp. 368, 289 A.2d 386, the parents of identical twins, age 7 years and 10 months, sought permission to have a kidney from the healthy twin transplanted into the body of the seriously ill twin who was suffering from a kidney disease. The parents brought a declaratory judgment action, as parents and natural guardians of the twins, seeking a declaration that they had the right to consent to the proposed operation. . . .

The *Hart* court reviewed the medical testimony presented concerning the kidney transplant which "indicate[d] that scientifically this type of procedure is a 'perfect' transplant." The court also noted that a psychiatrist examined the proposed donor and testified the proposed donor "has a strong identification with her twin sister." Further, the psychiatrist testified "that if the expected successful results are achieved they would be of immense benefit to the donor in that the donor would be better off in a family that was happy than in a family that was distressed and in that it would be a very great loss to the donor if the donee were to die from her illness." . . .

Both guardians ad litem gave their consent to the procedure. Both parents gave their consent to the procedure. A clergy person testified that the natural parents were "making a morally sound decision." The *Hart* court found the testimony of the parents showed they reached their decision to consent "only after many hours of agonizing consideration. The twin who would serve as the kidney donor "ha[d] been informed of the operation and insofar as she may be capable of understanding she desires to donate her kidney so that her sister may return to her."

The *Hart* court stated: "To prohibit the natural parents and the guardians ad litem of the minor children the right to give their consent under these circumstances, where there is supervision by this court and other persons in examining their judgment, would be most unjust, inequitable and injudicious. Therefore, natural parents of a minor should have the right to give their consent to an isograft kidney transplantation procedure when their motivation and reasoning are favorably reviewed by a community representation which includes a court of equity. It is the judgment of this court that [the parents] have the right, under the particular facts and circumstances of this matter, to give their consent to the operations." . . .

In Little v. Little (Tex. Civ. 1979), 576 S.W.2d 493, the mother of a 14-year-old mentally incompetent daughter petitioned the court to authorize the mother's consent to the removal of a kidney from her daughter for transplantation into her younger son, who suffered from a kidney disease. . . .

The *Little* court determined that "the testimony . . . conclusively establish[ed] the existence of a close relationship between [the proposed donor] and [her brother], a genuine concern by each for the welfare of the other and, at the very least, an awareness by [the proposed donor] of the nature of [her brother's] plight and an awareness of the fact that she is in a position to ameliorate [her brother's] burden." Both parents of the incompetent minor consented to the kidney donation; there was no evidence that the incompetent minor had been subjected to family pressure; and there were no medically preferable alternatives to the kidney transplant. The *Little* court also found that the dangers of the operation were minimal and there was evidence the incompetent minor would not suffer psychological harm. The kidney transplant would probably be substantially beneficial to the proposed recipient, and the trial court's decision was made "only after a full judicial proceeding in which the interests of [the incompetent minor] were championed by an attorney ad litem." The *Little* court concluded:

> Given the presence of all the factors and circumstances outlined above, and limiting our decision to such facts and circumstances, we conclude that the trial court did not exceed its authority by authorizing the participation of [the incompetent minor] in the kidney transplant as a donor, since there is strong evidence to the effect that she will receive substantial psychological benefits from such participation. Nothing in this opinion is to be construed as being applicable to a situation where the proposed [recipient] is not a parent or sibling of the incompetent.

In [In re Guardianship of Pescinski, 67 Wis. 2d 4, 226 N.W.2d 180 (1975)], the sister and guardian of an adult incompetent 39-year-old man petitioned the court for permission for the incompetent brother to donate a kidney to another sister suffering from a kidney disease. The incompetent, "classified as a schizophrenic, chronic, catatonic type" for over 17 years, was a mental patient at a State hospital.

A physician testified that the ward had a mental capacity of a 12-year-old child. The guardian ad litem for the incompetent person would not consent to the procedure.

In *Pescinski*, the supreme court of Wisconsin addressed the issue: "Does a county court have the power to order an operation to be performed to remove a kidney of an incompetent ward, under guardianship of the person, and transfer it to a sister where the dire need of the transfer is established but where no consent has been given by the incompetent or his guardian ad litem, nor has any benefit to the ward been shown?" The court answered that it did not. . . .

The Louisiana Court of Appeal in In re Richardson (La. App. 1973), 284 So. 2d 185, declined to adopt the doctrine of substituted judgment announced in *Strunk*. Both parents of a 17-year-old incompetent son with a mental age of three or four years consented to a kidney transplant from the son to his sister. . . . The *Richardson* court distinguished the case before it from the case in *Strunk*:

> We find the facts in [*Strunk*], particularly the conclusion relative to the "best inter-est" of the incompetent, are not similar to the facts in the instant case and we also find that both the procedural and the substantive aspects of the majority opinion are not in accord with Louisiana law.

Richardson, 284 So. 2d at 187.

The *Richardson* court stated that the law of its State "is designed to protect and promote the ultimate best interest of a minor." Louisiana law did not provide for the inter vivos donation of a minor's property either by the minor or by the minor's tutor (guardian). The *Richardson* court stated:

> Since our law affords this unqualified protection against intrustion [sic] into a com-paratively mere property right, it is inconceivable to us that it affords less protection to a minor's right to be free in his person from bodily intrusion to the extent of loss of an organ unless such loss be in the best interest of the minor. Of course, that state-ment and our conclusion are restricted to the facts of the present case.

Richardson, 284 So. 2d at 187. . . .

In each of the foregoing cases where consent to the kidney transplant was authorized, regardless whether the authority to consent was to be exercised by the court, a parent or a guardian, the key inquiry was the presence or absence of a benefit to the potential donor. Notwithstanding the language used by the courts in reaching their determination that a transplant may or may not occur, the standard by which the determination was made was whether the transplant would be in the best interest of the child or incompetent person.

The primary benefit to the donor in these cases arises from the relationship existing between the donor and recipient. In *Strunk*, the donor lived in a State institution. The recipient was a brother who served as the donor's only connection with the outside world. In both *Hart* and *Little*, there was evidence that the sibling relationship between the donor and recipient was close. In each of these cases, both parents had given their consent.

We hold that a parent or guardian may give consent on behalf of a minor daughter or son for the child to donate bone marrow to a sibling, only when to do so would be in the minor's best interest.

[Under Illinois law, Ms. Curran, as sole custodian of the twins, had authority to make decisions regarding them. However, Mr. Bosze, as a noncustodial parent, could petition the court for a limitation on her authority when her actions were contrary to the best interests of the children. Mr. Bosze argued that Ms. Curran's withholding of consent was contrary to the twins' best interests.]

In the case at bar, the circuit court heard extensive testimony from physicians concerning the status of Jean Pierre's condition, and the risks and benefits of donating bone marrow. . . .

The evidence reveals three critical factors which are necessary to a determination that it will be in the best interests of a child to donate bone marrow to a sibling. First, the parent who consents on behalf of the child must be informed of the risks and benefits inherent in the bone marrow harvesting procedure to the child.

Second, there must be emotional support available to the child from the person or persons who take care of the child. The testimony reveals that a child who is to undergo general anesthesia and the bone marrow harvesting procedure needs the emotional support of a person whom the child loves and trusts. A child who is to donate bone marrow is required to go to an unfamiliar place and meet with unfamiliar people. Depending upon the age of the child, he or she may or may not understand what is to happen. The evidence establishes that the presence and emotional support by the child's caretaker is important to ease the fears associated with such an unfamiliar procedure.

Third, there must be an existing, close relationship between the donor and recipient. The evidence clearly shows that there is no physical benefit to a donor child. If there is any benefit to a child who donates bone marrow to a sibling it will be a psychological benefit. According to the evidence, the psychological benefit is not simply one of personal, individual altruism in an abstract theoretical sense, although that may be a factor.

The psychological benefit is grounded firmly in the fact that the donor and recipient are known to each other as family. Only where there is an existing relationship between a healthy child and his or her ill sister or brother may a psychological benefit to the child from donating bone marrow to a sibling realistically be found to exist. The evidence establishes that it is the existing sibling relationship, as well as the potential for a continuing sibling relationship, which forms the context in which it may be determined that it will be in the best interests of the child to undergo a bone marrow harvesting procedure for a sibling. . . .

The primary risk to a bone marrow donor is the risk associated with undergoing general anesthesia. The risk of a life-threatening complication occurring from undergoing general anesthesia is 1 in 10,000. As noted by the circuit court, the risks associated with general anesthesia include, but are not limited to, "brain damage as a result of oxygen deprivation, stroke, cardiac arrest and death." The pain following the harvesting procedure is usually easily controlled with postoperative medication. Although there is a risk of infection at the needle puncture site, this is rare.

Ms. Curran has refused consent on behalf of the twins to the bone marrow transplant because she does not think it is in their best interests to subject them to the risks and pains involved in undergoing general anesthesia and the harvesting procedure. While Ms. Curran is aware that the risks involved in donating bone marrow and undergoing general anesthesia are small, she also is aware that when such risk occurs, it may be life-threatening. . . .

It is a fact that the twins and Jean Pierre share the same biological father. There was no evidence produced, however, to indicate that the twins and Jean Pierre are known to each other as family.

Allison and James would need the emotional support of their primary care-giver if they were to donate bone marrow. The evidence establishes that it would not be in a 3½-year-old child's best interests if he or she were required to go to a hospital and undergo all that is involved with the bone marrow harvesting proce-dure without the constant reassurance and support by a familiar adult known and trusted by the child.

Not only is Ms. Curran presently the twins' primary caretaker, the evidence establishes she is the only caretaker the twins have ever known. Ms. Curran has refused to consent to the twins' participation in donating bone marrow to Jean Pierre. It appears that Mr. Bosze would be unable to substitute his support for the procedure for that of Ms. Curran because his involvement in the lives of Allison and James has, to this point, been a limited one.

The guardian ad litem for the twins recommends that it is not in the best interests of either Allison or James to undergo the proposed bone marrow har-vesting procedure in the absence of an existing, close relationship with the recip-ient, Jean Pierre, and over the objection of their primary caretaker, Ms. Curran. Because the evidence presented supports this recommendation, we agree. . . .

This court shares the opinion of the circuit court that Jean Pierre's situation "evokes sympathy from all who've heard [it]." No matter how small the hope that a bone marrow transplant will cure Jean Pierre, the fact remains that without the transplant, Jean Pierre will almost certainly die. The sympathy felt by this court, the circuit court, and all those who have learned of Jean Pierre's tragic situation cannot, however, obscure the fact that, under the circumstances presented in the case at bar, it neither would be proper under existing law nor in the best interests of the 3½-year-old twins for the twins to participate in the bone marrow harvest-ing procedure.

On September 28, 1990, this court entered an order affirming the judgment of the circuit court, with opinion to follow, and now for the foregoing reasons, we reaffirm our previous order. For purposes of computing time limits for any fur-ther proceedings, the date of the filing of this opinion shall control. Circuit court affirmed.

NOTES AND QUESTIONS

1. A case similar to Hart v. Brown, which is discussed in *Curran*, is analyzed in Samuel J. Tilden, Ethical and Legal Aspects of Using an Identical Twin as a Skin Transplant Donor for a Severely Burned Minor, 31 Am. J.L. & Med. 87, 107-112 (2005). In that case, which did not go to an appellate court, the trial court author-ized the parents of a six-year-old to consent to her being a donor for her twin sister, who was severely burned and needed a skin transplant.

2. *Curran* and the cases that it cites all say that a child cannot be an organ donor if the donation will not benefit the child. Why not? In all these cases, the

alleged benefit to the child donor is psychological. What are the requirements that must be satisfied before a court finds psychological benefit to the child? Would the good feelings that come from being altruistic be a sufficient psychological benefit? Why or why not? The early organ transplants between twins during the 1950s also relied on psychological benefit to the donating sibling to justify approving the process as being in that child's best interests. Doriane Lambelet Coleman, Testing the Boundaries of Family Privacy: The Special Case of Pediatric Sibling Transplants, 35 Cardozo L. Rev. 1289, 1300-1307 (2014).

Professor Coleman argues that under a traditional best interests analysis, psychological benefits cannot be used to justify intentionally inflicted physical harm. 35 Cardozo L. Rev. at 1327-1331. She argues that the few cases authorizing sibling organ transplants either find that parents have the authority to balance the competing interests of their children when it is impossible for a parent to act in the best interests of all his or her children or when the parents act in the interests of the family as a collective. Id. at 1327-1341.

3. Would it ever be permissible for a child to be an organ donor without parental consent? Should the mature minor rule apply in this situation? For example, could a 16-year-old consent to be a blood donor? To give a kidney to a stranger? For a discussion of the role teenagers should play in deciding whether to be organ donors, see Rhonda Gay Hartman, Gault's Legacy: Dignity, Due Process, and Adolescents' Liberty Interests in Living Donation, 22 Notre Dame J.L. Ethics & Pub. Pol'y 67 (2008).

4. Do parents have a conflict of interest when they must decide whether to allow one child to be an organ donor for the other? For this reason, should proposed organ donations from a child always be subject to judicial review? How would a court decide whether the parents were adequately considering the interests of the would-be donor child?

5. According to the Organ Procurement and Transplant Network, between 1988 and 2019, 75 living children younger than 18 were organ donors in the United States; 42 donated a kidney, and 33 donated a liver lobe, and the other two donated a heart. Detailed information is available on the organization's website, optn.transplant.hrsa.gov/. The recipients of the organs were ordinarily siblings.

6. Because of advances in medical transplant technology and genetic testing, a number of diseases can now be treated with transplants if matching donors can be found. This development, in turn, has led parents of children with diseases or conditions that can be treated by transplants to conceive and bear children intended to become donors for their ill siblings—"savior siblings." Preimplantation genetic diagnosis allows selection of an embryo that will be a suitable match. Unlike in other western countries, these practices are largely unregulated by law in the U.S. For discussion of the medical, ethical, and legal issues, see Marley McClean, Note and Comment, Children's Anatomy v. Children's Autonomy: A Precarious Balancing Act with Preimplantation Genetic Diagnosis and the Creation of "Savior Siblings," 43 Pepp. L. Rev. 837 (2016); Amy T.Y. Lai, PhD, JD, To Be or Not To Be My Sister's Keeper?: A Revised Legal Framework Safeguarding Savior Siblings' Welfare, 32 J. Legal Med. 261 (2011); Richard F. Storrow, Therapeutic Reproduction and Human Dignity, 21 Law & Literature 257 (2009); Judith F. Daar, Embryonic Genetics, 2 St. Louis U. J. Health L. & Pol'y 81 (2008); Susannah Baruch, Preimplantation Genetic Diagnosis and Parental Preferences: Beyond

Deadly Disease, 8 Hous. J. Health L. & Pol'y 245 (2008); Michele Goodwin, My Sister's Keeper?: Law, Children, and Compelled Donation, 29 W. New Eng. L. Rev. 357 (2007); Susan M. Wolf et al., Using Preimplantation Genetic Diagnosis to Create a Stem Cell Donor: Issues, Guidelines, & Limits, 31 J.L. Med. & Ethics, 327 (2003).

PROBLEM

Jane and Don's oldest daughter, Anna, has leukemia. When she was first diagnosed, the doctors told them that her best chance for survival was to receive a bone marrow transplant, but neither Jane, Don, nor their other daughter, Betsy, was a match. Jane and Don had another child, hoping for a match. They successfully conceived, and their daughter Carrie, was indeed a match for Anna. At Carrie's birth, with the consent of Jane and Don, Anna's doctors took some of Carrie's cord blood to use in an experimental treatment for Anna. The treatment was successful for several years, but when Carrie was three, Anna's leukemia returned. Jane and Don consented for Carrie to be a white blood cell donor for Anna. Again, the treatment was successful for a few years, and again Anna relapsed. When Carrie was ten, her parents consented to her being a bone marrow transplant donor for Anna. Carrie is now 13, and Anna's kidneys are failing because of the years of cancer treatment that she has undergone. Jane and Don want Carrie to donate one of her kidneys to Anna. Carrie has found a sympathetic attorney, who has filed a suit on her behalf, seeking authority for Carrie to make her own decision about whether or not to continue to be a donor for her sister. Jane and Don have moved to dismiss the suit on the bases that recognizing Carrie's cause of action would unconstitutionally invade their parental rights and would be contrary to public policy. What arguments should be made?

2. *Research with Children*

Modern regulation of research with human beings traces its origins to the Nuremberg Code of 1949, which was written in response to the horrors of experiments that Nazi doctors conducted on inmates of concentration camps during World War II. One of the fundamental prerequisites for ethical research, expressed in the Code, is that a person cannot be a subject of research without his or her voluntary consent. This requirement would seem to preclude experiments involving children as subjects unless parents or legal guardians can give consent, an issue that both the next case and the federal regulations following it address.

GRIMES V. KENNEDY KRIEGER INSTITUTE, INC.

782 A.2d 807 (Md. 2001)

CATHELL, Judge. . . .[P]recious few courts in the United States have addressed the issues presented in the cases at bar. In respect to nontherapeutic research using minors, it has been noted that "consent to research has been virtually unanalyzed by courts and legislatures." Robert J. Katerberg, Institutional Review Boards, Research on Children, and Informed Consent of Parents: Walking the Tightrope Between Encouraging Vital Experimentation and Protecting Subjects' Rights, 24 J.C. & U.L. 545, 562, quoting National Commission for the Protection of Human Subjects of Biomedical and Behavioral Research, Report and Recommendations [National Commission]: Research Involving Children 79-80 (1977). Our research reveals this statement remains as accurate now as it was in 1977.

In these present cases, a prestigious research institute, associated with Johns Hopkins University, *based on this record*, created a nontherapeutic research program whereby it required certain classes of homes to have only partial lead paint abatement modifications performed, and in at least some instances, including at least one of the cases at bar, arranged for the landlords to receive public funding by way of grants or loans to aid in the modifications. The research institute then encouraged, and in at least one of the cases at bar, required, the landlords to rent the premises to families with young children. In the event young children already resided in one of the study houses, it was contemplated that a child would remain in the premises, and the child was encouraged to remain, in order for his or her blood to be periodically analyzed. In other words, the continuing presence of the children that were the subjects of the study was required in order for the study to be complete. Apparently, the children and their parents involved in the cases *sub judice* were from a lower economic strata and were, at least in one case, minorities.

The purpose of the research was to determine how effective varying degrees of lead paint abatement procedures were. Success was to be determined by periodically, over a two-year period of time, measuring the extent to which lead dust remained in, or returned to, the premises after the varying levels of abatement modifications, and, as most important to our decision, by measuring the extent to which the theretofore healthy children's blood became contaminated with lead, and comparing that contamination with levels of lead dust in the houses over the same periods of time. In respect to one of the protocols presented to the Environmental Protection Agency and/or the Johns Hopkins Joint Committee on Clinical Investigation, the Johns Hopkins Institutional Review Board (IRB), the researchers stated: "To help insure that study dwellings are occupied by families with young children, City Homes will give priority to families with young children when renting the vacant units following R & M [Repair and Maintenance] interventions."

The same researchers had completed a prior study on abatement and partial abatement methods that indicated that lead dust remained and/or returned to abated houses over a period of time. In an article reporting on that study, the very same researchers said: "Exposure to lead-bearing dust is particularly hazardous for children because hand-to-mouth activity is recognized as a major route of entry of lead into the body and because absorption of lead is inversely related to particle size." After publishing this report, the researchers began the present research project in which children were encouraged to reside in households where the possibility of lead dust was known to the researcher to be likely, so that the lead dust content of their blood could be compared with the level of lead dust in the houses at periodic intervals over a two-year period.

Apparently, it was anticipated that the children, who were the human subjects in the program, would, or at least might, accumulate lead in their blood from the dust, thus helping the researchers to determine the extent to which the various partial abatement methods worked. There was no complete and clear explanation in the consent agreements signed by the parents of the children that the research to be conducted was designed, at least in significant part, to measure the success of the abatement procedures by measuring the extent to which the children's blood was being contaminated. It can be argued that the researchers intended that the children be the canaries in the mines but never clearly told the parents. . . .

The researchers and their Institutional Review Board apparently saw nothing wrong with the search protocols that anticipated the possible accumulation of lead in the blood of otherwise healthy children as a result of the experiment, or they believed that the consents of the parents of the children made the research appropriate. Institutional Review Boards (IRB) are oversight entities within the institutional family to which an entity conducting research belongs. In research experiments, an IRB can be required in some instances by either federal or state regulation, or sometimes by the conditions attached to governmental grants that are used to fund research projects. Generally, their primary functions are to assess the protocols of the project to determine whether the project itself is appropriate, whether the consent procedures are adequate, whether the methods to be employed meet proper standards, whether reporting requirements are sufficient, and the assessment of various other aspects of a research project. One of the most important objectives of such review is the review of the potential safety and the health hazard impact of a research project on the human subjects of the experiment, especially on vulnerable subjects such as children. Their function is *not* to help researchers seek funding for research projects. . . .

Otherwise healthy children, in our view, should not be enticed into living in, or remaining in, potentially lead-tainted housing and intentionally subjected to a research program, which contemplates the probability, or even the possibility, of lead poisoning or even the accumulation of lower levels of lead in blood, in order for the extent of the contamination of the children's blood to be used by scientific researchers to assess the success of lead paint or lead dust abatement measures. Moreover, in our view, parents, whether improperly enticed by trinkets, food stamps, money or other items, have no more right to intentionally and unnecessarily place children in potentially hazardous nontherapeutic research surroundings, than do researchers. In such cases, parental consent, no matter how informed, is insufficient. . . .

The research relationship proffered to the parents of the children the researchers wanted to use as measuring tools, should never have been presented in a nontherapeutic context in the first instance. Nothing about the research was designed for treatment of the subject children. They were presumed to be healthy at the commencement of the project. As to them, the research was clearly nontherapeutic in nature. The experiment was simply a "for the greater good" project. The specific children's health was put at risk, in order to develop low-cost abatement measures that would help all children, the landlords, and the general public as well. . . .

The research project at issue here, and its apparent protocols, differs in large degree from, but presents similar problems as those in the Tuskegee Syphilis Study conducted from 1932 until 1972 (The Tuskegee Syphilis Study, 289 New England Journal of Medicine 730 (1973)), the intentional exposure of soldiers to radiation in the 1940s and 50s (Jaffee v. United States, 663 F.2d 1226 (3d Cir.1981), *cert. denied*, 456 U.S. 972 1982)), the tests involving the exposure of Navajo miners to radiation (Begay v. United States, 591 F. Supp. 991 (1984), *aff'd*, 768 F.2d 1059 (9th Cir. 1985), and the secret administration of LSD to soldiers by the CIA and the Army in the 1950s and 60s (United States v. Stanley, 483 U.S. 669 (1987); (Central Intelligence Agency v. Sims, 471 U.S. 159 (1985)). The research experiments that follow were also prior instances of research subjects being intentionally exposed to infectious or poisonous substances in the name of scientific research. They include the Tuskegee Syphilis Study, aforesaid, where patients infected with syphilis were not subsequently informed of the availability of penicillin for treatment of the illness, in order for the scientists and researchers to be able to continue research on the effects of the illness, the Jewish Hospital study,[21] and several other post-war research projects. Then there are the notorious use of "plague bombs" by the Japanese military in World War II where entire villages were infected in order for the results to be "studied"; and perhaps most notorious, the deliberate use of infection in a nontherapeutic project in order to study the degree of infection and the rapidity of the course of the disease in the Rose and Mrugowsky typhus experiments at Buchenwald concentration camp during World War II. These programs were somewhat alike in the vulnerability of the subjects; uneducated African-American men, debilitated patients in a charity hospital, prisoners of war, inmates of concentration camps and others falling within the custody and control of the agencies conducting or approving the experiments. In the present case, children, especially young children, living in lower economic circumstances, albeit not as vulnerable as the other examples, are nonetheless, vulnerable as well.

It is clear to this Court that the scientific and medical communities cannot be permitted to assume sole authority to determine ultimately what is right and appropriate in respect to research projects involving young children free of the limitations and consequences of the application of Maryland law. The Institutional Review Boards, IRBs, are, primarily, in-house organs. In our view, they are not designed, generally, to be sufficiently objective in the sense that they are as sufficiently concerned with the ethicality of the experiments they review as they are with the success of the experiments. . . .

We now discuss more specifically the two cases before us, and the relevant law.

Two separate negligence actions involving children who allegedly developed elevated levels of lead dust in their blood while participating in a research study with respondent, Kennedy Krieger Institute, Inc. (KKI), are before this Court. Both cases allege that the children were poisoned, or at least exposed to the risk of being poisoned, by lead dust due to negligence on the part of KKI. Specifically, they allege that KKI discovered lead hazards in their respective homes and, having a duty to notify them, failed to warn in a timely manner or otherwise act to prevent the children's exposure to the known presence of lead. Additionally, plaintiffs alleged that they were not fully informed of the risks of the research.

---

21. Generally known as the Jewish Chronic Disease Hospital study where chronically ill and debilitated patients were injected with cancer cells without their consent. *See* Zeleznik v. Jewish Chronic Disease Hosp., 47 A.D.2d 199, 366 N.Y.S.2d 163 (1975). And *see* Application of Hyman, 42 Misc. 2d 427, 248 N.Y.S.2d 245, *rev'd* Hyman v. Jewish Chronic Disease Hospital, 21 A.D.2d 495, 251 N.Y.S.2d 818 (1964), *rev'd* 15 N.Y.2d 317, 206 N.E.2d 338, 258 N.Y.S.2d 397 (1965).

In the first case, Number 128, appellant, Ericka Grimes, by her mother Viola Hughes, appeals from a ruling of the Circuit Court for Baltimore City granting KKI's motion for summary judgment based on the sole ground that as a matter of law there was no legal duty, under the circumstances here present, on the part of KKI, owed to the appellants. In the second case, Number 129, appellant, Myron Higgins, by his mother Catina Higgins, and Catina Higgins, individually, appeal from a ruling of the Circuit Court for Baltimore City granting KKI's motion for summary judgment based on the ground that KKI had no legal duty to warn them of the presence of lead dust. The parties, in their respective appeals, presented almost identical issues to the Court of Special Appeals. . . . .

V.   THE ETHICAL APPROPRIATENESS OF THE RESEARCH

The World Medical Association in its Declaration of Helsinki[22] included a code of ethics for investigative researchers and was an attempt by the medical community to establish its own set of rules for conducting research on human subjects. The Declaration states in relevant part:

"III. Non-therapeutic biomedical research involving human subjects (Non-clinical biomedical research)

1. *In the purely scientific application of medical research carried out on a human being, it is the duty of the physician to remain the protector of the life and health of that person on whom biomedical research is being carried out.*
2. The subjects should be volunteers—either healthy persons or patients for whom the experimental design is not related to the patient's illness.
3. The investigator or the investigating team should *discontinue the research if in his/her or their judgement it may, if continued, be harmful to the individual.*
4. *In research on man, the interest of science and society should never take precedence over considerations related to the well being of the subject.*" [Emphasis added.]

Adopted in Declaration of Helsinki, World Medical Assembly (WMA) 18th Assembly (June 1964), amended by 29th WMA Tokyo, Japan (October 1975), 35th WMA Venice, Italy (October 1983), and the 41st WMA Hong Kong (September 1989).

The determination of whether a duty exists under Maryland law is the ultimate function of various policy considerations as adopted by either the Legislature, or, if it has not spoken, as it has not in respect to this situation, by Maryland courts. In our view, otherwise healthy children should not be the subjects of nontherapeutic experimentation or research that has the potential to be

---

22. The Declaration of Helsinki was crafted by the international medical profession, as preferable to the Nuremberg Code crafted by lawyers and judges and adopted right after the Second World War. The Declaration, or, for that matter, the Nuremberg Code, have never been formally adopted by the relevant governmental entities, although the Nuremberg Code was intended to apply universally. The medical profession, and its ancillary research organs, felt that the Nuremberg Code was too restrictive because of its origins from the Nazi horrors of that era. Serious questions arise in this case under either code, even under the more general provisions of the Declaration of Helsinki apparently favored by doctors and scientists.

harmful to the child. It is, first and foremost, the responsibility of the researcher and the research entity to see to the harmlessness of such nontherapeutic research. Consent of parents can never relieve the researcher of this duty. We do not feel that it serves proper public policy concerns to permit children to be placed in situations of potential harm, during nontherapeutic procedures, even if parents, or other surrogates, consent. Under these types of circumstances, even where consent is given, *albeit* inappropriately, policy considerations suggest that there remains a special relationship between researchers and participants to the research study, which imposes a duty of care. This is entirely consistent with the principles found in the Nuremberg Code.

Researchers cannot ever be permitted to completely immunize themselves by reliance on consents, especially when the information furnished to the subject, or the party consenting, is incomplete in a material respect. A researcher's duty is not created by, or extinguished by, the consent of a research subject or by IRB approval. The duty to a vulnerable research subject is independent of consent, although the obtaining of consent is one of the duties a researcher must perform. All of this is especially so when the subjects of research are children. Such legal duties, and legal protections, might additionally be warranted because of the likely conflict of interest between the goal of the research experimenter and the health of the human subject, especially, but not exclusively, when such research is commercialized. There is always a potential substantial conflict of interest on the part of researchers as between them and the human subjects used in their research. If participants in the study withdraw from the research study prior to its completion, then the results of the study could be rendered meaningless. There is thus an inherent reason for not conveying information to subjects as it arises, that might cause the subjects to leave the research project. That conflict dictates a stronger reason for full and continuous disclosure.

In research, the study participant's "well-being is subordinated to the dictates of a research protocol designed to advance knowledge for the sake of future patients." In a recent report, the National Bioethics Advisory Commission recognized that this conflict between pursuit of scientific knowledge and the well-being of research participants requires some oversight of scientific investigators:

> However noble the investigator's intentions, when research involves human participants, the uncertainties inherent in any research study raise the prospect of unanticipated harm. In designing a research study an investigator must focus on finding or creating situations in which one can test important scientific hypotheses. *At the same time, no matter how important the research questions, it is not ethical to use human participants without appropriate protections.* Thus, there can be a conflict between the need to test hypotheses and the requirement to respect and protect individuals who participate in research. This conflict and the resulting tension that can arise within the research enterprise suggest a need for guidance and oversight.

National Bioethics Advisory Commission, Ethical and Policy Issues in Research Involving Human Participants, 2-3 (Dec. 19, 2000) (emphasis added). When human subjects are used in scientific research, the rights of the human subjects are afforded the protection of the courts when such subjects seek redress for any wrongs committed. . . . .

VI.   Parental Consent for Children to Be Subjects of Potentially Hazardous Nontherapeutic Research

The issue of whether a parent can consent to the participation of her or his child in a nontherapeutic health-related study that is known to be potentially hazardous to the health of the child raises serious questions with profound moral and ethical implications. What right does a parent have to knowingly expose a child not in need of therapy to health risks or otherwise knowingly place a child in danger, even if it can be argued it is for the greater good? The issue in these specific contested cases does not relate primarily to the authority of the parent, but to the procedures of KKI and similar entities that may be involved in such health-related studies. The issue of the parents' right to consent on behalf of the children has not been fully presented in either of these cases, but should be of concern not only to lawyers and judges, but to moralists, ethicists, and others. The consenting parents in the contested cases at bar were not the subjects of the experiment; the children were. Additionally, this practice presents the potential problems of children initiating actions in their own names upon reaching majority, if indeed, they have been damaged as a result of being used as guinea pigs in nontherapeutic scientific research. Children, it should be noted, are not in our society the equivalent of rats, hamsters, monkeys, and the like. Because of the overriding importance of this matter and this Court's interest in the welfare of children we shall address the issue.

Most of the relatively few cases in the area of the ethics of protocols of various research projects involving children have merely assumed that a parent can give informed consent for the participation of their children in nontherapeutic research. The single case in which the issue has been addressed, and resolved, a case with which we agree, will be discussed further, *infra*.

It is not in the best interest of a specific child, in a nontherapeutic research project, to be placed in a research environment, which might possibly be, or which proves to be, hazardous to the health of the child. We have long stressed that the "best interests of the child" is the overriding concern of this Court in matters relating to children. Whatever the interests of a parent, and whatever the interests of the general public in fostering research that might, according to a researcher's hypothesis, be for the good of all children, this Court's concern for the particular child and particular case, over-arches all other interests. It is, simply, and we hope, succinctly put, not in the best interest of any healthy child to be intentionally put in a nontherapeutic situation where his or her health may be impaired, in order to test methods that may ultimately benefit all children.

To think otherwise, to turn over human and legal ethical concerns solely to the scientific community, is to risk embarking on slippery slopes, that all too often in the past, here and elsewhere, have resulted in practices we, or any community, should be ever unwilling to accept.

We have little doubt that the general motives of all concerned in these contested cases were, for the most part, proper, albeit in our view not well thought out. The protocols of the research, those of which we have been made aware, were, in any event, unacceptable in a legal context. One simply does not expose otherwise healthy children, incapable of personal assent (consent), to a nontherapeutic research environment that is known at the inception of the research, might cause the children to ingest lead dust. It is especially troublesome, when a measurement of the success of the research experiment is, in significant respect, to be determined by the extent to which the blood of the children absorbs, and is contaminated by, a substance that the researcher knows can, in sufficient amounts, whether solely from the research environment or cumulative from all sources, cause serious and long-term adverse health effects. Such a practice is not legally acceptable. . . .

When it comes to children involved in nontherapeutic research, with the potential for health risks to the subject children in Maryland, we will not defer to science to be the sole determinant of the ethicality or legality of such experiments. The reason, in our view, is apparent from the research protocols at issue in the case at bar. Moreover, in nontherapeutic research using children, we hold that the consent of a parent alone cannot make appropriate that which is innately inappropriate.

In T.D. v. New York State Office of Mental Health, 165 Misc. 2d 62, 626 N.Y.S.2d 1015 (1995), that court was presented with a dispute as between which state agency had control over the approval of experiments using persons generally incapable of giving consent. Most were mental patients and included both adult and minor subjects. The trial court agreed with the representatives of the subjects, granting a partial summary judgment to that effect. In its opinion, it stated:

> The plaintiffs seek a declaratory judgment as to the validity of the OMH regulations promulgated November 7, 1990 which set forth the procedures to be followed for the nonconsensual participation by mental patients in potentially high-risk **experiments.** It is important to note at the outset that this action is not a broad-based challenge by the plaintiffs to any and all research performed on human subjects. It is limited to those procedures which may cause stroke, heart attack, convulsions, hallucinations, or other diseases and disabilities including death, and which, while possibly shedding light on possible future treatments to others, offer no direct therapeutic benefit to the participating subject. Plaintiffs contend that their challenge affects only approximately 10 studies which utilize incapable individuals or **children,** involve more than a minimal risk. . . .
>
> What is most objected to are the provisions for substituted . . . decision makers. Courts tread cautiously when third parties are relied on to make decisions for an incapable patient. When the proposed medical course does not involve an emergency and is not for the purpose of bettering the patient's condition, or ending suffering, it may be doubtful if a surrogate decision maker—a guardian, a committee, a health-care proxy holder, a relative, *or even a parent* could properly give consent to permitting a ward to be used in experimental research with no prospect of direct therapeutic benefit to the patient himself. 'Parents may be free to become martyrs themselves. But it does not follow they are free, in identical circumstances, to make martyrs of their children before they have reached the age of full and legal discretion when they can make that choice for themselves.'

The intermediate appellate court of New York, affirmed and modified the trial court's declaration, finding additional sections of the statute at issue inappropriate. In respect to the reasonableness of accepting parental consent for minors to participate in potentially harmful, nontherapeutic research, that court stated:

> We also find unacceptable the provisions that allow for consent to be obtained on behalf of minors for participation in greater than minimal risk[23] nontherapeutic research from the minor's parent or legal guardian, or, where no parent or guardian is available, from an adult family member involved in making treatment decisions for the child. . . .
>
> We are not dealing here with parental choice among reasonable treatment alternatives, but with a decision to subject the child to nontherapeutic treatments and procedures that may cause harmful permanent or fatal side effects. It follows therefore that a parent or guardian, . . . may not consent to have a child submit to painful and/or potentially life-threatening research procedures that hold no prospect of benefit for the child. . . . We do not limit a parent or legal guardian's right to consent to a child's participation in therapeutic research that represents a valid alternative and may be the functional equivalent of treatment.

T.D. v. New York State Office of Mental Health, 228 A.D.2d 95, 123-24, 650 N.Y.S.2d 173, 191-92 (1996). We concur with that assessment.

Additionally, there are conflicting views in respect to nontherapeutic research, as to whether consent, even of a person capable of consenting, can justify a research protocol that is otherwise unjustifiable.

> This 'justifying' side of consent raises some timeless and thorny questions. What if people consent to activities and results which are repugnant, or even evil? Even John Stuart Mill worried about consensual slavery. . . . Today, we wonder whether a woman's consent to appear in graphic, demeaning, or even violent pornography justifies or immunizes the pornographer. If she appears to consent to a relationship in which she is repeatedly brutalized, does her consent stymie our efforts to stop the brutality or punish the brute?
>
> These problems make us squirm a little, just as they did Mill. We have three ways out: We can say, first, 'Yes, consent justifies whatever is consented to—you consented, so case closed;' second, 'This particular consent is deficient—you did not really consent and so the result or action is not justified;' or third, 'You consented, but your consent cannot justify this action or result.' . . .
>
> Note the subtle yet crucial difference between these three options: In the first, consent is king, while the third option assumes a moral universe shaped and governed by extra-consensual considerations. The second option, however, reflects the tension between the other two. We might block the consented-to action, but we pay lip service to consent's justifying role by assuring ourselves that had the consent been untainted, had it been 'informed,' it would have had moral force. In fact, we pay lip service precisely because we often silently suspect that consent cannot and does not always justify. . . . Rather than admit that the consent does not and could not justify the act, we denigrate the consent and, necessarily, the consenter as well.

---

23. Minimal risk has been defined as "meaning 'that the probability and magnitude of harm or discomfort anticipated in the research are not greater in and of themselves than those ordinarily encountered in daily life or during the routine physical or psychological examinations or tests.' "

This is cheating; it is a subterfuge designed to hide our unease and to allow us to profess simultaneous commitment to values that often conflict.

Garnett, Why Informed Consent? Human Experimentation and the Ethics of Autonomy, 36 Catholic Lawyer 455, 458-60 (1996) (footnotes omitted). The article continues:

We should worry about the behavior of the experimenter, about our own culpability, and not about the subject's choosing capacities.

Such restrictions on consent, which aim at objective behaviors and results rather than at subjective decision-making processes, are common in the criminal law. For example, guilty pleas must usually be supported by a factual basis, and be knowing and voluntary. We recognize that defendants might quite rationally plead guilty to crimes they did not commit and that prosecutors might be willing to accept such pleas. However, because such pleas embroil the legal system in a monstrous falsehood, we refuse to accept them while admitting that they might indeed be in the defendant's correctly perceived best interests. . . .

Similarly, in contract and consumer law, we often balance our general preference for unfettered respect for consensual arrangements against other concerns . . . . One purpose of these rules is undeniably to substitute the supposedly better judgment of the legislature and the judiciary about what is really in a person's best interest. . . .

. . . The Nuremberg Code explicitly recognized the need to place non-paternalistic limits on the scope of experiments. The Code asks more of an experiment, a researcher, or society than mere consent.

Id. at 494-97. Based on the record before us, no degree of parental consent, and no degree of furnished information to the parents could make the experiment at issue here, ethically or legally permissible. It was wrong in the first instance. . . .

. . . Accordingly, we vacate the rulings of the Circuit Court for Baltimore City and remand these cases to that court for further proceedings consistent with this opinion.

NOTES AND QUESTIONS

1. Is the holding of *Grimes* consistent with principles that govern other parental choices regarding exposure of children to risks? For example, can a parent ethically transport an infant in a car seat over icy roads, exposing the child to the risks of an automobile accident, while the parent picks up an older child at school? Can a parent consent to one child donating an organ to a sibling? Why might these situations be treated differently?

2. Does *Grimes* forbid all research with children as subjects? Under *Grimes*, may a parent allow a child to be weighed and measured periodically for a medical study of growth, even though the study promises no benefit to the child? What if the research involved pricking the child's finger to take a blood sample? Administering drugs that have significant side effects? Why might these kinds of research be treated differently?

3. As the court in *Grimes* notes, lawsuits involving the ethics of human research are rare. As a practical matter, Institutional Review Boards have the

responsibility and authority to monitor research proposals to insure compliance with ethical rules. In an omitted part of the *Grimes* opinion, the court criticized the IRB's work in this case. The opinion reports that the IRB was concerned that the research offered no benefit to the children in the control groups. Therefore, it recommended that the informed consent forms be amended to say "that the 'control group' is being studied to determine what exposure outside the home may play in a total lead exposure; thereby, indicating that these control individuals are gaining some benefit, namely learning whether safe housing alone is sufficient to keep the blood-lead levels in acceptable bounds." *Grimes*, 782 A.2d at 814. The court then commented:

> While the suggestion of the IRB would not make this experiment any less nontherapeutic or, thus, less regulated, this statement shows two things: (1) that the IRB had a partial misperception of the difference between therapeutic and nontherapeutic research and the IRB's role in the process and (2) that the IRB was willing to aid researchers in getting around federal regulations designed to protect children used as subjects in nontherapeutic research. An IRB's primary role is to assure the safety of human research subjects—not help researchers avoid safety or health-related requirements. The IRB, in this case, misconceived, at least partially, its own role. *Id.*

Nationwide, much of the research involving children is conducted with federal funds or in federally funded institutions. All this research must comply with the ethical guidelines of the federal Department of Health and Human Services, which are codified at 45 C.F.R. 46. The guidelines impose requirements concerning review of proposed research and obtaining informed consent from research subjects that apply to all research. In addition, the guidelines impose additional protections for research involving children, which are excerpted here.

PART 46—PROTECTION OF HUMAN SUBJECTS, SUBPART D—ADDITIONAL PROTECTIONS FOR CHILDREN INVOLVED AS SUBJECTS IN RESEARCH

45 C.F.R. §§ 46.402 et seq.

§ 46.402 Definitions. The definitions in § 46.102 of Subpart A shall be applicable to this subpart as well. In addition, as used in this subpart:

a. Children are persons, who have not attained the legal age for consent to treatments or procedures involved in the research, under the applicable law of the jurisdiction in which the research will be conducted.

b. Assent means a child's affirmative agreement to participate in research. Mere failure to object should not, absent affirmative agreement, be construed as assent.

c. Permission means the agreement of parent(s) or guardian to the participation of their child or ward in research.

d. Parent means a child's biological or adoptive parent.

e. Guardian means an individual, who is authorized under applicable State or local law, to consent on behalf of a child to general medical care.

§ 46.404 Research not involving greater than minimal risk. HHS will conduct or fund research, in which the IRB finds that no greater than minimal risk to children is presented, only if the IRB finds that adequate provisions are made for soliciting the assent of the children and the permission of their parents or guardians, as set forth in § 46.408.

§ 46.405 Research involving greater than minimal risk, but presenting the prospect of direct benefit to the individual subjects. HHS will conduct or fund research, in which the IRB finds that more than minimal risk to children is presented by an intervention or procedure that holds out the prospect of direct benefit for the individual subject, or by a monitoring procedure that is likely to contribute to the subject's well-being, only if the IRB finds that:

 a. The risk is justified by the anticipated benefit to the subjects;

 b. The relation of the anticipated benefit to the risk is at least as favorable to the subjects as that presented by available alternative approaches; and

 c. Adequate provisions are made for soliciting the assent of the children and permission of their parents or guardians, as set forth in § 46.408.

§ 46.406 Research involving greater than minimal risk and no prospect of direct benefit to individual subjects, but likely to yield generalizable knowledge about the subject's disorder or condition. HHS will conduct or fund research, in which the IRB finds that more than minimal risk to children is presented by an intervention or procedure that does not hold out the prospect of direct benefit for the individual subject, or by a monitoring procedure which is not likely to contribute to the well-being of the subject, only if the IRB finds that:

 a. The risk represents a minor increase over minimal risk;

 b. The intervention or procedure presents experiences to subjects that are reasonably commensurate with those inherent in their actual or expected medical, dental, psychological, social, or educational situations;

 c. The intervention or procedure is likely to yield generalizable knowledge about the subjects' disorder or condition, which is of vital importance for the understanding or amelioration of the subjects' disorder or condition; and

 d. Adequate provisions are made for soliciting assent of the children and permission of their parents or guardians, as set forth in § 46.408.

§ 46.407 Research not otherwise approvable, which presents an opportunity to understand, prevent, or alleviate a serious problem affecting the health or welfare of children. HHS will conduct or fund research that the IRB does not believe meets the requirements of § 46.404, § 46.405, or § 46.406, only if:

 a. The IRB finds that the research presents a reasonable opportunity to further the understanding, prevention, or alleviation of a serious problem affecting the health or welfare of children, and

 b. The Secretary, after consultation with a panel of experts in pertinent disciplines (for example: science, medicine, education, ethics, law), and following opportunity for public review and comment, has determined either:

  1. That the research in fact satisfies the conditions of § 46.404, § 46.405, or § 46.406, as applicable, or

2. The following: (i) the research presents a reasonable opportunity to further the understanding, prevention, or alleviation of a serious problem affecting the health or welfare of children; (ii) the research will be conducted in accordance with sound ethical principles; (iii) adequate provisions are made for soliciting the assent of children and the permission of their parents or guardians, as set forth in § 46.408.

§ 46.408 Requirements for permission by parents or guardians and for assent by children.

a. In addition to the determinations required under other applicable sections of this subpart, the IRB shall determine that adequate provisions are made for soliciting the assent of the children, when in the judgment of the IRB the children are capable of providing assent. In determining whether children are capable of assenting, the IRB shall take into account the ages, maturity, and psychological state of the children involved. This judgment may be made for all children to be involved in research under a particular protocol, or for each child, as the IRB deems appropriate. If the IRB determines that the capability of some or all of the children is so limited that they cannot reasonably be consulted or that the intervention or procedure involved in the research holds out a prospect of direct benefit that is important to the health or well-being of the children and is available only in the context of the research, the assent of the children is not a necessary condition for proceeding with the research. Even where the IRB determines that the subjects are capable of assenting, the IRB may still waive the assent requirement under circumstances in which consent may be waived in accord with § 46.116 of Subpart A.

b. In addition to the determinations required under other applicable sections of this subpart, the IRB shall determine, in accordance with and to the extent that consent is required by § 46.116 of Subpart A, that adequate provisions are made for soliciting the permission of each child's parents or guardian. Where parental permission is to be obtained, the IRB may find that the permission of one parent is sufficient for research to be conducted under § 46.404 or § 46.405. Where research is covered by § 46.406 and § 46.407, and permission is to be obtained from parents, both parents must give their permission, unless one parent is deceased, unknown, incompetent, or not reasonably available, or when only one parent has legal responsibility for the care and custody of the child.

c. In addition to the provisions for waiver contained in § 46.116 of Subpart A, if the IRB determines that a research protocol is designed for conditions or for a subject population, for which parental or guardian permission is not a reasonable requirement to protect the subjects (for example, neglected or abused children), it may waive the consent requirements in Subpart A of this part and paragraph (b) of this section, provided an appropriate mechanism for protecting the children who will participate as subjects in the research is substituted, and provided further that the waiver is not inconsistent with Federal, state, or local law. The choice of an appropriate mechanism would depend upon the nature and purpose of the activities described in the protocol, the risk and anticipated benefit to the research subjects, and their age, maturity, status, and condition.

d. Permission by parents or guardians shall be documented in accordance with and to the extent required by § 46.117 of Subpart A.

e. When the IRB determines that assent is required, it shall also determine whether and how assent must be documented.

§ 46.409 Wards.

a. Children, who are wards of the state or any other agency, institution, or entity can be included in research approved under § 46.406 or § 46.407, only if such research is:

1. Related to their status as wards; or

2. Conducted in schools, camps, hospitals, institutions, or similar settings, in which the majority of children involved as subjects are not wards.

b. If the research is approved under paragraph (a) of this section, the IRB shall require appointment of an advocate for each child who is a ward, in addition to any other individual acting on behalf of the child as guardian or in *loco parentis*. One individual may serve as advocate for more than one child. The advocate shall be an individual, who has the background and experience to act in, and agrees to act in, the best interests of the child for the duration of the child's participation in the research, and who is not associated in any way (except in the role as advocate or member of the IRB) with the research, the investigator(s), or the guardian organization.

NOTES AND QUESTIONS

1. The federal regulations distinguish between research that promises direct benefit to the child and research that does not. What is the significance of this distinction?

2. Would the research in *Grimes* properly have been approved under the federal rules?

3. Under the federal rules, may a parent allow a child to be weighed and measured periodically for a medical study of growth, even though the study promises no benefit to the child? What if the research involved pricking the child's finger to take a blood sample? Administering drugs that have significant side effects? Why might these kinds of research be treated differently? What explains the differences between the federal rules and *Grimes*?

4. What is the difference between consent and assent? How is an IRB to know whether children are capable of assenting? If a child capable of assenting objects to participating, can the child be forced to be a research subject?

5. Controversy during the early 2000s about whether commonly prescribed antidepressant and antianxiety medications increase the risk of suicide in teenagers and younger children highlights the importance of medical research with child subjects. Until 1997, the FDA did not require that drugs be tested on children, though it prohibited drug companies from marketing drugs for use with children if they had not been tested. However, given the legal limitations on research with children, many drug manufacturers simply chose not to study the effects of drugs and other medical interventions on children. As a result, little information about the effect of many drugs is available, leaving physicians who want to prescribe untested medications for their child patients to guess about proper dosages. The

Pediatric Research Equity Act requires manufacturers to conduct testing on children unless they can show that this would be impossible or highly impracticable. *Id.* at 225. The Pediatric Medical Device Safety and Improvement Act encourages research on pediatric device development. For more information *see* Allan M. Joseph, Kid Test, FDA Approved: Examining Pediatric Drug Testing, 72 Food & Drug L. J. 543 (2017); Kathleen Hilton, Off-Label Prescribing in a Vulnerable Pediatric Marketplace, 10 J. Health & Biomedical L. 403 (2015).

6. Historically, children in institutions such as mental hospitals and reform schools were subjected to research that is today considered highly unethical. For example, the first smallpox vaccinations were conducted on children living in a poorhouse; a doctor in Hawaii studied germ theory by infecting children in a leprosarium with syphilis; in the 1950s, researchers at the Willowbrook State School infected mentally disabled children with hepatitis to study the course of the disease. For details, *see* Leonard H. Glantz, Research with Children, 24 Am. J.L. & Med. 211 (1998).

Why might children in institutions be particularly attractive as research subjects? Are the risks of abuse so great that such children should never be research subjects? Do the provisions of the federal regulations adequately protect these children against abuse?

Targeting of vulnerable children as research subjects continues. For example, between 1988 and 2001, foster children in Illinois, Louisiana, Maryland, New York, North Carolina, Colorado, and Texas were enrolled in studies of drugs for HIV/AIDS. The purposes of the studies were to determine the drug toxicity and side effects of the drugs, which had not been shown to be safe for adults or children. In response to complaints, the federal Office for Human Research Protections found that using these children was inequitable and sent letters to IRBs around the country, saying that approval of the studies had violated the federal rules, but it did not impose any sanctions. Ruqaiijah Yearby, Missing the "Target": Preventing the Unjust Inclusion of Vulnerable Children for Medical Research Studies, 42 Am. J. L. & Med. 797, 818-822 (2016).

7. For more information, *see* Heather L. Mullins-Owens et al, Protecting a Vulnerable Population with Little Regulatory Framework: A Comparative Analysis of International Guidelines for Pediatric Research Ethics, 29 J. Contemp. Health L. & Pol'y 36 (2012); Paul Litton, Non-Beneficial Pediatric Research and the Best Interests Standard: A Legal and Ethical Reconciliation, 8 Yale J. Health Pol'y & Ethics 359 (2008); Doriane Lambelet Coleman, The Legal Ethics of Pediatric Research, 57 Duke L.J. 517 (2007).

JUVENILE COURTS AND DELINQUENCY

Juvenile Courts and Juvenile Offenders

4

This section of the book examines legal responses to minors who break the law. This chapter considers jurisdictional issues—when does the juvenile court have authority to act, and when and how do adult criminal courts assert jurisdiction instead? Chapter 5 concerns the law that governs investigatory encounters and pretrial procedures, and Chapter 6 covers modern juvenile court practice and disposition.

A. DEVELOPMENT OF THE MODERN JUVENILE COURT

We have already observed the tension, and sometimes the conflict, between two notions of children's rights—as welfare claims and as autonomy claims. That conflict is acute in the debates over juvenile court jurisdiction over misconduct by minors, which was the original emphasis of the juvenile court and continued to be its dominant focus until the later part of the twentieth century. The emphasis placed on one or the other aspect of children's rights has shifted dramatically from time to time. At no point, however, has one aspect wholly supplanted the other, nor has a final adjustment in the tension between them been achieved. The development of the American juvenile court can be divided into four periods, beginning with the establishment of the Chicago Juvenile Court in 1899.

The Traditional Juvenile Court: 1899-1950. Before juvenile courts were established, minors accused of crime were treated much the same as adults. The procedural framework for determining the guilt of a child was the same as for an adult, and, if found capable of criminal intent, a minor defendant was subject in principle to the same range of penalties as an adult offender. The simplest way to see the juvenile court movement is as a reaction against the criminal court treatment of youthful offenders. Proponents of the juvenile court movement sharply criticized the treatment of young people as if they were "hardened" adult criminals, especially the incarceration of youthful with seasoned offenders.

However, the juvenile court, as it was conceived and implemented, was far more than a simple reform. The court arose during the Progressive period of

American history and reflects both the anxiety and the optimism of that remarkable era. Americans during the late nineteenth and early twentieth centuries found much to be anxious about. As early as the 1820s, the causes of crime were traced back to weaknesses in parental supervision, and by the middle of that century, perceptions of family weakness grew. An industry of books on child rearing emerged, which repeatedly described the average home with "words like 'disorder,' 'disobedience,' 'licentiousness,' and above all 'indulgence' (i.e., of the children)." John Demos & Virginia Demos, Adolescence in Historical Perspective, 31 J. Marriage & Fam. 632, 633 (1969).

Concern with the adequacy of home life and parental guidance was seemingly confirmed by a set of experiences that might independently have suggested weakness in the family as an institution. The waves of European immigration during the nineteenth century were seen as increasing the pauper and criminal populations. Not only were immigrants poor, but also, it was said, they came with values and goals that made it difficult for them to rear children in a "free" society without falling into licentiousness.

Nineteenth-century changes in the means of economic production also contributed to declining confidence in the family. Although women and children performed working roles during the seventeenth and early eighteenth centuries, those were typically carried out within the home. Early American factories were largely filled with women and children, changing their roles and capacities. As Arthur Calhoun observed:

> Long hours of factory labor abolished family life. Insufficient wages forced parents to set children prematurely to work. . . . [W]ith the passing of home industry woman had to go out into public work or remain a dangerous parasite. The man might go to work without upsetting the home center . . . but when woman ceased to be "housekeeper" the reality of the home came into question.

2 Arthur Calhoun, A Social History of the American Family from Colonial Times to the Present 197 (1917). The urbanization associated with the Industrial Revolution added to the perception of social decline, as families migrated from smaller communities in which churches and neighbors provided agencies for social control to crowded, anonymous, and corrupt cities in which mothers as well as fathers worked, leaving their children in unhealthy and dangerous circumstances.

The optimistic side of Progressivism, however, saw solutions for the problems created by these environmental conditions. Those solutions were founded on confidence in professional knowledge and skills. The compulsory school movement, together with progressive educational theory, substituted professional educators for parents who could or would not discharge that responsibility adequately. Social work, a profession that arose at the beginning of the twentieth century, offered expert assistance to families in distress. And the juvenile court provided a judicial vehicle for intervention in the lives of children who had gone, or had begun to go, "wrong." The link between the besetting problem identified by Progressives, family failure, and the juvenile court's role was explicit. As Judge Cabot of the Boston Juvenile Court observed, "Remember the fathers and mothers have failed, or the child has no business [in the court], and it is when they failed that the state opened this way to receive them, into the court, and said, 'This is the way in which we want you to grow up.'" Frederick P. Cabot, The Detention of Children as Part of Treatment, in The Child, the Clinic and the Court (Jane Addams, ed., 1925).

The ambition of the juvenile court movement, accordingly, went far beyond avoiding incarceration of youthful with adult offenders. Substitution of state for parental supervision of children carried significant implications for the scope of juvenile court jurisdiction and for its procedure as well as for the kind of treatment it would order. As we will see, the jurisdiction of the court was not limited, as criminal courts were, to specific acts creating harm but encompassed all conduct or circumstances indicating a need for official action. The court's process was conceived as informal, resembling the method by which parents deal with children in the home, rather than in terms of counsel, confrontation, and other characteristics of a criminal trial. And the treatment to be given was always understood in terms of therapeutic interventions rather than according to the criminal court's retributive or deterrent goals.

The scope, procedure, and sanctions of the juvenile court differed greatly from those of the criminal court, and, to mark these differences, even the vocabulary changed. Those subject to the juvenile court process were called "respondents" rather than "defendants." A respondent found to have committed misconduct was "adjudicated" rather than "found guilty," and labeled a "delinquent" rather than a "criminal" or "felon." Upon adjudication, the child was subject to "disposition" rather than "sentence."

It's important to remember, though, that these changes in the treatment of youthful offenders did not extend to African-American children, who were not fully included in the system for almost a century. Geoff K. Ward, The Black Child-Savers: Racial Democracy and Juvenile Justice (2012).

The Due Process Revolution: 1960-1985. For the first 50 years of the juvenile court's existence, this experiment was widely acclaimed. Although criticism did appear from time to time, it was too infrequent to upset the marriage of legal power and social work goals. Beginning in the 1950s, however, doubts about the operation and the goals of the juvenile court came to be expressed more frequently. These doubts took a number of forms.

At the most general level, the 1960s and 1970s saw increasing distrust of governmental power and sharply diminished confidence in the claims of professionals and agencies engaged in the enterprise of social control. A line of Supreme Court decisions impeached the methods by which police secured confessions and seized evidence from adults prosecuted for crime. *E.g.*, Mapp v. Ohio, 367 U.S. 643 (1961) (exclusion of illegally seized evidence); Miranda v. Arizona, 384 U.S. 436 (1966) (warnings prior to interrogation). At the level of principle, a critique of the therapeutic model itself emerged. This critique was given powerful voice by Professor Francis Allen in addressing the use of rehabilitative strategies for children (as well as mentally disturbed offenders):

> [T]he rise of the rehabilitative idea has often been accompanied by attitudes and measures that conflict, sometimes seriously, with the values of individual liberty and volition. . . . We are concerned here with the perennial issue of political authority: Under what circumstances is the state justified in bringing its force to bear on the individual human being? . . .

>The mere deprivation of liberty, however benign the administration of the place of confinement, is undeniably punishment. . . . Measures which subject individuals to the substantial and involuntary deprivation of their liberty are essentially punitive in character, and this reality is not altered by the fact that the motivations that prompt incarceration are to provide therapy or otherwise contribute to the person's well-being or reform. As such, these measures must be closely scrutinized to insure that power is being applied consistently with those values of the community that justify interference with liberty for only the most clear and compelling reasons.

Francis Allen, Criminal Justice, Legal Values, and the Rehabilitative Ideal, 50 J. Crim. L. Criminology & Police Sci. 226, 230 (1959).

This argument had special significance for juvenile courts. Doubts about the legitimacy of therapeutic intervention were supported by doubts about the extent to which those courts had realized in practice their claims to rehabilitative and nonpunitive intervention. Under these influences, the United States Supreme Court undertook an examination of the constitutional status of juvenile court procedure and, in a number of cases, held that juveniles charged with delinquency were entitled to procedural safeguards previously established for defendants in criminal prosecutions. State legislatures responded to the claim that delinquents were in fact subject to punishment and stigma by limiting the scope of delinquency jurisdiction to criminal misconduct and creating a new category and new dispositional options for "status offenders"—minors whose misbehavior would not be criminal if committed by an adult.

Although these developments dramatically affected the operation of the juvenile court, they were not conceived as rejections of the theory of the juvenile court or of its aspirations to nonpunitive responses to juvenile misconduct. A recurring note of regret in the juvenile court's inability to achieve its goals, and of hope that it can do better than the criminal justice system, is evident even as courts constitutionalized juvenile delinquency procedure.

Get Tough on Crime: 1985-2005. The mid-1980s and 1990s through the middle of the first decade of the twenty-first century saw a new approach to juvenile deviance, driven more by legislatures than by courts. Reformers of the 1960s and 1970s sought primarily to infuse procedural regularity into the juvenile court, without abandoning its pre- and post-trial differences from the criminal court. Accuracy of fact-finding and fairness in process were the principal goals of this initial reform. While delinquency matters were regarded as "comparable in seriousness to felony prosecutions," it did not follow that delinquents were comparable in dangerousness to felons.

Some of the juvenile court critics of the 1980s and 1990s instead challenged the principle that youthful offenders *should be* viewed differently from adults. They argued that since juveniles were entitled to many of the same rights as adults in delinquency proceedings, they should also be treated as adults for purposes of culpability and punishment. This position reflected concerns about increases in gang violence and juvenile homicide, finding expression in a literature that described a massive increase in juvenile violence led by juvenile offenders characterized as "super predators." Within juvenile court statutes, statements of purpose that once spoke only in terms of rehabilitating young people and strengthening families adopted deterrence, retribution, or both as justifying goals. Dispositional provisions were amended to employ determinate orders of confinement explicitly tied to the child's conduct rather than the individualized, indeterminate dispositions of the traditional juvenile court. More than half the states categorically excluded certain offenders from juvenile court jurisdiction, usually by a combination of minimum age and offense criteria. Explaining the rise of the get tough approach, Professor Feld wrote,"[T]he racial and structural transformation of American cities that accompanied the Great Migration of Blacks from the rural South to the urban North fueled the politics of race and crime and encouraged conservative politicians to use coded appeals to Whites' racial animus to crack down on youth crime." Barry C. Feld, My Life in Crime: An Intellectual History of the Juvenile Court, 17 Nev. L. J. 299, 319 (2017), citing Barry C. Feld, Bad Kids (1999).

The impetus to respond formally and severely to juvenile misconduct could be seen in connection with noncriminal conduct as well, especially conduct that suggested some kind of gang affiliation or activity. The number of status offense proceedings, which had declined from 1960 to 1980, increased, and virtually all of the increase was related to proceedings brought by police to enforce the juvenile curfew or gang affiliation statutes that had been adopted by hundreds of jurisdictions.

Recognition that Kids Are Different: 2005-Today. Supreme Court decisions ending the juvenile death penalty and juvenile life without parole sentences for non-homicides and holding that a child's age properly informs the *Miranda* custody analysis powered another shift in the approach of the legal system toward minors in conflict with the law. Between 2005 and 2017, 36 states and the District of Columbia passed 70 laws reducing the number of teens prosecuted, tried, and incarcerated in the adult criminal system, relying on social science research as well as a "common sense" understanding of the differences between adolescents and adults. Campaign for Youth Justice, Raising the Bar: State Trends in Keeping Youth Out of Adult Courts (2015-2017) (2017), http://cfyj.org/images/StateTrends_Repot_FINAL.pdf. A number of courts have reconfirmed the position that, even with changes in purposes and dispositional schemes, juvenile courts must continue to pursue rehabilitative and nonpunitive functions that distinguish them substantially from the criminal system. However, the tension observed throughout this book remains evident in judicial opinions as well as legislative action.

1.   The Origins and Method of the Traditional Juvenile Court

JULIAN W. MACK, THE JUVENILE COURT

23 Harv. L. Rev. 104, 106-107, 119-121 (1909)

Our common criminal law did not differentiate between the adult and the minor who had reached the age of criminal responsibility, seven at common law and in some of our states, ten in others. . . . The majesty and dignity of the state demanded vindication for infractions from both alike. The fundamental thought in our criminal jurisprudence was not, and in most jurisdictions is not, reformation of the criminal, but punishment; punishment as expiation for the wrong, punishment as a warning to other possible wrongdoers. The child was arrested, put into prison, indicted by the grand jury, tried by a petit jury, under all the forms and technicalities of our criminal law, with the aim of ascertaining whether it had done the specific act—nothing else—and if it had, then of visiting the punishment of the state upon it. . . .

Today, however, the thinking public is putting another sort of question. Why is it not just and proper to treat these juvenile offenders, as we deal with the neglected children, as a wise and merciful father handles his own child whose errors are not discovered by the authorities? Why is it not the duty of the state, instead of asking merely whether a boy or girl has committed a specific offense, to find out what he is, physically, mentally, morally, and then if it learns that he is treading the path that leads to criminality, to take him in charge, not so much to punish as to reform, not to degrade but to uplift, not to crush but to develop, not to make him a criminal but a worthy citizen.

And it is this thought—the thought that the child who has begun to go wrong, who is incorrigible, who has broken a law or an ordinance, is to be taken in hand by the state, not as an enemy but as a protector, as the ultimate guardian, because either the unwillingness or inability of the natural parents to guide it toward good citizenship has compelled the intervention of the public authorities; it is this principle, which . . . was first fully and clearly declared, in the Act under which the Juvenile Court of Cook County, Illinois, was opened in Chicago, on July 1, 1899. . . .

The problem for determination by the judge is not, Has this boy or girl committed a specific wrong, but what is he, how has he become what he is, and what had best be done in his interest and in the interest of the state to save him from a downward career. It is apparent at once that the ordinary legal evidence in a criminal court is not the sort of evidence to be heard in such a proceeding. A thorough investigation, usually made by the probation officer, will give the court much information bearing on the heredity and environment of the child. This, of course, will be supplemented in every possible way; but this alone is not enough. The physical and mental condition of the child must be known. . . . It is, therefore, of the utmost importance that there be attached to the court . . . a child study department, where every child, before hearing, shall be subjected to a thorough psycho-physical examination. In hundreds of cases the discovery and remedy of defective eyesight or hearing or some slight surgical operation will effectuate a complete change in the character of the lad.

The child who must be brought into court should, of course, be made to know that he is face to face with the power of the state, but he should at the same time, and more emphatically, be made to feel that he is the object of its care and solicitude. The ordinary trappings of the courtroom are out of place in such hearings. The judge on a bench, looking down upon the boy standing at the bar, can never evoke a proper sympathetic spirit. Seated at a desk, with the child at his side, where he can on occasion put his arm around his shoulder and draw the lad to him, the judge . . . will gain immensely in the effectiveness of his work.

DAVID S. TANENHAUS, *THE EVOLUTION OF JUVENILE COURTS IN THE EARLY TWENTIETH CENTURY: BEYOND THE MYTH OF IMMACULATE CONCEPTION*

A Century of Juvenile Justice 42, 42-45
(Margaret K. Rosenheim et al. eds., 2002)

The world's first juvenile court law was enacted during a tense centennial moment. The Illinois General Assembly had waited until April 14, 1899, the last day of the last legislative session of the nineteenth century, to approve "An Act for the Treatment and Control of Dependent, Neglected and Delinquent Children." The law, when it went into effect on July 1, 1899, established the Cook County Juvenile Court (more generally known as the Chicago Juvenile Court). Led by the visionary philanthropist Lucy Flower and her friend Julia Lathrop, a child-welfare expert who later became the first Chief of the United States Children's Bureau in 1912, the moral crusaders for juvenile justice could now breathe a temporary sigh of relief. After a decade of concerted work, they had finally succeeded in writing their ideals about childhood innocence and public responsibility into law. In Chicago, the nation's second largest and fastest growing city, the cases of dependent and neglected children as well as ones accused of committing crimes could now be heard in a separate children's court. A sympathetic judge could now use his discretion to apply individualized treatments to rehabilitate children, instead of punishing them. Yet, as Flower and Lathrop understood perfectly well, especially after the long struggle to pass the legislation, their efforts to secure justice for the child had only begun.

Illinois' pioneering juvenile court act read like a rough blueprint. Most of the features that later became the hallmarks of progressive juvenile justice—private hearings, confidential records, the complaint system, detention homes, and probation officers—were either omitted entirely from the initial law or were included without any provisions for public funding. As a result, the world's first juvenile court opened on July 3, 1899, with an open hearing, a public record, no means to control its calendar (i.e., no complaint system), and without public funds to pay either the salaries of probation officers or to maintain a detention home for children. It would, in fact, take more than eight years before the completion of the city's first juvenile court building, which would be located across from the famous social settlement, Hull House, on the city's Near West Side. Thus, the Chicago Juvenile Court had a rather inchoate beginning.

The juvenile court had such a tentative start partly because its invention raised fundamental questions about the role of legal institutions in the increasingly interdependent modern world of the early twentieth century. In Europe and America, progressive reformers had begun to question classical legal conceptions about the rule of law, free will, and the benefits of limited state intervention into social relations. The progressive efforts to extend the reach of the state into the everyday lives of predominantly working-class urban dwellers raised troubling questions about what the proper relationship of new institutions, such as the juvenile court, to "the public" should be. The inventors of the juvenile court designed this "new piece of social machinery" not only to remove children from the harsh criminal justice system, but also to shield them from stigmatizing publicity. In the juvenile court, its inventors envisioned, hearings would be closed to spectators and the press, a juvenile's record would remain confidential, and no private lawyers or juries would be part of the legal process. This vision of the juvenile court as a sheltered place to protect a child, especially during the storms of adolescence, would eventually become law in most states.

The process of making the juvenile court into a sheltered place, however, took many years (in some states, decades) to complete. The length of this construction process, which due to American federalism varied from state to state, is significant for two reasons. First, it challenges the common assumption that the history of juvenile justice has been a relatively simple story of decline, beginning with the juvenile court as a social welfare institution at the turn of the twentieth century and ending up as a quasi-criminal court by century's end. Instead . . . the juvenile court has been a work in progress and . . . many of the "defining features" of progressive juvenile justice—private hearings, confidential records, the complaint system, detention homes, probation officers—were additions. . . . Juvenile courts, including Chicago's model court, were not immaculate constructions; they were built over time.

Second, the initial failure in Illinois to close juvenile hearings to spectators and members of the press allowed for the first juvenile courts to become much more public spaces than their progressive inventors would have liked. The inaugural generation of juvenile court administrators struggled with the problem of how to shield the children in court from publicity while also desiring to publicize their plight in order to raise public consciousness and further the progressive crusade for social justice. Supporters of the court, including the presiding judges, adapted to the public nature of the early cases by using the free publicity to explain the rehabilitative mission of the court and helping to make the case for its benefits to the public. These efforts to educate the public about the court were critical to legitimizing the new institution. To help secure and sustain the legitimacy of the juvenile court, the early judges and staff delivered many public lectures, participated in child welfare exhibitions and, in the process, helped to spread the word about the benefits of the so-called new piece of social machinery.

. . . [T]he "idea" of a juvenile court was a historical phenomenon that crystallized a number of nineteenth-century trends in child welfare and corrections, but . . . twentieth-century juvenile courts had diverse and dynamic histories worth knowing. The fact that juvenile courts have always been statutory creations, which state legislatures can alter at will, has contributed to many differences among these courts. The most fundamental difference has been whether courts used chancery proceedings, the Chicago model of informal hearings, or continued to remain part of the criminal justice system, retaining most of the features of criminal procedure, as New York courts did until the 1930s. In addition, the emphasis on informal procedures in courts using chancery proceedings also accounted for the adoption of very different procedures by individual courts. By 1925, however, every state except for Maine and Wyoming at least had a juvenile court law, and juvenile courts were operating in all American cities with more than one hundred thousand people. Efforts to extend juvenile justice into the countryside began in the early twentieth century, but remained a troubling problem for most of the century. Since urban juvenile courts were built and then retrofitted over the course of the early twentieth century, these years offer especially promising sites for investigations into how earlier generations adjusted juvenile justice to meet pressing new conditions and concerns about the place of children and youth in American society.

2. *Traditional Juvenile Court Substance and Procedure*

The first Illinois juvenile code included the following definition of children over whom the court had jurisdiction:

> The words "delinquent child" shall mean any male child who while under the age of seventeen years or any female child who while under the age of eighteen years, violates any law of this State; or is incorrigible, or knowingly associates with thieves, vicious or immoral persons; or who without just cause and without . . . [the] consent of its parents, guardian or custodian absents itself from its home or place of abode, or is growing up in idleness or crime; or knowingly frequents a house of ill-repute; or knowingly frequents any policy shop or place where any gaming device is operated; or frequents any saloon or dram shop where intoxicating liquors are sold; or patronizes or visits any public pool room or bucket shop; or wanders about the streets in the night time without being on any lawful business or lawful occupation; or habitually wanders about any railroad yards or tracks or jumps or attempts to jump onto [any] moving train; or enters any car or engine without lawful authority; or uses vile, obscene, vulgar, profane or indecent language in [any] public place or about any school house; or is guilty of indecent or lascivious conduct.

Illinois Revised Statutes, ch. 23, § 169 (1907).

This provision employs a variety of strategies for extending juvenile court jurisdiction over both neglected and delinquent children. It defines a number of acts with considerable specificity (such as begging and patronizing pool halls or bucket shops). Other grounds for intervention, such as lacking "proper parental care or guardianship" or "growing up in idleness or crime" found in the definition of "dependent" and "neglected" child, are far more general. Moreover, the statute is addressed to a wide range of potential complainants who might categorize conduct variously. Parents whose children had run away could invoke court jurisdiction on the ground of incorrigibility. Neighbors who observed a child's presence on the street and thought that he was receiving inadequate care or engaging in dangerous activities might complain on various neglect or delinquency grounds. Police officers or social workers who saw a child in company with criminals or notorious persons might conclude that the child was dependent or neglected, or that he or she was delinquent as one who "knowingly associates with thieves, vicious or immoral persons" or was "growing up in idleness or crime."

The overlap among seemingly independent juvenile court jurisdictional categories such as neglect and delinquency is consistent with the social work emphasis of the juvenile court. It was important to reach all children in need of assistance, and the formal basis for doing so was not important. Moreover, the prevailing theory of delinquency emphasized at least a soft determinism, according to which dependency, neglect, delinquency, and crime were all considered stages of a developmental phenomenon. Because the juvenile court's concern was to arrest this phenomenon rather than to punish a child or parent, sharp distinctions among the stages did not seem important.

The traditional statutory scheme also permits broad charges to operate as residual categories when narrower allegations cannot be proved. If, for example, a child alleged to have been a party to burglary could not be shown to have participated knowingly in the theft, the petition might conveniently be amended to charge her with associating with criminals.

From the perspective of Progressive ideology, the scope of juvenile court jurisdiction was sensible. From the perspective of nineteenth- and twentieth-century American legal institutions, however, that scope seems nothing short of radical. While most American law purports to regulate by relatively clear rules established in advance of their application, the juvenile court deemphasized specific conduct in favor of attention to the "whole child," thereby approximating the kind of approach that Roberto Unger calls "substantive justice." Roberto M. Unger, Knowledge and Politics 88-92 (1975).

The theory of criminal law punishment rests heavily on principles of deterrence and retribution. Juvenile court intervention, by contrast, did not rely on either of these general justifying purposes. Rather, it sought to reform young people with a view toward their development as "upright citizens."

Theories of punishment have much to do with the ways in which sanctions are designed. General deterrence assumes that the appropriate measure of punishment is just that amount necessary to lead community members to avoid offending. Accordingly, the extent of punishment is directly related to the particular wrongdoing involved. In principle, the characteristics of the offender have nothing to do with general deterrence, which is intended to address the behavior of the community at large.

Penalties justified by retribution or "just deserts" are likewise specifically related to the offense committed. Punishment is justified by the social obligation to behave so as not to interfere with the freedom of others or to gain an unfair advantage over others who behave correctly. Sanctions restore equilibrium by removing the advantage otherwise associated with wrongful conduct and must, accordingly, be related to the wrong committed.

The link between principles of deterrence or retribution and the offense committed is reflected in criminal sentencing by the direct relation between the kind of offense committed and the kind and extent of punishment.

When intervention is justified by rehabilitation, however, the focus of concern is on the offender rather than on his or her offense. A correlative of this focus on the offender has been the individualization of judgments of culpability and imposition of sanctions.

Juvenile court statutes, therefore, expressly disassociated dispositions (as juvenile court sanctions are called) from the behavior bringing the child to court. Once an adjudication of delinquency was entered, the court could enter any statutorily authorized order that the circumstances seemed to make appropriate. Moreover, the length and character of the dispositional order were variable according to the child's circumstances and needs. Orders of probation and incarceration were typically indeterminate in length.

If the substantive scope of juvenile court jurisdiction reflects the social and political theory of the Progressive era, it would be sensible to expect that the procedure of the juvenile court would reflect the goals embodied in the substantive law of neglect, dependency, and delinquency. Most juvenile courts were established during the first two decades of the twentieth century, and their procedures differed markedly from both the criminal and the civil justice systems.

At that time the criminal trial in most states included many of the procedures we now expect. A charging paper was employed—an information or, in cases of felony, an indictment. Rules of evidence generally prohibited introduction of hearsay or evidence of prior offenses by the accused except for impeachment purposes. The privilege against self-incrimination was generally recognized in criminal matters, although with a somewhat more limited meaning than is now the case. Although indigents had no constitutional right to the assistance of counsel as of right, the criminal bar was well established and active on behalf of clients who could pay for their services and, to some extent, clients who could not. State constitutional provisions assured the right to jury trial for at least serious felonies and the right to public trial generally. The burden of proof was then, as it is now, proof beyond a reasonable doubt.

Some of these procedures also applied in ordinary civil litigation as well. The defendant was entitled to a complaint that was characterized by rather more specificity than is now generally required. The rules of evidence for civil cases were (and are) much the same as for criminal matters. Although civil defendants could be called to testify, many states created a practical disincentive to doing so through rules that required a party calling a witness (even the opposing party) to "vouch for" (that is, not impeach the testimony of) that witness. Civil litigants often had the services of counsel and, at least in substantial cases, access to trial by jury.

In the following case, the Supreme Court for the first time resolved constitutional challenges to juvenile court procedure. Consider the extent to which juvenile court proceedings had abandoned the procedural format of both criminal and civil trials by the time this case reached the court. Also consider the relationship between the substantive goals of the juvenile court and the procedures it used.

3. *Constitutional Domestication of the Juvenile Court*

In re Gault

387 U.S. 1 (1967)

Fortas, J. . . . On Monday, June 8, 1964, at about 10 a.m., Gerald Francis Gault and a friend, Ronald Lewis, were taken into custody by the Sheriff of Gila County. Gerald was then still subject to a six months' probation order which had been entered on February 25, 1964, as a result of his having been in the company of another boy who had stolen a wallet from a lady's purse. The police action on June 8 was taken as the result of a verbal complaint by a neighbor of the boys, Mrs. Cook, about a telephone call made to her in which the caller or callers made lewd or indecent remarks. It will suffice for purposes of this opinion to say that the remarks or questions put to her were of the irritatingly offensive, adolescent, sex variety.

At the time Gerald was picked up, his mother and father were both at work. No notice that Gerald was being taken into custody was left at the home. No other steps were taken to advise them that their son had, in effect, been arrested. Gerald was taken to the Children's Detention Home. When his mother arrived home at about 6 o'clock, Gerald was not there. Gerald's older brother was sent to look for him at the trailer home of the Lewis family. He apparently learned then that Gerald was in custody. He so informed his mother. The two of them went to the Detention Home. The deputy probation officer, Flagg, who was also superintendent of the Detention Home, told Mrs. Gault "why Jerry was there" and said that a hearing would be held in Juvenile Court at 3 o'clock the following day, June 9.

Officer Flagg filed a petition with the court on the hearing day, June 9, 1964. It was not served on the Gaults. Indeed, none of them saw this petition until the habeas corpus hearing on August 17, 1964. The petition was entirely formal. It made no reference to any factual basis for the judicial action which it initiated. It recited only that "said minor is under the age of eighteen years, and is in need of the protection of this Honorable Court; [and that] said minor is a delinquent minor." It prayed for a hearing and an order regarding "the care and custody of said minor." Officer Flagg executed a formal affidavit in support of the petition.

On June 9, Gerald, his mother, his older brother, and Probation Officers Flagg and Henderson appeared before the Juvenile Judge in chambers. Gerald's father was not there. He was at work out of the city. Mrs. Cook, the complainant, was not there. No one was sworn at this hearing. No transcript or recording was made. No memorandum or record of the substance of the proceedings was prepared. Our information about the proceedings and the subsequent hearing on June 15, derives entirely from the testimony of the Juvenile Court Judge, Mr. and Mrs. Gault and Officer Flagg at the habeas corpus proceeding conducted two months later. From this, it appears that at the June 9 hearing Gerald was questioned by the judge about the telephone call. There was conflict as to what he said. His mother recalled that Gerald said he only dialed Mrs. Cook's number and handed the telephone to his friend, Ronald. Officer Flagg recalled that Gerald had admitted making the lewd remarks. Judge McGhee testified that Gerald "admitted making one of these [lewd] statements." At the conclusion of the hearing, the judge said he would "think about it." Gerald was taken back to the Detention Home. He was not sent to his own home with his parents. On June 11 or 12, after having been detained since June 8, Gerald was released and driven home. There is no explanation in the record as to why he was kept in the Detention Home or why he was released. At 5 p.m. on the day of Gerald's release, Mrs. Gault received a note signed by Officer Flagg. It was on plain paper, not letterhead. Its entire text was as follows:

> Mrs. Gault:
>   Judge McGhee has set Monday June 15, 1964 at 11:00 a.m. as the date and time for further Hearings on Gerald's delinquency.
>
>   "/s/ Flagg"

At the appointed time on Monday, June 15, Gerald, his father and mother, Ronald Lewis and his father, and Officers Flagg and Henderson were present before Judge McGhee. Witnesses at the habeas corpus proceeding differed in their recollections of Gerald's testimony at the June 15 hearing. Mr. and Mrs. Gault recalled that Gerald again testified that he had only dialed the number and that the other boy had made the remarks. Officer Flagg agreed that at this hearing Gerald did not admit making the lewd remarks. But Judge McGhee recalled that "there was some admission again of some of the lewd statements. He—he didn't admit any of the more serious lewd statements." Again, the complainant, Mrs. Cook, was not present. Mrs. Gault asked that Mrs. Cook be present "so she could see which boy had done the talking, the dirty talking over the phone." The Juvenile Judge said "she didn't have to be present at that hearing." The judge did not speak to Mrs. Cook or communicate with her at any time. Probation Officer Flagg had talked to her once—over the telephone on June 9.

At this June 15 hearing a "referral report" made by the probation officers was filed with the court, although not disclosed to Gerald or his parents. This listed the charge as "Lewd Phone Calls." At the conclusion of the hearing, the judge committed Gerald as a juvenile delinquent to the State Industrial School "for the period of his minority [that is, until 21], unless sooner discharged by due process of law." An order to that effect was entered. It recites that "after a full hearing and due deliberation the Court finds that said minor is a delinquent child, and that said minor is of the age of 15 years."

No appeal is permitted by Arizona law in juvenile cases. On August 3, 1964, a petition for a writ of habeas corpus was filed with the Supreme Court of Arizona and referred by it to the Superior Court for hearing.

At the habeas corpus hearing on August 17, Judge McGhee was vigorously cross-examined as to the basis for his actions. He testified that he had taken into account the fact that Gerald was on probation. He was asked "under what section of . . . the code have you found the boy delinquent?"

. . . In substance, he concluded that Gerald came within ARS § 8-201-6(a), which specifies that a "delinquent child" includes one "who has violated a law of the state or an ordinance or regulation of a political subdivision thereof." The law which Gerald was found to have violated is ARS § 13-377. This section of the Arizona Criminal Code provides that a person who "in the presence or hearing of any woman or child . . . uses vulgar, abusive or obscene language, is guilty of a misdemeanor. . . . " The judge also testified that he acted under ARS § 8-201-6(d) which includes in the definition of a "delinquent child" one who, as the judge phrased it, is "habitually involved in immoral matters."

Asked about the basis for his conclusion that Gerald was "habitually involved in immoral matters," the judge testified, somewhat vaguely, that two years earlier, on July 2, 1962, a "referral" was made concerning Gerald, "where the boy had stolen a baseball glove from another boy and lied to the Police Department about it." The judge said there was "no hearing," and "no accusation" relating to this incident, "because of lack of material foundation." But it seems to have remained in his mind as a relevant factor. The judge also testified that Gerald had admitted making other nuisance phone calls in the past which, as the judge recalled the boy's testimony, were "silly calls, or funny calls, or something like that."

The Superior Court dismissed the writ, and appellants sought review in the Arizona Supreme Court. . . .

The Supreme Court handed down an elaborate and wide-ranging opinion affirming dismissal of the writ and stating the court's conclusions as to the issues raised by appellants and other aspects of the juvenile process. In their jurisdictional statement and brief in this Court, appellants . . . urge that we hold the Juvenile Code of Arizona invalid on its face or as applied in this case because, contrary to the Due Process Clause of the Fourteenth Amendment, the juvenile is taken from the custody of his parents and committed to a state institution pursuant to proceedings in which the Juvenile Court has virtually unlimited discretion, and in which the following basic rights are denied:

1. Notice of the charges;
2. Right to counsel;
3. Right to confrontation and cross-examination;
4. Privilege against self-incrimination;
5. Right to a transcript of the proceedings; and
6. Right to appellate review. . . .

We do not in this opinion consider the impact of these constitutional provisions upon the totality of the relationship of the juvenile and the state. We do not even consider the entire process relating to juvenile "delinquents." For example, we are not here concerned with the procedures or constitutional rights applicable to the pre-judicial stages of the juvenile process, nor do we direct our attention to the post-adjudicative or dispositional process. We consider only the problems presented to us by this case. . . .

From the inception of the juvenile court system, wide differences have been tolerated—indeed insisted upon—between the procedural rights accorded to adults and those of juveniles. In practically all jurisdictions, there are rights granted to adults which are withheld from juveniles. In addition to the specific problems involved in the present case, for example, it has been held that the juvenile is not entitled to bail, to indictment by grand jury, to a public trial or to trial by jury. It is frequent practice that rules governing the arrest and interrogation of adults by the police are not observed in the case of juveniles. . . .

[The benevolent aspects of juvenile court intervention] were to be achieved, without coming to conceptual and constitutional grief, by insisting that the proceedings were not adversary, but that the state was proceeding as *parens patriae*. The Latin phrase proved to be a great help to those who sought to rationalize the exclusion of juveniles from the constitutional scheme; but its meaning is murky and its historic credentials are of dubious relevance. The phrase was taken from chancery practice, where, however, it was used to describe the power of the state to act *in loco parentis* for the purpose of protecting the property interests and the person of the child. . . .

The right of the state, as *parens patriae*, to deny to the child procedural rights available to his elders was elaborated by the assertion that a child, unlike an adult, has a right "not to liberty but to custody." He can be made to attorn to his parents, to go to school, etc. If his parents default in effectively performing their custodial functions—that is, if the child is "delinquent"—the state may intervene. In doing so, it does not deprive the child of any rights, because he has none. It merely provides the "custody" to which the child is entitled. On this basis, proceedings involving juveniles were described as "civil" not "criminal" and therefore not subject to the requirements which restrict the state when it seeks to deprive a person of his liberty.

Accordingly, the highest motives and most enlightened impulses led to a peculiar system for juveniles, unknown to our law in any comparable context.

The constitutional and theoretical basis for this peculiar system is—to say the least—debatable. And in practice, as we remarked in [Kent v. United States, 383 U.S. 541 (1966)], the results have not been entirely satisfactory. Juvenile Court history has again demonstrated that unbridled discretion, however benevolently motivated, is frequently a poor substitute for principle and procedure. . . .

Failure to observe the fundamental requirements of due process has resulted in instances, which might have been avoided, of unfairness to individuals and inadequate or inaccurate findings of fact and unfortunate prescriptions of remedy. Due process of law is the primary and indispensable foundation of individual freedom. It is the basic and essential term in the social compact, which defines rights of the individual and delimits the powers which the state may exercise. As Mr. Justice Frankfurter has said: "The history of American freedom is, in no small measure, the history of procedure." But in addition, the procedural rules which have been fashioned from the generality of due process are our best instruments for the distillation and evaluation of essential facts from the conflicting welter of data that life and our adversary methods present. It is these instruments of due process which enhance the possibility that truth will emerge from the confrontation of opposing versions and conflicting data. . . .

It is claimed that juveniles obtain benefit from the social procedures applicable to them which more than offset the disadvantages of denial of the substance of normal due process. As we shall discuss, the observance of due process standards, intelligently and not ruthlessly administered, will not compel the States to abandon or displace any of the substantive benefits of the juvenile process. But it is important, we think, that the claimed benefits of the juvenile process should be candidly appraised.

[The Court found that recidivism among juvenile offenders was high, that there was "only slightly less stigma" associated with the term "delinquent" than with the term "criminal," and that police and court records were often available to law enforcement agencies, the armed forces, and private employers.]

Further, it is urged that the juvenile benefits from informal proceedings in the court. The early conception of the Juvenile Court proceeding was one in which a fatherly judge touched the heart and conscience of the erring youth by talking over his problems, by paternal advice and admonition, and in which, in extreme situations, benevolent and wise institutions of the State provided guidance and help "to save him from a downward career." Then, as now, goodwill and compassion were admirably prevalent. But recent studies have, with surprising unanimity, entered sharp dissent as to the validity of this gentle conception. They suggest that the appearance as well as the actuality of fairness, impartiality, and orderliness—in short, the essentials of due process—may be a more impressive and more therapeutic attitude so far as the juvenile is concerned. For example, in a recent study, the sociologists Wheeler and Cottrell observe that when the procedural laxness of the "*parens patriae*" attitude is followed by stern disciplining, the contrast may have an adverse effect upon the child, who feels that he has been deceived or enticed. They conclude as follows: "Unless appropriate due process of law is followed, even the juvenile who has violated the law may not feel that he is being fairly treated and may therefore resist the rehabilitative efforts of court personnel." Of course, it is not suggested that juvenile court judges should fail appropriately to take account, in their demeanor and conduct, of the emotional and psychological attitude of the juveniles with whom they are confronted. While due process requirements will, in some instances, introduce a degree of order and regularity to Juvenile Court proceedings to determine delinquency, and in contested cases will introduce some elements of the adversary system, nothing will require that the conception of the kindly juvenile judge be replaced by its opposite, nor do we here rule upon the question whether ordinary due process requirements must be observed with respect to hearings to determine the disposition of the delinquent child.

Ultimately, however, we confront the reality of that portion of the Juvenile Court process with which we deal in this case. A boy is charged with misconduct. The boy is committed to an institution where he may be restrained of liberty for years. It is of no constitutional consequence—and of limited practical meaning—that the institution to which he is committed is called an Industrial School. The fact of the matter is that, however euphemistic the title, a "receiving home" or an "industrial school" for juveniles is an institution of confinement in which the child is incarcerated for a greater or lesser time. His world becomes "a building with whitewashed walls, regimented routine and institutional hours. . . . " Instead of mother and father and sisters and brothers and friends and classmates, his world is peopled by guards, custodians, state employees, and "delinquents" confined with him for anything from waywardness to rape and homicide. . . .

If Gerald had been over 18, he would not have been subject to Juvenile Court proceedings. For the particular offense immediately involved, the maximum punishment would have been a fine of $5 to $50, or imprisonment in jail for not more than two months. Instead, he was committed to custody for a maximum of six years. . . .

In Kent v. United States, we stated that the Juvenile Court Judge's exercise of the power of the state as *parens patriae* was not unlimited. We said that "the admonition to function in a 'parental' relationship is not an invitation to procedural arbitrariness." With respect to the waiver by the Juvenile Court to the adult court of jurisdiction over an offense committed by a youth, we said that "there is no place in our system of law for reaching a result of such tremendous consequences without ceremony—without hearing, without effective assistance of counsel, without a statement of reasons." We announced with respect to such waiver proceedings that while "We do not mean . . . to indicate that the hearing to be held must conform with all of the requirements of a criminal trial or even of the usual administrative hearing; but we do hold that the hearing must measure up to the essentials of due process and fair treatment." We reiterate this view, here in connection with a juvenile court adjudication of "delinquency," as a requirement which is part of the Due Process Clause of the Fourteenth Amendment of our Constitution.

We now turn to the specific issues which are presented to us in the present case.

III.   Notice of Charges . . .

. . . Notice, to comply with due process requirements, must be given sufficiently in advance of scheduled court proceedings so that reasonable opportunity to prepare will be afforded, and it must "set forth the alleged misconduct with particularity." . . . The "initial hearing" in the present case was a hearing on the merits. Notice at that time is not timely; and even if there were a conceivable purpose served by the deferral proposed by the court below, it would have to yield to the requirements that the child and his parents or guardian be notified, in writing, of the specific charge or factual allegations to be considered at the hearing, and that such written notice be given at the earliest practicable time, and in any event sufficiently in advance of the hearing to permit preparation. Due process of law requires notice of the sort we have described—that is, notice which would be deemed constitutionally adequate in a civil or criminal proceeding. . . .

IV.   RIGHT TO COUNSEL

. . . The Supreme Court of Arizona . . . rejected the proposition that "due process requires that an infant have a right to counsel." It said that juvenile courts have the discretion, but not the duty, to allow such representation; it referred specifically to the situation in which the Juvenile Court discerns conflict between the child and his parents as an instance in which this discretion might be exercised. We do not agree. Probation officers, in the Arizona scheme, are also arresting officers. They initiate proceedings and file petitions which they verify, as here, alleging the delinquency of the child; and they testify, as here, against the child. And here the probation officer was also superintendent of the Detention Home. The probation officer cannot act as counsel for the child. His role in the adjudicatory hearing, by statute and in fact, is as arresting officer and witness against the child. Nor can the judge represent the child. There is no material difference in this respect between adult and juvenile proceedings of the sort here involved. In adult proceedings, this contention has been foreclosed by decisions of this Court. A proceeding where the issue is whether the child will be found to be "delinquent" and subjected to the loss of his liberty for years is comparable in seriousness to a felony prosecution. The juvenile needs the assistance of counsel to cope with problems of law, to make skilled inquiry into the facts, to insist upon regularity of the proceedings, and to ascertain whether he has a defense and to prepare and submit it. The child "requires the guiding hand of counsel at every step in the proceedings against him." . . .

We conclude that the Due Process Clause of the Fourteenth Amendment requires that in respect of proceedings to determine delinquency which may result in commitment to an institution in which the juvenile's freedom is curtailed, the child and his parents must be notified of the child's right to be represented by counsel retained by them, or if they are unable to afford counsel, that counsel will be appointed to represent the child. . . .

V.   CONFRONTATION, SELF-INCRIMINATION, CROSS-EXAMINATION . . .

Mrs. Cook, the complainant, and the recipient of the alleged telephone call, was not called as a witness. . . . Gerald was . . . questioned by the Juvenile Court Judge at each of the two hearings. The judge testified in the habeas corpus proceeding that Gerald admitted making "some of the lewd statements . . . [but not] any of the more serious lewd statements."

We shall assume that Gerald made admissions of the sort described by the Juvenile Court Judge, as quoted above. Neither Gerald nor his parents were advised that he did not have to testify or make a statement, or that an incriminating statement might result in his commitment as a "delinquent." . . .

. . . [W]e emphasize again that we are here concerned only with a proceeding to determine whether a minor is a "delinquent" and which may result in commitment to a state institution. Specifically, the question is whether, in such a proceeding, an admission by the juvenile may be used against him in the absence of clear and unequivocal evidence that the admission was made with knowledge that he was not obliged to speak and would not be penalized for remaining silent. In light of Miranda v. Arizona, 384 U.S. 436 (1966), we must also consider whether, if the privilege against self-incrimination is available, it can effectively be waived unless counsel is present or the right to counsel has been waived. . . .

The privilege against self-incrimination is, of course, related to the question of the safeguards necessary to assure that admissions or confessions are reasonably trustworthy, that they are not the mere fruits of fear or coercion, but are reliable expressions of the truth. The roots of the privilege are, however, far deeper. They tap the basic stream of religious and political principle because the privilege reflects the limits of the individual's attornment to the state and — in a philosophical sense — insists upon the equality of the individual and the state. In other words, the privilege has a broader and deeper thrust than the rule which prevents the use of confessions which are the product of coercion because coercion is thought to carry with it the danger of unreliability. One of its purposes is to prevent the state, whether by force or by psychological domination, from overcoming the mind and will of the person under investigation and depriving him of the freedom to decide whether to assist the state in securing his conviction. . . .

Against the application to juveniles of the right to silence, it is argued that juvenile proceedings are "civil" and not "criminal," and therefore the privilege should not apply. It is true that the statement of the privilege in the Fifth Amendment, which is applicable to the States by reason of the Fourteenth Amendment, is that no person "shall be compelled in any *criminal case* to be a witness against himself." However, it is also clear that the availability of the privilege does not turn upon the type of proceeding in which its protection is invoked, but upon the nature of the statement or admission and the exposure which it invites. The privilege may, for example, be claimed in a civil or administrative proceeding, if the statement is or may be inculpatory.

It would be entirely unrealistic to carve out of the Fifth Amendment all statements by juveniles on the ground that these cannot lead to "criminal" involvement. In the first place, juvenile proceedings to determine "delinquency," which may lead to commitment to a state institution, must be regarded as "criminal" for purposes of the privilege against self-incrimination. To hold otherwise would be to disregard substance because of the feeble enticement of the "civil" label-of-convenience which has been attached to juvenile proceedings. Indeed, in over half of the States, there is not even assurance that the juvenile will be kept in separate institutions, apart from adult "criminals." In those States juveniles may be placed in or transferred to adult penal institutions after having been found "delinquent" by a juvenile court. For this purpose, at least, commitment is a deprivation of liberty.

It is incarceration against one's will, whether it is called "criminal" or "civil." And our Constitution guarantees that no person shall be "compelled" to be a witness against himself when he is threatened with deprivation of his liberty—a command which this Court has broadly applied and generously implemented in accordance with the teaching of the history of the privilege and its great office in mankind's battle for freedom. . . .

It is also urged, as the Supreme Court of Arizona here asserted, that the juvenile and presumably his parents should not be advised of the juvenile's right to silence because confession is good for the child as the commencement of the assumed therapy of the juvenile court process, and he should be encouraged to assume an attitude of trust and confidence toward the officials of the juvenile process. This proposition has been subjected to widespread challenge on the basis of current reappraisals of the rhetoric and realities of the handling of juvenile offenders.

In fact, evidence is accumulating that confessions by juveniles do not aid in "individualized treatment," as the court below put it, and that compelling the child to answer questions, without warning or advice as to his right to remain silent, does not serve this or any other good purpose. . . . [I]t seems probable that where children are induced to confess by "paternal" urgings on the part of officials and the confession is then followed by disciplinary action, the child's reaction is likely to be hostile and adverse—the child may well feel that he has been led or tricked into confession and that despite his confession, he is being punished. . . .

We conclude that the constitutional privilege against self-incrimination is applicable in the case of juveniles as it is with respect to adults. We appreciate that special problems may arise with respect to waiver of the privilege by or on behalf of children, and that there may well be some differences in technique—but not in principle—depending upon the age of the child and the presence and competence of parents. The participation of counsel will, of course, assist the police, Juvenile Courts, and appellate tribunals in administering the privilege. If counsel was not present for some permissible reason when an admission was obtained, the greatest care must be taken to assure that the admission was voluntary, in the sense not only that it was not coerced or suggested, but also that it was not the product of ignorance of rights or of adolescent fantasy, fright, or despair.

The "confession" of Gerald Gault was first obtained by Officer Flagg, out of the presence of Gerald's parents, without counsel and without advising him of his right to silence, as far as appears. The judgment of the Juvenile Court was stated by the judge to be based on Gerald's admissions in court. Neither "admission" was reduced to writing, and, to say the least, the process by which the "admissions" were obtained and received must be characterized as lacking the certainty and order which are required of proceedings of such formidable consequences. Apart from the "admissions," there was nothing upon which a judgment or finding might be based. There was no sworn testimony. Mrs. Cook, the complainant, was not present. The Arizona Supreme Court held that "sworn testimony must be required of all witnesses including police officers, probation officers, and others who are part of or officially related to the juvenile court structure." We hold that this is not enough. No reason is suggested or appears for a different rule in respect of sworn testimony in juvenile courts than in adult tribunals. Absent a valid confession adequate to support the determination of the Juvenile Court, confrontation and sworn testimony by witnesses available for cross-examination were essential for a finding of "delinquency" and an order committing Gerald to a state institution for a maximum of six years. . . .

As we said in Kent v. United States, 383 U.S. 541, 554 (1966), with respect to waiver proceedings, "there is no place in our system of law for reaching a result of such tremendous consequences without ceremony. . . ." We now hold that, absent a valid confession, a determination of delinquency and an order of commitment to a state institution cannot be sustained in the absence of sworn testimony subjected to the opportunity for cross-examination in accordance with our law and constitutional requirements. . . .

STEWART, J., dissenting. . . . Juvenile proceedings are not criminal trials. They are not civil trials. They are simply not adversary proceedings. Whether treating with a delinquent child, a neglected child, a defective child, or a dependent child, a juvenile proceeding's whole purpose and mission is the very opposite of the mission and purpose of a prosecution in a criminal court. The object of the one is correction of a condition. The object of the other is conviction and punishment for a criminal act. . . .

I possess neither the specialized experience nor the expert knowledge to predict with any certainty where may lie the brightest hope for progress in dealing with the serious problems of juvenile delinquency. But I am certain that the answer does not lie in the Court's opinion in this case, which serves to convert a juvenile proceeding into a criminal prosecution. The inflexible restrictions that the Constitution so wisely made applicable to adversary criminal trials have no inevitable place in the proceedings of those public social agencies known as juvenile or family courts. And to impose the Court's long catalog of requirements upon juvenile proceedings in every area of the country is to invite a long step backwards into the nineteenth century. In that era there were no juvenile proceedings, and a child was tried in a conventional criminal court with all the trappings of a conventional criminal trial. So it was that a 12-year-old boy named James Guild was tried in New Jersey for killing Catharine Beakes. A jury found him guilty of murder, and he was sentenced to death by hanging. The sentence was executed. It was all very constitutional. . . .

NOTES AND QUESTIONS

1. Kent v. United States, 383 U.S. 541 (1966), decided the year before *Gault*, did not itself deal directly with the method by which children were found delinquent. Rather, it involved the procedure by which the District of Columbia Juvenile Court Act authorized transfer of a child from the original and exclusive jurisdiction of the juvenile court to criminal court for trial as an adult. *Kent* and this process are explored later in this chapter.

2. Does the majority in *Gault* hold that commitment to an industrial school is "punishment"? Does it adopt a method for resolving the much-disputed question of the kinds of intervention that constitute "punishment"?

To talk of deprivations of liberty supposes that the child is entitled to liberty. The Supreme Court plainly assumed such an entitlement. On what basis can one talk about a child's liberty interest?

How far is *Gault* inconsistent with the basic theory of the juvenile court? Does *parens patriae* remain available as a justification for juvenile court action? Is anything left of Judge Mack's view of the nature and function of the court?

3. The attack on the traditional juvenile court focused on questions of practice as well as questions of principle. One commentator has suggested that the opinion in *Gault* relies "as much on social science 'fact' as . . . on more fundamental principles of legal reasoning." W. Vaughan Stapleton, A Social Scientist's View of *Gault* and a Plea for the Experimenting Society, 1 Yale Rev. L. & Soc. Action 72 (Winter 1970).

What empirical claims were made by the traditional juvenile court about its operation and effects? What empirical claims are made by critics of the juvenile court, and by the majority in *Gault*, about the effects of a constitutionalized juvenile court procedure?

Consider in this connection a point made by Professor Stapleton: that a strategy can be said to have failed only if we have some basis for saying that the situation would not have been worse without that strategy. For example, an increase in crime among juveniles does not alone indicate a failure of the juvenile court method because it is possible that the juvenile crime rate would have been even higher had minors been tried as adults.

4. Is a juvenile's right to free counsel because of indigency determined by the child's own financial resources or those of the parents? Most appellate courts have held that the child's finances are controlling; if the parents' ability to pay was determinative, the child could be denied an attorney because of the parents' unwillingness to pay. *See, e.g.*, In the Interest of L.G.T., 216 So. 2d 54 (Fla. Dist. Ct. App. 1968); Gordon v. Copeland, 803 S.W.2d 153 (Mo. App. 1991); Opinion of the Justices, 431 A.2d 144 (N.H. 1981); Matter of Samy F., 33 Misc.3d 1209(A) (Fam. Ct. 2011); In re J.B., 603 A.2d 368 (Vt. 1991). *Contra*, State in Interest of W.B.J., 966 P.2d 295 (Utah App. 1998).

5. The *Gault* Court did not find it necessary to decide whether there was a constitutional right to appellate review and a transcript of proceedings.

———————————

On a first reading, *Gault* may appear to reject the central premises of the traditional juvenile court, but it is a limited decision. What does it imply when the Court says, "We do not mean . . . to indicate that the hearing to be held must conform with all of the requirements of a criminal trial or even the usual administrative hearing . . . "? The "usual administrative hearing" is not, after all, a highly formal process. Moreover, the Court addresses only certain aspects of the adjudicative procedure and makes clear that it is not addressing the pre-judicial or dispositional phases of the juvenile court process. The next two Supreme Court decisions concerning the juvenile court gave mixed messages about how closely its processes must adhere to those that the constitution requires in criminal cases.

In re Winship

397 U.S. 358 (1970)

Brennan, J. . . . During a 1967 adjudicatory hearing, a judge in New York Family Court found that appellant, then a 12-year-old boy, had entered a locker and stolen $112 from a woman's pocketbook. The petition which charged appellant with delinquency alleged that his act, "if done by an adult, would constitute the crime or crimes of Larceny." The judge acknowledged that the proof might not establish guilt beyond a reasonable doubt, but rejected appellant's contention that such proof was required by the Fourteenth Amendment. The judge relied instead on § 744(b) of the New York Family Court Act which provides that "any determination at the conclusion of [an adjudicatory] hearing that a [juvenile] did an act or acts must be based on a preponderance of the evidence." During a subsequent dispositional hearing, appellant was ordered placed in a training school for an initial period of 18 months, subject to annual extensions of his commitment until his 18th birthday—six years in appellant's case. The New York Court of Appeals then affirmed by a four-to-three vote, expressly sustaining the constitutionality of § 744(b). We noted probable jurisdiction. We reverse. . . .

The accused during a criminal prosecution has at stake interests of immense importance, both because of the possibility that he may lose his liberty upon conviction and because of the certainty that he would be stigmatized by the conviction. . . . "There is always in litigation a margin of error, representing error in factfinding, which both parties must take into account. Where one party has at stake an interest of transcending value—as a criminal defendant his liberty—this margin of error is reduced as to him by the process of placing on the other party the burden of . . . persuading the factfinder at the conclusion of the trial of his guilt beyond a reasonable doubt. Due process commands that no man shall lose his liberty unless the Government has borne the burden of . . . convincing the factfinder of his guilt." To this end, the reasonable-doubt standard is indispensable, for it "impresses on the trier of fact the necessity of reaching a subjective state of certitude of the facts in issue." . . .

We turn to the question whether juveniles, like adults, are constitutionally entitled to proof beyond a reasonable doubt when they are charged with violation of a criminal law. The same considerations that demand extreme caution in factfinding to protect the innocent adult apply as well to the innocent child. . . . The Court of Appeals indicated that a delinquency adjudication "is not a 'conviction'; that it affects no right or privilege . . . and a cloak of protective confidentiality is thrown around all the proceedings. . . . " The Court of Appeals also attempted to justify the preponderance standard on the related ground that juvenile proceedings are designed "not to punish, but to save the child." . . . *Gault* expressly rejected this justification. We made clear in that decision that civil labels and good intentions do not themselves obviate the need for criminal due process safeguards in juvenile courts, for "[a] proceeding where the issue is whether the child will be found to be 'delinquent' and subjected to the loss of his liberty for years is comparable in seriousness to a felony prosecution."

Nor do we perceive any merit in the argument that to afford juveniles the protection of proof beyond a reasonable doubt would risk destruction of beneficial aspects of the juvenile process. Use of the reasonable-doubt standard during the adjudicatory hearing will not disturb New York's policies that a finding that a child has violated a criminal law does not constitute a criminal conviction, that such a finding does not deprive the child of his civil rights, and that juvenile proceedings are confidential. Nor will there be any effect on the informality, flexibility, or speed of the hearing at which the factfinding takes place. And the opportunity during the post-adjudicatory or dispositional hearing for a wide-ranging review of the child's social history and for his individualized treatment will remain unimpaired. . . .

The Court of Appeals observed that "a child's best interest is not necessarily, or even probably, promoted if he wins in the particular inquiry which may bring him to the juvenile court." It is true, of course, that the juvenile may be engaging in a general course of conduct inimical to his welfare that calls for judicial intervention. But that intervention cannot take the form of subjecting the child to the stigma of a finding that he violated a criminal law and to the possibility of institutional confinement on proof insufficient to convict him were he an adult. . . .

Reversed.

NOTES AND QUESTIONS

1. Does *Gault* compel the outcome reached in *Winship*?

2. Compare *Winship* with Addington v. Texas, 441 U.S. 418 (1979), dealing with the standard of proof for involuntary commitment of a person determined to be mentally ill. The Court there held that while a preponderance of evidence was insufficient to justify such a "massive curtailment of liberty," proof beyond a reasonable doubt was not required. In concluding that the appropriate standard is clear and convincing evidence, the majority distinguished *Winship* on several grounds. The *Addington* Court said, "In a civil commitment state power is not exercised in a punitive sense. Unlike the delinquency proceeding in *Winship*, a civil commitment proceeding can in no sense be equated to a criminal prosecution." *Id.* at 428. Does this mean that the Court viewed delinquency proceedings as involving "punishment"? What are the differences between civil commitment (which may be very long in duration) and confinement in a state juvenile corrections institution?

3. The Court also distinguished the factual inquiry in a civil commitment proceeding from that in a delinquency or criminal prosecution. In the last two, the basic issue is described as a straightforward factual question: Did the accused commit the act alleged? Civil commitments, on the other hand, were said to turn not just on conduct but also on the meaning of the facts, which must be interpreted by expert psychiatrists and psychologists. *Id.* at 429. May one assume, then, that delinquency jurisdiction can now be founded only on proof of a particular offense? Is such a conclusion consistent with the central purpose of the juvenile court, as traditionally understood? What would Judge Mack have said?

McKeiver v. Pennsylvania

403 U.S. 528 (1971)

Mr. Justice BLACKMUN announced the judgments of the Court and an opinion in which THE CHIEF JUSTICE, Mr. Justice STEWART, and Mr. Justice WHITE join. These cases present the narrow but precise issue whether the Due Process Clause of the Fourteenth Amendment assures the right to trial by jury in the adjudicative phase of a state juvenile court delinquency proceeding. . . .

[In two of the cases before the Court, the respondents were charged with "garden variety" street crimes. The third case, In re Burrus, 168 S.E.2d 695 (N.C. App. 1969), arose from a series of demonstrations by African-American adults and children protesting school assignments and school consolidation plans. The juveniles were charged in petitions filed by state highway patrolmen with willfully impeding traffic. "The evidence as to the juveniles . . . consisted solely of testimony of highway patrolmen. No juvenile took the stand or offered any witness. The testimony was to the effect that on various occasions the juveniles and adults were observed walking along Highway 64 singing, shouting, clapping, and playing basketball. As a result, there was interference with traffic. The marchers were asked to leave the paved portion of the highway and they were warned that they were committing a statutory offense. They either refused or left the roadway and immediately returned. The juveniles and participating adults were taken into custody."]

All the litigants here agree that the applicable due process standard in juvenile proceedings, as developed by *Gault* and *Winship*, is fundamental fairness. As that standard was applied in those two cases, we have an emphasis on fact-finding procedures. The requirements of notice, counsel, confrontation, cross-examination, and standard of proof naturally flowed from this emphasis. But one cannot say that in our legal system the jury is a necessary component of accurate factfinding. There is much to be said for it, to be sure, but we have been content to pursue other ways for determining facts. Juries are not required, and have not been, for example, in equity cases, in workmen's compensation, in probate, or in deportation cases. Neither have they been generally used in military trials. In Duncan [v. Louisiana, 391 U.S. 145 (1968)], the Court stated, "We would not assert, however, that every criminal trial—or any particular trial—held before a judge alone is unfair or that a defendant may never be as fairly treated by a judge as he would be by a jury." . . .

We must recognize, as the Court has recognized before, that the fond and idealistic hopes of the juvenile court proponents and early reformers of three generations ago have not been realized. . . . The community's unwillingness to provide people and facilities and to be concerned, the insufficiency of time devoted, the scarcity of professional help, the inadequacy of dispositional alternatives, and our general lack of knowledge all contribute to dissatisfaction with the experiment. . . .

Despite all these disappointments, all these failures, and all these shortcomings, we conclude that trial by jury in the juvenile court's adjudicative stage is not a constitutional requirement. We so conclude for a number of reasons:

1. The Court has refrained, in the cases heretofore decided, from taking the easy way with a flat holding that all rights constitutionally assured for the adult accused are to be imposed upon the state juvenile proceeding.

2. There is a possibility, at least, that the jury trial, if required as a matter of constitutional precept, will remake the juvenile proceeding into a fully adversary process and will put an effective end to what has been the idealistic prospect of an intimate, informal protective proceeding. . . .

5. The imposition of the jury trial on the juvenile court system would not strengthen greatly, if at all, the fact-finding function, and would, contrarily, provide an attrition of the juvenile court's assumed ability to function in a unique manner. It would not remedy the defects of the system. Meager as has been the hoped-for advance in the juvenile field, the alternative would be regressive, would lose what has been gained, and would tend once again to place the juvenile squarely in the routine of the criminal process.

6. The juvenile concept held high promise. We are reluctant to say that, despite disappointments of grave dimensions, it still does not hold promise, and we are particularly reluctant to say, as do the Pennsylvania appellants here, that the system cannot accomplish its rehabilitative goals. So much depends on the availability of resources, on the interest and commitment of the public, on willingness to learn, and on understanding as to cause and effect and cure. In this field, as in so many others, one perhaps learns best by doing. We are reluctant to disallow the States to experiment further and to seek in new and different ways the elusive answers to the problems of the young, and we feel that we would be impeding that experimentation by imposing the jury trial. The States, indeed, must go forward. If, in its wisdom, any State feels the jury trial is desirable in all cases, or in certain kinds, there appears to be no impediment to its installing a system embracing that feature. That, however, is the State's privilege and not its obligation.

7. Of course there have been abuses. The Task Force Report has noted them. We refrain from saying at this point that those abuses are of constitutional dimension. They relate to the lack of resources and of dedication rather than to inherent unfairness.

8. There is, of course, nothing to prevent a juvenile court judge, in a particular case where he feels the need, or when the need is demonstrated, from using an advisory jury.

9. "The fact that a practice is followed by a large number of states is not conclusive in a decision as to whether that practice accords with due process, but it is plainly worth considering in determining whether the practice 'offends some principle of justice so rooted in the traditions and conscience of our people as to be ranked as fundamental.'" It therefore is of more than passing interest that at least 29 States and the District of Columbia by statute deny the juvenile a right to a jury trial in cases such as these. The same result is achieved in other States by judicial decision. In 10 States statutes provide for a jury trial under certain circumstances.

10. Since *Gault* and since *Duncan* the great majority of States, in addition to Pennsylvania and North Carolina, that have faced the issue have concluded that the considerations that led to the result in those two cases do not compel trial by jury in the juvenile court.

11. Stopping short of proposing the jury trial for juvenile proceedings are the Uniform Juvenile Court Act, § 24(a), approved in July 1968 by the National Conference of Commissioners on Uniform State Laws; the Standard Juvenile Court Act, Art. V. § 19, proposed by the National Council on Crime and Delinquency; and the Legislative Guide for Drafting Family and Juvenile Court Acts § 29(a).

12. If the jury trial were to be injected into the juvenile court system as a matter of right, it would bring with it into that system the traditional delay, the formality, and the clamor of the adversary system and, possibly, the public trial. . . .

13. Finally, the arguments advanced by the juveniles here are, of course, the identical arguments that underlie the demand for the jury trial for criminal proceedings. The arguments necessarily equate the juvenile proceeding—or at least the adjudicative phase of it—with the criminal trial. Whether they should be so equated is our issue. Concern about the inapplicability of exclusionary and other rules of evidence; about the juvenile court judge's possible awareness of the juvenile's prior record and of the contents of the social file; about repeated appearances of the same familiar witnesses in the persons of juvenile and probation officers and social workers—all to the effect that this will create the likelihood of pre-judgment—chooses to ignore, it seems to us, every aspect of fairness, of concern, of sympathy, and of paternal attention that the juvenile court system contemplates.

If the formalities of the criminal adjudicative process are to be superimposed upon the juvenile court system, there is little need for its separate existence. Perhaps that ultimate disillusionment will come one day, but for the moment we are disinclined to give impetus to it.

NOTES AND QUESTIONS

1. *McKeiver* is concerned not only with the importance of a jury trial to fact-finding but also with the jury's effect on juvenile court proceedings. In what ways does the imposition of trial by jury threaten the beneficial aspects of the juvenile court? Is it possible to view the adjudicative procedure as nonadversarial after In re Gault? At what point is it appropriate for the judge to conduct himself or herself with "paternal attention"?

The plurality opinion also observes that imposition of jury trial would effectively end the juvenile court experiment and suggests that "[i]f the formalities of the criminal adjudicative process are to be superimposed upon the juvenile court system, there is little need for its separate existence." Why does this follow?

2. Only three years before *McKeiver*, the Supreme Court had decided that jury trial was a necessary aspect of due process in criminal trials. Duncan v. Louisiana, 391 U.S. 145 (1968). Justice White, who wrote the opinion for the Court in *Duncan* and concurred in *McKeiver*, distinguished delinquency from criminal proceedings in several ways.

He first argued that while jury trial is an important buffer against corrupt or overzealous prosecution in the criminal system, the distinctive intake policies of the juvenile court lessen the importance of this function. Why is this so? Does it matter that, in many courts, the intake department does not have a veto over the decision to prosecute? Would it matter that, in many courts, the intake department is a part of the court administration itself and that intake officers are appointed by the judge?

Next, Justice White argued that the jury is a buffer against judicial bias in the criminal system but that the nonpunitive orientation of the juvenile court lessens the risk of such bias in that forum. Moreover, juvenile courts do not present the same invitation to political influence as do criminal courts. Why is this so? Is it clear that juvenile court decisions have no political significance?

Finally, Justice White said that the consequences of a delinquency adjudication are less severe than those of criminal proceedings. To what extent is this conclusion consistent with *Gault* and *Winship*? Note that, in Duncan v. Louisiana itself, the defendant was convicted of simple battery; the maximum sentence was two years in prison, and Duncan in fact was sentenced only to 60 days in jail.

3. *McKeiver* expresses concern that bringing jury trials to juvenile court would bring public clamor, perhaps even public trials. In the decades since the case was decided, juvenile delinquency trials have become much more open to the public. By 2011, in 3 states juvenile delinquency hearings were open without restrictions. In 15 states all hearings were presumptively open, subject to a judge's decision to close a hearing for good cause, and in 13 jurisdictions hearings were presumptively closed. In the remaining states whether hearings were open depended on the age of the child facing charges, the nature of the charges, or a combination of these factors. Office of Juvenile Justice and Delinquency Prevention, Statistical Briefing Book, Are Delinquency Hearings Confidential (2011), https://www.ojjdp.gov/ojstatbb/structure_process/qa04125.asp?qaDate=201.

As the Supreme Court recognized in *Gault*, the promise of confidentiality for delinquency records has long been "more rhetoric than reality." 387 U.S. at 24. All states allow access to information in juvenile court records to one or more of the following: prosecutors, law enforcement agencies, social service agencies, schools, victims, or the public. A recent survey of state statutes found that only seven statutes prohibit open, public access to law enforcement, probation, and court-related records relating to a delinquency case, though most of these allow schools, the accuser, or probational personnel to have access to the records. In more than a third of the states, some juvenile records receive this kind of protection, but others are open to the public. Most commonly records are open because of the juvenile's age or record or the seriousness of the charges. In addition, some of these states allow the media access to records. Finally, 9 states offer virtually no confidentiality, making juvenile records open to the public. Joy Radice, The Juvenile Record Myth, 106 Geo. L. J. 365, 402-407 (2018).

B.   JUVENILE COURT JURISDICTION OVER MISCONDUCT BY CHILDREN

1.   *Violations of the Criminal Law*

We have already observed that juvenile court statutes may reach a broad range of conduct and that, initially, juvenile delinquency was applied to the entire range of misconduct by minors. Most modern statutes, however, separate criminal from noncriminal misbehavior, labeling the former "delinquency." Children who engage in noncriminal misconduct are often labeled as "minors in need of supervision" (MINS), as "children in need of supervision" (CINS), or in some similar way. This section deals with the core notion of delinquency, allegations of criminal misconduct.

Until relatively recently, juvenile courts in almost all states retained exclusive original jurisdiction over all, or virtually all, criminal conduct by minors. The Pennsylvania code reflects a more limited scope for juvenile court jurisdiction over criminal misconduct.

Pa. Cons. Stat. § 6302 Definitions (2018)
"Child." An individual who:

    (1) is under the age of 18 years;

    (2) is under the age of 21 years who committed an act of delinquency before reaching the age of 18 years; . . . .

"Delinquent act." (1) The term means an act designated a crime under the law of this Commonwealth, or of another state if the act occurred in that state, or under Federal law, or an act which constitutes indirect criminal contempt under Chapter 62A (relating to protection of victims of sexual violence or intimidation) with respect to sexual violence or 23 Pa.C.S. Ch. 61 (relating to protection from abuse) or the failure of a child to comply with a lawful sentence imposed for a summary offense, in which event notice of the fact shall be certified to the court.

    (2) The term shall not include:

        (i) The crime of murder.

        (ii) Any of the following prohibited conduct where the child was 15 years of age or older at the time of the alleged conduct and a deadly weapon as defined in 18 Pa.C.S. § 2301 (relating to definitions) was used during the commission of the offense which, if committed by an adult, would be classified as:

        (A) Rape as defined in 18 Pa.C.S. § 3121 (relating to rape).

        (B) Involuntary deviate sexual intercourse as defined in 18 Pa.C.S. § 3123 (relating to involuntary deviate sexual intercourse).

        (C) Aggravated assault as defined in 18 Pa.C.S. § 2702(a)(1) or (2) (relating to aggravated assault).

        (D) Robbery as defined in 18 Pa.C.S. § 3701(a)(1)(i), (ii) or (iii) (relating to robbery).

        (E) Robbery of motor vehicle as defined in 18 Pa.C.S. § 3702 (relating to robbery of motor vehicle).

        (F) Aggravated indecent assault as defined in 18 Pa.C.S. § 3125 (relating to aggravated indecent assault).

        (G) Kidnapping as defined in 18 Pa.C.S. § 2901 (relating to kidnapping).

        (H) Voluntary manslaughter.

        (I) An attempt, conspiracy or solicitation to commit murder or any of these crimes as provided in 18 Pa.C.S. §§ 901 (relating to criminal attempt), 902 (relating to criminal solicitation) and 903 (relating to criminal conspiracy).

(iii) Any of the following prohibited conduct where the child was 15 years of age or older at the time of the alleged conduct and has been previously adjudicated delinquent of any of the following prohibited conduct which, if committed by an adult, would be classified as:

(A) Rape as defined in 18 Pa.C.S. § 3121.

(B) Involuntary deviate sexual intercourse as defined in 18 Pa.C.S. § 3123.

(C) Robbery as defined in 18 Pa.C.S. § 3701(a)(1)(i), (ii) or (iii).

(D) Robbery of motor vehicle as defined in 18 Pa.C.S. § 3702.

(E) Aggravated indecent assault as defined in 18 Pa.C.S. § 3125.

(F) Kidnapping as defined in 18 Pa.C.S. § 2901.

(G) Voluntary manslaughter.

(H) An attempt, conspiracy or solicitation to commit murder or any of these crimes as provided in 18 Pa.C.S. §§ 901, 902 and 903.

(iv) Summary offenses.

(v) A crime committed by a child who has been found guilty in a criminal proceeding for other than a summary offense.

"Delinquent child." A child ten years of age or older whom the court has found to have committed a delinquent act and is in need of treatment, supervision, or rehabilitation.

For the most part, when a minor is charged as a delinquent with an act forbidden by the state penal code, the substantive issues in juvenile court are the same as they would be in adult court. The next cases deal with some of the legal and policy questions that arise because those accused are minors, not adults.

In the Matter of M.K.

514 S.W.3d 369 (Tex. App. 2017)

Lee Gabriel, Justice. Appellant M.K. is now fifty-nine years old. The State alleges that on August 7, 1973 — when Appellant was fifteen years old — he murdered fourteen-year-old D.R. The State previously filed a delinquent-child petition in juvenile court against Appellant in 1973 alleging that he murdered D.R., but the juvenile court ultimately dismissed the case at the State's request because of insufficient evidence. . . .

. . . At some point on August 7, 1973, Appellant's parents and sisters left their house to go visit family. As they were leaving, Appellant's parents saw him playing basketball with D.R. in the driveway. When Appellant's family returned to the house later that day, they discovered that a large rock had been thrown through the sliding glass door leading to their back patio. One of Appellant's sisters went into a hallway bathroom and discovered D.R. dead on the floor. He had been shot in the face with a shotgun and stabbed multiple times with a kitchen knife, which had been left in his chest.

D.R.'s injuries were so severe that Appellant's mother, R.K., initially believed Appellant was the deceased victim, but she learned that was not the case after Appellant's uncle, E.M., called her and told her that Appellant was with him at his house, which was a couple of miles away. E.M. stated that Appellant had run to his house and told him that somebody had broken into his house and that his friend was dead. E.M. also called the police and then drove Appellant back to his house. By the time E.M. arrived back at the crime scene with Appellant, FWPD investigators were already on site, and an Officer Earl Ferguson spoke with Appellant. Appellant told Officer Ferguson that he and D.R. were playing basketball when D.R. asked Appellant to use the bathroom. Appellant stated that he escorted D.R. inside the house to the bathroom and then went back outside to continue playing basketball by himself. He said that he continued to play basketball by himself for a few minutes when he heard the sound of glass breaking coming from the back of his house. Appellant said he went to the back of the house, heard a gunshot, and then fled to his uncle's house.

Inside the house, officers discovered wadding belonging to a 16–gauge shotgun shell in the bathroom where D.R. was killed. They also found a 16–gauge shotgun in the master bedroom closet, which smelled like it had been recently fired. Investigators recovered the knife from D.R.'s chest, and R.K. confirmed that it was one of the knives from her kitchen. Officers further discovered that a large floor model console television had been turned over in front of the back patio door. Some of the broken glass from the back patio door was on top of the overturned television, but when officers picked up the television, there was no glass underneath it, suggesting that it had been overturned before the sliding glass door was broken.

Investigators interviewed a few individuals in the neighborhood. They interviewed two boys, R.H. and M.P., who were about the same age as Appellant. They told officers that the day before D.R. was killed, they were both at Appellant's house playing basketball with Appellant and that Appellant asked them separately to come inside his house. R.H. stated that when he walked into the house, Appellant pointed a shotgun at him, pulled the trigger, and said, "Talk noise now." M.P. stated that when he went in the house separately, Appellant pointed a shotgun at him and then later showed him another shotgun in a bedroom. Officers also interviewed fourteen- or fifteen-year-old C.G., who lived in a house about 400 yards behind Appellant's. C.G. stated that on the day of the homicide, he was outside in his yard when he heard a crash. He looked in the direction of the sound, which was the back of Appellant's house, and he saw a young black male walking away from the sliding glass door. Another neighbor told officers that her dogs were in her backyard and that they barked at everything. But her dogs did not bark until officers arrived at Appellant's house.

. . . [T] State filed a delinquent-child petition against Appellant in juvenile court on August 24, 1973, alleging that he had murdered D.R. with a shotgun. . . .

. . . [O]n January 22, 1974, the State moved to dismiss the case it filed against Appellant because "the evidence was insufficient." . . .

. . . [The cold case detective investigating the reopened case in 2015] spoke with Appellant's mother, R.K., who still resided at the house where D.R. had been killed. She relayed much of the same information that [he] had learned when reading over the original case file. However, she provided [him] with some additional information. . . . She also stated that after the police left, Appellant told her that D.R. had gone into the house to use the restroom. Appellant stated that D.R. had been in the restroom for a while, so Appellant went in the house to check on him. Appellant said he found D.R. in the restroom playing with a toy that belonged to Appellant's brother and that he told D.R. to drop the toy. Appellant said when

D.R. did not drop the toy, he went to the master bedroom closet, grabbed a shotgun, returned to the bathroom, pointed the shotgun at D.R., and again told him to drop the toy. Appellant told R.K. that D.R. still did not drop the toy, so he shot him. Appellant told R.K. that although he did not remember anything after he shot D.R., he must have also stabbed him. R.K. also told Detective McCormack that Appellant is the one who broke the sliding glass door. R.K. told Detective McCormack that she chose not to disclose to police the information Appellant told her because the police had already left and because one of the police officers was mean and believed Appellant had shot D.R. on purpose.

Based on the new information R.K. had provided, the FWPD arrested Appellant for murder. He was transported to the FWPD homicide office, where Detective McCormack informed him that he was under arrest for murder and read him his *Miranda* warnings. Detective McCormack informed Appellant that he had spoken to R.K. and asked Appellant if he wanted to hear what she told him, and Appellant said that he did. Detective McCormack played the portion of the taped interview with R.K. in which she stated that Appellant told her that he shot D.R., and Appellant stated that he did not want to hear any more of the taped interview. Appellant then told Detective McCormack that he did not mean to kill D.R. He stated that he and D.R. were in the house playing with guns, which was his idea. He stated that D.R. pointed a gun at him and pulled the trigger, but nothing happened. Then Appellant pulled the trigger on his gun and heard a blast. Appellant stated that he could not remember anything after that. When Detective McCormack told Appellant that he did not believe D.R. had a gun and that the evidence did not show that D.R. ever had a gun, Appellant admitted it was true D.R. did not have a gun. Appellant further acknowledged that he knew the shotgun was dangerous, and he admitted that he had pointed a shotgun at kids four or five times before he shot D.R.

The State filed a petition under section 54.02(j) of the Texas Family Code asking the juvenile court to waive its exclusive original jurisdiction over Appellant and to transfer him to the criminal district court for criminal proceedings. [After an evidentiary hearing the juvenile court granted the motion to transfer the case to criminal court in light of newly discovered evidence and because it was not practicable to proceed before M.K. turned 18. M.K. appealed.]

. . . [Appellant] challenges the juvenile court's findings under subsection 54.02(j)(4), which provides that before the juvenile court may waive its jurisdiction and transfer a person to criminal district court, it must

(4) . . . find from a preponderance of the evidence that:
    (A) for a reason beyond the control of the state it was not practicable to proceed in juvenile court before the 18th birthday of the person; or
    (B) after due diligence of the state it was not practicable to proceed in juvenile court before the 18th birthday of the person because:
        (i) the state did not have probable cause to proceed in juvenile court and new evidence has been found since the 18th birthday of the person;
        (ii) the person could not be found; or
        (iii) a previous transfer order was reversed by an appellate court or set aside by a district court.

As it exists today, the Juvenile Justice Code is codified as Title 3 of the Texas Family Code. The legislature did not add the current version of subsection 54.02(j)(4) to Title 3 until 1995. Before the current version of subsection 54.02(j)(4) went into effect, subsection 54.02(j)(4) of the Texas Family Code provided as follows:

> (j) The juvenile court may waive its exclusive original jurisdiction and transfer a person to the appropriate district court or criminal district court for criminal proceedings if:
> (4) the juvenile court finds from a preponderance of the evidence that after due diligence of the state it was not practicable to proceed in juvenile court before the 18th birthday of the person because:
>> (A) the state did not have probable cause to proceed in juvenile court and new evidence has been found since the 18th birthday of the person; or
>> (B) the person could not be found.

When comparing the current version of subsection 54.02(j)(4) with the previous version, it is evident that one change H.B. 327 made to subsection 54.02(j)(4) was to add for the first time the language that the State relies upon for the efficacy of the juvenile court's amended waiver and transfer order in this case—that is, it added the language authorizing a juvenile court to waive jurisdiction and transfer a person who is eighteen years of age or older and who committed an offense when he was a child to criminal district court by finding, by a preponderance of the evidence, that "for a reason beyond the control of the state it was not practicable to proceed in juvenile court before the 18th birthday of the person."

H.B. 327 expressly provided that the changes it made to the law, which included the addition of this new provision, became effective January 1, 1996. However, while the amended subsection became effective January 1, 1996, H.B. 327 also expressly limited the applicability of the changes it made in the following way:

> (a) Except as provided by Subsection (b) of this section, this Act applies only to conduct that occurs on or after January 1, 1996. Conduct violating a penal law of this state occurs on or after January 1, 1996, if every element of the violation occurs on or after that date. Conduct that occurs before January 1, 1996, is governed by the law in effect at the time the conduct occurred, and that law is continued in effect for that purpose.

It is undisputed that the conduct forming the basis of the State's waiver and transfer petition in this case occurred on August 7, 1973. Thus, under the plain terms of section 106 of H.B. 327, the changes made by that Act—which, as noted above, include the addition of the current subsection 54.02(j)(4)(A) language—do not apply to this case.. Rather, H.B. 327 mandates that because this case involves conduct that occurred before January 1, 1996, it is governed by the law in effect at the time the conduct occurred. Accordingly, we conclude that this case is governed by the law in effect on August 7, 1973, the date on which Appellant allegedly killed D.R.

Title 3 was first enacted by the 63d Legislature on May 25, 1973, but it did not become effective until September 1, 1973. Thus, Title 3 was not in effect on August 7, 1973. The predecessor statute to Title 3 was Article 2338–1 of the

Revised Civil Statutes of Texas. Accordingly, we conclude that Article 2338–1, as effective on August 7, 1973, is the law that governs this case. Having so concluded, the jurisdictional question presented here is whether, under that law, the juvenile court in this case had jurisdiction to conduct the waiver and transfer proceeding that is the subject of this appeal. We conclude that it did not.

As effective on August 7, 1973, section 5 of Article 2338–1 vested the juvenile courts with "exclusive original jurisdiction in proceedings governing any delinquent child." Section 3 of Article 2338–1 defined the term "child" as "any person over the age of ten years and under the age of seventeen years." The term "delinquent child" included any child who "violate[d] any penal law of this state of the grade of a felony[.]" Under these provisions of Article 2338–1, "[t]he juvenile court is one of limited jurisdiction, and it is confined to those persons 'over the age of ten years and under the age of seventeen years.'" In stark contrast to Title 3, which mandates that the jurisdiction of the juvenile courts is determined by a person's age at the time he allegedly engaged in the delinquent conduct at issue rather than his age at the time of trial, the settled law in applying Article 2338–1 provided the opposite: under Article 2338–1, the jurisdiction of the juvenile courts was determined by the person's age at the time of trial, not his age at the time he allegedly engaged in the delinquent conduct. Thus, for the juvenile court to obtain jurisdiction over a proceeding under Article 2338–1, two elements must be present: "[f]irst, [the person] must be within the age limits set by Section 3 of [Article 2338–1], and second, he or she must have committed one of the enumerated acts." . . . *see also Morgan*, 595 S.W.2d at 130 n.1 (explaining same and stating that "if a person had already turned 17 by the time criminal charges were initiated against him, he was not charged as a child but as an adult[;] [h]e was not made subject to the jurisdiction of the juvenile court because the first requirement [that he be a person over the age of ten years and under the age of seventeen years] was lacking").

At the time the State filed its waiver and transfer petition in the juvenile court, Appellant was fifty-eight years of age. He therefore was not a "child" under the terms of Article 2338–1. For that reason, in light of the authorities discussed above, we are compelled to conclude that the juvenile court lacked subject-matter jurisdiction to conduct the waiver and transfer proceeding and to render the amended waiver and transfer order that is the subject of this appeal. . . .

[Transfer order vacated.]

NOTES AND QUESTIONS

1. Texas law in 1973 allowed judges to transfer some serious cases over which the juvenile court had original jurisdiction to adult criminal court. Why did the prosecutor in *M.K.* seek to transfer the case to adult criminal court, rather than trying it in juvenile court? (The processes that may result in a minor being tried as an adult are covered later in this chapter.)

After this decision, M.K. pled guilty to murder in adult court and asked for probation but was sentenced to 40 years in prison. Deanna Boyd, Calling It a "Heinous Crime," Judge Gives Fort Worth Man 40 Years for 1973 Murder, Fort Worth Star Telegram, July 10, 2017.

2. As you might expect, the states are divided about whether juvenile court jurisdiction is determined by age at the time of the act or the time of the trial. Examine the language of the Texas juvenile court jurisdiction statute as it existed in 1973 (quoted in the case above). The Texas courts interpreted this language to mean that the relevant question was the child's age at the time of trial, not at the time the alleged act was committed. Is this meaning clear from the statutory language? The legislature later amended the statute to make the child's age at the time of trial determinative of the court's jurisdiction. What are the advantages and disadvantages of each approach? What would be the theory of maintaining juvenile court jurisdiction over someone clearly an adult at the time of prosecution? Would determining jurisdiction at the time of charging provide an incentive to strategic behavior by prosecuting attorneys?

3. Michael Skakel, a member of the extended Kennedy family, allegedly murdered a childhood friend when he was 15 years old. Evidence of his acts did not become known until 25 years later; under state law his case was initiated in juvenile court and then was transferred for trial to adult court. He was convicted of murder and sentenced to 20 years in prison. The state supreme court affirmed, rejecting, among other claims, his argument that trying him as an adult was erroneous. State v. Skakel, 888 A.2d 985 (Conn. 2005). *But see* State v. Cassidy D., 29 A.3d 190 (Conn. 2010) (distinguishing *Skakel* on its facts and finding that an adult defendant could be given a delinquency commitment for charges brought when he was 15, even though he did not admit guilt, receive a sentence, or violate probation until he was 18). In 2018 the Connecticut Supreme Court overturned Skakel's conviction upon finding that his attorney provided ineffective assistance of counsel by failing to obtain readily available evidence that was critical to an alibi defense. Skakel v. Comm'r of Corrections, 188 A.3d 1 (Conn. 2018).

In re Devon T.

584 A.2d 1287 (Md. Spec. App. 1991)

Moylan, Judge. . . . The juvenile appellant, Devon T., was charged with committing an act which, if committed by an adult, would have constituted the crime of possession of heroin with intent to distribute. In the Circuit Court for Baltimore City, Judge Roger W. Brown found that Devon was delinquent. The heart of the case against Devon was that when on May 25, 1989, Devon was directed to empty his pockets by the security guard at the Booker T. Washington Middle School, under the watchful eye of the Assistant Principal, the search produced a brown bag containing twenty zip-lock pink plastic bags which, in turn, contained heroin. . . .

At the time of the offense, Devon was 13 years, 10 months, and 2 weeks of age. He timely raised the infancy defense. Initially, we will look at the infancy defense in its original (and still primary) context of a criminal prosecution, before turning briefly to the applicability of the defense to juvenile delinquency proceedings.

The case law and the academic literature alike conceptualize the infancy defense as but an instance of the broader phenomenon of a defense based upon lack of moral responsibility or capacity. The criminal law generally will only impose its retributive or deterrent sanctions upon those who are morally blame-worthy — those who know they are doing wrong but nonetheless persist in their wrongdoing.

After several centuries of pondering the criminal capacity of children and experimenting with various cut-off ages, the Common Law settled upon its current resolution of the problem by late Tudor and early Stuart times. . .:

> At common law, children under the age of seven are conclusively presumed to be without criminal capacity, those who have reached the age of fourteen are treated as fully responsible, while as to those between the ages of seven and fourteen there is a rebuttable presumption of criminal incapacity. . . .

With the creation shortly after the turn of the present century of juvenile courts in America, diverting many youthful offenders from criminal courts into equity and other civil courts, the question arose as to whether the infancy defense had any pertinence to a juvenile delinquency adjudication. Under the initially prevailing philosophy that the State was acting in delinquency cases as *parens patriae* (sovereign parent of the country), the State was perceived to be not the retributive punisher of the child for its misdeeds but the paternalistic guardian of the child for its own best interests. Under such a regime, the moral responsibility or blameworthiness of the child was of no consequence. Morally responsible or not, the child was in apparent need of the State's rehabilitative intervention and the delinquency adjudication was but the avenue for such intervention. . . .

Over the course of the century, however, buffeted by unanticipated urban deterioration and staggering case loads, the reforming vision of Judge Julian Mack and the other founders of the movement faded. Although continuing to stress rehabilitation over retribution more heavily than did the adult criminal courts, delinquency adjudications nonetheless took on, in practice if not in theory, many of the attributes of junior varsity criminal trials. The Supreme Court, in In re Gault, 387 U.S. 1 (1967), and In re Winship, 397 U.S. 358 (1970), acknowledged this slow but inexorable transformation of the juvenile court apparatus into one with increasingly penal overtones. It ultimately guaranteed, therefore, a juvenile charged with delinquency most of the due process protections afforded an adult charged with crime. . . .

In terms of the applicability of the infancy defense to delinquency proceedings, the implications of the new dispensation are clear. A finding of delinquency, unlike other proceedings in a juvenile court, unmistakably connotes some degree of blameworthiness and unmistakably exposes the delinquent to, whatever the gloss, the possibility of unpleasant sanctions. Clearly, the juvenile would have as an available defense to the delinquency charge 1) the fact that he was too criminally insane to have known that what he did was wrong, 2) that he was too mentally retarded to have known that what he did was wrong, or 3) that he was too involuntarily intoxicated through no fault of his own to have known that what he did was wrong. It would be inconceivable that he could be found blameworthy and suffer sanctions, notwithstanding precisely the same lack of understanding and absence of moral accountability, simply because the cognitive defect was caused by infancy rather than by one of the other incapacitating mechanisms. . . .

The Court of Appeals . . . brought Maryland in line with the modern trend in In re William A., 548 A.2d 130 (1988). . . .

> A principal reason supporting the applicability of the defense is that juvenile statutes typically require, for a delinquency adjudication, that the child commit an act which constitutes a crime if committed by an adult, and if the child lacks capacity to have the requisite *mens rea* for a particular crime, he has not committed an act amounting to a crime. . . .

The infancy defense was not applied to all juvenile court proceedings but only to delinquency adjudications, where moral blameworthiness is an integral part of the wrongdoing. . . . With respect to other situations, where the conduct itself of the juvenile, irrespective of moral accountability, calls for some rehabilitative intervention on the part of the State . . . the State may still file a petition alleging a Child in Need of Supervision (CINS) or a Child in Need of Assistance (CINA).

As these proceedings are not necessarily based on the commission of acts constituting crimes, the infancy defense obviously has no relevance to them.

In a juvenile delinquency adjudication, however, the defense of infancy is now indisputably available in precisely the same manner as it is available in a criminal trial. . . .

Devon initially had the benefit of presumptive incapacity. The presumption having been generated, the State had the burdens (of both production and persuasion) of rebutting that presumption. . . .

To overcome the presumption of incapacity, then, what precisely was that quality of Devon's mind as to which the State was required to produce legally sufficient evidence? It was required to produce evidence permitting the reasonable inference that Devon — the Ghost of M'Naghten speaks: — "at the time of doing the act knew the difference between right and wrong." . . .

In short, when Devon walked around the Booker T. Washington Middle School with twenty zip-lock bags of heroin, apparently for sale or other distribution, could Devon pass the M'Naghten test? Was there legally sufficient data before him to permit Judge Brown to infer that Devon knew the difference between right and wrong and knew, moreover, that what he was doing was wrong?

As we turn to the legal sufficiency of the evidence, it is important to know that the only mental quality we are probing is the cognitive capacity to distinguish right from wrong. Other aspects of Devon's mental and psychological make-up, such as his scholastic attainments, his I.Q., his social maturity, his societal adjustment, his basic personality, etc., might well require evidentiary input from psychologists, from parents, from teachers or other school authorities, etc. On knowledge of the difference between right and wrong, however, the general case law, as well as the inherent logic of the situation, has established that that particular psychic phenomenon may sometimes permissibly be inferred from the very circumstances of the criminal or delinquent act itself. . . .

Before looking at the circumstances of the delinquent act in this case, as well as at other data pointing toward Devon's awareness that he was doing wrong, a word is in order about the quantity of proof required. In re William A quotes with approval from Adams v. State, in pointing out:

It is generally held that the presumption of *doli incapax* is "extremely strong at the age of seven and diminishes gradually until it disappears entirely at the age of fourteen . . . " Since the strength of the presumption of incapacity decreases with the increase in the years of the accused, the quantum of proof necessary to overcome the presumption would diminish in substantially the same ratio. . . .

We stress that the burden in that regard, notwithstanding the probabilities, was nonetheless on the State. The impact of the allocation of the burden of proof to the State is that the infant will enjoy the benefit of the doubt. The fact that the quantum of proof necessary to overcome presumptive incapacity diminishes in substantially the same ratio as the infant's age increases only serves to lessen the State's burden, not to eliminate it. The State's burden is still an affirmative one. It may not, therefore, passively rely upon the mere absence of evidence to the contrary.

We hold that the State successfully carried that burden. A minor factor, albeit of some weight, was that Devon was essentially at or near grade level in school. The report of the master, received and reviewed by Judge Brown, established that at the time of the offense, Devon was in middle school, embracing grades 6, 7, and 8. The report of the master, indeed, revealed that Devon had flunked the sixth grade twice, with truancy and lack of motivation as apparent causes. That fact nonetheless revealed that Devon had initially reached the sixth grade while still eleven years of age. That would tend to support his probable inclusion in the large majority of his age group rather than in a small and subnormal minority of it.

We note that the transcript of the hearing before the juvenile master shows that the master was in a position to observe first-hand Devon's receiving of legal advice from his lawyer, his acknowledgement of his understanding of it, and his acting upon it. His lawyer explained that he had a right to remain silent and that the master would not infer guilt from his exercise of that right. He acknowledged understanding that right. His lawyer also advised him of his right to testify but informed him that both the assistant state's attorney and the judge might question him about the delinquent act. Devon indicated that he wished to remain silent and say nothing. Although reduced to relatively simple language, the exchange with respect to the risk of self-incrimination and the privilege against self-incrimination forms a predicate from which an observer might infer some knowledge on Devon's part of the significance of incrimination. . . .

The transcript that was received and reviewed by Judge Brown revealed yet a further exchange between the juvenile master and Devon, also not without some significance. After Devon and his companion Edward had already been adjudicated delinquent and when no further risk of incrimination inhered, the master, prior to disposition, asked each of the two what, if anything, he would like to say and was met by "stonewalling":

Master Price: Edward, is there anything you want to say to me about whether or not you want to be on community detention? (inaudible) Get these drugs? Edward? Devon? Neither one of you want to tell me. Right? Which shows that you are hanging around with the wrong people and protecting them. Right?

This inferable allegiance to the Underworld's "Code of Silence" suggests that Devon and Edward were no mere babies caught up in a web they did not comprehend. The permitted inference, rather, was that they were fully conscious of the ongoing war between lawful authority and those who flout it and had deliberately chosen to adhere to the latter camp.

We turn, most significantly, to the circumstances of the criminal act itself. . . . [U]se of a secluded location or concealment was present in this case. The case broke when a grandmother, concerned enough to have had her own live-in grandson institutionalized, complained to the authorities at Booker T. Washington Middle School that several of her grandson's classmates were being truant on a regular basis and were using her home, while she was out working, as the "hide out" from which to sell drugs. Although the initial suspicion was directed toward Edward, it ultimately appeared that Edward and Devon were in the enterprise together. Children who are unaware that what they are doing is wrong have no need to hide out or to conceal their activities.

The most significant circumstance was the very nature of the criminal activity in which Devon engaged. It was not mere possession of heroin. It was possession of twenty packets of heroin with the intent to distribute. This was the finding of the court and it was supported by the evidence. There were no needle marks or other indications of personal use on Devon's body. Nothing in the information developed by the Juvenile Services Agency on Devon and his family gave any indication that this sixth grader, directly or indirectly, had the affluence to purchase drugs for himself in that amount. Indeed, a statement he gave to the interviewer from the Juvenile Services Agency acknowledged that he had been selling drugs for two days when the current offense occurred. His motivation was "that he just wanted something to do."

The evidence in this case affirmatively indicated that Devon and Edward and several other students had been regularly using the absent grandmother's home as a base from which to sell drugs. The circumstances clearly indicated that Devon and his companions were not innocent children unaware of the difference between games and crimes but "street wise" young delinquents knowingly involved in illicit activities. Realistically, one cannot engage in the business of selling drugs without some knowledge as to sources of supply, some pattern for receiving and passing on the money, some network of potential customers, and some *modus operandi* to avoid the eye of the police and of school authorities. It is almost inconceivable that such a crime could be engaged in without the drug pusher's being aware that it was against the law. That is, by definition, criminal capacity.

We hold that the surrounding circumstances here were legally sufficient to overcome the slight residual weight of the presumption of incapacity due to infancy. . . .

GARY B. MELTON, *TAKING GAULT SERIOUSLY: TOWARD A NEW JUVENILE COURT*

68 Neb. L. Rev. 146, 153-155, 157 (1989)

. . . [A] large body of recent psycholegal scholarship [indicates that] juveniles, especially adolescents, commonly are more competent decisionmakers than the law historically presumed. Piagetian theory implied that adolescents, at least

by age fourteen, would not differ from adults on average in their ability to comprehend and weigh risks and benefits of personal decisions. That general proposition
now has been supported by numerous laboratory and field studies of decisionmaking by youth in various legally relevant contexts.

In fact, if research contradicts the Piagetian hypotheses at all, it generally is
in the direction of competence of even younger minors to make personal decisions. . . . [R]esearch has indicated that children in the intermediate grades make
adult-like decisions about routine therapeutic and educational matters, even if
they are not as competent as adolescents and adults in comprehending and weighing the risks and benefits of the various alternatives. Stated somewhat differently,
children can imitate adult models in making decisions for themselves, even when
they are not prepared cognitively to explain the merits of their decisions. . . .

. . . [C]omprehension of physical causality occurs much earlier than children
are able to articulate their understanding of causality and, therefore, earlier than
Piaget believed was possible. "Adult-like" causal reasoning is well established by
age four or five and sometimes observable even among two- and three-year-old
children. Thus, concepts of agency and intentionality are within the repertoire
even of young children.

Although such bodies of research cast doubt on the historic presumption
of irresponsibility among juveniles, it is important not to oversell their significance. The capacity to perceive and evaluate the intentionality of behavior does
not translate directly into the capacity to form criminal intent. Moreover, some of
the research by Piagetian critics that shows children capable of higher-level reasoning than cognitive-developmental theorists typically assumed requires unusual
conditions. . . .

Similarly, research on juveniles' competence in decisionmaking is not completely apposite to questions of their responsibility. On the one hand, the cognitive
requirements for compliance with the criminal law probably are generally less
advanced than the information-processing skills needed to make rational decisions about one's physical and economic welfare. On the other hand, the threshold
for personal responsibility should be higher than the threshold for exercise of
self-determination. . . .

The age thresholds for recognition of autonomy and privacy, cessation of
special age-based entitlements, and establishment of criminal responsibility need
not be, indeed should not be, the same. Respect for personhood demands that we
err on the side of promotion of autonomy. Therefore, the presumption should
be in favor of self-determination . . . but doubt about criminal (or quasi criminal)
responsibility should be resolved in the direction of nonresponsibility.

DANIEL R. WEINBERGER ET AL., *THE ADOLESCENT BRAIN: A WORK IN PROGRESS 1-3*

June 2005, http://www.teenpregnancy.org/resources/reading/ pdf/BRAIN.pdf

Neuroscience, the scientific study of the biology of the brain, has made great
strides over the past decade in revealing that remarkable changes occur in the
brain during the second decade of life. Contrary to long-held ideas that the brain
was most grown-up—"fully cooked"—by the end of childhood, it is now clear

that adolescence is a time of profound brain growth and change. In fact, the brain of an early adolescent in comparison to that of a late adolescent differs measurably in anatomy, biochemistry, and physiology.

Between childhood and adulthood, the brain's "wiring diagram" becomes richer, more complex, and more efficient, especially in the brain's frontal lobe, . . . which is the seat of such higher order functions as learning and socialization. An important part of the frontal lobes is the prefrontal cortex, which is often referred to as the "CEO" or executive of the brain and is responsible for such skills as setting priorities, organizing plans and ideas, forming strategies, controlling impulses, and allocating attention. New research suggests that the PFC is one of the last areas of the brain to fully mature.

The brain produces a large number of neural connections just before puberty—connections that diminish in number throughout adolescence through a "use-it-or-lose-it" pruning. Through this process, the brain becomes leaner and more efficient. Like a sophisticated computer, the maturing brain also grows circuits that can perform several tasks simultaneously and with ever-greater efficiency. As circuits mature, they become coated with a layer of a white fatty substance, myelin, which speeds communication, much like the insulation on electric wire.

In addition, cells that use the chemical messenger dopamine—a neurotransmitter that, among other things, increases one's capacity to learn in response to reward—increase the density of their connections with the prefrontal cortex. Dopamine inputs to the prefrontal cortex grow dramatically during adolescence, probably representing one of the neuronal mechanisms that increase the capacity for more mature judgment and impulse control. Indeed, beginning in adolescence, the dopamine reward signal becomes especially important in the prefrontal cortex as ideas, *per se*, become increasingly reinforced and valued.

It is also apparent that regions of the cortex (i.e., the outer mantle layer of the brain) that handle abstract information and that are critical for learning and memory of such concepts as rules, laws, and codes of social conduct seem to become much more likely to share information in a parallel processing fashion as adulthood approaches. This increased information sharing is reflected in the patterns of connections between and among neurons in different regions of the cortex. For example, the branching of neurons in the prefrontal cortex becomes much more complex during adolescence, likely reflecting a more intricate web of information flow. It is as if the cells change their architecture in order to meet the increasingly difficult cognitive and emotional challenges that they are being asked to master. By the end of the twenties, the profile of cell-to-cell contacts reaches an adult pattern and the number of connections reaches a steady state that persists until old age. . . .

Impulse control, planning, and decision-making are largely frontal cortex functions that are still maturing during adolescence. One way that the functions of the frontal lobes have been understood is by observing changes in the cognitive processes and behavior of adults who have suffered injury to this key area of the brain. For example, adults whose frontal lobes are damaged often tend to be more uninhibited and impulsive. Often unable to suppress irrelevant information, people with this kind of damage are often easily distracted and falter at even the simplest tasks requiring sustained attention and short-term memory. Such observations suggest that one reason adolescents may have difficulty inhibiting inappropriate impulses is that the circuitry needed for such control is not fully mature in early adolescence, thereby making such tasks relatively difficult. . . .

Planning behavior is another case in point. Adults with damage to the prefrontal cortex tend to be inflexible in adapting to the environment. Studies show that the ability to plan improves with age until adulthood, since the process requires a temporary mental workspace—"working memory"—which is still developing throughout adolescence. Similar parallels can be drawn with regard to decision-making. Damage to the lower middle portion of the adult prefrontal cortex appears to impair the ability to imagine the future consequences of actions or to appropriately gauge their emotional significance. One needs to be able to estimate the probabilities of the possible outcomes of actions in order to make appropriate decisions and to appreciate the complex relationships of cause and effect. People with such damage tend to make decisions on the basis of immediate reward. And it has also been learned that teens are prone to certain types of flawed logic or to ignoring cues about how questions are framed in their decision-making. Again, such observations suggest that one reason adolescents may have limited cognitive ability to simultaneously process information about antecedents and outcomes, hold it in working memory, and use it to make decisions is likely traceable, in part, to brain circuitry not fully developed and still under construction, particularly in the prefrontal cortex of the frontal lobes.

In sum, a large and compelling body of scientific research on the neurological development of teens confirms a long-held, commonsense view: teenagers are not the same as adults in a variety of key areas such as the ability to make sound judgments when confronted by complex situations, the capacity to control impulses, and the ability to plan effectively. Such limitations reflect, in part, the fact that key areas of the adolescent brain, especially the prefrontal cortex that controls many higher order skills, are not fully mature until the third decade of life. Teens are full of promise, often energetic and caring, capable of making many contributions to their communities, and able to make remarkable spurts in intellectual development and learning. But neurologically, they are not adults. They are, as we say in this paper often, a work in progress.

NOTES AND QUESTIONS

1. Do *Gault* and its progeny require that the infancy defense be recognized in a delinquency proceeding? Besides *Devon T*, cases concluding that the infancy defense is available in delinquency proceedings include State v. Q.D., 685 P.2d 557, 560 (Wash. 1984) ("Being a criminal defense, [infancy] should be available to juvenile proceedings that are criminal in nature."). The Supreme Court of Kentucky held that the defense is not available in W.D.B. v. Commonwealth, 246 S.W.3d 448 (Ky. 2007), saying "Since the enactment of the Kentucky Unified Juvenile Code, the common law presumption that a child lacks criminal capacity is no longer necessary [because] a delinquency adjudication in juvenile court is not a criminal conviction [and] allowing the presumption would frustrate the clinical and rehabilitative purposes of the juvenile code." *See generally* Craig S. Lerner, Originalism and the Common Law Infancy Defense, 67 Am. U. L. Rev. 1577 (2018); Barbara

Kaban & James Orlando, Revitalizing the Infancy Defense in the Contemporary Juvenile Court, 60 Rutgers L. Rev. 33 (2007).

2. When juvenile codes incorporate a minimum age in their definitions of juvenile delinquency, that age functions in the same way that the age of 7 functioned at common law — it defines the point below which *mens rea* is said not to exist. Only 20 states have statutes that explicitly specify a minimum age for delinquency adjudication. The most common age is 10; North Carolina has set the lowest minimum age at 6 years old. In addition, a Minnesota appellate court held that the minimum age is 10. Matter of Welfare of S.A.C., 529 N.W.2d 517 (Minn. App. 1995). National Juvenile Defender Center, Minimum Age for Delinquency Adjudication – Multi-Jurisdiction Survey (last updated September 2016), http://njdc.info/practice-policy-resources/state-profiles/multi-jurisdiction-data/minimum-age-for-delinquency-adjudication-multi-jurisdiction-survey/

A finding that a child is incompetent to stand trial because of developmental immaturity prevents a trial and thus a finding of delinquency. Competence to stand trial is considered in Chapter 6. Since competence is determined on a case-by-case basis, it provides less consistent protection than a minimum jurisdictional age would. Elizabeth S. Barnert et al., Setting a Minimum Age for Juvenile Justice Jurisdiction in California, 13(1) Int. J. Prison Health 49 (2017); Laura S. Abrams et al., Is a Minimum Age of Juvenile Court Jurisdiction a Necessary Protection? A Case Study in the State of California, Crime & Delinquency, https://doi.org/10.1177/0011128718770817 (Apr. 21, 2018).

3. Does a state's creation of a juvenile court system mean that it has rejected the common law infancy defense for cases tried in adult criminal court? *Compare* Sen. v. State, 301 P.3d 106 (Wyo. 2013) (endorsing the argument), *with* Commonwealth v. Martz, 118 A.3d 1175 (Pa. Super. 144, 2015), *appeal dismissed as improv. granted* 150 A.3d 15 (Pa. 2016) (rejecting argument).

4. Is it clear from the decision in *Devon T.* that the insanity defense would also be recognized in delinquency proceedings? Cases are divided on this issue. *Compar*e Commonwealth v. Chatman, 538 S.E.2d 304 (Va. 2000) (no statutory or constitutional right to assert insanity defense in juvenile court), *with* In the Interest of H.C., 256 A.2d 322 (N.J. Super. 1969); Matter of L. J., 552 P.2d 1322, Or. App. 1976 (holding that defense is available).

Does the theoretical justification for recognizing the insanity defense matter? In one (utilitarian) view, insane persons are excused from criminal punishment on the ground that punishment, being an evil, can be justified only when it prevents some greater evil. Because insane persons do not calculate their behavior in rational terms, punishment cannot deter their misconduct and thus will serve no valid purpose. *See* Jeremy Bentham, An Introduction to the Principles of Morals and Legislation 162, 166 (Methuen Books, 1982) (1789). For those who follow a retributivist approach, criminal punishment is the appropriate and necessary societal response to those who make morally wrong choices or, it is sometimes said, fail to exercise self-restraint and thereby gain an advantage over those who follow the rules. *See* Herbert Morris, On Guilt and Innocence, 33-34 (1976). Because insane persons are not morally responsible for their choices, criminal punishment is not a just response.

5. The youth of an alleged offender can also affect how *mens rea* terms are applied. Most importantly, for some crimes the required mental state is criminal

negligence, requiring proof that the actor behaved unreasonably, and many affirmative defenses, such as self-defense, also require a reasonableness assessment. Youth can be a factor in defining the reasonable person standard against which an accused is charged. *But see* State v. Heinemann, 920 A.2d 278 (Conn. 2007) (refusing jury instruction to consider how adolescent decision-making affects assessment of reasonableness). For discussions *see* Jenny E. Carroll, Brain Science and the Theory of Juvenile *Mens Rea*, 94 N.C. L. Rev. 539 (2016); Christopher Northrop & Kristina Rothley Rozan, Kids Will Be Kids: Time for a "Reasonable Child" Standard for the Proof of Objective *Mens Rea* Elements, 69 Me. L. Rev. 109 (2016-2017).

STATE IN THE INTEREST OF C.K.

182 A.3d 917 (N.J. 2018)

Justice ALBIN delivered the opinion of the Court. Juveniles adjudicated delinquent of certain sex offenses are barred for life from seeking relief from the registration and community notification provisions of Megan's Law. That categorical lifetime bar cannot be lifted, even when the juvenile becomes an adult and poses no public safety risk, is fully rehabilitated, and is a fully productive member of society. . . .

. . . When C.K. was approximately fifteen years old, he began sexually assaulting his younger adopted brother, A.K., who was then seven years old. After A.K. turned sixteen, he disclosed his older brother's abuse to his priest and then to the police.

The State charged C.K. with committing, while he was a juvenile, the offense of aggravated sexual assault against his adopted brother. At the time of the charge, C.K. was twenty-three years old.

. . . In 2003, C.K. was sentenced to a three-year probationary term, conditioned on his attending sex-offender treatment and having no contact with his brother unless recommended by a therapist. The court also ordered C.K. to comply with the Megan's Law requirements and barred him from working with children without the court's permission.

The State classified C.K. as a Tier One offender — the lowest risk category for re-offense. As a Tier One offender, C.K. is required to register annually with the law enforcement agency in the municipality where he resides.

In the years after turning eighteen, C.K. received an undergraduate degree in psychology from Catholic University and a master's degree in counseling from Montclair State University. At the time of his arrest, C.K. was a teacher's assistant for children with autism. After his juvenile adjudication, C.K. stopped working with children. By age thirty-three, C.K. had worked for many years at a nonprofit agency that provides adults suffering from mental illness a range of services, such as securing psychiatric treatment and affordable housing. C.K. has turned down opportunities for professional advancement from fear that a background check might "out" his status as a Megan's Law registrant. It has now been more than twenty years since C.K. engaged in any unlawful conduct and more than fourteen years since his juvenile adjudication. . . .

In November 2012, C.K. filed [a post-conviction relief petition challenging the constitutionality of the registration requirement].

At the evidentiary hearing, . . . [a]ll of the expert witnesses asserted that juvenile sex offenders are more amenable to rehabilitation and less likely to reoffend than adult sex offenders. They stressed that juvenile offenders, because of their lack of maturity and delayed social and emotional development, are fundamentally different from adult offenders.

The experts pointed to multiple studies confirming that juveniles who commit sex offenses are more likely to act impulsively and be motivated by sexual curiosity, in contrast to adult sex offenders who are commonly aroused by deviant sexual behavior or engage in predatory or psychopathic conduct. Dr. Hiscox explained that "adolescent sex offense recidivism rates are relatively low" when compared "with higher sex offense recidivism rates of individuals who commit sex offenses as adults." Dr. Bosley and other experts also noted that previous assumptions about high rates of juvenile sex offender recidivism as adults are inaccurate.

One recent study—cited by all five expert witnesses—analyzed sixty-three data sets with information about more than 11,200 juvenile sex offenders. The study averaged the data sets, some of which followed juvenile sex offenders for less than five years and others for more than five years, and concluded that the overall juvenile sex re-offense rate was seven percent.

According to a report of psychologist Dr. Philip Witt, the recidivism rate for those falling into C.K.'s risk assessment category is 1.1% over a two-year period and 2.0% over a four-year period. In that report, he indicated that "a sibling incest offender whose offense [was] in his early to mid-teens has little bearing on his risk" many years later.

None of the risk assessment statistics accounted for a juvenile sex offender who had been offense-free for a period of fifteen or more years since his adjudication. The experts, however, explained that juvenile sex offenders who commit subsequent sex offenses generally do so within the first few years following their last offense. According to Dr. Hiscox, the longer a juvenile turned adult remains offense-free in the community, the lower the risk that he will re-offend.

The experts generally agreed that the best way to assess an offender's risk of recidivism is with individualized assessments. As Dr. Prentky explained, "Risk is not fixed, and it certainly can't be adequately captured by one single event in the life of . . . an adolescent who is constantly changing."

Ms. Pittman observed that categorical lifetime registration requirements based on an aggravated sex offense conviction disproportionately impact juveniles. That is so because juveniles commonly commit sex offenses against their peers or somewhat younger children.

Last, according to the experts, studies reveal that registration policies do not necessarily reduce recidivism among juvenile sex offenders. Correspondingly, Ms. Pittman expressed her concern that inflexible lifetime registration requirements imposed on juveniles impede their rehabilitation and their quest for normal and productive lives in welcoming communities.

The evidentiary hearing also focused on the experts' individualized risk assessments of C.K., now thirty-eight years old, and on the negative impact the registration requirements continue to have on his ability to lead a normal life.

C.K. participated in several psychological assessments, including two with Dr. Witt. In his 2003 assessment, made shortly after C.K.'s arrest, Dr. Witt did not find any indication that "[C.K.'s] sexual behavior with his brother was part of a broader pattern of illegal sexual behavior." He considered C.K. "a low risk."

In 2009, Dr. Witt reevaluated C.K., then twenty-nine years old, and observed that C.K. was "an adult with a productive, appropriate lifestyle and healthy sexual adjustment" who presented a low risk to reoffend. Dr. Witt noted that the "risk assessment is really just a reflection of commonsense: When an individual's risk is relatively low to begin with and the individual has had a stable, offense-free life-style for many years, his current risk is minimal."

At the evidentiary hearing, Dr. Hiscox testified that C.K.'s 2013 psycholog-ical evaluation was "completely consistent with Dr. Witt's two risk assessments." Dr. Hiscox further observed that C.K. had "gone 16 to 20 years in the community without a new sexual or non-sexual offense" and the research was clear: "the lon-ger an individual goes without committing a new sex offense while at liberty in the community, the lower his risk of reoffending."

That same year, in interviews with Ms. Pittman, C.K. expressed his feelings of isolation, anxiety, and depression resulting from his Megan's Law status. He also disclosed his sense of hopelessness, and his fear that his registrant status will inter-fere with his ability to one day be a normal parent who can attend his children's sports games and school conferences. . . .

The PCR court concluded, however, that any loosening of the strictures of Megan's Law must come from this Court in assessing the constitutionality of the registration scheme as applied to juveniles or from the Legislature, which has the paramount role in forging public policy. . . .

We granted certification to address the constitutionality of imposing the Megan's Law lifetime registration and notification requirements on juveniles adju-dicated of committing certain sex offenses, despite the peculiar procedural vehicle for doing so. . . .

We begin our analysis with the statute at issue, with our focus on juvenile sex offenders.

N.J.S.A. 2C:7–2(g) provides that

> [a] person required to register under this section who has been convicted of, *adju-dicated delinquent,* or acquitted by reason of insanity *for more than one sex offense as defined in subsection b. of this section* or who has been convicted of, *adjudicated delinquent,* or acquitted by reason of insanity *for aggravated sexual assault pursuant to subsection a. of [N.J.S.A.] 2C:14–2 or sexual assault [using physical force or coercion, without causing severe injury]* is not eligible under subsection f. of this section to make application to the Superior Court of this State to terminate the registration obligation.

N.J.S.A. 2C:7–2(g) is part of the registration and community notification provisions of Megan's Law. . . .

On adjudication of a sex offense identified in N.J.S.A. 2C:7–2(b), a juvenile offender must register with the police department in the municipality where he lives. Registration requires the collection of an offender's fingerprints and such information as his residence, school enrollment, and employment. The juvenile also must advise the appropriate law enforcement agency of whether he has access to a computer or device with internet capability, and any change in residence, employment, or other required information. A juvenile offender who fails to register or inform the appropriate law enforcement agency of a change of address or other status is guilty of a third-degree crime. . . .

The lifetime registration requirements imposed by N.J.S.A. 2C:7-2(g) are categorical. A juvenile, fourteen years or older, who has committed an enumerated sex offense, or multiple sex offenses, under subsection (g) cannot seek relief *ever* from those requirements—however successful his rehabilitation, however many his achievements, and however remote the possibility that he will reoffend.

Subsection (g) of N.J.S.A. 2C:7-2 was not part of the original legislative scheme that became Megan's Law in 1994. The Legislature enacted subsection (g) in 2002 with the intended purpose of conforming our State registration and notification scheme to Congress's 1996 amendments to the Jacob Wetterling Crimes Against Children and Sexually Violent Offender Registration Act of 1994 (Jacob Wetterling Act). The amended Jacob Wetterling Act—the federal counterpart to Megan's Law—required law enforcement agencies to notify the community when "necessary to protect the public." Under the Act, offenders who committed certain enumerated sex crimes were subject to lifetime registration requirements. . . .

The presence of subsection (g) of N.J.S.A. 2C:7-2 in our legislative scheme today, however, is not a precondition to the maintenance of federal funding. In 2006, Congress repealed the Jacob Wetterling Act and passed the Adam Walsh Child Protection and Safety Act (Adam Walsh Act). Title I of the Adam Walsh Act—known as the Sex Offender Registration and Notification Act (SORNA)—establishes a national baseline for sex offender registration and requires that states receiving federal crime funds substantially comply with the guidelines it outlines. In effect, SORNA serves as model legislation that can be adopted in part or in whole by the states. Nevertheless, most states, including New Jersey, have not substantially implemented SORNA.

SORNA classifies sex offenders into three risk tiers—Tiers I, II, and III—for registration and notification purposes, depending solely on the nature of the offense. If New Jersey strictly followed federal law, C.K. would be classified as a Tier III offender based on his juvenile aggravated sexual assault adjudication. The offender's tier assignment, in turn, determines the duration of his registration requirements. Unlike N.J.S.A. 2C:7-2(g), SORNA has no permanent lifetime registration provision for juveniles. A juvenile Tier III offender, although subject to presumptive lifetime registration, is eligible under SORNA to have his registration requirements terminated after twenty-five years if he has a "clean record." Although Tier I and II offenders are subject to fifteen-year and twenty-five-year registration periods, respectively, Tier I offenders are allowed to apply for a shortened registration period.

Currently, under SORNA, states have discretion whether to include juveniles on their public sex-offender registry websites. In 2016, the United States Attorney General implemented new SORNA guidelines governing juvenile offenders. Under those guidelines, states that do not register juveniles who have committed serious sex offenses may still be compliant with SORNA if the federal government finds that those states have nonetheless "substantially implemented SORNA's juvenile registration requirements" through other means.

Moreover, the United States Attorney General may exempt a state from implementing a provision of SORNA that "would place the jurisdiction in violation of its constitution, as determined by a ruling of the jurisdiction's highest court." In short, a state's highest court can declare unconstitutional a state's sex-offender registration provision without necessarily jeopardizing a state's federal funding.

Before the passage of subsection (g) of N.J.S.A. 2C:7–2 in 2002, subsection (f) governed the termination of registration requirements for all adult and juvenile sex offenders. N.J.S.A. 2C:7–2(f), which is still operative, provides that

> a person required to register under this act may make application to the Superior Court of this State to terminate the obligation upon proof that the person has not committed an offense within 15 years following conviction or release from a correctional facility for any term of imprisonment imposed, whichever is later, and is not likely to pose a threat to the safety of others.

Subsection (f) was part of the original Megan's Law registration and notification requirements, which we declared constitutional in *Doe*. . . .

In *J.G.*, this Court grappled with the implication of applying the presumptive lifetime registration requirements of N.J.S.A. 2C:7–2(f) to juveniles under the age of fourteen. In that case, J.G. pled guilty in family court to committing a second-degree sexual assault. At the time of the assault, J.G. was ten years old and the victim, his cousin, just eight years old. The family court imposed a suspended indeterminate custodial sentence not to exceed three years, ordered J.G. to attend a family counseling program, and advised J.G. that he was subject to the Megan's Law lifetime registration and community notification requirements. . . .

We emphasized our Juvenile Code's continued focus on rehabilitation as evidenced by such dispositional alternatives as individual and family counseling, academic and vocational education, work programs, and community service. We also acknowledged the goals of Megan's Law, which focus on the need to protect society from sex offenders by disseminating critical information to the public. In viewing the two statutory schemes, seemingly in conflict, we found "implausible and anomalous the notion that a child 'sex offender' such as J.G. should pursuant to Megan's Law be subject to a lifetime registration requirement merely on the basis of a delinquency adjudication that included no effort to assess his true culpability."

In reconciling the rehabilitative goals of the Juvenile Code and the public safety goals of Megan's Law, we held that for an adjudicated juvenile sex offender under age fourteen, the "registration and community notification orders shall terminate at age eighteen," provided the juvenile can establish in the Law Division by "clear and convincing evidence that [he] is not likely to pose a threat to the safety of others." . . .

Less than a year after our *J.G.* decision in 2001, for the reasons previously discussed, the Legislature enacted the permanent, irrevocable lifetime registration requirements in subsection (g) that are applicable to adult as well as juvenile offenders. In this case, our focus is only on those juveniles between the ages of fourteen and seventeen adjudicated delinquent in family court for sex offenses falling within the ambit of subsection (g). We agree with the Appellate Division's determination in In re Registrant L.E. that the Legislature did not intend to override the rights provided in *J.G.* to juvenile sex offenders under age fourteen who are authorized to seek termination of their registration and notification requirements at age eighteen. . . .

Our laws and jurisprudence recognize that juveniles are different from adults—that juveniles are not fully formed, that they are still developing and maturing, that their mistakes and wrongdoing are often the result of factors related to their youth, and therefore they are more amenable to rehabilitation and more worthy of redemption. Our juvenile justice system is a testament to society's judgment that children bear a special status, and therefore a unique approach must be taken in dealing with juvenile offenders, both in measuring culpability and setting an appropriate disposition. Indeed, the United States Supreme Court has explained that juvenile courts were created "to provide measures of guidance and rehabilitation for the child and protection for society, not to fix criminal responsibility, guilt and punishment." Kent v. United States, 383 U.S. 541, 554 (1966).

Among the purposes of the Juvenile Code, N.J.S.A. 2A:4A–20 to –92, is "to remove from children committing delinquent acts certain statutory consequences of criminal behavior, and to substitute therefor an adequate program of supervision, care and rehabilitation, and a range of sanctions designed to promote accountability and protect the public." Although rehabilitation, historically, has been the primary focus of the juvenile justice system, a second purpose—increasingly so in recent times—is protection of the public.

Nevertheless, rehabilitation and reformation of the juvenile remain a hallmark of the juvenile system, as evidenced by the twenty enumerated dispositions available to the family court in sentencing a juvenile adjudicated delinquent. The range of dispositional options signifies that a "'one size fits all' approach" does not apply in the juvenile justice system. The juvenile system's flexibility in selecting an appropriate disposition for a young offender allows the family court to take into account "the complex, diverse, and changing needs of youth" and to address "the unique emotional, behavioral, physical, and educational problems of each juvenile before the court."

In a series of landmark cases, the United States Supreme Court declared unconstitutional legal regimes that imposed capital punishment on juvenile offenders, Roper v. Simmons, 543 U.S. 551, 568–70 (2005); life without parole on juveniles convicted of non-homicide offenses, Graham v. Florida, 560 U.S. 48, 82 (2010); and mandatory life without parole on juveniles convicted of homicide offenses, Miller v. Alabama, 567 U.S. 460, 489 (2012). In striking down each of those statutory schemes, relying on the Eighth Amendment's ban on cruel and unusual punishment, the Court grounded its decisions on commonly accepted scientific and sociological notions about the unique characteristics of youth and the progressive emotional and behavioral development of juveniles. . . .

Based on scientific and sociological studies, the United States Supreme Court and this Court have acknowledged that (1) "[a] lack of maturity and an underdeveloped sense of responsibility are found in youth more often than in adults," (2) "juveniles are more vulnerable or susceptible to negative influences" and "have less control . . . over their own environment," and (3) the personality and character traits of juveniles "are more transitory, less fixed," and "not as well formed as that of an adult." Scientific studies reveal that "parts of the brain involved in behavior control continue to mature through late adolescence," accounting for one of the "fundamental differences between juvenile and adult minds." As a result, "[j]uve-niles are more capable of change than are adults, and their actions are less likely to be evidence of 'irretrievably depraved character.'" Because juveniles are in a state of becoming, they "'have a greater claim than adults to be forgiven for failing to escape negative influences in their whole environment,' and there is 'a greater possibility . . . that a minor's character deficiencies will be reformed.'"

In finding unconstitutional juvenile life sentences without parole in non-homicide cases, the United States Supreme Court concluded that just because a juvenile defendant "posed an immediate risk" at one point in his young life does not mean that he will "be a risk to society for the rest of his life.". . .

Other state courts of last resort that have addressed the constitutionality of long-term registration and notification requirements imposed on juvenile sex offenders offer guidance.

In In re C.P., the Ohio Supreme Court declared an Ohio statute that sub-jected certain juvenile offenders to automatic and mandatory lifetime sex-offender registration and notification requirements—with the potential for reclassification after twenty-five years—violative of the cruel-and-unusual-punishment and due-process clauses of the Federal and Ohio Constitutions. . . . Under an Ohio statute, which adopted federal SORNA, C.P. was automatically classified as a Tier III sex offender, which required him to register with the sheriff every ninety days and to comply with community notification requirements. . . .

In striking down the statute on constitutional grounds, the Ohio Supreme Court reasoned: (1) the lifetime registration and notification requirements are imposed at an age when the juvenile offender's character is not yet fixed; (2) the "statutory scheme gives the juvenile judge no role in determining how dangerous a child offender might be or what level of registration or notification would be adequate to preserve the safety of the public"; and (3) "the juvenile judge never gets an opportunity to determine whether the juvenile offender has responded to rehabilitation or whether he remains a threat to society." The Court observed that "[f]ew labels are as damaging in today's society as 'convicted sex offender'" and that sex offenders are "'the lepers of the criminal justice system.'" The Court determined that "[l]ifetime registration and notification requirements run con-trary to [the law's] goals of rehabilitating the offender and aiding his mental and physical development."

Similarly, the Pennsylvania Supreme Court declared that Pennsylvania's statute imposing lifetime registration and notification requirements on sexually violent juvenile offenders violated the state constitution's due process guarantee. In re J.B., 107 A.3d 1, 2, 10, 14–16 (2014). The Pennsylvania statute authorized termination of the registration requirements after twenty-five years, provided the juvenile could establish he did not reoffend within that period, successfully completed a rehabilitation program and court-ordered supervision, and was "not likely to pose a threat to the safety of any other person." Like the Ohio statute, Pennsylvania's statute is modeled after the federal SORNA statute. Nevertheless, the Pennsylvania high court held that the sex-offender registration statute vio-lated the due process rights of juvenile offenders "by utilizing the irrebuttable presumption that all juvenile offenders 'pose a high risk of committing additional sexual offenses.' The court explained that an irrebuttable presumption doctrine should not apply when a "presumption is not universally true and a reasonable alternative means currently exists for determining which juvenile offenders are likely to reoffend."

In *J.B.*, the Pennsylvania Supreme Court held that the registration statute's "presumption that sexual offenders pose a high risk of recidivating is not universally true when applied to juvenile offenders" because, as studies suggest, "many of those who commit sexual offenses as juveniles do so as a result of impulsivity and sexual curiosity, which diminish with rehabilitation and general maturation." The court concluded that the registration statute's other parts, authorizing individualized assessments for determining which juveniles posed a high risk of reoffending, provided a reasonable alternative to the use of a discredited presumption.

We now determine whether the categorical lifetime registration and notification requirements imposed on juvenile offenders by N.J.S.A. 2C:7–2(g) passes muster under the substantive due process guarantee of our State Constitution. . . .

. . . The guarantee of substantive due process requires that a statute reasonably relate to a legitimate legislative purpose and not impose arbitrary or discriminatory burdens on a class of individuals. . . .

N.J.S.A. 2C:7–2(g) is grounded on the irrebuttable presumption that juveniles adjudicated delinquent for committing certain sex offenses will forever pose a danger to society. That irrebuttable presumption disregards any individual assessment of whether a particular registrant is likely to reoffend, long after the adjudication and long after the juvenile has become an adult. Those juveniles are, in effect, branded as irredeemable—at a point when their lives have barely begun and before their personalities are fully formed. They must carry this stigma even if they can prove that they pose no societal threat. But that irrebuttable lifetime presumption is not supported by scientific and sociological studies or our jurisprudence and is not needed given the fifteen-year look back required by subsection (f). . . .

. . . Subsection (g) has the perverse effect of keeping on the sex-offender registry those juveniles who have completed their rehabilitation, not reoffended, and who can prove after a fifteen-year look-back period that they are not likely to pose a societal threat. When, in the case of juveniles, the remedial purpose of Megan's Law—rehabilitation of the offender and protection of the public—is satisfied, then the continued constraints on their lives and liberty pursuant to subjection (g), long after they have become adults, takes on a punitive aspect that cannot be justified by our Constitution. . . .

For the reasons expressed, we hold that N.J.S.A. 2C:7–2(g) is unconstitutional as applied to juveniles adjudicated delinquent as sex offenders.

NOTES AND QUESTIONS

1. How does the description of juvenile court in *C.K.* court differ from the description in *Devon T.*? What might explain the difference? What is the significance of the difference?

2. The *C.K.* court holds that a lifetime sex offender registration requirement for an offense committed while a minor violates due process, but a requirement that lasts a minimum of 15 years does not. Why? Note that Pennsylvania in *J.B.*,

which is discussed in *C.K.*, held that a requirement that lasted at least 25 years violated due process.

    3. In the Interest of T.H., 913 N.W.2d 578 (Iowa 2018), described the consequences of being required to register as a sex offender under Iowa law. While specific requirements vary some from jurisdiction to jurisdiction, this description is representative of most registration laws:

> T.H. must appear in person to register with the sheriff of each county where he resides, works, or attends. If T.H. changes his residence, employment, or school he must notify the county sheriff within five business days. If T.H. moves to, works in, or attends school in a new jurisdiction, he must notify the sheriff in the county of his principal residence of his presence in the new jurisdiction. If T.H. plans to leave the county for more than five days, he must notify the sheriff of his intentions and provide the location and period of time that he will be staying out of the county. Every three months, T.H. must appear in person to verify the location of his residence, employment, and school. He will also pay an annual registration fee of twenty-five dollars.
>
> Because T.H. committed an offense against a minor, he is subject to a number of exclusion zones and employment restrictions. He may not be present upon, nor loiter within 300 feet of, the property of an elementary or secondary school, except for the school he attends. He similarly may not be present upon, nor loiter within 300 feet of, the property of a public library, absent prior written permission by the library administrator. T.H. also may not be present upon, nor loiter within 300 feet of, the property of a child care facility, absent prior written permission by the facility. T.H. may not loiter on the premises of any facility for dependent adults, nor may he be present at an event that provides services or programming for dependent adults. Finally, T.H. may not be present upon nor loiter within 300 feet of any place intended primarily for the use of minors including but not limited to a playground available to the public, a children's play area available to the public, a recreational or sport-related activity area when in use by a minor, a swimming or wading pool available to the public when in use by a minor, or a beach available to the public when in use by a minor.
>
> Throughout the duration of his registration, T.H. may not work or volunteer for a "municipal, county, or state fair or carnival when a minor is present on the premises." He also may not work or volunteer at a "children's arcade, an amusement center having coin or token operated devices for entertainment, or facilities providing programs or services intended primarily for minors, when a minor is present." T.H. similarly may not work or volunteer at a "public or nonpublic elementary or secondary school, child care facility, or public library." He is also prevented from working or volunteering at "any place intended primarily for use by minors including but not limited to a playground, a children's play area, recreational or sport-related activity area, a swimming or wading pool, or a beach." He may not work or volunteer for any business that "operates a motor vehicle primarily marketing, from or near the motor vehicle, the sale and dispensing of ice cream or other food products to minors." As well, T.H. may not be employed by a "facility providing services for dependent adults or at events where dependent adults participate in programming."
>
> Because T.H. is a minor, he is not subject to any residency restrictions. However, if T.H. is still required to register after becoming an adult, he will not be permitted to reside within 2000 feet of a school or child care facility. As well, should

the juvenile court see fit, T.H. may be supervised by an electronic tracking and monitoring system.

T.H.'s registration information will be publicized on the sex offender registry website, which is searchable by "name, county, city, zip code, and geographic radius." The website will also publish T.H.'s full name, photographs, date of birth, home address, and physical description, including scars, marks, or tattoos. The website provides the statutory citation and text of his offense, as well as informs the public whether T.H. is subject to residence restrictions, employment restrictions, and exclusion zones.

Members of the general public may also contact the county sheriff's office and request additional information about T.H. A member of the public that contacts the sheriff and provides T.H.'s date of birth, which is publicized on the sex offender registry website, may request a list of schools T.H. has attended, the names and addresses of his current and former employers, locations and dates of any temporary lodging, and his vehicle information.

913 N.W.2d at 585-586.

4. While *C.K.* cites cases from Pennsylvania and Ohio that find juvenile sex offender registration requirements unconstitutional, the outcomes of recent constitutional challenges to juvenile sex offender registration statutes are mixed, as are the bases for the constitutional challenges. Other courts besides the Ohio Supreme Court have dealt with the claim that long registration requirements violate the Cruel and Unusual Punishments Clause, but several have held that the clause does not even apply because registration is not a punishment. In re J.C., 221 Cal. Rptr.3d 579 (Cal. App. 2017); In re A.C., 54 N.E.3d 952 (Ill. App. 2016); State v. Boche, 885 N.W.2d 523 (Nev. 2016). Similarly, In re Nick H., 123 A.3d 229 (Md. 2015), held that a registration statute is not an unconstitutional ex post facto law because registration is not a punishment. In contrast, In the Interest of T.H, *above*, held that registration is punishment but that it is not cruel and unusual. State v. Eighth Judicial Dist. Ct. (Logan D.), 306 P.3d 369 (Nev. 2013), rejected procedural due process, void for vagueness, and ex post facto challenges, and Vaughn v. State, 391 P.3d 1086 (Wyo. 2017), rejected equal protection, substantive and procedural due process, and ex post facto challenges. On the other hand, People in the Interest of Z.V., 757 N.W.2d 595 (S.D. 2008), held that its statute violated equal protection because, unlike the registration statute for adults, it did not provide juveniles an opportunity to have their names removed from the registry.

5. As of 2018, only eighteen states had substantially complied with the requirements of SORNA. Office of Sex Offender Sentencing, Monitoring, Apprehending, Registering, and Tracking, SORNA Implementation Status, https://smart.gov/sorna-map.htm.

6. The growing phenomenon of sexting, teenagers creating, sharing, and forwarding sexually suggestive nude or nearly nude images of minors, raises additional issues. Teens pictured in images or found with provocative images on their cell phones have been prosecuted for offenses ranging from disorderly conduct and open lewdness to illegal use of a minor, felony sexual abuse of children, and child pornography. A 2015 survey found that twenty states have specific laws about sexting, but they vary greatly. "For example, ten states, including Utah, Florida,

and Georgia, have felony provisions for sexting. Meanwhile, ten states, including Pennsylvania, Nevada, and Texas, have legal provisions to treat sexting as a violation. In these less serious states, judges order a fine, counseling, or community service. . . . When sexting occurs between two minors, again, there is much variation between states in how to prosecute these cases. Generally, however, the laws treat sexting between minors with more levity than in anti-child porn cases. For example, some states do not require sex offender registration, as is the case in Rhode Island, Vermont, and Nevada. . . . Consent can be a defense to sending or receiving sexts, but generally only between two adults. . . . [O]nly Nebraska treats consent as an affirmative defense if sexting occurred between two minors. Otherwise, like with statutory rape laws, minors cannot provide consent." Bark Technologies, State-by-State Differences in Sexting Laws (Dec. 1, 2017), citing Sameer Hinduja, Ph.D. & Justin W. Patchin, Ph.D., State Sexting Laws: A Brief Review of State Sexting and Revenge Porn Laws and Policies (July 2015), https://cyberbullying.org/state-sexting-laws.pdf.

7. Today an adjudication of delinquency has other collateral consequences in common with criminal convictions. All states except North Carolina include juvenile adjudications in criminal history scores for purposes of applying sentencing guidelines, though in some states they do not weigh as heavily as adult convictions. Rhys Hester et al., Prior Record Enhancements at Sentencing: Unsettled Justifications and Unsettling Consequences, 47 Crime & Just. 209, 216 (2018). In some jurisdictions, adjudication as a delinquent for a felony makes it illegal for the minor to possess firearms as an adult under statutes that prohibit possession by felons. A minor who has been adjudicated delinquent may be disqualified from military service, although waivers are sometimes available. Juvenile adjudications can also have adverse immigration consequences, even though they are not "convictions" under federal immigration law. Joanna C. Kloet, It's Not (Fundamentally) Fair!: The Right to Counsel on the Immigration Consequences of Juvenile Misconduct, 27 U. Fla. J. L. & Pub. Pol'y 329 (2016); Theo Liebmann, Adverse Consequences and Constructive Opportunities for Immigrant Youth in Delinquency Proceedings, 88 Temp. L. Rev. 869 (2016). On collateral consequences generally see Joy Radice, The Juvenile Record Myth, 106 Geo. L. J. 365 (2018).

A.J. v. Eighth Judicial District Court

394 P.3d 1209 (2017)

HARDESTY, J.: Petitioner A.J. has been in foster care for most of her life. When A.J. was 15 years old, she was recruited by an older man into the Las Vegas sex trade. In July 2015, A.J. was stopped by a Las Vegas Metropolitan Police Department (LVMPD) officer while she was walking back and forth on Tropicana Avenue. A.J. initially refused to provide her identifying information to the police officers but later provided the requested information. During the stop, A.J. admitted that she had been working as a prostitute for the last three months. A.J. was then arrested for soliciting prostitution and loitering for the purpose of prostitution and transferred to Clark County Juvenile Hall.

Due to the nature of her charges, A.J.'s case was transferred to the juvenile court's sexually exploited youth calendar. The State filed a delinquency petition charging A.J. with only obstructing an officer based on her refusal to provide identifying information (Petition 1). A.J. entered an admission to the charge and was adjudicated as a delinquent. She was placed on formal probation for a period of 12 months, with a suspended commitment to the Division of Child and Family Services (DCFS), and with various conditions, including no contact with persons and places involved in prostitution and home placement through the Clark County Department of Family Services (CCDFS).

A.J. was placed at St. Jude's Ranch for Children on GPS monitoring. Less than a month after placement, GPS monitoring was removed and A.J. ran away from St. Jude's. In September, LVMPD again stopped A.J. on Tropicana Avenue for suspected solicitation of prostitution. A.J. was subsequently arrested for soliciting prostitution after agreeing to perform a sexual act for a fee with an undercover police officer.

A.J. again appeared in juvenile court. A.J. was released to Child Haven because she lost her placement at St. Jude's after running away. The State filed a second petition (Petition 2), alleging a violation of probation for violating curfew and associating with places involved in prostitution. A.J. ran away again, resulting in the State filing a third petition (Petition 3), alleging violation of probation for being in an unauthorized location. The juvenile court then determined that A.J. would remain detained pending entry of a plea.

In October, A.J. admitted to a violation of probation on Petition 2, and Petition 3 was dismissed. A.J. was continued on formal probation and was released to CCDFS once placement was located. A placement home was located in November, and the GPS ankle monitor was removed. A.J. ran away from her placement, and a writ of attachment was issued. A.J. was arrested on the writ, and the State filed a fourth petition alleging another violation of probation (Petition 4). A.J. appeared in juvenile court again and was ordered detained. A formal report and disposition was set and the juvenile court subsequently committed A.J. to DCFS for placement at the Caliente Youth Center.

A.J. petitions this court for a writ of mandamus or prohibition directing the juvenile court to vacate its orders adjudicating her as a delinquent and apply the provisions of NRS 62C.240....

In 2015, the Legislature unanimously passed Assembly Bill (A.B.) 153, later codified as NRS 62C.240. NRS 62C.240 provides, in relevant part:

> 1. If the district attorney files a petition with the juvenile court alleging that a child who is less than 18 years of age has engaged in prostitution or the solicitation of prostitution, the juvenile court:
> (a) Except as otherwise provided in paragraph (b), shall:
> (1) Place the child under the supervision of the juvenile court pursuant to a supervision and consent decree, without a formal adjudication of delinquency; and
> (2) Order that the terms and conditions of the supervision and consent decree include, without limitation, services to address the sexual exploitation of the child and any other needs of the child, including, without limitation, any counseling and medical treatment for victims of sexual assault in accordance with the provisions of NRS 217.280 to 217.350, inclusive.

The parties agree that NRS 62C.240 was enacted to "ensure[] that children are treated as victims of commercial sexual exploitation rather than juvenile delinquents." The parties disagree, however, as to what would trigger the application of NRS 62C.240. The State argues that, under the plain language of the statute, the application of NRS 62C.240 depends on the charges alleged in the petition filed by the district attorney. Specifically, the State contends that, because the triggering event for the application of NRS 62C.240 is the district attorney charging prostitution or solicitation, the statute does not limit prosecutorial discretion, and the charges alleged in the petition control.

A.J. argues that the statute's legislative history does not support the State's interpretation as it would allow the district attorney to avoid triggering the statute by alleging fictitious conduct that does not involve prostitution or solicitation even if the juvenile's conduct puts her within the class of those intended to be protected. Therefore, A.J. argues, an interpretation of NRS 62C.240 in line with the legislative intent and public policy dictates that when the underlying circumstances of the arrest, the referral charge, or other persuasive evidence demonstrate that prostitution or solicitation was the basis for the juvenile's arrest, the court must apply NRS 62C.240. We agree. . . .

The legislative history of NRS 62C.240 indicates that the Legislature intended for the conduct and circumstances surrounding an arrest to trigger NRS 62C.240, not fictitious conduct the district attorney alleges in the petition. . . .

Here, the arresting officer stated in the declaration of arrest that A.J. was arrested for soliciting prostitution and loitering for the purpose of prostitution. The declaration of arrest does not indicate that A.J. was arrested for obstruction, yet that was the only charge the district attorney alleged in Petition 1. The circumstances leading to A.J.'s original delinquency adjudication are precisely those which the Legislature intended to trigger the application of NRS 62C.240.

The legislative history further demonstrates the intent for NRS 62C.240 was not to allow additional delinquency petitions to be filed for certain violations of the conditions of a consent decree. In contemplating a situation in which a juvenile was under court supervision and a consent decree pursuant to NRS 62C.240, Mr. Frierson testified that "[i]f conditions [of the consent decree] are violated, the district attorney *will not* be able to file a delinquent petition as a result of that violation." However, "[t]he district attorney *can* file an additional petition if it is an act not relating to the *circumstance surrounding the decree*." Here, as a result of Petition 1, A.J. was placed on formal probation, the terms of which included no contact with persons and places involved in prostitution. A.J. subsequently violated the terms of her probation, and the district attorney filed Petition 2. In the petition, the district attorney alleged that A.J. violated the terms of her probation by associating with places involved in prostitution. A.J. was then adjudicated as a delinquent for a second time based on an act that would have triggered NRS 62C.240 protection if she had been under court supervision pursuant to a consent decree rather than formal probation.

Finally, the Legislature also discussed prosecutorial discretion during hearings on NRS 62C.240. Assemblyman P.K. O'Neill asked John T. Jones, Jr., representing the Nevada District Attorneys Association, if NRS 62C.240 would help juveniles in circumstances where a police officer makes an arrest for engaging in prostitution, but charges a different, nonprostitution crime, "just to get [the juvenile] off the street." Mr. Jones replied: "What happens now in practice is that the officers book the kids under solicitation or some other type of prostitution-related crime. The district attorneys, especially in Clark County, will work with . . . [the] defense attorneys to find some other nonprostitution-related crime to plead them to." The situation Mr. Jones described is the exact situation in which A.J. finds herself. She was arrested for solicitation of prostitution but charged with obstruction to avoid the solicitation charge. Before the enactment of NRS 62C.240, exercising that type of prosecutorial discretion may have been in the juvenile's best interest. However, it is clear from the testimony cited above that the Legislature intended to make the practice of filing fictitious charges in lieu of charges for solicitation or prostitution unnecessary by enacting NRS 62C.240.

Liberally construing the statute with what reason and public policy dictate, we hold that the Legislature clearly intended for NRS 62C.240 to be triggered when circumstances surrounding the arrest plainly demonstrate that the juvenile was arrested for engaging in prostitution or solicitation of prostitution. We further hold that the protections of NRS 62C.240 apply to prostitution-related crimes committed contemporaneous to an act that would otherwise trigger those protections, including, without limitation, trespassing, loitering, or curfew violations. However, our decision should not be read to insulate juveniles from delinquency adjudication based on different, nonprostitution-related crimes committed contemporaneous to an act that would otherwise trigger NRS 62C.240. For example, NRS 62C.240 would not apply to a juvenile who engages in prostitution and commits a robbery in the course of such conduct. In that circumstance, a district attorney is not prevented from filing a delinquency petition based on the robbery charge, independent of any charges for engaging in prostitution. . . .

Accordingly, we grant A.J.'s petition for extraordinary relief and direct the clerk of this court to issue a writ of mandamus instructing the juvenile court to set aside its earlier orders adjudicating A.J. as a delinquent and to enter a supervision and consent decree that includes as part of its terms and conditions other services to address A.J.'s needs as specified in NRS 62C.240.[1]

---

1. We note that although NRS 62C.240 prevents a formal adjudication of delinquency for juveniles who fall within its purview, that statute does not appear to prevent a juvenile court from issuing an order for "any placement of the child that the juvenile court finds to be in the child's best interest," including commitment to a facility for detention of children. However, this appears to conflict with this court's caselaw regarding placement of nondelinquent children in detention facilities. *See* Minor v. Juvenile Div. of Seventh Judicial Dist. Court, 630 P.2d 245, 249–50 (1981) (specifically mentioning the training center located in Caliente, Nevada, and determining that "[t]raining centers are meant to house delinquents and delinquents only," and holding "that nondelinquent children coming within the jurisdiction of the juvenile court *may not be committed to the juvenile correctional institutions*" (emphasis added) (citation omitted)); *see also* NRS 63.030(1) (defining Caliente Youth Center as a "facility for the detention or commitment of children").

While we recognize this potential conflict, the issue is not before us in this case. Thus, we do not address it here.

NOTES AND QUESTIONS

1. Before Nevada enacted the statute prohibiting delinquency adjudications of minors for prostitution, police and prosecutors in Las Vegas often charged a minor picked up for prostitution with another offense not related to prostitution. In *A.J.* the prosecutor sought to continue this practice, rather than employing the procedure that the new statute created. Why might the prosecutor have preferred the older strategy, assuming that his or her goal was to protect minors who are victims of sex trafficking? Why did A.J. and her attorney object to this strategy as a practical matter? What approach does the "kids are different" argument support?

Some prosecutors claim that without the threat of a criminal conviction or imprisonment, young prostitutes will fail to appear at court hearings, resulting in the dismissal of charges against pimps. Law enforcement often echoes these concerns. Others support arresting, detaining, and prosecuting prostituted children to keep them off the streets and ensure their cooperation with social services. Proponents of this view reason that because strategies of persuasion and common sense have failed with these youth, it is necessary to place them in secure custody for their own protection.

2. After *A.J.*, when could a prosecutor charge a minor who was arrested for prostitution or soliciting prostitution with an offense that could result in a delinquency adjudication?

3. Of the almost 25,000 runaways reported to the National Center for Missing and Exploited Children in 2017, one in seven are believed to have been victims of child sex trafficking. NCMEC, Child Sex Trafficking (2017), http://www.missingkids.org/1in6. Children in foster care or group homes are at a particularly high risk of being trafficked. Studies estimate that 50 to more than 90 percent of children who were victims of child sex trafficking had been involved with child welfare services. Child Welfare Information Gateway, Human Trafficking and Child Welfare: A Guide for Child Welfare Agencies 4 (July 2017), https://www.childwelfare.gov/pubPDFs/trafficking_agencies.pdf.

4. Laws that require different treatment of minors who have been trafficked are broadly called safe harbor laws. The substance of safe harbor laws varies greatly. Some states prohibit prosecution; others permit prosecution but have diversion programs that are available at the discretion of the prosecutor. In a number of states prosecution is allowed, but minors may assert an affirmative defense that prevents conviction; some but not all of these statutes allow an affirmative defense only if the minor was subjected to fraud, force, or coercion. Sarah Wasch et al., An Analysis of Safe Harbor Laws for Minor Victims of Commercial Sexual Exploitation: Implication for Pennsylvania and Other States 2-4 (Field Center for Children's Policy, Practice & Research, University of Pennsylvania, Mar. 11, 2016), https://fieldcenteratpenn.org/wp-content/uploads/2013/05/SafeHarborWhitePaperFINAL.pdf.

New York enacted the first safe harbor law, which required offering services and which went into effect in 2010. As of 2017, 23 states and the District of Columbia prohibited criminal prosecution of minors for prostitution; two states limited the protection to minors younger than 16. Thirteen of the states extended the prohibition to other, related offenses such as solicitation of prostitution. Shared Hope International, National State Law Survey: Non-Criminalization of Child Sex Trafficking Victims (2018), http://sharedhope.org/wp-content/uploads/2016/03/NSL_Survey_Non-Criminalization-of-Juvenile-Sex-Trafficking-Victims.pdf. In 36 states and the District of Columbia, juvenile sex trafficking victims cannot be adjudicated as delinquent for prostitution but are instead referred to specialized services. National State Law Survey: Protective Responses of Juvenile Sex Trafficking (JuST) Victims (2018), http://sharedhope.org/wp-content/uploads/2016/03/NSL_Survey_Protective-Responses-for-Child-Sex-Trafficking-Victims.pdf.

PROBLEM

A petition filed in juvenile court alleges that William Randolph is a delinquent child because he committed murder on or about July 1. William is a member of the North Side Dragons, a youth gang some of whose members have engaged in criminal activities, including assaults resulting in serious injuries and death, as well as thefts of money, clothing, and cars.

Before July 1, William, like many other young people associated with the Dragons, had not committed any serious crimes with gang members, although he had a history of minor offenses committed on his own. On July 1, Ron Castle, the gang leader, told William that he, Ron, and three other members were going to rob a liquor store. William did not want to participate and offered an excuse; Ron, however, told him that a member who had refused to help in a gang activity was "a traitor, and we all know what happens to traitors." William knew that gang members said that loyalty was the first duty to the gang and that the penalty for disloyalty was death. He also knew that Ron had twice been arrested on suspicion of murder, although he had never been convicted.

Accordingly, William agreed to go along with the others and participated in the robbery of a liquor store. During the course of the robbery, Ron beat the owner, who suffered severe injuries from which he died three days later.

Ron and William have been charged with murder, Ron as the principal and William as an aider and abettor. What arguments should William's lawyer make in his defense, and how should the prosecutor respond? Consider the following materials, as well as those above.

LEGAL BACKGROUND

State Penal Code § 203
(1) Criminal homicide constitutes murder if the actor: . . .
(d) while in the commission . . . of aggravated robbery, robbery, rape, arson, burglary, or kidnapping, causes the death of another person.

§ 205 Criminal liability for conduct of another.
When one person engages in conduct which constitutes an offense, another person is criminally liable for such conduct when, acting with the

mental culpability required for the commission thereof, he solicits, requests, commands, importunes, or intentionally aids such person to engage in such conduct.

§ 240 Duress.

(1) In any prosecution for an offense, it is an affirmative defense that the defendant engaged in the proscribed conduct because he was coerced to do so by the use or threatened imminent use of unlawful physical force upon him or a third person, which force or threatened force a person of reasonable firmness in his situation would have been unable to resist.

(2) The defense of duress as defined in subdivision one of this section is not available when a person intentionally or recklessly places himself in a situation in which it is probable that he will be subjected to duress.

SOCIAL BACKGROUND

Robert K. Jackson & Wesley D. McBride, *Understanding Street Gangs* 25, 31, 34-36, 40-41 (1985): A gang member views gang activity differently from the general public. Traditions of solidarity and neighborhood cohesiveness run deep. Pride in one's neighborhood, however poor it may be, is intense. The gang member has a driving need to belong and will often profess it in his last, dying breath. He not only needs to belong, but needs to tell others where he is from. This becomes so important that the greeting "Where are you from?" (or, in Latin areas, "Deconde?") [sic] is the standard form of introduction on the street . . . . [A gang member] will proclaim the status of his *barrio* or gang as number one on almost any markable surface or wall. To a gang member, graffiti represents his pride in his neighborhood. . . .

The structure of Hispanic street gangs is similar throughout the western states. Codes of conduct have been established from which traditions have evolved over generations. These traditions are not written, but handed down orally from generation to generation and are referred to as *Movidas.* . . .

A gang member is loyal to the death to his gang. He is proud, even boastful of his membership. If for some reason the Hispanic gang member's family moves from his home gang's turf, he will not exchange loyalties with a gang in his new home. . . .

A traditional gang member will never inform or turn *rata* ("rat") on his home boys, even if faced with death or prison. Loyalty is given at any price. A gang member will seldom disgrace himself or his family by turning informant. . . .

Black street gangs have existed in the Los Angeles area for many years. In the 1920's the Boozie gang was very active, committing street crimes around 18th Street and Central Avenue. . . .

Presently, the number of black street gangs and their activity levels seem to follow varying cycles; at times almost non-existent, while at other times many gangs become active and violent. The most recent cycle began to emerge in the early 1970s.

At that time a group of young high school age thugs began to terrorize their local campus and the neighborhoods in which they lived. This gang called themselves the "Crips" and extorted money from other students and were involved in violence. . . . [I]t was not uncommon for a few of the members to approach another youth and ask him to join their gang. If his answer was no, he would be beaten senseless and left on the ground. Next day the gang would again approach the victim and repeat their offer. Each refusal to join resulted in some form of physical abuse.

Thus, four choices were left to the victim. He could join, flee, face repeated violence, or seek assistance. Unfortunately, school officials and the police were unable to provide continuous protection, and this led a number of victims to form their own gang for protection against the Crips. . . .

ARLEN EGLEY JR., ET AL *HIGHLIGHTS OF THE 2012 NATIONAL YOUTH GANG SURVEY* 2(OJJDP Dec. 2014), http://www.ojjdp.gov/pubs/248025.pdf.: Approximately 85 percent of larger cities, 50 percent of suburban counties, and 15 percent of rural counties have reported gang activity in each of the past four surveys. The greatest change in recent years has occurred in smaller cities, where the percentage of agencies reporting gang activity has significantly declined—approximately 25 percent reported gang activity in 2012, down from 34 percent in 2010. This is the lowest rate recorded in more than a decade. . . .

In terms of gang-related crime, law enforcement agencies report that they do not regularly record offenses as "gang related," with the exception of homicides. Thus, the NYGS can only report findings related to this one criminal offense type. . . . [R]espondents reported a total of 2,363 gang-related homicides in the United States in 2012. The Federal Bureau of Investigation's Uniform Crime Reports estimates that there were more than 14,800 homicides nationally in 2012. Taken together, these findings suggest that gangs were involved in approximately 16 percent of all homicides in the United States in 2012 and underscore the considerable overlap between gang activity and violent crime.

Compared with the previous 5-year average, the number of gang-related homicides that NYGS respondents reported increased by more than 20 percent in 2012. This increase is due to higher counts of reported gang homicides in certain larger cities in the NYGS sample and also to NYGS respondents reporting more completely compared with previous years (i.e., the increase in 2012 is partly an artifact of agencies reporting more complete data). Fifty-five percent of the responding agencies characterized their gang problems as "staying about the same" in 2012, an increase over the percentage of agencies in 2010 and 2011 and the largest percentage that the survey has ever recorded.

———————

A study published in 2015 found that more than one million youths are gang members—more than triple the number estimated by law enforcement. Gang members come from all backgrounds, with 40 percent identifying as non-Hispanic white. About 2 percent of youth in the U.S. belong to a gang; at age 14 about

5 percent are involved with a gang. Contrary to popular belief, about 400,000 youth leave gangs every year, to be replaced by about 400,000 who join. David C. Pyrooz & Gary Sweeten, Gang Membership Between Ages 5 and 17 Years in the United States, 56(4) J. Adolesc. Health 414 (2015), https://www.jahonline.org/article/S1054-139X(14)00756-3/fulltext.

2.   Offenses for Juveniles Only — Ungovernability, Curfews, and Other "Status Offenses"

Ohio Revised Code § 2151.022 (2018)

As used in this chapter, "unruly child" includes any of the following:

(A) Any child who does not submit to the reasonable control of the child's parents, teachers, guardian, or custodian, by reason of being wayward or habitually disobedient;

(B) Any child who is an habitual truant from school;

(C) Any child who behaves in a manner as to injure or endanger the child's own health or morals or the health or morals of others;

(D) Any child who violates a law . . . that is applicable only to a child.

LEE E. TEITELBAUM, *JUVENILE STATUS OFFENDERS*

3 Encyclopedia of Crime and Justice 983, 984-988
(Sanford H. Kadish, ed., 1983)

Ancient and common-law traditions. The rationale for asserting juvenile court jurisdiction over acts that are not, when committed by adults, considered sufficiently serious to warrant the exercise of public authority rests on norms and values with both ancient and modern aspects.

That part of status offense jurisdiction which enforces a child's obligation to obey parental commands embodies a norm of untraceable antiquity and perhaps of universal acceptance. The Analects of Confucius declare that "a young man's duty is to behave well to his parents at home and to his elders abroad." Prebiblical and pre-Islamic custom, like Roman law, accorded the father sole authority over the life and death of his children, a power which inherently conveyed the right to determine how a child should behave, as well as to judge the gravity of misbehavior. The Old Testament also demanded filial obedience, not only through the Fifth Commandment but in the Book of Deuteronomy (21:18-21), which provides for the execution by stoning of any son found by the elders of the community to have been "disloyal and defiant" to his parents. It says much about prebiblical paternal authority that the Mosaic law, as savage as it now seems, in fact limited a prior parental right by requiring that offending children be put to death only upon the judgment of the community rather than at the absolute discretion of their fathers. . . .

Stubborn-child laws in America. These traditional values also explain the development of American laws directed to stubborn or disobedient children, but only to a limited extent. The earliest American statute concerning unruly children was adopted by the Massachusetts Bay Colony in 1646 (*The Laws and Liberties of*

Massachusetts, p. 6). That ordinance incorporated almost verbatim the language of Deuteronomy and announced the death penalty for male children over the age of sixteen who were "stubborn or rebellious." While it does not appear that any child was in fact put to death by authority of this law, its enactment reflected not only the biblical literalism of Puritan colonists but their strong convictions about the importance of the family to effective social control. . . .

During the early 1800s, houses of refuge for unruly and delinquent children were established in the large cities, and courts were given special jurisdiction over disobedient and ungovernable youths who might for their better moral education be placed, along with children who had committed criminal acts, in reform or industrial schools. . . .

. . . Because the juvenile court was interested in reaching all children in need of help, juvenile codes uniformly incorporated broad jurisdictional definitions. "Delinquency" commonly included not only criminal acts but vagabondage, association with undesirable persons, presence in undesirable places, undesirable but noncriminal conduct, and disobedience to parents or teachers. . . .

Traditional juvenile court acts not only included status with criminal offenses for jurisdictional purposes but provided that all delinquents were subject to the entire range of statutory dispositions, from probation to commitment until majority in an industrial school. This flexible approach to dispositional decisions, like the definition of delinquency, followed from the principle that juvenile court intervention was not intended to measure guilt; the behavior bringing the child to the court's attention was only an indication of need for treatment, and in no way defined the court's dispositional authority. Moreover, the principle that choice of disposition bears no necessary relation to the youth's conduct was commonly followed in practice. In most jurisdictions, children found to be incorrigible or to have committed some other status offense were as likely to be placed in an industrial school as those who engaged in criminal misconduct. . . .

. . . [D]uring the 1950s and 1960s . . . a newly popular theory of deviance suggested that labeling a child as delinquent would promote rather than deter his becoming an offender in the future. According to this labeling theory, which still commands great support, once a person has been called a deviant, and particularly if he is publicly condemned and placed with a group considered deviant, a self-fulfilling prophecy is initiated. Members of the child's community will perceive and respond to such a youth as a delinquent, denying him opportunities that might otherwise be available. Moreover, placement with a deviant group, as by commitment to an institution for delinquents, makes the youth a member of a subculture which identifies itself as deviant or delinquent, and the child will accordingly develop deviant views of the world and of himself. These circumstances may ultimately lead to the commission of deviant acts that might have been avoided if the child had not been so labeled at the outset.

Although initially addressed to the inclusion of noncriminal misconduct within delinquency definitions, this theory suggested as well that treatment before and after adjudication should be differentiated. If juveniles who committed crimes were more serious offenders than those who did not, then commingling incorrigible children with delinquents during pretrial detention or upon commitment to an industrial school might lead to the corruption of the noncriminal offenders. . . . Moreover, if a delinquent identity was developed by placement with delinquents, as labeling theory has it, that consequence could be avoided only by separating criminal children from status offenders for detention and treatment purposes, as well as by adjudicative label.

The criticism of labeling status offenders as delinquents soon received sympathetic attention from legislatures. New York revised its Family Court Act in 1963 by reserving the "delinquency" category for children who committed crimes and by creating a new jurisdictional category, Person in Need of Supervision, to encompass all forms of behavior that were illegal only for children (New York Fam. Ct. Act § 712(b) (1981)). This pattern has been widely followed. By the late 1970s the once-universal commitment to undifferentiated treatment had so eroded that approximately one-half of the states had separated status offense from delinquency jurisdiction, and by 1980, only a handful of states retained the original definition of delinquency. . . .

Differentiation of preadjudicative and postadjudicative treatment of status offenders, however, did not appear as readily. Few states required separate services or facilities when they first drew a distinction between status offenders and delinquents. Children who had committed acts of noncriminal misconduct continued to comprise 30 percent or more of the population of industrial schools, with the rate of institutionalization particularly high for young women. Through most of the 1970s, some 70 percent of all institutionalized girls had been committed for status offenses.

The fact that separate treatment, unlike differentiation by label, involved questions of expense and resources probably deterred state legislative action in this area for some time. Although a few states during the 1970s prohibited commitment of some or all status offenders to state institutions for delinquent children, the greatest impetus for differentiated treatment came from the federal Juvenile Justice and Delinquency Prevention Act of 1974, Pub. L. No. 93-415, 88 Stat. 1109 (codified in scattered sections of 5, 18, 42 U.S.C.). This statute made continued federal funding of state and local juvenile offender programs, after a three-year grace period, contingent on action to deinstitutionalize juvenile status offenders.

In re Brandi B.

743 S.E.2d 882 (W. Va. 2013)

Workman, Justice: On October 11, 2011, the Pocahontas County Attendance Director filed a petition in Pocahontas County Circuit Court against the then 14-year–old petitioner, alleging that she had six unexcused absences from school between September 22 and October 6, 2011 and was therefore a "delinquent child" for committing the status offense of truancy. . . .

. . . [P]etitioner offered to stipulate that she was absent from school on nine days between September 22, 2011 and October 28, 2011, but that six of the nine days were due to an out-of-school suspension resulting from her involvement in a fight. As a result, petitioner denied that she was an habitual truant. Petitioner filed a "Motion for Judgment as a Matter of Law," arguing that the six absences due to suspension constituted "good cause" under West Virginia Code § 49–1–4(15)(C) and could not be used to adjudicate her an habitual truant. Petitioner argued that the three remaining non-suspension unexcused absences were insufficient to prove "habitual" truancy as required by statute.

The circuit court disagreed, reasoning that a student is expected to abide by the code of conduct while at school and that absences occasioned by a failure to do so did not constitute "good cause." The circuit court found that, although the three undisputed absences would not constitute "habitual" truancy, the total nine absences including the six suspension days did. The court then adjudicated petitioner to be a status offender, referred her to DHHR for services and placed her on probation[2] until she graduates from high school. As further part of its disposition, the court ordered that petitioner be placed in the legal custody of DHHR but remain in the physical custody of her biological mother. . . . This appeal followed. . . .

. . . West Virginia Code § 49–1–4(15) describes the conduct making a juvenile susceptible to adjudication as a "status offender." Subparagraph 15(C) provides the pertinent definition at issue herein, and defines "a juvenile who has been adjudicated as one . . . [w]ho is habitually absent from school without good cause" as a status offender. . . .

. . . This Court has historically held that "good cause" determinations prescribed by statute lie within the lower court's discretion.

Nevertheless, petitioner urges this Court to invade the province of the circuit court and decree that disciplinary absences *per se* constitute good cause and thereby judicially insert into the statute a definition which is not there. . . . We find that the statute at issue quite deliberately omits an enumerated list of absences for "good cause" to allow the circuit court to give full effect to the protective and rehabilitative goals of the status offender statutory scheme. . . .

In State ex rel. Harris v. Calendine, 233 S.E.2d 318, 325 (1977), this Court expressly found that "[t]he Legislature has vested the juvenile court with jurisdiction over children who commit [] status offenses so that the court may enforce order, safety, morality, and family discipline within the community." . . .

. . . [N]ot only does West Virginia Code § 49–1–4(15)(C) leave to the circuit court's discretion the determination as to whether absences which form the basis of a truancy petition are "without good cause," it further requires a determination by the court that such absences are "habitual." Although petitioner suggests that the Legislature did not intend for students subject to disciplinary suspensions to be treated as truants, we find nothing in the language of the statute or elsewhere which would demand exemption of students who are absent due to disciplinary suspensions from adjudication as habitual truants. To the contrary, regardless of whether a student is absent from school due to disciplinary suspension or merely lacks the discipline and guidance to ensure regular school attendance, our status

---

2. As part of her probation, the circuit court ordered that petitioner comply with the following terms and conditions: (1) that she not change her status of school unless approved by the circuit court; (2) that she have no unexcused absences/tardiness, failing grades, or disciplinary problems at school; (3) that she abide by her parents' supervision and the terms of her probation; (4) that she "cooperate with the MDT process by attending and participating in any and all meets [sic]"; (5) that she abstain from use/possession of alcohol, drugs, marijuana, controlled substances, or prescriptions not prescribed by a doctor; and (6) that she submit to random drug screens of blood, breath, or urine at the request of the Probation Officer and at her expense.

offender laws seek to address the core problems underlying the absences for the protection of both the juvenile and the public.

Accordingly, we hold that whether a juvenile's absences from school are "habitual" and are "without good cause," pursuant to West Virginia Code § 49–1–4(15)(C) is to be determined on a case-by-case basis. Such determination lies within the sound discretion of the circuit court and is subject to appellate review only upon an abuse of that discretion. In the case *sub judice*, we find no such abuse of discretion.

. . . [P]etitioner further argues that her adjudication under West Virginia Code § 49–1–4(15)(C) on the basis of suspension absences has resulted in an infringement of her constitutional rights to substantive and procedural due process. In that regard, petitioner advances an "as applied" constitutional challenge to West Virginia Code § 49–1–4(15)(C). . . .

. . . Although in *Harris*, this Court described due process as an "inherently elusive concept," we have nonetheless succinctly characterized the right to substantive due process as one of fundamental fairness: "[D]ue process ... is ultimately measured by the concept of fundamental fairness." Although petitioner's argument on this front is not fully developed, it appears that it is this notion of "fundamental fairness" upon which her substantive due process claim is based. In short, petitioner argues simply that it is fundamentally unfair to penalize her lawful compliance with the out-of-school suspension by using the absences occasioned thereby as a basis to adjudicate her an habitual truant.

For purposes of determining whether application of the status offender statutory scheme to petitioner violates substantive due process, it is instructive to note that this Court has held:

> The legislature is vested with a wide discretion in determining what the public interest requires, the wisdom of which may not be inquired into by the courts; however, to satisfy the requirements of due process of law, legislative acts must bear a reasonable relationship to a proper legislative purpose and be neither arbitrary nor discriminatory.

. . .

We therefore are left to determine if adjudicating a juvenile an habitual truant on the basis, in whole or in part, of absences occasioned by an out-of-school suspension is rationally related to a "proper legislative purpose" and further, whether such adjudication is arbitrary or discriminatory. West Virginia Code § 49–1–1(a) (1–3) states that the purpose of the chapter is to provide a "coordinated system of child welfare and juvenile justice," the goals of which are, in part, to "[a]ssure each child care, safety and guidance . . . [s]erve the mental and physical welfare of the child, [and] [p]reserve and strengthen the child's family ties[.]" More pointedly, the child welfare laws are designed to "[p]rovide for early identification of the problems of children and their families, and respond appropriately with measures and services to prevent abuse and neglect or delinquency" and "[p]rovide a system for the rehabilitation of status offenders and juvenile delinquents[.]"

In light of these purposes, we have little difficulty in finding that adjudicating a juvenile a status offender on the basis of absences occasioned by disciplinary suspension is rationally related to the Legislative purpose of "early identification of problems of children and their families" and commensurate rehabilitation of such juveniles. In point of fact, we find status offender adjudication even more critical for a juvenile subject to disciplinary suspension, who is not otherwise being aided or addressed by our child welfare or juvenile justice laws. Clearly, on the basis of the disciplinary action which gave rise to petitioner's suspension, a delinquency petition may have been available to the State. However, we find petitioner's adjudication as an habitual truant under the more lenient status offender laws to have been a measured and compassionate attempt by the State to exercise its sovereign *parens patriae* power to provide early intervention and rehabilitation to petitioner in the least restrictive means available. In light of these considerations, we find nothing arbitrary nor discriminatory about the use of an habitual truancy adjudication occasioned by disciplinary absences to bring petitioner within the ambit of the child welfare and juvenile justice laws; therefore, we find no substantive due process violation.

In addition to substantive due process rights, "[t]he Due Process Clause, Article III, Section 10 of the West Virginia Constitution, requires procedural safeguards against State action which affects a liberty or property interest." Petitioner contends that if absences occasioned by an out-of-school suspension are to be used as a basis for a truancy adjudication, procedural due process requires that she be provided all of the same due process rights at the school level *prior to suspension* to which she is entitled under the circuit court's juvenile jurisdiction. . . .

. . . [P]etitioner expresses concern that use of out-of-school suspension absences to form the basis of a truancy petition essentially leaves truancy adjudications to the whim of principals. Petitioner suggests that principals may indiscriminately use their authority under West Virginia Code § 18A–5–1a (2006) to suspend a student and thereby compel a student to become a "truant," while stripping the student of the due process rights afforded juveniles under West Virginia Code § 49–5–2 when being subjected to a truancy adjudication. We find this concern unfounded. Were this Court to adopt a *per se* rule that absences occasioned by suspension were necessarily lacking in "good cause," or further, that a certain number of such absences were *per se* "habitual," petitioner's argument may have merit. However, as discussed more fully *supra*, the determination of whether an absence is without "good cause" is left to the sound discretion of the circuit court. As such, a mere suspension at the school level does not an habitual truant make. The circuit court is left to determine, in its discretion, not only whether the absences which form the basis of the petition are "without good cause," but also whether such absences are "habitual." Accordingly, a juvenile receives the full benefit of the due process rights afforded by West Virginia Code § 49–5–2 at the instant of a truancy adjudication on the basis, in whole or in part, of suspension absences. Rather than being *denied* adequate due process, a juvenile subject to a truancy adjudication which involves suspension absences actually receives two levels of due process—once at the school level prior to suspension and again at the circuit court level upon adjudication. As such, the "precise nature" of the government functions at issue—enforcement of disciplinary rules at the school level and adjudication for purposes of integration into our juvenile justice system—do not require that school-level due process rise to the level of the procedural protections set forth in West Virginia Code § 49–5–2. . . .

Petitioner next assigns as error the circuit court's disposition arising from her adjudication as a status offender. . . .

West Virginia Code §§ 49–5–11 and –11a govern disposition for juveniles adjudicated as status offenders. West Virginia Code § 49–5–11(d) provides that if allegations alleging a status offense are sustained by clear and convincing proof, "the court shall refer the juvenile to the [DHHR] for services, pursuant to section eleven-a"; however, if the circuit operates a "truancy program," the judge may "in lieu of referring truant juveniles to the department, order that the juveniles be *supervised by his or her probation office.*" (emphasis added).

West Virginia Code § 49–5–11a provides further direction regarding disposition of status offenders. West Virginia Code § 49–5–11a(a) describes the types of services which may be provided by the DHHR and notes that such services "shall be designed to develop skills and supports with their families and to resolve problems related to the juveniles or conflicts with their families." Critically, West Virginia Code § 49–5–11a(b) provides that, if necessary, the DHHR may petition the court for a valid court order: 1) "to enforce compliance with a service plan or to *restrain actions that interfere with or defeat a service plan*"; and/or 2) "to place a juvenile out of home in a nonsecure or staff-secure setting, and/or to place a juvenile in custody of the department" (emphasis added). . . .

These provisions, read in *pari materia*, clearly evince a Legislative intent to permit the circuit court to place a status offender on probation and order terms and conditions of such probation as the court determines necessary to "enforce compliance with a service plan or to restrain actions that interfere with or defeat a service plan[.]"

As noted above, despite petitioner's concession that the statutory scheme grants the circuit court authority to order probation, she contends that the circuit court "threw the book at her" and therefore transformed the rehabilitative means and methods of disposition into "punishment" which was excessive in light of her "first-time" status offense. We are particularly sensitive to such an argument inasmuch as we have previously indicated that the cruel and unusual punishment concepts contained in Article III, Section 5 of the West Virginia Constitution should be broadly applied to status offenders "whom the State has pledged *not* to punish at all, but rather, to protect and rehabilitate."

In *Harris*, we expressly applied the proportionality principles of Article III, Section 5 of the West Virginia Constitution to treatment of status offenders and found that incarceration of status offenders in secure, prison-like facilities was unconstitutional. In reaching that conclusion, we examined three elements utilized by the Fourth Circuit in Hart v. Coiner, 483 F.2d 136 (4th Cir. 1973), to determine if certain "punishment" is constitutionally disproportionate: "(1) the nature of the offense itself; (2) the legislative purpose behind the punishment; and (3) what punishment would have been applied in other jurisdictions." As to the first element, we found that status offenders are "located on the extreme end of the spectrum of juvenile misconduct running from most serious to least serious offenses." As to the second, we reiterated the well-established legislative purpose of the status offender laws to "enforce[e] family discipline, protect[] children, and protect[] society from uncontrolled children[.]"We found that incarceration in prison-like facilities with children guilty of criminal conduct was not rationally related to that end. Finally, we found that other jurisdictions had eliminated incarceration of status offenders;

therefore, we held that incarceration of status offenders in secure, prison-like facilities violated Article III, Section 5 of the West Virginia Constitution.

However, unlike incarceration of status offenders, we find the imposition of a term of probation—even for a first-time status offender—to be not only statutorily authorized, but constitutionally proportionate. It is critical to view probation not under the lens of the criminal justice system, but rather the juvenile justice system. With respect to probationary terms and conditions in the adult, criminal context, "[e]very condition of probation constitutes a restriction of liberty[.]" However, as to juveniles, the United States Supreme Court has acknowledged,

> [J]uveniles, unlike adults, are always in some form of custody. Children, by definition, are not assumed to have the capacity to take care of themselves. They are assumed to be subject to the control of their parents, and if parental control falters, the State must play its part as *parens patriae*. In this respect, the juvenile's liberty interest may, in appropriate circumstances, be subordinated to the State's "*parens patriae* interest in preserving and promoting the welfare of the child."

Schall v. Martin, 467 U.S. 253, 265 (1984) (quoting Santosky v. Kramer, 455 U.S. 745, 766 (1982) (citations omitted)). Moreover, this Court, in reviewing the constitutionality of a curfew ordinance, quoted extensively from and found persuasive like reasoning expressed by the United States Court of Appeals for the District of Columbia in Hutchins v. District of Columbia, 188 F.3d 531 (D.C. Cir. 1999). In particular, we quoted with approval the District Court's findings that

> "[U]nemancipated minors lack some of the most fundamental rights of self-determination—including even the right of liberty in its narrow sense, *i.e.*, the right to come and go at will." . . . [I]t [is] anomalous to say that juveniles have a right to be unsupervised when they are always in some form of custody [and] the recognition of such a right would fly in the face of the state's well-established power of *parens patriae* in preserving and promoting the welfare of children. The state's authority over children's activities is unquestionably broader than that over like actions of adults[.]

We find that supervision by a probation officer and required compliance with terms and conditions designed to integrate with a juvenile's service plan is a tangible and effective means of fulfilling the laudatory goals of the juvenile justice system. . . .

Insofar as the particular terms and conditions of probation ordered by the circuit court are concerned, petitioner highlights only one for substantive attack—not surprisingly, the requirement that she stay enrolled in school until she graduates. Petitioner contends that since the compulsory school attendance statute permits her to withdraw at age seventeen, the circuit court's attempt to force her to remain enrolled beyond seventeen is erroneous. We disagree. First, we note that the circuit court's order does not wholesale prohibit petitioner from withdrawing from school; rather, it indicates that she may not "change her status of school *unless approved by the Court.*" (emphasis added). Secondly, we find that this particular term of probation, obviously, is exquisitely designed to give effect to the very purpose of the underlying adjudication and further does credit to the overall scheme of juvenile justice. We find more than adequate support within the parameters set forth in West Virginia Code § 49–5–11a permitting the court to enter an order "restrain[ing] actions that interfere with or defeat a service plan" to justify this term of probation in light of the basis upon which petitioner was adjudicated a status offender.

As such, subject to our holding set forth *infra* regarding the jurisdictional age limit of the circuit court's order of probation, we find no error in the circuit court's imposition of probation, nor in any of its terms and conditions, including but not limited to the requirement that petitioner stay enrolled in school until graduation, unless otherwise permitted by the circuit court.

Petitioner next argues that the circuit court erred in its disposition by transferring her legal custody to the DHHR without the requisite findings in support of such a transfer. . . .

Without question, status offenders are subject to out-of-home placement and/or a custody transfer. . . . However, as we first noted in *Harris*, committing juveniles to the custody of the state in the absence of a showing of necessity is an improper use of *parens patriae* power. . . .

To that end, this Court has previously articulated the requisite showing and commensurate findings and conclusions required of the circuit court before any such transfer of custody may occur. In Syllabus Point 2, in part, *State v. Damian R.*, 591 S.E.2d 168 (2003), this Court held:

> [A] petition seeking an order regarding transferring custody of the status offender to the Department and/or out-of-home placement under *W. Va.Code*, 49–5–11a(b) (2) [1998] . . . may only be granted upon a showing by clear and convincing evidence that such a custody or placement order is *actually necessary*; that the *effective provision of services cannot occur absent such an order*; and that *all reasonable efforts have been made to provide appropriate services without an out-of-home placement or custody transfer*; and orders granting such placement and/or transfer must be based on *specific findings and conclusions by the court with respect to the grounds for and necessity of the order.*

(emphasis added). As noted hereinabove, the circuit court's order states simply that "it is contrary to the welfare of [petitioner] for her legal custody to remain with her parents and it is in her best interest of the child [sic] to have her legal custody be with the Department[.]" Clearly, the lack of evidence adduced as to this issue and the court's conclusory finding are insufficient to comply with the requirements of *Damian R.* . . .

Finally, petitioner contends that the circuit court erred in ordering that her probation extend until she graduates from high school. Petitioner contends that the circuit court's juvenile jurisdiction over her extends only until the age of eighteen and inasmuch as she will reach the age of eighteen approximately one month prior to the customary commencement of graduating senior classes, the circuit court's order exceeds its jurisdiction. . . .

West Virginia Code § 49–1–2 (1997) provides, in part, that "[a]s used in this chapter, 'juvenile' or 'child' means any person under eighteen years of age." . . .

We therefore find that aspect of the circuit court's order placing petitioner on probation until she "graduates from high school" to be erroneous and remand this case to the circuit court for entry of an order providing that petitioner be placed on probation until the earlier of her eighteenth birthday or graduation from high school. . . .

ANNE R. MAHONEY, *PINS AND PARENTS*

in Beyond Control: Status Offenders in the Juvenile Court 161,
162-164 (Lee E. Teitelbaum & Aidan R. Gough, eds., 1977)

The acts of children who are adjudicated status offenders are not very different from the acts of most adolescents. Yet some adolescents come to court and others do not. One important difference between the two sets of youth is the fact that in PINS cases, the complainant typically is a parent or relative of the respondent rather than someone external to the family. In New York City, for example, the overwhelming majority of PINS petitions—over 80 percent—are brought by parents or guardians. In Rockland County, a suburban area near New York City, nearly a third of the PINS cases in 1972 were initiated by parents. Statistics for New York State for 1964 through 1970 show that petitions by parents, relatives, or guardians accounted for approximately 43 percent of all male PINS adjudications and between 65 percent and 70 percent of the PINS adjudications for girls.

Parental use of a PINS petition—involving subjection of one's own child to the juvenile court process and to the possibility of being institutionalized in a correctional facility—signals a crisis in parent-child relationships. Some theoretical and empirical work has been done on family response to certain kinds of crises, such as unemployment, alcoholism, separation because of war, and mental illness, but surprisingly little attention has been focused upon family response to juvenile misbehavior. Nevertheless, general theory about family reaction to stress provides a starting point in an attempt to understand why a parent might seek juvenile court intervention.

Family reaction to crisis has been described as a process of adaptation and reorganization. Initially a family may attempt to deny the existence of a crisis by denying the behavior or events which threaten the family, and try to handle the matter within the existing family structure in the hope that the situation is temporary and will soon resolve itself. . . . It is, however, more difficult for a family to conceal youthful "ungovernability" from the community than it is to conceal some other kind of deviant behavior. Attendance records, for example, are kept on youths under a certain age; they are supposed to be in school and accounted for. If they are not, inquiries are made. In addition, community members often feel freer to complain about a youth's behavior than they would about similar behavior by an adult. The child's behavior may precipitate recognition of a crisis when attempts at concealment fail and deviant behavior has become so visible that non-family members begin openly to react negatively to it. . . . If [the crisis is not resolved at this point,] a second stage of family response is reached in which the child's conduct is defined formally as a problem. One intake worker in Manhattan noted that parents tend to bring their children to court after they have received calls about the child's disruptive behavior from schools, teachers, or recreation centers. In such cases the youth's behavior may be defined as a problem by the family *because* it has become public. . . .

Although almost every PINS petition signals a crisis, setting in motion the process just described, it should not be assumed that all families attach the same meaning or expectations to the initiation of court proceedings. Some parents may use the petition to coerce children into compliant behavior. Other parents may hope to employ it as a dumping device to remove the youth physically from the family. Others may bring a PINS petition because they seek help for their child that they cannot themselves provide. To understand the significance of PINS proceedings for the families that use them, it is important to identify the motives and expectations that lead parents to file complaints against their children. . . .

[William] Goode suggests that parents of the lower class may be impelled to use overt force because they lack other resources that provide power to parents of higher status. Most people do not willingly choose overt force when they command other means of control because the costs of using force are high, especially in the family where its use can destroy spontaneous affection and respect. Furthermore, the utility of physical force diminishes when children begin to approach their parents in size and strength. One of the few resources available to lower class or minority parents is the legal power to take a child to court, with its threat of limitation of freedom. The parent, himself, may be unable to restrict his child's movement, but he has access to a coercive community agency—the juvenile court—which can. Access to legal coercive power may thus serve as a powerful resource for otherwise powerless parents. No one knows how many harassed and frustrated parents use this threat or how often they do so. Nor is there any systematic evidence to show whether or not such threats are effective. It may be, however, that for some youths the threat of court is sufficient to maintain parental control.

Some parents may seek a PINS petition against a child because they want to be rid of him. Difficult adolescents cause problems in families. They often cause strain in a parent's relationships with other adults, provide "bad" models for younger siblings, and limit parental ability to move upward. The initiation of a PINS petition may represent a family's attempt to legalize a parent-child split, much as a petition for divorce legalizes the split between husband and wife. . . .

JAMIE EDWARDS, *A LESSON IN UNINTENDED CONSEQUENCES: HOW JUVENILE JUSTICE AND DOMESTIC VIOLENCE REFORMS HARM GIRLS IN VIOLENT FAMILY SITUATIONS (AND HOW TO HELP THEM)*

13 U. Pa. J.L. & Soc. Change 219, 230, 232-234 (2009-2010)

Across the board, juvenile arrests have fallen in the last decade: the total number of juveniles arrested fell by about 24% from 1997 to 2006. However, girls' arrest rates for various offenses have risen, or dropped more slowly than boys' arrest rates, resulting in girls' increasing representation in the juvenile justice system since 1980. From 1980 to 2003, girls' arrests for simple assault increased by 269%, compared to a 102% increase for boys. From 1997 to 2006, boys' arrest rates fell for every type of offense, but girls' arrest rates rose for several categories, including a 19% increase for simple assault arrests compared to a 4% drop in boys' arrests for the same offense. The vast majority of arrests for violent offenses result in simple assault charges; moreover, simple assault charges are more likely to result in family violence offenses than in stranger violence offenses. This, and the fact that girls are more likely to engage in violence within the home, may help provide an explanation for the increase in simple assault arrests among girls. . . .

. . . Since at least the early 1970s, researchers have recognized the inequitable treatment of females in the juvenile justice system, criticizing the disproportionate number of girls brought in for status offenses and the differential treatment girls experience based upon community and parental intolerance of behaviors when manifested by girls as opposed to boys.

Today, girls account for 29% of all juvenile arrests and 19% of juveniles in detention. Girls are more likely than boys to be picked up and detained for minor offenses, including property, drug and status offenses, as opposed to person offenses. There are two offenses for which girls are more likely to be arrested than boys: prostitution and running away (a status offense). Girls are disproportionately arrested and detained for "violation[s] of a court order, probation violations, or contempt charges," a practice referred to as "bootstrapping," which is authorized by the 1980 amendment to the JJDPA. . . . It has been suggested that the gender differences in arrests can be accounted for, at least in part, due to the fact that parents, community members, law enforcement officers, and others are less tolerant of the deviance, aggression, non-cooperation, and non-compliance of females than males, probably due to gender role expectations.

Boys and girls are detained for different reasons: decision-makers tend to detain boys based upon public safety considerations, while girls are detained more often because of the problems they experience at home, or "for [their] own safety." Decisions to detain girls have been shown to be influenced by paternalistic attitudes and justified by the need to obtain services for the girls, protect them from sexual abuse, and to prevent sexual behavior and teen pregnancy. Although decision-makers in juvenile courts often rely on screening instruments to determine whether a given juvenile should be placed in detention, scores suggesting that detention is inappropriate are twice as likely to be overridden for girls than for boys. In other words, girls are more likely than boys to be placed in detention even when screening instruments indicate that detention is inappropriate. Half of the overrides that keep girls in detention are motivated by either family violence or a parent's refusal to take his or her daughter home. There is also a lack of community advocacy programs and detention alternatives for females compared to males; as a result, girls are often detained due to either a lack of appropriate alternatives or while awaiting placement at an over-utilized program.

Girls also have different risk factors for delinquency than boys. In one statistical model, the strongest predictive risk factors for boys were financial hardship, poor school behavior, prior offense history and poor peer groups; the strongest predictive factors for girls were special education placement, child abuse, running away, and prior person offense history.

Girls in detention have significant histories of trauma, abuse, and cross-system involvement. For example, one large study revealed that among juveniles in detention, 77.8% of girls had a documented history of physical abuse, but only 3% of boys did. A history of abuse increases the risk of being arrested for a violent crime for girls and women, but not for boys. Adolescent females have been found to be four times more likely than their male counterparts to be physically or verbally abused in the home, and 75% of sexually abused children are females. Up to 92% of girls in the juvenile justice system have experienced physical, sexual, or emotional abuse.

Exposure to violence in childhood has been associated with depression, aggression, anxiety, low self-esteem, traumatic stress, and self-destructive behaviors. Victims of abuse are more likely to have "distorted and deficient patterns of information processing," including attributing hostility to others. In what has been called "self-punishment syndrome," a victim of abuse is more likely to harm herself, for example through self-mutilation, and "is more likely to put herself in harm's way."

In part because of the strong correlation between past trauma and delinquency in girls, girls in the juvenile justice system are much more likely than their male peers to have mental health problems, most notably depression and PTSD. They are six times more likely to have PTSD, but are often misdiagnosed with Oppositional Defiant Disorder ("ODD"). In particular, aggressive or violent girls are more likely to have been both physically and sexually abused than non-violent girls. Girls also have higher rates of undiagnosed learning disorders than boys.

Girls have significant cross-system involvement. Girls are 44% more likely than boys to have a history of involvement with Child Protective Services ("CPS"). A girl with prior CPS involvement is four times more likely than the average juvenile, and twice as likely as a boy with CPS involvement, to become involved with the juvenile justice system. Children with foster care involvement are also more likely to become involved in the juvenile justice system than their peers; of those with foster care backgrounds, girls are twice as likely as boys to be detained. The cross-system involvement gives credence to the charge that girls are being "dumped" in detention by other social services. . . .

NOTES AND QUESTIONS

1. If you were a juvenile court judge applying the truancy statute in *Brandi B.*, how would you determine whether a student who had been suspended from school had good cause for being absent? Recall that under Goss v. Lopez, 419 U.S. 565 (1975), discussed in Chapter 2 at p. 123 a school can use very informal procedures before suspending a student for up to 10 days. In such a case due process is satisfied if the principal tells the student of the alleged misconduct and gives the student a chance to respond.

2. Other bases for finding that a child is a status offender can be even more indeterminate than "habitually truant." Consider, for example, the charge against the child in *Damian R.*, discussed in *Brandi B.*—that the child habitually and continually refused to obey the lawful supervision of a parent. Must a child always obey a parent? How often must a child disobey for the conduct to be habitual? The ostensible purpose of this strand of juvenile court jurisdiction is to support parental authority. However, some commentators have argued that whenever a parent appeals to a source of authority outside the family, the result is to "democratize" the family—that is, to weaken the authority of parents over their child. Phillip E. Slater, Social Change and the Democratic Family, in Warren E. Bennis & Phillip E. Slater, The Temporary Society 20, 47 (1968); Al Katz & Lee E. Teitelbaum, PINS Jurisdiction, the Vagueness Doctrine, and the Rule of Law, 53 Ind. L.J. 1, 17-20 (1977-1978). *See also* Randy Frances Kandel & Dr. Anne

Griffiths, Reconfiguring Personhood from Ungovernability to Parent Adolescent Autonomy Conflict Actions, 53 Syracuse L. Rev. 995 (2003). Why would that be so?

3. If Brandi B. later violated a condition of her probation, could the juvenile court remove her from home and place her in a state facility? The West Virginia statute allows a court to order a child placed out of the home only if this is actually necessary. What facts would make it necessary to place a child charged with a status offense in a secure out of home placement?

While the federal Juvenile Justice and Delinquency Prevention Act of 1974 forbids incarcerating children for status offenses, a 1984 amendment to the act allows incarceration of children who violate a valid court order, such as a probation order. More than half the states still allow detention for status offenses. Gary Gately, New Report Finds Incarceration for 'Status Offenses' Still Widespread, Juvenile Justice Information Exchange (Apr. 10, 2015), http://jjie.org/new-report-finds-incarceration-for-status-offenses-still-widespread/.

4. In 2014 there were 100,100 status offense cases filed in juvenile court, 1 of every 11 formally processed juvenile court cases. Sarah Hockenberry & Charles Puzzanchera, Juvenile Court Statistics 2014, at 68 (Nat'l Ctr. For Juv. Just., Apr. 2017), https://perma.cc/8XV4-G8F9. Courts adjudicated children to be status offenders in 42,500 cases. Id. at 82. The child was detained in about 7 percent of the cases filed; those charged as runaways were the most likely to be detained. Id. at 81. About 2,700 of those adjudicated were placed outside their homes, with charges of ungovernability and runaway most likely to result in this disposition. Id. at 84. The 2015 figures were much the same. Sarah Hockenberry & Charles Puzzanchera, Juvenile Court Statistics 2015 at 63-85 (Nat'l Center for Juv. Just., Apr. 2018), https://www.ojjdp.gov/ojstatbb/njcda/pdf/jcs2015.pdf.

5. The Coalition for Juvenile Justice has published best practice standards for those who work with youth charged with status offenses that are designed to reduce the numbers of these youth who are held in detention facilities through the valid court order (VCO) exception to the JJDPA. The Standards emphasize finding the most appropriate services for children in the least restrictive environments, reducing contact with the juvenile justice system, and avoiding the use of detention for status offenders. Coalition for Juvenile Justice, National Standards for the Care of Youth Charged with Status Offenses (2013), available at http://juv-justice.org/our-work/safety-opportunity-and-success-project/national-standards-care-youth-charged-status. *See also* Vera Institute of Justice, Keeping Kids Out of Court: Rethinking Our Response to Status Offenses, (Oct. 8, 2014), http://www.modelsforchange.net/publications/648 (describing the scope of the problem, highlighting states that are rethinking the current approach, and providing recommendations for community-based programs, rather than incarceration, to support youth and families who are struggling with status offenses).

6. Girls are more likely to be charged with status offenses than boys, half of all female status offenders are alleged to be runaways, and girls charged with status offenses typically have highly specialized needs as they have been sexually abused or come from families in discord. Cynthia Godsoe, Contempt, Status, and the Criminalization of Non-Conforming Girls, 35 Cardozo L. Rev. 1091 (2014). A 2016 report confirmed that girls are increasingly appearing in juvenile court, despite a decline in juvenile arrests over the past two decades. The report suggests that girls are disproportionately arrested and charged with offenses that pose

little to no threat to public safety, including intra-family in-home assaults. These arrests can be particularly traumatizing for girls who have a previous history of violence and abuse, yet there are few therapeutic programs specifically designed for girls. The report calls for an end to the criminalization of girls' coping behaviors. Francine T. Sherman, Unintended Consequences: Addressing the Impact of Domestic Violence Mandatory and Pro-Arrest Policies and Practices on Girls and Young Women (2016), http://nationalcrittenton.org/wp-content/uploads/2015/03/Unintended-Consequences-NGI.pdf.

NOTE: CONVERTING SCHOOL PROBLEMS TO JUVENILE OFFENSES – THE SCHOOL-TO-PRISON PIPELINE

Until the 1990s, infractions of school rules and minor violations of the law were usually handled internally by schools. As part of the general get tough approach to youth offending and in response to school shootings around the country, the federal Gun Free Schools Act of 1994 mandated the first zero tolerance policy; it requires schools to expel students for one year and report them to law enforcement authorities for bringing firearms and certain other kinds of weapons to school. 20 U.S.C. §§ 7151(b) and (h). Schools were quick to extend zero tolerance to other offenses; by 1998, 79 percent of public schools had zero tolerance policies for tobacco, 87 percent for alcohol, and 88 percent for drugs. The policies may also apply to tardiness, disrespect, and defiance. The vast majority of students who are expelled or suspended committed minor offenses such as smoking and truancy. Eric Blumenson & Eva S. Nilsen, One Strike and You're Out? Constitutional Constraints on Zero Tolerance in Public Education, 81 Wash. U. L.Q. 65, 70-72 (2003). In 2013-2014, 2.8 million students, about 6 percent of all public-school students, received out-of-school suspensions, and more than 220,000 were referred to law enforcement. Executive Office of the President, Report: The Continuing Need to Rethink Discipline 2, 4 (Dec. 2016), https://www.aclupa.org/files/9514/8493/3029/WH_-_Continuing_Need_to_Rethink_Discipline.pdf.

In addition, schools increasingly employ police officers to work in schools as "resource officers," often with federal funding. Trained in law enforcement rather than education and related areas, the officers tend to respond to violations of school rules as crimes rather than conduct to be expected from developing teens. Jason P. Nance, Students, Police, and the School-to-Prison Pipeline, 93 Wash. U. L. Rev. 919, 950-951 (2016).

In cases such as *Brandi B.*, being suspended itself can turn into a violation of a law, prompting a juvenile court referral, and sometimes the school directly refers a student who has broken a relatively minor school rule to the court. Even if the suspended student is not immediately referred to court, the student is at increased risk for more suspensions, for academic difficulties, and for dropping out of school, all of which increase the chances that the young person will become involved with the juvenile justice system. *Id.* at 952-956; Russell J. Skiba, Reaching a Critical Juncture for Our Kids: The Need to Reassess School-Justice Practices, 51 Fam. Ct. Rev. 380 (2013) (zero tolerance policies are associated with lower graduation rates, higher dropout rates, and increased contact with the juvenile justice system).

These laws and practices adversely affect students of color disproportionately. Data from the U.S. Department of Education shows racial disparities in suspensions, expulsions, referrals to law enforcement, and school-based arrests. African-American students are more than three times as likely as white students to receive out-of-school suspensions. Nance, above at 957, *see also* Elbert H. Aull IV, Zero Tolerance, Frivolous Juvenile Court Referrals, and the School-to-Prison Pipeline: Using Arbitration as a Screening-Out Method to Help Plug the Pipeline, 27 Ohio St. J. on Disp. Resol. 179, 206 (2012) (arguing that zero tolerance policies exacerbate school-to-prison-pipeline issues, have a disproportionate impact on students of color, and lead to violations of the Fourth, Fifth, and Fourteenth amendments); Erik J. Girvan, The Law and Social Psychology of Racial Disparities in School Discipline, (forthcoming in 4 Advances in Psychology and Law—, M. Miller & B. Bornstein, eds.) The data also show that from 2011 to 2012, African-American girls in public elementary and secondary schools were suspended at a rate of 12 percent, compared with a rate of just 2 percent for white girls, and more than girls of any other race or ethnicity. Tanzina Vega, Schools' Discipline for Girls Differs by Race and Hue, N.Y. Times (Dec. 10, 2014), http://www.nytimes.com/2014/12/11/us/school-discipline-to-girls-differs-between-and-within-races.html. *See also* Kimberlé Williams Crenshaw et al., Black Girls Matter: Pushed Out, Overpoliced and Underprotected, African American Policy Forum (2014), http://www.atlanticphilanthropies.org/sites/default/files/uploads/BlackGirlsMatter_Report.pdf.

Students with disabilities and LGBTQ students are also disproportionately disciplined in schools. American Bar Assn., School-to-Prison Pipeline Report 1-3 (Aug. 2016), https://www.americanbar.org/groups/child_law/resources/attorneys/school-to-prison-pipeline.htm. "According to the U.S. Department of Education's Office of Civil Rights, discipline and other disparities are based on race and cannot be explained by more frequent or serious misbehavior by minority students. . . . Substantial empirical research corroborates the U.S. Department of Education's conclusion. *School discipline records and students' self-reports also show that the concerning differences and disproportionality are not simply attributable to the stigmatized group behaving "badly" relative to their peers or to socioeconomic factors.*" *Id.* at 6 (emphasis in original).

Even though schools argue that safety concerns justify tighter limitations on students' freedoms, no evidence supports this claim, largely because most suspensions are for nonviolent offenses such as dress code violations and disruptive behavior. *Id.* at 10. The Departments of Justice and Education issued policy recommendations to reduce the use of suspension and expulsion as disciplinary tools in the schools and to focus instead on other strategies such as staff training, engaging families and communities, and helping students develop skills to avoid and de-escalate problems. U.S. Dept. Education, Guiding Principles: A Resource Guide for Improving School Climate and Discipline (Jan. 2014), https://www2.ed.gov/policy/gen/guid/school-discipline/guiding-principles.pdf.

While a number of states have introduced legislation to address these issues, results are mixed. For example, in California, out-of-school suspensions declined in all major racial and ethnic groups by 28 to 30 percent, but in Virginia they increased in 2015-2016, compared to 2014-2015. Education Comm'n of the States, Policy Snapshot: Suspension and Expulsion (Jan. 2018); Tom Loveless,

2017 Brown Center Report on American Education: Race and School Suspensions (Mar. 22, 2017); Amy Woolard, Suspended Progress 2017: An Update on the State of Exclusionary Discipline in Virginia's Public Schools (Oct. 2017).

A number of commentators have argued that restorative justice and other appropriate dispute resolution practices are more appropriate than juvenile justice referrals for resolving many of the problems that now find their way to juvenile court. *See* Elbert H. Aull IV, Zero Tolerance, Frivolous Juvenile Court Referrals, and the School-to-Prison Pipeline: Using Arbitration as a Screening-Out Method to Help Plug the Pipeline, 27 Ohio St. J. on Disp. Resol. 179, 206 (2012) (recommending that juvenile courts use mandatory arbitration to screen out frivolous juvenile court referrals); Aaron J. Curtis, Tracing the School to Prison Pipeline from Zero-Tolerance Policies to Juvenile Justice Dispositions, 102 Geo. L. J. 1251 (2014) (arguing for an end to zero tolerance policies and for alternatives to punitive juvenile court dispositions, including diversion to community-based alternatives that focus on rehabilitation); David Mitchell, Zero Tolerance Policies: Criminalizing Childhood and Disenfranchising the Next Generation of Citizens, 92 Wash. U. L. Rev. 271, 271-322 (2014) (arguing that referring non-serious infractions in a school setting to law enforcement harms students' perceptions of fairness of the rule of law and prepares them to be disenfranchised adults in the future, that zero tolerance policies may violate students' rights to free speech, privacy, and due process, and that school discipline should focus more on restorative justice than punishment).

DIAMOND V. DIAMOND

283 P.3d 260 (N.M. 2012)

SERNA, Justice. . . . Petitioner Jhette Diamond (Daughter), then sixteen years old, petitioned the district court in January 2007 for a declaration of emancipation pursuant to the Act. Daughter left the home of her mother Adrienne Diamond (Mother) at age thirteen and had been living with several different households since that time.

The district court held a hearing on Daughter's petition in February 2007. Mother did not appear at the hearing or otherwise oppose the petition. Daughter, represented by counsel, told the district court that she had moved out of Mother's home due to domestic violence and substance abuse issues. Daughter had been working since the age of eleven, including for the past several years as a restaurant server and busser, while maintaining a high grade-point average as a sophomore at Española Valley High School. Counsel described Daughter as "focused on her future," and thriving with the support of the couple with whom she was living. Daughter had no intention of returning to live with Mother, who maintained a relationship with the man whose violent behavior and substance abuse had contributed to Daughter's decision to leave Mother's home in the first place.

The district court concluded that by all accounts Daughter was capable of making appropriate choices for herself and covering her own expenses, describing Daughter's situation as "a classic case" for emancipation. Because Mother had not provided any financial support to Daughter before or after Daughter began living apart from Mother, Daughter asked if the emancipation order could be styled to reserve her right to pursue financial support from Mother. The court agreed provided that counsel could confirm that the Act authorized the court to do so.

The district court issued a "Declaration of Emancipation of Minor" in March 2007, finding that Daughter had been living independently and managing her own financial affairs without support from Mother, determining that emancipation would be in Daughter's best interest, and declaring Daughter "an emancipated minor in all respects, except that she shall retain the right to support from [Mother]" pursuant to Section 32A–21–5(D) of the Act. Mother filed a pro se motion to set aside the declaration because she had not received adequate notice of the original emancipation hearing. Mother additionally argued that she had supported Daughter even after Daughter moved out by paying for Daughter's traffic tickets, medical and dental care, and school clothes, and "[was] always giving [Daughter] spending money." Mother also disputed that Daughter was managing her own financial affairs.

The district court held a hearing on Mother's pro se motion in April 2007. Mother repeated her objections to Daughter's emancipation because, in her view, Daughter was not mature enough to act in her own best interest. The district court asked Mother for evidence or examples of Daughter's lack of maturity, and Mother could not think of any.

Consistent with her prior representations to the court, Daughter testified that she had been working since age eleven. Daughter added that during the time she was still living with Mother, her earnings went to household expenses such as utility bills, and stated that "whenever my mom asked me for money, I gave it to her." Daughter also reiterated that she had left Mother's home due to violence that Mother's boyfriend perpetrated against both Mother and Daughter, as well as the boyfriend's chronic alcohol and drug abuse.

The incident precipitating Daughter's decision to stop living with Mother, Daughter testified, took place in October 2003. One evening, in the course of an argument, Mother's boyfriend shook Mother and threw her against a bed. Mother began to have a panic attack, and her boyfriend departed. Although she was only thirteen years old at the time, Daughter drove Mother to the hospital. Some time after Mother and Daughter returned from the hospital, Mother's boyfriend reappeared at their home and demanded to see Mother. Daughter told him to leave. Mother's boyfriend pushed his way into the home, and when Daughter continued to block his access to Mother, the boyfriend picked Daughter up and threw her over a couch. Daughter kicked the boyfriend in the face and he again left the home.

After this altercation, Daughter told Mother that she did not want Mother's boyfriend to come over to their home anymore. Instead of asking her boyfriend to stay away, Mother went to live with him at his home, leaving Daughter alone in their trailer with no water, gas, or electricity service due to unpaid bills. Daughter remained in the trailer until being evicted several months later in the middle of winter. During this period, Daughter continued to work and attend school full time. Because there was no food at Mother's home, Daughter frequently obtained food from a woman who employed her at a local restaurant.

Daughter then lived for several months with neighbors, again while attending school full time and remaining employed. She later moved in with the brother of one of her neighbors, where she lived for several years, continuing to work at a local restaurant, paying for her own expenses and contributing to rent and other household expenses. Several months before filing her petition for emancipation, Daughter began living with members of the same extended family, a couple who allowed her to stay with them rent-free so that she could focus on school.

Disputing Mother's assertions about having covered certain expenses, Daughter testified that it was actually a concerned teacher who paid for her traffic ticket, that Daughter herself paid for dental care, and that Medicaid covered the cost of medical care when Daughter broke her arm at school. Daughter acknowledged that on a single occasion Mother had purchased several items of clothing for her, but that she could not recall Mother ever providing her with spending money, contrary to Mother's claim that she "always" did so. Daughter testified that since living apart from Mother, she would visit Mother at her home approximately once a month but that she could remember only a handful of occasions when Mother visited her or otherwise attempted to contact her, including once when Mother turned up at Daughter's school to ask her for money.

Daughter also explained why she was seeking emancipation. Although at that point in time she had already been living apart from her Mother for two to three years, paying her own expenses, attending school, and working, Daughter testified that she had difficulty obtaining medical insurance, accessing her school report cards, or applying for a driver's permit, all of which required parental consent. Emancipated status also would allow Daughter to open a bank account. Daughter stated that she would be uncomfortable if she were required to resume living with Mother, especially because Mother's abusive boyfriend remained a presence in Mother's home, and because she was doing well on her own.

After hearing testimony from Mother and Daughter, the district court ruled from the bench that even assuming that all of Mother's contentions were true, emancipation remained in Daughter's best interest. The district court then re-declared Daughter to be emancipated and issued a formal order to that effect, which included the same provision as the court's prior order that Daughter was "an emancipated minor in all respects, except that she shall retain the right to support from [Mother]" pursuant to Section 32A–21–D(5) of the Act.

As permitted by the district court's emancipation orders, in February 2008 Daughter filed a petition asking the district court to order Mother to pay retroactive and prospective child support to Daughter. . . .

. . . The hearing officer recommended that Mother be ordered to make support payments to Daughter in the amount of $390.00 per month from March 1, 2008 until Daughter reached the age of eighteen or graduated from high school, whichever event occurred later. . . . The district court affirmed the hearing officer's report over Mother's written objections, and in January 2009 directed that a portion of Mother's retirement benefit, her sole source of income, be garnished and paid to Daughter.

The parties filed several subsequent motions before the district court in summer and fall 2009, with Mother now represented by counsel. Mother principally argued that "New Mexico law does not allow child support for an emancipated minor." . . .

The district court reaffirmed its prior ruling that emancipation does not necessarily cut off a minor's right to child support. . . . Mother appealed the judgment entered against her in the support proceeding and a related order from the original emancipation proceeding. . . . Agreeing with Mother, the Court of Appeals held that "New Mexico law does not permit a minor emancipated pursuant to [the Act] to collect child support payments," . . .

Daughter subsequently petitioned this Court for writ of certiorari. . . .

. . . The Act defines an emancipated minor as any person sixteen years of age or older who "has entered into a valid marriage, whether or not the marriage was terminated by dissolution," who "is on active duty with any of the armed forces of the United States of America," or who "has received a declaration of emancipation" pursuant to the Act. The Act sets forth three prerequisites to emancipation by judicial declaration. "Any person sixteen years of age or older may be declared an emancipated minor for one or more purposes enumerated in the [Act] if he is [1] willingly living separate and apart from his parents, guardian or custodian, [2] is managing his financial affairs and [3] the court finds it in the minor's best interest."

In addition, the Act provides a procedural mechanism for a minor to obtain a declaration of emancipation. A minor seeking to be emancipated must file a verified petition with the children's court that "set[s] forth with specificity the facts" in support of such relief, and the court shall provide notice of the petition to the minor's parent, guardian, or custodian. If the court determines the minor to be sixteen years of age or older and to fulfill the preconditions for emancipation, "the court may grant the petition unless, after having considered all of the evidence introduced at the hearing, it finds that granting the petition would be contrary to the best interests of the minor." . . .

As for the legal effect of emancipation, under the Act [a]n emancipated minor shall be considered as being over the age of majority for one or more of the following purposes:

    A. consenting to medical, dental or psychiatric care without parental consent, knowledge or liability;
    B. his capacity to enter into a binding contract;
    C. his capacity to sue and be sued in his own name;
    D. his right to support by his parents;
    E. the rights of his parents to his earnings and to control him;
    F. establishing his own residence;
    G. buying or selling real property;
    H. ending vicarious liability of the minor's parents . . . or
    I. enrolling in any school or college.

. . . Emancipation confers on eligible minors some or all of "the rights and status of adults." In setting forth the nine possible legal effects of emancipation, the Act refers to "one or more of the [enumerated] purposes." . . .

The plain meaning of the phrase "one or more . . . purposes" is that a minor may be declared to be emancipated under the Act for a single enumerated purpose, for all nine enumerated purposes, or for any intermediate number of enumerated purposes. "As a rule of construction, the word 'or' should be given its normal disjunctive meaning unless the context of a statute demands otherwise," if "adherence to the literal use of the word leads to absurdity or contradiction." . . .

. . . Not only does the Act fail to evidence any legislative intent contrary to the plain meaning of "one or more purposes," the history of its enactment provides persuasive indications of the Legislature's intent that district courts should tailor emancipation orders to the best interests of the minor in each particular case.

As originally introduced, the legislation that ultimately became the Act included language consistent with Respondent's (and the Court of Appeals') interpretation, namely that "[a]n emancipated minor shall be considered as being over the age of majority *for the purpose of* "the nine specific grounds." The Legislature considered and rejected this phrasing, opting instead for the more flexible alternative of "one or more of the following purposes." . . .

. . . [W]e hold that the Act's directive that emancipation may be declared for "one or more purposes" expressly authorizes partial emancipation.

The Act requires that a minor must be living independently and "managing his own financial affairs" in order to be emancipated. . . .

The Act does not define the phrase "managing [one's] financial affairs," but that term logically would include obtaining income and transacting for the necessities of life. . . .Here, the district court determined that Daughter had been living independently and that Daughter had paid for all of her expenses out of her own earnings since March 2005, with no support from Mother. Daughter sought emancipation, in part, to obtain health insurance and open a bank account, further evidence of her intent and capacity to manage her own affairs but for certain legal impediments of minority.

The Court of Appeals agreed with Mother and found the district court's interpretation of the Act "paradoxical," explaining that "a minor cannot be 'managing his own financial affairs' if he is receiving financial and other support from his parents." We do not see management of one's financial affairs and entitlement to support as inherently contradictory. Certainly, in other proceedings courts routinely award support without any finding or implication that the recipient is incapable of managing his or her affairs.

The Act itself contemplates that an emancipated minor may receive public assistance: An emancipated minor "shall not be denied benefits from any public entitlement program which he may have been entitled in his own right prior to the declaration of emancipation." A minor entitled to public assistance is necessarily not entirely self-supporting, at least not after he or she begins to receive the assistance payments. Under the Court of Appeals' interpretation of the Act, Daughter would be managing her own financial affairs if she were receiving financial support from the State, but not if she were receiving support from Mother. Mother does not offer any explanation for why the *source* of the support should be determinative of Daughter's ability to manage her affairs, and indeed such an approach would be inconsistent with our "strong public policy" favoring parental support where appropriate. . . .

Although we find ample support for our interpretation of the Act in its plain language and legislative intent, a brief review of several other states' emancipation statutes, illustrative rather than exhaustive, indicates a diversity in approach to defining the legal effects of emancipation. Some states have determined that emancipation should always entail a fixed rather than a flexible set of legal consequences. For example, in contrast to the Act's provision that emancipation may be ordered for "one or more purposes," California's emancipation statute directs that an emancipated minor "shall be considered as being an adult for the following purposes, that is, for *all* of the seventeen purposes enumerated by the California statute, including "the minor's right to support by the minor's parents," and the minor's capacity to "establish [his or her] own residence." . . .

Consistent with California's approach and in contrast to ours, Vermont law provides that an emancipation order "shall recognize the minor as an adult for *all purposes* that result from reaching the age of majority, including ... terminating parental support and control of the minor and [parental] rights to the minor's income." Pennsylvania state law does not set forth a specific statutory mechanism for a minor to obtain a declaration of emancipation, but nonetheless expressly provides that "[a] court shall not order either or both parents to pay for the support of a child if the child is emancipated."

Other states, while perhaps not favoring parental support for emancipated minors, do not foreclose it either. Under Nevada law, for example, an emancipation decree confers the right of majority for six enumerated purposes, including entering into contracts or incurring debts, obtaining medical care without parental consent, and establishing the minor's own residence, but not elimination of support from a parent. Whether to award support, however, is left to the discretion of the court considering the emancipation petition, with the default under the statute for support to cease upon emancipation: "Unless otherwise provided by the [emancipation] decree, the obligation of support otherwise owed a minor by his or her parent or guardian is terminated by the entry of the decree."

On the other hand, New Mexico is far from the only state where a minor's emancipation does not presumptively extinguish a parent's support obligation. Montana's emancipation statute probably resembles New Mexico's most closely. If a Montana court grants a petition for emancipation, it must issue an order that "specifically set[s] forth the rights and responsibilities that are being conferred upon the youth[, which] may include but are not limited to one or more" of a list of six purposes. Purposes include the right to live in housing of the minor's choice, the right to enter into contracts and incur debts, the right to consent to medical care, and the right to "directly receive and expend money to which the youth is entitled and to conduct the youth's own financial affairs." The Montana statute, like ours, does not define emancipation to automatically end a parent's support obligation.

At least one state goes further than New Mexico by not merely permitting but *mandating* parental support for emancipated minors. Under Michigan's emancipation statute, a court may declare a minor emancipated "for the purposes of, but not limited to, all of the following [fourteen purposes]," a list that does not include child support. Instead, Michigan law explicitly provides that "[t]he parents of a minor emancipated by court order are jointly and severally obligated to support the minor," except that the parents are not liable for debt incurred by the minor during the period of emancipation. . . .

While our holding that the Act allows a district court to reserve a minor's right to financial support from a parent follows from the plain language of the Act, it is consistent with the treatment of emancipation under the common law. Historically, American courts recognized a "correlative" relationship between a parent's duty to support his or her minor child and the parent's entitlement to the child's services and earnings. 1 Homer H. Clark, Jr., The Law of Domestic Relations in the United States § 9.3, at 548–49 (2d ed. 1987). Under this approach, the father [was] entitled to the services and earnings of his minor children, because he [was] bound to support and educate them. The right grows out of the obligation, and is correlative to it. When one ceases the other ceases also. The helplessness of the infant, demanding the tutelage and support of the father, in contemplation of law terminates in ordinary cases at twenty-one [then the age of majority], and the child becomes emancipated from parental control and entitled to his own earnings.

More contemporary cases instead view the minor's reciprocal duty as submitting to the parent's control.

Emancipation developed largely to protect minors from claims against their wages asserted by their parents or by third parties. A minor could only be emancipated through parental consent, although that consent could be implied as well as expressed. A parent's abandonment of a minor, or even oral expressions of an intent to abandon the minor, could constitute an implied consent to emancipation. Courts have long recognized that common-law emancipation may be partial, that is, conferring some but not all of the aspects of adult status on the minor. While courts typically treated complete emancipation as "terminating the parent's legal duty to support the child," partial emancipation would not necessarily do so.

Prior to passage of the Act, New Mexico courts recognized emancipation under the common law. In contrast to the procedures provided by the Act for seeking emancipation, under our common law, as in other states, "[t]he power to emancipate a minor reside[d] in that parent or those parents having the duty to support the child." As in other states, common-law emancipation in New Mexico could be expressed, where "the parent freely and voluntarily agrees" to allow a minor child to live independently and control his or her own earnings, or implied, where "the child is no longer subject to parental care and discipline." . . .

Giving effect to the plain meaning of the Act is consistent with our state's public policy favoring judicial determination of the best interests of the minor. A district court could, for example, where appropriate declare a minor emancipated for a single purpose, such as "consenting to medical, dental or psychiatric care without parental consent, knowledge or liability," or attending college. Similarly, a district court has the discretion to declare a minor emancipated for a greater number of purposes, or all of the purposes, set forth in the Act. The critical inquiry remains the best interests of the minor, which the court determines on the basis of specific findings of fact. . . .

NOTES AND QUESTIONS

1. As *Diamond* indicates, most emancipation statutes treat emancipation as a comprehensive alteration of the parent–child relationship. What arguments support the comprehensive approach? What arguments support the approach that the New Mexico statute takes?

As of 2014, 28 states had enacted emancipation statutes, and almost half provided that emancipation automatically terminated parents' child support obligations. Mayra Alicia Cataldo, Safe Haven: Granting Support to Victims of Child Abuse Who Have Been Judicially Emancipated, 52 Fam. Ct. Rev. 592 (2014).

Emancipation statutes may allow for rescission of emancipation when the minor is indigent. *E.g.*, Cal. Fam. Code § 7130(b) (2018); Mich. Stat. Ann. § 722.4d(3)(a) (2018). Rescission does not affect rights or obligations that arose during the period that the declaration was in effect. Why should rescission be permitted? Should parental agreement be required?

2. Emancipated minors remain subject to many state and federal labor laws, including the hour and workplace limits of the Fair Labor Standards Act of 1938. This makes it difficult, if not impossible, for most minors to earn enough money to support themselves in states with comprehensive emancipation statutes. Dana M. Dohn & Amy Pimer, Child Labor Laws and the Impossibility of Statutory Emancipation, 33 Hofstra Lab. & Emp. L. J. 121, 122 (2015). Statutes that allow partial emancipation, such as New Mexico's, allow a court to grant an emancipation order even in such a case. When should a court do this?

3. The statutes generally provide that the minor will file the petition for emancipation. *E.g.*, Ariz. Rev. Stat. § 12-2451 (2018); Cal. Fam. Code § 7120 (2018); Conn. Gen. Stat. § 46b-150 (2018); Mich. Stat. Ann. § 722.4a (2011); Mont. Code Ann. § 41-1-501 (2018); Or. Rev. Stat. § 419B.552 (2018); Utah Code Ann. § 78A-6-803 (2018); Wash. Rev. Code Ann. § 13.64.010 (West 2018). What motives would lead a child to establish an independent home?

4. What would lead a parent to agree to that independence, especially for a child of 15 or 16? A study of emancipation in California found that parents often proposed emancipation to their children as a solution to family conflict. The uncontested petitions were generally granted, but emancipation did not turn out well for most of the teens. Within a short time many were struggling financially, lonely, and unhappy. "[A]t times emancipation may facilitate an abdication by parents of caretaking responsibilities, an abandonment of sorts." Carol Sanger & Eleanor Willemsen, Minor Changes: Emancipating Children in Modern Times, 25 U. Mich. J.L. Reform 239, 247 (1992).

Parents obligated to pay child support after a divorce or separation have tried to argue that their support duties should be terminated because their children are employed and so can be declared emancipated. This argument usually fails. *See, e.g.*, Anderson v. Loper, 689 So.2d 118, 120 (Ala. App. 1996); Tew v. Tew, 924 N.E.2d 1262 (Ind. App. 2010); Thomas B. v. Lydia D., 886 N.Y.S.2d 22 (N.Y. App. 2009); Purdy v. Purdy, 578 S.E.2d 30, 31 (S.C. App. 2003).

5. Could a child use a status offender statute to achieve the same result as in *Diamond*? re Snyder, 532 P.2d 278 (Wash. 1975), concerned Cynthia Nell Snyder, a 16-year-old high school student who had a very hostile relationship with her parents, strict disciplinarians who restricted her activities and choice of friends and refused to allow her to smoke, date, or participate in various extracurricular school activities. Her father, having decided that the juvenile court might be able to assist him in controlling his daughter, removed Cynthia from the family home and placed her in a receiving home. Cynthia then filed a petition in juvenile court alleging that she was incorrigible, hoping to avoid being returned to her home.

The juvenile court commissioner, after hearing from psychiatric witnesses chosen by the parents, placed Cynthia in a foster home under the supervision of the probation department and ordered her and her parents to participate in counseling. The commissioner's order was sustained by the superior court and, on appeal, by the Supreme Court of Washington. The Supreme Court concluded that there was substantial evidence to support a finding that the parent-child relationship had dissolved to the point where parental control was lost and that Cynthia had clearly and unambiguously declared her unwillingness to return home. It also noted the testimony of an expert witness who stated that counseling would not be beneficial until all of the parties had backed away from the positions they now held, which was the cause of the hostility between parents and child.

If counseling did not work, what should happen next?

6. Jhette Diamond graduated from the University of San Diego Law School and is an attorney practicing in California. Jhette Diamond's Emancipation, U. San Diego School of Law News Sept. 17, 2015, http://www.sandiego.edu/news/law/detail.php?_focus=52607; Jhette J. Diamond, Council of Parent Attorneys and Advocates, https://www.copaa.org/members/?id=52932033.

PROBLEMS

1. Damien is the 14-year-old son of a single mother. He was often truant and often got into trouble at school. His mother wasn't able to control him and contacted the county probation office, seeking help. The probation officer filed a status offender petition against Damien, and the court found that he was habitually truant and habitually disobedient of his parent. The court placed him on probation and ordered the probation office to provide family counseling and services to resolve the problems with school, but the agency did not comply. Damien continued to skip school frequently, and the state returned to court, seeking an order placing him in a semi-secure residential facility where he would receive counseling and have to go to school. Damien and his mother do not want him removed from the home; the mother just wants the agency to provide the services that the court ordered. Could a court find that it was necessary to remove the child from the home on these facts? Should it?

2. Raul, a 16-year-old young man, is gay, and his parents do not accept his sexual orientation. Raul has tried to talk about it with them, but they insist that he just needs counseling and have on several occasions arranged appointments with a counselor (which Raul has refused to keep). His parents have also insisted that he not socialize with his current friends, some of whom are openly gay, because, as his parents see it, these friends are responsible for his "problem." Raul is employed part-time at a hardware store and is sure that his employer would be glad to employ him full-time. He is an indifferent student and thinks he might continue in school on a part-time basis. Would a petition of emancipation be appropriate and successful in this case?

LEE E. TEITELBAUM, *STATUS OFFENSES AND STATUS OFFENDERS*

A Century of Juvenile Justice 158, 167-169 (Margaret Rosenheim et al., eds., 2002)

The reforms in status offense jurisdiction that occurred between the early 1960s and the 1980s can be considered social experiments in the same way that the original formulation of juvenile court jurisdiction and procedure can be thought of in that way. It would be good to be able to evaluate the success of this experiment. However, relatively scant information is available to that purpose.

Some things are surely true. One is that status offense jurisdiction now makes up a much smaller part of the juvenile court's business than previously. While PINS and their counterparts comprised up to one-quarter to one-half of the juvenile court's caseload at earlier times, between 1985 and 1995 the incidence of petitioned status offense cases was only about 15% of the incidence of petitioned delinquency matters. Another is that the institutionalization of children for status offenses is now far more uncommon than it was. These phenomena are, no doubt, related. The reduction in the number of states retaining status offense jurisdiction is far too small to account by itself for the reduction in status offense cases. It seems likely that parents, police, and court intake offices have concluded that formal juvenile court response to juvenile misconduct is so unlikely that either other community-based strategies are preferable or that no institutional response is available.

But what happened to those children who, prior to the reforms of the last thirty years, would have been treated as status offenders and often committed to secure institutions? Having regard to the wide variety of circumstances in which this jurisdiction was invoked, a variety of possibilities exist. To the extent that status offense jurisdiction was used by police as a residual category for proceedings that involved delinquency as well, some of these children may now be brought to juvenile court on delinquency charges alone. An evaluation of the effects of elimination of status offense jurisdiction in Washington state indicates some such effect, although it clearly appeared that status offense behavior had generally been eliminated from judicial concern.

However, many status offense cases—especially those alleging running away or incorrigibility—were brought by parents and did not involve any associated criminal misconduct. While these family conflicts came less often to juvenile courts, they remained crises for parents whose children were disobedient, had run away, had poor school attendance or performance, spent time with undesirable companions, stayed out past curfew, engaged in sexual relations, or used alcohol or drugs. If judicial agencies would not respond to these circumstances, other systems concerned with deviance might do so.

One alternate vehicle for parents seeking help was the mental health system. Mental health treatment for "emotionally disturbed" or chemically dependent children does not present the same procedural barriers or the same limits on institutionalization that parents now encounter in juvenile courts. Most states allow parents to commit their minor children "voluntarily" for residential mental health treatment without any judicial process. The United States Supreme Court has held that an informal commitment process by parents is constitutionally valid as long as a staff mental health professional evaluates the child and approves the admission.

In fact, parents would not need to look far for information about the availability of sources of help outside the juvenile justice system. The kinds of conduct that the juvenile court labeled status offenses could equally well be considered signs of emotional disturbance, personality disorders, or adjustment reactions to adolescence. And although mental health policy analysts, like juvenile court commentators, urged reduction in the inpatient care of children and youths during the 1980s, the number of hospital commitments in fact rose dramatically increasing approximately 400% during the decade when juvenile courts withdrew from institutionalization of status offenders.

The inference that the mental health system served as an alternative to juvenile court jurisdiction is suggested not only by the dramatic increase in admissions itself but by the conditions surrounding the increase in admissions. As we have just noted, there was no general call by mental health policy makers for increased hospital treatment of minors; rather, the contrary was true. Nor was there an increase in serious mental health problems among children. Although between one-half and two-thirds of adults admitted to mental hospitals suffered from serious disorders, less than one-third of juvenile admittees did so. Rather, their characteristics resembled those of status offenders more than they did severely disturbed children; they were young people who had experimented with drugs and/or alcohol, suffered from eating disorders, ran away, had school problems, and were generally in conflict with their parents or other authorities. If the juvenile court had become too legalistic to deal with these children, private mental health providers were ready to do so. And in fact they mounted an aggressive campaign to reach just those parents who might earlier have gone to juvenile court. The percentage of mental hospitals advertising in newspapers increased from 43% in 1982 to 75% in 1988, and many marketed their services to schools, juvenile probation officers, and social services agencies as well. . . .

There is another potential response to the reduction in the availability of status offense jurisdiction and of residential treatment for children in conflict with their parents that has not been much studied. Children who run away may simply stay away, and parents who cannot control their children may exclude them from the home by telling them to leave or by refusing to allow their return after some violation of parental rules. The popularity of "toughlove" approaches has given legitimacy to these exclusions. While the proponents of dejudicialization of status offense problems vigorously urged the creation of alternative, community-based residential and counseling programs that might have served these children, legislatures have proven generally unwilling to invest funds in creating and staffing resources of these kinds.

As of 2013, 413,000 children in the United States were runaways or 'thrownaways"—that is, abandoned or exiled by their parents. This amounts to 5.3 children per 1,000, a rate that is not statistically different from the rate found in 1999. Andrea J. Sedlak et al., National Estimates of Missing Children: Updated Findings from a Survey of Parents and Other Primary Caretakers (Office of Juvenile Justice and Delinquency Prevention, June 2017).

ANONYMOUS v. CITY OF ROCHESTER

915 N.E.2d 593 (N.Y. 2009)

JONES, J. . . . In 2006, the Rochester City Council (City Council) adopted chapter 45 of the Code of the City of Rochester (City Code) which established a nighttime curfew for juveniles. Under the curfew:

"It is unlawful for minors to be in or upon any public place within the City at any time between 11:00 P.M. of one day and 5:00 A.M. of the immediately following day, except that on Friday and Saturday the hours shall be between 12:00 midnight and 5:00 a.m. of the immediately following day."

A minor is defined as "[a] person under the age of 17[but][t]he term does not include persons under 17 who are married or have been legally emancipated" (Rochester City Code § 45–2). The curfew provides for certain exceptions which make the prohibition under the curfew inapplicable

"if the minor can prove that:

A. The minor was accompanied by his or her parent, guardian, or other responsible adult;

B. The minor was engaged in a lawful employment activity or was going to or returning home from his or her place of employment;

C. The minor was involved in an emergency situation;

D. The minor was going to, attending, or returning home from an official school, religious, or other recreational activity sponsored and/or supervised by a public entity or a civic organization;

E. The minor was in the public place for the specific purpose of exercising fundamental rights such as freedom of speech or religion or the right of assembly protected by the First Amendment of the United States Constitution or Article I of the Constitution of the State of New York, as opposed to generalized social association with others; or

F. The minor was engaged in interstate travel.[3]

The "Findings and purpose" with respect to the curfew were set forth by the City Council in section 45–1. They state that

A. A significant number of minors are victims of crime and are suspects in crimes committed during the nighttime hours, hours during which minors should generally be off the streets and getting the sleep necessary for their overall health and quality of life. Many of these victimizations and criminal acts have occurred on the streets at night and have involved violent crimes, including the murders of teens and preteens.

B. While parents have the primary responsibility to provide for the safety and welfare of minors, the City also has a substantial interest in the safety and welfare of minors. Moreover, the City has an interest in preventing crime by minors, promoting parental supervision through the establishment of reasonable standards, and in providing for the well-being of the general public.

C. A curfew will help reduce youth victimization and crime and will advance the public safety, health and general welfare of the citizens of the City.

---

3. A responsible adult is defined as "[a] person 18 years of age or older specifically authorized by law or by a parent or guardian to have custody and control of a minor" (Rochester City Code § 45–2).

Plaintiffs, father and son, commenced the instant action challenging the validity of the curfew. They seek a declaration that the ordinance is unconstitutional and to enjoin defendants, the City of Rochester (City) and other city officials, from enforcing the ordinance on the grounds that the curfew violated Jiovon's federal and state constitutional rights to freedom of movement, freedom of expression and association, and equal protection under the law, and Thomas' due process rights under the Federal and State Constitutions to raise his children without undue interference from the government. . . . The Supreme Court granted the City's motion to dismiss finding that the curfew . . . (2) did not violate the constitutional rights of the minor, (3) did not unreasonably interfere with the rights of the parent, and (4) was not facially defective.

Declaring the ordinance unconstitutional, the Appellate Division, with two Justices dissenting, reversed and enjoined its enforcement. . . . Defendants appealed to this Court as of right, and we now affirm . . .

Curfew ordinances have long been enacted in cities around the country and numerous cases, both state and federal, have addressed similar constitutional issues implicated by these curfews (*see, e.g.*, State v. J.P., 907 So. 2d 1101 [Fla. 2005]; Treacy v. Municipality of Anchorage, 91 P.3d 252 [Alaska 2004]; Ramos v. Town of Vernon, 353 F.3d 171 [2d Cir. 2003]; City of Sumner v. Walsh, 148 Wash. 2d 490, 61 P.3d 1111 [2003]; Hutchins v. District of Columbia, 188 F.3d 531 [C.A.D.C. 1999]; Schleifer by Schleifer v. City of Charlottesville, 159 F.3d 843 [4th Cir. 1998]; Nunez by Nunez v. City of San Diego, 114 F.3d 935 [9th Cir. 1997]; Qutb v. Strauss, 11 F.3d 488 [5th Cir. 1993]; Johnson v. City of Opelousas, 658 F.2d 1065 [5th Cir. 1981]). Recent decisions analyzing the constitutionality of curfews have differed as to the appropriate level of scrutiny to apply: some courts have favored intermediate scrutiny (*see, e.g.*, *Hodgkins*, 355 F.3d at 1057; *Ramos*, 353 F.3d at 181; *Hutchins*, 188 F.3d at 541; *Schleifer*, 159 F.3d at 847), while others have adopted strict scrutiny (*see, e.g.*, *J.P.*, 907 So. 2d at 1116; *Treacy*, 91 P.3d at 265-266; *Nunez*, 114 F.3d at 946; *Qutb*, 11 F.3d at 492). Regardless of the level of scrutiny ultimately applied, these cases highlight a number of important factors relevant to constitutional review of a curfew ordinance.

Initially, we note that a municipality has general police powers and, under the traditional powers of *parens patriae*, a strong interest in preserving and promoting the welfare of children. Plaintiffs do not dispute that the City Council, pursuant to its broad police powers, has the authority to enact a curfew ordinance. The issue, however, is whether that power was exercised in a manner consistent with the Federal and State Constitutions. We first turn to how the curfew may interfere with a minor's constitutional right to freely move about in public.

"[F]reedom of movement is the very essence of our free society, setting us apart. Like the right of assembly and the right of association, it often makes all other rights meaningful—knowing, studying, arguing, exploring, conversing, observing and even thinking." For an adult, there is no doubt that this right is fundamental and an ordinance interfering with the exercise of such a right would be subject to strict scrutiny (*see* Chicago v. Morales, 527 U.S. 41, 5, [1999]). The critical question, however, is whether a minor has a corresponding right that is equally fundamental, and therefore warrants the same restrictive level of scrutiny.

In many situations, children do not possess the same constitutional rights possessed by their adult counterparts; for example, children are afforded lesser freedom of choice than adults with respect to marriage, voting, alcohol consumption, and labor. On the other hand, a child's otherwise-criminal actions do not carry the same consequences as those of adults. The inherent differences between children and adults—specifically their immaturity, vulnerability, and need for parental guidance—have been recognized by the Supreme Court as the basis to justify treating children differently than adults under the Federal Constitution (*see* Bellotti v. Baird, 443 U.S. 622, 634-635 [1979]). "So 'although children generally are protected by the same constitutional guarantees . . . as are adults, the State is entitled to adjust its legal system to account for children's vulnerability' by exercising broader authority over their activities."

We find the rationale in *Bellotti* persuasive in the context of a curfew because it is hard to imagine that, even absent a curfew, the police may not take a vulnerable five-year-old child found alone at night on a city street into custody for the child's own safety and well-being. Even if we assume that the police may not do the same to a 17 year old under the *parens patriae* function, an unemancipated minor still does not have the right to freely "come and go at will." Moreover, "juveniles, unlike adults, are always in some form of custody" and their right to free movement is limited by their parents' authority to consent or prohibit such movement. As one court observed, "it would be inconsistent to find a fundamental right here, when the [Supreme] Court has concluded that the state may intrude upon the 'freedom' of juveniles in a variety of similar circumstances without implicating fundamental rights" (*Hutchins*, 188 F.3d at 539, citing Prince v. Massachusetts, 321 U.S. 158, 166-167 [1944] [prohibiting children from selling magazines on the street]; *Flores*, 507 U.S. 292, 301-303 [1993] [detention of deportable juveniles]; *Schall*, 467 U.S. at 263-264 [pretrial detention of juvenile delinquents]; Ginsberg v. New York, 390 U.S. 629, 637-643 [1968] [prohibiting sale of non-obscene material to minors]).

Rather than categorically applying strict scrutiny to a curfew which implicates a minor's right to free movement simply because the same right, if possessed by an adult, would be fundamental, courts have found that intermediate scrutiny is better suited to address the complexities of curfew ordinances—it is sufficiently skeptical and probing to provide rigorous protection of constitutional rights yet flexible enough to accommodate legislation that is carefully drafted to address the vulnerabilities particular to minors. In the context of juvenile curfews, we find persuasive the reasoning which recognizes that although children have rights protected by the Constitution, they can be subject to greater regulation and control by the state than can adults.

Next, we turn to the constitutional right asserted by the father. Our precedent has repeatedly emphasized the "primacy of parental rights" to the care and custody of the child absent abandonment, surrender, or unfitness. Although it is settled that parents have a fundamental due process right, in certain situations, to raise their children in a manner as they see fit (*see* Wisconsin v. Yoder, 406 U.S. 205, 213-214 [1972]; *see also Ginsberg*, 390 U.S. at 63), this is not the end of the analysis. Were the ordinance directly aimed at curbing parental control over their children, it might be that strict scrutiny would apply. However, that is not the case here.

Parental rights are not absolute and are subject to reasonable regulation. . . . The Supreme Court has stated that "the state has a wide range of power for limiting parental freedom and authority in things affecting the child's welfare" specifically when it concerns the government's interest in the "moral, emotional, mental, and physical welfare of the minor." Because the purpose of the juvenile curfew is, in part, to prevent victimization of minors during nighttime hours, it easily falls within the realm of the government's legitimate concern. . . .

Moreover, "to the extent that the curfew is enforced against minors moving about in public with no purpose or with an improper purpose," how it impinges on a parent's rights is surely less clear and more indirect. Because the curfew is aimed primarily at minors, only peripherally burdening parents' rights, the reflexive labeling of a fundamental right, and accompanying analysis under strict scrutiny, is inadequate for taking into account the complexities and governmental concerns of this kind of regulation. As with the minor's due process rights, we agree that a searching review of the curfew is required but that a strict scrutiny analysis is not. . . .

Under intermediate scrutiny, defendants must show that the ordinance is "substantially related" to the achievement of "important" government interests. Here, defendants assert that their governmental interest is to prevent minors from perpetrating and becoming victims of crime during nighttime hours. While this is clearly an important governmental interest, its expression does not end the intermediate scrutiny analysis. In addition to identifying an important governmental interest, defendants must show a substantial nexus between the burdens imposed by this curfew and the goals of protecting minors and preventing juvenile crime. The Supreme Court has explained that although the government need not produce evidence of this relationship to a scientific certainty, the "purpose of requiring [proof of] that close relationship is to assure that the validity of a classification is determined through reasoned analysis rather than through the mechanical application of traditional, often inaccurate, assumptions."

Quite simply, the proof offered by the City fails to support the aims of the curfew in this case. As the Appellate Division observed, "a common theme of the [affidavits of political officials and affidavits and reports of police officials] is that city officials perceived a pressing need to respond to the problem of juvenile victimization and crime as a result of the . . . tragic deaths of three minors." These incidents would not have been prevented by the curfew because two of the victims were killed during hours outside the curfew and the third, as a result of being adjudicated a person in need of supervision, was already subject to an individualized curfew. Thus, these incidents do not provide the necessary nexus between the curfew and the ordinance's stated purpose.

Further, we conclude that the crime statistics produced by defendants do not support the objectives of Rochester's nocturnal curfew. Although the statistics show that minors are suspects and victims in roughly 10% of violent crimes committed between curfew hours (11:00 P.M. to 5:00 A.M.), what they really highlight is that minors are far more likely to commit or be victims of crime outside curfew hours and that it is the adults, rather than the minors, who commit and are victims of the vast majority of violent crime (83.6% and 87.8% respectively) during curfew hours. The crime statistics are also organized by days of the week and despite that minors are 64% to 160% more likely to be a victim and up to 375% more likely to be a suspect of violent crimes on Saturdays and Sundays as compared to a given weekday, surprisingly, the curfew is less prohibitive on weekends. We also note that the methodology and scope of the statistics are plainly over-inclusive for purposes of studying the effectiveness of the curfew.

To be sure, minors are affected by crime during curfew hours but from the obvious disconnect between the crime statistics and the *nighttime* curfew, it seems that "no effort [was] made by the [City] to ensure that the population targeted by the ordinance represented that part of the population causing trouble or that was being victimized." If, as the dissent argues, it is enough that from 2000 to 2005 a number of juveniles were victimized at night, then the same statistics would justify, perhaps even more strongly, imposing a juvenile curfew during all hours outside of school since far more victimization occurs during those hours. . . .

We also conclude that the curfew imposes an unconstitutional burden on a parent's substantive due process rights. The City asserts that the ordinance promotes "parental supervision" of minors. But the curfew fails to offer parents enough flexibility or autonomy in supervising their children. Indeed, an exception allowing for parental consent to the activities of minors during curfew hours is of paramount importance to the due process rights of parents. "The . . . notion that governmental power should supersede parental authority in *all* cases because *some* parents abuse and neglect children is repugnant to American tradition." If a parental consent exception were included in this curfew, it would be a closer case — courts have upheld curfews having, among other things, such an exception as only minimally intrusive upon the parent's due process rights. . . .

Accordingly, the order of the Appellate Division should be affirmed without costs.

(The concurring opinion of Justice Graffeo is omitted.)

PIGOTT, J. (dissenting). . . . [B]ecause children often lack the capacity to make important decisions for themselves, "[t]hey are assumed to be subject to the control of their parents, and if parental control falters, the State must play its part as *parens patriae*. In this respect, the juvenile's liberty interest may, in appropriate circumstances, be subordinated to the State's *parens patriae* interest in preserving and promoting the welfare of the child." All states limit children's freedom of movement by requiring them to attend school for much of every weekday — a requirement never thought to call for either strict or intermediate scrutiny. As the Supreme Court has succinctly expressed it, "juveniles, unlike adults, are always in some form of custody" (Reno v. Flores, 507 U.S. 292, 302 [1993], quoting *Schall*, 467 U.S. at 265).

These well-established premises of constitutional jurisprudence lead to the conclusion that the fundamental right to travel or movement does not extend to unsupervised minors. Because parents have the right to control or forbid children's travel, there can be no such thing as a child's fundamental right to free movement. Quite simply, children do not have the right to wander the streets freely at night. Because the curfew ordinance does not impinge on any cognizable constitutional right of minors, its restriction of minors' movements should therefore be subject to rational basis review.

On the other hand, the majority's choice of intermediate scrutiny to evaluate plaintiffs' assertion that the curfew ordinance violates the substantive due process rights of *parents* to make decisions concerning the care, custody, and control of their children makes sense. The majority apparently does not dispute that preventing minors from committing or becoming the victims of nighttime crime is an important government interest. The only remaining question then is whether the curfew ordinance is substantially related to this important objective. I believe it is.

The record contains extensive affidavits of public officials who were involved in the adoption of the curfew ordinance, and the affidavits and reports of experienced police officials responsible for its enforcement, which describe the considerable amount of investigation and research that was carried out before the City Council adopted the ordinance. The record also contains crime statistics for the City, and information concerning the implementation of similar curfews in other municipalities. The decision to enact the curfew, while based in part on objective data, was also based in substantial part on the subjective judgment of experienced civic leaders, who believed the ordinance to be the best way of dealing with a very troubling problem. Their judgment is, in my opinion, entitled to considerable deference. The majority gives it none.

Instead, the majority focuses on the statistics, but does so in a selective manner. It does not mention the statistics which demonstrate that between 2000 and 2005 most of the 13 juvenile murder victims in Rochester would have been in violation of the ordinance at the time of the murders. Nor does it mention that 45% of homicides in Rochester occurred during the curfew hours, a surprisingly high percentage given that the curfew hours make up less than 25% of the hours in a week.

The majority casts a skeptical eye on the statistics, writing that they show "that minors are far more likely to commit or be victims of crime outside curfew hours and that it is the adults, rather than the minors, who commit and are victims of the vast majority of violent crime . . . during curfew hours." Here, I respectfully suggest, the majority jumbles together two platitudes. Of course minors are more likely to commit or be victims of crime outside curfew hours. For one thing, the curfew hours comprise only 40 out of the 168 hours in a week. As to the likelihood of becoming crime victims, most children are at home during the curfew hours, as the defendant Mayor noted. But it certainly does not follow that a child who goes out at night is less likely to become the victim of a crime than one who goes out during the day. Again, it is completely unsurprising that adults commit and are victims of most crimes during curfew hours. Adults commit more crimes than children at all hours. Indeed, this may simply be an instance of the general truth that adults, who make up some three quarters of the population, are more likely to do anything.

From these platitudes, the majority infers a "disconnect between the crime statistics and the *nighttime* curfew. . . ." But here, under the guise of assessing whether the curfew ordinance is substantially related to a government objective, the majority essentially withdraws its earlier concession that protecting minors from becoming the victims or perpetrators of crimes is an important government interest. In essence, the majority is asserting that if adults commit and become victims of more crimes than children, then protecting children from crime cannot be an important city objective, and that if more crimes are committed during the day than at night, then preventing nighttime crime cannot be an important city objective. The problem with that reasoning is obvious.

Putting aside the Rochester crime statistics, which suggest that a significant proportion of violent crime victims in that city are children, I do not believe that it is the judiciary's place to decide that protecting even a small number of minors from crime is an unimportant objective. I would have thought that protecting children from becoming the victims or perpetrators of violent crime is one of the most important goals a municipality could try to achieve, especially in the wake of a series of nighttime murders of minors.

Turning to plaintiffs' challenge based on parental authority, the majority observes that this would be a closer case if the curfew had included an exception for parental consent . . . However, even without that exception, I believe that the curfew ordinance in Rochester is merely a minimal intrusion on parents' rights. If the standard of review in this regard were strict scrutiny, I might conclude that the ordinance is not the least restrictive alternative means of achieving the City's purpose. But, applying intermediate scrutiny as the majority professes to, I believe that the curfew—which contains exceptions for minors who are accompanied by a parent, guardian, or other responsible adult, those engaged in lawful employment or en route to or from such employment, those facing emergency circumstances, those who are "going to, attending, or returning home from an official school, religious, or other recreational activity sponsored and/or supervised by a public entity or a civic organization," those who are in a public place "for the specific purpose of exercising fundamental rights such as freedom of speech or religion or the right of assembly protected by the First Amendment of the United States Constitution or Article I of the Constitution of the State of New York," and those engaged in interstate travel—is narrowly tailored to serve its important government purpose of preventing juvenile crime. . . .

For these reasons, I respectfully dissent.

NOTES AND QUESTIONS

1. In Chicago v. Morales, 527 U.S. 41, 54 (1999), which involved the constitutionality of an ordinance punishing loitering, the Supreme Court discussed the "right to move around":

> [T]he freedom to loiter for innocent purposes is part of the "liberty" protected by the Due Process Clause of the Fourteenth Amendment. We have expressly identified this "right to remove from one place to another according to inclination" as "an attribute of personal liberty" protected by the Constitution. Indeed, it is apparent that an individual's decision to remain in a public place of his choice is as much a part of his liberty as the freedom of movement inside frontiers that is "a part of our heritage" or the right to move "to whatsoever place one's own inclination may direct" identified in Blackstone's Commentaries. 1 W. Blackstone, Commentaries on the Laws of England 130 (1765).

The majority and dissent in Anonymous v. City of Rochester disagree about whether minors have this right. What is the source of their disagreement? The majority, unlike courts in some other states, applies intermediate scrutiny to assess the constitutionality of the statutes even though similar statutes affecting adults would be subject to strict scrutiny. Why does the court use the lower standard?

2. The majority also says that the statute affects constitutionally protected parental rights. If the statute had had a broader emergency errand exception, would it have survived this challenge? Why or why not?

3. While juvenile curfew laws have existed for more than a century, their popularity waned in the 1960s and 1970s and then resurged in the 1990s. By 2009, 84 percent of cities with populations of greater than 180,000 had curfew laws. Tony Favro, Youth Curfews Popular with American Cities but Effectiveness and Legality Are Questioned (City Mayors Society, July 21, 2009), http://www.city-mayors.com/society/usa-youth-curfews.html#Anchor-History-49575.

In 2016, more than 34,000 juveniles were arrested for curfew violations, a decrease of 51 percent from 2012 and of 24 percent from 2015. Office of Juvenile Justice and Delinquency Prevention, Statistical Briefing Book, Juvenile Arrests 2016, https://www.ojjdp.gov/ojstatbb/crime/qa05101.asp.

4. Two reviews of published empirical research about the effectiveness of juvenile curfews concluded that the evidence does not show that enforcing curfews causes a decrease in juvenile crime or in victimization of juveniles. David Wilson et al., Juvenile Curfew Effects on Criminal Behavior and Victimization (Campbell Collaboration, Mar. 23, 2016), https://www.campbellcollaboration.org/library/juvenile-curfew-effects-on-behaviour.html; Kenneth Adams, The Effectiveness of Juvenile Curfews at Crime Prevention, 587 Annals of Am. Acad. Pol. & Soc. Sci. 136, 141-148 (2003). On the other hand, a 2016 research review found that the studies of curfews found mixed results and that the studies that found positive effects used stronger methodologies than those that did not. The authors concluded, however, that because of the low number of high-quality studies, more research is needed before conclusions can be drawn about the effectiveness of curfews. Elyse R. Grossman & Nancy A. Miller, A Systematic Review of the Impact of Juvenile Curfew Laws on Public Health and Justice Outcomes, 49(6) Am. J. Prev. Med. 945 (2015).

C.   PROSECUTING MINORS IN ADULT CRIMINAL COURT

In 45 states, juvenile courts have original jurisdiction over most cases in which a person younger than 18 is charged with an offense. Five states—Georgia, Michigan, Missouri, Texas, and Wisconsin—prosecute juveniles as adults beginning at age 17. Nat'l Conf. of State Legislatures, Juvenile Age of Jurisdiction and Transfer to Adult Court Laws (Apr. 17, 2017), http://www.ncsl.org/research/civil-and-criminal-justice/juvenile-age-of-jurisdiction-and-transfer-to-adult-court-laws.aspx (Aug. 13, 2018). New York and North Carolina, the last two states that terminated juvenile court jurisdiction at 16, raised their age limits to 18 in 2017. Nat'l Conf. of State Legislatures, Juvenile Justice 2017 Year End Report (Jan. 19, 2018), http://www.ncsl.org/research/civil-and-criminal-justice/juvenile-justice-2017-year-end-report.aspx (Aug. 13, 2018).

All states have one or more means of transferring at least some cases involving minors younger than the maximum age limit from juvenile court to adult criminal court. Transfer provisions have been included in juvenile codes from the beginning; the Chicago juvenile court transferred fourteen children to the criminal justice system in 1903, only 5 years after the court's creation.

The differences between juvenile court and adult treatment reflect the traditional juvenile court scheme. Juvenile court adjudications still do not carry with them some of the collateral consequences associated with convictions for crime. Juvenile court hearings were traditionally closed, and court records were confidential—a practice that, when observed, reduced prejudice to a child's opportunities for employment and, in some cases, education. Besides facing the potential of much harsher sentences, minors tried as adults rather than juveniles receive little or no rehabilitative programming and have more difficulty expunging their criminal records. Minors transferred to adult court may be held in adult jails and prisons, where they are at greater risk of victimization and death than in juvenile facilities.

1.   The Processes for Transferring Cases to Adult Court

Until the 1960s, individual orders by the juvenile court judge were the means for transferring a case to adult court. The Supreme Court's first decision concerning juvenile court practices concerned this process.

KENT v. UNITED STATES

383 U.S. 541 (1966)

[Morris Kent was arrested for rape and theft. During interrogation, he admitted his involvement in these and other offenses. He was detained in the receiving home (detention facility) for almost a week, without arraignment. During this time, he was examined by two psychiatrists, one of whom diagnosed him as psychopathic and recommended hospitalization. The Department of Social Services, which presented the case in juvenile court matters at that time, requested waiver of jurisdiction, in connection with which Kent's lawyer asked for access to his client's Social Services file. The trial judge did not rule on this motion and did not hold a hearing or otherwise take evidence but entered an order reciting that after "full investigation, I do hereby waive" jurisdiction of the minor. Kent was tried as an adult and found not guilty of rape by reason of insanity but guilty of six counts of housebreaking and robbery. He was sentenced to a total of 30 to 90 years in prison. He was also committed to a mental hospital because of his acquittal by reason of insanity.]

FORTAS, J. . . . We do not consider whether, on the merits, Kent should have been transferred; but: there is no place in our system of law for reaching a result of such tremendous consequences without ceremony—without hearing, without effective assistance of counsel, without a statement of reasons. It is inconceivable that a court of justice dealing with adults, with respect to a similar issue, would proceed in this manner. It would be extraordinary if society's special concern for children, as reflected in the District of Columbia's Juvenile Court Act, permitted this procedure. We hold that it does not. . . .

It is clear beyond dispute that the waiver of jurisdiction is a "critically important" action determining vitally important statutory rights of the juvenile. . . . The statutory scheme makes this plain. The Juvenile Court is vested with "original and exclusive jurisdiction" of the child. This jurisdiction confers special rights and immunities. He is, as specified by statute, shielded from publicity. He may be confined, but with rare exceptions he may not be jailed along with adults. He may be detained, but only until he is 21 years of age. The court is admonished by the statute to give preference to retaining the child in the custody of his parents "unless his welfare and the safety and protection of the public can not be adequately safeguarded without . . . removal." The child is protected against consequences of adult conviction such as the loss of civil rights, the use of adjudication against him in subsequent proceedings, and disqualification for public employment.

The net, therefore, is that petitioner—then a boy of 16—was by statute entitled to certain procedures and benefits as a consequence of his statutory right to the "exclusive" jurisdiction of the Juvenile Court. In these circumstances, considering particularly that decision as to waiver of jurisdiction and transfer of the matter to the District Court was potentially as important to petitioner as the difference between five years confinement and a death sentence, we conclude that, as a condition to a valid waiver order, petitioner was entitled to a hearing, including access by his counsel to the social records and probation or similar reports which presumably are considered by the court, and to a statement of reasons for the Juvenile Court's decision. We believe that this result is required by the statute read in the context of constitutional principles relating to due process and the assistance of counsel. . . .

Meaningful review requires that the reviewing court should review. It should not be remitted to assumptions. It must have before it a statement of the reasons motivating the waiver including, of course, a statement of the relevant facts. It may not "assume" that there are adequate reasons, nor may it merely assume that "full investigation" has been made. Accordingly, we hold that it is incumbent upon the Juvenile Court to accompany its waiver order with a statement of the reasons or considerations therefor. We do not read the statute as requiring that this statement must be formal or that it should necessarily include conventional findings of fact. But the statement should be sufficient to demonstrate that the statutory requirement of "full investigation" has been met; and that the question has received the careful consideration of the Juvenile Court; and it must set forth the basis for the order with sufficient specificity to permit meaningful review.

Correspondingly, we conclude that an opportunity for a hearing which may be informal, must be given the child prior to entry of a waiver order. . . . These rights are meaningless—an illusion, a mockery—unless counsel is given an opportunity to function. The right to representation by counsel is not a formality. It is not a grudging gesture to a ritualistic requirement. It is of the essence of justice. Appointment of counsel without affording an opportunity for hearing on a "critically important" decision is tantamount to denial of counsel. There is no justification for the failure of the Juvenile Court to rule on the motion for hearing filed by petitioner's counsel, and it was error to fail to grant a hearing.

We do not mean by this to indicate that the hearing to be held must conform with all of the requirements of a criminal trial or even of the usual administrative hearing; but we do hold that the hearing must measure up to the essentials of due process and fair treatment. . . .

NOTES AND QUESTIONS

1. The kind of information relevant at a transfer hearing depends on the statutory standards for transfer, but the facts of the alleged offenses will always be relevant. After *Kent*, some jurisdictions conducted transfer hearings after the trial on the merits in the juvenile court, but the Supreme Court held that the constitutional prohibition on double jeopardy precludes trying the young person again in adult criminal court. Breed v. Jones, 421 U.S. 519 (1975). The Court said,

> We believe it is simply too late in the day to conclude, as did the District Court in this case, that a juvenile is not put in jeopardy at a proceeding whose object is to determine whether he has committed acts that violate a criminal law and whose potential consequences include both the stigma inherent in such a determination and the deprivation of liberty for many years. For it is clear under our cases that determining the relevance of constitutional policies, like determining the applicability of constitutional rights, in juvenile proceedings, requires that courts eschew "the 'civil' label-of-convenience which has been attached to juvenile proceedings," and that "the juvenile process . . . be candidly appraised.". . .
>
> We do not agree with petitioner that giving respondent the constitutional protection against multiple trials in this context will diminish flexibility and informality to the extent that those qualities relate uniquely to the goals of the juvenile-court system. We agree that such a holding will require, in most cases, that the transfer decision be made prior to an adjudicatory hearing. To the extent that evidence concerning the alleged offense is considered relevant, it may be that, in those cases where transfer is considered and rejected, some added burden will be imposed on the juvenile courts by reason of duplicative proceedings. Finally, the nature of the evidence considered at a transfer hearing may in some States require that, if transfer is rejected, a different judge preside at the adjudicatory hearing. . . .
>
> A requirement that transfer hearings be held prior to adjudicatory hearings affects not at all the nature of the latter proceedings. More significantly, such a requirement need not affect the quality of decisionmaking at transfer hearings themselves. In Kent v. United States, the Court held that hearings under the statute there involved "must measure up to the essentials of due process and fair treatment." However, the Court has never attempted to prescribe criteria for, or the nature and quantum of evidence that must support, a decision to transfer a juvenile for trial in adult court. We require only that, whatever the relevant criteria, and whatever the evidence demanded, a State determine whether it wants to treat a juvenile within the juvenile-court system before entering upon a proceeding that may result in an adjudication that he has violated a criminal law and in a substantial deprivation of liberty, rather than subject him to the expense, delay, strain, and embarrassment of two such proceedings. . . .

421 U.S. at 529, 535-538.

2. After *Kent* and *Breed*, what does a "full investigation" at the transfer hearing require? What evidence should the judge consider in a judicial waiver hearing? What is the burden of proof? Who is "amenable to treatment"? How can a judge

predict a youth's future "dangerousness"? *See generally* Barry C. Feld, Reference of Juvenile Offenders for Adult Prosecution: The Legislative Alternative to Asking Unanswerable Questions, 62 Minn. L. Rev. 151 (1978). *SEE ALSO* In re D.M., 18 N.E.3d 404, 406-407 (Ohio 2014) (holding that youth subject to transfer hearings, such as probable cause and amenability hearings in juvenile court, are entitled to discovery and the prosecution must hand over all evidence in the state's possession that is favorable to the juvenile and material to guilt, innocence, or punishment).

3. Apprendi v. New Jersey, 530 U.S. 466, 490 (2000), held that any fact other than a prior conviction that exposes a defendant to a sentence in excess of the statutory maximum must be established beyond a reasonable doubt and must be found by a jury, not a judge. Since transferring a child to adult court can extend the sentence beyond what the juvenile court could order, does *Apprendi* require that the findings justifying transfer be made by a jury under the beyond a reasonable doubt standard of proof? Courts have generally rejected this claim. Villalon v. State, 956 N.E.2d 697 (Ind. App. 2012); State v. Andrews, 329 S.W.3d 369 (Mo. 2011) (en banc); State v. Rudy B., 243 P.3d 726 (N.M. 2010); State v. Rice. 737 S.E.2d 485 (S.C. 2013). *See also* In re M.I., 989 N.E.2d 173 (Ill. 2013) (*Apprendi* does not require that findings necessary to apply extended juvenile court jurisdiction, which is discussed later in this chapter, be made by a jury).

NOTE: PROSECUTORIAL CONTROL OVER THE WAIVER DECISION

After *Kent* made clear that the Constitution requires procedural safeguards during transfer hearings, states began to enact laws that create other mechanisms that result in youth who are younger than the maximum age for juvenile court jurisdiction being tried as adults. Today most states have at least two methods.

As of 2016, judicial waiver remained the most common statutory provision, available in 45 states and the District of Columbia. Judicial waiver is initiated by prosecutorial motion, but most states limit waiver by age and offense. In all these states, judges have discretion over waiver decisions for some offenses; in 12 the statutes provide that waiver is rebuttably presumed to be correct for some offenses, and in 13 waiver is required once certain statutory criteria are proven. In 28 states "reverse waiver"—return of a minor charged in adult court to juvenile court based on an individual judicial decision—is also authorized. Office of Juvenile Justice and Delinquency Prevention, Statistical Briefing Book, Juveniles Tried as Adults, https://www.ojjdp.gov/ojstatbb/structure_process/qa04115.asp?qaDate=2016.

In 14 states, juvenile and adult courts have concurrent jurisdiction over some offenses for offenders older than prescribed ages; the prosecutor has discretion to choose where to file. In 28 states certain offenses, most often murder and other serious crimes against the person, must be tried in adult court. *Id.* While the latter kind of statute does not expressly grant prosecutors discretion, it does so effectively, since prosecutors have discretion whether to charge an offense that falls within these mandatory provisions or a lesser offense that may be tried in juvenile court. This kind of statute accounts for the largest number of minors tried as adults in the United States. In fact, more minors may reach adult court through this process than through the other transfer mechanisms combined. In recent years these transfer mechanisms have been eliminated or limited in several jurisdictions. "For example, in 2016, Illinois eliminated the direct or automatic transfer of all children below the age of 16, regardless of the crime charged, limiting the practice to juveniles ages 16 or 17 who are charged with first-degree murder, aggravated criminal sexual assault, or aggravated battery with a firearm. The same year, California voters approved a proposition that repealed direct filing completely, regardless of the youth's age or the crime charged. Other states that have eliminated or severely restricted direct filing include Vermont, New Jersey, and Indiana. Recent legislation will accordingly significantly diminish, though not abolish, the criminal prosecution of adolescents." Merril Sobie, The State of American Juvenile Justice, 33 (Spring) Crim. Just. 26, 27 (2018).

Constitutional challenges to legislatures' choices regarding type of waiver statutes and their specific terms have not been successful. Courts have generally accepted the argument that, since juveniles have no constitutional right to be tried in a separate court system at all, states may design their procedures for sorting minors into adult and juvenile court as they see fit, provided that the procedure comports with fundamental fairness. *E.g.*, United States v. Bland, 472 F.2d 1329 (D.C. 1972) (prosecutorial waiver is not subject to judicial review and does not have to meet the due process standards set out in *Kent*); Tate v. State, 864 So. 2d 44 (Fla. App. 2003) (11-year-old has no constitutional right to be tried in juvenile court, and subjecting him to adult penalties when older youth may receive juvenile or adult penalties in the judge's discretion does not violate equal protection); Commonwealth v. Wayne W., 606 N.E.2d 1323 (Mass. 1993) (statute that rebuttably presumes minor charged with murder will be tried as an adult does not violate due process); State v. Aalim, 83 N.E.3d 883 (Ohio 2017) (legislature has exclusive constitutional authority to define the jurisdiction of court of general jurisdiction, including granting it jurisdiction over limited class of juvenile cases and legislation does not violate due process or equal protection).

Barry C. Feld, *Juvenile and Criminal Justice Systems' Responses to Youth Violence*

24 Crime & Just. 189, 195-196, 199-202, 206, 208-212 (1998)

Public frustration with crime, fear of the recent rise in youth violence, and the racial characteristics of violent young offenders fuel the desire to "get tough" and provide political impetus to prosecute larger numbers of youths as adults. These initiatives simplify the transfer of young offenders to criminal courts and expose many waived youths to mandatory minimum sentences as adults, or require juvenile court judges to impose determinate or mandatory minimum sentences on youths. . . . [They] deemphasize rehabilitation and individualized consideration of the offender, stress personal and justice system accountability and punishment, and base waiver and sentencing decisions on the seriousness of the present offense and prior record. Sentencing young offenders as adults increases the number of chronological juveniles confined in adult prisons and poses substantial challenges for adult correctional officials. Juvenile institutional administrators confront similar challenges as judges confine more serious young delinquents for longer periods of time. . . .

In response to the resurgence of youth crime in the late 1980s, politicians, juvenile justice personnel, and criminologists debated extensively the relative merits of different strategies to prosecute some serious young offenders in criminal courts. . . . All of the theoretical differences between juvenile and criminal courts' sentencing philosophies become visible in transfer proceedings and in legislative policy debates. Transfer laws simultaneously attempt to resolve both fundamental crime control issues and the ambivalence embedded in our cultural construction of youth. The jurisprudential conflicts reflect current sentencing policy debates: the tensions between rehabilitation and incapacitation or retribution, between decisions based on characteristics of the offender or the seriousness of the offense, between discretion and rules, and between indeterminacy and determinacy. Waiver laws attempt to reconcile the contradictory impulses engendered when the child is a criminal and the criminal is a child. What processes best enable us to choose between competing conceptions of youths as responsible and culpable offenders and as immature and salvageable children? In the early stages of a criminal career and prospectively, what criteria best differentiate between adolescent-only offenders and life-course persistent offenders? . . .

Judicial waiver criteria framed in terms of amenability to treatment or dangerousness give judges broad, standardless discretion. Lists of substantive factors such as those appended in *Kent* do not provide adequate guidance. Rather, catalogues of contradictory factors reinforce judges' discretion and allow them selectively to emphasize one element or another to justify any decision. . . .

The subjective nature of waiver decisions, the absence of effective guidelines to structure outcomes, and the lack of objective indicators or scientific tools with which to classify youths allows judges to make unequal and disparate rulings without any effective procedural or appellate checks. Empirical analyses provide compelling evidence that judges apply waiver statutes in an arbitrary, capricious, and discriminatory manner. States' waiver rates for similar types of offenders vary extensively. Even within a single jurisdiction, judges do not administer, interpret, or apply waiver statutes consistently from county to county or court to court. Research in several states reports a contextual pattern of "justice by geography" in which, where youths lived rather than what they did, determined their juvenile or adult status. . . . These differences influence both the characteristics of youths waived and the sentences they receive.

A youth's race also may affect waiver decisions. In analyses in four states in which the U.S. General Accounting Office could control for the effects of race on judicial waiver decisions, it found that judges transferred black youths charged with violent, property, or drug offenses more readily than comparable white offenders. Differences in judicial philosophies, the location of a waiver hearing, a youth's race, or organizational politics may explain as much about transfer decisions as does a youth's offense or personal characteristics. . . .

Critics of offense exclusion question whether legislators can exclude offenses and remove discretion without making the process excessively rigid and overinclusive. In a get tough climate, politicians experience considerable difficulty resisting their own impulses to adopt expansive lists of excluded "crimes de jour." Once a legislature adopts an excluded-offense or presumptive waiver statute, the list of offenses often lengthens quickly and results in far more youths being tried as adults than would occur under a more flexible, discretionary system. California amended its presumptive waiver offense criteria seven times between 1977 and 1993 and increased the initial list of eleven serious violent crimes to twenty-three, including drug crimes, carjacking, and escape from a correctional facility. Critics of prosecutorial waiver strategies contend that locally elected prosecutors often succumb to the same get tough pressures that influence legislators. Prosecutors often lack the experience or maturity that judges possess, exercise their discretion just as subjectively and idiosyncratically as do judges, and introduce additional geographic variability.

In short, excluded-offense and prosecutor-choice waiver legislation may suffer from the rigidity, inflexibility, and overinclusiveness characteristic of mandatory sentencing statutes. In practice, offense exclusion transfers discretion from judges to prosecutors who determine delinquent or criminal status by manipulating their charging decisions. States that use a concurrent-jurisdiction prosecutor-choice strategy simply make the allocation of power and sentencing authority explicit. While a rule-of-law approach can improve on unstructured judicial discretion, offense exclusion and prosecutor-choice laws do not provide either a jurisprudentially satisfactory or politically practical solution. . . .

State legislatures in the past two decades have extensively modified their transfer laws. . . . One cannot overemphasize either the amount and scope of legislative activity or the rapidity with which these changes spread. Since 1992, forty-eight of the fifty-one states and the District of Columbia have amended provisions of their juvenile codes, sentencing statutes, and transfer laws to target youths who commit chronic, serious, or violent crimes. The overarching legislative theme is a shift from the principle of individualized justice to the principle of offense, from rehabilitation to retribution. . . .

Judicial waiver statutes that use offense criteria explicitly to target serious violent offenders and laws that grant prosecutors discretion to choose the forum or that exclude violent offenses from juvenile court jurisdiction increase the likelihood that young offenders will receive significant sentences as adults. Recall that until the recent spate of statutory amendments, prosecutors typically charged most judicially waived juveniles with property offenses, not violent crimes, and that criminal courts neither imprisoned most of these adult first offenders nor imposed sentences longer than those available in juvenile courts. The limited research on the adult sentences received by violent youths produces mixed results.

Restricting waiver to serious offenses and specifying special procedures apparently increases the likelihood that juvenile courts will waive and that criminal courts will impose significant adult sentences. Several studies examine the sentences that waived or excluded youths receive when tried as adults in jurisdictions that target them as serious offenders and found that their probabilities of significant adult sanctions increased. In 1976, California amended its judicial waiver statute, created a presumption that juvenile courts should waive youths charged with certain serious crimes, and shifted the burden of proof to the juvenile defendant. Initial evaluations indicated that the changes increased the number of youths tried, convicted, and sentenced as adults after being charged with one of the enumerated offenses. Criminal court judges in Los Angeles did not sentence juveniles tried as adults more leniently than they did other offenders, the gravity or violence of the crime rather than the age or record of the offender determined the sentence for more serious crimes, and the prior juvenile record influenced the severity of the first adult sentence for marginal crimes like burglary. A study in a northern California county reported that prosecutors filed waiver motions for four presumptive-transfer violent offenses for every one property offense, and judges waived about half the youths. Youths transferred and convicted as adults for crimes against the person received substantially greater punishment based solely on the seriousness of the present offense than did youths retained in juvenile court or transferred as chronic property offenders. As a result of the legislative changes, in 1990 and 1991 California juvenile courts waived the vast majority of youths (85.1 percent) to adult courts for violent offenses.

A number of studies have analyzed prosecutorial waiver practices in Florida. . . . They found that prosecutors charged a majority (55 percent) of direct-file youths with property felonies and less than one-third of youths with crimes against the person. Moreover, as legislative amendments expanded prosecutors' authority to direct file, the proportion of violent offenders transferred actually declined from 30 percent in 1981 to 20 percent in 1984. Prosecutors apparently transferred many youths simply because they neared the jurisdictional age limits of juvenile courts. Frazier compared the characteristics of youths against whom prosecutors direct filed with those retained and confined in the deep end of the juvenile system and found that the latter youths appeared to be more serious offenders than the transferred youths in terms of their present offense, amount and quality of prior records, and prior correctional dispositions. Bishop et al. compared the postconviction recidivism of youths whom prosecutors direct filed in 1987 for noncapital or life offenses with a matched sample of retained juveniles and found that, by all measures, the youths whom prosecutors tried as adults did worse—they committed additional and more serious offenses more quickly than did those youths retained in juvenile jurisdiction.

The transfer decision has profound consequences for waived violent youths even though the decision itself lacks any apparent or consistent rationale. A study of the dispositions received by waived and retained youths in four urban sites whom prosecutors charged with a violent offense and who had a prior felony conviction reported that criminal courts incarcerated over 90 percent and imposed sentences five times longer than those given to youths with similar offense characteristics but who remained in juvenile court. However, analysts could not identify the factors that juvenile court judges used initially to distinguish between the juveniles whom they waived or retained within this sample of violent youths.

A natural quasi-experiment compared young robbery and burglary offenders in New York, whose excluded offenses placed them in criminal court, with a similar sample of fifteen- and sixteen-year-old youths in matched counties in New Jersey whose age and offenses placed them in juvenile courts. The New York criminal courts convicted and incarcerated a somewhat larger proportion of youths, but both justice systems imposed sentences of comparable length. Although burglary offenders in both jurisdictions recidivated at about the same rate, adult robbery offenders in New York reoffended more quickly and at a higher rate than did the juveniles in New Jersey. Criminalizing adolescent crimes provides only symbolic benefits but allows youths to acquire criminal records earlier and thereby receive more severe sentences for subsequent adult offenses.[4]

Several studies consistently indicate that criminal courts imprison more often and impose longer sentences on violent youths tried as adults than do juvenile courts. Although violent offenders constituted a small subset of all juveniles judicially waived in Oregon, criminal courts incarcerated 75 percent of the violent juveniles and imposed prison sentences in excess of six years. In Hennepin County (Minneapolis), Minnesota, criminal courts convicted and incarcerated transferred youths at higher rates than juvenile courts did the retained juveniles. Although juvenile courts imposed longer sentences on young property offenders than did criminal courts, the latter sentenced the violent young adults to terms about five times longer than those received by violent juveniles sentenced as delinquents. In Arizona, criminal court judges incarcerated only 43 percent of all transferred juveniles but imprisoned youths convicted of violent crimes almost three times as often as they did youths convicted of other types of offenses (McNulty 1996).

Waiver laws, in all their guises, appear to confront two somewhat different but overlapping populations of offenders — persistent and violent youths. One group consists of chronic offenders currently charged with property crimes, but whose extensive delinquency histories, prior correctional exposures, and advancing age in relation to juvenile courts' maximum jurisdiction render them eligible for adult prosecution. A second group consists of violent offenders. While some violent youths also are chronic offenders, others have less extensive prior records or exposure to juvenile court correctional treatment. Judges appear more likely to waive violent offenders at younger ages than to waive property offenders. For example, while 71.9 percent of all youths whom Arizona juvenile court judges waived were seventeen years of age, prosecutors charged three-quarters (75 percent) of the youths transferred at age fourteen with violent crimes but only 43.7 percent of the oldest waived juveniles.

---

4. [Other empirical studies have also concluded that minors transferred to adult criminal court, particularly those charged with crimes against the person, are more likely to reoffend than those who are tried in the juvenile system. *See, e.g.,* Donna Bishop & Charles Frazier, Consequences of Transfer in The Changing Borders of Juvenile Justice: Transfer of Adolescents to the Criminal Court 27, 261-264 (Jeffrey Fagan & Franklin E. Zimring, eds., 2000); Kareem J. Jordan & David L. Myers, Juvenile Transfer and Deterrence: Reexamining the Effectiveness of a "Get-Tough" Policy, 57 Crime & Delinq. 247 (2011) (finding that of the three basic criteria necessary for deterrence, juvenile transfer achieves only *severity* of punishment, as there is no difference in *certainty* of punishment between the two court systems, and court processing occurred with more *speed* in juvenile court); Richard E. Redding, The Effects of Adjudicating and Sentencing Juveniles as Adults, 1 Youth Violence & Juv. Just. 128 (2003); Richard E. Redding, Adult Punishment for Juvenile Offenders: Does It Reduce Crime? in Handbook on Children, Culture and Violence 375 (Nancy Dowd, Dorothy Singer & Robin Fretwell Wilson, eds., 2006) (collecting and analyzing studies). *See also* Randi Hajalmarsson, Juvenile Jails: A Path to the Straight and Narrow or to Hardened Criminality?, 52 J.L. & Econ. 779 (2009) (finding that incarceration in juvenile facilities for 15–36 weeks, rather than probationary or non-incarcerative sentences, was effective in reducing recidivism rates).—Eds.]

In the Matter of J. C. N.–V.

380 P.3d 248 (Or. 2016)

WALTERS, J. . . . Youth was 13 years and eight months old when he allegedly participated in a violent murder and robbery. When he was taken into custody, youth was deemed to be within the exclusive jurisdiction of the juvenile court. The state, however, petitioned the juvenile court to waive youth into Washington County Circuit Court so that he could be tried as an adult for, among things, aggravated murder.

At a hearing on the state's petition, the parties presented evidence addressing the requirements for waiver. To show that youth possessed "sufficient sophistication and maturity to appreciate the nature and quality of the conduct involved," the state relied in large part on facts about youth's alleged participation in the murder. It presented evidence that Aguilar-Mandujano, the 20-year-old brother of youth's girlfriend, had solicited youth's assistance in a plan to rob and murder an adult acquaintance; that youth had agreed to participate; that youth had initiated the attack on the victim by striking him with a tire iron that Aguilar-Mandujano had provided; that youth had repeatedly hit the victim with the tire iron while Aguilar-Mandujano stabbed him with a knife; that Aguilar-Mandujano had given the knife to youth, who also had stabbed the victim in the chest and neck; that youth had assisted Aguilar-Mandujano in disposing of the murder weapons and in pushing the victim's body down to the river that ran next to the park where the murder occurred; and that youth had later returned to the river with another associate and, finding the victim's body still visible, had kicked the body completely into the river. The state suggested that the requisite "sophistication and maturity to appreciate the nature and quality of the conduct" was evident from youth's own admission that he had understood Aguilar-Mandujano's plan and what he was being asked to do, from his "high degree of participation" in the actual killing, from his efforts to conceal evidence of the murder, and from his own acknowledged apprehensions about being caught and going to jail for his participation in the murder.

The state also relied on an evaluation of youth submitted by a psychologist, Dr. Sebastian. Dr. Sebastian's report acknowledged youth's immaturity. She reported that, on a well-accepted "Sophistication-Maturity Scale" designed for use by courts in making waiver decisions, youth was immature in many ways: he "ha[d] not developed an internal locus of control," he was "influenced and led by older youth," and his "self-concept [was] not yet solidly developed." His "moral development [was] still immature in that he c[ould] identify the impacts of his behavior on his immediate family . . . but he was unable to appreciate the impact of his behavior on his victims." Dr. Sebastian's conclusion, however, was that youth exhibited average sophistication and maturity for his age and that he understood that his conduct was wrong:

> By structured interview, testing and collateral dat[a], it is this examiner's opinion that [youth] is as sophisticated and mature as one might expect of a thirteen/fourteen-year old. In other words, he is average in sophistication and maturity for his age. Using records, testing, and interview it is clear this young man has the ability to: (1) think

independently, (2) understand behavioral norms and expectations of adolescents in the larger picture, (3) weigh the risks and benefits of his action, (4) demonstrate age appropriate social skills, (5) anticipate the consequences of his actions, [and] (6) discern which of his behaviors are antisocial. When compared to his age mates, he is just as effective or more effective (because of his strong cognitive ability) in understanding that his crime was wrong and identifying alternatives to his actions. He is less able than his peers at understanding his emotions, resolving conflicts effectively and resisting the influence of other youth.

To counter the state's contention that, at the time of the murder, youth had sufficient "sophistication and maturity to appreciate the nature and quality of [his] conduct," youth presented neuro-scientific evidence about the limitations of adolescent brains in relation to those of adults. An expert, Dr. Nagel, testified about the undeveloped nature of the pre-frontal cortex in adolescents, and about how that neurological difference makes it harder for adolescents to access the brain's higher level, logical functions. Dr. Nagel also testified that not only do adolescents thus remain deficient in higher level thinking and decision-making, but the onset of puberty causes additional neurological "disequilibrium" by "turning up the volume" on the brain's emotional and reward centers. The result, Nagel testified, is that adolescents have significantly more trouble than both adults and younger children in making moral choices in emotionally-charged or social reward-based situations. Although adolescents may have the capacity to understand the act of killing someone in a cold situation, Nagel explained, that capacity is easily overridden in emotionally-laden situations.

Youth also presented the report of a psychologist, Dr. Bolstad, who had performed an intensive examination of youth and his history. Bolstad concluded that cognitively and in most other respects youth was "average" or "normal" for a 13-year-old. Bolstad noted, however, that young adolescents as a whole are considerably less capable of independent thinking than are adults; they are "vulnerable to turning their own decision making responsibilities over to their peers or leaders in their peer group." Based on his review of youth's testing record, Bolstad opined that youth was even more strongly affected in that respect than most adolescents; he had "an immature orientation toward peer group associations, even in comparison with his own same-aged group."

Bolstad also noted that, because of their immature brains, 13-year-olds generally lack sophistication in terms of understanding abstract principles and have difficulty in weighing alternatives and in anticipating the consequences of their actions and decisions. Bolstad added that, because empathy and remorse require abstract thinking, 13-year-olds generally have limitations in those areas as well. He opined that much of the deficits in empathy and remorse that he and others had observed in youth was a product of his young age. He suggested, too, that a family culture of not talking about feelings and youth's own personal strategies for distracting himself from difficult feelings also might play a role in those deficits. When pressed to speak to the "sophistication and maturity" requirement of ORS 419C.349(3), Bolstad seemed to acknowledge that, at the time that youth participated in the murder, he could understand that what he was doing was against the law and that it potentially was going to harm someone; he opined, however, that, although youth thus could appreciate the nature of the crime at some level, he

could not do so "at a level of having empathy because . . . that's a much more challenging task for a 13-year–old with an immature brain." Bolstad concluded that
the "cognitive deficits" associated with the typically undeveloped brain of adolescents "likely would have interfered with [youth's] capacity to appreciate the nature
and quality of the conduct involved."

The parties also offered evidence on another requirement for waiver—that
the juvenile court find that retaining jurisdiction over the youth would not serve
"the best interests of the youth and of society," that evidence addressed the considerations identified in the statute—youth's amenability to treatment, the seriousness of the offense and the aggressive, violent, premeditated or willful manner
in which it was committed, youth's history, including criminal history, the gravity
of the injury caused by the offense, etc. The state's evidence included Sebastian's
psychological evaluation, which suggested that youth was amenable to treatment;
an analysis of treatment resources that suggested that similar resources were available in the juvenile and adult criminal systems up until the age of 25, but that only
in the adult system would any sort of supervision or treatment extend beyond the
age of 25; evidence of the willful and violent nature of youth's involvement in the
murder; and evidence of youth's significant history of violent and delinquent acts,
beginning as early as age nine. Youth's evidence focused primarily on youth's personal history and his amenability to treatment: Through Bolstad's testimony and
the testimony of teachers, youth detention providers and the like, youth sought
to demonstrate that he had performed well in the past in more controlled environments, that he was a normal 13-year–old in many ways, although even more
susceptible to peer pressure than the typical youth of that age, and that, by the age
of 25 when the juvenile court would no longer have jurisdiction, treatment and the
simple maturation of his brain would transform him into a person who could be
released without endangering the community.

After hearing the parties' evidence, the juvenile court granted the state's
petition to waive youth into adult court. As required by ORS 419C.355, the
court . . . made the required determination . . . that youth had sufficient "sophistication and maturity to appreciate the nature and quality of the conduct
involved." . . . Ultimately, the juvenile court concluded that youth's conduct

> demonstrate[d] a degree of maturity consistent with Youth's biological age at the
> time of the event, and in several respects reflect[ed] a degree of maturity consistent
> with an older youth. Youth's response to the police in the interview was coherent
> and responsive. Youth was able to respond to questions of motivation and intent,
> explain his behavior, and the decisions behind his conduct. . . . Youth was aware of
> the criminality of his conduct and told police he did not want to 'get in trouble' or
> 'go to jail.' Although Youth's decisions were tragically flawed, his statements to police
> demonstrate awareness regarding the nature of the criminal act, the degree of his
> participation in the criminal act, and an awareness of the consequences of the crimi-
> nal act if apprehended by authorities.

In considering the issue of whether retention of the juvenile court's jurisdiction over youth was in the best interests of youth and of society, the juvenile
court paid considerable attention to youth's history of unlawful and sometimes
violent conduct, beginning at the age of nine. It also contrasted youth's behavioral

difficulties in public school with his exemplary behavior in the "structured and supportive environment" of juvenile detention facilities. Finally, the court considered whether youth's significant treatment needs, which youth's own expert had acknowledged, would be best met through juvenile or adult adjudication. It found that there would be no significant difference between the two adjudication paths until youth reached the age of 25, but that, at that point, the fact that only the adult adjudication system offered additional supervision made adult adjudication preferable. The court concluded that the interests of both youth and society would best be served by prosecution as an adult. . . .

Youth appealed . . . In an en banc decision, the Court of Appeals . . . opined that the legislature had drawn the provision's "nature and quality" wording from the common-law test for criminal capacity as it relates to the insanity defense, which has been held to require only that the person understand the physical nature and criminality of the act. further opined that the legislature's purpose in employing the "sophistication and maturity" wording was only to exclude children who are *less* sophisticated and mature than their same-age peers, such as children who are "mentally retarded," "extremely emotionally disturbed," or "too immature to understand the nature of the act." The Court of Appeals thus determined that ORS 419C.349(3) requires only that youths "understand what they are doing in a physical sense and understand that their actions are wrong or will likely have criminal consequences," a level of understanding that any normally-abled child of 12 to 14 years of age (or much younger) would possess and that, historically, was considered sufficient to establish criminal capacity. Consequently, the Court of Appeals affirmed.[5]

Youth is eligible for waiver under ORS 419C.352, which provides:

The juvenile court, after a hearing, . . . may waive a youth under 15 years of age at the time the act was committed to circuit court for prosecution as an adult if:

"(1) The youth is represented by counsel during the waiver proceedings;
"(2) The juvenile court makes the findings required under ORS 419C.349(3) and (4); and
"(3) The youth is alleged to have committed an act or acts that if committed by an adult would constitute one or more of the following crimes;
"(a) Murder or any aggravated form thereof . . .
"(b) Rape in the first degree . . .;
"(c) Sodomy in the first degree . . . or
"(d) Unlawful sexual penetration in the first degree[.]"

Subsection (2) of ORS 419C.352 refers to provisions from a different waiver statute, ORS 419C.349, that authorizes waiver of youths "15 years of age or older at

---

5. In the meantime, youth's criminal prosecution proceeded in Washington County Circuit Court. He was adjudged guilty of aggravated murder and other crimes and sentenced to life in prison with the possibility of parole after 30 years. The Court of Appeals has ordered that his appeal from that conviction and sentence be held in abeyance pending resolution of the present case.

the time of the commission of the alleged offense" who have committed any one of a number of specified criminal acts—but only if

> "(3) *The youth at the time of the alleged offense was of sufficient sophistication and maturity to appreciate the nature and quality of the conduct involved;* and
>
> "(4) The juvenile court, after considering the following criteria, determines by a preponderance of the evidence that retaining jurisdiction will not serve the best interests of the youth and of society and therefore is not justified."

Thus, the dispute in this case concerns the meaning of the italicized requirement set out in ORS 419C.349(3), as incorporated by reference in ORS 419C.352. . . .

Before we analyze the parties' arguments, we think it helpful to describe the relevant legal framework in place at that time that the legislature enacted ORS 419C.349, along with the changes that the legislature made in that framework. . . .

In 1985, when ORS 419C.349 was enacted, a youth could be considered lacking in criminal capacity either because the youth was too immature to be held criminally responsible or because the youth had a mental disease or defect that constituted a defense to criminal responsibility. . . .

. . . [T]he Oregon legislature adopted a statutory definition of insanity that negated criminal responsibility, and the common law rule and its "nature and quality of the act" wording fell out of usage in Oregon. The statutory formulation, which was imported from the Model Penal Code and which now is codified, as amended, at ORS 161.295(1), provides:

> A person is guilty except for insanity if, as a result of mental disease or defect at the time of engaging in criminal conduct, the person lacks substantial capacity either to appreciate the criminality of the conduct or to conform the conduct to the requirements of the law." . . .

In 1985, the legislature enacted the waiver provision at issue in this case. The 1985 statute, now codified as ORS 419C.349(3), permitted the juvenile court to "waive" a youth into adult court provided that the youth was 15 or older at the time an act was committed and that three additional conditions were met: (1) the youth was represented by counsel during the waiver proceedings, (2) the juvenile court made certain findings; and (3) the youth was alleged to have committed an act that if committed by an adult would constitute one or more of certain specified crimes. The two findings that the juvenile court was required to make were: (1) that "the youth at the time of the alleged offense was of sufficient sophistication and maturity to appreciate the nature and quality of the conduct involved," and (2) that, considering specified criteria, retaining jurisdiction in the juvenile court "will not serve the best interests of the youth and of society and therefore is not justified." . . .

Having set out the foregoing background, we return to the issue at hand. To determine what the legislature intended when it enacted ORS 419C.349(3) in 1985, we examine the statutory text in its context, along with its legislative history.

. . . In this case, the relevant text resolves naturally into three parts, which we analyze separately. The text requires that a youth have (1) "sufficient sophistication and maturity" to (2) "appreciate" the (3) "nature and quality of the conduct involved."

The words in part one of the text describe adult-like qualities. The term "maturity," when viewed in isolation, describes a quality that is associated with normal, well-adjusted adults. "Sophistication" is similar but carries with it a connotation of heightened worldliness and discernment. "Sufficient" sophistication and maturity refers to the amount of those qualities necessary to a particular situation or end—in the case of ORS 419C.349(3), to "appreciate the nature and quality of the conduct involved."

Part two of the text requires that the youth have the ability to "appreciate" the nature and quality of the conduct at issue. The word "appreciate" ordinarily means to "comprehend [it] with knowledge, judgment and discrimination" or "to judge [it] with heightened perception or understanding."

Part three of the text describes the object of the youth's appreciation—the "nature and quality of the conduct involved." In ordinary parlance, both "nature" and "quality" refer to a thing's "essential character." In this instance, the "thing" is the conduct that constituted the alleged offense.

Based on the dictionary definitions of the words used in ORS 419C.349(3), the state argues that that provision requires that a youth have a level of understanding equivalent to the common law concept of criminal capacity. The state uses the term "criminal capacity" to mean a minimal level of understanding of limited aspects of a criminal act—a mental grasp of the physical nature of an act and its wrongfulness. Thus, taking an example from LaFave, the state uses the term criminal capacity to mean that a person knows that he or she is holding a flame to a building, that holding a flame to a building will make it burn, and that burning a building is wrong. In making that argument, the state acknowledges that the words "maturity" and "sophistication" describe adult-like qualities. However, focusing on the qualifying word "sufficient," and the object of the understanding, the "nature and quality" of the conduct, the state contends that the statute requires no more than an adult-like mental grasp of the physical nature of an act and its wrongfulness.

There are two problems with that interpretation of the statute's text. First, an ability to have a mental understanding of the physical nature of an act and its wrongfulness is not an ability that is particular to adults, as the defense of immaturity makes clear. At a very young age, a child can know that she is holding a flame to a building, that the flame will burn the building and that burning a building is wrong. In 1985, when ORS 419C.349 was enacted, Oregon law conclusively presumed that all children 14 and older would have criminal capacity. At common law, it was understood that many children seven years of age and older also would have that capability: The presumption of incapacity that attached to that age group could be, and often was, rebutted. Thus, it is seems unlikely that the legislature used the words "maturity" and "sophistication" to describe capabilities that all youths over age 14 and many children under age 14 were expected to have.

Second, the understanding necessary to establish criminal capacity—a mental grasp of the physical nature of an act and its criminality—is a basic awareness that would be better described by the word "know" than the word "appreciate." As noted, the word "appreciate," describes an ability to comprehend with heightened understanding and judgment. The word "know" describes an awareness of a fact or concept. The statute's use of the word "appreciate" rather than "know" is an indication that the legislature intended to require that a youth have a deeper ability to understand than a basic mental awareness. . . .

In interpreting a statute we also consider context. A statute's context includes other provisions of the same statute as well as the common law and statutory framework within which the statute was enacted. . . .

The state argues that the statute's use of the words "nature and quality" is informed by the use of those terms in the insanity defense. As noted, the insanity defense was first described in an 1843 case, M'Naghten's Case, 10 Clark & Fin 200. And, as also noted, the original M'Naghten rule set out a two-part test, one having to do with knowledge of the "nature and quality" of the act and the other having to do with the actor's knowledge of the act's wrongfulness:

> "If at the time of committing an act, the party was laboring under such a defect of reason from disease of the mind as not to know the nature and quality of the act he was doing, or if he did know the nature and quality thereof, that he did not know that he was doing what was wrong, he should not be held responsible under the criminal law."

The state argues that the statute's use of the words "nature and quality" is drawn from that test and thus indicates an intent to require a minimal showing of criminal capacity as the state explains that concept.

As an initial matter, we note that, although the phrase "nature and quality" was used in M'Naghten to refer narrowly to the nature of the act and its physical consequences, later cases and commentators suggested (in an era when psychiatry was expanding notions of mental incapacity) that the phrase was not so limited. For example, some suggested that the phrase "gives important emphasis to the realization of the wrongfulness of the act." . . . Because the classic, narrow reading of the M'Naghten test had been tempered by many courts and commentators by the time that ORS 419C.349(3) was enacted, it seems unlikely that legislature had that narrow and specific conception in mind, and the state does not disagree. The state acknowledges that the phrase, "nature and quality" of the conduct involved, refers to both a physical act and its wrongfulness. However, the state argues, the phrase also captures the necessary degree of understanding of those concepts—a mental ability to grasp them.

We agree that the words "nature and quality" may well have roots in the M'Naghten rule and that that context is helpful to understanding what we have denominated as part three of the statutory phrase—the object of the youth's appreciation. However, we are not persuaded that, when it enacted ORS 419C.349(3), the legislature intended to use that phrase to require only the limited understanding of an act and its consequences described in the M'Naghten rule. We think it significant that, although M'Naghten and other common law criminal capacity cases referred almost uniformly to a capacity to "know" the nature and wrongfulness of the conduct, the Oregon legislature, in enacting ORS 419C.349(3), chose a different word—"appreciate." . . .

. . . [T]he Oregon Criminal Law Revision Commission had written commentary to accompany ORS 161.295, the 1971 statutory revision of the common law insanity defense. After explaining that the new statute was based on section 4.01(1) of the Model Penal Code, which in turn represented a modernized version of the M'Naghten rule, combined with the so-called "irresistible impulse" test, the commission noted that "the draft section substitutes 'appreciate' for M'Naghten's 'know,' thereby indicating a preference for the view that an offender must be emotionally as well as intellectually aware of the significance of his conduct." Particularly in light of the latter commentary, which was directed to the Oregon legislature, it seems reasonable to assume that, when the legislature later enacted a requirement that a juvenile "appreciate" the nature and quality of the conduct involved, it intended to require more than the minimal knowledge that was required to establish criminal capacity for purposes of the M'Naghten rule.

Youth argues that the words "sophistication and maturity" in ORS 419C.349(3) are informed by their use in a United States Supreme Court case, Kent v. United States, 383 U.S. 541 (1966). . . . The court appended to its decision a set of criteria that juvenile courts in the District of Columbia had used in deciding waiver issues, hinting that due process would be served if juvenile courts based their waiver decisions on such criteria. Included in those criteria were items like the seriousness and violent nature of the offense, the juvenile's record and previous history, and, notably, "[t]he sophistication and maturity of the juvenile as determined by consideration of his home, environmental situation, emotional attitude and pattern of living." After Kent, courts and legislatures around the country adopted the so-called Kent criteria as providing a helpful, and sometimes required, analytical framework for remand decisions.

Youth observes, quite correctly, that the Oregon legislature borrowed from the Kent criteria when it adopted the waiver criteria set out at ORS 419C.349(3) and (4). . . .

The "sophistication and maturity" criterion set out in Kent contemplated a fairly open and extensive examination of the mental, social, and emotional development of the youth in question: The broad group of sources that it instructed courts to consider ("[the juvenile's] home, environmental situation, emotional attitude and pattern of living") are evidence of that. Moreover, in Kent, the "sophistication and maturity" criterion was free standing. It required a court to consider "the sophistication and maturity of the juvenile" as an independent criterion relevant to a waiver decision, indicating that the court should consider the full panoply of a youth's capabilities that indicate "maturity" and "sophistication." Based on the ordinary meaning of those terms, those capabilities would be the capabilities of normal adults that evidence heightened worldliness and discernment. Because those terms were used to determine, among other things, whether a youth was sufficiently blameworthy to stand trial as an adult, it seems logical that they would include adult-like traits that relate to traditional notions of blameworthiness beyond those necessary to establish criminal responsibility, such as capacities for premeditation and planning, impulse control, independent judgment, and a more hardened personality and outlook. Given our understanding that the statutory phrase "sophistication and maturity" came from the Kent criteria, it is logical to understand the phrase as requiring an inquiry into the extent to which a juvenile's mental, social, and emotional developmental capabilities indicate adult-like capabilities indicative of blameworthiness. . . .

Youth also directs our attention to notions of the capacities of juveniles reflected in the law as it stood when ORS 419C.349(3) was enacted, and the logic of ORS 419C.349(3) in that context. In 1985, there was a broad understanding among jurists and lawmakers that, because youths are mentally, socially, and emotionally less formed, they are inherently less capable of making critical decisions and require society's protection. The case law of the time is replete with statements to that effect. A plethora of statutes placing age restrictions on the exercise of important privileges, in Oregon and elsewhere, also reflected that thinking. *See, e.g.,* ORS 482.110 (1983) (driving); ORS 109.640 (1983) (medical decisions); ORS 109.670 (1983) (donating blood); ORS 106.060 (1983) (marriage); ORS 247.002(2) (1983) (voting); ORS 471.430 (1963) (purchase of alcohol). And it is evident that those general sentiments about the lesser capacity of juveniles extended to their moral development and their capacity to be criminally culpable.

In fact, the idea that children are morally undeveloped and, therefore, less criminally culpable, has long been a feature of Oregon law. . . .

Significantly, although the law treats all youths 14 and older as being criminally responsible, it assumes that those under 18 generally will be held responsible for their conduct in juvenile, rather than adult, court. . . . ORS 419C.349, allows some youths under 18 to be waived into adult court, but only two things distinguish a 15- to 17-year-old youth who is eligible for adult adjudication from one who is not: the type of crime with which the youth is charged, ORS 419C.349(2), and the youth's possession, under ORS 419C.349(3), of "sufficient sophistication and maturity to appreciate the nature and quality of the conduct involved." Given that fact, it is logical to assume that that threshold "sophistication and maturity" requirement demands an ability to appreciate the nature and quality of the conduct involved that is different from the criminal capacity that all 15- to 17–year–olds already are deemed to have. . . .

The upshot of the foregoing discussion of text and context is that ORS 419C.349(3) represents a combination of terms and phrases, which, when given both their ordinary and specialized meanings and considered together, convey a requirement for waiver that is more demanding than the one that the state proposes. . . . To give meaning to each of those terms and phrases, as we must, we interpret the text of ORS 419C.349(3) to require that a youth have sufficient adult-like intellectual and emotional capabilities to appreciate the nature and wrongfulness of the conduct to justify his or her prosecution as an adult. . . .

. . . [T]he juvenile court's findings do not support a conclusion that youth possessed "sufficient sophistication and maturity to appreciate the nature and quality of the conduct involved," as we have interpreted that requirement. It follows that the case must be reversed and remanded to the juvenile court for further consideration under the proper standard. . . .

NOTES AND QUESTION

1. Traditionally, hearings under judicial waiver statutes like Oregon's have focused on the child's "amenability to treatment" and whether the juvenile court had the ability to enter orders to protect the community from the child. Much of the evidence at the hearing in *J.C.N.-V.*, which is described at the beginning of the case, was relevant to these issues. Applying these traditional criteria, the juvenile court judge ordered that the case be waived to adult court. Why, do you suppose?

2. The major issue in *J.C.N.-V.* is the meaning of the requirement that the youth have "sufficient sophistication and maturity to appreciate the nature and quality of the conduct involved," Does this factor relate to amenability to treatment or to community safety?

When the legislature enacted this standard in 1985, the information about adolescent brain development, which was used at trial, was not common knowledge and was not discussed in juvenile cases. Does that mean that the legislature intended for the juvenile judge to determine only whether the child had the capacity to know what he or she was doing, as the state argued?

3. States differ considerably in their approach to the relevance of "amenability to treatment" within the juvenile justice system to the transfer decision. Some regard capacity for rehabilitation as a sufficient ground for retaining juvenile court jurisdiction, while others consider amenability to treatment as either irrelevant to or a merely nominal element in the transfer decision. What are the differences in the theory of social response to juvenile crime reflected by these various formulations? What empirical propositions do they embody or assume?

4. Judges in one study told researchers that they rank dangerousness as the most important factor in the transfer decision, followed by amenability to treatment and then sophistication/maturity. R.T. Salekin et al., Juvenile Transfer to Adult Criminal Courts: Prototypes for Dangerousness, Sophistication-Maturity, and Amenability to Treatment Through a Legal Lens, 8 Psychol. Pub. Pol'y & L. 373 (2002).

During the mid-2000s, researchers surveyed 361 members of the National Council of Juvenile and Family Court Judges to learn how they evaluate transfer cases, based on hypothetical cases constructed to raise issues about dangerousness, amenability to treatment, and sophistication. The great majority of the judges said that they believe case-by-case decision making, rather than prosecutorial discretion or legislative waiver, is the best way to make the transfer decision. As expected, the study found that judges were most likely to transfer youths rated high in dangerousness and sophistication but low in treatment amenability and least likely to transfer those low in dangerousness and sophistication and high in amenability. Dia N. Brannen et al., Transfer to Adult Court: A National Study of How Juvenile Court Judges Weigh Pertinent *Kent* Criteria, 12 Psychol. Pub. Pol'y & L. 332, 346 (2006). The researchers found that dangerousness and sophistication were significant predictors of their decisions, but amenability to treatment was not. The study did not reveal why judges downplay amenability. *Id.* at 347.

5. The number of cases that judges waived to adult court rose 81 percent between 1985 and 1994 but then declined 47 percent through 2001. Benjamin Adams & Sean Addie, Delinquency Cases Waived to Criminal Court 2007 1-3 (OJJDP 2010). "Between 2005 and 2015, the number of delinquency cases waived to criminal court was at its highest in 2006 (6,800). By 2015, the number of cases waived had decreased by 53 percent, to its lowest level during that time period. . . . Historically, the number of cases judicially waived declined after 1994 and may be attributable in part to the large increase in the number of states that passed legislation excluding certain serious offenses from juvenile court jurisdiction and legislation." Sarah Hockenberry & Charles Puzzanchera, Juvenile Court Statistics 2015 (National Center for Juvenile Justice, 2018) at 38, https ://www. ojjdp.gov/ojstatbb/njcda/pdf/jcs2015.pdf. Although the proportions of waived

cases involving girls and younger juveniles increased between 1985 and 2015, the majority involved males 16 or older. *Id.* at 40.

2.   *The Blended Jurisdiction Alternative*

BARRY C. FELD, *JUVENILE AND CRIMINAL JUSTICE SYSTEMS' RESPONSES TO YOUTH VIOLENCE*

24 Crime & Just. 189, 239, 243 (1998)

Statutes that increase juvenile courts' punitive capacity or give criminal courts a juvenile sentencing option represent another offense-based sentencing strategy to respond to violent and persistent young offenders. These blended jurisdiction laws attempt to meld the sentencing authority of juvenile with criminal courts, to provide longer sentences for serious crimes than otherwise would be available to the juvenile court, or to increase the rehabilitative sentencing options available to criminal courts. These blended sentences provide juvenile courts with the option to punish as well as to treat and criminal courts with therapeutic alternatives to imprisonment for youths of certain ages charged with serious or repeated offenses. Several variants of youthful offender, blended, or extended jurisdiction sentences exist. The nature of the sanctions depends on whether the prosecutors try the youth initially in juvenile or in criminal court. . . .

Although [these] statutes differ in many details, the blended jurisdiction strategy shares several common features. Because they provide these intermediate offenders with adult criminal procedural safeguards, they can acknowledge the reality of juvenile punishment. Once a state gives a juvenile the right to a jury trial and other criminal procedural safeguards, then it retains the option to punish without apology and thereby gains greater flexibility to treat a youth as well. These various enhanced sentencing strategies recognize that age jurisdictional limits of juvenile courts create binary forced choices, either juvenile or adult, either treatment or punishment. By trying a juvenile with criminal procedural rights, these states preserve the option to extend jurisdiction for a period of several years or more beyond that available for ordinary delinquents. Finally, these statutes recognize the futility of trying to rationalize social control in two separate systems. These blended provisions embody the procedural and substantive convergence between juvenile and criminal courts, provide a conceptual alternative to binary waiver statutes, and recognize that adolescence constitutes a developmental continuum that requires an increasing array of graduated sanctions.

IN RE WELFARE OF T.C.J.

689 N.W.2d 787 (Minn. App. 2004)

LANSING, Judge. ... TCJ's assault charges stem from a confrontation between him and a teacher near Park Center High School. TCJ, a seventeen-year-old former student, visited the school with a friend, JH, who was seeking enrollment materials. When TCJ and JH entered the school through a side entrance to the gymnasium, a member of the faculty recognized TCJ and knew that he was not currently a student. The teacher ordered them to leave the school grounds.

The teacher saw TCJ and JH on the school grounds several times that day and each time told them to leave. TCJ and JH failed to comply, and after a final response that the teacher characterized as insubordinate and disrespectful, they suddenly fled through a set of doors, which the teacher stated was off limits to students. The teacher, suspecting wrongdoing, pursued them.

When he caught up with them, they were off school property, and the teacher told them that they must return to the school to deal with the problem "[t]he easy way or the hard way." He then grabbed JH by the shirt. TCJ testified at trial that the teacher mistook JH for a student at the school and repeatedly referred to JH by the wrong name. JH spun from the teacher's grip and out of the shirt, then snatched it away from the teacher, who testified that he was struck across the face with the garment and pushed against a nearby car.

The teacher testified that JH began to choke him, and the teacher, who taught self-defense at the high school, countered by grabbing JH's hands. TCJ testified that the teacher grabbed JH by the throat. According to the teacher, TCJ punched him on the left side of his head, and when he moved to resist, JH began to hit him on the other side of his head. TCJ admitted to hitting the teacher in the face to get him to let go, but he claimed that another student who joined the fray also punched the teacher. The teacher sustained multiple jaw fractures, bruises, and abrasions, and lost several teeth. He testified that, despite his knowledge of self-defense techniques, he did not retaliate. TCJ testified that, despite JH's being choked, neither he nor JH sustained injuries from the altercation. Several other witnesses corroborated aspects of the testimony of each of the principal participants.

TCJ's age and the gravity of the first-degree-assault charge resulted in a presumptive-certification to the district court. The district court determined that TCJ had presented evidence that overcame the presumption and designated the proceeding an EJJ prosecution. The jury acquitted TCJ of first-degree assault but found him guilty of third-degree assault. TCJ appeals. . . .

Finally, TCJ challenges the district court's decision to sentence him under the extended-juvenile-jurisdiction procedure in Minn. Stat. § 260B.130, subdivision 4(a) (2002), which requires the imposition of a stayed adult criminal sentence in addition to a juvenile disposition under Minn. Stat. § 260B.198 (2002). TCJ maintains that he should have been sentenced only to a juvenile disposition as provided by § 260B.130, subdivision 4(b). But that provision is limited to "a child prosecuted as an extended jurisdiction juvenile after designation *by the prosecutor*" who is convicted of an offense that would not, on its own, have justified an EJJ prosecution. (Emphasis added.) As the state indicated in its brief, TCJ's assault proceedings were designated as extended jurisdiction juvenile *by the juvenile court* after the prosecution unsuccessfully sought his certification to district court as an adult under Minn. Stat. § 260B.125 (2002). TCJ argues that the district court's application of the EJJ statute violated his right to equal protection under the law. While TCJ did not fully articulate this constitutional challenge at trial, we may consider issues not addressed by the district court when the interests of justice so require.

We begin by reviewing the procedural aspects of this case that led to the prosecution of TCJ under the EJJ statute. In its delinquency petition, the state charged TCJ with two counts of assault: third-degree assault . . . and first-degree assault. . . . Because the first-degree-assault charge satisfied the presumptive-certification requirement of the adult certification statute, as "an offense that would result in a presumptive commitment to prison under the sentencing guidelines and applicable statutes," the state moved for district court "certification" to try TCJ as an adult. Following an order establishing probable cause for the presumptive offense and subsequent extensive briefing and a hearing, the juvenile court found that TCJ had overcome the presumption of adult certification and granted TCJ's motion that the proceeding "be designated an extended juvenile jurisdiction case."

TCJ's case proceeded under Minn. Stat. § 260B.130, which governs EJJ prosecutions. A decision to prosecute a juvenile in the district court under the laws and procedures controlling adult criminal violations is termed a "certification"; the equivalent process under the EJJ statute is termed "designation." Although TCJ's case defaulted to EJJ upon the district court's designation, the EJJ process can also be instigated by the prosecutor under the same standard as the adult certification process if "the child is alleged to have committed an offense for which the sentencing guidelines and applicable statutes presume a commitment to prison." Unlike the adult certification statute, under which the prosecution proceeds "as if the jurisdiction of the juvenile court had never attached," the EJJ statute contains a provision to distinguish between those offenses that justify the extended jurisdiction and other offenses with which the defendant may have been charged.

Subdivision 4 of the EJJ statute governs the disposition of offenses. Subpart (a) of the subdivision requires the court to impose a bifurcated sentence following a guilty plea or finding of guilt: first, the child is given a juvenile disposition under Minn. Stat. § 260B.198; and second, the child receives "an adult criminal sentence, the execution of which shall be stayed on the condition that the offender not violate the provisions of the disposition order and not commit a new offense." Minn. Stat. § 260B.130, subdivision 4(a). But subpart (b) qualifies the second part of the bifurcated process: if the child is convicted as an EJJ of an offense for which the sentencing guidelines and applicable statutes *do not* presume a commitment to prison, then the court shall order only the juvenile disposition.

The provision is sensible and fair because it recognizes that the absence of guilt for the offense that increased the degree of seriousness in the child's prosecution should correspondingly permit the punishment for the nontriggering offenses to revert to the juvenile system. That result would apply to all EJJ prosecutions but for the phrase "after designation by the prosecutor in the delinquency petition" in subpart (b). We read this language to require a disparately more severe sentence for every EJJ conviction that results from the juvenile court's rejection of adult certification. In other words, under a literal reading of the EJJ statute, if TCJ's trial and conviction had followed a decision by the state to forego the adult certification process and a successful motion to designate his offense as an EJJ proceeding, he would only be subject to a juvenile disposition for the third-degree assault conviction. But because the state chose a more stringent approach of seeking adult certification—a decision entirely within the state's discretion and a choice which the court rejected—the statute mandates a stayed adult sentence for the third-degree assault *after the very same trial.* We find this result inconsistent with the protections afforded TCJ under the United States and Minnesota Constitutions.

The Equal Protection Clause of the Fourteenth Amendment provides, in relevant part, "No [s]tate shall . . . deny to any person within its jurisdiction the equal protection of the laws." U.S. Const. amend. XIV, § 1. Article I, Section 2, of the Minnesota Constitution provides, "[n]o member of this [s]tate shall be disenfranchised, or deprived of any of the rights or privileges secured to any citizen thereof, unless by the law of the land, or the judgment of his peers." While all similarly situated persons shall be treated alike, "only invidious discrimination is deemed constitutionally offensive."

Minnesota law presumes that all statutes are constitutional and should be declared unconstitutional only if it is established beyond a reasonable doubt that they violate a constitutional provision. Unless a constitutional challenge to the statute involves a suspect classification or a fundamental right, we review the challenge using a rational-basis standard under both the state and federal constitutions, and the statute will be sustained if the classification drawn by the statute is rationally related to a legitimate state interest. TCJ argues summarily that the imposition of a stayed adult sentence has deprived him of his liberty, a fundamental right, but he provides no legal support for this argument. We are not convinced that a fundamental right to liberty is affected when a stayed sentence is imposed concurrently with a juvenile sentence that already requires TCJ's commitment to a juvenile facility, and we thus examine the statute under the rational-basis standard.

We are guided in this equal-protection analysis by the Minnesota Supreme Court's recent holding that the classification imposed by another subdivision of the EJJ statute could not withstand a rational-basis test. In State v. Garcia, 683 N.W.2d 294 (Minn. 2004), the court applied the following test:

(1) The distinctions which separate those included within the classification from those excluded must not be manifestly arbitrary or fanciful but must be genuine and substantial, thereby providing a natural and reasonable basis to justify legislation adapted to peculiar conditions and needs; (2) the classification must be genuine or relevant to the purpose of the law; that is there must be an evident connection between the distinctive needs peculiar to the class and the prescribed remedy; and (3) the purpose of the statute must be one that the state can legitimately attempt to achieve.

Id. at 299. TCJ argues that separate sentencing of "identically situated juveniles" is a manifestly arbitrary distinction which this court must find unconstitutional.

We agree. We perceive no rational basis linking this classification to the underlying purpose of the statute, which provides the juvenile courts with a means to retain jurisdiction to try juveniles for adult crimes and thus serve public safety. *See* Minn. Stat. § 260B.130, subd. 2 (requiring a showing of "clear and convincing evidence that designating the proceeding an extended jurisdiction juvenile prosecution serves public safety"). There is no evident connection between: (1) juveniles who were originally subjected to the adult certification process but who are not convicted of the presumptive offense, and (2) a sentencing provision that subjects them to harsher punishment than others not convicted of a presumptive offense simply because the first group arrived in an EJJ court through the adult-certification route. We are convinced that, as written, the statute inevitably overweighs the prosecutor's discretion as an influence on the juvenile's sentence. This result, while clearly in violation of a juvenile's right to equal protection under the law, appears to have due process implications as well. If prosecutorial empowerment was the legislature's purpose in drafting subdivision 4 of the EJJ statute, it is not a purpose which "the state can legitimately attempt to achieve." Therefore, we hold that Minn. Stat. § 260B.130, subd. 4(b) is unconstitutional, and we vacate that part of TCJ's disposition that stays an adult sentence. . . .

NOTES AND QUESTIONS

1. *T.C.J.* considers the relationship between blended sentencing and transfer from the juvenile court. What purposes does each of these alternatives serve?

2. The legislation challenged in *T.C.J.* made EJJ status automatic after a juvenile court refuses to certify a case to adult court, regardless of the offenses of which the minor is found guilty, but if the case is initially prosecuted as an ordinary juvenile case, EJJ status attaches only if the minor is found guilty of an offense that presumptively carries prison time under the state's sentencing guidelines. Do you agree that this distinction is not rationally related to legitimate state ends? Recall that courts have generally upheld "prosecutorial waiver statutes" that allow prosecutors to decide whether to charge a minor in adult or juvenile court.

3. West Virginia adopted the first blended sentencing statute in 1985. By 2016 26 states had some form of blended sentencing. Shelly S. Schaefer & Christopher Uggen, 41 Law & Soc. Inquiry 435, 438 (2016). "Blended sentencing" laws take different forms. In 2016, 15 states had statutes that allow a juvenile court to impose a suspended adult sentence, in addition to the juvenile disposition. If the young person successfully completes the terms of the juvenile order, the adult sentence never goes into effect. Office of Juvenile Justice and Delinquency Prevention, Statistical Briefing Book, How Do Juvenile Court Blended Sentencing Provisions Vary by State? https://www.ojjdp.gov/ojstatbb/structure_process/qa04113.asp?qaDate=2016. In general, blended sentencing of this type increases the overall risk that juvenile-age offenders will be sanctioned as adults. *See* Anabel Cassady, Note: The Juvenile Ultimatum: Reframing Blended Sentencing Laws to Ensure Juveniles Receive a Genuine "One Last Chance at Success," 102 Minn. L. Rev. 391, 411-413 (2017). The other states allow a juvenile judge to impose an adult or a juvenile sentence, a juvenile disposition that lasts longer than the maximum age of juvenile court jurisdiction so that the child is transferred to the adult sentence to serve the rest of the sentence, or a juvenile disposition ordered by an adult court judge. Cassady, 102 Minn. L. Rev. at 406-407.

4. Does the adoption of dispositional schemes that can include adult sanctions simply reflect the harshness of current political thinking about juvenile offenders and offenses? Can it also be regarded as a politically acceptable alternative to even broader transfer for criminal prosecution than is now found?

5. In Minnesota, once a juvenile violates probationary conditions of a stayed adult sentence, the adult sentence must be executed unless the court makes findings justifying continuance of the stay, using the same criteria that it would ordinarily use to determine whether to revoke probation. *See* State v. B.Y., 659 N.W.2d 763 (Minn. 2003).

3. Reconsidering Minors' Culpability and Eligibility for the Most Severe Penalties

We come now to a series of cases that are central to the "kids are different" reforms of the early twenty-first century, cases that use the Eighth Amendment prohibition of cruel and unusual punishment to limit the death penalty and very long criminal sentences. Only criminal courts may impose the most serious penalties in the United States legal system: death and life imprisonment without the possibility of parole. Thus, a potential consequence for a minor tried as an adult is that he or she becomes eligible for these sentences. In Eddings v. Oklahoma, 455 U.S. 104 (1982), the Supreme Court held that in a capital murder trial the jury must be able to consider the offender's age as a mitigating factor, and in Thompson v. Oklahoma, 487 U.S. 815 (1988), the Court held that the Eighth Amendment prohibits imposing the death penalty on a defendant younger than 16, without a majority opinion. However, the next year in Stanford v. Kentucky, 492 U.S. 361 (1989), a majority rejected the argument that putting a 17-year-old to death is unconstitutional. Only 16 years later the Court revisited that issue and reached a different conclusion.

ROPER V. SIMMONS

543 U.S. 551 (2005)

Justice KENNEDY delivered the opinion of the Court. ... At the age of 17, when he was still a junior in high school, Christopher Simmons, the respondent here, committed murder. About nine months later, after he had turned 18, he was tried and sentenced to death. There is little doubt that Simmons was the instigator of the crime. Before its commission Simmons said he wanted to murder someone. In chilling, callous terms he talked about his plan, discussing it for the most part with two friends, Charles Benjamin and John Tessmer, then aged 15 and 16 respectively. Simmons proposed to commit burglary and murder by breaking and entering, tying up a victim, and throwing the victim off a bridge. Simmons assured his friends they could "get away with it" because they were minors.

The three met at about 2 A.M. on the night of the murder, but Tessmer left before the other two set out. (The State later charged Tessmer with conspiracy, but dropped the charge in exchange for his testimony against Simmons.) Simmons and Benjamin entered the home of the victim, Shirley Crook, after reaching through an open window and unlocking the back door. Simmons turned on a hallway light. Awakened, Mrs. Crook called out, "Who's there?" In response Simmons entered Mrs. Crook's bedroom, where he recognized her from a previous car accident involving them both. Simmons later admitted this confirmed his resolve to murder her.

Using duct tape to cover her eyes and mouth and bind her hands, the two perpetrators put Mrs. Crook in her minivan and drove to a state park. They reinforced the bindings, covered her head with a towel, and walked her to a railroad trestle spanning the Meramec River. There they tied her hands and feet together with electrical wire, wrapped her whole face in duct tape and threw her from the bridge, drowning her in the waters below.

By the afternoon of September 9, Steven Crook had returned home from an overnight trip, found his bedroom in disarray, and reported his wife missing. On the same afternoon fishermen recovered the victim's body from the river. Simmons, meanwhile, was bragging about the killing, telling friends he had killed a woman "because the bitch seen my face."

The next day, after receiving information of Simmons' involvement, police arrested him at his high school and took him to the police station in Fenton, Missouri. They read him his *Miranda* rights. Simmons waived his right to an attorney and agreed to answer questions. After less than two hours of interrogation, Simmons confessed to the murder and agreed to perform a videotaped reenactment at the crime scene.

The State charged Simmons with burglary, kidnapping, stealing, and murder in the first degree. As Simmons was 17 at the time of the crime, he was outside the criminal jurisdiction of Missouri's juvenile court system. He was tried as an adult. At trial the State introduced Simmons' confession and the videotaped reenactment of the crime, along with testimony that Simmons discussed the crime in advance and bragged about it later. The defense called no witnesses in the guilt phase. The jury having returned a verdict of murder, the trial proceeded to the penalty phase.

The State sought the death penalty. As aggravating factors, the State submitted that the murder was committed for the purpose of receiving money; was committed for the purpose of avoiding, interfering with, or preventing lawful arrest of the defendant; and involved depravity of mind and was outrageously and wantonly vile, horrible, and inhuman. The State called Shirley Crook's husband, daughter, and two sisters, who presented moving evidence of the devastation her death had brought to their lives.

In mitigation Simmons' attorneys first called an officer of the Missouri juvenile justice system, who testified that Simmons had no prior convictions and that no previous charges had been filed against him. Simmons' mother, father, two younger half brothers, a neighbor, and a friend took the stand to tell the jurors of the close relationships they had formed with Simmons and to plead for mercy on his behalf. Simmons' mother, in particular, testified to the responsibility Simmons demonstrated in taking care of his two younger half brothers and of his grandmother and to his capacity to show love for them.

During closing arguments, both the prosecutor and defense counsel addressed Simmons' age, which the trial judge had instructed the jurors they could consider as a mitigating factor. Defense counsel reminded the jurors that juveniles of Simmons' age cannot drink, serve on juries, or even see certain movies, because "the legislatures have wisely decided that individuals of a certain age aren't responsible enough." Defense counsel argued that Simmons' age should make "a huge difference to [the jurors] in deciding just exactly what sort of punishment to make." In rebuttal, the prosecutor gave the following response: "Age, he says. Think about age. Seventeen years old. Isn't that scary? Doesn't that scare you? Mitigating? Quite the contrary I submit. Quite the contrary."

The jury recommended the death penalty after finding the State had proved each of the three aggravating factors submitted to it. Accepting the jury's recommendation, the trial judge imposed the death penalty.

Simmons obtained new counsel, who moved in the trial court to set aside the conviction and sentence. . . .

The trial court . . . denied the motion for postconviction relief. In a consolidated appeal from Simmons' conviction and sentence, and from the denial of
postconviction relief, the Missouri Supreme Court affirmed. The federal courts
denied Simmons' petition for a writ of habeas corpus.

After these proceedings in Simmons' case had run their course, this Court
held that the Eighth and Fourteenth Amendments prohibit the execution of a
mentally retarded person. Atkins v. Virginia, 536 U.S. 304 (2002). Simmons filed
a new petition for state postconviction relief, arguing that the reasoning of *Atkins*
established that the Constitution prohibits the execution of a juvenile who was
under 18 when the crime was committed. . . .

The Eighth Amendment provides: "Excessive bail shall not be required, nor
excessive fines imposed, nor cruel and unusual punishments inflicted." The provision is applicable to the States through the Fourteenth Amendment. As the Court
explained in *Atkins*, the Eighth Amendment guarantees individuals the right not
to be subjected to excessive sanctions. The right flows from the basic "'precept
of justice that punishment for crime should be graduated and proportioned to
[the] offense.'" By protecting even those convicted of heinous crimes, the Eighth
Amendment reaffirms the duty of the government to respect the dignity of all
persons.

The prohibition against "cruel and unusual punishments," like other expansive language in the Constitution, must be interpreted according to its text, by
considering history, tradition, and precedent, and with due regard for its purpose
and function in the constitutional design. To implement this framework we have
established the propriety and affirmed the necessity of referring to "the evolving
standards of decency that mark the progress of a maturing society" to determine
which punishments are so disproportionate as to be cruel and unusual. . . .

Three Terms ago the [constitutionality of imposing the death penalty on
mentally retarded people] was reconsidered in *Atkins*. We held that standards of
decency have evolved since Penry v. Lynaugh, 492 U.S. 302 (1989), [which had
rejected this claim] and now demonstrate that the execution of the mentally
retarded is cruel and unusual punishment. . . .

Just as the *Atkins* Court reconsidered the issue decided in *Penry*, we now
reconsider the issue decided in *Stanford*. The beginning point is a review of objective indicia of consensus, as expressed in particular by the enactments of legislatures that have addressed the question. This data gives us essential instruction. We
then must determine, in the exercise of our own independent judgment, whether
the death penalty is a disproportionate punishment for juveniles.

The evidence of national consensus against the death penalty for juveniles
is similar, and in some respects parallel, to the evidence *Atkins* held sufficient
to demonstrate a national consensus against the death penalty for the mentally
retarded. . . . In the present case, too, even in the 20 States without a formal prohibition on executing juveniles, the practice is infrequent. Since *Stanford*, six States
have executed prisoners for crimes committed as juveniles. In the past 10 years,
only three have done so: Oklahoma, Texas, and Virginia. . . .

There is, to be sure, at least one difference between the evidence of consensus
in *Atkins* and in this case. Impressive in *Atkins* was the rate of abolition of the death
penalty for the mentally retarded. Sixteen States that permitted the execution of
the mentally retarded at the time of *Penry* had prohibited the practice by the time

we heard *Atkins*. By contrast, the rate of change in reducing the incidence of the juvenile death penalty, or in taking specific steps to abolish it, has been slower. Five States that allowed the juvenile death penalty at the time of *Stanford* have abandoned it in the intervening 15 years—four through legislative enactments and one through judicial decision.

Though less dramatic than the change from *Penry* to *Atkins*, we still consider the change from *Stanford* to this case to be significant. As noted in *Atkins*, with respect to the States that had abandoned the death penalty for the mentally retarded since *Penry*, "[i]t is not so much the number of these States that is significant, but the consistency of the direction of change." . . . Since *Stanford*, no State that previously prohibited capital punishment for juveniles has reinstated it. This fact, coupled with the trend toward abolition of the juvenile death penalty, carries special force in light of the general popularity of anticrime legislation, and in light of the particular trend in recent years toward cracking down on juvenile crime in other respects. . . .

The slower pace of abolition of the juvenile death penalty over the past 15 years, moreover, may have a simple explanation. When we heard *Penry*, only two death penalty States had already prohibited the execution of the mentally retarded. When we heard *Stanford*, by contrast, 12 death penalty States had already prohibited the execution of any juvenile under 18, and 15 had prohibited the execution of any juvenile under 17. If anything, this shows that the impropriety of executing juveniles between 16 and 18 years of age gained wide recognition earlier than the impropriety of executing the mentally retarded. . . .

As in *Atkins*, the objective indicia of consensus in this case—the rejection of the juvenile death penalty in the majority of States; the infrequency of its use even where it remains on the books; and the consistency in the trend toward abolition of the practice—provide sufficient evidence that today our society views juveniles, in the words *Atkins* used respecting the mentally retarded, as "categorically less culpable than the average criminal."

Because the death penalty is the most severe punishment, the Eighth Amendment applies to it with special force. Capital punishment must be limited to those offenders who commit "a narrow category of the most serious crimes" and whose extreme culpability makes them "the most deserving of execution." . . .

Three general differences between juveniles under 18 and adults demonstrate that juvenile offenders cannot with reliability be classified among the worst offenders. First, as any parent knows and as the scientific and sociological studies respondent and his *amici* cite tend to confirm, "[a] lack of maturity and an underdeveloped sense of responsibility are found in youth more often than in adults and are more understandable among the young. These qualities often result in impetuous and ill-considered actions and decisions." It has been noted that "adolescents are overrepresented statistically in virtually every category of reckless behavior." In recognition of the comparative immaturity and irresponsibility of juveniles, almost every State prohibits those under 18 years of age from voting, serving on juries, or marrying without parental consent.

The second area of difference is that juveniles are more vulnerable or susceptible to negative influences and outside pressures, including peer pressure. This is explained in part by the prevailing circumstance that juveniles have less control, or less experience with control, over their own environment.

The third broad difference is that the character of a juvenile is not as well formed as that of an adult. The personality traits of juveniles are more transitory, less fixed.

These differences render suspect any conclusion that a juvenile falls among the worst offenders. The susceptibility of juveniles to immature and irresponsible behavior means "their irresponsible conduct is not as morally reprehensible as that of an adult." Their own vulnerability and comparative lack of control over their immediate surroundings mean juveniles have a greater claim than adults to be forgiven for failing to escape negative influences in their whole environment. The reality that juveniles still struggle to define their identity means it is less supportable to conclude that even a heinous crime committed by a juvenile is evidence of irretrievably depraved character. From a moral standpoint it would be misguided to equate the failings of a minor with those of an adult, for a greater possibility exists that a minor's character deficiencies will be reformed. Indeed, "[t]he relevance of youth as a mitigating factor derives from the fact that the signature qualities of youth are transient; as individuals mature, the impetuousness and recklessness that may dominate in younger years can subside." . . .

Once the diminished culpability of juveniles is recognized, it is evident that the penological justifications for the death penalty apply to them with lesser force than to adults. We have held there are two distinct social purposes served by the death penalty: "'retribution and deterrence of capital crimes by prospective offenders.'" . . . Whether viewed as an attempt to express the community's moral outrage or as an attempt to right the balance for the wrong to the victim, the case for retribution is not as strong with a minor as with an adult. Retribution is not proportional if the law's most severe penalty is imposed on one whose culpability or blameworthiness is diminished, to a substantial degree, by reason of youth and immaturity.

As for deterrence, it is unclear whether the death penalty has a significant or even measurable deterrent effect on juveniles, as counsel for the petitioner acknowledged at oral argument. In general we leave to legislatures the assessment of the efficacy of various criminal penalty schemes. Here, however, the absence of evidence of deterrent effect is of special concern because the same characteristics that render juveniles less culpable than adults suggest as well that juveniles will be less susceptible to deterrence. . . .

In concluding that neither retribution nor deterrence provides adequate justification for imposing the death penalty on juvenile offenders, we cannot deny or overlook the brutal crimes too many juvenile offenders have committed. Certainly it can be argued, although we by no means concede the point, that a rare case might arise in which a juvenile offender has sufficient psychological maturity, and at the same time demonstrates sufficient depravity, to merit a sentence of death. Indeed, this possibility is the linchpin of one contention pressed by petitioner and his *amici*. They assert that even assuming the truth of the observations we have made about juveniles' diminished culpability in general, jurors nonetheless should be allowed to consider mitigating arguments related to youth on a case-by-case basis, and in some cases to impose the death penalty if justified. A central feature of death penalty sentencing is a particular assessment of the circumstances of the crime and the characteristics of the offender. The system is designed to consider both aggravating and mitigating circumstances, including youth, in every case. Given this Court's own insistence on individualized consideration, petitioner maintains that it is both arbitrary and unnecessary to adopt a categorical rule barring imposition of the death penalty on any offender under 18 years of age.

We disagree. The differences between juvenile and adult offenders are too marked and well understood to risk allowing a youthful person to receive the death penalty despite insufficient culpability. An unacceptable likelihood exists that the brutality or cold-blooded nature of any particular crime would overpower mitigating arguments based on youth as a matter of course, even where the juvenile offender's objective immaturity, vulnerability, and lack of true depravity should require a sentence less severe than death. In some cases a defendant's youth may even be counted against him. In this very case, as we noted above, the prosecutor argued Simmons' youth was aggravating rather than mitigating. While this sort of overreaching could be corrected by a particular rule to ensure that the mitigating force of youth is not overlooked, that would not address our larger concerns.

It is difficult even for expert psychologists to differentiate between the juvenile offender whose crime reflects unfortunate yet transient immaturity, and the rare juvenile offender whose crime reflects irreparable corruption. As we understand it, this difficulty underlies the rule forbidding psychiatrists from diagnosing any patient under 18 as having antisocial personality disorder, a disorder also referred to as psychopathy or sociopathy, and which is characterized by callousness, cynicism, and contempt for the feelings, rights, and suffering of others. If trained psychiatrists with the advantage of clinical testing and observation refrain, despite diagnostic expertise, from assessing any juvenile under 18 as having antisocial personality disorder, we conclude that States should refrain from asking jurors to issue a far graver condemnation—that a juvenile offender merits the death penalty. When a juvenile offender commits a heinous crime, the State can exact forfeiture of some of the most basic liberties, but the State cannot extinguish his life and his potential to attain a mature understanding of his own humanity.

Drawing the line at 18 years of age is subject, of course, to the objections always raised against categorical rules. The qualities that distinguish juveniles from adults do not disappear when an individual turns 18. By the same token, some under 18 have already attained a level of maturity some adults will never reach. For the reasons we have discussed, however, a line must be drawn. . . . The age of 18 is the point where society draws the line for many purposes between childhood and adulthood. It is, we conclude, the age at which the line for death eligibility ought to rest. . . .

Our determination that the death penalty is disproportionate punishment for offenders under 18 finds confirmation in the stark reality that the United States is the only country in the world that continues to give official sanction to the juvenile death penalty. This reality does not become controlling, for the task of interpreting the Eighth Amendment remains our responsibility. Yet at least from the time of the Court's decision in *Trop*, the Court has referred to the laws of other countries and to international authorities as instructive for its interpretation of the Eighth Amendment's prohibition of "cruel and unusual punishments."

As respondent and a number of *amici* emphasize, Article 37 of the United Nations Convention on the Rights of the Child, which every country in the world has ratified save for the United States and Somalia, contains an express prohibition on capital punishment for crimes committed by juveniles under 18. No ratifying country has entered a reservation to the provision prohibiting the execution of juvenile offenders. Parallel prohibitions are contained in other significant international covenants.

Respondent and his *amici* have submitted, and petitioner does not contest, that only seven countries other than the United States have executed juvenile offenders since 1990: Iran, Pakistan, Saudi Arabia, Yemen, Nigeria, the Democratic Republic of Congo, and China. Since then each of these countries has either abolished capital punishment for juveniles or made public disavowal of the practice. In sum, it is fair to say that the United States now stands alone in a world that has turned its face against the juvenile death penalty. . . .

It is proper that we acknowledge the overwhelming weight of international opinion against the juvenile death penalty, resting in large part on the understanding that the instability and emotional imbalance of young people may often be a factor in the crime. The opinion of the world community, while not controlling our outcome, does provide respected and significant confirmation for our own conclusions. . . .

NOTES AND QUESTIONS

1. Decisions about whether to impose the death penalty in individual cases require an evidentiary hearing in every case. Given that, why does Justice Kennedy reject the prosecution's argument that the jury should determine whether older minors are to be put to death, as would happen under *Stanford*? Is he saying that all youths who are younger than 18 actually are less culpable than all those older than 18 or that for some reason we should treat them as if they are? Is determining eligibility for the death penalty by drawing the line at any age indefensibly arbitrary?

2. What was the implication of the prosecutor's argument during Simmons' trial about his youth? Does the risk that juries may find a defendant's youth to be a reason to impose the death penalty justify the Court's decision? Should "youth" be an aggravating or mitigating factor during sentencing?

3. Justice Kennedy concludes the opinion with the statement, "It does not lessen our fidelity to the Constitution or our pride in its origins to acknowledge that the express affirmation of certain fundamental rights [including the rights or individual freedom and human dignity] by other nations and peoples simply underscores the centrality of those same rights within our own heritage of freedom." *Roper* at 578. Justice Scalia responds in dissent by stating, "Foreign sources are cited today . . . *to set aside* the centuries-old American practice—a practice still engaged in by a large majority of the relevant States—of letting a jury of 12 citizens decide whether, in the particular case, youth should be the basis for withholding the death penalty. What these foreign sources 'affirm,' rather than repudiate, is the Justices' own notion of how the world ought to be, and their diktat that it shall be so henceforth in America." *Id.* at 628. What is the significance of death penalty law and practice in other countries?

NOTE: LIFE WITHOUT PAROLE SENTENCES
FOR JUVENILES

The Court relied on Roper v. Simmons when it held in Graham v. Florida, 560 U.S. 48 (2010), that sentences of life without parole for juveniles (JLWOP) convicted of non-homicides violate the Eighth Amendment's Cruel and Unusual

Punishment Clause. Again writing for the majority, Justice Kennedy applied a form of Eighth Amendment comparative analysis that previously had been reserved only for capital cases to conclude that evolving standards of decency no longer support this type of sentence for this category of offenders. As in *Roper*, Justice Kennedy was unwilling to tolerate the risk that a judge or jury would sentence a minor to JLWOP based on a "discretionary, subjective" judgment that the youth was incorrigible. The Court held that states must provide young offenders sentenced to JLWOP with a "meaningful opportunity for release based on demonstrated maturity and rehabilitation," leaving the states to explore the "means and mechanisms for compliance."

Two years later in Miller v. Alabama, 567 U.S. 460 (2012), the Court held 5-4 that the Eighth Amendment does not categorically bar a life without parole sentence for a minor who committed murder, although it does not permit mandatory imposition of such sentences. Instead, states may retain the possibility of life without parole for juveniles who murder provided that in each case the sentencing authority must make an individualized decision about whether life without parole is warranted. The Court added,

> But given all we have said in *Roper*, *Graham*, and this decision about children's diminished culpability and heightened capacity for change, we think appropriate occasions for sentencing juveniles to this harshest possible penalty will be uncommon. That is especially so because of the great difficulty we noted in *Roper* and *Graham* of distinguishing at this early age between "the juvenile offender whose crime reflects unfortunate yet transient immaturity, and the rare juvenile offender whose crime reflects irreparable corruption." Although we do not foreclose a sentencer's ability to make that judgment in homicide cases, we require it to take into account how children are different, and how those differences counsel against irrevocably sentencing them to a lifetime in prison.

567 U.S. at 479. Montgomery v. Louisiana, 136 S. Ct. 718 (2016), held that Miller v. Alabama is retroactive, greatly expanding the number of people in prison who can have their cases reviewed. It permits states to comply with this requirement by considering prisoners serving juvenile life without parole sentences for parole, rather than resentencing them.

As of 2017, 28 states and the District of Columbia had amended their laws regarding the eligibility of juveniles convicted of murder to be sentenced to life without parole. The new laws provide mandatory minima with a chance of parole ranging from 15 years to 40 years. Thirty states still allowed life without parole sentences for juvenile murderers. Josh Rovner, Juvenile Life Without Parole: An Overview 3 (The Sentencing Project, Oct. 13, 2017), https://www.sentencing-project.org/publications/juvenile-life-without-parole/. *See also* Kimberly Thomas, Random if not "Rare"? The Eighth Amendment Weaknesses of Post-Miller Legislation, 68 S.C. L. Rev. 393 (2017).

In July 2017 the Associated Press published its review of how states are implementing the *Miller/Montgomery* requirement that courts reexamine the cases of people who had been sentenced to life without parole for offenses committed while they were juveniles. The survey found more than 3,100 people serving such sentences. The variation among the states was dramatic. Ten states had no prisoners serving such sentences (Alaska, Hawaii, Kansas, Maine, New Mexico, New York, Rhode Island, Vermont, West Virginia, and Wyoming), and 12 states had five or fewer serving this sentence (Delaware (1), Idaho (4), Indiana (5), Iowa (3), Kentucky (4), Montana (2), New Hampshire (5), North Dakota (1), Oregon (5), South Dakota (3), Utah (2), and Wisconsin (3)). At the other extreme were Florida (600), Louisiana (303), Michigan (363), and Pennsylvania (517). AP, Locked Up for Life 50-State Examination (July 31, 2017), https://www.ap.org/explore/locked-up-for-life/50-states. As the authors of the report wrote, the states' responses to the Miller/Montgomery mandate are very inconsistent.

> Pennsylvania, which long resisted reopening the old cases, has resentenced more than 1 in 5 of its 517 juvenile lifers and released 58 so far. . . .
>
> In Michigan, meanwhile, prosecutors want new no-parole terms for some 236 of 363 juvenile lifers, and there are wide variances from county to county, which has prompted lawsuits. . . .
>
> Louisiana lawmakers spent two sessions debating over that state's 303 juvenile lifers, with district attorneys lobbying against eliminating no-parole terms. The Louisiana Center for Children's Rights notes 18 of 23 juvenile offenders tried for murder since 2012 have gotten life without parole.
>
> In June, the state Legislature finally changed the law, making juvenile homicide offenders eligible for release after 25 years, though prosecutors can still petition a judge for a no-parole sentence in old cases and new cases of first-degree murder. . . .
>
> The AP also found that while many states have taken steps to make former teen criminals eligible for parole, in practice, officials regularly deny release.
>
> In Missouri, the parole board has turned down 20 of 23 juvenile lifers, according to the MacArthur Justice Center, which filed a federal lawsuit this year claiming the board is denying the state's juvenile life-without-parole inmates a meaningful chance for release as required by the Supreme Court.
>
> The lawsuit says these decisions were made after short hearings—some just 30 minutes long—before a three-person panel that includes just one of seven parole board members, and two corrections employees. Inmates can bring only one supporter, either a witness or lawyer, not both, and have been told their lawyers may not even take notes during hearings.
>
> The state's parole board has come under fire after an investigation revealed a board member had made a game out of hearings by repeating words like "armadillo" and "hootenanny" and trying to get inmates to say the words, too. The board member resigned in June.
>
> Maryland, meantime, has 271 juvenile lifers whose sentences have always given them a chance for release. But no such prisoner has won parole in more than 20 years, prompting a lawsuit by the American Civil Liberties Union.

Sharon Cohen & Adam Geller, Parole for Young Lifers Inconsistent Across U.S. (July 31, 2017), https://apnews.com/a592b421f7604e2b88a170b5b438235f. The Kansas Supreme Court extended the reasoning in *Graham* to hold that mandatory lifetime post-release supervision of a minor is categorically cruel and unusual punishment in violation of the Eighth Amendment, and the Washington Supreme Court reached the same conclusion under the state constitutional. State v. Dull, 351 P.3d 641 (Kan. 2015); State v. Bassett, 428 P.3d 343 (Wash. 2018). However, the state supreme courts of Nebraska and Iowa rejected this interpretation.

State v. Boche, 885 N.W.2d 523 (Neb. 2016); State v. Graham, 897 N.W.2d 476 (Iowa 2017).

Graham, Miller, and *Montgomery* give rise to a number of other questions. One of the most significant is whether a very long single term of years sentence (99 years, say) or an aggregated series of term-of-years sentences (for example, 50 or 60 years) that are in effect life sentences should be analyzed as if they were life without parole sentences. The courts are divided. Cases holding that *Graham* or *Miller,* as the case may be, does not apply to such sentences include Bunch v. Smith, 685 F.3d 546 (6th Cir. 2012); State v. Kasic, 265 P.3d 410 (Az. App. 2011); Lucero v. People, 394 P.3d 1128 (Colo. 2017); State v. Brown, 118 So.3d 332 (La. 2013) (aggregated sentences for term of years); State v. Nathan, 522 S.W.3d 881 (Mo. 2017) (en banc); Vasquez v. Commonwealth, 781 S.E.2d 920 (Va. 2016). Cases that have applied *Graham* or *Miller* on the theory that the sentence was the functional equivalent of life without parole include Moore v. Biter, 725 F.3d 1184 (9th Cir. 2013); People v. Contreras, 411 P.3d 445 (Cal. 2018); Casiano v. Comm'ner of Correction, 115 A.3d 10310 (Conn. 2015); Henry v. State, 175 So.3d 675 (Fla. 2015); State v. Null, 836 N.W.2d 41 (Iowa 2013); State v. Boston, 363 P.3d 453 (Nev. 2015); State v. Zuber, 152 A.3d 197 (N.J. 2017); Ira v. Janecka, 419 P.3d 161 (N.M. 2018); State v. Moore, 76 N.E.3d 1127 (Ohio 2016); Kinkel v. Persson, 417 P.3d 401 (Or. 2018); Commonwealth v. Batts, 163 A.3d 410 (Pa. 2017); State v. Ramos, 387 P.3d 650 (Wash. 2017); and Bear Cloud v. State, 334 P.3d 132 (Wyo. 2014). *See generally* Daniel Jones, Technical Difficulties: Why A Broader Reading of Graham and Miller Should Prohibit De Facto Life Without Parole Sentences for Juvenile Offenders, 90 St. John's L. Rev. 169 (2016).

Juvenile Offenders: Investigation and Pretrial Processes 5

A. INTERROGATIONS

In *Gault*, the Supreme Court held that the Fifth Amendment privilege against self-incrimination protects minors during official court proceedings. The opinion did not address minors' rights during pretrial interrogation. However, since the early days following *Gault*, courts have generally assumed that the basic rules governing police interrogation of adults apply to juveniles too. Therefore, if a juvenile's statement to the police is involuntarily given, it is not admissible in a delinquency proceeding against the juvenile. Whenever police question a suspect, there is some degree of coercion. The purpose of *Miranda* warnings, which tell a suspect in custody of the right to remain silent and to have an attorney before talking to the police, is to counteract the coercion that arises when police take a suspect into custody. If a suspect purports to waive *Miranda* rights and talks to the police, the statements are admissible in later proceedings only if the waiver was knowing, voluntary, and intelligent. How does this rule apply when the suspect is a minor?

FARE v. MICHAEL C.
442 U.S. 707 (1979)

BLACKMUN, J. . . . Respondent Michael C. was implicated in the murder of Robert Yeager. The murder occurred during a robbery of the victim's home on January 19, 1976. A small truck registered in the name of respondent's mother was identified as having been near the Yeager home at the time of the killing, and a young man answering respondent's description was seen by witnesses near the truck and near the home shortly before Yeager was murdered.

On the basis of this information, Van Nuys, Cal., police took respondent into custody at approximately 6:30 P.M. on February 4. Respondent then was 16 years old and on probation to the Juvenile Court. He had been on probation since the age of 12. Approximately one year earlier he had served a term in a youth corrections camp under the supervision of the Juvenile Court. He had a record of several previous offenses, including burglary of guns and purse snatching, stretching back over several years.

Upon respondent's arrival at the Van Nuys station house two police officers began to interrogate him. The officers and respondent were the only persons in the room during the interrogation. The conversation was tape-recorded. One of the officers initiated the interview by informing respondent that he had been brought in for questioning in relation to a murder. The officer fully advised respondent of his *Miranda* rights. The following exchange then occurred. . . .

Q: . . . Do you understand all of these rights as I have explained them to you?
A: Yeah.
Q: Okay, do you wish to give up your right to remain silent and talk to us about this murder?
A: What murder? I don't know about no murder.
Q: I'll explain to you which one it is if you want to talk to us about it.
A: Yeah, I might talk to you.
Q: Do you want to give up your right to have an attorney present here while we talk about it?
A: *Can I have my probation officer here?*
Q: Well, I can't get a hold of your probation officer right now. You have the right to an attorney.
A: How I know you guys won't pull no police officer in and tell me he's an attorney?
Q: Huh?
A: [How do I know you guys won't pull no police officer in and tell me he's an attorney?]
Q: Your probation officer is Mr. Christiansen.
A: Yeah.
Q: Well, I'm not going to call Mr. Christiansen tonight. There's a good chance we can talk to him later, but I'm not going to call him right now. If you want to talk to us without an attorney present, you can. If you don't want to, you don't have to. But if you want to say something, you can, and if you don't want to say something you don't have to. That's your right. You understand that right?
A: Yeah.
Q: Okay, will you talk to us without an attorney present?
A: Yeah, I want to talk to you.

Respondent thereupon proceeded to answer questions put to him by the officers. He made statements and drew sketches that incriminated him in the Yeager murder.

Largely on the basis of respondent's incriminating statements, probation authorities filed a petition in Juvenile Court alleging that respondent had murdered Robert Yeager. . . .

Respondent thereupon moved to suppress the statements and sketches he gave the police during the interrogation. He alleged that the statements had been obtained in violation of *Miranda* in that his request to see his probation officer at the outset of the questioning constituted an invocation of his Fifth Amendment right to remain silent, just as if he had requested the assistance of an attorney. Accordingly, respondent argued that since the interrogation did not cease until he had a chance to confer with his probation officer, the statements and sketches could not be admitted against him in the Juvenile Court proceedings. In so arguing, respondent relied by analogy on the decision in People v. Burton, 491 P.2d 793 (Cal. 1971), where the Supreme Court of California had held that a minor's request, made during custodial interrogation, to see his parents constituted an invocation of the minor's Fifth Amendment rights.

In support of his suppression motion, respondent called his probation officer, Charles P. Christiansen, as a witness. Christiansen testified that he had instructed respondent that if at any time he had "a concern with his family," or ever had "a police contact," he should get in touch with his probation officer immediately. The witness stated that, on a previous occasion, when respondent had had a police contact and had failed to communicate with Christiansen, the probation officer had reprimanded him. This testimony, respondent argued, indicated that when he asked for his probation officer, he was in fact asserting his right to remain silent in the face of further questioning.

In a ruling from the bench, the court denied the motion to suppress. It held that the question whether respondent had waived his right to remain silent was one of fact to be determined on a case-by-case basis, and that the facts of this case showed a "clear waiver" by respondent of that right. The court observed that the transcript of the interrogation revealed that respondent specifically had told the officers that he would talk with them, and that this waiver had come at the outset of the interrogation and not after prolonged questioning. The court noted that respondent was a "16 and a half year old minor who has been through the court system before, has been to [probation] camp, has a probation officer, [and is not] a young, naive minor with no experience with the courts." Accordingly, it found that on the facts of the case respondent had waived his Fifth Amendment rights, notwithstanding the request to see his probation officer.

On appeal, the Supreme Court of California took the case by transfer from the California Court of Appeal and, by a divided vote, reversed. . . .

The rule the Court established in *Miranda* is clear. In order to be able to use statements obtained during custodial interrogation of the accused, the State must warn the accused prior to such questioning of his right to remain silent and of his right to have counsel, retained or appointed, present during interrogation. "Once [such] warnings have been given, the subsequent procedure is clear."

> If the individual indicates in any manner, at any time prior to or during questioning, that he wishes to remain silent, the interrogation must cease. At this point he has shown that he intends to exercise his Fifth Amendment privilege; any statement taken after the person invokes his privilege cannot be other than the product of compulsion, subtle or otherwise. . . . If the individual states that he wants an attorney, the interrogation must cease until an attorney is present. At that time, the individual must have an opportunity to confer with the attorney and to have him present during any subsequent questioning. If the individual cannot obtain an attorney and he indicates that he wants one before speaking to police, they must respect his decision to remain silent.

Any statements obtained during custodial interrogation conducted in violation of these rules may not be admitted against the accused, at least during the State's case in chief. . . .

The California court in this case, however, significantly has extended this rule by providing that a request by a juvenile for his probation officer has the same effect as a request for an attorney. Based on the court's belief that the probation officer occupies a position as a trusted guardian figure in the minor's life that would make it normal for the minor to turn to the officer when apprehended by the police, and based as well on the state-law requirement that the officer represent the interest of the juvenile, the California decision found that consultation with a probation officer fulfilled the role for the juvenile that consultation with an attorney does in general, acting as a "protective [device] . . . to dispel the compulsion inherent in custodial surroundings."

The rule in *Miranda*, however, was based on this Court's perception that the lawyer occupies a critical position in our legal system because of his unique ability to protect the Fifth Amendment rights of a client undergoing custodial interrogation. Because of this special ability of the lawyer to help the client preserve his Fifth Amendment rights once the client becomes enmeshed in the adversary process, the Court found that "the right to have counsel present at the interrogation is indispensable to the protection of the Fifth Amendment privilege under the system" established by the Court. Moreover, the lawyer's presence helps guard against overreaching by the police and ensures that any statements actually obtained are accurately transcribed for presentation into evidence. . . .

. . . [T]he probation officer is not in a position to offer the type of legal assistance necessary to protect the Fifth Amendment rights of an accused undergoing custodial interrogation that a lawyer can offer. The Court in *Miranda* recognized that "the attorney plays a vital role in the administration of criminal justice under our Constitution." It is this pivotal role of legal counsel that justifies the *per se* rule established in *Miranda*, and that distinguishes the request for counsel from the request for a probation officer, a clergyman, or a close friend. A probation officer simply is not necessary, in the way an attorney is, for the protection of the legal rights of the accused, juvenile or adult. He is significantly handicapped by the position he occupies in the juvenile system from serving as an effective protector of the rights of a juvenile suspected of a crime. . . .

Nor do we believe that a request by a juvenile to speak with his probation officer constitutes a *per se* request to remain silent. As indicated, since a probation officer does not fulfill the important role in protecting the rights of the accused juvenile that an attorney plays, we decline to find that the request for the probation officer is tantamount to the request for an attorney. And there is nothing inherent in the request for a probation officer that requires us to find that a juvenile's request to see one necessarily constitutes an expression of the juvenile's right to remain silent. . . .

Miranda further recognized that after the required warnings are given the accused, "[i]f the interrogation continues without the presence of an attorney and a statement is taken, a heavy burden rests on the government to demonstrate that the defendant knowingly and intelligently waived his privilege against self-incrimination and his right to retained or appointed counsel." . . . Thus, the determination whether statements obtained during custodial interrogation are admissible against the accused is to be made upon an inquiry into the totality of the circumstances surrounding the interrogation, to ascertain whether the accused in fact knowingly and voluntarily decided to forgo his rights to remain silent and to have the assistance of counsel.

This totality-of-the-circumstances approach is adequate to determine whether there has been a waiver even where interrogation of juveniles is involved. We discern no persuasive reasons why any other approach is required where the question is whether a juvenile has waived his rights, as opposed to whether an adult has done so. The totality approach permits — indeed, it mandates — inquiry into all the circumstances surrounding the interrogation. This includes evaluation of the juvenile's age, experience, education, background, and intelligence, and into whether he has the capacity to understand the warnings given him, the nature of his Fifth Amendment rights, and the consequences of waiving those rights.

Courts repeatedly must deal with these issues of waiver with regard to a broad variety of constitutional rights. There is no reason to assume that such courts — especially juvenile courts, with their special expertise in this area — will be unable to apply the totality-of-the-circumstances analysis so as to take into account those special concerns that are present when young persons, often with limited experience and education and with immature judgment, are involved. Where the age and experience of a juvenile indicate that his request for his probation officer or his parents is, in fact, an invocation of his right to remain silent, the totality approach will allow the court the necessary flexibility to take this into account in making a waiver determination. At the same time, that approach refrains from imposing rigid restraints on police and courts in dealing with an experienced older juvenile with an extensive prior record who knowingly and intelligently waives his Fifth Amendment rights and voluntarily consents to interrogation.

In this case, we conclude that the California Supreme Court should have determined the issue of waiver on the basis of all the circumstances surrounding the interrogation of respondent. The Juvenile Court found that under this approach, respondent in fact had waived his Fifth Amendment rights and consented to interrogation by the police after his request to see his probation officer was denied. Given its view of the case, of course, the California Supreme Court did not consider this issue, though it did hold that the State had failed to prove that, notwithstanding respondent's request to see his probation officer, respondent had not intended to invoke his Fifth Amendment rights.

We feel that the conclusion of the Juvenile Court was correct. The transcript of the interrogation reveals that the police officers conducting the interrogation took care to ensure that respondent understood his rights. They fully explained to respondent that he was being questioned in connection with a murder. They then informed him of all the rights delineated in *Miranda*, and ascertained that respondent understood those rights. There is no indication in the record that respondent failed to understand what the officers told him. Moreover, after his request to see his probation officer had been denied, and after the police officer once more had explained his rights to him, respondent clearly expressed his willingness to waive his rights and continue the interrogation.

Further, no special factors indicate that respondent was unable to understand the nature of his actions. He was a 16½-year-old juvenile with considerable experience with the police. He had a record of several arrests. He had served time in a youth camp, and he had been on probation for several years. He was under the full-time supervision of probation authorities. There is no indication that he was of insufficient intelligence to understand the rights he was waiving, or what the consequences of that waiver would be. He was not worn down by improper interrogation tactics or lengthy questioning or by trickery or deceit.

On these facts, we think it clear that respondent voluntarily and knowingly waived his Fifth Amendment rights. Respondent argues, however, that any statements he made during interrogation were coerced. Specifically, respondent alleges that the police made threats and promises during the interrogation to pressure him into cooperating in the hope of obtaining leniency for his cooperative attitude. He notes also that he repeatedly told the officers during his interrogation that he wished to stop answering their questions, but that the officers ignored his pleas. He argues further that the record reveals that he was afraid that the police would coerce him, and that this fear caused him to cooperate. He points out that at one point the transcript revealed that he wept during the interrogation.

Review of the entire transcript reveals that respondent's claims of coercion are without merit. As noted, the police took care to inform respondent of his rights and to ensure that he understood them. The officers did not intimidate or threaten respondent in any way. Their questioning was restrained and free from the abuses that so concerned the Court in *Miranda*. The police did indeed indicate that a cooperative attitude would be to respondent's benefit, but their remarks in this regard were far from threatening or coercive. And respondent's allegation that he repeatedly asked that the interrogation cease goes too far: at some points he did state that he did not know the answer to a question put to him or that he could not, or would not, answer the question, but these statements were not assertions of his right to remain silent.

. . . On the basis of the record in this case, we hold that the Juvenile Court's findings that respondent voluntarily and knowingly waived his rights and consented to continued interrogation, and that the statements obtained from him were voluntary, were proper, and that the admission of those statements in the proceeding against respondent in Juvenile Court was correct.

The judgment of the Supreme Court of California is reversed, and the case is remanded for further proceedings not inconsistent with this opinion.

MARSHALL, J., with whom BRENNAN, J., and STEVENS, J., join, dissenting. . . . As this Court has consistently recognized, the coerciveness of the custodial setting is of heightened concern where, as here, a juvenile is under investigation. In Haley v. Ohio, 332 U.S. 596 (1948), the plurality reasoned that because a 15½-year-old minor was particularly susceptible to overbearing interrogation tactics, the voluntariness of his confession could not "be judged by the more exacting standards of maturity." The Court reiterated this point in Gallegos v. Colorado, 370 U.S. 49 (1962), observing that a 14-year-old suspect could not "be compared with an adult in full possession of his senses and knowledgeable of the consequences of his admissions." . . .

On my reading of *Miranda*, a California juvenile's request for his probation officer should be treated as a *per se* assertion of Fifth Amendment rights. The California Supreme Court determined that probation officers have a statutory duty to represent minors' interests and, indeed, are "trusted guardian figure[s]" to whom a juvenile would likely turn for assistance. In addition, the court found, probation officers are particularly well suited to assist a juvenile "on such matters as to whether or not he should obtain an attorney" and "how to conduct himself with police." Hence, a juvenile's request for a probation officer may frequently be an attempt to secure protection from the coercive aspects of custodial questioning. . . .

POWELL, J., dissenting. Although I agree with the Court that the Supreme Court of California misconstrued Miranda v. Arizona I would not reverse the California court's judgment. This Court has repeatedly recognized that "the greatest care" must be taken to assure that an alleged confession of a juvenile was voluntary. Respondent was a young person, 16 years old at the time of his arrest and the subsequent prolonged interrogation at the station house. Although respondent had had prior brushes with the law . . . the taped transcript of his interrogation—as well as his testimony at the suppression hearing—demonstrates that he was immature, emotional,[1] and uneducated, and therefore was likely to be vulnerable to the skillful, two-on-one, repetitive style of interrogation to which he was subjected. . . .

It is clear that the interrogating police did not exercise "the greatest care" to assure that respondent's "admission was voluntary."

NOTES AND QUESTIONS

1. Why did Michael C. ask to see his probation officer? Why does it matter that he apparently misunderstood the role the probation officer might be required to play? Who was in the best position to clarify this misunderstanding, and how could that have been most easily accomplished?

2. Juveniles are often encouraged to cooperate with probation officers, both before trial and after adjudication and disposition. In view of these practices and their potential benefits, should a rule be adopted that admissions made by a juvenile to a probation officer are not admissible in an adjudicatory hearing? *Compare* In re Wayne H., 596 P.2d 1 (Cal. 1979), and K.N. v. State, 203 S.W.3d 103 (2005). In dispositional hearings? *See* In re Randy G., 487 N.Y.S.2d 967, 969 (N.Y. Fam. Ct. 1985).

3. The totality of the circumstances approach to waiver inquires into every aspect of the child's circumstances and those of the interrogation. The child's age, experience, background, intelligence, prior dealings with the police and court, and maturity are among the relevant factors. His or her physical and mental conditions (especially drug or alcohol use) during the interrogation are also relevant, as are the presence of an adult, the length of the interrogation, and the lateness of the day when questioning occurred, among other factors.

Examining recent cases about the validity of waivers, Professor Paul Marcus found that the courts are "hardly consistent in applying apparently concrete constitutional mandates as to minors." Paul Marcus, The *Miranda* Custody Requirement and Juveniles, 88 Tenn. L. Rev. 253, 270 (2018). *Compare* K.A. ex rel. J.A. v. Abington Heights Sch. Dist., 28 F. Supp. 3d 356, 372-374 (M.D. Pa. 2014) (finding that school officials questioning a student for 7 hours about his possession of synthetic marijuana and his family's drug use was not "sufficiently

---

1. The Juvenile Court Judge observed that he had "heard the tapes" of the interrogation and was "aware of the fact that Michael [respondent] was crying at the time he talked to the police officers."

egregious so as to shock the conscience," and thus did not violate the student's substantive due process rights, because the juvenile did not suffer any physical harm and the school had a compelling reason to question him, even though it had violated its own policy requiring that a parent be contacted about drug use, and the juvenile had ADD and a dysthymic disorder), *with* In re K.C., 32 N.E.3d 988 (Ohio App. 2015) (finding that because of the vulnerability of youth, the state bears the burden of proving, by a preponderance of the evidence, that a juvenile made a knowing, voluntary, and intelligent waiver of his or her *Miranda* rights).

Thirty-three states and the District of Columbia follow *Fare* and apply a totality of the circumstances test in reviewing waivers by juveniles. The other 17 states have statutes providing additional protections for minors during interrogations. Brief of Amicus Curiae Human Rights Watch in Support of Petition for Writ of Certiorari at 8, Joseph H. v. California, 137 S. Ct. 34 (2016), http://www.scotus-blog.com/wp-content/uploads/2016/04/Joseph-H.-v.-California-Amicus-Brief.pdf. We will examine the protective statutes more closely later in this chapter.

4. Did Michael C. understand the *Miranda* warnings that the police read to him? Professor Thomas Grisso did early, pathbreaking research on the ability of minors to understand legal information provided to them and to make legal decisions for themselves. In one study, he asked his respondents to paraphrase in their own words each of the four basic *Miranda* warnings and to define six words found in the warnings (consult, attorney, interrogation, appoint, entitled, and right). In addition, subjects were given a true-or-false test asking them to say whether an accurate and a paraphrased version of the *Miranda* warnings were the same. The results of the survey showed that approximately 9 percent of the juveniles did not understand their right to remain silent, almost a quarter did not understand that their statements could be used against them in court, and almost half (45 percent) did not understand their right to have an attorney provided for them. Thomas Grisso, Juveniles' Capacities to Waive *Miranda* Rights: An Empirical Analysis, 68 Cal. L. Rev. 1134, 1144-1152 (1980). Professor Grisso also found, consistent with more recent studies, that younger juveniles are particularly likely not to understand the significance of their *Miranda* rights. *Id.* at 1166.

Professor Feld's study supports these findings:

Psychologists distinguish between youths' cognitive ability—capacity to understand— and ability to make mature decisions and exercise self-control. *Miranda* requires only the ability to understand words, which developmental psychologists conclude that most sixteen- and seventeen-year-old youths can do.

This study corroborates that sixteen- and seventeen-year-old juveniles appear to understand and exercise *Miranda* similarly to adults. This consistency inferentially bolsters research that younger juveniles increasingly lack ability to understand and competence to exercise rights. . . .

The Court in *Haley, Gallegos, Gault, Fare, Alvarado*, and *J.D.B.* excluded statements taken from youths fifteen years of age or younger and admitted those obtained from sixteen- and seventeen-year-olds. The Court's de facto line—fifteen and younger versus sixteen and older—closely tracks what psychologists have found about youths' ability to understand the warning and concepts. State courts and legislatures should formally adopt the functional line that the Court and psychologists discern between youths sixteen and older and those fifteen and younger.

Barry C. Feld, Real Interrogation: What Actually Happens When Cops Question Kids, 47 Law & Soc'y Rev. 1, 25 (2013).

In light of these findings, should *Miranda* warnings be adapted for minors? If so, how? In 2010, the American Bar Association House of Delegates adopted a recommendation urging federal, state, territorial, and local legislative bodies and governmental agencies to support the development of simplified *Miranda* warning language use with juvenile arrestees, including, but not limited to, slight word changes (e.g., "lawyer" rather than "counsel") and simplified sentence structure. A.B.A., Recommendation (Feb. 2010), https://www.americanbar.org/groups/ child_law/resources/attorneys/simplified_mirandawarningsforjuveniles.html. The King County (Seattle), Washington sheriff's office adopted Miranda warnings for juveniles in 2017:

1. You have the right to remain silent, which means that you don't have to say anything.
2. It's OK if you don't want to talk to me.
3. If you do want to talk to me, I can tell the juvenile court judge or adult court judge and Probation Officer what you tell me.
4. You have the right to talk to a free lawyer right now. That free lawyer works for you and is available at any time—even late at night. That lawyer does not tell anyone what you tell them. That free lawyer helps you decide if it's a good idea to answer questions. That free lawyer can be with you if you want to talk with me.
5. If you start to answer my questions, you can change your mind and stop at any time. I won't ask you any more questions.

Juvenile Waiver of Rights:

1. Do you understand? (If yes, then continue to number 2)
2. Do you want to have a lawyer? (If no, then continue to number 3)
3. Do you want to talk with me? (If yes, then proceed with questioning)

Sheriff news release, Sheriff's Office simplifies Miranda Warnings for Juveniles (Sept. 27, 2017), https://www.kingcounty.gov/depts/sheriff/news-media/ news/2017/September/Miranda-warnings-simplified-for-juveniles.aspx.   Would such changes solve the problems identified by Professor Grisso and others?

Would using these child-friendly *Miranda* warnings solve the problems that Professor Grisso describes? Would they have changed Michael C.'s decision to talk to the police?

Under New Mexico law, all statements by juveniles under 13 are inadmissible at trial, and statements by 13- and 14-year-olds are rebuttably presumed to be inadmissible, *i.e.*, not knowing, intelligent, and voluntary. N.M. Stat. Ann. § 32A-2-14(F) (West 2018).

5. The interrogation of Michael C. was recorded, as evidenced by the Court's quotation of the dialog between him and the police officers and the description of him crying during the interview. While the law did not require interrogations to be recorded in the 1970s, the number of jurisdictions requiring recording of all interrogations has grown every year in recent years. As of 2015, 20 states and D.C. had this requirement, and many law enforcement agencies that are not required to do so record at least some interrogations. Kevin Lapp, Taking Back Juvenile Confessions, 64 UCLA L. Rev. 902, 932 (2017). In addition, a few jurisdictions require at least some juvenile (but not necessarily adult) interrogations to be recorded. *See, e.g.*, Wis. Stat. § 938.195 (2018). Professor Lapp concludes that recording does not have much effect on how interrogations are conducted, however. *Id.* On the other hand, Professor Feld found that recording interrogations has virtually eliminated suppression motions, expedites the processing of routine cases, and reserves court resources for complex cases. Barry C. Feld, Kids, Cops, and Confessions: Inside the Interrogation Room (New York University Press, 2013); Barry C. Feld, Behind Closed Doors: What Really Happens When Cops Question Kids, 23 Cornell J. L. & Pub. Pol'y 395 (2013). *See also* Steven A. Drizin & Marisa J. Reich, Heeding the Lessons of History: The Need for Mandatory Recording of Police Interrogations to Accurately Assess the Reliability and Voluntariness of Confessions, 52 Drake L. Rev. 619, 646 (2004).

An Ohio statute provides that if an interrogation is recorded, it is presumed that the suspect's statement is voluntary. Ohio Rev. Code § 2933.81. However, the Ohio Supreme Court held that this provision does not apply to a waiver of *Miranda* rights and could not apply to a minor's waiver of *Miranda* rights without violating the constitution. State v. Barker, 73 N.E.3d 365 (Ohio 2016).

6. In Bellotti v. Baird, above, at page 163, and Parham v. J.R., above, at page 194, the Court assumed that at least younger teens require assistance in making important decisions and that parents will make decisions in their children's best interests. Is the approach in *Fare* consistent with these assumptions? Most states require that the parents of a juvenile subjected to interrogation be notified, though failure to do so is only a factor that may affect the voluntariness analysis. Consider these perspectives:

> Custodial interrogation of a child in his parents' absence infringes on their right to control his upbringing in two ways. First, a child who confesses to a delinquent act is very likely to a charged in juvenile court, adjudged delinquent, and subjected to sanctions up to and including incarceration for a period of years. Even if the court imposes a lesser punishment, such as a term of probation, its assertion of authority over the child necessarily diminishes the child's parents' freedom to control his life. Second, the decision to waive Miranda rights and confess constitutes a relinquishment of the right to refuse to provide evidence for one's own conviction. A child's parents may have strong principled views about how this decision should be made which they would want their child to consider.

Leslie J. Harris, Children's Waiver of *Miranda* Rights and the Supreme Court's Decisions in *Parham, Bellotti*, and *Fare*, 10 N.M. L. Rev. 379, 400-401 (1980).

The limitations and safeguards on child decision-making autonomy that are well rehearsed in other legal contexts are not brought to bear in the areas of juvenile and criminal law. But for the lawyer's possible intervention, the child rises or falls on her own in making decisions about the handling of her case. The conventional rule that parents have a constitutional right to make decisions of import for their minor children (absent a showing of unfitness, conflict with the child's ability to exercise her constitutional rights, or a strong countervailing policy reason) appears to go unheeded.

Several hypotheses might explain why we disallow parental intrusion into the life-altering decisions of their children, though there are apparent anomalies. Greater judicial oversight over juvenile cases leads us to worry less about reduced parental oversight. Our commitment to providing rights to the accused adult leads us to an exaggerated conception of individual autonomy for the accused minor. Society is unconcerned with juveniles charged with crimes and uninterested in helping them acquire more adult strategies to "game" the system. Parents of juvenile delinquents are either undeserving of the broad rights over their children's upbringing or are estopped from now trying to exert control over their children's lives. But if one or more of these hypotheses is correct, the cases have so far not said so explicitly. In the end, none of these possible explanations suffices to explain the nearly wholesale disregard for the legal rights of parents in these cases.

Margareth Etienne, Managing Parents: Navigating Parental Rights in Juvenile Cases, 50 Conn. L. Rev. 61, 81 (2018). Professor Etienne reports that four states require police to grant a juvenile's request to speak with a parent; one state says that police must grant the parent's request to speak with the child; three states say that an officer does not have to grant a request to speak from either the parent or child, seven states say that a minor's waiver of rights is not valid unless the child has access to an interested adult; 19 states use the totality of the circumstances rule; four states say that a juvenile may waive her rights without a parent being present; eight states say a minor cannot waive rights without the consent of a parent or guardian, and four states have no identified case law or statute on the issue. *Id.* at 84. *See also* Note, Juvenile *Miranda* Waiver and Parental Rights, 126 Harv. L. Rev. 2359 (2013).

In Crowe v. City of San Diego, 608 F.3d 406 (9th Cir. 2010), the court refused to dismiss parents' claim that police violated their right to familial companionship when their sons' continued detention was "wrongfully justified by their illegally coerced confessions." *Id.* at 441.

On the other hand, as Professor Etienne has said, "parents are generally lousy at protecting the rights of their children in the interrogation room." Margareth Etienne, Managing Parents: Navigating Parental Rights in Juvenile Cases, 50 Conn. L. Rev. 61, 85 (2018). The parent may not fully appreciate the rights at stake or may encourage the juvenile to "do the right thing" and admit to the allegation, regardless of the circumstances or ramifications. To further complicate matters, the parent may be an alleged victim in the case, a witness to the offense, a co-defendant, or in danger of being held in contempt because of failure to abide by a court order. *Id.*; *see also* Hillary B. Farber, The Role of the Parent/Guardian in Juvenile Custodial Interrogations: Friend or Foe?, 41 Am. Crim. L. Rev. 1277, 1288-1298 (2004).

Miranda warnings are required only if the person being questioned is "in custody." Because police must know when they have to give the warnings, the test for determining whether questioning was custodial is objective and examines all the circumstances surrounding the interrogation, including whether a "reasonable person" in the suspect's position would have felt free to leave. The subjective views and "actual mindset" of the suspect are not relevant, so as to give clear guidance to the police. In the next case the Supreme Court considered whether, if the suspect is a child, this test is modified.

J.D.B. v. North Carolina

564 U.S. 261 (2011)

SOTOMAYOR, J. . . . Petitioner J.D.B. was a 13-year-old, seventh-grade student attending class at Smith Middle School in Chapel Hill, North Carolina when he was removed from his classroom by a uniformed police officer, escorted to a closed-door conference room, and questioned by police for at least half an hour.

This was the second time that police questioned J.D.B. in the span of a week. Five days earlier, two home break-ins occurred, and various items were stolen. Police stopped and questioned J.D.B. after he was seen behind a residence in the neighborhood where the crimes occurred. That same day, police also spoke to J.D.B.'s grandmother — his legal guardian — as well as his aunt.

Police later learned that a digital camera matching the description of one of the stolen items had been found at J.D.B.'s middle school and seen in J.D.B.'s possession. Investigator DiCostanzo, the juvenile investigator with the local police force who had been assigned to the case, went to the school to question J.D.B. Upon arrival, DiCostanzo informed the uniformed police officer on detail to the school (a so-called school resource officer), the assistant principal, and an administrative intern that he was there to question J.D.B. about the break-ins. Although DiCostanzo asked the school administrators to verify J.D.B.'s date of birth, address, and parent contact information from school records, neither the police officers nor the school administrators contacted J.D.B.'s grandmother.

The uniformed officer interrupted J.D.B.'s afternoon social studies class, removed J.D.B. from the classroom, and escorted him to a school conference room. There J.D.B. was met by DiCostanzo, the assistant principal, and the administrative intern. The door to the conference room was closed. With the two police officers and the two administrators present, J.D.B. was questioned for the next 30 to 45 minutes. Prior to the commencement of questioning, J.D.B. was given neither *Miranda* warnings nor the opportunity to speak to his grandmother. Nor was he informed that he was free to leave the room.

Questioning began with small talk — discussion of sports and J.D.B.'s family life. DiCostanzo asked, and J.D.B. agreed, to discuss the events of the prior weekend. Denying any wrongdoing, J.D.B. explained that he had been in the neighborhood where the crimes occurred because he was seeking work mowing lawns. DiCostanzo pressed J.D.B. for additional detail about his efforts to obtain work; asked J.D.B. to explain a prior incident, when one of the victims returned home to find J.D.B. behind her house; and confronted J.D.B. with the stolen camera. The assistant principal urged J.D.B. to "do the right thing," warning J.D.B. that "the truth always comes out in the end."

Eventually, J.D.B. asked whether he would "still be in trouble" if he returned the "stuff." In response, DiCostanzo explained that return of the stolen items would be helpful, but "this thing is going to court" regardless. DiCostanzo then warned that he may need to seek a secure custody order if he believed that J.D.B. would continue to break into other homes. When J.D.B. asked what a secure custody order was, DiCostanzo explained that "it's where you get sent to juvenile detention before court."

After learning of the prospect of juvenile detention, J.D.B. confessed that he and a friend were responsible for the break-ins. DiCostanzo only then informed J.D.B. that he could refuse to answer the investigator's questions and that he was free to leave. Asked whether he understood, J.D.B. nodded and provided further detail, including information about the location of the stolen items. Eventually J.D.B. wrote a statement, at DiCostanzo's request. When the bell rang indicating the end of the school day, J.D.B. was allowed to leave to catch the bus home.

Two juvenile petitions were filed against J.D.B., each alleging one count of breaking and entering and one count of larceny. J.D.B.'s public defender moved to suppress his statements and the evidence derived therefrom, arguing that suppression was necessary because J.D.B. had been "interrogated by police in a custodial setting without being afforded *Miranda* warnings." . . . After a suppression hearing at which DiCostanzo and J.D.B. testified, the trial court denied the motion, deciding that J.D.B. was not in custody at the time of the school house interrogation. . . . As a result, J.D.B. entered a transcript of admission to all four counts, renewing his objection to the denial of his motion to suppress, and the court adjudicated J.D.B. delinquent.

A divided panel of the North Carolina Court of Appeals affirmed. The North Carolina Supreme Court held, over two dissents, that J.D.B. was not in custody when he confessed, "declin[ing] to extend the test for custody to include consideration of the age . . . of an individual subjected to questioning by police."

We granted certiorari to determine whether the *Miranda* custody analysis includes consideration of a juvenile suspect's age.

. . . The State and its *amici* contend that a child's age has no place in the custody analysis, no matter how young the child subjected to police questioning. We cannot agree. In some circumstances, a child's age "would have affected how a reasonable person" in the suspect's position "would perceive his or her freedom to leave." That is, a reasonable child subjected to police questioning will sometimes feel pressured to submit when a reasonable adult would feel free to go. We think it clear that courts can account for that reality without doing any damage to the objective nature of the custody analysis.

A child's age is far "more than a chronological fact." Roper v. Simmons, 543 U.S. 551, 569 (2005). It is a fact that "generates common-sense conclusions about behavior and perception." . . . Such conclusions apply broadly to children as a class. And, they are self-evident to anyone who was a child once himself, including any police officer or judge.

Time and again, this Court has drawn these commonsense conclusions for itself. We have observed that children "generally are less mature and responsible than adults"; that they "often lack the experience, perspective, and judgment to recognize and avoid choices that could be detrimental to them," Bellotti v. Baird, 443 U.S. 622, 635 (1979) (plurality opinion); that they "are more vulnerable or susceptible to . . . outside pressures" than adults, *Roper*, 543 U.S. at 569; and so on. . . . Addressing the specific context of police interrogation, we have observed that events that "would leave a man cold and unimpressed can overawe and overwhelm a lad in his early teens." Haley v. Ohio, 332 U.S. 596, 599 (1948) (plurality opinion); see also Gallegos v. Colorado, 370 U.S. 49, 54 (1962) ("[N]o matter how sophisticated," a juvenile subject of police interrogation "cannot be compared" to an adult subject). Describing no one child in particular, these observations restate what "any parent knows"—indeed, what any person knows—about children generally. Roper, 543 U.S. at 569.[2]

Our various statements to this effect are far from unique. The law has historically reflected the same assumption that children characteristically lack the capacity to exercise mature judgment and possess only an incomplete ability to understand the world around them. . . . Like this Court's own generalizations, the legal disqualifications placed on children as a class—e.g., limitations on their ability to alienate property, enter a binding contract enforceable against them, and marry without parental consent—exhibit the settled understanding that the differentiating characteristics of youth are universal.

Indeed, even where a "reasonable person" standard otherwise applies, the common law has reflected the reality that children are not adults. In negligence suits, for instance, where liability turns on what an objectively reasonable person would do in the circumstances, "[a]ll American jurisdictions accept the idea that a person's childhood is a relevant circumstance" to be considered. . . .

As this discussion establishes, "[o]ur history is replete with laws and judicial recognition" that children cannot be viewed simply as miniature adults. We see no justification for taking a different course here. So long as the child's age was known to the officer at the time of the interview, or would have been objectively apparent to any reasonable officer, including age as part of the custody analysis requires officers neither to consider circumstances "unknowable" to them, nor to "anticipat[e] the frailties or idiosyncrasies" of the particular suspect whom they question. The same "wide basis of community experience" that makes it possible, as an objective matter, "to determine what is to be expected" of children in other contexts, likewise makes it possible to know what to expect of children subjected to police questioning.

In other words, a child's age differs from other personal characteristics that, even when known to police, have no objectively discernible relationship to a reasonable person's understanding of his freedom of action. . . . Precisely because childhood yields objective conclusions like those we have drawn ourselves—among others, that children are "most susceptible to influence" and "outside pressures," considering age in the custody analysis in no way involves a determination of how youth "subjectively affect[s] the mindset" of any particular child.

In fact, in many cases involving juvenile suspects, the custody analysis would be nonsensical absent some consideration of the suspect's age. This case is a prime

---

2. Although citation to social science and cognitive science authorities is unnecessary to establish these commonsense propositions, the literature confirms what experience bears out. See, e.g., Graham v. Florida, 560 U.S. 48,_(2010) ("[D]evelopments in psychology and brain science continue to show fundamental differences between juvenile and adult minds").

example. Were the court precluded from taking J.D.B.'s youth into account, it would be forced to evaluate the circumstances present here through the eyes of a reasonable person of average years. In other words, how would a reasonable adult understand his situation, after being removed from a seventh-grade social studies class by a uniformed school resource officer; being encouraged by his assistant principal to "do the right thing"; and being warned by a police investigator of the prospect of juvenile detention and separation from his guardian and primary caretaker? To describe such an inquiry is to demonstrate its absurdity. Neither officers nor courts can reasonably evaluate the effect of objective circumstances that, by their nature, are specific to children without accounting for the age of the child subjected to those circumstances.

Indeed, although the dissent suggests that concerns "regarding the application of the *Miranda* custody rule to minors can be accommodated by considering the unique circumstances present when minors are questioned at school," the effect of the schoolhouse setting cannot be disentangled from the identity of the person questioned. A student—whose presence at school is compulsory and whose disobedience at school is cause for disciplinary action—is in a far different position than, say, a parent volunteer on school grounds to chaperone an event, or an adult from the community on school grounds to attend a basketball game. Without asking whether the person "questioned in school" is a "minor," the coercive effect of the schoolhouse setting is unknowable.

. . . Reviewing the question *de novo* today, we hold that so long as the child's age was known to the officer at the time of police questioning, or would have been objectively apparent to a reasonable officer, its inclusion in the custody analysis is consistent with the objective nature of that test. This is not to say that a child's age will be a determinative, or even a significant, factor in every test. It is, however, a reality that courts cannot simply ignore. . . .

The question remains whether J.D.B. was in custody when police interrogated him. We remand for the state courts to address that question, this time taking account of all of the relevant circumstances of the interrogation, including J.D.B.'s age at the time. The judgment of the North Carolina Supreme Court is reversed, and the case is remanded for proceedings not inconsistent with this opinion.

ALITO, J., with whom ROBERTS, C.J., SCALIA, J., and THOMAS, J., join, dissenting. . . . [The Court] may choose to limit today's decision by arbitrarily distinguishing a suspect's age from other personal characteristics—such as intelligence, education, occupation, or prior experience with law enforcement—that may also correlate with susceptibility to coercive pressures. Or, if the Court is unwilling to draw these arbitrary lines, it will be forced to effect a fundamental transformation of the *Miranda* custody test—from a clear, easily applied prophylactic rule into a highly fact-intensive standard resembling the voluntariness test that the *Miranda* Court found to be unsatisfactory.

For at least three reasons, there is no need to go down this road. First, many minors subjected to police interrogation are near the age of majority, and for these suspects the one-size-fits-all *Miranda* custody rule may not be a bad fit. Second, many of the difficulties in applying the *Miranda* custody rule to minors arise because of the unique circumstances present when the police conduct interrogations at school. The *Miranda* custody rule has always taken into account the setting in which questioning occurs, and accounting for the school setting in such cases will address many of these problems. Third, in cases like the one now before us, where the suspect is especially young, courts applying the constitutional voluntariness standard can take special care to ensure that incriminating statements were not obtained through coercion.

Safeguarding the constitutional rights of minors does not require the extreme makeover of *Miranda* that today's decision may portend. . . .

NOTES AND QUESTIONS

1. *J.D.B.* cited the Eighth Amendment cases of Roper v. Simmons (p. 398) and Graham v. Florida (p. 40) in support of its conclusion that "a reasonable child subjected to police questioning will sometimes feel pressured to submit when a reasonable adult would feel free to go." 564 U.S. at 271. Is this a valid extension of the holdings of *Roper* and *Graham*, or is the Court comparing apples with oranges?

2. The dissenting justices argue that the majority's position opens the floodgates to requiring that the determination of whether a suspect is in custody take into account many aspects of the suspect's personal characteristics and situation, such as "intelligence, education, occupation, or prior experience with law enforcement." Is this true? Can a police officer conducting an interrogation identify these characteristics in the same way that the officer can determine a suspect's age?

Would *J.D.B.* support a requirement that the officers take into account a suspect's gender in making the custody determination? If so, would it matter? A study of 307 interrogations of male and female youth, aged 16 or 17 and charged with a felony, found few quantitative differences in how police question boys and girls, despite the fact that interviews with juvenile justice personnel reported substantial differences in how they perceive boys and girls (e.g., "While some described girls as more cooperative than boys, most offered much more negative characteristics of females, describing them as emotional, confrontational, and verbally aggressive."). The study found that males and females waive *Miranda* rights at similar rates. Barry C. Feld, Questioning Gender: Police Interrogation of Delinquent Girls, 49 Wake Forest L. Rev. 1059, 1060-1105 (2014).

3. Professor Marcus concludes that *J.D.B.* has not had a great impact on courts' analyses of whether a minor is in custody because most juveniles who are interrogated are 16 or older, and the empirical evidence shows little difference between 16- and 18-year-olds in their understanding of their rights during an interrogation. Paul Marcus, The *Miranda* Custody Requirement and Juveniles, 88 Tenn. L. Rev. 253, 280-281 (2018). However, he found that *J.D.B.* tended to make a difference when the suspect was younger than 13. *Id.* at 282-289. On the other hand, he found that courts' rulings on whether children are "in custody" depending on whether the interrogation occurred at home or at school and on whether a friendly adult was present were "utterly irreconcilable." *Id.* at 289.

4. Some jurisdictions have statutes or case law requiring that minors be given *Miranda* warnings whenever they are questioned, without regard to whether they are "in custody." *See, e.g.*, N.M. Stat. § 32A-2-14 (C) (2018), which was interpreted in State v. Antonio T., 352 P.3 1172 (N.M. 2015), to require that warnings be given to a 17-year-old student questioned by an assistant principal in the presence of a police officer. However, the New Mexico court later held that a juvenile on probation

questioned by a probation officer about a possible probation violation was not entitled to *Miranda* warnings or to the protection of the statute because probationers, both juvenile and adult, are entitled to less protections than people interrogated by police as criminal suspects. State v. Taylor, 385 P.3d 639 (N.M. App. 2016).

5. Does *J.D.B.* change the way in which *Fare* should be applied? Or does it simply call for a totality of the circumstances test for analyzing the custody question similar to that endorsed in *Fare*? Consider In re Art T., 183 Cal. Rptr. 3d 784, 799-801 (2015) (applying *J.D.B.* to the invocation of the right to counsel by a juvenile and holding that a 13-year-old's statement, "Could I have an attorney? Because that's not me," made after watching a video of a shooting during the course of a custodial interrogation, was an unambiguous request for counsel and that failure to stop the interrogation until counsel was present was not harmless beyond a reasonable doubt).

DASSEY V. DITTMANN

877 F.3d 297 (7th Cir. 2017), *cert. denied*, 138 S. Ct. 2677 (2018)

HAMILTON, Circuit Judge. Petitioner Brendan Dassey confessed on videotape to participating in the 2005 rape and murder of Teresa Halbach and the mutilation of her corpse. The Wisconsin state courts upheld Dassey's convictions for these crimes, finding that his confession was voluntary and could be used against him. The principal issue in this habeas corpus appeal is whether that finding was based on an unreasonable application of Supreme Court precedent or an unreasonable view of the facts. . . .

After the state courts found the confession voluntary, a federal district court and a divided panel of this court found that the state courts' decision was unreasonable and that Dassey was entitled to a writ of habeas corpus. We granted *en banc* review to consider the application of the deferential standards of 28 U.S.C. § 2254(d) and the implications of the panel decision for interrogations of juvenile suspects. . . .

We first discuss our standard of review under the Antiterrorism and Effective Death Penalty Act of 1996 (AEDPA) and then describe the Supreme Court's clearly established law for when a confession, particularly a confession by a sixteen-year-old like Dassey, is deemed voluntary and admissible.

A. Deference Under AEDPA

In considering habeas corpus petitions challenging state court convictions, "our review is governed (and greatly limited) by" AEDPA . . . Section 2254(d) provides that a state court conviction cannot be overturned unless the state courts' adjudication of a federal claim on the merits:

(1) resulted in a decision that was contrary to, or involved an unreasonable application of, clearly established Federal law, as determined by the Supreme Court of the United States; or

(2) resulted in a decision that was based on an unreasonable determination of the facts in light of the evidence presented in the State court proceeding. . . .

The standard for legal errors under § 2254(d)(1) was meant to be difficult to satisfy. The issue is not whether federal judges agree with the state court decision or even whether the state court decision was correct. The issue is whether the decision was unreasonably wrong under an objective standard. Put another way, we ask whether the state court decision "was so lacking in justification that there was an error well understood and comprehended in existing law beyond any possibility for fairminded disagreement." . . .

B.   The Law of Confessions

The Due Process Clause of the Fourteenth Amendment forbids the admission of an involuntary confession in evidence in a criminal prosecution. . . .

This general standard has some specific requirements to guide courts. First, a person arguing his confession was involuntary must show that the police engaged in coercive practices. . . .

Interrogation tactics short of physical force can amount to coercion. The Court has condemned tactics designed to exhaust suspects physically and mentally. Such tactics include long interrogation sessions or prolonged detention paired with repeated but relatively short questioning.

The Supreme Court has not found that police tactics not involving physical or mental exhaustion taken alone were sufficient to show involuntariness. In several cases, the Court has held that officers may deceive suspects through appeals to a suspect's conscience, by posing as a false friend, and by other means of trickery and bluff. False promises to a suspect have similarly not been seen as *per se* coercion, at least if they are not quite specific.

False promises may be evidence of involuntariness, at least when paired with more coercive practices or especially vulnerable defendants as part of the totality of the circumstances. But the Supreme Court allows police interrogators to tell a suspect that "a cooperative attitude" would be to his benefit. Fare v. Michael C., 442 U.S. 707, 727 (1979) (reversing finding that confession was involuntary). Supreme Court precedents do not draw bright lines on this subject.

In assessing voluntariness, courts must weigh the tactics and setting of the interrogation alongside any particular vulnerabilities of the suspect. Relevant factors include the suspect's age, intelligence, and education, as well as his familiarity with the criminal justice system.

The interaction between the suspect's vulnerabilities and the police tactics may signal coercion even in the absence of physical coercion or threats. The Supreme Court has made it clear that juvenile confessions call for "special care" in evaluating voluntariness. E.g., Haley v. Ohio, 332 U.S. 596, (1948); *see also* J.D.B. v. North Carolina, 564 U.S. 261, 277 (2011); In re Gault, 387 U.S. 1, 45 (1967); *Gallegos*, 370 U.S. at 54. In juvenile cases, the law is particularly concerned with whether a friendly adult is present for or consents to the interrogation. Concerns about physical exhaustion, naïveté about friendly police in the context of an adversarial police interview, and intellectual disability also take on heightened importance for assessing whether a juvenile's will was overborne. . . .

In 2005, Teresa Halbach was a young photographer with her own business based in Calumet County, Wisconsin. On October 31, her last appointment of the day was at Avery's Auto Salvage to photograph a van for an advertisement. Halbach never returned from that appointment. A few days later during a missing-person search, her car was found at the salvage yard. Her blood stained the car's interior. A further search turned up Halbach's charred remains in a burn pit on the property, along with shell casings on the floor of Steven Avery's garage.

Police investigators spoke with a number of Avery's relatives in early November, including an hour-long interview of his sixteen-year-old nephew Brendan Dassey, who lived close by. Dassey said he had seen Halbach taking pictures at the salvage yard on the afternoon of October 31, but he resisted the suggestion that she had entered Avery's home. At that time, he provided no other useful information.

Several months later, though, investigators received word that Dassey had been crying uncontrollably and had lost about forty pounds of weight. They proceeded to interview him a total of three times on February 27, 2006. In these voluntary witness interviews, it became clear that Dassey knew much more about Teresa's murder. (Dassey was not in custody on February 27th. He signed and initialed a *Miranda* waiver, and his mother consented, though she did not sit in.) In those interviews, Dassey admitted that on October 31st, he had gone over to Avery's trailer around 9:00 p.m. to help with a bonfire. He told the police that he had seen parts of a human body in the fire. He also said that Avery had threatened to hurt him if he spoke to the police. When the police asked about a pair of bleach-stained jeans they had learned about from another family member, Dassey admitted that he had helped Avery clean up a spill on the garage floor late that night. But Dassey claimed to have had nothing to do with Teresa's death.

After those interviews, investigators thought Dassey had been a witness to at least the aftermath of a terrible crime and was struggling with the horror of what he had seen. On March 1st, the investigators (Mark Wiegert and Tom Fassbender) obtained his mother's permission for another interview. They took Dassey from his high school to a local sheriff's department, where he was questioned without the presence of a friendly adult. In the car the investigators gave Dassey standard *Miranda* warnings about his right to remain silent, his right to an attorney, and the possibility that statements he gave could be used against him. Dassey orally acknowledged the warnings, and he initialed and signed a written *Miranda* waiver form. . . .

The interview took place in a so-called "soft" interview room equipped for videotaping. Dassey sat on a couch facing two officers and a camera. Over the next three hours, Dassey was repeatedly offered food, drinks, restroom breaks, and opportunities to rest. At no point in the interview did the investigators threaten Dassey or his family. Nor did they attempt to intimidate him physically. They did not even raise their voices. Neither investigator tried to prevent Dassey from leaving the room, nor did they use any sort of force to compel him to answer questions. Dassey never refused to answer questions, never asked to have counsel or his mother present, and never tried to stop the interview.

One officer began by telling Dassey how he could help the investigation, since "this information and that information" from previous accounts needed "just a little tightening up." Sensing that Dassey "may have held back for whatever reasons," the officer assured Dassey "that Mark and I both are in your corner, we're on your side." Acknowledging Dassey's potential concern that talking to the police meant he "might get arrested and stuff like that," the investigator urged Dassey to "tell the whole truth, don't leave anything out." Talking could be in Dassey's best interest even though it "might make you look a little bad or make you look like you were more involved than you wanna be," because admitting to unfortunate facts would leave "no doubt you're telling the truth." The first investigator closed by saying that "from what I'm seeing, even if I filled" in some holes in Dassey's story, "I'm thinkin' you're all right. OK, you don't have to worry about things . . . [W]e know what Steven [Avery] did . . . we just need to hear the whole story from you." The other investigator went next:

> Honesty here Brendan is the thing that's gonna help you. OK, no matter what you did, we can work through that. OK. We can't make any promises but we'll stand behind you no matter what you did. OK. Because you're being the good guy here. . . . And by you talking with us, it's, it's helping you. OK? Because the honest person is the one who's gonna get a better deal out of everything.

After Dassey nodded in agreement, the investigator continued:

> You know. Honesty is the only thing that will set you free. Right? And we know, like Tom said we know, we reviewed those tapes. . . . We pretty much know everything that's why we're . . . talking to you again today. We really need you to be honest this time with everything, OK. . . . [A]s long as you be honest with us, it's OK. If you lie about it that's gonna be problems. OK. Does that sound fair?

Dassey again nodded and the questioning turned to the events of October 31st.

Over the course of the next three hours, with several breaks as the investigators conferred outside the room, Dassey told an even more disturbing and incriminating story about October 31st. In the first hour, Dassey admitted that he received a telephone call from Avery, went over to Avery's garage in the six o'clock hour, and found Teresa already dead in her car. Dassey then said he helped Avery lower Teresa's bound body onto a "creeper" (used to work underneath an automobile), which he and Avery used to take her body outside and throw her onto the already-burning bonfire.

At that point, less than an hour into the interview, Dassey's story pivoted dramatically. Dassey revised his story to say that he first noticed something amiss in the four o'clock hour. Dassey volunteered that when he was out getting the mail, he heard a woman screaming inside Avery's trailer. Dassey knocked on Avery's door, ostensibly to deliver a piece of mail, and a sweaty Avery answered the door.

Dassey said he then saw Teresa alive, naked, and handcuffed to Avery's bed. Dassey said he went inside at Avery's invitation and had a soda while Avery told him that he had raped Teresa. Dassey said that, at Avery's urging, he then raped Teresa . . .

In Dassey's telling, he next helped Avery subdue and kill Teresa and move her to the garage. In response to questioning and prodding, Dassey told a confusing story about these critical events. Dassey said that Avery stabbed Teresa with a large knife, that her handcuffs were removed, and that she was tied up with rope. He also said that Avery cut off some of her hair with that large knife, that he (Dassey) cut her throat with the same knife, and that at some point Avery choked or punched her. All these events reportedly happened by 6:00 or 6:30 p.m.

The details and sequence of these events changed repeatedly, however, as investigators pressed Dassey for more details. This portion of the interrogation provides the most support for Dassey's claim that his confession was both involuntary and unreliable. For example, because the recovered remnants of Teresa's skull contained trace amounts of lead, the investigators believed that Teresa had been shot in the head. They were eager for Dassey to describe what "else was done to her head" besides cutting and punching. In this exchange, Dassey did not provide the answer they were looking for. He offered what seemed like guesses. The investigators abandoned their vague admonitions to tell the truth. They lost patience and blurted out:

Wiegert:	All right, I'm just gonna come out and ask you. Who shot her in the head?
Brendan:	He did.
Fassbender:	Then why didn't you tell us that?
Brendan:	Cuz I couldn't think of it.
Fassbender:	Now you remember it? (Brendan nods "yes") Tell us about that then.

Dassey continued to do so over the whole course of the March 1st interview, revising upwards the number of times Teresa was shot from twice to three times, and then up to ten times. Dassey also revised the location of the shooting, first outside the garage, then inside Teresa's car, then on the floor of the garage. After this shifting exchange about the shooting, the first hour of the March 1st interview concluded with Dassey explaining how he and Avery put Teresa's body on the fire, how they moved her car, and finally how they cleaned up the stain in Avery's garage before Dassey went home.

The investigators then took a break to confer. During the break, Dassey had the opportunity to rest and to use the restroom. Before starting up again, Dassey and Wiegert had this exchange, indicating that Dassey did not understand the gravity of what he had told the investigators:

Brendan:	How long is this gonna take?
Wiegert:	It shouldn't take a whole lot longer.
Brendan:	Do you think I can get [back to school] before one twenty–nine?
Wiegert:	Um, probably not.
Brendan:	Oh.
Wiegert:	What's at one twenty–nine?
Brendan:	Well, I have a project due in sixth hour.

In the second hour of questioning, the investigators sought to confirm details from the first. They had only limited success. Dassey provided more confusing details about how Teresa was killed and the status of the bonfire. But in the main, Dassey largely confirmed his account from the first hour, especially about the details of his sexual assault of Teresa. His story regarding what he saw of Teresa in the fire — hands, feet, forehead, and part of a torso — also remained mostly consistent.

Signaling that the investigators did not overwhelm his will, Dassey resisted repeated suggestions by both investigators that he and Avery used the wires and cables hanging in the garage to torture Teresa. The investigators also tested Dassey's suggestibility. They told him falsely that Teresa had a tattoo on her stomach and asked if he had seen it. . . . In this exchange, Dassey stuck to what he thought he knew, despite being challenged and prodded by the investigators.

The investigators took another break, during which Dassey ate a sandwich and briefly fell asleep. The investigators returned to talk about the consequences Dassey was facing:

Fassbender: What do you think's gonna happen? What do you think should happen right now?
Brendan: I don't know.
Fassbender: You know obviously that we're police officers, OK. (Brendan nods "yes") And . . . because of what you told us, we're gonna have ta arrest you. Did you kinda figure that was coming? For . . . what you did we . . . can't let you go right now. The law will not let us. And so you're not gonna be able to go home tonight. All right?
Brendan: Does my mom know?
Fassbender: Your mom knows.

After briefly discussing some logistics, the exchange continued:

Fassbender: Did you kinda . . . after telling us what you told us you kinda figured this was coming? (Brendan nods "yes") Yeah? (Brendan nods "yes")
Brendan: Is it only for one day or?
Wiegert: We don't know that at this time, but let me tell ya something Brendan, you did the right thing. OK. (Brendan nods "yes") By being honest, you can at least sleep at night right now. . . .
Fassbender: Your cooperation and help with us is gonna work in your favor. I can't say what [it's] gonna do or where [you're] gonna end up but [it's] gonna work in your favor and we appreciate your continued cooperation. (Brendan nods "yes") . . .

Dassey was taken into custody after this interview, which he now contends was involuntary and should not have been used at his trial.

At trial, Dassey testified and denied any knowledge of or involvement in Teresa Halbach's murder. . . . According to his lawyer's version of events, Brendan came home from school at 3:45 p.m. on October 31st and played video games until having dinner with his brother and mother. After the others left, Dassey claimed, he fielded a phone call from his brother's boss and then shortly after that a call from Avery. At "about sevenish," Dassey claimed, he joined Avery for the bonfire, making four or five trips around the salvage yard picking up discarded items to throw on the flames. Around nine o'clock, Dassey helped Avery clean up a spill in his garage, and after a phone call from his mother, Dassey claimed, he returned home around 9:30 or 9:45 p.m. According to his trial testimony, none of the incriminating events related in his March 1st confession ever happened.

[At trial the judge denied Dassey's motion to suppress his confession as involuntary. While finding that Dassey was a minor, "an IQ level in the low average to borderline range," was in special education and had no prior record, the judge found that he was not in custody and that he knew he could stop answering questions and leave at any time. The judge also found that the police spoke in normal tones "with no raised voices, no hectoring, or threats of any kind." "Nothing on the video-tape visually depicts Brendan Dassey as being agitated, upset, frightened, or intimidated by the questions of either investigator," and he "displayed no difficulty in understanding the questions asked of him," the judge found. The judge also found that Dassey was not coerced and that the investigators made no promises of leniency. At trial the confession was the most incriminating evidence against Dassey, who was found guilty of rape, murder, and mutilation of a corpse. The Wisconsin Court of Appeals found that his confession was voluntary, and the Wisconsin Supreme Court denied a petition for review.]

Dassey filed a federal habeas corpus petition in the Eastern District of Wisconsin in 2014. In a detailed opinion, the district court granted habeas relief, finding that false promises of leniency were indeed made to Dassey and that his March 1st confession was not voluntary. We granted the State's petition to rehear the case *en banc* and now reverse with instructions to dismiss Dassey's habeas petition.

The state court decision that Dassey confessed voluntarily was not an unreasonable application of Supreme Court precedent. . . .

A number of relevant factors, we recognize, tend to support Dassey's claims about the March 1st confession. He was young. He was alone with the police. He was somewhat limited intellectually. The officers' questioning included general assurances of leniency if he told the truth, and Dassey may have believed they promised more than they did. At times it appeared as though Dassey simply did not grasp the gravity of his confession—after confessing to rape and murder, he asked the officers if he would be back at school that afternoon in time to turn in a project. Portions of the questioning also included leading and suggestive questions, and throughout the interrogation Dassey faced follow-up inquiries when the investigators were not satisfied with what he had told them, leading him at times to seem to guess. In addition, the confusion and contradictions in Dassey's account of the crimes of October 31st lend support to the view that his confession was the product of suggestions and/or a desire to tell the police what they wanted to hear.

At the same time, many other factors support the finding that Dassey's confession was indeed voluntary. Start with the circumstances of the interrogation. As stipulated by both sides, Dassey was not in custody when he admitted participating in the crimes of October 31st. He went with the officers voluntarily and with his mother's knowledge and consent. He was given *Miranda* warnings and understood them sufficiently. The interrogation was conducted during school hours and in a comfortable setting. Dassey showed no signs of physical distress. He had access to food, drinks, and restroom breaks. The interrogation was not particularly lengthy, especially with the breaks that were taken every hour. . . .

Turning to the techniques used in the interrogation, the investigators told Dassey many times that they already knew what had happened when in fact they did not. Such deception is a common interview technique. To our knowledge, it has not led courts (and certainly not the Supreme Court) to find that a subject's incriminating answers were involuntary. Also, most of the incriminating details in Dassey's confession were not suggested by the questioners. He volunteered them in response to open-ended questions.

When Dassey's story did not make sense, seemed incomplete, or seemed to conflict with other evidence, the questioners pressed Dassey with further questions. Those techniques are not coercive. Dassey responded to such questioning by modifying his story on some points, but he stuck to his story on others. . . .

Under AEDPA, the essential point here is that the totality-of-the-circumstances test gives courts considerable room for judgment in cases like this one, where the factors point in both directions. Given the many relevant facts and the substantial weight of factors supporting a finding that Dassey's confession was voluntary, the state court's decision was not an unreasonable application of Supreme Court precedent. . . .

The requirement that courts take "special care" in analyzing juvenile confessions does not call for habeas relief here. The state appellate court met the requirements for analyzing juvenile confessions by considering Dassey's age, his intellectual capacity, and the voluntary absence of his mother during the interrogation. The state court noted that the officers read Dassey his *Miranda* rights and that Dassey later remembered his rights and agreed to talk anyway. The court assessed coercion in relation to Dassey's vulnerabilities, including his "age, intellectual limitations and high suggestibility." The court did not limit its inquiry to only whether the most abusive interrogation techniques were used. The court examined the tones and volumes of the investigators' voices, finding that the officers "used normal speaking tones, with no hectoring, threats or promises of leniency," though they did prod Dassey to be honest and sought to establish a rapport with him. The court even considered Dassey's physical comfort by noting he sat on a sofa and was offered food, drink, and restroom breaks. . . .

Dassey also argues that he is entitled to relief under § 2254(d)(2) on the ground that the state courts made an unreasonable finding of fact: that the questioners made no false promises of leniency. . . . We reject this argument.

. . . The trial court here highlighted the key points for both sides, including the warning that the questioners could not make promises (which supports the State here) and the problematic assurance that honesty was the only thing that would set Dassey free (which helps Dassey's claim, especially in light of his limited intellect). Whether we treat the state court's decision on this point as a finding of fact or a conclusion of law, we find nothing unreasonable about it. . . .

The concerns expressed by our dissenting colleagues and the district court about the potential coercive effects of the police tactics here are understandable. Critics of Dassey's interrogation see evidence of fabrication through the confession's inconsistencies and lack of solid corroborating physical evidence. Some of the confession's inconsistencies are startling, particularly Dassey's shifting answers on the location of the shooting (outside the garage, on the garage floor, and in the car inside the garage), and his failure to recall consistently the order of attacks in the bedroom (stabbing, hair-cutting, and throat-slicing). Also, during the dialogue about Teresa's shooting, the investigators prodded Dassey and injected some critical facts into the discussion that corroborated evidence they already knew. . . .

The concerns about reliability echo the opinions of scholars who believe that certain interrogation tactics tend to produce false confessions. Some police departments and experts have acknowledged this criticism and have changed their interrogation practices in response. . . .

These debates over interrogation techniques have not resulted in controlling Supreme Court precedent condemning the techniques used with Dassey. Absent a clear declaration from the Court, we may not create new constitutional restraints on habeas review. . . .

Given the state courts' reasonable findings of fact and the absence of clearly established Supreme Court precedent that compels relief for Dassey, the district court's grant of habeas relief is reversed. The case is remanded to the district court with instructions to dismiss the petition.

The dissenting opinion of Justice Wood, joined by Justices Rovner and Williams, is omitted.

Rovner, Circuit Judge, and Wood, Chief Judge, and Williams, Circuit Judge, dissenting. I continue to believe . . . that the state court failed to fulfill the Supreme Court's mandate to review juvenile confessions with special care, and unreasonably held that Dassey's confession was voluntary. . . . I write separately simply to point out the chasm between how courts have historically understood the nature of coercion and confessions and what we now know about coercion with the advent of DNA profiling and current social science research. . . .

Half a century ago the Supreme Court held that police misrepresentations during interrogations, although relevant to a totality of the circumstances inquiry, were not in and of themselves sufficient to render an otherwise voluntary confession inadmissible. In other words, police may deceive, trick, conceal, imply, and mislead in any number of ways, provided that, under a totality of the circumstances evaluation, they do not destroy a suspect's ability to make a rational choice.

These cases, however, were born in an era when the human intuition that told us that "innocent people do not confess to crimes" was still largely unchecked. This belief is rooted in the mind's tendency to assume that statements made to a police officer that are against one's self interest can be trusted or, to put it simply, the thought that most of us have that "I would never confess to a crime I did not commit." Peer-reviewed studies confirm that jurors tend to have hard-to-dislodge beliefs that a suspect who is innocent could not be manipulated into confessing. And, in fact, this false notion is precisely what the state implored the jurors in Dassey's trial to believe, arguing in closing that "[p]eople who are innocent don't confess." We know, however, that this statement is unequivocally incorrect. Innocent people do in fact confess, and they do so with shocking regularity. As of June 7, 2016, The National Registry of Exonerations had collected data on 1,810 exonerations in the United States since 1989 (that number as of December 4, 2017 is 2,132), and that data includes 227 cases of innocent people who falsely confessed. This research indicates that false confessions (defined as cases in which indisputably innocent individuals confessed to crimes they did not commit) occur in approximately 25% of homicide cases.

In a world where we believed that "innocent people do not confess to crimes they did not commit," we were willing to tolerate a significant amount of deception by the police. Under this rubric, the thinking went, the innocent person (or at least the vast majority of healthy, sane, innocent adults of average intelligence) would not confess even in response to deception and cajoling. And so our case law developed in a factual framework in which we presumed that the trickery and deceit used by police officers would have little effect on the innocent.

If it is true that, except in extreme cases, innocent people do not confess, what difference does it make if detectives Fassbender and Wiegert made false assurances and used deception in interrogating Dassey? So what if they gave general assurances of leniency, used leading questions, fed Dassey information, lied about how much information they had, told Dassey that they were on his side, implored him that "honesty is the only thing that will set you free," suggested answers, and even went so far as to tell a confused and floundering Dassey that Teresa had been shot in the head? "Dassey was not subject to physical coercion or any sort of threats at all," the majority tells us, and "[g]iven the history of coercive interrogation techniques from which modern constitutional standards for confessions emerged, this is important."

But what do we do when the facts that supported our "modern constitutional standards" come from a fifty-year-old understanding of human behavior, and when what we once thought we knew about the psychology of confessions we now know not to be true? Our long-held idea that innocent people do not confess to crimes has been upended by advances in DNA profiling. We know now that in approximately 25% of homicide cases in which convicted persons have later been unequivocally exonerated by DNA evidence, the suspect falsely confessed to committing the crime. . . . The universe of people who falsely confess is undoubtedly larger than the subset of people who have confessed and then been fortunate enough to have been exonerated by objective, irrefutable evidence. But most importantly, as the majority concedes, even one coerced false confession is "very troubling." Indeed any coerced false confession is an affront to due process and cannot stand. . . .

Some of the factors that induce false confessions are internal. Studies have demonstrated that personal characteristics such as youth, mental illness, cognitive disability, suggestibility, and a desire to please others may induce false confessions. A survey of false confession cases from 1989-2012 found that although only 8% of adult exonerees with no known mental disabilities falsely confessed to crimes, in the population of exonerees who were younger than 18 at the time of the crime, 42% of exonerated defendants confessed to crimes they had not committed, as did 75% of exonerees who were mentally ill or mentally disabled. Overall, one sixth of the exonerees were juveniles, mentally disabled, or both, but they accounted for 59% of false confessions. Indeed, youth and intellectual disability are the two most commonly cited characteristics of suspects who confess falsely. Dassey suffered under the weight of both characteristics.

In addition to the factors specific to the suspect, some of the factors that induce false confessions are externally imposed. These include "isolation, long interrogation periods, repeated accusations, deception, presenting fabricated evidence, implicit/explicit threats of punishment or promises of leniency, and minimization or maximization of the moral seriousness or legal consequences of the offence." "Maximization" describes the technique whereby the interrogator exaggerates the strength of the evidence and the magnitude of the charges. Dassey's interrogators employed maximization by constantly reminding Dassey, "We already know everything." "Minimization" describes tactics that are designed to lull a suspect into believing that the magnitude of the charges and the seriousness of the offense will be downplayed or lessened if he confesses. Studies demonstrate that minimization causes suspects to infer leniency to the same extent as if an explicit promise had been made, increasing not only the rates of true confessions (from 46% to 81% in one experiment) but also the rate of false confessions (from 6% to 18%). Although a court must exclude a confession obtained by direct promise of leniency, the research demonstrates that minimization techniques are the functional equivalent in their impact on suspects. The investigators in this case employed classic minimization techniques by repeatedly telling Dassey that it was not his fault that he committed the crime because his uncle, Steven Avery, had made him do it. As Chief Judge Wood points out in her dissent, interrogators in this case, as in most police forces in the United States, used the Reid Technique to obtain Dassey's confession. This technique involves isolation, confrontation, maximization and minimization—the psychological strong-arm tactics that are known to produce coerced confessions even in adults of average intelligence.

Dassey's interrogation thus combined a perfect storm of these internal and external elements. He was young, of low intellect, manipulable, without a friendly adult, and faced repeated accusations, deception, fabricated evidence, implicit and explicit promises of leniency, police officers disingenuously assuming the role of father figure, and assurances that it was not his fault. . . .

No reasonable state court, knowing what we now know about coercive interrogation techniques and viewing Dassey's interrogation in light of his age, intellectual deficits, and manipulability, could possibly have concluded that Dassey's confession was voluntarily given. . . .

NOTES AND QUESTIONS

1. The Avery-Dassey case was the subject of the Netflix documentary *Making a Murderer*. Parts of Brendan Dassey's interrogation are available on YouTube. For commentary on the case, *see* Brian R. Gallini, The Interrogation of Brendan Dassey (2019), available at SSRN: https://ssrn.com/abstract=3249221.

2. In federal habeas corpus proceedings, the petitioner must carry the heavy burden of showing that the state court decision that affirmed the conviction was not merely wrong but was "so lacking in justification" that there cannot be "fairminded disagreement" about it. Even applying this standard, the Seventh Circuit was divided four to three. Where do the majority and dissenters disagree?

3. The interrogation techniques used in *Dassey* and in many other interrogations have long been criticized as creating a risk of false confessions. As the dissent says, minors are especially susceptible to these techniques and liable

to make false confessions. *See* Hayley M. D. Cleary, Police Interviewing and Interrogation of Juvenile Suspects: A Descriptive Examination of Actual Cases, 38 Law & Hum. Behav. 271, 273-81 (2014) (in a study of 57 electronic recordings of interrogations of juveniles from 17 police departments, the juvenile was physically positioned in such a way as to trigger authority cues over the juvenile; the median interrogation time was 46 minutes, with the longest session at nearly 5 hours; and very few juveniles directly invoked their *Miranda* rights); Steve Drizin & Richard Leo, The Problem of False Confessions in the Post-DNA World, 82 N.C. L. Rev. 891, 906-907 (2004) (in a study of 125 proven false confessions, 63 percent of the wrongfully accused were under the age of 25, and 35 percent were under 18); Barry C. Feld, Kids, Cops, and Confessions: Inside the Interrogation Room (New York University Press, 2013); Barry C. Feld, Behind Closed Doors: What Really Happens When Cops Question Kids, 23 Cornell J. L. & Pub. Pol'y 395 (2013) (in 307 juvenile felony interrogation recordings, the majority waived their *Miranda* rights and at higher rates than adults; juveniles did not require a lot of "persuasion or intimidation" to talk; and all the interrogations were 30 minutes or less); Thomas Grisso et al., Juveniles' Competence to Stand Trial: A Comparison of Adolescents and Adults Capacities as Trial Defendants, 27 Law & Hum. Behav. 333, 353-356 (2003) (children 15 years old and younger are more likely to comply with authority and confess than older teens); Lindsay C. Malloy et al., Interrogations, Confessions, and Guilty Pleas Among Serious Adolescent Offenders, 38 Law & Hum. Behav. 181 (2014) (in a study of juveniles in California, one-third reported having made either a false confession to police or a false guilty plea; a majority reported high-pressure interrogation tactics used by the police, and even occasionally by the juvenile's lawyer; half of the false confessions were the result of juveniles attempting to protect a family member or friend from more severe consequences; and the false confessions were associated with higher levels of duress, created by longer interrogation periods or the police officer's refusal to take a break); Eric Rassin & Han Israels, False Confessions in the Lab: A Review, 4 ELR 219, 219-222 (2014) (finding that it is surprisingly easy to persuade innocent people, particularly juveniles, to falsely confess to crimes); Joshua A. Tepfer et al., Arresting Development: Convictions of Innocent Youth, 62 Rutgers L. Rev. 887, 904 (2010) (in an examination of 103 factually innocent teenagers and children, over 31 percent involved a false confession as compared to 17.8 percent of wrongfully convicted adults).

3. As the dissent in *Dassey* also says, the Supreme Court has rejected repeatedly arguments that the criticized interrogation tactics are coercive in the constitutional sense. In response, many commentators have argued that courts or legislature should adopt rules to protect minors from their effects, in light of the empirical findings summarized above. The most common proposals are for recording interrogations, training law enforcement officers in less coercive interrogation techniques, time limits on interrogations, and most importantly, requiring that minors consult with attorneys before they are allowed to waive their *Miranda* rights. Authors supporting one or more of these reforms include Tamar R. Birckhead, The Age of the Child: Interrogating Juveniles after Roper v. Simmons, 65 Wash. & Lee L. Rev. 385 (2008); Barry C. Feld, Real Interrogation: What Actually Happens When Cops Question Kids, 47 Law & Soc'y Rev. 1, 25 (2013); Abigail

Kay Kohlman, Kids Waive the Darnedest Constitutional Rights: The Impact of J.D.B. v. North Carolina on Juvenile Interrogation, 49 Am. Crim. L. Rev. 1623, 1623-1643 (2012); Laurel LaMontagne, Children Under Pressure: The Problem of Juvenile False Confessions and Potential Solutions, 41 W. St. U. L. Rev. 29, 29-56 (2013); Lindsay C. Malloy et al., Interrogations, Confessions, and Guilty Pleas Among Serious Adolescent Offenders, 38 Law & Hum. Behav. 181 (2014).

4. Today at least four states have statutes requiring counsel for at least some children undergoing interrogation. Cal. Welf. & Inst. Code § 625.6 (2018) (child younger than 15 must consult with attorney before waiver of rights is valid); Ill. Comp. Stat. § 405/5-170 (2018) (child younger than 15 must be represented by counsel throughout the interrogation for listed offenses); Tex. Fam. Code. Ann. § 51.09 (West 2018) (waiver of a juvenile's rights must be made by a child and the attorney for the child); W. Va. Code Ann. § 49-4-701(l) (West 2018) (statements of juveniles under 14 years of age are inadmissible unless made in the presence of an attorney). In addition, a few states only admit the statements of some minors if a parent or attorney was present. *E.g.*, Ind. Code § 31-32-5-1 (2018) (unemancipated child may waive rights only with agreement of counsel or with agreement of parent who has no interest adverse to child; emancipated minors may waive rights without parent or counsel); N.C. Gen. Stat. § 7B-2101 (2018) (in-custody statements of juveniles younger than 16 are inadmissible unless made in presence of parent, guardian, custodian, or attorney).

5. In 2009, the Dutch Supreme Court ruled that all arrested suspects have a right to consult a lawyer prior to the first police interrogation and that juveniles have the additional right to have counsel present during the police interrogation. This followed a similar decision in the European Court on Human Rights in 2008. Tom Liefaard & Yannick van den Brink, Juveniles' Right to Counsel During Police Interrogations: An Interdisciplinary Analysis of a Youth-Specific Approach, with a Particular Focus on the Netherlands, 4 ELR 206, 206-218 (2014).

PROBLEM

The following evidence was elicited during a hearing on respondent's motion to suppress statements made to the police.

Several burglaries had been committed in the City of Lake Park. During the investigation, detectives from the Lake Park Police Department went to the home of W.M., then ten years old, and spoke to the child and his grandmother/guardian.

According to Detective Kevin Umphrey, he and Detective Lewis explained the reason for their visit to the grandmother, Juanita Williams, and informed her that they wanted to take W.M. to the police station. They asked if she wanted to go, and she declined.

W.M. was advised of his constitutional rights in the police car from a *Miranda* card. After each right was read to the child, the child acknowledged and nodded his head. Detective Umphrey testified that he made no threats to W.M. and also told the grandmother and W.M. that W.M. would not be arrested that day. The detectives took the child to the police station and again advised him of his rights.

W.M. was not handcuffed, and at no time did he either request a lawyer or state that he wished to remain silent. At the station, W.M. was taken into the detective's office. There was testimony that the temperature of the office was normal, that the detectives brought W.M. a Coke and some candy, and that the lighting condition was good. The detective testified that W.M. never requested to leave and that he again explained W.M.'s rights to him.

Detective Lewis assisted Detective Umphrey. He was present on December 19, 1989, when Detective Umphrey went to the child's home. Detective Lewis testified that he observed and heard Detective Umphrey explain the procedures and rights to W.M.'s grandmother and observed no threats. Detective Lewis further testified that W.M. went with the detectives in a "grid" pattern, observing various homes allegedly broken into by the defendant. Detective Lewis was taking notes about where the defendant said the burglaries were committed and writing down addresses and the descriptions of the way each house was entered and the property that was taken. Detective Lewis believed that the defendant was able to recall very well the situations and circumstances of each burglary. After having been read his rights, W.M. confessed to having committed the burglaries. He was then taken back to the station and ultimately back to his home. On the following day, December 20, W.M. was arrested at his residence. On the way to the police station, after his rights were read to him again, he admitted to other burglaries he had committed.

Neither of the detectives had W.M. sign a *Miranda* card or a waiver of rights card. No tape recordings were made of any of the interviews, nor was the child's grandmother present during any of the interviews. W.M. was transported to the Division of Youth Services Detention Center after being arrested.

Laurie Collins, a specific learning disability (SLD) teacher at Washington Elementary School, taught the child from August to December 5, 1989. An SLD child has a normal IQ but has problems performing at that IQ level. W.M. was at a third-grade level; however, his reading ability was at the beginning second-grade level, and his writing ability was at the first-grade level. According to Ms. Collins, W.M. is a "visual" learner and has an IQ of 70. She testified that an IQ of 69 is mildly disabled. The last IQ test given to W.M. was two years ago. Ms. Collins further testified that the child functions best in a one-on-one teaching situation.

Juanita Williams, the child's guardian and grandmother, was present when the police came to the child's home. Juanita Williams is an elderly woman who suffers from high blood sugar and nerves and has a heart problem. She doesn't recall the police asking her when they came to the home on December 19 if she wanted to go to the police station. However, she testified that at times she does have memory problems.

W.M. testified that he felt sad and scared at the police station and claimed that the police officer said, "If you don't show us the houses, we'll hang you by your neck." W.M. explained that he told the officers he did the burglary because he was "scared about what the officers would do" to him. The officers denied making these statements.

The trial court found that W.M. validly waived his *Miranda* rights and confessed voluntarily. What arguments would be made on appeal?

B. SEARCH AND ARREST

Courts hold that in most circumstances the Fourth Amendment limits on searches and arrests of adults apply to minors as well. Robert E. Shepherd, Jr., Juvenile Justice: Searches and Seizures Involving Juveniles, 5(1) Crim. Just. 27 (Spring 1990). This section examines exceptions to this general rule.

1. School Searches

The only Supreme Court cases that have addressed whether the Fourth Amendment is applied differently when the objects of the search are minors have concerned searches by school officials. These cases, then, are as closely or more closely related to cases that you read in Chapter 2—Tinker v. Des Moines Independent School District, Hazelwood School District v. Kuhlmeier, and Morse v. Frederick—as to In re Gault.

NEW JERSEY V. T.L.O.

469 U.S. 325 (1985)

WHITE, J. ... On March 7, 1980, a teacher at Piscataway High School in Middlesex County, N.J., discovered two girls smoking in a lavatory. One of the two girls was the respondent T.L.O., who at that time was a 14-year-old high school freshman. Because smoking in the lavatory was a violation of a school rule, the teacher took the two girls to the Principal's office, where they met with Assistant Vice Principal Theodore Choplick. In response to questioning by Mr. Choplick, T.L.O.'s companion admitted that she had violated the rule. T.L.O., however, denied that she had been smoking in the lavatory and claimed that she did not smoke at all.

Mr. Choplick asked T.L.O. to come into his private office and demanded to see her purse. Opening the purse, he found a pack of cigarettes, which he removed from the purse and held before T.L.O. as he accused her of having lied to him. As he reached into the purse for the cigarettes, Mr. Choplick also noticed a package of cigarette rolling papers. In his experience, possession of rolling papers by high school students was closely associated with the use of marihuana. Suspecting that a closer examination of the purse might yield further evidence of drug use, Mr. Choplick proceeded to search the purse thoroughly. The search revealed a small amount of marihuana, a pipe, a number of empty plastic bags, a substantial quantity of money in one-dollar bills, an index card that appeared to be a list of students who owed T.L.O. money, and two letters that implicated T.L.O. in marihuana dealing.

Mr. Choplick notified T.L.O.'s mother and the police, and turned the evidence of drug dealing over to the police. At the request of the police, T.L.O.'s mother took her daughter to police headquarters, where T.L.O. confessed that she had been selling marihuana at the high school. On the basis of the confession and the evidence seized by Mr. Choplick, the State brought delinquency charges against T.L.O. in the Juvenile and Domestic Relations Court of Middlesex

County. Contending that Mr. Choplick's search of her purse violated the Fourth Amendment, T.L.O. moved to suppress the evidence found in her purse as well as her confession, which, she argued, was tainted by the allegedly unlawful search. The Juvenile Court denied the motion to suppress. . . .

In determining whether the search at issue in this case violated the Fourth Amendment, we are faced initially with the question whether that Amendment's prohibition on unreasonable searches and seizures applies to searches conducted by public school officials. We hold that it does.

It is now beyond dispute that "the Federal Constitution, by virtue of the Fourteenth Amendment, prohibits unreasonable searches and seizures by state officers." Equally indisputable is the proposition that the Fourteenth Amendment protects the rights of students against encroachment by public school officials. . . .

These two propositions—that the Fourth Amendment applies to the States through the Fourteenth Amendment, and that the actions of public school officials are subject to the limits placed on state action by the Fourteenth Amendment—might appear sufficient to answer the suggestion that the Fourth Amendment does not proscribe unreasonable searches by school officials. On reargument, however, the State of New Jersey has argued that the history of the Fourth Amendment indicates that the Amendment was intended to regulate only searches and seizures carried out by law enforcement officers; accordingly, although public school officials are concededly state agents for purposes of the Fourteenth Amendment, the Fourth Amendment creates no rights enforceable against them.

. . . [T]his Court has never limited the Amendment's prohibition of unreasonable searches and seizures to operations conducted by the police. Rather, the Court has long spoken of the Fourth Amendment's strictures as restraints imposed upon "governmental action"—that is, "upon the activities of sovereign authority." Accordingly, we have held the Fourth Amendment applicable to the activities of civil as well as criminal authorities . . . . As we observed in Camara v. Municipal Court, . . ."[t]he basic purpose of this Amendment, as recognized in countless decisions of this Court, is to safeguard the privacy and security of individuals against arbitrary invasions by governmental officials." Because the individual's interest in privacy and personal security "suffers whether the government's motivation is to investigate violations of criminal laws or breaches of other statutory or regulatory standards," it would be "anomalous to say that the individual and his private property are fully protected by the Fourth Amendment only when the individual is suspected of criminal behavior."

Notwithstanding the general applicability of the Fourth Amendment to the activities of civil authorities, a few courts have concluded that school officials are exempt from the dictates of the Fourth Amendment by virtue of the special nature of their authority over schoolchildren. Teachers and school administrators, it is said, act *in loco parentis* in their dealings with students: their authority is that of the parent, not the State, and is therefore not subject to the limits of the Fourth Amendment.

Such reasoning is in tension with contemporary reality and the teachings of this Court. We have held school officials subject to the commands of the First Amendment, *see* Tinker v. Des Moines Independent Community School District, 393 U.S. 503 (1969), and the Due Process Clause of the Fourteenth Amendment, *see* Goss v. Lopez, 419 U.S. 565 (1975). If school authorities are state actors for purposes of the constitutional guarantees of freedom of expression and due process, it is difficult to understand why they should be deemed to be exercising parental rather than public authority when conducting searches of their students. More generally, the Court has recognized that "the concept of parental delegation" as a source of school authority is not entirely "consonant with compulsory education laws." Ingraham v. Wright, 430 U.S. 651, 662 (1977). Today's public school officials do not merely exercise authority voluntarily conferred on them by individual parents; rather, they act in furtherance of publicly mandated educational and disciplinary policies. . . . In carrying out searches and other disciplinary functions pursuant to such policies, school officials act as representatives of the State, not merely as surrogates for the parents, and they cannot claim the parents' immunity from the strictures of the Fourth Amendment. . . .

To hold that the Fourth Amendment applies to searches conducted by school authorities is only to begin the inquiry into the standards governing such searches. Although the underlying command of the Fourth Amendment is always that searches and seizures be reasonable, what is reasonable depends on the context within which a search takes place. The determination of the standard of reasonableness governing any specific class of searches requires "balancing the need to search against the invasion which the search entails." (citation omitted). On one side of the balance are arrayed the individual's legitimate expectations of privacy and personal security; on the other, the government's need for effective methods to deal with breaches of public order.

We have recognized that even a limited search of the person is a substantial invasion of privacy. We have also recognized that searches of closed items of personal luggage are intrusions on protected privacy interests, for "the Fourth Amendment provides protection to the owner of every container that conceals its contents from plain view." A search of a child's person or of a closed purse or other bag carried on her person,[3] no less than a similar search carried out on an adult, is undoubtedly a severe violation of subjective expectations of privacy.

Of course, the Fourth Amendment does not protect subjective expectations of privacy that are unreasonable or otherwise "illegitimate." To receive the protection of the Fourth Amendment, an expectation of privacy must be one that society is "prepared to recognize as legitimate." The State of New Jersey has argued that because of the pervasive supervision to which children in the schools are necessarily subject, a child has virtually no legitimate expectation of privacy in articles

---

3. We do not address the question, not presented by this case, whether a schoolchild has a legitimate expectation of privacy in lockers, desks, or other school property provided for the storage of school supplies. Nor do we express any opinion on the standards (if any) governing searches of such areas by school officials or by other public authorities acting at the request of the school officials. *Compare* Zamora v. Pomeroy, 639 F.2d 662, 670 (CA10 1981) ("Inasmuch as the school had assumed joint control of the locker it cannot be successfully maintained that the school did not have a right to inspect it"), *and* People v. Overton, 249 N.E.2d 366 (N.Y.2d 1969) (school administrators have power to consent to search of a student's locker), *with* State v. Engerud, 463 A.2d 934, 943 (N.J. 1983) ("We are satisfied that in the context of this case the student had an expectation of privacy in the contents of his locker. . . . For the four years of high school, the school locker is a home away from home. In it the student stores the kind of personal 'effects' protected by the Fourth Amendment").

of personal property "unnecessarily" carried into a school. This argument has two factual premises: (1) the fundamental incompatibility of expectations of privacy with the maintenance of a sound educational environment; and (2) the minimal interest of the child in bringing any items of personal property into the school. Both premises are severely flawed.

Although this Court may take notice of the difficulty of maintaining discipline in the public schools today, the situation is not so dire that students in the schools may claim no legitimate expectations of privacy. We have recently recognized that the need to maintain order in a prison is such that prisoners retain no legitimate expectations of privacy in their cells, but it goes almost without saying that "[t]he prisoner and the schoolchild stand in wholly different circumstances, separated by the harsh facts of criminal conviction and incarceration." Ingraham v. Wright, *supra*, at 669. We are not yet ready to hold that the schools and the prisons need be equated for purposes of the Fourth Amendment.

Nor does the State's suggestion that children have no legitimate need to bring personal property into the schools seem well anchored in reality. Students at a minimum must bring to school not only the supplies needed for their studies, but also keys, money, and the necessaries of personal hygiene and grooming. In addition, students may carry on their persons or in purses or wallets such nondisruptive yet highly personal items as photographs, letters, and diaries. Finally, students may have perfectly legitimate reasons to carry with them articles of property needed in connection with extracurricular or recreational activities. In short, schoolchildren may find it necessary to carry with them a variety of legitimate, noncontraband items, and there is no reason to conclude that they have necessarily waived all rights to privacy in such items merely by bringing them onto school grounds.

Against the child's interest in privacy must be set the substantial interest of teachers and administrators in maintaining discipline in the classroom and on school grounds. Maintaining order in the classroom has never been easy, but in recent years, school disorder has often taken particularly ugly forms: drug use and violent crime in the schools have become major social problems. . . .

How, then, should we strike the balance between the schoolchild's legitimate expectations of privacy and the school's equally legitimate need to maintain an environment in which learning can take place? It is evident that the school setting requires some easing of the restrictions to which searches by public authorities are ordinarily subject. The warrant requirement, in particular, is unsuited to the school environment: requiring a teacher to obtain a warrant before searching a child suspected of an infraction of school rules (or of the criminal law) would unduly interfere with the maintenance of the swift and informal disciplinary procedures needed in the schools. Just as we have in other cases dispensed with the warrant requirement when "the burden of obtaining a warrant is likely to frustrate the governmental purpose behind the search," we hold today that school officials need not obtain a warrant before searching a student who is under their authority.

The school setting also requires some modification of the level of suspicion of illicit activity needed to justify a search. Ordinarily, a search—even one that may permissibly be carried out without a warrant—must be based upon "probable cause" to believe that a violation of the law has occurred. However, "probable cause" is not an irreducible requirement of a valid search. The fundamental command of the Fourth Amendment is that searches and seizures be reasonable, and although "both the concept of probable cause and the requirement of a warrant bear on the reasonableness of a search, . . . in certain limited circumstances neither is required." Thus, we have in a number of cases recognized the legality of searches and seizures based on suspicions that, although "reasonable," do not rise to the level of probable cause. . . .

Determining the reasonableness of any search involves a twofold inquiry: first, one must consider "whether the . . . action was justified at its inception," second, one must determine whether the search as actually conducted "was reasonably related in scope to the circumstances which justified the interference in the first place." Under ordinary circumstances, a search of a student by a teacher or other school official[4] will be "justified at its inception" when there are reasonable grounds for suspecting that the search will turn up evidence that the student has violated or is violating either the law or the rules of the school.[5] Such a search will be permissible in its scope when the measures adopted are reasonably related to the objectives of the search and not excessively intrusive in light of the age and sex of the student and the nature of the infraction.[6]

This standard will, we trust, neither unduly burden the efforts of school authorities to maintain order in their schools nor authorize unrestrained intrusions

---

4. We here consider only searches carried out by school authorities acting alone and on their own authority. This case does not present the question of the appropriate standard for assessing the legality of searches conducted by school officials in conjunction with or at the behest of law enforcement agencies, and we express no opinion on that question. *Cf.* Picha v. Wielgos, 410 F. Supp. 1214, 1219-1221 (N.D. Ill. 1976) (holding probable-cause standard applicable to searches involving the police).

5. We do not decide whether individualized suspicion is an essential element of the reasonableness standard we adopt for searches by school authorities. In other contexts, however, we have held that although "some quantum of individualized suspicion is usually a prerequisite to a constitutional search or seizure[,] . . . the Fourth Amendment imposes no irreducible requirement of such suspicion." United States v. Martinez-Fuerte, 428 U.S. 543, 560-561 (1976). Exceptions to the requirement of individualized suspicion are generally appropriate only where the privacy interests implicated by a search are minimal and where "other safeguards" are available "to assure that the individual's reasonable expectation of privacy is not 'subject to the discretion of the official in the field.'" Delaware v. Prouse, 440 U.S. 648, 654-655 (1979). Because the search of T.L.O.'s purse was based upon an individualized suspicion that she had violated school rules, we need not consider the circumstances that might justify school authorities in conducting searches unsupported by individualized suspicion.

6. Our reference to the nature of the infraction is not intended as an endorsement of Justice Stevens' suggestion that some rules regarding student conduct are by nature too "trivial" to justify a search based upon reasonable suspicion. We are unwilling to adopt a standard under which the legality of a search is dependent upon a judge's evaluation of the relative importance of various school rules. The maintenance of discipline in the schools requires not only that students be restrained from assaulting one another, abusing drugs and alcohol, and committing other crimes, but also that students conform themselves to the standards of conduct prescribed by school authorities. We have "repeatedly emphasized the need for affirming the comprehensive authority of the States and of school officials, consistent with fundamental constitutional safeguards, to prescribe and control conduct in the schools." Tinker v. Des Moines Independent Community School District, 393 U.S. 503, 507 (1969). The promulgation of a rule forbidding specified conduct presumably reflects a judgment on the part of school officials that such conduct is destructive of school order or of a proper educational environment. Absent any suggestion that the rule violates some substantive constitutional guarantee, the courts should, as a general matter, defer to that judgment and refrain from attempting to distinguish between rules that are important to the preservation of order in the schools and rules that are not.

upon the privacy of school-children. By focusing attention on the question of reasonableness, the standard will spare teachers and school administrators the necessity of schooling themselves in the niceties of probable cause and permit them to regulate their conduct according to the dictates of reason and common sense. At the same time, the reasonableness standard should ensure that the interests of students will be invaded no more than is necessary to achieve the legitimate end of preserving order in the schools.

IV

There remains the question of the legality of the search in this case. We recognize that the "reasonable grounds" standard applied by the New Jersey Supreme Court in its consideration of this question is not substantially different from the standard that we have adopted today. Nonetheless, we believe that the New Jersey court's application of that standard to strike down the search of T.L.O.'s purse reflects a somewhat crabbed notion of reasonableness. Our review of the facts surrounding the search leads us to conclude that the search was in no sense unreasonable for Fourth Amendment purposes.

The incident that gave rise to this case actually involved two separate searches, with the first—the search for cigarettes—providing the suspicion that gave rise to the second—the search for marihuana. Although it is the fruits of the second search that are at issue here, the validity of the search for marihuana must depend on the reasonableness of the initial search for cigarettes, as there would have been no reason to suspect that T.L.O. possessed marihuana had the first search not taken place. Accordingly, it is to the search for cigarettes that we first turn our attention.

The New Jersey Supreme Court pointed to two grounds for its holding that the search for cigarettes was unreasonable. First, the court observed that possession of cigarettes was not in itself illegal or a violation of school rules. Because the contents of T.L.O.'s purse would therefore have "no direct bearing on the infraction" of which she was accused (smoking in a lavatory where smoking was prohibited), there was no reason to search her purse. Second, even assuming that a search of T.L.O.'s purse might under some circumstances be reasonable in light of the accusation made against T.L.O., the New Jersey court concluded that Mr. Choplick in this particular case had no reasonable grounds to suspect that T.L.O. had cigarettes in her purse. At best, according to the court, Mr. Choplick had "a good hunch."

Both these conclusions are implausible. T.L.O. had been accused of smoking, and had denied the accusation in the strongest possible terms when she stated that she did not smoke at all. Surely it cannot be said that under these circumstances, T.L.O.'s possession of cigarettes would be irrelevant to the charges against her or to her response to those charges. T.L.O.'s possession of cigarettes, once it was discovered, would both corroborate the report that she had been smoking and undermine the credibility of her defense to the charge of smoking. . . .

Of course, the New Jersey Supreme Court also held that Mr. Choplick had no reasonable suspicion that the purse would contain cigarettes. This conclusion is puzzling. A teacher had reported that T.L.O. was smoking in the lavatory.

Certainly this report gave Mr. Choplick reason to suspect that T.L.O. was carrying cigarettes with her; and if she did have cigarettes, her purse was the obvious place in which to find them. . . . Accordingly, it cannot be said that Mr. Choplick acted unreasonably when he examined T.L.O.'s purse to see if it contained cigarettes.

Our conclusion that Mr. Choplick's decision to open T.L.O.'s purse was reasonable brings us to the question of the further search for marihuana once the pack of cigarettes was located. The suspicion upon which the search for marihuana was founded was provided when Mr. Choplick observed a package of rolling papers in the purse as he removed the pack of cigarettes. Although T.L.O. does not dispute the reasonableness of Mr. Choplick's belief that the rolling papers indicated the presence of marihuana, she does contend that the scope of the search Mr. Choplick conducted exceeded permissible bounds when he seized and read certain letters that implicated T.L.O. in drug dealing. This argument, too, is unpersuasive. The discovery of the rolling papers concededly gave rise to a reasonable suspicion that T.L.O. was carrying marihuana as well as cigarettes in her purse. This suspicion justified further exploration of T.L.O.'s purse, which turned up more evidence of drug-related activities: a pipe, a number of plastic bags of the type commonly used to store marihuana, a small quantity of marihuana, and a fairly substantial amount of money. Under these circumstances, it was not unreasonable to extend the search to a separate zippered compartment of the purse; and when a search of that compartment revealed an index card containing a list of "people who owe me money" as well as two letters, the inference that T.L.O. was involved in marihuana trafficking was substantial enough to justify Mr. Choplick in examining the letters to determine whether they contained any further evidence. In short, we cannot conclude that the search for marihuana was unreasonable in any respect.

Because the search resulting in the discovery of the evidence of marihuana dealing by T.L.O. was reasonable, the New Jersey Supreme Court's decision to exclude that evidence from T.L.O.'s juvenile delinquency proceedings on Fourth Amendment grounds was erroneous. Accordingly, the judgment of the Supreme Court of New Jersey is [r]eversed.

NOTES AND QUESTIONS

1. Searches of students and their lockers present problems that are peculiar, if not unique, to minors. The *T.L.O.* decision answers some questions that arise out of the school situation, but hardly all. For example, the Court permitted searches by school officials that are "reasonably related to the objectives of the search and not excessively intrusive in light of the age and sex of the student and the nature of the infraction." What was the objective of the search in *T.L.O.*? Was the search of the purse "reasonably related" to that objective? What would finding cigarettes in a student's purse prove?

Is a search of a purse highly intrusive? Does the gender of the school official matter? Is there an analogous situation for male students?

2. In *T.L.O.*, which of the reasons for abandoning probable cause and warrant requirements applied?

3. The Court in *T.L.O.* emphasizes the need of schools to protect students and employees and explains why school searches are not subject to probable cause or warrant requirements. What picture of the school setting does the Court adopt? How does the school setting differ from a post office or a Burger King? Does the student-teacher relationship argue for or against probable cause and warrant requirements?

See Rachel N. Johnson, How Students Became Criminals: The Similarities Between "Stop and Frisk" and School Searches and the Effect on Delinquency Rates, 24 B.U. Pub. Int. L.J. 1, 14-23 (2015) (asserting that school searches produce an increase in delinquency rates and arguing for a more rigorous standard and method of execution of searches in a school setting than outside of schools); see also Alexis Karteron, Arrested Development: Rethinking Fourth Amendment Standards for Seizures and Uses of Force in Schools, 18 Nev. L.J. 863 (2018).

4. In general, the warrant requirement does not apply to "exigent" circumstances, calling for swift and immediate action. Why would that exception not provide sufficient protection when students are thought to have dangerous articles in schools?

5. Riley v. California, 573 U.S. 373 (2014), held that police may not search cell phones of people they arrest without a search warrant. Does that limitation apply to searches of students' cell phones by school officials? In a case decided before *Riley*, the Sixth Circuit applied *T.L.O.* to school officials' searches of students' electronic devices:

> A search is justified at its inception if there is reasonable suspicion that a search will uncover evidence of further wrongdoing or of injury to the student or another. Not all infractions involving cell phones will present such indications. Moreover, even assuming that a search of the phone were justified, the scope of the search must be tailored to the nature of the infraction and must be related to the objectives of the search. Under our two-part test, using a cell phone on school grounds does not automatically trigger an essentially unlimited right enabling a school official to search any content stored on the phone that is not related either substantively or temporally to the infraction.

G.C. v. Owensboro Pub. Sch., 711 F.3d 623, 633 (6th Cir. 2013). *See* Marc C. McAllister, Rethinking Student Cell Phone Searches, 121 Penn St. L. Rev. 309 (2016); Deborah Ahrens, Schools, Cyberbullies, and the Surveillance State, 49 Am. Crim. L. Rev. 1669 (2012); Amy Vorenberg, Indecent Exposure: Do Warrantless Searches of A Student's Cell Phone Violate the Fourth Amendment?, 17 Berkeley J. Crim. L. 62, 64 (2012).

6. If a police officer is stationed in a school as a school resource officer, do the *T.L.O.* standards apply to searches that he or she may conduct, or do the higher standards regarding warrants and probable cause apply? The presence of police officers in schools today is much greater than at the time when *T.L.O.* was decided. The Indiana Supreme Court analyzed cases from other states and found that standards vary depending on the level of police involvement in the search: "(1) where school officials initiate the search or police involvement is minimal, the reasonableness standard is applied; (2) where the search is conducted by the school resource

officer on his or her own initiative to further educationally related goals, the reasonableness standard is applied; and (3) where "outside" police officers initiate the search of a student for investigative purposes, the probable cause and warrant requirements are applied." Myers v. State, 839 N.E.2d 1154 (Ind. 2005). *See* Josh Gupta-Kagan, Reevaluating School Searches Following School-to-Prison Pipeline Reforms, 87 Fordham L. Rev. 2013 (2019); Kerrin C. Wolf, Assessing Students' Civil Rights Claims Against School Resource Officers. 38 Pace L. Rev. 215 (2018); Michael Pinard, From the Classroom to the Courtroom: Reassessing Fourth Amendment Standards in Public School Searches Involving Law Enforcement Authorities, 45 Ariz. L. Rev. 1067 (2003).

7. Safford Unified School District #1 v. Redding, 557 U.S. 364 (2009), concerns the constitutionality of school officials' strip search of a 13-year-old female student based on individualized suspicion that she possessed prescription-strength ibuprofen and over-the-counter naproxen without school permission, in violation of school rules. The Supreme Court was expected to revisit the test for school searches set out in *T.L.O.*, but instead it simply applied *T.L.O.* and held that the scope of the search was unreasonable. The Court said:

> Savana's subjective expectation of privacy against such a search is inherent in her account of it as embarrassing, frightening, and humiliating. The reasonableness of her expectation (required by the Fourth Amendment standard) is indicated by the consistent experiences of other young people similarly searched, whose adolescent vulnerability intensifies the patent intrusiveness of the exposure. The common reaction of these adolescents simply registers the obviously different meaning of a search exposing the body from the experience of nakedness or near undress in other school circumstances. Changing for gym is getting ready for play; exposing for a search is responding to an accusation reserved for suspected wrongdoers and fairly understood as so degrading that a number of communities have decided that strip searches in schools are never reasonable and have banned them no matter what the facts may be.
>
> The indignity of the search does not, of course, outlaw it, but it does implicate the rule of reasonableness as stated in T.L.O., that "the search as actually conducted [be] reasonably related in scope to the circumstances which justified the interference in the first place."
>
> Here, the content of the suspicion failed to match the degree of intrusion. Wilson knew beforehand that the pills were prescription-strength ibuprofen and over-the-counter naproxen, common pain relievers equivalent to two Advil, or one Aleve. She must have been aware of the nature and limited threat of the specific drugs he was searching for, and while just about anything can be taken in quantities that will do real harm, Wilson had no reason to suspect that large amounts of the drugs were being passed around, or that individual students were receiving great numbers of pills.
>
> Nor could Wilson have suspected that Savana was hiding common painkillers in her underwear. Petitioners suggest, as a truth universally acknowledged, that "students . . . hid[e] contraband in or under their clothing," Reply Brief for Petitioners 8, and cite a smattering of cases of students with contraband in their underwear. But when the categorically extreme intrusiveness of a search down to the body of an adolescent requires some justification in suspected facts, general background possibilities fall short; a reasonable search that extensive calls for suspicion that it will pay off.

But nondangerous school contraband does not raise the specter of stashes in intimate places, and there is no evidence in the record of any general practice among Safford Middle School students of hiding that sort of thing in underwear.

In sum, what was missing from the suspected facts that pointed to Savana was any indication of danger to the students from the power of the drugs or their quantity, and any reason to suppose that Savana was carrying pills in her underwear. We think that the combination of these deficiencies was fatal to finding the search reasonable.

557 U.S. at 374-376. However, the Supreme Court denied Savana's claim for damages and granted the school officials qualified immunity because the law was not clearly established at the time of the search.

Are the remedies available to students—the suppression of evidence in a delinquency prosecution or court-ordered relief in a civil suit—adequate? Do they effectively protect students' rights or impel school officials to respect them? *See* Barry Feld, *T.L.O.* and *Redding*'s Unanswered (Misanswered) Fourth Amendment Questions: Few Rights and Fewer Remedies, 80 Miss. L.J. 847 (2011); Kerrin C. Wolfe, Assessing Students' Civil Rights Claims Against School Resource Officers, 38 Pace L. Rev. 215 (2018).

8. Most of the lower court decisions finding violations of *T.L.O.* and *Safford* involve fairly extreme facts. Recent examples include Littell v. Houston Independent School Dist., 894 F.3d 616 (5th Cir. 2018) (strip search of all students in class to find missing money violated Fourth Amendment); E.W. ex rel. T.W. v. Dolgos, 884 F.3d 172 (4th Cir. 2018) (school resource officer who handcuffed calm, compliant 10-year-old for fighting with another student three days earlier violated the Fourth Amendment); D.H. v. Clayton Cty. Sch. Dist., 830 F.3d 1306 (11th Cir. 2016) (principal had authority under *Safford* to strip search 12-year-old student because other students reported he had drugs and principal found drugs on his friends, but doing search in front of other children violated Fourth Amendment); C.B. v. City of Sonora, 769 F.3d 1005 (9th Cir. 2014) (police violated Fourth Amendment when they handcuffed an 11-year-old with ADHD who was sitting quietly on the school after school officials called police because the boy, who had not taken his medication, had "shut down" and was not responsive to teachers' orders to go inside the school building). Although *E.W.* and *C.B.* are about seizure of the child's person rather than searches, the court applied the school-based standards of *T.L.O.* and *Safford*.

BOARD OF EDUCATION V. EARLS

536 U.S. 822 (2002)

Justice THOMAS delivered the opinion of the Court. . . . The city of Tecumseh, Oklahoma, is a rural community located approximately 40 miles southeast of Oklahoma City. The School District administers all Tecumseh public schools. In the fall of 1998, the School District adopted the Student Activities Drug Testing Policy (Policy), which requires all middle and high school students to consent to drug testing in order to participate in any extracurricular activity. In practice, the Policy has been applied only to competitive extracurricular activities sanctioned by the Oklahoma Secondary Schools Activities Association, such as the Academic Team, Future Farmers of America, Future Homemakers of America, band, choir, pom-pom, cheerleading, and athletics. Under the Policy, students are required to take a drug test before participating in an extracurricular activity, must submit to random drug testing while participating in that activity, and must agree to be tested at any time upon reasonable suspicion. The urinalysis tests are designed to detect only the use of illegal drugs, including amphetamines, marijuana, cocaine, opiates, and barbiturates, not medical conditions or the presence of authorized prescription medications. . . .

Together with their parents, Earls and James brought a 42 U.S.C. § 1983 action against the School District, challenging the Policy both on its face and as applied to their participation in extracurricular activities. They alleged that the Policy violates the Fourth Amendment as incorporated by the Fourteenth Amendment and requested injunctive and declarative relief. . . .

. . . Searches by public school officials, such as the collection of urine samples, implicate Fourth Amendment interests. We must therefore review the School District's Policy for "reasonableness," which is the touchstone of the constitutionality of a governmental search.

In the criminal context, reasonableness usually requires a showing of probable cause. . . . The Court has also held that a warrant and finding of probable cause are unnecessary in the public school context because such requirements "'would unduly interfere with the maintenance of the swift and informal disciplinary procedures [that are] needed.'" Vernonia [School District 47J v. Acton, 515 U.S. 545, 653 (1995)], (quoting *T.L.O.*, at 340-341).

Given that the School District's Policy is not in any way related to the conduct of criminal investigations, respondents do not contend that the School District requires probable cause before testing students for drug use. Respondents instead argue that drug testing must be based at least on some level of individualized suspicion. It is true that we generally determine the reasonableness of a search by balancing the nature of the intrusion on the individual's privacy against the promotion of legitimate governmental interests. But we have long held that "the Fourth Amendment imposes no irreducible requirement of [individualized] suspicion." "[I]n certain limited circumstances, the Government's need to discover such latent or hidden conditions, or to prevent their development, is sufficiently compelling to justify the intrusion on privacy entailed by conducting such searches without any measure of individualized suspicion." Therefore, in the context of safety and administrative regulations, a search unsupported by probable cause may be reasonable "when 'special needs, beyond the normal need for law enforcement, make the warrant and probable-cause requirement impracticable.'" . . .

Significantly, this Court has previously held that "special needs" inhere in the public school context. *See Vernonia, supra*, at 653; *T.L.O., supra*, at 339-340. While schoolchildren do not shed their constitutional rights when they enter the schoolhouse, *see* Tinker v. Des Moines Independent Community School District, 393 U.S. 503, 506, (1969), "Fourth Amendment rights . . . are different in public schools than elsewhere; the 'reasonableness' inquiry cannot disregard the schools' custodial and tutelary responsibility for children." In particular, a finding of individualized suspicion may not be necessary when a school conducts drug testing.

In *Vernonia*, this Court held that the suspicionless drug testing of athletes was constitutional. The Court, however, did not simply authorize all school drug testing, but rather conducted a fact-specific balancing of the intrusion on the children's Fourth Amendment rights against the promotion of legitimate governmental interests. . . .

We first consider the nature of the privacy interest allegedly compromised by the drug testing. . . .

A student's privacy interest is limited in a public school environment where the State is responsible for maintaining discipline, health, and safety. Schoolchildren are routinely required to submit to physical examinations and vaccinations against disease. Securing order in the school environment sometimes requires that students be subjected to greater controls than those appropriate for adults.

Respondents argue that because children participating in nonathletic extracurricular activities are not subject to regular physicals and communal undress, they have a stronger expectation of privacy than the athletes tested in *Vernonia*. This distinction, however, was not essential to our decision in *Vernonia*, which depended primarily upon the school's custodial responsibility and authority.

In any event, students who participate in competitive extracurricular activities voluntarily subject themselves to many of the same intrusions on their privacy as do athletes. Some of these clubs and activities require occasional off-campus travel and communal undress. All of them have their own rules and requirements for participating students that do not apply to the student body as a whole. For example, each of the competitive extracurricular activities governed by the Policy must abide by the rules of the Oklahoma Secondary Schools Activities Association, and a faculty sponsor monitors the students for compliance with the various rules dictated by the clubs and activities. This regulation of extracurricular activities further diminishes the expectation of privacy among schoolchildren. We therefore conclude that the students affected by this Policy have a limited expectation of privacy.

Next, we consider the character of the intrusion imposed by the Policy. Urination is "an excretory function traditionally shielded by great privacy." But the "degree of intrusion" on one's privacy caused by collecting a urine sample depends upon the manner in which production of the urine sample is monitored.

Under the Policy, a faculty monitor waits outside the closed restroom stall for the student to produce a sample and must "listen for the normal sounds of urination in order to guard against tampered specimens and to insure an accurate chain of custody." The monitor then pours the sample into two bottles that are sealed and placed into a mailing pouch along with a consent form signed by the student. This procedure is virtually identical to that reviewed in *Vernonia*, except that it additionally protects privacy by allowing male students to produce their samples behind a closed stall. Given that we considered the method of collection in *Vernonia* a "negligible" intrusion, the method here is even less problematic.

In addition, the Policy clearly requires that the test results be kept in confidential files separate from a student's other educational records and released to school personnel only on a "need to know" basis. Respondents nonetheless contend that the intrusion on students' privacy is significant because the Policy fails to protect effectively against the disclosure of confidential information and, specifically, that the school "has been careless in protecting that information: for example, the Choir teacher looked at students' prescription drug lists and left them where other students could see them." But the choir teacher is someone with a "need to know," because during off-campus trips she needs to know what medications are taken by her students. Even before the Policy was enacted the choir teacher had access to this information. In any event, there is no allegation that any other student did see such information. This one example of alleged carelessness hardly increases the character of the intrusion.

Moreover, the test results are not turned over to any law enforcement authority. Nor do the test results here lead to the imposition of discipline or have any academic consequences. Rather, the only consequence of a failed drug test is to limit the student's privilege of participating in extracurricular activities. Indeed, a student may test positive for drugs twice and still be allowed to participate in extracurricular activities. After the first positive test, the school contacts the student's parent or guardian for a meeting. The student may continue to participate in the activity if within five days of the meeting the student shows proof of receiving drug counseling and submits to a second drug test in two weeks. For the second positive test, the student is suspended from participation in all extracurricular activities for 14 days, must complete four hours of substance abuse counseling, and must submit to monthly drug tests. Only after a third positive test will the student be suspended from participating in any extracurricular activity for the remainder of the school year, or 88 school days, whichever is longer.

Given the minimally intrusive nature of the sample collection and the limited uses to which the test results are put, we conclude that the invasion of students' privacy is not significant.

Finally, this Court must consider the nature and immediacy of the government's concerns and the efficacy of the Policy in meeting them. This Court has already articulated in detail the importance of the governmental concern in preventing drug use by schoolchildren. The drug abuse problem among our Nation's youth has hardly abated since *Vernonia* was decided in 1995. In fact, evidence suggests that it has only grown worse. As in *Vernonia*, "the necessity for the State to act is magnified by the fact that this evil is being visited not just upon individuals at large, but upon children for whom it has undertaken a special responsibility of care and direction." The health and safety risks identified in *Vernonia* apply with equal force to Tecumseh's children. Indeed, the nationwide drug epidemic makes the war against drugs a pressing concern in every school.

Additionally, the School District in this case has presented specific evidence of drug use at Tecumseh schools. Teachers testified that they had seen students who appeared to be under the influence of drugs and that they had heard students speaking openly about using drugs. A drug dog found marijuana cigarettes near the school parking lot. Police officers once found drugs or drug paraphernalia in a car driven by a Future Farmers of America member. And the school board president reported that people in the community were calling the board to discuss the "drug situation." We decline to second-guess the finding of the District Court that "[v]iewing the evidence as a whole, it cannot be reasonably disputed that the [School District] was faced with a 'drug problem' when it adopted the Policy."

Respondents consider the proffered evidence insufficient and argue that there is no "real and immediate interest" to justify a policy of drug testing non-athletes. We have recognized, however, that "[a] demonstrated problem of drug abuse . . . [is] not in all cases necessary to the validity of a testing regime," but that some showing does "shore up an assertion of special need for a suspicionless general search program." The School District has provided sufficient evidence to shore up the need for its drug testing program.

Furthermore, this Court has not required a particularized or pervasive drug problem before allowing the government to conduct suspicionless drug testing. For instance, in *Von Raab* the Court upheld the drug testing of customs officials on a purely preventive basis, without any documented history of drug use by such officials. In response to the lack of evidence relating to drug use, the Court noted generally that "drug abuse is one of the most serious problems confronting our society today," and that programs to prevent and detect drug use among customs officials could not be deemed unreasonable. Likewise, the need to prevent and deter the substantial harm of childhood drug use provides the necessary immediacy for a school testing policy. Indeed, it would make little sense to require a school district to wait for a substantial portion of its students to begin using drugs before it was allowed to institute a drug testing program designed to deter drug use.

Given the nationwide epidemic of drug use, and the evidence of increased drug use in Tecumseh schools, it was entirely reasonable for the School District to enact this particular drug testing policy. We reject the Court of Appeals' novel test that "any district seeking to impose a random suspicionless drug testing policy as a condition to participation in a school activity must demonstrate that there is some identifiable drug abuse problem among a sufficient number of those subject to the testing, such that testing that group of students will actually redress its drug problem." Among other problems, it would be difficult to administer such a test. As we cannot articulate a threshold level of drug use that would suffice to justify a drug testing program for schoolchildren, we refuse to fashion what would in effect be a constitutional quantum of drug use necessary to show a "drug problem."

Respondents also argue that the testing of nonathletes does not implicate any safety concerns, and that safety is a "crucial factor" in applying the special needs framework. They contend that there must be "surpassing safety interests," or "extraordinary safety and national security hazards," in order to override the usual protections of the Fourth Amendment. Respondents are correct that safety factors into the special needs analysis, but the safety interest furthered by drug testing is undoubtedly substantial for all children, athletes and nonathletes alike. We know all too well that drug use carries a variety of health risks for children, including death from overdose.

We also reject respondents' argument that drug testing must presumptively be based upon an individualized reasonable suspicion of wrongdoing because such a testing regime would be less intrusive. In this context, the Fourth Amendment does not require a finding of individualized suspicion, and we decline to impose such a requirement on schools attempting to prevent and detect drug use by students. Moreover, we question whether testing based on individualized suspicion in fact would be less intrusive. Such a regime would place an additional burden on public school teachers who are already tasked with the difficult job of maintaining order and discipline. A program of individualized suspicion might unfairly target members of unpopular groups. The fear of lawsuits resulting from such targeted searches may chill enforcement of the program, rendering it ineffective in combating drug use. In any case, this Court has repeatedly stated that reasonableness under the Fourth Amendment does not require employing the least intrusive means, because "[t]he logic of such elaborate less-restrictive-alternative arguments could raise insuperable barriers to the exercise of virtually all search-and-seizure powers."

Finally, we find that testing students who participate in extracurricular activities is a reasonably effective means of addressing the School District's legitimate concerns in preventing, deterring, and detecting drug use. While in *Vernonia* there might have been a closer fit between the testing of athletes and the trial court's finding that the drug problem was "fueled by the 'role model' effect of athletes' drug use," such a finding was not essential to the holding. *Vernonia* did not require the school to test the group of students most likely to use drugs, but rather considered the constitutionality of the program in the context of the public school's custodial responsibilities. Evaluating the Policy in this context, we conclude that the drug testing of Tecumseh students who participate in extracurricular activities effectively serves the School District's interest in protecting the safety and health of its students. . . .

Justice GINSBURG, with whom Justice STEVENS, Justice O'CONNOR, and Justice SOUTER join, dissenting. Seven years ago, in Vernonia School District 47J v. Acton, 515 U.S. 646 (1995), this Court determined that a school district's policy of randomly testing the urine of its student athletes for illicit drugs did not violate the Fourth Amendment. In so ruling, the Court emphasized that drug use "increase[d] the risk of sports-related injury" and that *Vernonia*'s athletes were the "leaders" of an aggressive local "drug culture" that had reached "'epidemic proportions.'" Today, the Court relies upon *Vernonia* to permit a school district with a drug problem its superintendent repeatedly described as "not . . . major" to test the urine of an academic team member solely by reason of her participation in a nonathletic, competitive extracurricular activity—participation associated with neither special dangers from, nor particular predilections for, drug use.

"[T]he legality of a search of a student," this Court has instructed, "should depend simply on the reasonableness, under all the circumstances, of the search." New Jersey v. T.L.O., 469 U.S. 325, 341 (1985). Although "'special needs' inhere in the public school context," those needs are not so expansive or malleable as to render reasonable any program of student drug testing a school district elects to install. . . .

This case presents circumstances dispositively different from those of *Vernonia*. True, as the Court stresses, Tecumseh students participating in competitive extracurricular activities other than athletics share two relevant characteristics with the athletes of *Vernonia*. First, both groups attend public schools. "[O]ur decision in *Vernonia*," the Court states, "depended primarily upon the school's custodial responsibility and authority." Concern for student health and safety is basic to the school's caretaking, and it is undeniable that "drug use carries a variety of health risks for children, including death from overdose."

Those risks, however, are present for all schoolchildren. *Vernonia* cannot be read to endorse invasive and suspicionless drug testing of all students upon any evidence of drug use, solely because drugs jeopardize the life and health of those who use them. Many children, like many adults, engage in dangerous activities on their own time; that the children are enrolled in school scarcely allows government to monitor all such activities. If a student has a reasonable subjective expectation of privacy in the personal items she brings to school, *see T.L.O.*, surely she has a similar expectation regarding the chemical composition of her urine. Had the *Vernonia* Court agreed that public school attendance, in and of itself, permitted the State to test each student's blood or urine for drugs, the opinion in *Vernonia* could have saved many words.

The second commonality to which the Court points is the voluntary character of both interscholastic athletics and other competitive extracurricular activities. "By choosing to 'go out for the team,' [school athletes] voluntarily subject themselves to a degree of regulation even higher than that imposed on students generally." Comparably, the Court today observes, "students who participate in competitive extracurricular activities voluntarily subject themselves to" additional rules not applicable to other students.

The comparison is enlightening. While extracurricular activities are "voluntary" in the sense that they are not required for graduation, they are part of the school's educational program; for that reason, the petitioner (hereinafter School District) is justified in expending public resources to make them available. Participation in such activities is a key component of school life, essential in reality for students applying to college, and, for all participants, a significant contributor to the breadth and quality of the educational experience. Students "volunteer" for extracurricular pursuits in the same way they might volunteer for honors classes: They subject themselves to additional requirements, but they do so in order to take full advantage of the education offered them.

Voluntary participation in athletics has a distinctly different dimension: Schools regulate student athletes discretely because competitive school sports by their nature require communal undress and, more important, expose students to physical risks that schools have a duty to mitigate. For the very reason that schools cannot offer a program of competitive athletics without intimately affecting the privacy of students, *Vernonia* reasonably analogized school athletes to "adults who choose to participate in a closely regulated industry." . . . Interscholastic athletics similarly require close safety and health regulation; a school's choir, band, and academic team do not.

In short, *Vernonia* applied, it did not repudiate, the principle that "the legality of a search of a student should depend simply on the reasonableness, under all the circumstances, of the search." Enrollment in a public school, and election to participate in school activities beyond the bare minimum that the curriculum requires, are indeed factors relevant to reasonableness, but they do not on their own justify intrusive, suspicionless searches. . . .

Vernonia initially considered "the nature of the privacy interest upon which the search [there] at issue intrude[d]." The Court emphasized that student athletes' expectations of privacy are necessarily attenuated. . . .

Competitive extracurricular activities other than athletics, however, serve students of all manner: the modest and shy along with the bold and uninhibited. Activities of the kind plaintiff-respondent Lindsay Earls pursued — choir, show choir, marching band, and academic team — afford opportunities to gain self-assurance, to "come to know faculty members in a less formal setting than the typical classroom," and to acquire "positive social supports and networks [that] play a critical role in periods of heightened stress."

On "occasional out-of-town trips," students like Lindsay Earls "must sleep together in communal settings and use communal bathrooms." But those situations are hardly equivalent to the routine communal undress associated with athletics; the School District itself admits that when such trips occur, "public-like restroom facilities," which presumably include enclosed stalls, are ordinarily available for changing, and that "more modest students" find other ways to maintain their privacy.

After describing school athletes' reduced expectation of privacy, the *Vernonia* Court turned to "the character of the intrusion . . . complained of." Observing that students produce urine samples in a bathroom stall with a coach or teacher outside, *Vernonia* typed the privacy interests compromised by the process of obtaining samples "negligible." As to the required pretest disclosure of prescription medications taken, the Court assumed that "the School District would have permitted [a student] to provide the requested information in a confidential manner — for example, in a sealed envelope delivered to the testing lab." On that assumption, the Court concluded that *Vernonia*'s athletes faced no significant invasion of privacy.

In this case, however, Lindsay Earls and her parents allege that the School District handled personal information collected under the policy carelessly, with little regard for its confidentiality. Information about students' prescription drug use, they assert, was routinely viewed by Lindsay's choir teacher, who left files containing the information unlocked and unsealed, where others, including students, could see them; and test results were given out to all activity sponsors whether or not they had a clear "need to know." . . .

Finally, the "nature and immediacy of the governmental concern" faced by the *Vernonia* School District dwarfed that confronting Tecumseh administrators. *Vernonia* initiated its drug testing policy in response to an alarming situation: "[A] large segment of the student body, particularly those involved in interscholastic athletics, was in a state of rebellion . . . fueled by alcohol and drug abuse as well as the student[s'] misperceptions about the drug culture." Tecumseh, by contrast, repeatedly reported to the Federal Government during the period leading up to the adoption of the policy that "types of drugs [other than alcohol and tobacco] including controlled dangerous substances, are present [in the schools] but have not identified themselves as major problems at this time." . . .

Not only did the Vernonia and Tecumseh districts confront drug problems of distinctly different magnitudes, they also chose different solutions: Vernonia limited its policy to athletes; Tecumseh indiscriminately subjected to testing all participants in competitive extracurricular activities. Urging that "the safety interest furthered by drug testing is undoubtedly substantial for all children, athletes and nonathletes alike," the Court cuts out an element essential to the *Vernonia* judgment. Citing medical literature on the effects of combining illicit drug use with physical exertion, the *Vernonia* Court emphasized that "the particular drugs screened by [Vernonia's] Policy have been demonstrated to pose substantial physical risks to athletes." . . .

At the margins, of course, no policy of random drug testing is perfectly tailored to the harms it seeks to address. The School District cites the dangers faced by members of the band, who must "perform extremely precise routines with heavy equipment and instruments in close proximity to other students," and by Future Farmers of America, who "are required to individually control and restrain animals as large as 1500 pounds." For its part, the United States acknowledges that "the linebacker faces a greater risk of serious injury if he takes the field under the influence of drugs than the drummer in the halftime band," but parries that "the risk of injury to a student who is under the influence of drugs while playing golf, cross country, or volleyball (sports covered by the policy in *Vernonia*) is scarcely any greater than the risk of injury to a student . . . handling a 1500-pound steer (as [Future Farmers of America] members do) or working with cutlery or other sharp instruments (as [Future Homemakers of America] members do)." . . . Notwithstanding nightmarish images of out-of-control flatware, livestock run amok, and colliding tubas disturbing the peace and quiet of Tecumseh, the great majority of students the School District seeks to test in truth are engaged in activities that are not safety sensitive to an unusual degree. There is a difference between imperfect tailoring and no tailoring at all.

The Vernonia district, in sum, had two good reasons for testing athletes: Sports team members faced special health risks and they "were the leaders of the drug culture." No similar reason, and no other tenable justification, explains Tecumseh's decision to target for testing all participants in every competitive extracurricular activity. . . .

Nationwide, students who participate in extracurricular activities are significantly less likely to develop substance abuse problems than are their less-involved peers. Even if students might be deterred from drug use in order to preserve their extracurricular eligibility, it is at least as likely that other students might forgo their extracurricular involvement in order to avoid detection of their drug use. Tecumseh's policy thus falls short doubly if deterrence is its aim: It invades the privacy of students who need deterrence least, and risks steering students at greatest risk for substance abuse away from extracurricular involvement that potentially may palliate drug problems. . . .

. . . [Tecumseh's] policy was not shown to advance the "'special needs' [existing] in the public school context [to maintain] . . . swift and informal disciplinary procedures . . . [and] order in the schools." What is left is the School District's undoubted purpose to heighten awareness of its abhorrence of, and strong stand against, drug abuse. But the desire to augment communication of this message does not trump the right of persons — even of children within the schoolhouse gate — to be "secure in their persons . . . against unreasonable searches and seizures." . . .

It is a sad irony that the petitioning School District seeks to justify its edict here by trumpeting "the schools' custodial and tutelary responsibility for children." In regulating an athletic program or endeavoring to combat an exploding drug epidemic, a school's custodial obligations may permit searches that would otherwise unacceptably abridge students' rights. When custodial duties are not ascendant, however, schools' tutelary obligations to their students require them to "teach by example" by avoiding symbolic measures that diminish constitutional protections. "That [schools] are educating the young for citizenship is reason for scrupulous protection of Constitutional freedoms of the individual, if we are not to strangle the free mind at its source and teach youth to discount important principles of our government as mere platitudes."

For the reasons stated, I would affirm the judgment of the Tenth Circuit declaring the testing policy at issue unconstitutional.

The concurring opinion of Justice Breyer and the dissenting opinion of Justice O'Connor are omitted.

NOTES AND QUESTIONS

1. Does participation in Future Farmers of America or Future Homemakers of America amount to consent to suspicionless, random drug testing? Or does *Earls* actually hold that the school's "custodial responsibility and authority" limits students' privacy interests as a matter of law? Could a school constitutionally impose the drug testing program approved in *Earls* on all students, regardless of whether they participate in extracurricular activities?

2. Which is the more serious intrusion on privacy—the requirement to participate in drug testing or the school's failure to keep the test results confidential? Does the majority opinion in *Earls* adequately account for both intrusions?

3. If students who tested positive for drugs were referred to the police for prosecution in the juvenile court, would the court's analysis of the constitutionality of the drug testing program change?

4. If it could be shown that random drug testing of students does not reduce student drug use, should *Earls* be overruled? Or does *Earls* allow a school district to justify its random student drug testing merely by asserting that the United States is engaged in a "war on drugs"? For a review of the empirical data showing that drug testing programs have no statistical effect on student drug use, *see* Susan B. Stuart, When the Cure Is Worse Than the Disease: Student Random Drug Testing & Its Empirical Failure, 44 Val. U.L. Rev. 1055 (2010).

5. The Supreme Court in *T.L.O.* left open the constitutionality of searches of school lockers. Do students have a reasonable expectation of privacy in their lockers? Even if they do, would random locker searches be constitutional under *Earls*? Would it make a difference if a school adopted and posted the following policy?

> School lockers are the property of Milwaukee Public Schools. At no time does the Milwaukee school district relinquish its exclusive control of lockers provided for the convenience of students. Periodic general inspections of lockers may be conducted by school authorities for any reason at any time, without notice, without student consent, and without a search warrant.

Cases holding that students have no reasonable expectation of privacy in their lockers include In re Patrick Y., 746 A.2d 405 (Md. App. 2000); Commonwealth v. Cass, 709 A.2d 350 (Pa. 1998); Shoemaker v. State, 971 S.W.2d 178 (Tex. App. 1998); In re Interest of Isiah B., 500 N.W.2d 637 (Wis. 1993); Cases finding that students do have a reasonable expectation of privacy in their lockers include State v. Jones, 666 N.W.2d 142 (Iowa 2003); In re Interest of S.C., 583 So. 2d 188 (Miss. 1991); In re Adam, 697 N.E.2d 1100 (Ohio App. 1997); In re Dumas, 515 A.2d 984, 985–86 (Pa. Super. 1986).

Would a random search of backpacks be allowable on the same basis as a search of a school locker? How about sniff searches of students' cars parked at the school or students themselves by police dogs trained to detect drugs? Consider Jason P. Nance, Random, Suspicionless Searches of Students' Belongings: A Legal, Empirical, and Normative Analysis, 84 U. Colo. L. Rev. 367 (2013) (arguing that suspicionless searches violate the Fourth Amendment and raise concerns about disproportionate targeting of minority students).

6. Is the critical factor in school searches about schools or children? Suppose that a small state college instituted a policy of random searching of lockers in the classroom buildings. Would that policy be sustained? Would the publication of a notice such as the one quoted above make a difference?

7. As stricter security measures have become commonplace among low-income schools, some scholars have argued that the measures negatively affect the education that students receive and is at least partially responsible for the school-to-prison pipeline. As a result, one commentator has noted:

> The historical justification for diluting students' constitutional rights in schools—including their Fourth Amendment rights—is to promote students' educational interests by providing an environment that is conducive to learning. . . . [W]hen this justification no longer holds true—when conducting suspicionless searches or, worse, creating a prison-like environment contributes to a deteriorated learning climate and harms students' educational interests—students' Fourth Amendment rights should not be abridged, but strengthened. Accordingly, students should have the opportunity to submit evidence showing that strict security measures do not promote their educational interests but detract from an educational climate, and thus their privacy interests should be given greater consideration against the government's interest in conducting these searches. Such a test more closely aligns with the overall tenor of cases evaluating students' constitutional rights in schools and is more consistent with good education policy and practice. Further, because primarily students of color more often are subjected to intense surveillance environments, applying this test will help ameliorate the disproportionate use of strict security measures against minorities.

Jason P. Nance, School Surveillance and the Fourth Amendment, 2014 Wis. L. Rev. 79, 83-84 (2014).

PROBLEMS

1. William G. was adjudicated delinquent on a finding that he illegally possessed marijuana for purposes of sale. He was placed on probation for 3 years. At the time of the offense, William was 16 years old and a high school student. An assistant principal noticed William and two other male students walking through the center of campus. As the principal approached the students, he noticed that William was carrying a small vinyl calculator case, to which the students' attention was momentarily drawn. The case had what seemed to the

assistant principal an odd-looking bulge. Upon reaching the students, the assistant principal asked where they were heading and why they were late to class. William did not have any classes at the time, and the school official noticed that William placed the case behind his back. He asked what William had with him, and William responded, "Nothing." When the assistant principal attempted to look at the case, William said, "You can't search me." Following more discussion, William was taken by the arm to the assistant principal's office, where his case was searched. Inside were four baggies of marijuana, a gram weight scale, and some cigarette papers. This evidence was the basis for William's prosecution. What arguments can be made on each side regarding the legality of this search?

2. East High School has had a long history of drug use problems. After a series of meetings, at which both parents and school officials expressed grave concern about the incidence of substance abuse in the school, both groups agreed that routine supervision would be necessary for a while. To that end, the school prevailed upon the police department to allow them to use their K-9 corps, which included several dogs who had been trained to identify narcotics by smell. The dogs were to come at unannounced times to sniff both lockers and students. If the dogs indicated that either a student or his or her locker possessed narcotics, a school official would open the locker and inspect it.

On March 1 of this year, the K-9 corps officer came and conducted a search by sniffing. The dog identified the locker of Renee Jones as one containing narcotics. The principal opened the locker and discovered a quantity of marijuana. Renee has been charged with delinquency by reason of possession of marijuana and has moved to suppress the evidence against her. What arguments can be made at the hearing on the motion?

Assume instead that school officials were told by an unidentified student that someone was bringing pills into the school that would be "unsafe" to the students. In response, all of the students entering the school were strip searched, and oxycodone bills were found in Renee's bra. Renee has moved to suppress the pills. What arguments should be made on the motion?

2.   *Searches Outside School*

In Bell v. Wolfish, 441 U.S. 520 (1979), the Supreme Court held that a policy authorizing strip searches of all adult prisoners and pretrial detainees was justified by the state's interests in maintaining institutional security, safety, and regulation. The opinion did not authorize all such searches, though, holding instead that courts must balance the need for a particular search against the invasion of personal rights that the search entails. However, in Florence v. Bd. of Chosen Freeholders, 566 U.S.318 (2012), the Supreme Court rejected the argument that *Bell* should not apply to invasive searches of people arrested for minor, nonviolent offenses. The following case considers whether *Safford* provides greater protection to minors admitted to juvenile detention facilities.

MABRY V. LEE COUNTY

849 F.3d 232 (5th Cir. 2017)

EDITH BROWN CLEMENT, Circuit Judge: . . . T.M. was a twelve-year old student at Tupelo Middle School. She was in a physical altercation with a fellow student on school property. Pursuant to the school's zero-tolerance policy, the school principal consulted with the Tupelo police officer assigned to be the School Resource Officer ("SRO"). Following that conversation, the SRO determined there was probable cause to arrest T.M. on charges of assault, disorderly conduct, and disruption of a school session. He called the Lee County Youth Court's judicial designee and was given authorization, based on the designee's determination of probable cause, to transport T.M. to the Lee County Juvenile Detention Center ("Center"). He then removed T.M. from school property, handcuffed her, and patted her down. No weapons or contraband were found.

Center intake procedures dictated that all juveniles processed into the Center were to be searched for contraband using a metal detecting wand and a pat down. In addition, procedures required that juveniles charged with a violent, theft, or drug offense who were to be placed into the Center's general population be subjected to a visual strip and cavity search. All juveniles brought to the Center were processed for placement in the general population unless the Youth Court specifically informed the Center that the juvenile was to be held as a "non-detainee."

Pursuant to these policies, a female corrections officer searched T.M. when she arrived at the Center. The officer first used the metal detecting wand and patted T.M. down, finding no contraband. At that point, the officer had no reason to suspect T.M. was concealing any contraband in or on her person. Because T.M. was charged with a violent offense, however, Center policy required that the officer strip and cavity search T.M. In a private setting, T.M. was made to strip naked, bend over, spread her buttocks, display the anal cavity, and cough. At no point did the officer touch T.M. during the search. No contraband was found. Following the search, T.M. showered, dressed, moved to a holding cell for approximately twenty minutes, and then entered the general population. She was released from the Center later that evening. No charges against T.M. were pursued.

Mabry sued on T.M.'s behalf. The County filed two separate motions for partial summary judgment. The district court granted both motions. . . .

Mabry timely appealed. . . .

The Fourth Amendment to the United States Constitution reads in relevant part, "[t]he right of the people to be secure in their persons, houses, papers, and effects, against unreasonable searches and seizures, shall not be violated." Because "[t]he Fourth Amendment prohibits only *unreasonable* searches," it has been left to courts to draw the line between reason and unreason. There are many different kinds of searches, varying in relative intrusiveness and distinguishable by context. Unsurprisingly, search and seizure jurisprudence has been patchwork, composed of a number of different tests, to be applied to different kinds of searches and in different settings.

The question presented to us is whether Mabry has shown that the County's visual strip and cavity search of T.M., who was detained for simple assault pursuant to a probable cause determination by a judicial designee, violated the Fourth

Amendment. To answer, it is necessary to probe the Supreme Court's Fourth Amendment precedents to determine whether any bind us. Although there are myriad Supreme Court cases that are at least tangentially related to the issues raised here, three are especially pertinent. None is on all-fours with the facts here. We give a brief summary of each nonetheless, to properly situate our substantive analysis below in the context of governing Supreme Court case law.

A.   Bell v. Wolfish

Bell v. Wolfish, 441 U.S. 520 (1979), "is the starting point for understanding" how to evaluate the reasonableness of a search at a correctional facility. In *Bell*, a group of adult pretrial detainees brought a class action suit, challenging, among other things, a New York correctional facility's practice of strip and cavity searching all inmates "after every contact visit with a person from outside the institution." The searches were strictly visual; inmates were not touched. The Court announced a holistic balancing test to be applied when determining a search's reasonableness:

> The test of reasonableness under the Fourth Amendment is not capable of precise definition or mechanical application. In each case it requires a balancing of the need for the particular search against the invasion of personal rights that the search entails. Courts must consider the scope of the particular intrusion, the manner in which it is conducted, the justification for initiating it, and the place in which it is conducted.

Applying this test to the searches at issue in *Bell*, the Court "[b]alance[d] the significant and legitimate security interests of the institution against the privacy interests of the inmates," and concluded that the balance weighed in favor of the reasonableness of the searches.

B.   Safford v. Redding

The inmates in *Bell* were adults. Thirty years later, the Supreme Court addressed the constitutionality of strip searches of minor students by school officials on school property. *See* Safford Unified Sch. Dist. No. 1 v. Redding, 557 U.S. 364 (2009). In *Safford*, the principal of a middle school oversaw the search of a student who was required to "pull her bra out and to the side and shake it, and to pull out the elastic on her underpants, thus exposing her breasts and pelvic area to some degree." The Court, relying heavily on prior precedent in New Jersey v. T.L.O., 469 U.S. 325 (1985), held that, when assessing the constitutionality of "searches by school officials[,] a 'careful balancing of governmental and private interests suggests that the public interest is best served'" by applying "a standard of reasonable suspicion." In addition to having reasonable suspicion to conduct a search, the Court explained, school officials must also narrow the scope of the search such that "the measures adopted are reasonably related to the objectives of the search and not excessively intrusive in light of the age and sex of the student and the nature of the infraction." Importantly for present purposes, the Court emphasized that the Fourth Amendment's interest-balancing calculus outlined in *Bell* is necessarily different when applied to minors, in part because "adolescent vulnerability intensifies the patent intrusiveness" of a strip search.

C. *Florence v. Board of Chosen Freeholders*

The most recent relevant Supreme Court precedent came in Florence [v. Bd. of Chosen Freeholders of Cty. of Burlington, 566 U.S. 318 (2012)]. An adult pretrial detainee challenged strip and cavity searches conducted pursuant to routine intake procedures. The Court reiterated the *Bell* balancing test but further emphasized that "a responsible Fourth Amendment balance is not well served by standards requiring sensitive, case-by-case determinations of government need, lest every discretionary judgment in the field be converted into an occasion for constitutional review." Rather than directly applying *Bell*'s holistic balancing test, the Court applied a more deferential Fourth Amendment calculus.

The *Florence* Court held that "a regulation impinging on an inmate's constitutional rights must be upheld 'if it is reasonably related to legitimate penological interests.'" The Court further stressed the deference owed to correctional officials in designing search policies intended to ensure security, noting that, "in the absence of substantial evidence in the record to indicate that the officials have exaggerated their response . . . courts should ordinarily defer to their expert judgment in such matters." While taking pains to describe and apply the long-established reasonableness framework of *Bell* and other Fourth Amendment precedent, the Court in *Florence* nonetheless set up a high hurdle for inmates challenging the constitutionality of searches. The Court concluded that, in the correctional context, the burden is on the plaintiff to prove with substantial evidence that the challenged search does not advance a legitimate penological interest.

Although stressing the importance of deference to correctional officials, the Court suggested that substantial evidence could demonstrate that a correctional strip search policy is an exaggerated response to security concerns when, compared to the facts presented in *Florence*, the need for such a policy is lower, the justification weaker, the intrusiveness higher, or an alternative, less invasive policy more feasible. Justice Kennedy's majority opinion clarified that "[t]his case does not require the Court to rule on the types of searches that would be reasonable in instance where, for example, a detainee will be held without assignment to the general jail population and without substantial contact with other detainees. . . . The accommodations provided in these situations may diminish the need to conduct some aspects of the searches at issue." Similarly, Chief Justice Roberts stressed: "it is important for me that the Court does not foreclose the possibility of an exception to the rule it announces." Justice Alito highlighted that "the Court does not hold that it is always reasonable to conduct a full strip search of an arrestee whose detention has not been reviewed by a judicial officer and who could be held in available facilities apart from the general population. Most of those arrested for minor offenses are not dangerous, and most are released from custody prior to or at the time of their initial appearance before a magistrate. . . . For these persons, admission to the general jail population, with the concomitant humiliation of a strip search, may not be reasonable, particularly if an alternative procedure is feasible." Despite this cautionary language, the Court in *Florence* nonetheless made clear that the evidentiary burden rests with the plaintiff when challenging a correctional search policy. Without substantial evidence to the contrary, courts should defer to the reasonableness determinations of correctional officials.

As the district court noted, T.M.'s case "lies at the intersection" of *Safford* and *Florence*: both precedents share important similarities with the facts here, but neither is on all-fours. T.M.'s case is like *Safford* in that it involves the search of a minor student, and it is like *Florence* in that the search was conducted pursuant to routine intake procedures at a correctional facility. The first question we must address, then, is whether *Florence* or *Safford*—or neither—controls in cases when, as here, the inmate who is searched on intake into a correctional facility is a juvenile.

Only one of our sister circuits has addressed precisely this question since *Florence* was decided. In J.B. ex rel. Benjamin v. Fassnacht, 801 F.3d 336 (3d Cir. 2015), a minor was strip and cavity searched pursuant to routine intake procedures at a juvenile detention center. The Third Circuit held that *Florence* controlled for two reasons. First, focusing on the logic underlying *Florence*, the court asserted that "[t]here is no easy way to distinguish between juvenile and adult detainees in terms of the security risks cited by the Supreme Court in *Florence*." And, the court explained, because juveniles and adults pose the same security risks, it follows that the same constitutional test for reasonableness should apply in assessing searches meant to mitigate those risks. . . .

In explaining its motivation for shifting the burden of marshalling substantial evidence onto plaintiffs who challenge a search's reasonableness, the Court in *Florence* stressed the deference owed to correctional officers. The reason for that deference is because courts do not have "sufficient expertise . . . to mandate, under the Constitution . . . specific restrictions and limitations." "Maintaining safety and order" in correctional facilities "requires the expertise of correctional officials." Consequently, "determining whether a policy is reasonably related to legitimate security interests is peculiarly within the province and professional expertise of corrections officials." It is this expertise on the part of officials, and the lack thereof on the part of courts, that motivates the deferential test outlined in *Florence*.

Florence's argument as to institutional competence applies with equal force to juvenile detention centers as it does to adult correctional institutions. That is, we can discern no reason why designing and implementing measures to maintain safety and order in juvenile detention centers requires any less expertise than in adult correctional facilities, nor do we see why courts are more competent to achieve the task in the juvenile context. Importantly, the persuasiveness of this point is not undermined by the fact that the actual security concerns and privacy interests implicated in the juvenile detention center context may be different in important ways from those faced in adult correctional facilities. *See, e.g., Safford*, 557 U.S. at 375 (noting that "adolescent vulnerability intensifies the patent intrusiveness" of a search); *J.B.*, 801 F.3d at 343 (explaining that "juveniles pose risks unique from those of adults as the state acts as the minor's de facto guardian ... during a minor's detention period"). Nevertheless, we read *Florence* to mean that, in the correctional context—whether juvenile or adult—courts, which are not experts, should still defer to officials who are. The logic underlying *Florence*'s deferential test thus compels the conclusion that the deference given to correctional officials in the adult context applies to correctional officials in the juvenile context as well. . . .

The district court's ruling is affirmed.

NOTES AND QUESTIONS

1. The *Mabry* court says that it cannot distinguish juvenile detention facilities from adult jails for purposes of assessing the reasonableness of a policy allowing blanket strip searches of detainees. Could *Safford* support a distinction? *See* Emily J. Nelson, Custodial Strip Searches of Juveniles: How *Safford* Informs a New Two-Tiered Standard of Review, 53 B.C. L. Rev. 339, 372-73 (2011) (arguing for a two-tiered review of custodial strip searches of a juvenile in a juvenile detention center based on the level of the offense committed, with the first tier for minor offenses using the *Safford* and *T.L.O.* "reasonableness of the intrusion" standard, and the second tier, applied to more serious crimes, using a balancing test (comparing the level of the intrusion to the state's rationale for the intrusion) that gives extra weight to the state).

2. Before *Florence* was decided, most of the federal courts of appeals held that suspicionless strip searches of adults detained for minor offenses were unconstitutional. Miller v. Kennebec County, 219 F.3d 8, 12 (1st Cir. 2000) (failure to pay fine); Shain v. Ellison, 273 F.3d 56, 62-66 (2d Cir. 2001); Logan v. Shealy, 660 F.2d 1007, 1012-13 (4th Cir. 1981) (drunk driving); Kelly v. Foti, 77 F.3d 819, 821-22 (5th Cir. 1996) (motor vehicle violations); Masters v. Crouch, 872 F.2d 1248, 1253-55 (6th Cir. 1989) (failure to appear for motor vehicle violation); Mary Beth G. v. City of Chicago, 723 F.2d 1263, 1266, 1268-73 (7th Cir. 1983) (various misdemeanors); Jones v. Edwards, 770 F.2d 739, 740-42 (8th Cir. 1985) (refusal to sign complaint for leash law violation); Giles v. Ackerman, 746 F.2d 614, 615-19 (9th Cir. 1984) (motor vehicle violations); Chapman v. Nichols, 989 F.2d 393, 395-97 (10th Cir. 1993) (same). *Contra* Powell v. Barrett, 541 F.3d 1298 (11th Cir. 2009).

Two of these courts held that juvenile detention facilities could conduct suspicionless strip searches of all children admitted to the facilities, distinguishing the adult cases on the basis of the state's obligation to protect children. N.G. v. Connecticut, 382 F.3d 225 (2d Cir. 2004); Smook v. Minnehaha County, 457 F.3d 806 (8th Cir. 2006).

IN THE MATTER OF S.C.

523 S.W.3d 279 (Tex. App. 2017)

LUZ ELENA D. CHAPA, Justice . . . On a Friday evening in 2015, San Antonio Police Department Officer Charles Kholleppel received a report of a burglary on the west wide of San Antonio. He spoke with a person who witnessed the burglary, and this witness personally knew the individuals who broke into the house. The witness identified them as S.C. and his brother, V.C., and told Officer Kholleppel where they lived. The stolen property included a video game console, $10,000 in cash, and other "small items."

Officer Kholleppel went to S.C.'s home and spoke with a woman who said she was S.C.'s mother. She told Officer Kholleppel that S.C. was playing basketball down the street. Officer Kholleppel found S.C. and asked him several questions. S.C. told Officer Kholleppel he was fifteen years old and in the eighth grade. Officer Kholleppel and S.C. went back to the house, and Officer Kholleppel asked him about the burglary in the presence of his mother. During Officer Kholleppel's discussion with S.C. and his mother, two other SAPD officers arrived.

Officer Kholleppel observed S.C. "jumping around," "moving his hands around," and being "fidgety," and he therefore placed S.C. in handcuffs. He told S.C. he was "all over the place" and he was only being detained and not under arrest. Officer Hector Perez, one of the other officers who arrived, also told S.C. he was only being detained. Officer Kholleppel placed a handcuffed S.C. in the back of Officer Perez's patrol car and asked S.C.'s mother for consent to enter the house. S.C.'s mother expressly refused numerous times to allow the officers to go inside the house without a warrant. During their conversation with S.C. and his mother, the officers repeatedly stated the burglary victim would not press charges if all of the property were returned.

Approximately eight minutes after being placed in the patrol car, and after S.C.'s mother refused multiple times to allow the officers in the house, Officer Perez approached his patrol car and asked S.C. whether S.C. "wanted to talk" to him and S.C. stated he did. Officer Perez told S.C. that if he did not return the stolen property and the property was found inside the house, his grandmother, who owned the house, could be arrested. S.C. then told Officer Kholleppel the stolen property was inside the house. According to Officer Kholleppel, S.C. agreed to show him where the stolen property was.

Officer Perez removed S.C. from the patrol car and then removed the handcuffs. Officer Kholleppel followed S.C. into the house, and told his mother that S.C. was going to show him where the stolen property was to "save y'all a headache." S.C.'s mother did not further object at that time. Officer Kholleppel followed S.C. into his bedroom, where S.C. retrieved an Xbox, a video game, and DVDs, but not the $10,000 in cash. S.C. remained at the house and was not further detained or arrested that evening. . . .

The State filed a petition alleging S.C. was a juvenile who had engaged in the delinquent conduct of burglary of a habitation. . . . At the suppression hearing, the trial court denied S.C.'s motion. S.C. then pled true to the delinquency allegation, and the trial court signed orders of adjudication and disposition. S.C. timely filed this appeal. . . .

[The court held that S.C.'s statements were admissible even though the officers did not advise him of his *Miranda* rights because he was not in custody.]

S.C. argues the trial court erred by not suppressing evidence obtained from Officer Kholleppel's entry into his home because the entry violated his rights. . . .

. . . A warrantless police entry into a person's home is a presumptively unreasonable search "unless the entry falls within an exception to the warrant requirement."

. . . It is undisputed Officer Kholleppel entered the house without a warrant. Thus, the State had the burden to prove Officer Kholleppel's entry into the house was reasonable. The State argues Officer Kholleppel's search was reasonable because S.C. voluntarily consented to the officer entering his home.

Voluntary consent is generally an exception to the warrant requirement. *Schneckloth v. Bustamonte*, 412 U.S. 218, 219 (1973). A police officer may obtain voluntary consent from either the suspect or a third party who has actual or apparent authority to consent to the search. *Illinois v. Rodriguez*, 497 U.S. 177, 181 (1990). "[T]he typical third party consent case [is when] the police solicit the consent of *A* in order to search an area in which *B* has a privacy interest for the express purpose of finding evidence against *B*." Typically, third party consent cases arise when the suspect is not present and objecting to the search. Because "reasonableness" is the ultimate touchstone for any Fourth Amendment analysis, "'reasonableness' is also the touchstone for determining voluntary consent to search."

The Supreme Court of the United States has addressed the reasonableness of a search when there is "disputed consent," which is when one resident of a home expressly consents to the search and another resident is present and expressly objects to the search. *Georgia v. Randolph*, 547 U.S. 103, 120 (2006). In *Randolph*, an officer obtained a wife's consent to search a house for evidence of her husband's drug use, but the husband, who was present, unequivocally objected. The Supreme Court held the warrantless search was invalid "as to him" (the husband) given the great significance of "widely shared social expectations." The Court explained that "[w]ithout some very good reason, no sensible person would go inside" a residence "when a fellow tenant stood there saying, 'stay out.'"

The State notes the Court in *Randolph* repeatedly emphasized that when one resident is present and objecting to a search and another resident gives consent to the search, the search is not reasonable *as to the objecting party*. The State implies the Court thereby indicated the non-objecting resident's voluntary consent would make the search reasonable as to that party. But the Court in *Randolph* did not address whether a suspect who voluntarily consented to a search may rely on another physically present resident's objection to a search because those were not the facts before the Court. The Court did suggest, however, that the reasonableness of an officer's search when there is disputed consent may turn on whether "the people living together fall within some recognized hierarchy, like a household of parent and child or barracks housing military personnel of different grades."

Several courts in other jurisdictions have relied upon *Randolph*'s "recognized hierarchy" language to resolve disputed consent cases involving a parent and minor child. These courts have held the search of the child's room or belongings is reasonable when the parent consents, even if the minor child is present and objecting to the search. *In re D.C.*, 188 Cal. App. 4th 978, 115 Cal. Rptr. 3d 837, 842-43 (2010); *State v. S.B.*, 758 So. 2d 1253, 1255 (Fla. 4th Dist. Ct. App. 2000); *see In re Tariq A-R-Y*, 347 Md. 484, 701 A.2d 691, 692 (1997); *Vandenberg v. Superior Court*, 87 Cal. Rptr. 876, 879-80, 8 Cal. App. 3d 1048 (Ct. App. 1970). These courts generally rely on the superiority of parents' property rights to the entire residence and basic parental rights to make decisions for their minor children.

Although S.C.'s grandmother owned the house, Officer Kholleppel was informed the woman at the house was S.C.'s mother. If an officer's search is generally reasonable when a parent expressly consents to a search and her minor child expressly objects, then it logically follows that an officer's search is generally unreasonable when a parent objects to a search and her minor child expressly consents. Under Texas law, parents have "the right ... to make ... decisions of substantial legal significance concerning the child" and have the "duty of care, control, protection, and reasonable discipline of the child." Furthermore, "the interest of parents in the care, custody, and control of their children ... is perhaps the oldest of the fundamental liberty interests recognized by [the Supreme] Court." Troxel v. Granville, 530 U.S. 57, 65 (2000) (plurality). We must presume officers know the rights and duties of parents and understand the recognized hierarchy in the parent–child relationship. We therefore conclude it is generally unreasonable for an officer to rely on a minor child's consent to search a home when the child's parent is present and has objected to the search. . . .

The State also argues S.C.'s mother impliedly consented to Officer Kholleppel's search by remaining silent after S.C. consented and contends S.C.'s mother was required to object again or "impede [the officers'] efforts." In all of the "implied consent" cases the State cites, the suspect either initiated the investigation by calling the police or expressly consented to a search and failed to clarify or otherwise limit the scope of consent. This case is distinguishable because S.C.'s mother did not call the police and she did not give express consent to search. She expressly objected numerous times to the officers entering the house without a warrant. Despite her objections, Officer Kholleppel entered the house. Although S.C.'s mother did not reurge her objection after Officer Kholleppel entered the house, Officer Kholleppel knew at the time he entered the house she had repeatedly objected to the officers entering the house without a warrant. . . .

We conclude that under the specific facts of this case, Officer Kholleppel's entry into S.C.'s home was unreasonable. . . .

NOTES AND QUESTIONS

1. As *S.C.* says, most courts hold that a minor's parent has authority to consent to a search of the child's room and belongings. In addition to the cases that the court cites, *see* R.B. v. State, 43 N.E.3d 648 (Ind. App. 2015). Does it follow then, that a minor's consent cannot ever override a parent's refusal to consent to a search?

2. Courts often cite the dicta from Georgia v. Randolph, 547 U.S. 103 (2006), quoted in *S.C.* that absent "some recognized hierarchy, like a household of parent and child . . . there is no societal understanding of superior and inferior," and "[e]ach cotenant . . . has the right to use and enjoy the entire property as if he or she were the sole owner, limited only by the same right in the other cotenants." Is this right an inherent part of being a parent?

Professor Henning argues "that the Court's *dicta* in Georgia v. Randolph oversimplifies, and maybe even mischaracterizes, the Court's own analysis of children's rights in previous cases, and as a result has and will continue to distort the analysis of lower courts called upon to mediate the rights of children in competition with the rights and duties of their parents." She endeavors "to move courts away from the overbroad deference to parental authority and advocates for a more nuanced and faithful analysis of children's Fourth Amendment rights right-based cases involving minors." Kristin Henning, When Parental Authority Goes Too Far: The Fourth Amendment Rights of Minors in Their Parents' Homes, 53 Wm. & Mary L. Rev. 55 (2011).

3. Can a child claim a privacy interest in his or her room as against his or her parents in some circumstances? Assume, for example, that a parent authorized police to search a child's bedroom, and the police find a locked suitcase. Can the parent authorize the police to break the lock and search the suitcase?

4. The Oregon Court of Appeals held that a search and seizure of drug paraphernalia found in a youth's purse was unconstitutional under the Oregon Constitution when a "police officer [had] 'encouraged' youth's mother to empty the contents of youth's purse on the back seat of the police car." State ex rel. Juvenile Dep't of Jackson Cnty. v. S.L.M., 206 P.3d 283, 285 (Or. App. 2009). The court stated that the suggestion of the officer and the mother's compliance with that suggestion indicated that the mother was acting as an agent of the state, which required a search warrant. *Id.* at 284, 285. Because no search warrant was in place at the time of the seizure, the court ruled that the youth's motion to suppress should have been granted.

5. Minors can consent to searches of their persons and property, and courts take into account their youth when determining whether the consent was voluntary. However, courts are divided and inconsistent in their application of age as a factor in the voluntariness analysis. Megan Annitto, Consent Searches of Minors, 38 N.Y.U. Rev. L. & Soc. Change 1 (2014). *See also* Kristin Henning, The Reasonable Black Child: Race, Adolescence, and the Fourth Amendment, 67 Am. U. L. Rev. 1513 (2018).

3. *Arrest or Taking into Custody*

The traditional juvenile court terminology distinguished sharply between juvenile and criminal proceedings. Juveniles were "taken into custody," rather than "arrested," and the adult law of arrest was said not to apply. Since *Gault*, courts that have considered the issue have held that the Fourth Amendment limitations on police arrests apply to juveniles suspected of having committed crimes. *See, e.g.,* Lanes v. State, 767 S.W.2d 789 (Tex. Crim. App. 1989).

M.J. v. State

121 So. 3d 1151 (Fla. App. 2013)

WARNER, J. . . . On a Thursday about mid-day, Broward Deputy Sheriff Johnson, who was on road patrol, observed appellant, M.J., in front of a house in a high crime area of Broward County. Deputy Johnson knew M.J. from prior dealings, including the fact that he was seventeen and should have been in school at that time. The deputy made a u-turn in his vehicle to initiate a truancy investigation. By the time he turned around, he saw M.J. start running and disappear from his view. The deputy stopped at the house where he had seen M.J., went up to the porch, and found M.J. lying along the concrete wall inside the porch.

The deputy grabbed M.J. and told him to stand up. He then read M.J. *Miranda* rights. He asked M.J. what he was doing there. M.J. said he was at the house to see a friend. The deputy knocked on the door but no one answered.

A second deputy came on the scene and Deputy Johnson, being suspicious about the circumstances, walked around the house. In some bushes on the side of the house, he discovered three boxes containing new sports sneakers. At that point, about five or ten minutes after M.J. was detained, Deputy Johnson noticed the home's resident, whom he knew from prior dealings, at the home's window. Through the window, the resident told the deputy that M.J. had brought the shoes to his residence. The deputy knew that the resident had prior burglaries on his record. The deputy never asked the resident whether M.J. had permission to be on his property.

The officer arrested M.J. for loitering and prowling and transported him to the sheriff's office where an interrogation was conducted. At the time of the arrest, the deputy had "no idea that the sneakers were stolen." When he got to the station, however, a third deputy informed him that a burglary of shoes had been reported. M.J. ultimately confessed to that burglary during the interrogation.

Deputy Johnson admitted that generally a truancy investigation would result in the return of the child to school or the child's parents. He did not return M.J. to school because he arrested him for loitering and prowling. The circumstances Deputy Johnson identified as supporting the arrest were M.J.'s running and hiding from him when he turned his vehicle around and that M.J.'s explanation as to why he was on the porch—to see a friend—was not "valid," because when Deputy Johnson looked at the resident through the window, it appeared as though the resident had just awoken.

The trial court ruled that Deputy Johnson was authorized to commence a truancy investigation. Based upon the totality of the circumstances after Deputy Johnson observed M.J. fleeing from him, the court believed the circumstances were "suspicious" and justified Deputy Johnson's continued detention and investigation of M.J. The court then denied the motion to suppress.

M.J. reserved the right to appeal the denial of the motion to suppress, and the state did not contest the dispositive nature of the motion. Following the denial, he entered a no contest plea to the charge of burglary of a dwelling. The court withheld adjudication and sentenced M.J. to juvenile probation. This appeal follows.

. . . The trial court made the factual finding that the officer was authorized to conduct a truancy investigation when he stopped M.J. Section 984.13, Florida Statutes (2012), allows a law enforcement officer to take a child "into custody" when "the officer has reasonable grounds to believe that the child is absent from school without authorization . . . for the purpose of delivering the child without unreasonable delay to the appropriate school system site." The officer may also deliver the child to his parents if the student has been suspended or expelled from school. Therefore, Deputy Johnson had the authority to take M.J. into custody.

Truancy, however, is not a crime. While a law enforcement officer has the authority to take a juvenile into custody, that authority is limited to returning the child to school or the child's parents. The officer does not have the statutory authority to transport the child to a police station for further questioning based upon truancy.

Where the officer has reasonable suspicion that a person is involved in criminal activity, the officer may conduct an investigatory stop. That investigation should be limited and cannot extend beyond the place of initial encounter. To transport an individual for additional questioning, a law enforcement officer must have probable cause for an arrest.

> Where ... the detained individual is physically removed from the scene and involuntarily transported to the police station for questioning and/or investigation, the courts have had little difficulty in construing such a detention to be a de facto arrest requiring either probable cause or prior judicial authorization.

In this case, Deputy Johnson placed M.J. under arrest and transported him to the sheriff's office for questioning; therefore, the question we must answer is whether the totality of the circumstances provided him with probable cause to arrest M.J. for loitering and prowling.

Section 856.021, Florida Statutes (2012), provides: "It is unlawful for any person to loiter or prowl in a place, at a time or in a manner not usual for law-abiding individuals, under circumstances that warrant a justifiable and reasonable alarm or immediate concern for the safety of persons or property in the vicinity." When a person takes "flight upon appearance of a law enforcement officer" or "manifestly endeavors to conceal himself or herself or any object," this is a circumstance for consideration in determining the alarm or immediate concern element. Prior to arrest, a law enforcement officer must give the suspect the opportunity to explain his conduct.

We have explained, "[b]ecause of its potential for abuse, the loitering statute must be applied with special care." "It is not to be used as a 'catch-all' provision when there is an insufficient basis for another charge."

The statute is comprised of two elements. "To satisfy the first element, the state must prove that 'the defendant engaged in incipient criminal behavior which law-abiding people do not usually engage in due to the time, place, or manner of the conduct involved.'" "To satisfy the second element, the state must demonstrate that the loitering occurred under 'circumstances that warrant a justifiable and reasonable alarm or immediate concern for the safety of persons or property in the vicinity.'" In *P.R.*, we explained:

> "[T]he offense of loitering and prowling must be completed prior to any police action." And because flight from police comes *after* the officers' presence is made known, flight alone is insufficient to satisfy the elements of loitering and prowling. . . .

Deputy Johnson saw M.J. and suspected him of being a truant, not of committing a crime. M.J.'s flight after observing the deputy, who knew him, did not provide probable cause for a loitering and prowling arrest. Indeed, it may have been quite normal of a truant to flee from law enforcement. All other conduct on which the deputy relied in his decision to arrest M.J. occurred *after* stopping and detaining M.J. Even if the deputy were allowed to rely on the discovery of the sports shoes as part of the probable cause on which he based the arrest, he admitted that he had no idea that the shoes were the subject of a burglary. Assuming that M.J. had possessed them, he could have purchased them. Thus, the deputy had only a bare suspicion that M.J. was up to something. There was nothing at the time and place of M.J.'s detention to provide probable cause that any criminal activity had occurred, was occurring, or was about to occur.

Because Deputy Johnson did not have probable cause to support an arrest for loitering and prowling, M.J.'s detention and transport to the station for questioning was illegal, making his confession the fruit of an illegal arrest. The court erred in denying its suppression. As the issue is dispositive, we direct that the court dismiss the delinquency petition on remand.

NOTES AND QUESTIONS

1. Why did the officer believe that M.J. was a truant? Did the reasons amount to probable cause to believe that M.J. was truant? What facts would show probable cause to believe that a young person was a runaway?

The court holds that the officer did not have probable cause to believe M.J. was loitering and prowling. Why not? Recall that the juvenile court status offense categories, including incorrigibility, are closely related to the offenses of prowling and loitering. Would it be possible to have probable cause to believe a child was incorrigible?

2. Florida law allows a patdown search of a minor taken into custody for being truant but not a full search incident to arrest. What is the difference in the scope of these searches? Why is a patdown allowed but a full search is not?

Other cases making the same distinction regarding the scope of a search include State v. A.A, 349 P.3d 909 (Wash. App. 2015) (truancy), and Matter of Marrhonda G., 613 N.E.2d 568 (N.Y. 1998) (runaway).

3. If police have probable cause to believe a minor is truant or a runaway and the minor resists being taken into custody, can the minor be adjudicated delinquent for resisting arrest? In re Gabriela A., 12 N.E.3d 1054 (N.Y. 2014), held that a minor could not be convicted of resisting arrest when she resisted being taken into custody for having run away from her nonsecure status offender placement even though her behavior arguably posed a risk to herself, the probation officer, or her family. Her behavior, the court said, was simply a manifestation of being "beyond control," which is not a crime.

PROBLEM

On April 5, Port Authority Police Officer Joseph DeFelice observed respondent standing alone in the Port Authority Bus Terminal for several hours with a large knapsack-type bag. DeFelice approached and questioned respondent, concluding that she could be a runaway. Respondent was traveling alone, had initially lied about her age, had no identification with her, and appeared to be nervous. Moreover, respondent said that her mother could not be contacted, and while indicating that she was waiting for a relative, she could not give a local address or telephone number for that person.

DeFelice took respondent to the Port Authority Youth Services Unit office—a facility for investigating suspected runaways. Upon entering the office, respondent put her bag down on the floor and sat in a chair about 15 feet away from the bag. A few minutes later another officer picked up respondent's bag from the floor in order to move it out of the way. While holding the bag, the officer felt what he believed to be the butt and trigger guard of a gun. DeFelice also handled the bag and was able to feel what he believed to be the impression of a gun inside the bag. The officers then opened the bag and found four weapons and ammunition.

The respondent filed a motion to suppress the weapons seized in the bag. What arguments would be made for and against the motion?

C. PRE-ADJUDICATION PROCESSES

1. *Intake and Diversion*

Tamar R. Birckhead, *Closing the Widening Net: The Rights of Juveniles at Intake*

46 Texas Tech Law Review 157, 162-164 (2013)

Intake is the threshold screening and gate-keeping function of the juvenile court. Some jurisdictions authorize prosecutors to decide whether to file a petition, dismiss, or informally adjust a juvenile's case. Most jurisdictions have [juvenile probation officers] conduct the intake screening during which they make this determination. Typically the chief juvenile probation officer for each judicial district establishes the specific procedures governing intake services. . . .

Although each state follows the specific language of its own juvenile code, the general purpose of the intake process is to assess a combination of factors, including whether there are reasonable grounds to believe the facts alleged are true; whether the facts alleged constitute a delinquent or undisciplined offense; whether the facts alleged are sufficiently serious to warrant court action; and whether to obtain assistance from community resources when court referral is not necessary. This last option, also termed diversion, typically takes the form of police probation, community service, or participation in such programs as teen court.

Social scientists have identified a number of beneficial purposes of diversion. It has been found to "mitigate the rigidity of the criminal law, which reduces a vast variety of behaviors into relatively few categories." For example, although intentionally pushing someone in a school hallway can be prosecuted as assault, and taking a pencil from a teacher's desk without returning it as simple larceny, diversion provides an alternative avenue to hold children and adolescents responsible for such behavior without formal court involvement. It can also be understood as "a concession to the limits of judicial and community resources," as it is more efficient and cost-effective than court proceedings. In addition, diversion helps avoid the stigma and negative effects on youths that can result from appearing in the public forum of delinquency court and being formally adjudicated as "juvenile delinquents." This concern draws on "labeling theory," in which the juvenile defines herself as "deviant" or "dangerous" because others perceive her that way. Diversion has been shown to reduce recidivism rates, as data suggests that behavioral or skill-oriented methods delivered within the community are more successful than "scared-straight" or "shock incarceration" deterrence programs.

There are three basic critiques of diversion. Some juvenile justice advocates assert that it "widens the net" of court intervention, as it brings youth into the system for informal treatment who would not otherwise be processed. In fact, studies have shown that diverted youth experience as much intrusion into their lives as those whose cases are not diverted. Diverted youth may also experience labeling, as the types of services mandated during a diversion program (i.e., psychological counseling or drug treatment) can impose a harsher label on a young person (i.e., mentally ill or drug addicted) than referral to juvenile court, where the case may ultimately be dismissed or the child adjudicated not delinquent. As a result, social scientists have concluded that it is "[o]f particular importance [to] ensur[e] that youth presenting low levels of risk are provided minimal levels of intervention or none at all." A second critique, advanced by law enforcement and JPOs, asserts that diversion trivializes the seriousness of law breaking, as there is no formal acknowledgement of wrongdoing by the juvenile offender, and the case resolution is often a mere slap on the wrist. A third perspective contends that diversion does a disservice to crime victims, as often they are not involved in diversion schemes, precluding the victims, and the juveniles themselves, from the potential benefits of mediation and restorative justice programs.

Intake procedures vary considerably among states. While some JPOs make screening decisions based on internal policy or local custom (i.e., no diversion of felonies or automatic approval of the petition if the juvenile does not appear at her intake appointment), others conduct in-depth interviews, formal hearings, or both. Generally, all children are assessed during intake for any immediate needs, such as mental health or substance abuse problems. Most JPOs also consider other factors, such as the young person's prior record, his school attendance and conduct, and his home environment. Upon a finding of legal sufficiency, the JPO then determines whether the complaint should be filed as a petition, the juvenile should be diverted, or the case should be dismissed without further action. In some jurisdictions, the JPO makes a referral to the prosecutor who assesses whether a formal petition should be issued; in others, the prosecutor makes the screening decision without the JPO's input.

More than 80 percent of all delinquency cases referred to the juvenile court come from law enforcement agencies. Sarah Hockenberry & Charles Puzzanchera, Juvenile Court Statistics 2015, at 31 (April 2018), http://www.ncjj.org/pdf/jcsreports/jcs2015report.pdf. Juvenile cases are more likely to be handled formally than informally; in 2015, 55 percent of juveniles taken to juvenile court intake by police were referred to juvenile court. *Id.* at 36. The proportion of delinquency cases petitioned for formal handling changed little between 2005 and 2015. Nina Hyland, Delinquency Cases in Juvenile Court, 2014 (Jan. 2018), http://www.ncjj.org/pdf/251107.pdf. In 2014, of the 45 percent of all cases that were not referred for formal proceedings in juvenile court, 18 percent were dismissed at intake, usually for legal insufficiency, and in the remaining 27 percent, the juvenile agreed to a voluntary sanction, such as restitution or informal probation. *Id.*

Serious offenses are more likely to be handled formally than informally, and cases involving teens 16 and older are more likely to be petitioned than cases involving younger teens. Of all cases involving white, Hispanic, and Asian youth, 51 to 53 percent were handled formally, compared to 62 percent of black youths' cases, and 56 percent of Native American youths' cases. Almost 60 percent of males' cases were petitioned, compared to 47 percent of females' cases. Hockenberry & Puzzanchera at 36-37.

Intake is not considered to be a "critical stage" of the proceedings at which a juvenile is entitled to counsel under the federal constitution, and case law is mixed about whether juveniles are entitled to counsel under state law principles. The IJA-ABA Juvenile Justice Standards Project, Standards Relating to Counsel for Private Parties (1980), recommends that lawyers participate at this stage in order to address the legal sufficiency of the complaint, explore the availability of community services in place of referral to court, and explain to the child and his parents the child's situation and the consequences of any proposed nonjudicial disposition. *Id.* at 119-126. As a practical matter, though, even where juveniles have a right to counsel, most juveniles waive this right, and lawyers rarely participate in diversion discussions.

In some states, statements made during the intake or diversion process are inadmissible in evidence. *See, e.g.,* N.C. Gen. Stat. § 7B-2408 (2018) ("[N]o statement made by a juvenile to the juvenile court counselor during the preliminary inquiry and evaluation process shall be admissible prior to the dispositional hearing."). *See also* Lourdes M. Rosado & Riya S. Shah, Protecting Youth from Self-Incrimination when Undergoing Screening, Assessment and Treatment within the Juvenile Justice System 35, 40-41 (2007), available at http://www.jlc.org/sites/default/files/publication_pdfs/protectingyouth.pdf (listing statutes in Arkansas, Arizona, the District of Columbia, Hawaii, Iowa, Kentucky, Maine, Maryland, Mississippi, Missouri, New Mexico, North Carolina, Texas, and Virginia). *See also* In re Wayne H., 596 P.2d 1 (Cal. 1979) (holding that statement made during intake is not admissible as substantive evidence); In re Randy G., 487 N.Y.S.2d 967 (Fam. Ct. 1985) (same).

Breach of diversion conditions by the minor can result in a formal petition on the offense that originally brought the chil to the intake or prosecution office, and often the diversion agreement requires that the juvenile admit to the offense before entering into the agreement and provides that the admission is admissible in an adjudicatory hearing if the agreement is breached.

The Office of Juvenile Justice and Delinquency Prevention maintains a website with information about model diversion programs, https://www.ojjdp.gov/mpg-iguides/topics/diversion-programs/. Programs are surveyed in Literature Review, Diversion from Formal Juvenile Court Processing (Feb. 2017), https://www.ojjdp.gov/mpg/litreviews/Diversion_Programs.pdf.

2. Detention

When police take a child into custody, they may release the child to a parent or guardian or deliver the child to a detention facility pending a judicial hearing. The detention facility itself ordinarily decides whether detention is warranted and may either retain the child or arrange for release to the parent or guardian. Detention is typically justified when it appears that there is probable cause to believe the child has committed a delinquent act and there is reason to believe that he or she is a threat to run away or otherwise be unavailable for court proceedings, or reason to believe that if released the child will be harmed or cause harm to others' persons or property. The degree of confidence required for these judgments differs formally from jurisdiction to jurisdiction, though most states use probable cause.

After many years of rising rates, the number of delinquency cases in which minors were detained declined steadily between 2000 and 2015, when 48,043 juvenile offenders were housed in residential facilities (both pre- and post-trial). This is the lowest number since 1997, when 105,055 were held in out of home placements. Sarah Hockenberry, Juveniles in Residential Placement, 2015 (OJJDP, Jan. 2018), https://www.ojjdp.gov/pubs/250951.pdf. The number of juveniles detained pretrial dropped 44 percent between 2005 and 2015, although the proportion of delinquency cases in which the youth was detained rose from 23 percent in 2005 to 24 percent in 2015. Sarah Hockenberry & Charles Puzzanchera, Juvenile Court Statistics 2015, at 32 (April 2018), http://www.ncjj.org/pdf/jcsreports/jcs2015report.pdf. During this time period, the rate of detention fell for drug cases but rose slightly for all other categories of cases. The largest number of detained minors are charged with crimes against a person, and a minor is most likely to be detained for a crime against a person. In about 30 percent of cases involving an offense against a person the juvenile is detained, compared to a quarter of those charged with public order offenses and a fifth of those charged with property offenses. *Id.* As is true of other stages of juvenile delinquency processing, males are more likely to be detained than females, though the gender disparity has dropped significantly in recent years. In 2015, 20 percent of females charged as delinquents were detained, compared to 26 percent of males. Detention rates did not vary between teens younger and older than 16. Hispanic youth were statistically the most likely to be detained of all racial and ethnic groups; they accounted for 19 percent of all delinquency cases but 23 percent of those detained. In comparison, black youths accounted for 36 percent of all delinquency cases and 39 percent of all detentions, and white teens accounted for 43 percent of the delinquency caseload but only 36 percent of those detained. *Id.* at 33.

SCHALL V. MARTIN

467 U.S. 253 (1984)

REHNQUIST, J. [The New York Family Court Act authorizes pretrial detention of an accused delinquent child on a finding that there is a "serious risk" that the child might commit a future crime. This is a class action challenging preventive detention of juveniles.]

Appellee Gregory Martin was arrested on December 13, 1977, and charged with first-degree robbery, second-degree assault, and criminal possession of a weapon based on an incident in which he, with two others, allegedly hit a youth on the head with a loaded gun and stole his jacket and sneakers. Martin had possession of the gun when he was arrested. He was 14 years old at the time and, therefore, came within the jurisdiction of New York's Family Court. The incident occurred at 11:30 at night, and Martin lied to the police about where and with whom he lived. He was consequently detained overnight.

A petition of delinquency was filed, and Martin made his "initial appearance" in Family Court on December 14th, accompanied by his grandmother. The Family Court Judge, citing the possession of the loaded weapon, the false address given to the police, and the lateness of the hour, as evidencing a lack of supervision, ordered Martin detained. . . . A probable cause hearing was held five days later, on December 19th, and probable cause was found to exist for all the crimes charged. At the fact-finding hearing held December 27-29, Martin was found guilty on the robbery and criminal possession charges. He was adjudicated a delinquent and placed on two years' probation. He had been detained . . . between the initial appearance and the completion of the factfinding hearing, for a total of 15 days. . . .

On December 21, 1977, while still in preventive detention pending his fact-finding hearing, Gregory Martin instituted a habeas corpus class action on behalf of "those persons who are, or during the pendency of this action will be, preventively detained. . . . "

In an unpublished opinion, the District Court certified the class. . . .

There is no doubt that the Due Process Clause is applicable in juvenile proceedings. "The problem," we have stressed, "is to ascertain the precise impact of the due process requirement upon such proceedings." In re Gault. We have held that certain basic constitutional protections enjoyed by adults accused of crimes also apply to juveniles. But the Constitution does not mandate elimination of all differences in the treatment of juveniles. *See, e.g.*, McKeiver v. Pennsylvania, 403 U.S. 528 (1971) (no right to jury trial). The State has "a *parens patriae* interest in preserving and promoting the welfare of the child," Santosky v. Kramer, 455 U.S. 745 (1982), which makes a juvenile proceeding fundamentally different from an adult criminal trial. We have tried, therefore, to strike a balance—to respect the "informality" and "flexibility" that characterize juvenile proceedings, . . . and yet to ensure that such proceedings comport with the "fundamental fairness" demanded by the Due Process Clause.

The statutory provision at issue in this case permits a brief pretrial detention based on a finding of a "serious risk" that an arrested juvenile may commit a crime before his return date. The question before us is whether preventive detention of juveniles . . . is compatible with the "fundamental fairness" required by due process. Two separate inquiries are necessary to answer this question. First, does preventive detention under the New York statute serve a legitimate state objective? And, second, are the procedural safeguards contained in the Family Court Act adequate to authorize the pretrial detention of at least some juveniles charged with crimes?

Preventive detention under the [Family Court Act] is purportedly designed to protect the child and society from the potential consequences of his criminal acts. When making any detention decision, the Family Court judge is specifically directed to consider the needs and best interests of the juvenile as well as the need for the protection of the community. In Bell v. Wolfish [441 U.S. 520, 534 n.15 (1979)], we left open the question whether any governmental objective other than ensuring a detainee's presence at trial may constitutionally justify pretrial detention. As an initial matter, therefore, we must decide whether, in the context of the juvenile system, the combined interest in protecting both the community and the juvenile himself from the consequences of future criminal conduct is sufficient to justify such detention.

The "legitimate and compelling state interest" in protecting the community from crime cannot be doubted. We have stressed before that crime prevention is "a weighty social objective," and this interest persists undiluted in the juvenile context. . . . The harm suffered by the victim of a crime is not dependent upon the age of the perpetrator. And the harm to society generally may even be greater in this context given the high rate of recidivism among juveniles.

The juvenile's countervailing interest in freedom from institutional restraints, even for the brief time involved here, is undoubtedly substantial as well. . . .But that interest must be qualified by the recognition that juveniles, unlike adults, are always in some form of custody. Children, by definition, are not assumed to have the capacity to take care of themselves. They are assumed to be subject to the control of their parents, and if parental control falters, the State must play its part as *parens patriae*. In this respect, the juvenile's liberty interest may, in appropriate circumstances, be subordinated to the State's "*parens patriae* interest in preserving and promoting the welfare of the child." Santosky v. Kramer, *supra*, at 766.

The New York Court of Appeals, in upholding the statute at issue here, stressed at some length "the desirability of protecting the juvenile from his own folly." Society has a legitimate interest in protecting a juvenile from the consequences of his criminal activity—both from potential physical injury which may be suffered when a victim fights back or a policeman attempts to make an arrest and from the downward spiral of criminal activity into which peer pressure may lead the child.

The substantiality and legitimacy of the state interests underlying this statute are confirmed by the widespread use and judicial acceptance of preventive detention for juveniles. Every State, as well as the United States in the District of Columbia, permits preventive detention of juveniles accused of crime. A number of model juvenile justice acts also contain provisions permitting preventive detention. And the courts of eight States, including the New York Court of Appeals, have upheld their statutes with specific reference to protecting the juvenile and the community from harmful pretrial conduct, including pretrial crime. . . .

Of course, the mere invocation of a legitimate purpose will not justify particular restrictions and conditions of confinement amounting to punishment. It is axiomatic that "[d]ue process requires that a pretrial detainee not be punished.". . .

There is no indication in the statute itself that preventive detention is used or intended as a punishment. First of all, the detention is strictly limited in time. . . . [T]he maximum possible detention under § 320.5(3)(b) of a youth accused of a serious crime . . . is 17 days. The maximum detention for less serious crimes . . . is six days. These time-frames seem suited to the limited purpose of providing the youth with a controlled environment and separating him from improper influences pending the speedy disposition of his case.

The conditions of confinement also appear to reflect the regulatory purposes relied upon by the State. When a juvenile is remanded after his initial appearance, he cannot, absent exceptional circumstances, be sent to a prison or lockup where he would be exposed to adult criminals. Instead, the child is screened by an "assessment unit" of the Department of Juvenile Justice. The assessment unit places the child in either nonsecure or secure detention. Nonsecure detention involves an open facility in the community, a sort of "halfway house," without locks, bars, or security officers where the child receives schooling and counseling and has access to recreational facilities.

Secure detention is more restrictive, but it is still consistent with the regulatory and *parens patriae* objectives relied upon by the State. Children are assigned to separate dorms based on age, size, and behavior. They wear street clothes provided by the institution and partake in educational and recreational programs and counseling sessions run by trained social workers. Misbehavior is punished by confinement to one's room. We cannot conclude from this record that the controlled environment briefly imposed by the State on juveniles in secure pretrial detention "is imposed for the purpose of punishment" rather than as "an incident of some other legitimate governmental purpose.". . .

Given the legitimacy of the State's interest in preventive detention, and the nonpunitive nature of that detention, the remaining question is whether the procedures afforded juveniles detained prior to factfinding provide sufficient protection against erroneous and unnecessary deprivations of liberty. In Gerstein v. Pugh, we held that a judicial determination of probable cause is a prerequisite to any extended restraint on the liberty of an adult accused of crime. We did not, however, mandate a specific timetable. Nor did we require the "full panoply of adversary safeguards—counsel, confrontation, cross-examination, and compulsory process for witnesses." Instead, we recognized "the desirability of flexibility and experimentation by the States." *Gerstein* arose under the Fourth Amendment, but the same concern with "flexibility" and "informality," while yet ensuring adequate predetention procedures, is present in this context.

In many respects, the FCA provides far more predetention protection for juveniles than we found to be constitutionally required for a probable-cause determination for adults in *Gerstein*. The initial appearance is informal, but the accused juvenile is given full notice of the charges against him and a complete stenographic record is kept of the hearing. The juvenile appears accompanied by his parent or guardian. He is first informed of his rights, including the right to remain silent and the right to be represented by counsel chosen by him or by a law guardian assigned by the court. The initial appearance may be adjourned for no longer than 72 hours or until the next court day, whichever is sooner, to enable an appointed law guardian or other counsel to appear before the court. When his counsel is present, the juvenile is informed of the charges against him and furnished with a copy of the delinquency petition. A representative from the presentment agency appears in support of the petition.

The nonhearsay allegations in the delinquency petition and supporting depositions must establish probable cause to believe the juvenile committed the offense. Although the Family Court judge is not required to make a finding of probable cause at the initial appearance, the youth may challenge the sufficiency of the petition on that ground. Thus, the juvenile may oppose any recommended detention by arguing that there is not probable cause to believe he committed the offense or offenses with which he is charged. If the petition is not dismissed, the juvenile is given an opportunity to admit or deny the charges.

At the conclusion of the initial appearance, the presentment agency makes a recommendation regarding detention. A probation officer reports on the juvenile's record, including other prior and current Family Court and probation contacts, as well as relevant information concerning home life, school attendance, and any special medical or developmental problems. He concludes by offering his agency's recommendation on detention. Opposing counsel, the juvenile's parents, and the juvenile himself may all speak on his behalf and challenge any information or recommendation. If the judge does decide to detain the juvenile . . ., he must state on the record the facts and reasons for the detention.

As noted, a detained juvenile is entitled to a formal, adversarial probable-cause hearing within three days of his initial appearance, with one 3-day extension possible for good cause shown. The burden at this hearing is on the presentment agency to call witnesses and offer evidence in support of the charges. Testimony is under oath and subject to cross-examination. The accused juvenile may call witnesses and offer evidence in his own behalf. If the court finds probable cause, the court must again decide whether continued detention is necessary. . . . Again, the facts and reasons for the detention must be stated on the record. . . .

Appellees argue, however, that the risk of erroneous and unnecessary detentions is too high despite these procedures because the standard for detention is fatally vague. Detention . . . is based on a finding that there is a "serious risk" that the juvenile, if released, would commit a crime prior to his next court appearance. . . . [A]ppellees claim, and the District Court agreed, that it is virtually impossible to predict future criminal conduct with any degree of accuracy. Moreover, they say, the statutory standard fails to channel the discretion of the Family Court judge by specifying the factors on which he should rely in making that prediction. The procedural protections noted above are thus, in their view, unavailing because the ultimate decision is intrinsically arbitrary and uncontrolled.

Our cases indicate, however, that from a legal point of view there is nothing inherently unattainable about a prediction of future criminal conduct. Such a judgment forms an important element in many decisions, and we have specifically rejected the contention, based on the same sort of sociological data relied upon by appellees and the District Court, "that it is impossible to predict future behavior and that the question is so vague as to be meaningless." . . .

We have also recognized that a prediction of future criminal conduct is "an experienced prediction based on a host of variables" which cannot be readily codified. Judge Quinones of the Family Court testified at trial that he and his colleagues make a determination . . . based on numerous factors including the nature and seriousness of the charges; whether the charges are likely to be proved at trial; the juvenile's prior record; the adequacy and effectiveness of his home supervision; his school situation, if known; the time of day of the alleged crime as evidence of its seriousness and a possible lack of parental control; and any special circumstances that might be brought to his attention by the probation officer, the child's attorney, or any parents, relatives, or other responsible persons accompanying the child. The decision is based on as much information as can reasonably be obtained at the initial appearance. . . .

Justice MARSHALL, with whom Justice BRENNAN and Justice STEVENS join, dissenting. The New York Family Court Act governs the treatment of persons between 7 and 16 years of age who are alleged to have committed acts that, if committed by adults, would constitute crimes. The Act contains two provisions that authorize the detention of juveniles arrested for offenses covered by the Act for up to 17 days pending adjudication of their guilt. Section 320.5(3)(a) empowers a judge of the New York Family Court to order detention of a juvenile if he finds "there is a substantial probability that [the juvenile] will not appear in court on the return date." Section 320.5(3)(b), the provision at issue in these cases, authorizes detention if the judge finds "there is a serious risk [the juvenile] may before the return date commit an act which if committed by an adult would constitute a crime."

There are few limitations on § 320.5(3)(b). Detention need not be predicated on a finding that there is probable cause to believe the child committed the offense for which he was arrested. The provision applies to all juveniles, regardless of their prior records or the severity of the offenses of which they are accused. The provision is not limited to the prevention of dangerous crimes; a prediction that a juvenile if released may commit a minor misdemeanor is sufficient to justify his detention. Aside from the reference to "serious risk," the requisite likelihood that the juvenile will misbehave before his trial is not specified by the statute.

The Court today holds that preventive detention of a juvenile . . . does not violate the Due Process Clause. Two rulings are essential to the Court's decision: that the provision promotes legitimate government objectives important enough to justify the abridgment of the detained juveniles' liberty interests, and that the provision incorporates procedural safeguards sufficient to prevent unnecessary or arbitrary impairment of constitutionally protected rights. Because I disagree with both of those rulings, I dissent. . . .

In the typical case, the judge appoints counsel for the juvenile at the time his case is called. Thus, the lawyer has no opportunity to make an independent inquiry into the juvenile's background or character, and has only a few minutes to prepare arguments on the child's behalf. The judge ordinarily does not interview the juvenile, makes no inquiry into the truth of allegations in the petition, and does not determine whether there is probable cause to believe the juvenile committed the offense. The typical hearing lasts between 5 and 15 minutes, and the judge renders his decision immediately afterward.

Neither the statute nor any other body of rules guides the efforts of the judge to determine whether a given juvenile is likely to commit a crime before his trial. In making detention decisions, "each judge must rely on his own subjective judgment, based on the limited information available to him at court intake and whatever personal standards he himself has developed in exercising his discretionary authority under the statute." Family Court judges are not provided information regarding the behavior of juveniles over whose cases they have presided, so a judge has no way of refining the standards he employs in making detention decisions. . . .

NOTES AND QUESTIONS

1. Is the Court's discussion of the child's liberty interest closer to the analysis in In re Gault or in traditional juvenile court theory?

2. In support of the suggestion that juveniles, unlike adults, are "always in some form of custody" and thus his reliance on the *parens patriae* doctrine, Justice Rehnquist cites Santosky v. Kramer, 455 U.S. 745 (1982), which is set out

in Chapter 8 at page 752. *Santosky* involves an action to terminate parental rights because of parental neglect. The state asserts an interest in protecting the well-being of the children, and its opponents are the parents who have allegedly maltreated the children. When the Court talks about the child's "right" in *Santosky*, does that term have the same meaning that it has in *Gault* and other juvenile delinquency cases?

3. How does the majority reach the conclusion that secure detention does not count as punishment and thus is allowable? Is the understanding of punishment in *Schall* the same understanding employed by the Court in earlier delinquency cases?

4. Most courts have held that "fundamental fairness" under the Due Process Clause does not require that juveniles detained on delinquency charges be allowed to post bail. *E.g.*, State v. M.L.C., 933 P.2d 380 (Utah 1997); In re Gillespie, 782 N.E.2d 140 (Ohio App. 2002). However, several states allow some form of release on bond. *See, e.g.*, Ga. Code Ann. § 15-11-507(a) (2018); Mass. Gen. L. Ann. 119 § 68 (2018); Neb. Rev. Stat. § 43-253(5) (2018).

5. In Gerstein v. Pugh, 420 U.S. 103 (1975), the Supreme Court held for the first time that a judge must find probable cause to believe the defendant committed a criminal act before he or she can be detained for an extended period following arrest. The Court distinguished the application of the Fourth Amendment to arrest and detention in the following way:

> Maximum protection of individual rights could be assured by requiring a magistrate's review of the factual justification prior to any arrest, but such a requirement would constitute an intolerable handicap for legitimate law enforcement. Thus, while the Court has expressed a preference for the use of arrest warrants when feasible, it has never invalidated an arrest supported by probable cause solely because the officers failed to secure a warrant.
>
> Under this practical compromise, a policeman's on-the-scene assessment of probable cause provides legal justification for arresting a person suspected of crime, and for a brief period of detention to take the administrative steps incident to arrest. Once the suspect is in custody, however, the reasons that justify dispensing with the magistrate's neutral judgment evaporate. There no longer is any danger that the suspect will escape or commit further crimes while the police submit their evidence to a magistrate. And, while the State's reasons for taking summary action subside, the suspect's need for a neutral determination of probable cause increases significantly. The consequences of prolonged detention may be more serious than the interference occasioned by arrest. Pretrial confinement may imperil the suspect's job, interrupt his source of income, and impair his family relationships. Even pretrial release may be accompanied by burdensome conditions that effect a significant restraint of liberty. When the stakes are this high, the detached judgment of a neutral magistrate is essential if the Fourth Amendment is to furnish meaningful protection from unfounded interference with liberty. Accordingly, we hold that the Fourth Amendment requires a judicial determination of probable cause as a prerequisite to extended restraint of liberty following arrest.

Id. at 113-114.

However, the Court did not require that this judicial determination "be accompanied by the full panoply of adversary safeguards." The Court said that use of informal procedures "is justified not only by the lesser consequences of a probable cause determination [when compared with trial] but also by the nature of the determination itself. It does not require the fine resolution of conflicting evidence that a reasonable-doubt or even a preponderance standard demands, and credibility determinations are seldom crucial in deciding whether the evidence supports a reasonable belief in guilt." *Id.* at 121.

A determination that "probable cause" exists to believe a youth has committed an offense ordinarily requires sworn evidence, even though that evidence may be presented by affidavit or petition.

6. In *Gerstein*, the Supreme Court held that the Fourth Amendment requires a "*timely* judicial determination" of probable cause as a prerequisite to detention. The Court did not say what it meant by "timely." That question was partially answered in Riverside v. McLaughlin, 500 U.S. 44 (1991), where the Court held that a probable cause determination within 48 hours of arrest was presumptively reasonable and that a later probable cause determination is presumptively unreasonable. By "presumptively," the Court meant that the burden shifts to the government to demonstrate the existence of some extraordinary circumstance requiring longer than 48 hours.

In *Schall*, however, the Court appeared to hold that a 72-hour detention prior to the probable cause hearing did not violate the Fourth Amendment. The question becomes whether *McLaughlin*'s strict 48-hour rule, announced after the decision in *Schall*, applies to juvenile as well as adult hearings. The courts are divided. *See* Alfredo A. v. Superior Court, 865 P.2d 56 (Cal. 1994); Shaheem P. v. Carbone, In re Doe, 73 P.3d 29 (Hi. 2003); Matter of Jordan, 616 N.E.2d 388 (Ind. App. 1993); State ex rel. C.R., 976 So. 2d 243 (La. 2008); State v. K.K.H., 878 P.2d 1255 (Wash. App. 1994).

JEFFREY FAGAN & MARTIN GUGGENHEIM, *PREVENTIVE DETENTION AND THE JUDICIAL PREDICTION OF DANGEROUSNESS OF JUVENILES: A NATURAL EXPERIMENT*

86 J. Crim. L. & Criminology 415, 432-435, 437-439 (1996)

The Supreme Court in *Schall* allowed the preventive detention of juveniles once a judge concluded that there was a "serious risk" that the juvenile would commit any crime, no matter how trivial, if released. This breadth is obviously problematic. Several states allow for preventive detention under statutes that lack specific references to public safety concerns. In [United States v. Salerno, 481 U.S. 739 (1987)], however, the Court upheld a rather specific preventive detention law which authorized detention only for the following crimes: (1) a crime of violence; (2) a crime punishable by life imprisonment or death; (3) a major drug offense; or (4) a felony committed by a person previously convicted of two of the crimes listed. In *Salerno*, the Supreme Court characterized preventive detention as the "civil regulation of a dangerous person." This definition of dangerousness encompasses three dimensions of criminal behavior: (1) chronicity; (2) assaultive behavior; and

(3) particular crimes (in this case, drug offenses) that have been assigned a unique societal threat.

Most states define categories of defendants who are eligible for preventive detention. Eligibility entails a variety of criteria: charged offense, prior record, probation, or parole status at the time of arrest, pretrial release status at the time of arrest, threats to witnesses or jurors following arrest, and risk assessments of "dangerousness." Such criteria speak more to descriptions of defendants rather than the harms or acts they are anticipated to commit. Although it is not the sole determinant for defining eligibility for denial of release, the severity of the current charge is the primary criterion in most states. However, the states vary widely in the scope of the current charge. Moreover, specificity in the designation of classes of defendants eligible for preventive detention does not make these statutes specific with respect to standards. Even when "danger" or "public safety" concerns are explicit, most states fail to provide operational standards or definitions for these constructs. . . .

We assessed the validity of judicial predictions of dangerousness in two ways. First, the arrest histories of the *Schall* cases were examined to determine whether predictions of dangerousness during the pretrial period were accurate. Second, the base rates of rearrest were examined for a matched sample of juvenile offenders drawn from the time period when the *Schall* injunction was in effect. This group was identical to the *Schall* group and provided an estimate of the marginal gain in predictive efficiency from the judicial determination of dangerousness. These offenders were not detained during the pretrial period. . . .

Most offenders were males (over 92%), African-American (about 60%), and 14.5 years of age at the time of the sample arrest. About one-in-three were charged with a violent offense, and over half were charged with non-violent felony offenses. One-in-ten had no prior record. Defendants with at least one prior apprehension had an average of three prior apprehensions. Over 45% had at least one prior apprehension for a violent offense. Among both *Schall* and control cases, four-in-ten (42.9%) had neither a prior nor a current charge for a violent felony offense, suggesting that the assessment of their "dangerousness" was unrelated to their involvement in violent crimes.

There were no significant differences in any of the social or legal characteristics of the groups. *Schall* and control cases differed only on the judicial determination of risk that the accused would commit a crime if released. The bases for this determination may be reflected in data not available systematically: the defendant's physical appearance and demeanor in the courtroom, the presence of a family member at the detention hearing, presence or use of weapons, or injury to victims. . . .

Social and legal histories were constructed for the *Schall* and control samples from official records in the Kings County (Brooklyn) and Queens County Family Courts in New York City, and the City Probation Department and the Department of Juvenile Justice (the detention authority). Social histories were limited to social structural characteristics since other information (defendants' family composition, school performance, and other social behaviors) was not uniformly available from any of the data sources.

Complete juvenile and criminal histories were compiled for the interval from the subject's first family court appearance through October 31, 1987; those histories were segmented for the periods preceding and following the sample arrest. Family court histories were constructed from the same data sources. Adult criminal histories were constructed from two sources: New York City criminal court arraignments and state criminal justice records. Criminal history information included the dates, charges, and dispositions of all court appearances. . . .

. . . [T]he fairest measure of time within which a judge should be concerned with the juvenile's out-of-court behavior is the maximum time within which the trial must occur—the period from arraignment through the trial. Once the trial has been held, one of two things will occur which will materially change the status of the accused. If the accused is acquitted, the court's power to detain evaporates, even if there still remains reason to believe there is a "serious risk" that he or she will commit a crime. If the accused is convicted, the presumption of innocence has been overcome. If detention is continued, it no longer is pretrial. Detention after conviction, even before final sentencing, may be for punitive purposes. [In New York City,] the period from initial court appearance through final disposition for delinquency petitions is ninety days. Accordingly, the *Schall* and control groups were compared for all rearrests and specifically for violent offenses within ninety days. To further assess the validity of predictions of dangerousness, we have also looked at rearrests beyond ninety days. . . .

Schall defendants were more likely to be rearrested within the ninety day period, regardless of the type of rearrest. Over 40% of the *Schall* defendants were rearrested within ninety days, compared to only 15.6% of the controls (chi^2 = 16.18, p = .006). For violent offenses, 18.8% of the *Schall* defendants were rearrested, compared to 7.8% of the controls (chi^2 = 6.82, p = .033). Evidently, for all rearrests, judges accurately identified a group of defendants that posed a higher risk of subsequent rearrest during the ninety day period when their cases typically reached conclusion.

The marginal gain in predictive efficiency for the *Schall* cases is tempered by the high rate of false prediction. . . . Nearly six-out-of-ten (59.4%) of the *Schall* defendants were not rearrested within the ninety day period, compared to about five-out-of-six (84.4%) of the control cases. When violent felony offenses are applied as the standard for evaluating preventive detention decisions, consistent with the Bail Reform Act criteria for dangerousness, the false prediction rate for judicial decisions rises. More than eight-in-ten (81.2%) *Schall* defendants were not rearrested for violent offenses during the ninety day period, compared to more than nine-in-ten (92.2%) control cases. Accordingly, while predictions of subsequent crime within ninety days are effective, predictions of violence or danger are less accurate.

Statutes authorizing preventive detention commonly mention violence as a decision standard for assessing pretrial danger. After controlling for evidence of violence in both the current charge and prior violence, the results suggest even more modest differences. For rearrests for any offense, [the study] shows significant differences only for any rearrest; for violent felonies, differences exist with those current charges. Of the *Schall* defendants with both current and prior violence charges, 58.8% were rearrested for any crime within ninety days, compared to 20% of the controls (p[chi^2]= .040). None of the control defendants charged with violent crimes but with no history of violence were rearrested, compared to 41.7% of the *Schall* cases (p[chi^2]= .027]). For rearrests for violent offenses, the comparisons failed to produce significant differences.

For defendants charged with other felonies, there were no significant differences in rearrest within ninety days, regardless of prior record or type of rearrest. For defendants charged with misdemeanors, few were rearrested within the ninety day period. In fact, the rearrest rates within ninety days were zero for nearly all groups. The results show that even when defendants meet statutory standards for past dangerousness, predictions of their future dangerousness are unreliable.

On preventive detention in the adult criminal system, including analyses of the empirical data and policy analysis, *see* Sandra G. Mayson, Dangerous Defendants, 127 Yale L. J. 490 (2018).

In 1992 the Annie E. Casey Foundation launched the Juvenile Detention Alternatives Initiative to improve detention practices by establishing more effective, efficient, and fair ways of determining which alleged delinquents are detained pretrial. The program operates in more than 300 counties in 39 states and the District of Columbia. A number of states have revised their detention policies and practices in conjunction with JDAI or independently. The changes generally seek to limit the use of secure detention to only young people who are dangerous or who present a serious risk of not appearing that cannot be solved by other means. An important part of the reform is developing alternatives, such as home detention, electronic monitoring, and day and evening reporting centers. Reformers also call for guiding decisionmakers' discretion through the use of risk assessment tools that allow more systematic analysis of the risks that each child presents. Anne S. Teigen, Legislative Reforms in Juvenile Detention and the Justice System (NCSL 2015). In 2017, JDAI sites reported a reduction of 43 percent in the number of youths in detention on an average day, compared to the number detained before JDAI was implemented, and a 49 percent decrease in admissions to detention facilities. Levels of juvenile crime in the reporting communities declined by an average of more than 40 percent. Annie E. Casey Foundation, JDAI at 25 (2017), https://www.aecf.org/m/resourcedoc/aecf-jdaiat25-2017.pdf.

Other reforms include prohibition of solitary confinement of young people and limits on the use of shackles. In some states, shackles, which include a variety of physical restraints such as handcuffs, straitjackets, leg irons, belly chains and others, are automatically used on all minors coming from secure detention facilities, both while they are being transported and while they are in court. Statutes, court decisions, or court rules in 24 states and the District of Columbia prohibit the use of unnecessary restraints. Since early 2016, solitary confinement for juvenile offenders has been prohibited in the federal prison system, and 19 states also forbid it. Anne Teigen, States that Limit or Prohibit Juvenile Shackling and Solitary Confinement (July 16, 2018), http://www.ncsl.org/research/civil-and-criminal-justice/states-that-limit-or-prohibit-juvenile-shackling-and-solitary-confinement635572628.aspx.

NOTE: DETENTION OF UNDOCUMENTED CHILDREN

In Reno v. Flores, 507 U.S. 292 (1993), the Supreme Court invoked *Schall* in its analysis of the constitutionality of immigration rules that required the detention of unaccompanied minors unless they could be released to parents, close relatives, or legal guardians. Under other immigration rules, an adult could not be detained except on a finding that he or she was a threat to national security or a poor bail risk. The Court ruled that the right to freedom from physical restraint was not at issue because "juveniles, unlike adults, are always in some form of custody, and where the custody of the parent or legal guardian fails, the government may (indeed, we have said *must*) either exercise custody itself or appoint someone else to do so." 507 U.S. at 302, citing *Schall*.

The minors in *Flores* did not seek the right to be released on their own recognizance but rather claimed a right to be released to other institutional or individual custodians rather than being held in secure detention. The Court rejected this claim, saying, "We are unaware . . . that any court . . . has ever held that a child has a constitutional right not to be placed in a decent and humane custodial institution if there is available a responsible person unwilling to become the child's legal guardian but willing to undertake temporary legal custody. The mere novelty of such a claim is reason enough to doubt that 'substantive due process' sustains it. . . . Where a juvenile has no available parent, close relative, or legal guardian, where the government does not intend to punish the child, and where the conditions of governmental custody are decent and humane, such custody surely does not violate the Constitution." 507 U.S. at 303.

In 1996, the government and the petitioners entered into a settlement agreement that allows unaccompanied minors to be released to any adult who executes an agreement to care for the child and guarantees his or her presence at immigration proceedings. In 2001 the parties stipulated that the settlement would terminate 45 days after the government published final regulations applying the settlement, but that has not yet occurred. The settlement agreement and extension are available at https://www.aclu.org/legal-document/flores-v-meese-stipulated-settlement-agreement-plus-extension-settlement.

As more undocumented families entered the United States in 2014, the federal government briefly detained families, including children, rather than citing and releasing them as had been the earlier practice. However, Flores v. Lynch, 828 F.3d 898 (9th Cir. 2016), held that the agreement applied to children accompanied by their parents, and the office of Immigration and Customs Enforcement resumed the earlier policy of citation and release. In 2018, after abandoning the policy of deliberately separating undocumented children and parents, the Trump administration began looking for ways to supersede the Flores settlement. In September 2018 the Department of Homeland Security and Health and Human Services issued proposed rules to replace the settlement and allow detention of families, including children. 83 FR 45486 (Sept. 7, 2018).

Juvenile Delinquency Cases: Adjudication and Disposition

6

A. ADJUDICATION

As we saw in Chapter 4, United States Supreme Court decisions have addressed some, but by no means all, aspects of juvenile court adjudicatory proceedings. And, of course, the existence of a constitutional standard does not mean that all state proceedings will look alike, since states are free to adopt greater protections for juvenile court respondents than the federal Constitution requires. Even though the Supreme Court left open the possibility that procedural safeguards in juvenile court could differ from those in adult court without violating the Constitution, for the most part courts and legislatures have imported the adult court procedures to juvenile court. This section examines some of the major areas where differences remain. As you think about procedure in delinquency cases, consider the following perspectives on constitutional limits and state choices.

IN RE GAULT

---

387 U.S. 1, 68-72 (1967)

HARLAN, J., concurring in part and dissenting in part. . . . The central issue here, and the principal one upon which I am divided from the Court, is the method by which the procedural requirements of due process should be measured. It must at the outset be emphasized that the protections necessary here cannot be determined by resort to any classification of juvenile proceedings either as criminal or as civil, whether made by the State or by this Court. Both formulae are simply too imprecise to permit reasoned analysis of these difficult constitutional issues. The Court should instead measure the requirements of due process by reference both to the problems which confront the State and to the actual character of the procedural system which the State has created. The Court has for such purposes chiefly examined three connected sources: first, the "settled usages and modes of proceeding," second, the "fundamental principles of liberty and justice which lie at the base of all our civil and political institutions," and third, the character and requirements of the circumstances presented in each situation. Each of these factors is relevant to the issues here, but it is the last which demands particular examination. . . .

The foregoing considerations, which I believe to be fair distillations of relevant judicial history, suggest three criteria by which the procedural requirements of due process should be measured here: first, no more restrictions should be imposed than are imperative to assure the proceedings' fundamental fairness; second, the restrictions which are imposed should be those which preserve, so far as possible, the essential elements of the State's purpose; and finally, restrictions should be chosen which will later permit the orderly selection of any additional protections which may ultimately prove necessary. In this way, the Court may guarantee the fundamental fairness of the proceeding, and yet permit the State to continue development of an effective response to the problems of juvenile crime.

Measured by these criteria, only three procedural requirements should, in my opinion, now be deemed required of state juvenile courts by the Due Process Clause of the Fourteenth Amendment: first, timely notice must be provided to parents and children of the nature and terms of any juvenile court proceeding in which a determination affecting their rights or interests may be made; second, unequivocal and timely notice must be given that counsel may appear in any such proceeding in behalf of the child and its parents, and that in cases in which the child may be confined in an institution, counsel may, in circumstances of indigency, be appointed for them; and third, the court must maintain a written record, or its equivalent, adequate to permit effective review on appeal or in collateral proceedings. These requirements would guarantee to juveniles the tools with which their rights could be fully vindicated, and yet permit the States to pursue without unnecessary hindrance the purposes which they believe imperative in this field. Further, their imposition now would later permit more intelligent assessment of the necessity under the Fourteenth Amendment of additional requirements, by creating suitable records from which the character and deficiencies of juvenile proceedings could be accurately judged. I turn to consider each of these three requirements.

The Court has consistently made plain that adequate and timely notice is the fulcrum of due process, whatever the purposes of the proceeding. Notice is ordinarily the prerequisite to effective assertion of any constitutional or other rights; without it, vindication of those rights must be essentially fortuitous. So fundamental a protection can neither be spared here nor left to the "favor or grace" of state authorities. Provision of counsel and of a record, like adequate notice, would permit the juvenile to assert very much more effectively his rights and defenses, both in the juvenile proceedings and upon direct or collateral review. The Court has frequently emphasized their importance in proceedings in which an individual may be deprived of his liberty, this reasoning must include with special force those who are commonly inexperienced and immature. The facts of this case illustrate poignantly the difficulties of review without either an adequate record or the participation of counsel in the proceeding's initial stages. At the same time, these requirements should not cause any substantial modification in the character of juvenile court proceedings: counsel, although now present in only a small percentage of juvenile cases, have apparently already appeared without incident in virtually all juvenile courts; and the maintenance of a record should not appreciably alter the conduct of these proceedings.

The question remains whether certain additional requirements, among them the privilege against self-incrimination, confrontation, and cross-examination, must now, as the Court holds, also be imposed.... [T]here are compelling reasons at least to defer imposition of these additional requirements. First, quite unlike notice, counsel, and a record, these requirements might radically alter the character of juvenile court proceedings.... At the least, it is plain that these additional requirements would contribute materially to the creation in these proceedings of the atmosphere of an ordinary criminal trial, and would, even if they do no more, thereby largely frustrate a central purpose of these specialized courts. Further, these are restrictions intended to conform to the demands of an intensely adversary system of criminal justice; the broad purposes which they represent might be served in juvenile courts with equal effectiveness by procedural devices more consistent with the premises of proceedings in those courts. As the Court apparently acknowledges, the hazards of self-accusation, for example, might be avoided in juvenile proceedings without the imposition of all the requirements and limitations which surround the privilege against self-incrimination. The guarantee of adequate notice, counsel, and a record would create conditions in which suitable alternative procedures could be devised; but, unfortunately, the Court's haste to impose restrictions taken intact from criminal procedure may well seriously hamper the development of such alternatives....

TAMAR R. BIRCKHEAD, *TOWARD A THEORY OF PROCEDURAL JUSTICE FOR JUVENILES*

57 Buff. L. Rev. 1447, 1458-1459, 1476-1483 (2009)

[In *Gault*] the Court stated that [the procedural safeguards of the right to counsel, the privilege against self-incrimination, and the opportunity for cross-examination of witnesses] may, in fact, be "more impressive and therapeutic" for the juvenile than the long-assumed benefits of the juvenile system — namely, its informality and the benevolence and compassion of the judge. Citing a 1966 report on juvenile delinquency by sociologists Stanton Wheeler and Leonard Cottrell, the Court recognized that when harsh punitive measures come on the heels of "procedural laxness," a child may feel that she has been "deceived or enticed." As Wheeler and Cottrell have stated, "Unless appropriate due process of law is followed, even the juvenile who has violated the law may not feel that he is being fairly treated and may therefore resist the rehabilitative efforts of court personnel."...

Behavioral psychologists who have studied adolescent populations have generally focused on a question closely related to that of why people obey the law — what factors shape adolescent criminal behavior? While these researchers have agreed that children's compliance with the law is promoted by the processes of maturation and psychosocial development, some have recognized further that legal socialization is a process that is not static between childhood and adolescence but variable, changing over time and developing concurrently with a child's cognitive and moral maturation; it is profoundly affected by one's peers, family unit, and neighborhood culture; and it is interactive and integrative, a process in which children internalize information that is assimilated from their own experiences, from the attitudes and factual claims of others, and from the ways in which others react and respond to them. The core argument underpinning the literature in this area is that children develop an orientation toward the law and legal actors early in life, and that this orientation shapes their behavior towards authority from adolescence through adulthood.

Research in this area has shown that a myriad of factors combine to shape and influence the law-related behavior of children and adolescents, including institutional legitimacy, an obligation to obey the law from a normative perspective; legal cynicism, one's sense of whether it is acceptable to act outside the law and social norms; and the impact of moral ambiguity and disengagement, processes by which adolescents detach from the system of internal controls and moral values and become more open to illegal behavior. Additional factors shaping criminal behavior include the deterrent effect of punitive sanctions, in which punishment that is perceived to be "swift, certain, and severe" inhibits criminal activity, and the theory of rational choice, whereby behavior is determined by the weighing of the costs and benefits associated with violating the law. Research has suggested, however, that active adolescent offenders may be less sensitive to the threat of sanctions and rational choice theory than either adults or young people who have not previously engaged in criminal activity; the reasons are twofold — immaturity causes youth not only to underestimate the level of risk but also to downplay the threat of punishment that is oriented toward the future rather than the present. Intellectual and psychosocial deficits caused by developmental delays, mental illness, and drug dependency can also "impair or skew" rational calculations of risk and reward made by adolescents.

Not surprisingly, procedural justice also plays a significant role in the process of legal socialization, as social scientists have demonstrated that perceptions of fair treatment enhance children's evaluations of the law, while unfair treatment triggers negative reactions, anger, and defiance of the law's norms. Specifically, researchers have found that children's perceptions of fair procedures are based on the degree to which the child was given the opportunity to express her feelings or concerns, the neutrality and fact-based quality of the decision-making process, whether the child was treated with respect and politeness, and whether the authorities appeared to be acting out of benevolent and caring motives. In this way, procedural justice directly affects compliance with the law, while indirectly affecting whether one views the law as legitimate. . . .

In recent decades, social scientists have focused their research more deliberately upon the question of whether a causal connection between procedural justice and rates of reoffending by juveniles may be shown through data analysis . . . . The data from [recent studies in this area], which have focused to varying degrees on the relevance of adolescents' views of the legitimacy of legal institutions and legal actors, suggest a causal connection between procedural justice and recidivism that is not outcome-dependent. While all such studies have their limitations, a consistent trend based on multiple data sets may be seen. . . .

. . . However, while the United States Supreme Court recognized the import of procedural justice theory and its potential impact on juveniles' recidivism rates in 1967, this connection has not been advanced in Supreme Court jurisprudence since *Gault*. While a handful of lower federal courts and some state courts have referenced the work of social scientists when determining whether juveniles should be granted specific due process protections, this is only one of many areas in which lawmakers and legal authorities would benefit from a fuller understanding of social psychology.

MARK R. FONDACARO, CHRISTOPHER SLOBOGIN & TRICIA CROSS,
RECONCEPTUALIZING DUE PROCESS IN JUVENILE JUSTICE:
CONTRIBUTIONS FROM LAW AND SOCIAL SCIENCE

57 Hastings, L.J. 955, 984-986 (2006)

The upshot of the procedural justice research is that the automatic equation of adversarial procedures and "fairness" or accuracy is not warranted. It may well be that, in some settings, alternatives to a process in which parties represented by counsel are responsible for providing and challenging evidence better promote both subjective and objective justice, and will often cost less as well. The central question raised by this Article is whether the juvenile delinquency proceeding is one of those settings. . . .

[F]irst and foremost, . . . questions about the appropriate procedure in the juvenile justice system [must] be recast into empirical hypotheses rather than framed, as they have been up to now, by reference to adult criminal procedure requirements. Whether decisionmaking accuracy and fairness are best promoted by a judge, a hearing officer, or a layperson; multiple or single decisionmakers; and the rights to cross-examination, silence and the assistance of counsel are all empirical questions.

Of course, these questions are pertinent in the adult criminal justice setting as well. A fundamental fairness/performance-based approach to answering them requires, as Justices Harlan and Frankfurter emphasized, that any special attributes of the setting in question be taken into account. In the juvenile justice context, these special aspects might include the facts that juveniles tend to be dependent on and under the authority of others, are less likely than adults to be competent to make the types of decisions that arise in the legal arena, and are less willing than adults to reveal their thoughts and feelings. They may also be particularly sensitive to any failure on the part of legal actors to listen to their story and treat them with dignity. Taking these considerations into account, we should be open to the possibility that juveniles charged with crime will respond better to "social-worker" judges than distant, passive decisionmakers, and that informal hearings are more likely than public, jury trials to produce an environment conducive to obtaining relevant adjudicative and dispositional facts. We should also be willing to contemplate the possibilities that party control of evidence obfuscates rather than clarifies, that rigorous cross-examination is not the "greatest legal engine ever invented for the discovery of truth," and that unfamiliar defense counsel and rules of evidence curb juveniles' ability to tell their story. Research on "teen courts," for instance, suggests that an adjudicative process that mimics aspects of the European inquisitorial model might be more "therapeutic" for juveniles and more effective at curbing their antisocial behavior than the traditional adversarial model.

Finally, . . . the spirit of ongoing evaluation and feedback characterizes . . . assessment of the system's ability to promote substantive policy objectives, such as rehabilitation, crime prevention, deterrence, restitution, and retribution. As Mathews [v. Eldridge, 424 U.S. 319 (1976),] itself suggested, inquisitorial methods might be perceived as fairer and more accurate when the inquiry is "scientific," and thus might be preferable when the decision is a clinical judgment about whether a juvenile needs treatment to prevent recidivism (the principal goal of a preventive-rehabilitative system) rather than a moral judgment about blameworthiness and punishment. Even if, however, the juvenile justice system continues its trend toward a punitive regime, the choice between the traditional adversarial model and a more investigative approach is not a foregone conclusion, as the European example illustrates. The procedural choice should not be based, as it has largely been up to now, on whether the juvenile justice system is genuinely therapeutic (and therefore does not require more "protective" adversarial procedures), but rather should be driven primarily by an empirical assessment of which procedural mix best achieves the goals of the system, whatever they are. . . .

1.   *The Right to a Jury Trial*

Since McKeiver v. Pennsylvania was decided, most, if not all, states have revised their juvenile codes to incorporate policies reflecting concerns for deterrence and retribution in addition to or in place of traditional juvenile court concerns for individualized treatment and rehabilitation of offenders. This trend raises the questions of whether states that did adopt jury trial can now abandon it and whether states that followed *McKeiver* but have responded to the public concern over serious juvenile crime must now adopt trial by jury. The next case offers contrasting views about the impact of punitive changes in juvenile codes on the procedural rights of juveniles.

IN RE L.M.

---

186 P.3d 164 (Kan. 2008)

ROSEN, J. . . . Sixteen-year-old L.M. was charged and prosecuted as a juvenile offender on one count of aggravated sexual battery and one count of minor in possession of alcohol. The facts leading up to these charges involve a sexually suggestive confrontation between L.M. and a neighbor who was walking home. Further discussion of the facts is not relevant to the issue on appeal and will not be discussed herein. L.M. requested a jury trial, and the district court denied his request. After a trial to the bench, the district court found L.M. guilty as charged. The district court sentenced L.M. as a Serious Offender I to a term of 18 months in a juvenile correctional facility but stayed his sentence and ordered L.M. to be placed on probation until he was 20 years old. In addition, the district court ordered L.M. to complete sex offender treatment and register as a sex offender in accordance with K.S.A. 2005 Supp. 22-4906.

L.M. appealed to the Court of Appeals . . . . The Court of Appeals affirmed . . . . We granted L.M.'s petition for review.

L.M. is challenging the constitutionality of K.S.A. 2006 Supp. 38-2344(d), which provides that a juvenile who pleads not guilty is entitled to a "trial to the court," and K.S.A. 2006 Supp. 38-2357, and which gives the district court complete discretion in determining whether a juvenile should be granted a jury trial. . . .

Kansas has previously resolved this issue against L.M.'s position. Twenty-four years ago, under the statutes then controlling the disposition of juvenile offender cases, this court held that juveniles do not have a constitutional right to a jury trial under either the federal or state constitutions. *Findlay v. State*, 681 P.2d 20 (1984). Acknowledging that the Sixth Amendment applies only to criminal prosecutions, the *Findlay* court concluded that juvenile adjudications then were not criminal prosecutions based on K.S.A.1982 Supp. 38-1601, which provided:

> 'K.S.A.1982 Supp. 38-1601 through 38-1685 shall be known and may be cited as the Kansas juvenile offenders code and shall be liberally construed to the end that each juvenile coming within its provisions shall receive the care, custody, guidance, control and discipline, preferably in the juvenile's own home, as will best serve the juvenile's rehabilitation and the protection of society. *In no case shall any order, judgment or decree of the district court, in any proceedings under the provisions of this code, be deemed or held to import a criminal act on the part of any juvenile; but all proceedings, orders, judgments and decrees shall be deemed to have been taken and done in the exercise of the parental power of the state.*' (Emphasis supplied.)

The *Findlay* court also adopted the United States Supreme Court's reasoning in *McKeiver v. Pennsylvania*, 403 U.S. 528 (1971), where a plurality of the Court held that juveniles are not entitled to a jury trial under the Sixth and Fourteenth Amendments to the Constitution. . . .

We begin our analysis by noting that the Kansas Legislature has significantly changed the language of the Kansas Juvenile Offender Code (KJOC) since the *Findlay* court decided this issue 24 years ago. The juvenile code is now called the Revised Kansas Juvenile Justice Code (KJJC). . . .

In 1982, the KJOC was focused on rehabilitation and the State's parental role in providing guidance, control, and discipline. However, under the KJJC, the focus has shifted to protecting the public, holding juveniles accountable for their behavior and choices, and making juveniles more productive and responsible members of society. These purposes are more aligned with the legislative intent for the adult sentencing statutes, which include protecting the public by incarcerating dangerous offenders for a long period of time, holding offenders accountable by prescribing appropriate consequences for their actions, and encouraging offenders to be more productive members of society by considering their individual characteristics, circumstances, needs, and potentialities in determining their sentences.

In addition to being more aligned with the purpose of the criminal sentencing statutes, the KJJC also incorporates language similar to that found in the Kansas Criminal Code and the Kansas Code of Criminal Procedure. Under the KJOC, juveniles were required to admit or deny the allegations against them or plead nolo contendere. Under the KJJC, a juvenile is required to plead guilty, not guilty, or nolo contendere like adults charged with a crime. Although both the KJOC and the KJJC refer to an adjudication rather than a conviction, a "dispositional proceeding" under the KJOC is now referred to as a "sentencing proceeding" in the KJJC. The "State youth center" referred to in the KJOC is now called a "Juvenile correctional facility," which is more akin to an adult "correctional institution." Moreover, the KJJC emulates the language of the Kansas Criminal Code when it refers to the term of commitment to a juvenile correctional facility as a "term of incarceration." This conceptualization of juvenile offenders stresses the similarities between child and adult offenders far more than it does their differences.

The legislature also emulated the structure of the Kansas Sentencing Guidelines when it established a sentencing matrix for juveniles based on the level of the offense committed and, in some cases, the juvenile's history of juvenile adjudications. For example, a juvenile offender found guilty of committing an off-grid felony may be sentenced to "a juvenile correctional facility for a minimum term of 60 months and up to a maximum term of the offender reaching the age of 22 years, six months." A juvenile offender found guilty of committing a level 7, 8, 9, or 10 person felony with one prior felony adjudication may be sentenced to "a juvenile correctional facility for a minimum term of nine months and up to a maximum term of 18 months."

Like the adult sentencing guidelines, the KJJC allows the sentencing judge to depart from the juvenile placement matrix upon a motion by the State or the sentencing judge. The KJJC sentencing judge may consider the aggravating factors. If the sentencing judge departs from the presumptive sentence, he or she must state on the record the substantial and compelling reasons for the departure just as if he or she were sentencing an adult offender. Although any juvenile sentence within the presumptive sentencing range is not subject to appeal, juvenile departure sentences, like adult departure sentences, may be appealed.

The KJJC is also similar to the adult sentencing guidelines in imposing a term of after-care on any juvenile sentenced in accordance with the juvenile placement matrix. Another similarity between the KJJC and the adult sentencing guidelines is the juvenile offender's opportunity to earn good time credits to reduce his or her term of incarceration.

In addition to reflecting the provisions of the sentencing guidelines, the KJJC also establishes sentencing options that are similar to those available for adult offenders. Both adults and juveniles may be sentenced to probation; a community-based program; house arrest; a short-term behavior-modification program like a sanctions house or conservation camp; placement in an out-of-home facility; or incarceration in a correctional facility. The district court also has authority to order both adults and juveniles to attend counseling; drug and alcohol evaluations; mediation; or educational programs. In addition, the district court may require both adults and juveniles to perform charitable or community service; pay restitution; or pay a fine. Sentencing of juveniles has become much more congruent with the adult model.

Besides amending the 1982 version of the KJOC to reflect the purpose and provisions included in the adult criminal code, the legislature has removed some of the protective provisions that made the juvenile system more child-cognizant and confidential, a key consideration in the *McKeiver* plurality decision. In 1982, juvenile proceedings were confidential. . . .

However, under the KJJC, the official file must be open to the public unless a judge orders it to be closed for juveniles under the age of 14 based on finding that it is in the best interests of the juvenile. Similarly, law enforcement records and municipal court records for any juvenile age 14 and over are subject to the same disclosure restrictions as the records for adults. Only juveniles under the age of 14 may have their law enforcement and municipal records kept confidential. The legislature has also eliminated the presumption of confidentiality for hearings, opening all hearings to the public unless the juvenile is under the age of 16 and the judge concludes that a public hearing would not be in the juvenile's best interests.

These changes to the juvenile justice system have eroded the benevolent *parens patriae* character that distinguished it from the adult criminal system. The United States Supreme Court relied on the juvenile justice system's characteristics of fairness, concern, sympathy, and paternal attention in concluding that juveniles were not entitled to a jury trial. *McKeiver*. Likewise, this court relied on that *parens patriae* character in reaching its decision in *Findlay*. However, because the juvenile justice system is now patterned after the adult criminal system, we conclude that the changes have superseded the *McKeiver* and *Findlay* Courts' reasoning and those decisions are no longer binding precedent for us to follow. Based on our conclusion that the Kansas juvenile justice system has become more akin to an adult criminal prosecution, we hold that juveniles have a constitutional right to a jury trial under the Sixth and Fourteenth Amendments. As a result, K.S.A. 2006 Supp. 38-2344(d), which provides that a juvenile who pleads not guilty is entitled to a "trial to the court," and K.S.A. 2006 Supp. 38-2357, which gives the district court discretion in determining whether a juvenile should be granted a jury trial, are unconstitutional.

In reaching this conclusion, we are mindful of decisions in other jurisdictions rejecting the argument that changes to the juvenile justice system have altered its *parens patriae* character. *See* Valdez v. State, 33 Ark. App. 94, 801 S.W.2d 659 (1991); In re Myresheia *W.*, 61 Cal. App. 4th 734, 72 Cal. Rptr. 2d 65 (1998); In re L.C., 273 Ga. 886, 548 S.E.2d 335 (2001); State, ex rel. D.J., 817 So.2d 26 (La. 2002); State v. Gleason, 404 A.2d 573 (Me. 1979); State v. Lawley, 91 Wash.2d 654, 591 P.2d 772 (1979); State v. Schaaf, 109 Wash.2d 1, 10, 12-13, 743 P.2d 240 (1987).

We are also mindful that many of the state courts that have addressed this issue in one form or another have declined to extend the constitutional right to a jury trial to juveniles. *See, e.g.,* David G. v. Pollard ex rel. County of Pima, 207 Ariz. 308, 314, 86 P.3d 364 (2004); A.C., IV v. People, 16 P.3d 240, 244-45 (Colo. 2001); In re J.T., 290 A.2d 821 (D.C.), *cert. denied* 409 U.S. 98, (1972); McMullen v. Geiger, 184 Neb. 581, 584, 169 N.W.2d 431 (1969); R. v. Cory, 353 N.Y.S.2d 783, 44 App. Div. 2d 599 (1974); In re R.Y., 189 N.W.2d 644, 651-53, 655 (N.D. 1971; State v. Hezzie R., 219 Wis.2d 848, 887, 889-90, 919, 580 N.W.2d 660 (1998).

While there is wide variability in the juvenile offender laws throughout the country, it nevertheless seems apparent to us that the KJJC, in its tilt towards applying adult standards of criminal procedure and sentencing, removed the paternalistic protections previously accorded juveniles while continuing to deny those juveniles the constitutional right to a jury trial. Although we do not find total support from the courts in some of our sister states, we are undaunted in our belief that juveniles are entitled to the right to a jury trial guaranteed to all citizens under the Sixth and Fourteenth Amendments to the United States Constitution. . . .

The concurring opinion of Justice LUCKERT is omitted.

McFARLAND, C.J., dissenting. . . . The majority contends that the current juvenile system has changed to be more in line with the adult criminal system in four ways: (1) the policy goals of the juvenile system have shifted from rehabilitation to protection of the public and accountability, goals more akin to those underlying the criminal system; (2) the current juvenile code uses language similar to that used in the criminal codes; (3) juveniles are now subject to determinative sentencing that closely resembles the sentencing guidelines for adults, and the sentencing options available for juvenile offenders are analogous to those available in the adult sentencing system; and (4) some of the protective confidentiality features of the former juvenile system have been eliminated. . . .

The majority contends the amendments in the stated goals evidence a shift from rehabilitation and the State's parental role in providing care, custody, guidance, control, and discipline to protecting the public, holding juveniles accountable, and making juveniles more productive and responsible members of society. What the majority disregards, however, is that in 1982, protection of the public, along with rehabilitation, was an express goal of the juvenile system. . . . Similarly, protection of the public and rehabilitation remain primary goals of the juvenile justice system:

> This act shall be known and may be cited as the revised Kansas juvenile justice code. The primary goals of the juvenile justice code are to *promote public safety*, hold juvenile offenders accountable for their behavior *and improve their ability to live more productively and responsibly in the community*. To accomplish these goals, juvenile justice policies developed pursuant to the revised Kansas juvenile justice code shall be designed to: (a) Protect public safety; (b) recognize that the ultimate solutions to juvenile crime lie in the strengthening of families and educational institutions, the involvement of the community and the implementation of effective prevention and early intervention programs; (c) be community based to the greatest extent possible; (d) be family centered when appropriate; (e) facilitate efficient and effective cooperation, coordination and collaboration among agencies of the local, state and federal government; (f) be outcome based, allowing for the effective and accurate assessment of program performance; (g) be cost-effectively implemented and administered to utilize resources wisely; (h) encourage the recruitment and retention of well-qualified, highly trained professionals to staff all components of the system; (i) appropriately reflect community norms and public priorities; and (j) encourage public and private partnerships to address community risk factors. (Emphasis added.) K.S.A. 2006 Supp. 38-2301.

Although the new statute is much more specific about how its goals will be accomplished, the basic goals of protecting the public and rehabilitating juvenile offenders, *i.e.*, improving the ability of juveniles to live more productively and responsibly in the community, remain consistent.

Moreover, contrary to the majority's contention, these goals are nothing like those set out in the adult sentencing guidelines in K.S.A. 21-4601. . . . That statute makes it clear that in the adult sentencing system, the focus is on the protection of the public through long terms of confinement for dangerous offenders, with imposition of lesser sanctions only where consistent with public safety and the welfare of the offender. There is no language suggesting that rehabilitation is one of the goals of the adult sentencing system.

Language

The majority concludes that the current juvenile code incorporates language similar to that found in the adult system, thus stressing the similarities between juvenile and adult offenders over their differences. . . .

Clearly some of the terminology has changed. And labels are important to some extent — hence the retention of the term adjudication instead of the term conviction. Nevertheless, form must not be placed over substance. If a change in terminology does not reflect any substantive change in the thing or process described, then too much emphasis should not be placed on that terminology. The facilities denominated as state youth centers, and now juvenile correctional facilities, are one and the same. Regardless of their names, these facilities have always been institutions where juvenile offenders are sent to serve a period of court-ordered confinement.

Sentencing

The majority contends that the sentencing scheme and the options available are now more like those in the adult criminal system. . . . Significant differences remain between the two systems that are overlooked by the majority. First, the majority's analysis fails to take into account the difference in the severity of the sentences juveniles face under the matrix for the same crime committed by an adult offender. For example, a juvenile adjudicated for an offense which if committed by an adult would be classified as a nondrug severity level 1 felony offense, would face a minimum term of 24 months and a maximum term that could not extend beyond the juvenile reaching the age of 22 years, 6 months. An adult with no criminal history convicted of a nondrug severity level 1 felony would face a minimum term of 147 months and a maximum term of 165 months. The KJJC also does not allow imposition of consecutive sentences. Additionally, the maximum term of commitment of any juvenile to a juvenile correctional facility is age 22 years, 6 months.

Second, in contrast to the adult sentencing guidelines, the sentences provided under the juvenile sentencing matrix are not mandatory. Commitment to a juvenile correctional facility for a term under the matrix is only *one* of a number of sentencing alternatives available to a juvenile judge. Thus, the judge has discretion in deciding whether to sentence a juvenile to a juvenile correctional facility. If that option is chosen, however, the court must impose the applicable sentence specified in the matrix. While the court may depart upward, downward departures are not authorized, presumably because a commitment to a juvenile correctional facility is discretionary in the first instance.

Another compelling difference is the power given to the juvenile judge to modify the sentence after it has been imposed — a power that does not exist under the adult sentencing guidelines. . . .

The discretionary sentencing provisions and the modification provisions are unique to the juvenile system and are a clear expression of the legislature's continued belief in the juvenile system as an individualized, protective, and rehabilitative process.

Additionally, the majority notes that the current juvenile code imposes a term of aftercare on juveniles sentenced to a term of confinement under the matrix. This, the majority contends, reflects the adult sentencing guidelines postrelease provisions. A postrelease period of supervision is not new to the juvenile system. In 1982, the code required a period of conditional release for juvenile offenders who had completed a period of confinement at a state youth center. Under the KJOC,

the period of conditional release was determined by the youth center superintendent, while now, the sentencing matrix provides specified periods of aftercare.

The majority also mentions that the KJJC now provides the opportunity for
good time credits, just like the adult system. I fail to see how providing a benefit
to juveniles — even if it is the same benefit provided to incarcerated adult offenders — is really relevant to the issue of whether the new juvenile system is no longer
the individualized, protective, rehabilitative system that it was when *Findlay* was
decided. How would denying juveniles good time credits better serve a benevolent, paternalistic purpose?

The majority also fails to consider the importance of extended jurisdiction
juvenile prosecution under K.S.A. 2006 Supp. 38-2347. Extended jurisdiction
juvenile prosecution became effective in 1997, and is a mechanism whereby serious or repeat juvenile offenders who might otherwise have been waived up to
adult court may remain in the juvenile sentencing system. In an extended jurisdiction juvenile prosecution, the court imposes both a juvenile and an adult sentence.
The adult sentence is stayed as long as the juvenile complies with and completes
the conditions of the juvenile sentence. If, however, the juvenile violates the conditions of the juvenile sentence, the juvenile sentence is revoked, the adult sentence is imposed, and the juvenile court transfers jurisdiction of the case to adult
court. Because a juvenile in an extended jurisdiction prosecution may end up in
adult court with an adult sentence, the right to trial by jury is provided by statute. Extended jurisdiction juvenile prosecution is important to the issue at hand
because it evidences a last-ditch effort to extend the favorable protections of juvenile court and the benefits of its less severe sentences to juvenile offenders who
previously would have been waived to adult court.

Sentencing options

The majority contends that the sentencing options available to the juvenile
judge are much more akin to those available for adult offenders. . . .

This broad overview overlooks the many unique features of the juvenile system that emphasize family and community involvement early intervention diversionary procedures, flexibility to accommodate individualized needs of juveniles
upon intake into the system, preference for noncustodial placements, graduated
sanctions with preferences for the least-restrictive alternatives, and, above all,
rehabilitation.

The juvenile system has unique pre-charge intake and intervention procedures: the Juvenile Intake and Assessment Program and the intermediate intervention program. Under the Juvenile Intake and Assessment Program, a juvenile taken
into custody by law enforcement is taken to a local juvenile intake and assessment
program for evaluation. The program is operational in all 31 judicial districts, and
juvenile intake and assessment centers are open 24 hours a day, 7 days a week. The
intake and assessment worker administers assessments and gathers information
about the juvenile, including criminal history, abuse history, history of substance
abuse, educational history, and family history. After completing the assessment
process, the intake and assessment worker has several options. The worker may
release the juvenile to a parent or parents, or other legal guardian or appropriate
adult, with or without conditions, if the worker believes that is in the child's best
interests. The conditions may include counseling for the juvenile and/or the child's

family, participation by the juvenile, family members and other relevant persons in mediation, inpatient treatment, and referral to available community services. The worker may also refer the juvenile to the county or district attorney for the filing of charges and make recommendations concerning intermediate intervention programs that may be beneficial for the juvenile.

A juvenile may be taken directly to a juvenile detention facility rather than an intake and assessment program if specific criteria apply, including: the juvenile is a fugitive, has escaped from a juvenile detention facility, or has absconded from an ordered placement; the juvenile is alleged to have committed a sex offense; the juvenile has a history of violent behavior or a prior adjudication for a felony offense. However, before taking the juvenile to a detention facility, the officer must first consider whether taking the juvenile to a nonsecure facility is more appropriate.

The immediate intervention program is also unique to the juvenile code. It is a diversionary program designed to allow juveniles to avoid prosecution but, unlike adult diversion, is available even before charges are filed. In addition, the immediate intervention program statute authorizes the establishment of local programs which provide for intake and assessment workers or county or district attorneys to refer cases directly to youth courts, restorative justice centers, hearing officers, or other local programs sanctioned by the court.

The importance of these unique intake and intervention procedures to the issue at hand cannot be dismissed. As Justice White noted in *McKeiver:* "To the extent that the jury is a buffer to the corrupt or overzealous prosecutor in the criminal law system, the distinctive intake policies and procedures of the juvenile court system to a great extent obviate this important function of the jury." . . .

Additionally, and most importantly, the KJJC not only emphasizes, but requires, parental involvement in the entire process. Intake and assessment workers may require parents to participate in programs and services as a condition of the juvenile's release back home. The county or district attorney is authorized to require parents to be a part of any immediate intervention program. Parents served with a summons are required to attend all proceedings involving the juvenile unless excused by the court. The court has the power to require parents to participate in counseling, mediation, alcohol and drug evaluations and treatment programs, and parenting classes. The court also has the power to order parents to report violations of conditions of probation or conditional release and may order them to aid the court in enforcing the court's orders. Violation may result in contempt sanctions.

This emphasis on parental involvement is not merely incidental to the fact the juvenile offender is a child, but is, instead, part of the family and community centered approach to juvenile rehabilitation. As the Oregon Supreme Court found when it rejected the argument that the Oregon juvenile system had become so akin to the adult system that juveniles should be afforded the right to jury trial:

"Coupled with the juvenile code's focus on the best interests and welfare of the child, this policy of parental involvement in the rehabilitation of children distinguishes a delinquency proceeding from an adult criminal prosecution for purposes of Article I, section 11. The message of the juvenile code is clear and unequivocal — rehabilitation of children in trouble is a family affair. In no way is the adult criminal justice system comparable to that model." *State ex rel. Juv. Dept. v. Reynolds*, 317 Or. 560, 573-74, 857 P.2d 842 (1993).

Confidentiality and other protective provisions

The majority also contends that juvenile proceedings and records no longer have the confidentiality protections they did in 1982. The majority points to provisions concerning public access to juvenile court hearings and confidentiality of records. With respect to juvenile hearings, there is little practical difference between the KJOC provisions in 1982 and the current KJJC provisions. . . .

The changes to the juvenile code cited by the majority have not so eroded the features of the juvenile system that distinguish it from the adult system that it can be said that the rationale underlying *McKeiver* and *Findlay* is no longer valid. The new system continues to further the goals that have always characterized the modern juvenile system: protection of the public and rehabilitation. As the Criminal Justice Coordinating Council's Juvenile Task Force noted in its report to the legislature in 1995, these two goals are not incompatible. . . .

The dual goals of the juvenile system that commanded its process in 1982 are very much alive and well. The juvenile system still retains significant individualized, protective, rehabilitative, child-cognizant features that distinguish it from the adult system and which allow it to operate toward achieving those goals. . . .

For these reasons, I dissent.

NOTES AND QUESTIONS

1. The court in *L.M.* emphasized the similarities in the language and stated purpose of Kansas's juvenile and criminal codes. Does the terminology traditionally used in juvenile courts (e.g., "delinquent act" rather than "crime," "admission" rather than "guilty plea") have substantive meaning or is it merely window dressing?

The Kansas Supreme Court later rejected a juvenile's claim of entitlement to a preliminary hearing, as required in adult criminal prosecutions. The court distinguished *L.M.* on the basis that the right to a preliminary hearing is statutory, not constitutional. In the Matter of D.E.R., 225 P.3d 1187 (Kan. 2010), the court wrote:

> The recent confusion as to whether the preliminary examination statutorily mandated by the adult criminal code must also be conducted in proceedings under the Juvenile Code is a consequence of this court's decision in In re L.M. The actual holding in In re L.M. was that a juvenile has a right to a jury trial under the Sixth and Fourteenth Amendments to the United States Constitution and under § 10 of the Kansas Constitution Bill of Rights, notwithstanding statutory provisions in the Juvenile Code to the contrary which were declared unconstitutional. . . . In re L.M. essentially determined that the . . . rationales for denying juveniles a constitutional jury trial right were outdated and obsolete, given that the current Juvenile Code in Kansas "has become more akin to an adult criminal prosecution."
>
> Apparently, some have interpreted In re L.M. to mean that, because a juvenile proceeding is akin to a criminal prosecution for purposes of the right to a jury trial, juvenile proceedings must also utilize all of the same statutory procedures as a criminal prosecution. Such an interpretation reads too much into In re L.M. That decision was founded upon a juvenile's entitlement to a constitutional right. At most, In re

L.M.'s equating of juvenile proceedings and criminal prosecutions would support the proposition that juveniles are entitled to all of the constitutional rights which adult criminal defendants possess, not that juvenile proceedings must look exactly the same as a criminal prosecution. . . .

225 P.3d at 1191-1192.

2. The *L.M.* majority also supports its argument for extending the constitutional right to jury trial to the juvenile court by pointing out that juvenile court proceedings are no longer confidential. Records are accessible to the public, and the trial must be open to the public. What is the relationship between confidentiality and closed trials and the possibility of trial by jury?

3. The dissent, on the other hand, points out that many of the distinctive protections of the juvenile court process remain available in Kansas. What is the relation between jury trial and the lesser penalties available to the juvenile court? How is the extent of judicial discretion over disposition/sentencing related to jury trial?

4. As the dissent in *L.M.* observes, if a respondent in juvenile court faces the possibility of adult incarceration under the state's extended juvenile jurisdiction statute, the statute also requires that the right to jury trial be available. Other states have similar statutory provisions, and courts in some states have concluded that it is unconstitutional to expose a juvenile to adult sanctions without a jury trial right. In re C.B., 708 So. 2d 391 (La. 1998); State v. Hezzie R., 580 N.W.2d 660 (Wis. 1998). Is this distinction consistent with In re Gault? *See* In re M.I., 989 N.E.2d 173 (Ill. 2013) (although the juvenile was exposed to an adult sentence, his rights were not violated by the lack of a jury trial because the EJJ statute was dispositional in nature and did not apply to the determination of his guilt under *Gault*).

5. Since *L.M.* was decided, supreme courts in at least four states have rejected its reasoning and adhered to earlier decisions holding that respondents in juvenile court do not have a constitutional right to a jury trial. In re Jonathon C.B., 958 N.E.2d 227 (Ill. 2011); In re State ex rel. A.J., 27 So. 3d 247 (La. 2009); State in re A.C., 43 A.3d 454 (N.J. Super. Ct. Ch. Div. 2012); In the Interest of Kevin R., 762 S.E.2d 387 (S.C. 2014). Professor Gardner criticizes such decisions for failing to recognize the significance of the punitive orientation of modern juvenile courts. Martin R. Gardner, Punitive Juvenile Justice and Public Trials by Jury: Sixth Amendment Applications in a Post-*McKeiver* World, 91 Neb. L. Rev. 1, 3-5 (2012).

6. Where jury trial is available in delinquency cases, it is rarely used. *See* Barry C. Feld, Violent Youth and Public Policy: A Case Study of Juvenile Justice Law Reform, 79 Minn. L. Rev. 965, 1108 (1995) (jury trial used in less than 1 percent of cases in Oklahoma and Texas and less than 3 percent of cases in Wisconsin). What would account for so few requests for a jury trial?

7. A West Virginia statute seeking to enforce the traditional juvenile court promise of confidentiality by making it a crime to publish, without written approval of the court, the name of any youth charged as a juvenile offender was held unconstitutional in Smith v. Daily Mail Publishing Co., 443 U.S. 97 (1979). The Court held that whether the statute is viewed as a prior restraint or as a penal sanction for publishing lawfully obtained, truthful information is unimportant because in either case the most exacting scrutiny is required. Using that test, the Court found that the state interest in protecting the anonymity of the juvenile offender is insufficient.

2. *Statutory Time Limits and the Right to a Speedy Trial*

IN RE CRISTIAN A.

198 A.3d 1064 (Md. App. 2014)

NAZARIAN, J. . . . On October 26, 2012, shortly after Cristian's seventeenth birthday, his younger brother Ricardo was involved in a fight at a McDonald's in Silver Spring. Cristian was not implicated in the altercation and was not there when it occurred. Detective Jeffrey Bunge of the Montgomery County Police saw the fighting from the police station across the street. He witnessed Ricardo punching another individual and began to approach the scene.

The fight broke up as Detective Bunge arrived and the participants fled, including Ricardo. Detective Bunge and Officer Daniel Sassi found Ricardo approximately fifteen minutes later. They pursued him, and Detective Bunge eventually stopped him. Detective Bunge identified himself, drew his gun, and told Ricardo to get on the ground. Ricardo complied and as Detective Bunge began to put him in handcuffs, Cristian arrived at the scene. Cristian had heard that his brother was involved in a fight and had come looking for him. Cristian ran toward Detective Bunge and Ricardo yelling, "That's my brother, that's my brother, leave him alone." Detective Bunge and Corporal Tony Galladora, who had come to assist the other officers, told Cristian to stop, but he continued to approach his brother and Detective Bunge. Corporal Galladora stopped Cristian and brought him to the ground. According to the testimony of Corporal Galladora and Officer Jeffrey Rea, Cristian got back up, assumed a fighting stance, and said, "What's up? What's up?" Officer Rea, who was standing behind Cristian, subdued him with a Taser and then arrested him.

The State filed a complaint (the "Complaint") with the Department of Juvenile Services ("DJS") on November 15, 2012, twenty days after Cristian's arrest on October 26. A juvenile intake officer (the "Intake Officer") reviewed the Complaint that day and authorized the filing of a formal delinquency petition (the "Petition") without conducting an intake interview with Cristian. As luck would have it, Cristian was arrested for first-degree assault on that same day, November 15, 2012, in an unrelated incident (the "assault action"), although these charges were *nol prossed* on January 11, 2013.

The Intake Officer determined in the *delinquency* action that Cristian's detention in the *assault* action would likely last beyond the twenty-five-day timeline allotted for an intake officer to make a decision on whether to file a petition.[1] Accordingly, the Intake Officer authorized the filing of the Petition in keeping with CJP § 3–8A–10(c) and without conducting an intake interview with Cristian. The State filed the Petition on December 11, 2012, charging Cristian with

---

1. The statute sets limits on the amount of time an intake officer has to make a decision after the filing of a complaint:

(c)(1) Except as otherwise provided in this subsection, in considering the complaint, *the intake officer shall make an inquiry within 25 days* as to whether the court has jurisdiction and *whether judicial action is in the best interests of the public or the child.*

CJP § 3–8A–10(c) (emphasis added).

second-degree assault, disorderly conduct, conspiracy to commit disorderly conduct, resisting and interfering with arrest, attempting to resist and interfere with arrest, and attempting to obstruct and hinder a police officer.

Cristian moved to dismiss on February 13, 2013. He argued that the State had violated CJP § 3–8A–10(m), which requires law enforcement officers to file the initial complaint with DJS within fifteen days of when a juvenile is brought into custody. The State had filed the Complaint on November 15, 2012, twenty days after Cristian's arrest on October 26, 2012, and five days late under the statute. Cristian argued that the State's delay in filing violated "statutory timeliness" and due process, and "caused [him] actual prejudice," since he was not provided the opportunity for an intake interview, which might have convinced the Intake Officer to refrain from authorizing the filing of the Petition.

At an adjudication hearing on February 15, 2013, the circuit court denied the motion to dismiss, noting that "it's just too speculative to think that the case would have been not petitioned and there's really no showing of any prejudice to the defense. So if it was delayed four days or six days, or whatever, I don't think that's sufficient in and of itself to dismiss it." The circuit court found that Cristian was "involved"[2] in attempting to interfere with arrest and attempting to obstruct and hinder a police officer performing his lawful duties. At the disposition hearing on March 7, 2013, the court sustained Cristian's probation pursuant to the recommendation of DJS. Cristian filed a timely notice of appeal. . . .

After a juvenile is taken into custody, the State may file a complaint with DJS. The complaint must be filed within fifteen days from the date a juvenile is arrested. *See* CJP § 3–8A–10(m). In turn, the intake officer must review the complaint "within 25 days as to whether the court has jurisdiction and whether judicial action is in the best interests of the public or the child." CJP § 3–8A–10(c)(1). As part of this inquiry, "it is incumbent upon the intake officer to review *all* of the evidence reasonably available to him or her. . . . *Ordinarily* an intake interview is an essential part of the preliminary review unless the juvenile refuses to participate or is unable to participate." After this investigation, and within the twenty-five-day time period, the intake officer makes a recommendation to the State's Attorney and may "[a]uthorize the filing of a petition," "[p]ropose an informal adjustment of the matter," or decide not to authorize a petition at all. CJP § 3–8A–10(c)(3)(i)–(iii).[3] Violations of CJP § 3–8A–10 may result in dismissal of a petition, but "*only* if the respondent has demonstrated actual prejudice." CJP § 3–8A–10(n) (emphasis added).

---

2. "In juvenile proceedings the more precise term to use when referring to the plea of the respondent is 'not involved' [or involved] as opposed to 'not guilty' [or guilty]."

3. The statute describes the intake officer's potential courses of action after receiving a complaint and the timeframe for making a decision:

> Subject to the provisions of § 3–8A–10.1 of this subtitle, in accordance with this section, the intake officer may, after such inquiry and within 25 days of receiving the complaint:
>
> (i) Authorize the filing of a petition or a peace order request or both;
> (ii) Propose an informal adjustment of the matter; or
> (iii) Refuse authorization to file a petition or a peace order request or both.

Because Cristian's claims include a constitutional dimension (he alleges a violation of his due process rights), we review his contentions against "our own independent constitutional analysis." "We perform a *de novo* constitutional appraisal in light of the particular facts of the case at hand; in so doing, we accept a lower court's findings of fact unless clearly erroneous."

Cristian argues that the State's failure to file a timely complaint under CJP § 3–8A10(m) caused him actual prejudice. He contends that had the State filed the Complaint within the statute's timeframe, he could have participated in an intake interview and this interview might have convinced the Intake Officer not to authorize the filing of the Petition.

The Intake Officer reviewed the belatedly-submitted Complaint and decided to authorize the filing of the Petition without interviewing Cristian. The Intake Officer anticipated that Cristian couldn't participate in an interview, especially given the twenty-five-day timeframe allotted for a decision on whether or not to file a petition, because of Cristian's arrest, which the officer believed would result in a detention. Put differently, the Intake Officer assumed Cristian would be unavailable for an interview since he had been arrested.

Cristian contends that he *was* in fact available for an intake interview up until his arrest on November 15, 2012. He claims he was prejudiced by the delay in filing the Complaint, which deprived him of an interview, because there was "at least a reasonable possibility that a delinquency petition would not have been filed had an intake hearing been conducted." Cristian claims that in an intake interview, "he would have [had] the opportunity to persuade the [Intake Officer] to pursue an informal adjustment or deny authorization for the filing of a petition." He points to several mitigating factors that he would have discussed during the intake interview, including his abusive upbringing and his attempts to protect his younger brother, and that he contends may have convinced the Intake Officer not to file a petition. Cristian admits, however, that "there is no guarantee that the [Intake Officer] would have taken a different course had there been an opportunity for an intake hearing." . . .

We conclude that the Intake Officer in this case met his responsibility to review Cristian's case, even though he did not conduct an interview, and we agree with the State that Cristian has failed to establish actual prejudice. *First*, an intake officer's responsibility is to "review fully the case so as to determine whether it would be more appropriately handled through informal adjustment or even to recommend that no further action be taken." An intake interview may be a part of this review process, but the core requirement is that the officer conduct a thorough *investigation* of the juvenile's case.

The determination of whether dismissal of a petition is warranted in the absence of an intake interview depends on whether "under the circumstances . . . an intake interview is an indispensable part of the mandated preliminary inquiry, or whether the goals and objectives of the preliminary inquiry can be accomplished absent such an interview." "When faced with a situation where an interview with the child was not held, the court should inquire as to the reason and, if not satisfied with the intake officer's explanation, may take such action as it believes appropriate under the circumstances, including dismissal of the petition."

We have held that an intake interview is not required if the "juvenile refuses to participate or is unable to participate," and have noted that dismissal is *not* "a necessary, automatic sanction that must be applied in every case where an intake interview was not held." . . . Dismissal is appropriate if the State deliberately files a petition before an intake interview is conducted and without taking into account input from the Juvenile Services Administration. Similarly, a policy that "automatically recommend[s]" that the State file a petition, regardless of intake interviews, circumvents the statutory purpose. Overall, though, the rehabilitative purpose of juvenile statutes may well be better served by erring on the side of engagement rather than reflexive procedural dismissal:

> [T]he foremost consideration in the disposition of a juvenile proceeding should be a course of treatment and rehabilitation best suited to promote the full growth and development of the child. . . . [T]he judge must keep in mind the overriding purpose of the juvenile statute along with the fact that this purpose will ordinarily not be served by dismissal of the juvenile proceeding.

Keith W., 310 Md. at 109, 527 A.2d 35 (affirming lower court's refusal to dismiss a petition based on a violation of Maryland Rule 11–114, which prescribes the timing requirements for adjudicatory hearings).

This case presents no procedural failing or inappropriate policy that justified dismissal. . . . This case does not present an "extraordinary circumstance" warranting dismissal of the Petition simply because an intake interview was not conducted. To the contrary, the record reveals that Cristian had a lengthy history with DJS leading up to this incident, and the Intake Officer likely was already aware of Cristian's history and the circumstances surrounding this particular arrest. The Intake Officer readily could conclude from this record that Cristian needed the services DJS could provide him. His decision to authorize the Petition without an intake interview continued DJS's engagement with him, and the circuit court judge ultimately found that Cristian "is still . . . amenable to services" and properly continued Cristian's probation, pursuant to DJS's recommendation.

Second, even if Cristian was entitled to an intake interview and could have participated in one, there is no evidence that the five-day delay in the initial filing of the Complaint caused him actual prejudice. Under CJP § 3–8A–10(n), a court "may dismiss a petition or a peace order request for failure to comply with this section[, in this case filing the Complaint beyond the fifteen-day window,] *only if the respondent has demonstrated actual prejudice.*"

Although the statute does not define "actual prejudice," we look to the related area of speedy trial violations in criminal prosecutions. In Barker v. Wingo, 407 U.S. 514 (1972), the Supreme Court established four factors, including prejudice, that we analyze to determine whether a defendant's right to a speedy trial has been violated. Within the prejudice analysis, the Court indicated three "interests of defendants which the speedy trial right was designed to protect," namely: "(i) to prevent oppressive pretrial incarceration; (ii) to minimize anxiety and concern of the accused; and (iii) to limit the possibility that the defense will be impaired." The Court also recognized that out of these interests, the defendant's need to build a strong case is paramount because an impaired defense could threaten "the fairness of the entire system." Maryland courts have adopted the *Barker* test in both criminal and juvenile proceedings.

Cristian does not argue that he has faced oppressive pretrial incarceration, and he conceded that the five-day delay in the filing of the Complaint was "not an impairment to [his] defense." He did contend at the adjudicatory hearing that waiting for the State to file the Complaint caused him "anxiety and nervousness," though he does not mention this point in his brief. His primary argument is that had he had an opportunity to participate in an intake hearing, he might have persuaded the Intake Officer not to recommend the Petition at all. Beyond hopefulness or speculation, nothing in the record supports this argument and, as we discussed above, there is ample evidence to support the Intake Officer's decision to recommend the Petition. Cristian has admitted that he was prejudiced *only* if the Intake Officer would not have submitted the Petition after conducting an intake hearing with him, and the link between what could have happened and actual prejudice is too hypothetical and attenuated. . . .

NOTES AND QUESTIONS

1. The United States Supreme Court has never considered the applicability of the speedy trial requirement to juvenile court proceedings. Most courts that have passed on the issue have concluded that the requirement applies. *See, e.g.*, United States v. Furey, 500 F.2d 338 (2d Cir. 1974); P.V. v. District Court, 609 P.2d 110 (Colo. 1980). State v. Barksdale, 451 A.2d 1174 (Del. Fam. 1982); State v. Robinson, 434 P.3d 232 (Kan. App. 2018); In re Thomas J., 811 A.2d 310 (Md. 2002); Piland v. Clark Co. Juvenile Court Services, 457 P.2d 523 (Nev. 1969); In the Matter of Darcy S., 936 P.2d 888 (N.M. App. 1997); Commonwealth v. Dallenbach, 729 A.2d 1218 (Pa. Super. 1999). *See also* United States v. Doe, 571 F. App'x. 656, 659-61 (10th Cir. 2014) (holding that the juvenile's speedy trial rights were not violated).

2. Juvenile codes typically impose short time lines on decisions to file petitions in delinquency cases and in bringing cases to trial. For example, the Model Indian Juvenile Code provides that intake investigations must occur within 1 business day after the detention hearing if the child is in detention or 5 days if the child has been released, that adjudicatory hearings must occur within 10 days of the initial hearing if the child is in custody and 30 days if the child has been released, and that the disposition hearing must occur within 10 days of the adjudication hearing if the child is in custody and 20 days if the child has been released. Matthew T. Ficcaglia & Ron J. Whitener, Model Indian Juvenile Code §§ 2.05.130, 2.10.110, 2.12.110 (Center of Indigenous Research & Justice, University of Washington School of Law 2016 rev.), https://www.bia.gov/sites/bia.gov/files/assets/bia/ojs/ojs/pdf/idc2-047015.pdf. Why are these short timelines imposed? Should the sanctions for violating them be based on the same considerations that are used for speedy trial determinations?

3. *Adjudicative Competence*

At common law, trying a person who lacked the capacity to understand the proceedings, that is, the "competence to stand trial," was forbidden, 4 W. Blackstone Commentaries, *24. In Drope v. Missouri, 420 U.S. 162 (1975), the Supreme Court held that due process required reversal of a state court criminal conviction when the defendant was tried and convicted without an adequate inquiry into his competence. In the traditional juvenile court, competence to stand trial was not an issue because the purpose of the proceedings was to determine whether the child was in need of assistance and rehabilitation, rather than to punish wrongdoers. The Supreme Court has never addressed whether the competence to stand trial requirement applies in juvenile court, and as a practical matter, the issue was rarely raised even after *Gault*. However, as trying ever-younger juveniles as adults has become more common, greater attention has been focused on this issue. The following document summarizes recent important empirical research on this question.

SUMMARY, THE MACARTHUR JUVENILE ADJUDICATIVE COMPETENCE STUDY

(2002) (available from the MacArthur Foundation Research Network on Adolescent Development and Juvenile Justice, http://www.adjj.org/ downloads/58competence_study_summary.pdf/)

U.S. law has long required that defendants in criminal cases must be capable of understanding the trial process and contributing to their defense, indicating that they are "competent to stand trial." For example, defendants must understand the charges against them, have some rudimentary understanding of the court proceeding, be able to understand and answer questions posed to them by their attorney, and be able to make basic decisions about their trial, such as weighing the consequences of accepting or turning down a plea agreement. The U.S. Supreme Court has held that it is fundamentally unfair and in violation of the U.S. Constitution to try defendants who do not have these basic capacities.

Historically, virtually all defendants found incompetent to stand trial have been persons with mental illnesses or mental retardation. In recent years, however, an increase in the number of adolescents tried as adults and the number of younger children tried in juvenile court has raised questions about children's and adolescents' capacities to participate in their trials — not necessarily due to mental illness or mental retardation, but simply because of intellectual and emotional immaturity.

In order to address these questions, the MacArthur Foundation Research Network on Adolescent Development and Juvenile Justice conducted the first-ever large-scale study of age differences in competence to stand trial. The study was funded by grants from the John D. and Catherine T. MacArthur Foundation and the Open Society Institute, a nonprofit organization that is part of the Soros Foundations Network. The study was designed and carried out by some of the country's leading scientific and legal researchers in the area of children and the law.

HOW THE STUDY WAS CONDUCTED

Over 1,400 males and females between the ages of 11 and 24 participated in the study, which was conducted in four sites — Philadelphia, Los Angeles, Northern and Eastern Virginia, and Northern Florida — in order to obtain a sample with cultural, ethnic, and socioeconomic diversity. Half of the study participants were in jail or detained in juvenile detention centers at the time of the study, and half were individuals of similar age, gender, ethnicity, and social class but residing in the community.

These individuals were administered a standardized battery of tests designed to assess their knowledge and abilities relevant for competence to stand trial, their legal decision-making in several hypothetical situations (such as whether to confess a crime to the police, share information with one's attorney, or accept a proffered plea agreement), and measures of a number of other characteristics that could potentially influence these capacities, such as intelligence, symptoms of mental health problems, and prior experience in the justice system.

The primary measure of abilities relevant to competence to stand trial was an evaluation tool that has been used extensively in prior studies of competence among adults with mental illnesses. The evaluation does not label individuals as "competent" or "incompetent," but it does identify individuals whose knowledge, understanding, and reasoning are sufficiently impaired that they are at grave risk of being incompetent to stand trial in a criminal proceeding. Prior studies of adults with mental illness who have been found incompetent to stand trial were used to establish a threshold in the present study that served as the basis for identifying individuals' levels of ability as "impaired" or "seriously impaired." In the present study, individuals who were identified as "seriously impaired" performed at a level comparable to adult defendants with mental illness who would likely be considered incompetent to stand trial by clinicians who perform evaluations for courts.

It is important to note that our study examined only youths' competence to stand trial, not their criminal blameworthiness (i.e., whether someone should be held fully responsible for an offense). These are two separate issues. For example, a young inexperienced driver who accidentally skidded off the road and killed another person might be competent to stand trial for the wrongful death of another, but could be judged less than fully responsible for the death because it was accidental. Whether youths of a certain age have abilities suggesting competence or incompetence to stand trial does not tell us whether youths of that age should or should not be held as responsible as adults for their offenses.

WHAT THE STUDY FOUND

The study found that juveniles aged 11 to 13 were more than three times as likely as young adults (individuals aged 18 to 24) to be "seriously impaired" on the evaluation of competence-relevant abilities, and that juveniles aged 14 to 15 were twice as likely as young adults to be "seriously impaired." Individuals aged 15 and younger also differed from young adults in their legal decision-making. For example, younger individuals were less likely to recognize the risks inherent in different choices and less likely to think about the long-term consequences of their choices (e.g., choosing between confessing versus remaining silent when being questioned by the police).

In the present study, juveniles of below-average intelligence (i.e., with an IQ less than 85) were more likely to be "significantly impaired" in abilities relevant for competence to stand trial than juveniles of average intelligence (IQ scores of 85 and higher). Because greater proportion of youths in the juvenile justice system than in the community were of below-average intelligence, and because lower intelligence was related to poorer performance on abilities associated with competence to stand trial, the risk for incompetence to stand trial is even greater among adolescents who are in the justice system than it is among adolescents in the community. In fact, more than half of all below-average 11- to 13-year-olds, and more than 40 percent of all below-average 14- and 15-year-olds, were in the "significantly impaired" range on abilities related to competence.

Age and intelligence were the only significant predictors of performance on the evaluation of abilities relevant to competence to stand trial. Performance on the evaluation did not vary as a function of individuals' gender, ethnicity, socioeconomic background, prior experience in the legal system, or symptoms of mental health problems. Because mental illness and its impact on competence to stand trial was not the focus of this study, very few individuals with serious mental disorders were included in the sample, and the study's results do not answer questions about the competence of juveniles with serious mental illnesses. The study did not find differences between juveniles aged 16 and 17 and young adults in abilities relevant to their competence to stand trial. As noted above, however, this does not mean that juveniles of this age are equivalent to adults with respect to other capacities that are relevant to their adjudication, such as their criminal blameworthiness or likelihood of rehabilitation. The MacArthur Network is currently conducting further research to examine age differences in other capacities and abilities that are important in making decisions about the appropriate treatment of young offenders in the legal system.

WHAT THE RESULTS OF THIS STUDY MEAN

The results of this study indicate that, compared to adults, a significantly greater proportion of juveniles in the community who are 15 and younger, and an even larger proportion of juvenile offenders this age, are probably not competent to stand trial in a criminal proceeding. Juveniles of below-average intelligence are especially at risk of being incompetent to stand trial. States that transfer large numbers of juveniles who are 15 and under to the criminal justice system may be subjecting significant numbers of individuals to trial proceedings for which they lack the basic capacities recognized as essential for competent participation as a defendant.

Based on these findings, states should consider implementing policies and practices designed to ensure that young defendants' rights to a fair trial are protected. In some jurisdictions, this may mean requiring competence evaluations for juveniles below a certain age before they can be transferred to criminal court. States that permit juveniles 13 and under to be tried as adults may wish to re-examine this policy in light of the substantial proportion of individuals of this age who are at great risk for incompetence to stand trial.

More information about the MacArthur study is available at http://www.adjj.org/content/index.php. *See also* Thomas Grisso et al., Juveniles' Competence to Stand Trial: A Comparison of Adolescents' and Adults' Capacities as Trial Defendants, 27 Law & Hum. Behav. 333 (2001).

TATE V. STATE

864 So. 2d 44 (Fla. App. 2003)

STONE, J. Lionel Tate appeals his conviction of first-degree murder and the resulting mandatory sentence to life in prison. . . . Tate, age twelve at the time of the crime, was indicted by a grand jury and convicted of the first-degree murder of six-year-old Tiffany Eunick in 1999. The general verdict included charges of both felony murder, based on committing aggravated child abuse, and premeditated murder. The trial and sentence, in light of Tate's age, has been the focus of considerable public interest reflected in the multiple amicus briefs filed in this appeal.

The evidence was clear that the victim was brutally slain, suffering as many as thirty-five injuries, including a fractured skull, brain contusions, twenty-plus bruises, a rib fracture, injuries to her kidneys and pancreas, and a portion of her liver was detached. It was undisputed that it would take tremendous force to inflict these injuries. None of the experts, not even those for the defense, believed that the injuries were consistent with "play fighting," or that they were accidentally inflicted.

Post-trial, in addition to a motion for new trial, the defense requested an evidentiary hearing . . . challenging whether pretrial plea negotiations and an alleged proposal to jointly lobby the governor for clemency in the event of a conviction, were adequately explained to Tate. Tate's appellate counsel, who was representing him on the motion for new trial, for the first time, also sought a competency evaluation and hearing, asserting that Tate did not know or understand the consequences of proceeding to trial and that he was unable to assist counsel before and during trial. Such a post-trial evaluation and hearing would be the only remaining opportunity to establish Tate's mental condition at that point in time. . . .

[After hearing some evidence, the trial court refused to order a post-trial evaluation because the issue was not brought up before or during trial. Tate appealed.]

The question we resolve, here, is whether, due to his extremely young age and lack of previous exposure to the judicial system, a competency evaluation was constitutionally mandated to determine whether Tate had sufficient present ability to consult with his lawyer with a reasonable degree of rational understanding and whether he had a rational, as well as factual, understanding of the proceedings against him. We conclude that it was.

Tate's appellate lawyer advised the court, "[a]nd as [sic] officer of the court I'm standing next to Lionel drawing pictures, hasn't listened to one work [sic] and had no idea what's going on." Counsel added that Tate was not "assist[ing] us in assisting him, and there's no interaction that's going on," and continued,

> It's someone [Tate] sitting here playing with pencil, pen and drawing pictures in what's probably the most important proceeding of his life, and it is something that every [sic] needs to stop and step back.
>
> There were — there was [sic] great people involved in this case, very experienced doctors but never a competency evaluation done. And one of the things that was in [sic] original motion for new trial, I think we're glossing over here is did Lionel Tate know the consequences of going forward.

Counsel also pointed out that "his eyes are moving around," which counsel interpreted as indicating that he did not understand. The court, however, pointed out that Tate's lack of interest in the proceeding did not equate with incompetency. Counsel further related their concerns as to Tate's pretrial rejection of an apparently favorable plea offer, arguing that Tate's trial counsel never told him that if he lost at trial, there was only one possible sentence, life in prison without parole, and that since he did not understand this, he could not have knowingly and voluntarily rejected the state's plea offer.

At trial, neuropsychologist, Dr. Mittenberg, testified that Tate had a mental delay of about three to four years, "which means that Lionel has an age equivalent of nine or ten years old." It is undisputed that Tate's IQ is approximately 90. Dr. Joel Klass, a child psychiatrist, testified for the defense at trial that Tate had the social maturity of a six-year-old and delays in inferential thinking. Dr. Sheri Bourg-Carter, called by the state as a rebuttal witness, likewise acknowledged Tate's immaturity.

Tate's trial counsel wanted to testify further in support of the request for a post-trial competency hearing, but was concerned about his ability to do so without a waiver of the attorney-client privilege. Accordingly, the question then arose whether Tate would waive his privilege and allow his trial attorney to testify concerning competency. Apparently, Tate, after conferring with his mother, did not agree to the proposed waiver. On the record, it appears that he simply followed his mother's instruction not to waive his attorney-client privilege, despite his lawyers' positions that waiving the privilege was in Tate's best interest. Significantly, defense counsel wanted to reveal what led him to believe that Tate was not competent during trial, but was apparently precluded from doing so.

At the March 2nd hearing, . . . the state's witness, Dr. Bourg-Carter, stated that, in her opinion, Tate was "legally" competent and that Tate's trial lawyer knew the results of a pretrial evaluation she performed. . . . Dr. Bourg-Carter further testified that during her evaluation of Tate, he understood that the possible consequences of a conviction was to spend a "[l]ong time in prison."[4]

The state also drew the court's attention to the plea colloquy that was conducted five days before trial at which Tate, accompanied by his lawyer and court appointed psychiatrist, acknowledged that the state offered a plea of three years in a juvenile detention facility, followed by ten years of probation. Tate's lawyer stated at that time that, after consulting with Tate and his mother, he wanted to reject the plea offer and proceed to trial.

At the plea hearing, Tate did advise the trial court that he understood what his counsel told the court, that he had enough time to talk with his mother, and

---

4. We note that Tate contends that Dr. Bourg-Carter's testimony was over a defense objection and an uncontroverted record that her twenty minute pre-trial competency assessment was not authorized by a court order and violated the specialty guidelines for forensic psychology. Even state forensic expert Dr. Brannon admitted that with children, you must "go deeper" to test their insights to see if they really understand. Apparently Tate's trial counsel learned, after the fact, that Dr. Bourg-Carter claimed to have had the verbal consent of Lionel Tate, his mother, and a defense expert to confer with him for an evaluation.

that he wanted to proceed to trial. Further, Tate stated that no one forced or pressured him into going to trial, and he had no questions for the court. Accordingly, the trial court concluded, "I'm convinced that Mr. Tate has sufficient ability to make a decision in this very important matter." . . .

[T]he brief plea colloquy, taken alone, was not adequate to evaluate competency given his age, immaturity, his nine- or ten-year-old mental age, and the complexity of the proceedings. Even if a child of Tate's age is deemed to have the capacity to understand less serious charges, or common place juvenile court proceedings, it cannot be determined, absent a hearing, whether Tate could meet competency standards incident to facing a first-degree murder charge involving profound decisions regarding strategy, whether to make disclosures, intelligently analyze plea offers, and consider waiving important rights.

The record reflects that questions regarding Tate's competency were not lurking subtly in the background, but were readily apparent, as his immaturity and developmental delays were very much at the heart of the defense. It is also alleged that his I.Q. of 90 or 91 means that 75% of children his age scored higher, and that he had significant mental delays. . . .

In light of the fact based professional doubts expressed post-trial concerning Tate's competency, Tate was entitled to a complete evaluation and hearing at that time, if for no other reason than to clarify the record, notwithstanding that the trial court may have been correct in concluding that Tate's demeanor and disinterest did not necessarily mean that he did not understand the proceedings and that his incompetency was not previously raised despite defense counsel's continuing access to professional help. . . .

Upon remand, Tate is entitled to a new trial because a hearing at this late date to determine the present competency of a maturing adolescent cannot adequately retroactively protect his rights. . . .

NOTES AND QUESTIONS

1. A number of states have statutes requiring that juveniles be competent before they are tried in juvenile court. *See, e.g.,* Ark. Code Ann. § 9-27-502 (2018); Ariz. Rev. Stat. § 8-291.01 (2018); D.C. Code Ann. § 16-2315 (2018); Fla. Stat. § 985.19 (2018); Tex. Fam. Code § 55.31 (2018); Va. Code § 16.1-356 (2018); Wis. Stat. § 938.295(2) (2018). Most courts addressing the question have held that a minor must be competent to be tried in juvenile court. Elizabeth S. Scott & Thomas Grisso, Developmental Incompetence, Due Process and Juvenile Justice Policy, 83 N.C. L. Rev. 793, 801 n.27 (2005); Richard E. Redding & Lynda E. Frost, Adjudicative Competence in the Modern Juvenile Court, 9 Va. J. Soc. Pol'y & L. 353, 400-401(2001). *See also* In re T.S., 798 N.W.2d 649 (N.D. 2011). However, the Oklahoma Court of Criminal Appeals has held that juveniles can be tried regardless of whether they are competent because juvenile courts can consider and accommodate issues of mental health. G.J.I. v. State, 778 P.2d 485, 487 (Okla. Crim. App. 1989); *see* Mary Sue Backus, Achieving Fundamental Fairness for Oklahoma's Juveniles: The Role for Competency in Juvenile Proceedings, 65 Okla. L. Rev. 41, 41-42 (2012).

2. In Dusky v. United States, 362 U.S. 402 (1960), the Supreme Court held that the test for competence to stand trial is "whether [the defendant] has sufficient

present ability to consult with his lawyer with a reasonable degree of rational understanding — and whether he has a rational as well as factual understanding of the proceedings against him." 362 U.S. at 402. *See also* Drope v. Missouri, 420 U.S. 162 (1975). When competence to stand trial is raised in a criminal prosecution, ordinarily the question arises because the defendant has a mental illness or mental disability. In *Tate*, what was the basis for the claim that Lionel was incompetent?

Most of the relatively few courts that have faced the issue have held that developmental immaturity alone may be sufficient to establish incompetence to stand trial. In re Hyrum H., 328, 131 P.3d 1058 (Ariz. 2006); Timothy J. v. Superior Court, 58 Cal. Rptr. 3d 746 (Cal. App. 2007); In re W.A.F. 573 A.2d 1264, 1266 (D.C. 1990); In re J.K., 873 N.W.2d 289 (Iowa App. 2015). However, the Colorado Court of Appeals rejected a due process challenge to a statute requiring that a finding of incompetence to stand trial in juvenile court be based on mental illness or disability. People in Interest of A.C.E.-D., 433 P.3d 153 (Colo. App. 2018).

3. Many incarcerated juveniles and adults, as well as children and young adults with disabilities associated with later involvement in the juvenile or criminal justice system, "exhibit an uncommonly high rate of communication and language disorders or impairments. Moreover, research has also established a 'strikingly high' connection between those communication and language disorders and myriad psychological, emotional, and behavioral problems. . . . Language-impaired defendants face a daunting series of procedural and linguistic obstacles when they enter the juvenile or criminal process. While most litigants are perplexed by the arcane language and rituals of the legal process, the cognitive and communication difficulties encountered by the defendant with language deficits rise to another level altogether. These communication difficulties threaten his vital constitutional rights to be competent, to assist with his defense, to due process, and to make knowing and intelligent decisions about which rights to waive and which to assert." Michele LaVigne & Gregory Van Rybroek, Breakdown in the Language Zone: The Prevalence of Language Impairments Among Juvenile and Adult Offenders and Why It Matters, 15 U.C. Davis J. Juv. L. & Pol'y 37, 44, 66 (2011). *See also* Michele LaVigne & Gregory Van Rybroek, "He Got in My Face So I Shot Him": How Defendants' Language Impairments Impair Attorney Client Relationships, 17 CUNY L. Rev. (2014).

4. In many states the minor bears the burden of proving incompetence to stand trial; courts generally reject claims that this rule violates due process. In re R.V., 349 P.3d 68, 79 (Cal. 2015); People in Interest of A.C.E.-D., above; In re J.K., above; State v. P.E.T., 344 P.3d 689, 694 (Wash. App. 2015). *See also* David R. Katner, Eliminating the Competency Presumption in Juvenile Delinquency Cases, 24 Cornell J.L. & Pub. Pol'y 403, 403-437 (2015) (arguing that the legal presumption that a juvenile is fit to stand trial, premised on *Dusky*, is harmful to juveniles and should be eliminated based on recent Supreme Court decisions acknowledging the differences in the juvenile brain and research on the higher rates of incompetency to stand trial among children, and calling for the party seeking adjudication to be responsible for establishing that the accused juvenile is fit to stand trial or that the factors currently used to establish juvenile competency should be expanded to include developmental immaturity and mental illness).

5. The court in *Tate* indicates that after Lionel talked with his mother, he declined a plea offer that would have resulted in him serving three years in a

juvenile facility. Later, at the post-conviction hearing, Lionel also refused to waive his attorney-client privilege because his mother told him not to, even though his lawyer said this was in his best interests. His mother said she believed that he had only been playing. Would consultation with a parent adequately protect a child whose competence to stand trial was marginal?

6. At the time of his conviction, Lionel was the youngest person in the United States to be sentenced to life without parole. After the court reversed Lionel's conviction, he pled guilty to second degree murder and was sentenced to one year of house arrest and 10 years of probation. While he was on probation, he was charged with armed burglary and armed robbery, as well as probation violation. He pled guilty and was sentenced to 10 years in prison for the new counts, to run concurrently with the 30 years on the original count. Terry Aguayo, Youth Who Killed at 12 Will Return to Prison, But Not for Life, N.Y. Times, Mar. 2, 2006.

7. In a criminal proceeding, if a court finds that the defendant is incompetent to stand trial, the court typically orders that the defendant be held so that "restoration services" may be provided to make the defendant competent after which the trial can then proceed.

> For mentally ill defendants, restoration usually entails a relatively brief period of roughly six months of psychiatric hospitalization to stabilize and medicate the defendant so as to eliminate or reduce psychotic symptoms such as paranoia, thought disorder, loose associations, and delusions or hallucinations. For defendants with mental retardation, low educational levels, poor fluency in English, or few years in the United States, restoration to competency (or, more accurately, development of competency) may require outpatient psychoeducation that teaches defendants about the legal proceedings and any social or communication skills necessary to work with their attorney and comport themselves appropriately in court. . . .
>
> If, however, the defendant is found to be incompetent and likely to remain so for the foreseeable future, then in accord with Jackson v. Indiana, [406 U.S. 715 (1972)], the court shall order that the defendant be (1) dismissed, (2) civilly committed if mentally ill, or (3) civilly certified if mentally retarded (a voluntary procedure requiring the defendant's consent to institutionalization).

Richard E. Redding & Lynda E. Frost, above, 9 Va. J. Soc. Pol'y & L. at 367-368.

Can a minor who is incompetent to stand trial be held in custody until he or she is old enough to be considered competent? The states' approaches to this question vary widely. In In re K.G., 808 N.E.2d 631 (Ind. 2004), the Indiana Supreme Court held that the adult competency statute, which requires that a person found incompetent be committed to the state mental hospital, does not apply; instead, the juvenile court has discretion to fashion an appropriate remedy. In re A.B., 715 N.W.2d 767 (Iowa App. 2006), held that delinquency proceedings may be suspended for up to 18 months to allow efforts to make the respondent competent. Missouri's approach is especially unusual; if a juvenile court finds a respondent incompetent to stand trial, it appoints a guardian ad litem to advocate the child's best interests and proceeds to trial. In the Interest of: A.G.R., 359 S.W.3d 103 (Mo. App. 2011), held that this procedure does not violate due process.

The principal authors of the MacArthur Study address the questions raised in these notes in the following excerpt.

ELIZABETH S. SCOTT & THOMAS GRISSO, *DEVELOPMENTAL INCOMPETENCE, DUE PROCESS, AND JUVENILE JUSTICE POLICY*

83 N.C. L. Rev. 793, 831-832, 838-839 (2005)

The unique features of developmental incompetence create a dilemma for courts unless appropriate mechanisms are available for responding to youths who are incompetent to proceed under the conventional legal standard. To be sure, some youths may be found incompetent simply because they lack adequate understanding about the purposes and operation of a criminal trial. They may respond to focused "competence training" programs designed to provide instruction that will enable them to function in their assigned role with at least minimal effectiveness. The question is how to respond to youths whose developmental incapacity is not correctable with short-term remedial instruction.

It is critically important to find a satisfactory answer to this question. Consider the dilemma faced by a criminal court judge deliberating about the competence of a thirteen-year-old charged with aggravated assault and armed robbery. The charges arose from an incident in which the youth and his friends allegedly ran off with an elderly woman's purse after attacking her brutally with a tire iron, causing her to suffer serious injuries. The youth, because of his extreme immaturity and low IQ, fails to comprehend the seriousness of the charges or the consequences of conviction. He can provide little assistance to his attorney, and it seems highly unlikely that these deficits can be remedied in the near future. If the court decides, as it should, that the youth is incompetent, neither dismissal of the charges nor long-term indefinite confinement ("waiting for maturity") will be acceptable dispositions; the former sacrifices public safety and accountability, and the latter violates constitutional norms.

In our view, the disposition that is appropriate for this youth and for most developmentally incompetent youths is adjudication in a juvenile delinquency proceeding. If a juvenile court adjudicates the charges against the youth, it can determine whether he committed the crime and, if so, it can structure a disposition based on remediation, accountability, and public safety. This outcome is possible only if criminal and juvenile courts apply dual standards of competence, such that a youth who is found incompetent in a criminal proceeding can be adjudicated under more relaxed criteria in juvenile court. Such a regime largely resolves the dispositional quandary faced by courts dealing with immature youths charged with serious crimes. On the other hand, if a uniform standard is applied in both judicial contexts, the youth excluded from criminal court on grounds of incompetence would also be unable to participate in delinquency proceedings.

The application of dual competence standards in criminal and delinquency proceedings is important for another reason; it is the means to avoid profound disruption of juvenile delinquency proceedings. Although few thirteen-year-olds are subject to criminal charges, many face adjudication in juvenile court. The research evidence suggests that evenhanded application of adult competence criteria may well result in the disqualification of a substantial percentage of youngsters from adjudication in any court. This outcome is jarring in light of uncontroversial premises of juvenile court jurisdiction; few would challenge the appropriateness of delinquency proceedings for younger teens. Thus, as a policy matter, a strong case can be made for a relaxed juvenile court competence standard under which immature youths could be tried in delinquency proceedings, even though they are incompetent to stand trial under adult criteria. . . .

To elaborate a bit on the operation of a relaxed standard, a youth faced with a serious delinquency charge must understand why he faces a deprivation of liberty and the possible extent of that confinement. But, because the consequences are less far-reaching than those of a criminal proceeding, a lesser ability to foresee remote consequences would be sufficient. The youth must also understand that his attorney's role is to advocate for him, that the prosecutor aims to convict and punish him, and that the judge will decide whether he committed the crime based on the evidence. But he need not understand how advocacy is translated into practice in a way that would be required of an adult. He must also have the capacity to provide his attorney with an account of relevant events and to answer questions so that the attorney can plan and execute a defense. But he need not have the ability to weigh the value of defense strategies, or to advise counsel accordingly. In delinquency proceedings, attorneys will often have an additional burden of explanation and solicitation of assent in planning a defense. It seems likely, however, that in practice, attorneys already play this role with younger clients, whose questionable competence heretofore has not been expressly acknowledged.

This standard satisfies the purposes of the competence requirement sufficiently to protect the interests of youths in delinquency proceedings — assuming the pre-conditions are met. The dignity and integrity of the proceedings are preserved if youths are not confused about the jeopardy they face or bewildered at the purpose and nature of the proceedings. Accuracy is satisfied if a young client can describe relevant events to her attorney; this communicative role also satisfies the purpose of promoting participation by the youthful client. What may also be important in realizing these purposes is the development of a set of guidelines and practices by which young defendants' understanding and effective participation in delinquency proceedings can be enhanced. Such guidelines might include the creation of a process that provides adequate time for attorney–client consultation and the development of strategies for explaining trial-related concepts grounded in educational principles and developmental knowledge. If these goals are taken seriously, most youths should be capable of participating in delinquency proceedings with sufficient competence to satisfy due process.

The authors propose that youth who are found incompetent even under this relaxed standard may be subject to civil commitment if their incompetence stems from mental illness or may be found to be dependent because of their parents' inadequate supervision and control.

4. Waivers of Trial Rights and the Right to Counsel

At the first court appearance of a criminal defendant or juvenile respondent, the judge will describe the charges, advise the defendant/respondent of the right to counsel, and set a trial date. While most criminal defendants and many juvenile respondents accept the offer of counsel, in many places juveniles commonly decline the offer and plead guilty at the initial appearance. Of the juvenile cases that are not resolved at the initial appearance by an admission, the vast majority, like the great majority of all civil and criminal matters, do not go to trial. Instead, the parties reach an agreement to settle. In the criminal courts, this agreement takes the form of a guilty plea — an admission by the defendant to all or, most often, some of the charges against him or her. In juvenile court, the respondent's acceptance of responsibility may be called an admission, but it is in substance the same as a guilty plea. In either situation, the defendant or respondent waives numerous constitutional rights, and the record must reflect that the accused knowingly and voluntarily waived those rights. Courts ordinarily use a more or less formal ritual in which the defendant is asked whether he or she understands the charges, understands the right to contest the charges, has consulted with counsel (if represented), and understands the sanctions the court may impose. The prosecution may be required to call evidence to establish a prima facie case supporting the allegations, or a stipulation by the defendant to that effect may be sufficient.

In the following case, the juvenile respondent waived the right to counsel and all the trial rights at the initial appearance; the appellate court had to consider whether these waivers were legally valid.

In re C.S.

874 N.E.2d 1177 (Ohio 2007)

O'CONNOR, J. . . . Appellant, C.S., was brought before the Juvenile Division of the Licking County Court of Common Pleas on August 9, 2005. At that time, he was almost 14 years old. . . .

The facts of the theft case are largely undisputed; C.S. and one of his friends waived their rights to an attorney and made admissions to the police. Those admissions included statements that they had stolen two cars and had used them to traverse three central Ohio counties while committing various criminal acts from August 3, 2005, through August 7, 2005. Indeed, the magistrate hearing the case initially termed the boys' activities "a regular crime spree." The crime spree allegedly included the theft of the cars and the destruction of one, the repeated burglarizing of a trailer (stealing electronic equipment and a firearm from it), the procurement and use of alcohol and cocaine-laced marijuana, engaging in sexual relations with an adult woman, and cruelty to animals (shooting a cow and a horse multiple times). . . .

At some point prior to an initial hearing held on August 9, 2005, C.S. and his mother received the common pleas court's notice and order to appear. The document, entitled "Order to Appear and Explanation of Rights," sets forth seven pages of information.

Included on the first page of the document is a section captioned "Your Right to an Attorney." That section clearly states, that "[y]ou have the right to be represented by an attorney at all stages of this proceeding" and that an attorney will be appointed if "you cannot afford an attorney and you qualify under State guidelines."

The document further states, "You should contact the Clerk's Office seven (7) days in advance of your scheduled hearing and the Clerk will advise you how to apply for a Court-appointed attorney." Given that C.S. does not appear to have been taken into custody until August 7 or August 8, and that his hearing was held on August 9, he could not have complied with that notice provision.

On the page that follows, after a section that sets forth "Your Rights in Court," the papers contain a section entitled "Waiver of Attorney." That section states, "The undersigned have read the instructions concerning our right to an attorney and the right to a Court-appointed attorney, if applicable. Knowing and understanding these rights, we hereby waive our right to be represented by an attorney or Court-appointed attorney. We further understand that we can be represented by an attorney in the future simply by advising the Court of our intention to do so." Ms. S. and C.S. signed the lines designated for "parent" and "juvenile" in that section.

At the hearing, the magistrate stated in open court that he had "two sets of rights papers"—an apparent reference to the notice to appear and its explanation of rights. The magistrate verified that C.S. had received the papers, read them, and understood the rights set forth on them and that C.S. and his mother had signed the papers.

The magistrate also inquired of C.S. and his mother as follows:

THE COURT:	Do you understand that you have the right to be represented by an attorney at today's hearing?
C.S.:	Yes, sir.
THE COURT:	If you cannot afford an attorney and you qualify under state guidelines, I will appoint an attorney to represent you. Do you understand that?
C.S.:	Yes, sir.
THE COURT:	Do you wish to go forward with today's hearing without an attorney?
C.S.:	Yes, sir.
THE COURT:	Ms. S., do you agree with C.S.'s decision today to go forward without an attorney?
MS. S.:	Yes, sir."

The magistrate then explained the charges against appellant, including the degree of the offenses charged. After each offense was stated, the magistrate asked C.S. whether he understood the charge. Each time, C.S. answered that he did.

After each affirmative response, the magistrate asked whether C.S. admitted or denied the charge. C.S. admitted every charge. The magistrate then continued:

THE COURT:	If you admit these charges today, C.S., that's basically the same as pleading guilty. Do you understand that?
C.S.:	Yes, sir.
THE COURT:	As a result then we would not have an adjudicatory hearing or trial in either of these cases. Do you understand that?
C.S.:	Yes, sir.

"*THE COURT:*	Instead we would proceed directly to disposition, that is, for me to decide what punishment or conditions if any that should be imposed upon you. Do you understand that?
"*C.S.:*	Yes, sir.
"*THE COURT:*	By entering that plea you will be—well, first of all, that disposition in your case in A2005–0616 could include a commitment to the custody of the Ohio Department of Youth Services for a minimum period of six months or twelve months and a maximum period not to exceed age twenty-one. Do you understand that?
"*C.S.:*	Yes, sir.
"*THE COURT:*	Do you understand what the Ohio Department of Youth Services is?
"*C.S.:*	Yes, sir.
"*THE COURT:*	What is it?
"*C.S.:*	Juvenile prison, sir.
"*THE COURT:*	That's correct. By entering that plea of admit you will be waiving or giving up certain Constitutionally guaranteed rights that you would otherwise enjoy. Among the rights that you will be giving up is the right to remain silent. Do you understand that?
"*C.S.:*	Yes, sir.
"*THE COURT:*	You will also be giving up the right to call witnesses and to present evidence in your defense. Do you understand that?
"*C.S.:*	Yes, sir.
"*THE COURT:*	And you'll be giving up the right to question and to cross-examine prosecution witnesses. Do you understand that?
"*C.S.:*	Yes, sir.
"*THE COURT:*	Ordinarily, C.S., the State of Ohio would be required to prove these cases against you beyond a reasonable doubt. If you enter a plea of admit, however, the State of Ohio will not have to prove anything at all. Do you understand that?
"*C.S.:*	Yes, sir.
"*THE COURT:*	Have there been any promises or threats of any sort to cause you to enter these pleas?
"*C.S.:*	No, sir.
"*THE COURT:*	Ms. S., do you agree with C.S.'s decision today to enter pleas of admission to these charges?
"*MS. S.:*	Yes, sir.
"*THE COURT:*	Then, C.S., I'll accept the pleas of admission. Is there any statement about this situation that you wish to make?
"*C.S.:*	No, sir.

"THE COURT:	Have you talked with your mother since you got arrested?
"C.S.:	No, sir.
"THE COURT:	Ms. S., did you have an opportunity to read the police report?
"MS. S.:	No, sir.
"THE COURT:	I think it's safe to say, Ms. S. and C.S. . . . — it's safe to assume that there will be more . . . felony charges coming. I—I don't know when. It'll—it's going to be in the jurisdiction of Perry County. They'll transfer those cases up here so we'll deal with them, but in terms of the filing of the complaints, it'll be the Perry County Prosecutor that has to file those complaints. But we'll cross that bridge when we come to it. I just wanted you to know that because of the burglaries, the firearm thefts, the discharging of the firearm, animal cruelty, underage consumption, drug—felony drug possession charges—what else? What am I missing? That's probably it. Underage alcohol, possession of marijuana, possession of cocaine, burglary, animal cruelty, theft of a firearm. That pretty much covers it, doesn't it?
"C.S.:	Yes sir. B and E, sir.
"THE COURT:	And the B and E. Well, burglary. It'll be a burglary because it's a home. Did you do—oh, well, the trailer, was it—someone living in that trailer too?
"C.S.:	It—it was a camper, sir.
"THE COURT:	Okay. So that'd probably be a B and E so you'd get a B and E and a burglary. So all together, once those all get filed, you're probably looking at another three years on top of that once you add all those together. So that—that'll be coming at some time, Ms. S. A regular crime spree. Steals two cars. Basically totals them both. Shoots a cow. Shoots a horse. Steals a gun. Breaks into a house. Smokes dope. Has sex with an adult woman. Alcohol. Cocaine. Hope it was worth it. Ms. S., is there anything that you wish to say?
"MS. S.:	No, sir.
"THE COURT:	Do you know what I think, C.S., is the biggest injustice in this whole situation? Do you know?
"C.S.:	No, sir.
"THE COURT:	Well, I'll tell you what I think is the biggest injustice in the whole situation. The biggest injustice . . . is that I can only give you a year in prison. Based on what you've done over the past week, you ought to stay in prison until you're twenty-one years of age in my opinion, but I can't do that. To me, that's wrong. That's a disservice to every other taxpaying, law-abiding citizen of the state of Ohio that I can't lock you up [until you turn] twenty-one based on what you've been doing

for the past week. The biggest injustice in this case is that I can only give you a year in prison. . . . [T]he way this commitment works is I'm going to commit you to [DYS] today for a minimum of a year. Okay. But at the end of that year, however, that doesn't mean you automatically get out. The end of that year means simply that your case goes before the review authority to decide whether or not you should get out on parole. They don't have to let you out. So based on the nature of the offense, based on the opinion of our probation director . . . and based on your conduct in [DYS], it's entirely possible that you will do more than a year. But the only thing that I can guarantee that you'll do is a year. . . . So you're looking at another two and a half years on top of that once those charges are filed by Perry County. C.S., based upon your pleas of admission and the facts contained in the report in A2004–0329, I'll adjudicate you a probation violator as alleged in the motion. I'll order that you be released unsuccessfully in that—in that and all other cases. I'll order that you be released from probation unsuccessfully in all cases. Do you understand that?

"*C.S.:* Yes, sir.

"*THE COURT:* In A2005–0616, based upon your pleas of admission and the facts contained in the report, I'll adjudicate you delinquent on both counts. . . . On both counts, I'll order you committed to the custody of the Ohio Department of Youth Services for a minimum period of six months and a maximum period not to exceed your twenty-first birthday. I'll order that those two counts run consecutive to each other for an initial minimum commitment of twelve months. And . . . the Department of Youth Services is to ensure that [C.S.'s older brother] and C.S. are not in the same facility. I know that was your plan. Your plan was that they be in—you were—you were anxious to be arrested on these felonies so that you could go to [DYS] and be with your brother again. You're going to [DYS] but I'll ensure you're not in the same facility."

C.S. and his mother were informed of their right to object to the magistrate's decision and acknowledged receipt of the magistrate's decision. They waived objections and consented to the magistrate's decision.

After the trial court accepted the magistrate's decision, C.S. appealed on various grounds. One of those claims is pertinent here. C.S. argued that the trial court violated his rights to counsel and due process as those rights are conferred by the Fifth, Sixth, and Fourteenth Amendments to the United States Constitution, Sections 10 and 16, Article I of the Ohio Constitution, R.C. 2151.32, and Juv. R. 4 and 29.

After the court of appeals rejected that claim of error, we accepted C.S.'s discretionary appeal. . . .

Our analysis here must be placed in the context of the juvenile courts, which occupy a unique place in our legal system.

Juvenile courts are legislative creations, "rooted in social welfare philosophy rather than in the *corpus juris*." The juvenile courts were premised on profoundly different assumptions and goals than a criminal court, and eschewed traditional, objective criminal standards and retributive notions of justice. Instead, a new civil adjudication scheme arose, with a focus on the state's role as *parens patriae* and the vision that the courts would protect the wayward child from "evil influences," "save" him from criminal prosecution, and provide him social and rehabilitative services.

Not surprisingly then, the juvenile courts adopted proceedings that were less formal and more inquisitorial than adversarial, and a new lexicon that denoted differences between the two court systems. As one Ohio court explained, "Delinquency has not been declared a crime in Ohio, and the Ohio juvenile act is neither criminal nor penal in its nature, but is an administrative police regulation of a corrective character; and while the commission of the crime may set the machinery of the juvenile court in motion [,] the accused was not tried in that court for his crime but for incorrigibility."

Considered "a monument to the enlightened conviction that wayward boys may become good men," juvenile courts were lauded as "'one of the most significant advances in the administration of justice since the Magna Carta.'" They were widely left to operate without legal oversight for the first half of the 20th century. But with time, much of the beneficence that underlay the genesis of juvenile courts eroded. And with that erosion came increased constitutional oversight.

By midcentury, it was clear that the juvenile courts not only had the authority to impose significant penalties but that they frequently did so. Amid increasing disaffection with juvenile courts and some of their judges during the 1960s and 1970s came increasing recognition of due process rights and constitutional scrutiny of police action.

By that era, the Supreme Court recognized that a juvenile could "receive[] the worst of both worlds" in the juvenile court system by being provided "neither the protections accorded to adults nor the solicitous care and regenerative treatment postulated for children." In a series of cases, the court addressed that concern.

Although the court had recognized a due process interest in juvenile court proceedings as early as 1948, the understanding that the Due Process Clause of the Fourteenth Amendment applied to juvenile proceedings because of the juvenile's liberty interests was more fully developed in *Kent* (recognizing that "the admonition to function in a 'parental' relationship is not an invitation to procedural arbitrariness" and holding that a juvenile is entitled to a hearing on the issue of whether juvenile court jurisdiction should be waived before being released to a criminal court for prosecution), and crystallized in In re Gault (1967), 387 U.S. 1. . . .

In the wake of *Gault* and its progeny, we also found that "numerous constitutional safeguards normally reserved for criminal prosecutions are equally applicable to juvenile delinquency proceedings and overruled prior decisions that held to the contrary."

As a result of those cases, juveniles secured more of the rights afforded to adults, and juvenile court proceedings became more formal. Although some suggest that those changes, and the revisions to the juvenile delinquency laws themselves, indicate a criminalization of juvenile law, we have found that the General Assembly has adhered to the core tenets of the juvenile system even as it has made substantive changes to the Juvenile Code in a get-tough response to increasing juvenile caseloads, recidivism, and the realization that the harms suffered by victims are not dependent upon the age of the perpetrator.

Despite the inherent tension in the juvenile court system between the goals of juvenile rehabilitation and protection of society, the Supreme Court has suggested that the system should remain. "[O]ur decisions in recent years have recognized that there is a gap between the originally benign conception of the system and its realities. . . . That the system has fallen short of the high expectations of its sponsors [however] in no way detracts from the broad social benefits sought or from those benefits that can survive constitutional scrutiny." Contemporary juvenile courts thus remain "'an uneasy partnership of law and social work.'" We, too, abide by the principles that underlie the founding of the juvenile courts, but we do so with pragmatism and an understanding of modern realities.

For example, although we often characterize juvenile proceedings as civil rather than criminal, we recognize that "[w]hatever their label, juvenile delinquency laws feature inherently criminal aspects that we cannot ignore." "[J]uvenile delinquency laws feature inherently criminal aspects," and the state's goals in prosecuting a criminal action and in adjudicating a juvenile delinquency case are the same: "to vindicate a vital interest in the enforcement of *criminal* laws."

Given the state's valid interests in enforcing its criminal laws against juveniles and, in at least some cases, in requesting that the juvenile court impose significant penalties in their dispositions, we must also remain cognizant of the nature of the juvenile's right to representation by counsel.

In declaring that the juvenile facing commitment to an institution has a right to counsel "'at every step in the proceedings against him,'" the Supreme Court reinforced its belief that the appointment of counsel for a juvenile is not a mere formality or "a grudging gesture to a ritualistic requirement"; it is a venerable right at the core of the administration of justice and due process.

Indeed, it was the understanding of the right to due process that drove the court's holdings in *Kent*, *Gault*, and *Winship*. Those cases make clear that the right to counsel in a juvenile case flows to the juvenile through the Due Process Clause of the Fourteenth Amendment, not the Sixth Amendment. And although modern juvenile proceedings share some indicia of the criminal courts, juvenile proceedings are not considered criminal prosecutions for purposes of Sixth Amendment analyses.

Because the juvenile's right to counsel is predicated on due process, it is malleable rather than rigid. As the Supreme Court has explained, "For all its consequence, 'due process' has never been, and perhaps can never be, precisely defined. . . . [D]ue process 'is not a technical conception with a fixed content unrelated to time, place and circumstances.' Rather, the phrase expresses the requirement of 'fundamental fairness,' a requirement whose meaning can be as opaque as its importance is lofty. Applying the Due Process Clause is therefore an uncertain enterprise which must discover what 'fundamental fairness' consists of in a particular situation by first considering any relevant precedents and then by assessing the several interests that are at stake."

The flexibility of due process lies in its scope after it has been determined that some process is due, and due process doctrine recognizes that "not all situations calling for procedural safeguards call for the same kind of procedure." A court's task is to ascertain what process is due in a given case, while being true to the core concept of due process in a juvenile case—to ensure orderliness and fairness. We proceed in our analysis with that understanding at the fore.

The fact that the right to counsel in a juvenile case arises from due process does not diminish its importance. A juvenile typically lacks sufficient maturity and good judgment to make good decisions consistently and sufficiently foresee the consequences of his actions. *See, e.g.,* Roper v. Simmons (2005), 543 U.S. 551, 569–570; Planned Parenthood of Cent. Missouri v. Danforth (1976), 428 U.S. 52, 102 (Stevens, J., concurring in part and dissenting in part). Thus, "[t]he juvenile needs the assistance of counsel to cope with problems of law, to make skilled inquiry into the facts, to insist upon regularity of the proceedings and to ascertain whether he has a defense and to prepare and submit it."

Given the importance of counsel in juvenile proceedings, the General Assembly codified a juvenile's constitutional right to appointed counsel in the wake of *Gault.* Indeed, through R.C. 2151.352, the legislature provided a statutory right to appointed counsel that goes beyond constitutional requirements.

Former R.C. 2151.352 provided that a child "is entitled to representation by legal counsel at all stages of the proceedings . . . and if, as an indigent person, any such person is unable to employ counsel, to have counsel provided for the person." The statute mandated that "[i]f a party appears without counsel, the court shall ascertain whether the party knows of the party's right to counsel and of the party's right to be provided with counsel if the party is an indigent person." . . .

We have also incorporated constitutional safeguards in our rules of procedure. According to Juv.R. 4(A), "[e]very party shall have the right to be represented by counsel and every child * * * the right to appointed counsel if indigent." Similarly, Juv.R. 29(B) mandates that "[a]t the beginning of the hearing," the court inform unrepresented parties of their rights to counsel. The rules also recognize that, like an adult, a juvenile may waive his right to counsel. . . .

We believe that the fifth sentence of the statute reflects the General Assembly's understanding that *Gault* held that the juvenile may waive his rights, including his right to counsel, and that it codifies that right of waiver but only if the juvenile is advised by a parent in considering waiver. . . .

We are also persuaded by the reasoning of the Supreme Court of Connecticut in its rejection of the notion of nonwaiver. As that court noted, "a per se rule of nonwaivability might actually frustrate a principal goal of juvenile law of encouraging children to accept responsibility for their transgressions and take an active role in their rehabilitation. . . . Without minimizing the significance of this inevitable tension [between the juvenile courts' roles of protecting society and nurturing and rehabilitating juveniles], we are persuaded that allowing a child to make an informed and deliberate choice about legal representation, if properly supervised by the trial court, can advance both the goal of control and that of treatment. . . . To mandate the presence of counsel . . . might serve to reduce the child's own sense of involvement and might enhance his perception of his own role as merely that of spectator. . . . [W]e believe that the waiver of counsel decision, *in itself*, can be a significant rehabilitative moment for the child."

. . . We further hold that in a delinquency proceeding, a juvenile may waive his constitutional right to counsel, subject to certain standards articulated below, if he is counseled and advised by his parent, custodian, or guardian. If the juvenile is not counseled by his parent, guardian, or custodian and has not consulted with an attorney, he may not waive his right to counsel. . . .

In light of the sixth sentence of R.C. 2151.352, we hold that a judge must appoint counsel for a juvenile if there is a conflict between the juvenile and his parent, custodian, or guardian on the question of whether counsel should be waived. In so doing, we recognize that no case in Ohio has held that a parent can waive the constitutional right of a juvenile in a delinquency proceeding, and we make clear that no parent has that authority.

Our holdings here comport with similar decisions in other state courts that have addressed this issue, with Juv.R. 3 (which expressly countenances waiver) and with the precepts of *Gault*, which were concerned with the fundamental fairness of juvenile proceeding for all parties concerned, including the juvenile, his parents, and the state. . . .

In holding that the constitutional right to counsel may be waived by a juvenile, we apply the definition of waiver used in State v. Foster—an "intentional relinquishment or abandonment of a known right." As in cases involving adults, there is a strong presumption against waiver of the constitutional right to counsel.

An effective waiver of the right to counsel by a juvenile must be voluntary, knowing, and intelligent. In a juvenile court proceeding in which the judge acts as *parens patriae*, the judge must scrupulously ensure that the juvenile fully understands, and intentionally and intelligently relinquishes, the right to counsel.

In the discharge of that duty, the judge is to engage in a meaningful dialogue with the juvenile. Instead of relying solely on a prescribed formula or script for engaging a juvenile during the consideration of the waiver, the inquisitional approach is more consistent with the juvenile courts' goals, and is best suited to address the myriad factual scenarios that a juvenile judge may face in addressing the question of waiver.

We agree with the Supreme Court of Nebraska's recent holding that a totality-of-the-circumstances analysis is the proper test to be used in ascertaining whether there has been a valid waiver of counsel by a juvenile. The judge must consider a number of factors and circumstances, including the age, intelligence, and education of the juvenile; the juvenile's background and experience generally and in the court system specifically; the presence or absence of the juvenile's parent, guardian, or custodian; the language used by the court in describing the juvenile's rights; the juvenile's conduct; the juvenile's emotional stability; and the complexity of the proceedings.

In cases such as this one, in which a juvenile is charged with a serious offense, the waiver of the right to counsel must be made in open court, recorded, and in writing. If a written waiver has been executed, the juvenile court judge must consider the form used and the juvenile's literacy level to ensure that the juvenile has an intelligent understanding of the document and an appreciation of the gravity of signing it.

Though it is not dispositive, a key factor in the totality of the circumstances is the degree to which the juvenile's parent is capable of assisting and willing to assist the juvenile in the waiver analysis. . . .

The juvenile court judge must be guided by Juv.R. 29 in the process of considering a waiver of counsel and in accepting an admission. Juv.R. 29(B) mandates that the juvenile court judge must advise a juvenile, at the commencement of the adjudicatory hearing, of certain rights, including the rights to counsel. Juv.R. 29(D) further mandates that before an admission can be accepted, the juvenile court judge must be satisfied that the admission is voluntarily made with the understanding of the nature of the allegations and the consequences of the admission and that by entering the admission, the juvenile is waiving the rights to confront witnesses and challenge evidence, to remain silent, and to introduce his own evidence.

As many Ohio courts of appeals recognize, "An admission in a juvenile proceeding, pursuant to Juv.R. 29, is analogous to a guilty plea made by an adult pursuant to Crim.R. 11 in that both require that a trial court personally address the defendant on the record with respect to the issues set forth in the rules." . . .

We hold that in a juvenile delinquency case, the preferred practice is strict compliance with Juv.R. 29(D). We further hold, however, that if the trial court substantially complies with Juv.R. 29(D) in accepting an admission by a juvenile, the plea will be deemed voluntary absent a showing of prejudice by the juvenile or a showing that the totality of the circumstances does not support a finding of a valid waiver. For purposes of juvenile delinquency proceedings, substantial compliance means that in the totality of the circumstances, the juvenile subjectively understood the implications of his plea. . . .

We now turn to the facts of this case.

Although the magistrate secured representations from C.S. and his mother that they had signed the "rights papers," the record is not clear as to the knowingness of the waiver and the intelligent relinquishment of rights. At the time C.S. waived his rights, with his mother's assent, there were clear portents of additional, significant charges that would have been felony offenses had they been committed by an adult. In fact, after C.S. had waived counsel, the magistrate specifically mentioned the possibility that additional felony charges could be forthcoming.

There is ample evidence in the record to suggest that from the time C.S. first spoke to police until he waived his right to counsel in the courtroom, his focus was on being committed so that he could be close to his older brother, who had previously been committed to the custody of the Department of Youth Services. His rationale for the admission cannot be said to be intelligent, as evidenced by the judge's conclusion that the two youths should not be housed together.

An important aspect of our consideration in this case is our concern that there was not any meaningful advice rendered to C.S. in his decision to waive counsel. We acknowledge that an inference can be drawn that this family, through its past dealings with the juvenile courts, may have had an understanding of the process in which C.S. was engaged. But we are not satisfied that there was a sufficient showing that Ms. S. was in a position to render any meaningful advice to her son in this case.

Ms. S. had not spoken with her son since his arrest, and she had not had an opportunity to read the police report detailing his prodigious criminal activity before agreeing that he should waive his right to legal counsel. The magistrate did not ask about those facts until after he had secured the waiver of counsel and accepted C.S.'s admissions. We would not condone an attorney's failure to meet with a client prior to advising him to waive his rights to counsel or appearing before a judge for a plea hearing, and we are not satisfied that any meaningful advice was offered by Ms. S. in this matter.

Ms. S.'s only inquiry during the hearing related not to the evidence against her son, to the controlling law, or to her son's rights. Rather, like her son, she was focused on whether C.S. could be placed in the same facility in which his brother was housed. Her focus on the place of confinement was not based on the services available to her son in a particular facility but, rather, on a pragmatic concern: her means of transportation were limited, and it would be easier for her to visit her children if they were in the same institution.

In the circumstances before us, we are not persuaded that the waiver of counsel was valid. We thus vacate the court of appeals' judgment to the extent that it held that there was a sufficient showing of a valid waiver of counsel, and we remand the cause to the juvenile court. . . .

Judgment reversed and cause remanded.

The dissenting opinion of Justice O'DONNELL is omitted.

LANZINGER, J., dissenting. . . . The record reveals that C.S. acknowledged reading and signing a form that included the statement "You have the right to be represented by an attorney at all stages of this proceeding" and informed him that an attorney will be appointed if "you cannot afford an attorney and you qualify under State guidelines." The waiver of attorney that C.S. and his mother signed stated, "The undersigned have read the instructions concerning our right to an attorney and the right to a Court-appointed attorney, if applicable. Knowing and understanding these rights, we hereby waive our right to be represented by an attorney or Court-appointed attorney. We further understand that we can be represented by an attorney in the future simply by advising the Court of our intention to do so." During a colloquy with the magistrate regarding his rights, C.S. answered "yes" to the question "Do you understand that?" at least nine times. The magistrate in juvenile court determined that a valid waiver of counsel was made in accepting the plea.

Despite this record of the proceedings, the majority holds that the waiver of counsel was invalid because C.S.'s mother was not "in a position to render any meaningful advice to her son," even though she was present at the delinquency adjudication hearing. . . .

I agree that the totality of circumstances should be considered to ascertain the validity of the waiver but disagree with the majority's emphasis on C.S.'s mother's intent. "Meaningful advice" from a parent was not required for a valid waiver until now, and any assistance that C.S.'s mother offered him would have been considered part of the totality of the circumstances the court would consider in determining whether C.S. validly waived the right to counsel. Nothing in rule or statute requires "a sufficient showing that [the parent is] in a position to render . . . meaningful advice to her son." Besides being unnecessary, such an ambiguous standard will be difficult to apply.

C.S.'s mother's motivation in having her two children placed in the same facility should not invalidate C.S.'s waiver when, as the record shows, he waived his right to counsel and admitted to the charges against him after a colloquy with the judge that occurred in open court. . . .

NOTES AND QUESTIONS

1. Why did the court hold that C.S.'s waiver was not legally sufficient? If C.S.'s mother had had more time to talk with him before the court hearing, would that have validated C.S.'s waiver? If not, what more would have to have been shown to support a finding that the waiver was valid?

While most courts that allow waivers examine the totality of circumstances to determine if the respondent acted voluntarily and knowingly, the application of this very discretionary test varies significantly. For example, to the principal case compare In re Interest of Dalton S., 730 N.W.2d 816 (Neb. 2007), where the court upheld the waiver of a 9-year-old diagnosed as mildly mentally handicapped and suffering from bipolar disorder, attention deficit disorder, and posttraumatic stress syndrome. A factor weighing in favor of the finding, according to the court, was the mother's support for the waiver, even though she "had demonstrated some failings in caring for Dalton," did not pursue a diversion offer from the prosecution, and told Dalton at the hearing, "You don't need a lawyer. Say no [to the question of whether you want a lawyer]. Say it."

2. The juvenile court judge's colloquy with C.S. is typical; was it sufficient for determining if he had knowingly and voluntarily waived his right to counsel? If you were a judge required to decide whether a child was making a knowing and voluntary waiver of the right to counsel, what would you consider in making a decision? When would such a decision be knowing and intelligent for an adult?

3. As the court's discussion indicates, C.S. and his mother were also advised of the right to counsel in writing before they appeared before the judge. In a recent study, researchers analyzed the content and comprehensibility of such forms from a number of jurisdictions. They found that the forms varied greatly from jurisdiction to jurisdiction and were likely to "exceed the reading comprehension" of most adult and juvenile defendants. The juvenile and adult forms were indistinguishable. Allison D. Redlich & Catherine L. Bonventre, Content and Comprehensibility of Juvenile and Adult Tender-of-Plea Forms: Implications for Knowing, Intelligent, and Voluntary Guilty Pleas, 39 Law & Hum. Behav. 162 (2015). In light of researchers' findings about minors' understanding of their rights during police encounters and at trial, discussed in Chapter 5 and earlier in this chapter, what kind of tender-of-plea forms should be used in juvenile court, if any?

4. A recent study found that juveniles are twice as likely to plead guilty when they are factually innocent as adults. Age did not affect willingness to plead guilty when the subjects were factually guilty. The principal reason for juveniles being more willing to plead guilty when innocent is that they are less likely to consider the short- and long-term consequences of their plea decisions. Allison D. Redlich & Reveka V. Shteynberg, To Plead or Not to Plead: A Comparison of Juvenile and Adult True and False Plea Decisions, 40 J. L. & Human Behavior 611 (2016).

5. The degree to which adolescents understand the role of the defense attorney has long been a topic of study by social scientists. A recent report focuses on whether juveniles understand the concepts of attorney-client privilege and zealous representation, finding that factors that impact a youth's understanding are demographics, previous exposure to the legal system, attitudes regarding the fairness of court proceedings, and the outcome of her own case. The study's authors argue that because even some of the most experienced juveniles do not fully understand these concepts, juveniles are more likely to devalue the right to counsel. The authors argue further for mandatory warnings that give children substantive information about a lawyer's role in a way that is catered to their needs. M. Dyan McGuire et al., Do Juveniles Understand What an Attorney Is Supposed to Do Well Enough to Make Knowing and Intelligent Decisions About Waiving Their Right to Counsel?: An Exploratory Study (2015) http://npjs.org/jajjs/wp-content/uploads/2015/02/JAJJS-Article-McGuire.pdf

Should states adopt a rule forbidding a juvenile to waive the right to counsel at trial? The court in *C.S.* rejects such a rule. Why? What other arguments support the court's position?

Some states permit waiver of counsel only with the advice of an attorney. *See, e.g.*, State ex rel. J.M. v. Taylor, 276 S.E.2d 199 (W. Va. 1981); In re Appeal No. 544, 332 A.2d 680 (Md. Spec. App. 1975); 10 Del. Code § 1007C (2019); N.Y. Fam. Ct. Act § 249-a (2019); Or. Rev. Stat. § 419C.200 (2019); Tex. Fam. Code Ann. § 51.09 (2019). Delaware also forbids waiver by a minor accused of a felony or who is younger than 16. The most restrictive view is that of the Institute for Judicial Administration-American Bar Association, Juvenile Justice Standards Project, Standards Relating to Pre-Trial Court Proceedings 88-95 (allowing pro se representation only in "exceptional circumstances" and requiring appointment of standby counsel).

6. When a criminal defendant pleads guilty with the advice of counsel, most of the time the prosecutor and defense attorney have bargained for this result. In return for the defendant's waiver of trial rights, the defendant may receive one or more benefits: dismissal of some of the charges, substitution of less serious charges for those initially lodged, or prosecutorial agreement to a recommendation for sentence that is less severe than the maximum punishment associated with the offense to which defendant pleads.

In principle, it is hard to see how plea negotiations could be carried out in the traditional juvenile court. In its classic form, the parties bargain around the charges because the penalty that the defendant receives results directly from the offense for which he is convicted. Disposition (sentencing) in juvenile court, however, traditionally was not determined by the offense committed but rather by the totality of the child's circumstances. While reducing a felony charge to a misdemeanor would benefit the criminal accused in precisely calculable terms, this same reduction might not affect a juvenile court judge's dispositional order in any way.

Nonetheless, a considerable amount of plea bargaining did occur even in the traditional juvenile court despite the lack of relationship between the dispositional order and the offense charged or committed. *See* W. Vaughan Stapleton & Lee E. Teitelbaum, In Defense of Youth: A Study of the Role of Counsel in American Juvenile Courts 134-138 (1972). Bargaining is more common in juvenile courts with relatively formal and adversarial procedures than in more informally structured juvenile courts. *Id.* With the adoption of a process that more closely resembles the criminal justice system and the greater possibility of transfer, plea bargaining has become as standard a feature of juvenile court representation as it is in adult prosecutions.

7. Any minor, but especially a preadolescent or young teen, may rely heavily on a parent for advice about whether to accept his or her lawyer's recommendations. How should the child's attorney handle the problem of a parent giving a child advice that seems contrary to the child's legal interests?

B. DISPOSITION

1. *The Tradition of Judicial Discretion*

HERBERT H. LOU, *JUVENILE COURTS IN THE UNITED STATES*

143-145 (1927)

The real test of the value of the juvenile court lies in the character of legal treatment in the form of court orders or judgments, and social treatment in the form of constructive work with the child or the family. . . . The juvenile court prescribes methods of treatment, not according to any set forms, but according to individual needs of the child as revealed by social, physical, and mental diagnoses regarding the child himself, his environment, and the essential causal factors responsible for his behavior, and according to a constructive plan arrived at by conference of the judge, probation officer, physician, psychologists, and the psychiatrist. The essential consideration in the disposition of cases and the treatment that follows is the welfare of the child. . . . The existence of the juvenile court is to be justified not by any theory but by its intelligent administration of treatment and its actual success in saving the child. . . .

There are, in substance, four ways in which a juvenile-court judge may dispose of a children's case and administer treatment: (1) dismissal, (2) probation, (3) home placement, and (4) commitment; that is, he may discharge the child, put him on probation, place him in a foster-family home, or commit him to an institution. An order of dismissal may be made upon a hearing or after "continuance," unaccompanied by probation order. In delinquency cases, orders of dismissal and probation may be accompanied by orders for restitution or reparation. . . .

An order of the juvenile court, unlike that of a criminal court, may usually be vacated or set aside or modified as the facts of the case and the welfare of the child may, from time to time, require. . . .

Other methods of disposition [such as corporal punishment, jail sentence, or commitment to a state reformatory], although sometimes necessary, . . . do not have any positive value. . . . Of course, there is preference of one form of order and treatment to another but, at all events, it should be given as the most logical means of helping the individual child. It should be a matter of the individual and his social needs rather than the kind of offense and punishment for it.

As we saw in the first part of Chapter 4, addressing the origin and theory of the American juvenile court, the disassociation of offense from treatment was an essential aspect of a "therapeutic" and noncriminal approach to juvenile misconduct. This disjunction could, in principle, operate in two directions. Most commonly, the effect was to increase the ambit of the court's authority. Principles of preventive penology and child-saving justified intervention in cases where no offense had been proved but where the child's uncooperative behavior with parents or teachers gave rise to concern. As Judge Harvey Baker of the Boston Juvenile Court pointed out:

> . . . [T]he court does not confine its attention to just the particular offense which brought the child to its notice. For example, a boy who comes to court for some such trifle as failing to wear his badge when selling papers may be held on probation for months because of difficulties at school; and a boy who comes in for playing ball in the street may . . . be committed to a reform school because he is found to have habits of loafing, stealing or gambling which cannot be corrected outside.

Harvey H. Baker, Procedure of the Boston Juvenile Court, 23 Survey 643, 649 (1910). You will recall that Gerald Gault was committed to the Arizona state industrial school for his minority because of an obscene telephone call that would have resulted in a sentence of no more than 6 months for an adult. Courts generally hold that sentencing disparities of this kind between juvenile and adult court do not violate equal protection, emphasizing the very different orientation and purposes of the two systems. *See, e.g.*, Matter of Appeal, in Maricopa Cty. Juvenile No. J-86509, 604 P.2d 641 (Ariz. 1979); People in Interest of M.C., 774 P.2d 857 (Colo. 1989); In re T.D., 401 N.E.2d 275 (Ill. App. 1980); In re Interest of A.M.H., 447 N.W.2d 40 (Neb. 1989); State in Interest of K.V.N., 283 A.2d 337 (N.J. Sup. 1971), *aff'd*, 291 A.2d 577 (N.J. 1972); People ex rel. Cromwell v. Warden, 345 N.Y.S.2d 381 (1973); Wilson Appeal, 264 A.2d 614 (Pa. 1970); State v. Rice, 655 P.2d 1145 (Wash. 1982); In re Interest of J.K., 228 N.W.2d 713 (Wis. 1975).

A diminished emphasis on offense could also mean that a child proved to have engaged in serious criminal misconduct might receive a probationary sanction or, at least in principle, would receive no sanction if it appeared that even therapeutic intervention was unnecessary. The latter possibility is explicitly recognized in juvenile code provisions creating explicitly or implicitly a "dual condition" — that is, requiring that the court find that the child both had committed an offense and was in need of care, rehabilitation, or treatment before adjudication and disposition. *See, e.g.*, In re Johnson, 174 N.E.2d 907 (Ill. App. 1961) ("If every juvenile misdemeanor is to result in the State taking charge, few parents are secure in the custody of their children."); In the Matter of Edwin R., 323 N.Y.S.2d 909 (Fam. Ct. 1971) (homicide charges dismissed); Uniform Juvenile Court Act § 2(3) (1969). The North Dakota Supreme Court has held that if a juvenile court dismisses a petition on the basis that the juvenile does not need treatment or rehabilitation, the state cannot appeal because allowing an appeal would violate the double jeopardy clause. Interest of M.H.P., 830 N.W.2d 216 (N.D. 2013). The next case is an example of a contemporary use of this kind of statute.

In re T. Q. N.

365 P.3d 1112 (Or. App. 2015)

EGAN, J. Youth appeals an adjudication judgment that found him within the juvenile court's jurisdiction on allegations that, if committed as an adult, would

constitute sexual abuse in the first degree and attempted sexual abuse in the first
degree . . . .

To provide context, we begin with a description of the Washington County
conditional postponement program. A conditional postponement program agreement provided by the court to youth states:

> The juvenile court conditional postponement program allows eligible persons charged
> with a sex offense petition to avoid adjudication trial by successfully completing a sex
> offender treatment program. If you satisfactorily complete treatment and comply with
> all of the terms of the conditional postponement program, the juvenile petition will be
> dismissed and a new petition could not be filed on those same charges. If you do not
> successfully complete the conditions of this agreement, you have waived your right to
> a hearing and a judge will proceed directly to disposition (sentencing). Juvenile condi-
> tional postponement is a privilege you may exercise only once.

The agreement then lists factors that automatically render a person ineligible
for the program such as a history of repeated sex offenses or the use of a weapon
during the charged incident. It also states that postponement lasts 18 months subject to extension by the agreement of the parties. The agreement also provides that
a participating youth must fully complete the sex offender treatment recommended
in a psychosexual evaluation and approved of by a juvenile counselor during the
postponement period and comply with all other conditions. Last, the agreement
states that, to participate in the program, the youth must admit to the offense.

We turn to the facts of this case. In July 2011, a Washington County Juvenile
Department counselor filed a petition alleging that youth had committed one
count of sexual abuse in the first degree and one count of attempted sexual abuse
in the first degree. In August 2011, youth completed a psychosexual evaluation.
At a pretrial conference held on October 24, 2011, youth informed the court that
he would be filing a motion for conditional postponement and, the following day,
youth filed that motion accompanied by a memorandum of law. In his memorandum, youth argued that the court has authority to grant his motion under
ORS 419C.261. The state opposed the motion, arguing only that the Washington
County conditional postponement program is unlawful and not that the youth was
an inappropriate candidate for the program.

On January 12, 2012, the court held a contested jurisdictional hearing and,
the following day, the court issued an order finding youth within the jurisdiction
of the juvenile court. On January 31, the court signed an amended order relating
to the January 12 contested jurisdictional hearing. The amended order stated, in
part, "[M]otion for conditional postponement to be addressed at [contested jurisdictional hearing] . . . set [contested jurisdictional hearing] 1-12-12 9 AM[.]"

In February 2012, the court held a dispositional hearing. During that hearing, youth renewed his motion for conditional postponement filed in October
2011. In response, the following exchange occurred:

COURT:	All right, I will include as part of the written order from today's hearing that the condi-tional postponement was denied.
[YOUTH'S COUNSEL]:	I would ask the court to [inaudible] whether the court [is] exercising its discretion in deciding that [youth] was not an appropriate

	candidate for the conditional postponement program, or whether the court—
COURT:	I don't think there's legal basis for this 'conditional postponement.'
[YOUTH'S COUNSEL]:	Will that be included in your written order?
COURT:	No, it's on the record.

On appeal, youth argues that the juvenile court erred when it concluded that it lacked authority to grant youth's motion for conditional postponement. The state responds that the juvenile court was correct that it lacked the authority to grant youth's motion because, although the legislature gave juvenile courts broad power to dismiss a petition, there is no specific statutory grant of power to juvenile courts to postpone adjudication of a petition subject to conditions. . . .

The parties' dispute presents a question of statutory construction, which we review for legal error. "We ascertain the legislature's intentions by examining the text of the statute in its context, along with relevant legislative history, and, if necessary, canons of construction."

ORS 419C.261(2)(a) provides:

> The court may set aside or dismiss a petition filed under ORS 419C.005 in further-ance of justice after considering the circumstances of the youth and the interests of the state in the adjudication of the petition. . . .

. . . [W]e turn to the state's argument that the court lacks authority to set conditions upon the completion of which the court would dismiss a juvenile peti-tion. The state concedes that a juvenile court's powers to dismiss a petition under ORS 419C.261 are "broad." However, the state asserts that youth's motion for conditional postponement "did not ask the court to amend, dismiss, or set aside the delinquency petition without taking jurisdiction." That is incorrect. To be sure, youth's motion did not ask the court to dismiss the petition immediately; however, youth, indeed, asked for dismissal. Youth's memorandum in support of his motion concludes:

> This court is authorized by the juvenile code to consider a dismissal of this case pursuant to ORS 419C.261. [Youth] is asking the court to allow a conditional post-ponement in order to allow him time to complete the recommendations of the psy-chosexual evaluation he completed, with the understanding that if he successfully completes the requirements his case will be dismissed.

We agree with the state that Oregon appellate courts have interpreted ORS 419C.261 to grant broad discretion to juvenile courts to dismiss petitions. *See, e.g.*, Dreyer, 328 Ore. 332, 976 P.2d 1123 (concluding that, under ORS 419C.261, a juvenile court can dismiss a petition before or after a youth has been found within the jurisdiction of the court); State v. L. M. W., 275 Ore. App. 731, 734, 365 P.3d 1181 (concluding that, under ORS 419C.261, a juvenile court can dismiss a petition for conduct that would otherwise subject a youth to sex-offender reg-istration requirements); State v. C. E. B., 254 Ore. App. 353, 295 P3d 118 (2012) (concluding that, under ORS 419C.261, the juvenile court's authority to dismiss a petition is not limited to cases in which the person continues to be within the juvenile court's jurisdiction). Furthermore, we conclude that the legislature's grant of authority to juvenile courts to dismiss petitions "in the furtherance of justice after considering the circumstances of the youth and the interests of the state in the adjudication of the petition" is broad enough to encompass the Washington County conditional postponement program as presented in this case. Accordingly, we reverse and remand for the juvenile court to consider merits of youth's motion.

NOTES AND QUESTIONS

1. The dual condition jurisdictional requirement was originally intended for cases of "good kids" whose parents were regarded as able to handle the (usually minor) problem. Would the facts of *T.Q.N.* fit this paradigm?

2. Recall that state and federal laws require juveniles convicted of many sex offenses to register for many years or even for life. The local procedure implemented under the dual condition statute in *T.Q.N.* provides relief from such requirements. Is this use within the legislative intent?

2. *Structuring Dispositional Discretion*

Probation is the most frequently ordered disposition in juvenile court. In 2014, juvenile judges ordered probation in 63 percent of the cases in which a minor was found delinquent and residential placement in 26 percent of the cases. Nina Hyland, Delinquency Cases in Juvenile Court, 2014 at 3 (OJJDP Jan. 2018).

In 2015, juvenile residential placement facilities held 48,043 youths, down from a peak of 120,006 in 1999. Most of those in custody, 85 percent, were male, and 69 percent were minority youth, with the largest share being black males. Nationwide, the detention rate for black youth was six times the rate for white youth, and their commitment rate was nearly five times that of white youth. Sarah Hockenberry, Juveniles in Residential Placement, 2015 (U.S. Dept. Justice, OJJDP Jan. 2018). *See also* Kareem L. Jordan & Tina L. Freiburger, Examining the Impact of Race and Ethnicity on the Sentencing of Juveniles in Adult Court, 21 Crim. Just. Pol'y Rev. 185 (2010); Mark Soler, Reducing Racial and Ethnic Disparities in the Juvenile Justice System (2014), http://www.ncsc.org/~/media/Microsites/Files/Future%20Trends%202014/Reducing%20Racial%20and%20Ethnic%20Disparities_Soler.ashx; The Marshall Project, Our Prisons in Black and White (Nov. 18, 2015) https://www.themarshallproject.org/2015/11/18/our-prisons-in-black-and-white#.IDMLBCuz2.

Bias, explicit and implicit, explains much of the racial disparity in juvenile delinquency dispositions, and reduction of discretion is often recommended as at least a partial solution.

In re P.O.

200 Cal. Rptr. 3d 841 (Cal. App. 2016)

HUMES, P. J. P.O. appeals from a juvenile court order declaring him a ward of the court and placing him on probation after he admitted to a misdemeanor count of public intoxication. He claims that a condition of his probation requiring him to submit to warrantless searches of his "electronics including passwords" is unreasonable under People v. Lent (1975) 15 Cal. 3d 481 (Lent) and unconstitutionally overboard. . . .

In November 2014, the principal of P.O.'s Pleasanton high school observed that P.O., who was 17 years old at the time, appeared to be under the influence of drugs. P.O. admitted to using hashish oil earlier that morning, and a search revealed 11 tablets of Xanax in his pockets.

A few months later, the Alameda County District Attorney filed a petition under Welfare and Institutions Code section 602, subdivision (a) seeking to have P.O. declared a ward of the court. The petition alleged one misdemeanor count of unlawful possession of a controlled substance, and P.O. ultimately admitted to an amended allegation that he committed a misdemeanor count of public intoxication.

At the dispositional hearing, the juvenile court declared P.O. a ward of the court and placed him on probation with various conditions, three of which are at issue in this appeal. The first requires him to "[s]ubmit person and any vehicle, room[,] or property, electronics including passwords under [his] control to search by Probation Officer or peace office[r] with or without a search warrant at any time of day or night." We shall refer to the portion of this condition permitting searches of "electronics including passwords" as the "electronics search condition." The other two require him to "attend classes or job on time and regularly; be of good behavior and perform well" and "be of good citizenship and good conduct." We shall refer to these conditions as the "good-behavior conditions." A number of other conditions that P.O. does not challenge were also imposed, including conditions that he not use or possess illegal drugs, not "associate with anyone [he] know[s] to use, deal[,] or possess illegal drugs," and submit to drug testing.

P.O. objected to the electronics search condition on the basis that there was no evidence to suggest he was buying or selling drugs. In response, the juvenile court emphasized the need to help P.O. avoid substance abuse. It then stated, "[T]o properly supervise these drug conditions, we need to go on your web sites, check what you may be presenting as far as your ability to purchase, to sell drugs, your ability to—we have people who present themselves on the Internet using drugs or . . . in possession of paraphernalia, and that's the only way we can properly supervise these conditions . . ."

A. *Although Reasonable Under Lent, the Electronics Search Condition Is Unconstitutionally Overbroad. . . .*

When a minor is made a ward of the juvenile court and placed on probation, the court "may impose and require any and all reasonable conditions that it may determine fitting and proper to the end that justice may be done and the reformation and rehabilitation of the ward enhanced." (Welf. & Inst. Code, § 730, subd. (b); *see also id.*, § 202, subd. (b).) "'In fashioning the conditions of probation, the . . . court should consider the minor's entire social history in addition to the circumstances of the crime.'" The court has "broad discretion to fashion conditions of probation," although "every juvenile probation condition must be made to fit the circumstances and the minor." We review the imposition of a probation condition for an abuse of discretion, taking into account "the sentencing court's stated purpose in imposing it."

A juvenile court's discretion to impose probation conditions is broad, but it has limits. Under *Lent*, which applies to both juvenile and adult probationers, a condition is "invalid [if] it '(1) has no relationship to the crime of which the offender was convicted, (2) relates to conduct which is not in itself criminal, and (3) requires or forbids conduct which is not reasonably related to future criminality.'" "This test is conjunctive—all three prongs must be satisfied before a reviewing court will invalidate a probation term." . . .

The first prong under *Lent*, that must be met to invalidate a probation condition requires the condition to have no relationship to the offender's crime. P.O. argues that the electronics search condition has no relationship to his crime because the record contains no evidence about his use of electronic devices, much less his use of "electronics or social media to display drug use." The Attorney General effectively concedes that the first prong is met, and we agree that the challenged condition has no relationship to P.O.'s crime of being intoxicated in public.

The second prong required to invalidate a probation condition—that the condition relates to conduct that is not itself criminal—is also met here, because there is nothing inherently illegal about using electronic devices. The Attorney General agrees that "as a general matter, using electronic devices is not illegal," and she does not contest that the second prong is met.

We conclude that the third prong required to invalidate a probation condition is not met, however, because the electronics search condition is reasonably related to future criminality. Under *Olguin*, 45 Cal. 4th 375, a probation condition that enables probation officers "to supervise [their] charges effectively is . . . 'reasonably related to future criminality.'" This is true "even if [the] condition . . . has no relationship to the crime of which a defendant was convicted." Here, the condition reasonably relates to enabling the effective supervision of P.O.'s compliance with other probation conditions. Specifically, the condition enables peace officers to review P.O.'s electronic activity for indications that P.O. has drugs or is otherwise engaged in activity in violation of his probation. We cannot say that the juvenile court's given reason for imposing the condition—that minors are apt to use electronic devices to show off their drug use or ability to procure drugs—was speculative or otherwise constituted an abuse of discretion.

Another published opinion holding that an electronics search condition was unreasonable under *Len*, has been issued since our prior opinions on the same subject. In *Mark C.*, Division Two followed its earlier decision in In re Erica R., 240 Cal.App.4th 907 and held that the third prong of *Lent* was not satisfied because the condition was not reasonably related to future criminality. In reaching this holding, *Mark C.* made two primary points with which we disagree.

First, *Mark C.* distinguished *Olguin* on the basis that the probation condition in *Olguin*—which required the probationer to disclose any pets he kept at his home—"did not extend the scope of the warrantless search of the probationer's residence, rather it facilitated the search of the residence by mitigating the potential of any pet residing with the probationer 'to distract, impede, and endanger probation officers in the exercise of their supervisory duties.' Thus, it enabled the 'probation officer to supervise his or her charges effectively.'" The court continued, "We do not read *Olguin* to hold that *every* condition that might enable a probation officer to supervise his or her minor charges more effectively is necessarily 'reasonably related to future criminality.' Such a reading would effectively eliminate the reasonableness requirement that the court in *Olguin* discusses at some length. Requiring [the minor] to copy his probation officer on all his e-mails, and forward all his postings on social media to his probation officer might also facilitate his probation officer's supervision of him, as would requiring him to wear a body camera. But *Olguin* no more justifies these hypothetical probation conditions than the actual electronics search condition in this case."

In our view, this point misconstrues the reasonableness requirement discussed in *Olguin*. *Olguin*'s mention of reasonableness occurred during a discussion of the burden that compliance with the probation condition imposed on the probationer. It is this burden that must be reasonable, not the condition itself. It may well be that a probation condition requiring a minor to forward all electronic communications to the probation officer or to wear a body camera would be unreasonable under *Lent*, but it would be so because of the burden it imposed on the minor—not because it invaded the minor's privacy (a constitutional concern better addressed by the overbreadth doctrine), and certainly not because it lacked a connection to preventing future criminality.

Second, *Mark C.* distinguished *Olguin* because *Olguin* involved an adult probationer, stating, "Adults, but not minors, have the right to refuse probation. Accordingly, search conditions that apply to a minor must be tailored to fit the minor's particular rehabilitative needs; if they [do] not, they are invalid under *Lent*." *Mark C.* considered the electronics search condition not to be so tailored because there was "nothing in [the minor's] offense or personal history show[ing] a connection between his use of electronic devices or social media and any criminal activity" and thus "there [was] no reason to believe that the . . . condition [would] serve the rehabilitative function of preventing [the minor] from committing future criminal acts."

If this reasoning were correct, then juvenile courts would be unable to impose standard search conditions permitting warrantless searches of a minor's person, residence, vehicle, and other physical locations without a showing that those locations were all connected to past criminal conduct. In fact, such conditions are routinely imposed despite their potential to invade minors' privacy. Although "a minor cannot be made subject to an automatic search condition," this requires a court to consider whether a search condition is appropriate under the circumstances before imposing it, not to find a connection between the locations to be searched and the minor's past conduct. And to the extent the concern with the reasonableness of electronics search conditions stems from the impact electronic searches have on privacy, the fact that a probationer is a minor justifies *more* intrusive probation conditions, as we discuss further below.

In sum, we conclude that the electronics search condition is valid under *Lent* because it is reasonably related to future criminality. . . .

When a probation condition imposes limitations on a person's constitutional rights, it "'must closely tailor those limitations to the purpose of the condition'"—that is, the probationer's reformation and rehabilitation—"'to avoid being invalidated as unconstitutionally overbroad.'" "The essential question in an overbreadth challenge is the closeness of the fit between the legitimate purpose of the restriction and the burden it imposes on the [probationer]'s constitutional rights—bearing in mind, of course, that perfection in such matters is impossible, and that practical necessity will justify some infringement." "Even conditions which infringe on constitutional rights may not be invalid [as long as they are] tailored specifically to meet the needs of the juvenile."

A probation condition imposed on a minor must be narrowly tailored to both the condition's purposes and the minor's needs, but a condition . . . that would be unconstitutional or otherwise improper for an adult probationer may be permissible for a minor under the supervision of the juvenile court. This is because juveniles are deemed to be more in need of guidance and supervision than adults, and because a minor's constitutional rights are more circumscribed. The state, when it asserts jurisdiction over a minor, stands in the shoes of the parents. And a parent may curtail a child's exercise of . . . constitutional rights . . . [because a] parent's own constitutionally protected "liberty" includes the right to "bring up children" [citation] and to "direct the upbringing and education of children." Whether a probation condition is unconstitutionally overbroad presents a question of law reviewed de novo. . . .

P.O.'s claim is that the electronics search condition infringes upon his constitutional right to privacy in the way it impacts his cell phone use. We agree with P.O. that the electronics search condition is overbroad in its authorization of searches of cell phones and electronic accounts accessible through such devices because it is not narrowly tailored to its purpose of furthering his rehabilitation. According to the juvenile court, the condition's purpose is to allow monitoring of P.O.'s involvement with drugs, but the condition does not limit the types of data that may be searched in light of this purpose. Instead, it permits review of all sorts of private information that is highly unlikely to shed any light on whether P.O. is complying with the other conditions of his probation, drug-related or otherwise.

In reaching this conclusion, we are aware that Division Four recently held that a substantively identical probation condition was not overbroad. The court determined that the condition in that case was sufficiently tailored to its rehabilitative purpose in light of the case's "rather unique constellation of facts"— including the minor's "serious mental illnesses, . . . dysfunctional family life, . . . significant gap in her educational training, and poor social choices." In contrast, the condition here is not sufficiently tailored because P.O.'s needs are less severe and the condition's purpose is accordingly less expansive.

Although we disagree with P.O. that no electronics search condition is warranted at all because other conditions of his probation constitute "less restrictive alternatives to meet the state's goal[s] of rehabilitation and public safety," we hold that the condition must be modified to limit authorization of warrantless searches of P.O.'s cell phone data and electronic accounts to media of communication reasonably likely to reveal whether he is boasting about drug use or otherwise involved with drugs. In addition, while P.O. must disclose to peace officers passwords necessary to gain access to these accounts, to the extent any other types of digital accounts maintained by him are password protected, he is not required to disclose those passwords.

B. *The Good-behavior Conditions Are Unconstitutionally Vague.*

P.O. claims that the good-behavior conditions are unconstitutionally vague because they are too "imprecise" and "subjective" to provide sufficient notice of the conduct they require. The Attorney General concedes that these conditions are vague, and we accept her concession.

As noted above, juvenile courts have "broad discretion to fashion conditions of probation" to further a minor's rehabilitation, but "[a] probation condition 'must be sufficiently precise for the probationer to know what is required of him, and for the court to determine whether the condition has been violated,' if it is to withstand a challenge on the ground of vagueness." "[T]he underpinning of a vagueness challenge is the due process concept of 'fair warning.' The rule of fair warning consists of 'the due process concepts of preventing arbitrary law enforcement and providing adequate notice to potential offenders' protections that are 'embodied in the *due process clauses of the federal* and *California Constitutions.*'" We review vagueness claims de novo.

We agree with the parties that the good-behavior conditions are not "'sufficiently precise'" to give P.O. notice of the conduct expected of him. Reasonable minds can differ about what it means to "be of good behavior and perform well" at school or work and to "be of good citizenship and good conduct," and the conditions are therefore vague.

P.O. suggests that the "perform well" language can be modified to require him to get "'passing grades in each graded subject'" and should not be read to apply to his employment, but he does not address the "good behavior" language. He contends that the "good citizenship and good conduct" language should be stricken. The Attorney General contends that we should remand to the juvenile court for it to decide whether to strike or modify the good-behavior conditions. We believe the best course is to strike all the challenged language, leaving the court free to impose, if it wishes, substitute conditions that are sufficiently clear to comply with constitutional requirements.

The search condition in the minute order for the May 7, 2015 hearing, which currently reads, "Submit person and any vehicle, room or property, electronics including passwords under your control to search by Probation Officer or peace office[r] with or without a search warrant at any time of day or night," is modified to read: "Submit your person and any vehicle, room, or property under your control to a search by the probation officer or a peace officer, with or without a search warrant, at any time of the day or night. Submit all electronic devices under your control to a search of any medium of communication reasonably likely to reveal whether you are boasting about your drug use or otherwise involved with drugs, with or without a search warrant, at any time of the day or night, and provide the probation or peace officer with any passwords necessary to access the information specified. Such media of communication include text messages, voicemail messages, photographs, e-mail accounts, and social media accounts."

The document listing probation conditions and court orders, signed by P.O. on May 7, 2015, is modified as follows. The condition requiring him to "attend classes or job on time and regularly; be of good behavior and perform well" is modified by striking the phrase "be of good behavior and perform well." The condition requiring P.O. to "be of good citizenship and good conduct" is stricken.

As so modified, the juvenile court's order is affirmed.

NOTES AND QUESTIONS

1. Why did the court conclude that a juvenile probationer may be subject to intrusions on privacy that would be unconstitutional for an adult? How would you argue that a juvenile's right to privacy in this context should be equal to or greater than an adult's claim?

2. How does *Lent* restrict a judge's discretion to fashion conditions of probation? All three prongs of *Lent* must be satisfied before a probation condition is invalid. This means a court can impose conditions that have no relationship to the crime of which a juvenile is convicted or that forbid conduct that is not criminal or that are not reasonably related to future criminality. How significant is the *Lent* limitation, then?

3. Having concluded that the probation condition regarding P.O.'s electronic media was not invalid under *Lent*, the court nevertheless concludes that the condition is unconstitutionally overbroad. How does the overbreadth analysis differ from the *Lent* analysis? Examine the condition regarding electronic media as the court says it should be rewritten. What content on his electronic devices is P.O. entitled to withhold from his probation officer?

4. The court also holds that the good conduct probation condition is unconstitutional because it is so vague. Considering the purpose of the prohibition against overly vague statutes, how would you advise the juvenile court judge to redraft this condition?

5. Probation conditions related to school attendance and school performance are commonly imposed and upheld. *See, e.g.,* In re Gerald B., 164 Cal. Rptr. 193 (Ct. App. 1980) (attendance); In re Angel J., 11 Cal. Rptr. 2d 776 (Ct. App. 1992) (passing grades). Terms requiring the probationer to associate only with persons approved by his or her parents or the probation officer have also been upheld. *E.g.,* L.M. v. State, 587 So. 2d 648 (Fla. Dist. App. 1991). However, courts have often invalidated orders requiring religious attendance on First Amendment grounds, although they may be upheld if tied to parental commands. *Id.* Courts have also invalidated certain probation conditions that they believe are not reasonably related to rehabilitation of the delinquent juvenile. For example, a prohibition on two juveniles participating in organized sports was held to be unacceptable in J.H. v. State, 107 So. 3d 1249 (Fla. App. 2013).

6. A large percentage of minors adjudicated delinquent are eligible for special education services under the Individuals with Disabilities Education Act, which you studied in Chapter 1. Generally, completion of an Individual Education Plan (IEP) is not a prerequisite to juvenile court disposition, but the IDEA's requirements of a free appropriate public education do apply to juveniles in state custody. *See* In re C.S., 804 A.2d 307 (D.C. 2002). If the parent of a child subject to juvenile court jurisdiction is not available to participate in creating the IEP, the court must appoint a surrogate parent to fill this role. 20 U.S.C. § 1415(b)(2)(A).

M.J. v. State

212 So. 3d 534 (Fla. App. 2017)

PER CURIAM. In these consolidated cases, the juvenile appellant, M.J., argues that the trial court reversibly erred in deviating from the Department of

Juvenile Justice's recommendation without complying with the requirements of E.A.R. v. State, 4 So. 3d 614 (Fla. 2009). We agree and reverse.

In November 2015, after admitting to a violation of probation in four prior cases, M.J.'s probation was continued with a special condition that he successfully complete the AMI program. In March 2016, M.J. admitted to violating probation again, this time by not attending AMI. Upon the trial court's directive, the Department prepared a pre-disposition report (PDR), which found M.J. was a "high risk" to reoffend, but stated the Department's belief that M.J. had not had the proper services in place to facilitate his successful completion of probation. The Department continued to recommend probation as the least restrictive setting necessary to ensure public safety. The PDR further provided, "But in compliance with the Court's expressed intention to commit the youth, and its demand for a restrictiveness level, the Department would offer minimum-risk as the most appropriate commitment alternative."

At the disposition hearing, the State objected, arguing that M.J. had already violated probation for not attending AMI, rendering the Department's recommendations futile. The State requested that M.J. be committed to a nonsecure residential level facility. See § 985.03(44), Fla. Stat. (2016) (defining the four restrictiveness levels of juvenile commitment). During the hearing, the trial court heard from M.J.'s probation officer that she had no reason to believe he would comply with probation and also heard that M.J. had not attended AMI because he was fearful of some people in the program.

The trial court found that probation was not appropriate. The trial court also found commitment to AMI was not appropriate based upon M.J.'s articulated fear. The trial court announced it would deviate from the Department's recommendation, adjudicated M.J. delinquent in each case, and committed him to the Department under concurrent nonsecure residential placements. The State attempted to bolster the trial court's ruling by stating for the record that the deviation was valid because the Department did not take into consideration the welfare of the community and the welfare of the child. The trial court agreed with this statement, and again stated that probation was "simply not an option" for M.J. and there was no reason to believe he was going to comply with the probation. The trial court did not enter a written order.

On appeal, M.J. argues that the trial court improperly deviated from the Department's recommendation solely based on its disagreement and, in so doing, failed to comply with the requirements of E.A.R. This Court reviews the trial court's decision for an abuse of discretion. Whether the trial court exercised appropriate discretion depends on "(1) whether the trial court employed the proper legal standard as set forth in E.A.R. and (2) whether the court's departure reasons are supported by the evidence." Whether the trial court employed the proper legal standard is reviewed de novo.

Section 985.433, Florida Statutes (2016), governs the disposition hearing in delinquency proceedings. Under subsection (6), the first determination to be made is "the suitability or nonsuitability for adjudication and commitment of the child to the [D]epartment." This Court has recognized that subsection (6) gives wide discretion to the trial court in determining whether to commit a child to the Department and that the rigorous analysis in E.A.R. does not apply to this initial determination. Here, the trial court apparently advised the Department in advance that it intended to commit M.J. and requested an alternative commitment recommendation.

The trial court's decision to deviate from the Department's minimum-risk commitment recommendation is what triggers the application of the *E.A.R.* in this case. Under *E.A.R.*, a trial court may not depart from the Department's recommendation merely because it disagrees; instead, it must provide reasons that are supported by a preponderance of the evidence. The standards the trial court must meet are as follows:

(1) Articulate an understanding of the respective characteristics of the opposing restrictiveness levels *including* (but not limited to) the type of child that each restrictiveness level is designed to serve, the potential "lengths of stay" associated with each level, and the divergent treatment programs and services available to the juvenile at these levels; and

(2) Then logically and persuasively explain why, in light of these differing characteristics, one level is better suited to serving both the rehabilitative needs of the juvenile—in the least restrictive setting—and maintaining the ability of the State to protect the public from further acts of delinquency.

The trial court's stated reasons must provide a "legally sufficient foundation" for departing from the Department's recommendation, which is accomplished "by identifying significant information that [the Department] has overlooked, failed to sufficiently consider, or misconstrued with regard to the child's programmatic, rehabilitative needs along with the risks that the unrehabilitated child poses to the public." These measures insure "fulfillment of the Legislature's comprehensive scheme and its stated intent that the juvenile courts of this state exercise appropriate discretion with the ultimate aim of providing the juvenile offender the most appropriate dispositional services in the least restrictive available setting."

Here, the trial court did not articulate an understanding of the respective characteristics of the different restrictiveness levels as required under *E.A.R.* Nor did it explain why the nonsecure residential level was better suited to serving both M.J.'s rehabilitative needs—in the least restrictive setting—and maintaining the ability of the State to protect the public from further acts of delinquency than the Department's minimum-risk recommendation. While the trial court may have relied on its experience and personal knowledge to determine that a nonsecure residential program was more suitable, it did not provide a full reasoning and understanding on the record. Without such elucidation, this Court is not able to provide a meaningful review and determine whether the rigorous requirements of *E.A.R.* were complied with.

We agree with M.J. that this case is similar to *B.L.R.* in which the majority recognized that the trial court had a legally sufficient basis to deviate from the Department's recommendation, but held the trial court's failure to articulate its understanding of the restrictiveness levels and failure to explain why a maximum-risk facility was better suited to the juvenile's needs and the safety of the public compelled reversal under *E.A.R.* Much like *B.L.R.*, the trial court in this case did not articulate a sufficient basis for deviating from the Department's recommendation of minimum-risk commitment. We disagree with the State's argument that the trial court implicitly set out reasons for the deviation and relied on pieces of information that the Department overlooked. First, implicit reasoning does not satisfy the court's duty under *E.A.R.* as the trial court's reasoning must be placed on the record. Second, the information identified by the State primarily relates to M.J.'s suitability for probation and not why a nonsecure residential placement was more suitable than the Department's minimum-risk recommendation. We also note the trial court's general agreement with the State's attempt to bolster its analysis for the record by using magic buzzwords does not meet the strict requirements under *E.A.R.* As stated by this Court in M.H. v. State,

> [I]t is important for trial courts to understand that deviating from a [Department] recommendation is a difficult matter pursuant to the dictates of *E.A.R.* In order to deviate lawfully, a trial court must do more than place generalized reasons on the record; it must engage in a well-reasoned and complete analysis of the PDR and the type of facility to which the trial court intends to send the child. This is no easy task and will take time and consideration.

Accordingly, we reverse the trial court's dispositions and remand for resentencing with instructions to either enter a disposition order that includes the requisite *E.A.R.* findings or, if such findings cannot be made, enter an order committing M.J. to a minimum-risk facility as recommended by the Department.

NOTES AND QUESTIONS

1. In most jurisdictions statutes or case law requires the judge to make findings to support a dispositional order, especially one involving placement in a residential facility, but the Florida approach is notable for the specific findings it requires. What are the purposes of requiring a trial court to make specific findings to justify its decision? How does this requirement limit the court's discretion to determine a placement? In D.V. v. State, 216 So. 3d 3, 16-17 (Fla. App. 2017), the court observed,

> Following *E.A.R.*, courts have reversed sentencing rationales that would easily have passed muster in adult court. In S.B. v. State, we reversed a trial court's deviation from the DJJ recommendation that was based on the "seriousness of offense to community; protection of community requires commitment; offense was aggressive, premeditated and willful; record and previous criminal history; no prospect for adequate protection of public and no likelihood for rehabilitation in a community service program." 16 So. 3d 256, 257 (Fla. 4th DCA 2009); *see also* D.B. v. State, 12 So. 3d 875 (Fla. 4th DCA 2009) (relying on *E.A.R.* to reverse a departure sentence citing only the seriousness of the offense and protection of the community from such crimes); L.A.G. v. State, 58 So. 3d 393, 394 (Fla. 2d DCA 2011) (recognizing that "the nature of the charge is not a sufficient reason to depart from the D.J.J.' s recommendation.").

2. The Florida courts previously held that juvenile courts have much more discretion to decide whether to place a child on probation or to commit the child to a secure custodial placement than to deviate from the probation department's recommendation about what level of custodial placement to use. J.B.S. v. State, 90

So.3d 961, 967 (Fla. 1st DCA 2012); B.K.A. v. State, 122 So. 3d 928, 930 (Fla. 1st DCA 2013). Thus, in *M.J.*, the juvenile court did not have to justify the decision to reject the department's recommendation for continued probation beyond finding that probation was not "suitable." Why would the legislature grant juvenile judges more discretion to determine whether to remove the child from home for placement in a residential facility than over the type of facility?

3. The Florida Supreme Court decision in *E.A.R.* requires a juvenile court to explain its conclusion that a child requires placement in a more restrictive setting than the probation department recommends. Fla. Stat. § 985.03(44) (2019), defines the four levels of restrictive placements. The statutory definitions are set out below. In *M.J.* the department recommended minimum-risk placement, and the judge instead chose nonsecure residential placement. What are the differences between the two? Why were the trial court's findings in *M.J.* insufficient? What kind of findings would a juvenile court have to make to justify deviating from the recommendation for minimum-risk placement and choosing nonsecure residential instead?

(a) Minimum-risk nonresidential. — Programs or program models at this commitment level work with youth who remain in the community and participate at least 5 days per week in a day treatment program. Youth assessed and classified for programs at this commitment level represent a minimum risk to themselves and public safety and do not require placement and services in residential settings. Youth in this level have full access to, and reside in, the community. Youth who have been found to have committed delinquent acts that involve firearms, that are sexual offenses, or that would be life felonies or first degree felonies if committed by an adult may not be committed to a program at this level.

(b) Nonsecure residential. — Programs or program models at this commitment level are residential but may allow youth to have supervised access to the community. Facilities at this commitment level are either environmentally secure, staff secure, or are hardware-secure with walls, fencing, or locking doors. Residential facilities at this commitment level shall have no more than 90 beds each, including campus-style programs, unless those campus-style programs include more than one treatment program using different treatment protocols, and have facilities that coexist separately in distinct locations on the same property. Facilities at this commitment level shall provide 24-hour awake supervision, custody, care, and treatment of residents. Youth assessed and classified for placement in programs at this commitment level represent a low or moderate risk to public safety and require close supervision. The staff at a facility at this commitment level may seclude a child who is a physical threat to himself or herself or others. Mechanical restraint may also be used when necessary.

(c) High-risk residential. — Programs or program models at this commitment level are residential and do not allow youth to have access to the community, except that temporary release providing community access for up to 72 continuous hours may be approved by a court for a youth who has made successful progress in his or her program in order for the youth to attend a family emergency or, during the final 60 days of his or her placement, to visit his or her home, enroll in school or a career and technical education program, complete a job interview, or participate in a community service project. High-risk residential facilities are hardware-secure with perimeter fencing and locking doors. Residential facilities at this commitment level shall have no more than 90 beds each, including campus-style programs, unless those campus-style programs include more than one treatment program using different treatment protocols, and have facilities that coexist separately in distinct locations on the same property. Facilities at this commitment level shall provide 24-hour awake supervision, custody, care, and treatment of residents. Youth assessed and classified for this level of placement require close supervision in a structured residential setting. Placement in programs at this level is prompted by a concern for public safety that outweighs placement in programs at lower commitment levels. The staff at a facility at this commitment level may seclude a child who is a physical threat to himself or herself or others. Mechanical restraint may also be used when necessary. The facility may provide for single cell occupancy, except that youth may be housed together during prerelease transition.

(d) Maximum-risk residential. — Programs or program models at this commitment level include juvenile correctional facilities and juvenile prisons. The programs at this commitment level are long-term residential and do not allow youth to have access to the community. Facilities at this commitment level are maximum-custody, hardware-secure with perimeter security fencing and locking doors. Residential facilities at this commitment level shall have no more than 90 beds each, including campus-style programs, unless those campus-style programs include more than one treatment program using different treatment protocols, and have facilities that coexist separately in distinct locations on the same property. Facilities at this commitment level shall provide 24-hour awake supervision, custody, care, and treatment of residents. The staff at a facility at this commitment level may seclude a child who is a physical threat to himself or herself or others. Mechanical restraint may also be used when necessary. Facilities at this commitment level shall provide for single cell occupancy, except that youth may be housed together during prerelease transition. Youth assessed and classified for this level of placement require close supervision in a maximum security residential setting. Placement in a program at this level is prompted by a demonstrated need to protect the public.

4. There is a growing recognition that judges, especially those who work with children and families, must be informed about Adverse Childhood Experiences, so that they are better able to meet the needs of those who come into their courtroom. Best practices include making courtrooms less threatening to defendants, recognizing that trauma is passed on generationally, and taking a solution-oriented response to the impact of childhood trauma. *See* Ed Finkel, Social Justice Solutions, Trauma-Informed Judges Take Gentler Approach, Administer Problem-Solving Justice to Stop Cycle Of ACEs (Apr. 8, 2015), http://www.socialjusticesolutions. org/2015/04/08/trauma-informed-judges-take-gentler-approach-administer-problem-solving-justice-stop-cycle-aces/.

PROBLEMS

1. Lauren, a 16-year-old girl, was found delinquent because she knowingly or intentionally was possessing a controlled substance, cocaine. She appeals the juvenile court order committing her to the Texas Youth Commission for custodial placement, based on the following finding:

The court further finds that the best interest of the child and the best interest of society will be served by committing her to the care, custody, and control of the Texas

Youth Commission because there exists in the community of Lockhart, Texas, where this conduct occurred, a great public awareness and concern about the problem of drug abuse in both the schools and the community at large. Because of the findings stated above [reciting the facts that the juvenile had been found guilty of using cocaine which had been acquired at school in school], the court believes that the best interests of society in insuring that conduct of the nature involved in this case is not to be tolerated, particularly in the school system, far outweigh any interests to be served by placing the child on probation.

The juvenile probation report recommended that Lauren be placed on probation. The probability of Lauren successfully completing probation was rated as good. This prediction was based on several factors, including the existence of a supportive family, the lack of any prior juvenile referrals, and the existence of a stable academic school record. The report also shows that in high school Lauren served as president of the Future Homemakers of America during her sophomore and junior years and engaged in activities such as tennis, volleyball, and baseball.

Under the Florida system described in *M.J.*, what arguments could be made on behalf of her appeal, and what arguments would the state make?

2. David's parents separated shortly after his birth, and he did not know his father. His mother died when he was 12, and he lived for a year with his maternal grandmother. Then he moved to Florida to live with his father, stepmother, and their children. The arrangement did not go well. David was depressed and did poorly in school. He did not adapt to the rules of the household, and his father and stepmother punished him, accusing him of laziness. They took away all his privileges and possessions until he was left with only his schoolwork and a dreary bedroom. David began to act out, stealing from his stepsiblings. The parents put locks on the doors to guard against him. Eventually the family stopped interacting with him, and he was left alone much of the time.

One day at school David wrote a note with a friend in which David promised to pay the friend $1,200 for murdering his father and stepmother. The friend thought David was joking and did nothing more about it. The boys never discussed it again. Three weeks later the father found the note in David's pants and called the police. During five hours of interrogation David said things about his family that one might say to a therapist but normally not to the police. He was charged with three counts of solicitation to commit first degree murder.

After a contested adjudicatory hearing, the juvenile court judge found David guilty of all the charges. The probation department submitted a recommendation that David remain at home on probation with individual, group, and family therapy. However, the father made clear at the hearing that he would not participate in therapy, and the stepmother submitted a letter expressing her intense dislike for and resentment of David and her belief that he was dangerous. David's maternal grandmother offered to take him back to live with her and to participate in therapy. Staff from the detention center testified that David was cooperative, respectful, and "a nice kid." The state's attorney played portions of the video of David's interrogation and submitted the testimony of a social worker who said that David needed residential treatment. The juvenile court judge did not follow the department's recommendation for probation but instead committed him to level 4, maximum risk residential custody based on the severity of the charges and the need to protect the community. The judge refused to send David to the grand-mother because "It would give David what he looked for from the beginning. He would win by committing criminal acts." David has appealed from the disposition. What arguments should be made on his behalf and on behalf of the state, which supports the court's order?

3. *Renewed Emphasis on Rehabilitation*

DANIEL M. FILLER & AUSTIN E. SMITH, *THE NEW REHABILITATION*

91 Iowa L. Rev. 951, 952-954, 968-970, 973-975 (2006)

Juvenile courts were created for the express purpose of rehabilitating offenders. Most histories of modern American juvenile justice begin in 1899, when Illinois established the first separate juvenile court for prosecuting delinquent children. Over the course of the next twenty-five years, virtually every other state adopted a similar tribunal for juveniles charged with crimes. According to the accepted history of American juvenile justice, this commit-ment to rehabilitation began to wane in the second half of the twentieth cen-tury, particularly after the United States Supreme Court extended many crimi-nal procedural rights to children during the civil rights revolution of the 1960s. States narrowed the jurisdiction of the juvenile courts, exporting thousands of children into adult criminal courts. For those children remaining in the juvenile system, judges exercised less individualized judgment and served up increas-ingly punitive sentences.

Progressive critics mourn the demise of this rehabilitative ideal, citing the Warren Court's extension of rights to child offenders as a catalyst for this shift. They contend that the Supreme Court's extension of adult rights to child defendants led those suspicious of rehabilitation to argue that juvenile courts had been rendered ineffective, since they could no longer intervene, treat, and rehabilitate the wayward child at an early stage. Progressives have been so frustrated by juvenile courts in recent years that several leading scholars have argued that it is time to junk the juvenile justice system because it offers incomplete procedural protections paired with the brutality of adult criminal sanctions. These critics thus join the chorus of liberals worried that the civil rights revolution has backfired.

It turns out, however, that the accepted progressive critique of juvenile courts is incomplete. Over the past decade, a major new development has occurred within the American juvenile justice system that undermines the dominant view that juvenile rehabilitation is on its deathbed. Across the nation, in every state, local courts are creating new juvenile tribunals that explicitly seek to treat and rehabilitate juvenile offenders. These specialty courts, including drug, gun, and mental health courts, are specifically created to change children's lives so that they do not re-offend. . . .

The most pervasive form of juvenile specialty courts is the drug court. Like adult drug courts, after the news of the perceived success of the first programs in 1995 began to spread, programs started to pop up across the country. There are also juvenile courts that address drug and alcohol abuse by children, drug use by parents whose children are processed by dependency courts, gun possession, truancy, violent acts committed by juveniles, and even teen courts that are intended to impose peer pressure on young offenders for minor violations.

While the general jurisdiction of courts is usually authorized by a state legislature, these specialty courts are typically homegrown creations. Local courts carve out specialty dockets from their general court business. The impetus for forming these new courts often comes from a local judge. The idea of a specialty court may surface for a variety of reasons, including particular local case management issues (such as court overloading), the concerns of juvenile court judges or other players in the juvenile court system seeking better outcomes in particular cases, or the growing notoriety of such courts in other jurisdictions. In many cases, the availability of federal grant money to fund such projects may focus attention on these types of courts and help motivate players to organize them. . . .

Juvenile specialty courts appear, at first, anachronistic. Juvenile courts were designed, originally, to provide individualized rehabilitative justice for children. Specialty courts are supposed to provide the same thing. Why, then, are they necessary? Because legislatures have worked diligently to undermine rehabilitative juvenile courts, existing court structures have difficulty delivering rehabilitative services. Specialty courts create new forums where delinquency cases can be funneled to receive the individualized attention once dedicated to all children charged with delinquency. One purpose of specialty courts is to "abandon[] conventional adversarial roles in the interest of providing a more therapeutic and less contentious environment for the resolution of issues."

Specialty courts pull cases out of the general delinquency docket and subject them to special, intensive handling on a smaller docket. Frequently, a defendant must enter a guilty plea — or its juvenile court equivalent — to become eligible for the special jurisdiction. Depending on the jurisdiction, it may be more or less difficult to divert the most serious cases from a punitive to a rehabilitative docket. In many states, the decision of whether to prosecute a child in adult court belongs to either a judge or district attorney. In these cases, judges and prosecutors committed to specialty courts retain the power to divert suitable children to a rehabilitative regime. Even in states with juvenile sentencing guidelines, it may be possible for children to enter conditional pleas that may be withdrawn later if they successfully complete a treatment program. In these ways, specialty courts may remain open even to offenders explicitly targeted by legislators for tough sentences.

Once in these tribunals, offenders are subject to a unique sanction and reward regime that often bears little resemblance to the main line of delinquency cases. Instead of a hands-off probation, or a bid at the state "industrial school," children are brought back to court regularly so that judges can check on their progress. The offenders receive stepped sanctions to punish small transgressions and rewards to affirm small successes. They often undergo intensive, self-conscious treatment and therapeutic counseling programs. The roles of actors within the juvenile justice process have been fluid over the past quarter century. Until the civil rights revolution in the Supreme Court, juvenile courts were driven primarily by judges, their professional staff (such as probation officers and social workers), and prosecutors. Lawyers, if they were present at all, had a peripheral role. With *Gault* and its progeny, juvenile courts began to more closely resemble adult criminal courts. They became adversarial, with a more clearly defined role for the defense attorney, and the judge became more of a fact-finder and sentencer than a parent. The advent of specialty courts has, to a significant extent, turned back the clocks, and it has done so while remaining consistent with the procedural safeguards of *Gault*. Specialty courts have "all but abandoned conventional adversarial roles in the interest of providing a more therapeutic and less contentious environment for the resolution of issues." Juvenile specialty courts have once again redefined the roles of court personnel, expert witnesses, defense attorneys, prosecutors, juvenile probation officers, and a host of others. The nonadversarial, treatment-based approach of most specialty courts has shifted the power structure by placing the decision-making in the hands of a few key participants, while reducing the roles of those who are accustomed to actively participating in criminal and juvenile court proceedings.

NOTES AND QUESTIONS

1. Are specialized juvenile treatment courts really necessary, given the traditional rehabilitative orientation of juvenile courts? This question is raised but not answered in National Institute of Justice, Drug Court Intervention for Juveniles, in Drug Courts: The Second Decade 21 (June 2006), https://www.ncjrs.gov/pdf-files1/nij/211081.pdf. The report also questions whether all minors referred to drug courts are actually substance abusers, rather than casual experimenters without long-term problems. *Id.* at 22.

2. As of 2015, at least one juvenile court drug program was operating in every state, for a total of 409. There were also 312 family drug courts. National Institute of Justice, Drug Courts (Aug. 23, 2018), topics/courts/drug-courts/pages/welcome.aspx. While most drug court programs operate as dispositional alternatives, after a juvenile has been adjudicated delinquent, some are pretrial diversionary programs. *E.g.*, Fla. Stat. Ann. § 985.345 (2019).

Before 2006, the available analyses concluded that juvenile drug courts had a modest impact, reducing delinquency by 3 to 5 percent on average. Wes Huddleston & Douglas B. Marlowe, Painting the Current Picture: A National Report on Drug Courts and Other Problem-Solving Court Programs in the United States 11 (Nat'l Drug Court Institute 2006). Two more recent studies have found greater impacts, particularly in reducing drug use and rearrest. *Id.*

3. Following the enthusiastic response to juvenile drug courts, local officials have established juvenile gun courts in Detroit, Indianapolis, New York City, Washington, D.C., Baltimore, and Birmingham. Filler & Smith, above, 91 Iowa L. Rev. at 979-981. Yakima County, Washington, established the first Juvenile Gang Court in June of 2011. Michelle Young & Robert L. Thornton, Gang Courts: An Innovative Strategy for Gang-Involved Offenders (U.S. Dept of Justice, Bureau of Justice Assistance, Apr. 2014), http://www.communitycorrections.org/images/publications/CCI_Gang_Court_Pub.pdf.

4. Tens of thousands of the youth in the juvenile justice system have unmet mental health needs. In many jurisdictions, court and probation staff cannot adequately screen or identify such youth. The lack of services and programs means that juveniles often languish in detention centers and correctional facilities without treatment or support. A longitudinal study of 1,829 youth detained in the juvenile justice system between 1995 and 1998 concluded that the mental health needs of youth in the juvenile justice system are much greater than those of the general population, but that these needs go largely untreated in detention. It found that 66 percent of male detainees and 74 percent of females met the criteria for at least one disorder, and many of these detainees exhibited two or more disorders; 93 percent had been exposed to one or more traumas before or during detention, and 80 percent had been physically abused. Only 23 percent of those detainees with major psychiatric disorders and functional impairment received treatment (15 percent while in detention, 8 percent when back in the community), and 85 percent of youth with disorders reported at least one perceived barrier to accessing services. Linda A. Teplin et al, The Northwestern Juvenile Project: Overview (U.S. Dept, of Justice, Office of Juvenile Justice and Delinquency Prevention, February 2013), http://www.ojjdp.gov/pubs/234522. pdf. *See also* Thomas Grisso, Adolescent Offenders with Mental Disorders, in The Future of Children: Juvenile Justice 143 (2008); Michael Perlin, "Yonder Stands Your Orphan with His Gun": The International Human Rights and Therapeutic Jurisprudence Implications of Juvenile Punishment Schemes, 46 Tex. Tech L. Rev. 301, 308-16 (2013).

In more than 30 states juvenile detention centers hold mentally ill children, some younger than 10, without charges. Today there are more than 40 juvenile mental health courts nationwide. They divert mentally ill children from the juvenile justice system and into community-based treatment centers when possible. Patrick Gardner, An Overview of Juvenile Mental Health Courts (ABA Center on Children and the Law, Jan. 9, 2018), https://www.americanbar.org/groups/child_ law/resources/child_law_practiceonline/child_law_practice/vol30/september_ 2011/an_overview_of_juvenilementalhealthcourts/.

4. *The Right to Treatment and Conditions in Institutions*

Between 2006 and 2015, almost 90 percent of states cut the rates at which they held youth in residential placements by half or more. Of those detained in 2015, 95 percent were held for delinquency offenses, and 5 percent for a status offense. Less than 40 percent were held for a person offense. Almost half the facilities were private, and they held 31 percent of all juveniles in placement. While rehabilitation has always been defined as a major justification for residential placement, in reality many institutions have been very similar to adult prisons, offering little to no therapy and harsh conditions.

REED V. PALMER

906 F.3d 540 (7th Cir. 2018)

FLAUM, Circuit Judge. . . . In January 2014, the State of Iowa closed the Iowa Girls State Training School in Toledo, Iowa. Defendant Charles Palmer, Director of the Iowa Department of Human Services, subsequently contracted with the State of Wisconsin to use the Wisconsin Girls State Training School (also known as "Copper Lake") in Irma, Wisconsin. Under the terms of the agreement, Iowa agreed to pay Wisconsin $301 per day for each child.

According to plaintiffs, Copper Lake comes with a disreputable history. They claim that, since its opening in 2011, it "has had a very high turnover rate of employees," leading to "over worked and untrained staff." They further assert that between 2012 and 2016, the facility received criticism from multiple Wisconsin circuit court judges regarding its "sordid" and "inhumane" treatment of juveniles. Plaintiffs claim a state criminal probe into Copper Lake began in 2015.

Iowa juvenile courts ordered plaintiffs Paige Ray-Cluney and Laura Reed to be placed at Copper Lake on March 10 and June 4, 2015, respectively. At the time, both girls were sixteen years old. Plaintiffs claim that during their stays, Copper Lake staff subjected them to prolonged periods of "isolation," which involved spending approximately twenty-two out of twenty-four hours each day in a seven-foot by ten-foot concrete cell furnished with only a metal cot and a thin mattress. They allege these isolation cells had urine stains on the floor and wall, and only one window "covered by a thick cage reducing light that [could] pass through." They claim that during their limited periods of release, they were only allowed to "shower, clean [their] room[s], receive 15 minutes to exercise, receive 10-15 minutes to write a letter, and use the restroom." If any time remained, they were required to sit in chairs by themselves and were "not allowed to speak." They allege they were not released from isolation for meals and received little or no educational instruction. Both plaintiffs attempted suicide.

In addition to solitary confinement, plaintiffs also claim they were subjected to excessive force. Reed alleges that, during one of her periods of isolation, a security guard pulled her "fingers through the food tray slot in the cell door," causing "scrapes and bleeding." She further asserts that, on an occasion when she attempted self-harm by placing her head underneath her cot, the same security guard stood on top of the cot in order to tighten it against her neck. She also alleges the security guard "slammed her against [her] cell wall with such force as to leave a contusion on her head and a laceration on her lips." Meanwhile, Ray-Cluney alleges she was "placed in restraints so tight that they left her arm purple" and "had her head rammed against the wall of the cell." Finally, both plaintiffs claim Copper Lake staff sprayed them with mace on multiple occasions.

B. PROCEDURAL BACKGROUND

Plaintiffs separately filed suit in the Western District of Wisconsin on August 1, 2017. They each asserted violations of the Fourth, Eighth, and Fourteenth Amendments under 42 U.S.C. § 1983 for cruel and unusual punishment, excessive force, and deprivation of due process. They additionally brought common law claims for intentional infliction of emotional distress and negligence. Finally, Reed alleged multiple violations of the Iowa state constitution.

The named defendants in both cases were almost entirely Wisconsin officials associated with Copper Lake. The lone exception was Palmer. . . .

Palmer moved to dismiss the claims against him in both cases. He raised multiple legal objections, including . . . qualified immunity. . . .

The district court concluded that it "need not address" Palmer's personal jurisdiction defense because it could "resolv[e] the suit on the merits." Specifically, the court found that no law clearly established "what the [C]onstitution requires of a government official in [Palmer's] position under similar circumstances." As a result, the court held qualified immunity barred plaintiffs' federal constitutional claims. . . .

"The doctrine of qualified immunity protects government officials 'from liability for civil damages insofar as their conduct does not violate clearly established statutory or constitutional rights of which a reasonable person would have known.'" "Qualified immunity balances two important interests—the need to hold public officials accountable when they exercise power irresponsibly and the need to shield officials from harassment, distraction, and liability when they perform their duties reasonably." "The defense provides 'ample room for mistaken judgments' and protects all but the 'plainly incompetent and those who knowingly violate the law.'"

"A state official is protected by qualified immunity unless the plaintiff shows: '(1) that the official violated a statutory or constitutional right, and (2) that the right was "clearly established" at the time of the challenged conduct.'" "If *either* inquiry is answered in the negative, the defendant official" is protected by qualified immunity. "In order to avoid '[u]nnecessary litigation of constitutional issues' and expending scarce judicial resources that ultimately do not impact the outcome of the case," courts "may analyze the 'clearly established' prong without first considering whether the alleged constitutional right was violated." The district court adopted that approach here.

Under the clearly established prong, "the burden is on plaintiffs to demonstrate the alleged violation of their [constitutional] right[s] was 'clearly established.'" "To be clearly established at the time of the challenged conduct, the right's contours must be sufficiently clear that every reasonable official would have understood that what he is doing violates that right . . . ." "[T]he crucial question [is] whether the official acted reasonably in the *particular circumstances* that he or she faced."

Ordinarily, to show that the law was "clearly established," plaintiffs must point to a "closely analogous case" finding the alleged violation unlawful. They need not point to an identical case, "but existing precedent must have placed the statutory or constitutional question beyond debate." "[W]e look first to controlling Supreme Court precedent and our own circuit decisions on the issue." If no controlling precedent exists, "we broaden our survey to include all relevant caselaw in order to determine 'whether there was such a clear trend in the caselaw that we can say with fair assurance that the recognition of the right by a controlling precedent was merely a question of time.'"

Alternatively, "[i]n some rare cases, where the constitutional violation is patently obvious, the plaintiffs may not be required to present the court with any analogous cases." Instead, plaintiffs can demonstrate clearly established law by proving the defendant's conduct was "so egregious and unreasonable that . . . no reasonable [official] could have thought he was acting lawfully." Outrageous conduct "obviously will be unconstitutional." "But even as to action less than an outrage, 'officials can still be on notice that their conduct violates established law . . . in novel factual circumstances.'"

Importantly, "[b]efore we can determine if the law was clearly established, 'the right allegedly violated must be defined at the appropriate level of specificity.'" "The Supreme Court has 'repeatedly told courts . . . not to define clearly established law at a high level of generality.'" Instead, "[t]he dispositive question is 'whether the violative nature of *particular* conduct is clearly established.'" In other words, "the clearly established law must be 'particularized' to the facts of the case." . . .

Given this backdrop, the district court acted prematurely in deciding Palmer's entitlement to qualified immunity at the motion to dismiss stage. The court found that, during the time period alleged in the complaints, no law clearly established "what the [C]onstitution requires of a government official in [Palmer's] position under similar circumstances."

Palmer's position is determined with reference to the well-pleaded factual allegations in plaintiffs' complaints, which are taken as true and considered in the light most favorable to plaintiffs on a Rule 12(b)(6) motion to dismiss. According to the complaints, Palmer contracted with the state of Wisconsin to place juveniles, including plaintiffs, in the Copper Lake facility. The complaints further allege that both plaintiffs were in Palmer's custody pursuant to state court orders. Moreover, Palmer monitored and received reports concerning Reed's and Ray-Cluney's conditions of confinement at Copper Lake. Based on these reports, plaintiffs allege Palmer "knew or should have known of the systemic and excessive use of isolation cells at Copper Lake," and "[d]espite such knowledge, Palmer failed to remove the Iowa girls placed at Copper Lake and acted with deliberate indifference in doing so." These allegations are sufficient to withstand a Rule 12(b)(6) motion to dismiss.

Plaintiffs have sufficiently alleged that their constitutional rights were violated through excessive use of isolation cells at Copper Lake. Supreme Court precedent is not clear about whether state juvenile detention facility conditions should be judged under the Eighth Amendment's Cruel and Unusual Punishment Clause or the Fourteenth Amendment's Due Process Clause. Indeed, the Court expressly avoided deciding this question in Ingraham v. Wright, 430 U.S. 651, 669 n.37 (1977).

In a case over forty years ago, we applied the Eighth Amendment's cruel and unusual punishment standard to evaluate the use of corporal punishment and tranquilizing drugs at a juvenile correctional institution. *See* Nelson v. Heyne, 491 F.2d 352, 354-357 (7th Cir. 1974). Under that test, a prison's deprivation must be an "objectively, 'sufficiently serious' . . . denial of 'the minimal civilized measure of life's necessities,'" and the state actor "must have a 'sufficiently culpable state of mind.'" Using this standard, a district court recently held, in the context of a preliminary injunction motion, that juvenile isolation is likely unconstitutional. *See* V.W. ex rel. Williams v. Conway, 236 F. Supp. 3d 554, 584 (N.D.N.Y. 2017) ("[T]he use of disciplinary confinement on juveniles [was] not *reasonably* calculated to restore prison safety and, even when it [was], disciplinary isolation at the [detention center] continue[d] long after any safety concerns had been abated.").

Meanwhile, other circuits have applied the Fourteenth Amendment's "more protective" Due Process Clause in evaluating juvenile detention center conditions. *Gary H.*, 831 F.2d at 1432 (evaluating management of facility for adolescent wards of the juvenile court); *see also* A.J. ex rel. L.B. v. Kierst, 56 F.3d 849, 854 (8th Cir. 1995) (juvenile pretrial detainees); H.C. v. Jarrard, 786 F.2d 1080, 1084-1085 (11th

Cir. 1986) (same); *Santana*, 714 F.2d at 1179-81 (juvenile residents of industrial school); Milonas v. Williams, 691 F.2d 931, 942 & n. 10 (10th Cir. 1982) (private school for juvenile boys with behavioral and mental health problems). This standard is more protective in that "Eighth Amendment scrutiny is appropriate only after the State has complied with the constitutional guarantees traditionally associated with criminal prosecutions." *Ingraham*, 430 U.S. at 671 n. 40. "Where the State seeks to impose punishment without such an adjudication, the pertinent constitutional guarantee is the Due Process Clause of the Fourteenth Amendment."

To determine "the constitutionality of conditions or restrictions of pretrial detention" using a Fourteenth Amendment due process inquiry, courts must first evaluate "whether those conditions amount to punishment of the detainee," because "a detainee may not be punished prior to an adjudication of guilt in accordance with due process of law." Bell v. Wolfish, 441 U.S. 520, 535, 99 S. Ct. 1861, 60 L. Ed. 2d 447 (1979). Still, "restrictions on liberty" are permissible so long as they are "reasonably related to legitimate government objectives and not tantamount to punishment." Youngberg v. Romeo, 457 U.S. 307, 320, 102 S. Ct. 2452, 73 L. Ed. 2d 28 (1982). To make this determination, courts "weigh [ ] the individual's interest in liberty against the State's asserted reasons" for their restraint.

At the time plaintiffs were allegedly in Palmer's custody, isolation of pre-trial juvenile detainees not "reasonably related to a legitimate governmental objective" could rise to the level of a constitutional violation. Here, plaintiffs' complaints plausibly allege that they were kept in isolation at Copper Lake for excessive amounts of time. Caselaw clearly establishes that such conduct could violate the Fourteenth and/or the Eighth Amendment.

On the present record, however, it is impossible to determine whether such a constitutional violation occurred in plaintiffs' cases. We know the respective complaints allege plaintiffs spent an inordinate amount of time at Copper Lake in isolation. However, we do not know the reasons behind their seclusion. We therefore cannot evaluate, under the Fourteenth Amendment, whether Palmer — or the other defendants — acted reasonably pursuant to a "legitimate governmental objective" or instead unlawfully "punished" plaintiffs. Nor can we determine, under the Eighth Amendment, whether Palmer had a "sufficiently culpable state of mind." In sum, as one district court recently concluded in denying a motion to dismiss Eighth and Fourteenth Amendment claims arising from a plaintiff's isolated confinement at an Iowa juvenile home:

> Whether the alleged actions herein were "reasonably related to a legitimate institutional interest," or were for the "legitimate purpose" of containing Plaintiff's violent behavior, *requires a factual inquiry that cannot be accomplished at this stage of proceedings* so long as Plaintiff has alleged facts that generate a plausible claim. Taking the complaint in its entirety, Defendants' current legal arguments [did] not render implausible the allegations in the complaint. Additionally, . . . even if a legitimate purpose for isolating a detainee is provided, a due process violation may still occur if the conditions imposed are excessive in relation to the nonpunitive purpose, *a further factual inquiry* . . . . Accordingly, Defendants have not shown that they are entitled to qualified immunity on the face of the compliant.

The same reasoning applies here. Plaintiffs have plausibly alleged their constitutional rights were violated at Copper Lake when they were placed in isolation "without justification." On the face of plaintiffs' complaints alone, Palmer has not shown he is entitled to qualified immunity.

This case involves the added wrinkle that plaintiffs were housed in Wisconsin, not in Iowa. In other words, Palmer was not one of the Copper Lake officials placing plaintiffs in isolation. Rather, plaintiffs allege Palmer only contracted with Wisconsin to send juveniles to Copper Lake and later "received" and "monitored" reports regarding the juveniles sent there. According to the district court, this made the claims against Palmer "completely different" from other cases where the defendants "actually controlled and operated the institution in which the abuse had occurred and 'oversaw the use of the isolation cells in which [the] plaintiff was confined.'" In the district court's view, no law clearly establishes what the Constitution requires of an official in Palmer's unique posture.

Palmer's additional degree of separation is a distinguishing feature of this litigation, but at the motion to dismiss stage, our conclusion does not change. Under DeShaney v. Winnebago County Department of Social Services, it is clearly established that the Due Process Clause "forbids the State itself to deprive individuals of life, liberty, or property without 'due process of law,'" but does not "impose an affirmative obligation on the State to ensure that those interests do not come to harm through other means." It is equally established, however, that an exception to the *DeShaney* principle arises "if the state has a 'special relationship' with a person, that is, if the state has custody of a person, thus cutting off alternate avenues of aid." In such cases, the State "assumes at least a rudimentary duty of safekeeping."

On multiple occasions, we have applied the "special relationship" exception to cases where "the State removes a child from her natural parents." Thus, "once a state removes a child from her parents' custody," it "assumes a duty of safekeeping" due to the restraints it places on the liberty of the child. Such a duty is violated when the State "place[s] a child in custody with foster parents it knows are incompetent or dangerous."

This case differs from [the foster care cases]. Nevertheless, in *K.H.*, we defined the relevant constitutional right as "the right of a child in state custody not to be handed over by state officers to a foster parent *or other custodian, private or public*, whom the state knows or suspects to be a child abuser." This language encompasses Palmer's alleged role here.[5] Allegations against Palmer are not limited to his role in signing the contract that led to plaintiffs' placement at Copper Lake: Plaintiffs further allege that Palmer retained custody and received reports detailing their excessive isolation, yet took no steps to remove them from the facility and was deliberately indifferent in doing so. . . .

---

5. The D.C. Circuit's decision in Smith v. District of Columbia, 413 F.3d 86 (D.C. Cir. 2005), reinforces this conclusion. There, the District of Columbia placed delinquent youths in so-called "independent living programs" run by private companies: such placements were made, and could only be changed by, court order. One such youth placed in this program was murdered while living at his assigned apartment. The deceased's grandmother filed due process claims against not only the private apartment complex and the independent living program, but also the District. The District argued it was not liable because the deceased could not "meaningfully be said to have been in the District's custody when he was murdered" given this contractual relationship with the private company housing the deceased. The D.C. Circuit disagreed: "[T]he District's *legal* custody over [the deceased

Of course, the above discussion does not preclude Palmer from securing qualified immunity later. It is entirely possible, for example, that plaintiffs did not endure the extent of isolation that they allege. It is equally feasible that such solitary confinement was ordered pursuant to a legitimate governmental objective, or that plaintiffs will be unable to marshal evidence to show that defendants' actions substantially departed from accepted standards. Plaintiffs might also overstate Palmer's true level of involvement or his actual or constructive knowledge of the allegedly unconstitutional activity. If so, the district court would possess the authority to revisit the issue. In the meantime, however, this case is one that would greatly benefit from a more robust record. In short, although qualified immunity defenses should be decided at "the earliest possible stage in litigation," the determination whether qualified immunity exists for Palmer depends on "particular facts" that are not yet in the record. . . .

For the foregoing reasons, we REVERSE the judgment of the district court in favor of Palmer on plaintiffs' claims against him and REMAND for further proceedings consistent with this opinion.

NOTES AND QUESTIONS

1. The key questions in determining whether a state officer is entitled to qualified immunity for conduct are whether the officer violated an individual's constitutional rights and, if so, whether that right was clearly established at the time of the officer's conduct. What actions do the plaintiffs in *Reed* claim violated their constitutional rights while they were confined in the Wisconsin Girls State Training School? Is it clear that these actions violated the girls' constitutional rights? That these rights were clearly established at the time the defendants acted?

2. Beyond a right not to be harmed, do minors in state training schools have an affirmative right to treatment? Some courts have concluded that they so. For example, in Alexander S. v. Boyd, 876 F. Supp. 773 (D.S.C. 1995), the court wrote:

> Traditionally, courts that have recognized a constitutional right to rehabilitative treatment have generally employed two basic theories to divine such a right. These theories were initially developed in the context of mentally ill or retarded persons

---

was] a good indicator that it had a duty to look after him." It analogized the case to decisions "holding that children in foster care are in state custody for substantive due process purposes and . . . that in placing them in foster homes and monitoring their progress, the state owes them a constitutional duty of care." According to the court, "[l]ike such children, [the deceased] not only looked to the government as primary guardian of his needs, but, absent District approval, also lacked freedom to seek alternate arrangements—precisely the two circumstances courts have found create . . . custody in the foster care situation."

This case closely resembles *Smith*. Just as the District retained legal custody of the deceased in *Smith*, plaintiffs here allege that Palmer and the Iowa Department of Human Services retained legal custody for their well-being. Although Palmer argues that plaintiffs' placement was technically made—and controlled—by judicial rather than executive order, that same fact did not prevent the *Smith* court from holding the District liable. Nor did the fact that the District contracted its day-to-day hands-on responsibilities to an outside entity, which is precisely what Palmer did here, change the court's decision.

committed to state mental institutions or hospitals. Courts extended these theories to the context of juveniles incarcerated in training schools, because juveniles, like mentally incompetent or retarded individuals, generally fall within the same *parens patriae* authority of the state. *See generally* Santana v. Collazo, 533 F. Supp. 966, 972 (D.P.R. 1982) (discussing the development of "right to treatment" theories, although eventually rejecting them), *aff'd*, 714 F.2d 1172 (1st Cir. 1983), *cert. denied*, 466 U.S. 974 (1984). The first theory, which is adopted by this court, finds support in the Supreme Court's pronouncement in Jackson v. Indiana, 406 U.S. 715, 738 (1972), that "due process requires that the nature and duration of confinement bear some reasonable relation to the purpose for which the individual is committed." As stated previously, when a state incarcerates juveniles for the purposes of treatment or rehabilitation, as does South Carolina, due process requires that the conditions of confinement be reasonably related to that purpose.

The second theory is known as the *quid pro quo*, or mutual compact, theory. Under this approach, courts have held that states are required to rehabilitate juveniles as a consideration for affording juveniles fewer procedural safeguards than those afforded to adult criminal defendants....

The validity of the *quid pro quo* theory is now quite suspect. In O'Connor v. Donaldson, 422 U.S. 563 (1975) [dealing with patients confined in state mental hospitals], Chief Justice Burger's concurring opinion specifically rejects the theory.... Burger concluded that this premise is flawed because the state's traditional authority as *parens patriae* allows it to confine individuals for reasons other than treatment, such as providing them with a more humane place of confinement. In Santana v. Collazo, the First Circuit Court of Appeals applied Chief Justice Burger's concurring opinion in O'Connor v. Donaldson and concluded ... that no constitutional right to rehabilitation exists for incarcerated juvenile delinquents. *See also* Morales v. Turman, 562 F.2d 993, 997-98 (5th Cir. 1977) (in dictum, rejecting constitutional right to treatment for juvenile offenders). 876 F. Supp. at 796-97, n.43.

Some courts have recognized a state law-based right to treatment or rehabilitation. *E.g.*, In re D.F., 351 A.2d 43 (N.J. Juv. & Dom. Rel. 1975); Nelson v. Heyne, 355 F. Supp. 451 (N.D. Ind. 1972) (state and federal rights). *But see* Hughes v. Judd, No. 8:12-CV-568-T-23MAP, 2015 WL 1737871, at 72-76 (M.D. Fla. Apr. 16, 2015) (finding that sheriff has no obligation to provide rehabilitative services to juvenile detainee and was not statutorily or constitutionally required, or even permitted, to rehabilitate a juvenile detainee not convicted of any crime).

3. Though solitary confinement is linked to stress-related, dysfunctional, and destructive behavior in both adults and juvenile inmates, it continues to be used under the rationale that it is necessary for the protection of prison staff and inmates who are vulnerable. Despite the Supreme Court's recent findings on the vulnerability of youth, no court has ruled that solitary confinement of juveniles is per se unconstitutional and it is a practice that has been justified in at least 57 nations across the world. Although there have been efforts to reform this practice through legislation and litigation, progress has been slow. The implementation of best practice standards in juvenile detention centers and removal of children under 18 from adult facilities would be a step in the right direction toward ending the practice of isolating children. *See* Tamar R. Birckhead, Children in Isolation: The Solitary Confinement of Youth, 50 Wake Forest L. Rev. 1 (2015). *See also* Laura

Anne Gallagher, More Than a Time Out: Juvenile Solitary Confinement, 18 U.C. Davis J. Juv. L. & Pol'y 244, 246-265 (2014).

In 2016 President Obama adopted Department of Justice recommendations forbidding solitary confinement of juveniles in federal prisons. Michael D. Shear, Obama Bans Solitary Confinement of Juveniles in Federal Prison (N.Y. Times, Jan. 25, 2016). This policy change affected very few individuals, but it sent a symbolic message to the states.

4. Justice Department investigations of complaints about conditions in juvenile residential facilities have become the most important means of remedying conditions in juvenile facilities. The department gets its authority from the Civil Rights of Institutionalized Persons Act of 1980 (CRIPA) and the Violent Crime Control and Law Enforcement Act of 1994. Douglas E. Abrams, Reforming Juvenile Delinquency Treatment to Enhance Rehabilitation, Personal Accountability, and Public Safety, 84 Or. L. Rev. 1001, 1004-1005, 1010 (2005). Most recently, the department opened an investigation of the South Carolina Broad River Road Complex I, South Carolina's long-term juvenile commitment facility, including whether the Department of Juvenile Justice fails to protect youth from physical abuse by other youth and by staff, and subjects youth to prolonged solitary confinement. "The investigation will also review whether the Department of Juvenile Justice violates the Americans with Disabilities Act in decisions where it has the sole authority to determine whether to place youth with disabilities in its pre-sentencing residential evaluation centers, and whether the Department of Juvenile Justice reasonably modifies its pre-sentencing evaluation system to avoid disability-based discrimination." Department of Justice Activities Under the Civil Rights of Institutionalized Persons Act Fiscal Year 2017 at 7 (March 2018), https://www.justice.gov/crt/case-document/file/1081841/download.

C.   THE ROLE OF COUNSEL FOR CHILDREN

INSTITUTE FOR JUDICIAL ADMINISTRATION — AMERICAN BAR ASSOCIATION, JUVENILE JUSTICE STANDARDS PROJECT, STANDARDS RELATING TO COUNSEL FOR PRIVATE PARTIES

1-8 (1979)

There has always been sharp controversy regarding the propriety and role of counsel in juvenile court proceedings. Traditionally, cases involving children were considered "nonadversarial" with respect to both the relationship of the parties and the forms of procedure employed. The child's interest in the proceeding was assumed to be identical with that of the state, which claimed to seek only the child's welfare and not his or her punishment. There did not exist, accordingly, that adversity of interest among the parties which characterizes other civil or criminal proceedings. Given this premise, modes of trial and methods of protecting legal rights designed for cases involving frankly conflicting interests seemed inappropriate. Juvenile hearings were viewed not as a contentious process but as a therapeutic one. Informality and direct communication between judge and child replaced demonstration by ordinary rules of procedure and evidence as vehicles for eliciting needed information concerning the child's circumstances and, as well, for imparting to children, or sometimes their parents, a sense of social responsibility. . . .

[After In re Gault], however, expressions of good intentions and references to parens patriae could no longer justify denial of access to counsel to juveniles. . . . The case did not, however, entirely clarify the nature of juvenile court proceedings nor the role of counsel participating in them. Judges and others have pointed to the limits placed by the Court on its holding, and to the desire expressed in *Gault* (and in subsequent decisions) for retention of the benevolent aspects of the juvenile justice system, as support for maintaining as far as possible the traditional nonadversary approach.

The post-*Gault* effort to accommodate traditional juvenile court theory and the requirement of counsel resulted, for some, in a fundamental redefinition of counsel's function. Many have suggested that attorneys for children abandon the sharply defined role of the advocate for a "guardianship" theory of representation. As a "guardian," counsel is primarily concerned with ascertaining and presenting the plea and program best calculated to serve the child's perceived welfare. *E.g.* Isaacs, "The Role of Counsel in Representing Minors in the New Family Court," 12 Buff. L. Rev. 501, 506-507 (1963). Others have urged an "amicus curiae" function, in which counsel acts largely as an intermediary between the participants and explains the significance of proceedings to the client. *See* Cayton, "Relationship of the Probation Officer and the Defense Attorney after Gault," 34 Fed. Prob. 8, 10 (1970). *See also* Skoler & Tenney, "Attorney Representation in Juvenile Court," 4 J. Fam. L. 77 (1964). It is apparent that both guardianship and amicus curiae approaches involve radical modification of the rules governing a lawyer's professional role. At the very least, either approach places on counsel responsibility for decisions ordinarily allocated to the client. For example, whether to admit or contest the charges may become a matter to be determined by the attorney, perhaps in consultation with probation staff and parents, rather than by the respondent. *E.g.*, Edelstein, "The Duties and Functions of the Law Guardian in the Family Court," 45 N.Y.S. B.J. 183, 184 (1973). Either of these approaches may also shift from client to counsel responsibility for the exercise of the privilege against self-incrimination, as suggested by the statement, "A sensitive lawyer, like a sensitive judge or a sensitive social worker, knows when confession is good for the soul." Coxe, "Lawyers in Juvenile Court," 13 Crime & Delinq. 488, 490 (1967). Moreover, a lawyer who seeks to block presentation of complete and accurate information to the court through, for example, a motion to suppress illegally obtained evidence might be accused by proponents of this redefined role of frustrating the court's proper functioning. *See* Kay & Segal, "The Role of the Attorney in Juvenile Court: A Non-Polar Approach," 61 Geo. L.J. 1401, 1412-1413 (1973). . . .

The standards set forth in this volume generally reject both guardianship and amicus curiae definitions of counsel's role and require instead that attorneys in juvenile court assume those responsibilities for advocacy and counseling which obtain in other areas of legal representation. Accordingly, counsel's principal function is a derivative one; it lies in furthering the "lawful objectives of his client through all reasonably available means permitted by law." ABA, Code of Professional Responsibility DR 7-101(A). Generally, determination of those objectives — whether to admit or deny, to press or abandon a claim, and the like — is the responsibility of the client whose interests will be affected by the proceeding.

Attorneys may urge one course or another, but may not properly arrogate the final decision to themselves. . . .

[The] political and instrumental goals [of the legal system, and the lawyer's role within it], and hence the rules they generate, are as important to juvenile court proceedings as to other civil or criminal matters. While the juvenile justice system retains a number of distinctive and significant features, it cannot still be maintained that juveniles facing deprivation of liberty have no cognizable claim under law apart from those asserted by the state on their behalf. By necessary implication, the traditional juvenile court view claiming identity of interest between the state and the accused juvenile has been rejected in favor of recognition of a privilege in juvenile respondents to withhold cooperation in proceedings that may affect their liberties. In this connection, it is important that the Supreme Court, in extending the privilege against self-incrimination to delinquency proceedings, did so not only out of concern for untrustworthy confessions, but because children, like adults, may claim a measure of distance from the state in actions which may result, however benevolent the motivation, in a substantial restriction of freedom. . . . The respondents' right to decide whether to assist the state necessarily assumes that they are entitled to define their own interest in the proceeding different from that urged by the state. . . . And, most recently, the Supreme Court has held that both the function and the consequences of delinquency proceedings are virtually identical to those characterizing criminal prosecutions. Each system is "designed 'to vindicate [the] very vital interest in enforcement of criminal laws,'" Breed v. Jones, 421 U.S. 519 (1975), a goal clearly independent of that held by the accused. . . .

Once the traditional premise of identity of interest between the state and the juvenile in delinquency proceedings is impeached, the related notion — that adversarial procedures ought to be avoided in a noncontentious forum — becomes flawed as well. . . .

While most of the decisional law concerning rights of persons before the juvenile court is concerned with delinquency proceedings, the same rationales apply to the role of counsel in other juvenile court matters. As in prosecutions for crime or delinquency, respondents alleged to be in need of supervision are subject to deprivations of liberty, including institutional commitment, for what may be the duration of their minority. And while stigmatization may be of a different or less aggravated kind, it presumably still exists since a disadvantageous label is applied to the child as a result of the adjudication. In child protective proceedings as well, the respondent — here the parent or guardian — faces a grave penalty in the substantial restriction of his or her constitutionally recognized interest in the custody of a child. . . . Again, as with delinquency and supervision matters, it is little more than wordplay to insist that the interests of the state and respondent — one seeking to take custody and the other to maintain it — are coincidental rather than frankly adverse. Nor, of course, could it be urged that accuracy in factual and legal decisions is less important in these areas.

THE RELEVANCE OF THE CLIENT'S YOUTH

It has sometimes been suggested that all or most of a juvenile court lawyer's clients are not sufficiently mature to instruct counsel in any usual sense and that counsel must therefore usually act as guardian or amicus curiae. The proponents of this view often tend, however, to equate competence with capacity to weigh accurately all immediate and remote benefits or costs associated with the available options. In representing adults, wisdom of this kind is not required; it is ordinarily sufficient that clients understand the nature and purposes of the proceeding, and its general consequences, and be able to formulate their desires concerning the proceeding with some degree of clarity. Most adolescents can meet this standard, and more ought not be required of them. To do so would, in effect, reintroduce the identification of state and child by imposing on respondents an "objective" definition of their interests.

It is, of course, true that "the responsibilities of a lawyer may vary according to the intelligence, experience, mental condition or age of a client . . . or the nature of the particular proceeding." ABA, Code of Professional Responsibility EC 7-11. Attorneys will sometimes be required, by reason of their clients' youth and inexperience, to take special pains in explaining the nature and potential results of the action and to investigate formal and informal dispositional alternatives in their clients' interest. . . . And, particularly where counsel represents a very young client (ordinarily but not always in connection with a child protective, custody, or adoption matter), it will in some cases happen that the client is incapable of rational consideration regarding the proceeding. Where this is true, attorneys may be required to abandon their role as advocate. . . . However, the occasions for doing so are rare — particularly in delinquency and supervision cases — and may not properly be extended through manipulation of the general standard for competence.

IN THE INTEREST OF LDO

858 P.2d 553 (Wyo. 1993)

THOMAS, Justice. The issue presented in this case is whether, because of the failure to investigate the circumstances surrounding the interrogation of the juvenile concerning the underlying delinquency charge and the failure to move to suppress unlawful admissions prior to the hearing, a juvenile had the benefit of effective assistance of counsel in a juvenile proceeding. . . .

In August of 1992, LDO, a fifteen-year-old minor, ran away from a crisis center in Casper where he had been placed. He returned to Gillette and resumed living with his aunt and her family. LDO had lived with the aunt's family for about three years prior to his placement at the crisis center in Casper. On the afternoon of August 14, 1992, the aunt discovered LDO had not gone to his community service job, and she reported him to the police as a runaway. An officer went to the aunt's home for the purpose of obtaining a report from the aunt and, during the course of their discussion, the aunt noticed a CD player was missing from her home. . . .

On the following day, the officer made a traffic stop and found LDO as a passenger in the vehicle. At that juncture, LDO was placed in custody as a runaway, and he was first taken to the police station. Later, he was transported to the Campbell County Detention Center. On August 16, an officer interviewed LDO about the CD player. The officer did not advise LDO of his constitutional rights in the form of a *Miranda* warning, or in any other way, prior to questioning him.

LDO told the officer he had taken the CD player from the aunt's home without permission and had left it at a friend's house. The officer then went to the friend's house and retrieved the CD player. LDO then was interviewed again about the CD player, still without advice as to his constitutional rights, and he admitted he had asked his friend to pawn it.

At the adjudicatory hearing, after his admissions had been received in evidence, LDO testified and admitted the aunt had purchased the CD player. He also admitted he took it from the aunt's home, left it at a friend's house, and he did intend to pawn it. On October 27, 1992, LDO was adjudicated a delinquent minor. . . . LDO was committed temporarily to the custody of the Department of Family Services, for placement at Sky Ranch, Buffalo, South Dakota. This appeal is taken from the adjudication.

The dispositive issue in this case is whether LDO had the benefit of effective assistance of counsel. A juvenile in delinquency proceedings has a right to the assistance of counsel, which is guaranteed by the Sixth Amendment to the Constitution of the United States, made applicable to the states through the Fourteenth Amendment.

The standard for appellate review of a claim of ineffective assistance of counsel is the same under the state and federal constitutions. *See* Strickland v. Washington, 466 U.S. 668 (1984). The fact counsel was assigned does not satisfy the constitutional requirement; effective assistance must be provided by counsel in the preparation of the case for trial. The standard for review of a claim of ineffective assistance of counsel demands LDO demonstrate both that counsel's performance was deficient, and LDO was prejudiced as a result of that deficient performance. . . .

We first adopted this standard in Frias v. State, 722 P.2d 135 (Wyo. 1986), and we recently had occasion to revisit it. . . . [W]e summarized the two-prong test found in *Strickland* as follows:

> First, the defendant must show that counsel's performance was deficient. This requires showing that counsel made errors so serious that counsel was not functioning as the "counsel" guaranteed the defendant by the Sixth Amendment. Second, the defendant must show that the deficient performance prejudiced the defense. This requires showing that counsel's errors were so serious as to deprive the defendant of a fair trial, a trial whose result is reliable. Unless a defendant makes both showings, it cannot be said that the conviction or death sentence resulted from a breakdown in the adversary process that renders the result unreliable.

. . . The Supreme Court of the United States has articulated the duty of counsel to investigate in this way:

> In other words, counsel has a duty to make reasonable investigations or to make a reasonable decision that makes particular investigations unnecessary. In any ineffectiveness case, a particular decision not to investigate must be directly assessed for reasonableness in all the circumstances, applying a heavy measure of deference to counsel's judgments.

The court also said: "[I]nquiry into counsel's conversations with the defendant may be critical to a proper assessment of counsel's investigation decisions. . . ."

In this case, it is clear the attorney failed to contact LDO prior to the adjudicatory hearing. Counsel advised the court he had attempted to visit LDO in the Campbell County Detention Facility, but he was told LDO already had been sent to Buffalo, South Dakota to the Sky Ranch. Counsel acknowledged he could have contacted LDO in South Dakota by telephone, but he did not do so. If LDO had been interviewed, counsel readily could have ascertained LDO had made inculpatory statements to the police officer while he was in the Campbell County Juvenile Detention Center. In light of the exclusionary rules that pertain today, the follow-up question as to whether, prior to the interrogation, LDO had been advised of his constitutional rights pursuant to the *Miranda* decision was obvious. Counsel then would have been aware of the violation of LDO's constitutional rights and would have recognized that a motion to suppress was indicated.

LDO argues the juvenile court, in essence, found he was denied effective assistance of counsel when the court determined counsel failed to show cause for not moving to suppress the evidence prior to trial. Again, there is no dispute about whether a pre-trial motion was filed in this case. Counsel did not file the pre-trial motion to suppress the statements as required by Wyo. R. Crim. P. 12(b), which provides:

> *Pretrial motions.* — Any defense, objection, or request which is capable of determination without the trial of the general issue may be raised before trial by motion. Motions may be written or oral at the discretion of the judge. The following must be raised prior to trial:
>
> . . .
>
> (3) Motions to suppress evidence; . . .

The same rule makes provision for the failure to make a motion to suppress:

> *Effect of failure to raise defenses or objections, or to make requests.* — Failure by a party to raise defenses or objections or to make requests which must be made prior to trial, at the time set by the court pursuant to subdivision (d), or prior to any extension thereof made by the court, shall constitute waiver thereof, but the court for cause shown may grant relief from the waiver.
>
> These rules are specifically made applicable to juvenile proceedings. . . .

The juvenile court judge considered the objection to the evidence at the adjudicatory hearing, but then overruled the objection because of the failure to make a timely motion to suppress. In effect, the court held that a motion to suppress *must* be made prior to the adjudicatory hearing unless good cause is demonstrated as to why the motion was not filed on time. The rule affords discretion to the court to grant relief from the failure to make the motion for good cause shown. In this instance, the juvenile court did not abuse its discretion because counsel for LDO did not show good cause, or any cause, for failing to make the motion prior to trial.

Our conclusion is that ineffective assistance of counsel has been demonstrated. Counsel should have interviewed his client prior to the adjudicatory hearing. Had that been done, counsel would have known that a motion to suppress the inculpatory statements for failure to advise LDO of his constitutional rights was in order. If the admissions by LDO, which clearly were inculpatory, had been excluded from evidence, LDO might well have decided not to testify, and he would not have confirmed the information testified to by the interviewing officer.

[We agree] with the conclusion of the Supreme Court of the United States "that the failure to file a suppression motion does not constitute ineffective assistance of counsel *per se*." It is necessary, in addition to the failure to file the motion, to evaluate that failure from the perspective of counsel at the time of the alleged error and in light of all the circumstances. We conclude LDO has demonstrated his counsel's performance was deficient for failure to investigate the circumstances surrounding his interrogation about the facts of the underlying charge and the failure to pursue the rule requirements with respect to a motion to suppress the unlawful information. LDO has demonstrated prejudice as a result of this failure and comes within the two-prong test articulated in *Strickland*. We hold LDO did not receive effective assistance of counsel in connection with his adjudication of juvenile delinquency, and that adjudication must be reversed. Such a failure to prepare, even in a juvenile proceeding, places at risk not only the rights of the juvenile, but the reliability of the adversarial process. . . .

NOTES AND QUESTIONS

1. *LDO* emphasizes the importance of active representation at an early stage. Standard 4.1 of the IJA-ABA Standards Relating to Counsel for Private Parties (1980) notes that "[m]any important rights of clients . . . can be protected only by prompt advice and action. The lawyers should immediately inform clients of their rights and pursue any investigatory or procedural steps necessary to protection of their clients' interests." Standard 4.3 calls for prompt investigation and preparation, which "should always include efforts to secure information in the possession of prosecution, law enforcement, education, probation and social welfare authorities. The duty to investigate exists regardless of the client's admissions. . . ." As *LDO* points out, failure to investigate promptly can lead to failure to take essential steps to secure the client's rights.

Demonstration of a failure to investigate may well indicate poor professional conduct. It does not, however, establish ineffective assistance of counsel unless the respondent can demonstrate prejudice as a result of that failure. What prejudice was shown in *LDO*? Must it appear that (1) the inculpatory statements would have been suppressed and (2) the prosecution would have been unable to establish a prima facie case without those statements? Or must it appear that (1) the statements would have been suppressed, (2) LDO would not have testified, and (3) without his testimony, the case would have been dismissed?

2. Early interviews with the client and investigation of the child's circumstances may also be valuable for seeking nonjudicial resolution of a complaint. As we have seen, a substantial proportion of delinquency and status offense matters are settled through diversion at intake. *See* IJA-ABA Standards, above, at Standard 4.3(b). In what circumstances might early investigation promote a diversionary rather than a judicial resolution of a complaint?

3. A frequent basis for challenges to competence of counsel arises when one lawyer represents multiple clients in the same matter. Cuyler v. Sullivan,

446 U.S. 335 (1980), presented the question of ineffective assistance where counsel actively represented multiple parties in a criminal case. The Court required the defendant to show both that counsel actively represented conflicting interests and that the conflict "adversely affected" counsel's performance. However, unlike cases involving claims of ineffective assistance generally, the defendant is not required to show "prejudice" (that is, that the result would have been different except for the conflict). *Cf.* Strickland v. Washington, 466 U.S. 668 (1984).

Multiple representation in criminal cases is strongly disfavored by ethics rules and case law generally. *See, e.g.*, Model Rules of Professional Responsibility, Comment to Model Rule 1.7; Fed. R. Crim. P. 44(c). Standard 3.2 of the IJA-ABA Standards Relating to Counsel for Private Parties (1980) takes the same position:

> Subsection [3.2(i)] incorporates the traditional definition of conflict of interest . . . : "[A] lawyer represents conflicting interests when, on behalf of one client, it is his duty to contend for that which duty to another client requires him to oppose." Subsection (ii) extends this rule to instances where the demands of strategy or advocacy require an attorney to argue on one client's behalf a proposition which, if accepted by the judge or jury, would prejudice another client's position. . . . This form of adversity is, perhaps, most likely to arise during dispositional hearings, although it may do so at any stage of proceedings. As the California Supreme Court observed in People v. Chacon, 69 Cal. 2d 765, 447 P.2d 106, 112 (1968), one lawyer "cannot simultaneously argue with any semblance of effectiveness that each defendant is most deserving of the lesser penalty." And, even during the course of trial, counsel representing co-respondents may effectively be disabled from stressing evidence that points to one of his clients as less culpable than the other. *Ibid*.
>
> Careful application of these principles ordinarily should lead counsel to avoid representation of both parent and child or more than one party in juvenile court matters. . . .

Id. at 85.

4. An increasing number of states are requiring more rigorous mandatory legal education training for juvenile public defenders. Massachusetts, which is viewed by many states as the leader in juvenile defense, is one of 20 states that has a statewide juvenile public defense system that can regulate the training of juvenile public defenders. *See* Rebecca Beitsch, The Pew Charitable Trusts, States Push Tougher Standards for Juvenile Public Defenders (May 5, 2016) http://www. pewtrusts.org/en/research-and-analysis/blogs/stateline/2016/05/05/states-push-tougher-standards-for-juvenile-public-defenders. *See also* Assembly Bill No. 703 (2015) http://www.leginfo.ca.gov/pub/15-16/bill/asm/ab_0701-0750/ab_703_bill_20150930_chaptered.pdf (a California bill that recognizes the importance of juvenile defenders and clarifies their ethical duties, requiring defenders to represent the minor's expressed interests, honor the duty of confidentiality with the client, maintain meaningful contact with the client, consult with social workers and other experts as appropriate, and meet minimum standards of training or experience. This legislation, which went into effect on July 1, 2016, was developed in light of statistics showing that half of the appointed counsel in juvenile court have

no juvenile defense specific training.); Kansas Juvenile Justice Workgroup Final Report (Nov. 2015) (finding, after a comprehensive analysis of the state's juvenile courts and corrections systems, that the juvenile justice system has not kept pace as the crime rate has fallen, and issuing forty consensus-based recommendations, including the need to improve the quality of juvenile defense via specialization, oversight and juvenile-specific training, and a payment structure that encourages specialization), https://www.doc.ks.gov/juvenile-services/workgroup/report/Final/view.

5. Appellate courts have assumed the authority to hear juvenile appeals based on arguments of ineffective assistance of counsel, and national standards state that appellate attorneys have an ethical obligation to review the record for trial counsel's adequacy and to make an ineffective assistance of counsel claim when one is warranted. *See* Barbara Fedders, Losing Hold of the Guiding Hand: Ineffective Assistance of Counsel in Juvenile Delinquency Representation, 14 Lewis & Clark L. Rev. 771, 802-803 (2010). Yet, the reality is that such claims are brought infrequently. Between 1995 and 2005, over six million youths were adjudicated delinquent. In that period, only 290 adjudicated juveniles filed ineffective assistance claims that resulted in opinions published in Westlaw or Lexis. Among those cases, only 41 claims yielded appellate relief. For a discussion of why the legal doctrine and rules governing ineffective assistance claims make accessing the appellate system particularly difficult for juveniles, *see id.* at 802-813. *See also* Joshua A. Tepfer & Laura H. Nirider, Adjudicated Juveniles and Collateral Relief, 64 Me. L. Rev. 553 (2012) ("[s]ome states explicitly make collateral relief unavailable to defendants who are tried as juveniles, even while granting such access to adults. In many other states, legislatures have drafted laws governing the availability of post-conviction relief that are vague and ambiguous, leading to uncertainty about whether adjudicated juveniles may take advantage of such proceedings. This disparity exists despite the fact that those tried in juvenile court need access to collateral remedies just as much as those tried in adult court." *Id.* at 554.)

TAMAR R. BIRCKHEAD, *CULTURE CLASH: THE CHALLENGE OF LAWYERING ACROSS DIFFERENCE IN JUVENILE COURT*

62 Rutgers L. Rev. 959, 962-963, 970, 971-979, 980-982, 990-991 (2010)

. . . Professional guidelines direct attorneys who represent youth in juvenile delinquency court to advocate based on their young client's "expressed interest" (what the youth says she wants), rather than relying on what the attorney believes is "best" for the child. Yet, this basic premise is often more challenging to follow than is commonly acknowledged. The standards of effective criminal defense practice emphasize rigorous oral and written advocacy with little mention of whether the client has learned a lesson from the experience. This is in direct conflict with the informal culture that exists in most juvenile courtrooms in the United States, where delinquency court judges fail to apply the beyond-a-reasonable-doubt standard of proof, prosecutors neglect to respond meaningfully to discovery motions filed by the defense, and probation officers recommend punitive sentences regardless of the child's actual needs. In such instances, defense attorneys are confronted with hurdles that are difficult to overcome. Furthermore, the parents of juvenile clients may have priorities that differ greatly from those of the attorney, a serious problem that is compounded when the parent is a co-defendant, witness, or alleged victim of the offense. Likewise, even defense attorneys who are firmly committed to their role and to rigorous representation may feel conflicted, as their young clients can be impulsive, unreliable, and incapable of mature decision-making.

A.   JUDGES

"We don't pay much attention to the fact-portion of the case. We just want to get these kids help.
— Juvenile court judge, North Carolina

. . . Some [juvenile court] judges persist in focusing on the needs of the juvenile without first determining whether a criminal offense has been committed. Furthermore, most jurisdictions do not provide juveniles with the right to a jury trial, and the bench trial model typically employed in juvenile court, in which the judge alone hears the evidence, has problematic features that perpetuate unfairness. It has been found, for example, that juvenile court judges are inclined to evaluate evidence in a manner that favors the prosecution. This may follow from the judge's desire to protect the community by erring on the side of conviction, to avoid being perceived as soft on crime, or to ensure that troubled youth receive services as mandatory conditions of probation. It may also arise from instances of individual bias on the part of the trial judge. As a result, although the United States Supreme Court held in 1970 that the high standard of proof used in criminal cases ("beyond a reasonable doubt") also applies to juvenile delinquency cases, this is inconsistently reflected in practice.

In addition, juvenile court judges managing heavy dockets or operating in jurisdictions in which all pending matters must be handled within a single court session face systemic pressures to resolve cases. This can give rise to judges' impatience and distain for defense attorneys who file motions or request adjudicatory hearings rather than advise their young clients to admit to the charges. Defense attorneys who fail to cooperate may face both subtle and direct forms of retaliation, including reduction in fees and removal from court-appointed lists. Such an attitude on the part of judges can be exacerbated by the prevailing view that the youth charged as a delinquent may not have committed the offense charged, but she must have done *something*. In jurisdictions in which juvenile court judges are elected and therefore compelled to campaign on their record in order to win the popular vote, such views are even more likely to predominate.

Further, juvenile court is frequently used as a training ground or brief rotation for judges, many of whom are unfamiliar with the state juvenile code or the ways in which adolescent development, mental health, and special education needs can impact a child's behavior. These judges may have distorted views of the delinquency court system and the young people who are in it. When a juvenile's lawyer is also untrained and inexperienced — a not-uncommon occurrence — a power imbalance can develop in the courtroom that results in an over-reliance by all parties on the probation officer. This, too, compromises the system's commitment to justice and contributes to the risk of wrongful convictions.

B. Prosecutors

"Suppression motions are disruptive. Motions and defense attorneys interfere with the process."
— Juvenile court prosecutor, Georgia

Prosecutors who are assigned to juvenile delinquency court are a second contributing factor in the calculus. They commonly receive minimal supervision and training. They are saddled with unwieldy caseloads, and they — like judges — are under pressure to resolve matters quickly and efficiently. As a result, many juvenile court prosecutors have little understanding or tolerance for defense attorneys who practice with more than the barest amount of diligence. They are annoyed when expected to provide discovery in advance of a hearing. They are perplexed and sometimes resentful when juvenile defenders file written motions, although the practice is, of course, allowable under the rules of criminal procedure and juvenile code of every state. They are offended when the defense interviews prosecution witnesses prior to the trial ("adjudicatory hearing") and have suggested that such a practice is unethical and burdens the alleged victim.

Likewise, juvenile court prosecutors benefit from the structural realities of the system. They typically have access to investigative resources that the defense lacks. They have the discretion to file certain cases in adult court, and they use the threat of transfer to extract admissions from juveniles who otherwise would have requested a hearing. In addition, prosecutors often share the mistaken view of the judge that juvenile court is not an adversarial forum and that no negative consequences to the child will result. Thus, given the distain with which prosecutors treat those few attorneys who are committed to rigorous, client-directed representation, it is not surprising when defenders assume the posture of one who is seen and not heard.

C. Probation Officers

"I could take my client to my office to talk, but then I would get behind on court call — the court does not wait."
— Juvenile probation officer, Florida

Probation officers who work with juveniles in delinquency court often face a dilemma when making sentencing ("dispositional") recommendations on behalf of juveniles. In theory, they can recommend a comprehensive package of services that includes psychological treatment, anger-management counseling, and academic tutoring. However, because of the resource-strapped budgets of many juvenile courts, mental health agencies, and school systems, often the only real choice is some form of incarceration. Even in jurisdictions in which funding is not at issue, probation officers make harsh recommendations because of a fear of appearing soft and losing credibility with the judge and prosecutor. Likewise, it is not uncommon for probation officers to become burned out after years in the trenches with heavy caseloads and little support. Some become tired of fighting the more punitive aspects of the system, while others internalize the clichés and stereotypes perpetuated about juveniles and buy into the warehousing of "bad kids." The result is that a juvenile probation officer may privately acknowledge to a defender that her client's family is dysfunctional and that the child has serious psychological, developmental, or learning issues that have never been properly addressed. Yet, in the courtroom the officer will recommend the most punitive sanction: the child's commitment to what is euphemistically known as a "detention home," "training school," or "youth development center."

The problematic role of juvenile probation officers is compounded by the fact that they are often the best informed people in the courtroom and have the most sustained contact with the child. This results in an overreliance on their judgments by the judge and prosecutor that can make the facts of the case and the applicable law only minimally relevant to the ultimate disposition. In jurisdictions in which juveniles commonly waive their right to counsel, probation officers often provide procedural as well as substantive legal advice to juveniles. In such instances, they arguably cross the line into the unlicensed practice of law. The failure of defense counsel to question the nearly unfettered discretion of the probation officer or to challenge the accuracy of the facts contained within probation reports serves to further the department's influence in juvenile court. This phenomenon is particularly troublesome in complex cases in which the juvenile has serious mental health or drug treatment needs or has been found delinquent of a sex offense, the potential consequences of which can be particularly severe.

D.   DEFENDERS

"I don't always listen to what [the clients] say. Mine is not the role of the typical defense attorney; I must consider what is best for the child, and I do not take the position that I must 'get the child off at all costs.' "
— Juvenile defense attorney, Mississippi

Before the *Gault* decision in 1967, fewer than 10 percent of children in juvenile court received *any* legal assistance. Traditionally, the lack of counsel for juveniles was justified by the view that attorneys serve neither the interests of the child nor the interests of justice, and that the judge is "the defender as well as corrector of the child." In fact, pre-*Gault* judges were encouraged to discuss the special nature of juvenile court with counsel and to instruct them that they had a professional obligation to *assist in* the child's supervision, rehabilitation, and treatment.

Forty years later, state assessments of juvenile court practice have established that the model of client-directed robust defense is infrequently put into practice. Some juvenile defenders are experienced and have received high-quality training and supervision, but many are new to the practice of law and have been placed there by under-staffed public defender offices. Others accept assignments in juvenile court out of their own misguided belief that it is an appropriate learning ground because the stakes are low. Meanwhile, there are some who are crossovers from family court or abuse, neglect, and dependency court (also known as "DSS" or Department of Social Services court). They have no criminal defense training but have developed delinquency caseloads as a result of being regulars in these corollary courts — or sometimes merely because they happen to be warm bodies who practice in the local district or even traffic court.

Systemic barriers also contribute to the challenges faced by today's defenders. It is not unusual, for instance, when courthouses lack adequate space and resources for the defense bar. This means that lawyers and their young clients must forego private discussion or attempt to consult in whispers in order to speak in confidence before, during, or after court hearings. In addition to these types of physical limitations, the complacent attitude of the local defense bar can serve as a deterrent to effective representation. If most of the lawyers in an office put little effort into their juvenile cases, it is likely that the diligent few will gradually lower their standards. Likewise, the fact that most juvenile cases are resolved by guilty plea ("admission") further supports the misconception that preparation is unnecessary and an impediment to judicial economy. In fact, it is not uncommon for a lawyer to negotiate a plea agreement without first speaking to her juvenile client. She may briefly discuss it with the youth in the moments before the hearing and then immediately proceed into the courtroom with the client to enter the plea. It is also not unusual for salary disparities to exist between those attorneys who represent juveniles in delinquency court and their higher paid counterparts who represent defendants in adult criminal court, further reinforcing the message that juvenile defenders are worth less than "real lawyers." The same discrepancies in compensation, however, are not typically found between juvenile court and adult criminal court prosecutors.

Therefore, lawyers defending children are particularly susceptible to the negative message conveyed by others in the juvenile court system: don't investigate, don't talk to state's witnesses, don't file motions, don't make the state meet its burden, and — in short — don't be zealous, hard-working advocates. As a result, many assume that their only role is to work in partnership with the judge and prosecutor in order to get "help" for the child.

E. PARENTS

"If he didn't do it, then he needs a lawyer."
— Parent of juvenile, Indiana

"I believe it's what the parents want; so I cannot really argue against it."
— Juvenile defense attorney responding to the judge regarding the possibility of detaining his client, Maryland

Juvenile courts have jurisdiction over the parents or guardians of children in the system, establishing a formal role for them in delinquency cases. The defense attorney, therefore, often has little choice but to interact with and gain the cooperation and trust of her client's parents. As a result, the interests and attitudes of the parents can conflict and interfere with the defender's role in relation to her juvenile client.

While many parents of children charged with criminal offenses in juvenile delinquency court have constructive — even amicable — working relationships with their child's attorney, others stand in direct opposition to the defense lawyer's goals and objectives. Some parents pressure their child to "do the right thing," which usually translates to admitting to the crime and taking responsibility for what they did, regardless of the consequences. They believe that in this way their son or daughter will emerge from the experience a better person. They insist that the youth make amends and show remorse, despite a lack of evidence. Others, however, do not accept that their child could have been capable of committing the act alleged. They insist upon an adjudicatory hearing and refuse even to consider allowing the youth to admit to the charge — again, regardless of the consequences for the juvenile.

In general, most parents of juveniles are, at best, conflicted. Parenting involves conveying positive values, providing support and encouragement, and utilizing constructive forms of discipline. It can be difficult to helplessly stand by as one's child is labeled a juvenile delinquent or taken to detention in shackles and leg irons. To further complicate matters, the parent may be the alleged victim in the case, a witness to the offense, a co-defendant, or in danger of being held in contempt because of her failure to abide by a court order. Further, many parents are unable to escape the lingering question that inevitably arises when a youth is accused of violating the law: how does my child's case reflect upon me as a parent and as an individual?

Because of the parent's established role in delinquency matters, in many ways the juvenile court pits the child's lawyer against the parent, as the goals and objectives of each group may not only differ but may be diametrically opposed. The parent is determined either to keep her child out of the system (which may be rational but unrealistic) or to get her child into the system (as a result of the parent's frustration or lack of resources). Meanwhile, the child's lawyer stands at the other end of the spectrum working, at least in theory, for the least punitive result for her client — nothing more and nothing less.

Further, even defense lawyers who are committed to their role and to the most rigorous form of advocacy are not immune from feeling conflicted themselves. They are adults, but their clients are children or adolescents whose brains are not fully formed. Juvenile clients can be impulsive, unpredictable, and incapable even of providing a clear account of what happened. Further, the role of the adult in relation to the child is intended to be that of mentor, counselor, and protector — one who offers direction and guidance for children to live by as they mature. Yet any defender who is worth her salt will admit that this familial function can be in direct opposition to the blunt legal counseling that may be needed by a juvenile defendant.

The result is that the child's lawyer is caught in the middle and gradually worn down by all sides. Accurate fact-finding stops being a priority. Advocacy, both oral and written, falters. The quality of representation suffers, and wrongful convictions, among other harms, occur. Further, while this Article's focus is on juvenile delinquency court, this same dynamic can also develop and predominate among attorneys who represent youth in adult criminal court. Young people transferred to that forum for prosecution may face longer terms of imprisonment, but the fact of their immaturity and developmental incompetence remains.

CONCLUSION

Even the best juvenile defense attorney will acknowledge that she has occasionally been caught between acting as an aggressive, win-at-all-costs trial lawyer and serving as a counselor who gives advice based only on what she believes would be best for her young clients. Unfortunately, there is no magic bullet for resolving this dilemma. Defenders must try to build meaningful relationships with juveniles and help them make decisions that are both legally savvy and beneficial for their personal growth. However, it is not always easy. When heavy caseloads, court pressure, and concerns regarding expedience take over, lawyers operate on autopilot. Facts are overlooked, laws are misconstrued, and mistakes inevitably are made. Perhaps by recognizing the challenges faced by juvenile defenders, we can take proactive steps to change the culture of juvenile court and, as a result, lower the risk of wrongful convictions of youth.

PROBLEM

The following case file was maintained by an attorney representing juveniles in Cook County.
Case File L 77
Date Opened: August 29, 2018

Interview with Client: I met the respondent, Charles North, at court. He is a thirteen-year-old boy, charged with burglary of a building at 1216 South Halsdale Street. Charles freely admitted that he had been outside the building at the time, in an alley alongside, and that he had been trying to break in order to steal a television set. Charles said that he had been asked by a man known to him as Frank to get a television set, and he had agreed to do so. Charles does not know Frank's last name, nor where he lives. At the time of the arrest, it appears, Charles was outside the building. The owner of the building had apparently called the police; Charles heard the police car pulling up in front of the house, had taken the crowbar and hid it in a trash can, and was doing nothing except standing in the alley when the policeman came back and saw him. The crowbar has not been found, so far as he knows.

According to Charles, he is presently on probation, a fact confirmed by his mother. He is not sure why he was placed on probation but remembers having been in court on at least one prior occasion. Both Charles and his mother express the firm desire that Charles not be held in custody or committed to an institution. Charles appears to be very close to his mother and protective of her.

Charles has a very large scarred area on top of his head, which he usually covers by wearing a hat. He received this scar as a result of a blow suffered during childhood. He also complains of a ringing in his ears, particularly when he attends school.

At this point, I excused myself and asked the court police liaison officer for a copy of the police arrest report, which contained the following:

POLICE REPORT

Record:

Curfew	1/18/16	AAS
Curfew	8/10/16	AAS
Curfew	11/10/16	AAS
Curfew	12/22/16	AAS
Curfew	1/16/17	AAS
Curfew	2/11/17	AAS
Missing	4/25/17	AAS
Burglary	7/02/17	AAS
Not specified (Berwyn PD)	8/15/17	AAS
Burglary	11/15/17	AAS
At Theft Auto	1/31/17	AAS
Burglary	4/14/17	AAS
Burglary	6/26/17	RCD
Burglary	7/06/17	RCD
Curfew	2/20/17	AAS
Curfew	2/29/17	AAS
Curfew	3/11/17	AAS
Burglary	8/30/17	AAS
Burglary	6/20/18	AAS

* AAS: Adjusted at station; not referred to intake

Charge: Charles committed offense of burglary in that he intentionally, without authority, knowingly entered into the building at 1216 South Springfield (basement) with the intent to commit the crime of theft.

Statement: None

Narrative: On 26 August, 2018, at about 1230 hours beat 1002 responded to call at 1216 South Springfield. Patrolman Vincent met Ms. Wilson who stated her son heard noises in the vicinity of basement door at above location. Upon investigation by Officer Vincent Charles was apprehended trying to break into the building. Upon questioning of Officer, Charles stated a man named Frank offered him $50.00 USC to break in and steal a TV. A search by arresting officer for person named Frank was to no avail.

I spoke with Charles' probation officer, Willard Moore, who said that Charles had been in continuous difficulty before and after his adjudication of delinquency. Moore further indicated that, in his experience, Charles was simply suggestible, and that he had said on several occasions that he would do anything for a friend. It appears, according to the probation officer, that Charles feels socially handicapped by his scar, and has been subject to vicious teasing in school and on the street. It is to this teasing, in part, that Mr. Moore attributes Charles' poor school attendance record and his willingness to do whatever he is asked by someone appearing as a "friend." We made an appointment to discuss the case further and agreed that a request would be made for a psychological examination of Charles, since none had ever been prepared.

We appeared before Judge Johnson of the Juvenile Court, and I indicated that because there had not been sufficient time to consult with Charles no plea would be entered at this time. I also asked the Court to order a psychological examination for the respondent, on the basis of what the boy told me about ringing in his ears, and what his mother and probation officer say about Charles' extreme suggestibility and his feeling that if anybody was friendly to him, he would do whatever he was told. Judge Johnson agreed to order a psychological examination, and continued the case for six weeks (since that is the time required for completion of an examination by court services when the respondent is not held in custody).

9/1/18

I received a copy of the psychological evaluation prepared by clinical services. It reads:

PSYCHOLOGICAL REPORT

Identifying Information: This is a 13-year-old boy, who was arrested on a charge of burglary in August 2018. The Social Investigation indicates that he has twelve other station adjustments since January of 2016. School report from Spring of 2018 indicated that his scholarship, neatness and deportment are poor and that he attends school only about one day out of every two weeks. His attitude at school is described as belligerent and ill mannered. Charles lives with his mother and five siblings. The father died in 2011. Records attached to the Social Investigation indicate that this family has deteriorated steadily since the father's death in 2011. Mother is said to have had an alcoholic problem. Several children have had emotional problems manifesting in school truancy and behavior disorders.

Interview with the Mother: Mother is at a loss to explain the delinquent behavior of Charles. She says that he goes with the wrong bunch of boys and probably follows their lead. He is no trouble at home and she indicates that he is helpful in doing household chores. He seems to know right from wrong but does not realize the seriousness of what he does. She feels that an important part of his emotional problem is related to a scalp burn in infancy which required a skin graft at about age 7. Charles has a bald spot and is very self-conscious of this. Mother feels that the children are cruel and tease him about this baldness and this leads to a temper outburst in Charles. Mother tells how Charles constantly wears a hat and that he puts this hat on as soon as he arises in the morning.

Interview with the Boy: Charles is a small thirteen-year-old boy who appears and behaves much younger than his stated age. Throughout the interview he wears his hat. His speech is very difficult to understand and he has a great deal of difficulty in understanding questions. There is no evidence for a psychotic thought disorder and it's my impression that Charles' intelligence is in the low average range. In explaining his behavior related to burglaries Charles says that he does not know why he does these things except that he wants to be with his friends and therefore does what his friends do. As he describes his stealing activity he seems not to feel guilty about such activity. Initially he says he attends school regularly and does all right and when confronted with the report of the school he rationalizes his poor performance and attendance. When the teacher talks to him his ears hurt and he cannot hear. He explains his misbehavior at school by stating that the teacher calls him a baby for wanting to sleep in class and Charles then becomes angry at the teacher and refuses to listen. He explains much of his truancy on the basis of his sensitivity of his baldness and scarring. He tells how the other children tease him and he gets angry and doesn't want to go to school. Sometimes he fights the other children if he gets very angry. Charles has very little to say about his family except that he gets along well with his mother and siblings. His ambition in the future is to be a fireman or a policeman and if he were a policeman he would do as he is told. He tells how he would like driving a bicycle and play ball for fun.

10/2/18
Interview with Officer Vincent: I interviewed Officer Vincent, the arresting officer, at the police station. He remembered the arrest well, and his recollection is consistent both with the police report and with Charles' story. He received a radio call concerning a reported burglary at 1216 South Halsdale. He immediately drove to that address, which required approximately fifteen minutes. The owner of the house, Mrs. Rose Jarrett, answered the door in a wheelchair, and said that she had heard "noises" like a scratching or banging on the window of the basement, toward the back of the house. She was not able to investigate herself, since there are stairs which she cannot negotiate with her wheelchair between the front and back sections of the house. Officer Vincent then went to the side alley to check, and found Charles North leaning against the wall across from a basement window which was partially opened. When asked why he was not in school, Charles initially had no answer, nor did he explain what he was doing in the alley or how long he had been there. Officer Vincent thereupon took Charles to the police station and further interrogated the boy there. Charles then admitted trying to break into the building and stated "Frank" offered him $50 to break in and steal the television. Officer Vincent then told Charles he could call his mother; this was, he said, the only "advice" of rights offered, since Officer Vincent did not really expect the case to come to court. When asked why he felt that way, Officer

Vincent explained that Mrs. Jarrett is housebound, and has already indicated that she cannot physically make a trip to the courthouse.

10/7/18

Interview with Mrs. North: After having read the psychological evaluation, I spoke with Mrs. North about some parts of it. She confirmed much of what might have been speculation on the psychologist's part with regard to the other children in the family. I noticed today, as I had on our first meeting, a strong odor of alcohol on her breath, and did not think it necessary to pursue the report concerning her drinking. In view of the emotional problems revealed by the evaluation, and the observation that Charles has not internalized societal norms, I raised the question of seeking institutional or non-institutional psychiatric assistance. She was unalterably opposed to the former, wanting very much for Charles to remain at home. She did not oppose out-patient treatment with any rigor, but also did not display any interest in the idea. Indeed, she did not seem to think that Charles needed any special help in this regard. She repeated several times, with great emphasis, that she did not want Charles "sent away" to any institution.

10/7/18

Interview with Charles North: After having spoken with his mother, I spent some time talking with Charles. We discussed, at considerable length, the problems Charles has had with school and with his classmates and neighbors; his previous conduct; his relations with his mother and the rest of the family. After careful exploration, I raised with him the question of psychiatric assistance. His reaction was very much the same as his mother's. He knows that his mother is not well and feels that he must protect her. Accordingly, he does not like the idea of commitment to a mental institution, even though he fairly clearly would prefer that to commitment to the state training school. He is somewhat less adamant than his mother, but still would like a result which did not separate him from his home for any period of time. I discussed the legal aspects of the case with Charles and made an appointment to see him again two days before our scheduled court hearing.

I should add that these interviews took place at the North apartment. They live with a sister, who has two children of her own; Mrs. North has three: Charles, Alfred (age 11) and Cynthia (age 15). The apartment has four rooms: 2 bedrooms, living room, kitchen. The apartment was littered and dirty when I visited; the children all sleep together in the living room, and vodka bottles were opened and apparently in use. Mrs. North claims to dislike the living arrangements and says she will move as soon as possible. The children have not been going to school for the last semester, while she is looking for a new apartment, because arranging for transfers between school districts is very difficult.

10/8/18

Interview with Willard Moore, Probation Officer: Mr. Moore and I met, as we had previously arranged. Our discussion covered the entire North family. He said, and I accepted from my own visit, that Mrs. North was drunk a great deal of the time and not capable of taking care of the family. There was, however, no other family member better situated. His own feeling was that Charles was not responding to probation, and that he had no reason to believe that he would become more responsive in the future. He had considered out-patient treatment for Charles, but the several appointments he made were never kept. When he had discussed this with Charles and his mother, they apologized for forgetting, but did not urge that new appointments be made.

We further discussed facilities available to Charles. Mr. Moore was of the view that Charles would not be accepted by the state school for the developmentally disabled, since he had learned from several experiences that that school does not ordinarily take children who are only marginally disabled. He raised the notion of commitment to a state mental hospital but was not sure whether Charles would be accepted there on the basis of the psychological evaluation. Mr. Moore did strongly feel that nothing was realistically to be expected from further supervision by the probation staff and was pessimistic about the chances of cooperation with community family counseling services.

---

1. Consider this case file in light of Professor Birckhead's article on the challenges faced by lawyers who represent juveniles in delinquency court. In what ways is it consistent with her observations?

2. What pleas might be entered in the case? What principles or other considerations influence the choice of plea?

The IJA-ABA Standards Relating to the Role of Counsel for Private Parties, at 79-80, takes the following position:

3.1(b) Determination of Client's Interests.
(i) Generally.

In general, determination of the client's interests in the proceedings, and hence the plea to be entered, is ultimately the responsibility of the client after full consultation with the attorney.

(ii) Counsel for the juvenile.

[a] Counsel for the respondent in a delinquency or in need of supervision proceeding should ordinarily be bound by the client's definition of his or her interests with respect to the admission or denial of the facts or conditions alleged. It is appropriate and desirable for counsel to advise the client concerning the probable success and consequences of adopting any posture with respect to those proceedings.

Rule 1.14 of the ABA Model Rules of Professional Conduct deals with clients "under a disability." Rule 1.14(a) provides that,

When a client's ability to make adequately considered decisions in connection with the representation is impaired, whether because of minority, mental disability or for some other reason, the lawyer shall, as far as reasonably possible, maintain a normal client-lawyer relationship with the client.

3. The attorney learned a great deal from the conversations with the client and the client's mother. Some of that information is relevant to both adjudicative and treatment issues. To what extent can counsel disclose that information to, for example, the probation officer or the judge if he or she believes disclosure will facilitate an accurate finding of fact or a beneficial treatment program for the client? Should counsel be able to disclose information from the client to the parent if he or she believes that doing so will assist the parent in understanding or dealing with the child?

The IJA-ABA Standards assert that an attorney should not reveal confidential information concerning a client to anyone else, including the parent. Standard 3.3(b)(i). Do you agree?

What about the information from Ms. North? Suppose that there is competent evidence establishing counsel's client's responsibility. The lawyer considers encouraging the probation officer to file a neglect petition against the mother in the hope that the court will decide that the respondent is better treated as a neglected rather than a delinquent child and therefore will not commit the child to the industrial school. Can the lawyer disclose information to the probation officer or the court about Ms. North's failings as a parent that was either told to or observed by him or her? *See* IJA-ABA Standards, above, Standard 3.3(c). If some or all such information is disclosable, how should counsel approach a parent or guardian in the course of investigation?

4. What recommendations would you expect the probation officer to make to the court? What recommendations, if any, would you consider making to the court?

5. What further action might you consider undertaking?

6. Suppose that Ms. North were not indigent and had hired you to represent her son in the pending delinquency proceeding. Unlike the Problem situation, she believes that Charles needs direction of a kind she cannot supply: an understandable belief in view of Charles's record. Charles, however, wants to be at liberty. Can you take Ms. North's desires into account in deciding how to represent Charles? What should you tell Ms. North when she approaches you to represent her son? *See* IJA-ABA Standard 3.2(a)(iii), defining adversity of interest to exist where lawyers "[f]ormally represent one client but are required by some third person or institution, including their employer, to accommodate their representation of that client to factors unrelated to the client's legitimate interests." *See also* ABA Model Rule of Professional Conduct 1.8(f), providing that,

> A lawyer shall not accept compensation for representing a client from one other than the client unless: (1) the client consents after consultation; (2) there is no interference with the lawyer's independent professional judgment . . .; and (3) information relating to representation of a client is protected [as required by confidentiality rules].

On conflicts between children and their parents, *see* Kristin Henning, It Takes a Lawyer to Raise a Child?: Allocating Responsibilities Among Parents,

Children, and Lawyers in Delinquency Cases, 6 Nev. L.J. 836 (2006); Norman Lefstein, W. Vaughan Stapleton & Lee E. Teitelbaum, In Search of Juvenile Justice: *Gault* and Its Implementation, 3 Law & Soc'y Rev. 491, 548-549 (1969); Wallace J. Mlyniec, Who Decides: Decision Making in Juvenile Delinquency Proceedings, *in* Ethical Problems Facing the Criminal Defense Lawyer, 115 (1995).

CHILD ABUSE AND NEGLECT

Defining and Discovering Child Abuse and Neglect

7

This is the first of three chapters concerning legal responses to child abuse and neglect. This chapter deals with issues that arise regardless of whether a case is handled in juvenile court, criminal court, or both. The first section of this chapter returns to a topic that we explored in the first chapter and that is at the core of this unit—the constitutional right of parents to raise their children and the limits on that right. The second section examines the major legal categories of abuse and neglect—physical abuse, physical and emotional neglect, and sexual abuse—and difficult definitional issues that arise within each category. The third section covers child abuse reporting laws and investigation of allegations of abuse or neglect. Chapter 8 takes us into the child welfare system, whose fundamental purpose is to protect the child from harm, to help parents correct the situation if possible, and, if not, to provide an alternate permanent home for the child. Chapter 9 considers issues that arise in the criminal prosecution of child abuse and neglect, particularly where the defendants are a child's parents or other caregivers.

A. PARENTAL RIGHTS AND THE CHILD MISTREATMENT LIMIT

TROXEL V. GRANVILLE

530 U. S. 57 (2000)

Justice O'CONNOR announced the judgment of the Court and delivered an opinion, in which THE CHIEF JUSTICE, Justice GINSBURG, and Justice BREYER join. . . . Tommie Granville and Brad Troxel shared a relationship that ended in June 1991. The two never married, but they had two daughters, Isabelle and Natalie. Jenifer and Gary Troxel are Brad's parents, and thus the paternal grandparents of Isabelle and Natalie. After Tommie and Brad separated in 1991, Brad lived with his parents and regularly brought his daughters to his parents' home for weekend visitation. Brad committed suicide in May 1993. Although the Troxels at first continued to see Isabelle and Natalie on a regular basis after their son's death,

Tommie Granville informed the Troxels in October 1993 that she wished to limit their visitation with her daughters to one short visit per month.

In December 1993, the Troxels . . . [petitioned for visitation under Washington law.] Section 26.10.160(3) [of the Wash. Rev. Code] provides: "Any person may petition the court for visitation rights at any time including, but not limited to, custody proceedings. The court may order visitation rights for any person when visitation may serve the best interest of the child whether or not there has been any change of circumstances.". . . In 1995, the Superior Court issued an oral ruling and entered a visitation decree ordering visitation one weekend per month, one week during the summer, and four hours on both of the petitioning grandparents' birthdays.

Granville appealed, during which time she married Kelly Wynn. Before addressing the merits of Granville's appeal, the Washington Court of Appeals remanded the case to the Superior Court for entry of written findings of fact and conclusions of law. On remand, the Superior Court found that visitation was in Isabelle and Natalie's best interests. . . .

The Washington Supreme Court granted the Troxels' petition for review and, after consolidating their case with two other visitation cases, affirmed. . . .

The demographic changes of the past century make it difficult to speak of an average American family. The composition of families varies greatly from household to household. While many children may have two married parents and grandparents who visit regularly, many other children are raised in single-parent households. In 1996, children living with only one parent accounted for 28 percent of all children under age 18 in the United States. . . . Understandably, in these single-parent households, persons outside the nuclear family are called upon with increasing frequency to assist in the everyday tasks of child rearing. In many cases, grandparents play an important role. For example, in 1998, approximately 4 million children—or 5.6 percent of all children under age 18—lived in the household of their grandparents.

The nationwide enactment of nonparental visitation statutes is assuredly due, in some part, to the States' recognition of these changing realities of the American family. Because grandparents and other relatives undertake duties of a parental nature in many households, States have sought to ensure the welfare of the children therein by protecting the relationships those children form with such third parties. The States' nonparental visitation statutes are further supported by a recognition, which varies from State to State, that children should have the opportunity to benefit from relationships with statutorily specified persons—for example, their grandparents. The extension of statutory rights in this area to persons other than a child's parents, however, comes with an obvious cost. For example, the State's recognition of an independent third-party interest in a child can place a substantial burden on the traditional parent–child relationship. Contrary to Justice STEVENS' accusation, our description of state nonparental visitation statutes in these terms, of course, is not meant to suggest that "children are so much chattel." Rather, our terminology is intended to highlight the fact that these statutes can present questions of constitutional import. . . .

The liberty interest at issue in this case—the interest of parents in the care, custody, and control of their children—is perhaps the oldest of the fundamental liberty interests recognized by this Court. More than 75 years ago, in Meyer v. Nebraska, we held that the "liberty" protected by the Due Process Clause includes the right of parents to "establish a home and bring up children" and "to control the education of their own." Two years later, in Pierce v. Society of Sisters, we again held that the "liberty of parents and guardians" includes the right "to direct the upbringing and education of children under their control." We explained in Pierce that "[t]he child is not the mere creature of the State; those who nurture him and direct his destiny have the right, coupled with the high duty, to recognize and prepare him for additional obligations." We returned to the subject in Prince v. Massachusetts, and again confirmed that there is a constitutional dimension to the right of parents to direct the upbringing of their children. "It is cardinal with us that the custody, care and nurture of the child reside first in the parents, whose primary function and freedom include preparation for obligations the state can neither supply nor hinder."

Section 26.10.160(3), as applied to Granville and her family in this case, unconstitutionally infringes on that fundamental parental right. The Washington nonparental visitation statute is breathtakingly broad. According to the statute's text, "[a]ny person may petition the court for visitation rights *at any time*," and the court may grant such visitation rights whenever "visitation may serve *the best interest of the child.*" § 26.10.160(3) (emphases added). That language effectively permits any third party seeking visitation to subject any decision by a parent concerning visitation of the parent's children to state-court review. Once the visitation petition has been filed in court and the matter is placed before a judge, a parent's decision that visitation would not be in the child's best interest is accorded no deference. Section 26.10.160(3) contains no requirement that a court accord the parent's decision any presumption of validity or any weight whatsoever. Instead, the Washington statute places the best-interest determination solely in the hands of the judge. Should the judge disagree with the parent's estimation of the child's best interests, the judge's view necessarily prevails. Thus, in practical effect, in the State of Washington a court can disregard and overturn any decision by a fit custodial parent concerning visitation whenever a third party affected by the decision files a visitation petition, based solely on the judge's determination of the child's best interests. The Washington Supreme Court had the opportunity to give § 26.10.160(3) a narrower reading, but it declined to do so. . . .

Turning to the facts of this case, the record reveals that the Superior Court's order was based on precisely the type of mere disagreement we have just described and nothing more. The Superior Court's order was not founded on any special factors that might justify the State's interference with Granville's fundamental right to make decisions concerning the rearing of her two daughters. To be sure, this case involves a visitation petition filed by grandparents soon after the death of their son — the father of Isabelle and Natalie — but the combination of several factors here compels our conclusion that § 26.10.160(3), as applied, exceeded the bounds of the Due Process Clause.

First, the Troxels did not allege, and no court has found, that Granville was an unfit parent. That aspect of the case is important, for there is a presumption that fit parents act in the best interests of their children. . . .

Accordingly, so long as a parent adequately cares for his or her children (i.e., is fit), there will normally be no reason for the State to inject itself into the private realm of the family to further question the ability of that parent to make the best decisions concerning the rearing of that parent's children.

The problem here is not that the Washington Superior Court intervened, but that when it did so, it gave no special weight at all to Granville's determination of her daughters' best interests. More importantly, it appears that the Superior Court applied exactly the opposite presumption. In reciting its oral ruling after the conclusion of closing arguments, the Superior Court judge explained:

> The burden is to show that it is in the best interest of the children to have some visitation and some quality time with their grandparents. I think in most situations a commonsensical approach [is that] it is normally in the best interest of the children to spend quality time with the grandparent, unless the grandparent, [sic] there are some issues or problems involved wherein the grandparents, their lifestyles are going to impact adversely upon the children. That certainly isn't the case here from what I can tell.

The judge's comments suggest that he presumed the grandparents' request should be granted unless the children would be "impact[ed] adversely." In effect, the judge placed on Granville, the fit custodial parent, the burden of disproving that visitation would be in the best interest of her daughters. The judge reiterated moments later: "I think [visitation with the Troxels] would be in the best interest of the children and I haven't been shown it is not in [the] best interest of the children."

The decisional framework employed by the Superior Court directly contravened the traditional presumption that a fit parent will act in the best interest of his or her child. In that respect, the court's presumption failed to provide any protection for Granville's fundamental constitutional right to make decisions concerning the rearing of her own daughters. . . . In an ideal world, parents might always seek to cultivate the bonds between grandparents and their grandchildren. Needless to say, however, our world is far from perfect, and in it the decision whether such an intergenerational relationship would be beneficial in any specific case is for the parent to make in the first instance. And, if a fit parent's decision of the kind at issue here becomes subject to judicial review, the court must accord at least some special weight to the parent's own determination.

Finally, we note that there is no allegation that Granville ever sought to cut off visitation entirely. Rather, the present dispute originated when Granville informed the Troxels that she would prefer to restrict their visitation with Isabelle and Natalie to one short visit per month and special holidays. In the Superior Court proceedings Granville did not oppose visitation but instead asked that the duration of any visitation order be shorter than that requested by the Troxels. . . .

Considered together with the Superior Court's reasons for awarding visitation to the Troxels, the combination of these factors demonstrates that the visitation order in this case was an unconstitutional infringement on Granville's fundamental right to make decisions concerning the care, custody, and control of her two daughters. The Washington Superior Court failed to accord the determination of Granville, a fit custodial parent, any material weight. . . . As we have explained, the Due Process Clause does not permit a State to infringe on the fundamental right of parents to make childrearing decisions simply because a state judge believes a "better" decision could be made. Neither the Washington nonparental visitation statute generally—which places no limits on either the persons who may petition for visitation or the circumstances in which such a petition may be granted—nor the Superior Court in this specific case required anything more. Accordingly, we hold that § 26.10.160(3), as applied in this case, is unconstitutional. . . .

NOTES AND QUESTIONS

1. *Troxel* is more relevant to this and the next two chapters than are *Meyer*, *Pierce*, and *Yoder*, since it deals directly with parents' custodial rights. What level of scrutiny does the plurality opinion use to analyze the constitutionality of limits on these rights?

2. Is the problem with the Washington statute that it permitted courts to override parents' decisions based on the "best interests of the child"? That it did not impose the burden of proof on those who challenge the parents' decisions? That it gave judges too much discretion to override parental decisions?

3. *Troxel* emphasizes that Tommie Granville was a "fit" parent; what does the case tell us about the rights of "unfit" parents?

3. Prince v. Massachusetts, 321 U.S. 158 (1944), set out at page 46, which observes that "the state has a wide range of power for limiting parental freedom and authority in things affecting the child's welfare," is often cited as recognizing the constitutionality of state child abuse and neglect laws. What limits on this authority does *Troxel* suggest?

4. The Supreme Court has also held in two cases regarding termination of parental rights that right to maintain the very existence of the parent-child relationship is constitutionally protected. Lassiter v. Department of Social Services, 452 U.S. 18 (1981); Santosky v. Kramer, 455 U.S. 745 (1982). We will examine these cases in Chapter 8.

B.   THE MEANINGS OF CHILD ABUSE AND NEGLECT

"Social meanings of events flow from analyses of the intentions of actors, the consequences of acts, the value judgments of observers, and the source of the standard for that judgment. These four elements—intentionality, effect, evaluation, and standards—present the fundamental issues in defining abuse. . . . 'Abuse' is a socially mediated conclusion drawn about family life, and it must be based on a mixture of community standards and professional knowledge." James Garbarino, The Incidence and Prevalence of Child Maltreatment, in Family Violence 219, 222 (Lloyd Ohlin & Michael Tonry, eds., 1989).

The definition of child abuse or neglect may vary, depending on the context. For example, people discussing the child-rearing practices of someone in the neighborhood may have a very different understanding of "abuse" than does an emergency medical technician deciding whether a child needs medical treatment. And both these definitions may be different from a legal definition of child abuse or neglect. Indeed, the legal definition may vary from one situation to another.

The law in one state may define child abuse and neglect differently for purposes of determining (1) when harm or risk of harm to a child must be reported to the authorities, (2) whether a juvenile court may intervene into a family to protect a child, or (3) whether a parent who has harmed a child should be criminally punished.

This chapter examines legal definitions of child abuse and neglect and includes criminal cases, juvenile court cases, and child abuse reporting act cases. These differences in context are not central to this chapter, since the issues that we will look at could arise in any of these kinds of proceedings. As a general matter, though, it seems likely that reporting act definitions of child abuse and neglect would be the broadest, since their purpose is to bring situations that may endanger children to the attention of authorities for the purposes of further investigation. Juvenile court definitions should identify circumstances in which services should be offered to protect the child or, if necessary, to remove the child to safety. And, of course, criminal definitions should be crafted to identify those who should be punished.

Before considering particular categories of child abuse and neglect, we will look at two overarching issues that Garbarino identifies: whether a child must already have been harmed to be regarded as abused or neglected and how to define the community whose standards are used to define adequate parenting.

1.   *Harm and Risk of Harm*

ANDREA J. SEDLAK ET AL., *EXECUTIVE SUMMARY OF THE FOURTH NATIONAL INCIDENCE STUDY OF CHILD ABUSE AND NEGLECT (NIS-4)*

1-5 (2010)

The NIS serves as the nation's needs assessment on child abuse and neglect. It offers a unique perspective on the scope of the problem beyond the children that child protective service (CPS) agencies investigate. While the NIS includes children who were investigated by CPS agencies, it also obtains data on other children who were not reported to CPS or who were screened out by CPS without investigation. These additional children were recognized as maltreated by community professionals. Thus, the NIS estimates include both abused and neglected children who are in the official CPS statistics and those who are not.

The NIS follows a nationally representative design, so the estimates reflect the numbers of abused and neglected children in the United States who come to the attention of community professionals. The fact that there have been three previous cycles using comparable methods and definitions means that one can compare NIS-4 estimates with those from the earlier studies in order to identify changes over time in the incidence and distribution of abused and neglected children. . . .

Like the earlier NIS cycles, the NIS-4 employed sentinel survey methodology. In this approach, community professionals who work in certain categories of agencies and who typically encounter children and families in the course of their job duties serve as lookouts for victims of child abuse and neglect. In each county, these professionals, called "sentinels," represent all staff that have contact with children and families in police and sheriffs' departments, public schools, day care centers, hospitals, voluntary social service agencies, mental health agencies, the county juvenile probation and public health departments, public housing, and shelters for runaway and homeless youth and for victims of domestic violence. . . .

The NIS uses standard definitions of abuse and neglect, so its estimates of the numbers of maltreated children and incidence rates have a calibrated, standard meaning across the various sites (multiple states and agencies), sources (CPS and community professionals), and NIS cycles. As in previous cycles, children submitted by sentinels and those described in the CPS sampled cases were evaluated according to standard study definitions of abuse and neglect, and only children who fit the standards were used in generating the national estimates. . . .

The NIS applies two definitional standards in parallel: the Harm Standard and the Endangerment Standard. The Harm Standard has been in use since the NIS-1. It is relatively stringent in that it generally requires that an act or omission result in demonstrable harm in order to be classified as abuse or neglect. It permits exceptions in only a few specific maltreatment categories, where the nature of the maltreatment itself is so egregious that one can infer that the child was harmed. The chief advantage of the Harm Standard is its strong objectivity. Its principal disadvantage is that it is so stringent that it provides a perspective that is too narrow for many purposes, excluding even many children whom CPS substantiates or indicates as abused or neglected.

The Endangerment Standard has been in use since the NIS-2. It includes all children who meet the Harm Standard but adds others as well. The central feature of the Endangerment Standard is that it counts children who were not yet harmed by abuse or neglect if a sentinel thought that the maltreatment endangered the children or if a CPS investigation substantiated or indicated their maltreatment. In addition, the Endangerment Standard is slightly more lenient than the Harm Standard in allowing a broader array of perpetrators, including adult caretakers other than parents in certain maltreatment categories and teenage caretakers as perpetrators of sexual abuse. . . .

The findings of the Fourth National Incidence Study of Child Abuse and Neglect (NIS-4) show an overall decrease in the incidence of maltreatment since the NIS-3, as well as decreases in some specific maltreatment categories and increases in others.

Incidence of Harm Standard maltreatment. Using the stringent Harm Standard definition, more than 1.25 million children (an estimated 1,256,600 children) experienced maltreatment during the NIS-4 study year (2005-2006). This corresponds to one child in every 58 in the United States. A large percentage (44%, or an estimated total of 553,300) were abused, while most (61%, or an estimated total of 771,700) were neglected. The NIS classifies children in every category that applies, so the components (here and throughout the NIS findings) sum to more than 100%. Most of the abused children experienced physical abuse (58% of the abused children, an estimated total of 323,000). Slightly less than one-fourth were sexually abused (24%, an estimated 135,300), while slightly more than one-fourth were emotionally abused (27%, an estimated 148,500). Almost one-half of the neglected children experienced educational neglect (47% of neglected children, an estimated 360,500 children), more than one-third were physically neglected (38%, an estimated 295,300 children), and one-fourth were emotionally neglected (25%, an estimated 193,400 children).

Unlike the dramatic increase in the incidence of Harm Standard maltreatment that occurred between the NIS-2 and NIS-3, where the rate increased by 56%, the NIS-4 reveals a smaller change since the NIS-3, in the opposite direction. The NIS-4 estimate of the incidence of overall Harm Standard maltreatment in the 2005-2006 study year reflects a 19% decrease in the total number of maltreated children since the NIS-3 in 1993. Taking into account the increase in the number of children in the United States over the interval, this change is equivalent to a 26% decline in the rate of overall Harm Standard maltreatment per 1,000 children in the population. This decrease is close-to significant, meaning the probability that it is due to chance factors is less than 10%. This decrease returned the incidence of Harm Standard maltreatment to a level that does not differ from the NIS-2 estimate for 1986.

The number of children who experienced Harm Standard abuse declined significantly, by 26%, from an estimated 743,200 in the NIS-3 to 553,300 in the NIS-4. This reflects a 32% decrease in the rate of Harm Standard abuse per 1,000 children in the nation. Moreover, the incidence of all specific categories of abuse decreased: The incidence of sexual abuse decreased significantly, while the declines in physical abuse and emotional abuse were both close-to-significant:

- The estimated number of sexually abused children under the Harm Standard decreased from 217,700 in 1993 to 135,300 in 2005-2006 (a 38% decrease in the number of sexually abused children and a 44% decrease in the rate of sexual abuse);
- The number of children who experienced Harm Standard physical abuse decreased from an estimated 381,700 at the time of the NIS-3 to an estimated 323,000 in the NIS-4 (a 15% decrease in number and a 23% decline in the rate);
- The estimated number of emotionally abused children under the Harm Standard was 204,500 at the time of the NIS-3, which decreased to 148,500 during the NIS-4 (a 27% decrease in number; a 33% decline in the rate).

The incidence of Harm Standard neglect showed no statistically reliable changes since the NIS-3, neither overall nor in any of the specific neglect categories (physical, emotional, and educational neglect).

Classifying these abused and neglected children according to the level of injury or harm they suffered from Harm Standard maltreatment revealed only one change: a significant decrease in the incidence of children for whom injury could be inferred due to the severe nature of their maltreatment. This group declined from 165,300 children in the NIS-3 to 71,500 in the NIS-4 (a 57% decrease in number; a 60% decline in the rate in the population).

Incidence of Endangerment Standard maltreatment. Defining maltreatment according to the more inclusive Endangerment Standard provides a very different picture of the incidence and distribution of child abuse and neglect. Nearly

3 million children (an estimated 2,905,800) experienced Endangerment Standard maltreatment during the NIS-4 2005-2006 study year. This corresponds to one child in every 25 in the United States. While 29% (an estimated 835,000 children) were abused, more than three-fourths (77%, an estimated 2,251,600 children) were neglected. Most abused children (57%, or 476,600 children) were physically abused, more than one-third (36%, or 302,600 children) were emotionally abused, and less than one-fourth (22%, or 180,500 children) were sexually abused. Under the Endangerment Standard definitions, more than one-half of the neglected children were physically neglected (53%, or 1,192,200 children) and a similar percentage were emotionally neglected (52%, or 1,173,800), whereas 16% (an estimated 360,500) were educationally neglected.

Between 1993 and 2005-2006, the overall incidence of children who experienced Endangerment Standard maltreatment showed no statistically reliable change. However, within Endangerment Standard maltreatment, counterbalancing changes occurred in the incidence of abuse and neglect. Significant decreases in the incidence of abuse and all specific categories of abuse contrast with a significant increase in the incidence of emotional neglect:

- The estimated number of children who experienced Endangerment Standard abuse decreased from 1,221,800 to 835,000 (a 32% decrease in number, a 38% decline in the rate);
- The estimated number of physically abused children decreased from an estimated 614,100 children to 476,600 (a 22% decrease in number, a 29% decline in the rate);
- The incidence of children with Endangerment Standard sexual abuse decreased from 300,200 in 1993 to 180,500 in 2005-2006 (reflecting a 40% decrease in number and a 47% decline in the rate);
- The incidence of emotionally abused children decreased from 532,200 to 302,600 (a 43% decrease in number, a 48% decline in the rate); and
- The estimated number of emotionally neglected children more than doubled in the interval between the studies, rising from 584,100 in 1993 to 1,173,800 in 2005-2006 (a 101% increase in number, an 83% increase in the rate).

Classifying these children according to the severity of harm they suffered as a result of their Endangerment Standard maltreatment revealed no significant changes in the incidence of children with any specific level of injury or harm. . . .

Race/ethnicity. Unlike previous NIS cycles, the NIS-4 found strong and pervasive race differences in the incidence of maltreatment. In nearly all cases, the rates of maltreatment for Black children were significantly higher than those for White and Hispanic children. These differences occurred under both definitional standards in rates of overall maltreatment, overall abuse, overall neglect, and physical abuse and for children with serious or moderate harm from their maltreatment. They also occurred in the incidence of Harm Standard sexual abuse, in the incidence of children who were inferred to be harmed by Harm Standard maltreatment, and in Endangerment Standard rates for physical neglect, emotional maltreatment, and children who were endangered but not demonstrably harmed by their maltreatment.

In part, the emergence of race/ethnicity differences in the NIS-4 may stem from the greater precision of the NIS-4 estimates. Statistical tests are able to detect more of the underlying differences when estimates are more precise. However, the recently identified race/ethnicity differences are also consistent with changes in maltreatment rates since the NIS-3. While general declines in rates of maltreatment were noted since the NIS-3, these declines did not occur equally for all races and ethnicities. Rather, under both definitional standards, rates of maltreatment for White children declined more than the rates for Black and Hispanic children in the incidence of abuse, physical abuse, and children seriously harmed by maltreatment. For Harm Standard emotional neglect, maltreatment rates for White children declined while rates for Black and Hispanic children increased. For Endangerment Standard emotional neglect, rates for White children increased less than the rates for Black and Hispanic children. . . .

U.S. DEPT. OF HEALTH AND HUMAN SERVICES, ADMINISTRATION ON CHILDREN, YOUTH, AND FAMILIES, *CHILD MALTREATMENT 2016*

ii, 20 (2018)
https://www.acf.hhs.gov/cb/research-data-technology/statistics-research/
child-maltreatment

The national estimate of children who received a child protective services investigation response or alternative response increased 9.5 percent from 2012 (3,172,000) to 2016 (3,472,000).

The number and rate of victims have fluctuated during the past 5 years. Comparing the national rounded number of victims from 2012 (656,000) to the national estimate of victims in 2016 (676,000) shows an increase of 3.0 percent.

. . .

Three-quarters (74.8%) of victims were neglected, 18.2 percent were physically abused, and 8.5 percent were sexually abused. In addition, 6.9 percent of victims experienced such "other" types of maltreatment as threatened abuse or neglect, drug/alcohol addiction, and lack of supervision. . . .

Polyvictimization in child welfare refers to children who experienced multiple types of maltreatment. In FFY 2016, 86.0 percent of victims suffered a single type of maltreatment, although they could suffer that single type multiple times. The remaining victims (14.0%) experienced a combination of maltreatments. A child is considered to have suffered a combination of maltreatments if:

The child had two different types of maltreatment in a single report.
The child suffered different maltreatment types in several reports (e.g., neglect in one report and physical abuse in a second report).

The most common combination was neglect and physical abuse (5.2%). The other common combinations included neglect and "other"/unknown at 3.5 percent, neglect and psychological maltreatment at 1.9 percent, and neglect and sexual abuse at 1.4 percent.

PROBLEM

Jason and Kristen lived in a second-floor apartment with their son, A.J., who was two years and nine months old. One day Jason left for work at about 5:30 A.M. Kristen soon awoke with a migraine headache. When she got up to take pain medication, A.J. woke up. Before Kristen went back to bed, she tied A.J.'s bedroom door almost shut with a cord, leaving a gap of about two inches so that he could call for her. She did this because A.J. liked to climb out of his bed and wander around, and she was afraid that he would leave his room and possibly go outside. Kristen fell sound asleep.

Around 10 A.M. a neighbor saw A.J. leaning out of his second-story window and tried unsuccessfully to persuade him to move away from it. She called the apartment manager for help. The manager went to Kristin's apartment and rapped loudly on the door, but got no answer. He used his key to open the door, saw the cord tied to A.J.'s door, and untied it. He rushed into the bedroom and pulled A.J. away from the window. As he was doing this, Kristin awoke and walked groggily into the room.

The apartment manager called child protective services, and the worker investigating the case learned that the bedroom window was shut and locked when Jason left for work. Kristin and Jason did not know that A.J. could open the window by himself.

Are the facts sufficient to show that Kristin neglected A.J.? Was A.J. harmed? At risk of serious harm? Does it matter whether Kristin knew of the risk?

2.   *The Cultural Meanings of Child-Rearing Practices*

STATE v. KARGAR

---

679 A.2d 81 (Me. 1996)

DANA, J. MOHAMMAD KARGAR, an Afghani refugee, appeals from the judgments entered in the Superior Court (Cumberland County, Crowley, J.) convicting him of two counts of gross sexual assault ...

On June 25, 1993, Kargar and his family, refugees since approximately 1990, were babysitting a young neighbor. While the neighbor was there, she witnessed Kargar kissing his eighteen-month-old son's penis. When she was picked up by her mother, the girl told her mother what she had seen. The mother had previously seen a picture of Kargar kissing his son's penis in the Kargar family photo album. After her daughter told her what she had seen, the mother notified the police.

Peter Wentworth, a sergeant with the Portland Police Department, went to Kargar's apartment to execute a search warrant. Wentworth was accompanied by two detectives, two Department of Human Services social workers, and an interpreter. Kargar's family was taken outside by the social workers and the two detectives began searching for a picture or pictures of oral/genital contact. The picture of Kargar kissing his son's penis was found in the photograph album. Kargar admitted that it was him in the photograph and that he was kissing his son's penis. Kargar told Wentworth that kissing a young son's penis is accepted as common practice in his culture. Kargar also said it was very possible that his neighbor had seen him kissing his son's penis. Kargar was arrested and taken to the police station.

Prior to the jury-waived trial Kargar moved for a dismissal of the case pursuant to the de minimis statute. With the consent of the parties, the court held the trial phase of the proceedings first, followed by a hearing on the de minimis motion. The de minimis hearing consisted of testimony from many Afghani people who were familiar with the Afghani practice and custom of kissing a young son on all parts of his body. Kargar's witnesses, all relatively recent emigrants from Afghanistan, testified that kissing a son's penis is common in Afghanistan, that it is done to show love for the child, and that it is the same whether the penis is kissed or entirely put into the mouth because there are no sexual feelings involved. The witnesses also testified that pursuant to Islamic law any sexual activity between an adult and a child results in the death penalty for the adult. Kargar also submitted statements from Professor Ludwig Adamec of the University of Arizona's Center for Near Eastern Studies and Saifur Halimi, a religious teacher and Director of the Afghan Mujahideen Information Bureau in New York. Both statements support the testimony of the live witnesses. The State did not present any witnesses during the de minimis hearing. Following the presentation of witnesses the court denied Kargar's motion and found him guilty of two counts of gross sexual assault.

Maine's de minimis statute provides, in pertinent part:

1. The court may dismiss a prosecution if, . . . having regard to the nature of the conduct alleged and the nature of the attendant circumstances, it finds the defendant's conduct:

A. Was within a customary license or tolerance, which was not expressly refused by the person whose interest was infringed and which is not inconsistent with the purpose of the law defining the crime; or

B. Did not actually cause or threaten the harm sought to be prevented by the law defining the crime or did so only to an extent too trivial to warrant the condemnation of conviction; or

C. Presents such other extenuations that it cannot reasonably be regarded as envisaged by the Legislature in defining the crime.

The court analyzed Kargar's conduct, as it should have, pursuant to each of the three provisions of section [1]. The language of the statute itself makes it clear that if a defendant's conduct falls within any one of these provisions the court may dismiss the prosecution. We agree with the State that trial courts should be given broad discretion in determining the propriety of a de minimis motion. In the instant case, however, Kargar asserts that the court erred as a matter of law because it found culture, lack of harm, and his innocent state of mind irrelevant to its de minimis analysis. We agree. . . .

In order to determine whether this defendant's conduct was anticipated by the Legislature when it defined the crime of gross sexual assault it is instructive to review the not-so-distant history of that crime. 17-A M.R.S.A. § 253(1)(B) makes criminal any sexual act with a minor (non-spouse) under the age of fourteen. A sexual act is defined as, among other things, "direct physical contact between the genitals of one and the mouth . . . of the other." Prior to 1985 the definition of this type of sexual act included a sexual gratification element. The Legislature removed the sexual gratification element because, "given the physical contacts described, no concern exists for excluding 'innocent' contacts." Thus, the 1985 amendment to section 251(1)(C) illuminates the fact that an "innocent" touching such as occurred in this case has not forever been recognized as inherently criminal by our own law. The Legislature's inability to comprehend "innocent" genital-mouth contact is highlighted by reference to another type of "sexual act," namely, "any act involving direct physical contact between the genitals . . . of one and an instrument or device manipulated by another." The Legislature maintained the requirement that for this type of act to be criminal it must be done for the purpose of either sexual gratification or to cause bodily injury or offensive physical contact. Its stated reason for doing so was that "a legitimate concern exists for excluding 'innocent' contacts, such as for proper medical purposes or other valid reasons."

All of the evidence presented at the de minimis hearing supports the conclusion that there was nothing "sexual" about Kargar's conduct. There is no real dispute that what Kargar did is accepted practice in his culture. The testimony of every witness at the de minimis hearing confirmed that kissing a young son on every part of his body is considered a sign only of love and affection for the child. This is true whether the parent kisses, or as the trial court found, "engulfs" a son's penis. There is nothing sexual about this practice. In fact, the trial justice expressly recognized that if the State were required to prove a purpose of sexual gratification it "wouldn't have been able to have done so."

During its sentencing of Kargar, the court stated: "There is no sexual gratification. There is no victim impact." The court additionally recognized that the conduct for which Kargar was convicted occurred in the open, with his wife present, and noted that the photograph was displayed in the family photo album, available for all to see. The court concluded its sentencing by recognizing that this case is "not at all typical [but instead is] fully the exception. . . . The conduct was unequivocally criminal, but the circumstances of that conduct and the circumstances of this defendant call for leniency." Although the court responded to this call for leniency by imposing an entirely suspended sentence, the two convictions expose Kargar to severe consequences independent of any period of incarceration, including his required registration as a sex offender pursuant to 34-A M.R.S.A. § 11003 (Supp. 1995), and the possibility of deportation pursuant to 8 U.S.C.A. § 1251(a)(2)(A)(i)(I) (West Supp. 1996). These additional consequences emphasize why the factors recognized by the court during the sentencing hearing were also relevant to the de minimis analysis.

Although it may be difficult for us as a society to separate Kargar's conduct from our notions of sexual abuse, that difficulty should not result in a felony conviction in this case. The State concedes that dismissing this case pursuant to the de minimis statute would pose little harm to the community. The State is concerned, however, with the potential harm caused by courts using the factors of this case to allow for even more exceptions to the criminal statutes. It argues that exceptions should be made by the Legislature, which can gather data, debate social costs and benefits, and clearly define what conduct constitutes criminal activity. The flaw in the State's position is that the Legislature has already clearly defined what conduct constitutes gross sexual assault. It has also allowed for the adjustment of the criminal statutes by courts in extraordinary cases where, for instance, the conduct cannot reasonably be regarded as envisaged by the Legislature in defining the crime.

As discussed above, the Legislature removed the sexual gratification element previously contained within the definition of a sexual act because it could not envision any possible innocent contacts, "given the physical contacts described." In virtually every case the assumption that a physical touching of the mouth of an adult with the genitals of a child under the age of fourteen is inherently harmful is correct. This case, however, is the exception that proves the rule. Precisely because the Legislature did not envision the extenuating circumstances present in this case, to avoid an injustice the de minimis analysis set forth in section 12(1)(C) requires that Kargar's convictions be vacated.

NOTES AND QUESTIONS

1. Considering the legislative history of the statute that Kargar was charged with violating, was the court correct to conclude that the charges against him should be dismissed?

The *Kargar* court concludes that the child was not harmed by the father's conduct. If, when the child grows older, he learns about this incident, might he suffer psychological harm? If so, should the court have taken this into consideration?

2. Would a father raised in the United States who found the Afghani custom appealing be able to claim the defense that Kargar did? Why or why not? The court indicates that now that Kargar knows his conduct was not consistent with mainstream American mores, he is no longer free to follow Afghani custom and kiss his son's genitals. Why not?

On similar facts involving a mother from the Dominican Republic, State v. Ramirez, 2005 WL 3678032 (Me. Sup. Ct. 2005), reached the same conclusion as *Kargar*.

3. The leading scholar on cultural differences in child-rearing is Dr. Jill Korbin, an anthropologist at Case Western Reserve University. Her book, Child Abuse and Neglect: Cross-Cultural Perspectives (1981), is considered the seminal text on the subject. She points out that the common American practices of putting small children to sleep in their own beds and bedrooms and allowing them to cry rather than immediately responding to their needs are considered abusive in much of the rest of the world. *Id*. at 4. For a discussion of her work and that of others, *see* Alison Dundes Renteln, Corporal Punishment and the Cultural Defense, 73 Law & Contemp. Probs. 253 (2010).

4. Cultural differences also arise every day in middle America. During the 1980s and 1990s, many parents became very protective of their children, monitoring them closely and tightly structuring their lives, in response to perceived dangers such as stranger child abduction, physical dangers on the streets, and such. A countermovement, "free-range parenting," advocates allowing children more freedom to encourage and reward their independence. David Pimentel, Criminal Child Neglect and the "Free Range Kid": Is Overprotective Parenting the New Standard of Care?, 2012 Utah L. Rev. 947. A leading proponent of free-range parenting, Lenore Skenazy, allowed her 9-year-old child to ride the New York

City subway home alone in a carefully planned adventure and then wrote a column about it. Why I Let My 9-Year-Old Ride the Subway Alone (Apr. 1, 2008, NY Sun). She was promptly dubbed "America's Worst Mom." 2012 Utah L. Rev. at 956-957. Professor Pimentel points out that all parenting decisions protect against some risks but create others, e.g., protecting children from the dangers of the street by keeping them inside creates risks to their health from lack of exercise as well as diminishing their chances to develop independence, responsibility, and self-reliance. Substantial evidence shows that keeping children in highly sanitized environments has caused a great increase in childhood allergies as children's immune systems turn on the children's own bodies. Id. at 958-959. The age at which children can be left at home alone is a question of cultural values with widely varying answers. For example, in Illinois, it is illegal to leave a child younger than 14 unsupervised "for an unreasonable period of time," but in Maryland a 13-year-old is old enough to babysit infants. Id. at 952. See also David Pimentel, Protecting the Free-Range Kid: Recalibrating Parents' Rights and the Best Interest of the Child, 38 Cardozo L. Rev. 1 (2016).

5. Twice state child welfare agencies have raided isolated communities of fundamentalist Mormons and seized hundreds of children, alleging that the children were abused. In the most recent case, Texas officials took more than 450 children in the Fundamentalist Church of Jesus Christ of Latter Day Saints (FLDS) community of Yearning for Zion and placed them into foster care. At the juvenile court hearing after the seizures, the judge ruled that all the removals were proper, based on the following evidence:

> Interviews with investigators revealed a pattern of girls reporting that "there was no age too young for girls to be married";
> Twenty females living at the ranch had become pregnant between the ages of thirteen and seventeen;
> Five of the twenty females identified as having become pregnant between the ages of thirteen and seventeen are alleged to be minors, the other fifteen are now adults;
> Of the five minors who became pregnant, four are seventeen and one is sixteen, and all five are alleged to have become pregnant at the age of fifteen or sixteen;
> The Department's lead investigator was of the opinion that due to the "pervasive belief system" of the FLDS, the male children are groomed to be perpetrators of sexual abuse and the girls are raised to be victims of sexual abuse; . . .
> Department witnesses expressed the opinion that there is a "pervasive belief system" among the residents of the ranch that it is acceptable for girls to marry, engage in sex, and bear children as soon as they reach puberty, and that this "pervasive belief system" poses a danger to the children.

In re Steed No. 03-08-00235-CV, 2008 WL 2132014, at 1-2 (Tex. App.–Austin May 22, 2008, orig. proceeding), mand. denied sub nom. In re Tex. Dep't of Family & Protective Servs., 255 S.W.3d 613, 613-614 (Tex. 2008). On appeal, both the intermediate appellate court and Texas Supreme Court held that the evidence did not establish the grounds for emergency removal and remanded the cases. The trial judge then returned all but one of the children to their parents, and the juvenile court cases were dropped. Five men, including the leader of the FLDS community, Warren Jeffs, were later indicted for sexual assault of minor girls, based on evidence that girls as young as 14 had been spiritually married to much older men and borne children conceived while they were under the age of consent. Other men in the community were charged with various offenses, including bigamy, sexual assault, performing an illegal marriage, and failure to report child abuse.

More than 50 years earlier, child welfare officials in Utah and Arizona raided the community in which the same religious group was living and took more than 200 children into custody, based on allegations that their parents neglected them by raising them in an immoral environment, i.e., one in which plural marriage was practiced and advocated. (At this time, the group practiced marriage of underage girls to older men, but this was not the basis for the allegation of neglect.) All the Arizona children were returned home after their mothers promised not to return to their fathers and not to teach their children to violate the state law against bigamy. Similar cases were filed in Utah, and one, In re Black, 283 P.2d 887 (Utah 1955), was appealed to the state supreme court. The court upheld the juvenile court finding that the children were neglected and ruled that state intervention into the families did not violate the parents' rights to freedom of religion.

Are these cases of moral neglect? If not, what was the basis for removing all of the children in each case, many of whom were boys and preadolescent girls?

For discussion of these cases, *see* Martin Guggenheim, Texas Polygamy and Child Welfare, 46 Hous. L. Rev. 759 (2009); Linda F. Smith, Kidnapped from that Land II: A Comparison of Two Raids to Save the Children from the Polygamists, 30 Child. Legal Rts. J. 32 (2010).

PROBLEMS

1. Alhaji is a 26-year-old native of Nigeria studying medicine in the United States. He brought Rabi, his 13-year-old wife, whom he had married in Nigeria, to a local clinic to obtain birth control pills. The two are validly married according to Nigerian law. According to local statutory rape law, anyone older than 18 who has sexual intercourse with a minor younger than 14 is guilty of a felony, and neither boys nor girls may marry before age 16. If Alhaji is charged with statutory rape, should the charges against him be dismissed on the authority of *Kargar*? Can Alhaji and Rabi live together as spouses from now on?

2. "For centuries, several societies—primarily located in Muslim Africa—have engaged in a practice that is often, perhaps euphemistically, referred to as female circumcision. Some call it genital mutilation. Others use more specific and technical language to describe the particular form the practice takes, such as clitoridectomy or infibulation.

"The subjects (some would say objects) of this procedure are young girls ranging in age from several days to just prior to marriage, depending on the particular cultural practices of the region involved. Clitoridectomy serves largely as a prerequisite, if not a direct rite of passage, to a girl's adulthood, or womanhood. A woman who has not participated in the ritual is likely to be denied the possibility of marriage and is thereby foreclosed access to certain privileges of her society. The procedure is almost universally performed by women, either trained or lay. It often proves to be dangerous, sometimes fatal, because it is not always done in hygienic circumstances. . . .

"For others, including other feminists, clitoridectomy poses a more complex set of issues. The complexity arises in part from the fact that women perform the operation on other females and that girls, if old enough to consider it, often claim to desire the procedure. That the practice is deeply rooted in culture also poses difficulties. . . ." Karen Engle, Female Subjects of Public International Law: Human Rights and the Exotic Other Female, 26 New Eng. L. Rev. 1509, 1509-1511 (1992). *See also* Michael Freeman, The Morality of Cultural Pluralism, 3 Intl. J. Child. Rts. 1, 6 (1995).

Female circumcision of minors has been outlawed in several western countries, including the United States. Section 116 of 18 U.S.C. provides:

(a) Except as provided in subsection (b), whoever knowingly circumcises, excises, or infibulates the whole or any part of the labia majora or labia minora or clitoris of another person who has not attained the age of 18 years shall be fined under this title or imprisoned not more than 5 years, or both.
(b) A surgical operation is not a violation of this section if the operation is—
    (1) necessary to the health of the person on whom it is performed, and is performed by a person licensed in the place of its performance as a medical practitioner; or
    (2) performed on a person in labor or who has just given birth and is performed for medical purposes connected with that labor or birth by a person licensed in the place it is performed as a medical practitioner, midwife, or person in training to become such a practitioner or midwife.
(c) In applying subsection (b)(1), no account shall be taken of the effect on the person on whom the operation is to be performed of any belief on the part of that person, or any other person, that the operation is required as a matter of custom or ritual.

Legislation has been proposed in your state to outlaw circumcision of male minors as well. The proponents argue that the procedure is, at best, elective from a medical perspective. They cite the most recent policy statement from the American Academy of Pediatrics (AAP), which concludes that there are no clear medical benefits from the routine practice of circumcision and that circumcision is not essential to a child's well-being. American Academy of Pediatrics, Circumcision Policy Statement (RE9850), 103(3) Pediatrics 686 (1999), available from the academy's policy website, http://www.aappolicy.aappublications.org. The AAP policy statement also says that considerable evidence shows that newborns experience pain and physiologic stress from the procedure and that it is possible for the procedure to be done later, under general anesthesia.

The supporters of the proposed legislation argue that parents should not be permitted to subject their sons to an unnecessary and painful medical procedure, any more than parents may submit their daughters to such procedures. They also argue that choices about circumcision should be left for individuals to make after they become adults.

What arguments should be made in favor of and against this proposed legislation?

3. Mother and Father divorced while Mother was pregnant with Son, who is now two weeks old. The divorce decree provided that Mother and Father would have joint legal custody of Son and that Mother would have physical custody, with Father having visitation rights. Mother's religious beliefs require that male children be circumcised shortly after birth. Father belongs to a different religion, which imposes no such obligation, and he does not want Son to be circumcised. In this jurisdiction, if parents with joint legal custody cannot agree, the court is to decide the issue "in the best interest of the child." How should the court resolve this dispute and why?

Now assume that the court initially ruled in Father's favor, prohibiting the circumcision. When Son was nine years old, Mother decided to have him circumcised because the boy had suffered bouts of painful infections, and she wanted him to have the procedure to prevent the infections. Father again sues to stop the surgery, arguing that performing it at this point in the boy's life could cause significant psychological harm. How should the court resolve this dispute and why?

3. Specific Types of Maltreatment

a. Physical Abuse

The core definition of "physical abuse" is the intentional infliction of physical injury on a child. Ordinarily, cases of physical abuse involve repeated courses of conduct, though one act can surely be enough to constitute legal "abuse" if it is serious enough. In many cases of physical abuse, the disputed issue is whether a child's injuries were inflicted intentionally or accidentally. This evidentiary issue is covered in Chapter 9. The most common definitional issue arises from the social acceptance of corporal punishment, a form of deliberate infliction of pain upon a child. Most Americans support corporal punishment, and almost half of American parents have used corporal punishment on their children. The rates vary with the child's age and sex. Murray A. Straus, Prevalence, Societal Causes, and Trends in Corporal Punishment and Parents in World Perspective, 3 Law & Contemp. Problems 1, 3-6, 15-16 (2010). The next case explores the boundary between acceptable physical punishment and unacceptable physical abuse.

CARTER V. STATE

67 N.E.3d 1041 (Ind. App. 2016)

RILEY, Judge. . . . On August 24, 2015, Carter observed that his fourteen-year-old daughter, M.C., had altered her eyebrows. When Carter questioned M.C. about this, she initially denied that she had made any changes to herself. However, M.C. eventually admitted the truth. As punishment for her dishonesty, Carter confiscated M.C.'s cellphone. After taking possession of M.C.'s cellphone, Carter checked his daughter's social media accounts and was very upset by what he discovered. M.C. had posted photographs of herself wearing only "her panty and bra," and "she was talking to boys, [trying to] . . . like actually offer herself to them." In conjunction with these photographs, M.C. had published their address, as well as her grandmother's address, online.

The next day, August 25, 2015, M.C. woke up and readied herself for school while Carter was still asleep. Before walking out the door, M.C. retrieved her cellphone and grabbed a pair of Carter's shoes. When Carter awoke, he discovered that M.C. had taken her cellphone without permission. Carter walked to the bus stop, where he observed M.C. listening to music on her cellphone and wearing his shoes. Carter informed M.C. that she had disrespected him and that they needed to return home "to take [his] shoes off" because his feet are bigger "and she was looking like a clown."

Although M.C. resisted at first, she eventually heeded Carter's demands to walk home with him. On the way, Carter, who was still upset by the content of M.C.'s social media accounts, broke M.C.'s cellphone. M.C. threatened to run away, to which Carter responded by stating that he would call the police to bring her back. M.C. also responded that she would call the police over her broken phone. When they arrived home, there is no dispute that Carter determined that it was necessary to discipline M.C. However, Carter and M.C. offered varying accounts as to the extent and severity of the punishment.

According to Carter, when they arrived home, Carter instructed M.C. to start cleaning the apartment while he called his father to discuss M.C.'s behavior. While on the phone with his father, Carter was also "telling [M.C.] how she was doing me [*sic*] and how wrong she was what she was doing and I was telling her the consequences and I told her, that I was going to discipline [her] physically." Based on the fact that M.C. was fourteen years old, Carter determined that he was "going to discipline her [fourteen] times." Carter instructed M.C. "to bend over and touch the couch." Instead, Carter described that M.C. "jumped up off the couch and she raised her hand up at me." Still on the phone, Carter's father advised him to go take a shower before punishing M.C. so that he would be "level headed." Carter stated that after he showered, he spanked M.C. fourteen times with his belt.

On the other hand, according to M.C., as soon as they arrived home from the bus stop, Carter directed her "to take off my sweater and everything and my shoes that I had on and stuff. I still had on clothing and stuff and . . . he had told me, he was like bent over the couch." Carter started hitting her with his belt on her back, legs, and buttocks. She stated that he shoved her against a wall and pressed his forearm across her neck to the point that it was "hard to breathe in air." After hitting her again with the belt, Carter ordered her to clean the entire apartment. When M.C. finished cleaning, Carter asked her whether she wanted "the whoop-ing now or later" and she "said later." Carter then showered. When he returned, Carter "hit [M.C.] a couple times" and then had a conversation with her "[a]bout stuff [she] should have did [*sic*]." After their conversation, Carter continued with "the rest of this whooping." Even though M.C. begged for a reprieve of "two second[s]" or "two minutes," Carter told her to "take it like God did when they beat him." Also, at one point, M.C. stated that she had balled up her fist, and even though she claimed that she "wasn't going to hit him," Carter saw it and smacked her across the face. M.C. stated that it hurt when Carter hit her with his belt "because he was hitting [her] with all his force."

. . . When M.C. returned to school on August 26, 2016, she informed her guidance counselor that her "arm was hurting." The guidance counselor observed a bruise on M.C.'s shoulder and inquired as to what happened. After gleaning some details of the incident from M.C., the guidance counselor informed the school nurse about the situation and contacted the Indiana Department of Child Services (DCS). The nurse provided M.C. with ice packs to treat her pain. A DCS assessment worker arrived at the school and took photographs of bruises on M.C.'s body, which she opined to be the result of being hit with a belt. M.C. sustained bruises to her buttocks, inner and outer thigh, upper arm, forearm, and lower shoulder.

On August 31, 2015, the State filed an Information, charging Carter with Count I, strangulation, a Level 6 felony, and Count II, battery resulting in bodily injury, a Class A misdemeanor. At the close of the evidence, the trial court entered a judgment of conviction for battery resulting in bodily injury, a Class A misdemeanor. The trial court found Carter not guilty of strangulation. Immediately thereafter, the trial court sentenced Carter to 114 days—*i.e.*, his time already served with applicable credit time.

Carter now appeals. Additional facts will be provided as necessary....

It is well established that "[a] parent has a fundamental liberty interest in maintaining a familial relationship with his or her child." Willis v. State, 888 N.E.2d 177, 180 (Ind. 2008). Included within this fundamental liberty interest is "the right of parents 'to direct the upbringing and education of children,' including the use of reasonable or moderate physical force to control behavior." However, the State also "has a powerful interest in preventing and deterring the mistreatment of children[,]" and "the potential for child abuse cannot be taken lightly." Thus, prosecutors and courts are left with the difficult task of determining "when parental use of physical force in disciplining children turns an otherwise law-abiding citizen into a criminal."

In order to convict Carter of battery resulting in bodily injury, the State was required to prove that Carter "knowingly or intentionally . . . touche[d] [M.C.] in a rude, insolent, or angry manner," which "result[ed] in bodily injury to [M.C.]" In this case, Carter asserted the affirmative defense of the parental discipline privilege. Indiana Code section 35–41–3–1 provides that "[a] person is justified in engaging in conduct otherwise prohibited if he has legal authority to do so." Indiana courts have construed this provision "as including reasonable parental discipline that would otherwise constitute battery." "The defense of parental privilege, like self-defense, is a complete defense. That is to say a valid claim of parental privilege is a legal justification for an otherwise criminal act." . . .

In order to convict a parent for battery where parental privilege is asserted, "the State must prove that either: (1) the force the parent used was unreasonable or (2) the parent's belief that such force was necessary to control [his or] her child and prevent misconduct was unreasonable." *[Willis]*, (citing Restatement of the Law (Second) Torts, § 147 (1965)). Here, the State does not contest the reasonableness of Carter's *belief* that the use of force was necessary. Rather, the State maintains that Carter exerted unreasonable force in disciplining M.C., such that the parental privilege is negated.

While there "are no bright-line rules" as to what is considered "proper and reasonable parental discipline of children[,]" the Indiana Supreme Court has adopted the view that "[a] parent is privileged to apply such reasonable force or to impose such reasonable confinement upon his [or her] child as he [or she] reasonably believes to be necessary for [the child's] proper control, training, or education." In determining the reasonableness of a punishment, the following factors are to be considered and "balanced against each other, giving appropriate weight as the circumstances dictate":

(a)   whether the actor is a parent;

(b)   the age, sex, and physical and mental condition of the child;

(c)   the nature of his offense and his apparent motive;

(d)   the influence of his example upon other children of the same family or group;

(e)   whether the force or confinement is reasonably necessary and appropriate to compel obedience to a proper command;

(f)   whether it is disproportionate to the offense, unnecessarily degrading, or likely to cause serious or permanent harm.

[Willis] at 182 (quoting Restatement, *supra*, § 150). In addition to this non-exhaustive list of factors, "[t]here may be other factors unique to a particular case that should be taken into consideration." Similarly, "not all of the listed factors may be relevant or applicable in every case."

On appeal, Carter asserts that the State failed to rebut his parental privilege defense beyond a reasonable doubt, in part, because the evidence establishes that "[t]he force used was reasonable under the *Willis* factors." It is not apparent from the record which specific factors — *Willis* or otherwise — the trial court considered in finding Carter guilty of battery. However, looking to the first two *Willis* factors, the evidence establishes that Carter is M.C.'s biological father, and M.C. was fourteen years old at the time of the incident. The trial court noted that M.C., a female, was "as big as" Carter. The State directs our attention to M.C.'s testimony that she takes anti-anxiety medicine as evidence of her emotional instability.

Regarding the nature of her offense, ... According to Carter, it was the culmination of M.C.'s "escalating misbehavior and disrespect for her father's authority" that resulted in his choice of disciplinary measures. As to the influence of M.C.'s example upon other children in the family, no evidence was presented at the trial except that M.C.'s younger brother was in the apartment at the time and did not witness the punishment.

The last two *Willis* factors require an examination of whether the parent's force is reasonably necessary to compel obedience and whether that force is disproportionate to the offense, unnecessarily degrading, or likely to cause serious permanent harm. A parent "is not privileged to use a means to compel obedience if a less severe method appears to be likely to be equally effective." In this case, Carter argues that, prior to spanking M.C. with his belt, he "used progressive forms of discipline," including confiscating M.C.'s cellphone; asking his mother to speak with M.C.; and requiring M.C. to clean the apartment, which she failed to do in a satisfactory manner. According to Carter, none of these disciplinary measures were sufficient to deter M.C.'s misbehavior. Carter acknowledges that he doled out a "painful" punishment, but he maintains that it was an appropriate response as "M.C. was engaging in dangerous activity and [he] saw her defiance and disrespect escalating quickly." Carter argues that he "repeatedly took steps to ensure the discipline was not imposed hastily or in anger" such as by walking outside, calling his father, and taking a shower. Carter also points out that his punishment was not unnecessarily degrading because M.C. was fully clothed, and they were "in the privacy of their home." As a result of Carter's punishment, M.C. had bruises on her buttocks, inner and outer thigh, upper arm, forearm, and lower shoulder. One day after the whipping, M.C. was sore and was treated with ice packs at school, but there is no evidence that she suffered any serious or permanent harm.

Carter likens his case to *Willis*, 888 N.E.2d at 183, where the Supreme Court found the parent's punishment of striking her child five to seven times "with either a belt or an extension cord" was reasonable after the mother had previously "used progressive forms of discipline" such as sending the child to his room; grounding him; and withholding television, games, and time spent outdoors, all of which were insufficient to deter the child from committing additional offenses. Furthermore, the supreme court found "nothing particularly degrading" about an eleven-year-old boy receiving "five to seven swats on his buttocks, arm, and thigh for what many parents might reasonably consider a serious offense." Even though the swats hurt, the child returned to school the following day without any pain, and despite apparent bruising, "there is no indication that the school nurse provided any medical attention or even suggested that medical attention was necessary."

The State counters that M.C.'s offenses did not merit Carter's "brutal" punishment and argues that Carter should have taken "numerous steps" to punish M.C. instead of hitting her with his belt. Because M.C. complied with Carter's demands to return home and clean the apartment and because she accepted the discipline in a "docile" manner, the State contends that "M.C. was not an errant child who could not be reasoned with." The State further asserts that M.C.'s beating "was unnecessarily degrading, particularly because it was not limited to M.C.'s buttocks and back." Rather, "M.C. sustained severe bruising to her shoulders, arms, forehead, buttocks, back, and legs." The State concedes that the punishment did not lead to any permanent damage but nonetheless contends that Carter "used all of his force" and caused so much pain that M.C. "was unable to sit in school the next day."

The State posits that the present case is more akin to Smith v. State, 34 N.E.3d 252, 253–54 (Ind. Ct. App. 2015), where a parent beat her thirteen-year-old daughter with two different belts ten to twenty times on her arms, shoulder, and legs. There, as in the present case, the mother discovered that her teenaged daughter "was having conversations with boys on social media sites that were 'very sexual in nature'" among other dangerous behaviors. Prior to whipping her child, the mother imposed a substantial number of progressive disciplinary measures, including withdrawing the child from public school and replacing the child's wardrobe with more modest clothing. We found that the parent had inflicted an unreasonable punishment, and in so finding, we emphasized the fact that the mother had "engaged in a fighting match" with her child. The State also relies on Smith v. State, 489 N.E.2d 140, 141 (Ind. Ct. App. 1986), wherein a parent whipped his fifteen-year-old daughter with a belt approximately fifteen times, resulting in a facial laceration and numerous contusions on her buttocks, arms, legs, and shoulder. We held the privilege of parental discipline did not apply because the defendant "cruelly beat his daughter."

In this case, there is no question that Carter was justified in his assessment that some form of punishment was necessary in order to control and deter M.C.'s escalating defiance and dangerous behavior. As to Carter's choice of disciplinary measures, it is apparent that the trial court struggled with ascertaining the line between reasonable and unreasonable force. Prior to imposing a sentence, the trial court remarked to Carter:

> . . . [N]ot only do I believe that you um, had cause [] to discipline her, I do. . . . I also strongly believe that—that kids should be subject to discipline punishment under certain circumstances, I do. I have boys myself. If I had a girl who was posing half necked [*sic*] on social media, I would also be wearing orange because you would not be able to hold me back from her. So, I totally understand why you were as angry as you were, and why you did what you did. Because I'm assuming you were trying to prevent her from living a life you don't want her to live. . . . Which is, getting pregnant at a young age, dropping out of school, getting her[]self physical[ly] assaulted, things like that. I assumed why you did what you did. . . . Um, unfortunately, I think we're in this universe now, where parents don't just get to do whatever they want. And when they make decision[s] like you did, they subject themselves to going to jail for it. I would go to jail for it, if I thought it was going to help my kids, I really would. Um, and [if] some little girl was posting on my son[']s Facebook page, pictures half necked [*sic*], I probably would be after her too. I think under these circumstances though, I don't know what you['re] supposed to do. I'm not—I can't give you any guidance because I don't know what you do. That girl was as big as you are, she was definite (Phonetic), she probably did look like a clown wearing your shoes, um and I'm not sure what you['re] supposed to do. Because taking away her phone is not going to do the trick. You may have done the trick but you got yourself put in jail doing it. So, I think that um, I think it was over the top but I don't have—I don't have the solution for you. I[am] going to find you NOT GUILTY for [s]trangulation; I'm going to find you GUILTY for [b]attery as a Class A[m]isdemeanor. Giving [*sic*] all of that, I will take everything I heard in consideration during sentencing because I don't—there is not [an] easy solution to this problem. I'm not sure what you do. Cause if you allow them to act that way and they become bad people you get blamed for that too. So, I don't know what you do. . . .

Ultimately, the trial court concluded that Carter's use of force—*i.e.*, at least fourteen strikes with a belt which resulted in significant bruising and lasting pain—exceeded reasonableness, and on appeal, we are mindful of the trial court's role in weighing the evidence and assessing witness credibility to determine whether a parent's actions were justified as reasonable parental discipline. Although we are troubled by the lack of clear guidance for parents to be able to distinguish between reasonable discipline and battery, it was the trial court's duty to balance the *Willis* factors, and we decline to reweigh the evidence. Thus, we conclude that there is sufficient evidence to support Carter's conviction for battery resulting in bodily injury. . . .

Affirmed.

Crone, Judge, concurring. As noted above, "prosecutors and courts are left with the difficult task of determining 'when parental use of physical force in disciplining children turns an otherwise law-abiding citizen into a criminal.'" I write separately to suggest that our Supreme Court made that task much more difficult by importing the vague reasonableness standard of the Restatement of Torts into the criminal arena.

When does reasonable punishment become unreasonable? The trial court clearly struggled with this question, as have we at the appellate level. Would thirteen strikes with a belt have been reasonable? Or perhaps fifteen strikes with less bruising and pain? What if Carter had inflicted the same punishment with a rolled-up newspaper? What if M.C.'s transgressions had been slightly more egregious, or what if her brother had witnessed her punishment? With the possible exception of sentencing, I cannot think of any other area in criminal law that is so fraught with subjectivity. Everyone agrees that a line needs to be drawn, but current caselaw offers little guidance as to where that line is.

There may not be any area where reasonable minds differ more in our current society than corporal punishment of children. Attitudes vary dramatically by and within generations and cultures. If the purpose of the criminal law is to put a person on notice of what conduct is proscribed and what is permitted, then how can one's guilt or innocence depend upon how someone else disciplines his or her children when there is no consensus about what is appropriate?

That being said, courts must step in where legislatures decline to tread, so unless and until the General Assembly enacts clearer guidelines for parental discipline (or our Supreme Court adopts a more workable standard), trial judges and jurors must rely on their experience and judgment to determine when parents cross over the blurry line that separates lawful from unlawful conduct, and appellate courts must give those determinations significant deference. For that reason, I reluctantly concur in my colleagues' affirmance of Carter's battery conviction.

NOTES AND QUESTIONS

1. As *Carter* says, the parental privilege to discipline is said to "justify" what would otherwise be a criminal offense. Justification claims express the judgment that the actor's conduct was correct, not simply excusable, behavior. Why is using physical force to discipline a child regarded as correct?

Professor James Dwyer argues that normative arguments in favor of the parental prerogative to use corporal punishment differ from arguments in support of the general right of parents to decide how to raise their children:

. . . Parents' rights-based arguments against substantive restrictions on religious schooling rest on claims that according parents plenary rights to control children's education (1) is best for children because parents are in the best position to make decisions about children's schooling, given that parents care most about and know best their own children; (2) protects parents' interest in exercising their religion and living by their own lights; and (3) serves society's collective interest in cultural diversity. Parents' rights-based claims are also prominent in arguments for continuing to permit parents to have their baby boys circumcised, against objections that this violates the boys' basic right to bodily integrity, and they generally rest solely on parents' interests—predominantly, the interests of Jewish or Muslim parents in following the dictates of their religions and fathers' interests in making their sons' privates look like theirs. Parents' rights-based arguments in the corporal-punishment context, in contrast, are . . . secondary to a debate over the best way to raise children, and the arguments are generally limited to claims that according parents a right to spank is necessary to serve children's welfare.

James G. Dwyer, Parental Entitlement and Corporal Punishment, 73 Law & Contemp. Probs. 189, 196 (2010). Why isn't a parent's choice to use corporal punishment supported in terms of parents' own autonomy rights or societal interests?

2. Empirical research shows that corporal punishment is not a very effective method of discipline and is associated with harm to children's mental health and with children engaging in more aggressive and antisocial behavior. Elizabeth T. Gershoff & Andrew Grogan-Kaylor, Spanking and Child Outcomes: Old Controversies and New Meta-Analyses, 30 J. Fam. Psychol. 13 (2016). Courts most commonly justify parents' privilege to use corporal punishment by reference to tradition, and some cite their own experiences and beliefs about childrearing, as did the trial judge in *Carter*. Are these rationales sufficient? *See* Cynthia Godsoe, Redefining Parental Rights: The Case of Corporal Punishment, 32 Const. Comment. 281, 293-294 (2017); Cynthia Godsoe, Redrawing the Boundaries of Relational Crime, 69 Ala. L. Rev. 169 (2017).

3. Parents who use spanking as a means of disciplining their children are more likely to be reported to child protective services for child neglect than those who do not spank. Kristin Shook Slack et al., Understanding the Risks of Child Neglect: An Exploration of Poverty and Parenting Characteristics, 9 Child Maltreatment 395, 404 (2005).

The American Academy of Pediatrics Committee recommends, for purposes of physicians' duty to report suspected child abuse, that any nonaccidentally inflicted injury that goes beyond temporary reddening of the skin should be considered abuse. American Academy of Pediatrics, When Inflicted Skin Injuries Constitute Child Abuse, 110 Pediatrics 64 (2002).

4. *Carter* uses the Restatement of Torts(2d) definition of the parental privilege, even though it is a criminal case. Does the court's application of this test require that the parent be angry at the child for the use of force to cross the line from discipline to abuse? Did Carter use force because he was angry at her for raising her first to him? For defying him?

Some states use the Model Penal Code rule, which provides that a parent's use of force is not criminal if the force is used for the purpose of promoting the child's welfare and the force "is not designed to cause or known to create a substantial risk of causing death, serious bodily injury, disfigurement, extreme pain or mental distress or gross degradation." Model Penal Code 3.08(1). Under this formulation, would Carter have committed abuse?

5. The father in Carter used a belt to inflict the punishment. Does this make the use of force more or less questionable? In State in Interest of K.T., 424 P.3d 91(Utah 2017), parents used a belt to spank their children, and the juvenile court judge ruled that as a matter of law that hitting a child with an object is child abuse. The Utah Supreme Court reversed, saying that to support a finding of abuse, the evidence must show that the child was physically, emotionally, or psychologically harmed or threatened with such harm. In the absence of any evidence of harm, the finding was reversed. The court explained that it rejected the per se rule to avoid the conclusion that a parent who threw a pillow or a pair of socks at a child had committed abuse. In support of the juvenile court judge's ruling, how would you respond to this argument?

6. In State v. Crouser, 911 P.2d 725 (Haw. 1996), the court held that a statute that required a court to "consider the age and size of the recipient and whether a reasonable relationship exists between the force used" and the purpose of discipline in determining the lawfulness of a parent's use of corporal punishment was not unconstitutionally vague. The court said:

> An ordinary reading of [the statute] gives sufficient notice to a reasonable person that there are limits to both the purpose and degree of force that may justifiably be used against a minor and defines those limits with reasonable clarity. Thus, the statute cannot be said to be unconstitutionally vague.
>
> Crouser also argues that [the statute] is overbroad because it proscribes constitutionally protected conduct as well as unprotected conduct. The argument is without merit. The law long ago abandoned the view that children are essentially chattels of their parents without independent legal rights. Crouser points to no constitutional provision that protects his right to inflict upon a child, especially one not his own, force that the legislature has deemed to be excessive and harmful to the child's welfare.

911 P.2d at 735. Would it violate parents' constitutional rights to ban corporal punishment altogether? Sixteen years after *Crouser*, the Hawaii Supreme Court held that parents have a constitutional right to use corporal punishment to discipline their children as an inherent part of their right to the care, custody, and control of their children under the due process clause of the state constitution. Hamilton ex rel. Lethem v. Lethem, 270 P.3d 1024, 1032 (Hi. 2012). Other cases holding that corporal punishment is part of parents' constitutional rights in addition to *Carter* include Doe v. Heck, 327 F.3d 492, 523 (7th Cir. 2003); State v. Wilder, 748 A.2d 444 (Me. 2000); State v. Rosa, 6 N.E.3d 57 (Ohio App. 2013).

7. For an overview of state laws, *see* Doriane Lambelet Coleman, Kenneth A. Dodge & Sarah Keeton Campbell, Where and How to Draw the Line Between Reasonable Corporal Punishment and Abuse, 73 Law & Contemp. Probs. 107, 114-119 (2010). This article also reports on the authors' survey of child protective workers from around the country about the ways they draw the line when they are investigating allegations of child abuse. *Id.* at 119-128.

8. In 1979, Sweden enacted the first national law forbidding parents to use corporal punishment. As of 2018, 54 countries had banned all corporal punishment of youth. They include Nepal, Lithuania, Mongolia, Montenegro, Paraguay, Slovenia, Benin, Ireland, Peru, Andorra, Estonia, Nicaragua, San Marino, Argentina, Bolivia, Brazil, Malta, Cabo Verde, Honduras, North Macedonia, South Sudan, Albania, Republic of Congo, Kenya, Tunisia, Poland, Liechtenstein, Luxembourg, Republic of Moldova, Costa Rica, Togo, Spain, Venezuela, Uruguay, Portugal, New Zealand, Netherlands, Greece, Hungary, Romania, Ukraine, Turkmenistan, Iceland, Germany, Israel, Bulgaria, Croatia, Latvia, Denmark, Cyprus, Austria, Norway, Finland, and Sweden. An up-to-date list is available from the website of the Global Initiative to End All Corporal Punishment of Children, http://www.endcorporalpunishment.org/. For an analysis of the various countries' laws *see* Benjamin Shmueli, Corporal Punishment in the Educational System versus Corporal Punishment by Parents: A Comparative View, 73 Law & Contemp. Probs. 281 (2010).

In Sweden and Germany, after bans were enacted, corporal punishment, particularly severe punishment, was reduced significantly. Straus, 73 Law & Contemp. Probs., *above*, at 14.

Swedish parents who belonged to a church whose tenets include use of corporal punishment challenged the ban as violating the European Convention for the Protection of Human Rights and Fundamental Freedoms, particularly provisions protecting respect for private family life, freedom of religion, and the right of parents to control the education of their children. In X, Y, and Z v. Sweden, 5 Eur. H.R. Rep. 147 (1983), the European Commission on Human Rights rejected the challenges. It found that "the actual effects of the law are to encourage a positive review of the punishment of children by their parents, to discourage abuse and prevent excuses which could properly be described as violence against children. . . . The Commission does not regard the effects of the amendment which are the subject of this application as constituting an interference which amounts to a lack of respect for the applicants' family life."

In A v. United Kingdom (Human Rights: Punishment of Child), [1988] 2 FLR 959, the European Court of Human Rights found that a severe beating, which was protected under English law as within the bounds of legitimate parental discipline, violated a child's human rights. The court concluded, therefore, that English law was in conflict with Article 3 of the European Convention for the Protection of Human Rights and Fundamental Freedoms 1950, which prohibits "torture or inhuman or degrading treatment or punishment."

NOTE: EMOTIONAL ABUSE AND APPROPRIATE DISCIPLINE

Based on a nationally representative survey of 991 parents, personnel from the University of New Hampshire Family Research Laboratory concluded that verbal abuse as a means of discipline is "so prevalent as to be just about universal." Murray A. Straus & Carolyn J. Field, Psychological Aggression by American Parents: National Data on Prevalence, Chronicity, and Severity, 65 J. Marriage & Fam. 665, 666 (2003). These researchers defined psychological aggression as "a communication intended to cause the child to experience psychological pain." *Id.* at 797. The acts included in this definition including shouting, yelling, or screaming at a child, threatening to spank the child, swearing at a child, calling a child a name, and threatening to kick a child out of the house. *Id.* at 801-802. Psychological aggression began when children were infants and peaked at age seven. However, severe psychological aggression, defined as swearing, name calling, and threatening to kick the child out of the house, was very low for young children and increased steadily until more than half of all 17-year-olds experienced it. *Id.* at 802.

Using data from LONGSCAN, a multisite longitudinal study of the long-term effects of maltreatment on children, other researchers found that children exposed to verbally aggressive discipline were more likely to be anxious or depressed, have attention problems, exhibit delinquent behaviors and have somatic complaints. However, because the study based its findings about children's behaviors on the reports of their caregivers, "it is not clear to what degree these differences reflect actual functional impairment rather than, possibly, caregivers' misperceptions of child behavior. . . . We also acknowledge that the direction of causality underlying the association of verbal aggression with behavior problems is not known; not only might problem behaviors be caused by verbal aggression, but also problem behaviors on the part of a child may provoke aggressive verbal reactions from caregivers." Diana J. English et al., Toward a Definition of Neglect in Young Children, 10 Child Maltreatment 190, 202 (2005).

In light of these data, how should emotional abuse be defined for purposes of legal intervention into a family?

LGBTQ youth are much more likely than straight youth to have experienced physical abuse before being removed from home by a social worker. Gender nonconforming and transgender youth are almost four times more likely to have experienced physical abuse before removal than conforming youth. They are also more likely to run away or be kicked out of their homes because of conflicts with their parents before becoming involved with the juvenile justice system. Often the family's response to nonheterosexual or nonconforming identity drives the child into the child welfare system. Angela Irvine & Aisha Canfield, The Overrepresentation of Lesbian, Gay, Bisexual, Questioning, Gender Nonconforming and Transgender Youth within the Child Welfare to Juvenile Justice Crossover Population, 24 Am. U. J. So. Pol'y & L. 243 (2016). Are these cases of physical or emotional abuse? How should the child welfare system respond in such a case?

PROBLEMS

1. A mother, who is also a physician, struck her 7-year-old son, one of four children, on the buttocks six times with an imitation leather belt because he would not obey her and was shouting at her. The next day the boy had several bruises on his lower back. The mother believes in corporal punishment and insists that she will continue to use it. Has she committed abuse under the *C.F.* test? Under the MPC? The Restatement (2d) of Torts? What if, instead, she had washed his mouth out with soap?

2. The parents of 13-year-old Sam punished him by putting him in a three-by four-foot dog cage once a week for two hours at a time. Sam had learned how to get out of the cage and actually spent the time in the basement, as the parents knew. Are Sam's parents physically abusing him? What if Sam's parents chained him to his bed at night to keep him from climbing out the window to hang out with his friends?

b.   *Sexual Abuse*

CAROL S. LARSON ET AL., *SEXUAL ABUSE OF CHILDREN: RECOMMENDATIONS AND ANALYSIS*

4 The Future of Children: Sexual Abuse of Children 4, 8-11 (1994)

Child sexual abuse is generally defined as sexual activities involving a child and an adult or significantly older child. Although some societies have traditions of culturally sanctioned sexual conduct with children, . . . this country does not, and there is considerable consensus about proscribed sexual activities with children. . . .

It is important to acknowledge that a wide range of activities, varying greatly in type, frequency, duration, and intensity, can meet the [statutory definitions of sexual abuse]—for example, a single incident of inappropriate touching of an adolescent girl by a friend of the family; repeated sexual intercourse between a father and his daughter over a number of years; a stranger rubbing up against a young boy while standing in line at a shopping mall. Each of these activities meets the statutory definition of sexual abuse and is legally actionable; but, because these activities vary so in degree, they are often responded to very differently by the victims, the agencies investigating the activities, and the courts hearing cases based on them. . . .

Unfortunately, neither the criminal or child protection system maintains comprehensive data about cases of sexual abuse of children. . . . The most recent estimate of incidence looks only at the child protection system and finds that, in 1993, there were 330,000 reports of child sexual abuse, of which 150,000 were substantiated. Approximately 11% of the 2,984,000 reports of child abuse and neglect received by child protective services agencies in 1993 were for sexual abuse. . . .

It is important to remember, however, that these numbers may include duplicated reports, that is, one or more reports about the same incident and/or about the same child. Furthermore, these numbers include only reports made to child protective services. The incidence number would be higher if those sexual abuse cases that are handled by the criminal justice system were included, but currently there is no national data collection system that provides data on sexual crimes against children.

Because sexual abuse often goes undisclosed, a more comprehensive picture of the scope of the problem is obtained by asking adults whether they were sexually abused as children. The article by Finkelhor reviews 19 such adult retrospective studies. These studies vary in their definition of abuse, methodological approach, and quality. They often leave room for considerable interpretation by the respondent. Some include noncontact exploitation or exhibitionism, others do not. The findings from these studies are also highly varied. The percentage of adults disclosing histories of sexual abuse in these studies ranges from 2% to 62% for females and 3% to 16% for males. Finkelhor and many others believe that the better studies suggest that at least 20% of American women and 5% to 10% of American men experienced some form of sexual abuse as children. . . .

Finkelhor draws a number of estimates from adult retrospective surveys about the characteristics of abuse. He finds that most sexual abuse is committed by men (90%) and by persons known to the child (70% to 90%), such as family members, friends of the family, or acquaintances. Retrospective studies show that family offenders constitute 30% to 50% of the offenders against girls and 10% to 20% of the offenders against boys. The peak age of vulnerability is 7 to 13 years of age.

As discussed above, between the third and fourth National Incidence of Child Abuse Studies, the number of children reported to be in danger of sexual abuse decreased from 300,200 in 1993 to 180,500 in 2005-2006, a 40 percent decrease in number and a 47 percent decline in the rate. The number of children actually harmed by sexual abuse declined during the same period from 217,700 to

135,300 in 2005-2006, a 38 percent decrease in number and a 44 percent decrease in the rate. Executive Summary of Fourth National Incidence Study, at page 602 above. In an earlier examination of declining child sex abuse rates, the authors found that between 1992 and 2000, the number of reported child sex abuse cases declined by 40 percent. The authors evaluated possible reasons for the decline and concluded that it was both real and statistically significant. David Finkelhor & Lisa M. Jones, Explanations of the Decline in Child Sexual Abuse Cases (U.S. Justice Dept. 2004).

John D. v. Department of Social Services

744 N.E.2d 659 (Mass. App. 2001)

Jacobs, J. . . . This case arises from a report made to the DSS . . . which alleged sexual abuse and neglect by John D. of his fifteen-year-old stepdaughter. . . . After an investigation and report, . . . DSS supported that report, referred the allegation of sexual abuse to the district attorney, and listed John D.'s name on its registry of alleged perpetrators. An administrative hearing, termed a "fair hearing," was held . . . to consider John D.'s challenge to the DSS decision. After that decision was upheld by the administrative hearing officer, John D. obtained a review in the Superior Court. . . . The Superior Court judge affirmed the DSS decision.

We condense the factual background, as determined by the administrative hearing officer. John D. is the stepfather of the older and the biological father of the younger of the two alleged victims. He had been married to their mother for about six years at the time the mother reported that the older daughter disclosed that John D. had told her he needed to examine her genitals because he suspected she had been sexually active with her eighteen-year-old boyfriend. The stepdaughter told the DSS investigator that John D. is a nudist, that she does not like seeing him nude, and that she disliked his entering the bathroom and starting conversations with her while she was in the bathtub. She reported that he asked her if she knew "how to give a 'blow job'" and if she had gone beyond kissing, and that he stated he would help her with kissing if she needed help. He also asked if he could see her hymen, while noting it would be alright if she declined, and telling her that she should not tell her mother of the request. She indicated that he regularly said things that were "weird." There also was evidence of incidents of physical confrontation between John D. and his wife, including that of the wife hitting him in the presence of the children.

In her decision, the administrative hearing officer stated that John D.'s "actions . . . coupled with his pattern of engaging in conversations replete with sexual themes and sexual activities constitute sexual contact." She also opined that sexual contact was not limited by DSS regulations to physical touching and that John D. engaged in "verbal sexual contact" with his stepdaughter. The principal issue in this case is the interpretation by DSS of its regulation at 110 Code Mass. Regs. § 2.00 (1996), defining abuse as:

> the non-accidental commission of any act by a caretaker upon a child under age 18 which . . . constitutes a sexual offense under the laws of the Commonwealth or any sexual contact between a caretaker and a child under the care of that individual.

Because the validity of the regulation is not challenged, and there is no claim of unlawful procedure, the precise issue is whether the hearing officer correctly ruled that John D.'s "verbal sexual contact" in the context of his conduct with his stepdaughter and in the absence of physical contact, constitutes abuse. While the noun "contact" is defined in Webster's Third New International Dictionary 490 (1993), as the "union or junction of body surfaces," it also is defined as "association or relationship," and "a condition or an instance of . . . communicating." In the somewhat analogous circumstances of interpreting G.L. c. 209A protective orders, we have given a broad interpretation to the word "contact." We also do so here, using the nonphysical definition, because our focus is not limited to the precise nature of the interaction between parent and child, but additionally takes into account the purpose of that interaction and its potential effect upon the child.

That there is a broad range of possible communication between a parent (or caretaker) and a child on sexual subjects, is apparent from general experience and the dictionary definitions of "sexual." On the facts of this case, we need not declare particular standards as to what sexual communications may be improper between children and their caretakers. It is enough that we determine that the sexually oriented communications at issue constitute abuse, within the reach of the regulation, if they are not reasonably intended to provide information and direction for the child's education and physical and emotional well-being. Here, the hearing officer concluded that John D. was not acting "out of concern for [the stepdaughter's] physical well-being" when he discussed oral sexual acts and asked his stepdaughter whether he could examine her genital area to determine whether she was a virgin. The administrative hearing officer appears not to have credited his explanations because she concluded he "offered so many different accounts of what occurred indicating that he is not being truthful." This determination was hers to make.

John D. argues that while some of his discussions with his stepdaughter may have been "inappropriate," they did not "rise to the level of sexual abuse within the definition set forth in [G.L.] c. 119, § 51A." Two DSS supervisory staff members testified that "there is almost no situation in which an adult male, a stepfather especially, father included, as far as this office is concerned, [in which it] would in any way be appropriate to look at the genitals or discuss the genitals" and that a "show and tell atmosphere" in sex education is "clearly not appropriate." This testimony, based on agency experience, constitutes the kind of evidence upon which the hearing officer could rely in concluding that John D. did not act out of concern for his stepdaughter's well-being. The administrative hearing officer noted that the DSS regulations "do not limit sexual contact to physical touching." She concluded that John D.'s "verbal sexual contact" constituted abuse within the meaning of the regulation. "The court shall give due weight to the experience, technical competence, and specialized knowledge of the agency."

Moreover, there was evidence of a risk of harm to the stepdaughter from these inappropriately sexually laden communications. The stepdaughter told the investigator that she didn't "feel comfortable" with John D.'s nude conduct and his asking to see her hymen. She also stated that John D. thought he could say anything without offending her and that she felt he should move away. The evidence that John D.'s conduct was not only inappropriate but unwanted, reasonably gives rise to an inference of a substantial risk of emotional injury to the stepdaughter. While there was no direct or expert evidence of emotional harm presented at the fair hearing, we do not think such proof was required to justify the conclusion that the kind of inappropriate and unwanted conduct and sexually explicit remarks and questions as occurred in this case constitute the type of abuse the regulation encompasses. Section 51A speaks of a "substantial risk of harm," and the definition of abuse in 110 Code Mass. Regs. § 2.00 (1996), includes "a substantial risk of . . . emotional injury." The DSS need not wait until a risk is actuated before intervening. The statutes under which it operates are "intended to apply to threatened harm to children as well as actual harm."

Accordingly, we agree with the Superior Court judge that John D.'s "engaging his stepdaughter in sexually explicit conversations and suggesting sexual contact with her, such as examining her genitals and [offering to help her with] romantic kissing, is thus consistent with the plain and ordinary meaning of the word contact." We further find support in the record for the judge's conclusion that this was conduct "potentially causing emotional harm to a child" and, therefore, that such behavior reasonably is within the cognizance of the regulation. Beyond the considerable deference we accord to an agency's interpretation of its own regulation, we conclude that the interpretation by DSS of its regulation in this case was rational, reasonable, and consistent with its plain terms. Moreover, we conclude the regulation has been applied in a manner consistent with the purposes of c. 119, § 51A.

NOTES AND QUESTIONS

1. The definition, frequency, and causes of sexual abuse have been described in dramatically varying ways. According to the court in *John D.*, what must be established to prove sexual abuse, at least for purposes of the registry statute? What theory about the harm caused by sexual abuse supports this definition? The stepfather argued that sexual abuse could not occur without physical contact. What theory of harm supports this definition? What arguments support a narrow definition of sexual abuse? A broader definition?

Applying the definition in *John D.*, did Mohammad Kargar have "sexual contact" with his son?

2. Another problem of definition is when the risk of sex abuse exists and is severe enough to warrant some kind of state intervention. A common situation presenting this issue is the presence in a child's household of an adult who was convicted of a sex offense. Is that alone sufficient to show a risk of sex abuse justifying a finding that the child is within the juvenile court's jurisdiction and should be removed from the home? In In re Afton C., 950 N.E.2d 101 (N.Y. 2011), five children lived with their father, who had pled guilty to engaging in sexual intercourse with a minor younger than 15 and to patronizing a prostitute younger than 17, and who had not gone through sex offender treatment. The father had been designated a "level three SORA offender," meaning that he was considered likely to reoffend. The New York Court of Appeals ruled that the evidence was insufficient to find the children neglected because the simple fact of his convictions was not enough to show that he presented a substantial risk of harm to the children.

What additional evidence would show that the children were sufficiently at risk? Does it matter whether the adult is the child's parent or is unrelated to the child? Whether the adult has gone through sex offender treatment? Whether the sex offense was committed against children in the adult's care? The New York courts have upheld findings that untreated sex offenders presented unacceptable risks to children when their offenses were crimes against children rather than adults. *See, e.g.,* In re Cashmere S., 4 N.Y.S.3d 190 (App. Div. 2015); In re Lillian SS, 987 N.Y.S.2d 482 (App. Div. 2014). The California Supreme Court held in In re I.J., 299 P.3d 1254 (Cal. 2013), that proof that a father severely sexually abused his own child (a girl who at the time of the petition was 14) was sufficient to support a jurisdictional finding that all his other children (a boy aged 8, twin boys who were 12, and a girl who was 9) were at risk of harm. Lower California courts had been divided about whether proof of sexual abuse of a daughter supports jurisdiction over sons.

3. A survey of research on children and adults who had been sexually abused reported that they suffer various problems, including posttraumatic stress disorder, chronic perceptions of helplessness and danger, guilt, low self-esteem, self-blame, depression, anxiety, anger, impaired sense of self, and avoidance behaviors including "spacing out" or amnesia about painful abuse-related memories, substance abuse, suicide, indiscriminate sexual behavior, self-mutilation, bingeing and purging, and difficulties in interpersonal relationships. John N. Briere & Diana M. Elliott, Immediate and Long-Term Impacts of Child Sexual Abuse, 4 The Future of Children: Sexual Abuse of Children 54 (1994). However, "although child and adult survivors tend, as groups, to have more problems than their non-abused peers, there is no single universal or uniform impact of sexual abuse, and no certainty that any given person will develop any posttraumatic responses to sexual abuse." *Id.* at 63.

4. Even though most child sex abusers are friends or acquaintances of the victim, the law in some ways treats these offenders as less dangerous. Most states have criminal incest statutes under which relatives can be charged and which carry smaller penalties than child rape statutes. In several states offenders who had prior relationships with their victims do not have to register as sex offenders. Carissa Byrne Hessick, Violence Between Lovers, Strangers, and Friends, 85 Wash. U. L. Rev. 343 (2007). What might explain this more favorable treatment?

5. Sigmund Freud believed that many reports of sexual abuse were the product of girls' and women's fantasies and concluded that most claims of abuse were false. This perspective was given notorious expression in Wigmore's Evidence, which used these beliefs to justify evidentiary rules such as the requirement that the testimony of the complaining witness in a prosecution for sexual assault or rape be corroborated. 3A Wigmore, Evidence § 924a (James H. Chadbourn rev., 1978).

In 1979, Vincent DeFrancis's Protecting the Child Victim of Sex Crimes Committed by Adults argued that, in fact, sexual abuse of children is widespread. He conceptualized sexual abuse as the product of family dysfunction—fathers are often described as apparently normal men, often religious, conservative in sexual matters, and family oriented; mothers are often portrayed as collaborating in their daughters' abuse because they have withdrawn from the role of wife and implicitly acceded to the daughters' substitution; and daughters are sometimes described as seductive and provocative. For a summary of this theory, *see* Cynthia Ahlgren, Maintaining Incest Victims' Support Relationships, 22 J. Fam. L. 483, 494-497 (1983-1984).

Attacks on both these views argue that sexual abuse is widespread, that children rarely lie about its occurrence, and that they are not morally responsible for it. Some feminists add that sexual abuse/incest is most of all a method of gaining power over women beginning in childhood, the product of "physical and economic inequality between the sexes, power inequality between adults and children, and a lack of respect for children's right to bodily integrity." *Id.* at 499.

Does it matter whether the child is perceived as an innocent victim or as a seductress? Is it meaningful to attribute moral blame to the child? Do judgments about the appropriateness of the child's behavior affect the blameworthiness of the adult's?

6. Sexual abuse cases also frequently involve difficult evidentiary problems, such as whether abuse occurred at all and, if so, who the perpetrator was. These evidentiary issues are covered in Chapter 9.

PROBLEM

Your state has enacted the following definition of child sexual abuse:

> The term "sexual abuse" includes the following activities under circumstances which indicate that the child's health or welfare is harmed or threatened with harm: The employment, use, persuasion, inducement, enticement, or coercion of any child to engage in, or having a child assist any other person to engage in, any sexually explicit conduct (or any simulation of such conduct) for the purpose of producing any visual depiction of such conduct; or the rape, molestation, prostitution, or other form of sexual exploitation of children, or incest with children. With respect to the definition of sexual abuse, the term "child" or "children" means any individual who has not attained the age of eighteen.

Under this statute, is it sexual abuse to allow a 7-year-old to watch an X-rated movie? To allow a 14-year-old to watch an R-rated movie? To allow a 17-year-old to watch an X-rated movie?

Does a parent violate this statute by taking a bear-rug photograph of a baby? How about sexually suggestive photographs of older children? Are these art? Pornography? Sexual child abuse?

c. *Failure to Protect*

Many neglect cases can be described generally as instances of "failure to protect"—from dangerous conditions in the home, for example, although they are not described with that term. Instead, "failure to protect" is usually alleged when someone physically or sexually abuses a child and the child's parent does not act effectively to take the child to safety. Commonly that parent is the child's mother who is herself a victim of the person who has attacked the child. The next case is the first case of this type in New York in which courts admitted evidence of battered woman syndrome on behalf of the mother. Adriana Kohler, The Battered Mother's Struggle in New York: The Laws and Policies that Led to the Removal of Children from Their Abused Mothers Based on the Child's Exposure to Domestic Violence, 13 U. Pa. J.L. & Soc. Change 243, 253 (2009-2010).

In the Matter of Glenn G.

587 N.Y.S.2d 464 (Fam. Ct. Kings Cty. 1992)

Sara P. Schechter, J. ... This case came to the attention of the authorities on April 12, 1991 when the respondent mother went to the 68th Police Precinct to seek assistance after an incident of domestic violence. There she was referred to a worker with the Victim Services Agency, Barbara Anselmo. Ms. Anselmo testified that upon arrival respondent mother was pale, shaking, crying and incoherent. After about an hour, respondent mother became calm enough to speak and, in the ensuing discussion, asked if it was normal for a father to grab his children in the groin area, dance naked with them and take photos of them naked. Ms. Anselmo said, "No." After further discussion respondent mother was relocated to a battered women's shelter. The children were medically examined at Bellevue Hospital on April 19, 1991, following which a report of suspected child abuse or maltreatment (hereinafter 2221) was called in by the Bellevue social worker. . . .

The CWA [Child Welfare Administration] caseworker, Edris Juandoo, interviewed the respondent mother and the children on April 22, 1991. . . . Respondent mother recounted to the caseworker the same sort of touching she had described to Ms. Anselmo, and she told the caseworker that when she confronted the father about it, he threatened to kill her. . . .

Respondent mother is charged with sexual abuse, and, in the alternative, neglect, based on her failure to protect the children from the father's conduct described above. She asserts as a defense that she was a battered woman during the period when the abuse was occurring and asks that the charges against herself be dismissed. CWA and the Law Guardian argue that whether the mother was a battered woman is irrelevant, since they contend that the Family Court Act child protective article is a strict liability statute. . . .

The analysis of respondent mother's defense must commence with a preliminary review of the legal responsibility of the passive parent of a child who has been sexually abused. The passive parent is guilty of child abuse when she "allows" the abuse to be inflicted. Petitioner and the Law Guardian urge this court to adopt an objective standard for the conduct of the passive parent, by which the passive parent would be held to have "allowed" the abuse if she failed to act as a reasonable and prudent parent would have acted to protect the child. This argument fails to distinguish between a finding of abuse and one of neglect, however, and in several of the cases cited by petitioner and the Law Guardian in support of their strict liability argument the passive parent was actually found to have neglected rather than abused the child.

In a recent case which addresses the distinction between abuse and neglect it was held that when the passive parent is merely careless or negligent or inattentive, and by her failure to exercise a minimum degree of care leaves the child unprotected from the abusive parent, her conduct constitutes child neglect. "Neglect," as defined by Family Court Act § 1012(f)(i)(B) encompasses conduct which is not deliberate. Indeed, the definition of neglect includes failure to provide minimally adequate care due to the parent's mental illness or retardation, conditions for which the parent is entirely without fault.

The conduct of the passive parent of a sexually abused child may range across a wide spectrum. At one extreme is the parent who actually instigates the abuse or encourages the abuser; at the other extreme is the parent who has failed to notice nonspecific symptoms in the child such as frequent rashes or recurrent urinary tract infections. In between lie countless scenarios—a child who tries to confide in the passive parent and is rebuffed, a child who does confide and is disbelieved—through endless permutations of secrecy and deception. To label such variegated behavior as monolithic "abuse" would be arbitrary and insensitive and, in many instances, would needlessly stigmatize the passive parent without providing any greater protective or dispositional alternatives than would be available upon a finding of neglect. Instead, in determining where on the abuse-neglect spectrum the liability of a particular respondent lies, the court should use two coordinates: the passive parent's knowledge or awareness of the actions of the abusive parent, and second, the passive parent's actual ability to intervene to protect the child.

The first is not in dispute in the instant case, as respondent mother testified that she had witnessed numerous instances of improper touching of both children by the father over a period of years. The issue of her ability to protect the children, however, is heavily contested. Unlike the issue of a passive parent's degree of knowledge, which has been extensively litigated, the question of the parent's ability to protect has received little judicial attention. In the case at bar, respondent mother does not claim that she was afflicted with a mental illness or a physical disability which rendered her unable to protect the children. Rather, she asserts that she was unable to take appropriate action because she was suffering from "Battered Woman's Syndrome."

Respondent mother established by convincing evidence that during her relationship with respondent father she was a battered woman. She testified to an escalating pattern of abuse, which began soon after the couple began living together. . . .

After the birth of the first child, Mr. G. became more menacing. Although he sent Mrs. G. out to shop and do laundry, he would never permit her to take the baby because he believed that the child would be kidnapped. He lacked patience to care for the baby himself, however, so that when Mrs. G. returned from some errand, he would scream at her for having been gone too long. The first instance of actual physical abuse occurred when Mrs. G. returned from such an errand and found Mr. G. inappropriately touching Josephine. When she grabbed the baby away and began to yell at the father, he hit her in the mouth, causing her lip to bleed. At that point Mrs. G. realized that she should get away, and within a few weeks, in May 1987, she took Josephine and went to the home of her sister in Florida.

While in Florida she gave birth to the second child, Glenn. Mr. G., who had located the mother by phoning around to hospitals in the area but told the mother he had hired a detective to find her, arrived at the mother's bedside the day after Glenn's birth. He was tearful and apologetic, said he knew the problems were his fault and that he was getting counseling. After the mother returned to her sister's house, he kept up such a campaign of telephonic harassment that the mother finally felt she was imposing on her sister. Mr. G. sent a ticket, and Mrs. G. and the children returned to New York around the end of June 1987.

Following the return to New York, the domestic situation worsened. Mrs. G. learned that Mr. G. was not in therapy and neither did he plan to be. The physical abuse became more frequent and more intense. Mrs. G. described Mr. G. as being "like a time bomb." Mr. G. would throw objects at Mrs. G., would punch and kick her, would bang her head against the wall. He threatened to do worse, and bragged about his strength and his mastery of martial arts, boasts which he reiterated during his testimony at trial. . . .

Respondent mother's efforts to protect herself and the children after her return from Florida were meager. She began to call 911 once, but did not give the operator her address. She confided in her mother-in-law, who said she should just endure her situation and that Mr. G.'s father had been the same way. She stayed for days at a time at her mother-in-law's home with the children. She mentioned Josephine's frequent vaginal rashes to the pediatrician, but did not tell him of any sex abuse. She attempted to intervene when Mr. G. was behaving inappropriately with the children, but he told her, "Butt out, that's how you get hurt so much." . . .

Respondent mother produced two expert witnesses who testified about the condition known as "Battered Woman's Syndrome." Ms. Anselmo, qualified as an expert by virtue of her experience, described the syndrome as "a breaking down of a woman's self confidence and self respect to a point where she no longer knows if she is crazy or not." She stated typically the cycle begins with psychological abuse, as it did with the Gs., builds to extreme tension followed by a violent episode and then a "honeymoon period," in which the batterer apologizes, promises to do better and begs the woman not to leave. Mr. G.'s behavior when he found Mrs. G. in Florida is typical of the contrite phase. Over time the honeymoons get shorter and the violent periods expand. The battered woman experiences a sense of isolation, and often actually is socially isolated and confined to the home, which was true in Mrs. G.'s case. As the syndrome progresses, the woman loses confidence in her judgment, as Mrs. G. did, and starts to believe that she must be the one who is crazy. Based on her observations of Mrs. G. in the police station and in the days immediately following, Ms. Anselmo testified that in her opinion Mrs. G. had been a battered woman for a long period of time.

The second expert on the subject was Valerie Bryant, a certified social worker and doctoral candidate at New York University who has for six years run a therapy group for battered women. Ms. Bryant was qualified as an expert by virtue of both her education and experience. Ms. Bryant testified that Mrs. G. is definitely a battered woman, who experienced much abuse on many levels—verbal, physical, and sexual. . . .

Ms. Bryant described the cycle of domestic violence as Ms. Anselmo had done, and stated her opinion that the role of the mother-in-law in urging Mrs. G. to "bear with it" was very instrumental in undermining respondent mother's sense of self-worth and in reinforcing her sense of helplessness, particularly because she was estranged from her own family. Mrs. G., therefore, came to see herself as having few options. She lost the ability to protect herself, and thus lost the ability to protect the children as well. Ms. Bryant also noted that Mrs. G.'s dilemma is not uncommon, as a correlation between spousal abuse and child abuse is generally recognized among professionals who work with battered women and that in her opinion the two forms of abuse share very similar psychodynamics.

Several State and Federal courts have admitted evidence concerning Battered Woman's Syndrome. Most often such evidence has been offered in support of some form of self-defense claim by a woman who assaulted or killed the man who had been battering her. Occasionally it has been used to establish a lack of criminal intent (*mens rea*) or to assist the jury in assessing the credibility of the battered woman's testimony, as when, for example, she may have recanted her charges against the abusive man. Although accounts have appeared from time to time in the news media of a "Battered Woman's Syndrome defense" being offered in cases where a mother has been criminally charged for having failed to protect her children from an abusive father or live-in lover, these cases do not appear to have resulted in reported judicial decisions.

Although no New York decisions have been reported in which respondent asserted the Battered Woman's Syndrome defense in the context of a child protective case, there are a few such decisions from other States. The Supreme Court of Appeals of West Virginia ruled in Interest of Betty J.W. (179 W. Va. 605, 371 S.E.2d 326 [1988]) that it was error to terminate the parental rights of a mother who had failed to protect her children from physical and sexual abuse by their father. The court held that the child protective agency should have provided services to help the mother attempt to overcome the effects of "classic spouse abuse," particularly her tendency to place the children at renewed risk by reconciling with the abusive spouse.

This court is in accord with those who have recognized that Battered Woman's Syndrome is a condition which seriously impairs the will and the judgment of the victim. The abused should not be branded as abuser. Respondent mother in the case at bar clearly did not condone the sexual abuse of the children by the respondent father, but rather, due to her affliction with Battered Woman's Syndrome, was powerless to stop it. She cannot be said to have "allowed" the abuse within the meaning of Family Court Act § 1012(e)(iii). Accordingly, the child abuse charges against the respondent mother herein are dismissed. The neglect statute, however, imposes strict liability. As respondent mother's actions were manifestly inadequate to protect the children from the father's ongoing abuse, of which she was well aware, a finding of neglect must be entered against her.

BRYAN A. LIANG & WENDY L. MACFARLANE, *MURDER BY OMISSION: CHILD ABUSE AND THE PASSIVE PARENT*

36 Harv. J. on Legis. 397, 440-443 (1999)

The parent/child relationship exhibits a unique paradox—children are most vulnerable to abuse by the very persons who have the highest duty to protect them, their parents. As one court has stated,

> [A] parent's failure to take appropriate steps to protect their child from the abuse of the other parent is tantamount to neglect of that child, not to mention moral complicity with the base crime being perpetrated upon the child by the other parent. In

a situation where it is the other parent perpetrating the abuse upon the child, the non-abusing parent is under an even greater duty to take steps necessary to prevent the abuse. First, the parent has a higher probability of knowing about the abuse because he or she lives with both the victim and the abuser. Second, the relationship of the child-victim to the parent-abuser presents additional problems that do not arise when the abuser is a stranger. Due to the added problems inherent in a parent-child abuse situation, the non-abusing parent, as the only advocate for the child, has a greater responsibility to prevent such abuse when it becomes or should have become evident to that parent. . . .

The parent who fails to protect her child must be held accountable for her omission. When there is a history of child abuse, BWS should be no defense. The law holds much more attenuated parties, such as physicians, educators and other third parties, responsible for not reporting child abuse. Those with the highest duty and the most special relationship to the child should be accountable. . . .

A parent who fails to protect her child from abuse is no more a "loving and good parent" than the abuser. . . . One who intentionally places herself in an abusive relationship should not be characterized as a victim of that relationship.

G. KRISTIAN MICCIO, *A REASONABLE BATTERED MOTHER? REDEFINING, RECONSTRUCTING, AND RECREATING THE BATTERED MOTHER IN CHILD PROTECTIVE PROCEEDINGS*

22 Harv. Women's L.J. 89, 93, 109 (1999)

. . . [T]he socially constructed paradigm of mothering leaves no accommodation for the battered mother. Within this construct, the "good mother" is selfless and deferential. The needs and desires of fathers and children define her existence. The "bad" or "evil" mother is one who insinuates her independent self into the familial picture, permitting her needs to co-exist with those of familial members.

Cultural inscriptions of the "good mother" require women to place themselves outside the ambit of self-concern. Consequently, a woman who constructs a self independent from that of her children or from the father or husband does not conform to socially accepted notions of mothering or of motherhood. Battered women, then, who struggle for individual survival, as well as for the survival of their children, are bad mothers and transformed into cultural pariahs. . . .

We know that violence against mothers and children escalates at the point of separation from the batterer. Homicides and serious injury to mothers and children occur when battered mothers attempt to leave or to assert a self independent from that of the batterer. Thus, a mother's decision to remain in an abusive relationship may be based strategically on the inherent dangers that leaving the abuser may pose to both mother and child. The "positive value placed on leaving ignores the fact that domestic violence is a struggle for control and overlooks the extreme dangers of separation." Yet, judicial inquiry that focuses solely on "the results of [maternal] efforts" rather than on efforts made to protect children within the context of the violence, places mothers and children at greater risk of harm—harms that society is still loathe to *prevent*.

NOTES AND QUESTIONS

1. The juvenile court has jurisdiction over both abused and neglected children, and, as we will see in the next section, the court's authority in both kinds of cases is similar. The distinction may have great significance in other legal contexts, as, for example, where a parent is criminally prosecuted for failure to protect a child. *See* Chapter 9.

2. The *Glenn G.* court says that children may be found neglected and so subject to state control even if their parents are *unable* to protect them. Why is this so?

If a parent was not even aware that a child was in danger, could the court still find the child neglected on a failure-to-protect theory?

3. Is a mother who suffers from battered woman syndrome unable to protect her children? If she has not decided to leave? If she is ready to leave but lacks the resources?

PROBLEM

When Mother and Father were divorced, Mother was awarded custody, and Father was granted visitation rights every Saturday afternoon. Last Saturday when Father came for his weekly visit, he was visibly intoxicated. Mother tried to convince him to come back later after he was sober, but Father became angry, grabbed the children, and drove off in his car. Two miles away his automobile was in an accident caused by his intoxication, and he and the children were seriously injured. Is Mother guilty of failure to protect the children? If Mother and Father were not divorced and were living together and this was just the most recent of many incidents in which Father had driven with the children while he was intoxicated, would your answer change? Why or why not?

d. *Exposure to Domestic Violence*

In the Interest of K.M.

889 N.W.2d 701 (Iowa App. 2016)

Danilson, Chief Judge. . . . The mother came to the attention of the department of human services (DHS) in August 2015, after P.B.'s father, N.B., assaulted the mother and injured P.B. in the process. The mother was holding P.B. when the father hit the mother and pushed her onto a bed. P.B., who was only a few months old at the time, received a mark on her forehead in the altercation. K.M. was also present during the assault. A confirmed child-abuse assessment was completed naming the father as the person responsible.

DHS completed another child-abuse assessment after a January 2016 incident during which the father hit the mother across the face at a laundromat. P.B. was present during the altercation. The mother called the police. While being arrested, the father resisted and forcefully hit an officer in the face, causing the officer to become unconscious. The resulting child-abuse assessment was founded for denial of critical care, lack of adequate supervision, with the father named as the person responsible.

Voluntary services began in March 2016. The mother participated in Family Safety, Risk, and Permanency (FSRP) and Partners United for Supportive Housing (PUSH) services. Although she was encouraged to do so, the mother did not immediately seek counseling services to address the domestic violence issues. The mother initially stated she did not understand how domestic violence could be child abuse. The mother shared with DHS social workers that her relationship with K.M.'s father had also been violent and she had also witnessed her mother involved in violent relationships when she was a child.

In May 2016, the mother and the father were involved in another violent altercation. During an argument, the father pushed the mother onto the floor and held his hands over her nose and mouth until she could not breathe. The father also received minor scratches to his face and neck in the altercation. The mother was pregnant with the father's child at the time of the incident. Both K.M. and P.B. were present during the assault. The mother notified a DHS social worker of the incident, and the DHS social worker completed a safety check. The DHS social worker reported that K.M. stated he was scared and he saw his mother get hurt. The mother also called the police. Both the mother and the father were arrested for domestic abuse, but the charges against the mother were later dropped. DHS completed another founded child-abuse assessment as a result of the altercation, citing the mother and the father as the persons responsible.

After each of the August 2015, January 2016, and May 2016 domestic-violence incidents, no-contact orders were put into place to protect the mother and the children from the father. Each time, the mother filed requests to cancel the no-contact orders.

The mother began counseling services sometime after the May 2016 incident. Despite the mother's initial steadfast refusal to begin counseling, her counselor testified at the adjudication hearing that the mother was very engaged in the counseling services. However, also sometime after the May 2016 incident, the mother and the father married. DHS was not aware of the marriage until June 2016, when the children's maternal grandmother reported the marriage due to her concern regarding the mother's continuing relationship with the father.

The CINA petition was filed on May 17, 2016. A combined adjudicatory/dispositional hearing was held July 28, 2016.

At the time of the adjudicatory/dispositional hearing, the father was incarcerated. His attorney opined, twenty-one months "would be the absolute earliest he could realistically expect to be paroled." The mother maintains her relationship with the father; communicates with him regularly; and is seeking to be a placement for another child who is a CINA, born to the father and another woman.

In its adjudicatory and dispositional order, the juvenile court determined:

It is critical to the safety of her children that [the mother] engages in domestic violence counseling and internalizes how incidents of domestic violence impact her children. [The mother] has a long history of exposure to domestic violence from her own childhood exposure through her mother's poor relationships to her own domestically violent adult relationships with [N.B.] and [K.M.'s father]. The fact that [N.B.] is in jail does not cure the issue. It is concerning that [the mother] . . . had no-contact orders put into place for her protection but very quickly lifted so she could resume a relationship with her attacker. [The mother] does not believe her children are negatively impacted by exposure to domestic violence. She lacks an understanding of the trauma it causes her children to be exposed to violence.

The court also noted a DHS social worker's testimony that she believed without the CINA adjudication and judicial oversight, the mother would not continue participating in voluntary services. The court held the State established by clear and convincing evidence K.M. and P.B. should be adjudicated as CINA pursuant to section 232.2(6)(c)(2).

Our review of CINA proceedings is de novo. "In reviewing the proceedings, we are not bound by the juvenile court's fact findings; however, we do give them weight." "Our primary concern is the children's best interests."

The mother asserts the juvenile court erred in adjudicating the children as CINA pursuant to section 232.2(6)(c)(2). She argues because the father was incarcerated at the time of the adjudicatory hearing, the State could not present clear and convincing evidence the children were imminently likely to suffer harm. She also argues there was no indication she would not continue participating in voluntary services if the children were not adjudicated CINA.

Section 232.2(6)(c)(2) provides a child in need of assistance is one who "has suffered or is imminently likely to suffer harmful effects as a result of ... [t]he failure of the child's parent, . . . to exercise a reasonable degree of care in supervising the child." CINA adjudication determinations must be based upon clear and convincing evidence.

We agree with the juvenile court and find there is clear and convincing evidence establishing grounds for adjudication under section 232.2(6)(c)(2). P.B. was physically injured during the August 2015 domestic-abuse altercation. Although the mother was the victim in all three incidents, she has an obligation to provide reasonable care to her children, including providing for their safety. The mother knew P.B. was injured in the first reported abuse incident. She was also supervising the children when K.M. was present during two of the documented incidents of domestic violence, and P.B. was present for all three. Further, K.M. expressed understanding of the events he had witnessed stating directly after the May 2016 incident and again at a family team meeting held to discuss the incident that he saw his mother get hurt.

Notwithstanding these facts, the mother has been unable to overcome the cycle of violence and continues to maintain a relationship with the abuser, the father, who is now incarcerated. In fact, she married him. Because she has maintained her relationship with the father and sought cancellation of three no-contact orders in spite of continued abuse in the presence of the children, along with the injury to one child, the mother has failed to exercise a reasonable degree of care in supervising the children. P.B. has suffered harmful effects, and K.M. is imminently likely to suffer harmful effects as a result of the mother's failure to exercise a reasonable degree of care in supervising the children by ensuring they are protected from being injured during domestic altercations. Thus, we find clear and convincing evidence supports ground for adjudication under section 232.2(6)(c)(2).

By all accounts the mother is a good mother to her children. We commend the mother's participation in voluntary services and engagement in domestic-violence counseling. We sympathize with the mother's own history, but she needs to fully understand and overcome the cycle of violence she has experienced. We find little solace in the father's incarceration because, without fully addressing her issues with perpetrators of domestic violence, the mother lacks the ability to safeguard her children and prevent another abuser from entering her life in the father's absence. . . .

AFFIRMED.

JANET E. FINDLATER & SUSAN KELLY, *CHILD PROTECTIVE SERVICES AND DOMESTIC VIOLENCE*

9(3) Future of Children 84, 87-88 (1999)

For years, domestic violence service programs and CPS have worked with families experiencing both forms of abuse, but until recently they had not begun working together to create safe, appropriate, and effective responses to family violence. The relationship between child welfare workers and battered women's advocates has been difficult, at best. Mistrust has been common, noncollaboration the rule.

A significant obstacle to collaboration has been the tension caused by the different historical developments and missions of the domestic violence and child welfare movements. As stated above, the domestic violence movement began less than 30 years ago in order to provide safety to battered women because public institutions were not doing so. The criminal justice system did not treat domestic violence as a crime. Batterers were not being held accountable for their abuse. Some battered women and their advocates viewed CPS as yet another public institution that overlooked domestic violence and the needs of battered women, or blamed battered women for the harm their batterers caused to their children.

The mistrust has existed on both sides. Because of CPS's focus on the safety of the child, caseworkers did not consider the identification of domestic violence to be important to accomplishing CPS goals. When domestic violence was identified, CPS workers have often misunderstood its dynamics and held battered mothers responsible for ending it. Furthermore, as the domestic violence movement has focused primarily on the needs of battered women, and been slower to directly address the needs of these women's children, CPS workers have not viewed battered women's advocates as potential allies in their efforts to protect children.

NOTES AND QUESTIONS

1. What harm or risk of harm did the children face that justified juvenile court intervention?

Defining child maltreatment to include allowing children to witness domestic violence, even though they themselves are not hit, is based on the following claims:

(a) Being in a household in which adults abuse each other increases the risk that the child will be physically abused. Estimates of the overlap between children who witness men battering the children's mothers and children who are themselves battered by the men range from 30 to 60 percent. Jeffrey L. Edelson, The Overlap Between Child Maltreatment and Woman Battering, 5(2) Violence Against

Women, 134 (1999); Anne E. Appel & George W. Holden, The Co-Occurrence of Spouse and Physical Child Abuse: A Review and Appraisal, 12 J. Fam. Psych. 578 (1998). Battered women are much more likely to use harsh physical punishment or to be abusive physically than other mothers are. Murray A. Straus, Richard J. Gelles & Suzanne K. Steinmetz, Behind Closed Doors: Violence in the American Family 216-217 (1988). Women are eight times more likely to abuse children when the women are being battered than when they are not. Lenore Walker, The Battered Woman Syndrome 60 (1984). Fifty-three percent of men who abused their mates abused their children, and 28 percent of women who were abused abused their children. *Id.* at 59. The National Survey of Children's Exposure to Violence found that more than a third of children who had witnessed domestic violence had been maltreated in the past year, compared to 8.6 percent of children who had not witnessed such violence. Sherry Hamby et al., The Overlap of Witnessing Partner Violence with Child Maltreatment and Other Victimizations in a Nationally Representative Survey of Youth, 34 Child Abuse & Neglect 734 (2010).

(b) Children in violent homes may be neglected by parents who are focused on their partners or unresponsive to their children due to their own fears. Child Welfare Information Gateway, In Harm's Way: Domestic Violence and Child Maltreatment (1999).

(c) Children who witness parental violence have more aggressive, antisocial, and fearful behavior; more anxiety, aggression, depression, and temperamental problems; less empathy and self-esteem; and lower verbal, cognitive, and motor abilities. They may also carry violence and acceptance of violence into their adult relationships. Susan Schechter & Jeffrey L. Edleson, In the Best Interest of Women and Children: A Call for Collaboration Between Child Welfare and Domestic Violence Constituencies (1994), available at http://www.mincava.umn.edu/papers/wingsp.htm, reprinted at 11(3) Protecting Children 6-11 (1995) (surveying literature). On the other hand, studies also show that a majority of children who are exposed to domestic violence are not harmed. One study found that more than 80 percent of children "retain their overall psychological integrity," and the effects of harm tend to dissipate over time if the batterer is removed. Evan Stark, The Battered Mother in the Child Protective Service Caseload: Developing an Appropriate Response, 23 Women's Rts. L. Rep. 107, 116 (2002).

2. What more should the mother be required to do, and why?

3. In 1999 the National Council of Juvenile and Family Court Judges published a set of guidelines (called the Greenbook for its green cover) intended to define best practices for child welfare agencies, domestic violence service providers, and juvenile courts to work together when it was alleged that children were exposed to domestic violence at home. A key proposal was that "As a way to ensure stability and permanency for children, child welfare administrators and juvenile court personnel should try to keep children affected by maltreatment and domestic violence in the care of their non-offending parent (or parents), whenever possible. Making adult victims safer and stopping batterers' assaults are two important ways to remove risk and thereby create permanency for children." Principle I, Recommendation 2, Effective Intervention in Domestic Violence and Child Maltreatment Cases: Guidelines for Policy and Practice 14 (1999), https://rcdvcpc.org/resources/resource/effective-intervention-in-domestic-violence-child-maltreatment-cases-guidelines-for-policy-and-pract.html.

In 2000, the Departments of Justice and Health and Human Services awarded grants to demonstration projects in six counties to implement the Greenbook principles. The final evaluation report, which was never officially published, found that people at the sites undertook "major collaborative efforts" to implement the recommended practices. Child welfare agencies increased screening for domestic violence and identified more cases. However, the evaluation found little change in how juvenile courts handled the cases, and generally "[c]hange was challenging to achieve and sustain." The Greenbook National Evaluation Team, The Greenbook Initiative Final Evaluation Report, Ch. 1 (Feb. 2008), https://www.ncjrs.gov/pdffiles1/nij/grants/233290.pdf.

4. Following an appeal in a lawsuit challenging how the City of New York's child welfare system responded to domestic violence cases, particularly policies to remove children from custodial parents upon a finding of domestic violence in the home, the parties settled the case. Since the litigation's completion, the city child welfare agency has removed fewer children and charged fewer mothers with neglect solely because the children were exposed to domestic violence. Courts have reversed findings of neglect that were not supported by specific findings about the kind and extent of domestic violence to which children were exposed and the impact on the children, and the state is more frequently charging batterers with neglect for exposing children to domestic violence. Kathleen A. Copps, Comment: The Good, the Bad, and the Future of Nicholson v. Scoppetta: An Analysis of the Effects and Suggestions for Further Improvements, 72 Alb. L. Rev. 497, 510-512 (2009). *See also* Jaime Perrone, Failing to Realize Nicholson's Vision: How New York's Child Welfare System Continues to Punish Battered Mothers, 20 J.L. & Pol'y 641 (2012); Myrna S. Raeder, Preserving Family Ties for Domestic Violence Survivors and Their Children by Invoking a Human Rights Approach to Avoid the Criminalization of Mothers Based on the Acts and Accusations of Their Batterers, 17 J. Gender Race & Just. 105 (2014); Evan Stark, Nicholson v. Williams Revisited: When Good People Do Bad Things, 82 Denv. U. L. Rev. 691 (2005).

5. Many more children are exposed to domestic violence than are the subjects of juvenile court child protection cases. The National Survey of Children's Exposure to Violence (a nationally representative telephone survey) found that 26 percent of all children are exposed to family violence at least once during their lives; each year about 11 percent are exposed to some kind of family violence incident, and 6.6 percent are exposed to violence between parents or a parent and the parent's partner. Sherry Hamby et al., Children's Exposure to Intimate Partner Violence and Other Family Violence 1 (Office of Juvenile Justice and Delinquency Prevention, Oct. 2011), https://www.ncjrs.gov/pdffiles1/ojjdp/232272.pdf. A study based on 2001 data estimated that about 30 percent of all children younger than 18 lived in households in which at least one incident of domestic violence between adults occurred during their lifetimes. About 13 percent of all children experienced severe violence, defined as one or more of the following acts: "kicked, bit, or hit"; "hit or tried to hit with something"; "beat up"; "choked"; "burned or scalded"; "forced sex"; "threatened with a knife or gun" or "used a knife or gun." Renee McDonald et al., Estimating the Number of American Children Living in Partner-Violent Families, 20 J. Fam. Psych. 137, 138 – 139 (2006).

PROBLEM

Mr. and Mrs. Vulon and their three children—Maurice, 13; Marie, 10; and Michelle, 8—immigrated to New York City from Haiti. One day when Mr. Vulon was at work and Mrs. Vulon was next door at the neighbor's, Marie heard Michelle exclaim from the bathroom and saw she was bleeding. Marie ran to get Mrs. Vulon, who took Michelle to the hospital. The emergency room doctor found that Michelle's vagina was lacerated, and he suspected some kind of sexual abuse. Suspicion fell on Maurice, who had been in the bathroom with Michelle. Mr. and Mrs. Vulon refused to believe that Michelle had been raped and refused to discuss the incident with their children, explaining that in their country, children did not learn about sex until they were 15 years old. The hospital reported the case to the child protective services. When the case was more fully investigated, it turned out that Michelle had not been raped and that her wound could have been self-inflicted. However, the worker could not get any further information about the incident from anyone in the family. The worker recommended that Michelle be examined by a juvenile court-affiliated psychologist, but the parents declined. The worker also learned that Maurice aspires to be a priest and that he is the apple of his parents' eye. The worker is concerned that Mr. and Mrs. Vulon may be covering up wrongdoing by Maurice and is particularly suspicious of their refusal to cooperate with the investigation. Should the state intervene to protect Michelle? How?

e.   *Physical and Emotional Neglect*

The great majority of children reported and found to be maltreated are neglected rather than abused. Physical neglect is typically said to include abandonment, inadequate supervision, failure to protect children from hazards, and failure to provide adequate food, clothing, or shelter (including "empty cupboards" and cold or dirty houses). By way of illustrating the potential breadth of this category, the Children's Bureau includes in its definition of physical neglect "the desertion of a child without arranging for his reasonable care or supervision, . . . the blatant refusal of custody, such as the permanent or indefinite expulsion of a child from the home, without adequately arranging for his care by others or the refusal to accept custody of a returned runaway, shuttling—when a child is repeatedly left in the custody of others for days or weeks at a time, possibly due to the unwillingness of the parent or the caregiver to maintain custody, nutritional neglect—when a child is undernourished or is repeatedly hungry for long periods of time, which can sometimes be evidenced by poor growth, . . . clothing neglect—when a child lacks appropriate clothing, such as not having appropriately warm clothes or shoes in the winter, and other physical neglect—includes inadequate hygiene and forms of reckless disregard for the child's safety and welfare (e.g., driving while intoxicated with the child, leaving a young child in a car unattended)," Diane DePanfilis, Child Neglect: A Guide for Prevention, Assessment and Intervention (2006), available at https://www.childwelfare.gov/pubs/usermanuals/neglect/.

"Emotional neglect" includes "failure to thrive" cases, in which very young children literally waste away, apparently because their parents emotionally reject them and withhold physical contact and other expressions of affection from them. *See generally* Dexter M. Bullard, Jr., et al., Failure to Thrive in the "Neglected" Child, 37 Am. J. Orthopsychiatry 680 (1967). More broadly, "emotional neglect" includes ignoring, rejecting, verbally assaulting, isolating, terrorizing, or corrupting or exploiting a child. American Humane Assn., Child Neglect, available at www.americanhumane.org/children/stop-child-abuse/fact-sheets/child-neglect. html. Because of this category's vagueness and obvious potential for intrusiveness, it is not as popular a criterion for legal intervention as it once was. However, in the view of people who believe that healthy emotional development is among the most important needs of a child, the kind of parental behavior included here is potentially the most damaging.

STATE IN THE INTEREST OF B.M.

201 So.3d 974 (La. App. 2016)

CARAWAY, J. . . . On November 27, 2015, a person reported to the State of Louisiana, Department of Child and Family Services ("DCFS"), regarding physical abuse/tying or confinement of a two-year-old boy, B.M. In the report, it was alleged that B.M.'s parents left him in a bedroom 90% of the day. It was further alleged that the parents reside in a travel trailer and that the room in which B.M. is locked is only big enough for a full-size bed. It was asserted that the parents neglect B.M. by not caring for his hygiene and that he has very poor speech because the parents do not communicate with him.

On December 1, 2015, LaShunda Prim ("Prim"), a child protection investigator at the DCFS, escorted by Caddo Parish Sheriff Deputy Mike McConnell, went to the address of B.M.'s parents as provided in the report. When they entered the trailer, Deputy McConnell arrested the parents after marijuana was found inside. The mother was charged with possession of marijuana, illegal use of a controlled dangerous substance in the presence of a child under 17 years, and prohibited acts-use/possession of drug paraphernalia. The father was charged with the same offenses, except he was charged with a second possession of marijuana offense.

As Deputy McConnell arrested B.M.'s parents, Prim contacted and placed B.M. with his paternal grandmother and step-grandfather. The following day, December 2, 2015, the DCFS filed an instanter order, attached with the affidavit of Prim. The instanter order specified that B.M. would remain placed with his paternal grandmother and step-grandfather pending the custody hearing. The trial court granted this order, issuing temporary custody to the DCFS. . . .

On January 6, 2016, the DCFS filed a petition seeking to have B.M. adjudicated as a child in need of care as defined by La. Ch. C. art. 606, *et seq*. On March 7, 2016, the DCFS presented the case plan to the juvenile court. In the case plan, the DCFS stated that the goal was reunification. At the March 15, 2016 adjudication hearing, Prim, Deputy McConnell, and B.M.'s paternal grandmother each testified.

Prim testified that when she and Deputy McConnell arrived at the address, she saw that the front property was inhabited by B.M.'s paternal grandfather and step-grandmother and that B.M. and his parents resided in a travel trailer in the back of the property. Thereafter, she stated that she noticed that the ground leading to the back of the property and up to the trailer was wet. She said that upon further inspection, she realized that the wetness covering the ground was raw sewage and that it was coming from underneath the trailer. She also claimed that it was impossible to avoid as they walked up to the trailer.

Upon entry, she testified that she saw that the parents were sitting in camping chairs and that B.M. was crawling on the floor. Prim stated that she felt that the trailer was very small and noticed that it had only a living room and a bedroom. She also stated that she saw dirty dishes in the kitchen sink. She testified that the entrance into the bedroom was a half door that stopped at her waist, which she felt would prevent a small child from leaving the room. Inside the bedroom, she stated that there was a mattress and a small pallet next to the mattress. She testified that she believed that due to the small size of the trailer, she did not feel it was a fit location for B.M. to be living. However, she stated that B.M. appeared to be healthy. She testified that B.M. was examined by a pediatrician on December 8, 2015, and his examination revealed he was healthy. She also stated that after the arrest, the parents and B.M. were tested for drugs and the father tested positive for T.H.C., but the mother and B.M. tested negative.

Deputy McConnell also testified that he saw the raw sewage leading to the trailer and his description of the trailer matched Prim's. He stated that as soon as he entered the trailer, he noticed that B.M.'s father quickly placed his cell phone on what Deputy McConnell suspected was a marijuana cigarette. He testified that he immediately seized the marijuana cigarette and arrested the parents. Consequently, he stated that they waived their *Miranda* rights and elected to give statements. Deputy McConnell testified that the father told him that the marijuana cigarette belonged to him, not the mother, and that they never smoked in the presence of B.M. However, Deputy McConnell stated that the mother told him that they had smoked marijuana the day before in B.M.'s presence. Additionally, Deputy McConnell testified that the father gave him a Ziploc bag containing about 3 ½ grams of marijuana. Similar to Prim, Deputy McConnell also stated B.M. appeared to be well taken care of, describing him as a "little chubby little thing."

The paternal grandmother testified that when B.M. came into her care on December 1, 2015, he was healthy and did not have poor hygiene. She testified that she took B.M. to the doctor a week after he arrived and that there were no health concerns. She further stated that she had no concerns about B.M. being returned to his parents and that he cries when his parents leave after visitation.

After hearing the testimonies, the court requested the position of the attorney representing B.M.:

> [B.M.'s attorney]: The child's position is that this child is not in need of care. When the State initially went out to investigate this matter, they went out to investigate some report of physical abuse, tying, or confinement. [Your honor] heard the evidence. None was presented. There was no finding indicating that physical abuse or tying or confinement of this child occurred.

Thereafter, the juvenile court determined that B.M. was not in need of care, vacated the DCFS's custody, and returned custody to B.M.'s parents. The court reasoned as follows:

> The court does not find that the evidence warrants an adjudication in this case.
> There was a moment, a moment, when the child was in need of care in order to transit from the parents, as they were being arrested[,] to [B.M.'s paternal

grandmother]; but I don't find that the evidence in this case warrants a child in need of care adjudication at this time.

I would caution [the parents] that if you have not fixed that sewage problem by this time, B.M. need not to be there. So you need to make sure that B.M. stays with [his paternal grandmother] until you have a suitable place for the child to live.

The DCFS has appealed this judgment. . . . [The appellate court affirmed the trial court order, and DCFS appealed. The court granted rehearing.]

ON REHEARING

CARAWAY, J. We now grant rehearing for reconsideration of the juvenile court's failure to enter an adjudication order. The juvenile court's judgment was incomplete, being conditioned upon the sanitation status of the parents' trailer and home for the child. The State argues on rehearing that the burden of proof rested on the parents in defense to prove that the current state of the dwelling had changed from its prior condition with raw sewage in violation of the Sanitation Code. We agree. The juvenile court's judgment left that important issue unresolved and therefore requires the entry of an adjudication order and the continued monitoring by the State for the child's welfare, which is the overriding purpose of the child in need of care proceeding. That proceeding should therefore continue. The juvenile court judgment is therefore reversed, and it is hereby ordered that the evidence warrants a child in need of care adjudication for this child. ...

PITMAN, J., concurring in the decision reversing the trial court. . . . [In addition to restating the facts set out above, this opinion adds other facts from the record:] [Prim] testified that she . . . visited both parents in jail. B.M.'s father admitted that the marijuana was his, that it did not belong to his wife and that he had never smoked marijuana around B.M. The father submitted to a drug test, which was positive for marijuana. She stated that B.M.'s mother appeared not to know what was going on and was placed in the mental health unit of the jail due to suffering from depression. The mother submitted to a drug test and the results were negative. She stated that B.M. was also tested for drugs and that the test results were negative. She noted that B.M. appeared to be healthy but that there was not enough room in the travel trailer for him to move around.

On cross-examination, Ms. Prim stated that B.M. was not locked in the bedroom when she arrived at the trailer. She testified that B.M. received an examination from a state physician and was declared healthy. . . .

On cross-examination, B.M.'s paternal grandmother stated that she does have concerns about drugs being used around B.M. She noted that B.M. and his parents had lived in the travel trailer for approximately nine months and that it was supposed to be temporary housing. She stated that when his parents leave after their visitation, B.M. cries and looks for them. . . .

The grounds for finding a child to be in need of care are set forth in La. Ch. C. art. 606. Allegations that a child is in need of care must assert one or more of the grounds. In the case of B.M., it was alleged that he was a victim of neglect. La. Ch. C. art. 603(18) defines "neglect," in part, as follows:

> "Neglect" means the refusal or unreasonable failure of a parent or caretaker to supply the child with necessary food, clothing, shelter, care, treatment, or counseling for any injury, illness, or condition of the child, as a result of which the child's physical, mental, or emotional health and safety is substantially threatened or impaired.... Consistent with Article 606(B), the inability of a parent or caretaker to provide for a child due to inadequate financial resources shall not, for that reason alone, be considered neglect.

Adjudication of a child in need of care is warranted when a parent shows a repeated pattern of placing a child at risk and exposing a child to a lack of adequate shelter. At the adjudication hearing, the state bears the burden of proving by a preponderance of the evidence that the child is a child in need of care. . . .

The physical health, welfare, and safety of B.M. were substantially at risk of harm due to the conditions in which he was living while in the custody of his parents. Raw sewage surrounded the entry into the travel trailer, B.M.'s father possessed marijuana inside the travel trailer and B.M.'s mother admitted that she and his father had smoked marijuana when B.M. was present.

The trial court did not adjudicate B.M. a child in need of care, but it admonished B.M.'s parents that B.M. should not return to the travel trailer until the sewage problem was fixed and that B.M. should remain with his paternal grandmother until they had a "wholesome, appropriate" place for B.M. to live. These actions by the juvenile court are inconsistent.[1]

The juvenile court was clearly concerned with B.M.'s living conditions and did not want B.M. to return to a home surrounded by sewage. Although it instructed B.M.'s parents that B.M. should remain with his paternal grandmother until they could provide an appropriate living situation for him, it did not put in place any procedures to ensure that the parents would comply with its admonition. We do not know if the living conditions of B.M. have improved. We do not know if the sewage problem has been remediated. We do not know if B.M.'s parents continue to use illegal drugs in his presence.

Therefore, the juvenile court should have adjudicated B.M. a child in need of care and implemented available procedures to protect his safety by ensuring that the living situation with his parents improved before returning him to their custody. If parents neglect to provide a safe environment for their child, it is incumbent on our courts with jurisdiction over families to do so.

I agree with this court's reversal of the juvenile court and determination that B.M. is a child in need of care. . . .

---

1. In coming to its decision, the juvenile court considered and accepted the attorney for B.M.'s argument that B.M. was not a child in need of care. However, the arguments made by B.M.'s attorney were not in B.M.'s best interest.

NOTES AND QUESTIONS

1. Was B.M. being harmed by his parents? If so, how? Was he at risk of harm? What kind of harm?

2. Should poor housekeeping be a basis for finding a child neglected? How should the "minimally adequate" standard be determined? What other concerns might support a finding of neglect in *B.M.*? Why weren't these other concerns charged and proven?

Using data from a multisite longitudinal study of the long-term effects of maltreatment on children, researchers found that dirty, unsafe houses were correlated with children being at risk for impaired language and communication development. Failure to provide food was associated with a mix of "withdrawn, social, aggressive, and delinquent behaviors and thought problems. Moreover, failure to provide adequate hygiene was associated with some symptoms of anxiety and depression as well as attention problems." Diana J. English et al., Toward a Definition of Neglect in Young Children, 10 Child Maltreatment 190 (2005).

Courts routinely uphold adjudications of neglect where the facts show that the child is living in a very dirty house strewn with trash and garbage. *See, e.g.*, In the Interest of L.M., 57 So. 3d 518 (La. App. 2011); In re D.H., 2010 WL 447060 (Ohio App. 2010); In re J.A., 2009 WL 325636 (Ohio App. 2009). *But see* In re M.O., 2010 WL 4110911 (Ohio App. 2010) (adjudication of neglect reversed for insufficient evidence; house dirty and had an odor, walls had holes in them). In South Carolina Dept. of Social Services v. Scott K, 668 S.E.2d 425 (S.C. App. 2008), the court reversed a finding of neglect where the house was very cluttered — but not "dirty."

3. A group of professors from a range of disciplines with expertise in early childhood and early brain development has proposed that neglect be defined as "the ongoing disruption or significant absence of caregiver responsiveness." National Scientific Council on the Developing Child, The Science of Neglect: The Persistent Absence of Responsive Care Disrupts the Developing Brain 2 (Harvard Center on the Developing Child Dec. 2012), available at developingchild.harvard. edu/index.php/download_file/-/view/1249/. They argue that this kind of deprivation can cause cognitive delays, impairments in executive functioning, and disruption of the body's stress response and can ultimately be more harmful than physical abuse. The researchers further point out that intermittent, occasional disruption of attentive caregiving presents no cause for concern, in contrast to chronic deprivation. They also say that much of the research in this area was done with children who were profoundly neglected in institutional settings, which present much greater risks than what occurs in most homes. However, both children who are chronically and severely neglected in families and children raised in institutions are at greater risk for emotional, behavioral, and interpersonal relationship problems.

4. Poverty is correlated with an increased risk of every form of child abuse and neglect, and the relationship with neglect is especially high. Kristen Shook Slack et al., Understanding the Risks of Child Neglect: An Exploration of Poverty and Parenting Characteristics, 9 Child Maltreatment 395 (2004). Studies have found that states with welfare policies that impose stricter work requirements and

sanctions have higher rates of substantiated child abuse reports. *Id.* at 397, citing studies. Among the factors associated with poverty that may increase the danger of neglect are unemployment, single parenthood, housing instability or frequent moves, household crowding, limited access to health care, and exposure to environmental hazards such as lead paint or dangerous neighborhoods. National Clearinghouse on Child Abuse and Neglect Information, Acts of Omission: An Overview of Child Neglect 3 (Apr. 2001) (citing studies).

> "[I]n the presence of these conditions [such as environmental hazards and dangerous neighborhoods], impoverished parents have little leeway for lapses in responsibility, whereas in middle-class families, there is some leeway for irresponsibility, a luxury that poverty does not afford." *Id.* (quoting L.H. Pelton, The Role of Material Factors in Child Abuse and Neglect in Protecting Children from Abuse and Neglect: Foundations for a New National Strategy (G.B. Melton & F.D. Barry eds., 1994)).

5. Is smoking marijuana in a child's presence neglect? How about smoking marijuana outside the child's presence while being responsible for the child? How about drinking alcohol?

Parental substance abuse is reported to be a factor in one-third to two-thirds of cases of child maltreatment. Jill Goldman et al., A Coordinated Response to Child Abuse and Neglect: The Foundation for Practice 28 (DHHS, Children's Bureau 2003) (Parents who abuse drugs or alcohol may expose their children to dangerous people and situations or become emotionally or physically unavailable to their children and unable to supervise them well.).

In People v. Tennyson, 790 N.W.2d 354 (Mich. 2010), the Michigan Supreme Court reversed a conviction of an offense that required proof that the defendant did an act that "tended to cause a minor child to become neglected or delinquent" for insufficient evidence. The police found a baggie of heroin in the adults' bedroom, but no evidence showed that the child was aware of the drugs. The court said,

> To decide otherwise would render a conviction under MCL 750.145 an increasingly routine appendage to a broad array of other criminal charges in instances in which a child is merely present in a home where evidence of a crime has been uncovered. Moreover, to decide otherwise would have considerable implications for the process by which parental rights are terminated in this state, for, as the facts of this case demonstrate, a conviction under MCL 750.145 would almost certainly constitute a trigger at least for the *initiation* of the termination process by the Department of Human Services. Because this result has never before been reached by courts of this state, and because we believe that such result was never intended by the Legislature, we reverse in part the judgment of the Court of Appeals. . . .

790 N.W.2d at 356. On the other hand, a Texas appellate court affirmed a termination of parental rights order based on evidence that the parents had drugs in their homes, were arrested for drug possession, and "allowed others to live in the home." The court said, "The law does not require that a child suffer actual injury; rather, it is enough when the parental conduct produces an endangering

environment. In fact, a parent's abuse of drugs while having custody of children supports termination under [the TPR statute]. Additionally, unlawful conduct by persons who live with the child or with whom the child must associate on a regular basis is a part of the child's conditions or surroundings for purposes of [the statute]." Interest of M.Y.G., 423 S.W.3d 504, 511 (Tex. Civ. App. 2014). *See also* In re Carrdale H. II, 781 N.W.2d 622 (Neb. App. 2010) (reversing juvenile court adjudication of neglect for insufficient evidence where the state proved that the father possessed a small amount of crack cocaine but nothing else to support the allegation that the child was at definite risk of future harm, rejecting arguments that father might have been arrested and incarcerated because not supported by evidence); Department of Human Services v. C.Z., 236 P.3d 791 (Or. App. 2010) (juvenile court adjudication of neglect reversed for insufficient evidence where state proved only that mother admitted to having used marijuana at a party a week or two before dirty urinalysis, that she failed to attend a meeting with child welfare worker, and that she failed to do a second urinalysis; evidence did not show a reasonable likelihood of harm to the welfare of the child).

6. The Child Abuse Prevention and Treatment Act was amended in 2010 to require states to require reporting substance-exposed newborns to CPS. 42 U.S.C. § 5106a(b). . . . Approximately 19 states and the District of Columbia have reporting statutes, and 14 states and the District of Columbia include drug or alcohol exposure in their definitions of child abuse or neglect. Approximately 34 states and the U.S. Virgin Islands have criminal statutes regarding exposing children to illegal drug activity. In 20 states manufacturing or possessing methamphetamine in the presence of a child is a felony, and in 10 states, manufacturing or possessing any controlled substance in the presence of a child is a felony. Exposing children to the manufacture, possession, or distribution of illegal drugs is child endangerment in 11 states. Exposing a child to drugs or drug paraphernalia is a crime in eight states and the Virgin Islands. Child Welfare Information Gateway, Parental Drug Use as Child Abuse (2016), https://www.childwelfare.gov/pubPDFs/drugexposed.pdf#page=1&view=Introduction.

7. The West Virginia Supreme Court in State v. Louk, 786 S.E.2d 219 (W. Va. 2016), reversed the conviction of a woman for child neglect, based on prenatal ingestion of methamphetamine, ruling that the word "child" in the criminal statute does not include an unborn fetus. However, the next year the same court held that a child born with drugs in his or her system is an abused or neglected child for purposes of juvenile court jurisdiction. In re A.L.C.M., 801 S.E.2d 260 (W. Va. 2017). What might explain the different outcomes?

The supreme courts of South Carolina and Alabama have interpreted their criminal child endangerment statutes as applying to viable fetuses. Whitner v. State, 492 S.E.2d 777 (S.C. 1997); Hicks v. State, 153 So. 3d 53 (Ala. 2014). In 2014 Tennessee enacted the first statute criminalizing using illegal narcotics during pregnancy, but it sunsetted in 2016. Cortney E. Lollar, Criminalizing Pregnancy, 92 Ind. L. J. 947, 949 (2017). This article discusses empirical evidence showing that these statutes are enforced mostly against poor women of color and that babies born with illegal drugs in their systems do not tend to have long-lasting problems. *Id.* at 954-955.

PROBLEMS

1. Two parents working at a minimum wage job leave a 10-year-old and a 2-year-old alone in a locked car at night in 20-degree weather because they cannot find a babysitter and fear losing their jobs if they stay at home themselves. If either loses his or her job, they fear, with reason, that they will become homeless. Are they neglecting their children? If the parents worked during the day and asked neighbors to check on the children, whom they left alone in the apartment, would this amount to neglect?

2. Sara is the mother of two children who were 4 years old and 20 months old at the time of the juvenile court hearing. Eight months earlier, she had moved to Georgia with the children and her fiancé, who had a job offer there. Two months ago they returned to their home in this state to attend a relative's funeral. However, they did not have enough money to go back to Georgia, and neither Sara nor her fiancé could find work. The fiancé applied for and got transitional housing in a hotel, and Sara and the children moved in too. However, Sara and the children had to leave because the children could not live in the transitional housing. Sara then took her children to the child welfare agency and asked it to take temporary custody of them because she was homeless. The agency agreed but also filed a neglect petition. The juvenile court judge found the children were neglected, saying the family lacked housing because of the mother's "unbelievably poor planning," and criticized her for following her fiancé without due regard for her children's well-being and then leaving Georgia where she did have permanent housing without a plan to return or means to find housing in New Jersey. Sara has appealed. What arguments should be made on her behalf and on behalf of the state?

C.   DISCOVERY AND INVESTIGATION OF CHILD ABUSE AND NEGLECT

1.   *Child Abuse Reporting Statutes*

Statutes in every state require that suspected abuse or neglect be reported to the police or to the state child welfare agency. Most child abuse reporting statutes impose this duty only on specific groups, such as health care workers and school employees. A minority of states require anyone who knows about or suspects child abuse to make a report. Almost all states impose criminal penalties on required reporters who knowingly or willfully fail to make reports, and most provide immunity from civil and criminal liability for reports made in good faith. In some states, a mandatory reporter's failure to make a required report can also be the basis for loss of employment. *See, e.g.*, Struble v. Blytheville Sch. Dist., 516 S.W.3d 269 (Ark. 2017); Meier v. Salem-Keizer Sch. Dist., 392 P.3d 796 (Or. App. 2017).

The federal Child Abuse Prevention and Treatment Act, 42 U.S.C. §§ 5101 et seq., set minimum standards for reporting statutes. Section 5106(g)(2) of 42 U.S.C. provided that child abuse must be defined to include "any recent act or failure to act on the part of a parent or caretaker, which results in death, serious physical or emotional harm, sexual abuse, or exploitation, or an act or failure to act which presents an imminent risk of serious harm." For current state-by-state analyses of reporting laws, *see* the Child Welfare Information Gateway Web site at https://www.childwelfare.gov/topics/systemwide/laws-policies/.

Between 2012 and 2016, the number of child abuse reports to child protective services increased 14.7 percent, to an estimated 4.1 million in 2016. U.S. Dept. of Health and Human Services, Administration on Children, Youth and Families, Child Maltreatment 2016 at 6 (2018), available at https://www.acf.hhs.gov/cb/research-data-technology/statistics-research/child-maltreatment. All studies find that the highest number of reports comes from school employees. In 2016, school personnel made 18.9 percent of the reports, legal and law enforcement personnel made 18.4 percent, social services personnel made 11.2 percent, and medical personnel made 9.5 percent. Of the remaining 18.1 percent, relatives made 6.8 percent of the reports, parents made 6.6 percent, and friends and neighbors made 4.2 percent. The remaining sources were unclassified. *Id.* at 8.

Empirical studies have documented both over- and underreporting of suspected cases of abuse and neglect, particularly among professional reporters. Seth C. Kalichman & Cheryl L. Brosig, Mandatory Child Abuse Reporting Laws: Issues and Implications for Policy 153, 155-163 (1992). *See also* James Garbarino, The Incidence and Prevalence of Child Maltreatment in Family Violence 243-244, 246-248 (L. Ohlin & M. Tonry eds., 1989). Kalichman and Brosig suggest that the way reporting laws are drafted contributes to this phenomenon. In addition, studies show that professionals exercise discretion in reporting, with the likelihood of reporting increasing with the level of certainty that abuse occurred and with its severity. Finally, the researchers found that professionals do not report suspected abuse if they believe that reporting would damage their relationship with their client. Kalichman & Brosig, above. *See also* Dale Margolin Cecka, Abolish Anonymous Reporting to Child Abuse Hotlines, 64 Cath. U. L. Rev. 51 (2014).

The courts are divided about whether failure of a mandated reporter to report gives rise to a tort action by or on behalf of the alleged victim of abuse or neglect, although most have concluded that their legislatures did not intend the reporting statutes to be bases for private causes of action. *See* C.T. v. Gammon, 928 N.E.2d 847 (Ind. App. 2010), and cases cited therein. *Contra*, Beggs v. State, 247 P.3d 421 (Wash. 2011) (en banc). For an overview of case law, *see* Danny R. Veilleux, Validity, Construction, and Application of State Statute Requiring Doctor or Other Person to Report Child Abuse, 73 A.L.R.4th 782 (originally published in 1989, with weekly updates).

2. *Agency Response to Reports*

Child abuse reporting statutes typically provide that reports will be made to the police, to state child welfare authorities, or both. Ordinarily, if reports come to the police, the police will notify child welfare authorities, though the reverse is not always true. Agencies exercise discretion to determine which reports appear substantial enough to warrant further investigation. Two recent analyses show that agencies do not follow up many reports, though the analyses differ greatly in their specifics. The Fourth National Incidence Study suggests that the cases of most maltreated children are not investigated by child protective services. It reported that CPS investigated the mistreatment of only 32 percent of children that the study counted as having been "harmed" and 43 percent of children that were counted as "endangered." (For a discussion of the difference between the NIS harm and endangerment standards, *see* Section B.1 of this chapter, above.) Andrea J. Sedlak et al., above, at 16-17. On the other hand, analysis of actual CPS decision making shows that 58 percent of reports are investigated further, while the others are screened out. U.S. Dept. of Health and Human Services, Administration on Children, Youth and Families, Child Maltreatment 2016 at 6 (2018).

Many state statutes do not provide much detail about the nature of the investigation that the child welfare agency should undertake, though they usually contemplate that a caseworker will see the child and the place where the child lives. Some statutes explicitly authorize workers to interview children without parental consent, *e.g.*, Wis. Stat. § 48.981(3)(c)(1)(b) (2018), while others require parental consent, *e.g.*, Ind. Code § 31–33–8–6 (2018). Under the latter kind of statute, a court may grant an order allowing the interview if the parent refuses to grant permission. *See also* Jennifer Kwapisz, Note, Fourth Amendment Implications of Interviewing Suspected Victims of Abuse in School, 86 St. John's L. Rev. 963 (2012).

In 2016 CPS determined that 676,000 reports of maltreatment were substantiated. Child Maltreatment 2016 at 18. If a report is substantiated, the child welfare worker has substantial discretion regarding further action, ranging from doing nothing to removing the child to shelter care immediately and instituting legal action against the parent. If a child is removed from home before the adjudicatory hearing, the juvenile court will hold a shelter care hearing to determine whether the child's safety requires that he or she remain out of the home until after the adjudicatory hearing.

Because of inherent difficulties in conducting investigations, strained agency resources, and human failure, agencies sometimes make decisions that, in hindsight, are erroneous—children who have not been mistreated are subjected to examination and may even be removed from home; other children who are in danger are left at home and suffer serious injury. In either instance, the child or parents, seeking damages for the results of the error, may sue the agency.

NOTE: AGENCY LIABILITY FOR FAILURE TO REMOVE A CHILD: DESHANEY V. WINNEBAGO COUNTY AND STATE TORT PRINCIPLES

In DeShaney v. Winnebago County Department of Social Services, 489 U.S. 189 (1989), the Supreme Court held that the Constitution provides no remedy for a child protective services agency's negligent failure to remove a child from a dangerous home because the state does not, as a matter of federal law, owe a duty to protect children from other people under these circumstances. The opinion left open the possibility that state law might provide a tort remedy; since *DeShaney* was decided, many state courts have considered this issue, with mixed results.

Joshua DeShaney and his mother sued the agency for leaving him in his father's home, where he was severely beaten. According to the facts set out in *DeShaney*, workers in the department appear to have known that Joshua was at risk of serious injury in his father's home. Over a two-year period, the department received several credible reports indicating that he was being physically abused. The department did not initiate formal child protection proceedings, but a social worker visited Joshua's home regularly under a voluntary agreement. She observed suspicious injuries to Joshua's head and wrote in her files that she suspected Joshua was being abused and even that she feared he would be killed, but she did nothing more. In March 1984, four-year-old Joshua was severely beaten by his father, suffering such severe brain damage that he will probably spend the rest of his life in an institution.

A majority of the Supreme Court held that Joshua's 42 U.S.C. § 1983 action against the agency should be dismissed for failure to state a claim. The Court distinguished cases holding that due process requires the state to protect incarcerated prisoners and mental hospital patients on the basis that in those situations the state has rendered a person unable to care for himself or herself. Justice Rehnquist for the majority wrote:

> Judges and lawyers, like other humans, are moved by natural sympathy in a case like this to find a way for Joshua and his mother to receive adequate compensation for the grievous harm inflicted upon them. But before yielding to that impulse, it is well to remember once again that the harm was inflicted not by the State of Wisconsin, but by Joshua's father. The most that can be said of the state functionaries in this case is that they stood by and did nothing when suspicious circumstances dictated a more active role for them. In defense of them it must also be said that had they moved too soon to take custody of the son away from the father, they would likely have been met with charges of improperly intruding into the parent-child relationship, charges based on the same Due Process Clause that forms the basis for the present charge of failure to provide adequate protection.

489 U.S. at 202-203. Justice Brennan dissented, arguing that prior cases established that "if a State cuts off private sources of aid and then refuses aid itself, it cannot wash its hands of the harm that results from its inaction." *Id.* at 207. The dissent continued:

> Wisconsin has established a child-welfare system specifically designed to help children like Joshua. Wisconsin law places upon the local departments of social services such as respondent (DSS or Department) a duty to investigate reported instances of child abuse. . . . Wisconsin law invites — indeed, directs — citizens and other governmental entities to depend on local departments of social services such as respondent to protect children from abuse.
>
> The specific facts before us bear out this view of Wisconsin's system of protecting children. Each time someone voiced a suspicion that Joshua was being abused, that information was relayed to the Department for investigation and possible action. . . .
>
> Even more telling than these examples is the Department's control over the decision whether to take steps to protect a particular child from suspected abuse. . . .
>
> In these circumstances, a private citizen, or even a person working in a government agency other than DSS, would doubtless feel that her job was done as soon as she had reported her suspicions of child abuse to DSS. Through its child-welfare program, in other words, the State of Wisconsin has relieved ordinary citizens and governmental bodies other than the Department of any sense of obligation to do anything more than report their suspicions of child abuse to DSS. If DSS ignores

or dismisses these suspicions, no one will step in to fill the gap. Wisconsin's child protection program thus effectively confined Joshua DeShaney within the walls of Randy DeShaney's violent home until such time as DSS took action to remove him. Conceivably, then, children like Joshua are made worse off by the existence of this program when the persons and entities charged with carrying it out fail to do their jobs.

Id. at 208-210. In City of Castle Rock v. Gonzales, 545 U.S. 748 (2005), the Supreme Court reaffirmed the principle underlying *DeShaney*. The Court held that a woman who had obtained a domestic violence restraining order had no constitutionally protected right to have the restraining order enforced because a well-established tradition gives police discretion not to arrest, despite mandatory arrest statutes. As a result, the woman had no federal cause of action against the state for the death of her children at the hands of their father when police failed to enforce the restraining order. Gonzales took her case to the Inter-American Commission on Human Rights, which in 2011 ruled that the U.S. had violated her human rights and those of her daughters by failing to protect them from domestic violence. It recommended that she be paid full reparations and that the laws about enforcement of restraining orders be improved. The Commission's report is available at www.oas.org/en/iachr/decisions/2011/USPU12626EN.doc.

Under state law, a social worker and child welfare agency may be liable if the agency has a "special relationship" to the child giving rise to a duty to protect the child. In the context of reports of child abuse or neglect, a critical question is whether the agency has a duty to the children who are the subjects of the reports. The court in Beebe v. Fraktman, 921 P.2d 216 (Kan. App. 1996), held that the agency's duty to investigate is owed to the public generally rather than to a child as to whom an abuse report has been filed. *See also* Teresa T. v. Ragaglia, 865 A.2d 428 (Conn. 2005) (statute authorizing child welfare agency to remove child from home based on probable cause to believe that child is in imminent risk of physical harm and that immediate removal is necessary to ensure the child's safety does not impose a duty to remove under such circumstances). However, most state courts have held to the contrary, finding that the duty runs to the child and can give rise to a cause of action. Rees v. Idaho Department Health & Welfare, 137 P.3d 397 (Idaho 2006); M.W. v. Department of Social & Health Services, 70 P.3d 954 (Wash. 2003) (en banc) (both discussing cases). Even if the agency has a duty to the child to investigate competently, negligent failure may not be actionable because the caseworker has immunity. *See, e.g.*, Stratton v. Commonwealth, 182 S.W.2d 516 (Ky. 2006); Rees v. Idaho Department Health & Welfare, above.

NOTES AND QUESTIONS

1. According to the majority in *DeShaney*, why didn't Joshua have a § 1983 cause of action against the state? How does the dissent recast the facts to conclude that he should have an action?

2. Why do you suppose that the worker in *DeShaney* didn't take more decisive action to protect Joshua?

3. If the state agency removed a child from one parent's home and placed the child in the other parent's home, and the second parent harmed or killed the child, would the agency be liable under § 1983? *Compare* Currier v. Doran, 23 F. Supp. 2d 1277 (D.N.M. 1998), and Ford v. Johnson, 899 F. Supp. 227 (W.D. Pa. 1995) (distinguishing *DeShaney* by saying that the agency may have created the danger), *with* K.H. v. Morgan, 914 F.2d 846 (7th Cir. 1990), and Weller v. Dept. of Soc. Servs. for the City of Baltimore, 901 F.2d 387 (4th Cir. 1990) (holding that *DeShaney* prevents recovery).

4. In addition to being an occasion for determining whether further coercive intervention into a family is warranted, a child welfare investigation could also provide an opportunity to determine whether a child was at risk for future harm and, if so, to offer services to protect the child. However, a longitudinal study of 595 families at high risk for child maltreatment suggests that investigations do not serve the latter function. The study found no significant differences in most areas between families that underwent CPS investigations and those that did not. The study found no differences in social support, family function, poverty, maternal education, or child behavior problems. The only difference was that in investigated families "maternal depressive symptoms" were worse. Kristine A. Campbell et al., Household, Family, and Child Risk Factors After an Investigation for Suspected Child Maltreatment, 164 Archives of Pediatrics & Adolescent Med. 943 (2010). The researchers commented that the results are not surprising, since investigations do not focus on poverty and social support, and when services are offered, they are usually focused at immediate threats to a child's safety, such as substance abuse or domestic violence, even though it is not clear that this kind of intervention has much effect on future violence or abuse.

HERNANDEZ EX REL. HERNANDEZ V. FOSTER

---

657 F.3d 463 (7th Cir. 2011)

TINDER, Circuit Judge. . . . In the morning of September 8, 2008, Crystelle and Joshua Hernandez took their fifteen-month-old son, Jaymz Hernandez, to Sherman Hospital, stating that they thought he had fallen out of his crib, a distance of approximately three to four feet to the tiled floor. Nurse Lisa Luebke noted that she asked the parents if Jaymz was walking or climbing, and Crystelle said that he "is not walking or climbing, but [she] doesn't know how he fell out of [his] crib," which had its side rails up and was locked. The parents also told the treating physician, Dr. Natalie Kostinsky, that Jaymz was not walking or climbing. X-rays were taken, and the radiologist diagnosed a torus fracture of the distal right radius and ulna. This type of fracture is not a complete fracture and is also referred to as a buckle fracture. It is a common injury in children and can be sustained by a fall of a few feet onto a tiled floor. Dr. Kostinsky concurred with the diagnosis.

Nurse Luebke noted in the hospital record that the parents' "story doesn't sound correct." Around 12:00 p.m., she called the DCFS hotline, reporting that Jaymz had a right forearm fracture and a "story inconsisten[cy]." Nurse Luebke advised that Jaymz was not yet walking or climbing, but the parents claimed he fell out of his crib, although the crib railing was up and locked and neither parent saw him fall. (The mattress was not in its lowest position, but the record does not disclose that the nurse was aware of this fact.) The record of the initial report indicates that Nurse Luebke stated that the parents' "story d[id] not fit Jaymz's fracture." She also reported that Jaymz had old bruises above his left eyelid and it was unknown how he got them. DCFS advised Dr. Kostinsky to release Jaymz to his parents. Dr. Kostinsky testified that she felt Jaymz was not in immediate danger, but the case needed to be investigated. After Nurse Luebke notified Crystelle and Joshua that a report had been made to DCFS, Crystelle claimed, "Oh, [Jaymz] can walk," but denied that he could climb.

DCFS assigned an investigation into the hotline call's allegations to the team of defendant Pamela Foster–Stith, a DCFS supervisor. Foster–Stith promptly interviewed Nurse Luebke and Dr. Kostinsky by telephone. Nurse Luebke reported that Jaymz's radius and ulna were broken and he had bruising above his left eyelid. Foster–Stith's note of the interview stated that Nurse Luebke said "the story the family gave didn't match the injury." Nurse Luebke stated that the mother said the railing was up and locked and no one witnessed the incident. The nurse also reported that the father originally said he was called home from work, and then changed and said he was home when the incident occurred. Dr. Kostinsky reported that both parents said Jaymz fell out of the crib and was alone in the room. She said that she noted some bruising above Jaymz's eye from a prior injury, but the parents did not report how it occurred. Dr. Kostinsky told DCFS that the parents stated there was nothing in the crib that Jaymz could have used to climb out of the crib. Dr. Kostinsky reported that she was suspicious of abuse because both parents told her that they were at home at the time of the incident, but told Nurse Luebke that the mother was home alone. The doctor added that the age and size of the child and his ability to climb up the railing and fall out of the crib also made her suspicious.

Foster–Stith prepared a plan of action and early that afternoon contacted Foster about the matter. . . . It said that the child needed to be seen at home and instructed Foster to "[r]ule out Protective custody and/or Safety Plan" and "assess for safety and risk." Shortly after preparing the action plan, Foster–Stith met with DCFS Assistant Regional Manager, defendant Mike Ruppe, to discuss the case, including the medical providers' concerns. Ruppe advised her on how to proceed, including that they needed to rule out protective custody, which we understand as meaning to eliminate this as a requirement to ensure Jaymz's safety.

Foster–Stith next contacted Nurse Luebke and Dr. Kostinsky about the exact type of fracture Jaymz had, and they reported that he had a "buckle" fracture. Foster–Stith could not recall the significance of a buckle fracture: whether this type of fracture indicated a more serious situation or an accidental injury.

At about 4:00 p.m., Foster visited the Hernandez home. She observed Jaymz walking and climbing, playing with toys, and interacting with his mother and grandfather. She noted that his right arm was in a partial cast and he had a light scratch above his left eyelid. Foster interviewed Crystelle who reported that she, Joshua, and her father were upstairs while Jaymz was downstairs in his crib taking a nap. She said that the video baby monitor had been on, but she didn't sit and watch it the entire time. She heard Jaymz crying in an unusual manner and found him standing in front of his crib. He wouldn't calm down and frowned when he tried to use his right hand. After returning home from the hospital, she lowered the crib mattress to the lowest position.

Foster . . . completed a home safety checklist and screenings for substance abuse and domestic violence, finding no evidence of either issue.

Around 4:30 p.m., Foster called Foster–Stith and reported that Jaymz was able to walk and climb and was actively engaged in the home. According to Crystelle, Foster stated that "everything looks fine; there's nothing that seems suspicious or anything like that," and the supervisor responded that Foster needed to treat it just like every other protective custody case. Foster . . . advised Foster–Stith that the parents really didn't know what happened and that Jaymz must have climbed up and fallen out of his crib. Foster did not comment on whether she believed the parents' explanation. Foster–Stith testified that she asked Foster to talk to the family about implementing a safety plan based on Jaymz's age, his injury, and the fact that two medical professionals said that the parents' explanation "wasn't consistent" with the injury. Foster–Stith added that she and Foster discussed implementing a safety plan with the family, and the family was resistant to a safety plan at that time. Foster could not remember if she discussed a safety plan with the Hernandezes during this visit, and her notes do not document whether or not she did.

At about 4:45 p.m., Foster–Stith met with Ruppe to discuss the case. . . . Ruppe concluded that Jaymz was unsafe without either a safety plan or protective custody because there was conflicting information about his mobility and who was home at the time of the injury. Ruppe explained that protective custody had to be taken because the parents would not agree to a safety plan. The "driving force" behind his decision to take protective custody was the "allegation of [a] bone fracture" to a fifteen-month-old child with "no significant or sufficient [or consistent] explanation of how that injury occurred." Ruppe approved of Foster–Stith's decision to take protective custody of Jaymz.

Right after the conversation with Ruppe, Foster–Stith contacted Foster, who was still at the Hernandez home, by phone and directed her to take protective custody of Jaymz and determine whether he could go stay with a family member. . . .

At about 5:45 or 6:00 p.m., Foster took Jaymz into protective custody. She advised Crystelle (Joshua was not home) that Jaymz had to be taken into protective custody for forty-eight hours, during which time Crystelle and Joshua could not see him. Foster explained what protective custody was. She also explained that if the state's attorney were to file a petition, there would be a court hearing; but if the state's attorney did not file a petition, protective custody would lapse and they would be contacted. Foster stated that Crystelle and Joshua could have no contact with Jaymz while he was in protective custody and out of the home. She provided Crystelle with a notification of the investigation and an investigations brochure, explaining the investigation process. At Crystelle's request and with Foster–Stith's approval, DCFS placed Jaymz in relative foster care with his great-grandparents. Foster first took Jaymz to be examined by a physician (standard procedure when a child is taken into protective custody) and then to his great-grandparents' home, accompanied by Crystelle's stepmother, who stayed there for "[a] couple of days."

Early the next day on September 9, Foster contacted Nurse Luebke who again reported that Crystelle said Jaymz could not walk or climb and that he fell out of his crib. The nurse said that the two assertions were inconsistent. She also stated that Crystelle said there was nothing in the crib for Jaymz to climb up on, "which again does not match" the claim that Jaymz fell out of his crib.

Later that morning, Jaymz was seen by an orthopedist, Dr. Arnold Herbstman, who determined that he needed a cast on his arm for three weeks. DCFS allowed Crystelle and Joshua to accompany him to this appointment. Dr. Herbstman informed Foster that the injury "did not look like any abuse or neglect . . . this type of fracture is a torus type (a little buckle) not from a twisting of the arm, it is consistent with the history of child falling from a crib, it is sustain[ed] from direct contact and there were no finger marks on his arm."

At Foster's request, Jaymz was examined later that day by an emergency medicine physician, Dr. Marcy Zirlin. The doctor noted the wrist fracture; the physical exam was otherwise normal. She ordered a skeletal survey, which is an X-ray of all the bones in a child's body that can be used to detect bone fractures. Dr. Zirlin indicated that there were no clinical or radiographic signs of abuse. The radiologist did not disagree. In mid-afternoon, Foster informed a detective that the doctors who performed the full skeletal X-ray saw no reason to believe that Jaymz had been abused and believed the fracture was consistent with a fall from a crib.

Early that afternoon, Foster spoke with an assistant state's attorney, Julia Almeida, who told her that "there is not enough to file a petition." . . . Foster apparently shared this information with Foster–Stith. A short time later, Foster–Stith emailed Ruppe that Almeida didn't think there was enough for shelter care (a court hearing on protective custody). . . .

At about 1:00 or 2:00 p.m., Foster contacted the Hernandezes by phone. Foster testified that she told Crystelle that protective custody lapsed and there would be no court hearing in the case. Crystelle stated that Foster said there was not enough evidence to take it to court. Crystelle asked Foster whether that meant Jaymz could come home, and Foster said, "No, we still have to do investigating." So Crystelle asked when Jaymz could come home, and Foster said she did not know; she had to talk to her supervisor. According to Crystelle, she asked if she could go see Jaymz, and Foster said everything had to stay the same because the forty-eight-hour period wasn't up yet. Foster testified that she asked Crystelle whether there was a possibility of doing a safety plan until they got further into the investigation, and Crystelle was willing to discuss it. . . .

Early on September 10, Foster–Stith and Ruppe agreed to allow protective custody to lapse and decided to try to implement a safety plan under which Jaymz would remain with his great-grandparents and the parents would have supervised contact with him. At approximately 10:00 a.m., Foster visited the Hernandez home and presented the safety plan to Crystelle and Joshua. . . . Foster told Crystelle and Joshua that once they signed it, they could see Jaymz, but they could not be alone with him or take him anywhere. She said that they could stay at Crystelle's grandmother's house but could not have unsupervised contact with Jaymz. Foster also informed them that Crystelle's grandmother still had custody over Jaymz and they did not have their parental rights. Crystelle testified that Foster said if they "didn't sign it, [they] couldn't see him. So we were signing it." Crystelle did not ask Foster any questions about the safety plan, explaining, "I heard her say I can go see my kid, so I really didn't care." Joshua did not read the safety plan and signed it because Crystelle did. Foster also obtained Jaymz's great-grandmother's signature on the safety plan.

Immediately after signing the safety plan, Crystelle went to her grandmother's house to stay with Jaymz. She stayed there overnight for the eight days that the safety plan remained in effect. Joshua stayed there when he wasn't working.

. . . On September 16, Crystelle met with a lawyer and told him what happened with Jaymz and that DCFS would not give him back unless she went through a lot of hoops. The lawyer called DCFS and left a message, which "raised hell" and challenged the decision not to release Jaymz to his parents.

On September 17, Foster and Foster–Stith discussed the case, noting that the safety plan needed to be updated. Foster informed Foster–Stith that the family was somewhat resistant to the safety plan and had hired an attorney. They decided that Foster would contact the attorney and explain the situation. So Foster spoke with the attorney that day and advised him that Jaymz's X-rays had been sent to a forensic physician for a determination of whether there was evidence of prior breaks and a history of abuse. The attorney reported back to Crystelle that the investigation was progressing and hopefully she would get Jaymz back right away. That evening, Foster visited Jaymz at his great-grandmother's house to monitor the safety plan and had the great-grandmother sign a new safety plan, which contained terms strikingly similar to the first.

On the morning of September 18, Foster obtained the Hernandezes' agreement to the new safety plan . . . That afternoon, Foster discussed the case with DCFS supervisor Joseph Becerra, including whether the safety plan should be extended or terminated. Foster advised him that Jaymz had seen three physicians who reported his injury was consistent with an accident and the family had hired an attorney who believed there was no longer a need for a safety plan. Foster and Becerra agreed that the safety plan could be terminated. Foster also consulted with Foster–Stith, noting the findings of Dr. Rosado, Dr. Zirlin, and Dr. Herbstman that supported the conclusion that Jaymz's injury was not due to abuse and was consistent with a history of a fall out of a crib. Foster–Stith agreed to terminate the safety plan. That evening, Foster obtained Joshua's signature on a safety plan termination agreement, thus terminating the safety plan that the Hernandezes had signed earlier that same day.

DCFS's investigation continued and ultimately concluded on November 7, 2008, with a declaration that the allegation of child abuse was unfounded—there was no credible evidence of abuse or neglect.

The plaintiffs, Jaymz, Crystelle, and Joshua Hernandez, filed a complaint under 42 U.S.C. § 1983 against Foster, Foster–Stith, and Ruppe (along with another DCFS employee Andrew Polovin, not a part of this appeal), alleging violations of their rights under the Fourth and Fourteenth Amendments. The defendants moved to dismiss for failure to state a claim, or alternatively, on qualified immunity grounds. The motion was granted with respect to Polovin only. The defendants moved for summary judgment on qualified immunity grounds, and the district court granted their motion. . . .

. . . The Hernandezes appealed. . . .

Qualified immunity shields "government actors from liability for civil damages where their conduct does not violate clearly established statutory or constitutional rights of which a reasonable person would have been aware." When making a qualified immunity determination, a court considers (1) whether the plaintiff's allegations show that the defendant violated a constitutional right, and (2) whether that right was "clearly established" at the time of the defendant's conduct. . . .

The plaintiffs bear the burden of proving that the constitutional right was clearly established. A right is clearly established "when, at the time of the challenged conduct, '[t]he contours of [a] right [are] sufficiently clear' that every 'reasonable official would have understood that what he is doing violates that right.'" The plaintiffs need not identify "a case directly on point, but existing precedent must have placed the statutory or constitutional question beyond debate."

Jaymz brings a Fourth Amendment claim against Foster, Foster–Stith, and Ruppe, alleging that they violated his right to be free from unreasonable seizures when they removed him from the care and custody of his parents. All three plaintiffs bring a substantive due process claim premised on (1) Jaymz's seizure or initial removal, (2) the continued withholding of Jaymz in temporary protective custody after probable cause had dissipated (the "continued withholding" claim), and (3) conditioning the parents' contact with him on the acceptance of restrictions on their familial rights and coercing their agreement to the safety plan (the "coerced safety plan" claim). The plaintiffs do not challenge the district court's determination that Jaymz's claim premised on his initial removal should be analyzed under the Fourth Amendment. However, they argue that the court erred in granting summary judgment on these other claims.

"In the context of removing a child from his home and family, a seizure is reasonable if it is pursuant to a court order, if it is supported by probable cause, or if it is justified by exigent circumstances, meaning that state officers 'have reason to believe that life or limb is in immediate jeopardy.'" Removing Jaymz from his home and parents and taking him into protective custody qualifies as a seizure. Since Jaymz's seizure was not pursuant to a court order and the defendants do not assert that it was justified by exigent circumstances, the seizure must have been supported by probable cause to have been reasonable.

The probable cause analysis is an objective inquiry. The "focus is on the facts and circumstances known to defendants at the time they decided to remove [the child], and whether a prudent caseworker (meaning one of reasonable caution) could have believed that [the child] faced an immediate threat of abuse based on those facts." We need not decide whether Jaymz's removal was supported by probable cause, however; we can decide the claim on qualified immunity grounds. As long as a reasonable DCFS investigator, supervisor, and manager "'could have believed [Jaymz's removal] to be lawful, in light of clearly established law and the information [they] possessed,'" the defendants are entitled to qualified immunity. . . .

Under the Illinois Abused and Neglected Child Reporting Abuse Act, Dr. Kostinsky and Nurse Luebke were "mandated reporters," meaning that if they had "reasonable cause to believe" that a child in their care may have suffered abuse, they had a legal duty to report it to the DCFS. And they did notify DCFS about their suspicions of abuse but did not take Jaymz into temporary protective custody, apparently because they did not believe that he was in imminent danger. In fact, DCFS advised Dr. Kostinsky to release Jaymz to his parents, and the defendants have not asserted that exigent circumstances justified Jaymz's later removal. As for the type of fracture that Jaymz sustained, Foster–Stith did not recall the significance of a buckle fracture, and the plaintiffs do not point to any evidence to establish that Foster or Ruppe appreciated the significance of a buckle fracture in terms of suspected abuse. Foster did observe that Jaymz could walk and climb and reported this to Foster–Stith, and this observation corroborates the parents' suspicion that Jaymz had fallen out of his crib. But it does not explain why the parents initially denied that he could walk and climb. Their seemingly inconsistent statements as to Jaymz's abilities may support a reasonable belief that further investigation is necessary. We do not intend to imply that Crystelle and Joshua gave intentionally false statements. It is enough that their statements about Jaymz's abilities were reasonably understood to be inconsistent.

The plaintiffs assert that a telephone call to Dr. Kostinsky explaining that Jaymz could walk and climb may have cleared up the concern that prompted the initial call to DCFS. BeVier v. Hucal, 806 F.2d 123 (7th Cir. 1986), cited as support, is distinguishable. There, parents were arrested for child neglect, and the arresting officer knew about the children's condition which "weakly supported an inference" of neglect, but he did not question the parents, the medical personnel who had seen one of the children, or the babysitter who was watching them. The officer acted unreasonably in not asking questions; with "[a] few questions" he would have learned that the parents were not guilty of child neglect. We concluded that the officer did not have probable cause to arrest the parents: "A police officer may not close her or his eyes to facts that would help clarify the circumstances of [a seizure]. Reasonable avenues of investigation must be pursued especially when . . . it is unclear whether a crime had even taken place." And the officer was not entitled to immunity because no reasonably well-trained officer would have believed there was probable cause to arrest the parents.

Here, in contrast, Foster did conduct an investigation before taking Jaymz into protective custody. . . .

Although this is a close question, we conclude that a reasonable DCFS investigator, supervisor, and manager could have believed that removing Jaymz from his home and family was supported by probable cause given the following facts: (1) fifteen-month-old Jaymz suffered a fractured arm; (2) no one actually observed how he was injured and Jaymz could not verbalize what had happened; (3) Jaymz had an unexplained, older bruise above his left eyelid; (4) Dr. Kostinsky and Nurse Luebke suspected abuse because Jaymz's injury didn't fit with the parents' statements that he could not climb and there was nothing in his crib to climb on; (5) the parents gave conflicting reports about who was home at the time of the incident to Dr. Kostinsky and Nurse Luebke, and one could expect that they would be accurate in reporting what happened to the medical professionals; (6) Crystelle first denied that Jaymz could walk or climb, but when she was told that DCFS had been contacted, she claimed he could walk but could not climb; (7) Jaymz was observed later that same day to have the ability to walk and climb; and (8) the parents denied that anything was in the crib, but Foster observed objects in the crib. This was enough that under the circumstances a reasonable DCFS official would not have understood that taking Jaymz into temporary protective custody violated his Fourth Amendment rights. . . .

Based on our review of the record, the defendants are entitled to qualified immunity on Jaymz's Fourth Amendment claim based on taking him into protective custody. Thus, the district court did not err in granting them summary judgment on this claim. . . .

As noted, the plaintiffs assert substantive due process claims, alleging violations of their right to familial relations. A family's right "to remain together without the coercive interference of the awesome power of the state" is "the most essential and basic aspect of familial privacy." The fundamental right to familial relations is an aspect of substantive due process. This includes the parents' right "to bear and raise their children" and the child's right "to be raised and nurtured by his parents." This right is not absolute, but "must be balanced against the state's interest in protecting children from abuse." To achieve the proper balance, caseworkers must have "some definite and articulable evidence giving rise to a reasonable suspicion" of past or imminent danger of abuse before they may take a child into protective custody. "'A reasonable suspicion requires more than a hunch but less than probable cause.'" . . .

The plaintiffs argue that the district court erred in granting summary judgment on the substantive due process claims arising from Jaymz's continued withholding from the time he was taken into protective custody until the morning of September 10 when the defendants obtained the signed safety plan. The plaintiffs assert that even if the defendants had reason to believe that probable cause existed to take protective custody on September 8, probable cause dissipated by September 9, but the defendants continued to hold Jaymz and refused to release him to his parents.

The defendants respond by arguing that the plaintiffs are challenging a single seizure, not two separate ones. They further argue that the plaintiffs offer no authority for the proposition that they can assert separate "duration of custody" claims. The defendants overlook *Brokaw*, 235 F.3d at 1018–19, which analyzed a child's claim based on a nearly four-month period of government-forced separation from his parents under substantive due process. . . .

We find additional guidance in *BeVier*, in which an officer arrested parents for child neglect and later was advised by an experienced DCFS investigator that his description of the children's situation did not appear to establish child neglect. Nevertheless, the officer did not release the parents from custody. We held that he violated the parents' constitutional rights, stating that "[t]he continuation of even a lawful arrest violates ... [constitutional rights] when the police discover additional facts dissipating their earlier probable cause." That Jaymz's initial removal and continued holding in temporary protective custody formed one seizure is of little moment. The issue is whether the defendants could have believed that continuing to hold Jaymz in protective custody was lawful. Resolution of this issue turns on the facts and circumstances known to them at the relevant time. As they obtained additional information that eroded any reasonable basis for believing that Jaymz was abused or was in imminent danger of abuse, keeping him in protective custody became unreasonable.

Whether challenged under the Fourth Amendment or substantive due process, the plaintiffs allege that holding Jaymz in protective custody beyond the point that the defendants knew they had no reason to do so violated their constitutional rights. But are the plaintiffs' claims properly analyzed under the Fourth Amendment or substantive due process? In *Heck*, we stated: "[I]f a plaintiff's sole purpose in bringing a familial relations claim is to recover damages for a physical seizure, then that claim is more appropriately analyzed under the Fourth Amendment. On the other hand, if . . . a familial relations claim specifically alleges that the government's physical seizure coincided with other conduct amounting to an interference with the parent-child relationship, the plaintiff may also maintain a substantive due process claim. Jaymz complains about his seizure, specifically including the continued holding of him in protective custody. Other than the passage of time, the harm he complains of is no different than the harm he alleges was caused by his initial removal. He does not assert that any other conduct interfered with his right to familial relations. Therefore, Jaymz's continued withholding claim is analyzed under the Fourth Amendment. Crystelle and Joshua were not seized; their continued withholding claims are properly analyzed under substantive due process.

The evidence raises genuine issues of material fact as to when a reasonable DCFS investigator, supervisor, or manager would have known that the continued withholding of Jaymz violated clearly established constitutional rights. The morning of September 9, orthopedist Dr. Herbstman, who cast Jaymz's arm, informed Foster that the injury "did not look like any abuse or neglect" and that "this type of fracture is a torus type (a little buckle) not from a twisting of the arm . . . [and] is consistent with" a fall from a crib. He also advised that this type of fracture "is sustain[ed] from direct contact and there were no finger marks on [Jaymz's] arm." Although Dr. Herbstman did not further explain the significance of this last fact, the context raises a reasonable inference that such marks would be expected if the fracture was caused by abuse. Later that day, Jaymz had a full skeletal survey and was examined by Dr. Zirlin, who reported to Foster that other than the fracture, Jaymz's physical exam was normal and there were no clinical or radiographic signs of abuse. The radiologist did not disagree. Foster understood that Dr. Zirlin saw no reason to believe that Jaymz had been abused and, like Dr. Herbstman, believed the fracture was consistent with a fall from a crib. Furthermore, the assistant state's attorney had told Foster that there was not enough to file a petition; they did not have evidence of an "immediate and urgent [need to remove a child]." Foster apparently relayed at least the state's attorney's opinion to Foster–Stith, who conveyed it to Ruppe that afternoon. Finally, Foster advised Crystelle that protective custody had lapsed and there would be no court hearing because there was not enough evidence of abuse.

The record raises a genuine issue as to when on September 9 probable cause dissipated and the defendants no longer had a reasonable suspicion that Jaymz had been abused or was in imminent danger of abuse. At that time, the state had no interest in keeping him in protective custody and away from his parents. Nonetheless, the defendants continued to hold Jaymz in protective custody and he was not released to his parents. And Foster told Crystelle that everything had to stay the same just because the forty-eight hours wasn't up—she couldn't even go see Jaymz. The evidence raises a genuine dispute of fact about whether a reasonable person in the defendants' positions would have understood that continuing to hold Jaymz in protective custody violated the plaintiffs' clearly established constitutional rights.

The defendants argue that Illinois law authorizes them to keep a child in temporary protective custody for a full forty-eight hours. The federal Constitution is the supreme law of the land; state law cannot trump federal constitutional rights.

Even if it could, the Illinois Juvenile Court Act does not provide the state with blanket authority to hold a child in protective custody regardless of the circumstances, specifically where probable cause and reasonable suspicion have dissipated. Rather, the Act requires that "[u]nless sooner released, a minor . . . taken into temporary protective custody must be brought before a judicial officer within 48 hours . . . for a temporary custody hearing. . . ." Thus, the Act contemplates cases in which a minor may be released before he is brought before a judicial officer, and before the expiration of the forty-eight-hour period. Such cases would include those in which the discovery of additional facts dissipated the probable cause to hold a child in temporary protective custody. That is precisely this case. Probable cause is determined on the basis of the facts and circumstances known to the defendants at the time of the conduct in issue, whether it is the child's removal or the decision to continue holding a child in protective custody. The defendants' assertion that they could keep Jaymz in protective custody for up to forty-eight hours regardless of what came to be known to them in the meantime cannot be reconciled with the probable cause analysis. . . .

Therefore, the district court erred in concluding that the defendants were entitled to qualified immunity on Jaymz's Fourth Amendment continued withholding claim and the parents' substantive due process continued withholding claims.

The plaintiffs also raise substantive due process claims against all three defendants based on the safety plan. The state may, instead of immediately removing a child from his parents, offer the parents the option of agreeing to a "safety plan," which imposes certain restrictions pending completion of the state's investigation into suspected abuse. For example, a safety plan may require that a child be sent to live with other family members. Although such restrictions on familial rights are "less extreme than removing the child from parental custody altogether, . . . they may be invasive enough to count as deprivations of liberty, thus triggering the right to a hearing." We have likened a safety plan to an interim settlement agreement, stating that "the decision to agree to a safety plan is optional with the parents." In *Dupuy*, we concluded that there is no right to a hearing before the parents are offered a safety plan. We reasoned:

> Parents are entitled to a hearing if their parental rights are impaired, but the offer of a settlement [does not] impair[] those rights. . . .
> . . . Because the safety plan is voluntary, no hearing of any kind is necessary; hearings are required for deprivations ordered over objection, not for steps authorized by consent.

We added that "[i]t is not a forbidden means of 'coercing' a settlement to threaten merely to enforce one's legal [authority]." However, it is improper to obtain consent to a safety plan through duress or other illegal means. Exerting pressure "to obtain a result to which the party applying the pressure had no right" is an example of duress. . . .

. . . [W]here an official makes a threat to take an action that she has no legal authority to take, that is duress; and it is improper to obtain consent to a safety plan through duress or other illegal means. According to Crystelle, Foster presented the safety plan to them and said that once they signed it, they could see

Jaymz, but they "couldn't be alone with him or take him anywhere . . . can't be unsupervised. My grammy still has the custody over him; . . . I don't have . . . my parental rights." Crystelle stated that Foster informed them that "[i]f we didn't sign it [the safety plan], we couldn't see him." When Foster presented the safety plan to Crystelle and Joshua the morning of September 10, however, she could have had no reasonable suspicion that Jaymz had been abused or was in imminent danger of abuse. She therefore had no proper legal authority to tell them that they could not see Jaymz or exercise other parental custody rights unless they agreed to a safety plan.

The district court determined that in context Foster's statements could not reasonably be construed as threats or coercion. But a threat that parents cannot see their child unless they agree to something is extremely coercive. . . . At oral argument, counsel for defendants persisted in ignoring a material fact in this case: Crystelle and Joshua did not have custody of Jaymz when Foster "offered" the safety plan to them and represented that if they didn't sign the plan, they couldn't even see Jaymz. It is one thing for parents to question a caseworker's authority to impose a safety plan when they have custody of their child; it is entirely another when the parents don't have custody. In the former situation, the parents' resistance may create the risk that the child will be taken away from them, whereas in the latter, the child has already been removed—the risk is certain. Defense counsel failed to appreciate this critical difference. In asserting that it was not reasonable for the Hernandezes to sign the safety plan without reading it or questioning Foster's authority, despite "knowing" that temporary custody would end within a few hours and no court hearing would be held, the defendants fail to view the facts and reasonable inferences in favor of the plaintiffs, as we and the district court must. The record raises a genuine issue of fact as to whether Crystelle and Joshua were coerced into signing the safety plan. . . .

All plaintiffs in this case bring procedural due process claims, alleging that the defendants violated their due process rights by taking protective custody of Jaymz in the absence of an emergency or pre-deprivation hearing and coercing Crystelle and Joshua into accepting the safety plan. . . .

"The fundamental requirement of due process is the opportunity to be heard 'at a meaningful time and in a meaningful manner.'" Mathews v. Eldridge, 424 U.S. 319, 333 (1976). "The amount and timing of the process due . . . varies with circumstances." We stated in *Brokaw*, long before the events at issue in this case, that due process "at a minimum . . . requires that government officials not misrepresent the facts in order to obtain the removal of a child from his parents" and "also means that governmental officials will not remove a child from his home without an investigation and pre-deprivation hearing resulting in a court order of removal, absent exigent circumstances."

The plaintiffs assert that *Brokaw* placed any reasonable DCFS investigator, supervisor, or manager on notice that taking Jaymz into temporary custody without a hearing, absent exigent circumstances, violated the plaintiffs' procedural due process rights. We disagree. First, in *Brokaw* we concluded that "[b]ecause [the plaintiff] claims that he was removed based on knowingly false statements of child neglect, and that the defendants removed him from his home without an investigation, a pre-deprivation hearing, or exigent circumstances, he has stated a procedural due process claim[.]" Thus, the conclusion that the plaintiff stated a due process claim was not based solely on the absence of a predeprivation hearing and exigent circumstances. It is a bit unclear whether the plaintiff still would have stated a claim if he had not alleged that he was removed based on misrepresentations.

Furthermore, our decisions contain conflicting language regarding when a pre-deprivation hearing is required before a child's removal. For example, in *Jensen v. Foley*, 295 F.3d 745 (7th Cir. 2002), decided almost two years after *Brokaw*, we stated:

> So long as a post-deprivation hearing is held within 2 business days of removal, DCFS agents constitutionally may remove a child from her home and family without a pre-deprivation hearing if they are acting pursuant to a court order, if the taking is supported by probable cause to believe that the child would be subject to the danger of abuse if not removed, or if exigent circumstances require them to do so.

. . .

When *Jensen* is understood in its factual context, however, it is consonant with *Brokaw*. In *Jensen*, the state court found at a temporary custody hearing that there was probable cause to believe that the removed child was at risk of physical harm in her home *and* that keeping her out of her father's custody was "a matter of immediate and urgent necessity." Thus, in essence the state court found exigent circumstances, which justified the child's removal without a pre-deprivation hearing.

Another decision containing ambiguous language regarding a pre-removal hearing requirement is Lossman v. Pekarske, 707 F.2d 288 (7th Cir. 1983). There, we considered whether a father and his children were denied due process when the children were removed from the father's custody based on an ex parte order. We said that "[w]hen a child's safety is threatened, that is justification enough for action first and hearing afterward." This seems to be an implicit appeal to exigent circumstances, but the language is broad and arguably reaches situations in addition to those in which a child is in imminent danger.

We think it asks too much of reasonable child protection workers to expect them to conduct nuanced legal analysis of the situations they face in the field. Nor do we expect reasonable child protection workers to parse the language of our case law along such fine lines as we have just done. The conflicting language in our decisions may have left them with uncertainty about the procedural due process consequences of the situation confronted in our case.

When read together, our cases such as *Brokaw* and *Jensen*, imply that government officials may remove a child from his home without a pre-deprivation hearing and court order if the official has probable cause to believe that the child is in imminent danger of abuse. Our sister circuits are in accord with this view. *See, e.g.,* Gomes v. Wood, 451 F.3d 1122, 1129 (10th Cir. 2006) (collecting cases); *Kearney*, 329 F.3d at 1295–96 (same). It does not suffice for the official to have probable cause merely to believe that the child was abused or neglected, or is in a general danger of future abuse or neglect. The danger must be imminent, or put another way, the circumstances must be exigent.

At the time of Jaymz's removal, our case law did not put a reasonable DCFS investigator, supervisor, or manager on notice that removing Jaymz without a pre-deprivation hearing violated the plaintiffs' clearly established procedural due process rights. *Jensen* had indicated that the removal was lawful as long as there was probable cause to believe that Jaymz would be subject to the danger of abuse if not removed, and a post-deprivation hearing was held within two business days. We have concluded that a reasonable DCFS worker could have believed there was probable cause to remove Jaymz. No hearing was held in this case, but the defendants did not know at the time of removal that there would be no hearing. And the parents ultimately signed a safety plan before the end of the second day. (We address the procedural due process concerns that arise from the safety plan below.) As we have stated, "the amount of process due varies with the particular situation[.]" It is not insignificant that Jaymz was taken into temporary protective custody and placed with family members, and his parents were allowed some minimal contact with him, all of which lessened the intrusion on the family's rights. Therefore, the defendants are entitled to qualified immunity on the due process claim arising from Jaymz's initial removal. But the process due with respect to the allegedly coerced safety plan is another matter.

Due process "requires that government officials not misrepresent the facts in order to obtain the removal of a child from his parents." This conclusion applies equally in the context of obtaining parental consent to a restrictive safety plan. Under *Dupuy*, the state may not threaten to infringe parental custody rights when the state has no legal right to carry through on the threat. If Foster misrepresented the facts and Crystelle's and Joshua's legal rights in order to obtain their consent to the safety plan, their agreement to the safety plan was not voluntary and they were illegally coerced into signing the plan. Hence, they would have been denied due process. The plaintiffs have created a triable issue as to whether a reasonable parent in their situation would have felt free to refuse to sign the safety plan. Therefore, they have enough evidence to raise a genuine issue as to whether they were coerced into agreeing to the safety plan. . . .

For the foregoing reasons, the grant of summary judgment is AFFIRMED with respect to the Fourth Amendment, substantive due process, and procedural due process claims premised on Jaymz's initial removal, and VACATED with respect to the Fourth Amendment and substantive due process claims premised on the continued withholding of Jaymz as well as the substantive due process and procedural due process claims premised on the safety plan. This case is REMANDED to the district court for proceedings consistent with this opinion.

NOTES AND QUESTIONS

1. The Hernandezes alleged that the state child welfare agency violated Jaymz's Fourth Amendment right and his parents' substantive due process right when agency workers took him into custody the evening of the day that the agency received the child abuse report. Why did the court of appeals affirm the trial court's grant of summary judgment to the defendants on these claims?

Most of the federal courts of appeals have decided cases on these issues, and the majority say that a child can be removed when there is reasonable suspicion that the child has been abused or is in imminent peril of abuse. The Ninth and Eleventh Circuits require reasonable or probable cause of imminent danger. Gomes v. Wood, 451 F.3d 1122, 1129 (10th Cir. 2006) (discussing cases).

2. Jaymz and his parents also claimed that the agency violated their procedural due process rights when the workers took custody without a court order or a pre-removal hearing. What standard does the court use to determine when a court order or hearing is required before a child can be removed from home on the basis of alleged child abuse? Why does the court hold that the agency is entitled to qualified immunity on these claims?

Tenenbaum v. Williams, 193 F.3d 581, 594 (2d Cir. 1999), expresses a strong preference for a prior court order:

> While there is a sufficient emergency to warrant officials' taking a child into custody without a prior hearing if he or she is immediately threatened with harm, the converse is also true. If the danger to the child is not so imminent that there is reasonably sufficient time to seek prior judicial authorization, ex parte or otherwise, for the child's removal, then the circumstances are not emergent; there is no reason to excuse the absence of the judiciary's participation in depriving the parents of the care, custody and management of their child. If, irrespective of whether there is time to obtain a court order, all interventions are effected on an emergency basis without judicial process, pre-seizure procedural due process for the parents and their child evaporates.

This position was rejected by the Tenth and Eleventh Circuits as placing an unreasonable burden on caseworkers. However, failure to seek a court order is a factor in determining the reasonableness of the workers' action in removing the child. Gomes, 451 F.3d at 1130; Doe v. Kearney, 329 F.3d 1286, 1297-98 (11th Cir. 2003). What is the purpose of requiring or at least preferring a court order? If you were advising a caseworker about complying with the *Hernandez* standard, when would you say a prior court order is required?

3. The *Hernandez* court reversed the grant of summary judgment in favor of the defendants on Jaymz's and his parents' claims that workers acted unconstitutionally when they continued to hold him over the next two days after multiple doctors had said that the evidence did not indicate abuse and the state's attorney declined to file a petition because the evidence was insufficient. What standard did the court use to determine whether holding Jaymz was constitutionally permissible?

4. The appellate court also reversed grants of summary judgment to the defendants on the claims that the workers violated the parents' substantive and procedural due process during the process of securing the parents' consent to the "safety plan." Why?

Courts consistently hold that child welfare workers who fabricate evidence or make false statements during an investigation, whether to parents or to a court, are not entitled to qualified immunity. *See, e.g.*, Hardwick v. Cnty. of Orange, 844 F.3d 1112, 1118 (9th Cir. 2017) ("No official with an IQ greater than room temperature in Alaska could claim that he or she did not know that the conduct at the center of this case violated both state and federal law.").

5. As we have seen, the trial court in *Hernandez* granted the defendants' motion for summary judgment on the ground of qualified immunity as to all the claims. Although qualified immunity is an affirmative defense that logically becomes relevant only after the plaintiffs have established a claim that government officials violated their constitutional rights in some way, courts often address

qualified immunity claims first, since a finding of immunity resolves the suit in favor of the officials regardless of whether they violated the constitution. Hernandez says that the determinative issue of whether defendants are entitled to qualified immunity, assuming their conduct violated the constitution, is "whether that right was "clearly established" at the time of the defendant's conduct." Some courts add a second inquiry: "whether, in spite of the fact that the law was clearly established, "extraordinary circumstances"—such as reliance on the advice of counsel or on a statute—"so prevented [the official] from knowing that [her] actions were unconstitutional that [she] should not be imputed with knowledge of a clearly established right." Gomes, 451 F.3d at 1134.

6. An Indiana statute authorized the child welfare agency to seek a court order requiring that a child's parent make the child available for an interview or an order requiring that child welfare investigators be admitted to the home, school, or other place where the child may be located, provided that permission for the interview or admission had been denied and the agency showed good cause. Ind. Code § 31–33–8–7 (2018). In the Matter of A.H., 992 N.E.2d 960 (Ind. App. 2013), rejected a mother's argument that granting an order for an interview under the statute violated procedural due process in the absence of evidence given under oath showing that the child was being abused or neglected. Applying the balancing test of Mathews v. Eldridge, 424 U.S. 319 (1976), the court upheld the process used in that case because of the state's compelling interest in protecting children and in determining whether child abuse reports are substantiated. However, three years later the court held that an interview order that was issued based solely on reports of suspected child mistreatment that the agency made no attempt to investigate violated due process. In the Matter of F.S., 53 N.E.3d 582 (Inc. App. 2016).

7. The Ninth Circuit has held that a parent with legal custody has a protected interest at stake in a child abuse investigation, even if the parent does not have physical custody. Burke v. County of Alameda, 586 F.3d 725 (9th Cir. 2009). The court wrote, "We note, however, that the [constitutional test] is flexible and must take into account the individual circumstances. For example, if the parent without physical custody does not reside nearby, and a child is in imminent danger of harm, it is probably reasonable for a police officer to place a child in protective custody without attempting to place the child with the geographically distant parent." 586 F.3d at 733. In Kirkpatrick v. Cty. of Washoe, 843 F.3d 784 (9th Cir. 2016), the court applied this test to conclude that a biological father whose legal paternity had not been established, who was unsure if he was the biological father, and who had minimal contact with a newborn child did not have constitutionally protected rights that were violated when protective service workers placed the child in state custody.

8. Commentary on the standards and procedures for removing children from their parents' homes upon allegations of abuse includes Mark R. Brown, Rescuing Children from Abusive Parents: The Constitutional Value of Pre-Deprivation Process, 65 Ohio St. L.J. 913 (2004); Doriane Lambelet Coleman, Storming the Castle to Save the Children: The Ironic Costs of a Child Welfare Exception to the Fourth Amendment, 47 Wm. & Mary L. Rev. 413 (2005); Alyson Oswald, Comment: They Took My Child! An Examination of the Circuit Split over Emergency Removal of Children from Parental Custody, 53 Cath. U. L. Rev. 1161 (2004).

9. In some abuse cases, the court orders a child removed because the child cannot safely remain at home as long as the abusive parent is there also, even though if that parent were gone, the child would be safe with the other parent. Often, however, juvenile courts lack authority to order parents to leave their homes before a full adjudicatory hearing. *E.g.*, In re Macomber, 461 N.W.2d 671 (Mich. 1990). Even domestic abuse protection acts that do authorize judges to order people to leave their homes because of their abusive behavior often fail to solve this problem because of their limited scope. For example, they may apply only to abuse of an adult partner, not a child, or only to physical abuse.

PROBLEMS

1. MD is a 14-year-old girl who lives with her mother and stepfather. She told her older sister that the stepfather had sexually molested her, and the sister called the child abuse hotline. The next day a police officer contacted MD's mother about the claim. Mother said that MD often made things up and expressed her belief that MD was lying. Two weeks later a child welfare worker visited MD's home and talked to MD and her mother. MD told the worker that no further acts had occurred, and Mother again said that nothing had happened and that MD was a liar. The worker believed that MD may have been abused and that Mother pressured her to change her story. However, the worker left MD in the home and returned to her office to discuss the case with her supervisor. An agency committee reviewed the case four days later, and the committee recommended that MD be removed from the home and that a petition be brought in juvenile court. Under the *Gomes* standard, does the agency have sufficient evidence to justify removing MD from the home before a trial on the merits? Under the Doe v. Kearney standard discussed in *Gomes*? If so, must the agency obtain a court order before removing MD?

2. You are the assistant attorney general assigned to the state's child protective services agency. The head of the agency has asked you for help in drafting a policy to govern removal of a child from the parents' home in the course of investigation of a report of abuse or neglect. The agency head is particularly concerned about adverse publicity and potential tort liability when a worker misjudges the danger to the child, as will inevitably happen sometimes. Based on what you have read so far, what advice would you give and why?

NOTE: CHILD ABUSE REGISTRIES

All states maintain records of reported cases of child abuse or neglect; most have a centralized database. Child Welfare Information Gateway, U.S. Dep't of Health & Hum. Servs., Establishment and Maintenance of Central Registries for Child Abuse Reports: Summary of State Laws 1 (2014), available at www.childwelfare.gov/topics/systemwide/laws-policies/statutes/centreg/. The registries were originally created to help in investigations of child maltreatment reports and to generate statistical information for staffing and funding purposes.

In 31 states the registries are used to screen people applying to be youth or child care workers, and other employers can use them to screen people who work with children. Most states also use them in background checks of foster and adoptive parent applicants. *Id.*

In most states all reported cases are included in registries, although some of these remove unsubstantiated reports after a period of time ranging from 30 days to 10 years. Thomas L. Hafemeister, Castles Made of Sand? Rediscovering Child Abuse and Society's Response, 36 Ohio N.U. L. Rev. 819, 896 (2010). The amount of evidence required for a report to be classified as "substantiated" varies, with most states using something like probable cause.

The extent of procedural safeguards available to protect individuals who claim they are erroneously listed in a registry varies from state to state. In some cases challenging the adequacy of the safeguards, criminal or juvenile court charges against the person suing had been dropped or not proven at trial, and yet reports remained in the registry. Most courts have found that an individual listed in a registry has a protected liberty interest in not being falsely named, in light of the employment and other consequences that can come from listing. *See, e.g.,* Valmonte v. Bane, 18 F.3d 992 (2d Cir. 1994); Dupuy v. McDonald, 141 F. Supp. 2d 1090 (N.D. Ill. 2001); Jamison v State, 218 S.W.3d 399 (Mo. 2007); In re W.B.M., 690 S.E.2d 41 (N.C. App. 2010). *But see* Smith ex rel. Smith v. Siegelman, 322 F.3d 1290 (11th Cir. 2003) (no protected liberty interest). At a minimum, courts finding a liberty interest have held that people must have notice that they have been or will be listed and a meaningful opportunity to contest. Much of the litigation has focused on whether a pre-listing hearing is required and the standard of proof the state must bear.

For more information, *see* Kate Hollenbeck, Between a Rock and a Hard Place: Child Abuse Registries at the Intersection of Child Protection, Due Process, and Equal Protection, 11 Tex. J. Women & L. 1 (2001); John Sherman, Note: Procedural Fairness for State Abuse Registries: The Case for the Clear and Convincing Evidence Standard, 14 J. Gender Race & Just. 867 (2011); Shaudee Navid, They're Making a List, But Are They Checking It Twice? How Erroneous Placement on Child Offender Databases Offends Procedural Due Process, 44 U.C. Davis L. Rev. 1641 (2011).

The Child Welfare System

8

PATRICIA A. SCHENE, *PAST, PRESENT, AND FUTURE ROLES OF
CHILD PROTECTIVE SERVICES*

8(1) Future of Children 23, 24-29 (1998)

The history of the nation's response to child abuse and neglect has been marked by a tension between two missions: an emphasis on rescuing children from abusive or neglectful families on the one hand, and efforts to support and preserve their families on the other. The contemporary debate over the priority given to these competing goals, waged in the press and in scholarly journals, is actually more than 100 years old. The child rescue orientation is reflected in a longstanding tendency to see child maltreatment as arising from poverty and parental irresponsibility, and so to emphasize the removal of children from their homes to protect them. The family support approach, by contrast, focuses on ameliorating the social and environmental factors that contribute to parental stress and child maltreatment. The child rescue orientation was evident even in colonial times, while the family support philosophy's earliest roots can be found in the social services orientation of the progressive movement in the early twentieth century.

The legal basis for efforts to protect needy children in colonial times rested on the English Poor Law of 1601, which placed public responsibility for the poor in the hands of local townspeople. The doctrine known as *parens patriae*, or the ruler's power to protect minors, was viewed as justification for governmental intervention into the parent–child relationship, either to enforce parental duty or to supply substitute care for the child. The attention of community leaders, philanthropists, and social reformers who were concerned about child abuse and neglect focused primarily on the children of the poorest families and on those who were orphaned, abandoned, or unsupervised. Children of the "unworthy poor" were saved from developing slothful ways by separation from their parents through indenture or placement in institutions. Actions taken on behalf of those children were typically justified on moral grounds, but they also served as potent instruments of social control.

During most of the nineteenth century, destitute children were sent to institutions operated by private, charitable organizations. For instance, foundling hospitals to care for unwanted babies opened in some communities in the early nineteenth century. Many more poor or abandoned children were sent to live in almshouses—facilities established in the 1800s in many large cities to house the very poor of all ages. Almshouses provided a minimal standard of care to orphaned or needy children and to impoverished, insane, or diseased adults. Typically, when the children reached 9 or 10 years of age, they were either indentured to families as servants or apprenticed out to learn a skill and pay for their care by their free labor.

The second half of the nineteenth century saw increasing criticism of the impacts that the unsanitary, chaotic almshouses had on children, especially the very young, who suffered high mortality rates there. Private charities and religious groups established orphanages or children's asylums to separate needy children from adults and protect them from the disease, maltreatment, and exploitation that faced them in almshouses.

A number of states passed laws requiring that children be moved from almshouses to such children's institutions. The care of needy children was considered a public responsibility and so was financed with public dollars, although private agencies provided the care.

The demands that urbanization, industrialization, and immigration placed on poor and working-class families in the late nineteenth century left many children unattended.

Child vagrancy became an increasingly visible problem. In 1853, a young minister named Charles Loring Brace responded to the huge numbers of homeless, ragged, hungry children prowling the streets of New York City by forming the Children's Aid Society to rescue those children. During a span of 75 years, the Children's Aid Society sent more than 150,000 orphans by train to live in Christian homes in rural areas, often in the Midwest, where their labor was valued by farm families. Rural states also relied on family placements to care for their own homeless or dependent children. For instance, between 1866 and 1899, the state of Ohio established 50 homes in which farm families cared for wards of the county at a cost of one dollar per week per child. These homes can be seen as precursors of today's foster care system.

In the eighteenth and nineteenth centuries, poor and immigrant parents were rarely treated with compassion. Those facing hard times received little help. When there was a lack of supervision, a home was unsafe, or a family was not economically viable, the children were often removed. Some resourceful families escaped detection by the authorities, and others received help through ties to religious communities, assistance societies for ethnic immigrant groups or the nascent political machines in urban areas. Most families, however, faced their troubles on their own because help was not readily available, or because they wanted to avoid the risk of losing their children.

The forerunners of the child protective services (CPS) agencies that today investigate and respond to child abuse and neglect were private associations known as "anticruelty societies." The New York Society for the Prevention of Cruelty to Children was the first to be formed, following a famous case in New York City. A visiting nurse made headlines by demanding the same intervention for a severely abused child (called Mary Ellen) that would be afforded an animal in similar circumstances. In that same year, 1877, New York State passed a law to protect children and punish wrongs done to them, giving the anticruelty societies a legal foundation and a mandate to identify children who were being mistreated by their families. More states passed laws protecting children as the twentieth century began, laying the groundwork for the nation's juvenile court system.

By the early twentieth century, more than 300 Societies for the Prevention of Cruelty to Children (SPCCs) operated in cities in the Northeast and the Midwest under the umbrella of the American Humane Association. These private agencies, supported by public and private funds, investigated reports of child abuse and neglect, filed complaints against the perpetrators in court, and aided the courts in the prosecution of those complaints. Some SPCCs were given police powers and could take custody of children pending the investigation. In the nineteenth century only one state, Indiana, relied on a governmental body to perform these duties.

The philosophies of the SPCCs that developed in different states varied in the emphasis they placed on the mission of rescuing children from unhealthy environments or neglectful families, compared with that of helping families to provide more appropriate care for their offspring. Initially, many SPCCs adopted a punitive emphasis on the investigation and prosecution of charges of maltreatment, which dismissed parents as, in the words of the director of the New York SPCC, "cruelists." In other states, the SPCCs attempted to assist families instead. For instance, when it began in 1878, the Massachusetts SPCC operated "primarily as an arm of the law," but by 1907 it came to stress family rehabilitation and community reform under C.C. Carstens, its new executive director. Under his leadership, the MSPCC helped to address the environmental issues children and families faced, such as poor housing; lack of food, clothing, and child care; and harmful neighborhood conditions. He thought the SPCCs had to organize not only against individual cases of abuse and neglect, but also to prevent what he called "community neglect." His ideas placed child protective work firmly in the camp of progressive social action.

As a general progressive agenda of social reform was adopted in the early years of the twentieth century, the approach of assisting parents to care for their children was more widely endorsed. For instance, in 1909, the first White House Conference on Children issued the following policy statement: "No child should be removed from the home unless it is impossible so to construct family conditions or to build and supplement family resources as to make the home safe for the child. . . ."

A leader in the American Humane Association, Dr. Vincent de Francis, explained the emerging philosophy this way: "The best way to rescue a child is to rescue the family for the child." In 1920, the newly established Child Welfare League of America worked with the American Humane Association and other agencies to promote the idea of a national (though largely private) child welfare program that would stress temporary out-of-home care for dependent children, and would attempt to preserve the natural family home whenever possible.

During the mid-twentieth century, the issue of child protection was transformed in the eyes of professionals from one of law enforcement to one of rehabilitation through social services. Efforts to protect children gradually became part of the growing array of human services provided by governmental agencies. By the 1930s and 1940s, the functions once performed by the humane societies were taken over by a variety of public and voluntary organizations such as juvenile courts, juvenile protective associations, family welfare societies, and some newly formed governmental bodies. The growing acceptance by states, counties, and municipalities of the responsibility for child protection, although uneven, marked a new era in the child welfare movement.

The federal government first ventured into the child welfare arena with the passage of the Social Security Act of 1935. That law established the Aid to Dependent Children program, which offered cash assistance to enable poor, single mothers to care for their children rather than lose custody of them. A lesser-known part of that legislation (Title IV-B, Child Welfare Services) provided limited federal funding to encourage states to develop preventive and protective services for vulnerable children. . . .

OVERVIEW—THE LIFE HISTORY OF AN ABUSE OR NEGLECT CASE

The fundamental mission of the juvenile court/child welfare agency system is defined in therapeutic terms—to protect children from harm, to identify causes of family dysfunction, and to work with parents to solve the problems that lead to dysfunction.

If the child welfare agency determines that an allegation of abuse or neglect is well founded, no further formal action may be taken if the parents cooperate with child welfare agency staff. The agency must make reasonable efforts to avoid removing the child from the parents' home, and often will work with the parents on an informal basis. If the parents are uncooperative or if the worker thinks that services are needed that are unavailable without a court order, such as extended foster care for the child, the worker initiates formal court action.

In all states, jurisdiction for the purpose of child protection is vested in a specialized juvenile or family court with broad discretionary powers. The child welfare worker or the state's attorney will ordinarily review the case for legal sufficiency and, if further legal action is warranted, prosecute the case in juvenile court. The trial on the merits, called the adjudicatory hearing, is conducted before a judge or referee sitting without a jury. The state bears the burden of proof, usually by a preponderance of the evidence. Most evidentiary rules apply, and in most states, parents have a statutory right to appointed counsel. Children may be represented by a lawyer or by a court-appointed lay advocate. In the great majority of cases, courts find that the evidence is sufficient to support the allegations at the fact-finding hearing. If the allegations of abuse or neglect are proven, the court moves to the dispositional phase, which is analogous to sentencing following a criminal conviction.

Traditionally, juvenile court judges have had broad discretion to make a disposition "in the best interests of the child." An agency or court-affiliated social worker conducts a social study before disposition, which analyzes the problems that led to the finding of jurisdiction, reviews available resources, and recommends a disposition. Statutes typically authorize the judge to dismiss the case outright; leave the child at home on certain conditions, including agency supervision (protective supervision); or remove the child and grant custody to a friend or relative or to the state child welfare agency, which places the child in foster care or in a treatment facility if need be. If custody is granted to the child welfare agency, the agency continues in most cases to have a responsibility to make reasonable efforts to make it possible to reunify the parent and child, pursuant to a case plan, which also requires the parents to participate in activities intended to solve the problems that led to state intervention.

Following disposition, cases are reviewed by the court or by an administrative agency at least every six months for progress toward achieving the goals of the case plan. If sufficient progress is made, the child returns home; if this is not possible, an alternate permanent plan must be devised for the child, such as termination of parental rights followed by adoption or some other arrangement.

A.   PRETRIAL CUSTODY, THE SHELTER HEARING, AND REASONABLE EFFORTS

In most cases, children have been removed from their parents' custody by the time a child abuse and neglect petition is filed in juvenile court. In Chapter 7 we examined the constitutional standards that govern when a state child welfare agency may remove a child from the parents' custody without a full hearing on whether the removal is justified. State juvenile codes define when children can be removed from their parents' custody before the adjudicatory hearing on the state's allegations. In addition, state and federal laws provide that the child welfare agency must have made "reasonable efforts" to prevent removal, and a judge must then make a finding about whether the agency made reasonable efforts. The federal Adoption Assistance and Child Welfare Act of 1980 established these requirements by making compliance with them a condition of the state's eligibility to receive federal money for a child in foster care. The Adoption and Safe Families Act (ASFA) of 1997 modifies the requirements by requiring that the child's safety be the first concern in decisions about the child's placement. 42 U.S.C. §§ 671(a)(15), 672(a)(1).

Implicit in the reasonable efforts requirements is a preference for leaving the child in the parents' custody if possible. Explaining this preference, the Connecticut Supreme Court wrote:

> . . . [C]ourts and state agencies must keep in mind the constitutional limitations imposed on a state which undertakes any form of coercive intervention in family affairs. The United States Supreme Court has frequently emphasized the constitutional importance of family integrity. "The rights to conceive and to raise one's children have been deemed 'essential,' 'basic civil rights of man,' and '[r]ights far more precious . . . than property rights.' . . . The integrity of the family unit has found protection in the Due Process Clause of the Fourteenth Amendment, the Equal Protection Clause of the Fourteenth Amendment, and the Ninth Amendment." It must be stressed, however, that the right to family integrity is not a right of the parents alone, but "encompasses the reciprocal rights of both parents and children. It is the interest of the parent in the 'companionship, care, custody and management of his or her children,' and of the children in not being dislocated from the 'emotional attachments that derive from the intimacy of daily association,' with the parent." This right to family integrity includes "the most essential and basic aspect of familial

privacy—the right of the family to remain together without the coercive interference of the awesome power of the state." . . .

Studies indicate that the best interests of the child are usually served by keeping the child in the home with his or her parents. "Virtually all experts, from many different professional disciplines, agree that children need and benefit from continuous, stable home environments." Institute of Judicial Administration-American Bar Association, Juvenile Justice Standards Project, Standards Relating to Abuse and Neglect, p. 45 (Tentative draft, 1977) (IJA-ABA, STDS). The love and attention not only of parents, but also of siblings, which is available in the home environment, cannot be provided by the state. Unfortunately, an order of temporary custody often results in the children of one family being separated and scattered to different foster homes with little opportunity to see each other. Even where the parent–child relationship is "marginal," it is usually in the best interests of the child to remain at home and still benefit from a family environment.

In re Juvenile Appeal (83-CD), 455 A.2d 1313, 1318-1319 (Conn. 1983). The preference for leaving children at home if possible is also supported by evidence that many children are traumatized by removal and that foster care placements themselves are sometimes not adequate. Michael S. Wald, New Directions for Foster Care, 68 Juv. & Fam. Ct. J. 7 (2017).

State laws provide that if a child is taken into state custody, the agency must file a petition seeking juvenile court jurisdiction over the child within a short time. After the petition is filed, the parents are summoned to appear at an initial hearing, the shelter hearing, where the judge decides whether to return the child or keep the child in out-of-home care pending the adjudicatory hearing. At this hearing the judge typically makes the first reasonable efforts finding. A finding that the child welfare agency has not made reasonable efforts before removing a child from home does not mean that the child will be returned to the parents immediately, since the child's safety is the overriding concern. However, the state cannot receive federal foster care funds for the child if a judge finds that removal was not necessary to protect the child's welfare or that reasonable efforts to enable the child to remain at home were not made. Therefore, judges face something of a dilemma if they conclude that an agency has not made reasonable efforts. On the one hand, just making the finding has the effect of depriving the agency and thus the children of needed funds. On the other hand, failure to make the finding when the facts warrant it undermines the purposes of the law.

The federal statutes do not define "reasonable efforts," and most state statutes do not define the term either. The next case examines the requirement that a judge makes the reasonable efforts determination as well as the meaning of "reasonable efforts."

CARE AND PROTECTION OF WALT

84 N.E.3d 803 (Mass. 2017)

GANTS, C.J. . . . .[I]n June, 2016, the department received a report alleging that Walt, then three years old, was being neglected by his mother and father at the home of Walt's paternal grandmother in Worcester, where they were then living. On June 1, at approximately 4:30 P.M., a department investigator made an unannounced visit to the home, and subsequently prepared a written report as required by G. L. c. 119, § 51B. As she went upstairs, where Walt and his parents were residing, she smelled the strong odor of marijuana and saw that the upstairs hallway was littered with trash. She went to the parents' bedroom and saw a curtain hanging as a door. After she knocked on the door jamb, the mother opened the curtain and the investigator reported the allegations to her; the father was lying in bed. The investigator asked where Walt was, and the mother said he was in his room, which was next to the parents' bedroom. When the investigator visited Walt's bedroom, she observed that the floor was so covered with boxes, clothing, trash, and debris that there was no room to walk. She saw items piled taller than the dresser and various safety hazards. The investigator returned to the parents' bedroom and asked the parents about smoking marijuana in their bedroom with Walt in the next bedroom. The mother insisted she did not smoke in front of Walt. The investigator observed trash and debris littering the floor of the parents' bedroom, including dirty plates, cups, cigarette butts, and a chicken bone.

The investigator informed the parents that she was going to call her supervisor, and that she was taking custody of Walt "as I was not leaving him in this mess." The investigator telephoned her supervisor, who agreed that emergency removal of the child was necessary at that time. The investigator then telephoned the Worcester police department and asked for assistance in removing the child from the home.

After the investigator informed both parents that the department was taking custody of their son, the mother asked if she could call her aunt to take Walt rather than have him go to a foster home. The investigator told her that that could not happen, because the department office was closed and she therefore could not complete the process required to determine whether a family member qualified as a caregiver. The investigator offered to take down the name of the aunt and other household members to see if they would qualify.

The father was upset that the department was taking custody of his son and grabbed Walt and walked downstairs. The investigator told him that he could not leave with Walt because the department now had custody and, if he did, he could be arrested for parental kidnapping. He remained with Walt downstairs.

The maternal aunt then arrived and attempted to take Walt with her. The investigator told her she could not take him because the department had custody. The investigator wrote down her identifying information and explained that, if there were no issues, a home study would have to be done. The investigator said that Walt was going to a foster home that day and that the department would begin the process of evaluating the maternal aunt as a "resource" the next day.

The investigator then spoke with the mother and father. The mother said that she worked at a supermarket and that the father worked at an automobile body shop down the street. She did not have a set work schedule; the father watched Walt when she was working. As to the condition of the upstairs portion of the house, she said it was in that condition when they moved to the paternal grandmother's home in October, 2015. When the investigator asked why they had not cleaned the rooms, the mother said that the paternal grandmother would not allow it. The mother said that they had attempted to obtain public housing, but had been denied. The mother admitted to smoking marijuana a few times per week, but said she usually did not smoke upstairs; she explained that she did that day because she was "stressed out." The father said he smoked marijuana a "couple of times a day," but generally only at his workplace. The father denied having any adult criminal record, and both denied using any other controlled substance. The mother provided the name of Walt's pediatrician, and the parents reported that Walt had no health issues, except that he had a cold with fever, for which they were giving him Tylenol.

On June 2, a care and protection petition was filed in the Worcester County Division of the Juvenile Court Department (Worcester Juvenile Court) for emergency custody of Walt pursuant to G. L. c. 119, § 24, as well as a sworn affidavit in support of the application. The affidavit signed by the investigator and her supervisor briefly summarized the investigator's observations regarding the condition of the two rooms and hallway on the second floor of the parental grandmother's home and noted that the mother appeared to be "high" on marijuana. The affiants declared that the department "believes that the child is at risk for neglect by his parents and requests custody of" Walt pending a hearing on the merits, adding that it would be contrary to Walt's welfare "at this time" to return home. The affiants also stated, "In light of the emergency circumstances and risk to the child's health and safety, reasonable efforts by the [d]epartment were attempted. However, the parents have either not participated or have only minimally participated."

That same day, a judge, as authorized under § 24, issued an ex parte emergency order transferring custody of Walt to the department for up to seventy-two hours pending a hearing as to whether temporary custody should continue, and ordered that counsel be appointed for the mother, father, and child. Based on the affidavit, the judge signed a Trial Court form entitled, "Reasonable efforts—initial custody," certifying that "the continuation of the child in his[] home is contrary to the child's best interests." The judge also checked two of the three boxes, reflecting her determination both that the department "has made reasonable efforts prior to the placement of the child with the [department] to prevent or eliminate the need for removal from the child's home," and that "the existing circumstances indicate that there is an immediate risk of harm or neglect which precludes the provision of preventive services as an alternative to removal; consequently, the [department's] efforts were reasonable under the circumstances."

During the early evening of June 2, Walt was placed in the home of the maternal aunt, but the department retained custody of the child.

The seventy-two hour hearing was held on June 3 before another judge to determine whether the department's temporary custody of Walt would continue beyond seventy-two hours. The mother stipulated to continued custody of Walt by the department, and waived her right to a hearing. The father exercised his right to a hearing, which was rescheduled to June 7 and concluded on June 9. At the hearing, the judge heard the testimony of the investigator, the father, the mother, the maternal grandmother, and the maternal aunt, and considered the exhibits offered in evidence, which included the investigator's redacted § 51B report and photographs of the home taken by the investigator on June 2.

The investigator admitted at the hearing that she did not know whether the department was able to provide families with homemaking or babysitting services, whether the family support services the department provides included "chore services," or whether counselling and management services were available to prevent the removal of children from their parents by the department.[1] She also testified that, as an investigator, it was not her job to make reasonable efforts to prevent or eliminate the need for removal before removing a child to the custody of the department. As to Walt, she admitted that she decided to remove Walt within ten minutes of being in the home, before she spoke with the father. She also admitted that, before she placed Walt in the custody of the department, she did not explore with the family possible alternatives to avoid the need for foster care. She explained that her "job is to make sure children are safe," and she "did not feel the child was safe in the place that he was living." She later clarified that she meant "physically safe"; she said she did not remove Walt from the home simply because it was dirty and messy.

On June 9, the judge ruled that custody would remain with the department pending a final hearing on the merits, finding that the department had met its burden of proving by a preponderance of the evidence that, if Walt were returned to the home, he would be in immediate risk of serious abuse or neglect. The judge made no determination as to whether the department made reasonable efforts to prevent or eliminate the need for removal from the home before taking custody. Instead, he found that the department had no obligation "to do anything other than remove the child."

The father petitioned for interlocutory relief under G. L. c. 231, § 118, challenging both the judge's order that allowed the department's temporary custody of Walt to continue and his finding that the department was not obligated to make reasonable efforts to prevent or eliminate the need to remove Walt from his parents' custody. On August 1, 2016, a single justice of the Appeals Court determined that the judge erred in his June 9 ruling when he concluded that the department had no obligation to make reasonable efforts before removing the child from the parents' custody. The single justice declared that the department had an obligation to adhere to the mandates of G. L. c. 119, § 29C, including the obligation to make reasonable efforts to eliminate the need for removal from the home . . . The single justice further found that "[t]he [d]epartment did not make reasonable efforts to eliminate the need for removal prior to removing [Walt]; rather, it summarily removed the child from the premises."

The single justice remanded the case to the Worcester Juvenile Court Department "for a further hearing as to what reasonable efforts will be made by the [d]epartment to eliminate the need to remove [Walt] from the home." The single justice also ordered that (1) daily supervised visitation between the father and Walt, that is, parenting time, shall be permitted by the department; (2) the father shall be permitted to participate in Walt's special education meetings; (3) the department shall explore alternative housing options for Walt and his parents to facilitate their reunification; and (4) Walt shall remain in the custody of

---

1. Each of these services is available to the department to support struggling parents in need of such services. See 110 Code Mass. Regs. §§ 7.020–7.025 (2008) (homemaker services); 110 Code Mass. Regs. §§ 7.030–7.035 (2008) (family support services); 110 Code Mass. Regs. §§ 7.040–7.046 (2008) (babysitting services); 110 Code Mass. Regs. §§ 7.060–7.064 (2008) (parent aide services).

the department until the father has found alternative housing for the family and, once he has found such housing, the Juvenile Court shall determine whether Walt should be reunified with his parents.

The department moved for reconsideration of the single justice's order and for a stay. The single justice denied both motions but, at the request of the child's attorney, modified his order regarding visitation, reducing visits to four per week. The single justice also reported his order to a panel of the Appeals Court to determine the legal issues. We transferred the case to this court on our own motion. . . .

Statutory framework. To understand the legal issues presented on appeal, we need first to set forth the statutory framework governing care and protection proceedings. In 1954, the Legislature, through its enactment of G. L. c. 119, § 1, declared it "to be the policy of this commonwealth to direct its efforts, first, to the strengthening and encouragement of family life for the care and protection of children; to assist and encourage the use by any family of all available resources to this end; and to provide substitute care of children only when the family itself or the resources available to the family are unable to provide the necessary care and protection to insure the rights of any child to sound health and normal physical, mental, spiritual, and moral development." In 1999, the Legislature made clear that, where the interests of parents and children are in conflict, "[t]he health and safety of the child shall be of paramount concern and shall include the long-term well-being of the child." The legislative policy that removal of a child from the family is a last resort is implemented through three provisions: G. L. c. 119, §§ 24, 29C, and 51B. Where the department has reasonable cause to believe both that "a child's health or safety is in immediate danger from abuse or neglect," and that "removal is necessary to protect the child from abuse or neglect," the department "shall take a child into immediate temporary custody" and "shall file a care and protection petition under section 24 on the next court day."

On the day a petition is filed, a judge will conduct an emergency hearing which, like a hearing for a temporary restraining order, is usually ex parte, with the department's petitioner present but not the parents. "If the court is satisfied after the petitioner testifies under oath that there is reasonable cause to believe that: (i) the child is suffering from serious abuse or neglect or is in immediate danger of serious abuse or neglect; and (ii) that immediate removal of the child is necessary to protect the child from serious abuse or neglect, the court may issue an emergency order transferring custody of the child for up to [seventy-two] hours to the department . . . ." Upon entry of this emergency order, notice of the seventy-two hour hearing is given to the parents and, where they are indigent, counsel is appointed to represent the parents and the child.

The seventy-two hour hearing, like a hearing for a preliminary injunction, is an adversarial evidentiary hearing where the department and the parents have an opportunity to present evidence and to be heard. At this hearing, the judge "shall determine whether temporary custody shall continue beyond [seventy-two] hours until a hearing on the merits of the petition for care and protection is concluded. . . ." Because temporary custody is generally substantially longer than emergency custody, the department's burden of proof to continue temporary custody is a "fair preponderance of the evidence," not reasonable cause.

At the emergency hearing, if the judge grants custody of the child to the department, the judge must make both a written certification and a determination: the judge "shall certify that the continuation of the child in his home is contrary to his best interests and shall determine whether the department or its agent, as appropriate, has made reasonable efforts prior to the placement of a child with the department to prevent or eliminate the need for removal from the home." Under § 29C, the determination regarding reasonable efforts is separate and distinct from the certification regarding the child's best interests. . . .

The department's obligation to make reasonable efforts does not end once the department takes temporary custody of a child, but the purpose of those efforts shifts from preventing or eliminating the need for removal from the home to making it "possible for the child to return safely to his parent or guardian."

These State statutes must be understood in the context of Federal legislation, first enacted in 1980, that, among other things, expanded Federal foster care assistance payments and conditioned such funding on the State's development of a plan for the provision of foster care in accordance with the requirements in the Federal statute. *See* Adoption Assistance and Child Welfare Act of 1980, Pub. L. No. 96–272, 94 Stat. 500 (June 17, 1980) (1980 act). The bill established "a comprehensive set of child welfare services procedures and safeguards . . . [to] protect children and families against unwarranted removal of children from their homes and inappropriate and unnecessarily prolonged foster care placement."

Relevant for purposes of this case, Congress provided that "[e]ach State with a plan approved under this part shall make foster care maintenance payments" on behalf of each child who has been removed from the home into foster care where, among other requirements, there is "a judicial determination to the effect that continuation therein would be contrary to the welfare of such child and . . . that reasonable efforts of the type described in [42 U.S.C. § 671(a)(15)] have been made." Section 671(a)(15) provided that "reasonable efforts will be made (A) prior to the placement of a child in foster care, to prevent or eliminate the need for removal of the child from his home, and (B) to make it possible for the child to return to his home."

In 1997, Congress amended the reasonable efforts requirement with the passage of the Adoption and Safe Families Act, Pub. L. No. 105–89, 105th Cong., 1st Sess. (Nov. 19, 1997). . . .

. . . [T]he 1997 act made clear that, "in determining reasonable efforts to be made with respect to a child . . . and in making such reasonable efforts, the child's health and safety shall be the paramount concern."

Although the State policy announced in G. L. c. 119, § 1, that essentially declared that removal of a child from his or her parents is a last resort, predates the enactment of both the Federal 1980 and 1997 acts, the enactment of G. L. c. 119, § 29C in 1984 and the amendments to §§ 1 and 24 that followed those two acts ensured that Massachusetts remains eligible to receive Federal financial assistance for foster care maintenance payments. The department's obligation to make reasonable efforts, therefore, is both a duty owed by statute consistent with a State policy that dates back to 1954, and a duty with substantial financial consequences for Federal reimbursement of foster care maintenance payments.

Discussion. 1. *Must the judge make a reasonable efforts determination at the seventy-two hour hearing?* The department contends that, where the determination that the department made reasonable efforts prior to removal of the child from the home was made by the judge at the emergency hearing, the judge at the seventy-two hour hearing was not required to make such a determination, and the single justice erred in ruling otherwise. We disagree.

Section 24 plainly states that, where a judge determines at a seventy-two hour hearing that temporary custody of a child shall continue beyond seventy-two hours, the judge "shall also consider the provisions of [§] 29C and shall make the written certification and determinations required by said [§] 29C." Where the meaning of the statutory language is plain and unambiguous, and where a literal construction would not "yield an absurd or unworkable result," we need not look to extrinsic evidence to discern legislative intent.

It is equally plain that the Legislature's imposition of this obligation on the judge at the seventy-two hour hearing is consistent with the State policy that removal of a child from his or her parents is a last resort, albeit one that sometimes is necessary because "[t]he health and safety of the child shall be of paramount concern." The judge at the emergency hearing generally receives information only from the department petitioner; the parents are usually neither present nor at that time represented by counsel. The emergency nature of the hearing means that the hearing, "in the interest of expediency, most likely cannot be exhaustive." The judge's determination at that emergency hearing regarding the department's reasonable efforts therefore is generally based on information obtained solely from the department, whose efforts are the subject of the judge's evaluation, regarding a removal that occurred the previous day.

Much as a judge deciding a preliminary injunction must revisit his or her findings issued upon the grant of an ex parte temporary restraining order, so, too, must a judge at the seventy-two hour hearing revisit the determination of reasonable efforts made earlier at the ex parte emergency hearing. "[A] primary function of the seventy-two hour hearing is to discover and correct any errors that may have occurred during the initial hearing . . ."

The circumstances of this case illustrate the Legislature's wisdom in requiring that the determination of reasonable efforts also be made by the judge who conducts the seventy-two hour hearing. The judge who made the reasonable efforts determination at the emergency hearing wrote that she based her determination on the affidavit submitted by the investigator and her supervisor, which attested that "reasonable efforts by the [d]epartment were attempted; however, the parents have either not participated or have only minimally participated." In fact, as emerged at the seventy-two hour hearing, the investigator admitted that she had removed Walt from his parents' custody within ten minutes of entering the home, after only a brief conversation with the mother and before even speaking with the father. She also admitted that she did not explore possible alternatives to avoid the need for foster care with either the mother or the father. Therefore, it was simply not true that the investigator attempted to make reasonable efforts but was thwarted by the failure of the parents to participate with her in those efforts. The emergency judge's determination of reasonable efforts rested on materially inaccurate information. The judge at the seventy-two hour hearing was in a far better position, as a result of the adversarial evidentiary hearing, to make an informed determination of reasonable efforts.

2. . . . *[M]ay exigent circumstances excuse the department from making reasonable efforts to prevent or eliminate the need for a child's removal from his or her parents' custody?* . . . [T]he department claims that, where there are exigent circumstances,

such as those it contends were present in this case, the department is excused from making reasonable efforts to prevent or eliminate the need for removal of the child from parental custody. We disagree, but we recognize that a judge must determine what is reasonable in light of the particular circumstances in each case, that the health and safety of the child must be the paramount concern, and that no child should remain in the custody of the parents if his or her immediate removal is necessary to protect the child from serious abuse or neglect. . . .

What constitutes reasonable efforts, therefore, must be evaluated in the context of each individual case, considering any exigent circumstances that might exist. Where the department had prior involvement with the family before the exigency arose, those efforts may be considered in determining whether reasonable efforts were made. Where there was little or no prior involvement prior to the exigency, reasonable efforts are still required but they need only be reasonable in light of the exigency. We recognize that there might be exigent circumstances where there is nothing the department reasonably could have done to prevent or eliminate the need for removal from the home, but these do not excuse the department from its obligation reasonably to explore the possibility of reasonable alternatives to removal of the child; it simply means that in those circumstances, after such alternatives were considered, no reasonable alternatives were possible.

This case illustrates how reasonable efforts were possible in a situation that the department deemed exigent. The department's investigator here was so concerned about the sanitary conditions in the home and the mother's use of marijuana that she immediately took custody of the child after a brief conversation with the mother and before she had spoken with the father, who was ill but present. As a result, apart from what she had seen within ten minutes of her arrival at the home, when she took custody on behalf of the department, she knew almost nothing about the relationship between the parents and the child, about whether the parents had obtained appropriate medical care for the child and acted appropriately to address his speech issues, about why they were living with the paternal grandmother, about whether there were other housing arrangements that could be made that day for the child, and about whether there were other trusted members of the family who might care for Walt while the home was cleaned. The investigator had already taken custody of Walt before the maternal aunt arrived at the home and offered to take Walt to her home. As the single justice essentially found, reasonable efforts would have required the investigator at least to speak with the parents and obtain more information *before* making the decision to take custody of the child and put him in foster care.

As we have noted, and as § 29C makes clear, the judge's determination regarding reasonable efforts is separate and distinct from the judge's certification regarding the child's best interests that decides whether the child should remain in the custody of the department. "A determination by the court that reasonable efforts were not made shall not preclude the court from making any appropriate order conducive to the child's best interest." . . .

3. *Did the single justice exceed his authority by ordering the department to permit the father to visit with Walt four times each week, to permit his participation in Walt's special education meetings, and to explore alternative housing for the family?* The department contends that the single justice's order regarding visitation, participation in special education meetings, and exploration of alternative housing exceeded his

authority and that of any Juvenile Court judge. We disagree. Where, as here, the single justice found that the department failed to fulfil its duty to make reasonable efforts before taking custody of Walt, he had the equitable authority to order the department to take reasonable remedial steps to diminish the adverse consequences of its breach of duty.

As noted earlier, the single justice found that "[t]he department did not make reasonable efforts to eliminate the need for removal prior to removing Walt; rather, it summarily removed the child from the premises." The department contends that the only adverse consequence of its failure to obtain a reasonable efforts determination is the potential loss of Federal reimbursement for the foster care maintenance payments in this case.[2] But the single justice was entitled to conclude from the evidence in the record that the department's failure to make reasonable efforts also adversely affected Walt and his family and that reasonable equitable relief was needed to diminish that adverse impact. When the matter reached the single justice, it was too late to order the department to fulfil its duty to make reasonable efforts to eliminate the need for removal, but it was not too late to ensure that the department fulfilled its duty to make it possible for the child to return safely to his father or to attempt to hasten the time when that reunification would become practicable.

When the single justice entered his initial order, the department was allowing the father to visit his son only twice each month, for one hour per visit. We have recognized the critical importance of parenting time to the parent-child relationship:

> Visitation, like custody, is at the core of a parent's relationship with a child; being physically present in a child's life, sharing time and experiences, and providing personal support are among the most intimate aspects of a parent-child relationship. For a parent who has lost (or willingly yielded) custody of a child temporarily to a guardian, visitation can be especially critical because it provides an opportunity to maintain a physical, emotional, and psychological bond with the child during the guardianship period, if that is in the child's best interest; and in cases where the parent aspires to regain custody at some point, it provides an opportunity to demonstrate the ability to properly care for the child.

L.B. v. Chief Justice of the Probate & Family Court Dep't, 474 Mass. 231, 242, 49 N.E.3d 230 (2016). Where the department had so limited the father's opportunity to visit with his three-year-old son as to imperil the father-child bond that was essential if custody were to be restored, the single justice did not exceed his authority or abuse his discretion by ordering a visitation schedule that would enable that bond to remain intact. Nor did the single justice exceed his authority or abuse his discretion in ordering the department to permit the father to participate in Walt's special education meetings so that he could remain involved in his son's education.

---

2. Where a judge grants the department temporary custody but determines that reasonable efforts were not made by the department prior to removal, the department is ineligible for Federal reimbursement for the child's foster care maintenance payments for the duration of the child's stay in foster care. See 42 U.S.C. § 672(a)(2)(A)(ii) (2012); 45 C.F.R. § 1356.21(b)(1)(ii) (2016).

Another adverse consequence of the department's failure to make reasonable efforts prior to removal was that, with Walt in the department's custody, the family would potentially face greater difficulties in securing public housing benefits, which might have made it harder for the family to obtain the alternative housing that was likely a prerequisite to family reunification. The single justice did not exceed his authority or abuse his discretion in ordering the department to explore alternative housing options to facilitate that reunification. . . .

NOTES AND QUESTIONS

1. Massachusetts law requires that when the child welfare agency removes a child without a prior court order (the usual practice in most states), it must submit the case to a judge on the next court day for an ex parte determination of whether the removal was justified. Many states skip this step and go straight to the shelter hearing at which the parents are entitled to be present, which Massachusetts calls the 72-hour hearing. What are the advantages of having two hearings? Why would a state choose to have only one hearing (which would probably occur earlier than 72 hours after removal if possible)?

2. What standard governs emergency removal of a child under Massachusetts law? Was that standard met in Care and Protection of Walt?

3. Upon what basis did the juvenile court judge make the ex parte finding that the agency had made reasonable efforts to avoid having to remove Walt? Why did the single appellate justice (and then the Supreme Judicial Court) disagree? What meaning does the *Walt* opinion give to reasonable efforts?

4. Does *Walt* stand for the proposition that if the reason the child welfare agency proposes to remove a child is filthy conditions in the home, the agency must instead hire a housekeeping service to clean up the place? On similar facts, an Iowa court held that the agency made reasonable efforts when it simply told the parent that the house was unacceptably dirty and that she needed to clean it up. In the Interest of N.M.W., 461 N.W.2d 478 (Iowa App. 1990).

If you were the agency's lawyer, how would you argue cleaning goes beyond *reasonable* efforts? If you were the parents' lawyer, how would you argue for a weekly housekeeper if that were needed? Does it matter why the parents kept the house so dirty in the first place?

5. If a child is found neglected because the family is homeless and living in a car, does the reasonable-efforts requirement obligate the child welfare agency to find housing for the family? If so, does this mean that the agency must command another public entity, the housing authority, to move the family to the top of the waiting list for publicly subsidized housing? Must the child welfare agency pay rent for private housing? Why would the agency resist such obligations?

6. *Walt* also suggests that exploring the possibility that the child could stay with relatives while the house was being cleaned was part of the reasonable efforts requirement. How could this be regarded as furthering the goals of preventing the child's removal from home and, if the child is removed, reunifying the parents and child?

7. In addition to finding the agency had not made reasonable efforts to prevent removal, the appellate justice also ordered that Walt's father be allowed to visit him frequently and continue to participate in his special education programs. As the court says, regular, high-quality visitation helps children adjust to out of home care, greatly increases the chances of reunification, and if reunification is not possible, increases the chances that the children will be adopted. Judge Leonard P. Edwards, Judicial Oversight of Parental Visitation in Family Reunification Cases, 54 Juv. & Fam. Ct. J. 1 (2003).

8. Despite the expressed preference for leaving children in their homes and providing their families services, in-home services are often limited in extent and quality, and many children left at home are the subject of new abuse or neglect reports.

At the national level, comprehensive assessments of family-preservation efforts commissioned by the federal government paint a fairly dismal picture of family-preservation services in practice. The overarching conclusion of one report is that despite AACWA's promises, the child-welfare system still falls short of the goal of keeping children in their homes when possible. The report found that although there are some quality programs, there are considerable challenges in the delivery of services. Part of the problem is that of the four different program areas—family preservation, community-based support, adoption support, and reunification services—many states spend their funds on adoption support and family reunification, not family preservation. In other words, instead of working to keep children from entering foster care, states are using the funds to help children exit foster care, often to adoptive homes.

Additionally, there is considerable resistance to family-preservation efforts in agencies, particularly after a high-profile abuse case. Even when child-fatality cases had not gone through the family-preservation system, for example, the report found there was still a sense among child-welfare agencies that the family-preservation mentality was responsible for children's deaths in such abuse cases. Finally, the report found that family-preservation programs do little to address the multiple and complex problems facing families at risk of involvement in the child-welfare system.

The choice not to invest in family-preservation services is understandable in light of the mixed evidence about the effectiveness of such late-stage interventions. Family-preservation programs typically aim to prevent foster-care placement and also to strengthen family functioning and improve child safety.

A national assessment of family-preservation efforts conducted a randomized study of three programs based on the Homebuilders model, as well as one less intensive but still home-based program. The assessment tracked foster-care placement, child safety, family functioning, and the closure rate for child-welfare cases. After following these outcomes for families in the experimental and control groups, the evaluators concluded that there was no statistically significant difference in foster-care placement between families receiving the services and the control group, nor was there a difference in case-closure rates. Additionally, families that received the intensive services did not reunify with their children more quickly following a placement. Looking at child safety, the study found no significant differences in maltreatment rates for children in the two groups. Family functioning was somewhat higher for the families receiving intensive treatment, but these improvements were not sustained over time.

Clare Huntington, The Child Welfare System and the Limits of Determinacy, 76 L. & Contemp. Probs. 221, 231-234 (2014). The lack of in-home services has often been attributed to the federal funding scheme, which provided much more money for foster care than for these services. After years of criticism for this, in 2018 Congress enacted the Family First Prevention Services Act, which allows the largest source of federal funds to be used to pay for in-home services. More information is available on the National Conference of State Legislatures website, http://www.ncsl.org/research/human-services/family-first-prevention-services-act-ffpsa.aspx. While this change was strongly supported by many commentators, the emphasis on family preservation also has been strongly criticized as elevating parents' interests above children's interests in safety and permanency. *See, e.g.,* Elizabeth Bartholet, Differential Response: A Dangerous Experiment in Child Welfare, 42 Fla. St. U. L. Rev. 573 (2015).

9. About 10 percent of all children removed during the initial investigation are returned home within 30 days; the average length of stay nationally is 6 days, and 75 percent of these children are discharged within 2 weeks. Three-quarters are returned to their parents, and most of the rest are placed with relatives. Vivek S. Sankaran & Christopher Church, Easy Come, Easy Go: The Plight of Children Who Spend Less Than Thirty Days in Foster Care, 9 U. Pa. J. L. & Soc. Change 207, 217 (2016). Empirical studies show that very few judges ever make a finding that the agency failed to make reasonable efforts, even when they believe this to be the case. *Id.* at 227-228, citing studies.

PROBLEMS

1. Donna, a 28-year-old single mother, left her 8-year-old daughter and 22-month-old son alone at night for five hours while she went to a party. A fire started, probably because the children were playing with matches. Donna returned just as the firefighters were finishing to find child welfare workers with the children. Would emergency removal of the children be justified under the Massachusetts standard? What efforts to prevent removal, if any, should agency workers make?

2. Consider the facts of Hernandez ex rel. Hernandez v. Foster, p. 641, above. Did the child welfare agency workers make reasonable efforts to prevent removing Jaymz from his parents' custody?

B. JURISDICTION AND DISPOSITION

1. *Jurisdiction*

Colorado Revised Statutes § 19-3-102. Neglected or dependent child (2018)
(1) A child is neglected or dependent if:
(a) A parent, guardian, or legal custodian has abandoned the child or has subjected him or her to mistreatment or abuse or a parent, guardian, or

legal custodian has suffered or allowed another to mistreat or abuse the child without taking lawful means to stop such mistreatment or abuse and prevent it from recurring;

(b) The child lacks proper parental care through the actions or omissions of the parent, guardian, or legal custodian;

(c) The child's environment is injurious to his or her welfare;

(d) A parent, guardian, or legal custodian fails or refuses to provide the child with proper or necessary subsistence, education, medical care, or any other care necessary for his or her health, guidance, or well-being;

(e) The child is homeless, without proper care, or not domiciled with his or her parent, guardian, or legal custodian through no fault of such parent, guardian, or legal custodian;

(f) The child has run away from home or is otherwise beyond the control of his or her parent, guardian, or legal custodian;

(g) The child tests positive at birth for either a schedule I controlled substance, as defined in section 18-18-203, C.R.S., or a schedule II controlled substance, as defined in section 18-18-204, C.R.S., unless the child tests positive for a schedule II controlled substance as a result of the mother's lawful intake of such substance as prescribed. ...

In the Interest of J.G.

370 P.3d 1151 (Colo. 2016)

Justice BOATRIGHT delivered the Opinion of the Court. . . . M.L. is the mother of five children, J.W.G., J.G., J.P., C.L., and S.L., four of whom are interested parties in this dependency or neglect appeal. The events leading to this case began when S.L. informed her mother and father ("B.L.") that J.W.G., her half-brother, had touched her in a sexual manner while she was trying to sleep. The parents immediately contacted law enforcement officials, who discovered during their investigation that J.W.G. had also inappropriately touched another sister, J.P. As a result, J.W.G. was charged with unlawful sexual contact and sexual assault on a child. Initially, J.W.G. remained in the home while his siblings stayed with family members. Within a week, the Fremont County Department of Human Services ("DHS") placed J.W.G. in an offense-specific foster home, and the remaining children returned to the family home.

In response to J.W.G.'s actions, the State filed a dependency or neglect petition concerning all of the children pursuant to section 19-3-502, C.R.S. (2015). The petition named M.L. and the children's fathers as respondents. In pertinent part, it alleged that the children were dependent or neglected under three statutory bases: (1) the children lacked proper parental care; (2) the children were homeless, without proper care, or not domiciled with a parent through no fault of the parent; and (3) the children's environment was injurious to their welfare. M.L. and G.G., J.W.G.'s father, admitted the allegations in the dependency or neglect petition as to J.W.G., but M.L. and the fathers of the remaining four children denied the allegations as to those children and requested a jury trial. The case thus proceeded to jury trial.

At the conclusion of the evidence, the State proffered several jury instructions to which M.L. and the fathers objected. Specifically, M.L. objected to the questions in Jury Instruction 17, the State's proffered instruction regarding the injurious environment provision. Jury Instruction 17 (and a corresponding special verdict form) included a total of thirteen questions, twelve of which asked the jury to decide whether each child was dependent or neglected based on one of the three statutory bases alleged by the State. In objecting, M.L. argued that the trial court should require the jury to find that the children's environment was injurious to their welfare due to the actions or omissions of the parents, as per the pattern instruction for the injurious environment provision.

The trial court rejected M.L.'s argument and gave the State's proffered instruction, which was consistent with the injurious environment provision's statutory language. Notably, it excluded the parental fault language found in the pattern instruction. Therefore, the jury was not required to make findings as to parental fault regarding the State's injurious environment allegation. . . .

In reaching its verdicts, the jury responded to the questions in the special verdict form and Instruction 17. Specifically, the jury answered "no" to the questions asking (1) whether the children lacked parental care through the actions or omissions of the parents and (2) whether the children were homeless, without proper care, or not domiciled with their parents through no fault of the parents. But, it responded "yes" to the third question for the children, finding their environment injurious to their welfare. Based on the jury's conclusion that the children's environment was injurious, the court adjudicated the children dependent or neglected and continued the case for a dispositional hearing. At that hearing, the court entered an order adopting a treatment plan and granted legal custody of J.W.G. to DHS. It granted the parents legal custody of the four other children subject to DHS's protective supervision.

M.L. appealed. . . .

The court of appeals reversed. . . .

In reversing the trial court's adjudication of dependency or neglect as to each of the four children, the court of appeals relied on *Troxel*. The court of appeals held that, "because a fit parent has a fundamental right to the care, custody, and control of his or her children, free from state intervention," a child cannot be dependent or neglected if at least one parent is available, able, and willing to provide reasonable parental care. We now consider whether the court of appeals properly relied on *Troxel* in reaching its holding in this case.

We begin with the bedrock principle that the right to parent one's children is a fundamental liberty interest. Thus, intervening in "[t]he fundamental liberty interest of natural parents in the care, custody, and management of their child" requires "fundamentally fair procedures." *Troxel* emphasized that statutory procedures must protect parents' due process rights by requiring the State to justify its reasons for interfering with a family. . . .

Relying on *Troxel*, the court of appeals in this case created an additional factor that the State must prove before a child can be adjudicated dependent or neglected: that neither parent is available, able, and willing to provide reasonable parental care. We determine that this is unnecessary, as the court of appeals' analysis extends *Troxel* beyond its holding. . . .

Rather, the dependency or neglect statute, as drafted, satisfies due process. The purpose of adjudication is to determine whether State intervention is necessary to serve the best interests of the children, but to do so in a manner that protects parental rights. Thus, parents are afforded robust due process rights during the adjudicatory stage of dependency or neglect proceedings. Specifically, the statute protects against the erroneous deprivation of parental rights by putting the burden on the State to prove at least one of its allegations by a preponderance of the evidence to the satisfaction of the fact-finder. Those factual allegations must meet statutory criteria that can be described as "special factors" as that term is used in *Troxel*. Thus, the State justifies intervening into the parent-child legal relationship by proving special factors. . . .

In this case, the special factor warranting the State's intervention is the children's injurious environment. In other words, the State may intervene when a child is in a situation that is likely harmful to that child. The fact finder can find an injurious environment only after hearing and weighing evidence from all parties and after the court has ensured that the parents received all of the due process rights that the statute guarantees. For these reasons, *Troxel* does not require modifying what the State must prove in dependency or neglect proceedings. . . .

On the second issue, the State argues that the court of appeals erred in requiring the trial court to instruct the jury that it must make findings as to the fault of each parent before determining whether a child is dependent or neglected under the injurious environment provision of the dependency or neglect statute. . . .

Dependency or neglect proceedings are the State's method of "assist[ing] the parents and child in establishing a relationship and home environment that will preserve the family unit." Although the State may base its allegations that a child is dependent or neglected on any of the grounds contained in section 19–3–102(1), only paragraph (c), the injurious environment provision, is at issue in this case. Paragraph (c) provides that a child is dependent or neglected if "[t]he child's environment is injurious to his or her welfare." That paragraph differs from the others in the statute in two important ways. First, it is one of only two paragraphs that does not contain the words "parent, guardian, or legal custodian." This omission indicates the General Assembly's intent to focus on the *existence* of an injurious environment rather than who caused it. Thus, the legislature explicitly acknowledged that a child may be dependent or neglected for reasons that are distinct from the parents' conduct or condition.

Paragraph (c) also differs from most of the other bases for a finding of dependency or neglect in that it contains no language concerning fault. Specifically, paragraph (a) concerns situations where a parent has "abandoned" the child, "subjected [the child] to mistreatment or abuse," or "suffered or allowed another to mistreat or abuse the child without taking lawful means to stop such mistreatment or abuse and prevent it from recurring." Paragraph (b) contains the language, "through the actions or omissions of the parent." Similarly, paragraph (d) concerns when a parent "fails or refuses to provide the child with" appropriate care. Paragraph (e) specifically includes the language "through no fault of [a] parent." Paragraph (f) considers the child's actions as opposed to the parents', including when the child has run away or is beyond the parents' control. Like paragraph (c), paragraph (g) also contains no language concerning fault. However, it concerns children who test positive for unlawful controlled substances at birth, which necessarily requires some parental action. In contrast, paragraph (c) simply concerns when a child's environment is injurious to his or her welfare. . . .

M.L. asserts that paragraph (c) necessarily requires findings of parental fault because, unlike paragraph (e), it does not explicitly state that the child's environment may be injurious "through no fault of [the] parent." We reject such a reading because it adds words to the statute. . . . Moreover, it improperly narrows the statute's scope to focus on the parents' conduct rather than on the child's environment, contrary to the fundamental purpose of dependency or neglect proceedings. "At all times [during a dependency or neglect proceeding], the best interest of the child or children is paramount." The Children's Code exists to protect children and ensure that they have a safe and healthy environment. It does *not* exist to punish parents or ascribe fault. . . .

M.L. also asserts that in addition to the statute, *Troxel* mandates that the jury make findings as to parental fault before it can determine that a child's environment is injurious. But just as *Troxel* does not require the State to prove that both parents could not or would not provide reasonable parental care at the adjudication stage of dependency or neglect proceedings, it does not require that the jury make findings as to parental fault at the adjudication stage. As we discussed above, our dependency or neglect procedures satisfy *Troxel*'s due process requirements. Therefore, *Troxel* necessitates no additional findings beyond those contained in the statute, and the statute does not require the State to prove parental fault. . . .

Justice GABRIEL, dissenting. . . . [A]lthough the adjudication focuses on the status of the child, the process subjects the parents to the jurisdiction and orders of the court from the time the petition is filed and the summonses are issued throughout the pendency of the case. Accordingly, although courts sometimes laud the "helpful and remedial" purposes of dependency or neglect proceedings "in preserving and mending familial ties," adjudicatory proceedings can have a substantial impact on the lives of respondent parents, and the orders resulting from an adjudication can significantly interfere with the "fundamental liberty interest of natural parents in the care, custody, and management of their child."

For example, an adjudication suggests failures of parenting by respondent parents, and prior adjudications are often cited in subsequent dependency or neglect proceedings in support of the need for continued state intervention in a family's life.

Similarly, an adjudication has real legal consequences for a parent, who at best must comply with a court-ordered treatment plan and at worst faces the termination of his or her parent-child legal relationship.

In my view, to justify imposing such consequences and obligations on a parent, due process demands that we interpret the Children's Code in a way that requires the fact finder to consider and make findings regarding the acts or omissions (or, if pertinent, the fault or lack thereof) of each respondent parent. . . .

For the reasons set forth by the majority, however, I would not require the State to prove that a child lacks at least one parent who is available, able to give the child reasonable parental care, and willing to provide such reasonable parental care. Like the majority, I do not believe that either the Children's Code, the constitution, or our precedent mandates such additional requirements. . . .

Because it has been the subject of much confusion, the principle that adjudications of dependency or neglect are not made "as to" the parent but rather relate only to the "status of the child" warrants comment.

The phrase "as to the parent" does not appear in the Children's Code, although many cases from both this court and divisions of the court of appeals have recited the principle that adjudications are not made as to the parent but rather relate to the status of the child. In many instances, however, the very same cases that have reiterated this principle have also stated that the adjudication was made as to the respondent parents.

Although the juxtaposition of the concepts "the status of the child" and "as to the parent" is perhaps unfortunate, I understand these concepts to concern distinct findings in the above-mentioned cases. Specifically, when a juvenile court makes findings relating to "the status of the child," it is referring to the circumstances surrounding the child that require the State's intervention. The phrase "as to the parent," in contrast, refers to the resolution of the petition's allegations against that parent as a respondent. . . .

For these reasons, I respectfully dissent.

NOTES AND QUESTIONS

1. After reading the *J.G.* court's interpretation of the provision of the juvenile code providing that the court has jurisdiction if "the child's environment is injurious to his or her welfare," could you advise a client about what parenting practices are likely to result in a child being found neglected? If you were the state's attorney, could you advise a social worker how to apply the statute when deciding whether to file a petition?

2. Since the parents in *J.G.* immediately called the police when they learned that J.W.G. had sexually touched his sister and arranged for the other children to live with family members until an alternate placement was found for J.W.G., what made the other children's environment injurious to them, requiring juvenile court jurisdiction? Were they being harmed? Were they at risk of harm? What should the parents be required to do before the case is closed?

3. Most juvenile court jurisdiction statutes contain at least one provision that, like Colorado's injurious environment clause, is very broad and indeterminate. While a few courts have held that very broadly drafted juvenile court statutes are unconstitutionally vague, *see, e.g.,* Roe v. Conn, 417 F. Supp. 769 (M.D. Ala. 1976); *see also* In re Juvenile Appeal (83-CD), 455 A.2d 1313 (Conn. 1983) (narrowly construing statute to avoid constitutional problems), most vagueness challenges have failed. Note, Child Neglect: Due Process for the Parent, 70 Colum. L. Rev. 469-470 & n.30 (1970); Noah Weinstein, Legal Rights of Children 6-8 (1974). The constitutional prohibition against vague statutes is intended to (1) ensure that people have notice of the circumstances in which their behavior may lead to coercive state intervention, (2) decrease the opportunity for arbitrary or discriminatory enforcement of the law, and (3) avoid chilling the exercise of fundamental constitutional rights. Which of these dangers are created by vague juvenile court statutes? Why do courts tolerate vaguely drafted juvenile court statutes?

4. The practice of drafting juvenile court statutes very broadly has been criticized by many commentators. *See, e.g.,* Martin Guggenheim, The Political and Legal Implications of the Psychological Parenting Theory, 12 N.Y.U. Rev. L. & Soc. Change 549, 554 (1983-1984); Michael S. Wald, State Intervention on Behalf of "Neglected" Children: A Search for Realistic Standards, 27 Stan. L. Rev. 985, 993 (1975); Michael S. Wald, State Intervention on Behalf of "Neglected" Children: Standards for Removal of Children from Their Homes, Monitoring the Status of Children in Foster Care, and Termination of Parental Rights, 28 Stan. L. Rev. 623 (1976); Douglas J. Besharov, "Doing Something" About Child Abuse: The Need to Narrow the Grounds for State Intervention, 8 Harv. J.L. & Pub. Pol'y 539, 550-581 (1985). A few states have amended their jurisdictional statutes to be more specific, in line with the recommendations of these critics. California's statute, which was adopted in 1987 and which has kept the same format since then, although it has been amended, is an example. Relevant sections of the statute are set out below. Under this statute, would you be better able to advise parents about how to avoid state intervention or social workers about when intervention is warranted?

California Welfare and Institutes Code § 300

A child who comes within any of the following descriptions is within the jurisdiction of the juvenile court which may adjudge that person to be a dependent child of the court:

(a) The child has suffered, or there is a substantial risk that the child will suffer, serious physical harm inflicted nonaccidentally upon the child by the child's parent or guardian. For purposes of this subdivision, a court may find there is a substantial risk of serious future injury based on the manner in which a less serious injury was inflicted, a history of repeated inflictions of injuries on the child or the child's siblings, or a combination of these and other actions by the parent or guardian that indicate the child is at risk of serious physical harm. For purposes of this subdivision, "serious physical harm" does not include reasonable and age-appropriate spanking to the buttocks if there is no evidence of serious physical injury.

(b)(1) The child has suffered, or there is a substantial risk that the child will suffer, serious physical harm or illness, as a result of the failure or inability of his or her parent or guardian to adequately supervise or protect the child, or the willful or negligent failure of the child's parent or guardian to adequately supervise or protect the child from the conduct of the custodian with whom the child has been left, or by the willful or negligent failure of the parent or guardian to provide the child with adequate food, clothing, shelter, or medical treatment, or by the inability of the parent or guardian to provide regular care for the child due to the parent's or guardian's mental illness, developmental disability, or substance abuse. . . .

(c) The child is suffering serious emotional damage, or is at substantial risk of suffering serious emotional damage, evidenced by severe anxiety, depression, withdrawal, or untoward aggressive behavior toward self or others, as a result of the conduct of the parent or guardian or who has no parent or guardian capable of providing appropriate care. . . .

(d) The child has been sexually abused, or there is a substantial risk that the child will be sexually abused, as defined in Section 11165.1 of the Penal Code, by his or her parent or guardian or a member of his or her household, or the parent or guardian has failed to adequately protect the child from sexual abuse when the parent or guardian knew or reasonably should have known that the child was in danger of sexual abuse. . . .

5. In recent years, some state courts have interpreted their traditional broadly worded dependency jurisdiction statutes to require proof that parents' acts or failures to act cause a substantial risk of specific harm. *See, e.g.,* In re Carrdale H. II, 781 N.W.2d 622 (Neb. App. 2010) (evidence that father possessed crack cocaine did not prove that children "lacked property parental care and supervision by reason of the habits" of the parent); In Interest of P.T.D., 903 N.W.2d 83 (N.D. 2017) (proof of children's exposure to domestic violence and mother's use of drugs and mental health issues did not establish that children "were without proper parental care or control" in absence of findings to harm or risk of harm to children); Dept. Hum. Servs. v. A.F., 259 P.3d 957 (Or. App. 2011) (proof that father possessed pornography alone does not establish jurisdiction over child whose "conditions or circumstances are such as to endanger" the child's welfare).

6. Colorado is unusual, though not unique, in providing for jury trials in child abuse and neglect cases.

PROBLEMS

1. Under the Colorado statute as interpreted in *J.G.*, would a juvenile court have jurisdiction based on the facts of Care and Protection of Walt, above? Under the California statute set out in Note 4 above?

2. Marta's home is very messy, with piles of clothes, trash, and other items all over the floor. The kitchen and bathroom are very dirty, and the whole apartment has a bad odor. Marta's oldest child, Darwin, who was quite emotionally troubled, hanged himself in the apartment a month ago. Darwin had very poor hygiene and was teased mercilessly by the other children at school. Police investigating his death reported the condition of the apartment to the state child welfare authorities, who removed Marta's two younger children from the home. The state juvenile code includes a provision giving the court jurisdiction over children whose parents or custodians "cause or permit" them "to be placed in such a situation that the health of the child is likely to be injured." The state filed a petition alleging that Marta's two surviving children are within the court's jurisdiction under this statute because she has "permitted them to live in such a situation that their life or physical or mental health may be endangered." At the close of the state's evidence, Marta's attorney moved to dismiss, arguing that the evidence was insufficient to establish neglect under the statute. In the alternative, the attorney argued that the statute as applied to Marta is unconstitutionally vague. How should the judge rule on these motions and why?

2. *Disposition*

IN RE M.M.

---

72 N.E.3d 260 (Ill. 2016)

Justice FREEMAN delivered the judgment of the court, with opinion.... On July 31, 2013, DCFS filed separate juvenile petitions seeking wardship of 9-year-old J.M. and 10-year-old M.M. The petitions claimed that the minors were neglected because their environment was injurious to their welfare. At that time, the minors lived with their father, Larry. Each petition alleged as follows. Between July 1 and July 3, 2013, Larry was taking care of the children of his girlfriend, who was not respondent. One of those children, who was six years old, had a bedwetting accident. Larry "struck [the child] on the buttocks and slapped his face leaving multiple bruises on [the child's] buttocks and face." Also, Larry had a criminal history that consisted of a charge of battery in 2003 and charges of driving under the influence in 2003 and 2008. Each petition asserted that respondent's whereabouts were unknown.

Larry entered into an agreed order of protection with DCFS, which provided, *inter alia*, that the minors would reside with their paternal grandparents, Larry's visits with the children would be supervised, and Larry could not live with the minors or stay with them overnight. Respondent was not a signatory to the order of protection. Larry subsequently disclosed respondent's name. The trial court appointed legal counsel for respondent, and she filed an answer to the juvenile petition. The court also appointed a guardian *ad litem* for the minors.

The trial court held an adjudicatory hearing in which the parties stipulated to the petition's allegations. The hearing consisted essentially of the State's proffer as to what evidence would have been introduced had there been no stipulations. There was no evidence or other information presented concerning respondent. At the close of the adjudicatory hearing, the court found that the minors were neglected due to an injurious environment not involving physical abuse. The court specifically found that respondent did not contribute to this injurious environment. . . .

Respondent's [Luther Social Services of Illinois (LSSI)] dispositional hearing report . . . stated that she had stable housing in Peoria and had obtained a certified nursing assistant certificate and training in phlebotomy. Respondent was not addicted to alcohol or illegal substances, had passed a random drug screening, and had never been arrested. Respondent takes prescription medication for bipolar disorder, anxiety disorder, and depression. In 2011 and 2012, respondent completed a parenting class and a domestic violence class as part of an intact family service program and had recently engaged in an intact family program through LSSI and indicated a willingness to participate in services. Further, respondent was cooperating with the LSSI caseworker. The report opined: "Both of the minors are completely aware of why their family is involved with LSSI/DCFS. This worker feels that the children would benefit from counseling services. This worker feels that the children are safe in their paternal grandparents' home and care at this time." The report concluded that respondent would be able to provide a safe, loving, and nurturing environment in which to raise her children if she continued to cooperate and participate in services as requested. The report recommended that respondent continue to be found fit. The report made no guardianship or placement recommendation regarding the minors.

At the dispositional hearing, the LSSI caseworker took no position as to who should be appointed guardian for J.M. and M.M. Both the State and the guardian *ad litem* agreed that respondent was a fit parent. However, both the State and the guardian *ad litem* argued that the minors should be made wards of the court and DCFS should be appointed guardian. The State provided no basis for this assertion. The guardian *ad litem* stated: "She [respondent] has some mental health issues; I hope those can be addressed."

Respondent agreed that she was a fit parent and that the minors should be made wards of the court. She also agreed with the LSSI assessment and recommendations. However, she contended that placement with DCFS was not necessary and asked that the court grant her custody and guardianship of her children.

At the close of the dispositional hearing, the trial court found Larry unfit as a parent. The court further found: "DCFS is appointed guardian of these children, although I do find the mother, [respondent], to be fit. I also find that placement is necessary, based on all that was presented in the materials for my review for this disposition and upon considering argument." The court's written dispositional order reflected the court's oral findings and also required respondent to perform various tasks "to correct the conditions that led to the adjudication and/or removal of the children." In addition to generally cooperating with DCFS or its designee, these tasks included taking a mental health assessment to determine if counseling was needed. If so, then respondent was ordered to undergo counseling. The form order indicated that respondent was fit and did not indicate that she was unable or unwilling to care for her children, and the order lacked any written basis to support a finding of inability or unwillingness.

Respondent appealed to the appellate court. The State conceded that the trial court "did not articulate specific reasons for its decision and did not state that the respondent was unable or unwilling to care for the children." The appellate court concluded that the trial court thereby violated section 2-27(1) of the Act. The appellate court explained that the trial court was not authorized to grant custody of the minors to DCFS without a finding of unfitness or a properly supported finding that respondent was unable or unwilling to care for the minors. Accordingly, the appellate court held that the trial court committed reversible error in awarding custody of the minors to DCFS. The appellate court remanded the case "so that the trial court may enter explicit, specific findings consistent with the requirements of section 2--27(1)." . . .

The State appeals to this court. . . .

The Act sets forth the procedures that must be followed in determining whether a minor should be removed from his or her parents' custody and be made a ward of the court. . . . An agreed order placed J.M. and M.M. in the temporary custody of their paternal grandparents. Subsequently, the parties stipulated that the minors were neglected due to an injurious environment not involving physical abuse, to which respondent did not contribute. Thereafter, the Act required the trial court to hold a dispositional hearing, in which the court must first determine whether it is in the best interests of the minor and the public that the minor be made a ward of the court. At the instant dispositional hearing, respondent agreed that J.M. and M.M. should be made wards of the court.

However, respondent sought custody of J.M. and M.M., contending that placement with DCFS was not necessary. Pursuant to the Act, if a minor "is to be made a ward of the court, the court shall determine the proper disposition best serving the health, safety and interests of the minor and the public." The trial court may make four basic types of dispositional orders with respect to a ward of the court. The minor may be (1) continued in the care of the minor's parent, guardian, or legal custodian; (2) restored to the custody of the minor's parent, guardian, or legal custodian; (3) ordered partially or completely emancipated; or (4) "placed in accordance" with section 2-27 of the Act. Section 2-27 provides in relevant part:

> (1) If the court determines and puts in writing the factual basis supporting the determination of whether the parents, guardian, or legal custodian of a minor adjudged a ward of the court are unfit or are unable, for some reason other than financial circumstances alone, to care for, protect, train or discipline the minor or are unwilling to do so, *and* that the health, safety, and best interest of the minor will be jeopardized if the minor remains in the custody of his or her parents, guardian or custodian, the court may at this hearing and at any later point:
> . . . (d) commit the minor to the Department of Children and Family Services for care and service . . . (Emphasis added.) . . .

In the case at bar, the trial court placed the minors with DCFS without articulating a factual basis for its order. Holding that the trial court committed reversible error, the appellate court explained: "The statutory scheme and case law interpreting it dictate that a trial court cannot move on to a best interest determination until it finds the natural parents unfit, unwilling, or unable to care for their minor child." The appellate court stated that section 2-27(1) requires explicit findings by the trial court that the respondent is unfit, unable, or unwilling to care for her children.

Before this court, the State contends ... that the Act authorizes a trial court to place an abused, neglected, or dependent child with someone other than a parent if that placement is necessary based on the best interests of the child, even absent a finding that both parents are unfit, unable, or unwilling to care for the child. We reject this contention.

We begin with the plain language of section 2-27(1). Prior to committing a minor to the custody of a third party, such as DCFS, a trial court must first determine whether the parent is unfit, unable, or unwilling to care for the child, *and* whether the best interest of the minor will be jeopardized if the minor remains in the custody of his or her parents. "The word 'and' has been defined in our courts as meaning 'in addition to.' . . .

The State argues that the appellate court's literal reading of section 2-27(1) is contrary to the legislature's own stated purpose and policy of the Act. The State points to section 1-2 of the Act, which provides, in pertinent part, that the purpose of the Act "is to secure for each minor subject hereto such care and guidance, preferably in his or her own home, as will serve the safety and moral, emotional, mental, and physical welfare of the minor and the best interests of the community." Moreover: "The parents' right to the custody of their child shall not prevail when the court determines that it is contrary to the health, safety, and best interests of the child." Further:

> (1) At the dispositional hearing, the court shall determine whether it is in the best interests of the minor and the public that he be made a ward of the court, and, if he is to be made a ward of the court, the court shall determine the proper disposition best serving the health, safety and interests of the minor and the public.

According to the State: "These provisions demonstrate that the best interests of the child are paramount."

We cannot accept the State's argument. We initially observe that section 1-2 of the Act provides that the purpose of the Act is also "to preserve and strengthen the minor's family ties whenever possible, removing him or her from the custody of his or her parents only when his or her safety or welfare or the protection of the public cannot be adequately safeguarded without removal." "It is apparent that the preferred result under the Juvenile Court Act is that a child remain in his or her home, in the custody of his or her parents. This is a clarification of the child's best interests." . . .

. . . [T]o adopt the State's interpretation of section 2-27(1) would upset the careful balance the legislature has crafted. There is nothing to suggest that an accurate reading of "and" in section 2-27(1) would defeat the main intent and purpose of the Act, and there is nothing "dubious" about reading "and" conjunctively. Accordingly, section 2-27(1) must be applied as written.

Moreover, this court must construe a statute in a manner that upholds its constitutionality if it reasonably can be done. It is beyond discussion that parents have a fundamental liberty interest in the care, custody, and control of their children. Troxel v. Granville, 530 U.S. 57, 65-66 (2000) (and cases cited therein). Further, as a matter of constitutional law, "there is a presumption that fit parents act in the best interests of their children." Troxel, 530 U.S. at 68. "Accordingly, so long as a parent [is fit], there will normally be no reason for the State to inject itself into the private realm of the family to further question the ability of that parent to make the best decisions concerning the rearing of that parent's children." Id. at 68-69.

In Troxel, the United States Supreme Court invalidated a visitation statute that allowed a petition to go directly to a best interests determination, without any deference to the decision of a fit parent. . . .

The State's argument that the best interest standard trumps all would run afoul of Troxel. The plain language of section 2-27(1) respects the constitutional rights of parents while also insuring to protect the best interests of children. . . .

Additionally, respondent observes that the trial court has found her to be fit and did not indicate that she was unable or unwilling to care for her children. Respondent posits that, on remand, she would remain a fit parent. Respondent characterizes this status as "the law of the case" and asserts that there is no proper procedure for evidence to be introduced that could prove she is unable or unwilling.

Therefore, respondent contends that remand is unnecessary and asks us to "order immediate placement" with her.

Respondent cites no authority and presents no argument beyond this bare contention. This court will consider only fully briefed and argued issues. A court of review is entitled to have the issues clearly defined with pertinent authority cited and cohesive arguments presented. Accordingly, respondent has forfeited this contention, and we do not consider it.

We hold that section 2-27(1) of the Act does not authorize placing a ward of the court with a third party absent a finding of parental unfitness, inability, or unwillingness to care for the minor. . . .

MARTIN GUGGENHEIM, SOMEBODY'S CHILDREN: SUSTAINING THE FAMILY'S PLACE IN CHILD WELFARE POLICY

113 Harv. L. Rev. 1716, 1724-1726 (2000)

. . . [S]tudies have consistently found that the great majority of children in foster care could remain safely at home. Professor Duncan Lindsey, a leading child welfare researcher, concluded that "studies clearly demonstrate that child abuse is not the major reason children are removed from their parents"; he found instead that "inadequacy of income, more than any other factor, constitutes the reason that children are removed." In fact, when Lindsey evaluated placements of children in foster care, he found that 48 percent of the children did not require placement.

A study of Boston placement decisions led one team of researchers to conclude that:

[A]mong a group of children referred for suspected abuse in the emergency and surgical units of a hospital, the best predictor of removal of the child from the family was not severity of abuse, but Medicaid eligibility, which we might interpret as a proxy variable for the income status of the family.

Likewise, Lindsey found that "inadequacy of income increased the odds for placement by more than 120 times."

The evidence also clearly suggests that many children regularly remain in foster care merely because their parents are unable to secure adequate housing without assistance from the state. This seems to be a regular practice in Chicago and New York City. The court-appointed administrator of the District of Columbia's foster care system also found that between one-third and one-half of the children in foster care could have been returned immediately to their parents but for a lack of adequate housing.

In her recent book, Jane Waldfogel asserts that the current foster care population may be grouped into three categories. First, the most serious category, constituting about 10 percent of current caseloads, includes "serious and criminal cases." The second group encompasses serious cases that do not require criminal justice intervention. The final group of cases are those in which a child is at a relatively lower risk of serious harm, and the parents may be willing to work with an agency to secure needed services. Together, the latter two groups comprise

90 percent of the caseload. Typically, these cases involve less serious physical abuse (for example, a single, minor injury such as a bruise or a scratch) or less severe neglect (such as parental drug or alcohol abuse with no other apparent protective issues, dirty clothes or a dirty home, lack of supervision of a school-age child, or missed school or medical appointments). Many of these lower-risk neglect cases are poverty-related, resulting from inadequate housing or inappropriate child-care arrangements while a parent works.

Other data on entry into foster care are also inconsistent with the notion that our child welfare system carefully monitors foster children and insists upon a compelling reason to remove a child from his or her family. Specifically, placement rates vary widely from one state to another even in the absence of any material difference between known rates of abuse or neglect. For example, "[a] child is twice as likely to be placed in foster care in Vermont as in New Hampshire [and] [t]he placement rate in Minnesota is double the rate in Wisconsin." There is also significant evidence to suggest that placements can reflect the politics of particular administrations and have little to do with child safety. States appear to use very flexible standards depending on the policy of local child welfare officials, which can change dramatically from one administration to the next.

For example, New York City's foster care population soared in the aftermath of a notorious and highly publicized case of child abuse. In the four-year period from 1995 to 1998, the number of new child abuse and neglect petitions filed rose 55 percent, from 6658 to 10,395. Even more significantly, the number of children removed from their families and placed in foster care over parental objection rose by nearly 50 percent between 1995 and 1997. During this same period, however, there was no known change in the base rate of child abuse. This striking rise in prosecution suggests a change in the philosophy of the prosecutors rather than a change in the conditions of children's homes. One study found, for example, that "[i]ncreasingly in New York City, abuse and neglect proceedings are brought against battered mothers whose children are removed from them where the only allegation is their children's exposure to domestic violence." This also suggests that family and juvenile courts "rubber stamp" agency recommendations to remove children from their parents, even in circumstances that do not constitute true emergencies.

Further circumstantial proof that foster care has not been reserved for those cases in which children suffer extreme forms of abuse is the dramatic underutilization of the services established to prevent foster care placement. Studies consistently find that preventive and reunification services — services designed specifically to keep children out of foster care or to return them promptly to their homes after placement — are underused by child welfare agencies.

Richard J. Gelles & Ira Schwartz, *Children and the Child Welfare System*

2 U. Pa. J. Const. L. 95, 102-111 (Dec. 1999)

There is, at the very least, a theoretical tension between parents' rights and child protection. Because the underlying ideology of the child welfare system is that the best placement for children is with their parents, permanency, while theoretically allowing for a number of alternative placements (such as legal guardianship, adoption, congregate care), is typically conceptualized as keeping a child with his or her biological parents or achieving a reunification with them. Similarly, although child welfare institutions promote the ideology of making decisions that are in "the best interests of the child," almost always the best interests are assumed to be achieved if the child is raised by his or her biological caregivers. . . .

The mandate for child welfare agencies and family, juvenile, or dependency courts is to find a balance between parents' constitutional rights and children's rights. There appears to be a level playing field in achieving this balance; however, appearances are not only deceiving, they are false. . . .

1. The notion that all parents want to and can change is countered by a substantial body of research that demonstrates that people in general, including abusive and neglectful parents, are difficult to change. . . .

2. Although there is a general belief that change can be achieved if there are sufficient soft and hard resources, as yet, there is no empirical evidence to support the effectiveness of child welfare services in general, or in the newer, more innovative, intensive family preservation services. . . .

3. Although preserving families is certainly a worthy goal, it is a difficult one to accomplish. For all the reasons noted above (the individual and social problems confronting maltreating families, the limited quantity and quality of services available, and the reluctance and difficulty individuals have changing their behavior) reunifications are fragile and often fail. Research indicates that approximately 50% of children reunified with their families after a stay in foster care are put back into out-of-home placement within 18 months.

4. Although adoption is considered a last resort by many in the child welfare and child advocacy community, of all the placement possibilities for children, adoption is the least likely to fail.

5. Resources have been added to the child welfare system for the past two decades without a measurable improvement.

6. What little research exists on out-of-home-placement has found that children who reside in foster care fare neither better nor worse than children who remain in homes in which maltreatment occurred.

7. The current child welfare system is quite variable in how it provides counsel and legal representation for children involved in child welfare cases. . . .

For at least 100 years the main thrust of the child welfare system has been to provide social and psychological resources so that children can be raised without interference from the government. While the child welfare system is criticized from all directions, one consistent concern is that children are often removed from families without cause or that families that can be helped are not afforded that opportunity. Those who demonstrate concern for children harmed even after they have been identified by the child welfare system are labeled "child savers," a pejorative term in this context.

The child welfare system has been in crisis for nearly three decades. The response to the crisis is a "round up the usual suspects" call for more resources, more workers, and reorganization of child welfare bureaucracies. . .

. . . What is clear, however, is that currently children and their "best interests" have only a minimal voice in child welfare proceedings. The child welfare system remains a system where the client is the parent, where the parent's legal rights are primary, and where a child's developmental best interests are rarely represented or given careful and appropriate weight.

NOTES AND QUESTIONS

1. The statutory interpretation issue in *M.M.* is whether a juvenile court can deprive a parent of custody during the dispositional phase of a dependency case without finding that the parent is unfit, unable, or unwilling to care for the child. Does the statute make the answer to this question clear?

Why does the court conclude that this finding is required? Does this finding automatically follow from a finding that a child is within the jurisdiction of the juvenile court?

2. Ordinarily when a court removes a child from the parents' custody, it grants legal custody to the state child welfare agency, which then decides who will have physical custody. As legal custodian, the agency has authority to make major decisions for the child, including those regarding schooling and health care. However, state statutes may provide that parents must be consulted or even that they have the authority to make some of these decisions, that only courts may make major decisions such as for surgery, or a combination.

One of the most litigated issues is whether agencies with legal custody may have children vaccinated against common childhood illnesses over parental objection, often based on religious beliefs. Some courts have held that parents found to have neglected or abused their children forfeit their right to make these decisions for their children. *E.g.*, In re Deng, 887 N.W.2d 445 (Mich. App. 2016); Dept. Human Serv. v. S.M., 300 P.3d 1254 (Or. App. 2013). Other courts have concluded that agencies do not have authority to make decisions about immunization under statutes allowing agencies to provide children with medical care. *E.g.*, In re Elianah T.-T., 165 A.3d 1236 (Conn. 2017); Diana H. v. Rubin, 171 P.3d 200 (Ariz. App. 2007).

In recent years, children's advocates have become particularly concerned that foster children receive too much of one kind of medical care — psychotropic medications. While foster children have a higher incidence of mental health problems than children in the general population, the rate at which foster children are prescribed these medications very likely exceeds what the children need. *See* A. Rachel Camp, A Mistreated Epidemic: State and Federal Failure to Adequately Regulate Psychotropic Medications Prescribed to Children in Foster Care, 83 Temp. L. Rev. 369, 381 (2011). In most states parents' consent is not obtained before a foster child is given psychotropic medication. *Id.* at 388-392. *See also* M.B. v. Corsi, 2018 WL 327767 (W.D. Mo. 2018).

3. The underlying dispute in *M.M.* is the nature of the rights of a parent who is not found at the adjudicatory hearing to have neglected or abused the child. This issue typically arises when the child is living with only one parent, against whom the child maltreatment claim is made, though it can also happen when the

parents are both living with the child, but allegations are made with regard to only one of them. In such a case, *M.M.* allows a juvenile court to take jurisdiction over the child but requires that the parent who was not found neglectful be awarded custody. New Hampshire takes a similar approach. In re Bill F., 761 A.2d 470 (N.H. 2000), held that if a court finds that one parent has abused or neglected a child, the other parent is entitled to a hearing regarding his or her suitability to claim custody. "At that hearing, a parent must be provided the opportunity to present evidence pertaining to his or her ability to provide care for the child and shall be awarded custody unless the State demonstrates, by a preponderance of the evidence, that he or she has abused or neglected the child or is otherwise unfit to perform his or her parental duties." *Id. See also* In re Parental Rights as to A.G., 295 P.3d 589 (Nev. 2013); Cal. Welf. & Inst. Code § 361.2 (West 2018).

In comparison, Pennsylvania and Maryland courts have held that a juvenile court may not assert jurisdiction based on evidence that one parent neglected or abused a child if the other parent is ready, willing, and able to take custody. In re M.L., 757 A.2d 849 (Pa. 2000); In re Russell G., 672 A.2d 109, 114 (Md. Ct. Spec. App. 1996). After *Russell G.* was decided, the Maryland legislature enacted a statute that codifies this result and gives the juvenile court limited authority to enter a custody order:

> [I]f the allegations in the petition are sustained against only one parent of a child, and there is another parent available who is able and willing to care for the child, the court may not find that the child is a child in need of assistance, but, before dismissing the case, the court may award custody to the other parent.

Md. Code Ann., Cts. & Jud. Pro. § 3-819(e) (2018).

What are the practical differences between the approaches of *M.M.* and the Pennsylvania and Maryland courts? Does either approach adequately protect the noncustodial parent's rights? Ensure the child's safety?

4. If state law provides that the juvenile court has no jurisdiction without making findings against both parents, as in Maryland or Pennsylvania, or that a parent against whom no findings are made is entitled to custody, the state child welfare agency is likely to try to establish jurisdiction grounds against both parents. That can be difficult, though, if one parent has not had custody. Could the state successfully argue that the noncustodial parent failed to protect the child from the dangers in the home? *See* Russell G, above, 672 A.2d at 116 (reversing finding against father for lack of proof that he knew the mother was not caring for the child properly); In Interest of JB, 390 P.3d 357 (Wyo. 2017) (a noncustodial parent can be adjudicated neglectful, but only if the parent knows of the problems in the custodial parent's home and had the opportunity to solve them but failed or refused to do so); In re J.S., 324 P.3d 486 (Or. App. 2014) (court could not find that children were within the court's jurisdiction because their father, who was separated from their custodial mother, did not have a custody order; lack of the order did not present a current risk of harm to the children); M.H. v. Indiana Dept. Child Servs., 15 N.E.3d 602, 611 (Ind. App. 2014) (reversing finding that a two-year-old child was within the court's jurisdiction because the father had not been present in the child's life while in the military and lacked parenting skills, saying

"If it were sufficient for the purposes of CHINS adjudications that a parent has no prior parenting experience or training, then *all* new parents would necessarily be subject to DCS intervention."

5. At the other extreme from *M.L.* and *Russell G.*, Ohio allows the juvenile court to take jurisdiction over a child based on evidence of the custodial parent's abuse or neglect alone and gives no special placement preference to the child's other parent. In re C.R., 843 N.E.2d 1188, 1190 (Ohio 2006). Michigan for many years adhered to the one-parent doctrine, which allowed the juvenile court to take jurisdiction based only on findings relating to one parent and to order the other parent to participate in drug testing, classes, and the like if that parent ever wanted to have custody. In 2014 the Michigan Supreme Court held that the one-parent doctrine violates the procedural due process rights of the parent who was not adjudicated to be unfit and thus that a juvenile court cannot require a parent to satisfy treatment requirements imposed at a dispositional hearing if court has not previously found that the parent neglected or mistreated the child. In re Sanders, 852 N.W.2d 524 (Mich. 2014).

6. If the juvenile court does take jurisdiction over a parent who did not have custody of the child, what obligation do the court and the child welfare agency have to work with that parent? In Dept. Human Serv. v. J.F.D., 298 P.3d 653 (Or. App. 2013), the court ruled that a juvenile court erroneously found that the child welfare agency had satisfied its obligation to make reasonable efforts to return the child to the parents when it worked with the mother extensively but provided no services to the noncustodial father.

7. If a juvenile court finds that a child is not within its jurisdiction because no allegations have been proven against the noncustodial parent, the state will have no obligation to work with the former custodial parent to solve the problems that led to removal. If a jurisdiction approaches this issue like the *Bill F.* court, may the juvenile court place the child with the former noncustodial parent and order the agency to work with the former custodial parent with an eye toward return? *Compare* In re Interest of Ethan M., 723 N.W.2d 363 (Neb. App. 2006) (rejecting placement with former noncustodial parent because of the impediment this poses to reunification with former custodial parent), *to* In the Matter of T.S., 74 P.3d 1009 (Kan. 2003), *disapproved of on other grounds*, In re B.D.-Y., 286 Kan. 686, 187 P.3d 594 (2008) (juvenile court at least has option of placing child with noncustodial parent without ordering reintegration services for former custodial parent).

8. Often legally recognized parents (most often fathers) who do not share custody of a child do not know when their children are taken into custody based on allegations of abuse or neglect against the custodial parent. Best practices manuals say that efforts should be made to identify both of a child's parents as soon as a petition is filed and that both should be involved in the case from the outset. *E.g.*, National Council of Juvenile and Family Court Judges, Adoption and Permanency Guidelines: Improving Court Practice in Child Abuse and Neglect Cases 10 (2000). The Ninth Circuit has held that a state may violate a noncustodial parent's procedural due process rights by taking a child into protective custody without notifying the parent and giving the parent the opportunity to take the child. James v. Rowlands, 606 F.3d 646 (9th Cir. 2010).

However, in practice, noncustodial parents frequently do not receive timely notice of juvenile court proceedings involving their children, much less an opportunity to participate.

A study published in 2006 found that in 40% of almost 2,000 cases examined, the caseworker knew who the child's father was and where he could be found when the case was opened. In another 31%, his identity was known within thirty days, or his identity was known when the case was opened but his location was not. By the time a case had been in the system for at least three months but not more than thirty-six months, the caseworker knew the identity of the father 88% of the time. Nevertheless, paternity had not been established for 37% of the children.

The agency's awareness of the father's identity and location did not guarantee that he would be included in the case. Agencies reported contact with 55% of the fathers, but 20% whose identity and location were known were never contacted by the agency. Fathers who were identified early were much more likely to have contact with the agency than those identified later. Eighty percent of the fathers whose identity and location were known at the outset of the case were contacted by the agency, but only 13% of the fathers identified after the child had been in foster care for more than thirty days were contacted.

The study also found that when the agency did not know the father's identity, it did not necessarily use all available resources to find him. In only 20% of the cases in which the father had not been found did the caseworker ask the state child support agency for help, even though cooperation between the agencies is encouraged and child support agencies have a very high success rate in finding missing fathers.

Leslie Joan Harris, Involving Nonresident Fathers in Dependency Cases: New Efforts, New Problems, New Solutions, 9 J.L. & Fam. Stud. 281, 284-285 (2007), citing U.S. Dep't of Health & Hum. Serv., What About the Dads? Child Welfare Agencies' Efforts to Identify, Locate and Involve Nonresident Fathers 2 fig.1 (2006), available at https://aspe.hhs.gov/pdf-document/what-about-dads-child-welfare-agencies-efforts-identify-locate-and-involve-nonresident-fathers-research-summary. The delayed appearance of a legal parent may derail the case, since that parent will at least have a claim to be considered for custody of the child. *See also* Josh Gupta-Kagan, The Strange Life of Stanley v. Illinois: A Case Study in Parent Representation and Law Reform, 41 N.Y.U. Rev. of L. & Soc. Change 569 (2017); Vivek S. Sankaran, Parens Patriae Run Amuck: The Child Welfare System's Disregard for the Constitutional Rights of Nonoffending Parents, 82 Temp. L. Rev. 55 (2009).

NOTE: WHO IS A PARENT FOR PURPOSES OF JUVENILE COURT DEPENDENCY CASES?

The fathers in *M.M.* and in the other cases discussed in the notes above apparently were legal fathers because they were married to the children's mothers at birth or had established their paternity in some other way. Similarly, the wife of a woman who gives birth during their marriage will be presumed to be the legal parent of the child. On legal parentage when same-sex couples marry, *see* Leslie

Joan Harris, *Obergefell*'s Ambiguous Impact on Legal Parentage, 92 Chi.-Kent L. Rev. 55 (2017).

In many dependency cases, though, the child's biological father has not established legal paternity, or the child is living with an unrelated adult who functions as the child's parent but who was not the spouse of the child's mother at birth. In both cases, questions can arise about who should be treated as the child's parent during the dependency proceedings. Traditionally, unmarried fathers were simply ignored in juvenile court. Indeed, the first Supreme Court case concerning unmarried fathers' due process rights was such a case. Stanley v. Illinois, 405 U.S. 645 (1972), held that state juvenile court practice and law that do not protect the rights of any unmarried father, regardless of his actual relationship to his children, may violate due process. Supreme Court cases decided since *Stanley* establish that states may constitutionally distinguish between unmarried fathers who have tried to assume responsibility and those who have not. Fathers who have stepped forward to assume parental obligations are entitled to the procedural and substantive safeguards that other parents receive, but fathers who have not made such a commitment have far less constitutional protection. Quilloin v. Walcott, 434 U.S. 246 (1978); Caban v. Mohammed, 441 U.S. 380 (1979); Lehr v. Robertson, 463 U.S. 248 (1983). Today, some states give all unmarried fathers full legal protection, while others give fathers who have not assumed parental responsibility less protection.

The appellate courts are divided about the rights of biological fathers whose paternity has not been established and who appear late in the dependency proceedings and do not pursue their parental obligations vigorously. In re Chezron M., 698 N.W.2d 95 (Wis. 2005), upheld an order terminating the parental rights of a father for abandonment, based on his failure to maintain contact with the child during the two years before the petition was filed, rejecting his claim that he had no parental duty until his paternity was established. *See also* State ex rel. S.H., 119 P.3d 309 (Utah App. 2005); In re Involuntary Termination of Parent-Child Relationship of S.M., 840 N.E.2d 865 (Ind. App. 2006). *Compare* State ex rel. DHS v. Rardin, 134 P.3d 940 (Or. 2006), reversing a termination order on similar facts; the court said that a finding of unfitness could not be based on the father's failure to take responsibility when he had reason to believe the child might not be his.

Statutes in some states treat some stepparents as parents for purposes of dependency cases. *E.g.*, Colo. Rev. Stat. § 19-3-502(5) (2018) (giving state discretion to include stepparent or spousal equivalent in juvenile court proceeding); Neb. Rev. Stat. § 43-245(18) (2018) ("parent" includes stepparent living with a custodial parent). In some states an adult who is not a child's legal or biological parent but who has lived in a parent-child relationship with the child may be treated as a parent for purposes of child welfare proceedings. California has the most highly developed body of case law on the issue. Under California law, a man is presumed to be the father of a child if he takes the child into his home and holds out to the world that the child is his. Cal. Fam. Code § 7611(d) (2018). The leading cases on the application of this provision in juvenile court are In re Jesusa V., 85 P.3d 2 (Cal. 2004), and In re Nicholas H., 46 P.3d 923 (Cal. 2002). Together, these cases establish that this presumption is not necessarily rebutted by proof that the man is not the child's biological father and that the juvenile court has discretion to determine whether it is appropriate in a particular case to find that the presumption has been rebutted. In re K.S., 93 A.3d 687 (Me. 2014), held that the former husband of a child's mother who had been declared a "de facto parent" was entitled to the rights of a parent when the child was found neglected shortly after the divorce. Other states have statutes or case law that allow unrelated adults who have lived in a parent-child type relationship with a child to petition to intervene in juvenile court proceedings. These statutes do not, however, confer all the rights of a parent on the petitioner. *See, e.g.*, Or. Rev. Stat. § 419B.116 (2018).

NOTE: THE INDIAN CHILD WELFARE ACT LIMITATIONS ON JURISDICTION AND PROCEEDINGS IN STATE COURTS

Congress enacted the Indian Child Welfare Act (ICWA), 25 U.S.C. §§ 1901-1963, in 1978 because of "rising concern in the mid–1970s over the consequences to Indian children, Indian families, and Indian tribes of abusive child welfare practices that resulted in the separation of large numbers of Indian children from their families and tribes through adoption or foster care placement, usually in non-Indian homes." Mississippi Band of Choctaw Indians v. Holyfield, 490 U.S. 30, 32, (1989). "Congress found that 'an alarmingly high percentage of Indian families [were being] broken up by the removal, often unwarranted, of their children from them by nontribal public and private agencies.' 25 U.S.C. § 1901(4). This 'wholesale removal of Indian children from their homes' prompted Congress to enact the ICWA, which establishes federal standards that govern state-court child custody proceedings involving Indian children." Adoptive Couple v. Baby Girl, 570 U.S. 637, 641 (2013).

ICWA applies to any proceeding involving the custody of an "Indian child," which is defined as "any unmarried person who is under age eighteen and is either (1) a member of an Indian tribe or (2) is eligible for membership in an Indian tribe and is the biological child of a member of an Indian tribe." 25 U.S.C. § 1903. The tribe of which the child may be a member has the exclusive authority to determine whether the child is an Indian child. 25 CFR § 23.108. Several courts have held that statutes or rules that extend ICWA protections to more children than those covered by the federal act violate equal protection or are inconsistent with the federal act and fail under the Supremacy Clause. *E.g.*, In re Abbigail A., 375 P.3d 879 (Cal. 2016); In the Interest of A.W., 741 N.W.2d 793 (Iowa 2007).

ICWA regulations require state courts to inquire at the beginning of a custody proceeding whether any party knows or has reason to know that the child is an Indian child. 25 CFR 23.107. If the question is not resolved during the initial inquiry, it is critical for courts to continue to inquire until the issue is resolved because a custody order may be challenged at any time on the ground that ICWA applies but was not complied with. 25 U.S.C. § 1914.

If an Indian child is domiciled on the tribe's reservation, tribal courts have exclusive jurisdiction over proceedings concerning the child's custody. 42 U.S.C. § 1911(a). Under Section 1911(b), state and tribal courts have concurrent jurisdiction over Indian children not domiciled on the reservation; on the petition of a parent or the tribe, state-court proceedings must be transferred to the tribal court, except in cases of "good cause," objection by either parent, or declination of jurisdiction by the tribal court.

ICWA establishes numerous requirements that custody proceedings in state court must satisfy.[3] We will examine them in this chapter as they become relevant. Requirements that must be addressed during the early stages of a child welfare case include these:

1. Before a state court may remove a child from the legal or physical custody of a parent involuntarily, the court must find that active efforts were made to provide services to prevent the breakup of the family and that these efforts were unsuccessful. 25 U.S.C. § 1912. Regulations issued in 2016 define "active efforts" for the first time. 25 CFR § 23.2. The regulations with comments are available at http://www.indianaffairs.gov/cs/groups/public/documents/text/idc1-034238.pdf.

2. In an involuntary foster care or termination of parental rights proceeding, the state court must notify the child's parent and tribe, appoint counsel for the parent, and allow parties to examine all reports and documents. 25 U.S.C. § 1912(a). The child's tribe has the right to intervene in any state court proceeding for foster care placement or termination of parental rights. 25 U.S.C. § 1911(c).

3. Before an involuntary foster care placement can be ordered, the state must prove by clear and convincing evidence, including testimony of a qualified expert, that continued custody by the parent is likely to result in serious emotional or physical damage to the child. 25 U.S.C. § 1912(e). The 2016 ICWA regulations explain this requirement, providing that the evidence must show "a causal relationship between the particular conditions in the home and the likelihood that continued custody of the child will result in serious emotional or physical damage to the particular child who is the subject of the child-custody proceeding." They continue, "evidence that shows only the existence of community or family poverty, isolation, single parenthood, custodian age, crowded or inadequate housing, substance abuse, or nonconforming social behavior does not by itself constitute clear and convincing evidence or evidence beyond a reasonable doubt that continued custody is likely to result in serious emotional or physical damage to the child." 25 CFR § 223.121(c), (d).

---

3. In Adoptive Couple v. Baby Girl, 570 U.S. 637 (2013), the Supreme Court held that some requirements of ICWA do not protect a parent who has not had legal or physical custody (mostly commonly an unmarried father whose legal paternity has not been established). For more information, *see* Shreya A. Fadia, Note: Adopting "Biology Plus" in Federal Indian Law: Adoptive Couple v. Baby Girl's Refashioning of ICWA's Framework, 114 Colum. L. Rev. 2007 (2014); Kevin Heiner, Note: Are You My Father? Adopting a Federal Standard for Acknowledging or Establishing Paternity in State Court ICWA Proceedings, 117 Colum. L. Rev. 2151 (2017).

C. POST-DISPOSITION: CASE PLANNING, REVIEWS, AND THE SEARCH FOR PERMANENCY

Most children in the United States who are found dependent by a juvenile court are placed in foster care. During fiscal year 2016, 273,539 children entered and 250,248 left foster care. On September 30, 2016, 437,465 children were in foster care. In comparison, 4 years earlier, there were about 41,000 fewer children in foster care, 20,000 fewer entered care, and 10,000 fewer left care. *Id.* The 2010 figures were the lowest in 30 years. U.S. Dep't of Health & Hum. Serv., Children's Bureau, Administration for Children, Youth and Families, The AFCARS Report: Preliminary FY 2016 Estimates as of Oct. 20, 2017 at 1-2.

In FY 2016, about half of children entering foster care were 5 or younger; a quarter were 6 to 11 years old, and the other quarter were 12 to 17. These proportions have remained stable over several years. Twenty-three percent of all children in foster care were Black/African American, 21 percent were Hispanic, 2 percent were Native American, 1 percent were Asian, 44 percent were White, and 7 percent were mixed race. The AFCARS Report: Preliminary FY 2016 Estimates as of Oct. 20, 2017 at 1-2. About 10 percent of African-American children and 15 percent of Native American children will be in foster care at some point before they turn 18. Michael S. Wald, New Directions for Foster Care, 68 Juv. & Fam. Ct. J. 7 (2017).

The federal Adoption Assistance and Child Welfare Act of 1980 and the Adoption and Safe Families Act of 1997 require case planning for all children in foster care. These laws provide that if a child is removed from the home and the child's permanency goal is to return home, the child welfare agency must make reasonable efforts to achieve this goal. In compliance with federal law, state laws also provide for periodic reviews of each case to ensure that the child is still safe and to determine whether progress toward achieving the goals of the case plan is being made.

This phase of a dependency case is often the most practically significant but typically has very low visibility. In many states the bases for judicial review of agency actions are limited, reviews in some states are done by administrative bodies rather than courts, and many orders issued after a review are not subject to appellate review because they are not "final orders." *See* Alicia LeVezu, The Illusion of Appellate Review in Dependency Proceedings, 68 Juv. & Fam. Ct. J. 83 (2017).

1. Case Plans and More Reasonable Efforts

The child welfare agency must make reasonable efforts to reunify the parent and child after disposition, and in collaboration with the parents it must create a written case plan for every child in foster care within 60 days of the child's removal from the home that includes a goal for the child's permanent placement. (Later in this chapter we will examine the limited situations in which reasonable efforts are not required and the permanency goal is not reunification.) Case plans should describe the efforts that the agency must make in an attempt to reunify the family and will also impose obligations on the parent(s). Case law about reasonable efforts shows that the most prominent factors in courts' determinations of the adequacy of state efforts are "(1) whether the case plan and services address the problems that caused the child to be removed from the home; (2) whether the time period for the efforts was reasonable and the specific efforts during that period timely; and (3) whether there were arrangements for visitation." Kathleen S. Bean, Reasonable Efforts: What State Courts Think, 36 U. Tol. L. Rev. 321, 344 (2005). *See also* Will L. Crossley, Defining Reasonable Efforts: Demystifying the State's Burden under Federal Child Protection Legislation, 12 B.U. Pub. Int. L.J. 259 (2003). A researcher who studied parents' responses to case plans and the legal consequences commented:

> . . . The child-protection agency wants to insure that parents have ameliorated the situation that contributed to the children's harm. It is thus incumbent upon the worker to develop a case plan that requires changes in behavior rather that attendance at meetings. For example, compliance would more meaningfully be related to risk reduction in a case plan that required a period of sobriety rather than one requiring weekly attendance at Alcoholics Anonymous meetings. . . .
>
> Similarly, parents' attorneys have a responsibility to insure that case plans are responsive to the underlying problems that have contributed to safety issues and are reasonable in terms of the parents' ability to comply. Not only should parents' attorneys advocate for services that are related to the risks, they should insure that services are likely to result in behavior change that will mitigate risks. Parents' attorneys may need to utilize experts who can report on the effectiveness of various services for each parents' unique problems. Otherwise, attorneys may see their clients lose their parental rights not because they were unfit, but simply failed to comply with an ineffective or an unreasonable court ordered plan.

Eve M. Brank et al., Parental Compliance: Its Role in Termination of Parental Rights Cases, 80 Neb. L. Rev. 335, 351 (2001).

Federal law also authorizes "concurrent planning" as a tool to facilitate the ultimate goal of permanency. 65 Fed. Reg. § 1356.21(4) (Jan. 25, 2000). Concurrent planning is the practice of simultaneously planning for and making efforts to return a child home and planning for the child's permanent placement outside the parents' home, through adoption, permanent guardianship, or other planned arrangement. The idea of concurrent planning is that if the reunifications efforts fail, progress toward the alternative will already be well underway.

NOTE: SERVICES TO CHILDREN

Removing children from homes in which they have experienced severe deprivation is often not enough to protect them. They typically need therapeutic, supportive care; without it, they remain at risk for learning and behavioral problems and physical and mental illness. National Scientific Council on the Developing Child, The Science of Neglect: The Persistent Absence of Responsive Care Disrupts the Developing Brain 9-10 (Harvard Center on the Developing Child Dec. 2012), available at developingchild.harvard.edu/index.php/download_file/-/view/1249/. As part of its reasonable efforts and planning obligations, the state must provide health and educational services to children in its custody and develop plans to provide for the mental health and medical care of foster children. 42 U.S.C. 622(b)(15). These services are important to the well-being of the child and may also be an important part of efforts to reunite parent and child, since alleviating a child's health or behavioral problems may improve the parents' chances of raising the child successfully.

Almost all foster children are eligible for Medicaid, the state-federal program that provides health care to low-income people. As a condition of receiving federal funding for the program, states must provide services required by the federal program, including Early and Periodic Screening, Diagnostic, and Treatment (EPSDT) services for all participating children younger than 21. 42 U.S.C. §§ 1396a(a)(10)(A), -(a)(43), 1396d(r)(5), -(a)(4)(B) (2005). These services must include physical examinations; immunizations; treatment and diagnosis of vision problems, including glasses; dental care; hearing and treatment of hearing problems, including hearing aids; and other health care necessary to correct or ameliorate defects, physical and mental illnesses, and other conditions discovered by screening. Based on partial data, about 67 percent of children younger than three who were eligible for these services were actually referred to the appropriate agencies. U.S. Dept. of Health and Human Services, Administration on Children, Youth and Families, Child Maltreatment 2016 at 81 (2018), available at https://www.acf.hhs.gov/cb/research-data-technology/statistics-research/child-maltreatment.

Courts have held that required services include early intervention day treatment when recommended by a doctor, Pediatric Specialty Care, Inc. v. Arkansas Department of Human Services, 293 F.3d 472, 480 (8th Cir. 2002); long-term treatment in psychiatric residential treatment facilities to children with mental illnesses, Collins v. Hamilton, 349 F.3d 371, 376 n.8 (7th Cir. 2003); behavioral and psychological services for autistic children, Chisholm v. Hood, 133 F. Supp. 2d 894 (E.D. La. 2001), and long-term, in-home support services for children with serious emotional disturbances, as well as crisis intervention services, Rosie D. v. Romney, 410 F. Supp. 2d 18 (D. Mass 2006). In Katie A. vs. Los Angeles Cty., 481 F.3d 1150 (9th Cir. 2007), the court held that all required EPSDT services must be provided in an effective manner, but they do not have to be "bundled" into a wraparound package.

All children who are the subject of a substantiated report of abuse or neglect must be referred to early intervention for screening. 20 U.S.C. §§ 1437(a)(6)(A), 5106a(b)(2)(A). Eligible children and their families receive a range of services, including assistive technology devices, hearing services, vision and mobility services, family training, family counseling and home visits, health and medical services for diagnostic or evaluation purposes, nutrition counseling, occupational therapy, physical therapy, psychological services, service coordination, social work services, special instruction, speech and language services, and transportation services. 20 U.S.C. § 1432(4). Before the child turns 3 years old, he or she must be referred to the local school to determine eligibility for regular special education services.

Many foster children are also eligible for special education services. The basics of special education requirements for school-age children are discussed in Chapter 1, above. The special education statutes provide that a team that includes the child's parents devises an educational plan adapted to the child's particular needs. If a child has been found abused or neglected, however, the parents are very likely to be unavailable or unsuitable for serving this function. In such cases, federal and state law requires juvenile court judges to appoint educational surrogates for the children. Often foster parents are appointed. For more information *see* Rebekah Gleason Hope, Foster Children and the IDEA: The Fox No Longer Guarding the Henhouse?, 69 La. L. Rev. 349 (2009); Margaret Ryznar & Chai Park, The Proper Guardians of Foster Children's Educational Interests, 42 Loy. U. Chi. L.J. 147 (2010).

The federal special education law also requires early intervention services for children younger than 3 years old who are developmentally delayed or who have a physical or mental condition that is highly likely to result in developmental delay. 20 U.S.C. §§ 1419, 1432(4), (5). For more information *see* Jessica Goldberg, Note: Rethinking Continuity for Young Children under the IDEA, 50 Harv. J. on Legis. 491 (2013).

Homeless children, particularly teens, face numerous legal problems; the problems and potential solutions are discussed in Yvonne Vissing, Homeless Children and Youth: An Examination of Legal Challenges and Directions, 13 J. L. Soc'y 455 (2012). The McKinney-Vento Homeless Assistance Act, which guarantees a right to a free, appropriate public education to homeless children, also protects some foster children. 42 USC §§ 11431-11435. For more information, *see* the website of the National Center for Homeless Education, www.serve.org/nche. An enterprising foster child in California claimed that the agency was obliged to pay for automobile liability insurance for her so that she could get a driver's license. However, the California Supreme Court upheld the lower court's ruling in favor of the agency. In re Corrine W., 198 P.3d 1102 (Cal. 2009).

Under the Preventing Sex Trafficking and Strengthening Families Act of 2014, Pub L. 113-183, § 111, states must require foster parents to abide by the "reasonable and prudent parent standard" as they make decisions about the children in their care and to train foster parents in the skills and knowledge necessary for them to satisfy the standard. The act defines "reasonable and prudent parent standard" as "the standard characterized by careful and sensible parental decisions that maintain the health, safety, and best interests of a child while at the same time encouraging the emotional and developmental growth of the child, that a caregiver shall use when determining whether to allow a child in foster care under the responsibility of the State to participate in extracurricular, enrichment, cultural, and social activities." Foster parents must use the standard to decide whether to allow a child in foster care to participate in activities such as learning to drive or playing football. 42 U.S.C. 675. Foster children have sometimes been denied these opportunities because of concerns about liability.

PROBLEMS

1. Consider again the facts of Care and Protection of Walt, above, at p. 664. Assume that the juvenile court takes jurisdiction in this case and removes Walt from his parent's home, with a goal of reuniting him with his parents. What should the components of the case plan be? Be sure to consider the obligations of the state agency and of the parents.

2. When Erin, a 17-year-old high school student, became pregnant, her parents kicked her out of the house, and she became homeless. The state child welfare agency provided her housing assistance and filed a petition alleging that both she and the baby, Mary, were dependent when the baby was born. The agency proposes that Mary's permanent plan will be living with Erin and that Erin will become independent. Its proposed service plan requires Erin to complete her senior year of high school, work to support herself and the baby, and successfully complete independent living classes. To earn the money that she will need, Erin will have to work at least 20 hours per week. The foster mother will not provide child care, but she will help Erin arrange for a baby sitter. Erin will have to get up by 5:30 or 6 A.M. to get herself and the baby ready, and she will pick up the baby at 9 P.M. After that, she will put the baby to bed and do household chores and her homework. If you were the attorney for Erin, would you agree to this case plan? What changes would you propose? Representing the agency, how would you argue in support of the plan?

2. *Case Reviews and the Supervisory Role of the Juvenile Court*

When a child is removed from home, states must require reviews of the case at least every six months by a court or the state child welfare agency. At the six-month review, the judge or hearing officer must consider the child's safety, the continuing necessity for and appropriateness of the child's placement, the extent of compliance with the case plan, the extent of progress that has been made toward alleviating or mitigating the problems that prompted the child's removal from home, and the likely date by which the child will be returned home or placed for adoption or legal guardianship. 65 Fed. Reg. § 1355.20(a).

The court must conduct a more complex proceeding, called the permanency hearing, within 12 months of the time the child entered foster care to determine the goal for the child's permanent placement. Permanency hearings must be held every 12 months, for so long as the child is in state care. At this hearing, the court must make a finding as to whether the agency has made reasonable efforts to finalize a permanent plan for the child. For purposes of this requirement, the child is considered to have entered foster care at the earlier of two dates: (1) the date of the first judicial finding that the child was abused or neglected or (2) 60 days after the child was first removed from home. States may start the clock earlier, *e.g.*, from the date the child is actually first removed from the home. *Id.*

Federal law provides that "a permanency hearing shall determine the permanency plan for a child," 42 U.S.C. § 675(c), suggesting a strong supervisory role for the judge. However, interpretive guidance issued by the Department of Health and Human Services says that a state may allow the agency "to alter the permanency plan outside a permanency hearing and will not require the court to approve such a plan before the state agency can act on it." 65 Fed. Reg. 4052 (2000). Thus, states have substantial leeway in determining how much authority to give courts.

Defining the proper role of the juvenile court in reviewing agency decisions is difficult because they have two potentially inconsistent obligations. On the one hand, courts must insure that children and families who are subject to juvenile court jurisdiction receive meaningful treatment and services. On the other, courts may not intrude too deeply into the functioning of the treatment agencies for several reasons. Judges cannot see how decisions in individual cases affect an agency's ability to provide services to all its clients, agencies cannot function effectively if their every decision is subject to being overridden, and in some instances agency personnel are better than judges at deciding what kinds of services are most likely to solve the problems of children and their parents. For proposed rules, *see* Bruce A. Boyer, Jurisdictional Conflicts Between Juvenile Courts and Child Welfare Agencies: The Uneasy Relationships Between Institutional Co-Parents, 54 Md. L. Rev. 377 (1995) (courts should have power to make decisions concerning placement and services but they should take into account areas of agency expertise and the limits of judicial time); Leonard P. Edwards, The Juvenile Court and the Role of the Juvenile Court Judge, 43 Juv. & Fam. Ct. J. 1 (1992) (courts should be able to specify foster placements, visitation, and services whenever necessary to protect the best interests of the child); Leslie J. Harris, Rethinking the Relationship Between Juvenile Courts and Treatment Agencies—An Administrative Law Approach, 28 J. Fam. L. 217 (1989-1990) (courts should defer to agency decisions based on sound factfinding and reasoning); Jerald A. Sharum, The Arkansas Supreme Court's Unconstitutional Power Grab in Arkansas Department of Human Services v. Shelby and the Judiciary's Authority in Child-Welfare Cases, 37 U. Ark. Little Rock L. Rev. 391 (2015) (critique of judicial activism from the point of view of the agency); Jane M. Spinak, Judicial Leadership in Family Court: A Cautionary Tale, 10 Tenn. J. L. & Pol'y 47, 48 (2014) (courts should focus on traditional judicial functions).

State law must also require procedural safeguards for parents whenever a child is removed from their home, the child's placement is changed, or the parents' visitation rights are affected. In addition, states must provide that a child will be consulted "in an age appropriate manner" about plans at the permanency hearing. 42 U.S.C. § 675(5)(C)(iii). *See* Andrea Khoury, Seen and Heard: Involving Children in Dependency Court, 25(10) ABA Child Law Practice 145 (Dec. 2006); Andrea Khoury, With Me, Not Without Me: How to Involve Children in Court, 26(9) ABA Child Law Practice 129 (Nov. 2007). The next case considers what procedural safeguards are required at a permanency hearing.

KC v. State

351 P.3d 236 (Wyo. 2015)

DAVIS, Justice. . . . On May 20, 2013, Casper police officers and a Department of Family Services (DFS) representative responded to a report that a small child (GC) was wandering outside, alone and near a busy street. GC, age two at the time, was only wearing a t-shirt and socks. He was very cold and wet, and was initially unresponsive, but became more alert as he warmed up inside a neighbor's house. After the police officer and DFS child welfare worker arrived, his mother KC (Mother) came out of a house four doors down. She told them that she had been staying at the residence down the street for the last two weeks, but that she planned to return to Douglas shortly. She indicated that she did not know the names of the people she was staying with, and also said that she could not authorize the officer to enter the home to check on the conditions in which the child was living. The officer therefore took GC into protective custody because Mother could not demonstrate that he had a safe and appropriate living environment.

The State, through the district attorney's office, filed a petition alleging that Mother had neglected GC. The juvenile court held a shelter care hearing on May 22, 2013, and it placed the child in the temporary legal and physical custody of the State. The court appointed a guardian *ad litem* (GAL) for GC, an attorney to represent Mother, and a multi-disciplinary team (MDT) consisting of Mother,[4] a representative of DFS, counselors, the GAL, and various other individuals, including the assistant district attorney who filed the petition. A drug test on samples taken from Mother on May 24, 2013 came back positive for methamphetamine and THC, the active ingredient in marijuana. . . .

An adjudication hearing was scheduled for July 26, 2013, but at the hearing the parties stipulated to a consent decree. Mother admitted the allegations of neglect and agreed to complete a case plan with DFS, and the State agreed that the court should hold the neglect proceedings in abeyance in order to allow Mother time to comply with the plan and demonstrate that she could provide a safe environment for GC. . . .

The DFS case plan required Mother to attend visits with GC, demonstrate adequate parenting skills, complete a psychological evaluation, and follow the recommendations of that evaluation. She was also required to complete the testing necessary to evaluate her on the Addiction Severity Index (ASI), and to obtain the treatment required, which included, *inter alia*, substance abuse counseling. She was required to report for random urinalysis testing and to maintain a drug and alcohol free environment, to obtain safe and stable housing and maintain stable employment, and to attend appointments for GC. She was also obligated to provide various information and updates to DFS. The case plan's permanency goal was family reunification.

Mother initially complied with the case plan. She had a stable residence, completed an ASI, and complied with the ASI's recommendation for medium intensity group counseling. Visitation with GC also went well. However, in August Mother had two urinalysis tests which were positive for methamphetamine, and her compliance with the case plan and cooperation with DFS began to wane. Nevertheless, the MDT continued to recommend family reunification as the permanency goal after its second meeting in October of 2013.

Despite the positive drug tests and Mother's declining compliance with the case plan, she was first allowed unsupervised daytime visits with GC, and then unsupervised overnight visits. However, on November 9, 2013, Mother tested positive for methamphetamine the same day she had GC for an overnight visit. Her counselor indicated that she was in denial about her substance abuse. In addition, on five separate occasions before December, she failed to report for urinalysis

---

4. GC's father had no involvement with GC, and he did not participate in the proceedings resulting in this appeal. After the State and GAL requested a change in the permanency plan, he contacted DFS and expressed some interest in getting involved in his son's life. He was evidently reluctant to return to Wyoming from Kansas because of an outstanding arrest warrant here.

testing, and on three other occasions, she reported for testing but failed to provide or dumped her samples. Finally, while a second ASI was not required by the terms of the case plan, she was asked by the State to have the testing done to update the index, but did not.

Because of these violations of the case plan, the State moved that the consent decree be set aside and that an adjudication of neglect be entered . . . in December of 2013. The court held a review hearing and a hearing on the State's motion on January 8, 2014. It orally granted the State's motion for reinstatement of the proceeding and adjudicated GC as neglected by Mother. It did not issue a written order following the hearing until June 6, 2014, evidently due to delay on the part of the State in preparing it. Despite the delay, the order was consistent with the oral ruling. The court also set the case for review in six months, reconfirmed the permanency goal of reunification of GC with his mother, and continued the physical and legal custody of GC with the State.

Following the January hearing, the MDT conducted its third and fourth meetings. The third meeting was held in January 2014. At that meeting, despite continuing problems with missed urinalysis tests and denial of substance abuse problems, the MDT again recommended family reunification for GC's permanency plan.

At the fourth meeting held in April of 2014, the MDT again noted that there were continued problems with urinalysis, including a positive test for methamphetamine in March, and other missed tests and diluted samples. The report described some progress on Mother's mental health issues, but noted that she continued to miss group and individual counseling sessions. Consistent employment was also an issue. Mother stated that she was working inconsistent and sporadic hours at another new job, and that she was working for a temporary service as well. However, she failed to provide pay stubs and indicated that she was being paid "under the table" for at least one job. The majority recommendation after the April meeting was to change GC's permanency plan to termination of parental rights and adoption.

On May 6, 2014, consistent with the MDT's recommendation, the GAL filed a motion for an order which would allow DFS to cease reunification efforts and change the permanency plan to adoption. Ten days later, the State also filed a motion to waive reunification efforts. Mother objected to the motions and requested that the court require DFS to pay for hair follicle testing because of claimed irregularities with drug testing. She claimed, among other things, that employees at the drug testing center were tampering with her samples.

On June 4, 2014, the court held another review hearing in conjunction with a hearing on the pending motions relating to the permanency plan. At the hearing, neither the GAL nor the State presented any evidence, but instead based their arguments solely on the MDT reports. Mother did not offer any evidence to refute the findings or factual information in the reports, but her attorney implied that she would have objected to the foundation of the drug test reports referred to in the MDT reports if the hearing had been a trial, and she argued that hair follicle testing could refute the laboratory reports finding methamphetamine in the samples Mother gave.

The court orally granted the motions filed by the GAL and the State, changed the permanency plan to termination of parental rights and adoption, and denied Mother's request that the State be required to pay for hair follicle testing. It found that because of Mother's continued use of methamphetamine and a lack of progress on her case plan, it was in GC's best interest to cease efforts at reunification. The court entered a written order consistent with the oral ruling on August 19, 2014. The order changed the permanency plan to adoption. Mother timely appealed from this order. . . .

. . . The statutes provide little specific guidance regarding evidence to be considered by the court or the process that is due to the child or the parents at a permanency hearing. However, the statute does require DFS to provide certain information at the permanency hearing:

> [T]he department of family services shall present to the court the efforts made to effectuate the permanency plan for the child, address the options for the child's permanent placement, examine the reasons for excluding other permanency options and set forth the proposed plan to carry out the placement decision, including specific times for achieving the permanency plan. The [DFS] shall provide the court a compelling reason for establishing a permanency plan other than reunification, adoption, or legal guardianship.

At the permanency hearing, the court must determine whether the permanency plan is in the best interests of the child and whether DFS has made reasonable efforts to finalize the plan. If the court finds that reasonable efforts to reunite the child with his parent are not required (or are no longer required), and that the child's best interests require something other than family reunification, it will change the permanency plan accordingly. The State must justify the change in the permanency plan by a preponderance of the evidence.

If the permanency plan is adoption or any other alternative arrangement requiring the parents' rights to be severed, the next step will normally be for the State to file an action for termination of parental rights on the grounds stated in Wyo. Stat. Ann. § 14–2–309(a)(i)–(viii). The termination action is not conducted in the juvenile court, but is rather a separate action which must be filed in district court.

The statutes list grounds which justify termination. At the termination-of-parental-rights (TPR) hearing, a full gamut of procedural rights and processes come into play: the Wyoming Rules of Civil Procedure, including the right to a jury trial, and the Wyoming Rules of Evidence apply. At least one ground for termination must be proven by clear and convincing evidence.

Wyoming's statutes thus provide for a full evidentiary hearing or trial at the beginning of the abuse/neglect case when the juvenile court must determine whether there has been abuse or neglect and decides whether to return the child to the custody of his parents or to put the child in the State's custody to protect him from further abuse or neglect. They also provide for a full evidentiary hearing or trial in the district court when, at the end of the process, the State seeks to terminate a parent's parental rights.

Between the bookends of the initial adjudication and the TPR hearing, a number of review and permanency hearings regarding the progress made by the parents toward reunification and the ultimate permanency plan may be held. Those hearings look nothing like the typical evidentiary hearing or trial. In fact,

Rule 1101(b)(3) of the Wyoming Rules of Evidence expressly states that the rules of evidence "do not apply in . . . juvenile proceedings other than adjudicatory hearings." Moreover, the statutes provide little guidance as to the nature of the process required at these interim hearings.

Nevertheless, at review and permanency hearings, the juvenile court makes decisions that impact children and their families, in varying ways. For example, the juvenile court may decide to continue foster care, or it may conclude that the requirements of the permanency and DFS plans have been met and return the child to the custody of his or her parents. The juvenile court can also establish what services will or will not be provided to a parent to facilitate reunification, and the court can change aspects of the permanency plan as the parent and child adapt to their new situations. All of these decisions can affect the parents' relationship with the child and ongoing efforts at reunification, and they may also affect the TPR proceeding if the permanency plan is changed to require termination.

In the case of a change in the permanency plan to an alternative that requires termination of parental rights, the effect of the passage of time on the later TPR proceeding is often significant. As one commentator has pointed out, "[t]he time that passes between a permanency plan change away from reunification and any later permanency trial heightens [the] state power and increases the likelihood that a termination of parental rights, adoption, or guardianship motion will both be filed and granted, thereby permanently eliminating parents' rights to care, custody, and control of their children." Josh Gupta–Kagan, Filling the Due Process Donut Hole: Abuse and Neglect Cases between Disposition and Permanency, 10 Conn. Pub. Int. L.J. 13, 38 (2010). By the time the TPR hearing takes place, the child may have been living in foster care (sometimes with potential adoptive parents) for years, and the court will inevitably consider how well he or she is doing there and the bonds formed between the child and his foster family as a factor in determining whether to terminate parental rights. In addition, the juvenile court will examine the child's relationship with his parent, which will necessarily have been affected by the passage of time and separation from them. The State controls the timing of filing the proceeding.

II. Due Process Rights in Permanency and Review Hearings

Few courts have recognized the effect of a change in permanency to termination in any meaningful way. Yet the question of whether parents have a due process right to participate meaningfully in permanency hearings occurring long before hearings on termination of parental rights is a significant one. The Wyoming Constitution provides that "[n]o person shall be deprived of life, liberty or property without due process of law." The touchstone of our due process guarantee is the belief that parties are entitled to notice and an opportunity to be heard when their rights are at stake. However, the process due at any given time must reflect the nature of the proceeding and the interests involved.

We have held that a parent's substantial rights are affected when the permanency plan is changed from reunification to termination and adoption. In *In re HP*, we considered whether a juvenile court order stemming from a review hearing changing the permanency plan from reunification to termination and adoption was an appealable order. We held that because an order at a permanency hearing halting reunification efforts affects substantial rights, it is appealable:

> [U]nder W.R.A.P. 1.05(b), an order affecting a substantial right made in a special proceeding is an appealable order. Proceedings in juvenile court are special proceedings and both adjudication and disposition affect substantial rights. As discussed above, the court adjudicated neglect following the initial hearing. This order did however follow a dispositional review hearing and appears to be a dispositional order because it orders DFS to begin termination proceedings. **In any event, the order certainly affects Mother's substantial rights as it has the effect of halting reunification attempts.** Therefore, we treat it as an appealable order.

Not all review hearings have the same impact. At one end of the spectrum, a review hearing at which an ongoing permanency plan is reviewed and continued pending some required action by the parents will have relatively minor impact on the parties. At the other end of the spectrum, a permanency hearing in which a court changes the permanency plan from reunification to termination of parental rights has significant impacts, not only on parents, but on children as well.

Of course, one core constitutional interest at stake in all abuse and neglect cases is the parents' interest "in the care, custody, and control of their children." *Troxel v. Granville*, 530 U.S. 57, 65 (2000) . . . "Permanency hearings not only threaten substantial prejudice to parental rights, they bear a direct relation to the TPR hearing. The motion to terminate is based largely on conduct between the petition and the permanency hearing."

There is also the reciprocal interest of the child in maintaining his relationship with his parents. Finally, the State has an interest in providing for the best interest of the child, which includes resolution in a speedy fashion to avoid what has become known as "foster care limbo."

Because "termination proceedings are largely based on the parent's conduct from the time the child is taken into custody until the court decides further assistance to the parent is futile . . ., [i]f parents are not afforded an early opportunity to defend against charges of abuse and neglect before the end state, termination may very well be a foregone conclusion." . . .

However, we must also be mindful that proceedings after adjudication and prior to the TPR hearing substantially impact the rights of the parties, as discussed above. "Even though parental rights are not irrevocably decided at a permanency hearing, the general purpose of these hearings 'is to compel a resolution of the case so the child does not remain indefinitely in the system.'" It is usually a foregone conclusion that once a permanency plan is changed from family reunification to adoption or other permanent placement outside the home, an action to terminate parental rights will eventually be filed. Moreover, at the permanency hearing, the State will often rely on facts justifying termination, even though a formal TPR hearing follows. We therefore conclude that parents have a due process right to meaningful participation at permanency hearings when the State seeks to change permanency from family reunification to another status that will require termination of parental rights.

The process due at such hearings must be evaluated in light of the process received throughout the proceedings and must be proportionate to the issues at stake. Indeed, as the United States Supreme Court recounted, "'(d)ue process,' unlike some legal rules, is not a technical conception with a fixed content unrelated to time, place and circumstances. . . . [It] is flexible and calls for such procedural protections as the particular situation demands." Mathews v. Eldridge, 424 U.S. 319, 334 (1976).

In *Maria C.*, the New Mexico Court of Appeals was faced with the question of what type of procedure ought to be provided in a permanency hearing involving a change that would result in termination of parental rights. That court concluded that "notice and the opportunity to participate in a permanency hearing would contribute to the overall fairness of the procedure by giving parents an opportunity to present their side of the story, prepare a defense if termination is in the offing, or avoid the TPR hearing altogether by having the case dismissed." The New Mexico court recognized that "[e]ffective counsel might also expose weaknesses in the State's case and cross examination could be useful as an impeachment tool. Testimony from the parents regarding their efforts to rehabilitate might influence the court's decision" as well.

We generally agree with the New Mexico approach. Permanency hearings, when there may be a change in the plan from reunification to termination of parental rights, implicate substantial rights and thus require meaningful due process.

We take this opportunity to define the process due at such a hearing. Due process requires that if a change in permanency plan includes adoption or permanent placement other than reunification, the parents must have the right to request, and on request must be provided with, an evidentiary hearing. The parent must request the hearing if he or she desires one, because there may be instances in which parents do not dispute a recommendation or are content with a non-evidentiary hearing. The failure to request such a hearing waives that right.

As we have already noted, Wyoming Rule of Evidence 1101 specifically states that the Rules of Evidence do not apply to "juvenile proceedings other than adjudicatory hearings." Wyoming's Rules of Evidence do not apply in probation revocation proceedings in criminal cases. However, probationers are entitled "to appear in person and by counsel, to confront and examine adverse witnesses, and at the dispositional stage to make a statement in mitigation of revocation."

A similar process is sufficient to protect the rights of the parents in change-of-permanency hearings. The parent requesting a hearing is entitled to put the State to its proof, to be present, to confront and cross-examine witnesses, to call witnesses, and to present a case in support of a continued plan of reunification or dismissal of the case. Hearsay evidence that is probative, trustworthy, and credible may be received at the hearing. Finally, we reiterate that at the permanency hearing the State has the burden of establishing by a preponderance of the evidence that a change in the permanency plan is in the best interests of the child. Although these procedures are not as protective of parental rights as those which must be employed in a later TPR hearing, they provide realistic and meaningful protection against an erroneous decision at a critical point in the process. . . .

III.   DUE PROCESS IN THIS CASE

While this Court's aforementioned ruling will be applied prospectively, we must still determine whether Mother's rights to due process were violated. She contends that it was error for the juvenile court to apply W.R.E. 1101(b)(3) and rely solely on the MDT reports, which contained hearsay evidence, in spite of what she characterizes as an objection to that procedure and a request for follicle testing. In essence, Mother claims that the procedure was flawed because it did not allow her to meaningfully challenge the evidence contained in the MDT reports, and that her right to due process was violated as a result. . . .

W.R.E. 1101(b)(3) states that the rules of evidence do not apply in "juvenile proceedings other than adjudicatory hearings." The juvenile court followed that rule. We hold in this case that an evidentiary hearing utilizing procedures like those employed in probation revocation proceedings satisfies due process in these circumstances. That was not the rule when the juvenile court made its decision, and it was therefore not clear or unequivocal at the time. Accordingly, there was no plain error in conducting the permanency hearing as the court did. . . .

V.   SUFFICIENCY OF EVIDENCE

Finally, Mother challenges the sufficiency of the evidence to support the juvenile court's finding that a change in the permanency plan was warranted, and that the recommended permanency plan of adoption would be in GC's best interests. We must determine whether the juvenile court abused its discretion.

Mother argues that she complied with her case plan because she had adequate housing and a job, and because visitation with GC was going well. She takes the position that the court relied solely upon the MDT reports showing that she failed to report for drug testing and that some tests were positive for methamphetamine to change the permanency plan. She claims that because the positive results in the reports were hearsay and because there were irregularities with the testing, the State failed to meet its burden and the court abused its discretion by finding that reunification efforts should cease.

At the hearing, the court explained its reasoning:

> [In July of 2013] I communicated that the mother needed to make a pretty tough decision and pretty substantial commitment to her child rather than methamphetamine. And unfortunately, I do not believe she has complied with taking care of that problem. . . .
>
> . . . We have multiple violations of [the] Family Service Plan because of the UAs on the several and numerous dates over the extended almost year period of time that's involved here.
>
> In addition, a very strong component of the Family Service Plan is to make sure there's ongoing drug testing. And . . . the record documents an ongoing failure to appear to Day Reporting, and so we don't even know what some of those test results may be. Additionally, I didn't put much weight on the housing concern; but it does appear there's been ongoing instability with employment, with counseling, with other components of the Family Service Plan. . . . [T]here needs to be substantial progress made towards any reunification effort; and I do not see that in this case.

In the case of In re ARC, 258 P.3d 704 (Wyo. 2011), we considered whether termination of parental rights was justified under similar circumstances. There the mother "only occasionally showed up for UAs, many of which were positive for illegal drug use." At her TPR hearing, however, the mother testified that she had become sober. We affirmed the termination of her parental rights based upon missed and failed drug tests and her ultimate failure to address her substance abuse problems. . . .

We find that the court did not abuse its discretion in ordering a change in the permanency plan for GC. The court's finding that Mother failed to comply with her case plan is well-supported by the record, and was proven by a preponderance of the evidence presented. Of major significance were her repeated failures to appear for required drug testing. While Mother alleged there were "irregularities" with the drug testing, she has not even attempted to explain her repeated failure to appear for tests. Moreover, Mother failed a number of tests, indicating that she had an ongoing substance abuse problem. Finally, there were also other ongoing problems with maintaining steady employment and cooperating with the counseling required by the plan. . . .

NOTES AND QUESTIONS

1. Why was the mother's failure to comply with the requirement that she be drug-free a sufficient reason to change the permanency goal from reunification to adoption? What if she had complied with the condition but failed to visit regularly? What if she were drug-free and visited but had not secured adequate housing?

A survey of attorneys and state child welfare workers found that a parent's failure to comply with the requirements of the service plan significantly increased the chances that the attorney or worker would recommend filing a termination of parental rights petition. Eve M. Brank et al., Parental Compliance: Its Role in Termination of Parental Rights Cases, 80 Neb. L. Rev. 335 (2001). This held true regardless of whether or not the parent had a condition that was regarded as highly treatable (depression vs. mental retardation) and regardless of whether the plan was broadly or narrowly focused.

Nevertheless, failure to comply with a plan is not, in itself, a basis for termination. In the Interest of S.J.H., 124 S.W.3d 63 (Mo. App. W.D. 2004). *See also* State ex rel. Dept. Hum. Servs. V. D.T.C., 219 P.3d 610 (Or. App. 2009) (juvenile court found children dependent where father failed to comply with court-ordered alcohol treatment in an earlier case, but instead got effective treatment on his own because "it wasn't right" that he should get away with flouting court order; reversed for insufficient evidence).

2. In times of general economic hardship, community resources that might help parents, such as treatment programs, as well as child welfare agency resources, may be drastically reduced. How should a court respond to the agency's position that it cannot provide services that would be offered in better economic times because of current budget cuts? *See* Bruce A. Boyer & Amy E. Halbrook, Advocating for Children in Care in a Climate of Economic Recession: The

Relationship Between Poverty and Child Maltreatment, 6 Nw. J.L. & Soc. Pol'y 300 (2011).

3. The District of Columbia Court of Appeals also discussed the practical importance of the permanency hearing in In re TA.L., 149 A.3d 1060 (D.C. 2013). Holding that a court order changing the permanency goal from reunification is appealable, the court said, effectively agreeing with the argument of the parties and amici that

> when a trial court changes the goal of a neglect proceeding from reunification to adoption, it informally terminates the pending neglect case and effectively puts the case on an almost unalterable path to adoption. . . . While it is ostensibly possible for the biological parents to attain reunification notwithstanding a decision by the trial court to grant a permanency goal change, this very rarely occurs in practice. More often, the parents' efforts to build or maintain a positive relationship with their child is severely hampered by the trial court's permanency decision and by the time a parent is given the ability to challenge that decision, the passage of time and the child's resulting attachment to the custodial adoption petitioner tends to make the granting of the adoption petition and the consequent termination of parental rights a *fait accompli*.

149 A.3d at 1074.

3.   Foster Care Placements

Foster care is supposed to be a short-term placement for children while their parents work on resolving the problems that led to a court taking the children from the parents. For many decades, though, reality has not coincided with this theory. On average, in 2016 foster children had been in care more 20.1 months, with a median time in care of 12.7 months, and 20 percent had been in foster care for 30 months or more. U.S. Dep't of Health & Hum. Serv., Children's Bureau, Administration for Children, Youth and Families, The AFCARS Report: Preliminary FY 2016 Estimates as of Oct. 20, 2017 at 2.

In addition, many foster care placements are of poor quality; research shows that half of all teens in care reported having been abused or neglected. A major problem is lack of qualified foster parents, particularly for children with mental health or behavior problems. Michael S. Wald, New Directions for Foster Care, 68 Juv. & Fam. Ct. J. 7 (2017). A child welfare supervisor with 30 years of experience who also taught in the Washington School of Social Work observed, "The chronic shortage of homes leads to risky practices such as placing children wherever there is an opening regardless of the fit between a child's needs and the strengths of foster parents, overcrowding homes, placing physically aggressive or sexually acting out children in homes or facilities with younger or weaker children unable to protect themselves, having children sleep in child welfare offices or in hotel rooms, moving children from home to home every 24 hours and ignoring children's needs unless they are severe or immediate." Dee Wilson, "Is Foster Care Safe?" (2016), quoted in Wald, above.

Partly in response to this lack of foster homes, state and federal law express strong preferences for placing foster children with relatives. Federal law requires states to "consider[] giving preference to an adult relative over a non-related caregiver when determining a placement for a child, provided that the relative caregiver meets all relevant state child protection standards." 42 U.S.C. § 671(a)(18). The state must use the same standards to license foster homes provided by family members that it uses for other foster homes. 65 Fed. Reg. 1355.34(7) (January 25, 2000). Child welfare agencies are to exercise due diligence to identify and notify all adult relatives within 30 days of a child's placement in state care. The Act also requires states to provide enhanced financial assistance and other help to relative caregivers and allows states to waive non-safety-related foster care licensing requirements for relatives. State laws and their variations are analyzed in Child Welfare Information Gateway, Children's Bureau, U.S. Dept. Health & Hum. Servs., Placement of Children with Relatives (2018).

About a third of foster children live in kinship care.[5] The percentage of foster children living with relatives increased from about 25 percent in 2010 to 32 percent in 2016. 2016 AFCARS report, above, at 1; U.S. Dep't of Health & Hum. Serv., Children's Bureau, Administration for Children, Youth and Families, The AFCARS Report: Preliminary FY 2010 Estimates as of June 30, 2011, at 1.

Proponents of kinship care argue that it is inherently better for children because it helps them maintain family and community connections, provides them with a sense of stability, and minimizes the trauma and loss from being separated from their parents. Children in kinship care adjust better than children in stranger foster care and have fewer behavioral and mental health problems, and their schooling is less likely to be disrupted. Annie E. Casey Foundation, Stepping Up for Kids 3-4 (2012).

On the other hand, critics argue that children are placed with relatives without appropriate safeguards and supportive services, agencies are too hasty in sending children to live with kin rather than working with and providing services to parents that could keep children at home, and relatives are pressured into taking children without knowing what they are committing to. Some jurisdictions and workers are opposed to licensing relatives as foster parents because they are philosophically opposed to paying relatives to provide care. Annie E. Casey Foundation, The Kinship Diversion Debate 1-5 (2013); *see also* Rob Geen, The Evolution of Kinship Care Policy and Practice, 14(1) Future of Children 131 (2004).

Empirical studies show that kinship care is more heavily used by families of color than white families, and they find wide variation in associations between kinship care and children's legal permanency. Many studies found fewer placement changes and lower rates of re-entry into foster care but also lower rates of adoption. Findings regarding child safety were mixed. William Vesneski et al.,

---

5. An estimated 2.7 million children live with kin, most in informal arrangements. Annie E. Casey Foundation, Stepping Up for Kids 1 (2012). Some of these arrangements are orchestrated by child welfare agencies in response to reports of child maltreatment, and others are arranged solely by families themselves. One of every 11 children, including 20 percent of African-American children, will live in kinship care for at least three consecutive months. *Id*. at 2.

An Analysis of State Law and Policy Regarding Subsidized Guardianship for Children: Innovations in Permanency, 21 UC Davis J. Juv. L. & Pol'y 27, 36-37 (2017).

ADOPTION OF PAISLEY

178 A.3d 1228 (Me. 2018)

ALEXANDER, J. . . . In this appeal, we consider the application of the consent to adoption statute, 18–A M.R.S. § 9–302 (2017), to contested adoption proceedings heard in the District Court following a District Court judgment terminating parental rights concerning that child. . . .

As relevant to this appeal, 18–A M.R.S. § 9–302(a) states:

(a) Before an adoption is granted, written consent to the adoption must be given by:

. . . .

(3) The person or agency having legal custody or guardianship of the child or to whom the child has been surrendered and released, except that the person's or agency's lack of consent, if adjudged unreasonable by a judge . . . may be overruled by the judge. In order for the judge to find that the person or agency acted unreasonably in withholding consent, the petitioner must prove, by a preponderance of the evidence, that the person or agency acted unreasonably. The court may hold a pretrial conference to determine who will proceed. The court may determine that even though the burden of proof is on the petitioner, the person or agency should proceed if the person or agency has important facts necessary to the petitioner in presenting the petitioner's case. The judge shall consider the following:

(i) Whether the person or agency determined the needs and interests of the child;

(ii) Whether the person or agency determined the ability of the petitioner and other prospective families to meet the child's needs;

(iii) Whether the person or agency made the decision consistent with the facts;

(iv) Whether the harm of removing the child from the child's current placement outweighs any inadequacies of that placement; and

(v) All other factors that have a bearing on a determination of the reasonableness of the person's or agency's decision in withholding consent.

. . . .

A petition for adoption must be pending before a consent is executed.

Here, Paisley's parents' rights had been terminated, and because the Department had legal custody of Paisley, section 9–302(a)(3) required that, before any adoption could be granted, the Department's written consent had to be obtained. The Department's refusal to grant consent to adoption by the appellees and its consent to adoption by the appellants was the focus of the District Court hearing. After the hearing, the court, applying section 9–302(a)(3), found that the appellees—the foster parents—had met their burden to prove "by a preponderance of the evidence" that the Department had acted unreasonably in withholding its consent to their adoption of Paisley. . . .

The following findings, all of which are fully supported by the record, were made by the court in its decision. Paisley was born in October 2015. When she was just twelve days old, the Department took custody of her and placed her into the home of licensed foster parents, the appellees.

Title 22 M.R.S. § 4036–B requires the Department to notify relatives when a child enters foster care. *See* 22 M.R.S. § 4036–B(3–A) (2017) (requiring the Department to notify the following relatives: all grandparents of the child; all parents of a sibling of the child who have legal custody of the sibling; and other adult relatives of the child).

When Paisley was placed in foster care, the appellants, who had previously adopted two of Paisley's biological siblings and who live in Massachusetts, received the Department's notification, pursuant to 22 M.R.S. § 4036–B(3–A). They immediately contacted the Department, stating their interest in serving as a placement for Paisley.

At that time, the Department's plan for Paisley was reunification with her mother, who resided in mid-coast Maine. Accordingly, the Department chose to leave Paisley in the care of her foster parents. The record indicates that the Department was concerned that placing Paisley with the appellants in southern Massachusetts would make its efforts toward reunification with the mother in mid-coast Maine much more difficult.

While Paisley resided with her foster parents, the Department engaged in reunification efforts with Paisley's mother.[6] During this time, the appellants were in regular contact with the Department, seeking to set up visitation with Paisley and to make the Department aware that they were interested in being the permanent adoptive placement for Paisley. In January of 2016, a Department supervisor notified the appellants that the Department was "going to look into getting an Interstate Compact on Placement of Children ('ICPC')" evaluation started. The Department initiated that process in March of 2016.

On June 1, 2016, the Department filed its petition for termination of the parents' rights and, in that month, the appellants had their first visit with Paisley. Despite the filing of the termination petition, reunification efforts continued, and the Department remained "hopeful" that the mother would be able to reunify. In December of 2016, however, the mother relapsed, was incarcerated, and reunification efforts with the mother ceased.

On December 16, 2016, a Department supervisor directed the caseworker to tell Paisley's foster parents that, if the mother's rights were terminated, the Department intended to place Paisley in Massachusetts with the appellants. The foster parents told the caseworker that they had called an attorney "to possibly fight DHHS's placement decision." The Department attempted to have the two families meet but, when that meeting did not occur, and "with the threat of litigation looming," the Department backed off on any firm decision about Paisley's placement. Soon thereafter, both the appellants and the appellees moved to intervene

---

6. Paisley's father was incarcerated and did not participate in any reunification efforts with Paisley.

in the child protection action. In February of 2017, before any termination order issued, the foster parents filed a petition for adoption.

Paisley's parents consented to a termination of their parental rights on March 6, 2017, and the permanency plan for Paisley became adoption.[7] The appellants filed a competing petition to adopt Paisley on April 10, 2017.

On April 24, 2017, the court issued a case management and pretrial order that listed all three docket numbers: the child protection docket number and the two family matter docket numbers assigned to the competing adoption petitions. The order granted intervenor status to both the appellees and the appellants. The matters were then set for a contested adoption hearing.

In late May, approximately two weeks before the date set for the contested adoption hearing, the Department decided that Paisley should be placed with the appellants in Massachusetts with two of her siblings and that it would not consent to adoption by the foster parents. . . .

On June 6 and June 7, 2017, the District Court held a hearing on the competing petitions for adoption. During the hearing, all prospective adoptive parents testified and described their plans and commitment to the care of Paisley. The Department's witnesses testified that the decision that Paisley should be placed with the appellants and that it would not consent to adoption by the foster parents was made in late May, approximately two weeks before the date set for the contested adoption hearing. In its decision, the court noted that the supervisor who testified about this issue did "not know who actually made the decision but understood that it was made because of DHHS's sibling policy."[8]

The appellees called their expert witness, a specialist in early childhood attachment. . . .

Paisley's guardian ad litem recommended that the court grant the foster parents' petition to adopt Paisley. In its decision, the court quoted from the GAL's most recent report, in which she stated that Paisley "regards her foster parents as her parents . . . ."

On June 29, 2017, the District Court issued a single order that was entered in all three cases: (1) finding that the Department unreasonably withheld its consent to the foster parents' adoption petition; (2) granting their petition to adopt Paisley; and (3) denying the appellants' petition to adopt Paisley. In the order, the court found:

> [The Department's] consideration of Paisley's needs and best interest was, at best, narrowly confined to the fact that the [appellants] have adopted two of Paisley's biological siblings. There is no evidence that [the Department] gave weight to any other factor relevant to Paisley's best interest, including the bond that had formed between Paisley and the [foster parents]. This conclusion is reinforced by [the

---

7. At the termination hearing, both parents expressed to the court their belief that Paisley should stay with the appellees because of Paisley's bond with the appellees' family.

8. This policy states: "Placement of siblings together should be made a priority in case planning and implementation of the case plan. Valid reasons must be identified and documented for not placing siblings together."

permanency supervisor's] admission that she did not even read the GAL report and recommendation. . . .

The court finds that the harm of removing Paisley from the [foster parents'] home outweighs any inadequacies of that placement, specifically the fact that Paisley will not be living with biological siblings. Paisley has formed a strong attachment to the [foster parents'] family . . . . For Paisley, [the foster parents] are her parents and their two children are her siblings. . . .

While the court recognizes the importance and purpose of [the Department's] sibling policy, the court notes that some of the important reasons for that policy are not present in this case. . . . Here, the policy is being applied to unite Paisley with some of her biological siblings at the cost of separating her from those persons with whom she has come to know as her family. Here, Paisley can still have a meaningful sibling relationship with her biological siblings and the [appellants'] entire family without subjecting her to the trauma of separating her from the [foster parents], the family that she has come to know as her own. . . .

Paisley's relationship with [the foster parents] is one of parent and child. Paisley does not have the same depth of bond with the [appellants]. The court finds that it would be in Paisley's best interest for [the foster parents] to adopt her.

The appellants timely filed a notice of appeal. . . .

The Department's refusal to consent to an adoption can be overridden by the court if the court finds that the Department acted unreasonably in withholding consent.

Pursuant to 18–A M.R.S. § 9–302(a)(3), the court must consider the following factors in determining whether the Department acted unreasonably in withholding consent: (1) whether the Department determined the needs and interests of the child; (2) whether the Department determined the ability of the petitioner and other prospective families to meet the child's needs; (3) whether the Department's decision was consistent with the facts; (4) whether the harm of removing the child from the child's current placement outweighs any inadequacies of that placement; and (5) all other factors that have a bearing on a determination of the reasonableness of the Department's decision in withholding consent. The adoption petitioner, from whom the Department has withheld consent, bears the burden of proving, "by a preponderance of the evidence," that the Department acted unreasonably.

The appellants argue that the court erred by finding that the Department acted unreasonably when it withheld consent from the foster parents to adopt Paisley. We review findings of fact for clear error and discretionary determinations for an abuse of discretion. . . .

The court's finding that the Department acted unreasonably is supported by competent evidence in the record. The court applied 18–A M.R.S. § 9–302(a)(3), addressed each statutory factor individually, and made findings as to each factor that support the court's ultimate finding that the Department acted unreasonably in withholding its consent to adoption by the foster parents.

The court specifically found that (1) the Department's decision that Paisley should be placed with the appellants was primarily based on the Department's policy of placing siblings together; (2) the Department failed to consider other factors relevant to Paisley's needs and best interest, including the bond between Paisley and her long-term foster family; and (3) the Department failed to give adequate consideration to the harm Paisley would experience if removed from the care of the foster parents. The court found that "the harm of removing Paisley from [her current home] outweighs any inadequacies of that placement, specifically the fact that Paisley will not be living with biological siblings." Additionally, the court found that Paisley, if adopted by her foster parents, will be able to have a meaningful relationship with her biological siblings without being subjected to the trauma of being removed from the appellees, the only caregivers she has known. . . .

The court demonstrated that it understood the distinct roles it and the Department played in this proceeding. The Department, as the child's legal guardian, has an obligation to find an appropriate adoptive home for the child. Having done so, it is then in a position solely to offer its expertise to assist the court in determining whether the actual adoption of that child into that home is in the child's best interest. In the end, however, only the court may grant an adoption based on its independent determination of what is in a child's best interest. . . .

Judgment affirmed.

SAUFLEY, C.J., concurring. I must reluctantly concur in the court's opinion, particularly given the child's attachment to her foster family in Maine. I write separately, however, because the State's delays in establishing a solid contact schedule with the Massachusetts family have led to the sad result that Paisley will be deprived of the opportunity to grow up in an available family with her biological siblings.

I do not underestimate the complexity of scheduling visits between an infant and a family that is not local, nor do I question the reasons for placing a child in a location close to her parent for reunification purposes. And Paisley is certainly fortunate to have been placed in a foster home where she is loved and has been well cared for.

Nonetheless, had the Department acted more expeditiously and more assertively to establish a relationship between Paisley and the family of her sisters, she could have been adopted into the same family and had the benefit of a childhood and adolescence spent with her own sisters. The value of that family connection appears to have been lost in the Department's slow response to the Massachusetts family's availability, and those actions have cost this child dearly.

The Legislature has explicitly established kinship placement as a high priority for children who cannot be raised by their parents: "Recognizing that the health and safety of children must be of paramount concern and that the right to family integrity is limited by the right of children to be protected from abuse and neglect and recognizing also that uncertainty and instability are possible in extended foster home or institutional living, it is the intent of the Legislature that this chapter ...[p]lace children who are taken from the custody of their parents with an adult relative when possible." By urging the consideration of kinship care, the Legislature has certainly signaled that a home where a child's siblings reside should be considered for placement when possible.

Especially in light of the tragedies caused by the opioid addiction epidemic, it is important to honor the Legislature's purpose to provide for the early placement of children whose parents cannot care for them with other family members so that the children can grow up with a strong sense of family identity and are not deprived of the lifetime connection that a childhood and adolescence shared with siblings or other relatives can provide.

NOTES AND QUESTIONS

1. The problem in *Paisley*— how much weight to give to the relative preference when the child has been in foster care with an unrelated person and the time has come to choose an adoptive home—is relatively common. *See, e.g.* In the Interest of SO, 382 P.3d 51 (Wyo. 2016) (upholding trial court order favoring foster parents); In the Interest of AS, 322 P.3d 263 (Hi. 2014) (same). Is the relative preference based only on the child's interests? How is a relative placement in the child's best interests on facts like those in *Paisley*? Do the relatives have an interest that should be protected as well? What countervailing vision of the child's best interests supports allowing the foster parents to adopt?

Should it matter why the child was not placed with relatives early in the case? What if the agency simply failed to seek the relatives? What if the relatives were contacted earlier but initially refused to take the child? What if, as in *Paisley*, the agency chose not to place the child with relatives because of the difficulty that would pose for efforts to reunify the parent and child?

2. As *Paisley* says, an important factor in this kind of case is the state's law on the extent of judicial authority to override the agency's placement decisions. What was the standard in the Maine statute used in *Paisley*? Under this standard, what weight does the agency's decision carry? Compare the Hawaii standard:

> . . .HRS § 587A–31(c)(2) (Supp. 2010), entitled "Permanency hearing," provides the following (with emphasis added): "At each permanency hearing, the court shall make written findings pertaining to: . . . Whether the current placement of the child continues to be appropriate and in the best interests of the child or if another in-state or out-of-state placement should be considered. . . ." This statutory provision requires the family court to make its own independent determination of the child's best interests in a permanent placement. . . .
>
> . . . [W]here a party challenges DHS's permanent placement determination, that party bears the burden of proving, by a preponderance of the evidence, that DHS's permanent placement determination is not in the best interests of the child. This is because DHS is charged with administering child welfare services in the state, and its social workers are presumed to be experts on child protection and child welfare. . . .
>
> "[U]pon the termination of parental rights, discretion to determine an appropriate custodian is vested in DHS. . . . After termination of rights, custody is given to DHS which is charged with finding a suitable home for the child." As explained, *supra*, in Section III.A, this placement determination is, however, subject to review by the family court, which is authorized and required by law to determine whether the placement is in the child's best interests.

Interest of AS, above, 322 P.3d at 272-273. How does this standard differ from the Maine standard?

In Interest of SO, above, the Wyoming Supreme Court held that the juvenile court should review the agency's placement decision for an abuse of discretion. How does this standard differ from the Maine and Hawaii standards?

3. Among the relatives entitled to placement consideration under federal law are the legal parents of the siblings of a child. Federal law further protects sibling relationships by requiring state agencies to exercise due diligence in attempting to place siblings together in foster care. Where siblings are not placed together, states must make reasonable efforts to allow them to visit. 42 U.S.C. § 671(a)(31). In 35 states and Puerto Rico, statutes encourage placing siblings together in foster care or protect their relationship by providing for visitation. Child Welfare Information Gateway, Children's Bureau, U.S. Dept. Health & Hum. Servs., Placement of Children with Relatives (2018).

In several recent cases children in foster care have sought orders allowing them to visit with siblings over the objections of the children's parents or guardians, with mixed results. The Massachusetts Supreme Judicial Court held in Care and Protection of Jamison, 4 N.E.3d 889 (Mass. 2014), that court-appointed guardians of children are not entitled to the same deference that parents are in such a dispute, but that the juvenile court must determine whether visitation is in the best interests of the children who are not in state care as well as the petitioning child before ordering visitation. The Maryland high court held in In re Victoria C., 88 A.3d 749 (Md. 2014), that the request of an adult who had recently aged out of foster care for visitation with her half-siblings was governed by the third-party visitation statute which requires proof that lack of visitation with the children had a significant deleterious effect on them.

4. Paisley's parents expressed a preference for her to be adopted by her foster parents rather than her aunt. Some courts take the view that parents have no role in choosing who should adopt their children after their rights are terminated. *See, e.g.*, In Interest of L-MHB, 401 P.3d 949 (Wyo. 2017) (parent's residual rights do not include designating who will adopt child). However, In re Ta.L., 149A.3d 1060 (D.C. 2013), held that parents' constitutionally protected rights include the right to choose an adoptive parent unless the court finds by clear and convincing evidence that "placement with that caregiver is 'clearly contrary' to the best interests of the children, rather than simply not in the children's best interests." Nevertheless, the court upheld a juvenile court order allowing the child to be adopted by foster parents rather than the relative selected by the parents because of the children's close relationship to the foster parents and the risk of psychological harm to them if that relationship were severed.

5. The Indian Child Welfare Act (ICWA) contains substantive placement preferences that bind state courts. If the child is being placed in foster care, a state court must give preference to the child's extended family or to an Indian home. If the child is being placed for adoption, a state court, in the absence of good cause to the contrary, must give preference to a member of the child's extended family, to other members of the child's tribe, or to other Indian families. 25 U.S.C. § 1915. An implementing regulation provides, "A placement may not depart from the preferences based solely on ordinary bonding or attachment that flowed from time spent in a non-preferred placement that was made in violation of ICWA." 25 CFR § 23.132(e). This regulation is discussed at length in In re Alexandria P, 204 Cal.Rptr.3d 617 (Cal. App. 2016).

The policy underlying the ICWA provisions emphasizes the interests of the tribe in maintaining its identity and vitality by retaining its children, distinguishing this law from the more general relative preference laws.

6. The *Paisley* court mentions at one point that the state agency had begun the process of having an Interstate Compact on the Placement of Children evaluation done on the siblings' parents. The compact is an agreement among all states to coordinate the transfer and placement of children across state lines. All states are members of the compact and have enacted uniform legislation to implement the compact. The compact applies when a child is in state custody of a public or private agency involved in placing the child for adoption. The compact process is notoriously slow and cumbersome. Vivek Sankaran, Foster Kids in Limbo: The Effects of the Interstate Compact on the Placement of Children on the Permanency of Children in Foster Care (2014), http://xa.yimg.com/kq/groups/3808685/678201127/name/FinalSummary.pdf.

D.   TERMINATION OF PARENTAL RIGHTS AND OTHER PERMANENCY ALTERNATIVES

Of the children who left foster care in fiscal year 2016, only half were reunited with their parents. About a third left for another home pursuant to court orders that protected the permanency of that placement; 23 percent were adopted, and 10 percent were placed with guardians.[9] Of the remainder, 7 percent lived with a relative who was not an adoptive parent or guardian, 8 percent attained the age of majority and aged out of foster care, and 2 percent were transferred to another agency.

Federal law provides that permanent guardianship is an acceptable, though not a preferred, permanency option. Many states have enacted statutes that require that adoption be ruled out as an alternative before proceeding to other permanent alternatives, including legal guardianship and other planned permanent living arrangements. *E.g.*, Cal. Welf. & Inst. Code § 366.26(b)(2018); Md. Code, Family Law § 5-525(f)(2)(2018).

Federal funds are available to provide financial assistance to parents who adopt children with special needs from foster care. 42 U.S.C. §§ 471, 473, 475; 45 C.F.R. § 1356.40. States may provide financial assistance to relatives who become children's permanent guardians after having been their foster parents. As of 2017, 32 states, the District of Columbia, and six tribes used federal funds to subsidize relative guardianships. [William Vesneski et al., An Analysis of State Law and Policy Regarding Subsidized Guardianship for Children: Innovations in Permanency, 21 UC Davis J. Juv. L. & Pol'y 27, 33 (2017) (surveying state laws).] Many states allow guardians to receive more funding and services than the minimum required by federal law. In 10 states only relatives related by blood, marriage, or adoption can be a guardian for these purposes, while in 41 jurisdictions fictive kin can also be guardians. *Id.* at 43. In 2014 the number of guardianships and adoptions remained

---

9. 42 U.S.C. § 675(7) defines "legal guardianship" as a judicially created relationship between a child and a caretaker intended to be permanent and self-sustaining in which the caretaker has custody, care, and control of the child; responsibility for the child's protection and education; and decision-making authority with regard to the child.

about the same as in 2008. Josh Gupta-Kagan, The New Permanency, 19 U.C. Davis J. Juv. L. & Pol'y 1, 4 (2015).

Long-term foster care is a less-favored permanent alternative that is supposed to be used only when guardianship and adoption have been ruled out. The least-favored alternative, called Another Planned Permanent Living Arrangement (APPLA), usually assumes that the child will simply age out of foster care and is used for children for whom it is difficult to find permanent homes, particularly older children. Federal legislation enacted in 2014 limits the use of AAPLA as a permanency goal to children who are 16 and older. Planning for children aging out of care is considered further later in this chapter.

1.   Grounds for Terminating Parental Rights

Traditionally and still today, if a child cannot be reunited with his or her parents, the preferred permanent alternative is to terminate the child's legal relationship with the parents, allowing other adults to adopt the child. Termination of parental rights may be the result of the parents' voluntary choice. If parents voluntarily relinquish their rights to the state child welfare agency, the agency will have legal authority to act as an adoption agency and to place the child. If the parents will not relinquish their rights voluntarily, would-be adoptive parents may seek to terminate the birth parents' parental rights as part of an adoption proceeding. However, traditionally child welfare agencies rarely placed foster children for adoption before their parents' rights had been terminated. Largely for this reason, in the 1950s states began to enact separate termination of parental rights statutes, usually as part of their juvenile codes.

The grounds for termination of parental rights under early statutes were much the same as those for adoption without parental consent—abandonment or gross neglect. The most common grounds for termination of parental rights under modern statutes are "severe or chronic abuse or neglect, sex abuse, abuse or neglect of other children in the household, abandonment of the child, long-term mental illness or deficiency of the parent(s), long-term alcohol or drug-induced incapacity of the parent(s), failure to support or maintain contact with the child, and involuntary termination of rights of the parent to another child." Child Welfare Information Gate, Children's Bureau, U.S. Dept. Health & Hum. Servs., Grounds for Involuntary Termination of Parental Rights (current through Dec. 2016), https://www.child-welfare.gov/pubPDFs/groundtermin.pdf#page=2&view=Grounds%20for%20termination%20of%20parental%20rights. In addition to finding grounds, statutes also ordinarily require that the court find that termination of parental rights is in the child's best interests.

Statutes in a few states permit termination of parental rights without a finding of unfitness to protect the child's relationship with a long-term caregiver. In In re Guardianship of Ann S., 202 P.3d 1089 (Cal. 2009), the California Supreme Court rejected a constitutional challenge to a statute authorizing a court to terminate parental rights without finding that the parent was unfit so that the child could be adopted by a person who had been the child's guardian for at least two years. The court read cases, including Supreme Court decisions, that suggest that termination of parental rights without a finding of unfitness would be unconstitutional as applying only to parents with custody at the time of the hearing. 202 P.3d at 1101-1107. In a companion case, the California Supreme Court suggested that the statute might be unconstitutional as applied in a particular case, for example, when a fully committed, responsible, and capable parent finds an extended probate guardianship unavoidable under exigent circumstances. In re Charlotte D., 202 P.3d 1109, 1111, 1114 (Cal. 2009). In re D.H., 222 Cal. Rptr.3d 305 (Cal. App. 2017), declined to extend the standard in the guardianship statute to termination of parental rights cases in juvenile court, saying it would be unconstitutional to do so. A Maryland statute authorizes a court to terminate parental rights upon a finding of exceptional circumstances without a finding that the parent is unfit. The Maryland court of appeals interpreted this statute in In re Adoption of K'Amora K., 97 A.3d 169 (Md. App. 2014), to allow a child to remain with the foster family she had lived with since birth.

a. Termination After a Period of Foster Care

Termination of parental rights petitions are most commonly filed after the child has been in foster care for some period of time while the parent attempts to resolve the problems that led to loss of custody. Complying with federal law, state laws require child welfare agencies to file a petition to terminate parental rights and concurrently identify, recruit, process, and approve a qualified adoptive family for children who have been in foster care for 15 of the most recent 22 months. The 22-month clock begins to run on the earlier of the date of the first finding that the child has been abused or neglected or 60 days after the child was removed from home.

42 U.S.C. § 675(5)(E) provides three exceptions to the requirement of filing a termination petition:

1) When the child is being cared for by a relative;
2) When the child welfare agency has documented in the case plan a compelling reason for determining that filing would not be in the child's best interests, or
3) When reasonable efforts to reunify were required and the state did not provide timely services necessary for the safe return of the child.

H.B. v. MOBILE COUNTY DEPARTMENT OF HUMAN RESOURCES

236 So.3d 875 (Ala. Civ. App. 2017)

MOORE, Judge. . . . In 2008, when the child was approximately 18 months old, DHR removed the child from the one-bedroom apartment the mother shared with her mother ("the maternal grandmother") and the child. . . . The mother testified that, on that occasion, she was on the front porch of the apartment while the child was inside the apartment in a high chair within the mother's sight. The mother said that she became stressed when DHR arrived to take the child away. When the child was removed, the mother said, she asked for an ambulance, which took the mother to a local hospital. Natasha Dysert, a DHR worker who was "not on the scene that day," testified that DHR had been called due to the mother's erratic behavior and that, upon arrival at the mother's apartment, DHR workers discovered the child unattended in the doorway of the apartment; according to Dysert, drug paraphernalia had also been found inside the apartment. At that time, the mother, who, according to Dysert, was in the parking lot, reported that she had been shot in the head and that people were trying to run over her with a car.

The mother testified that she had been hospitalized following the 2008 incident. Dysert testified that, at the time of that incident, the mother was off the medication she had been prescribed for her mental illness but that changes in her medication had been made by the doctors who treated her. The mother testified that the doctors had stabilized her medication. Dysert testified that the mother had complied with DHR's family-reunification plan, which included a psychiatric evaluation, and the child was returned to the custody of the mother in 2010.

The child resumed living with the mother and the maternal grandmother in the same one-bedroom apartment. When the family planned to move from those premises in 2012, the management inspected the apartment and found 28 or more cats and a dog living there. DHR investigated and determined that the apartment was unsanitary and unsuitable for the child, so the child was again removed from the custody of the mother. The maternal grandmother testified that the mother was overly compassionate to animals and had regularly taken in strays. Charlene Clemons, the DHR social worker who oversaw the 2012 case, testified that DHR had established goals for the mother, including obtaining alternative housing and maintaining her mental health. According to Clemons, the mother had met those goals and the child was returned to the custody of the mother in December 2013 subject to DHR's supervision for the following six months. At that time, the mother and the maternal grandmother were residing in a three-bedroom house that the maternal grandmother had begun renting in 2012.

On August 31, 2015, DHR was called to the family's house by police officers who were serving an arrest warrant on the mother for theft of property. Natasha Reyes, the DHR social worker who responded to that call, testified that, when she arrived at the house, the house did not have running water or electricity and was in an unsanitary condition due to trash, cat waste, and bugs. The mother testified that the electric and water services to the house had been cut off for approximately six months after the maternal grandmother had lost her employment and could not afford to pay the bills. DHR removed the child from the mother's custody and placed the child into foster care. DHR requested that the mother undergo a psychological evaluation, attend parenting classes, and work with "FOCUS" in-home services, which the mother initially declined; the mother did, however, visit with the child.

On January 19, 2016, DHR changed its permanency plan from reunification with the mother to adoption. Sarah Jernigan, a DHR social worker, took over the case on March 8, 2016. Jernigan testified that the mother had begun cooperating with DHR's requests by undergoing a psychological evaluation in May 2016 and by participating in "Tools of Choice" in-home services. The mother testified that she had completed parenting classes. Jernigan testified that she had allowed the child to visit with the mother in the rental house in which the mother and the maternal grandmother resided after concluding that the house was suitable for the child. The maternal grandmother testified that she had resumed gainful employment and that she had paid all the necessary fees to restore electric and water services to the house. Jernigan testified that, at the time of the trial, the mother had made progress and was nearing completion of all of the goals DHR had set for her. The mother testified that she was given two years' probation on the theft-of-property criminal charge and that she was ready, willing, and able to regain custody of the child.

There was no evidence of harm to the child, which the mother denied and which DHR did not attempt to prove. The mother testified that she had taken pre-natal vitamins when she was pregnant with the child and that the child had been born "in perfect health." Dysert testified that, in 2008, the child had been found in a high chair, which, she admitted, was an appropriate place for the child to be. The mother testified that the child was never in danger. DHR discovered that the child had not yet been immunized, but no one testified that the child's immu-nization treatment was overdue. The mother testified that she and the maternal grandmother had paid to have the child immunized during the time the child was in DHR's custody between 2008 and 2010. The mother also testified that she had attended all of the child's medical appointments during that period.

Although DHR removed the child due to the conditions of the apartment in 2012, no witness testified that the health of the child had been adversely affected by those conditions. The mother testified that the child had slept in the bedroom "away from the cats," which, she testified, had stayed in the front room of the apart-ment. The mother testified that after the child was returned to her custody, the mother and the maternal grandmother had cared for the child by feeding, clothing, entertaining, and educating the child. The mother and the maternal grandmother celebrated birthdays and other holidays with the child by giving her toys and pres-ents. No one from the child's school ever questioned the care the child received.

Reyes testified that when she removed the child from the mother's custody in 2015, the child was in good physical condition and was clean. The mother testified that the child was never ill or malnourished, but was at a healthy weight. Although the family's house was without electric service and running water for a period, the child had informed Reyes that, during that time, she had been eating out and had also eaten frozen dinners that had thawed to room temperature. The maternal grand-mother and the mother testified that they had improvised by using gallons of water to flush the toilet as well as occasionally staying at a motel to bathe. They both tes-tified that, despite the lack of electricity and running water, the child had been kept well-groomed, had never missed a meal, had always had shelter, had always attended school on time, and had received help with her homework. According to the maternal grandmother, the child had earned good grades while in her and the mother's care, maintaining a "B" average. Jernigan testified that the child is bonded with the mother and the maternal grandmother and that they display love for one another.

The mother was 37 years old at the time of the trial. She has been regularly taking two Haldol tablets per day for her mental illness, as well as undergoing ther-apy once a year at Altapointe, a mental-health facility. She also visits Altapointe every three months for the purpose of monitoring her medication. Veronica Davis, a licensed professional counselor who was called as an expert witness by DHR, testi-fied that the mother was "stabilized" at the meeting they had had on May 18, 2016. The mother testified that she had not had a mental-health crisis since 2008, when DHR first removed the child from her custody. The mother testified that her mental illness does not impair her ability to care for the child. The maternal grandmother and the mother both testified that the mother could care for the child independently.

On appeal, the mother argues that the evidence does not support the juvenile court's findings that she failed to successfully rehabilitate herself and adjust her circumstances to meet the needs of the child or that termination of her parental rights serves the best interests of the child. . . .

Section 12–15–319, Ala. Code 1975, provides, in pertinent part:

"(a) If the juvenile court finds from clear and convincing evidence, competent, material, and relevant in nature, that the parent[] of a child [is] unable or unwilling to discharge [his or her] responsibilities to and for the child, or that the conduct or condition of the parent[] renders [him or her] unable to properly care for the child and that the conduct or condition is unlikely to change in the foreseeable future, it may terminate the parental rights of the parent[]."

In order to terminate parental rights under § 12–15–319, a juvenile court must be clearly convinced from the evidence that the parent cannot or will not provide adequate care for the child.

In deciding whether a parent is unable to properly parent a child, the juvenile court must consider, among other factors, "[t]hat reasonable efforts by the Department of Human Resources or licensed public or private child care agencies leading toward the rehabilitation of the parents have failed" and the "[l]ack of effort by the parent to adjust his or her circumstances to meet the needs of the child in accordance with agreements reached, including agreements reached with local departments of human resources or licensed child-placing agencies, in an administrative review or a judicial review." In its judgment, the juvenile court found that DHR's efforts at rehabilitation had failed and that the mother had not adjusted her circumstances to meet the needs of the child. The record does not contain clear and convincing evidence to sustain those findings. . . .

The mother argues that DHR removed the child solely because of the lack of electric service and running water at the family's house. Actually, Reyes testified that DHR had removed the child from the custody of the mother "[d]ue to inadequate shelter and [the mother's] being arrested for stealing. . . ." By "inadequate shelter," Reyes explained that she meant not only the absence of electric service and running water, but also the "deplorable" unsanitary condition of the house. Although Alabama law has not been clear on this point, other states have recognized that a child can be permanently removed from the custody of a parent who allows chronic, recurring unsanitary conditions to endanger the health of the child. A fair reading of the record indicates that DHR removed the child primarily for that reason.

In her brief to this court, the mother correctly notes that DHR did not assist her with restoring the utilities, which the maternal grandmother independently accomplished, but the mother overlooks that DHR did schedule classes and in-home services designed to improve the mother's housekeeping abilities, the main obstacle to family reunification. Even after the mother initially refused those services, DHR continued to offer them to the mother. Thus, we conclude that DHR used reasonable efforts to reunite the family in this case.

The real issue in this case is not whether DHR used reasonable efforts, but whether those efforts failed. Rehabilitation efforts succeed when those circumstances that led to the removal of the child have been resolved, so that the child can safely be returned to his or her parent's custody. Conversely, if DHR has proven by clear and convincing evidence that the parent remains unable to adequately care for the child after reasonable efforts have been expended to rehabilitate the parent, the juvenile court may find that those reasonable efforts have failed.

In this case, the evidence in the record indicates that DHR had not yet completed the rehabilitation process at the time of the trial. Nevertheless, the mother had adjusted her circumstances to alleviate the conditions that had led to the removal of the child. The house from which the child was removed was no longer in the "deplorable" condition that existed in 2015. Jernigan testified that the house was suitable for the child. DHR did not present any evidence suggesting that the mother lacks the mental or physical ability to maintain the house in a suitable condition. To the contrary, Jernigan testified that the mother had made considerable progress by the time of the trial. The record does not contain clear and convincing evidence indicating that the mother remained unable to properly care for the child.

"[T]he existence of evidence of *current* conditions or conduct relating to a parent's inability or unwillingness to care for his or her children is implicit in the requirement that termination of parental rights be based on clear and convincing evidence."

> Although a juvenile court certainly can consider a parent's past child-rearing history, legislative policy, as well as constitutional due-process concerns, require that a parent's parental rights be terminated based on clear and convincing evidence of that parent's present inability or unwillingness to care for the children that is likely to persist in the foreseeable future.

The conditions at the time of the trial showed that the child could safely be returned home.

A juvenile court can terminate parental rights in situations in which it is convinced that a parent has only temporarily corrected a recurring condition that threatens the welfare of the child. Although the juvenile court expressed concerns about the number of times the child had been removed from the custody of the mother, "in each instance, DHR's decision to remove the child from the mother's custody appears to have been taken as a precautionary measure and not as a result of actual threats or allegations of abuse or neglect of the child." The undisputed evidence in the record shows that the child has never been harmed by the mother. Despite her poor housekeeping skills, the mother had always safeguarded the child from the squalor around her. Reyes specifically testified that the child was in good physical condition and was clean when taken into DHR's custody in 2015. DHR did not present any admissible evidence to contradict the testimony of the mother that the child has always been healthy and well-groomed despite her otherwise poor living conditions.

To be sure, a child should not be subjected to living in unsanitary conditions, but the termination of a loving relationship between a child and his or her parent should occur only in the most egregious of circumstances. The evidence shows that the child has thrived under the care of the mother, having bonded with her maternal grandmother, making good grades, and celebrating milestones. The child, who is now 10 years old, shares an emotional and loving relationship with the mother. Jernigan even testified that DHR had scheduled counseling to prepare the child for the possibility that the juvenile court would terminate the mother's parental rights. A parent should not lose his or her fundamental right to the custody of his or her child, and a child should not be forced to undergo the anguish of losing his or her parent and extended family, just because the parent is not a model homemaker. In these circumstances, it is hard to see how termination of the mother's parental rights would serve the best interests of the child. Therefore, we conclude that the juvenile court erred in terminating the parental rights of the mother. We therefore reverse the juvenile court's judgment and remand the cause for the entry of a judgment consistent with this opinion. In light of our disposition of this issue, we pretermit the remaining issues raised by the mother.

THOMPSON, Presiding Judge, dissenting. . . . In offering the mother reunification services in 2015, DHR asked the mother to complete another psychological evaluation; Reyes explained that that evaluation was to determine if the mother was experiencing another mental-illness incident and whether she needed treatment. DHR also offered the mother in-home services through "FOCUS," as well as parenting classes. Reyes testified that the mother did not take advantage of those services during the time she worked on the case. Reyes testified that the case was transferred to another worker immediately following a January 19, 2016, Individualized Service Plan ("ISP") meeting. Reyes testified that although the mother went to DHR's offices for that ISP meeting, the mother refused to go upstairs to an office to take part in the meeting because her attorney, although invited to the meeting, had not shown up to attend the meeting. During that January 19, 2016, ISP meeting, the permanency plan for the child was changed from "return to parent" to "adoption." Reyes testified that she showed the January 19, 2016, ISP to the mother, and it is undisputed that the mother signed that ISP document.

Sarah Jernigan, the DHR social worker assigned to the child's case on March 8, 2016, testified that in the time between Reyes's leaving the case and Jernigan's being assigned to it, Jernigan's supervisor had managed the child's case. Jernigan testified that when she was first assigned to the case, she had difficulty communicating with the mother because the mother did not return her telephone calls. However, at some point, the mother indicated her willingness to accept reunification services, and in May 2016 the mother submitted to the recommended psychological evaluation. By the time of the termination hearing, DHR had provided in-home parenting classes to the mother, who had taken part in one of those classes. Jernigan also asked the mother to submit to a hair-follicle drug test in the week before the termination hearing, but the mother had not gone to the appointment at the testing facility because, she said, she was ill. Jernigan testified that, although her job as a social worker in this case was to provide adoptive services for the child, she had worked with the mother to provide the reunification services even though the mother had rejected those services for the first nine months that the child was in foster care after her removal from the home in 2015. Jernigan stated that, at the time of the August 1, 2016, termination hearing, the mother was making progress toward the reunification goals.

Jernigan testified that, shortly before the termination hearing, the mother had progressed sufficiently to allow a one-hour visit with the child to occur in the mother's house. That visit occurred on July 19, 2016, and was supervised by the in-home services provider; Jernigan stated that the in-home visit had gone well.

However, the mother had not had additional in-home visits with the child, apparently because the termination hearing occurred so soon after that first in-home visit. . . .

The mother challenges the evidence supporting the termination judgment. Specifically, the mother argues that the evidence does not support a determination that DHR made reasonable efforts to reunite the mother with the child.

> Whether DHR has made reasonable efforts to reunite a parent and a child is a fact-dependent inquiry. '[T]he efforts actually required by DHR in each case, whether the court is considering rehabilitation or reunification, depend on the particular facts of that case, the statutory obligations regarding family reunification, and the best interests of the child.'

DHR has removed the child from the mother's custody on three occasions. In B.J.K.A. v. Cleburne County Department of Human Resources, 28 So.3d 765 (Ala. Civ. App. 2009), a mother had lost custody of her children to the Cleburne County DHR for a third time, and the Cleburne County DHR did not make any further attempt to provide reunification services. The juvenile court in that case entered a judgment terminating the parental rights of the mother in that case, and this court affirmed, concluding that the Cleburne County DHR had complied with the requirements of Alabama law in providing its earlier attempts at reunification.

> We reject [the mother's] characterization of DHR's failure to resume efforts at rehabilitation that have proven futile as a failure to fulfill its statutory duty to make reasonable efforts to rehabilitate her and to reunify her family. As we have said before:
>   "'Based on these circumstances, the juvenile court reasonably could have concluded that an adequate amount of time and effort had been expended in an attempt to rehabilitate the mother but that further time and effort would not help achieve the goal of family reunification in light of the mother's lack of progress over a [five]-year period. We note that the law speaks in terms of "reasonable" efforts, not unlimited or even maximal efforts. In this case, DHR used reasonable efforts to rehabilitate the mother, and the juvenile court did not err in concluding that it would be unreasonable to prolong those efforts.'"

I believe that in this case, as in B.J.K.A., supra, the juvenile court could have reasonably concluded that DHR made reasonable efforts toward reuniting the mother and the child. In 2015, during the third time that the child was removed from the mother's custody, the mother made no efforts to accept DHR's offered reunification services until the child had been in foster care for nine months. The mother was informed in January 2016 that the permanency plan for the child had changed, and DHR filed its termination petition in February 2016. However, the mother did not begin to cooperate with reunification services until May 2016. I note that the record indicates that the child was transferred to live with a potential adoptive resource in May 2016.

I further note that the mother had <u>begun</u> to take part in reunification services at the time of the termination hearing, but had not completed those services. The fact that the mother's participation in the earlier reunification process did not enable her to maintain custody of her child, together with the mother's failure to cooperate with DHR's services for so long in this case, supports the conclusion that the juvenile court properly determined that DHR had provided appropriate reunification services and that further services would not have been successful in preventing the termination of the mother's parental rights. . . .

The juvenile court, which received ore tenus evidence and had the advantage of observing the demeanor of the mother and the other witnesses as they testified, could reasonably have determined that the mother's attempts to comply with the reunification goals were "'late, incomplete and, therefore, unconvincing [] measures taken only in anticipation of the termination-of-parental-rights hearing.'"

The majority opinion concludes that the evidence does not indicate that the child suffered harm from the mother's conduct. I note, first, that there is no statutory requirement that, in a termination-of-parental-rights case, DHR prove that a parent's conduct has harmed a child, and I question whether the majority opinion might be interpreted in the future as adding an additional requirement of demonstrable harm that is different from the factors set forth by our legislature in § 12–15–319, Ala. Code 1975, for a juvenile court to consider in an action involving the termination of parental rights. I note that this court has reviewed cases in which a child has been removed from a parent's custody because of issues such as a parent's drug use and that we have not required DHR or a juvenile court to wait to intervene until harm to a child has occurred or been demonstrated. DHR and the courts may, and have a duty to, seek to protect children from the serious potential for harm and to act to protect the best interests of children; I believe that, in most circumstances, DHR and the courts may act to <u>prevent</u> harm to a child.

I further note that I disagree with the conclusion that there has been no harm demonstrated in this case. At the time the child in this case was taken into foster care for the third time in August 2015, the child was 8 years old and had already spent a total of 40 months, or more than 3 years of her life, in foster care. At the time of August 1, 2016, termination hearing, the child was 9 years old and had spent 52 months, or more than 4 years (i.e., almost half her life) in foster care. The evidence supports a conclusion that, in 2008, the mother's erratic behavior left her unable to properly supervise the young child. The maternal grandmother, with whom the mother and the child resided, had not intervened to protect the child from the filth found repeatedly in the family's home environment. In spite of the mother's testimony that the family no longer had animals after the child had been removed from her custody in 2012, cat feces were listed as a part of the detritus that rendered the mother's house unsanitary in 2015, when the child was again taken into protective custody.

Given the facts, the applicable caselaw, and the presumption in favor of the juvenile court's judgment afforded after the juvenile court has had the advantage of receiving ore tenus evidence, I cannot agree with the majority that the mother has demonstrated that the juvenile court erred in determining that DHR had made reasonable efforts toward reunification. . . .

NOTES AND QUESTIONS

1. Between the time that H.B.'s child was 18 months old and 10 years old, the child welfare agency removed her from her mother's custody three times and

returned her twice. What was the reason for each removal? Could reasonable efforts have prevented the need to remove? Did the agency provide reasonable efforts to reunite the mother and child?

2. The majority and dissent disagree about whether H.B. had finally overcome the chronic problems that led to state intervention or whether she just made temporary efforts to solve the problems only when confronted with the threat of termination. How can a court tell which interpretation is correct?

3. Recall that federal law says that the agency can be excused from filing a termination of parental rights petition if it was required to provide reasonable efforts and failed to do so. Does this mean that federal law requires that state law forbid termination if the agency fails to provide reasonable efforts? *See* In the Interest of D.C.D., 105 A.3d 662 (Pa. 2014) (rejecting the argument because the purpose of the filing requirement is to prevent foster care drift by encouraging agencies to act).

4. Statutes in some states require that the court find the agency provided reasonable efforts before ordering termination. Interpreting such a statute, the Washington Supreme Court recently held that "futile" efforts are not required by the statute. What make efforts "futile"? *See* In re Parental Rights to K.M.M., 379 P.3d 75(Wash. 2016) (en banc) (agency need not provide family therapy and bonding and attachment services when child refused to participate in them after long period of estrangement); *see also* P.S. v. Jefferson Dept. Human Res., 143 So.3d 792 (Ala. Civ. App. 2013) (state must tell parent what conditions must be corrected before parental rights can be terminated; telling her what services to complete does not satisfy this requirement).

If a statute does not require that the court find that reasonable efforts were made before terminating, would the agency's failure to provide needed services nevertheless be relevant?

A survey of 20 judges from 18 states found that judges are most concerned about whether parents have complied with the case plan, whether the agency has made reasonable efforts, whether the parent and child are in regular contact, and the severity of the original maltreatment. The child's age and the child's opinion are less important, as is whether there is an identified adoptive placement. Raquel Ellis, Karin Malm, & Erin Bishop, The Timing of Termination of Parental Rights: A Balancing Act for Children's Best Interests (Sept. 2009), available from the Child Trends website, www.childtrends.org.

5. Should a parent's compliance with the specifics of the treatment plan entitle the parent to have his or her child returned? Should compliance preclude termination of the parent's rights? Most courts faced with this issue have held that compliance alone does not preclude termination if the parent is still unable to take responsibility for the care of the child. *E.g.*, In re A.G., 996 P.2d 494 (Okla. App. 1999).

6. If the juvenile and appellate courts find that grounds for terminating parental rights have not been proven, does that necessarily mean the child will be returned to the parent's custody?

7. Besides requiring that the state file a termination of parental rights petition after a child has been in foster care for 15 of the last 22 months unless an exception exists, Illinois legislation provided that it was presumed that a parent is unfit if the child has been in foster care for this period of time. The parent had

the burden to disprove this presumption by a preponderance of the evidence. In re H.G., 757 N.E.2d 864 (Ill. 2001), held the provision unconstitutional, concluding that passage of time alone did not indicate that a parent is unfit. The court distinguished other termination statutes that use passage of time as evidence of some other ground of unfitness.

A South Carolina statute provides a parent's rights may be terminated on the basis that the child has been in foster care for 15 of the most recent 22 months and the court finds that termination is in the child's best interests. S.C. Code Ann. § 63-7-2570(8) (2018). In Charleston County Department of Social Services v. Marccuci, 721 S.E.2d 768 (S.C. 2011), the court interpreted this statue as requiring proof that the delay in resolving the case is attributable to the parent's inability to provide for the child, rather than actions of the state. South Carolina Dept. Soc. Serv. v. Sarah W., 741 S.E.2d 739 (S.C. 2013), indicates that this interpretation is necessary for the statute to be constitutional.

8. The Americans with Disabilities Act (ADA) requires public entities to make "reasonable accommodation to allow the disabled person to receive services or to participate in the public entity's programs." 28 C.F.R. § 35.130(b)(7). It also prohibits a public entity from discriminating against a disabled person by excluding the person from participation or by denying him or her the benefits of public services, programs, or activities. 42 U.S.C. §§ 12101-12213, 12132. Courts holding that the ADA applies to child welfare services include In re Elijah C., 165 A.3d 1149 (Conn. 2017); In re H.D., 187 A.3d 1254 (D.C. 2018); State in Interest of K.C., 362 P.3d 1248 (Ut. 2015). Cases holding that the ADA does not apply include Stone v. Daviess Cty. Div. of Children & Family Servs., 656 N.E.2d 824 (Ind. App. 1995); J.T. v. Arkansas Dept. of Human Servs., 947 S.W.2d 761 (Ark. App. 1997); In re C.M.S., 646 S.E.2d 592 (N.C. App. 2007); In re B.S., 693 A.2d 716 (Vt. 1997); S.G. v. Barbour Cty. Dept. of Human Resources, 148 So.3d 439 (Ala. Civ. App. 2013); In re Terry, 610 N.W.2d 563 (Mich. App. 2000); In re Kayla N., 900 A.2d 1202 (R.I. 2006); In re Doe, 60 P.3d 285 (Hi. 2002), In re V.A., 73 N.E.3d 1156 (Ohio App. 2016). See also In re Hicks/Brown, 893 N.W.2d 637 (Mich. 2017) (Termination order reversed for lack of reasonable efforts when case plans for mother with borderline intellectual functioning who lived with her own mother never included services for assisting a cognitively impaired parent, including allowing her and the baby to live with an aunt).

In 2015 the Civil Rights Division of the U.S. Dept. of Justice found that the Massachusetts state child welfare agency violated the ADA and § 504 of the Rehabilitation Act by discriminating against a mother on the basis of her developmental disability, denying her the opportunity to benefit from services to enable her to raise her child. The opinion suggests the kind of efforts that may be required when parents have mental disabilities that go beyond what many agencies typically offer. The state removed the newborn baby from the mother in the hospital and placed her in foster care because of the mother's difficulties in caring for the baby in the hospital, notwithstanding that the mother, who lived with her own parents, planned to raise the baby with her parents' assistance. Over the next two years the agency provided minimal services, including visitation for one hour each week at agency offices and assistance from a parenting aide which only began when the child was 8 months old and the agency had already changed the child's permanent goal to adoption. The aide only worked with the mother during 30 minutes of each weekly visit. A variety of professionals, including the state's foster care review panel, supported placing the child with the mother in the grandparents' home with the grandparents as guardians, but the agency did not change the plan from adoption. The department found that the state agency failed to provide the mother the opportunity to use her family resources and individualized, in-home parenting supports, including visiting nurse assistance or a home health aide, homemaker services, and parent aides. It further found that the agency did not appropriately modify its services to accommodate her learning disabilities, that it denied her frequent, meaningful visitation with support, and that it failed to consider the progress she was making after the permanency goal was changed to adoption. The department also found that the agency failed to train its social workers adequately. The department ordered the agency to withdraw the termination petition, immediately implement services and supports to help the mother seek reunification, evaluate the case after an appropriate amount of time, pay compensatory damages to the mother, and develop policies and procedures to implement the ADA and § 504 and training programs for agency employees. The department's letter of findings is available on the Civil Rights Division's website. The child was returned to the mother's custody two months after the letter was issued. Elizabeth Picciuto, Mom with Disabilities and Daughter Reunited After Two-Year Court Battle, Daily Beast, Mar. 16, 2015. For a comprehensive analysis of the use of ADA in termination cases based on parents' mental disabilities, *see* Charisa Smith, Making Good on an Historic Federal Precedent; Americans with Disabilities Act (AD) Claims and the Termination of Parental Rights of Parents with Mental Disabilities, 18 Quinnipiac Health L. J. 191 (2015). On parents with mental disabilities in the child welfare system generally, *see* Charisa Smith, The Conundrum of Family Reunification: A Theoretical, Legal, and Practical Approach to Reunification Services for Parents with Mental Disabilities, 26 Stan. L. & Pol'y Rev. 307 (2015).

9. For information on the particular difficulties parents in rural areas have in complying with case plans and the problems of providing adequate services to them, *see* Lisa R. Pruitt & Janet L. Wallace, Judging Parents, Judging Place: Poverty, Rurality and Termination of Parental Rights, 77 Mo. L. Rev. 95 (2011).

PROBLEM

The state child welfare agency became involved with Clara, who had two preschool children, three years ago. The agency provided parenting classes for Clara and early childhood intervention services for the older child, Sam, who is developmentally delayed. However, the family moved so often that it was difficult for the agency to provide services. Two years ago, the children were removed from home and placed in temporary foster care because of allegations that their father had sexually abused the children. The agency and Clara entered into a service agreement with reunification as a goal. It provided that Clara was to visit the children regularly, submit to a psychological exam, obtain services from the local mentally retarded developmentally delayed (MRDD) program, establish a stable residence, and improve her parenting skills. Clara visited the children faithfully, took the psychological exam, and stabilized her residence, but she did not work with the

MRDD program or do anything to improve her parenting skills. Eighteen months ago, she became pregnant and lost contact with the agency, fearing that it would take the baby from her, too. When the baby was born, he was also removed from her custody. At that point, Clara began to work with the MRDD program.

The child welfare workers in charge of the case have asked the state's attorney to file a termination of parental rights petition as to the two older children because they have been in foster care more than 15 of the last 22 months. They say that Clara angers easily, does not interact with the children appropriately, and worked with the MRDD program only after the termination petition was filed. One psychologist who has examined Clara says that she is slow intellectually but that she could learn to take care of her children. Another psychologist is less optimistic, saying that Clara is mildly mentally retarded, has a dependent and schizoid personality disorder, and would have difficulty providing the children a stable and nurturing environment. An MRDD counselor says Clara now recognizes that she needs help to care for her children and that the children can be reunited with her in 12 to 18 months.

As an assistant state's attorney, would you file the termination petition? Why or why not? If not, what would you advise the agency workers to do now?

b.   "Aggravated Circumstances" Cases

Federal legislation promotes early termination of parental rights in "aggravated circumstances cases," that is, cases in which facts suggest that requiring the state to try to reunite a child with the parents is very likely to be unsafe for the child. To this end, states must have legislation that addresses three issues: (a) when the child welfare agency can forego reasonable efforts to reunite, (b) when the agency must file termination of parental rights petitions must be filed, and (c) substantive grounds for termination.

Under 42 U.S.C. § 671(a)(15)(D), a juvenile court may relieve the agency of the requirement to make reasonable efforts to reunify the parent and child if the court finds:

> (i) the parent has subjected the child to aggravated circumstances (as defined in State law, which definition may include but need not be limited to abandonment, torture, chronic abuse, and sexual abuse);
> (ii) the parent has—
>> (I) committed murder or manslaughter of another of his or her children;
>> (III) aided or abetted, attempted, conspired, or solicited to commit such a murder or such a voluntary manslaughter; or
>> (IV) committed a felony assault that results in serious bodily injury to the child or another child of the parent; or
> (iii) the parental rights of the parent to a sibling have been terminated involuntarily.

42 U.S.C. § 675(5)(E) provides that the child welfare agency is required to file a petition to terminate parental rights when a court has determined that:

> 1. the child has been abandoned;
> 2. the parent has committed murder or voluntary manslaughter of another of his or her children;

3. the parent has been convicted of aiding or abetting, attempting, conspiring to commit, or soliciting such a murder or manslaughter;
4. the parent has been convicted of felony assault resulting in serious bodily injury to the child or another of the parent's children.

However, the same exceptions to the requirement of filing a petition to terminate after a child has been in foster care for 15 of the last 22 months also apply to petitions based on aggravated circumstances. Thus, the agency may decline to file if the child is being cared for by a relative, the agency has documented in the case plan a compelling reason for determining that filing would not be in the child's best interests or, when reasonable efforts to reunify were required, the state failed to provide the necessary services. 42 U.S.C. § 675(5)(E).

Finally, 42 U.S.C. § 5106a(b)(2)(B)(xvi), (xvii) provides that the following must be grounds for termination of parental rights:

1. the parent has been convicted of murder or manslaughter of another of his or her children;
2. the parent has been convicted of aiding or abetting, attempting, conspiring to commit, or soliciting such a murder or manslaughter;
3. the parent has been convicted of felony assault resulting in serious bodily injury to the child or another of the parent's children;
4. the parent has been convicted of sexual abuse against the child or another of the parent's children; or
5. the parent is required to register with a sex offender registry.

In re Welfare of the Child of R.D.L.

853 N.W.2d 127 (Minn. 2014)

Gildea, Chief Justice. . . . On September 15, 2011, respondent Hennepin County Human Services and Public Health Department filed a Petition for Children in Need of Protection or Services ("CHIPS") on behalf of four children of parents J.W. (father) and appellant R.D.L. (mother). The petition alleged, among other things, that the mother was engaging in prostitution out of a Brooklyn Center hotel in the children's presence, that the father had physically abused the mother in front of their children, and that the mother used illegal drugs in front of the children. The juvenile court found that the children were in need of protection and services and issued an order placing them in foster care.

Eight months later, on May 3, 2012, the County filed a petition to terminate the parents' rights to the four children, alleging that the parents failed to comply with the case plans designed to reunite them with their children. The case plans required that the parents follow recommendations made after chemical dependency, mental health, and parenting assessments; provide random urine tests to demonstrate sobriety; and obtain safe, stable, and suitable housing. The mother's case plan required her to cut off contact with the father, and the father's case plan required that he seek anger management treatment. The mother took advantage of some of the services the County offered, but ultimately did not complete any components of her case plan. The father also did not comply with the case plan, and he refused to accept any of the services.

A few weeks after the County filed its petition to terminate the parents' rights to the four children, the mother gave birth to a fifth child, who is the subject of this action. On July 27, 2012, less than a week before trial began on the County's petition to terminate parental rights to the four older children, the County made an offer to the mother concerning her fifth child. The County proposed to agree "on the record" that if the mother would seek to voluntarily terminate her rights to the four older children, the County would not use that termination as a basis to seek termination of parental rights to her newborn child, "absent a separate reason for child protection involvement." The mother rejected the County's offer.

After a two-day trial, the juvenile court terminated the parents' rights to the four older children. Minnesota Statutes § 260C.301, subd. 1(b) (2012), provides that parental rights can be involuntarily terminated if the court finds that at least one of nine conditions exist. The court found by clear and convincing evidence that reasonable efforts had failed to correct conditions leading to the children's out-of-home placement, under Minn. Stat. § 260C.301, subd. 1(b)(5) and terminated the parents' rights. The mother appealed, and the court of appeals affirmed the termination.

Two days after the juvenile court's decision, the County filed a CHIPS petition on behalf of the fifth child, the newborn. After the County located and placed the baby into protective care, the County filed a petition to terminate the parents' rights to the newborn, alleging that four of the statutory grounds for termination existed, including, as relevant here, that the mother was "palpably unfit to be a party to the parent and child relationship." A parent is presumed to be "palpably unfit to be a party to the parent and child relationship" if "the parent's parental rights to one or more other children were involuntarily terminated."

At a subsequent hearing, the father offered some, "albeit scant," evidence in an effort to overcome the presumption. The mother offered no evidence to rebut the presumption. Instead, she argued that the statutory presumption, Minn. Stat. § 260C.301, subd. 1(b)(4), is unconstitutional. The mother argued that the presumption of unfitness violates due process and equal protection under the United States and Minnesota Constitutions because the presumption applies only to parents whose parental rights are terminated involuntarily and excludes those parents who voluntarily agree to terminate their parental rights.

The juvenile court rejected the mother's constitutional challenge and found that the father failed to overcome the presumption. The court found by clear and convincing evidence that both parents failed to overcome the presumption of unfitness and that it was in the child's best interests to terminate their parental rights. The court of appeals affirmed.

The mother filed a petition for review with our court. . . .

The question presented in this case is whether the statutory presumption in Minn. Stat. § 260C.301, subd. 1(b)(4), violates equal protection guarantees in the United States and Minnesota Constitutions. The Equal Protection Clause of the Fourteenth Amendment guarantees that no state can "deny to any person within its jurisdiction the equal protection of the laws." The equal protection provision of the Minnesota Constitution guarantees that "[n]o member of this state shall be disfranchised or deprived of any of the rights or privileges secured to any citizen thereof, unless by the law of the land or the judgment of his peers." Although the text of the provisions is different, claims made under them are analyzed using the same principles. . . .

We have required that a party establish that he or she is similarly situated to persons who have been treated differently in order to support an equal protection claim. We have explained that "the Equal Protection Clause does not require the State to treat things that are different in fact or opinion as though they were the same in law." In order to determine whether two groups are similarly situated, we focus on whether the groups are alike in all relevant respects. . . .

. . . Minnesota Statutes § 260C.001, subd. 2 (2012), provides that "[t]he paramount consideration in all juvenile protection proceedings is the health, safety, and best interests of the child." The statute also declares that one purpose of juvenile protection proceedings is "to provide judicial procedures that protect the welfare of the child." Accordingly, when addressing whether the two groups are alike in all relevant respects, we must address whether they are similarly situated in a way that is relevant to protecting the welfare and best interests of the child. We conclude that the parents at issue here are similarly situated. . . .

Minnesota Statutes § 260C.301 (2012), which addresses the termination of parental rights, undoubtedly classifies parents into two different groups. A parent can "voluntarily" terminate parental rights by giving written consent supported by "good cause." Minn. Stat. § 260C.301, subd. 1(a). By contrast, a court can involuntarily terminate a parent's rights if it finds clear and convincing evidence that at least one of nine statutory factors is present. Minn. Stat. § 260C.301, subd. 1(b). These factors include that the parent has abandoned the child, or that the parent has substantially, continuously, or repeatedly refused or neglected to comply with the duties imposed upon him or her by the parent and child relationship.

Despite these differences, we conclude that the two groups of parents before us are similarly situated, at least with respect to the purposes of Minn. Stat. § 260C.301. When we focus on the best interests of the children, which is the "paramount consideration" under the statute, the two classes of parents are the same. This is true because in both circumstances, whether parental rights were terminated voluntarily or involuntarily, the juvenile court must have concluded that the best interests of the children required termination.

Concluding that the two sets of parents are similarly situated, we next consider what level of scrutiny the statute, Minn. Stat. § 260C.301, subd. 1(b)(4), must satisfy if it is to survive an equal protection challenge. We have held that statutory classifications are generally permissible as long as they rationally further some legitimate state purpose. If, however, a statute classifies based on a suspect class or impinges on fundamental rights, the classification must meet strict scrutiny, meaning that it must be narrowly tailored to serve a compelling government interest.

The U.S. Supreme Court has long recognized the fundamental nature of parental rights. In Santosky v. Kramer, the Supreme Court noted that the "fundamental liberty interest of natural parents in the care, custody, and management of their child does not evaporate simply because they have not been model parents or have lost temporary custody of their child to the State." We have similarly held that a parent's right to make decisions concerning the care, custody, and control of his or her children is a protected fundamental right. Because the right to parent is a fundamental one, we will subject the statute at issue, Minn. Stat. § 260C.301, subd. 1(b)(4), to strict scrutiny.

Once a statute is subject to strict scrutiny, it is "not entitled to the usual presumption of validity." Rather, the County must carry a "heavy burden of justification," to show that the classification is narrowly tailored to serve a compelling government interest.

In the due process context, we have held that the government has a compelling interest in its role as *parens patriae* in promoting relationships among those in recognized family units in order to protect the general welfare of children. The government also has a compelling interest in "identifying and protecting abused children," and in "safeguarding the physical and psychological well-being" of children.

The mother does not dispute that the government has a compelling interest in protecting children. But she argues that the government interest served by the presumption at issue here is not generally to protect children, but rather to "conserve litigation resources and spare the County the time and expense of an actual trial," and she contends that such an interest is not compelling. We disagree. Proceedings involving endangered children are not expedited so that the government is able to conserve government resources. These proceedings are expedited because a quick resolution is essential for the best interests of children who are in need of protection. In fact, that resources are saved through operation of the statutory presumption in Minn. Stat. § 260C.301, subd. 1(b)(4), is merely a byproduct of the overarching objective of the child protection system—protecting the best interests of children by extricating them from dangerous situations quickly.

The statutory presumption directly serves the compelling government interest of protecting children because it facilitates the more expeditious resolution of cases involving children in need of protection. The principle that child protection cases are to receive priority and be resolved quickly is a thoroughly engrained policy that both the legislative and executive branches endorse and support. Under our law, children are not to be kept waiting, uncertain who will raise them or where they will grow up. The statutory presumption in Minn. Stat. § 260C.301, subd. 1(b)(4), which provides a mechanism to shorten a termination trial in the narrow instance in which clear and convincing evidence supported a previous finding that a child's best interests required termination, directly serves the compelling government interest of protecting these children.

But, the mother argues, the statutory presumption cannot survive strict scrutiny because it is not narrowly tailored to serve the government's compelling interest in protecting children. To survive strict scrutiny, a statute can be neither overinclusive nor underinclusive; rather, it must be "precisely tailored to serve the compelling state interest." The Supreme Court has repeatedly sought to "dispel the notion that strict scrutiny is 'strict in theory, but fatal in fact.'" And the Court has held that narrow tailoring "does not require exhaustion of every conceivable . . . alternative," nor does it require a "dramatic sacrifice" of the compelling interest at stake.

The mother argues that the statutory presumption in Minn. Stat. § 260C.301, subd. 1(b)(4), does not meet the narrow tailoring requirement because it is underinclusive in that there are "demonstrably unfit" parents who voluntarily terminated their rights, but in a subsequent termination proceeding are not subject to the operation of a presumption of parental unfitness. She argues that the government's compelling interest "is at least as compelling when a palpably unfit parent voluntarily terminates as when a palpably unfit parent chooses to litigate." No matter how "abusive or neglectful a parent may have been," she says, the parent avoids later application of the presumption by choosing to voluntarily terminate his or her parental rights. The mother's argument is not convincing.

To be sure, the presumption of unfitness in Minn. Stat. § 260C.301, subd. 1(b)(4), does not apply to those parents who voluntarily seek to end their parent-child relationship. It is also true that parents may seek to terminate their rights for any number of reasons that may have nothing to do with their fitness to be parents. That the "palpably unfit" presumption in subdivision 1(b)(4) does not apply to such parents therefore does not equate to a conclusion that the statute is not narrowly tailored. The purpose of the narrow tailoring requirement is to "ensure that the means chosen fit th[e] compelling goal so closely that there is little or no possibility that the motive for the classification was illegitimate." The statutory classification at issue here is closely tied to the government's goal of protecting children, and it meets the narrow tailoring requirement.

A natural parent is presumed to be suitable "to be entrusted with the care of his child" and it is "in the best interest of a child to be in the custody of his natural parent." When, however, the government has, in an initial proceeding, overcome that presumption of fitness through clear and convincing evidence that a parent cannot be entrusted to care for his or her children, the statutory presumption of unfitness in Minn. Stat. § 260C.301, subd. 1(b)(4), relieves the government of its burden to again overcome the natural parent's presumption of fitness, at least until the parent produces evidence warranting a finding of fitness. In other words, Minn. Stat. § 260C.301, subd. 1(b)(4), is narrowly drawn to operate only when the juvenile court has already once concluded based on clear and convincing evidence establishing one or more of nine specific statutory reasons, that the actions of the parent warrant severing the parent-child relationship. Given the presumption's limited operation, "there is little or no possibility that the motive for the classification was illegitimate."

We recognize that the statutory presumption, standing alone, may not meet the heavy burden of narrow tailoring. The U.S. Supreme Court has noted that "[p]rocedure by presumption is always cheaper and easier than individualized determination," and has said that in family law matters, presumptions that foreclose individual determinations on determinative issues can "needlessly risk [] running roughshod over the important interests of both parent and child." But the presumption we are faced with today does not forsake an individual determination. To the contrary, several factors establish that even when the presumption in Minn. Stat. § 260C.301, subd. 1(b)(4), operates, an individualized determination is still required and still made.

First, termination of parental rights is always discretionary with the juvenile court. Language throughout the juvenile protection laws emphasizes that the court "may," but is not required to, terminate a parent's rights when one of the nine statutory criteria is met. Accordingly, even if the presumption of unfitness in Minn. Stat. § 260C.301, subd. 1(b)(4), operates and is not rebutted, termination of parental rights is still a matter of discretion for the juvenile court.

Second, the presumption is easily rebuttable. The court of appeals has held that when the presumption of unfitness applies, a parent rebuts the presumption by introducing evidence that would "'justify a finding of fact' that [the parent] is not palpably unfit," and whether the evidence satisfies the burden of production is determined on a case-by-case basis. This standard, which is a much lower bar than the "clear and convincing" standard shouldered by the County, Minn. Stat. § 260C.317, subd. 1, is the appropriate standard. For the statute to survive under a strict scrutiny analysis, the burden imposed by the presumption cannot be a heavy one. Rather, the parent needs to produce only enough evidence to support a finding that the parent is suitable "to be entrusted with the care" of the children.

Third, we have made clear that an involuntary termination of parental rights is proper only when at least one statutory ground for termination is supported by clear and convincing evidence *and* the termination is in the child's best interest. Here, while the juvenile court relied on the presumption of parental unfitness in its order terminating the mother's rights to her fifth child, the court also separately found "[c]lear and convincing evidence" that it was "in the best interests of the child that any and all parental rights be terminated." This separate statutory requirement for a best-interests consideration, Minn. Stat. § 260C.301, subd. 7, ensures that a termination is not ordered simply because a parent introduces no evidence to overcome the presumption. In other words, and to be clear, just as termination based solely on the child's best interests is improper, termination based solely on a statutory presumption is improper. The juvenile court also must independently find in each case, even with a presumption of unfitness, that termination is in the child's best interests.

Together, these procedural protections ensure that the Minn. Stat. § 260C.301, subd. 1(b)(4), is narrowly tailored, that the child's best interests remain the paramount consideration, and that the presumption does not improperly encompass those who have had their parental rights terminated previously merely because those parents are not able to present evidence establishing that they are fit parents.

Based on our analysis, we conclude that Minn. Stat. § 260C.301, subd. 1(b)(4), is narrowly tailored to serve the government's compelling interest. We therefore hold that the statute does not violate the equal protection provisions of the United States or Minnesota Constitutions.

Affirmed.

PAGE, Justice (dissenting). . . . We typically review equal protection challenges under the rational basis standard. If the classification involves a suspect class or fundamental right, however, we apply the strict scrutiny standard. Because this case involves a fundamental right—the right of parents to make decisions on "the care, custody, and control" of their children—strict scrutiny applies. Strict scrutiny is the most rigorous standard applied in equal protection cases. Strict scrutiny in the context of fundamental rights focuses on whether the classification itself serves a compelling government interest, not whether the statute as a whole serves such an interest.

Here, the classification is between parents who have in the past voluntarily terminated their parental rights and parents who have previously had their parental rights involuntarily terminated. Under Minn. Stat. § 260C.301, subd. 1(b)(4), parents in the latter group are presumed to be palpably unfit to parent their children while no such presumption applies to parents in the former group. The court identifies the compelling government interest in having the presumption as the prompt and permanent removal of children from unsafe parents. The court concludes that the classification is narrowly tailored because the district court retains discretion over whether to terminate parental rights, the parent can easily rebut the presumption, and the presumption does not shift the burden of proof from the County. Essentially, the court reasons that because the impact of the presumption is what the court concludes is minimal and, because procedural protections are in place, the statute is narrowly tailored. The court ignores the fact that encompassed within the narrowly tailored requirement is the additional requirement that a statute can be neither overinclusive nor underinclusive.

R.D.L. argues that the classification in Minn. Stat. § 260C.301, subd. 1(b)(4), is underinclusive because it does not include parents who have voluntarily terminated their parental rights to other children. A statute is "overinclusive" if it "burden[s] more persons than necessary to cure the problem." A statute is underinclusive if it excludes persons that it should not.

I conclude that the classification in Minn. Stat. § 260C.301, subd. 1(b)(4), is underinclusive because there is no compelling reason to exclude from the presumption of palpable unfitness parents who have in the past voluntarily terminated their parental rights. First, many parents who voluntarily terminate their rights satisfy the standards for involuntary termination. In such cases, the only distinction between the two classes of parents is that parents whose rights were involuntarily terminated invoked their right to a hearing. Second, it is not uncommon that parents voluntarily relinquish their rights to a child for reasons that would support an involuntary termination.

Perhaps the best example of the lack of distinction between the two classifications as it relates to the asserted government interest in creating the two classes is R.D.L. herself. Had R.D.L. agreed to Hennepin County's proposal and voluntarily waived her parental rights to her four older children, the statutory presumption of palpable unfitness would not have applied to her newborn child. But having rejected the offer, the presumption applied. In both cases, however, the facts with respect to R.D.L.'s ability to parent her newborn are exactly the same. Thus, I can see no compelling reason or government interest in treating the two classifications of parents differently. Indeed, it would appear that the only reason for treating the two classes of parents differently is to put pressure on parents to voluntarily terminate their parental rights rather than asserting their right to a hearing and putting the government to its proof. Put another way, R.D.L. could have fit into either classification without any impact on her parental fitness or circumstances. This illustrates that the principal distinction between parents who voluntarily terminated their parental rights and parents, like R.D.L. here, whose rights are involuntarily terminated, is that parents in the latter group simply refuse to voluntarily terminate their rights. Because the distinction between the two classes of parents is marginal at best, the presumption of palpable unfitness in Minn. Stat. § 260C.301, subd. 1(b)(4), should apply to parents who have voluntarily terminated their rights. Since it does not, the presumption is underinclusive.

Even if a statute is underinclusive, "'perfection is by no means required.'" The U.S. Supreme Court has upheld an underinclusive or overinclusive statute if the statute otherwise meets the appropriate level of scrutiny. As indicated above, the applicable level of scrutiny here is strict scrutiny, which requires that the classification be narrowly tailored and reasonably necessary to meet a compelling governmental interest.

According to the court, the compelling government interest served by the statutory presumption at issue is "protecting children" by "facilitat[ing] more expeditious resolution of cases involving children in need of protection." While the protection of children is a compelling government interest, the court ignores the well-recognized principle that the classification itself, not the statute, must serve a compelling government interest. Thus, the County must articulate a compelling government interest that is furthered by applying Minn. Stat. § 260C.301, subd. 1(b)(4), to one class of parents and not the other. I surmise that if the State has a compelling interest in quickly removing children from parents whose rights have been involuntarily terminated, the State has an equally compelling interest in quickly removing children from parents who voluntarily terminated their rights since parents who voluntarily terminate their rights often satisfy the standards for involuntary termination. This case illustrates why the State's interests do not change simply because a parent has voluntarily terminated her parental rights. The juvenile court presumed R.D.L. to be palpably unfit to care for her newborn because R.D.L.'s parental rights with respect to her oldest children had been involuntarily terminated. The County advocates that it had a compelling government interest in expeditiously protecting the newborn from an unsafe situation. But, had R.D.L. accepted the County's offer to voluntarily terminate her parental rights to her oldest children, the palpably unfit presumption would not have applied with respect to her newborn. Nevertheless, if the newborn needed protection from an unsafe environment, that need would not have dissipated simply because R.D.L. had agreed to voluntarily terminate her parental rights to her other children. R.D.L.'s history and parental fitness, and the newborn's need for protection, were the same irrespective of how R.D.L.'s rights to her other children were terminated. Thus, if the State has an interest in protecting children when the presumption applies, I see no reason for the State's interest to be any less simply because a parent had in the past accepted the County's offer to voluntarily terminate his or her rights to other children. Since the State has an equal interest in quickly removing children from parents who voluntarily terminated their rights to other children, there is no compelling government interest that is furthered by applying Minn. Stat. § 260C.301, subd. 1(b)(4), to one class of parents and not the other.

Moreover, despite the articulated goal of expediting the removal of children in need of protection, the classification simply does not accomplish that goal. Here, R.D.L. faced two separate termination proceedings, one relating to her four oldest children in which the presumption was not applicable and one relating to her newborn child in which the presumption was applicable.

With respect to R.D.L.'s four oldest children, the County filed a child in need of protection or services (CHIPS) petition on September 15, 2011. The court terminated R.D.L.'s parental rights to her four oldest children on August 28, 2012, 11 months after the petition was filed. With respect to R.D.L.'s newborn child, the County filed a CHIPS petition on August 30, 2012. At this point, the County had the benefit of having already gathered ample evidence regarding R.D.L.'s parental fitness, and the County could rely on Minn. Stat. § 260C.301, subd. 1(b)(4), to help prove that R.D.L. was palpably unfit to care for her newborn child. However, even with sufficient evidence and with the presumption in place, the process of terminating R.D.L.'s parental rights was anything but prompt. The hearing to consider the termination of R.D.L.'s parental rights did not occur until July 31, 2013, and R.D.L.'s parental rights were not finally terminated until August 16, 2013, one year after the petition was filed. Given the fact that it took longer to terminate R.D.L.'s parental rights to her newborn with the presumption in place than it did to terminate R.D.L.'s parental rights to her older children without the presumption, it is fair to say that neither the statutory presumption nor the classification did anything to expedite the termination of R.D.L.'s parental rights to her newborn child. Thus, it is clear that the classification as applied to the presumption is not reasonably necessary to meet a compelling government interest.

NOTES AND QUESTIONS

1. When, if ever, should reasonable efforts be required despite the existence of statutory grounds to dispense with such efforts? For example, should the fact that a parent's relationship with regard to another child was terminated ten years ago necessarily mean that no efforts should be made to preserve the parent's relationship with another child today?

2. If reasonable efforts to reunite child and parent are not required, does this necessarily mean that a petition to terminate parental rights will be filed?

Professor James Dwyer has sharply criticized the common agency practice of seeking to reunite parents and children even when grounds for forgoing reasonable efforts and going straight to termination of parental rights exist. He particularly argues that early termination should be sought when the child is a newborn and that states should enact laws that provide additional grounds for excusing reasonable efforts. His rationale is that the circumstances in which reasonable efforts can be excused place infants at risk not only of harm from their parents but also of disruption of relationships at crucial times in the children's development. James G. Dwyer, The Child Protection Pretense: States' Continued Consignment of Newborn Babies to Unfit Parents, 93 Minn. L. Rev. 407 (2008).

3. Courts have generally rejected substantive due process challenges to state laws implementing the federal no reasonable efforts provisions. *See, e.g.,* G.B. v. Dearborn County Division of Family and Children, 754 N.E.2d 1027 (Ind. App. 2001); In re Child of P.T., 657 N.W.2d 577 (Minn. App. 2003). Matter of S.G. v. Indiana Dept. Child Servs., 67 N.E.3d 1138 (Ind. App. 2017).

4. Recall that ICWA requires "active efforts" to reunite the parent and child. Cases are mixed about whether active efforts can be excused on facts that would justify dispensing with reasonable efforts in other cases. People in Interest of J.S.B., 691 N.W.2d 611 (S.D. 2005), concluded that active efforts are still required because ICWA contains no exception for aggravated circumstances cases and is the more specific statute. *See also* In re JL, 770 N.W.2d 853 (Mich. 2009). However, the Alaska Supreme Court held in J.S. v. State, 50 P.3d 388 (Alaska 2002), that AFSA relieves the state of the ICWA obligation to attempt to reunify the family when a parent has sexually abused a child. In re E.G.M., 750 S.E.2d 657 (N.C. App. 2013), held that a statute allowing a court to cease reunification efforts based on a finding

that they "would be futile or inconsistent with the child's health, safety, and need for a safe, permanent home within a reasonable time" applies in an ICWA case. The court discussed the division in state law about whether aggravated circumstances excuse the ICWA active efforts requirement but said that courts agree that courts do not have to continue active efforts when they are "futile." *Id.* at 866 (citing cases).

5. The involuntary termination of parental rights with regard to another child must be a ground for dispensing with reasonable efforts under the federal statutes, but it does not have to be a ground for terminating parental rights. Would a statute authorizing termination on the basis of prior termination alone survive a due process challenge? Sampson v. Division of Family Services, 868 A.2d 832 (Del. 2005), upheld such a statute, reasoning that termination can be ordered only if the court finds clear and convincing evidence of grounds and that termination is in the best interests of the child, which gives a parent sufficient opportunity to show that he or she is able to care for the child. In contrast, In re Gach, 89 N.W.2d 707 (Mich. App. 2016), held that such a statute violated procedural due process. The court said that the statute, in conjunction with another statute that provides that if a ground to terminate is proven by clear and convincing evidence, the parent's rights should be terminated if the court finds by a preponderance of the evidence that to do so is in the child's best interest, effectively creates an irrebutable presumption of unfitness as to a parent whose rights have previously been terminated.

6. Instead of providing that a prior involuntary termination is itself a ground for terminating parental rights, the Minnesota statute provides that it is presumptive proof that the parent is "palpably unfit." However, no such presumption arises if the parent's rights are voluntarily terminated, i.e., if the parent relinquishes his or her rights. The majority and dissent in *R.D.L.* disagree about whether parents whose rights are involuntarily terminated after a trial in juvenile court and parents who voluntarily relinquish their rights are so similar that treating them differently violates equal protection. What is the basis of their disagreement?

Why do you suppose that federal and state law attach such different consequences to voluntary and involuntary terminations of parental rights?

7. A number of states have enacted termination statutes that create presumptions based on proof of aggravated circumstances. Challenges to their constitutionality have had mixed outcomes.

The Illinois termination statute provided that a parent was conclusively presumed to be unfit if he or she had been "criminally convicted of aggravated battery, heinous battery, or attempted murder of any child." The Illinois Supreme Court held that this statute violated due process because the parent was denied the opportunity to present evidence on the substantive issue of his or her fitness as a parent. In re D.W., 827 N.E.2d 466 (Ill. 2005). The court rejected the state's argument that a parent's interests were adequately protected by the additional requirement that the state prove that termination was in the child's best interests because the state's burden of proof on the latter issue was lower. The statute now provides for a rebuttable presumption of unfitness upon proof of physical abuse resulting in death of any child. 750 ILCS 50/1(D)(f) (2018).

A Florida statute provided that upon proof of conviction of one of several crimes against a child, a parent was rebuttably presumed to be unfit. Florida Department Children & Families v. F.L., 880 So. 2d 602 (Fla. 2004), said that if such a statute shifted the burden of persuasion on the issue of current fitness to the parent, it would be unconstitutional. The court construed the statute as merely allowing the state to file a termination petition without providing reasonable efforts but still requiring it to prove that "reunification would be a substantial risk to the child and that termination is the least restrictive way to protect the child." 880 So. 2d at 609-610.

In re Evelyn A., 169 A.3d 914 (Me. 2017), held that a statute providing that upon proof that a parent had committed manslaughter of another child, the court "may presume that the parent is unwilling or unable to protect the child . . . and these circumstances are unlikely to change within a time which is reasonably calculated to meet the child's needs" allowed the court to make an inference but did not shift the burden of persuasion to the parent, avoiding the constitutional problem identified by some other courts.

8. 42 U.S.C. § 671(a)(15)(D) requires that states allow a court to dispense with the reasonable efforts requirement when there are "aggravated circumstances." Some states define that term more fully, while others just use the federal language. After surveying case law from around the country on the meaning of "aggravated circumstances," the New Jersey intermediate appellate court said,

> Although there are a wide variety of approaches among the states, there are common threads, or themes, that are underpinned by the intent and purposes of AFSA, as implemented by our Legislature. We conclude that the term "aggravated circumstances" embodies the concept that the nature of the abuse or neglect must have been so severe or repetitive that to attempt reunification would jeopardize and compromise the safety of the child, and would place the child in a position of an unreasonable risk to be reabused.
>
> Moreover, any circumstances that increase the severity of the abuse or neglect, or add to its injurious consequences, equates to "aggravated circumstances." Whether couched as "severe child abuse or neglect," "serious child abuse or neglect," or "severe physical injury" of a singular, chronic, recurrent, or repetitive nature, where the circumstances created by the parent's conduct create an unacceptably high risk to the health, safety and welfare of the child, they are "aggravated" to the extent that the child welfare agency, here DYFS, may bypass reasonable efforts of reunification. Moreover, where the parental conduct is particularly heinous or abhorrent to society, involving savage, brutal, or repetitive beatings, torture, or sexual abuse, the conduct may also be said to constitute "aggravated circumstances." Additionally, whether the offer or receipt of services would correct the conditions that led to the abuse or neglect within a reasonable time may also be considered.

New Jersey Div. of Youth and Family Serv. v. A.R.G., 824 A.2d 213, 233-234 (N.J. Super. 2003), aff'd in part, modified in part, 845 A.2d 106, 118 (N.J. 2004). For an analysis of cases interpreting the "aggravated circumstances" catchall provision, *see* Kathleen S. Bean, Aggravated Circumstances, Reasonable Efforts, and ASFA, 29 B.C. Third World L.J. 223 (2009).

9. Abandonment of a child is also a basis for expedited termination proceedings under the federal legislation and implementing state statutes. "Safe haven laws," which have been enacted in all states, allow parents to, in legal and practical effect, abandon newborns in safe places, typically hospitals or police stations, without fear of adverse legal consequences. The first law was enacted in Texas after a series of widely publicized cases in which very young parents gave birth secretly and then abandoned the babies in trash receptacles, where they were found dead. Other states quickly followed suit with little or no opposition. Susan Ayres, *Kairos* and Safe Havens: The Timing and Calamity of Unwanted Birth, 15 Wm. & Mary J. Women & L. 227 (2009).

Professor Sanger argues that the laws are principally symbolic and part of the wider struggle over abortion and the "culture of life." She and other critics argue that the parents most likely to abandon their infants are unlikely to use the laws because they are often in denial about their pregnancies in the first place. Further, the laws are often not well-publicized, it may be difficult to reach a safe haven without being detected, and not all laws promise absolute anonymity and legal immunity. Carol Sanger, Infant Safe Haven Laws: Legislating in the Culture of Life, 106 Colum. L. Rev. 753, 792 (2006). The laws are also criticized for ignoring fathers' parental rights. Jeffrey A. Parness, Deserting Mothers, Abandoned Babies, Lost Fathers: Dangers in Safe Havens, 24 Quinnipiac L. Rev. 335 (2006). Responding to these arguments, Professor Ayers argues that judgments about the laws' effectiveness are premature and that the laws should be understood as providing women with another way for dealing with unwanted pregnancies, rather than as simply a tool in the abortion debate. Ayres, above.

PROBLEM

The state child welfare agency has filed to terminate the parental rights of Mother and Father on the basis that the children have been removed from the parents' custody three times and returned twice, all because of unsafe conditions in the home. Most recently, the children were removed six months before the hearing on the TPR petition. At that hearing the state showed that the parents' house had broken windows, exposed wires, and a flea infestation. The youngest child had severe diaper rash. The earlier removals were based on similar conditions. Each time the children were removed the agency told the parents to clean the house, get rids of their dogs, and repair broken doors and windows. Each of the previous two times the parents had remedied conditions, only to have them deteriorate within a few months. The agency repeatedly offered the parents counseling services; only three months ago the parents had begun going and reported that they found the sessions helpful. While in foster care the children have thrived. The parents have once again cleaned up the house and made repairs, and the state does not allege that the parents present any other kind of risk to the children. If the basis for the termination of parental rights petition is aggravated circumstances, is the evidence sufficient? What if the basis for the petition is failure to remedy conditions in the home despite the agency's reasonable efforts?

2. The Best Interests Determination

After the court has found a substantive basis for terminating parental rights has been proven, the court must also find that termination is in the child's best interests.

IN RE THE INVOLUNTARY TERMINATION OF THE PARENT–CHILD RELATIONSHIP OF R.S.

56 N.E.3d 625 (Ind. 2016)

DAVID, Justice. . . . R.S. (Father) and L.H. (Mother) are the parents of ten-year-old R.S., II (R.S.). In December 2009, Father pled guilty to a Class B felony and a no contact order was entered between Father and Mother. During Father's incarceration, Mother cared for R.S., but Father stayed in contact by writing letters to R.S. on a weekly basis and sending gifts. Father was released on probation in March 2013.

In April 2014, the Department of Child Services (DCS) alleged that R.S. was a child in need of services (CHINS) because of Mother's drug use and Father's lack of involvement. R.S. was placed with his maternal grandmother (Grandmother). Father requested that R.S. be placed with him, but DCS objected based upon an alleged no contact order between Father and R.S. Father informed the court that there was not a no contact order between himself and R.S., and he had documentation to support his claim. However, because the court and DCS believed otherwise, no parenting time was ordered for Father. In the meantime, DCS took no action to assess whether there was a valid no contact order between Father and R.S. It was not until June 10, 2015, when the Guardian Ad Litem (GAL) brought to the trial court's attention that there was not a no contact order between Father and R.S., that Father was ordered parenting time.

Subsequently, R.S. was found to be a CHINS as to Mother and Father. Father was ordered to participate in various services, including parenting classes, parenting assessment, and a Father Engagement Program. Father did not attend the disposition hearing, and he claimed to be unaware of any order to participate in services. Father also failed to appear for several of the subsequent court proceedings involving R.S. Thus, Father was largely absent during the CHINS action.

Despite his failure to complete the programs ordered by the court in relation to the CHINS proceeding, while incarcerated, Father completed various parenting and self-improvement courses. Father also successfully completed the Commercial Driver's License Course and successfully completed probation as of March 30, 2015. As a condition of probation, Father completed substance abuse evaluation and treatment, fifty-two weeks of domestic violence counseling, and a mental health evaluation.

On March 19, 2015, DCS filed a petition to terminate Father's parental rights. Even after the termination petition was filed, Father requested that he again be referred to services. His request for services was denied, but the court granted him supervised visitation. Mother consented to R.S.'s adoption. Therefore, a termination hearing was held as to Father only.

At the termination hearing, it became apparent that while the CHINS action was pending, Father had, in fact, been seeing R.S. on a regular basis, despite Father's absence from court proceedings and a couple of the court-ordered supervised visitations. Father had been visiting with R.S. two to three times a week, taking him swimming and paying for swimming activities, exercising overnights with R.S. on the weekends, and going to Grandmother's house upon her request to help resolve issues Grandmother was having with R.S.'s behavior.

The DCS case manager, the home-based therapist, and the GAL, all agreed that adoption by Grandmother was in R.S.'s best interests. However, there was a general consensus that R.S. and Father shared a close bond. The GAL believed that continued visitation between R.S. and Father was in R.S.'s best interests. Nevertheless, the trial court concluded that continuation of the parent-child relationship posed a threat to R.S.'s well-being by depriving him of permanency, and that termination was in the best interests of R.S.

Father appealed the termination of his parental rights, but the Court of Appeals affirmed the trial court. We now grant transfer . . .

As this Court and the United States Supreme Court have reiterated many times, "[a] parent's interest in the care, custody, and control of his or her children is 'perhaps the oldest of the fundamental liberty interests.'" Although parental interests are not absolute, "the parent-child relationship is 'one of the most valued relationships in our culture.'" Due to this, the Indiana statute governing termination of parental rights sets a high bar for severing this constitutionally protected relationship.

Under Indiana Code section 31–35–2–4(b), a petition seeking to terminate the parent-child relationship must allege the following:

(A) that one (1) of the following is true:
    (i) The child has been removed from the parent for at least six (6) months under a dispositional decree. . . .
(B) that one (1) of the following is true:
    (i) There is a reasonable probability that the conditions that resulted in the child's removal or the reasons for placement outside the home of the parents will not be remedied.
    (ii) There is a reasonable probability that the continuation of the parent-child relationship poses a threat to the well-being of the child. . . .
(C) that termination is in the best interests of the child; and
(D) that there is a satisfactory plan for the care and treatment of the child.

The State must prove each element by clear and convincing evidence.

On appeal, Father argued that there was insufficient clear and convincing evidence supporting the trial court's conclusion that termination was in the R.S.'s best interests and that there was not a satisfactory plan for the care of R.S. after termination. Because we are persuaded that the findings do not support the conclusion that termination is in R.S.'s best interests, we do not reach the issue of whether there was a satisfactory plan for the care and treatment of R.S.

In reaching this determination, we consider the trial court's findings regarding the best interests of R.S.:

> 26. Although there was confusion regarding a No Contact Order, [Father] had consistent contact with [R.S.] as a result of [R.S.] visiting or staying overnight with his paternal grandmother with whom [Father] now resides. . . .
> 28. [Father] did not see [R.S.] during his incarceration but kept in contact with him.
> 29. While incarcerated [Father] took several courses or programs to better him [sic], including the Therapeutic Community designed for people with a history of substance abuse.
> 30. As a condition of probation, [Father] completed a[sic] fifty-two weeks of domestic violence counseling in June of 2014. . . .
> 36. [Father] and [R.S.] share a bond. [R.S.] does love his father.
> 37. [R.S.] would like to stay with his grandmother and likes to visit with his father. . . .
> 48. Continuation of the parent-child relationship poses a threat to [R.S.]'s well-being in that it would pose a barrier to obtaining the permanency that he needs and strives through an adoption. To do otherwise could threaten the great progress [R.S.] has made in his special needs. Given additional time, and if [Father] was to follow through with services, he would have to complete therapy with [R.S.], still undergo a parenting assessment and obtain stable housing and an adequate income. After having the ChINS [sic] matter pend for fifteen month [sic], [Father] would be just beginning.
> 49. Termination of the parent-child relationship is in the best interests of [R.S.]. Termination would allow him to be adopted into a stable and permanent home where his needs will continue to be met. *It would be best for [R.S.] to be able to keep visiting his father* and paternal grandmother but staying in his placement is in his long term interests.
> 50. Family Case Manager Deen, who has been on the ChINS [sic] case since it was filed, believes adoption is in [R.S.]'s best interests given that he is bonded and comfortable with his grandmother. She does not believe [Father] would follow up if given more time and adoption would provide permanency for [R.S.]. . . .

These findings do not demonstrate clearly and convincingly that termination is in R.S.'s best interests. Rather, it is overwhelmingly apparent through the trial court's own findings and testimony provided at the termination hearing that Father and R.S. both love one another and have a close bond. Additionally, Father exercised parenting time with R.S. two to three times a week, including overnights with R.S., and it is the trial court's own conclusion that continued visitation with Father is in R.S.'s best interests. Father's failure to attend every scheduled supervised visitation or attend hearings during the course of the CHINS proceedings is not clear and convincing evidence that Father is uninterested or unwilling to parent R.S. While we strongly encourage parents to comply with the procedures and practices set out by the court and DCS when a child has been found a CHINS, we cannot ignore the fostered relationship, parenting, and individual improvement efforts that Father has personally undertaken.

Moreover, establishing permanency for R.S. was repeatedly expressed as a reason for termination. R.S. does currently have a stable home environment with Grandmother. However, when a child is in relative placement, and the permanency plan is adoption into the home where the child has lived for years already, pro-longing the adoption is unlikely to have an effect upon the child. Further, even when a father has had a "troubled past" and "failings as a parent," our courts will also recognize "the positive steps [a] [f]ather has taken to turn his life around for the sake of himself and his children." This is true even if the parent is not ready to "undertake full care" of the child and admits as much, but still wants a "chance to establish himself in the community and to participate in services . . . to make him a better person and parent." In the present case, Father has repeatedly expressed his desire and willingness to continue to develop as a person and a parent for R.S. . . .

. . . Father has demonstrated the desire and ability to achieve a meaning-ful reunification with his child. Since Father's release from incarceration, he has repeatedly demonstrated a desire to parent R.S. and has made progress by his suc-cessful completion of probation and maintaining clear drug screens. Accordingly, termination is not in R.S.'s best interests at this time.

While we understand the obstacles presented when a parent fails to appear for hearings or does not participate in referred services, "[t]ermination is intended as a last resort, available only when all other reasonable efforts have failed." Given the loving bond that R.S. and Father share, Father's successful completion of multiple self-improvement and parenting courses, Father's successful completion of proba-tion, his repeatedly expressed desire to parent R.S., and his exercise of regular visi-tation with R.S., "we do not believe that this case has reached the 'last resort' stage."

However, if in the future it becomes apparent that reunification is not a viable option, a subsequent petition for termination of parental rights or the appointment of a legal guardian could be pursued. Under Indiana Code section 31–34–21–7.5(c)(1)(E), a legal guardian serves as a "caretaker that is intended to be permanent and self-sustaining." Specified parental rights with respect to the child are transferred to the guardian, which include, "care, custody, and control of the child," along with "decision making concerning the child's upbringing." Given R.S.'s bond with both Father and Grandmother, this may be a suitable alternative. . . .

NOTES AND QUESTIONS

1. Maintaining ties with a parent or parents is one of the most commonly asserted reasons that termination is not in a child's best interests. Why did the court in *R.S.* accept this argument? Would it have reached the same conclusion if the child were living with unrelated foster parents who wanted to adopt and who were not willing to become the child's guardians? How would a court know whether continuing contact with a parent would benefit a child more than being adopted?

Some critics of a strong preference for adoption argue that children have interests in maintaining ties with their parents even if they are not strongly attached to them, which the law should recognize.

> Cutting a child off from her parents can cause her to have misconceptions about the absent parent(s). For example, absent parents may be idolized, and thus become a barrier to intimacy with other caregivers, or they may be demonized and thus neg-atively impact the child's self-esteem. Further, if the surrogate caregiver does not support the absent parent, the child may face a 'loyalty conflict,' further complicating her normal individuation process.

Eliza Patten, The Subordination of Subsidized Guardianship in Child Welfare Proceedings, 29 N.Y.U. Rev. L. & Soc. Change 237, 241 (2004). This issue is particularly likely to arise for older children.

2. What arguments support a legal preference in favor of adoption over a legal guardianship? When would legal guardianship be a better alternative? Should it be necessary to prove that it is highly unlikely that a child will be adopted before legal guardianship can be pursued? Some courts have held that maintaining a child's placement with a relative willing to offer the child a permanent home but who does not want to adopt supports the conclusion that termination is not in the child's interest. *E.g.*, In the Matter of B.A., 705 N.W.2d 507 (Iowa 2005); In re K.H., 133 Cal. Rptr.3d 797 (Cal. App. 2011) (interpreting statute). For discussions of the arguments for and against preferring adoption to legal guardianship, *see* Mark F. Testa, The Quality of Permanency—Lasting or Binding? Subsidized Guardianship and Kinship Foster Care as Alternatives to Adoption, 12 Va. J. Soc. Pol'y & L. 499 (2005); Sacha Coupet, Wells Conference on Adoption Law: Swimming Upstream Against the Great Adoption Tide: Making the Case for "Impermanence," 34 Cap. U. L. Rev. 405 (2005); Libby S. Adler, The Meanings of Permanence: A Critical Analysis of the Adoption and Safe Families Act of 1997, 38 Harv. J. on Legis. 1 (2001).

3. An adoption decree with an agreement or court order allowing post-adoption contact between the child and the biological parents or other members of the family of origin may also be used in about half the states to allow a child to maintain contact with family members when the court terminates parental rights. In some states, courts can order contact, while in others the court's power is limited to enforcing agreements between the adoptive parents and the biological family members. In either case, courts usually retain authority to decline to require contact if they find this to be contrary to the child's best interests. Annette Ruth Appell, Reflections on the Movement Toward More Child-Centered Adoption, 32 W. New Eng. L. Rev. 1 (2010); Carol Sanger, Bargaining for Motherhood: Postadoption Visitation Agreements, 41 Hofstra L. Rev. 309 (2012).

In a Washington case, a developmentally disabled father sought to relinquish his parental rights voluntarily because only then would he be allowed to negotiate a post-adoption visitation arrangement. However, the juvenile court judge, relying on the father's attorney's representation that the father could not competently relinquish his rights and the state's apparent argument that this guardian could not do this for him, involuntarily terminated his rights. The father appealed, and the Washington Court of Appeals held that constitutionally protected parental rights include the right to decide whether to relinquish a child voluntarily, that the father's attorney could not concede his incompetence, and that he was entitled to a hearing on the issues of his competence and whether he had authorized the attorney to concede his incompetence. In re Welfare of H.Q., 330 P.3d 195 (Wash. App. 2014).

4. Courts have also found that termination is not in a child's best interests when it would likely disrupt the child's established relationship to siblings. In re D.O., 201 Cal. Rptr.3d 642 (Cal. App. 2016); In re Naomi P., 34 Cal. Rptr. 3d 236 (Cal. App. 2005). However, courts have generally held that siblings have no constitutionally protected right to maintain a relationship and no standing to object

to the termination of the parental rights of a sibling to protect their relationship. *See, e.g.,* In re Meridian H., 798 N.W.2d 96 (Neb. 2011); In re J.T., 124 Cal. Rptr. 3d 716 (Cal. App. 2011). Despite statutory mandates to facilitate placing children with siblings, children lack standing to seek placement of siblings with them, and they cannot appeal from orders that do not place their siblings with them. State v. Kristopher E., 889 N.W.2d 362 (Neb. 2016); State v. Rodney P., 887 N.W.2d 45 (Neb. 2016).

5. Should the termination of the parental rights of the mother in *R.S.* be rescinded, since the court reversed the termination of the father's rights? Unless both parents' rights are terminated, the child will not be adopted. For this reason, some states do not allow termination of only one parent's rights. (Given this rationale, these statutes allow termination of the rights of a child's sole surviving parent.) Those states that permit termination of only one parent's rights do so to keep the child away from a parent who is a real source of risk to the child, while allowing the other parent to continue to have a relationship with the child.

6. More than five million American children, 7 percent of all U.S. children, have had one or both parents in prison at some time during their childhoods. The proportion is higher among African American, poor, and rural children. The most recent point-in-time estimate in 2007 found that 1.7 million had a parent currently in prison. (Oct. 2015), https://www.childtrends.org/wp-content/uploads/2015/10/2015-42ParentsBehindBars.pdf. Statutes in many states provide that a parent's incarceration may be a factor in determining whether to terminate parental rights. For detailed analysis of the statutory approaches, *see* Deseriee A. Kennedy, Children, Parents & the State: The Construction of a New Family Ideology, 26 Berkeley J. Gender L. & Just. 78 (2011). *See also* Sarah Abramowicz, Rethinking Parental Incarceration, 82 U. Colo. L. Rev. 793 (2011); Chesa Boudin, Children of Incarcerated Parents: The Child's Constitutional Right to the Family Relationship, 101 J. Crim. L. & Criminology 77 (2011); Mindy Herman-Stahl, Marni L. Kan & Tasseli McKay, Incarceration and the Family (2008), available at http://aspe.hhs.gov/hsp/08/MFS-IP/Incarceration&Family/index.shtml. Can it be assumed that a continuing relationship with an incarcerated parent is inherently harmful to a child? What obligations, if any, should the state have to preserve and promote the relationship between a child and an incarcerated parent?

PROBLEM

Marilyn was convicted of fraud, her second nonviolent felony conviction, and was sentenced to prison for two to ten years. The earliest she will be eligible for release is 18 months from now. After Marilyn was arrested, her two children stayed with Marilyn's mother, Ana, but Ana is ill and cannot care for them any longer. The children's father is dead. Marilyn has not been able to make other arrangements for the children, and they have been placed in foster care. The children are 18 months and three years old. How should Marilyn's attorney argue against termination of her parental rights? What arguments should the State make? What if the children were eight and ten? What if Marilyn had been convicted of aggravated assault and could not be released for five years?

3.   *Procedural Issues*

SANTOSKY V. KRAMER

455 U.S. 745 (1982)

BLACKMUN, J. . . . New York authorizes its officials to remove a child temporarily from his or her home if the child appears "neglected," within the meaning of Art. 10 of the Family Court Act. Once removed, a child under the age of 18 customarily is placed "in the care of an authorized agency," usually a state institution or a foster home. At that point, "the state's first obligation is to help the family with services to . . . reunite it. . . ." But if convinced that "positive, nurturing parent-child relationships no longer exist," the State may initiate "permanent neglect" [termination of parental rights] proceedings to free the child for adoption.

The State bifurcates its permanent neglect proceeding into "factfinding" and "dispositional" hearings. At the factfinding stage, the State must prove that the child has been "permanently neglected." . . . The Family Court judge then determines at a subsequent dispositional hearing what placement would serve the child's best interests.

At the factfinding hearing, the State must establish, among other things, that for more than a year after the child entered state custody, the agency "made diligent efforts to encourage and strengthen the parental relationship." The State must further prove that during that same period, the child's natural parents failed "substantially and continuously or repeatedly to maintain contact with or plan for the future of the child although physically and financially able to do so." Should the State support its allegations by "a fair preponderance of the evidence," the child may be declared permanently neglected. The declaration empowers the Family Court judge to terminate permanently the natural parents' rights in the child. . . .

New York's permanent neglect statute provides natural parents with certain procedural protections. But New York permits its officials to establish "permanent neglect" with less proof than most States require. Thirty-five States, the District of Columbia, and the Virgin Islands currently specify a higher standard of proof, in parental rights termination proceedings, than a "fair preponderance of the evidence." The only analogous federal statute of which we are aware permits termination of parental rights solely upon "evidence beyond a reasonable doubt." Indian Child Welfare Act of 1978, Pub. L. 95-608, § 102(f), 92 Stat. 3072, 25 U.S.C. § 1912(f) (1976 ed., Supp. IV). The question here is whether New York's "fair preponderance of the evidence" standard is constitutionally sufficient. . . .

. . . Whether the loss threatened by a particular type of proceeding is sufficiently grave to warrant more than average certainty on the part of the factfinder turns on both the nature of the private interest threatened and the permanency of the threatened loss.

Lassiter [v. Department of Social Services, 452 U.S. 18 (1981),] declared it "plain beyond the need for multiple citation" that a natural parent's "desire for and right to 'the companionship, care, custody, and management of his or her children'" is an interest far more precious than any property right. When the State initiates a parental rights termination proceeding, it seeks not merely to infringe that fundamental liberty interest, but to end it. "If the State prevails, it will have worked a unique kind of deprivation. . . . A parent's interest in the accuracy and justice of the decision to terminate his or her parental status is, therefore, a commanding one." . . .

Thus, the first [Mathews v. Eldridge, 424 U.S. 319, 335 (1976)] factor—the private interest affected—weighs heavily against use of the preponderance standard at a state-initiated permanent neglect proceeding. We do not deny that the child and his foster parents are also deeply interested in the outcome of that contest. But at the factfinding stage of the New York proceeding, the focus emphatically is not on them.

The factfinding does not purport—and is not intended—to balance the child's interest in a normal family home against the parents' interest in raising the child. Nor does it purport to determine whether the natural parents or the foster parents would provide the better home. Rather, the factfinding hearing pits the State directly against the parents. The State alleges that the natural parents are at fault. The questions disputed and decided are what the State did—"made diligent efforts,"—and what the natural parents did not do—"maintain contact with or plan for the future of the child." The State marshals an array of public resources to prove its case and disprove the parents' case. Victory by the State not only makes termination of parental rights possible; it entails a judicial determination that the parents are unfit to raise their own children.

At the factfinding, the State cannot presume that a child and his parents are adversaries. After the State has established parental unfitness at the initial proceeding, the court may assume at the dispositional stage that the interests of the child and the natural parents do diverge. But until the State proves parental unfitness, the child and his parents share a vital interest in preventing erroneous termination of their natural relationship. Thus, at the factfinding, the interests of the child and his natural parents coincide to favor use of error-reducing procedures. . . .

Under Mathews v. Eldridge, we next must consider both the risk of erroneous deprivation of private interests resulting from use of a "fair preponderance" standard and the likelihood that a higher evidentiary standard would reduce that risk. Since the factfinding phase of a permanent neglect proceeding is an adversary contest between the State and the natural parents, the relevant question is whether a preponderance standard fairly allocates the risk of an erroneous factfinding between these two parties. . . .

At such a proceeding, numerous factors combine to magnify the risk of erroneous factfinding. Permanent neglect proceedings employ imprecise substantive standards that leave determinations unusually open to the subjective values of the judge. In appraising the nature and quality of a complex series of encounters among the agency, the parents, and the child, the court possesses unusual discretion to underweigh probative facts that might favor the parent. Because parents subject to termination proceedings are often poor, uneducated, or members of minority groups, such proceedings are often vulnerable to judgments based on cultural or class bias.

The State's ability to assemble its case almost inevitably dwarfs the parents' ability to mount a defense. No predetermined limits restrict the sums an agency may spend in prosecuting a given termination proceeding. The State's attorney usually will be expert on the issues contested and the procedures employed at the factfinding hearing, and enjoys full access to all public records concerning the family. The State may call on experts in family relations, psychology, and medicine to bolster its case. Furthermore, the primary witnesses at the hearing will be the agency's own professional caseworkers whom the State has empowered both to investigate the family situation and to testify against the parents. Indeed, because the child is already in agency custody, the State even has the power to shape the historical events that form the basis for termination.

The disparity between the adversaries' litigation resources is matched by a striking asymmetry in their litigation options. Unlike criminal defendants, natural parents have no "double jeopardy" defense against repeated state termination efforts. If the State initially fails to win termination, as New York did here, it always can try once again to cut off the parents' rights after gathering more or better evidence. Yet even when the parents have attained the level of fitness required by the State, they have no similar means by which they can forestall future termination efforts.

Coupled with the "fair preponderance of the evidence" standard, these factors create a significant prospect of erroneous termination. A standard of proof that by its very terms demands consideration of the quantity, rather than the quality, of the evidence may misdirect the factfinder in the marginal case. Given the weight of the private interests at stake, the social cost of even occasional error is sizable.

Raising the standard of proof would have both practical and symbolic consequences. The Court has long considered the heightened standard of proof used in criminal prosecutions to be "a prime instrument for reducing the risk of convictions resting on factual error." . . . "Increasing the burden of proof is one way to impress the factfinder with the importance of the decision and thereby perhaps to reduce the chances that inappropriate" terminations will be ordered. . . .

. . . [W]e cannot agree with [the New York Appellate Division's] conclusion that a preponderance standard fairly distributes the risk of error between parent and child. Use of that standard reflects the judgment that society is nearly neutral between erroneous termination of parental rights and erroneous failure to terminate those rights. For the child, the likely consequence of an erroneous failure to terminate is preservation of an uneasy status quo. For the natural parents, however, the consequence of an erroneous termination is the unnecessary destruction of their natural family. A standard that allocates the risk of error nearly equally between those two outcomes does not reflect properly their relative severity.

C

Two state interests are at stake in parental rights termination proceedings—a *parens patriae* interest in preserving and promoting the welfare of the child and a fiscal and administrative interest in reducing the cost and burden of such proceedings. A standard of proof more strict than preponderance of the evidence is consistent with both interests.

"Since the State has an urgent interest in the welfare of the child, it shares the parents' interest in an accurate and just decision" at the factfinding proceeding. As *parens patriae*, the State's goal is to provide the child with a permanent home. Yet while there is still reason to believe that positive, nurturing parent-child relationships exist, the *parens patriae* interest favors preservation, not severance, of natural familial bonds. "[T]he State registers no gain towards its declared goals when it separates children from the custody of fit parents." Stanley v. Illinois, 405 U.S., at 652.

The State's interest in finding the child an alternative permanent home arises only "when it is clear that the natural parent cannot or will not provide a normal family home for the child." At the factfinding, that goal is served by procedures that promote an accurate determination of whether the natural parents can and will provide a normal home.

Unlike a constitutional requirement of hearings or court-appointed counsel, a stricter standard of proof would reduce factual error without imposing substantial fiscal burdens upon the State. As we have observed, 35 States already have adopted a higher standard by statute or court decision without apparent effect on the speed, form, or cost of their factfinding proceedings.

Nor would an elevated standard of proof create any real administrative burdens for the State's factfinders. New York Family Court judges already are familiar with a higher evidentiary standard in other parental rights termination proceedings not involving permanent neglect. . . .

We, of course, express no view on the merits of petitioners' claims. At a hearing conducted under a constitutionally proper standard, they may or may not prevail. Without deciding the outcome under any of the standards we have approved, we vacate the judgment of the Appellate Division and remand the case for further proceedings not inconsistent with this opinion.

It is so ordered.

(The dissenting opinion of Justice Rehnquist is omitted.)

NOTES AND QUESTIONS

1. Does *Santosky* apply to temporary removal of children from their parents' homes following a juvenile court finding of abuse or neglect? Most courts have held that a state may constitutionally require only proof by a preponderance of the evidence at the dispositional stage of a case. *See, e.g.*, People in Interest of O.E.P., 654 P.2d 312 (Colo. 1982); In re Juvenile Appeal (83-CD), 455 A.2d 1313 (Conn. 1983); In re Sabrina M., 460 A.2d 1009 (Me. 1983); In re Linda C., 451 N.Y.S.2d 268 (App. Div. 1982); Wright v. Arlington County Dept. of Social Services, 388 S.E.2d 477 (Va. App. 1990). In State in Interest of A.C., 643 So. 2d 743 (La. 1994), the Louisiana Supreme Court applied the analysis in *Santosky* to a statute that requires a court to cut off visitation and contact between a child and a sexually abusing parent unless the parent successfully completes a treatment program. Even parents who successfully go through treatment can have only supervised visitation with their children. *See* La. Rev. Stat. Ann. §§ 9:364, 9:341 (2018). The

court held that due process requires that the allegations of sexual abuse be proven by clear and convincing evidence.

2. In at least 15 jurisdictions a ruling dispensing with the requirement to make reasonable efforts must be supported by clear and convincing evidence, since that ruling makes termination of parental rights so much more likely. Division of Family Services v. Falkner, 2014 WL 2466461 (Fam Ct. 2014) (citing cases and statutes).

3. Under ICWA, a child's parent may voluntarily consent to termination of parental rights, but the consent may be given no earlier than ten days after the birth. Consent must be written and recorded before a judge, who must certify that the terms and consequences of the consent were fully explained and understood. Consent to termination of parental rights or adoption can be withdrawn at any time before a final decree is entered, and a final decree of adoption can be collaterally attacked for fraud or duress. 25 U.S.C. § 1913.

4. Lassiter v. Department of Social Services, 452 U.S. 18 (1981), held as a matter of due process that counsel must be appointed for indigent parents in termination proceedings on a case-by-case basis. Both *Lassiter* and *Santosky* focus on the importance of procedural safeguards to accurate fact-finding. Which is more critical to accurate development of the facts, the allocation of the burden of proof or the assistance of counsel? How does a lawyer help ensure accurate fact-finding? Do burdens of proof ensure *accurate* fact-finding? Or do they, as *Santosky* indicates, allocate the risk of error? What is the difference? For example, does requiring the State to prove the grounds for termination of parental rights by clear and convincing evidence increase the number of cases that are correctly decided? Indeed, what does "factual accuracy" even mean here?

In support of its conclusion that due process does not require the state to provide counsel for parents in all termination cases, *Lassiter* cited the state's interests in preserving the informality of proceedings and in avoiding the costs associated with an absolute right to counsel. Should termination proceedings be informal? Is the real issue cost?

Most states give parents an absolute right to counsel in termination of parental rights proceedings. However, in Delaware, Mississippi, Nevada, Vermont, and Wyoming courts are authorized to appoint counsel on a case-by-case basis. National Coalition for a Civil Right to Counsel, Status Map: Termination of Parent Rights (State)-Parents, available at http://civilrighttocounsel.org/map. *See also* Blakeney v. McRee, 188 So.3d 1154 (Miss. 2016).

5. In M.L.B. v. S.L.J., 519 U.S. 102 (1996), the Supreme Court ruled that an indigent parent cannot be barred from appealing an order terminating parental rights by a state rule requiring the payment of filing fees and costs. In addition to *Lassiter* and *Santosky*, the Supreme Court relied on prior decisions in civil and criminal cases holding that due process and equal protection are violated if access to the courts in cases affecting fundamental rights depends on a person's ability to pay.

6. Cases involving a parent with mental illness or disability can present a thorny procedural problem. As a matter of due process, a trial against the parent cannot proceed if the parent is unable to aid and assist his or her lawyer. State ex rel. Juv. Dept. v. Evjen, 813 P.2d 1092 (Or. App. 1991). In the comparable situation in a criminal case, the defendant can be held and treated until he or she regains

competence to stand trial, although if the defendant never regains competence, he or she can be held no longer than the maximum prison term authorized for the crime charged. Jackson v. Indiana, 1406 U.S. 715 (1972). This solution is not available in a termination of parental rights case, though, because of the child's interest in having his or her status resolved. Therefore, a guardian ad litem may be appointed for the parent so that the litigation can go forward. Oregon has enacted a statute regularizing the process of appointing a GAL for a parent that provides that the GAL must consult with the parent and take the position that the parent would take if the parent were not disabled. Or. Rev. Stat. § 419B.234 (2018). Attorneys for parents in Oregon virtually never seek the appointment of a GAL for even their most difficult clients because they believe that it is all but impossible to avoid a finding that the parent is unable to care for the child if the parent is unable even to direct his or her attorney.

AMY SINDEN, *"WHY WON'T MOM COOPERATE?": A CRITIQUE OF INFORMALITY IN CHILD WELFARE PROCEEDINGS*

11 Yale J.L. & Feminism 339, 348-349, 351 (1999)

State statutes and case law interpreting constitutional due process protections direct trial courts to conduct dependency and termination proceedings at an intermediate level of formality. These proceedings therefore include most of the standard trappings of the traditional adversarial model of dispute resolution. The state must set forth its allegations in a petition and serve it on the parent. Cases are heard by judges. Witnesses testify under oath. A court reporter transcribes the proceedings. Rules of evidence apply, with some exceptions. The parties may be represented by lawyers and may appeal adverse decisions.

However, parents in dependency and termination proceedings do not receive many of the procedural rights that criminal defendants—even those facing minor charges—enjoy. . . . Although termination and dependency cases generally provide the parent an opportunity to confront and cross-examine witnesses (with exceptions for child witnesses), courts in many instances apply relaxed evidentiary rules. For example, many jurisdictions allow social workers' hearsay reports to be admitted into evidence. Courts do not construe the due process rights of parents and children in dependency and termination proceedings to include rights analogous to the criminal prohibition on double jeopardy or the right against self-incrimination contained in the Fifth Amendment. . . .

A mother subpoenaed to court on allegations of abuse or neglect is likely to feel particularly vulnerable and insecure as she enters this environment. In light of the allegations against her, she may be especially eager to be accepted and viewed as normal and respectable. She may be particularly sensitive to any cues she receives from professionals as to how she should act to fit in with the norms of this microsocial setting. Race and class often exacerbate this outsider dynamic. The professionals in the system are by and large well-educated, middle-class, and predominantly white. Meanwhile, many of the accused parents and their children are members of racial minority groups and virtually all are extremely poor with little formal education.

In the negotiations leading up to and surrounding courtroom proceedings, a mother may often find herself the only outsider in a room full of professionals. Indeed, the sheer number of lawyers and social workers involved in a single family's case can be mind-boggling. In addition to the state agency social worker, there may be a social worker from a private agency contracted to provide more intensive social work services to the family, a social worker with the foster care agency (or in cases with more than one child in different foster homes, several social workers from different foster care agencies), a social worker working for the child advocacy organization, a guardian ad litem, a court-appointed special advocate, a lawyer representing the state child welfare agency, a lawyer representing the child, a lawyer representing the mother, and in some cases a lawyer representing one or more fathers or other involved family members. With some exceptions, all of these people speak with the intonation and dialect of the professional, educated class. This is usually not the native tongue of the mother. Additionally, as in any insular microsocial setting in which a limited group of people interact repeatedly, a host of catch phrases, acronyms, short-hands, and jargon develop that are unknown to outsiders.

Social work norms and discourse predominate in this setting. Perhaps this is due to the considerable power wielded by social workers, who initially exercise the discretion as to whether the coercion of the court process will be invoked against a family and to whom judges are often inclined to defer once a case gets to court. Perhaps it is also attributable to the tendency of both lawyers and social workers to view these cases in therapeutic terms, as an emotional crisis or breakdown in communication, rather than a legal question about whether the allegations of abuse are true and warrant state intervention.

In any case, the predominance of social work norms and discourse creates significant pressure on parents to resolve these cases through non-adversarial, informal means. Social workers are trained to be effective by building non-adversarial relationships characterized by cooperation and trust. From a social worker's point of view, she fails professionally if her relationship with her client becomes adversarial. While lawyers' training steeps them in the discourse of individual rights and prepares them to operate in formal, procedure-bound environments, social workers are steeped in the discourse of relationships and cooperation and trained to value informality over formality as a means of gaining trust and building rapport.

A key word in the prevailing social work discourse is thus "cooperation." This word often forms the focal point of the meetings and conversations that take place in the hallways of the courthouse: "If mom would just cooperate. . . ." Running as an undercurrent to this refrain are powerful cultural stereotypes and expectations attached to motherhood. Mothers are supposed to be nurturing, loving, and above all, protective of their children. Conflict is viewed as harmful to the child, and therefore the mother accused of child abuse who creates conflict by failing to "cooperate" harms her child a second time. This language of "cooperation" cloaks the substantial power differential that exists between the child welfare agency and the accused mother. The word "cooperation" implies a collaboration between equals in which each party contributes and makes compromises. In the child welfare context, however, "cooperation" is frequently just a code word for the parent doing whatever the social worker tells her to do. Where there is disagreement between the parties, it is the mother, not the social worker, who is labeled "uncooperative," and therefore blamed for creating conflict.

Another common element of this social work discourse is the claim: "we're all really on the same side; we just want what is best for the children." By creating an illusion of shared goals, this claim makes cooperation the obvious best solution. Two people working toward a shared goal clearly work more effectively if they cooperate. Conflict is again subverted and the power dynamic hidden. The fallacy, of course, is that this claim treats the "best interests of the child" as some objectively determinable absolute, when in fact it is an extremely malleable and subjective standard. In fact, the parent and the agency social worker may have two entirely different ideas of what is in the child's "best interests." In such a case, their goals are not shared and "cooperation" may be an impossibility.

These dynamics — operating either within the hallways of the courthouse or in families' homes or social workers' offices before court involvement has even been initiated — create pressure to cooperate rather than to assert rights, and to resolve cases through a process of compromise and agreement rather than through litigation. This is not simply to say that the parties tend to resolve these cases through negotiation rather than contested hearings. Where negotiation occurs against the backdrop of the formal procedures and rights afforded by the adversarial process, it reflects — at least roughly — the likely outcome of that process. Accordingly, such negotiation is a product of the formal rules and procedures that would apply if the case went to a hearing. For example, a litigant might gain concessions from her opponent by pointing out in negotiations that a particular witness's testimony would be barred as hearsay, and thus gain the protection against unreliable evidence afforded by the rules of evidence without actually invoking those rules in a contested hearing.

But the dynamics I describe above do more than simply push participants to resolve cases through negotiated settlement rather than trial. Instead, they serve to devalue and suppress rights talk, treating any effort to frame problems in an adversarial context as unmotherly and harmful to the child. Accordingly, they discourage participants from asserting, either in negotiations or contested hearings, the rights and procedural protections that are available to them. As such, these dynamics push the actual day-to-day functioning of these proceedings to an even lower level of formality than that proscribed by the due process analyses of courts and legislatures.

4. An Unresolved Problem: Permanency for Older Foster Children

Many children whose parents' rights have been terminated or whose permanency goal is adoption are never adopted. In FY 2016, about a fourth of the children in foster care, 117,794, were waiting for adoption; this proportion was unchanged from prior years. The rights of the parents of 65,274 of these children had been terminated. In the same year, 57,208 children were adopted from public foster care. On average, foster children waiting to be adopted had been in care for 31.2 months, and their average age was 7.7 years. About 45 percent of them were 7 years old or older. U.S. Dep't of Health & Hum. Serv., Children's Bureau, Administration for Children, Youth and Families, The AFCARS Report: Preliminary FY 2016 Estimates as of Oct. 20, 2017 at 1, 4, 5. In light of these statistics, a mother argued that it is unconstitutional to terminate parental rights if an imminent adoption placement for the child has not been identified. The appellate court rejected the claim, observing that the state statute requires the state to prove that "continuation of the parent and child relationship 'clearly diminishes the child's prospects for early integration into a stable and permanent home.'" Matter of Dependency of M.-A.F.-S., 421 P.3d 482, 496-497 (Wash. App. 2018), citing Rev. Code Wash. 13.34.180(1)(f) (2018).

Older children are especially at risk for neither returning home nor being adopted. A quarter of all children in foster care are 14 years old or older, and 44 percent of this group are 17 or older. Half of older teens who leave foster care age out instead of being reunited with their families of origin or placed with a new permanent family. Annie E. Casey Foundation, Youth Transition from Foster Care Findings & Stats in Fostering Youth Transitions: Using Data to Drive Policy and Practice Decisions (Nov. 13, 2018), https://www.aecf.org/resources/fostering-youth-transitions/.

Leslie Joan Harris, *Challenging the Overuse of Foster Care and Disrupting the Path to Delinquency and Prison*

in Justice for Kids: Keeping Kids Out of the Juvenile Justice System 62, 63-64, 65-66 (Nancy E. Dowd ed., 2011)

Almost 20 percent of the U.S. prison population under the age of 30 and 25 percent of those with prior convictions are former foster children. A recent large-scale study of foster children, conducted by the Chapin Hall research center at the University of Chicago, explores this connection in detail. The Chapin Hall researchers compared data about youth who had been in foster care homes in several states in the Midwest to a very large control data set.

More than half the young people in the Chapin Hall study who had been in foster care had been arrested, over one-third had spent a night in jail, and one-third had been convicted of a crime. For most offenses, the proportion of former foster care youth 17 to 18 years old committed offenses at twice or more the rate of the control group. The offenses considered were damaging property, stealing, going into a building to steal something, selling drugs, hurting someone badly enough to need medical care, using or threatening to use a weapon, participating in a group fight, pulling a knife or gun on someone, and shooting or stabbing someone. For 19-year-old young people, the Chapin Hall researchers found much smaller differences in offending, although youth who had been in foster care reported that they were significantly more likely to damage property, steal something worth more than $50, take part in a group fight, and pull a weapon on someone. More significantly, the 19-year-olds who had been in foster care faced much higher rates of arrest; 57 percent of the males reported that they had been arrested at least once, compared to 20 percent of the control group, and 36 percent reported having been arrested since age 18, compared to 2 percent of the control group. The percentage of female foster youth reporting that they had ever been arrested was not only higher than that of the female control group but also than the male control group. . . .

. . . By the time they turned 21 years old, nearly a quarter of the Chapin Hall foster care alumni had not obtained a high school diploma or a GED; they were more than twice as likely to lack either credential compared to similar young people in the general population. Only 30 percent had completed any college, compared to 53 percent of 21-year-olds in the general population. Just over half were currently working, compared with nearly two-thirds of 21-year-olds nationally. Doyle also found that children who were removed were less successful in the employment market; they worked 11 percent fewer quarters and earned $850 less than those who were left in their homes.

The findings from another large-scale study of former foster children from Oregon and Washington, conducted by the Casey Family Programs in Seattle, are similar. The proportion of Casey alumni who had a high school diploma or a GED was comparable to that of the general population (84.8 percent), but the alumni were much more likely to have only a GED—28.5 percent compared to 5 percent of the general population. While more than a quarter of the general population aged 20 to 34 had completed a bachelor's degree, only 1.8 percent of the foster care alumni had. (Pecora et al. 2005) Not counting people who were not in the workforce, only 80 percent of the Casey foster care alumni aged 20 to 34 were employed, compared to 95 percent in the general population. A third of the foster care alumni had household incomes at or below the poverty level, double the national average for people 18 to 34, and 22 percent experienced homelessness after leaving foster care.

Perhaps the most striking information from the Casey study was the very high incidence of mental health problems among former foster children. Within the 12 months before the study was conducted, more than half the foster care alumni (54 percent) had had clinical levels of at least one mental health problem, and 20 percent had had three or more such problems. In contrast, less than a quarter of the general population had mental health problems in the same time period. Twenty-five percent of the foster care alumni had been diagnosed with post-traumatic stress disorder within the previous 12 months, a rate twice as high as that of U.S. war veterans.

———————

Congress has responded to the problem of children "aging out" of foster care several times, beginning in 1986:

- The Independent Living Initiative of 1986, codified at 42 U.S.C. § 677, requires planning to help children 16 and older before they age out of foster care.
- The Foster Care Independence Act of 1999, Pub. L. No. 106-169, amended by Pub. L. No. 106-169, § 101(b) (1999), requires that services be available until a foster child is 21 (although states may opt for lower age limits) and that additional kinds of services be offered.
- The Fostering Connections Act of 2008, P.L. 110-351, extends adoption and subsidized guardianship subsidies to youths between 18 and 21. It also requires states to extend independent living services and education and

training vouchers to youths older than 16 who leave state custody to be adopted or live with a guardian.

- The Preventing Sex Trafficking and Strengthening Families Act of 2014, Pub.L. 113-183, increases funding for the foster care independence program and requires states to insure that children who are likely to remain in care until 18 have regular, ongoing opportunities to engage in age or developmentally-appropriate activities. The legislation also eliminates APPLA as a permanency goal for children under 16. State child welfare agencies must provide foster youth aging out of care at 18, or greater if the state elects, with a birth certificate, a Social Security card, health insurance information, medical records, and a driver's license or a state identification card. The state must consult with foster children age 14 and older in the development of or revision of their case plans. Case plans must include a document describing the rights of children to education, health, visitation, and court participation, and the right to stay safe and avoid exploitation. Children whose goal is APPLA are also entitled to a free annual credit report and help. The agency must:
  - Document intensive, ongoing, and unsuccessful efforts for family placement, including efforts to locate biological family members using search technologies such as social media,
  - Ensure youth are asked about their desired permanency outcomes,
  - Explain why APPLA is the best permanency plan for the youth and why reunification, adoption, guardianship, or placement with a fit relative are not in the youth's best interest,
  - Specify steps the agency is taking to ensure the reasonable and prudent parent standard (RPPS) is being followed and provide regular, ongoing opportunities for the youth to engage in age-appropriate and developmentally appropriate activities.

At each permanency hearing, the court must:
  - Determine whether the agency has documented the intensive, ongoing, unsuccessful efforts to achieve reunification, adoption, guardianship, or placement with a fit and willing relative
  - Ask youth about their desired permanency outcome
  - Make a judicial determination explaining why, as of the date of the hearing, APPLA is the best permanency plan and provide compelling reasons why reunification, adoption, legal guardianship, or placement with a fit and willing relative are not in the youth's best interest
  - Confirm that the agency is taking steps to ensure the RPPS is being exercised and the agency has documented that the youth has regular and ongoing opportunities to engage in age-appropriate and developmentally appropriate activities.

Child Welfare Information Gateway, Pathways to Permanency: Expanding on APPLA Provisions and Youth Engagement to Improve Permanency (1) (undated). For more information, *see* Bruce A. Boyer, Foster Care Reentry Laws: Mending the Safety Net for Emerging Adults in the Transition to Independence, 88 Temp. L. Rev. 837 (2016) (discussing the reluctance of many youth to remain in foster care and reentry laws in some states that allow former foster youth to come back into foster care if they exit and then decide they would like to have the continued support provided by the system); Randi Mandelbaum, Re-Examining and Re-Defining Permanency from a Youth's Perspective, 43 Cap. U. L. Rev. 259 (2015) (proposing redefining goals for older children, with a focus on stability and long-term connections rather than on "permanency" as that term is usually understood in the child welfare system).

Studies repeatedly show that foster youth maintain connections with, and often return to live with, their relatives once they are discharged from care, even if their parents' rights were legally terminated. *See, e.g.*, Mark Courtney et al., Midwest Evaluation of the Adult Functioning of Former Foster Youth: Outcomes at Age 21, Executive Summary 3 (2007). For this reason and because so many older foster children whose parental rights are terminated are never adopted, a number of states have enacted statutes that allow termination orders to be reversed in some circumstances. By 2017, statutes had been enacted in 18 states allowing parental rights to be reinstated. Meredith L. Schalick, The Sky Is Not Falling: Lessons and Recommendations from Ten Years of Reinstating Parental Rights, 51 Fam L. Q. 219, 220 (2017). All the statutes require that the child have been in post-termination state care for a period of time, ranging from one to three years, without being permanently placed. Some allow the child, the child welfare agency, or both to file the petition; most do not allow the parent to file. LaShanda Taylor, Backward Progress Toward Reinstating Parental Rights, 41 N.Y.U. Rev. L. & Soc. Change 507 (2017). *See also* Cynthia Godsoe, Parsing Parenthood 17 L. &. C. L. Rev. 113 (2013). In North Carolina, reinstatement of parental rights is authorized as a permanency goal for foster children. N.C. Gen Stat. § 7B-1114 (2018).

E.   CHILDREN'S ADVOCATES IN ABUSE AND NEGLECT CASES

Section 5106a of the Child Abuse Prevention and Treatment Act (CAPTA), requires states to provide children who are the subject of abuse or neglect proceedings with "a guardian ad litem, who has received training appropriate to the role, and who may be an attorney or a court appointed special advocate who has received training appropriate to that role (or both) . . . (I) to obtain first-hand, a clear understanding of the situation and needs of the child; and (II) to make recommendations to the court concerning the best interests of the child." 42 U.S.C. § 5106a(b)(2)(A)(xiii).

All but one of the states and the District of Columbia use trained volunteer lay advocates, typically called CASAs (court-appointed special advocates) to make recommendations to the court about the child's best interests. National CASA Program, CASA: A Guide to Program Development, http://www.casaforchildren. org/site/c.mtJSJ7MPIsE/b.5421109/k.C96D/CASA_A_Guide_to_Program_ Development__Introduction.htm. However, few if any jurisdictions have enough CASAs to appoint one for every dependent child in juvenile court. Most CASAs are middle-class white women over 30. Caliber Associates, Evaluation of CASA Representation, Final Report 2-3 (2004).

A national evaluation of CASA programs found that in 80 percent of the cases studied, the court accepted some or all of the CASA's recommendations. *Id.* at 47. In cases with CASAs, children and their parents received significantly more services than in cases without CASAs. However, the same percentage of the needs of children identified by child welfare caseworkers were met, regardless of whether the child had a CASA. Researchers suggest that CASAs may have successfully sought services for their children and families beyond those that the workers identified as necessary. *Id.* at 46. On the other hand, "[t]he well-being of children who had a CASA volunteer was largely no different from those who did not have a CASA volunteer, with the one exception that children who had a CASA volunteer reported fewer adult supports than children who did not have a CASA volunteer." *Id.* at 48. The researchers commented:

> . . . In this study children who were assigned a CASA volunteer were typically involved in more serious cases of maltreatment and faced more risky circumstances at the time the report was made that brought them into this sample. . . . Moreover, children who had a CASA volunteer were far more likely than children who did not have a CASA volunteer to already be in out of home care by the time of the first . . . interview, which took place only a few months after the initial report.
>
> Selection is a problem in this analysis because children in more difficult or more risky circumstances are more likely to experience negative outcomes, regardless of whether or not a CASA volunteer is involved. If an analysis does not "level the playing field" of those with CASA volunteers and those without at the outset of the case, the findings will reflect these vast differences in who gets a CASA volunteer and who does not, rather than the true impact of having a CASA volunteer. The current analysis includes a wide range of factors as statistical controls, attempting to level this playing field to the greatest extent possible. . . . However, even with a wide range of variables accounted for, it still appears that selection is playing a role in the findings of this study. Given this, we might have expected that children with a CASA volunteer may have looked significantly worse than children without a volunteer. For the most part, this was not the case.

Id. For criticism of the CASA model, *see* Amy Mulzer & Tara Urs, However Kindly Intentioned: Structural Racism and Volunteer CASA Programs, 20 CUNY L. Rev. 23, 24-25 (2016).

In most states, a lawyer is appointed for a child instead of or in addition to a CASA. A 2008 study found that children who have attorneys are much more likely to exit foster care to permanent placements than those who do not. Andrew Zinn & Jack Slowriver, Expediting Permanency: Legal Representation for Foster Children in Palm Beach County (Chapin Hall 2008).

The role of the child's lawyer is the subject of debate. Most fundamentally, the question is whether the lawyer's relationship to the child is client-directed or whether the lawyer advocates for the child's best interests as the lawyer determines them. Most commentators and professional organizations argue that lawyers' relationships to child clients should be consistent with the relationships of attorneys and adult, competent clients, at least where the children are competent. A number of professional organizations have issued statements regarding the role of lawyers appointed for children in child protection proceedings, all rejecting the best interests role. The American Bar Association's Standards of Practice for Lawyers

Representing a Child in Abuse and Neglect Cases (1996) (ABA Standards)[10] "express a clear preference for the appointment" of a lawyer who takes the role of the "child's attorney," which is defined as "a lawyer who provides legal services for a child and who owes the same duties of undivided loyalty, confidentiality, and competent representation to the child as [are] due an adult client." *Id.* §§ A-1, A-2. The National Association of Counsel for Children has also endorsed the approach of the ABA Standards.[11]

If the child is unable to or does not want to express a preference, the ABA Standards provide that the attorney is to advocate for the child's legal interests, ABA Standards § B-4(1) and (2). Addressing "one of the most difficult ethical issues of lawyers representing children," the Standards say that if the lawyer believes that the child's preference would be "seriously injurious to the child, the lawyer may request appointment of a separate guardian ad litem and continue to represent the child's expressed preference, unless the child's position is prohibited by law or without any factual foundation." ABA Standards § B-4(3).

Where a lawyer is required to represent the "best interests" of the child, the ABA Standards emphasize that he or she is functioning in a nontraditional role and should not rely on his or her "personal values, philosophies, or experiences." Instead, "determination of the child's interests should be based on objective criteria addressing the child's specific needs and preferences, the goal of expeditious resolution of the case so the child can remain or return home or be placed in a safe, nurturing, and permanent environment, and the use of the least restrictive/detrimental alternatives available." *Id.* § B-5.

The Uniform Representation of Children in Abuse and Neglect and Custody Proceedings Act,[12] approved by the National Conference of Commissioners on Uniform State Laws, recommends the creation of two categories of children's attorneys, the child's attorney and the best interests attorney. The prefatory note to the Act explains:

> The child's attorney is in a traditional attorney-client relationship with the child and is therefore bound by ordinary ethical obligations governing that relationship. Under the Act, the child's attorney is a client-directed representative and should function within that role rather than advocating for what the lawyer believes to be in the child's best interests. The Act authorizes, however, a limited exercise of substituted judgment by the child's attorney in taking positions in the proceeding. Under Section 12, when the child is incapable of directing or refuses to direct representation as to a particular issue, the child's attorney may take a position that is in the child's best interests so long as the position is not in conflict with the child's expressed objectives. The child's attorney may also request appointment of a court-appointed advisor or a best interests attorney. In contrast, if a child's expressed goals would put the child at risk of substantial harm and the child persists in that position despite the attorney's advice and counsel, the attorney *must* request a court-appointed advisor or

---

10. The ABA Standards are available online from the Web site of the ABA Center on Children and the Law at http://www.abanet.org/child/childrep.html.

11. The NACC revised version of the standards is available at https://www.naccchildlaw.org/page/StandardsOfPractice.

12. The act is available online at http://www.uniformlaws.org/shared/docs/representation%20of%20children/urcancpa_final_07.pdf.

best interests attorney for the child or withdraw from representation and request the appointment of a best interests attorney. . . .

The best interests attorney, in contrast, is a legal representative of the child but is not bound by the child's expressed wishes in determining what to advocate. Instead, the best interests attorney has the substantive responsibility of advocating for the child's best interests based on an objective assessment of the available evidence and according to applicable legal principles. Often the best interests attorney's position and the child's stated position will coincide, particularly in light of the attorney's duty to take the child's expressed wishes into account in determining what to advocate and to present the child's wishes to the court if the child so desires. Moreover, the availability of a best interests model of representation is particularly important for those children who are unable or unwilling to direct counsel.

In presiding over abuse, neglect, and custody cases, judges must resolve the proceedings in the best interests of the child, but the parties' presentations in an adversarial setting may not be adequate to provide the court with necessary information. Because of the potential impact of these proceedings on the lives of children, many courts want the participation of a best interests lawyer to ensure that they receive a comprehensive presentation of evidence that includes but is not limited to the child's stated objectives. . . .

Section 13 of the Act directs the best interests attorney to advocate for a resolution of the proceeding that is consistent with the child's best interests "according to criteria established by law." In other words, the best interests attorney is not free to rely on subjective bias but should adhere to recognized legal standards, such as those found in statutes, case law, and procedural rules, and should formulate a position that reflects the child's unique circumstances. Unlike the child's attorney, the best interests attorney is not bound by the client's expressed objectives, but neither should the best interests attorney disregard the child's preferences. Instead, the best interests attorney has an explicit duty to take into account the child's objectives and the reasoning underlying those objectives, in light of the child's developmental level, in determining what to advocate.

Statutes or court rules in a number of states provide that the attorney appointed for the child is supposed to represent both the child's expressed wishes and the lawyer's understanding of the child's best interests.

DEPARTMENT OF HEALTH AND HUMAN SERVICES, CHILDREN'S BUREAU, ADOPTION 2002: THE PRESIDENT'S INITIATIVE ON ADOPTION AND FOSTER CARE GUIDELINES FOR PUBLIC POLICY AND STATE LEGISLATION GOVERNING PERMANENCE FOR CHILDREN (DONALD N. DUQUETTE & MARK HARDIN, PRINCIPAL AUTHORS)

available at http://www.archive.org/details/guidelinesforpub00duqu

The vast majority of legal scholars who have addressed this issue recommend that a lawyer should take direction from her or his child client (only) if the child is determined to have developed the cognitive capacity to engage in reasoned decision-making. These scholars disagree, however, about how that capacity should be assessed. Some propose a bright-line age rule and some propose a case-by-case assessment by the lawyer or by the appointing judge. Supporters of this approach focus on the following arguments. The adversary system produces its best results when all positions are argued forcefully before the court. Lawyers are ill-trained to make best interest decisions and well-trained to serve as zealous advocates for their clients' positions. Children's judgments are not consistently worse than those of adults, particularly when all options presented are fraught with risks, and, children benefit from being given an opportunity to be heard and taken seriously in the courts.

Those who favor adopting a best interest approach for all but the oldest children seek to avoid imposing the adult-like responsibility of decision-making on children, and to ensure that the court has the benefit of all relevant information before making its decisions. The burden of having to take a position and instruct the attorney to influence judicial decision-making may be inappropriately placed on the child victim. This approach places the child, who simply by virtue of being in a court proceeding is vulnerable, in a position which potentially elevates distress due to feelings of guilt, fear, divided loyalty, etc. There is real danger of re-victimization of which we must be aware and cautious. The impact on self-esteem, particularly in younger children, can be damaging. From a developmental perspective, children's cognitive perception of the world is quite egocentric until age eight or so. The child sees self as the center and cause of all that happens, which—when traumatic events such as severe sexual and physical abuse are occurring, being removed from one's home, etc.—is terrifying. Telling the child to take on even more responsibility and "direct" his or her adult attorney may be overwhelming and traumatic for the child and exacerbate feelings of blame.

Many would argue that children are under tremendous pressure to misidentify and/or misarticulate their own interests because of pressure from their families, the court process, and the circumstances leading to the court process. Haralambie notes that, "Children's wishes may be based on threats, bribes, and other questionable bases. . . ." Buss interprets Perry as "suggesting that children's communications with their lawyers are hampered by, among other things, their difficulty in dealing with the emotional and social pressure connected with the proceeding, their feelings of guilt, their difficulty understanding and framing responses to lawyer's questions, and their lack of understanding of court proceedings." Melton notes that, "The necessity of making choices can be anxiety provoking for children."

Many would argue that the lawyer does not have to be the expert in all disciplines in order to determine the best interests of the child. Rather we should strongly encourage multidisciplinary training and collaboration, and advocate for legal utilization of the expertise of other professionals in providing assessments, determining competence, and making recommendations to the court. The bottom line is that the child should be heard and considered, but should also feel safe and protected by a caring, adult attorney who will represent what is best for the child. In this situation, the child will not feel burdened by additional responsibilities that are beyond his or her emotional capacity.

To some extent, these differences in approach, as stark as they may appear when presented side by side, are more apparent than real. Under either standard, the child's wishes are to be elicited and taken seriously, and under either standard the lawyer is expected to play a counseling role—advising the client of the risks and benefits of various options and, particularly, the likely consequences of the client's expressed choices. This discussion and counseling will, in many cases, produce agreement between client and lawyer about what they perceive to be in the client's best interests.

In some fraction of cases, however, the lawyer and the child client will not agree on what the child's interests are. In those cases, the role the lawyer assumes will have a significant effect on how the lawyer represents her or his client. Both because such cases will arise, and because lawyers need to be able to explain their role, from the outset of representation in a manner that can be understood and relied upon by their clients, the development and articulation of standards of representation is critical.

The deficiencies in legal representation in child welfare cases are certainly not universal; some jurisdictions generally achieve high quality attorney performance in these cases. In many courts, however, legal counsel for children, parents, and agencies does not achieve a minimal threshold of performance, much less the higher standard of legal representation that would be optimal. Yet, many practitioners, advocates, and others are concerned about the poor legal representation in child welfare cases nationally. In a survey by the National Council of Juvenile and Family Court Judges, the vast majority of court improvement specialists (84 percent) identified legal representation as a problematic aspect of case processing in child abuse and neglect cases. Of 25 Court Improvement Project self-assessments, most identified legal representation or the need for improved legal training as an item for reform. "Lack of experience, skills, training, and adequate compensation were cited as issues for parents' attorneys and children's representatives. Frequent rotation and high caseloads were problematic for many prosecutors and agency attorneys. Reports noted a lack of statutory or court rule imposing minimum requirements and qualifications for court-appointed attorneys."

Poor quality legal representation results from a variety of factors ranging from the pressure of high caseloads to poor customs and low expectations of representation in the jurisdiction. The old reputation of juvenile and family courts as a lesser "kiddie court" persists in some places, despite the increased sophistication and complexity of both the law and the underlying interdisciplinary perspective required to handle these cases effectively. Child welfare is a unique and highly specialized area of practice, yet many advocates have not received training in handling such cases.

Criminal Prosecution of Child Abuse and Neglect

9

Many kinds of child abuse and neglect come within the definition of conduct prohibited by criminal statutes of general applicability, such as those punishing assaults, homicides, and sexual assaults. In addition, during the 1980s and 1990s, all states enacted statutes that expanded the scope of parents' criminal liability for child abuse and neglect. The first section in this chapter considers issues that arise in determining how these substantive statutes apply when parents allegedly have harmed their children. The second section looks at problems that arise when criminal prosecution occurs simultaneously with child welfare proceedings in juvenile court. The final section examines evidentiary problems that may arise in these cases.

A. WHEN TO PUNISH AND WHY?

As we have seen, the purpose of the child welfare system is to protect children from being harmed by their own families. While parents who are drawn into the system may experience juvenile court intervention as negative, even painful, the ultimate purpose of that intervention is not to punish or harm the parents. In comparison, the purpose of criminal prosecution is to punish defendants who are convicted of crimes. Punishment, in turn, is usually justified on the theory that punishing an offender prevents future crimes. In particular, punishment may deter the offender or others from future lawbreaking, it may authorize the incarceration of a very dangerous offender, or it may enable the state to force the offender to undergo rehabilitative treatment. Punishment may also be justified on the basis that the offender simply deserves punishment; this idea may also limit the imposition of punishment. For example, an offender who is criminally insane is not punished because he or she is not morally culpable and so cannot justly be punished. (Of course, some also argue that such a person cannot be deterred by punishment either.)

As the following excerpts suggest, though, determining when parents and other adults who harm their children should be punished can be difficult because of complex questions about the adults' culpability, as well as concerns that in some situations prosecuting the adults may conflict with the desire to protect the children, at least in some respects.

U.S. ATTORNEY GENERAL'S TASK FORCE ON FAMILY VIOLENCE, FINAL REPORT

4-5 (1984)

. . . *The legal response to family violence must be guided primarily by the nature of the abusive act, not the relationship between the victim and the abuser:* The Task Force recommends that the legal system treat assaults within the family as seriously as it would treat the same assault if it occurred between strangers. . . . Law enforcement officers do not arrest two strangers who have shoved each other; neither ought they ordinarily arrest two family members engaged in similar behavior. But when an officer enters a home and finds a mother or child who is the victim of an assault, the officer is dealing with a crime — a crime with its own distinctive characteristics, but first and foremost a crime. When a prosecutor considers a criminal complaint arising out of an arrest for child, spouse or elder abuse, incest, or molestation, the first consideration is the nature of the violation of law that has occurred. When an offender has been convicted, the judge, as in all cases, may consider all sorts of extenuating circumstances in reaching a sentence. A judge should prescribe a sentence that takes the special nature of the victim's needs into account. But the fact that the offender is related to the victim may not in and of itself be a reason for being lenient.

Simple justice is the major justification for taking a harder stand toward family violence. The American legal system should not countenance one person doing physical harm to another person. But there is also a practical justification in terms of preventing family violence in the future, derived from two special characteristics of family violence.

One of the main reasons that the deterrent effects of punishment are diminished is the criminal's justified doubt that he will be caught or that the evidence will be strong enough to convict; in the case of family violence, the offender cannot hide his identity. Because family violence is the only crime in which the victim knows the identity of the offender, the deterrent effects of legal sanctions against the offender are potentially greater than for any other crime. If family violence were always reported and if the legal system always acted on the basis of its knowledge, the deterrent effects of swift and certain legal penalties would be great.

Unfortunately, this potentially important preventive effect is thwarted at present by the second key characteristic of family violence: A large proportion of family violence is committed by people who do not see their acts as crimes against victims who do not know they are victims. The first, indispensable step in preventing family violence is to ensure that abusers and victims alike recognize that a crime is involved and that, when appropriate, the legal system will intervene on the victim's behalf. Many segments of the population are unaware that beating one's wife or children is a crime. It is essential that every response of the legal system convey this message: child abuse, spouse abuse, and abuse of the elderly, incest and child molestation are not matters of personal belief on how to deal with children or keep order in the house. They are crimes. They are prohibited.

JOHN E.B. MYERS, *THE LEGAL RESPONSE TO CHILD ABUSE: IN THE BEST INTEREST OF CHILDREN*

24 J. Fam. L. 149, 178-184, 245-246 (1985)

Criminal prosecution is undoubtedly warranted in many cases. Egregious and sadistic abuse is appropriately dealt with through the criminal justice system, and the goals of criminal law are furthered by such prosecution. Furthermore, when abuse comes to official attention, the threat of prosecution may compel some individuals, who would otherwise deny abuse, to agree to therapy. Finally, incarceration may be the only method of keeping some abusers away from children.

While the positive aspects of the legal response to abuse are important, the negative consequences of increased reliance on prosecution and the adversarial process often outweigh the benefits. . . .

. . . The threat of legal action attaches the moment abuse comes to official attention and makes it very unlikely that the problem will ever surface voluntarily. There are tremendous incentives to hide the truth and none to reveal it. The legal and social consequences of revelation are so devastating that adults involved in abuse have no alternative but to hide the problem in the darkest corners of secrecy. To secure the truth, it must be wrenched out through reporting laws. Families or individuals involved in abuse are deterred from seeking therapy or guidance because the professionals to whom they would turn are under a duty to report, and once a report is made, the full force of the law swings into operation.

The blaming, punitive and accusatory approach of the criminal justice system can be destructive. Once in the system, families may be damaged or destroyed by incarceration, loss of employment and reputation, divorce, alienation and other negative influences. If it were accurate to categorize all adults who abuse children as criminals, invoking the legal system would be logical. However, if the complexity of abuse is recognized it becomes apparent that the legal response is appropriate only part of the time. In some cases the harm caused by adversarial intervention outweighs any benefit.

Involvement in the legal system is hard on children. The trauma of abuse may be compounded by the trauma of the criminal justice system. Several courts and commentators have described the effect of the legal system on abused children as a "second victimization." The child is subjected to multiple interviews in which the details of the abuse must be described repeatedly. The delay, anxiety, and fear associated with litigation and cross-examination are repeated at the grand jury, pretrial and trial stages. If juvenile court proceedings are underway, the child goes through a similar, if less adversarial gauntlet in that court. There is the embarrassment of appearing in court where the details of an excruciatingly private event or series of events must be recounted in public and, finally, there is the requirement that the child face the defendant.

. . . When a prosecutor is sensitive to the special needs of children and is willing to take the time necessary to assist the child through the process, trauma can be reduced and in some cases eliminated. In the majority of cases, however, involvement in the legal system is an unpleasant and traumatic experience which does not assist the healing process. . . .

[The accused has a] tremendous incentive to deny the alleged abuse, pin the blame elsewhere, or paint the child a liar. The defendant has little reason to cooperate with the state in its effort to protect society and the child unless cooperation lessens the threat of prosecution or punishment. On the contrary, the defendant is motivated to deny wrongdoing and seek to remain at home with the victim. The result is that the adversary system is unlikely to generate voluntary cooperation focused on the best interest of the child. The child's interests are more likely to be forgotten in the heat of battle between the defendant and the state.

Children are traumatized by abuse, and there is no question of the state's police and *parens patriae* authority to protect them. Unfortunately, when the response to child abuse is focused primarily on the criminal justice system and the prosecutive merit of individual cases, the interests of the child take second place. In criminal litigation, the parties are the state and the defendant, and while the victim is not forgotten, protecting the child's interests is not the primary concern of the prosecutor. So too, the accused concentrates her resources on defending against the alleged abuse. The child becomes an opposing witness whose testimony and credibility must be controverted and undermined. Despite praiseworthy efforts to reduce the trauma of litigation, the very nature of criminal prosecution renders such a goal largely unattainable, and the process remains difficult for children, causing them anxiety, fear, guilt, and embarrassment. . . .

The dynamics of intrafamily abuse are complex. Intervention may have far-reaching psychological effects on family members, and deciding how to proceed raises important nonlegal as well as legal questions. Is the family salvageable? Is the alleged perpetrator likely to benefit from treatment? Will involvement in judicial proceedings exacerbate psychological trauma already inflicted on the victim? Under the legal system as presently constituted, the prosecutor is the professional charged with ultimate decisionmaking responsibility on both the legal and nonlegal implications of the state's response. While the conscientious prosecutor considers the psychological implications of various alternatives, nothing in the lawyer's training or expertise qualifies him to make psychological assessments or judgments. . . . The prosecutorial monopoly on decisionmaking is appropriate with respect to most criminal behavior. In the context of child abuse, however, the psychological implications of the various alternatives take on extraordinary significance. It is here that the expertise of the mental health professional is particularly important. The psychiatrist, psychologist, and social workers can provide invaluable input on the non-legal factors that should form an important part of the decision in every case. Yet, as greater emphasis is placed on criminal prosecution and punishment of the child abuser, the likelihood that nonlawyers will have a meaningful impact on decisionmaking decreases. . . .

Though the legal issue in the next case is presented as whether certain evidence should be admitted, the real questions are whether the mother's blameworthiness for the death of her child depends on the facts underlying the evidence, and, if so, whether the law should take account of these facts in determining whether to punish her.

STATE V. RICHTER

424 P.3d 798 (Ariz. 2018)

Chief Justice BALES, opinion of the Court: . . . Early one morning in November 2013, two sisters, ages twelve and thirteen, escaped out the window of their bedroom and fled to their neighbors' house, shouting that their stepfather had broken down their bedroom door and threatened them with a knife. The neighbors, who did not know the two girls lived in the neighborhood, let them in and called 911. The neighbors described the girls as disheveled, with matted hair and body odor.

Police went to the girls' house, where they found the parents, Sophia and Fernando Richter. Inside the house, police found Sophia's seventeen-year-old daughter locked inside a separate bedroom. They confirmed that the younger sisters' bedroom door was kicked in and the doorknob damaged. During their search, they found video cameras and covered air-conditioning vents in the girls' rooms, an internal alarm system, a knife near the master bedroom, and a five-gallon bucket containing pasta mixed with meat and food scraps in the refrigerator.

The three girls described horrible living conditions. They were always confined to their rooms and were monitored by video camera. They had to ask permission to use the bathroom and occasionally were not let out in time. They ate their meals, which mostly consisted of the pasta mix, in their rooms. They had piles of soiled clothing and bedding in their closets. They rarely brushed their teeth or bathed, and they described being spanked and hit with various objects. Recorded music was continually played in their rooms to mask any noise they made. After being removed from school years earlier, they never returned. The younger sisters had not seen their older sister in over a year despite living in the same house.

A grand jury indicted Sophia and Fernando on separate counts of kidnapping and child abuse for each of the three girls (six counts total) alleged to have occurred between September 1, 2013, and November 26, 2013, the dates they lived in Pima County. Fernando was also charged with two counts of aggravated assault for his attacks on the younger sisters.

Before trial, Sophia gave notice that she intended to raise a duress defense. She and Fernando filed separate motions to sever their trials. The State opposed the motions and characterized Sophia's proposed duress defense and supporting expert testimony from psychologist Dr. Perrin as "diminished capacity" evidence that is prohibited by *Mott*, 931 P.2d at 1050–51. Additionally, the State argued that Sophia's proposed evidence failed to demonstrate a threat of immediate physical force as required by A.R.S. § 13-412(A). Agreeing with the State, the trial court ruled that Dr. Perrin's proposed testimony "was essentially that Sophia was a battered woman" and was prohibited by *Mott*. The court also found that Sophia failed to offer evidence in support of a duress defense and denied the request to sever her trial.

During trial, the State moved in limine to preclude Sophia from presenting evidence that Fernando physically or emotionally abused her. . . . The court granted the State's motion and again precluded the duress defense, finding no immediacy of threat when the dates for the alleged offenses spanned eighty-six days from September through November 2013. Sophia objected to the court's ruling and, near the close of trial, again sought to testify about Fernando's abuse, making an offer of proof through counsel's avowal of proposed testimony and photographs showing numerous scars from knife wounds inflicted by Fernando. The trial court found her proffer insufficient and again precluded her from testifying about Fernando's abuse and introducing the photographs.

Fernando and Sophia were ultimately convicted as charged. Fernando's convictions and sentences were affirmed on appeal. . . .

Sophia appealed, arguing that the trial court erred by restricting her trial testimony, precluding her duress defense, and preventing her expert from testifying. The court of appeals agreed, determining that the proposed testimony of Sophia and her expert was "admissible to show that she committed the charged offenses under duress." Furthermore, the court concluded that "to the extent that Perrin's proposed testimony addressed *mens rea*, . . . it would be properly characterized as 'observation evidence,' which is not precluded by *Mott*." The court explained that such evidence is admissible under *Clark*, 548 U.S. at 770-71. Finally, the court concluded that Sophia and Perrin's proposed testimony provided a legal basis for the duress defense.

We granted review . . . .

At trial, Sophia sought to introduce photographic and testimonial evidence regarding specific abusive events and the pattern of abuse that she experienced. She would have used such evidence to establish that she was "compelled to engage in the proscribed conduct by the threat or use of immediate physical force against" her or her children. However, the trial court precluded her from introducing the evidence, concluding it constituted prohibited diminished capacity evidence under *Mott*.

In *Mott*, a defendant sought to introduce "expert psychological testimony that as a battered woman, she was unable to form the requisite mental state necessary for the commission of the charged offenses." This Court barred the expert testimony, holding that "Arizona does not allow evidence of a defendant's mental disorder short of insanity either as an affirmative defense or to negate the *mens rea* element of a crime." . . .

But Sophia did not seek to negate the *mens rea* of the charged crimes. Instead, she sought to argue that her intentional illegal conduct was justified because she was compelled to abuse her children by the threat or use of immediate physical force against her or her children. The Arizona Legislature has codified duress as a justification defense in § 13-412(A):

> Conduct which would otherwise constitute an offense is justified if a reasonable person would believe that he was compelled to engage in the proscribed conduct by the threat or use of immediate physical force against his person or the person of another which resulted or could result in serious physical injury which a reasonable person in the situation would not have resisted. . . .

Because Sophia sought to assert a justification defense, the evidence of duress she would have introduced in support of that defense did not constitute "diminished capacity" evidence and was not prohibited by *Mott*. The trial court therefore erred by ruling that *Mott* precluded Sophia from presenting evidence in support of her duress defense to the jury.

IV.

. . . [T]he State urges us to affirm the trial court's determination that Sophia's proffered evidence failed to establish the requisite immediacy under § 13-412(A), which provides that illegal conduct committed under duress is justified only when the harm threatened is immediate. We have previously characterized immediate threatened harm as "present, imminent, and impending."

Although we have had few opportunities to consider what constitutes "present, imminent, and impending," other courts have found that an ongoing threat can satisfy that description for purposes of a duress defense. . . .

These cases persuade us that an ongoing threat of harm can be sufficiently immediate and present for purposes of a duress defense even when the threat precedes the illegal conduct by several days, the coercing party is physically removed from the defendant, or the threat is initiated and then repeatedly renewed over several years

To be sure, the "present, imminent, and impending" standard includes only conduct that would compel a "reasonable person in the situation," § 13-412(A), to act in duress. Therefore, a threat may not be vague or undetailed, and generalized fear does not suffice. . . .

Through counsel, Sophia proffered that "she was under immediate threat of physical harm to herself and/or to her children," and that this threat was ongoing. She stated that even when she went grocery shopping, she was accompanied by Fernando's mother and "[Sophia's] phone was required to be on at all times in order that he could hear what was going on." She further proffered that "she believed that if she resisted, that she would either be seriously harmed or killed, or that her children would as well." She submitted evidence of wounds and blood on her body that police documented on the day of her arrest. She also would have introduced evidence that, when she stood up to Fernando on a family trip, he threw her out of the hotel room by her hair. (Although the court of appeals considered Dr. Perrin's report as part of Sophia's proffer of duress evidence, we decline to do so. Sophia did not refer to Dr. Perrin's report or his potential testimony during her proffer of duress at trial and only did so during her earlier motion to sever.)

"[A] defendant is entitled to an instruction on any theory of the case reasonably supported by the evidence." In the context of justification, we have articulated a low threshold for evidentiary sufficiency: a justification instruction is warranted "if the record contains the 'slightest evidence'" of justification. Here, Sophia supported her claim that she and her children were under the threat of immediate physical harm with proffered evidence of specific injuries and abuse. In so doing, she provided the slightest evidence of duress, and her proffer was therefore sufficient to support a duress defense. Thus, the trial court erred when it precluded her from raising a duress defense and from introducing evidence in support of that defense. . . .

The State argues that admitting evidence of Fernando's abusive acts would transform the duress defense from an objective standard to a subjective standard. Sophia responds that evidence of abuse is relevant to informing the inquiry of whether a reasonable person in her situation would have likewise felt compelled to act under duress. *See* A.R.S. § 13-412(A). Amicus agrees, positing that an objective standard still requires consideration of the defendant's circumstances when determining the reasonableness of his or her conduct.

Justification defenses in Arizona "use objective standards that depend on the beliefs of a 'reasonable person' in the defendant's circumstances rather than the defendant's subjective beliefs." As an example, "Arizona courts have long held that a murder defendant who defends on the basis of justification should be permitted to introduce evidence of specific acts of violence by the deceased if the defendant either observed the acts himself or was informed of the acts before the homicide." This evidence demonstrates the defendant's knowledge of the victim's violent tendencies and shows that the defendant was "justifiably apprehensive" of the victim.

This same logic applies to establishing a duress defense. Knowledge of the circumstances under which the defendant committed the alleged crimes is essential to the jury's determination of whether the defendant's actions were reasonable. . . .

To be sure, the introduction of evidence of past incidents of abuse should not transform the duress defense into a subjective inquiry of whether a specific defendant was unusually susceptible to succumbing to otherwise implausible threats. Therefore, the proper inquiry for the jury here is whether a reasonable person subjected to the same threats and pattern of abuse would have believed he or she was compelled to engage in the same illegal conduct.

Noting that A.R.S. § 13-415 provides for the admission of evidence of past acts of domestic abuse for other justification defenses (self-defense, defense of a third party, defense of property), but not for duress, the State argues that the legislature intended to preclude such evidence from duress cases. The State's argument is unpersuasive. Section 13-415 concerns only defenses in which the perpetrator of domestic violence is the crime victim. It is therefore unsurprising that § 13-415 does not refer to the duress defense, which applies only when third parties are the victims. Consequently, we decline to construe this statute's codification of the admissibility of domestic violence evidence for self-defense as implicitly barring the admission of such evidence for duress.

V.

Just as the trial court precluded Sophia from presenting her own testimony regarding Fernando's abuse, it also determined that testimony from her expert, Dr. Perrin, would be inadmissible under *Mott* as so-called "psychological evidence." The court of appeals concluded, however, that "to the extent that Perrin's proposed testimony addressed *mens rea*, . . . it would be properly characterized as 'observation evidence.'"

In *Clark*, the United States Supreme Court concluded that *Mott* does not prohibit the introduction of "observation evidence" "to rebut the prosecution's evidence of *mens rea*." The Court framed its definition of observation evidence in the context of the defendant's alleged crime of homicide of a police officer:

> [T]here is "observation evidence" in the everyday sense, testimony from those who observed what [the defendant] did and heard what he said; this category would also include testimony that an expert witness might give about [the defendant's] tendency to think in a certain way and his behavioral characteristics. This evidence may support a professional diagnosis of mental disease and in any event is the kind of evidence that can be relevant to show what in fact was on [the defendant's] mind when he fired the gun.

The Court gave several examples of observation evidence in *Clark*: "[the defendant's] behavior at home and with friends, his expressions of belief around the time of the killing that 'aliens' were inhabiting the bodies of local people . . ., [and] his driving around the neighborhood before the police arrived." The Court clarified that "observation evidence can be presented by either lay or expert witnesses," explaining that "an expert witness might offer . . . descriptions of a defendant's tendency to think in a certain way or his behavioral characteristics." The Court admitted, however, that its broad definitions of the evidentiary categories discussed in *Mott* did not delineate the margins of those categories. Instead, it left that task for Arizona courts.

This Court has permitted a defendant to introduce observation "evidence about his [or her] behavioral tendencies to show that he [or she] possessed a character trait of acting reflexively in response to stress."

The record does not clearly identify what testimony Sophia would have elicited from Dr. Perrin. He prepared an abbreviated initial report of his psychological examinations of Sophia for the limited purpose of Sophia's motion to sever. The report detailed a horrific pattern of physical and psychological abuse that was, in a word, devastating. However, because the trial judge ruled before trial that this expert testimony was precluded by *Mott*, Sophia failed to further develop at trial what her expert would have testified to.

Based on the limited record before us, Dr. Perrin's report does not match the reflexive or impulsive observation evidence that this Court concluded was admissible [in prior cases]. Although observation evidence is broader than testimony about impulsivity, Dr. Perrin's testimony, as proffered, would not have been admissible as "observation evidence." We add that, even if his expert testimony were admissible, Dr. Perrin could not present hearsay testimony on direct examination about what Sophia told him months after being charged. That is, Dr. Perrin should not, under the guise of observation evidence, be permitted to serve as a mere conduit for otherwise inadmissible testimony.

We note that [prior cases] all uphold the admissibility of observation evidence to rebut *mens rea*, which is necessarily a subjective element. Because duress requires an objective inquiry, and because evidence of "a defendant's tendency to think in a certain way or his [or her] behavioral characteristics" is inherently subjective, we conclude that observation evidence is likely not admissible to support a duress defense. If Dr. Perrin's testimony is again proffered, we leave it to the trial court on remand to decide, consistent with this opinion, whether he can offer any admissible evidence. . . .

[Reversed and remanded.]

[The dissenting opinion of Justice Lopez is omitted.]

NOTES AND QUESTIONS

1. In a number of criminal prosecutions, mothers have successfully offered evidence that they had been battered and that they had battered spouse syndrome to support their claims that they did not intend to harm their child (where the *mens*

rea of the alleged crime was purpose or knowledge) or that they did not perceive the risk or the severity of the risk of injury to their children (where the *mens rea* of the alleged crime was recklessness or negligence). *See, e.g.,* Pickle v. State, 635 S.E.2d 197 (Ga. App. 2006); Barrett v. State, 675 N.E.2d 1112 (Ind. App. 1996). *See also* Kathy Luttrell Garcia, Battered Women and Battered Children: Admissibility of Evidence of Battering and Its Effects to Determine the *Mens Rea* of a Battered Woman Facing Criminal Charges for Failing to Protect a Child from Abuse, 24 J. Juv. L. 101 (2003-2004).

The Arizona Supreme Court rejected this use of evidence in State v. Mott, 931 P.2d 1046 (Ariz. 1997), holding that evidence of a "mental disorder" short of legal insanity is not admissible to disprove *mens rea* because the legislature had not authorized this use of evidence. In Clark v. Arizona, 548 U.S. 735 (2006), the Supreme Court ruled that the *Mott* rule does not violate due process. It affirmed that due process requires that defendants be able to offer evidence to disprove elements of an offense, but because states vary so much in how they structure the relationship between mental disorders and criminal responsibility, due process does not require that states treat evidence of mental disorders as negating *mens rea*. In contrast, the Court observed that Arizona law does not exclude "everyday observation evidence" of what a defendant did or said, which may support the professional diagnoses of disease and can be relevant to show what was on the defendant's mind at the time of the alleged offense. Is expert testimony about battered spouse syndrome and about whether a woman displays the symptoms of that syndrome evidence of a mental disorder that is not admissible to disprove *mens rea* under *Mott*, or is it observational evidence about what the defendant did or said that is relevant to whether she had *mens rea*?

2. Sophia Richter did not offer the expert testimony about battered spouse syndrome to show that she lacked *mens rea* but rather to support her affirmative defense of duress or coercion. The court expresses doubt that the evidence should be admitted for this purpose on remand. Why?

3. What purpose or purposes are served by criminally prosecuting a mother in Sophia Richter's situation? As we saw in Chapter 7, questions about the relevance of battered women's syndrome can arise in a child protective proceeding as well as in a criminal prosecution. In what ways is the analysis in these two kinds of cases similar? Why and how does it differ?

4. Professor Jennifer Collins studied criminal charging decisions in cases in which children died from overheating when they were left for extended periods in automobiles. She found that parents were prosecuted for involuntary homicide in more than half the cases, and nonrelatives were prosecuted more than 88 percent of the time. Parents in blue collar jobs or who were unemployed were four times more likely to be prosecuted than white collar parents. Jennifer M. Collins, Crime and Parenthood: The Uneasy Case for Prosecuting Negligent Parents, 100 Nw. U. L. Rev. 807, 809 (2006). One of the most common arguments against prosecuting parents, she found, is that they have already "suffered enough." What does this argument assume? If you favored prosecuting parents, how would you respond?

PROBLEMS

1. Should a criminal prosecution be brought against parents who leave young children alone in a locked car at night while the parents, who are too poor to pay a babysitter, work?

2. Should a custodial parent who allows a child to ride in a car with a visibly intoxicated adult be convicted of homicide when the driver has a fatal automobile accident?

B. COORDINATING CRIMINAL AND JUVENILE COURT PROCEEDINGS

Marcia Sprague & Mark Hardin, Coordination of Juvenile and Criminal Court Child Abuse and Neglect Proceedings

35 U. Louisville J. Fam. L. 239, 245-250 (1997)

There are several basic reasons why related criminal and juvenile child maltreatment [sic] must be coordinated: (1) ensuring complete information is available to both courts; (2) preventing conflicting or inconsistent court orders; (3) avoiding needless trauma to child victims; and (4) harmonizing the goals of state intervention. In short, case coordination avoids harmful, illogical, and wasteful inconsistencies in strategies and approach. . . .

. . . [L]ack of [communication between the juvenile and criminal systems] can lead to ill-informed or even inconsistent court orders. For example, a criminal court might order a parent to have no contact with a child while the juvenile court orders the same parent to attend therapy and visit with the child. Both courts may be unaware of the inconsistency.

Perhaps the most extreme example of inconsistency occurs when the family has successfully completed a rehabilitation plan and the juvenile court judge allows the child to be returned to the perpetrator, but the criminal court sentences the perpetrator to prison. Such inconsistencies can result from a lack of communication and a gross lack of consensus concerning case strategies.

When orders are complementary, the unique resources of one proceeding can reinforce the purposes of the other proceeding. If a parent sexually abuses a child and does not cooperate with juvenile court orders to stay away from the home, the criminal proceeding can be used to punish the offending parent. Furthermore, therapy provided to the child through the juvenile court can help prevent trauma to the child from testifying in the criminal proceeding.

3. Avoiding Repetitious Questioning of the Child

Repeated questioning and reliving the crime can be hard on children. A child may be repeatedly questioned by different interviewers concerning specific incidents of maltreatment. The child protection worker who makes the initial contact with the child, the police officer who responds to an emergency call, the child's attorney, a guardian ad litem, service providers such as a child therapist, the criminal prosecutor, and the victim's advocate in the criminal proceeding may all need to know the circumstances of the abuse.

Repeated questioning is not only difficult for the child, but it increases the likelihood of unclear and inconsistent answers. In addition, it is harmful to the child and wastes resources. Joint interviews conducted by trained interviewers can minimize the number of interviews and improve their quality.

4.   Coordination in Case Goals

The above example in which a juvenile court is ready to authorize a child's return home and a criminal court is ready to send the parent to prison presents a profound issue that demonstrates the need for coordination. When the state intervenes in the life of a child and his or her family, different parts of the government should not be pursuing inconsistent goals.

While the fundamental purposes of the proceedings are different — protection of the child in juvenile court and punishment of the perpetrator in the criminal proceeding — outright contradictions should be avoided. In most cases, child protection agencies should not work for the child's return to an alleged perpetrator while the criminal prosecutor is pursuing a strategy intended to lead to long-term imprisonment of the perpetrator. If the crime against a child is serious enough to merit long-term imprisonment, return of the child is unrealistic and termination of parental rights may be appropriate. If, on the other hand, the safe return of the child is realistic and in the best interests of the child, the prosecutor's goal of long-term imprisonment should at least be re-examined.

Alienation sometimes exists between those involved in the investigation and prosecution of criminals and those charged with child protection. Some individuals in the criminal justice system do not believe the child protection goals are valid, while some individuals in child protection do not believe in criminal sanctions except in rare cases. This alienation and inconsistency in case goals leads to less efficient and less effective state intervention on behalf of the public and on behalf of children. . . .

Individuals involved in both criminal justice and child protection need to acknowledge the complementary nature of juvenile and criminal court proceedings. As a first step, participants should agree that both the juvenile court and the criminal court proceedings serve useful and important purposes, and often even assist each other.

The consensus must recognize that strategies from both proceedings, such as seeking criminal sanctions, offering rehabilitative services, and seeking to terminate parental rights, are all appropriate in some cases. The most effective approach will probably incorporate a combination of strategies from both proceedings. Criminal sanctions can be used not only to punish and deter the perpetrator, but also to protect the child and reinforce family rehabilitation. Therapeutic resources available through child protection proceedings often can help prepare the child for court. Information from each proceeding can be useful to the other. Participants must agree that the gains from coordination outweigh the occasional minor tactical sacrifices required of both the criminal prosecutor and the agency attorney. . . .

Coordination requires basic consensus between the child protection agency and law enforcement, in principles and in approach. Such consensus should be possible because (a) rehabilitation and punishment are not mutually exclusive goals, and (b) the coercive effects of the criminal justice system are sometimes needed to ensure the safety of the child.

Without consensus, coordination efforts can break down. If, for example, there is disagreement in a particular jurisdiction between the child protection agency and law enforcement on whether persons who seriously abuse children can be rehabilitated, and thus whether many families of such offenders can be kept intact, then it may be substantially more difficult to coordinate law enforcement and child protective services efforts. If the criminal prosecutor does not believe rehabilitation is likely or appropriate, the criminal disposition or sentencing is less likely to mandate or reinforce a treatment plan directed at rehabilitation. . . .

While there are clear practical benefits from information sharing between the criminal justice system and child protection systems in child maltreatment cases, there is also a complex tangle of private interests and concerns. In some instances protection of these private interests creates legal barriers to an information exchange. . . .

As described below, parents and their defense attorneys face difficult choices in deciding whether to testify in juvenile court or participate in therapy which may involve disclosure of criminal behavior. In making such choices, they must weigh the risk of losing parental rights as a result of not testifying or participating in therapy against the risk of incrimination from their testimony or participation in therapy.

Routinely forcing these choices on parents also presents a complex policy choice for lawmakers, prosecutors, agency attorneys, and judges. If parents must risk incrimination from testifying or participating in therapy, they are far less likely to cooperate with the child protection agency before the criminal matter is resolved. On the other hand, if parents who testify in juvenile court or participate in juvenile court-ordered therapy do not face the risk of incrimination, then there is a possibility the prosecutor's criminal case could be weakened. . . .

When the juvenile court case precedes the completion of the criminal proceeding, the parents' dilemma in choosing whether to testify is as follows. If they wish to avoid imprisonment, they may, pursuant to their right against self-incrimination under the Fifth and Fourteenth Amendments, refuse to testify in juvenile court. On the other hand, if parents wish to avoid long-term or permanent loss of their children, they may need to make such admissions of wrongdoing. In the event a parent refuses to testify and claims the privilege against self-incrimination, the juvenile court may make adverse inferences against the parent. . . .

Another context in which a defendant can potentially give incriminating testimony is during a psychiatric exam or therapy as part of the juvenile court treatment process. In some cases an exam or therapy is court-ordered. Therapeutic treatment is generally ordered to keep the family intact or make progress toward reunification. It also helps the juvenile court gather evidence to make an informed disposition of the matter. Although a court-ordered evaluation or therapy sometimes ultimately reveals that reunification is not possible, the purpose of the service is not to gather evidence for a future criminal proceeding. . . .

In the Matter of the Parental Rights as to A.D.L.

402 P.3d 1280 (Nev. 2017)

By the Court, HARDESTY, J.: . . . In April 2010, respondent Clark County Department of Family Services (DFS) received an anonymous call through its child abuse hotline alleging that Keaundra's children were being abused and neglected. The caller alleged that the face of Keaundra's infant child had been burned. During an interview with a DFS investigator, Keaundra stated that she was the only adult at home when C.L.B., Jr. was burned. Her two children, A.D.L. and C.L.B., Jr., were in the master bedroom while she was preparing for work in the attached bathroom. She had recently ironed her clothes and had placed the iron on her dresser. Keaundra heard the iron fall and when she came out to investigate, A.D.L. told her that C.L.B., Jr. had "tried to kiss the iron." Keaundra then called her mother, a nurse, who told her to put ointment on the injury and to take C.L.B., Jr. to the emergency room if the burn blistered.

Following the initial contact with DFS, Keaundra moved her family to Louisiana, where her father was stationed with the U.S. Air Force. Upon learning that Keaundra moved to Louisiana, DFS sought help from U.S. Air Force authorities to gain protective custody of the children. The children were removed from Keaundra's care, and C.L.B., Jr. was taken to see Dr. Thomas A. Neuman, a physician in Louisiana. Dr. Neuman reported that the injury was well healed and that there was no evidence of abuse.

In May 2010, DFS filed a petition for protective custody of A.D.L. and C.L.B., Jr. under NRS Chapter 432B, alleging that Keaundra had either physically abused or negligently supervised C.L.B., Jr. A plea hearing was held wherein Keaundra entered a denial, and DFS requested placement of the children with their maternal grandmother.

At a subsequent adjudicatory hearing, the hearing master took testimony from Dr. Neha Mehta, a medical examiner who had reviewed photographs of C.L.B., Jr.'s injuries. Dr. Mehta opined that the shape of the injury was not consistent with an accident and that the iron had been deliberately held to C.L.B., Jr.'s face. Keaundra offered Dr. Neuman's report to rebut Dr. Mehta's testimony. The hearing master excluded the report on the ground that the report was not a certified copy. The hearing master found that Keaundra had physically abused C.L.B., Jr., had medically neglected him, and had absconded. Based on those findings, the hearing master recommended sustaining the abuse and neglect petition and that A.D.L. and C.L.B., Jr. remain in DFS custody. The juvenile court affirmed the hearing master's recommendation and concluded that C.L.B., Jr.'s injury was nonaccidental.

In light of these findings, Keaundra received a case plan which required that she maintain stable housing and income, keep in contact with DFS, and complete parenting classes. She was also required to complete a physical abuse assessment and "be able to articulate in dialogue with the Specialist and therapist(s) the sequence of events which result[ed] in physical abuse, as sustained by the Court, and how he/she will be able to ensure that no future physical abuse to [C.L.B.,] Jr. occurs." One month after giving Keaundra the case plan, DFS recommended termination of parental rights as the goal for the children. DFS then filed a petition to terminate Keaundra's parental rights as to A.D.L. and C.L.B., Jr.

At her six-month review, DFS reported that Keaundra had completed her parenting classes, maintained housing, held regular jobs, and completed both her assessment and therapy. At that point, the children had been placed with their maternal grandmother in Louisiana, where Keaundra was also living. DFS stated that it was satisfied with Keaundra's progress. DFS further stated that Keaundra had "successfully completed her case plan and has the knowledge and tools to effectively parent her children." Despite DFS's satisfaction with Keaundra's progress, it nonetheless maintained its recommendation that her parental rights be terminated because she had not admitted that she abused C.L.B., Jr. by holding an iron to his face. DFS later stated at trial that, with such an admission, it would not have sought termination of parental rights.

At the next six-month review, DFS again noted that Keaundra had completed her case plan in all other regards and that she acknowledged that negligence and improper supervision caused C.L.B., Jr.'s injury. Again, DFS maintained its recommendation to terminate parental rights due to Keaundra's refusal to admit that she held the iron to C.L.B., Jr.'s face.

In the meantime, Keaundra moved to South Carolina and was referred to a new therapist, who was in regular contact with a DFS caseworker. At the parental termination trial, the new therapist testified that therapy resulted in a marked change in Keaundra's behavior and demeanor. She noted that despite signs of depression and anxiety at the start of therapy, Keaundra's demeanor had substantially changed over the course of treatment and her risk to reoffend was low. The therapist saw no signs that she would expect to see in an abusive parent.

At the conclusion of the trial, the district court issued a decision terminating Keaundra's parental rights as to C.L.B., Jr. and A.D.L. The district court relied on the hearing master's findings, as affirmed by the juvenile court, that Keaundra was at fault for C.L.B., Jr.'s injuries and that his injuries were not accidental. Because Keaundra was unable to remedy the "circumstances, conduct or conditions" leading to C.L.B., Jr.'s removal, the district court terminated her parental rights based on token efforts, failure of parental adjustment, and unfitness. The district court further found that termination was in the best interests of the children.

Keaundra appealed that decision to this court. We reversed the district court's order based on the failure to admit the report of Dr. Neuman and remanded the matter for a new trial on the issue of parental fault and consideration of additional evidence. . . .

Before the second trial, the parties stipulated to admission of all evidence from the prior termination trial, retaining only the issue of the inappropriate finding of parental fault based on the exclusion of Dr. Neuman's report. At the new parental termination trial, the district court admitted Dr. Neuman's report over the objection of DFS, and Dr. Mehta again testified over the objection of Keaundra's counsel. Dr. Mehta once again opined that the injury to C.L.B., Jr.'s face was inconsistent with the explanation given, but she admitted that this opinion was based only on viewing the photographs before the initial trial. Dr. Mehta testified that generally her practice in ascertaining the nature of an injury would be to obtain as much information as possible. Dr. Mehta only recalled being told of an iron and a child kissing the iron; she did not interview any witnesses to the incident, did not see the child in person, and was unaware of the previous report from Dr. Neuman stating that there was no sign of abuse. Dr. Mehta noted that although an accidental cause of injury was possible, she could not conceive of such an explanation.

After closing arguments, the district court inquired as to whether any offer of immunity had been given to Keaundra, as well as why that immunity was not offered in order to further reunification efforts. The district court further opined that because the court's purpose in protective custody proceedings is to reunify children, parents need to be open and honest, and, as such, the judge's practice is to offer immunity from statements made to treatment providers or DFS. DFS acknowledged that Keaundra was not offered immunity. DFS further indicated that it was unaware of any legal authority that would preclude the offer of immunity. While acknowledging that the offer of immunity would cure any Fifth Amendment concerns, DFS indicated that immunity did not apply in Keaundra's case.

The district court ultimately reaffirmed its prior decision to terminate Keaundra's parental rights, due largely to Dr. Mehta's credentials and compelling testimony. The district court ended its decision by noting that Keaundra "continued to insist that the burn was accidental in nature in spite of all physical evidence being to the contrary." Keaundra now appeals. . . .

The district court's termination of Keaundra's parental rights constituted a violation of her Fifth Amendment right against self-incrimination.

Keaundra contends that the district court abused its discretion by finding that she did not exhibit behavioral changes that would warrant the return of her children since that finding was based solely on her noncompliance with her case plan because she refused to admit that she abused C.L.B., Jr. Thus, she argues, reunification and the avoidance of the termination of her parental rights were conditioned on her admitting a criminal act, in violation of her Fifth Amendment right against self-incrimination. We agree.

The Fifth Amendment right against self incrimination, which applies to the states through the Fourteenth Amendment, states that "[n]o person . . . . shall be compelled in any criminal case to be a witness against himself." *See* Estelle v. Smith, 451 U.S. 454, 462 (1981) (quoting U.S. Const. amend. V). The Fifth Amendment not only protects individuals in criminal proceedings, "but also privileges him not to answer official questions put to him in any other proceeding, civil or criminal, formal or informal, where the answers might incriminate him in future criminal proceedings." Lefkowitz v. Turley, 414 U.S. 70, 77 (1973). Further, an individual cannot be penalized for invoking his Fifth Amendment right. Spevack v. Klein, 385 U.S. 511, 514–515 (1967).

The United States Supreme Court has held that the state may not compel a person to choose between the Fifth Amendment privilege against self-incrimination and another important interest because such a choice is inherently coercive. Lefkowitz v. Cunningham, 431 U.S. 801, 805–808 (1977). This court has recognized that "the parent-child relationship is a fundamental liberty interest. Thus, we agree with other courts that have held that a parent may not be compelled to admit a crime under the threat of the loss of parental rights. *See, e.g.*, In re A.W., 896 N.E.2d 316, 326 (Ill. 2008); In re Amanda W., 705 N.E.2d 724, 727 (Ohio App. 1997); Dep't of Human Servs. v. K.L.R., 230 P.3d 49, 54 (Or. App. 2010); In re M.C.P., 571 A.2d 627, 641 (Vt. 1989).

The state, on the other hand, has an important interest in protecting the welfare of children. When a child has been removed from a parent's custody because of abuse, the court must consider whether the parent has adjusted the circumstances for the child's safe return.

In balancing a parent's Fifth Amendment right against self-incrimination and the need for meaningful rehabilitation in cases where a child has been removed from the parent's custody because of alleged child abuse, courts have generally concluded that while a court can require a parent to complete therapy as part of a family reunification plan, courts cannot explicitly compel a parent to admit guilt, either through requiring a therapy program that specifically mandates an admission of guilt for family reunification, or otherwise through a direct admission, because that violates the parent's Fifth Amendment right. In re A.W., 896 N.E.2d at 326 ("[A] trial court may order a service plan that requires a parent to engage in effective counseling or therapy, but may not compel counseling or therapy requiring the parent to admit to committing a crime."); In re C.H., 652 N.W.2d 144, 150 (Iowa 2002); ("The State may require parents to otherwise undergo treatment, but it may not specifically require an admission of guilt as part of the treatment."); In re J.W., 415 N.W.2d 879, 883 (Minn. 1987) ("While the state may not compel therapy treatment that would require appellants to incriminate themselves, it may require the parents to otherwise undergo treatment."); *see also* Minh T. v. Ariz. Dep't of Econ. Sec., 202 Ariz. 76, 41 P.3d 614, 617–18 (Ariz. Ct. App. 2001) ("[T]he State may require therapy and counseling for the parents. . . . However, there is a distinction between a treatment order that requires parents to admit criminal misconduct and one that merely orders participation in family reunification services.").

Accordingly, there is a distinction between a court-ordered case plan that mandates admission of culpability for family reunification and one that requires meaningful therapy for family reunification. Invoking the Fifth Amendment may have consequences and "[o]ne such consequence may be a person's failure to obtain treatment for his or her problems," and a failure to participate in meaningful therapy may result in the termination of parental rights without a violation of the Fifth Amendment, so long as the court did not mandate an admission of guilt. In re C.H., 652 N.W.2d at 150; In re P.M.C., 902 N.E.2d 197, 203 (Ill. App. 2009) (observing that where a parent fails to comply with an order to complete meaningful therapy because the refusal to admit guilt inhibits rehabilitation, there is no constitutional violation); K.L.R., 230 P.3d at 54 (concluding that "terminating or limiting parental rights based on a parent's failure to comply with an order to obtain meaningful therapy or rehabilitation, perhaps in part because a parent's failure to acknowledge past wrongdoing inhibits meaningful therapy, may not violate the Fifth Amendment").

We need not resolve the tension created by a parent's exercise of his or her Fifth Amendment right and its importance to meaningful therapy or rehabilitation. Notably, in Keaundra's case, DFS's six-month report confirmed that Keaundra's therapy was indeed effective without the need for an admission of guilt.

This approach is consistent with existing Nevada caselaw regarding the invocation of the Fifth Amendment in civil proceedings. Because Keaundra's case plan required her to admit that she intentionally caused C.L.B., Jr.'s injury, she could not fully comply with the case plan without admitting that she committed a criminal act. And, in terminating Keaundra's parental rights, the court based its decision on its finding that Keaundra "continued to insist that the burn was accidental in nature." Accordingly, we conclude that the district court violated Keaundra's Fifth Amendment rights by terminating her parental rights based on her refusal to admit that she intentionally caused C.L.B., Jr.'s injury. *See* In re J.W., 415 N.W.2d at 882–883 (holding that conditioning termination on compliance with a court-ordered case plan that requires admission to criminal conduct is a threat that triggers the Fifth Amendment). . . .

In reaffirming its decision that terminating Keaundra's parental rights was in the best interests of A.D.L. and C.L.B., Jr., the district court based its findings squarely on the fact that Keaundra refused to admit that she caused C.L.B., Jr.'s injury, which we conclude was a violation of Keaundra's Fifth Amendment rights. . . . Accordingly, we conclude that the district court's order terminating Keaundra's parental rights was an abuse of discretion and we thus reverse.

NOTES AND QUESTIONS

1. The Fifth Amendment prevents a juvenile court from ordering a parent to testify to facts that could be used as evidence against the parent in a criminal proceeding. If the parent refused to testify, could the juvenile court draw adverse inferences against the parent because of the parent's silence without offending the Constitution? Some courts have held that a court could draw this inference without violating the Fifth Amendment. Matter of Welfare of J.W., 391 N.W.2d 791 (Minn. 1986). *See also* New York City Commr. of Soc. Serv. v. Elminia E., 521 N.Y.S.2d 283 (App. Div. 1987). As a practical matter, if an adverse inference is allowed, do the parents have any choice but to testify?

2. The court in Parental Rights as to A.D.L. says that requiring a parent to participate in meaningful therapy which may be impossible if the parent does not admit to criminal conduct may not violate the Fifth Amendment. How is this requirement different from the requirement that the juvenile court actually imposed in this case?

In Dept. Human Serv. v. K.L.R., 230 P.3d 49 (Or. App. 2010), the juvenile court ordered parents to take a polygraph test in a case involving unexplained injuries to their child. If the purpose of the order was to clarify exactly what had happened, would it violate the Fifth Amendment? The court held that where the purpose was investigation, the order violated the Fifth Amendment. What if the purpose was to tailor the case plan to the parent's circumstances so as to insure that the child could be safely returned? *See* In the Matter of the Parental Rights as to S.L., 422 P.3d 1253, 1258 (Nev. 2018) ("The risk of losing one's children for failure to undergo meaningful therapy is not a penalty imposed by the state but 'is simply a consequence of the reality that it is unsafe for children to be with parents who are abusive and violent.'")

3. Lefkowitz v. Turley, 414 U.S. 70 (1973), held that denying a government contract to anyone who refused to waive immunity or testify concerning a contract with the state violates the Fifth Amendment. Lefkowitz v. Cunningham, 431 U.S. 801 (1977), held that the Fifth Amendment was violated when a man was removed from political party office and barred for five years from any party or public office for refusing to answer potentially incriminating questions. In contrast, in McKune v. Lile, 536 U.S. 24 (2002), the Court held that a voluntary

prison program for convicted sex offenders that required participants to sign admissions of all prior sexual activity, including uncharged criminal offenses, without giving them immunity from prosecution, did not violate the Fifth Amendment. While the program was voluntary, if a defendant refused to participate, his prison privileges would be reduced, and he would be transferred to a potentially more dangerous maximum security unit. The Court assessed the privilege claim in light of the general lessening of prisoners' privileges and rights and concluded that the program served legitimate penological purposes. The Court distinguished Garrity v. New Jersey, 385 U.S. 493 (1967), which held that police officers' statements given under threat of job forfeiture are "compelled" for purposes of the Fifth Amendment, and Uniformed Sanitation Men Assn., Inc. v. Commr. of Sanitation, 392 U.S. 280 (1968), which prohibited the state from firing state employees who refused to waive their privilege against self-incrimination and answer questions, on the basis that the petitioners in those cases were not imprisoned.

4. In some states, case law or statutes authorize prosecutors or courts to grant immunity to parents, allowing them to testify in juvenile court proceedings without fear that their testimony will be used against them in a criminal trial. Immunity is of two types; either is constitutionally sufficient to protect a person's Fifth Amendment rights. "Transactional immunity" prevents criminal prosecution of the immunized person for any crime that is part of the transaction that the person testifies about. "Use immunity," which is more common, does not preclude criminal prosecution. Instead, it protects the immunized person only from having his or her testimony used against him or her in a criminal trial. A grant of use immunity permits the prosecutor to present evidence in the criminal trial that is not derived from the parent's immunized testimony. The prosecutor bears the burden to prove that the evidence has an independent source. For more on immunity, *see* Wayne R. LaFave et al., Criminal Procedure § 8.11 (6th ed. 2017).

Should statutes require that use immunity be granted to any parent who wishes to testify in juvenile court proceedings involving the child, or should the judge or prosecutor, as the case may be, have discretion to decide whether to grant immunity? How should the decision maker decide how to exercise this discretion?

> . . . "[P]rosecutors often do not call upon parents to testify in contested adjudications because their testimony is not helpful in proving the case. This reasoning, however, does not apply in connection with the courts' decisions concerning custody, visitation, and treatment. The primary impact of an immunity statute is likely to be in the dispositional and post-dispositional phases where the judge decides upon or revises orders concerning the child's care, custody, and treatment."

Sprague & Hardin, above, at 305.

Some statutes also provide that parents' revelations in pre- or post-dispositional psychological evaluation or therapy cannot be used against them in a criminal proceeding. If a state has such a statute, may a court refuse to return children to parents who will not make admissions during evaluation or therapy? Could a court terminate parental rights on this basis?

5. Cases holding that ordering a parent to admit criminal conduct during therapy would violate the parent's privilege against self-incrimination implicitly assume that the disclosure would not be privileged. Whether such disclosures are privileged varies from state to state. In some states that recognize such a privilege, the therapist may be required to report a parent's admissions under the state's child abuse reporting law. For a detailed discussion, *see* Sprague & Hardin, at 311-313.

6. Would refusal to continue juvenile court proceedings pending the outcome of criminal proceedings violate a parent's privilege against self-incrimination or right to a hearing? Cases rejecting such a claim include In the Matter of Emily I., 854 N.Y.S.2d 792 (App. Div. 2008); In re Melissa M. 506 A.2d 324 (N.H. 1986). In contrast, In re Dolly A., 222 Cal. Rptr. 741 (Ct. App. 1986), held that denial of a continuance of the juvenile court proceeding, forcing the parent to choose between his privilege against self-incrimination and his right to testify in his own behalf in proceedings involving custody of his child, was an abuse of discretion. After *Dolly A.* was decided, the California statute was amended to provide that a pending criminal prosecution is not in and of itself good cause for granting a continuance in a juvenile court proceeding. Cal. Welf. & Inst. Code § 352. In 2014 the Alabama Court of Appeals affirmed the continuing vitality of a decision holding that a juvenile court termination of parental rights proceeding should be stayed pending the outcome of a parallel criminal proceeding because of the threat to a parent's privilege against self-incrimination if the parent is questioned during the termination trial. Ex parte S.B., 164 So.3d 599 (Ala. Civ. App. 2014).

7. Recall that federal law requires states to require that a termination of parental rights petition be filed once a child has been in foster care for 15 of the last 22 months in many cases. Given this rule, can parents afford to seek a delay in the juvenile court proceedings?

8. If a parent is acquitted in a criminal trial, could she successfully raise a *res judicata* or collateral estoppel defense to a juvenile court proceeding based on the same facts? If the juvenile court charges were found not proven, would that preclude prosecution of the parent on criminal charges?

> An affirmative finding of abuse in juvenile court does not collaterally estop a later criminal proceeding because of the higher standard of proof required for a criminal conviction. By contrast, a finding in a juvenile court proceeding that abuse was not proved logically seems to bar relitigation of the same issues in a criminal proceeding. Less proof is required to prevail in juvenile court than in a criminal proceeding; therefore, the failure to prove the case in juvenile court arguably demonstrates there is insufficient evidence in the criminal case.
>
> Some courts, however, have determined for policy reasons that collateral estoppel does not apply in these circumstances. Because of the differing natures of the juvenile and criminal court proceedings, application of the doctrine would be unfair or would result in injustice. Another public policy argument for making the doctrine inapplicable is that in most states the contested juvenile court case can be resolved by a judge in a bench trial while the criminal defendant is entitled to a trial by jury.
>
> In addition, the issues in the two proceedings might not be identical. The issue of child maltreatment typically takes into account a broader and different set of facts than allegations in the criminal case. Child maltreatment allegations might not include the specific elements of criminal charges. Under these circumstances, because issue identity is an element of collateral estoppel, the doctrine arguably will

not apply and there will be no issue preclusion. This result might not occur, however, in certain cases in states where the juvenile court act imports definitions from the criminal code, such as definitions of sexual abuse.

Sprague & Hardin, above, at 289-290.

9. Should a court routinely place a child in temporary shelter care pending the conclusion of the criminal trial to protect the child's testimony? If the parent who allegedly harmed the child leaves the home, is removal of the child warranted to avoid the risk that the other parent will pressure the child about his or her testimony?

> The juvenile court case may regulate contacts between the child and the alleged perpetrator, thereby affecting the outcome of the criminal proceeding as well. If no criminal charges have been brought, but a child is removed from the home pursuant to the juvenile court proceeding, the child may be less vulnerable to pressure from the alleged perpetrator to recant the accusations. On the other hand, if the juvenile court allows and encourages contact between the defendant and the child victim pursuant to a reunification plan, this contact could adversely affect the criminal prosecutor's case because it could weaken the child's testimony. . . .

Id. at 295.

C. SPECIAL EVIDENTIARY PROBLEMS

In some kinds of cases, abuse or neglect can be proven by physical evidence or eyewitness testimony from third parties. Sometimes, however, such evidence is unavailable or is insufficient to support a verdict, especially in criminal cases, where the prosecution must prove allegations beyond a reasonable doubt. The following cases and notes examine several types of evidence that prosecutors may attempt to use — expert testimony, testimony about children's out-of-court statements, and testimony from the children themselves. Consider how the tension between child protection and the goals of the criminal justice system plays out in these contexts.

CAVAZOS V. SMITH

565 U.S. 1(2011)

PER CURIAM. The opinion of the Court in Jackson v. Virginia, 443 U.S. 307 (1979), makes clear that it is the responsibility of the jury—not the court—to decide what conclusions should be drawn from evidence admitted at trial. A reviewing court may set aside the jury's verdict on the ground of insufficient evidence only if no rational trier of fact could have agreed with the jury. What is more, a federal court may not overturn a state court decision rejecting a sufficiency of the evidence challenge simply because the federal court disagrees with the state court. The federal court instead may do so only if the state court decision was "objectively unreasonable." . . .

This case concerns the death of 7-week-old Etzel Glass. On November 29, 1996, Etzel's mother, Tomeka, put Etzel to sleep on a sofa before going to sleep herself in another room. Respondent Shirley Ree Smith — Tomeka's mother — slept on the floor next to Etzel. Several hours later, Smith ran into Tomeka's room, holding Etzel, who was limp, and told her that "[s]omething [was] wrong with Etzel." By the time emergency officials arrived, Etzel was not breathing and had no heartbeat. Smith reported that she thought Etzel had fallen off the sofa. The officials' efforts to resuscitate Etzel failed.

Doctors initially attributed Etzel's death to sudden infant death syndrome (SIDS), the customary diagnosis when an infant shows no outward signs of trauma. But after an autopsy, the coroner concluded that the cause of death was instead shaken baby syndrome (SBS). When a social worker informed Smith of that finding, Smith told her that Etzel had not responded to her touch while sleeping, so she had picked him up and given him "a little shake, a jostle" to wake him. According to the social worker, Smith then said something to the effect of, "Oh, my God. Did I do it? Did I do it? Oh, my God." In an interview with the police a few days later, Smith said that she had shaken Etzel, but then she corrected herself and said that she had twisted him to try to elicit a reaction. Smith was arrested and charged with assault on a child resulting in death.

At trial, the jury heard seven days of expert medical testimony on the cause of Etzel's death. The prosecution offered three experts, each of whom attested that Etzel's death was the result of SBS — not SIDS, as the defense contended. The first expert, Dr. Eugene Carpenter, was the medical examiner for the Los Angeles County Coroner who had supervised Etzel's autopsy. Dr. Carpenter is board certified in forensic, anatomic, and clinical pathology. He testified that Etzel's autopsy revealed recent hemorrhages in the brain, and he opined that the bleeding and other features of Etzel's pathology, including a bruise and abrasion on the lower back of the baby's head, were consistent with violent shaking. Dr. Carpenter identified two means by which shaking can result in a baby's death: The first is that the shaking causes blood vessels in the brain to tear, creating a pool of blood that pushes the brain downward into the spinal canal, resulting in death but little direct damage to the brain. The second is that the shaking itself is sufficiently severe that the brain directly tears in vital areas, causing death with very little bleeding. Dr. Carpenter testified that Etzel's injuries were consistent with the latter pathology. He also explained that the injuries could not be attributed to either a fall from the sofa or the administration of cardiopulmonary resuscitation. Nor, according to Dr. Carpenter, was it possible that Etzel perished from SIDS, given the signs of internal trauma. Dr. Carpenter did testify, however, that while SBS victims often suffer retinal hemorrhaging, Etzel's autopsy revealed no such injury.

The prosecution's second expert, Dr. Stephanie Erlich, was the associate deputy medical examiner who actually performed Etzel's autopsy. She is board certified in anatomic pathology and neuropathology. She corroborated Dr. Carpenter's testimony about the autopsy findings, and added that a followup neuropathological examination of Etzel's brain confirmed the existence of recent hemorrhaging. Noting only a minimal amount of new blood in Etzel's brain, she testified that the cause of death was direct trauma to the brainstem. On cross-examination, she agreed with defense counsel that retinal hemorrhaging (absent in Etzel's case) is present in 75 to 80 percent of SBS cases.

The third prosecution expert, Dr. David Chadwick, is board certified in pediatrics and the author of articles on childhood death by abusive trauma. He testified that Etzel's injuries were consistent with SBS and that old trauma could not have been the cause of the child's death.

The defense called two experts to dispute these conclusions. The first, pathologist Dr. Richard Siegler, testified that Etzel died from brain trauma, but that it was not the result of SBS, given the lack of retinal hemorrhaging. He admitted on cross-examination, however, that an absence of retinal hemorrhaging does not exclude a finding of SBS. He also acknowledged that he did not believe the cause of Etzel's death was SIDS. According to Dr. Siegler, Etzel died from old trauma, an opinion he reached on the basis of studying photographs of the neuropathological examination.

The other defense expert, pediatric neurologist Dr. William Goldie, testified that Etzel's death *was* due to SIDS. He noted that Etzel was born with jaundice, a heart murmur, and low birth weight—making him more susceptible to SIDS. Dr. Goldie testified that pathologists had not been able to determine the cause of Etzel's death and that the bleeding could be attributed to the resuscitation efforts.

The jury found Smith guilty. Concluding that the jury "carefully weighed" the "tremendous amount of evidence" supporting the verdict, the trial judge denied Smith's motion for a new trial and sentenced her to an indeterminate term of 15 years to life in prison.

On direct review, Smith contended that the evidence was not sufficient to establish that Etzel died from SBS. After thoroughly reviewing the competing medical testimony, the California Court of Appeal rejected this claim, concluding:

> "The expert opinion evidence we have summarized was conflicting. It was for the jury to resolve the conflicts. The credited evidence was substantial and sufficient to support the jury's conclusions that Etzel died from shaken baby syndrome. The conviction is supported by substantial evidence."

The California Supreme Court denied review.

Smith then filed this petition for a writ of habeas corpus with the United States District Court for the Central District of California, renewing her claim that the evidence was insufficient to prove that Etzel died of SBS. Under the Antiterrorism and Effective Death Penalty Act of 1996 (AEDPA), 110 Stat. 1214, that court had no power to afford relief unless Smith could show either that the California Court of Appeal's decision affirming the conviction "was contrary to, or involved an unreasonable application of," clearly established federal law as reflected in the holdings of this Court's cases or that it "was based on an unreasonable determination of the facts" in light of the state court record.

The Magistrate Judge to whom the case was assigned issued a report acknowledging that "[t]his is not the typical shaken baby case" and that the evidence against Smith "raises many questions." But the Magistrate Judge nevertheless concluded that the evidence was "clearly sufficient to support a conviction." The District Court adopted the Magistrate Judge's report and denied the petition.

On appeal, the Ninth Circuit reversed with instructions to grant the writ. Despite the plenitude of expert testimony in the trial record concluding that sudden shearing or tearing of the brainstem was the cause of Etzel's death, the Ninth Circuit determined that there was "no evidence to permit an expert conclusion one way or the other" on that question because there was "no physical evidence of . . . tearing or shearing, and no other evidence supporting death by violent shaking." The court said that the State's experts "reached [their] conclusion because *there was no evidence in the brain itself of the cause of death*." The court concluded that because "[a]bsence of evidence cannot constitute proof beyond a reasonable doubt," the California Court of Appeal had "unreasonably applied" this Court's opinion in Jackson v. Virginia in upholding Smith's conviction.

That conclusion was plainly wrong. *Jackson* says that evidence is sufficient to support a conviction so long as "after viewing the evidence in the light most favorable to the prosecution, *any* rational trier of fact could have found the essential elements of the crime beyond a reasonable doubt." It also unambiguously instructs that a reviewing court "faced with a record of historical facts that supports conflicting inferences must presume—even if it does not affirmatively appear in the record—that the trier of fact resolved any such conflicts in favor of the prosecution, and must defer to that resolution." When the deference to state court decisions required by § 2254(d) is applied to the state court's already deferential review, there can be no doubt of the Ninth Circuit's error below. . . .

Justice GINSBURG, with whom Justice BREYER and Justice SOTOMAYOR join, dissenting. The Court's summary disposition of this case, in my judgment, is a misuse of discretion. I set out below my reasons for concluding that discretion, soundly exercised, would have occasioned denial of California's petition for review.

The Magistrate Judge who reviewed respondent Shirley Ree Smith's habeas corpus petition in the first instance concluded, as the Court does today, that relief was unwarranted. He observed, however, that the evidence, "though clearly sufficient to support a conviction, raises many questions":

> Grandmothers, especially those not serving as the primary caretakers, are not the typical perpetrators [in shaken baby cases]. Further, [Smith] was helping her daughter raise her other children (a [4-year–old] and a 14-month–old) and there was no hint of [Smith] abusing or neglecting these other children, who were in the room with Etzel when he died. Still further, there was no evidence of any precipitating event that might have caused [Smith] to snap and assault her grandson. She was not trapped in a hopeless situation with a child she did not want or love. Nor was she forced to single-handedly care for a baby that had been crying all day and all night. In fact, there is no evidence that Etzel was doing anything other than sleeping the night he died. In addition, [Smith's] daughter [Tomeka], Etzel's mother, was in the room next door when Etzel died. The medical evidence was not typical either, in that some of the telltale signs usually found in shaken baby cases did not exist in this case.

The District Court adopted the Magistrate Judge's recommendation to deny Smith's petition, but granted a certificate of appealability, recognizing that "reasonable jurists would find the [court's] assessment of [Smith's] claims debatable."

After full briefing and argument, the Ninth Circuit reversed the District Court's judgment. . . .

I turn first to the medical evidence presented at trial. Dr. Carpenter, the autopsy supervisor, testified that the following symptoms are consistent with, but not required for, a diagnosis of SBS: cerebral edema, subdural hemorrhage, retinal hemorrhage, bleeding at the joints of the back of the neck, bruises on the arms, fractures of the ribs, and internal injuries to the buttocks, abdominal organs, and chest organs. Few of these signs of SBS were present here. Etzel's subdural hemorrhage and subarachnoid hemorrhage were "minimal," insufficient to cause death. There was no brain swelling and no retinal hemorrhage in either eye. Similarly absent were any fractures, sprains, bleeding in the joints, or displacement of joints. A "tiny" abrasion on the skin and a corresponding bruise under the scalp did not produce brain trauma.

These findings led Dr. Carpenter, the autopsy supervisor, and Dr. Erlich, who performed Etzel's autopsy, to rule out two commonly proffered causes of death in SBS cases: massive bleeding and massive swelling that create pressure and push the brain downward. Instead, they opined, Etzel's death was caused by direct injury—shearing or tearing of the brainstem or the brain itself. The autopsy revealed no physical evidence of such injury, either grossly or microscopically. Dr. Carpenter was unable to state which particular areas of the brain were injured, and the neuropathologist found no evidence of specific brain injury. No doctor located any tear. Indeed, the examining physicians did not cut open Etzel's brainstem, or submit it to neuropathology, because, in their own estimation, "[w]e wouldn't have seen anything anyway."

Neither doctor testified to ever having performed an autopsy on an infant in which a similar conclusion was reached. Nor did either physician point to any medical literature supporting their belief that shearing or tearing of the brainstem or the brain itself caused Etzel's death. Dr. Carpenter nevertheless maintained that when there is subdural hemorrhage without signs of external trauma to the head or skull, the injury is necessarily caused by violent shaking. Smith's conviction thus turned on, as Dr. Erlich put it, "direct trauma which we don't see to the brainstem." That this gave the Ninth Circuit pause is understandable. Dr. Erlich herself conceded that "[i]t is a difficult concept to absorb."

Reason to suspect the Carpenter-Erlich thesis has grown in the years following Smith's 1997 trial. Doubt has increased in the medical community "over whether infants can be fatally injured through shaking alone." *See, e.g.,* Donohoe, Evidence-Based Medicine and Shaken Baby Syndrome, Part I: Literature Review, 1966-1998, 24 Am. J. Forensic Med. & Pathology 239, 241 (2003) (By the end of 1998, it had become apparent that "there was inadequate scientific evidence to come to a firm conclusion on most aspects of causation, diagnosis, treatment, or any other matters pertaining to SBS," and that "the commonly held opinion that the finding of [subdural hemorrhage] and [retinal hemorrhage] in an infant was strong evidence of SBS was unsustainable."); Bandak, Shaken Baby Syndrome: A Biomechanics Analysis of Injury Mechanisms, 151 Forensic Sci. Int'l 71, 78 (2005) ("Head acceleration and velocity levels commonly reported for SBS generate forces that are far too great for the infant neck to withstand without injury. . . . [A]n SBS diagnosis in an infant . . . without cervical spine or brain stem injury is questionable and other causes of the intracerebral injury must be considered."); Minns, Shaken Baby Syndrome: Theoretical and Evidential Controversies, 35 J. Royal College of Physicians of Edinburgh 5, 10 (2005) ("[D]iagnosing 'shaking' as a mechanism of injury . . . is not possible, because these are unwitnessed injuries that may be incurred by a whole variety of mechanisms solely or in combination."); Uscinski, Shaken Baby Syndrome: An Odyssey, 46 Neurol. Med. Chir. (Tokyo) 57, 59 (2006) ("[T]he hypothetical mechanism of manually shaking infants in such a way as to cause intracranial injury is based on a misinterpretation of an experiment done for a different purpose, and contrary to the laws of injury biomechanics as they apply specifically to the infant anatomy."); Leestma, Case Analysis of Brain-Injured Admittedly Shaken Infants, 54 Cases, 1969-2001, 26 Am. J. Forensic Med. & Pathology 199, 211 (2005) ("[M]ost of the pathologies in allegedly shaken babies are due to impact injuries to the head and body."); Squier, Shaken Baby Syndrome: The Quest for Evidence, 50 Developmental Med. & Child Neurology 10, 13 (2008) ("[H]ead impacts onto carpeted floors and steps from heights in the 1 to 3 feet range result in far greater . . . forces and accelerations than shaking and slamming onto either a sofa or a bed.").

In light of current information, it is unlikely that the prosecution's experts would today testify as adamantly as they did in 1997. . . . What is now known about SBS hypotheses seems to me worthy of considerable weight in the discretionary decision whether to take up this tragic case.

I consider next the State's meager nonmedical evidence. There was no evidence whatever that Smith abused her grandchildren in the past or acted with any malicious intent on the night in question. Instead, the evidence indicated that Smith was warm hearted, sensitive, and gentle. As earlier observed, the Magistrate Judge noted the absence of any motive or precipitating event that might have led Smith to shake Etzel violently. Although shaking may quiet a crying child, no evidence showed that Etzel was crying in the hours before he died. To the contrary: Any loud crying likely would have woken Etzel's siblings, Yondale, age 14 months, and Yolanda, age 4, asleep only feet away, even Etzel's mother, Tomeka, asleep in the neighboring room. Yet no one's slumber was disturbed.

The prosecution relied on the testimony of a social worker, who asserted that Smith, after hearing that the cause of Etzel's death had been changed from Sudden Infant Death Syndrome (SIDS) to shaken baby syndrome and after stating that she had given Etzel "a little shake, a jostle to awaken him" when she found him unresponsive, asked "something like 'Oh, my God. Did I do it? Did I do it? Oh, my God.'" Etzel's mother, Tomeka, contradicted this account. According to Tomeka, after the social worker accused Smith of killing Etzel, Smith started crying and responded, "No, I didn't." Taking the social worker's version of events as true, Smith's distraught and equivocal question fairly cannot be equated to a confession of guilt. Giving a baby "a little shake, a jostle to wake him" after finding him unexpectedly unresponsive, surely is not an admission to shaking a child violently, causing his brainstem to tear.

Moreover, Smith's counsel, Ubiwe Eriye, represented her poorly at trial. In a case as trying as this one, competent counsel might have persuaded the jury to disbelieve the prosecution's case. A few examples from the record are illustrative. At the suppression hearing, the presiding judge was so disturbed about Eriye's preparation for trial that he remarked to the defendant, "Miss Smith, I'm scared." Eriye badly misportrayed the burden of proof when he declared, both at the suppression hearing and in his opening remarks, that he would prove, beyond a shadow of a doubt, that Smith was not guilty. The two experts Eriye called presented testimony that hardly meshed.

For the reasons stated, justice is not served by the Court's exercise of discretion to take up this tragic, fact-bound case. I would therefore deny the petition for review.

NOTES AND QUESTIONS

1. Shaken baby syndrome evidence is based on the work of medical doctors seeking to discover the causes of unexplained head injuries in small children. Drs. Norman Guthkelch and John Caffey developed the theory of shaken baby syndrome, and Caffey named it. Caitlin M. Plummer & Imran J. Syed, "Shifted Science" Revisited: Percolation Delays and the Persistence of Wrongful Convictions Based on Outdated Science, 64 Clev. St. L. Rev. 483, 511-512 (2016); John Caffey, The Whiplash Shaken Infant Syndrome: Manual Shaking by the Extremities with Whiplash-Induced Intracranial and Intraocular Bleedings, Linked with Residual Permanent Brain Damage and Mental Retardation, 54 Pediatrics 396 (1974). Evidence that a child's head injuries fit the description of the syndrome has been crucial in hundreds of prosecutions. Professor Deborah Tuerkheimer described how the evidence is commonly used:

> With rare exception, the case turns on the testimony of medical experts. Unlike any other category of prosecution, all elements of the crime — *mens rea* and *actus reus* (which includes both the act itself and causation of the resulting harm) — are proven by the science. Degree of force testimony not only establishes causation, but also the requisite state of mind. Unequivocal testimony regarding timing — i.e., that symptoms necessarily would appear instantaneously upon the infliction of injury — proves the perpetrator's identity. In its classic formulation, SBS comes as close as one could image to a medical diagnosis of murder: prosecutors use it to prove the mechanism of death, the intent to harm, and the identity of the killer.

Deborah Tuerkheimer, The Next Innocence Project: Shaken Baby Syndrome and the Criminal Courts, 87 Wash. U. L. Rev. 1, 5 (2009).

Within a short time after the publication of Caffey's papers, the theory became widely accepted by courts and legislatures. Edward J. Imwinkelried, Shaken Baby Syndrome: A Genuine Battle of the Scientific (And Non-Scientific) Experts, 46(1) Crim. L. Bull. ART 6 at text accompanying nn. 93-107 (Jan.-Feb. 2010). However, by the early 2000s, new research challenged some of the most important early claims.

2. Courts' responses to collateral attacks on old convictions based on shaken baby syndrome evidence vary; the stringent legal standard that the challenger must meet in a collateral attack explains many of the rejections, as in *Cavazos*. In cases in which the jury has been presented with the testimony of dueling experts about shaken baby syndrome, convictions are still common, and they are usually upheld on review when sufficiency of the evidence is challenged. Deborah Tuerkheimer, Science-Dependent Prosecution and the Problem of Epistemic Contingency: A Study of Shaken Baby Syndrome, 62 Ala. L. Rev. 513, 524-527 (2011).

In addition to the sources cited, for more information, *see* Keith A. Findley et al, Shaken Baby Syndrome, Abusive Head Trauma, and Actual Innocence: Getting It Right, 12 Hous. J. Health L. & Pol'y 209 (2012); Joëlle Anne Moreno & Brian K. Holmgren, Dissent into Confusion: The Supreme Court, Denialism, and the False "Scientific" Controversy Over Shaken Baby Syndrome, 2013 Utah L. Rev. 53; Sandeep Narang, A Daubert Analysis of Abusive Head Trauma/Shaken Baby Syndrome, 11 Hous. J. Health L. & Pol'y 505, 505 (2012); Sandeep K. Narang, M.D.,

J.D. et al., A Daubert Analysis of Abusive Head Trauma/Shaken Baby Syndrome — Part Ii: An Examination of the Differential Diagnosis, 13 Hous. J. Health L. & Pol'y 203 (2013); Daniel G. Orenstein, Shaken to the Core: Emerging Scientific Opinion and Post-Conviction Relief in Cases of Shaken Baby Syndrome, 42 Ariz. St. L.J. 1305 (2011). Deborah Turkheimer, Flawed Convictions: "Shaken Baby Syndrome" and the Inertia of Justice (2014).

3. Shaken baby syndrome is related to battered child syndrome. Evidence of that syndrome is also commonly admitted in trials alleging physical abuse of a child. Battered child syndrome evidence is ordinarily used to prove that a child's injuries were not accidental and were probably inflicted by the child's caretaker(s). Even when defendants do not dispute that a child's injuries were not accidental, courts often admit it on the issue of who probably hurt the child. In Estelle v. McGuire, 502 U.S. 62 (1991), the Supreme Court held that admission of battered child syndrome evidence in a criminal homicide prosecution did not violate due process even though the defendant did not claim that the child died accidentally because the evidence of prior injuries was relevant to prove that whoever had harmed her had acted intentionally.

4. Surveying cases about the admissibility of expert testimony in child sex abuse prosecutions, the New York Court of Appeals wrote, "[T]he majority of states 'permit expert testimony to explain delayed reporting, recantation, and inconsistency,' as well as 'to explain why some abused children are angry, why some children want to live with the person who abused them, why a victim might appear 'emotionally flat' following sexual assault, why a child might run away from home, and for other purposes' (see 1 Myers on Evidence § 6.24, at 416–422 [collecting cases and noting that Kentucky, Pennsylvania and Tennessee are the only apparent exceptions])." People v. Spicola, 947 N.E.2d 620, 635 (N.Y. 2011). However, a number of courts have held that expert testimony that a child was sexually abused is not admissible, at least in the absence of physical evidence of abuse, because it adds little to the jury's understanding and is highly prejudicial. State v. Buchholtz, 841 N.W.2d 449 (S.D. 2013), citing and discussing cases. For a current survey of cases, see Elizabeth Trainor, Admissibility of Expert Testimony on Child Sexual Abuse Accommodation Syndrome (CSAAS) in Criminal Case, 85 A.L.R.5th 595 (originally published in 2001, updated weekly). See also Kamala London et al., Disclosure of Child Sexual Abuse: What Does the Research Tell Us About the Ways That Children Tell?, 11 Psychol. Pub. Pol'y & L. 194 (2005); John E.B. Myers, Expert Testimony in Child Sexual Abuse Litigation: Consensus and Confusion, 14 U.C. Davis J. Juv. L. & Pol'y 1, 44 (2010).

In many cases, important or even critical evidence of exactly what happened must come from the child. "To testify as a witness, a child must possess certain characteristics, including: the capacity to observe, sufficient intelligence, adequate memory, the ability to communicate, an awareness of the difference between truth and falsehood and an appreciation of the obligation to speak the truth. A child of any age who possesses the requisite characteristics may testify. There is no minimum age below which children are automatically disqualified from serving as witnesses." John E.B. Myers, The Testimonial Competence of Children, 25 J. Fam. L. 288-289 (1986-1987). *See also* Laurie Shanks, Evaluating Children's Competency to Testify: Developing a Rational Method to Assess a Young Child's Capacity to Offer Reliable Testimony in Cases Alleging Child Sex Abuse, 58 Clev. St. L. Rev. 575 (2010).

Testifying is itself a terrifying and traumatic experience for many children. Much thought has been given to ways to make testifying in court less frightening and humiliating for children. Creation of "child-friendly" courtrooms is often recommended. "Prior to testimony, the judge should take the child into chambers, introduce the attorneys and explain how the proceedings will be conducted. When testifying, the child should be allowed to use a smaller version of the adult witness chair or sit at a table with the judge and attorneys. The child also should be allowed to use drawings or anatomically correct dolls to describe the victimization if appropriate. Language that children can understand must be used for all questions. Prior videotaping of testimony must be used whenever possible." U.S. Attorney General's Task Force on Family Violence, Final Report 39 (1984). The next case and the following notes consider common law and constitutional challenges to devices and rules intended to ease the burden on child witnesses.

CORONADO V. STATE

351 S.W.3d 315 (Tex. Crim. App. 2011)

COCHRAN, J., delivered the opinion of the Court in which PRICE, WOMACK, JOHNSON and ALCALA, JJ., joined. . . . Three-year-old R.D. stayed with her great-grandmother for childcare. Appellant is R.D.'s great-uncle who, with his wife, moved into the great-grandmother's home in the spring of 2007. In August of that year, R.D. started acting "strange" and "walking around like a zombie." Her father asked her if anyone had touched her "cookie" — R.D.'s word for her vagina — and he named off various people that she had been around. When he named appellant, R.D. said, "Yes."[1] R.D.'s parents called the police.

A week later, R.D.'s family took her to The Bridge Advocacy Center, where a forensic interviewer videotaped an interview with R.D. Throughout most of the interview, R.D. was looking down at the pictures that she was vigorously coloring. She correctly answered some of the interviewer's questions concerning her body parts and the identification of animals and colors, but she answered others incorrectly. She seemed uninterested in many of the interviewer's questions and several times said that she wanted to go watch Spiderman on TV. When she couldn't leave, she folded her arms and, at first, would not cooperate.

Eventually, she said that her aunt saw appellant touch her "cookie" and that her grandmother saw him do it and "spanked" him for it. In fact, neither the aunt nor the grandmother had seen appellant touch the victim. R.D. was also examined

---

1. R.D.'s hearsay statement was admitted under Article 38.072, which provides for the admissibility of a child's initial "outcry" to an adult only when "the child . . . testifies or is available to testify at the proceeding in court or in any other manner provided by law." Tex. Code Crim. Proc. art. 38.072, § 2(b)(3).

by a sexual-assault nurse who found that her hymen was irregular and that this healed injury had been caused by penetration.

Before trial, the State filed a motion to request the trial court to find R.D. — now five years old — unavailable to testify and to admit the videotaped interview instead. R.D.'s therapist testified and said that she believed that testifying in front of the appellant or testifying via closed circuit television would be harmful. She thought that submitting written interrogatories through a female interviewer was the "best option." Over the appellant's objection, the trial court ruled that R.D. was unavailable to testify and that defense counsel could submit written interrogatories to the forensic interviewer, who would ask those questions and any "follow up" ones in a second recorded interview.

At this second interview — conducted fifteen months after the first one — the forensic interviewer began by discussing the difference between the truth and a lie, and R.D. appeared to understand the difference. Nonetheless, she said more than once that truthful statements were lies. During this interview, R.D. said that appellant put his finger in her "cookie" (as opposed to touching it as she had said fifteen months earlier). This time she said that neither her aunt nor her grandmother saw any sexual contact between her and appellant.

R.D. did not testify at trial, but the two videotaped interviews were admitted over appellant's confrontation objection. The jury convicted appellant of both touching R.D.'s genitals and penetrating her genitals and sentenced him to life in prison on both counts.

On appeal, appellant argued that the denial of rigorous cross-examination denied him his right to confront the witness. The court of appeals agreed that R.D.'s out-of-court statements were testimonial, but concluded that the trial court did not err in allowing "cross-examination through written questions only."

II.

a.   pre-CRAWFORD *law on the right to confrontation.*

The Confrontation Clause gives a criminal defendant the right "to be confronted with the witnesses against him." In Coy v. Iowa,[2] Justice Scalia explained that "[w]e have never doubted, therefore, that the Confrontation Clause guarantees the defendant a face-to-face meeting with witnesses appearing before the trier of fact." In Maryland v. Craig,[3] decided just two years later, the Supreme Court pulled back from that absolute position. It held that in *some* special cases, when the specific facts showed that there was a "compelling" state interest, the witness need not actually confront the defendant face-to-face as she testified, although the defendant must be able to see her as she testified and must be able to contemporaneously cross-examine her.

---

2. 487 U.S. 1012 (1988).
3. 497 U.S. 836 (1990).

Both *Coy* and *Craig* involved prosecutions for sexually assaulting a child. Coy was accused of molesting two thirteen-year-old girls who were having an outdoor sleepover in a neighboring yard. An Iowa statute allowed prosecutors to use a screen to shield child witnesses from seeing the defendant as they testified. Most of the elements of the right of confrontation were preserved through this procedure, but the witnesses could not see the defendant and the defendant could not see the witnesses as they testified. And, perhaps most importantly, the jury could not see how the witnesses and the defendant interacted when each confronted the other. In a 6-2 decision, the Supreme Court held that this procedure violated the right to confrontation. Justice Scalia noted the compelling state interest of protecting fragile children and other witnesses:

> That face-to-face presence may, unfortunately, upset the truthful rape victim or abused child; but by the same token it may confound and undo the false accuser, or reveal the child coached by a malevolent adult. It is a truism that constitutional protections have costs.

In *Craig*, however, the Supreme Court, in a 5-4 decision, upheld the use of a one-way closed-circuit television for questioning a six-year-old child in lieu of face-to-face confrontation in the courtroom itself. A Maryland statute authorized this procedure if the trial judge determined that "testimony by the child victim in the courtroom will result in the child suffering serious emotional distress such that the child cannot reasonably communicate." Under this procedure, the defendant could see the child as she testified, but she could not see the defendant.

According to Justice O'Connor, this procedure did not violate the Confrontation Clause because that provision can be reduced to its "central concern," which is "to ensure the reliability of the evidence against a criminal defendant by subjecting it to rigorous testing in the context of an adversary proceeding before the trier of fact." Rigorous and contemporaneous cross-examination could, under some special circumstances, alleviate the need for face-to-face confrontation. The Court stressed that only the witness's ability to confront the defendant face-to-face was affected—no other portion of the Sixth Amendment right of confrontation was compromised:

> [The one-way closed-circuit television procedure] "(1) insures that the witness will give his statements under oath—thus impressing him with the seriousness of the matter and guarding against the lie by the possibility of a penalty for perjury; (2) forces the witness to submit to cross-examination, the 'greatest legal engine ever invented for the discovery of truth'; [and] (3) permits the jury that is to decide the defendant's fate to observe the demeanor of the witness in making his statement, thus aiding the jury in assessing his credibility."

Thus, the "combined effect of these elements of confrontation — physical presence, oath, cross-examination, and observation of demeanor by the trier of fact — serves the purposes of the Confrontation Clause by ensuring that evidence admitted against an accused is reliable and subject to the rigorous adversarial testing that is the norm of Anglo-American criminal proceedings."

Justice SCALIA, the author of *Coy* just two years earlier, wrote a scathing dissent. . . .

. . . The Supreme Court has never overturned the holding in *Craig*, but, beginning with Crawford v. Washington,[4] the Supreme Court has nibbled it into Swiss cheese by repeating the categorical nature of the right to confrontation in every one of its more recent cases.[5]

b.   the right to confrontation under CRAWFORD

Fourteen years after *Craig*, in Crawford v. Washington, the Supreme Court reiterated the categorical right of confrontation that it had set out in *Coy*. Justice Scalia, speaking for seven members of the Court, concluded that, "[w]here

---

4. 541 U.S. 36 (2004).

5. Academics have noted the enormous impact that the *Crawford* line of cases has had upon both domestic-violence and child-abuse cases. Such prosecutions have become much more difficult because the victim must almost always testify at trial to satisfy the Confrontation Clause. *See, e.g.*, David M. Wagner, The End of the "Virtually Constitutional"? The Confrontation Right and Crawford v. Washington as a Prelude to Reversal of Maryland v. Craig, 19 Regent U. L. Rev. 469, 469 (2006) (noting that — after *Crawford* — a "forthright holding that the government may deny a criminal defendant a confrontation with his accuser because a 'compelling state interest' is present, in, say, combating child abuse, would invite obvious and well-founded objections of the 'slippery slope' variety" in arguing that the Supreme Court will overturn its prior decision in *Craig* based upon the constitutional analysis of *Crawford*); Myrna S. Raeder, Comments on Child Abuse Litigation in a "Testimonial" World: The Intersection of Competency, Hearsay, and Confrontation, 82 Ind. L.J. 1009, 1023 (2007) (discussing the use of forensic interviews in child-abuse cases; stating that "*Crawford* appears to doom the use of multidisciplinary teams in child abuse as a way of introducing statements of children who do not testify" and lamenting that "*Crawford* has turned these best practices into a textbook for creating testimonial statements when the child does not testify."); Kimberly Y. Chin, "Minute and Separate": Considering the Admissibility of Videotaped Forensic Interviews in Child Sexual Abuse Cases After *Crawford* and *Davis*, 30 B.C. Third World L.J. 67 (2010) (noting that, under *Crawford*, child-abuse forensic videotapes are generally inadmissible when the child is unavailable to testify at trial, and suggesting that some videotapes could be redacted to eliminate all testimonial statements); Prudence Beidler Carr, Comment: Playing By All the Rules: How to Define and Provide a "Prior Opportunity for Cross-Examination" in Child Sexual Abuses Cases After Crawford v. Washington, 97 J. Crim. L. & Criminology 631 (2007) (noting the enormous impact that the *Crawford* decision has had upon child-sexual-abuse cases, but arguing that pretrial videotapes may still be admissible under both *Crawford* and *Craig* if the defendant is given an appropriate opportunity for prior confrontation and cross-examination). *Cf.* State v. Stock, 361 Mont. 1, 256 P.3d 899, 905 (Mont. 2011) (defendant's confrontation rights under *Crawford* were not violated when six-year-old child testified via two-way closed-circuit television); People v. Buie, 285 Mich. App. 401, 775 N.W.2d 817, 825-27 (Mich. Ct. App. 2009) (applying *Craig* to the issue of whether expert testimony given via two-way interactive technology violated the defendant's confrontation rights); State v. Henriod, 131 P.3d 232 (Utah 2006) (rejecting the argument that *Crawford* implicitly abrogated *Craig*); State v. Blanchette, 35 Kan. App. 2d 686, 134 P.3d 19, 29 (Kan. Ct. App. 2006) (same).

testimonial statements are at issue, the only indicium of reliability sufficient to satisfy constitutional demands is the one the Constitution actually prescribes: confrontation." The Court overruled its prior decision in Roberts v. Ohio,[6] which allowed admission of "*ex parte* testimony upon a mere finding of reliability," because that "malleable standard" failed to protect against "paradigmatic confrontation violations." . . .

In *Crawford*, the Court explained that "[t]he text of the Sixth Amendment does not suggest any open-ended exceptions from the confrontation requirement to be developed by the courts." Social policy, public policy, even grave practical difficulties of obtaining the witness for trial do not trump the categorical requirement. Rather, under *Crawford*,

> Admitting statements deemed reliable by a judge is fundamentally at odds with the right of confrontation. To be sure, the Clause's ultimate goal is to ensure reliability of evidence, but it is a procedural rather than a substantive guarantee. It commands, not that evidence be reliable, but that reliability be assessed in a particular manner: by testing in the crucible of cross-examination.

The *Crawford* Court stated, "It is not enough to point out that most of the usual safeguards of the adversary process attend the statement, when the single safeguard missing is the one the Confrontation Clause demands." Thus, when testimonial statements are at issue, and the declarant is not making those statements from the witness stand at trial, "the Sixth Amendment demands what the common law required: unavailability and a prior opportunity for cross-examination." . . .

c.   *testimonial statements under* CRAWFORD *and its progeny.*

The question then became, "What out-of-court statements are 'testimonial' for purposes of the right of confrontation?" In *Crawford*, the Court did not fully resolve that issue, recognizing that there would be some "interim uncertainty" interpreting and applying the distinction between testimonial and nontestimonial statements. Two years later, in Davis v. Washington,[7] the Supreme Court elaborated on that distinction:

> Statements are nontestimonial when made in the course of police interrogation under circumstances objectively indicating that the primary purpose of the interrogation is to enable police assistance to meet an ongoing emergency. They are testimonial when the circumstances objectively indicate that there is no such ongoing emergency, and that the primary purpose of the interrogation is to establish or prove past events potentially relevant to later criminal prosecution.

Under *Davis*, (as well as the Supreme Court's more recent confrontation decision, Michigan v. Bryant[8]) the primary focus in determining whether an out-of-court statement is "testimonial" is on the objective purpose of the interview or

---

6. 448 U.S. 56 (1980).

7. 547 U.S. 813 (2006).

8. ____ U.S. ____, 131 S. Ct. 1143, 179 L. Ed. 2d 93 (2011).

interrogation, not on the declarant's expectations. If the objective purpose of the interview is to question a person about past events and that person's statements about those past events would likely be relevant to a future criminal proceeding, then they are testimonial.

> d. *child-abuse forensic interview statements and videotapes*
> *are testimonial and are inadmissible unless the child testifies*
> *or the defendant had a prior opportunity to cross-examine the child.*

Virtually all courts that have reviewed the admissibility of forensic child-interview statements or videotapes after the *Davis* decision have found them to be "testimonial" and inadmissible unless the child testifies at trial or the defendant had a prior opportunity for cross-examination.[9] Indeed, in this case, the State does not dispute that R.D.'s statements, made during her two interviews at The Bridge Children's Advocacy Center, were testimonial, and the court of appeals explicitly held that they were testimonial.

---

9. *See, e.g.,* Bobadilla v. Carlson, 575 F.3d 785, 791-93 (8th Cir. 2009) (holding, on defendant's federal writ of habeas corpus, that state supreme court made an "unreasonable application of federal law" under *Crawford* in concluding that child's videotaped statement to social worker in sex-abuse case was admissible when child did not testify at trial and defendant had no opportunity to cross-examine child; affirming district court's ruling granting habeas relief); State v. Contreras, 979 So. 2d 896, 905-12 (Fla. 2008) (harmful error to admit child-victim's videotaped statement to child-abuse coordinator when child was declared unavailable for trial and defense counsel's discovery deposition of child did not afford defendant sufficient opportunity for cross-examination); State v. Hooper, 145 Idaho 139, 176 P.3d 911, 917-18 (Idaho 2007) (holding that videotaped statements the child victim made to nurse during interview at a sexual-trauma abuse-response center were testimonial because the circumstances surrounding the interview indicated that the primary purpose of the interview was to establish past events potentially relevant to later criminal prosecution as opposed to meeting the child's medical needs; reversible error to admit them when child did not testify at trial and defendant had no prior opportunity for cross-examination); State v. Henderson, 284 Kan. 267, 160 P.3d 776, 785-93 (Kan. 2007) (reversible error to admit three-year-old child's videotaped statement to social worker taken at government facility to gather evidence against alleged perpetrator when child did not testify at trial and defendant did not have prior opportunity to cross-examine); State v. Justus, 205 S.W.3d 872, 880-81 (Mo. 2006) (while social worker's job was to protect child, "primary purpose" of videotaped statements was to establish past events; reversible error to admit four-year-old child's videotaped interview when defendant did not have opportunity to cross-examine her); State v. Blue, 717 N.W.2d 558, 564-67 (N.D. 2006) (videotaped statement to forensic interviewer at child advocacy center inadmissible because defendant did not have opportunity to cross-examine; irrelevant that trial judge found the child's statement reliable and trustworthy because Confrontation Clause requires cross-examination); State v. Pitt, 209 Or. App. 270, 147 P.3d 940, 943-46 (Or. Ct. App. 2006) (reversible error to admit "testimonial" videotaped statements made by two children to social worker at child-abuse assessment center when children did not testify at trial); In re S.R., 920 A.2d 1262, 1266-69 (Pa. Super. Ct. 2007) (reversible error to admit videotape of four-year-old child's statement to forensic DHS interviewer for the purpose of investigation and possible prosecution when child did not testify at juvenile's adjudication hearing).

1.   A prior opportunity to cross-examine means an opportunity for full personal adversarial cross-examination, including attacks on credibility.

Therefore, the Confrontation Clause question in this case is whether appellant had "a prior opportunity to cross-examine" R.D., as is required under *Crawford*. The court of appeals quite appropriately cited Davis v. Alaska[10] for the proposition that the right of confrontation includes "not only the right to face-to-face confrontation, but also the right to meaningful and effective cross-examination." And the court aptly cited Dean Wigmore, who had explained that the "'main and essential purpose'" of confrontation is "the opportunity for cross-examination through the process of putting direct and personal questions to the witnesses and the obtaining of immediate answers." . . . .

Cross-examination means

[t]he questioning of a witness upon a trial or hearing by the party opposed to the party who called the witness to testify. The purpose of cross-examination is to discredit a witness before the factfinder in any of several ways, as by bringing out contradictions and improbabilities in earlier testimony, by suggesting doubts to the witness, and by trapping the witness into admissions that weaken the testimony.

It is an examination by the opposing party, not a "neutral" interviewer. It occurs in the formal setting — a trial or a hearing. . . .

2.   Ex parte submission of written interrogatories does not qualify as cross-examination.

The State argues that it "has an important public policy interest in protecting the physical and psychological well-being of children and, in particular, child abuse victims." Therefore, argues the State, the trial court was "justified in requiring cross-examination by written interrogatories for the safety and protection of the child." Although the State argues that there should be more flexibility in child-abuse cases, the Supreme Court has rejected the notion that there should be more flexibility concerning the Confrontation Clause in certain types of cases, such as domestic-abuse prosecutions. In *Davis*, Justice Scalia said:

Respondents in both cases [*Davis* and *Hammon*], joined by a number of their *amici*, contend that the nature of the offenses charged in these two cases — domestic violence — requires greater flexibility in the use of testimonial evidence. This particular type of crime is notoriously susceptible to intimidation or coercion of the victim to ensure that she does not testify at trial. When this occurs, the Confrontation Clause gives the criminal a windfall. We may not, however, vitiate constitutional guarantees when they have the effect of allowing the guilty to go free. . . .

III.

The court of appeals in this case, without citing to any of the *Crawford* line of cases, concluded that written interrogatories, propounded by a forensic

---

10. 415 U.S. 308 (1974).

child-sexual-abuse examiner some fifteen months after the child's initial video-taped interview that the State wished to introduce, were a sufficient substitute for live, adversarial cross-examination to satisfy a defendant's right to confrontation. But we are "not free to conduct a cost-benefit analysis of clear and explicit constitutional guarantees, and then to adjust their meaning to comport with our findings." Cross-examination means personal, live, adversarial questioning in a formal setting. It cannot have one meaning for some witnesses and another meaning for others. . . .

There was no "rigorous adversarial testing" of R.D.'s testimonial statements by that greatest legal engine for uncovering the truth: contemporaneous cross-examination. The written-interrogatories procedure used in this case does not pass muster under our English common-law adversarial system or our United States Constitution. The constitutional requirement of confrontation and cross-examination "may not [be] disregard[ed] . . . at our convenience," regardless of the prediction of dire consequences.

We therefore reverse the judgment of the court of appeals and remand this case to that court for further proceedings consistent with this opinion.

NOTES AND QUESTIONS

1. The child's out-of-court videotape was undoubtedly testimonial hearsay evidence that could not be admitted under *Crawford* unless the child was available for cross-examination at trial or the defendant had a prior opportunity to cross-examine her about the statement. In what ways was the procedure used in this case different from what is usually meant by an opportunity to cross-examine? Of what importance are the differences?

In some states, the right to confrontation includes the right of a defendant to examine witnesses personally. For a discussion of the implications of such a right in child sex abuse trials *see* Tyler D. Carlton, Comment: A Balancing Act: Providing the Proper Balance Between a Child Sexual Abuse Victim's Rights and the Right to Personal Cross-Examination in Arizona, 49 Ariz. St. L. J. 1453 (2017).

2. In most states today, multidisciplinary teams of police, psychologists, social workers, and health care personnel investigate allegations of child abuse, usually in child advocacy centers affiliated with the local prosecutor's office. Office of Juvenile Justice and Delinquency Prevention, Evaluating Children's Advocacy Centers' Response to Child Sexual Abuse (Aug. 2008). This investigatory approach is intended to save children from repetitious and traumatizing interrogations. It also allows the state to procure evidence from children that is untainted by leading questioning and other inept investigatory practices that cast doubt on the reliability of children's statements. The centers were developed during the pre-*Crawford* era when the test for the admissibility of hearsay statements required that the judge find them to be "reliable." Anna Richey-Allen, Note: Presuming Innocence: Expanding the Confrontation Clause Analysis to Protect Children and Defendants in Child Sexual Abuse Prosecutions, 93 Minn. L. Rev. 1090, 1099 (2009). *See* Ohio v. Roberts, 448 U.S. 56 (1980) (establishing the reliability test). However, under *Crawford*, most courts have held that children's

statements taken at child advocacy centers are clearly testimonial. Richey-Allen, 93 Minn. L. Rev. at 1101-1116; Myrna S. Raeder, Comments on Child Abuse Litigation in a "Testimonial" World: The Intersection of Competency, Hearsay, and Confrontation, 82 Ind. L. J. 1009, 1023-1025 (2007); Robert P. Mosteller, *Crawford*'s Impact on Hearsay Statements in Domestic Violence and Child Sexual Abuse Cases, 71 Brook. L. Rev. 411 (2005).

3. *Crawford* rejected the Confrontation Clause mode of analysis upon which Maryland v. Craig is based. However, *Crawford* did not overrule *Craig*, and a number of courts have ruled that it is still good law. *See* Jessica Brooks, Two-Way Video Testimony and the Confrontation Clause: Protecting Vulnerable Victims after *Crawford*, 8 Stan. J. Civ. Rts. & Civ. Liberties 183 (2012).

4. Justice Scalia argued in *Craig* that, because children are more susceptible to suggestion and less able to sort reality from fantasy than adults, face-to-face confrontation is essential to a fair trial in child abuse prosecutions. Does face-to-face confrontation help solve the problems he identifies? Assuming the truth of his assertions, what might be done about it?

It seems in fact that the question of whether children's testimony is inherently less reliable than adults' is considerably more complex than Justice Scalia indicates. *See* Carol S. Larson et al., Sexual Abuse of Children: Recommendations and Analysis, 4 The Future of Children: Sexual Abuse of Children 4, 17-19 (1994); The Suggestibility of Children's Recollections: Implications for Eyewitness Testimony (Am. Psych. Assn., John Doris ed., 1991); John E.B. Myers, The Testimonial Competence of Children, 25 J. Fam. L. 288-289 (1986-1987). For more on children's testimony generally, *see* John E.B. Myers, Myers on Evidence in Child Abuse, Domestic, and Elder Abuse Cases (4th ed. 2010).

5. The National Conference of Commissioners on Uniform State Laws has promulgated the Uniform Child Witness Testimony by Alternative Methods Act to provide procedures for judges to determine when a child should testify by an alternative method. Section 4 of the Act requires the judge to hold a hearing on the record if a party, the child, or the child's representative moves to allow the child to testify by an alternative method. Section 5(a) provides that in a criminal proceeding the motion should be granted only if the judge finds by clear and convincing evidence that the child "would suffer serious emotional trauma that would substantially impair the child's ability to communicate with the finder of fact" if the child were required to testify in an open forum or face to face with the defendant. In a noncriminal proceeding, the motion should be granted if the judge makes the same finding by a preponderance of the evidence. Section 5(b). The Act has been adopted in Idaho, Nevada, New Mexico, and Oklahoma. Uniform Law Commission, Child Witness Testimony by Alternative Methods Act, Enactment Map, https://my.uniformlaws.org/committees/community-home?CommunityKey=fa810ffb-3194-417c-a79b-bf4100f02f2d.

Initial reports of child abuse frequently come from statements by children to parents, police, medical personnel, or teachers. If those statements are offered at trial because they themselves establish the fact of abuse ("I was spanked with a belt") or its perpetrator ("by my father"), they will be subject to challenge under the Confrontation Clause and the hearsay rule.

Several traditional exceptions to the hearsay rule can justify admission of some statements by children in abuse or neglect cases. A statement to a doctor or nurse consulted for diagnosis or treatment will be admissible to the extent that the content of the statement is pertinent to diagnosis or treatment. Frequently, however, any part of the statement not relevant to medical care will not be admitted. Classically, the statement "I was spanked" would be considered important to treatment, but the statement "by my father" would be excluded. *See* Federal Rule of Evidence 803(4) and Advisory Committee Note.

Two other traditional hearsay exceptions may also be invoked in child abuse cases. Federal Rule 803(1) permits introduction of hearsay statements that qualify as "present sense impressions": that is, statements describing or explaining an event or condition made while the speaker was perceiving the event or condition or immediately thereafter. Rule 803(2) allows receipt of statements made under the stress of an exciting event that relate to that event. Unlike present sense impressions, no particular time frame applies for excited utterances. They may be made hours after the event, as long as the court finds that the witness was still in the grip of the excitement. *See, e.g.,* Moore v. State, 338 A.2d 344 (Md. App. 1975) (doctor testified that excited three-year-old patient said, "Daddy was mad, Daddy did it"). However, where the witness has calmed down, this exception is unavailable. *See* Goldade v. State, 674 P.2d 721 (Wyo. 1983) (no evidence that child was still excited when statement made).

In addition to these traditional exceptions, the Federal Rules of Evidence include two residual hearsay exceptions. Rules 803(24) and 804(b)(5) permit the admission of statements not covered by a specific exception if they have "comparable guarantees of trustworthiness" and the evidence they provide is more cogent than other available kinds of proof. In most cases, the two rules will operate identically. A majority of states have also enacted statutes creating a child sexual abuse hearsay exception to facilitate criminal prosecution of sex abuse cases.

The admissibility of children's hearsay statements (indeed, any out-of-court statements) in a criminal trial is further limited by the Confrontation Clause of the Constitution. The next case considers the application of the *Crawford* test to a kind of out-of-court statement commonly offered in child abuse cases.

OHIO V. CLARK

135 S. Ct. 2173 (2015)

ALITO, J. . . . Darius Clark, who went by the nickname "Dee," lived in Cleveland, Ohio, with his girlfriend, T.T., and her two children: L.P., a 3-year-old boy, and A.T., an 18-month-old girl. Clark was also T.T.'s pimp, and he would regularly send her on trips to Washington, D.C., to work as a prostitute. In March 2010, T.T. went on one such trip, and she left the children in Clark's care.

The next day, Clark took L.P. to preschool. In the lunchroom, one of L.P.'s teachers, Ramona Whitley, observed that L.P.'s left eye appeared bloodshot. She asked him "'[w]hat happened,'" and he initially said nothing. Eventually, however, he told the teacher that he "'fell.'" When they moved into the brighter lights of a classroom, Whitley noticed "'[r]ed marks, like whips of some sort,'" on L.P.'s face. She notified the lead teacher, Debra Jones, who asked L.P., "'Who did this? What happened to you?'" According to Jones, L.P. "'seemed kind of bewildered'" and "'said something like, Dee, Dee.'" Jones asked L.P. whether Dee is "big or little," to which L.P. responded that "Dee is big." Jones then brought L.P. to her supervisor, who lifted the boy's shirt, revealing more injuries. Whitley called a child abuse hotline to alert authorities about the suspected abuse.

When Clark later arrived at the school, he denied responsibility for the injuries and quickly left with L.P. The next day, a social worker found the children at Clark's mother's house and took them to a hospital, where a physician discovered additional injuries suggesting child abuse. L.P. had a black eye, belt marks on his back and stomach, and bruises all over his body. A.T. had two black eyes, a swollen hand, and a large burn on her cheek, and two pigtails had been ripped out at the roots of her hair.

A grand jury indicted Clark on five counts of felonious assault (four related to A.T. and one related to L.P.), two counts of endangering children (one for each child), and two counts of domestic violence (one for each child). At trial, the State introduced L.P.'s statements to his teachers as evidence of Clark's guilt, but L.P. did not testify. Under Ohio law, children younger than 10 years old are incompetent to testify if they "appear incapable of receiving just impressions of the facts and transactions respecting which they are examined, or of relating them truly." After conducting a hearing, the trial court concluded that L.P. was not competent to testify. But under Ohio Rule of Evidence 807, which allows the admission of reliable hearsay by child abuse victims, the court ruled that L.P.'s statements to his teachers bore sufficient guarantees of trustworthiness to be admitted as evidence.

Clark moved to exclude testimony about L.P.'s out-of-court statements under the Confrontation Clause. The trial court denied the motion, ruling that L.P.'s responses were not testimonial statements covered by the Sixth Amendment. The jury found Clark guilty on all counts except for one assault count related to A.T., and it sentenced him to 28 years' imprisonment. Clark appealed his conviction, and a state appellate court reversed on the ground that the introduction of L.P.'s out-of-court statements violated the Confrontation Clause.

In a 4-to-3 decision, the Supreme Court of Ohio affirmed. . . .

The Sixth Amendment's Confrontation Clause, which is binding on the States through the Fourteenth Amendment, provides: "In all criminal prosecutions, the accused shall enjoy the right . . . to be confronted with the witnesses against him." In Ohio v. Roberts, 448 U.S. 56, 66, (1980), we interpreted the Clause to permit the admission of out-of-court statements by an unavailable witness, so long as the statements bore "adequate 'indicia of reliability.'" Such indicia are present, we held, if "the evidence falls within a firmly rooted hearsay exception" or bears "particularized guarantees of trustworthiness."

In Crawford v. Washington, 541 U.S. 36 (2004), we adopted a different approach. We explained that "witnesses," under the Confrontation Clause, are those "who bear testimony," and we defined "testimony" as "a solemn declaration or affirmation made for the purpose of establishing or proving some fact." The Sixth Amendment, we concluded, prohibits the introduction of testimonial statements by a nontestifying witness, unless the witness is "unavailable to testify, and the defendant had had a prior opportunity for cross-examination." Applying that definition to the facts in *Crawford*, we held that statements by a witness during police questioning at the station house were testimonial and thus could not be admitted. But our decision in *Crawford* did not offer an exhaustive definition of "testimonial" statements. Instead, *Crawford* stated that the label "applies at a minimum to prior testimony at a preliminary hearing, before a grand jury, or at a former trial; and to police interrogations.

Our more recent cases have labored to flesh out what it means for a statement to be "testimonial." In Davis v. Washington and Hammon v. Indiana, 547 U.S. 813 (2006), which we decided together, we dealt with statements given to law enforcement officers by the victims of domestic abuse. The victim in *Davis* made statements to a 911 emergency operator during and shortly after her boyfriend's violent attack. In *Hammon*, the victim, after being isolated from her abusive husband, made statements to police that were memorialized in a "'battery affidavit.'"

We held that the statements in *Hammon* were testimonial, while the statements in *Davis* were not. Announcing what has come to be known as the "primary purpose" test, we explained: "Statements are nontestimonial when made in the course of police interrogation under circumstances objectively indicating that the primary purpose of the interrogation is to enable police assistance to meet an ongoing emergency. They are testimonial when the circumstances objectively indicate that there is no such ongoing emergency, and that the primary purpose of the interrogation is to establish or prove past events potentially relevant to later criminal prosecution." Because the cases involved statements to law enforcement officers, we reserved the question whether similar statements to individuals other than law enforcement officers would raise similar issues under the Confrontation Clause. . . .

. . . But that does not mean that the Confrontation Clause bars every statement that satisfies the "primary purpose" test. We have recognized that the Confrontation Clause does not prohibit the introduction of out-of-court statements that would have been admissible in a criminal case at the time of the founding. Thus, the primary purpose test is a necessary, but not always sufficient, condition for the exclusion of out-of-court statements under the Confrontation Clause.

B

In this case, we consider statements made to preschool teachers, not the police. We are therefore presented with the question we have repeatedly reserved: whether statements to persons other than law enforcement officers are subject to the Confrontation Clause. Because at least some statements to individuals who are not law enforcement officers could conceivably raise confrontation concerns, we decline to adopt a categorical rule excluding them from the Sixth Amendment's reach. Nevertheless, such statements are much less likely to be testimonial than statements to law enforcement officers. And considering all the relevant circumstances here, L.P.'s statements clearly were not made with the primary purpose of creating evidence for Clark's prosecution. Thus, their introduction at trial did not violate the Confrontation Clause.

L.P.'s statements occurred in the context of an ongoing emergency involving suspected child abuse. When L.P.'s teachers noticed his injuries, they rightly became worried that the 3-year-old was the victim of serious violence. Because the teachers needed to know whether it was safe to release L.P. to his guardian at the end of the day, they needed to determine who might be abusing the child. Thus, the immediate concern was to protect a vulnerable child who needed help. Our holding in *Bryant* is instructive. As in *Bryant*, the emergency in this case was ongoing, and the circumstances were not entirely clear. L.P.'s teachers were not sure who had abused him or how best to secure his safety. Nor were they sure whether any other children might be at risk. As a result, their questions and L.P.'s answers were primarily aimed at identifying and ending the threat. Though not as harried, the conversation here was also similar to the 911 call in *Davis*. The teachers' questions were meant to identify the abuser in order to protect the victim from future attacks. Whether the teachers thought that this would be done by apprehending the abuser or by some other means is irrelevant. And the circumstances in this case were unlike the interrogation in *Hammon*, where the police knew the identity of the assailant and questioned the victim after shielding her from potential harm. . . .

As a historical matter, moreover, there is strong evidence that statements made in circumstances similar to those facing L.P. and his teachers were admissible at common law. And when 18th-century courts excluded statements of this sort, they appeared to do so because the child should have been ruled competent to testify, not because the statements were otherwise inadmissible. It is thus highly doubtful that statements like L.P.'s ever would have been understood to raise Confrontation Clause concerns. Neither *Crawford* nor any of the cases that it has produced has mounted evidence that the adoption of the Confrontation Clause was understood to require the exclusion of evidence that was regularly admitted in criminal cases at the time of the founding. Certainly, the statements in this case are nothing like the notorious use of *ex parte* examination in Sir Walter Raleigh's trial for treason, which we have frequently identified as "the principal evil at which the Confrontation Clause was directed."

Finally, although we decline to adopt a rule that statements to individuals who are not law enforcement officers are categorically outside the Sixth Amendment, the fact that L.P. was speaking to his teachers remains highly relevant. Courts must evaluate challenged statements in context, and part of that context is the questioner's identity. Statements made to someone who is not principally charged with uncovering and prosecuting criminal behavior are significantly less likely to be testimonial than statements given to law enforcement officers. It is common sense that the relationship between a student and his teacher is very different from that between a citizen and the police. We do not ignore that reality. In light of these circumstances, the Sixth Amendment did not prohibit the State from introducing L.P.'s statements at trial.

III

Clark's efforts to avoid this conclusion are all off-base. He emphasizes Ohio's mandatory reporting obligations, in an attempt to equate L.P.'s teachers with the police and their caring questions with official interrogations. But the comparison is inapt. The teachers' pressing concern was to protect L.P. and remove him from harm's way. Like all good teachers, they undoubtedly would have acted with the same purpose whether or not they had a state-law duty to report abuse. And mandatory reporting statutes alone cannot convert a conversation between a concerned teacher and her student into a law enforcement mission aimed primarily at gathering evidence for a prosecution.

It is irrelevant that the teachers' questions and their duty to report the matter had the natural tendency to result in Clark's prosecution. The statements at issue in *Davis* and *Bryant* supported the defendants' convictions, and the police always have an obligation to ask questions to resolve ongoing emergencies. Yet, we held in those cases that the Confrontation Clause did not prohibit introduction of the statements because they were not primarily intended to be testimonial. Thus, Clark is also wrong to suggest that admitting L.P.'s statements would be fundamentally unfair given that Ohio law does not allow incompetent children to testify. In any Confrontation Clause case, the individual who provided the out-of-court statement is not available as an in-court witness, but the testimony is admissible under an exception to the hearsay rules and is probative of the defendant's guilt. The fact that the witness is unavailable because of a different rule of evidence does not change our analysis. . . .

We reverse the judgment of the Supreme Court of Ohio and remand the case for further proceedings not inconsistent with this opinion. *It is so ordered.*

NOTES AND QUESTIONS

1. Would it be likely that a child's report of abuse to a parent or babysitter would be considered "testimonial"? What about the child's responses to questions posed by the parent or babysitter? Courts consistently rule that children's statements to law enforcement officers are testimonial "because they conclude that there are no credible alternative interpretations." Robert P. Mosteller, Confrontation in Children's Cases: The Dimensions of Limited Coverage, 20 J. L. & Pol'y 393, 406 (2012). On the other hand, statements to parents, family members, and friends are consistently labeled nontestimonial, on the assumption that the primary purpose of the questioners is ensuring the child's wellbeing, not investigation. Some courts have even found that statements made to child abuse investigators are not testimonial if the interviewer is working on the case from a child protection angle, rather than as part of a potential criminal prosecution. However, most courts have rejected this argument if the interview was conducted after the immediate emergency upon discovery of the child's abuse had passed. *Id.* at 409-410.

2. *Clark* dismisses out of hand the argument that the teachers' motivation for questioning was to gain information to help discharge their duty to report child abuse. What arguments support the court's position? The opposite view? *See* Myrna Raeder, Comments on Child Abuse Litigation in a "Testimonial" World: The Intersection of Competency, Hearsay, and Confrontation, 82 Ind. L.J. 1009, 1024-1026 (2007); Myrna Raeder, Remember the Ladies and the Children Too: *Crawford's* Impact on Domestic Violence and Child Abuse Cases, 71 Brook. L. Rev. 311, 377 (2005).

A review of cases found that most courts hold that statements to medical personnel are not testimonial, despite the child abuse reporting obligation. Robert

P. Mosteller, Testing the Testimonial Concept and Exceptions to Confrontation: "A Little Child Shall Lead Them," 82 Ind. L.J. 917, 944-965 (2007).

3. In Giles v. California, 554 U.S. 353 (2008), the Supreme Court discussed the forfeiture doctrine, which allows a court to admit evidence that would otherwise violate the Confrontation Clause when the defendant has wrongfully caused the declarant of the out-of-court testimony to be unavailable. The Court held that the state must prove that the defendant engaged in the conduct at least in part for the purpose of preventing the witness from testifying. For discussion of how this doctrine might be applied in child abuse cases, *see* Clifford S. Fishman, The Child Declarant, the Confrontation Clause, and the Forfeiture Doctrine, 16 Widener L. Rev. 279 (2010); Tom Lininger, Kids Say the Darnedest Things: The Prosecutorial Use of Hearsay Statements by Children, 82 Ind. L.J. 999, 1005-1007 (2007); Thomas D. Lyon & Julia A. Dente, Child Witnesses and the Confrontation Clause, 102 J. Crim. L. & Criminology 1181 (2012).

Table of Cases

Principal cases are in italics.

Index